A Review of the Events of 1982

The 1983 World Book Year Book

The Annual Supplement to The World Book Encyclopedia

World Book, Inc.
a Scott Fetzer company
Chicago London Sydney Toronto

Staff

Editorial Director
William H. Nault

Editorial Staff
Editor
A. Richard Harmet

Executive Editor
Wayne Wille

Associate Editor
Sara Dreyfuss

Senior Editors
David L. Dreier
Marsha F. Goldsmith
Barbara A. Mayes
Jay Myers

Staff Editors
William T. Graham
Karin C. Rosenberg

Research Editor
Irene B. Keller

Cartographic Editor
H. George Stoll

Statistical Editor
Katherine Norgel

Staff Indexer
Claire Bolton

Editorial Assistant
Lettie Zinnamon

Art Staff
Executive Art Director
William Hammond

Art Director
Roberta Dimmer

Senior Artist
Nikki Conner

Artists
Rosa Cabrera
Alice F. Dole

Photography Director
John S. Marshall

Photographs Editors
Karen M. Koblik
Sandra M. Ozanick
Randi E. Sherman

Editorial Services
Director
Susan C. Kilburg

Head, Research Services
Mary Norton

Researchers
Edna Capehart
Robert Hamm

Head, Library Services
Mary Kayaian

Product Production
Executive Director
Peter Mollman

Director of Manufacturing
Joseph C. LaCount

Director of Pre-Press
J. J. Stack

Production Control Manager
Barbara Podczerwinski

Assistant Product Manager
Madelyn Krzak

Film Separations Manager
Alfred J. Mozdzen

Film Separations Assistant Manager
Barbara J. McDonald

Research and Development Manager
Henry Koval

World Book, Inc.
Robert H. King, Chairman of the Board and Chief Executive Officer

Executive Vice-Presidents
John E. Frere — Finance
Michael J. Goodkin — Direct Response/Distributors
James L. Jackson — Marketing
Peter Mollman — Manufacturing
William H. Nault — Editorial

Printed in the United States of America
ISBN 0-7166-0483-3
ISSN 0084-1439
Library of Congress Catalog Card Number: 62-4818

Preface

A group of tiny islands became a battlefield in a war between two countries in 1982. If you can identify the islands and the countries, you will have the correct answer to one of the 50 questions in a new YEAR BOOK feature — The Year on File Quiz on pages 176 and 177. The quiz will give you an opportunity to have some fun while you test your knowledge of some of the events of 1982.

If you know what is going on in the picture below, you have another correct answer. The picture has no descriptive caption, because we don't want to give you too much help. Other questions in the quiz pertain to some people in the news in 1982 — Bashir Gemayel, Sir Ranulph Twisleton-Wykeham-Fiennes, Kate Smith, John Z. De Lorean, Wayne Gretzky, and Richard M. Nixon, to name a few. There also are questions about events in such countries as Canada, Japan, and Libya. All 50 questions are based on information in Year on File articles, and the answers are on page 531.

We also have added a two-page essay to the Chronology section and have renamed that section The Year in Brief. The essay — on pages 10 and 11 — will give you a fast overview of the year, capturing some of the main events and the spirit of 1982 in brief narrative form. The familiar Chronology — a month-by-month listing of events — follows on pages 12 through 23.

To get back to the quiz — here's a hint. The name of those battle-scarred islands mentioned above begins with an F. WAYNE WILLE

Contents

A tear-out page of cross-reference tabs for insertion in THE WORLD BOOK ENCYCLOPEDIA appears after page 16.

Contributors

Contributors not listed on these pages are members of THE WORLD BOOK YEAR BOOK editorial staff.

Adachi, Ken, B.A., M.A.; Literary Critic, *The Toronto Star.* [LITERATURE, CANADIAN]

Alexiou, Arthur G., B.S., M.S.; Associate Director, Office of Sea Grant. [OCEAN]

Alridge, Ron, B.A.; Television and Radio Critic, *Chicago Tribune.* [RADIO; TELEVISION]

Anderson, Virginia E., B.A., M.S.W.; Free-Lance Writer. [COMMUNITY ORGANIZATIONS; HANDICAPPED; NATIONAL PTA (NATIONAL CONGRESS OF PARENTS AND TEACHERS); SOCIAL SECURITY; VETERANS; WELFARE; YOUTH ORGANIZATIONS]

Apseloff, Marilyn Fain, B.A., M.A.; Assistant Professor of English, Kent State University. [LITERATURE FOR CHILDREN]

Barber, Peggy, B.A., M.L.S.; Director, Public Information Office, American Library Association. [AMERICAN LIBRARY ASSOCIATION]

Beckwith, David C., A.B., M.S., J.D.; Correspondent, *Time* Magazine. [COURTS AND LAWS; COURTS AND LAWS (Close-Up); CRIME; PRISON; SUPREME COURT OF THE UNITED STATES]

Benson, Barbara N., A.B., M.S., Ph.D.; Associate Professor, Biology, Cedar Crest College. [BOTANY; ZOOLOGY]

Berkwitt, George J., B.S.J.; Chief Editor, *Industrial Distribution Magazine.* [MANUFACTURING]

Biggar, Jeanne C., Ph.D.; Associate Professor of Sociology, University of Virginia. [POPULATION]

Blackadar, Alfred K., A.B., Ph.D.; Professor of Meteorology, The Pennsylvania State University. [WEATHER]

Bradsher, Henry S., A.B., B.J.; Foreign Affairs Analyst. [ASIA and Asian Country Articles]

Brown, Kenneth, Editor, *United Kingdom Press Gazette.* [EUROPE; EUROPE (Close-Up); European Country Articles]

Brown, Lester R., B.S., M.S., M.P.A.; President, Worldwatch Institute. [Special Report: THE COMING CROPLAND CRISIS]

Brown, Merrill, B.A.; New York Financial Correspondent, *The Washington Post.* [COMMUNICATIONS]

Cain, Charles C., III, A.B.; former Automotive Editor, Associated Press. [AUTOMOBILE]

Camper, John, B.A.; Editorial Writer, Chicago *Sun-Times.* [CHICAGO; CITY]

Campion, Owen F., A.B.; Editor, *The Tennessee Register.* [ROMAN CATHOLIC CHURCH]

Carlson, Eric D., M.S., Ph.D.; Senior Astronomer, Adler Planetarium. [ASTRONOMY]

Clancy, Katherine L., B.S., Ph.D.; Associate Professor, Syracuse University. [FOOD]

Clark, Phil, B.A.; Free-Lance Garden Writer and Photographer. [GARDENING]

Cormier, Frank, B.S.J., M.S.J.; former White House Correspondent, Associated Press. [U.S. Government Articles]

Cromie, William J., B.S.; Executive Director, Council for the Advancement of Science Writing. [BUILDING AND CONSTRUCTION; HOUSING; SPACE EXPLORATION]

Cuscaden, Rob, Editor, *Home Improvement Contractor* Magazine. [ARCHITECTURE]

Cviic, Chris, B.A., B.Sc.; Leader Writer and Correspondent, *The Economist.* [Eastern European Country Articles; DEATHS (Close-Up)]

Datre, Donna M., B.A.; Public Information Manager, Toy Manufacturers of America, Inc. [GAMES AND TOYS]

Deffeyes, Kenneth S., M.S.E., Ph.D.; Professor of Geology, Princeton University. [GEOLOGY]

DeFrank, Thomas M., B.A., M.A.; White House Correspondent, *Newsweek* Magazine. [ARMED FORCES]

Dent, Thomas H., Executive Director, The Cat Fanciers' Association, Inc. [CAT]

Dewey, Russell A., B.A., Ph.D.; Assistant Professor of Psychology, Georgia Southern College. [PSYCHOLOGY]

Dixon, Gloria Ricks, A.B.J.; Vice-President, Magazine Publishers Association. [MAGAZINE]

Eaton, William J., B.S.J., M.S.J.; Washington Correspondent, *Los Angeles Times.* [U.S. Political Articles]

Esseks, J. Dixon, A.B., A.M., Ph.D.; Associate Professor, Public Affairs Division, Department of Political Science, Northern Illinois University. [AFRICA and African Country Articles]

Farr, David M. L., D.Phil.; Professor of History and Director, Paterson Centre for International Programs, Carleton University, Ottawa. [CANADA; CANADA (Close-Up); Canadian Province Articles; SCHREYER, EDWARD RICHARD; TRUDEAU, PIERRE ELLIOTT]

Feather, Leonard, Author, Broadcaster, Composer. [MUSIC, POPULAR; RECORDINGS]

Fireman, Ken, B.A.J.; City-County Bureau Chief, *Detroit Free Press.* [DETROIT]

Fisher, Robert W., B.A., M.A.; Supervisory Economist, U.S. Bureau of Labor Statistics. [LABOR]

Francis, Henry G., B.S.; Executive Editor, *Contract Bridge Bulletin,* American Contract Bridge League. [BRIDGE, CONTRACT]

French, Charles E., B.S., A.M., Ph.D.; Director, Institute of Agribusiness, University of Santa Clara. [FARM AND FARMING]

Goldner, Nancy, B.A.; Dance Critic, *The Christian Science Monitor, Dance News.* [DANCING]

Goldstein, Jane, B.A.; Director of Publicity, Los Angeles Turf Club. [HORSE RACING]

Graham, Jarlath J., B.A.; Vice-President, Communications and Editorial Development, Crain Communications, Inc. [ADVERTISING]

Hales, Dianne, B.A., M.S.; Writer, Contributing Editor, *American Health Magazine.* [DRUGS; HEALTH AND DISEASE; HOSPITAL; MEDICINE; MENTAL HEALTH; PUBLIC HEALTH]

Haverstock, Nathan A., A.B.; Director, The Latin American Service. [LATIN AMERICA and Latin American Country Articles; WORLD BOOK SUPPLEMENT: BELIZE]

Hechinger, Fred M., B.A.; President, *The New York Times* Company Foundation, Inc. [EDUCATION]

Huenergard, Celeste, B.A.; Midwest Editor, *Editor & Publisher* Magazine. [NEWSPAPER; PUBLISHING]

Jacobi, Peter P., B.S.J., M.S.J.; Vice-President and Director of Instructional Services, Jack Hilton, Inc. [MUSIC, CLASSICAL]

Johanson, Donald C., B.A., M.A., Ph.D.; Director, Institute of Human Origins. [ANTHROPOLOGY]

Joseph, Lou, B.A.; Senior Science Writer, Hill and Knowlton. [DENTISTRY]

Kaiman, Arnold G., M.A.H.L., D.D.; Rabbi, Congregation Kol Ami. [JEWS AND JUDAISM]

Karr, Albert R., M.S.; Reporter, *The Wall Street Journal.* [TRANSPORTATION and Transportation Articles]

Kind, Joshua B., B.A., Ph.D.; Associate Professor of Art History, Northern Illinois University. [VISUAL ARTS]

Kisor, Henry, B.A., M.S.J.; Book Editor, Chicago *Sun-Times.* [LITERATURE]

Kitchen, Paul, B.A., B.L.S.; Executive Director, Canadian Library Association. [CANADIAN LIBRARY ASSOCIATION]

Knapp, Elaine Stuart, B.A.; Editor, Council of State Governments. [STATE GOVERNMENT]

Koenig, Louis W., B.A., M.A., Ph.D., L.H.D.; Professor of Government, New York University. [CIVIL RIGHTS]

Kolgraf, Ronald, B.A., M.A.; Director of Marketing and Communication, Morgan-Grampian Publishing Company. [MANUFACTURING]

Langdon, Robert, Executive Officer, Pacific Manuscripts Bureau, Australian National University. [PACIFIC ISLANDS]

Larsen, Paul A., P.E., B.S., Ch.E.; Member: American Philatelic Society; Collectors Club of Chicago; Royal Philatelic Society, London. Past President, British Caribbean Philatelic Study Group. [STAMP COLLECTING]

Lawrence, Al, A.B., M.Ed., M.A.; Assistant Director, United States Chess Federation. [CHESS]

Lawrence, Richard, B.E.E.; Washington Correspondent, *The Journal of Commerce.* [INTERNATIONAL TRADE AND FINANCE]

Levy, Emanuel, B.A.; Editor, *Insurance Advocate.* [INSURANCE]

Litsky, Frank, B.S.; Assistant Sports Editor, *The New York Times.* [Sports Articles]

Maki, John M., B.A., M.A., Ph.D.; Professor Emeritus, University of Massachusetts. [JAPAN]

Mangold, Mark A., B.A., M.A., Public Affairs Specialist, U.S. Bureau of the Census. [CENSUS]

Manning, Winton H., A.B., Ph.D.; Senior Vice-President for Development and Research, Educational Testing Service. [Special Report: THE ABC'S OF TESTING]

Martin, Lee, Director of Advertising and Associate Editor, Behn-Miller Publications. [COIN COLLECTING]

Marty, Martin E., Ph.D.; Fairfax M. Cone Distinguished Service Professor, University of Chicago. [PROTESTANTISM; RELIGION]

Mather, Ian, B.A., M.A.; Defense Correspondent, *The Observer.* [GREAT BRITAIN; IRELAND; NORTHERN IRELAND]

Mathews, Thomas G., B.A., M.A., Ph.D.; Secretary-General, Association of Caribbean Universities. [WORLD BOOK SUPPLEMENT: ANGUILLA; ANTIGUA AND BARBUDA; SAINT CHRISTOPHER-NEVIS]

Maugh, Thomas H., II, Ph.D.; Senior Science Writer, *Science.* [BIOCHEMISTRY]

Merina, Victor, A.A., B.A., M.S.; Staff Writer, *Los Angeles Times.* [LOS ANGELES]

Miller, J. D. B., M.Ec., M.A.; Professor of International Relations, Australian National University. [AUSTRALIA]

Moritz, Owen, B.A.; Urban Affairs Editor, *New York Daily News.* [NEW YORK CITY]

Morris, Bernadine, B.A., M.A.; Chief Fashion Critic, *The New York Times.* [FASHION]

Mullen, Frances A., Ph.B., M.A., Ph.D.; Secretary-General Emeritus, International Council of Psychologists. [CHILD WELFARE]

Murray, G. E., B.A., M.A.; Poetry Columnist, Chicago *Sun-Times.* [POETRY]

Newman, Andrew L., A.B., M.A.; Senior Information Officer, U.S. Department of the Interior. [CONSERVATION; ENVIRONMENT; FISHING; FISHING INDUSTRY; FOREST AND FOREST PRODUCTS; HUNTING; INDIAN, AMERICAN; WATER]

Oatis, William N., United Nations Correspondent, Associated Press. [UNITED NATIONS]

Pawelek, Richard, B.A.; Managing Editor, *Senior Scholastic.* [Special Report: THE HIGH COURT: AT THE CENTER OF A STORM AGAIN]

Phillips, Herbert P., A.B., Ph.D.; Professor of Anthropology, University of California at Berkeley. [WORLD BOOK SUPPLEMENT: THAILAND]

Pollock, Steve, B.A.; Features Editor, *Popular Photography.* [PHOTOGRAPHY]

Price, Frederick C., B.S., Ch.E.; Manager of Proposals, Crest Engineering. [CHEMICAL INDUSTRY]

Pyle, Kenneth B., Ph.D.; Professor of History and Director of the School of International Studies, University of Washington. [WORLD BOOK SUPPLEMENT: JAPAN]

Rabb, George B., B.S., M.A., Ph.D.; Director, Chicago Zoological Park. [ZOOS AND AQUARIUMS]

Reed, Pat, B.S.; Assistant Metropolitan Editor, *Houston Chronicle.* [HOUSTON]

Robinson, Michael, Ph.D.; Assistant Professor, History, University of Southern California. [WORLD BOOK SUPPLEMENT: JAPAN]

Rowse, Arthur E., I.A., M.B.A.; President, Consumer News, Inc. [CONSUMER AFFAIRS; SAFETY]

Roy, David, B.A., D.P.A.; Manager, Census Marketing and Promotion, Statistics Canada. [CANADA (Close-Up)]

Rubin, Jay, A.B., Ph.D.; Associate Professor of Japanese Literature, University of Washington. [WORLD BOOK SUPPLEMENT: JAPAN]

Schaffer, Jan, B.S.J., M.S.J.; Business Writer, *The Philadelphia Inquirer.* [PHILADELPHIA]

Schmemann, Alexander, S.T.D., D.D., LL.D., Th.D.; Dean, St. Vladimir's Orthodox Theological Seminary, New York. [EASTERN ORTHODOX CHURCHES]

Schubin, Mark, B.E.Ch.E.; Technological Consultant. [Special Report: THE VIDEO REVOLUTION]

Shand, David A., B.C.A., B.Com.; Director of Research, Parliament of Victoria. [NEW ZEALAND]

Shaw, Robert J., B.S., B.A.; former Editor, *Library Technology Reports,* American Library Association. [LIBRARY]

Shearer, Warren W., A.B., A.M., Ph.D., J.D.; Attorney; former Chairman, Department of Economics, Wabash College. [ECONOMICS]

Solomon, Neil, B.A., M.S., M.D., Ph.D.; Medical Doctor. [Special Report: FOOD, FADS, FAT, AND FITNESS]

Spencer, William, A.B., A.M., Ph.D.; Professor of History Emeritus, Florida State University. [MIDDLE EAST; MIDDLE EAST (Close-Up); Middle Eastern Country Articles; North Africa Country Articles]

Stasio, Marilyn, M.A.; Theater Critic, *New York Post.* [THEATER]

Stauffer, Gary D., B.S., M.S., Ph.D.; Fishery Biologist, National Marine Fisheries Service. [WORLD BOOK SUPPLEMENT: FISHING INDUSTRY]

Swanton, Donald, B.S., M.S., Ph.D., M.B.A.; Chairman, Department of Finance, Roosevelt University. [Finance Articles]

Teeley, Sandra Evans, B.S.J.; Staff Writer, *The Washington Post.* [WASHINGTON, D.C.]

Thompson, Ida, Ph.D.; Associate Research Professor, Center for Coastal and Environmental Studies, Rutgers University. [PALEONTOLOGY]

Tiegel, Eliot, B.A.; Managing Editor, *Billboard Magazine.* [MUSIC, POPULAR; RECORDINGS]

Verbit, Lawrence, Ph.D.; Professor of Chemistry, State University of New York at Binghamton. [CHEMISTRY]

Vesley, Roberta, A.B., M.L.S.; Library Director, American Kennel Club. [DOG]

Voorhies, Barbara, B.S., Ph.D.; Associate Professor, Department of Anthropology, University of California at Santa Barbara. [ARCHAEOLOGY]

Weininger, Jean, A.B., M.S., Ph.D.; Research Fellow, Department of Nutritional Sciences, University of California at Berkeley. [NUTRITION]

White, Thomas Otis, B.S., Ph.D.; University Lecturer in Physics, Cambridge University, Cambridge, England. [PHYSICS]

Windeyer, Charles Kendal, Transport Editor, *The Gazette,* Montreal, Canada. [MONTREAL]

Wolff, Howard, B.S.; Associate Managing Editor, *Electronics.* [ELECTRONICS]

Woods, Michael, B.S.; Science Editor, *The Toledo Blade.* [COAL; ENERGY; MINES AND MINING; PETROLEUM AND GAS; STEEL INDUSTRY]

Woodward, Ralph Lee, Jr., A.B., M.A., Ph.D.; Professor of Latin American History, Tulane University. [Special Report: WHAT WENT WRONG IN CENTRAL AMERICA?]

Wuntch, Philip, B.A.; Film Critic, *The Dallas Morning News.* [MOTION PICTURES]

The Year in Brief

1977
1978
1979
1980
1981
1982

A short essay captures the spirit of 1982, and a month-by-month listing highlights some of the year's significant events.

See November 10, page 22.

The Year in Brief

A review of some of the major trends and events that touched many of our lives during 1982

Worldwide recession and armed conflict dominated the news in 1982. Government leaders tried a variety of programs to lift their nations out of recession, but none could be judged a brilliant success. On the other hand, at least three military operations were highly successful.

A massive Israeli attack on forces of the Palestine Liberation Organization (PLO) in Lebanon in June erased the PLO threat against Israel's northern border and may have destroyed the Arab dream of overcoming Israel by force. However, the drive ended in a nightmare of death as Lebanese militiamen slaughtered Palestinian civilians, including women and children. (For more information on the Israeli-PLO conflict, see the MIDDLE EAST article in The Year on File, beginning on page 174. The Year on File section describes events according to the country, field, or general subject area in which they occur. The Chronology, which starts on page 12, lists major events month by month.)

President Reagan

Great Britain won a quick military victory after an old dispute with Argentina over tiny islands in the South Atlantic Ocean turned violent in April. Argentine troops overwhelmed a small contingent of British marines defending the Falkland Islands, a British dependency. Great Britain dispatched a huge task force to the Falklands and recaptured the islands after heavy fighting in June.

Poland's armed conflict against its own people appeared to reach a successful, repressive conclusion in 1982. The military government quelled sporadic disturbances in the early months, arrested more than 4,000 demonstrators during a nationwide protest in August, and declared the independent labor union Solidarity illegal in October. After a November call for demonstrations failed, the government felt secure enough to release Lech Walesa, the head of Solidarity, who had been detained since December 1981.

Other armed conflicts dragged on. Iraq, which had invaded Iran in 1980, suffered setbacks and withdrew its troops. Iran invaded Iraq but failed to win a decisive battle. Russian and Afghan troops continued to pursue Afghan rebels, and Vietnamese soldiers continued to fight Cambodian guerrillas along the Cambodia-Thailand border.

Leftist guerrillas in El Salvador received a sharp setback in March elections for a national constituent assembly as voters turned out in unexpectedly large numbers. El Salvador's election marked a turn away from rule by civilian-military junta. Other Latin American nations made similar moves. In January, Honduras got its first civilian president since 1972, and Bolivia ended military rule in October.

The recession forced some governments to take drastic action and put other governments out of power. Belgium and France adopted harsh austerity measures. Denmark installed a center-right government and adopted an austerity program. West Germany ousted Chancellor Helmut Schmidt and replaced him with the more conservative Helmut Kohl, who promised to invest in the economy while curbing debt by reducing social programs. Spain elected a Socialist government that promised to create 800,000 jobs.

Brezhnev and Andropov

The Netherlands' center-left government collapsed over a plan to cut federal spending and gave way to a center-right coalition. A stand-off over government spending toppled Italy's government.

Mexico faced financial ruin in 1982. The global recession and a worldwide drop in oil prices put Mexico's peso under pressure. As the peso began to buckle, the government nationalized the banks and implemented foreign exchange controls.

In the United States, rising unemployment, a skyrocketing deficit, and a Republican defeat in congressional elections put pressure on President Ronald Reagan to modify his economic program. On the international political scene, the United States failed in an effort to enforce economic sanctions against Russia for that country's role in Poland's imposition of martial law in December 1981. The United States slapped an embargo on equipment for a gas pipeline that Russia was building from Siberia to Central Europe. However, U.S. allies in Western Europe refused to cancel contracts that they had signed to supply parts for the pipeline. The United States ended the ban in November.

The two superpowers — the Soviet Union and the United States — jousted verbally about disarmament as a nuclear-freeze movement gathered momentum in the West. And a new combatant entered the fray: Yuri V. Andropov, successor to Russian leader Leonid I. Brezhnev, who died in November.

The year 1982 also brought the birth of Prince William of Wales and the death of Princess Grace of Monaco; the launching of a Constitution in Canada and the sinking of the Equal Rights Amendment in the United States; the inspiring flights of the space shuttle orbiter *Columbia* and the sickening crash of a jetliner into a Potomac River bridge in Washington, D.C.; an exciting World Cup soccer tournament and a greatly abbreviated U.S. professional football season; an intruder in a royal bedchamber and an extraterrestrial visitor to our small planet (on film, at least).

In 1982, the lives of many of the inhabitants of our small planet took a turn for the worse as the effects of armed conflict and recession touched them. Nevertheless, the world as a whole remained at peace, and the economy seemed capable of a recovery that would make life better in 1983.

Jay Myers

Jan. 13

Jan. 26

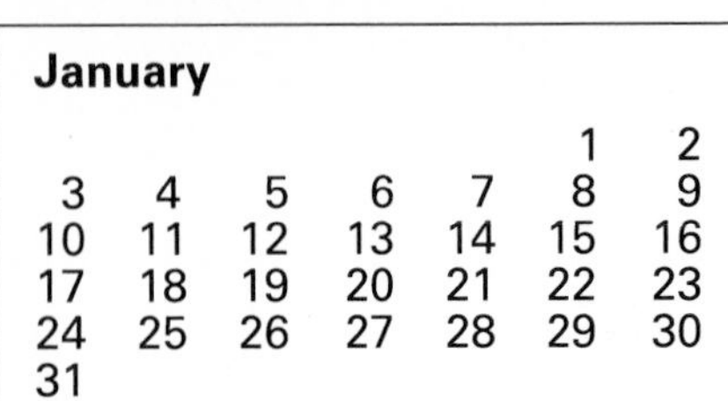

January

					1	2
3	4	5	6	7	8	9
10	11	12	13	14	15	16
17	18	19	20	21	22	23
24	25	26	27	28	29	30
31						

4 **Richard V. Allen resigns** as President Ronald Reagan's national security adviser and is replaced by William P. Clark.

5 **An Arkansas** law requiring equal time in public schools for so-called creation science when the theory of evolution is taught is overturned by a federal court.

8 **American Telephone & Telegraph Company** agrees to divest itself of 22 telephone companies.

9-17 **Frigid blast** of arctic air brings record low temperatures to the United States.

10 **The late Liu Shao-chi (Liu Shaoqi),** China's discredited former chief of state, is restored to favor as government authorities allow his memoirs to go on sale in Peking (Beijing).

11 **Reagan Administration announces** that it will continue to help Taiwan produce F-5E fighter planes, but will not sell more advanced models. China issues a strong protest.

12 **Canada creates** a Ministry of State for Economic Development, reorganizes other federal agencies.

13 **Air Florida jetliner** crashes into a Potomac River bridge after taking off from Washington National Airport. Seventy-eight people die as a result of the crash.

16 **The Vatican and Great Britain** re-establish full diplomatic relations, ending a rift that occurred when King Henry VIII broke with Roman Catholicism in 1532.

17-18 **Finnish voters elect** acting president Mauno H. Koivisto president, succeeding Urho Kekkonen, who resigned in October 1981.

20 **Montreal's 6,800** public transit workers vote to end an illegal six-day strike.

23 **France agrees** to buy 282.5 billion cubic feet (8 billion cubic meters) of natural gas from Russia every year for 25 years.

24 **San Francisco 49ers win** football's Super Bowl XVI, defeating the Cincinnati Bengals, 26-21.

25 **Mikhail A. Suslov,** 79, Russia's chief ideologist, dies.

26 **President Reagan proposes** a "new federalism" — a transfer of social programs to the states — in his State of the Union message.

27 **Roberto Suazo Córdova,** a civilian, is installed as president of Honduras, ending nine years of military rule.

28 **Italian antiterrorist forces** rescue U.S. Brigadier General James L. Dozier, held hostage by the leftist Red Brigades in Padua, Italy.

President Reagan certifies to the Congress of the United States that El Salvador is making progress in human rights.

29 ***The Bulletin*** ceases publication in Philadelphia after 134 years.

Feb. 27

Feb. 24

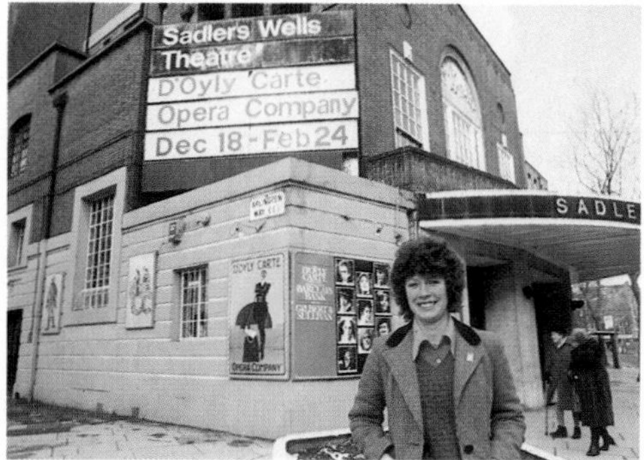

Feb. 27

February

	1	2	3	4	5	6
7	8	9	10	11	12	13
14	15	16	17	18	19	20
21	22	23	24	25	26	27
28						

2 **Belgium's Senate grants** the government power to enact reforms by decree to deal with the country's economic crisis.

3 **Russia calls for a reduction** in medium-range nuclear arms in Europe.

4 **Reagan announces a plan** for removing all nuclear missiles from Europe.

5 **Great Britain imposes** economic sanctions against Poland and Russia in a protest against martial law in Poland.

Bolivia devalues the peso, announces other measures to alleviate its economic problems.

Laker Airways declares bankruptcy. The British company had inaugurated cut-rate transatlantic passenger service in 1977.

6 **Reagan Administration unveils** a $757.6-billion federal budget for fiscal year 1983.

7 **Costa Rican voters elect** Luis Alberto Monge Alvarez president.

10 **Chan Sy becomes premier** of Cambodia (Kampuchea), succeeding Pen Sovan.

11 **France nationalizes** five groups of major industries and 39 banks.

12-13 **Polish police crackdown** turns up 145,000 violators of martial law rules.

12-19 **Pope John Paul II visits** West Africa in his first trip abroad since the May 1981 attempt on his life.

15 **Offshore oil rig Ocean Ranger sinks** about 175 nautical miles off Newfoundland, killing 84 crew members.

17 **Prime Minister Robert Mugabe** dismisses Joshua Nkomo from the Cabinet of Zimbabwe.

Mexico withdraws support of peso in international exchange markets. By February 24, the peso's value plunges 41 per cent against the U.S. dollar.

22 **Syria admits** for the first time that intense fighting is taking place against the rebel Muslim Brotherhood in the city of Hama.

22-24 **Belgium, Japan, and Canada** announce sanctions against Poland and Russia.

23 **Greenlanders vote** to withdraw from the European Community (EC or Common Market).

24 **Wayne Gretzky** of the Edmonton Oilers breaks the National Hockey League season-scoring record of 76 goals. By end of the season, he has set a new mark of 92 goals.

Reagan proposes a $996-million aid plan for Caribbean and Central American nations for fiscal 1982.

27 **Wayne B. Williams is convicted** of murdering two of 28 young blacks killed during a two-year period in Atlanta, Ga.

The D'Oyly Carte Opera Company goes out of business after presenting Gilbert and Sullivan operettas for more than 100 years.

28 **Auto workers** at Ford Motor Company approve major concessions in wages and benefits.

March 9

March 23

March 28

March 29

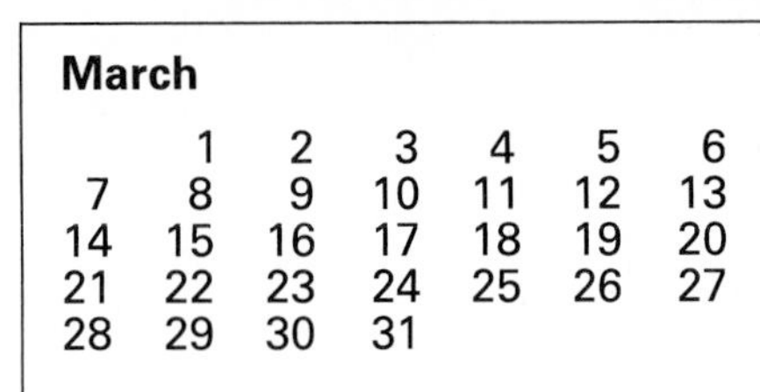

March

	1	2	3	4	5	6
7	8	9	10	11	12	13
14	15	16	17	18	19	20
21	22	23	24	25	26	27
28	29	30	31			

1-5 **Two unmanned Russian space probes** land on Venus and radio information to Earth.

4 **Bertha Wilson** becomes the first woman appointed to Canada's Supreme Court.

5 **Comedian John Belushi,** 33, dies of a drug overdose.

8 **China approves** sweeping changes in its central bureaucracy, cutting its ministerial staff from 49,000 people to 32,000.

The Dow Jones industrial average dips to 795.47, its lowest level since April 23, 1980.

9 **Charles J. Haughey is elected** prime minister of Ireland, succeeding Garret FitzGerald.

United States releases photographs of military build-up in Nicaragua.

11 **Senator Harrison A. Williams, Jr.** (D., N.J.), resigns as the Senate prepares to vote on expelling him for his conduct during the Abscam probe.

13-20 **Rivers overflow** in Michigan, Ohio, and Indiana, causing those states' worst floods since 1913.

14 **Mexico is authorized by the** Reagan Administration to make proposals for renormalizing U.S. relations with Cuba and Nicaragua.

16 **Russia announces** a halt in its deployment of new nuclear missiles in Europe.

20 **An oil-production cut** of 700,000 barrels per day is announced by the Organization of Petroleum Exporting Countries (OPEC).

22 **U.S. Department of State** releases a report charging that Russia and its allies have been waging chemical warfare in Afghanistan and Southeast Asia.

22-30 **U.S. space shuttle *Columbia*** flies its third mission.

23 **Guatemalan army officers** oust President Fernando Romeo Lucas García and install a three-man junta in his place.

24 **General H. M. Ershad** removes Bangladesh's President Abdus Sattar from office, appoints himself martial law head.

Russia is willing to resume border talks with China, declares Soviet leader Leonid I. Brezhnev.

28 **Five right wing parties** win a majority in national elections to El Salvador's constituent assembly.

29 ***Chariots of Fire,*** a British film about two Olympic athletes, wins Oscar as the best picture. Best actor and actress awards go to Henry Fonda and Katharine Hepburn, shown above.

The University of North Carolina wins the championship of college basketball with a 63-62 score against Georgetown University.

31 **Russia has a "definite margin** of superiority" over the United States in nuclear weapons, President Reagan declares.

April 2

April 17

April

				1	2	3
4	5	6	7	8	9	10
11	12	13	14	15	16	17
18	19	20	21	22	23	24
25	26	27	28	29	30	

1-10 **Storm sweeps** across the United States, killing 64 people and injuring hundreds.

2 **Argentina seizes** the Falkland Islands, a British dependency in the South Atlantic Ocean, and the nearby South Georgia Island and South Sandwich Islands.

4-5 **Suriname's President** and Prime Minister Henk R. Chin A Sen resigns. The country's armed forces take control of the government.

5 **British assault force** puts to sea for the Falkland Islands.

14 **The EC bans** imports from Argentina for one month, supporting Great Britain in the Falkland Islands conflict.

17 **New Canadian Constitution** is proclaimed by Queen Elizabeth II, making Canada completely independent of Great Britain.

19 **Two Australian Cabinet ministers** resign in a customs scandal.

21 **Israeli planes attack** Palestinian strongholds in Lebanon after an Israeli soldier is killed by a land mine in Lebanon. The violence ends a nine-month-long cease-fire.

April 25

22 **Nuclear freeze is rejected** by West Germany's ruling Social Democratic Party at a national congress.

24 **Vietnam reshuffles** its Cabinet, apparently because of economic problems.

25 **Israel completes its withdrawal** from the Sinai Peninsula as pledged in the Egyptian-Israeli peace treaty of 1979. Israelis opposed to the withdrawal were forcibly removed from buildings in the Sinai, as shown above.

Great Britain recaptures South Georgia Island.

John Cardinal Cody, 75, archbishop of Chicago, dies of congestive heart failure.

26 **Progressive Conservatives** win by a landslide in Saskatchewan's general elections, ending 11 years of rule by the New Democrats.

27 **China proposes** a new constitution that would radically alter the structure of the national government.

28 **Poland frees** 1,000 prisoners and announces plan to lift some martial law restrictions on May 1.

29 **El Salvador's constituent assembly** elects Alvaro Magaña Borja, a moderate conservative, as provisional president.

30 **Treaty on the use of the seas** is approved by the United Nations (UN) Law of the Sea Conference, ending eight years of bargaining. The United States votes against the treaty.

The Alsands project to recover oil from tar sands in Alberta is doomed by the withdrawal of the last two private investors.

May 1

May 7-12

May 13

May

						1
2	3	4	5	6	7	8
9	10	11	12	13	14	15
16	17	18	19	20	21	22
23	24	25	26	27	28	29
30	31					

1 **World's Fair opens** in Knoxville, Tenn. Theme is "Energy Turns the World."

4 **Poland reinstates** harsh security measures in several cities after three days of antigovernment demonstrations.

7-12 **Evangelist Billy Graham** is in Moscow to attend a religious leaders conference on nuclear disarmament. He says he saw no evidence of religious repression.

9 **President Reagan proposes** that the United States and Russia reduce the number of their nuclear missile warheads by one-third.

12 **South Africa unveils** a plan that would give voting rights to citizens of Asian and Colored, or mixed-race, descent, but not to blacks.

13 **Braniff International Corporation,** the eighth largest U.S. airline, files for bankruptcy.

14 **Australia's Arbitration Commission** rejects a union claim for a wage increase for 1.7 million workers that would compensate for inflation.
Abscam conviction of former Representative Richard Kelly (R., Fla.) is upset by a federal judge.

16 **Yugoslavia's Federal Assembly** elects Milka Planinc prime minister, the first woman to hold the post.
New York Islanders win professional hockey's Stanley Cup for the third consecutive year, defeating Vancouver.
Voters in the Dominican Republic elect Salvador Jorge Blanco president.

18 **Russia's Brezhnev** terms Reagan's arms proposals "absolutely one-sided," calls for an immediate nuclear freeze.
South Korean evangelist Sun Myung Moon is found guilty of tax evasion by a U.S. federal court.

21 **Great Britain invades** East Falkland Island.
Eleven of the 22 ministers in South Korea's Cabinet quit in the wake of a loan scandal.
California's parole board revokes a 1984 parole date scheduled for Sirhan B. Sirhan, who assassinated Robert F. Kennedy in 1968.
Constantin Dascalescu becomes Romania's prime minister, replacing Ilie Verdet.

24 **Yuri V. Andropov,** head of Russia's intelligence and security agency and mentioned as a possible successor to Brezhnev, is named to the secretariat of the Communist Party Central Committee.
Iran recaptures the city of Khorramshahr, which Iraq has held since October 1980. Iraqi troops fall back to the border.

30 **Spain becomes** the 16th member of the North Atlantic Treaty Organization (NATO).
Gordon Johncock wins the Indianapolis 500 auto race by 16-hundredths of a second, the closest finish ever.
Colombian voters elect Belisario Betancur president.

Here are your

1983 Year Book Cross-Reference Tabs

For insertion in your World Book

Each year, The World Book Year Book adds a valuable dimension to your World Book set. The Cross-Reference Tab System is designed especially to help youngsters and parents alike *link* The Year Book's new and revised World Book articles, its Special Reports, and its Close-Ups to the related World Book articles they update.

How to Use These Tabs

First, remove this page from The Year Book. Begin with the bottom Tab, "THAILAND."

Turn to the *T Volume* of your World Book set and find the first page of the "THAILAND" article. Moisten the gummed Tab and affix it to that page.

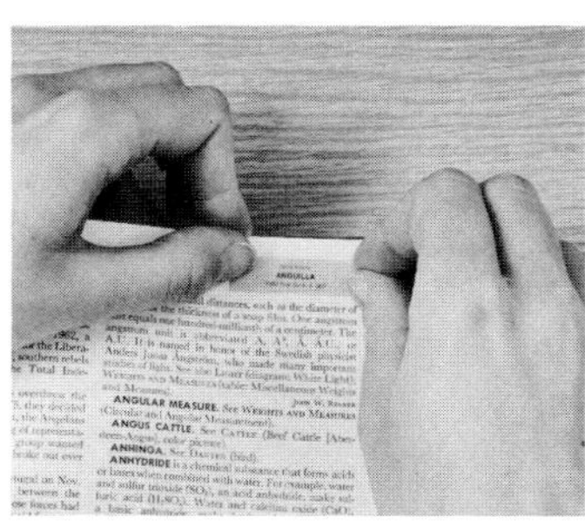

There is no "ANGUILLA" article in your World Book. So for the New Article on "ANGUILLA," affix the first Tab in the *A Volume* where it should appear in its alphabetical sequence.

New Article
ANGUILLA
1983 Year Book, p. 569

New Article
ANTIGUA AND BARBUDA
1983 Year Book, p. 569

New Article
BELIZE
1983 Year Book, p. 570

Year Book Close-Up
BREZHNEV, LEONID ILYICH
1983 Year Book (Deaths)

Year Book Close-Up
CANADA
1983 Year on File (Canada)

Year Book Close-Up
CANADA, GOVERNMENT OF
1983 Year on File (Canada)

Special Section
CENSUS
1983 Year on File (Canada)

Special Report
DIET
1983 Year Book, p. 142

New Article
FISHING INDUSTRY
1983 Year Book, p. 572

Year Book Close-Up
INSANITY
1983 Year on File (Courts and Laws)

New Article
JAPAN
1983 Year Book, p. 534

Year Book Close-Up
LEBANON
1983 Year Book (Middle East)

Year Book Close-Up
NORTH ATLANTIC TREATY ORG.
1983 Year Book (Europe)

Special Report
NUTRITION
1983 Year Book, p. 142

New Article
SAINT CHRISTOPHER-NEVIS
1983 Year Book, p. 571

Special Report
SOIL
1983 Year Book, p. 126

Special Report
SUPREME COURT OF THE U.S.
1983 Year Book, p. 56

Special Report
TELEVISION
1983 Year Book, p. 106

Special Report
TESTING
1983 Year Book, p. 90

New Article
THAILAND
1983 Year Book, p. 562

June 2

June 21

June 6

June 25

June

		1	2	3	4	5
6	7	8	9	10	11	12
13	14	15	16	17	18	19
20	21	22	23	24	25	26
27	28	29	30			

2 **Pope John Paul II** ends a six-day trip to Great Britain. He is the first pope to visit Britain.

4-6 **Economic summit meeting** in Versailles, France, is attended by leaders of France, Canada, Great Britain, Italy, Japan, the United States, and West Germany.

6 **Israel invades Lebanon** with the stated goal of driving the forces of the Palestine Liberation Organization (PLO) back 25 miles (40 kilometers). The UN Security Council demands that Israel withdraw its troops, but Israel rejects the demand.

7 **The UN opens** a special session on disarmament.

8 **Los Angeles Lakers** win the National Basketball Association championship, defeating Philadelphia, four games to two.

9 **José Efraín Ríos-Montt** dissolves Guatemala's ruling junta and names himself president.

11 **Heavyweight boxing champion** Larry Holmes knocks out Gerry Cooney.

12 **Some 750,000 people** take part in a peace and disarmament rally in New York City.

13 **King Khalid of Saudi Arabia** dies of a heart attack. His half-brother, Fahd Ibn Abdulaziz al-Saud, succeeds him.

14 **Argentine troops surrender** in the Falklands.
Israeli troops encircle Beirut, trapping PLO leaders.

15 **Russia pledges** not to be the first to use nuclear weapons in a future conflict.

17 **Leopoldo Fortunato Galtieri** resigns as president of Argentina.

18 **Reagan widens a ban** on sales of U.S. oil and gas equipment to Russia, which is building a gas pipeline from Siberia to Central Europe. Ban now includes equipment made by foreign subsidiaries and licensees of U.S. firms.
U.S. Senate approves renewal of the 1965 Voting Rights Act.

21 **A son is born** to the Prince and Princess of Wales.
John W. Hinckley, Jr., is found not guilty by reason of insanity on all charges of shooting President Reagan and three others in March 1981.

22 **New Zealand announces** a 12-month freeze on prices and wages.
Reynaldo Benito Bignone is appointed president of Argentina by the military government. He takes office on July 1.

22-23 **Compromise budget** of $769.82 billion, with a $103.9-billion deficit, for fiscal year 1983 is approved by Congress.

25 **U.S. Secretary of State** Alexander M. Haig, Jr., shown above, resigns. Reagan names George P. Shultz to succeed him.

29 **Strategic arms** reduction talks (START) between the United States and Russia begin in Geneva, Switzerland.

July 11

July 4

July

				1	2	3
4	5	6	7	8	9	10
11	12	13	14	15	16	17
18	19	20	21	22	23	24
25	26	27	28	29	30	31

1 **A mass wedding** by the Unification Church in New York City's Madison Square Garden joins more than 2,000 couples.

Starch blocker diet pills are declared to be "unapproved new drugs" by the U.S. Food and Drug Administration and are ordered off the market.

2 **Child pornography** is not automatically entitled to First Amendment safeguards, the U.S. Supreme Court rules.

3-4 **Martina Navratilova and Jimmy Connors** win Wimbledon tennis championships.

4 **Mexican voters elect** Miguel de la Madrid Hurtado president.

Antonio Guzmán Fernández, president of the Dominican Republic, dies of a self-inflicted gunshot wound. Vice-President Jacobo Majluta Azar succeeds him.

U.S. space shuttle *Columbia* completes the last of four scheduled test flights.

9 **An intruder** breaks into Great Britain's Buckingham Palace and enters the bedroom of Queen Elizabeth II.

A Pan American World Airways jetliner crashes after taking off from New Orleans International Airport, killing 153 people.

10 **A 30-day box-office record** of $102.6 million is set by the motion picture *E.T.: The Extra-Terrestrial.*

11 **Italy wins** soccer's World Cup, defeating West Germany, 3-1.

12 **Debate** on a proposed constitutional amendment requiring a balanced federal budget begins in the U.S. Senate.

Peru places three provinces in a state of emergency following violence by leftist guerrillas.

Australia announces a record current account deficit of $9.3 billion for the year ending on June 30, 1982.

13 **Iran invades Iraq** for the first time in their 22-month conflict.

15 **Bolivia's President** Celso Torrelio Villa resigns. Guido Vildoso Calderón succeeds him six days later.

20 **IRA terrorist** bombs explode in two London parks, killing 11 soldiers and wounding 59 soldiers and civilians.

22 **France orders** French licensees of U.S. firms to honor all contracts for the Siberian gas pipeline.

30 **Panama's President** Aristides Royo resigns and Vice-President Ricardo de la Espriella, Jr., succeeds him.

William P. Tavoulareas, president of Mobil Oil Corporation, wins a $2-million libel suit against *The Washington Post.*

31 **Yugoslavia imposes** a six-month freeze on prices.

Aug. 9

Aug. 31

Aug. 21

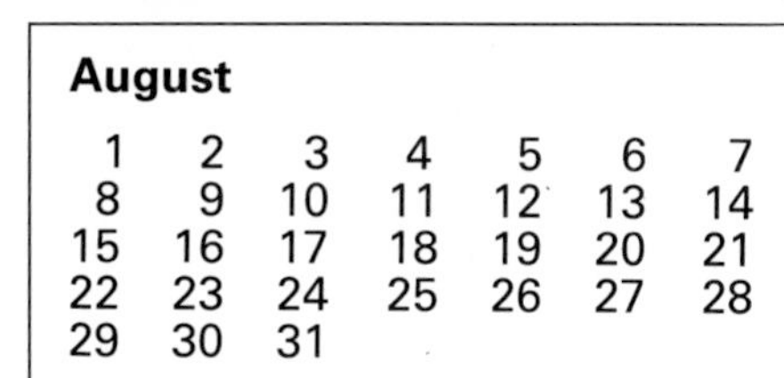

August

1	2	3	4	5	6	7
8	9	10	11	12	13	14
15	16	17	18	19	20	21
22	23	24	25	26	27	28
29	30	31				

1 **Attempted coup d'état** by members of Kenya's air force fails.

1-4 **China and South Korea** protest revisions in Japanese history texts that, they charge, gloss over Japanese military aggression in the 1930s and 1940s.

2 **Michael Somare succeeds** Julius Chan as prime minister of Papua New Guinea following parliamentary elections.

4 **Israeli troops** push into West Beirut.

5 **Nuclear freeze resolution** is rejected by the U.S. House of Representatives.

5-13 **The Mexican peso's value** in money markets drops from 49 to 85 pesos to U.S. $1.

6 **Italy liquidates** the scandal-ridden Banco Ambrosiano S.p.A. of Milan.

9 **A kosher restaurant** in a Jewish neighborhood in Paris is bombed, killing six people and wounding 22.

12 **Portugal's Parliament** dissolves the Council of the Revolution, which had broad veto power over legislation.

Mexico temporarily suspends all foreign exchange operations, sets a rate of 69.50 pesos to U.S. $1 for all foreign currency accounts.

Israeli jets bomb West Beirut for 11 hours. President Reagan says that the attacks caused "needless destruction and bloodshed."

13-20 **Major U.S. banks** lower their prime interest rate from 15 to 13.5 per cent.

17 **The United States and China** issue a communiqué in which the U.S. promises to reduce arms sales to Taiwan.

19 **A tax increase** of $98.3 billion is approved by Congress.

Svetlana Savtiskaya, a Russian test pilot, becomes the second woman to go into space.

20 **Russia agrees to buy grain** from the United States for another year.

21 **PLO guerrillas** begin an evacuation of Beirut.

25 **Representative Frederick W. Richmond** (D., N.Y.) pleads guilty of tax evasion and resigns from Congress.

26 **The United States imposes sanctions** on two French companies for sending equipment to Russia for the Siberian gas pipeline.

Manville Corporation files for bankruptcy to gain relief from health lawsuits filed against it. The company produces asbestos, which has been linked to lung cancer.

Canada's provincial premiers reject a federal program to limit price and wage increases to 6 per cent in 1982 and 5 per cent in 1983.

29 **Actress Ingrid Bergman,** 67, winner of three Academy Awards, dies of cancer.

31 **Riot police clash** with demonstrators in major Polish cities, arrest 4,050. Police fire on demonstrators in Lubin, killing at least five.

Sept. 16-18

September

			1	2	3	4
5	6	7	8	9	10	11
12	13	14	15	16	17	18
19	20	21	22	23	24	25
26	27	28	29	30		

1 **"Self-government** by the Palestinians of the West Bank and Gaza in association with Jordan" is advocated by President Reagan.
Mexico nationalizes private banks. The value of the peso falls to 140 pesos to U.S. $1 in money markets.

9 **Mideast peace plan** proposed by the Arab League calls for the UN to guarantee peace "among all the states of that region, including the independent Palestinian state."
Swiss police storm the Polish Embassy in Bern, capturing four men who held the building for three days.

9-10 **Congress overrides** President Reagan's veto of a $14.1-billion appropriations bill.

10 **Poul Schlüter** becomes Denmark's prime minister, heading a center-right coalition. Schlüter succeeds Anker Henrik Jorgensen, who resigned on September 3.
***Ariane,* a rocket** built by several European companies, plunges into the Atlantic Ocean 14 minutes into its first operational mission.

12 **Hua Kuo-feng** (Hua Guofeng), China's former premier and Communist Party chairman, is dropped from the ruling Politburo.

13 **Raymond J. Donovan,** U.S. secretary of labor, is cleared by a special federal prosecutor of alleged illegal payoffs and ties to organized crime.

14 **Princess Grace of Monaco,** former screen actress Grace Kelly, dies following an automobile accident in France.
A bomb blast in East Beirut kills Lebanon's President-elect Bashir Gemayel. He is succeeded by his brother Amin on September 21.

15 **Israeli troops push** into West Beirut. The United States demands a pullback the next day.
An Iranian firing squad executes the nation's former foreign minister, Sadegh Ghotbzadeh.
Pope John Paul II grants an audience to PLO leader Yasir Arafat.

16-18 **Christian militiamen massacre** hundreds of Palestinian men, women, and children in refugee camps in West Beirut.

21 **National Football League (NFL) players** strike, two weeks into the season, as negotiations for a basic labor agreement fail.

22 **Reagan signs** special legislation that forces 26,000 striking locomotive engineers back to work.

29-30 **Cyanide-laced capsules** of Extra-Strength Tylenol, a pain reliever, kill seven people in the Chicago area.

30 **Canada's Cabinet** is reshuffled, with 13 ministers changing posts.
12th Commonwealth Games open in Brisbane, Australia, and run until October 9.

Oct. 28

Oct. 1

Oct. 20

October

					1	2
3	4	5	6	7	8	9
10	11	12	13	14	15	16
17	18	19	20	21	22	23
24	25	26	27	28	29	30
31						

1 **Epcot Center,** Walt Disney Productions' $800-million theme park, opens in Lake Buena Vista, Fla.

Helmut Kohl is elected chancellor of West Germany in a vote of the *Bundestag* (parliament) that simultaneously ousts Chancellor Helmut Schmidt.

A proposed constitutional amendment requiring a balanced federal budget is defeated in the U.S. House of Representatives.

5-21 **China and Russia** hold their first high-level talks in almost three years.

7 **Olof Palme is sworn in** as prime minister of Sweden following a victory by his Social Democratic Party in September elections.

7-12 **The prime rate** of major U.S. banks is cut from 13.5 to 12 per cent.

8 **Poland outlaws** the independent labor union Solidarity.

10 **Hernán Siles Zuazo** becomes president of Bolivia as the nation returns to civilian rule.

15 **Halley's Comet** is sighted for the first time since 1911.

16 **U.S. warns** that it would withdraw from any UN organization, including the General Assembly, that voted to exclude Israel.

19 **Automobile executive** John Z. De Lorean is arrested in Los Angeles and charged with possession of cocaine and conspiracy to distribute it.

20 **The St. Louis Cardinals** win the World Series, defeating the Milwaukee Brewers, four games to three. Cardinal catcher Darrell Porter, shown above, is named series Most Valuable Player.

21 **Steel-export agreement** limits shipment of steel from nations of the European Community to the United States.

Discovery of a huge oil field off California's coast is announced by two U.S. petroleum companies.

26 **New Polish law** calls for forced labor for "social parasites" who cannot prove they have gainful employment.

27 **China announces** that its population is 1,008,175,288, after the largest census in history.

United States threatens "to push the world into the flames of nuclear war," Brezhnev tells Russian military leaders.

28 **Spain's Socialists,** led by Felipe González Márquez, shown above, win a parliamentary majority in general elections, ending 40 years as an opposition party, much of that time an illegal one.

29 **The sale of synthetic human insulin** for human use is approved by the U.S. Food and Drug Administration. This is the first substance made by gene-splicing techniques to be approved.

Nov. 10

Nov. 13

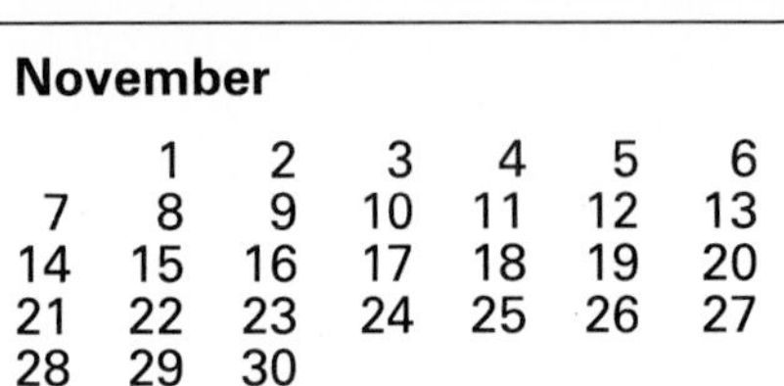

November

	1	2	3	4	5	6
7	8	9	10	11	12	13
14	15	16	17	18	19	20
21	22	23	24	25	26	27
28	29	30				

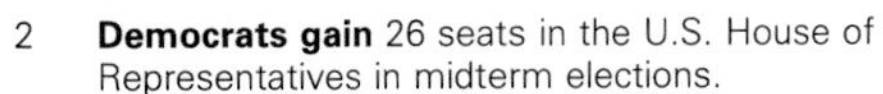

2 **Democrats gain** 26 seats in the U.S. House of Representatives in midterm elections.

2? **A tunnel blast** in Afghanistan kills hundreds of Russian soldiers and Afghan civilians.

3 **The Dow Jones industrial average** gains a record 43.41 points and reaches its highest closing in history — 1,065.49.

4 **Ruud Lubbers takes the oath** as prime minister of the Netherlands. He succeeds Andreas A. M. van Agt, who resigned.
A single-day record for volume of stock trading is set as 149.35 million shares change hands on the New York Stock Exchange.

5 **U.S. Social Security** retirement fund borrows money for the first time.
United Auto Workers strike at six Ontario plants of Chrysler Canada Limited.

6 **Cameroon's President** Ahmadou Ahidjo, who led the nation to independence in 1960, turns the presidency over to Prime Minister Paul Biya.

7 **Turkish voters approve** a new Constitution.

10 **Russian leader** Leonid Ilich Brezhnev, 75, dies of a heart attack. Following a four-day period of national mourning, his funeral is held on November 15, shown above.
New Zealand announces an agreement with Australia to phase out almost all tariffs and duties between the two countries.
Geoffrey Arthur Prime, who had worked for Great Britain's electronic intelligence agency, pleads guilty to charge of spying for Russia.

11-16 ***Columbia* space shuttle** performs its first operational mission, including the deployment of two communications satellites.

12 **Yuri V. Andropov** succeeds Brezhnev in the Soviet Union's most powerful post — general secretary of the Central Committee of the Communist Party.

13 **Reagan lifts sanctions** aimed at Russia's gas pipeline project, citing "an agreement with our allies for stronger and more effective measures."
Vietnam Veterans Memorial is dedicated in Washington, D.C.

14 **Lech Walesa,** former head of Poland's outlawed Solidarity labor union, returns home after 11 months of internment.

15 **U.S. draft registration law** is invalid, a federal district judge rules in Los Angeles.

16 **NFL players' strike ends.** Games resume on November 21.

19 **Wu Xueqian** replaces China's Foreign Minister Huang Hua, and Zhang Aiping replaces Defense Minister Geng Biao.

22 **A dense-pack installation** of 100 MX intercontinental nuclear missiles in Wyoming is proposed by President Reagan.

26 **Yasuhiro Nakasone** becomes prime minister of Japan.

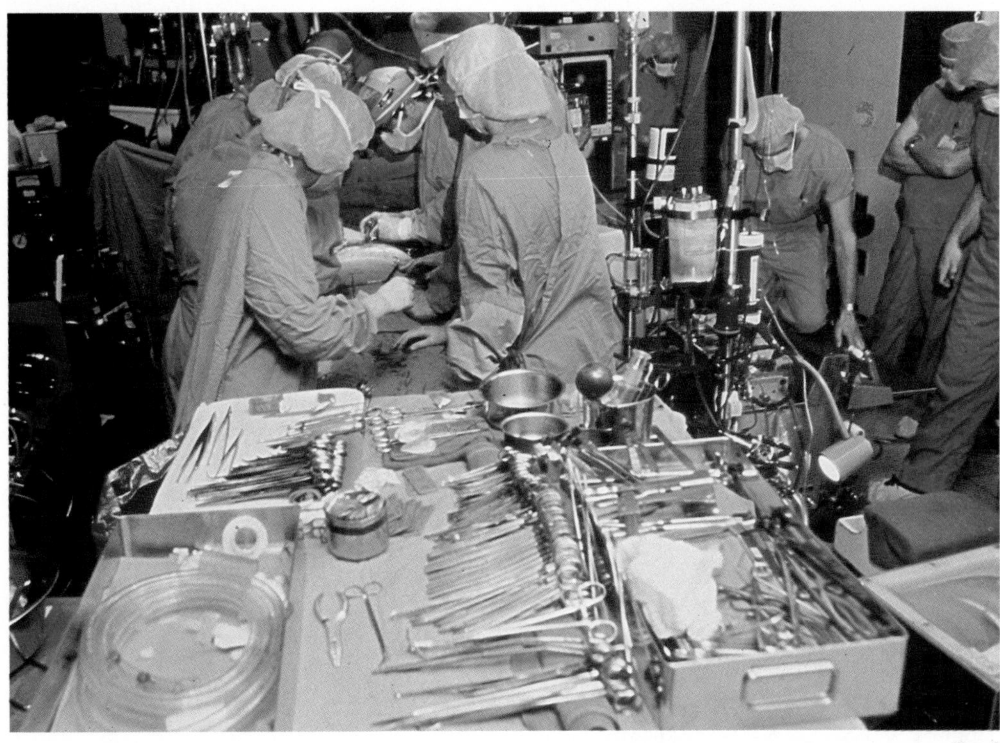

Dec. 2

December

			1	2	3	4
5	6	7	8	9	10	11
12	13	14	15	16	17	18
19	20	21	22	23	24	25
26	27	28	29	30	31	

1 **Senator Edward M. Kennedy** (D., Mass.) says he will not run for President in 1984.
Amintore Fanfani takes office as prime minister of Italy, succeeding Giovanni Spadolini, who resigned on November 13.

2 **A permanent artificial heart** is implanted inside the chest of a 61-year-old man in Salt Lake City, Utah, in the first such operation in history.

3 **U.S. unemployment rate** reached 10.8 per cent in November, the U.S. Department of Labor announces. The rate is the highest since 1940.

4 **Spain devalues** its peseta by 8 per cent.
China's new Constitution is ratified by the National Party Congress.

6 **A bomb explodes** in a disco and bar in Ballykelly, Northern Ireland, killing 17 people, including 11 British soldiers.

7 **A murderer is executed** in Huntsville, Tex., by injection of anesthetics, the first such execution in U.S. history.

8 **A man threatens** to blow up the Washington Monument in Washington, D.C., unless there is "a national dialogue on the nuclear weapons question." He is killed by police gunfire.

10 **Soviet cosmonauts** Anatoly Berezovoy and Valentin Lebedev land safely after a record 211 days in space.
Law of the Sea Treaty is signed by 117 nations, but not by the United States.

11 **Chemical tank explodes** in Taft, La. More than 20,000 area residents evacuate their homes.
Robbers take at least $9.9 million from a New York City armored car service, the largest robbery in U.S. history.

13 **Earthquake kills** more than 2,800 people in Yemen (Sana).

14 **Spain opens its border** with Gibraltar, allowing road travel back and forth for the first time since 1969.

15 **Roy L. Williams,** president of the International Brotherhood of Teamsters, is convicted of conspiring to bribe a United States senator.
Brazil is granted a $4.5-billion loan by the International Monetary Fund.

23 **U.S. Congress approves** a gasoline tax increase of 5 cents per gallon (3.8 liters).

27 **A stock exchange record** is set as the Dow Jones industrial average closes at 1,070.55, the highest ever.

28 **Andrew L. (Drew) Lewis, Jr.,** resigns as U.S. secretary of transportation, effective on Feb. 1, 1983.

30 **Poland "suspends" martial law** at midnight, but retains many of its repressive features.

The Year in Focus

The meaning of some of the important events and trends of 1982 is discussed by the members of The Year Book Board of Editors:

Harrison Brown, Director, the East-West Resource Systems Institute, the East-West Center, Honolulu, Hawaii.
Lawrence A. Cremin, President, Teachers College, Columbia University.
James J. Kilpatrick, columnist for the Universal Press Syndicate.
Sylvia Porter, columnist for the Universal Press Syndicate.
Carl T. Rowan, columnist for the Field Newspaper Syndicate.

Seated: Brown, Porter; standing, left to right, Rowan, Kilpatrick, Cremin.

NEW
CLAIMS

ДОМ СОЮЗОВ

Old Problems in America, a New Leader in Russia

In America — high unemployment, schools that may not be preparing students for the world of tomorrow, and a troubled Social Security system. In Russia — a new leader

Only weeks before THE YEAR BOOK Board of Editors met in Washington, D.C., in November 1982, the United States held a mid-term election, an election that comes halfway through a presidential term. During their discussion, the board members looked at that election. Was it a referendum on President Ronald Reagan's first two years in office? They then turned their attention to the schools and their role in preparing students for the world — specifically, the jobs — of tomorrow. Finally, after examining the troubled Social Security system, they speculated on the possible effects of the new leadership in the Soviet Union. Joining the discussion were Ralph Schey, chairman and chief executive officer of The Scott Fetzer Company; William H. Nault, editorial director of World Book, Inc.; and Wayne Wille, executive editor of THE YEAR BOOK.

Harrison Brown

Ralph Schey

Sylvia Porter

James J. Kilpatrick

William H. Nault: A few weeks ago, about halfway through President Ronald Reagan's first term, the United States held a midterm election. We want to briefly examine the results and significance of that election. Tied in with that, of course, is the state of the U.S. economy. Inflation has been reduced significantly. But, according to public opinion polls, the unemployment rate is now our main double-digit worry, with 1 out of every 10 workers jobless. Was the election a referendum on so-called Reaganomics? And what about the unaddressed issue of how our Social Security system can be saved? We want to talk about all of that. We also want to take a look at a subject that is related to the question of unemployment and employment, and that is the present and future state of education in America. Are we doing an adequate job of educating and training people for the kinds of jobs that will be available? Finally, on the international scene, we will speculate on the possible effects of the death of the Soviet Union's leader, Leonid Brezhnev.

First, the election. The Republican Party maintained its control of the U.S. Senate, while the Democrats increased their majority in the House of Representatives and picked up a number of governors' seats. Can that result be viewed as a national referendum on Reagan's first two years, or was it instead a series of state elections that were determined primarily by local concerns? Jack Kilpatrick, did the election provide any clear message?

James J. Kilpatrick: No. As I read the election returns, Bill, they were pretty much in the pattern of by-elections of the past. I did a little calculation on the by-elections that we have held since 1938, and it turned out that the party in power in the White House lost on the average about 14½ per cent of its strength in the House. If you apply that 14½ per cent to the 192 members that the Republicans had in the House, you come up with a loss of 26 or 27 seats, which is exactly what the Republicans experienced. It wasn't good for the Republicans, but it wasn't disastrous. Was it a referendum on Reagan's economic program? Not in my judgment. As you sug-

Wayne Wille

Lawrence A. Cremin

Carl T. Rowan

William H. Nault

gested, it was indeed a series of 435 local elections and 33 state elections, and in many of the districts local issues predominated and determined the outcome. So, looking at the country as a whole, I can't read this as any referendum on Reagan at all. It was a moderate shift to the left within the center of our political spectrum, and that is about all it amounted to.

Carl T. Rowan: It was more than that. I think the voters said as clearly as it can be said, "We want something done about jobs. We want something done about this economy." You already are seeing Republicans in both the House and the Senate scrambling to produce a jobs program. And very clearly, Reagan also has read the message, and he is going to do some things he swore he would never do to try to produce some jobs.

Kilpatrick: Well, is that a bad thing, making this course correction?

Rowan: No, I think it is a good thing, and it is long overdue. But I don't think he would have done it had he not read that election as a message for him to make a change in course.

Sylvia Porter: Rarely in modern times has economics governed an election as much as economics governed this one. This was a complete repudiation of Reaganomics, to the point where, during the campaign, its most ardent backers—the so-called supply-siders—kept quiet and left it up to Reagan's personal popularity to win votes. To understand this repudiation, let's look at what Reaganomics or supply-side economics was and is. It is a combination of very commendable goals that cannot be put together to make a cohesive whole. Specifically, Reagan asked for and got from Congress a huge three-year tax cut intended to increase consumer spending, to spur business to go out and invest in new plants and equipment, and to make jobs. This business expansion is supposed to provide additional tax revenues that will make up for the tax cut and help balance the budget. The balanced budget is supposed to reduce the rate of inflation to reasonable levels and restore faith in the dollar.

Now, all of those goals are commendable, as I've said, and I would like to add that some good will come out of Reagan's policies. Along with his Reaganomics he has made some worthwhile efforts to lessen the concentration of power in Washington and to reduce the regulations that are strangling business and other areas of our lives. But, those exceptions aside, Reaganomics couldn't work. It made no sense. Business didn't buy it, and the voters didn't buy it. A three-year tax cut was not needed, and the cuts so far have helped to throw the budget even further out of balance; we're looking at record annual deficits of $150 billion or more. And instead of increasing, investments in new plants are running at very low levels.

What happened was that the Federal Reserve Board adopted a tight money policy. The result was that interest rates soared. The housing industry couldn't take that. The automobile industry couldn't take it. The smokestack industries — the heavy industries — were on their way down anyway. The rate of inflation went down, but Reagan gets little credit for that. The Federal Reserve Board gets the credit. But at the same time, and as a result, unemployment went way up. Why shouldn't it? In the history of modern economics, there has always been one certain way to push inflation down: Raise the number of unemployed. You don't go out and raise prices for your product if few people are earning the money to buy it.

So, no matter how much you look at the details, you come back to the basic point: This election was a condemnation by the American public of what had happened to the economy during the two years that Reagan was in charge of policy.

Ralph Schey: Sylvia, I think the real culprit that Reaganomics was attacking was inflation, which historically is the number-one peril for an economy in the long run. Granted, he was attempting to do it with something that didn't turn out the way it was supposed to. He was attempting, with supply-side economics, to divert more of our country's resources into capital formation and away from consumption. That was the real thrust of Reaganomics, because we have a serious problem in the rate at which capital is being formed to support the kind of private-sector economy that is needed to provide the jobs for the increasing number of workers. As for what the public was saying to Reagan in the election, and is saying now, I think it is saying, "We want you to do the things you are doing." I think the public in general says, "Reduce government expenditures, reduce inflation, reduce interest rates." They are also saying that they want more jobs. I understand that. But, you know, between the end of 1980 and August 1982, almost 4 million new jobs were created — despite the fact that unemployment increased.

Kilpatrick: I will give you one more statistic. We tend to concentrate excessively on the 27,000 bankruptcies that we will experience in 1982 without saying a word about the 600,000 new businesses that will be created. That is a figure that is worth keeping in mind. The rate of formation of new businesses in 1982 will approach the record.

Rowan: Despite the new jobs and the new businesses, I think we have to acknowledge that there are a lot of jobs out there that are never going to come back — in the automobile and steel industries, for example. At least a million jobs will never come back.

Harrison Brown: Yes, we have to face that fact. And we have to examine carefully how we are going to handle ourselves in the future with respect to working. To a large extent the new jobs that Ralph mentioned are service jobs — in computers, medicine, and so on. Clearly, those jobs are going to continue to multiply. But there is a limit, because even in the service jobs we are getting more efficient, thanks to the use of computers, and so forth. So I suspect we are entering a period when — if we insist on an eight-hour day, 40-hour week, with a month-long vacation every year — we are not going to have enough jobs to employ all the people. We are going to have to change our philosophy as to how people work.

Porter: "This election was a condemnation by the American public of what had happened to the economy during the two years that Reagan was in charge of policy."

Lawrence A. Cremin: One of the reasons the unemployment figures are growing is that there have been some significant changes in the work force. Today, people are looking for work and are at work who would not have been there 30 years ago. More than half the married women with children under age 18 are now in the work force, working full-time or looking for full-time employment. Another large group that was assumed to be out of the work force is the group over age 65. It is no longer seen as progressive to force these people to retire, as we once did. People are living longer, and staying healthier, and — indeed — there are moves in Congress to prevent the mandatory retirement of anyone.

Wayne Wille: Sylvia used to tell us about the underlying rate of inflation, that level below which we probably can never get inflation. Does this suggest that there might be an underlying rate of unemployment, that despite all our best efforts there is some level of unemployment we are just going to have to learn to live with?

Porter: "We could reduce unemployment to 8 per cent or less and have only a moderate increase in inflation."

Brown: It is an organizational problem. If you organize yourself properly, there is no reason why you should have much unemployment, except for the totally unemployable people, those who can't be trained to do anything at all. You might have to have a four-hour day or a five-hour day — and a four-day workweek, perhaps — however you want to organize it. This means that companies have to employ more people, obviously. The question is, what does it do to wages? It could lead to enormous problems.

Rowan: You know, for a lot of years, 4 per cent unemployment was actually considered full employment. Now the Reagan Administration is talking about 6 or 6½ per cent unemployment as possibly being full employment. That is a terrible thought, to assume that you are never going to get unemployment under 6 per cent.

Nault: Sylvia, you mentioned the classic theory that if you raise the number of unemployed, inflation will go down, and we have seen that happening. But do you think it is possible that we could raise the level of employment and still keep inflation at a tolerable level?

Porter: I think it is possible, but so far it has not been proved. I mentioned that Reagan has turned the country toward deregulation. Many of the regulations were strangling the economy, and he is changing that. Now, as a result of deregulation, plus what the Federal Reserve has shown that it can do, I believe we are heading into a period when we can afford an increase in employment and still not reawaken inflation to the point that we are all frightened of. To use numbers, I think we could reduce unemployment to 8 per cent or less and have only a moderate increase in inflation.

Nault: I mentioned earlier that we wanted to expand our discussion of unemployment to talk about the status of education in America, because people have to be equipped for the jobs that are available today and those that will be available tomorrow. The Bureau of Labor Statistics says that during the remainder of the 1980s the most promising job outlook will be for such people — and Harrison mentioned this earlier — as doctors, lawyers, systems analysts, dentists, computer programmers, accountants, and so forth. Now, many of these jobs require a sound knowledge of math, many require science, and many require both. The National Science Board, which is the policymaking body of the National Science Foundation, has set up a commission on precollege education in math, science, and technology. The purpose is to improve how these subjects can be taught. And it appears that improvement is needed. The board has said, "We appear to be raising a generation of Americans many of whom lack the understanding and the skills necessary to participate fully in the technological world in which they will live and work." Harrison, how would you respond to that appraisal?

Brown: You have raised an issue that—from the point of view of the strength of the United States—is one of the more critical issues

Rowan: "Now the Reagan Administration is talking about 6 or 6½ per cent unemployment as possibly being full employment. That is a terrible thought."

Kilpatrick: "I will give you one more statistic. We tend to concentrate excessively on the 27,000 bankruptcies that we will experience in 1982 without saying a word about the 600,000 new businesses that will be created. That is a figure worth keeping in mind."

that we face today. The fact of the matter is that we are becoming increasingly a nation of what has been called "scientific illiterates."

It is not that we can't produce enough scientists and engineers from the pool of graduates from our very best high schools. Every year, we produce many thousands of very competent young people who go into science and engineering and will take their places in the research laboratories. What we lack is scientific-technological literacy in the great mass of the people. And we have been sliding downhill very rapidly in this regard. Now, there are a number of reasons for this. The first is a very real shortage of science and mathematics teachers. This has reached crisis proportions. If my memory serves me correctly, about half of the people entering mathematics teaching in recent years have gone in under emergency certification. That is, they do not have the diploma training that is needed. It is appalling to me to see what high schools are turning out these days. In some schools, a student can get by with only one math class and one science course. Further, our school year is considerably shorter than the school years in Japan, the Soviet Union, West Germany, and so forth. And in those countries, students are required to take solid subjects: chemistry, physics, mathematics, biology, geography, several years of them. It is no wonder that Japan, for example, with half our population, is turning out twice as many engineers as we are.

The question is, what can we do about it? There are 16,000 school districts in the United States. And only one-third of them require more than one year of science and a year of math for graduation. This is all left up to the local people. You say, well, we have to raise the salaries of physics teachers, and raise the salaries of math teachers, to lure more people. The unions won't have it; they say it is inequitable. So what do you do? Frankly, this is one of the toughest nuts to crack that we have faced for a long time.

Cremin: I agree totally with the data Harrison has just set forth. I would add only that in a number of our states, fewer than 20 qualified math and science teachers are produced in any given year. I think our school system is at a turning point now, as evidenced by the fact that there are now some 15 to 20 studies going forward on the state of American public schooling in general, and particularly the state of the high schools. Now, what can we say about high schools. First, we have to acknowledge that our school system has been loaded down with social goals and social purposes. Indeed, educational policy in the United States—perhaps more than in any other free society—has been a tool of political policy. So, we ask our schools to accomplish racial integration. We ask them to accomplish the economic upgrading of an underclass. We ask them to bring into the mainstream handicapped children. We ask them quickly to integrate into the population millions of immigrants. We have asked the schools to do an awful lot. I am not trying to be an apologist for the schools. I am simply saying that we need to be aware of what we have asked the schools to do.

Nault: "The National Science Board has said . . . 'We appear to be raising a generation of Americans many of whom lack the understanding and the skills necessary to participate fully in the technological world in which they will live and work.' "

Second, one of the most interesting phenomena in high schools since the 1960s is the proliferation of electives. It is one thing to say that every child will take math for four years or three years, that math will be taught in different ways depending upon the needs of the youngster and the ability of the youngster. It is another thing to say that if you don't want to take math, you can take mystery stories, film making, or whatever else you want. This decline both within the high school and as handed down by the universities in terms of what they require for entry has led to a flabbiness in the curriculum.

Third, as Harrison points out, our best people have not been attracted to teaching. The best mathematicians go into industry. The best scientists go into industry and into laboratories. We are not attracting to teaching the share of able people we need at every level.

Wille: Not only at every level, but in every discipline? We've been talking almost entirely about math and science so far.

Cremin: Yes, we have been concentrating on math and the sciences, and I think we are wrong in doing so, because the problem is that the entire school system is in trouble. If the students can't read the math problems, they are not going to do well in math. We have to look at the education system as a whole—at the work in English and in foreign languages as well as in math and science. We are going to fool ourselves if we think a crash program in getting able math and science teachers is going to produce the kind of school system we need for the 1980s and the 1990s.

Just one other thing. For many years, one of the prime sources of the supply of teachers and nurses has been women. For years, American schools were able to make do because they had marvelously qualified and underpaid women in teaching. The fact is that women are now avoiding teaching and nursing. Women are now going to law school and medical school in greater numbers, and we are unable to rely on that social discrimination of an earlier period to staff our schools. Simply to get the number of teachers we need is going to take an effort beyond what we are thinking about if we think only of crash programs for math and science.

Cremin: "The problem is that the entire school system is in trouble. If the students can't read the math problems, they are not going to do well in math. We have to look at the education system as a whole – at the work in English and in foreign languages as well as in math and science."

Nault: I am wondering if some of what we've said or implied doesn't strike at the heart of the concept of the comprehensive high school, at the idea that kids ought to enjoy the so-called common experiences. In other words, that you should not have a high school that specializes in science or math as do some of our outstanding ones. When I visited the Soviet Union, I saw a lot of schools that took gifted students only, but there is a feeling in the United States that it is undemocratic to segregate students in terms of intellect.

Cremin: I believe in the comprehensive high school. When you look at the great American high schools, you find that many of them are comprehensive high schools producing first-rate people. I believe that within the comprehensive high school, you need a common curriculum, but that that common curriculum needs to be taught in different ways to different youngsters. And, I'm happy to say, a recent Gallup poll of parent and public opinion indicates that the public is ready for sensibly administered requirements for the fundamental subjects that teach students what they need to know.

Brown: To me, what is happening in the science and engineering and math areas is far more important to our national security than whether we develop some new weapons system. It is far more important. What is happening today in education can kill us—not just from a military point of view; it can kill us economically. It can kill us competitively, with respect to our export capacity versus other nations in the world. So it seems to me that a legitimate function of the federal government is to examine those things that jeopardize U.S. security and to take remedial action, whatever remedial action is necessary. And, just as we don't leave the military aspect of national defense up to the school boards or up to the states, I feel that

Schey: "The value of great teachers was that . . . they motivated the learner to want to learn. And that motivation has to start before the student enters school. There has to be an alliance for learning that starts in the home."

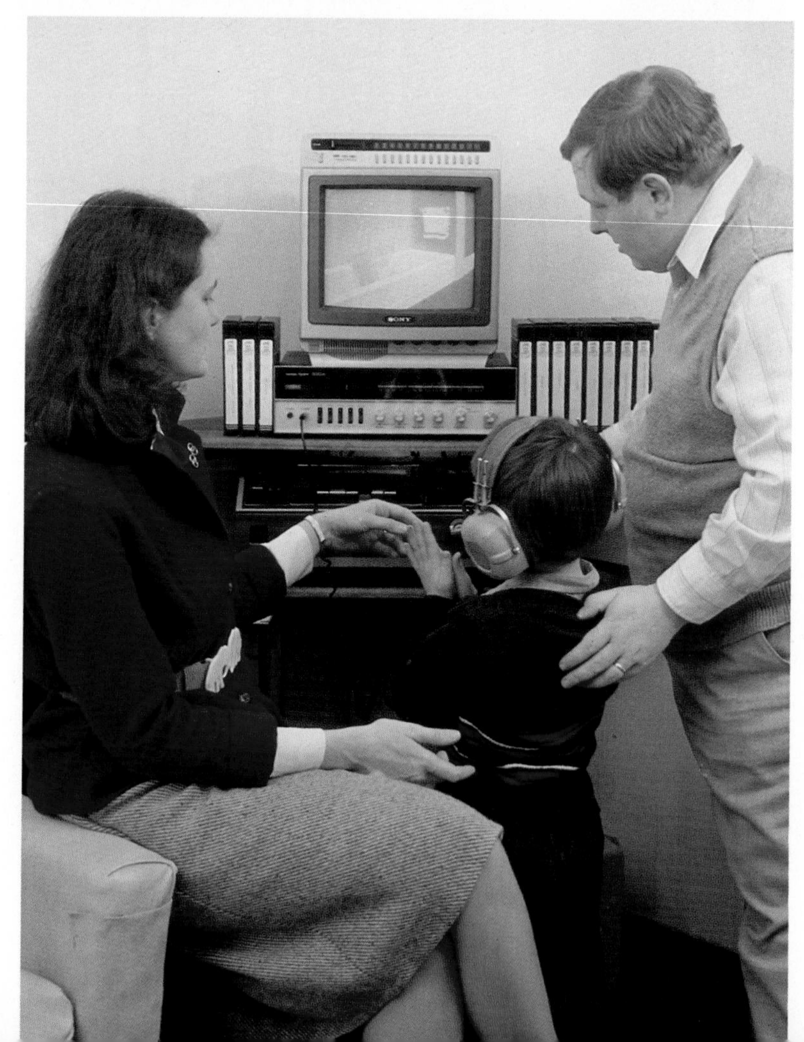

this educational problem is something that the federal government must be heavily involved with.

Porter: I think the funds for that kind of national effort can be found with relative ease. I speak here from a personal point of view, but I think I represent a large percentage of average men and women when I say that missiles and the MX this and the something or other that make no sense to me. They make no sense, but having a solid, sensible, required curriculum in a high school makes sense to me. And I think I am speaking for a large percentage of the people when I say we will find the money to finance the curriculum. We will find it. It is there. I go back to what we were talking about earlier, why I got a three-year tax cut. I didn't say I needed it. I didn't say I wanted it. I would have accepted a tax increase.

Rowan: Sylvia, I would have, too, but I cannot share your optimism that the money is going to be found. I don't see it in the way people vote when they vote down bond issues for their schools, and I don't see it in terms of what the federal government is doing. Reagan has proposed large cuts in the budget for education.

Kilpatrick: To me, national defense, national security—weapons systems, the army, the navy—has to come first. That is the top priority. There can't be any other, because if we fail to keep this country secure, then forget about your free society, forget about your education system, forget about all the values that we hold dear.

Rowan: But, Jack, you are not a strong nation if your people are not sufficiently educated to use the sophisticated weapons that you are producing.

Kilpatrick: Granted. I don't quarrel with that.

Schey: I believe that too frequently our response to an old problem is to try an old solution. I think the idea of a centralized school system with its curriculum, in effect, influenced and administered by the federal government is an outmoded notion. I think if we are going to get the motivation for people to learn, it is not going to come about by the kinds of programs that are envisioned. The value of great teachers was that they were motivators, not that they imparted knowledge to the learner, but that they motivated the learner to want to learn. And that motivation has to start before the student enters school. There has to be an alliance for learning that starts in the home. If it doesn't, it isn't going to do anything for us, no matter how much money we pour into it.

Cremin: I would build on what Ralph says about having to begin learning in the home. With the tumbling in the prices of microcomputers, with what cable television already brings into the home, with the software that is available now to feed home learning centers, you have a revolution in what can be done by an interested family.

Kilpatrick: I hope we don't leave an impression that almost all of our schools are failing at their job. There are many fine teachers and fine high schools throughout the country, and bright youngsters who are getting a good education in the public school system. The situation is by no means hopeless.

Brown: "I just tried to think through the problems of retraining a person who's been working . . . in a steel mill or in any of the other heavy industries. If, for example, we say we're going to retrain them to . . . work with computers, it's far easier to take young people and train them to do that than it is to retrain an older person."

Cremin: No, it is not hopeless. One could mention a hundred schools, a hundred school systems, that have begun to shape up and are producing results in a way that was not the case five to 10 years ago. And one of the things we have to do is learn from what those systems are doing.

We've talked about the lamentable omissions and problems in the education of the young. But a lot of what we were saying earlier about unemployment implies that we're going to have to develop as rigorous, as carefully planned, and as widespread an adult and continuing education effort as we have for the young. We have to do that if we are going to retrain the people who are machinists in New York or in Detroit who now have to become computer operators, the people in what you call the smokestack industries who now have to enter the knowledge industries. The country needs an unprecedented massive effort in the re-education and retraining of its adults. And, indeed, in this regard we are behind a number of West European countries that have made arrangements whereby persons in the work force can initiate their own re-education in collaboration with the government, the local community, and their employers and unions. Unless we do that promptly, we're going to be left far behind in the conversion of our economy into the kind of modern economy that can compete fully on the international scene.

Nault: The U.S. secretary of the Treasury, Donald Regan, said recently that a national retraining program is the only way to bring the unemployment rate under 6 per cent. There is an enormous mismatch between the skills of many of today's workers and the job demands in the new fields. One estimate is that as many as 90 per cent of all new jobs are in the service and technical fields, and they call for skills far different from the ones that many of these persons have, particularly in the disappearing manufacturing jobs.
Schey: I think retraining absolutely has to be one of our top priorities. The difficulty I see is that industry generally has abandoned training programs. This is because one of the things that happened when we had general purpose training programs — and by that I mean when we took students out of college into entry-level training programs — was that the turnover rate of those people was extremely high. Once they were trained, they found they could get a job with some other company for 15 or 20 per cent more than you could pay them right at that moment because you didn't have the equivalent kind of job available. So companies such as General Motors and General Electric found that they were paying for training programs for the entire industry. And, as companies became pinched financially, they began to drop the training programs. It is a two-way street. While the employer has to have more responsibility to the

employee for providing long-term employment, the employee in turn has to have more loyalty to the employer. And unless that occurs, I don't see that industry is going to pick up the slack and provide the training — or retraining — that is required. I believe that the individual is going to have to do more things to seek out his own training and improvement in the future.

Cremin: "We're going to have to develop as rigorous, as carefully planned, and as widespread an adult and continuing education effort as we have for the young."

Brown: I raise the question whether massive retraining programs are feasible. I just tried to think through the problems of retraining a person who's been working on an automobile assembly line for years or working in a steel mill or in any of the other heavy industries. I mean, what do we retrain them *for*? If, for example, we say we're going to retrain them to help produce microchips or microcircuitry or to work with computers, it's far easier to take young people and train them to do that than it is to retrain an older person. I suspect that in the long run, people whose jobs are disappearing will have to take on whatever jobs are available, even though they might not be particularly desirable from their point of view. They will have to go into more hand labor work and have to go into jobs that don't particularly require a lot of training. Admittedly, I'm pessimistic about this, but I suspect that is true.

Rowan: I share your pessimism. In fact, all my idealism and dreaming vanish when you get into that subject, because I think we have a good portion of a generation that is virtually lost in terms of it ever playing a meaningful role in this new economy. And because of that, we will be paying a pretty substantial bill in terms of the various welfare and social programs that will be required. I give great priority to trying to do something to see that we don't produce another generation with just as large a number of people who are totally out of kilter with the economy and the job market.

Kilpatrick: Bill, in your opening remarks you mentioned the question of how our Social Security system could be rescued, and that is something that ought to be explored. It figures in the depressing scenario that Harrison was sketching a moment ago, looking to the next century when there will not be enough jobs, or the kinds of jobs we know now, and we may have a four-hour day. We may have all kinds of economic changes that would be profoundly disturbing. As Larry says, people are living longer now, and this idea of retirement at 65 under Social Security is no longer supportable. We are at the point where only about 2½ or 3 productive workers are paying for the person on retirement, and that retired person, if he quits work at 65, may easily live another 20 years. How do you finance it?

Wille: Before we get further into the Social Security problem, let me try to give our young readers a better picture of what we're talking about. By Social Security we mean, basically, the old-age, survivors, and disability benefits financed by a payroll tax on both workers and their employers. About 9 out of every 10 workers in the United States are covered by these programs — that's about 92 million or 94 million workers. And as Jack said, every 2½ or 3 of those workers are paying for one person's benefit. That means that some 36 million or 38 million people are getting monthly Social Security benefits today. That low ratio of workers to retirees is getting steadily lower, and it's a matter of grave concern. Over the next seven years — 1983 through 1989 — the Social Security program faces a cumulative deficit of $150 billion to $200 billion. As Jack asked, how do you finance it? Basically, one — you raise more money; two — you spend less; or three — you do a combination of both. How you go about doing this is, of course, the big question.

Porter: One way to help solve the problem would be to put all government employees in the entire country under Social Security, which will be one of the options recommended by the National Commission on Social Security Reform when it issues its report soon. That step is long overdue. Federal and state employees should not have separate systems, and when they come into the Social Security system, they will help its financial picture, at least temporarily.

Increasing the age of retirement gradually over a period of years is another option for the long-term that must be considered, and it is one that almost surely will be adopted. You have to do it over a number of years so that people who are about to retire won't feel that we are at the very last moment grabbing something away from them. I think imposing a tax on Social Security benefits of those who are above a certain income level is a desirable option. I see no reason why I, at my income level, should get a tax-free benefit. I don't need it. I have worked; I have accumulated a pension fund of my own; and I don't need Social Security tax free. So tax me on it. I also think increasing the payroll tax that finances the system is certainly an option to be considered. There are so many ways in which Social Security could be shored up. The options are so clear and so many. And assuming that Congress gets the courage to adopt some of them in the next session, the system will again be viable.

Kilpatrick: One option Sylvia did not mention is adjustment of the cost-of-living increase for Social Security beneficiaries. It is so out of whack now that people in the work force are receiving less in the form of annual increases than those in retirement. Also, if the annual cost-of-living increase were delayed from July to October of each year, you could save a bundle of money simply because of the enormous number of people involved.

But the problem is, none of these options that Sylvia suggested or that the commission will come up with is politically attractive — except perhaps the one to tax us fat cats who have substantial outside income. That will have a political appeal, to tax our Social Security benefits when we are 65. In speeches I have made over the past several months, I have mentioned this phasing in of a higher retirement age, say 68. I find, to my dismay, as I found just the other day when I spoke to a fairly elderly audience in Michigan, that the idea has no appeal to them. They want to retire at 62. They don't want to wait until 66 or 68. That option is going to be politically tough to sell. None of these options is attractive, but Congress has to come up with some of them.

Schey: "While the employer has to have more responsibility to the employee for providing long-term employment, the employee in turn has to have more loyalty to the employer. And unless that occurs, I don't see that industry is going to pick up the slack and provide the training — or the retraining — that is required."

Rowan: Let me talk about some of the things being proposed that I think ought *not* to be done. There are a number of people who say that participation in the Social Security system ought to be voluntary. That, in my view, is the surest way to kill the program, which I regard as the best of all the social legislation passed in this country since 1932. If you made it voluntary, obviously a lot of people would opt out, and that would leave too few people in it and paying the taxes that support it, and it would never be a viable program.

Porter: "There are so many ways in which Social Security could be shored up. And assuming that Congress gets the courage to adopt some of them in the next session, the system will again be viable."

There are also the people who say there ought to be a means test; that it is, for example, not fair for me to collect Social Security because I don't really need it to live on. Well, I don't want to see Social Security made just a welfare program. I think all the people who have put into the program have a right to collect from it. And

I could swallow the idea of taxing Social Security benefits of people above a certain income. But, rather than that, I would much prefer to see the ceiling on the amount of annual income that is taxed to fund the system lifted from the current $32,400 to $50,000 or more. I don't think it would be terribly painful to anybody to tax income up to $60,000, and you would raise a lot of money that way.

So you lift the ceiling of taxed income; you bring in all the federal workers, which I agree is a step that ought to be taken; you tangle with Medicare costs, because medical costs are a tremendous chunk of the Social Security outlay; and you deal with the cost-of-living adjustment. Then you are on your way toward making Social Security able to do what it is supposed to be doing in this society.

Nault: Ralph, have you found many employees staying on past 65 since the law that passed in 1978 raising the mandatory retirement age from 65 to 70 for most workers? Or do they opt to leave at 65?

Schey: We have some people who stay on, but not very many. A distinct minority stay on past 65.

Cremin: It is very difficult to generalize from us and from people we know. We are professionals, we know professionals, we are in knowledge industries where people take pleasure in their work. The people who want out at 62 are the people in humdrum work who can't stand another year of it.

Rowan: Or they're people with physically crippling jobs, which is another reason I wouldn't want to extend it to 68 on any mandatory basis.

Kilpatrick: Carl, there are actuarial problems here that I think just have to be considered. People are living so much longer. If you permit full benefits at 65 and people live another 20 or 25 years, which is by no means unusual, you have to finance those retirement payments over that longer period of time.

Rowan: I am aware of that.

Kilpatrick: And that's not easy. I also want to disagree profoundly with Carl on the matter of phasing in the voluntary aspect of Social Security. This to me is what ought to be done in a free society, so that people have something of their own. If we put into a retirement account what we pay in Social Security taxes and then get to 65 or 70, we have something that can be inherited, it has tangible value. But with Social Security, you die at age 66 and there it goes.

Rowan: But, Jack, the reason we have the Social Security system is because history has shown us that most Americans would not take that money that they put into Social Security and put it into their own retirement plan. And then what you have when they reach 65 is a bunch of people with nothing, asking society to support them.

Kilpatrick: Those you keep in a Social Security program.

Rowan: But then you have narrowed the pool of people in Social Security to a point where the program cannot be financed. It needs people like you and me paying into the system. If we're out, there's no way to finance that program. You cannot finance Social Security on the payments of people earning $15,000 a year.

Rowan: "Older people vote in far greater percentages than do young people, and the politicians who somehow have to rescue the Social Security system know it. But they are just absolutely going to have to cast some tough votes in Congress."

Kilpatrick: I am certain that smart actuaries could figure out a way to do it.

Brown: I suspect that in the long run we are going to want to change the nature of the system. I have been impressed throughout my entire academic career by something that was forced on me when I first became an instructor at Johns Hopkins University. This was the Teachers Insurance and Annuity Association. I had to contribute so much a month, and the university contributed so much a month. But the thing is, the money is invested. It earns dividends for you, but you cannot take them out, and the amount of money in your fund grows. I moved from Johns Hopkins to another place—and I took my annuity with me, and they did the same. I moved to the University of Chicago—they did the same. I moved to the East-West Center—they are doing the same. So now that money represents quite a large sum of money by my poor standards. And—just as important—it has been helping the economy because it has been invested in stocks and bonds. When I retire, I will convert it to a lifetime annuity. Now, I have had no choice about this. I just had to do it, and I am grateful for it.

Schey: I would like to pick up on that point because a crucial fact about Social Security that tends to get ignored is that it started out as simply a supplementary retirement benefit. It was not intended

Kilpatrick: "The young people . . . don't think they ever will get any Social Security. And the old people are determined to cling to what they have and try to get some more. It's going to be a pretty tough political battle."

to provide all of a person's income during retirement, yet that is exactly what many people today expect it to do. As we've all seen, the difficulty with the Social Security system is that it is not funded. In our company's pension plan — as in the retirement plan Harrison described — there is a compounding effect of the contribution we pay in each year on behalf of our employees. So, over a period of time, a good fund reserve builds up. Then, when a person retires from our company at age 65 with 25 years of service, he gets 45 per cent of what he was earning each year during his last five years of employment. He gets Social Security payments in addition to that, of course. Now, under the Social Security program, a worker at the lower end of the income scale might get 70 per cent or more of what he received while he worked. There are even situations where he could get more from Social Security than he received on the job. Under a private pension program, that kind of payment would be extremely costly. On the average, it costs us 10 per cent of a person's annual gross income to fund the retirement program I described — namely, 45 per cent of a worker's base pay. But if you had a private program that wanted to fund, say, 70 per cent of base pay, the cost would be unbelievable, even assuming you had 25 years of compounding at between 6 and 8 per cent a year.

The fact that Social Security isn't funded and gets no compound-

Rowan: "I think the one most significant thing we could do would be to change the rhetoric of the United States."

ing effect has two negative results. One is that it penalizes the future payees; my kid is never going to get out of it what he started to pay into it at age 25. The second result is that Social Security funds are not invested in the economy, as funds in private programs are. They are not helping to build America's capital base.

Rowan: You know, one of the ironies is that the graying of America, the increasing numbers of older people in our population, which makes the system more and more costly, also makes the politics of it more difficult. Older people vote in far greater percentages than do young people, and the politicians who somehow have to rescue the Social Security system know it. We have a situation where it will be very difficult for a congressman from Florida, for example, to vote for some of these things we have been talking about, given the tremendous number of elderly and retired people living in Florida. But they are just going to have to cast some tough votes in Congress.

Kilpatrick: Well, Carl points to the political dichotomy that we can expect over the next 20 years — not between city and farm people, which used to be one of the historic splits, but between young people and old people. The young people, as the public opinion polls show, don't think they ever will get any Social Security. And the old people are determined to cling to what they have and try to get some more. It's going to be a pretty tough political battle.

Porter: Yes, it is going to be a tough battle, Jack. But I want to stress that one of the great problems is the increasing and unwarranted lack of faith in the Social Security system over the long term. The lack of faith that the system will be there for today's young people who are paying ever more and more into it. Ralph mentioned his son who'll never get as much out as he pays into it. You, Jack, mentioned the opinion polls. Well, I think that we *will* reach a solution. This country is going to insist that Social Security — no matter how it might be changed — continue to exist. I think the people of this country, on whom the ultimate decision rests, will insist that the Social Security system continue. We will find the solutions to its problems. We will find the answers. There are so many options. We will study them, and we will agree on them, and we will put the system back together again. And then it will be up to people like us who write daily columns to rebuild confidence in the system.

Nault: Let's turn to the international scene. One of the major events in 1982 on the world scene — perhaps it was *the* major event — was the death of Soviet Union leader Leonid Brezhnev. He had been head of Russia's Communist Party, which made him the most powerful man in the country, since 1964. Predicting anything about the Soviet Union is difficult, I know, but, Carl, I'd like you to speculate on the effects of Brezhnev's death and the advent of new leadership in Russia.

Rowan: Well, first of all, I do not believe that there will be any appreciable degree of change in the Soviet Union because of the succession of Yuri Andropov to the post of Communist Party leader. We have to remember that this is a 68-year-old man who is seized by the same fears that all the other Soviet leaders have about what may happen in the countries bordering on or around the Soviet Union. This is the man who was ambassador to Hungary at the time of Russia's great crackdown on that country in 1956. This is the man who headed the KGB — the secret police — until six months before Brezhnev's death.

I happen to think the Soviet Union is going to continue to pursue what it believes to be its own vital interests. And they will perceive those interests to be to crack down in Poland, to crack down in Afghanistan, to do whatever they have to do to keep their borders safe. I do not believe they are going to dismantle any of their major missile emplacements in Western Europe. I think the arms-control talks with the United States will go on, they will drag on, but I do not see any real prospect for any significant change in Soviet policy.

Wille: Early in 1982 when Andropov was added to the Secretariat, the 10-member group that handles the day-to-day work of the Communist Party, many experts on the Soviet Union said that the head of the KGB could never become the leader of the country because of the bad image of the secret police. Of course, there were other experts who disagreed with that appraisal, but it did seem to be the opinion of the majority of the experts. Apparently they were wrong. Is there any significance to the fact that Andropov was head of the KGB and is now going to be running the country?

Rowan: Well, I think it may simply reflect the power you can get — and wield — when you know where the bodies are buried. Lyndon Johnson exercised tremendous power in this country, and was a very effective President, because he knew how to twist arms. He knew where the bodies were buried on Capitol Hill. You can bet that Andropov knows where the bodies are buried in the Soviet Union, having headed the KGB for 15 years.

Kilpatrick: Knows where they're buried literally as well as metaphorically.

Rowan: And I just cannot conceive of this man suddenly becoming a great Soviet liberal in the American meaning of liberal. Now, he might figure that he's got perhaps seven years to go, and he might want to make some record of his own, in his own name in that time. How he will go about doing that we can only speculate on in the wildest kind of way. I am happy to say, however, that there are some restraints on him that I am glad exist. One of these is the fact that every day two ships leave some U.S. port loaded with 20,000 tons of grain for the Soviet Union. This dependence on the United States to help bail the Soviet Union out of its terrible economic problems, and particularly its terrible agricultural problem, may put some considerable restraints on Andropov in terms of how confrontational he wants to be or can be. But beyond that, I think we are going to have the same old rocky going for as far ahead as I can see.

Kilpatrick: I agree with that. I don't expect any major show of new force or any dramatic action on the part of the Andropov government. I think that is also the view of the White House and the view

Kilpatrick: "I don't expect any major show of new force or any dramatic action on the part of the Andropov government."

of most of the intelligence community. They expect, just as Carl says, pretty much a continuance of the policies we have seen.

Porter: Is there anything the United States could do to make whatever Russia is considering turn out better for us?

Rowan: I think the one most significant thing we could do would be to change the rhetoric of the United States. I would not change our basic policy, but I see absolutely no point in continuing some of the confrontational talk that the Reagan Administration has indulged in, particularly when the policies have not matched the rhetoric. Reagan's rhetoric has been far harsher than that of Jimmy Carter, but strangely enough, Carter's policies as President were harsher than those of Ronald Reagan. I'm thinking, for example, of Carter's economic measures against Russia when the Soviets invaded Afghanistan. In fact, this is one of the reasons for the growing conservative disenchantment with Reagan. They claim he talks tough but doesn't act tough. He sells the Soviets grain, lifts Carter's grain embargo, and so forth. And, of course, now he has lifted the embargo on materials for Russia's new natural-gas pipeline. If you are going to do these things, I think you should cool the tough talk a bit. Otherwise, all you get back is the kind of rhetoric that Brezhnev was uttering almost up to his deathbed—about how with their military might they were going to teach American adventurists a lesson.

Brown: You are quite correct that we cannot look toward any in-

Brown: "For us in the United States, I think the key to all of this is to develop and maintain communications with the Soviets at all levels. To arbitrarily cut off communications channels could be disastrous."

stantaneous changes in the Soviet Union because of Andropov. But I think we have to recognize that a very important evolutionary process has been taking place there. I have been in and out of the Soviet Union about 20 or 25 times over the last 20 years. I remember that on my first visit I didn't see any dissenters. And women didn't wear lipstick. Now, that might seem trivial, but it is important. On my next visit, women were wearing lipstick. The visit after that, there were lines in front of beauty parlors, and I also saw my first dissenters at that time. You saw them here and there surreptitiously. Not that I sought them out, but they sought me out. And this has been continuing. Today, despite the KGB, there are many, many dissenters in the Soviet Union. Most of them are very low-keyed, but they are ready to come out into the open, given a time they judge to be opportune. This, as I've said, is a change that has gone on and on and on. You cannot compare the Soviet Union today to the Soviet Union 20 years ago from this point of view. And if you combine the growing desire for consumer goods with these political desires, you have a situation that the Soviet government, no matter how repressive, is not going to be able to cope with. I think it is in the cards that there will be a continuing slow evolutionary process in the Soviet Union. For us in the United States, the key to all of this is to develop and maintain communications with the Soviets at all levels. To arbitrarily cut off communications channels could be disastrous.

Rowan: "I see absolutely no reason to believe that Andropov will follow any doctrine other than the Brezhnev Doctrine, which says that the Soviet Union has the right to intervene in the affairs of its neighbors. . . ."

Kilpatrick: Are you suggesting there will be some turning inward toward domestic problems under Andropov?
Brown: I think there certainly will be a turning inward toward domestic problems. At the same time, I would hope—and this is a hope more than a rational kind of forecast—that there will be some small liberalization in the area of external problems as well.
Kilpatrick: In the arms-limitation talks?
Brown: In the arms talks.
Rowan: I am with you 100 per cent, Harrison, in saying we must not cut off communications. We must not cease to have hope that we can have a better relationship. And I know there have been changes in the Soviet Union, as you say, but I have seen nothing to convince me that these changes will have enough impact on the Kremlin to force it to modify its attitude toward Poland or Czechoslovakia or Hungary or Afghanistan. What I am saying is that I see absolutely no reason to believe that Andropov will follow any doctrine other than the Brezhnev Doctrine, which says that the Soviet Union has the right to intervene in the affairs of its neighbors if those neighbors are deemed by the Kremlin to be any kind of threat to the Soviet Union. I wish I could see something else, but I just don't, no matter what you may see in terms of the desires of the average Soviet citizen. I just don't believe Yuri Andropov is going to pay any more attention to the desires of the average Soviet citizen than Leonid Brezhnev did.
Brown: I don't think that is correct. I think it would be disastrous were he to cut off the lipstick supply.
Kilpatrick: You say that both literally and metaphorically, of course.
Brown: Yes. The desire for consumer goods is there, and lipstick, naturally, is merely one small example of that desire. I have seen the long lines of shoppers. The Soviet citizens want more consumer goods, and I don't think they are going to be satisfied much longer without them.
Cremin: We ought to keep another consideration about this anti-Soviet rhetoric in mind. And that is the fact that while the rhetoric is produced largely for domestic consumption, it is heard by our allies, and it does not do us much good with our allies.
Kilpatrick: I don't object to the rhetoric, Larry. I don't think it is particularly strong, and certainly it is not as strong as the rhetoric that the Soviet Union has thrown at us.
Cremin: No doubt about that.
Kilpatrick: And it seems to me that it kind of clears the air. The Russians know where we stand, and we know where they stand. It is a lot better than the indecisiveness that characterized the rhetoric of the Carter Administration for four years.
Cremin: I am not in favor of indecisiveness, but I am not in favor of gratuitously alienating large numbers of Frenchmen or Englishmen or West Germans.
Rowan: As we sit here, we have to recognize that we are always in a guessing game, trying to figure out when the other side is sending

a signal. We are sitting here at the very moment Lech Walesa has been let go in Poland, allowed to go home to his wife and kids after 11 months of incarceration. Is that purely a coincidence?
Porter: It is a signal, is it not? It is highly unlikely that it is only a coincidence.
Rowan: I don't know. Maybe the Kremlin decided after Brezhnev's death and the oncoming of the new man, let's let Lech Walesa go. Maybe it is a total coincidence. These are the kinds of things diplomats sit around and guess about.
Kilpatrick: But there certainly is no change basically as to Poland, Carl. The Soviet Union has this grip on Poland, and it seems unlikely to let it go. I think the Lech Walesa thing, coincidence or planned, doesn't mean a great deal in that situation.
Rowan: I think one of the major developments of the past 35 or 40 years was the re-establishing of relations between the United States and China and the breaking up of the Sino-Soviet monolith. I think it serves U.S. interests immensely for the Soviets to have to keep all those army divisions on the border with China and for China to be making overtures toward capitalism and inviting in American corporations and American students and professors.

When the argument began over whether the Reagan Administration was keeping its promises toward Taiwan, some of us warned that we could do some things that would put that Sino-Soviet monolith back together, which would be a calamity. We are seeing, as of this date, some little inklings. The Chinese foreign minister, for example, went to Brezhnev's funeral and asked Andropov to make some gestures so that the Soviet Union and China could get a little closer. I think it behooves the United States to conduct its foreign policy so that we cannot be accused of doing anything to push a billion Chinese back into a tight alliance with the Soviet Union.
Porter: Hear, hear.
Cremin: Hear, hear, indeed.
Kilpatrick: Amen.
Brown: I have no problem with that.
Kilpatrick: We have consensus, a unanimous vote.
Nault: And that note of unanimity—rare for us, I think you'll agree—is a good point at which to end today's discussion. We've taken a look at a number of important issues, at some vexing problems that will not be solved easily. We've given our readers a good number of things to think about and to discuss among themselves, and I want to thank all of you for your contributions today.

For further reading:

Numerous articles in THE WORLD BOOK ENCYCLOPEDIA provide background information on some of the matters discussed by THE YEAR BOOK Board of Editors in this Focus article. These articles include CAREERS; EDUCATION (Current Issues in U.S. Education); EMPLOYMENT; MEDICARE; PENSION; RUSSIA (Government; History/Russia Today); SOCIAL SECURITY; and UNEMPLOYMENT.

Special Reports

1977 1978 1979 1980 1981 1982

Six articles give special treatment to subjects of current importance and lasting interest.

See "The ABC's of Testing," page 90

EQUAL·JUSTICE·UNDER·LAW

The High Court: at the Center of a Storm Again

By Richard Pawelek

Attempts to curb the U.S. Supreme Court are only the latest chapter in a long history of controversy

The Supreme Court of the United States, the heart of what Alexander Hamilton called "the least dangerous branch of government," came under attack by some members of Congress in 1981 and 1982. The 97th Congress had before it more than 30 bills that would restrict the authority of the high court and other federal courts by limiting their power to rule on certain highly controversial social issues.

Such limits would please those Americans who have been deeply disturbed by a number of major decisions handed down by the Supreme Court during the past 20 years. Chief among them have been decisions forbidding mandatory prayer in public schools, promoting busing to desegregate schools, and upholding a woman's right to an abortion. But other Americans, including many members of Congress, saw the attempts to limit the court as a serious threat to the court's role as the "balance wheel" in the U.S. constitutional system of checks and balances.

No doubt the nine justices of the Supreme Court were concerned. But, following tradition, they refused to comment publicly on pending legislation. As the controversy raged, they quietly carried on their work.

The time: nearly 10 A.M. *The place:* the mammoth courtroom of the United States Supreme Court Building in Washington, D.C. Attorneys are shuffling through papers or talking quietly with one another. Observers are watching the attorneys or studying the friezes—the marble bands of decoration—high up on the chamber's 44-foot (13-meter) walls. The carved figures in the friezes symbolize the giving of laws and the power of justice and government.

Promptly at 10, the court marshal pounds his gavel and cries out, "Oyez! Oyez! Oyez!" (Hear ye! Hear ye! Hear ye!), the Anglo-French call for attention used for centuries in English courts. "All persons having business before the honorable, the Supreme Court of the United States, are admonished to draw near and give their attention, for the court is now sitting. God save the United States and this honorable court," he continues. Everyone stands.

Then, the nine justices of the Supreme Court, robed in black, make their entrance. In groups of three, they step out from one of three openings in the long red drapes that provide a backdrop for four huge marble pillars and step up to the long mahogany bench. The gavel falls again. Each justice sits in a chair made especially for him or her. The chief justice of the United States, Warren E. Burger, sits in the center of the bench, with four associate justices on each side. After everyone is seated, Burger tells the attorneys to "proceed whenever you are ready."

For the next two hours and again for two hours after lunch, the justices listen intently as attorneys present their arguments in the cases that have wound their long way through lower courts to America's highest tribunal. Each case is allotted only one hour, giving each side only 30 minutes to present its arguments. And at exactly 3 o'clock, the justices quietly leave the bench and disappear behind the red drapes.

This traditional scene was repeated some 40 times during the court's term, which begins on the first Monday in October and ends in April, as the court held "hearing days." Those hearing days are just the most visible part of the long decision-making process in which the justices study and answer thorny constitutional questions. Their decisions affect the procedures of government and law enforcement agencies, the practices of public institutions and private businesses, and the lives of citizens across the United States. They also create news and—in many cases—controversy.

Controversy over court decisions is almost an American tradition. And quite often, the controversy begins within the court itself—when one or more justices do not agree with the majority vote, which makes a decision binding on lower federal and state courts. Statements of disagreement, or dissenting opinions, were issued time and again in the 1981-1982 term as the court grappled with such difficult constitutional questions as:

- Is a 40-year prison sentence for possession and sale of just 9

The author:
Richard Pawelek is the managing editor of *Senior Scholastic Magazine,* a national social studies magazine for high school students.

Nine empty chairs await the justices of the U.S. Supreme Court. In this dignified chamber, the justices hear arguments in the cases that have wound their way to America's high court. Figures in the friezes high on the walls symbolize the majesty and power of the law.

ounces (255 grams) of marijuana "cruel and unusual punishment" (*Hutto v. Davis*)?

■ Can a state deny free public education to alien children who are in the United States illegally (*Plyler v. Doe* and *Texas v. Certain Undocumented Alien Children*)?

■ Can a male student be refused admission to a school of nursing founded as a school for women only (*Mississippi University for Women v. Hogan*)?

A majority of justices voted no in each of those three cases. But the vote tally — 6-3, 5-4, 5-4, respectively — revealed how sharply divided the justices sometimes are. Such judicial disagreement often mirrors profound divisions in public opinion. And some Supreme Court decisions in recent years, particularly those involving controversial social issues, have aroused a storm of angry criticism. Severely attacked have been a number of rulings in criminal cases that have expanded the rights of criminals while, some people believe, hampering the effectiveness of the police and ignoring the safety of law-abiding citizens. But the targets of the most vehement criticism have been the decisions on school busing, abortion, and school prayer.

In 1981, some members of the 97th Congress, generally a more conservative body than those of recent years, decided to do something about these decisions. The time seemed ripe because they believed that many members of Congress agreed with them and that the conservative President, Ronald Reagan, would be more likely to sign bills curbing the power of the court.

THE LEGISLATIVE BRANCH MUST CONFIRM NOMINEES TO THE SUPREME COURT. CAN IMPEACH AND REMOVE JUDGES FROM OFFICE. CAN AMEND THE CONSTITUTION.
CAN OVERRIDE A PRESIDENTIAL VETO. CAN IMPEACH AND REMOVE THE PRESIDENT FROM OFFICE. MUST APPROVE GOVERNMENT APPROPRIATIONS.
CONGRESS
THE JUDICIAL BRANCH CAN DECLARE LAWS AND EXECUTIVE ORDERS UNCONSTITUTIONAL. APPOINTED FOR LIFE. DECISIONS BINDING ON LOWER COURTS AND OTHER BRANCHES OF THE GOVERNMENT.
CHECKS AND BALANCES
THE SUPREME COURT

Many people want to limit the jurisdiction of the Supreme Court, believing that the constitutional system of checks and balances has been warped by a too-powerful court.

How does one go about curbing the power of the courts through congressional action? One way is to amend the U.S. Constitution. If the court rules that a certain law is unconstitutional, then Congress can propose an amendment to make that law a part of the Constitution. However, ratifying an amendment is a difficult and time-consuming process. The most commonly used procedure requires approval by a two-thirds vote in both houses of Congress, then ratification by three-fourths (38) of the 50 states.

Congressional critics of the court decided instead on what they believed was a faster, easier way—legislation that would limit the court's jurisdiction by stripping the court of its power to rule on certain types of cases. Several dozen such bills were introduced in the House of Representatives, and at least six others were before the Senate in 1982.

The sponsors of these bills hoped not only to prevent the Supreme Court from reviewing cases involving abortion, school prayer, and school busing, but also to keep lower federal courts from ruling on these matters. The legislation would give state courts final responsibility for judging such cases. The sponsors believed state courts might be more responsive to local opinion, especially since many state judges are elected, rather than appointed for life the way Supreme Court justices are.

Such a strong move in one branch of government—the legislative—against another branch—the judicial—has raised questions, controversy, and fears. The fundamental question in the argument is: According to the Constitution, how much power does Congress really have over the court? People on both sides of the dispute were soon doing what the Supreme Court does all the time—they were reading the Constitution.

Article III of the Constitution establishes the Supreme Court; authorizes it to rule on cases "arising under" the Constitution, federal laws, and treaties; and gives Congress the right to set up lower federal courts. Article III also grants the Supreme Court two types of jurisdiction — original and appellate. *Original jurisdiction* means that a case goes directly to the Supreme Court; no other court hears it first. The court has original jurisdiction in cases involving a representative of a foreign country and cases in which a state is one of the parties. Under its *appellate jurisdiction*, the court can review, then confirm or reverse, the decisions of lower federal and state courts.

According to the Constitution, Congress does have undisputed control over some matters affecting the Supreme Court. For example, the Senate must approve all nominations to the court and has, in fact, rejected 11 of the 140 people nominated to serve as justices. Congress may also impeach justices for "treason, bribery, or other high crimes and misdemeanors."

Congress also sets the schedule, or term, of the court. In 1802, it used that power to delay a ruling on a case by setting no term at all. Finally, Congress controls the size of the court. Although the number of justices has been fixed at nine since 1869, Congress had previously changed the size of the court seven times. The number of justices was increased several times to reflect the westward expansion of the United States and increases in the country's population. But at other times Congress reduced the number of justices to prevent an outgoing President from filling a vacancy on the court.

According to the Constitution, Congress lacks the power to expand or limit the original jurisdiction of the court. Most experts also agree — like it or not — that Article III probably gives Congress the authority to limit the jurisdiction of lower federal courts. But like Supreme Court justices in split-decision cases, legal experts disagree vehemently about Congress's power over the appellate jurisdiction of the nation's highest court.

At the center of the argument is Section 2, Paragraph 2, of Article III of the Constitution. Known as the "exception clause," it states that the Supreme Court has appellate jurisdiction "*with such exceptions, and under such regulations as the Congress shall make.*" Proponents of court-curbing bills believe those words clearly give them the green light. And, they point out, Congress *has* limited and expanded the jurisdiction of the court. For example, in 1889, Congress gave the court the right to hear appeals in criminal cases. In 1914, Congress gave it the right to review lower state court decisions finding state laws unconstitutional or contrary to federal law. The Judiciary Act of 1925 sharply limited the types of appeals cases the court is required to hear and gave it more power to choose cases it wanted to hear.

Attempts to limit the court's jurisdiction date back to 1821, when a member of the Senate introduced a bill forbidding the court to review decisions made by the states' highest courts. In 1867, after

This oak-paneled room is where the justices meet, in great secrecy, to decide whether to accept cases for review and to vote on the cases they do review.

the Civil War, Congress prevented the court from ruling on the constitutionality of the Reconstruction Acts of 1867 by passing legislation repealing the court's appellate jurisdiction over the acts.

In an 1868 case dismissing a challenge to the constitutionality of the Reconstruction Acts, Chief Justice Salmon P. Chase wrote in the court's unanimous decision, "We are not at liberty to inquire into the motive of the legislature. We can only examine into its power under the Constitution, and the power to make exceptions to the appellate jurisdiction of this Court is given by express words." However, former justices and other legal experts disagreed vigorously with the opinion.

Modern opponents of the court-curbing bills also disagree. They argue that interpreting the exceptions clause literally is taking a very narrow view of the Constitution. They believe one must consider the intent of that section and how other parts of the Constitution would be affected.

David R. Brink, former president of the American Bar Association, points out that Article III also states that the court's judicial power extends to "all cases . . . arising under this Constitution." How then can Congress remove cases from the court's jurisdiction without amending the Constitution?

Furthermore, Brink contends, the Fifth Amendment guarantees

If *You* Sat on the Court

What kind of Supreme Court justice would you make? Test your understanding of the United States Constitution and your decision-making ability with these 10 Supreme Court cases, some old, some recent. How would you rule? And why? Turn to pages 72 and 73 for the actual decisions made by the court.

1. The Broken Electric Chair

Willie Francis, sentenced to die in the electric chair in Louisiana, received an unexpected reprieve when the switch was thrown and nothing happened. Stymied temporarily by faulty wiring, Louisiana officials then set another date for the execution. Francis appealed to the Supreme Court. He argued that to try to electrocute him twice was "cruel and unusual punishment" and thus forbidden by the Eighth Amendment. How would you have ruled on his appeal?

2. The Religious Factory Worker

Factory worker Eddie C. Thomas belonged to a religious group that forbids any activity that supports war. Transferred to a department where war materials were made, he decided to quit rather than violate his conscience and religious beliefs. When he sought unemployment payments, he was told that a religious reason was not a "good cause" for quitting a job. A state court agreed. It said that paying Thomas unemployment benefits would violate the First Amendment's prohibition against "an establishment of religion," because the state would be supporting a religious belief. Would you let the state court ruling stand?

3. The President and the Falkland Islands

A dispute between Argentina and Great Britain over ownership of the Falkland Islands spilled over to the U.S. government when the President refused to recognize Argentina's claim. Members of Congress who favored Argentina argued that the President had no right to make such a decision. Was Congress correct? (The President was Martin Van Buren, and his dispute with Congress took place in the late 1830s.)

4. Lincoln and the Prize Ships

Congress was not in session when the Civil War broke out in April 1861 with the firing on Fort Sumter. To preserve the Union and the Constitution, President Abraham Lincoln ordered bold action, including a blockade of Southern ports. Several neutral ships that tried to run the blockade were seized as "war prizes." Some congressmen challenged Lincoln's assumption of broad wartime powers by claiming that the seizure of the vessels was illegal. They insisted only Congress could control war policy. Were the congressmen justified in their attempt to restrict the President?

5. Muddied Waters

A wharf owner named Barron became alarmed when so much mud and debris clogged Baltimore Harbor that boats could no longer tie up easily at his wharf. Barron claimed that by paving its streets, the city of Baltimore had changed the course of streams and muddied the harbor as well as his future and livelihood. He sued for compensation under the Fifth Amendment, which says that a person may not be deprived of private property without payment or due process of law. How would you rule?

6. Sexism in Help-Wanted Ads?

The *Pittsburgh Press* took its case to the Supreme Court when the Pittsburgh Commission on Human Relations ordered it to stop headlining help-wanted ads with such phrases as "Jobs—Female Interest" and "Jobs—Male Interest." The paper claimed this order interfered with First Amendment guarantees of freedom of the press. Was the paper right?

7. The Name-Caller

"Racketeer!" and "Fascist!" were some of the names an angry New Hampshire man called a police officer who arrested him for causing a disturbance. The man was also charged with violating a state law forbidding use of "fighting words" in public. He claimed the law violated his freedom of speech under the First Amendment. Do you agree with the rowdy man?

8. The Stationery Seller's Fine

Sabine Robbins sold stationery made by a company in Ohio. While displaying samples and taking orders in Tennessee, Robbins was fined for not having a license to sell goods manufactured out of state. Robbins challenged the law, saying that requiring such a license interfered with interstate commerce. Do you agree?

9. Privacy of Car Trunks

After arresting a motorist in Washington, D.C., police searched his car and found a bag in the trunk that contained heroin. Convicted for possession of drugs and imprisoned, the man appealed. He argued that his Fourth Amendment protection against unreasonable search and seizure without a warrant was violated. Were the police wrong?

10. The Whites-Only Railroad Car

In July 1890, Louisiana passed a law requiring "equal but separate accommodations for the white and colored races" on railroad cars. In June 1892, Homer Plessy, a member of a group fighting the law, boarded a train in New Orleans. Letting it be known that he had "one-eighth African blood," Plessy sat in the whites-only car and was arrested when he refused to move to an all-black car. Does the 14th Amendment, which forbids the states to deny equal rights to all citizens, also forbid "equal but separate" accommodations for different races?

that no person shall be "deprived of life, liberty, or property without due process of law"—that is, without proper legal procedures. Therefore, Brink says, many citizens might be deprived of their rights if the Supreme Court could not review their cases. And, he adds, "if state legislatures followed the example of Congress and deprived state courts of constitutional jurisdiction, we would have no judicial review at all." That situation, he says, would leave the United States "without either an enforceable written Constitution or a court having the power to declare the process unconstitutional."

Among those who take a similar view is one of the nation's leading conservatives, Senator Barry Goldwater (R., Ariz.). In a Senate speech, Goldwater said that "to make a frontal assault on the independence of the courts is a dangerous blow to the foundations of a free society. In my view, the Supreme Court has erred. But we should not meet judicial excesses with legislative excesses. Now it is busing and abortion and prayer. But what will be next?"

The attempts to limit the court's jurisdiction raise another interesting question. What if a new law restricting court jurisdiction came before the court—and was ruled unconstitutional? The result could be a stalemate between branches of government and a serious constitutional crisis.

There would be irony in such a decision because the Constitution does not give the court the power of judicial review—that is, the power to overturn acts of Congress. Nor did Congress ever give the court such power. The Supreme Court simply took over that role beginning with a landmark decision in 1803 in a case called *Marbury v. Madison* and started a tradition that has never been seriously challenged. At the same time, however, many legal scholars agree that the writers of the Constitution clearly wanted an independent court system and intended the Supreme Court to take such a role. Before the Constitution was ratified, Alexander Hamilton wrote: "The courts were designed to be an intermediate body between the people and the legislature [Congress] in order . . . to keep the latter within limits [of their] authority."

Nevertheless, many storms have broken over court decisions. The first came after the court issued its first major ruling, in a case called *Chisholm v. Georgia.*

In 1792, a resident of South Carolina named Chisholm sued the state of Georgia demanding payment for property seized during the Revolutionary War. Chisholm based his case on Article III of the Constitution, which gave the Supreme Court jurisdiction over suits between a state and citizens of another state. Georgia insisted that the court had no jurisdiction over the case. In 1793, the Supreme Court upheld Chisholm's right to sue Georgia and found the state in breach of contract.

The storm that followed the announcement of that ruling probably seems incomprehensible to most Americans in 1982. But in 1793, the decision "fell upon the country with a profound shock," according to historian Charles Warren. In Georgia, legislators considered a bill to hang "without benefit of clergy" anyone who dared try to enforce the ruling. And in Congress, both the House and the Senate moved immediately to curb Supreme Court jurisdiction by passing a constitutional amendment barring such suits. Three-fourths of the states approved the 11th Amendment in less than one year.

Why such an uproar? One reason was that people held very strong feelings about the independence and rights of the states. There was also a lingering suspicion of the new federal government. The Constitution had been ratified only five years earlier and only after a hard-fought campaign to convince Americans that despite the establishment of a powerful central government, their liberties would be protected. The Chisholm decision suddenly made many people feel that they had been betrayed. The federal government could now haul a state into court against its will.

Over the next few years, the Supreme Court seemed content to let the dust settle. But in 1801, court power began to rise again when President John Adams appointed John Marshall as chief justice. One of the Marshall court's most important decisions, *Marbury v. Madison,* established the power of judicial review, the ability of the court to declare acts of Congress unconstitutional.

On his last night in office, President John Adams appointed William Marbury, a member of his party, justice of the peace in the District of Columbia. When James Madison, President-elect Thomas Jefferson's new secretary of state, withheld the appointment, Marbury asked the Supreme Court to order Madison to deliver his commission. Marbury contended that Section 13 of the Judiciary Act of 1789, which expanded the jurisdiction of the court, gave the court the power to act in the case.

Chief Justice Marshall and a majority of the justices ruled that Marbury's appointment was valid. But they also found that the court did not have the authority to force Madison to grant the commission. The justices said that Section 13 went beyond the Constitution in expanding the court's jurisdiction and therefore was unconstitutional. The case marked the first time the court had declared its power to overturn legislation passed by Congress.

The most controversial court decision of the 1800s probably was the 1857 case *Scott v. Sandford,* better known as the Dred Scott decision. In a 7-2 vote, the court declared that Congress could not ban slavery in United States territories and that blacks—free or slave—could not claim U.S. citizenship. The case greatly divided the nation and became a rallying cry for abolitionists.

In the early 1900s, liberal reformers were outraged by Supreme Court decisions striking down laws that regulated child labor, promoted the growth of labor unions, and provided compensation to workers who were unable to work because of accidental injury or

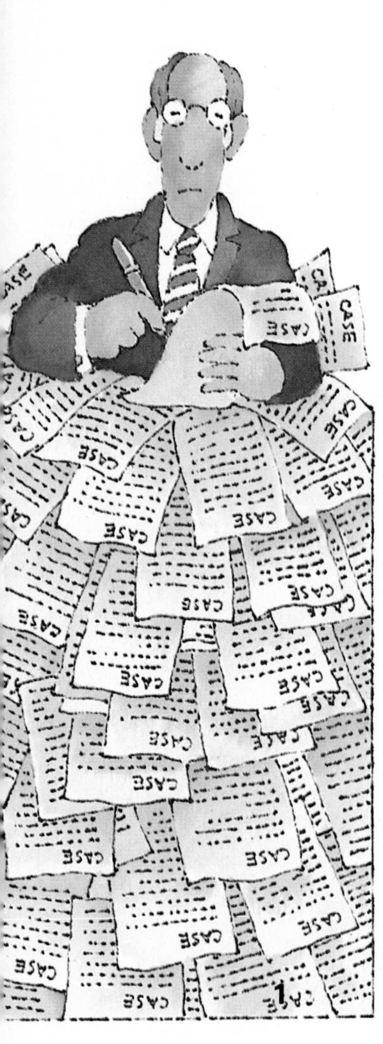

From the thousands of petitions for appeal received by the Supreme Court each year **(1)**, the justices agree to review fewer than 200 **(2)**. Following presentations of oral arguments in court **(3)**, the justices meet to discuss and vote on each case **(4)**. Written opinions explaining the decisions **(5)** may be revised many times before they are announced to the public **(6)**.

illness. In response, some members of Congress introduced bills that would have required the approval of six of the justices to overturn legislation. Beginning in the mid-1950s, the situation was reversed, and many conservatives complained about what they considered abuses of judicial power in cases involving school prayer, abortion, criminal rights, and school busing.

Through it all, the justices have carried on their work with little public notice of the winds of controversy sometimes swirling around them. Anyone who sees news reports on the number of appeals made to the Supreme Court each year and the number of decisions issued might wonder what a justice's workday is like. They might also wonder about the procedures and traditions that ensure the smooth operation of what one legal scholar called "the most extraordinarily powerful court of law the world has ever known."

During the 1981-1982 term, 4,172 appeals were filed with the

court. These petitions asking the court to review a case are called petitions for *certiorari*. The court agreed to hear only 184 of the cases, most of which came under the discretionary appellate jurisdiction of the court.

The court has two types of appellate jurisdiction—obligatory and discretionary. Losers in some types of cases have the right of direct appeal to the court. Such cases include those involving reapportionment of congressional districts and some civil rights and voting rights matters. These cases of obligatory jurisdiction, however, make up only a small fraction of the court's workload.

In all other cases, the court has discretionary jurisdiction — the right to decide whether it will review a case. By selecting only a small percentage of the appeals filed, generally those it considers the most important, the court can keep its caseload manageable.

Reading through more than 4,000 appeals sounds like a monumental task—and it is. But a trained staff helps smooth the process by seeing that each petition is in the proper legal order. They are assisted by computers that can quickly summon up background information on the cases and provide information on similar cases from the past. In the end, however, each justice must study each appeal. One former justice estimated that all the pleadings, briefs, and other papers coming to each justice to read average 3,700 pages a day.

Exactly how does this mill of justice grind out its decisions? The case history that follows, the 1982 ruling on whether illegal alien children are entitled to a free public education, is probably typical. The account includes information from former Justice Potter Stewart, whose retirement from the court in 1981 paved the way for appointment of Justice Sandra Day O'Connor, the first woman justice.

In 1975, the Texas legislature decided to do something about the flood of illegal alien children seeking free education in the state's public schools. It passed laws that forbade the use of state tax money for their education and allowed schools to deny the children enrollment. Two lawsuits challenging the constitutionality of the laws were filed in Texas courts. After lower courts ruled the laws were unconstitutional, Texas appealed to the Supreme Court.

Texas' petition was filed with the Supreme Court in 1981. Each justice received a copy of this petition along with copies of all the other appeals that had been made. "Each justice," Justice Stewart explains, "without any consultation with his or her colleagues, then reaches a tentative conclusion whether the petition should be granted or denied. I went through that process every recent summer with respect to almost a thousand petitions."

The petition in the Texas case was among about 200 placed on a "discuss list" by the chief justice. This list is really an agenda for the conferences that take place nearly every Wednesday and Friday during the court's term. The cases on the list usually involve important constitutional questions. Most petitions filed never make the discuss list. But no case is denied review without an examination by the justices, who may add any petition to the list submitted by the chief justice.

The conferences at which the discuss lists are reviewed are held in great secrecy. Only the justices are present. The junior justice acts as the guardian of the door to prevent unauthorized persons from entering. After shaking hands with one another as they enter, the justices sit around a long rectangular table. The chief justice, following the "discuss list" for that day, presents his thoughts on each case. Then each justice, in order of seniority, discusses the case. The junior justice speaks last, and then votes on whether to accept the case. The others now vote in opposite order from which they spoke. The chief justice votes last. A case must receive four "yes" votes to be granted certiorari.

The Texas petition was selected as one involving important and far-reaching questions. Congress had passed no federal law and taken no other definite action regarding the education of illegal alien children. Many persons in states with a large number of illegal aliens wondered why their tax money should be used to educate children who are not American citizens. The case also raised constitutional issues. The 14th Amendment says that no state shall "deny to any person within its jurisdiction the equal protection of the law." Is an illegal alien a *person* to which that amendment refers? And is a state responsible for the care of such a person?

Oral arguments in a case are presented during a hearing day about four months after a petition is approved in conference. During that time, attorneys for both sides submit legal papers to the court and each justice studies them.

Four months after the court granted the petition in the Texas case, it heard arguments. During his 30 minutes, an assistant attorney general for Texas argued that the state had a right to charge tuition or deny an education to the estimated 11,500 illegal alien children in Texas. Some of the justices, as often happens, asked questions.

"Doesn't the Texas statute punish children for something over which they have no control?" asked Justice O'Connor.

The Supreme Court has been called "the most extraordinarily powerful court of law the world has ever known."

Answers

1. The Broken Electric Chair

The court ruled 5-4 that Francis was wrong. The majority opinion was that the electric chair had been devised as a "method employed to extinguish life humanely." If the method is humane, then cruelty is not involved (*Louisiana ex rel. Francis v. Resweber,* 1947).

2. The Religious Factory Worker

The Supreme Court reversed the state court decision. It ruled 8-1 that this was not a matter of "an establishment of religion" at all but a matter of "free exercise" of religion, also guaranteed in the First Amendment. By making violation of conscience or religious beliefs a requirement for receiving an important benefit available to others, the state law had pressured Thomas in a way that was unconstitutional, the court said (*Thomas v. Review Board, Indiana Unemployment Security Division,* 1981).

3. The President and the Falkland Islands

The court refused to consider this challenge to a President's authority to determine whether a foreign nation has jurisdiction over a territory. The Constitution gives the President the right to recognize—and the power to refuse to recognize—foreign governments by giving him authority to appoint and receive ambassadors. The court ruled that Van Buren's decision fell under this provision and that Congress had no say in the matter (*Williams v. Suffolk Ins. Co.,* 1839).

4. Lincoln and the Prize Ships

The court ruled 5-4 that the Constitution grants Congress the power to declare war against another nation but not against a state or group of states. On the other hand, the President, as commander in chief, can call up the militia, even though he may not start a war or declare war. The court ruled in Lincoln's favor because, it said, the President must be able to take immediate action if the nation is attacked or invaded (*Prize Cases,* 1863).

5. Muddied Waters

The court ruled unanimously that it could not order Baltimore to pay Barron. The Fifth Amendment, it said, applies only to federal government action and the court has no constitutional authority to take action against a city or state (*Barron v. Baltimore,* 1833).

"They're going to be part of the community. . . . So you'd rather have them uneducated than educated?" asked Justice John Paul Stevens.

Following the arguments in open court, the justices hold one or more other conferences at which they discuss the case. Again, only the justices are present and there is absolute secrecy. When all the justices have had their say, a vote is taken. The junior justice votes first, followed by the other justices in order of seniority. The chief justice casts his vote last.

At any time, a justice can elect to stay out of a case altogether without announcing any reason to the public. Justice Thurgood Marshall, for example, removes himself from many cases in which the National Association for the Advancement of Colored People is involved because he once worked on its staff and argued its cases before the Supreme Court.

The next step is writing the opinions. These are statements explaining the legal issues in a case and the reasons for the decision. When the chief justice votes with the majority, he assigns one of the justices who agreed with him to write the majority opinion unless he wishes to do it himself. The minority justices then decide among themselves who will write the dissenting opinion. If the chief justice votes with the minority, the senior member of the majority writes the opinion or assigns it to another member of the majority. Each justice, however, can write a separate opinion. For example, justices who agree with the majority, but for different reasons, can write their own opinion explaining their views.

Writing an opinion can take weeks or even months as the justices sift through the sometimes complex issues in a case. During that time, the justices may change their mind and a new vote may be taken, with a new result.

Drafts of opinions are printed in great secrecy in the basement of the court building, then circulated among the justices for review. At this point, too, justices may be swayed by the arguments and change their vote. "Before everyone finally approves an opinion," says retired Justice Stewart, "a constant interchange goes on—by written memorandum, by telephone, in lunch table conversation. There was one case in my last term on the court in which I circulated 10 printed drafts before one was finally approved as the opinion of the court."

But finally the finished opinions are approved and printed and the decision is ready to be announced. In the Texas case, the court ruled on June 15, 1982, that laws restricting the education of illegal alien children were unconstitutional. Texas had lost its appeal. The vote was 5-4—with the chief justice voting with the minority.

How are the decisions announced? News reporters covering the Supreme Court are told in advance that decisions will be announced on a certain day. But they are never told what those decisions will be.

At exactly 10 A.M. each decision day, the justices file into the courtroom. The chief justice introduces the justice who has written the majority opinion and who will announce the decision. In the Texas case, that justice was William J. Brennan, Jr.

The justice giving the majority opinion sometimes speaks extemporaneously, explaining the opinion briefly. At other times, the justice may read a prepared statement or use extensive notes. Dissenting justices also present their views.

Afterward, the reporters pick up a complete set of printed facts about the case at a press desk. Before long, stories about the decisions are being telephoned to newspaper offices for the latest editions or being broadcast over television and radio stations. Then the decisions begin to create whatever change—or controversy—they will.

For further reading:

Abraham, Henry J., and Doherty, Grace. *Freedom and the Court: Civil Rights and Liberties in the United States.* 3rd ed. Oxford, 1977.

Baum, Lawrence. *The Supreme Court.* Congressional Quarterly, Inc., 1981.

Equal Justice Under Law: The Supreme Court in American Life. The Supreme Court Historical Society, 1981.

Witt, Elder, ed. *Guide to the U.S. Supreme Court.* Congressional Quarterly, Inc., 1979.

Woodward, Bob, and Armstrong, Scott. *The Brethren: Inside the Supreme Court.* Simon & Schuster, 1979.

6. Sexism in Help-Wanted Ads?

The paper was wrong, the court ruled 5-4, because the discriminatory headlines are "commercial speech," which is not protected by the First Amendment (*Pittsburgh Press Co. v. Pittsburgh Commission on Human Relations,* 1973).

7. The Name-Caller

Because "fighting words" can inflict injury and are not "essential" to the communication of ideas, they are not protected by the First Amendment, the court said in a unanimous decision (*Chaplinsky v. New Hampshire,* 1942).

8. The Stationery Seller's Fine

The court agreed with Robbins, ruling that taxing the sale of out-of-state goods or charging a fee for a license to sell goods before the goods are brought into the state is a tax on interstate commerce. And only Congress can set or allow such taxes. This decision still affects Americans today. A mail-order firm, for example, cannot charge a state sales tax on goods sold to persons out of state (*Robbins v. Shelby County Taxing District,* 1887).

9. Privacy of Car Trunks

In a 6-3 ruling, the court reversed its decision in a similar case made the year before. It decided that police may search car trunks, suitcases, paper bags, and other containers found in a car at time of arrest without obtaining a warrant—if they have probable cause to believe the car contains illegal substances (*United States v. Ross,* 1982).

10. The Whites-Only Railroad Car

The court ruled 8-1 that segregated railroad cars traveling *within* a state could not be forbidden by the federal government's power to control *interstate* commerce. It also ruled that the Louisiana law requiring separate but equal facilities for whites and blacks in the railroad cars did not violate the 13th or 14th amendments by creating inequality (*Plessy v. Ferguson,* 1896). However, in 1954, the Supreme Court ruled that segregated schools violate the equal protection clause of the 14th Amendment and therefore "separate but equal" facilities for different races are unconstitutional (*Brown v. Board of Education of Topeka,* 1954).

What Went Wrong in Central America?

By Ralph Lee Woodward, Jr.

A long history of violence, poverty, and political chaos lies behind today's turmoil

The setting sun cast a golden glow over a landscape that included dense tropical forests, a smoking volcano, a coffee plantation shaded by banana trees, and an array of brilliant flowers and exotic fruit trees. This was the view from the veranda of the palatial home of a Nicaraguan rancher and coffee planter with whom I was discussing the Sandinista revolution. The Sandinista National Liberation Front, a leftist group, had seized the government of Nicaragua several years before, in 1979.

"This is a crisis like when William Walker took over Nicaragua in 1856," the rancher told me. "And the result may be the same." My first impression was that there was little similarity between the Sandinistas and Walker, a military adventurer from Tennessee who came to power in the 1850s. At that time, two rival political parties — one liberal and the other conservative — struggled for control of Nicaragua. The liberals asked Walker for help. He went to Nicaragua in 1855 and quickly captured the city of Granada, a center of conservatism, for the liberals. But the next year, to the dismay of the people who invited him, Walker seized control of the government and had himself elected president of Nicaragua. He ruled for almost a year. Finally, in a surge of unity rare for Central America, Nicaraguans joined with conservative forces from Costa Rica, El Salvador, Guatemala, and Honduras, and drove out the invader.

"A crisis like Walker's take-over . . . what do you mean?" I asked.

"Well, it is the same in that the Sandinistas have brought a foreign power, actually two powers, to control Nicaragua, and it is having repercussions throughout Central America."

After the Sandinistas took over, those two powers—Cuba and the Soviet Union—sent thousands of military and technical advisers to Nicaragua and provided arms and training for Sandinista troops. The growing Cuban and Soviet presence in Nicaragua affected other Central American countries. Terrorism and violence increased throughout the region as leftist guerrillas, with Cuban-Soviet support, renewed their efforts to overthrow moderate or right wing governments. Indeed, I thought, all five Central American nations were being drawn into the conflict. Guerrilla warfare had raged intermittently in Guatemala for 20 years, but had reached new levels of violence during the past year. In El Salvador, a state of civil war had developed between government troops and leftist guerrilla forces, and the fighting had not ended with the election of a new government in 1982. There was new violence in Honduras amid charges that its military was intervening in El Salvador and Nicaragua. Just two days before my talk with the rancher, a bomb had shattered the offices of the Honduran national airline in San José, the capital city of Costa Rica. Only the night before, bombs had shut down electric power in Tegucigalpa, the Honduran capital. "But just as Central America united in the great national campaign to drive out Walker in the 1850s," the rancher continued, "I think it will again unite to liberate Nicaragua."

Revolution, of course, is not new to Central America. In 1821, amid glowing promises of a bright future, a small Creole aristocracy—people of Spanish ancestry born in the Americas—declared the area independent of Spain. The region, called the Kingdom of Guatemala in colonial times, had been a Spanish colony since the 1500s. Early in 1822, the new government in Guatemala annexed the Central American provinces to the newly formed Mexican Empire. The Mexican emperor was soon overthrown, however.

The Central American provinces quickly shed their ties to Mexico and in 1823 formed their own federal republic, the United Provinces of Central America, consisting of Costa Rica, El Salvador, Guatemala, Honduras, and Nicaragua. Although many of the inhabitants spoke Maya or other Indian dialects, the Spanish language, religion,

The author:
Ralph Lee Woodward, Jr., is professor of Latin American history at Tulane University in New Orleans.

and customs united the ruling classes. (Two other nations, Belize and Panama, are usually considered part of Central America. But in this Special Report, the term *Central America* refers to the five nations, linked by geography and history, that formed the United Provinces. Belize, a long-time British colony, and Panama, a former Colombian province, had different histories.)

The new nation had the good will of the major powers, and British merchants and bankers stood ready to invest in the development of Central American production and trade. Moreover, a United States company and other firms proposed to build a canal across Nicaragua that would enable ships to travel between the Atlantic and Pacific oceans without sailing around South America. Such a canal, Central Americans believed, would draw the commerce of the world to their country and make it the crossroads of the Americas.

But Central America did not become the model republic or prosperous nation that its founders had predicted. Instead, poverty persisted, political chaos and mismanagement became the rule, and the United Provinces disintegrated into five quarreling states whose independence was increasingly jeopardized by economic reliance on foreign investors. What went wrong? And why is there so much violence and social division in Central America today?

Jealous regional rivalries created problems from the start, but more important were differences in political beliefs among the elite regarding how best to develop Central America. These differences led to the development of two political groups, the liberals and the conservatives. The liberals generally favored the establishment of civil rights and wanted to end the special privileges of powerful landowners and the Roman Catholic Church. The conservatives wanted to maintain the privileges of the landowning elite and the church. Conflicts between the two groups divided the ruling families and the union in destructive turmoil. By 1840, the union had collapsed, and conservative dictators arose in each country. Although they joined forces to defeat Walker in 1857, efforts at permanent reunification failed, and Central America remains fragmented to this day.

After about 1870, the liberals came to power in what has been called the Liberal Revolution. They established governments in which most of the economic and political power was held by a few wealthy families. Such governments, known as oligarchies, have dominated Central America ever since.

The liberal oligarchies stripped the Roman Catholic Church of its former political power, seized many of its extensive landholdings, and took away its control of education. Without its former wealth and power, the church could not continue its traditional role as protector of the poor. Parishes went without priests, and church buildings fell into ruin.

The new liberal regimes maintained their power with professional military forces, trained by European and later North American

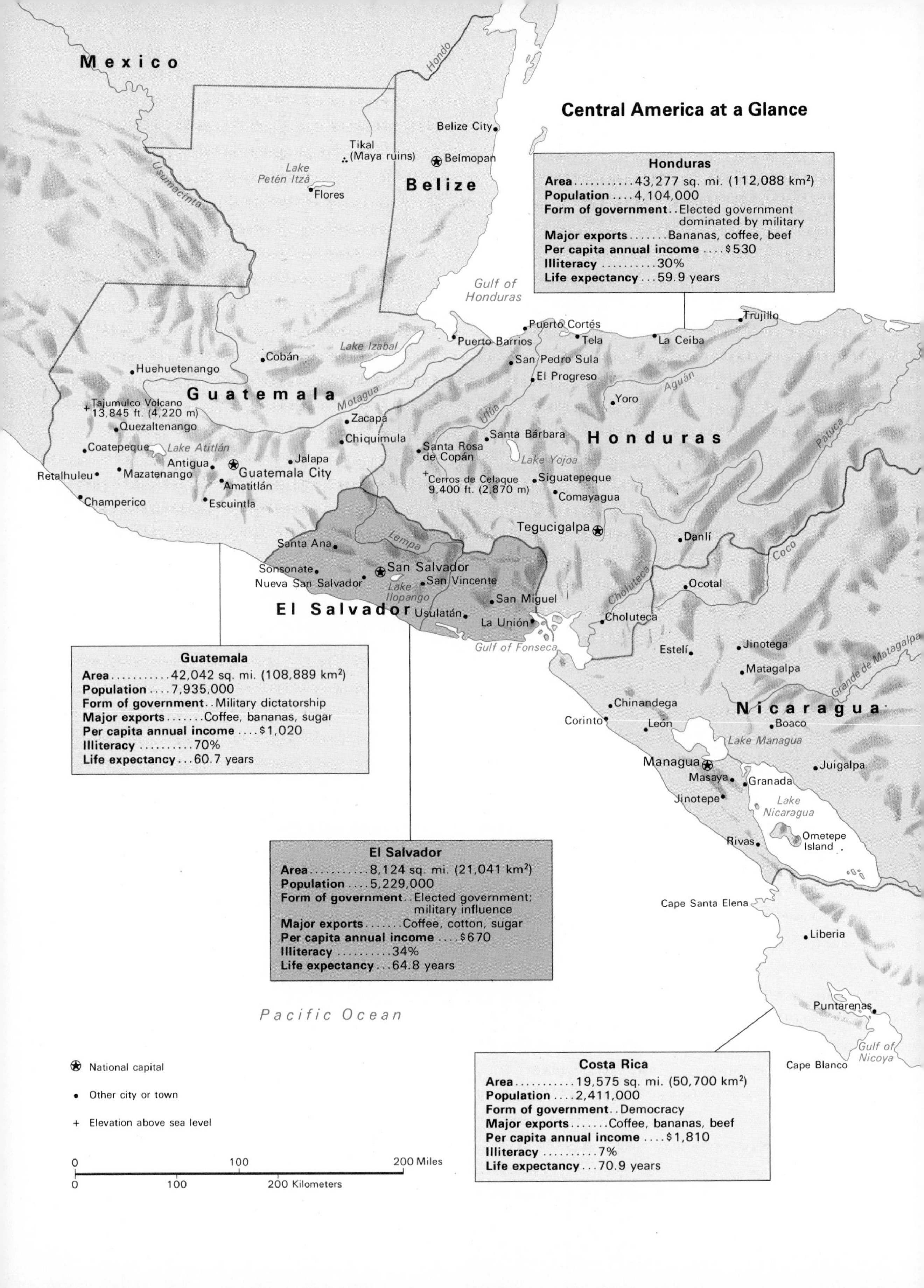
Central America at a Glance
Mexico
Belize
Guatemala
Honduras
El Salvador
Nicaragua
Hondo
Usumacinta
Belize City
Belmopan
Tikal
(Maya ruins)
Lake
Petén Itzá
Flores
Gulf of
Honduras
Puerto Cortés
Puerto Barrios
Tela
La Ceiba
Trujillo
Lake Izabal
Cobán
Huehuetenango
San Pedro Sula
El Progreso
Yoro
Aguán
Motagua
Tajumulco Volcano
13,845 ft. (4,220 m)
Quezaltenango
Zacapa
Chiquimula
Ulúa
Santa Bárbara
Santa Rosa
de Copán
Lake Yojoa
Patuca
Coatepeque
Lake Atitlán
Antigua
Guatemala City
Jalapa
Retalhuleu
Mazatenango
Amatitlán
Champerico
Escuintla
Cerros de Celaque
9,400 ft. (2,870 m)
Siguatepeque
Comayagua
Tegucigalpa
Danlí
Lempa
Santa Ana
Sonsonate
San Salvador
Nueva San Salvador
San Vincente
Lake
Ilopango
San Miguel
Usulatán
La Unión
Gulf of Fonseca
Coco
Choluteca
Ocotal
Choluteca
Estelí
Jinotega
Matagalpa
Grande de Matagalpa
Chinandega
Corinto
León
Boaco
Lake Managua
Managua
Masaya
Granada
Juigalpa
Jinotepe
Lake
Nicaragua
Rivas
Ometepe
Island
Cape Santa Elena
Liberia
Puntarenas
Gulf of
Nicoya
Cape Blanco
Pacific Ocean
National capital
Other city or town
Elevation above sea level
0
100
200 Miles
0
100
200 Kilometers
Honduras
Area...........43,277 sq. mi. (112,088 km²)
Population....4,104,000
Form of government..Elected government dominated by military
Major exports.......Bananas, coffee, beef
Per capita annual income....$530
Illiteracy..........30%
Life expectancy...59.9 years
Guatemala
Area...........42,042 sq. mi. (108,889 km²)
Population....7,935,000
Form of government..Military dictatorship
Major exports.......Coffee, bananas, sugar
Per capita annual income....$1,020
Illiteracy..........70%
Life expectancy...60.7 years
El Salvador
Area...........8,124 sq. mi. (21,041 km²)
Population....5,229,000
Form of government..Elected government; military influence
Major exports.......Coffee, cotton, sugar
Per capita annual income....$670
Illiteracy..........34%
Life expectancy...64.8 years
Costa Rica
Area...........19,575 sq. mi. (50,700 km²)
Population....2,411,000
Form of government..Democracy
Major exports.......Coffee, bananas, beef
Per capita annual income....$1,810
Illiteracy..........7%
Life expectancy...70.9 years

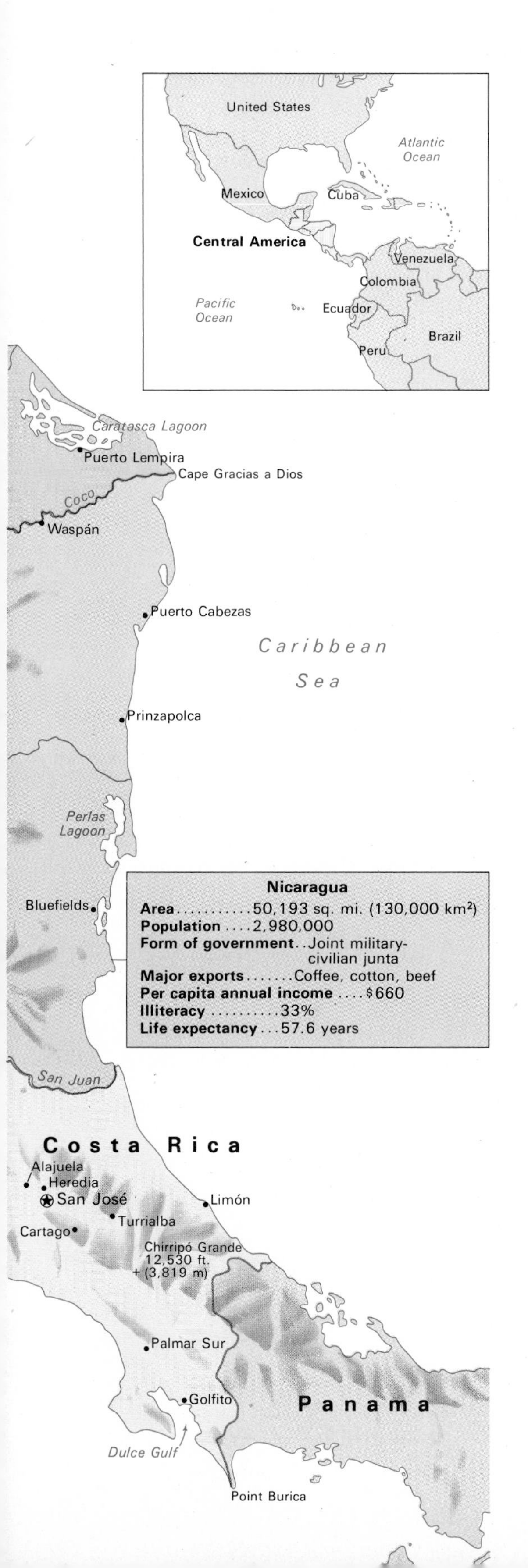

military instructors. These internal security forces became the key to the dictatorships that have characterized Central America in the 20th century.

The liberal dictator-presidents promoted economic development and sought to incorporate Central America more fully into the North American and European economies. A trickle of exports had flowed from Central American plantations to world markets since the 16th century, but most farmers produced goods chiefly for their own families. The liberal governments forced a major shift from such small-scale subsistence farming to large-scale production of coffee, bananas, sugar, and other tropical crops for export sale. Foreign capital financed much of this production.

The liberal regimes developed especially close political, economic, and cultural ties with the United States. Central American constitutions and judicial systems copied those of the United States. United States firms, such as the giant United Fruit Company (now United Brands Company), financed economic development and brought technology to the tropics. United Fruit began growing bananas in Central America during the late 1800s. The company cleared forests and drained swamps for plantations, and built railroads and ports to get the fruit to market. The firm also established hospitals and schools for its workers — and exported millions of dollars worth of Central American crops without giving local people much share in the profits.

Sometimes, the United States government sent troops to Central America to protect U.S. economic interests. In 1911, for example, two U.S. banks granted Nicaragua a loan under an agreement that gave them control over the country's finances until the debt was repaid. The next year, rebels opposed to U.S. control tried to overthrow the Nicaraguan government. At the request of the banks and the Nicaraguan president, U.S. Marines landed in Nicaragua in 1912 to put down the rebellion. They stayed almost continuously until 1933. Elsewhere, smaller interventions, gunboat diplomacy, and training of Central American militia and police forces by U.S. military advisers contributed to the Americanization process.

New universities served the expanding Central

American middle class, and some wealthy parents sent their children to U.S. schools. But the education of the masses, formerly provided mainly by the church, was virtually ignored, especially in rural areas. High rates of illiteracy retarded economic and technological growth. The elimination of many epidemic diseases, meanwhile, led to startling population increases, reaching about 3 per cent a year in most of the region. That rate of growth almost doubles the population every 25 years. The population explosion further strained the already inadequate educational and social services. Moreover, as the oligarchies put more good farmland into production of export crops, there was less and less for the peasants.

In the spring of 1982, I walked one day through a fertile valley in Guatemala. Coffee trees and cattle occupied all of the good land, producing coffee and beef destined for export. Only near the rugged hilltops surrounding the valley was there any sign of food production for local consumption. There, the land sloped so steeply that the peasants sometimes had to tie themselves to trees with ropes around their waists to cultivate their corn patches. I asked one man why they did not grow corn on some of the better land in the valley, where the yield would be much higher, and leave the hilltops for the cattle. The peasant shrugged, his eyes lowered submissively, and answered, "The *patrón* [boss] wouldn't let us do that."

Because most of Central America's best farmland is used for export crops, many peasants struggle to raise food for their families on rugged hills or other infertile land.

A week later, in the hills of northwestern Honduras, I met a family of seven who occupied a one-room hut made of bamboo and dried mud. They eked out a living selling eggs from a few chickens and working for the cattle rancher on whose land they lived. The wife told me she had given birth to 20 children, but most had died or gone to the city to work. A mango tree and other fruit trees supplied much of the family's diet, supplemented by freshwater shellfish from a nearby stream. The children had no shoes and only a few rags for clothing. They received no formal education.

That scene of poverty could be duplicated, with minor variations, throughout much of Central America. The poverty of the peasants stands in brutal contrast to the lavish wealth of the few who own the land. These oligarchs have luxurious houses in town and magnificent estates in the country. They wear the latest fashions from New York City, Paris, and Rome; and many send their children to Harvard, Yale, and other U.S. universities.

This unequal distribution of wealth and the growth of urban middle classes who were denied effective political participation and greater economic opportunity led to the serious challenges that now threaten the oligarchs and their military regimes. Modernization of the cities, combined with the conversion of subsistence agriculture to export production, stimulated a migration of rural people into the cities. Miserable slums and shantytowns developed in every Central American capital, testifying to the failure of the system to provide adequate jobs, housing, and social services for the displaced peasants and their families. Two groups especially, students and urban labor unions, urged reform. Their leaders often encouraged revolution. Thus, although the basic problems developed in the countryside, stemming from unfair land use and the failure to develop a stronger peasant class, most revolts occurred in the cities, calling for an end to the oligarchies established by the Liberal Revolution.

The Liberal Revolution had produced the best results in Costa Rica, in many ways an exception to generalizations about Central America. Both coffee, developed by relatively small Costa Rican landholders, and bananas, developed later by the United Fruit Company, contributed to growing prosperity. The nation had a small population of mostly Spanish descent, thus lacking the large numbers of Indians or Africans that were exploited in other Central American states. As a result, Costa Rica had fewer social and racial tensions. Wages were higher, land distribution was more equitable, and a stronger urban and rural middle class developed. Although the military played a role in supporting the liberal government, the Costa Ricans began early to put more emphasis on education than armaments. A democratic process developed, in which opposition parties could win elections and take office. In the mid-20th century, modern political parties, promising reform and social services, replaced the old liberals and conservatives.

Wealth and poverty exist side by side in Central American cities, where needy families inhabit shantytowns, *above,* and rich landowners live in luxurious houses, *right.*

In 1948, however, the Costa Rican government refused to step aside for its democratically elected successor. José Figueres, a Costa Rican farmer, headed a revolt and took over the presidency after a brief civil war. He disbanded the army, established social welfare programs, and after a year handed over the government to the actual winner of the 1948 election. Costa Rican voters later brought Figueres back to power. Over the years, his party—the Party of National Liberation (PLN)—has often lost the presidency in free elections to more conservative candidates, but it has been the dominant force in maintaining Costa Rican democracy and economic growth for the past 35 years. In 1982, Costa Rica faced the most serious economic crisis in its history. A rise in world oil prices, coupled with a drop in coffee prices and too large a foreign debt, had left the nation strapped. During this time of trouble, voters again elected the PLN after it had been out of power for four years.

Elsewhere in Central America, the revolution against liberalism and U.S. domination has been more violent and less productive. In the 1920s, the Nicaraguan rebel leader Augusto César Sandino launched a stubborn guerrilla war against the U.S. Marines in his country. Nationalists throughout Latin America heralded Sandino as a symbol of resistance to "Yankee imperialism." The Marines left in 1933, but not before they had trained a tough Nicaraguan National Guard, which assassinated Sandino in 1934. The guard suppressed political opposition and maintained the power of Anastasio Somoza García and his two sons, who controlled the government of Nicaragua directly or indirectly from the mid-1930s to 1979.

In 1944, a group of Guatemalan students, military officers, and professionals overthrew that country's dictator. The new revolutionary government carried out many social and economic reforms. After 1950, the government turned further left and began to take over privately owned land, including United Fruit Company plantations. The United States began to fear Soviet influence in Guatemala and supported a revolt against the government. The rebels invaded from Honduras in 1954 and established a regime more favorable to landholding, capitalist, and U.S. interests.

United States fears about the region increased when Fidel Castro led a revolution that took over Cuba in 1959 and, two years later, declared his government to be Communist. Castro's shift to the left prompted a right wing reaction throughout Central America during the 1960s. U.S. military assistance helped maintain repressive right wing rule in Guatemala, El Salvador, Nicaragua, and Honduras.

On the positive side, the 1960s witnessed the remarkable growth of the Central American Common Market (CACM), an economic union formed to lower tariffs and stimulate trade among its members. El Salvador, Guatemala, Honduras, and Nicaragua established the CACM in 1960, and Costa Rica joined in 1963. The common market prompted industrial expansion and enormously increased trade among the Central American nations. Many factories sprang up on the outskirts of Guatemala City, Guatemala; San Salvador, El Salvador; and other cities. However, many of the new industrial plants belonged to U.S. firms or multinational corporations, causing leftists to brand the CACM as a tool of "Yankee imperialism."

There can be no doubt that the CACM contributed to the expansion of the middle class, created new jobs, and generally raised per capita income. Unfortunately, the benefits were mixed. Guatemala and El Salvador, which were already more industrialized than the other states, gained even more. Honduras, on the other hand, imported more than it exported and suffered serious trade deficits. Moreover, liberalized immigration rules caused a large number of landless Salvadoran peasants to settle in the sparsely populated countryside across the border in Honduras. Hondurans resented the take-over of land and jobs by aggressive Salvadorans. Tension mounted, aggravated by a Honduran land-reform law that forced many Salvadorans living in Honduras to give up their land. In 1969, a riot that broke out at a soccer match between the two countries led to a conflict called the Soccer War. El Salvador invaded Honduras in July. Within a week, the two nations reached a cease-fire.

Central America has a shortage of schools and teachers. A Nicaraguan woman learns to read, *below left,* as part of a Sandinista government literacy program. The Roman Catholic Church still dominates the lives of Central Americans, *below right,* but most of them have had little schooling since the church lost its control of education in the 1800s.

After the war, Honduras withdrew from the CACM, which lost much of its earlier momentum. The decline of the CACM, a rise in world oil prices, and dropping coffee and sugar prices worsened the economic situation in all five nations during the 1970s. The political structures were under great strain.

Geology has also played a role in Central American affairs. Central America is a region of much volcanic and earthquake activity, and natural disasters have often compounded economic and political problems. In 1972, an earthquake devastated the city of Managua, Nicaragua. In the hard times that followed, it became evident that the ruling Somoza family was profiting handsomely from international relief efforts and from its monopoly on the building materials needed for reconstruction. Angry opposition arose both from business and landholding interests and from the Sandinista guerrilla organization. The Sandinistas had their roots in student movements and organized labor, and were named in honor of Augusto Sandino, the guerrilla hero of the 1920s and 1930s. In 1978, Pedro Joaquín Chamorro, editor of the opposition newspaper *La Prensa*, was assassinated. The murder shocked Nicaragua profoundly and touched off rioting, general strikes, and open warfare between the Sandinista

An urban middle class has begun to develop in many Central American cities. Members of the Nicaraguan middle class live in a comfortable neighborhood in Managua, *left,* and prosperous Costa Ricans shop in San José, *below.*

guerrillas and the Somoza regime. President Anastasio Somoza Debayle was almost alone, without support and barricaded in his bunker near the presidential palace, before he decided to flee the country on July 19, 1979. In 1980, he was assassinated in Paraguay.

After Somoza left Nicaragua, efforts to erect a moderate regime failed, and the Marxist-oriented Sandinistas seized power with Cuban and Soviet support. The war left the country economically crippled, but the Sandinistas began a bold revolutionary program. They provided new housing and health facilities for the poor, and sponsored a literacy campaign that was a notable success, though their record of economic achievement was otherwise bleak. They also carried out a military build-up that alarmed their neighbors and the United States. In 1982, U.S. officials estimated that Nicaragua's armed forces had grown to nearly 100,000 troops. In contrast, Somoza had a national guard of about 10,000 troops.

As it had been for Nicaragua, the year 1972 also was a crucial one for El Salvador, where José Napoleón Duarte, the leader of a moderate group called the Christian Democratic Party, apparently won the presidency after gaining much support among peasant and urban groups at the grass-roots level. But the government refused to

The Sandinista National Liberation Front, *left,* celebrates the third anniversary of the 1979 revolution in which it seized control of Nicaragua. Nationalists throughout Central America demand an end to "Yankee imperialism"—political and economic domination by the United States—symbolized by such U.S. firms as McDonald's Corporation, *above.*

recognize Duarte's victory. Violence escalated as the opposition turned to guerrilla warfare against the government. Right wing death squads loyal to the government murdered thousands of political opponents, calling them Communist. By the late 1970s, a state of civil war existed between the guerrillas and the government. The left wing Sandinista victory in Nicaragua alarmed moderates as well as rightists in El Salvador, and in October 1979 a group of young military officers and civilians seized power in a coup and declared a program of peace and reform. Duarte soon returned from exile in Venezuela to head the new government. He launched a sweeping land-reform program, trying to deprive the leftist guerrillas of a major issue—unfair land distribution—that had won them much peasant support. To some degree Duarte succeeded, but he also alienated the old oligarchy and elements of the military, which embarrassed his government with frequent and flagrant violations of human rights. By early 1982, the country was exhausted, the economy at a near standstill. Elections, which the guerrillas boycotted but failed to disrupt, gave the Christian Democrats the largest number of votes but not enough for a majority of seats in the legislature. A coalition of right wing parties joined forces to form a government

United States military aid has supported right wing governments in El Salvador, Guatemala, and Honduras. A U.S. military adviser helps train Honduran soldiers, *right.*

and brought to power a former army major named Roberto D'Aubuisson. Many people blamed D'Aubuisson for the assassination of Roman Catholic Archbishop Oscar Arnulfo Romero y Galdamez, one of Central America's most outspoken and respected clergymen. Romero had been killed by gunfire in 1980 as he celebrated Mass. The new Salvadoran government was officially headed by Alvaro Magaña, a moderate. With the assistance of U.S. military advisers, the government continued its war against the guerrillas.

Meanwhile, there was growing opposition to the Sandinistas both inside and outside Nicaragua. The governments of the other four Central American states began to work together to defend themselves against the threat of Marxist revolution spreading from Nicaragua. Skirmishes occurred along the country's borders. United States military aid to Nicaraguan exiles and to right wing governments in Honduras, El Salvador, and Guatemala strained U.S.-Nicaraguan relations, and Central America appeared braced for a showdown that might involve the entire region.

Perceptions of the turmoil in Central America vary considerably. To a substantial degree, the conflict is an internal one, in which lower- and middle-class interests are challenging the oligarchies established a century ago. Yet much of the leadership in this struggle still comes from the elite. As they did during the 19th century, the leading families are quarreling among themselves, often violently, over how best to develop their countries. Moderate Social Democratic and Christian Democratic parties might be able to make the transition from the old oligarchies to more modern democracies while resisting Communist solutions. But to date, except in Costa Rica, the polarization between right and left extremes has excluded moderate parties from real power.

The struggle in Central America is also strongly nationalistic, aimed at freeing the region from its dependency on the major powers — a goal referred to as "national liberation." This dimension of the conflict is strongly anti-American, because the United States has been the dominant power in the region for the last century and has been closely identified with the oligarchies that are resisting change. This anti-American character makes it especially difficult for the United States to play an active role in solving Central America's problems. Some experts think that the United States should leave such neighbors as Mexico and Venezuela to serve as mediators and leaders in the region. In a larger sense, the anti-U.S. feeling in Central America is part of the North-South conflict, the struggle between the wealthy, industrialized nations of the Northern Hemisphere and the developing countries of the Southern Hemisphere.

These varying perceptions reflect the complexity of events in Central America and the difficulty in solving them. Within Central America, there seems to be a new popular opposition to revolutionary solutions and guerrilla warfare. Whether this will favor extremists or will encourage moderate parties remains to be seen. There is growing recognition that the problems are regional and not confined to single states. A united and stronger Central America could better face the difficulties that modernization has presented. Despite recent setbacks, there is still much support for reunification, and the present crises make the need clearer than ever before.

For further reading:

Ameringer, Charles D. *Don Pepe: A Political Biography of José Figueres of Costa Rica*. University of New Mexico Press, 1978.

Browning, David. *El Salvador: Landscape and Society*. Clarendon Press, 1971.

Gettleman, Marvin E., et al., eds. *El Salvador: Central America in the New Cold War*. Grove, 1981.

Millett, Richard. *Guardians of the Dynasty: A History of the U.S. Created Guardia Nacional de Nicaragua and the Somoza Family*. Orbis Books, 1977.

Walker, Thomas, ed. *Nicaragua in Revolution*. Praeger, 1982.

Webre, Stephen. *José Napoleón Duarte and the Christian Democratic Party in Salvadoran Politics, 1960-1972*. Louisiana State University Press, 1979.

Woodward, Ralph Lee, Jr. *Central America: A Nation Divided*. Oxford University Press, 1976.

The ABC's of Testing

By Winton H. Manning

First as students and later as workers, Americans face a lifetime of standardized examinations designed to evaluate their abilities and assess their progress

Alphabet soup might make the ideal meal to nourish all those who face a lifetime of participation in the great American testing experience. From SAT to ACT, GED to GRE, and LSAT to MCAT, students are subject to a wide range of examinations designed to determine their skills, knowledge, intelligence, and interests. The days when a high school senior's hardest task was to score 75 out of 100 per cent on Miss Smith's own supertough English exam to earn a C are long gone. People today — young and not so young — are continually required to measure themselves against others or against a standard in a broad variety of tests in school and business. There are tests to measure your progress through grade school and high school. Tests to get you into college and tests before you can get out of college. Tests to get a driver's license. Tests to get a job and sometimes tests to keep a job. There are always tests. How did all this testing come about? What is the purpose? Where can we expect it all to lead?

Tests have been used in education and employment since ancient times. More than 3,000 years ago, for example, the emperors of China established a system of examinations to select young men for government service. The system assured that entry into at least some

Starting in kindergarten, testing – sometimes with the use of electronic gear – becomes an integral part of the life of every student.

levels of government would depend on test performance rather than on the influence of powerful patrons. During the 1700s, the British government adopted the Chinese idea of civil service examinations. By the end of the 1800s, nearly every Western nation had a similar program. The basis for appointing public servants thus had shifted from class patronage to individual merit.

The growth of civil service exams in the 1800s occurred at a time when many biologists and other scientists began to develop an interest in the individual differences among people. These scientists studied variations in such simple functions as reaction time and devised techniques to measure individual differences over a wide range of human performance and physical characteristics. The scientists then began to reason that if obvious differences among people, such as differences in height and weight, followed certain statistical or mathematical laws, perhaps those laws also governed other human characteristics. They thus began to study mental abilities, such as a person's ability to recall a string of numbers or how quickly a person could respond to a signal.

Scientific interest in individual differences was also closely associated with the development of statistics as a field of study. To this day, the effort to *quantify* (measure) aspects of human performance is intertwined with mathematical theory and statistical methods. The field of science that deals with the mathematical foundation of testing is called *psychometrics*. In the past 50 years, psychometrics has contributed greatly to the improvement of testing.

The author:
Winton H. Manning is senior vice-president for development and research of the Educational Testing Service, Princeton, N.J.

The earliest studies of individual differences were mainly *descriptive;* that is, scientists were interested in measuring human abilities or knowledge quantitatively and studying the systematic distribution, or arrangements, of their measurements. Soon, however, they began to wonder whether, or how well, various measures of individual differences were related to one another. In particular, scientists began to wonder whether tests could be *predictive;* that is, if it would be possible to predict how well a person would perform one task by knowing how well that person had done on another task. If investigators could show a sufficiently close relationship between test results and later performance on a job or in school, they could then use test scores to identify those who were likely to do best on the job or in school.

In the early 1900s, such psychologists as Alfred Binet and Theodore Simon of France and Lewis M. Terman and Edward L. Thorndike of the United States discovered that tests of memory, perception (the ability to recognize patterns or visualize objects in various situations), and the ability to learn quickly were useful predictors of later performance. Scientific work on the development of intelligence tests then progressed rapidly. Soon after World War I started in 1914, a committee of psychologists began to devise paper-and-pencil intelligence tests for use in selecting recruits for the United States armed services. These tests — the Army alpha and Army beta — became widely known. In the years that followed, American educators and employers enthusiastically embraced the use of tests.

During World War II (1939-1945), complex physical and mental tests, backed by massive research, played a significant role in the placement of men and women in all the military services, but especially in the Army Air Forces. The enormous cost of training pilots and such other skilled personnel as navigators and bombardiers proved the need for testing to decide who should be selected for training. The success of testing during World

Students in Florida must pass competency tests – achievement tests designed to measure their knowledge of material at a given grade level – before they can pass to the next higher grade.

Florida Student Assessment Test
Sample items/Grade 5 Reading

1. Look at the sign and choose the answer that best tells what the sign means.

   a. People
   b. Men
   c. Women
   d. In

2. Choose the sign that means "School Crossing."

a.

b.

c.

d.

3. When you see this sign on the door of a store, what does it mean?

   OPEN

   a. There is a sale in the store.
   b. You may go in the store now.
   c. You may not go in the store.
   d. You must push to open the door of the store.

4. When you see this sign on a street corner, what does it mean?

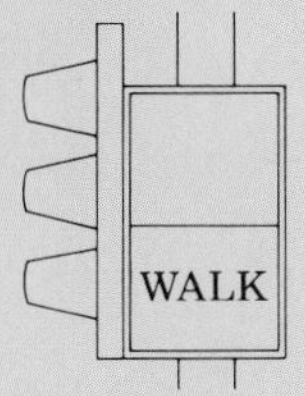

   a. It is safe to cross the street now.
   b. It is not safe to cross the street.
   c. Be sure to stay in the crosswalk.
   d. This is the way to walk to school.

5. If you did not know the meaning of a word, where would be the best place to look?

   a. in a dictionary
   b. on a map
   c. in a newspaper
   d. in a telephone book

(Answers on page 105)

War II intensified interest in using tests by an increasingly large number of businesses and schools.

Testing today is widespread, particularly in the United States and Western Europe. So many kinds of tests are used for so many purposes that a testing industry has developed. The industry consists of dozens of research, development, and publishing firms. The examinations the industry has devised are fundamentally different from the tests a classroom teacher makes up to determine whether students have learned the course material. The main difference is that professionally developed tests are *standardized*. Standardized tests have been used, revised, and used again until they show consistent results. Carefully specified conditions have been developed for administering and scoring the tests. For example, one of the largest sources of unreliability in tests is the varying standards different teachers use for grading essays. For this reason, multiple-choice questions are used in standardized tests. They eliminate the judgment involved in evaluating "free response" questions.

Why has testing become so widespread? The reasons are complex and debatable, but three major factors were certainly contributory:

■ The scientific development of testing occurred at a time when the practical needs of people in the United States and other Western democracies began to change. Rapid industrialization created many new jobs, and formal education was expanded to include a wider range of subjects. Urbanization and better use of the limited work force called for more efficient methods of evaluating human abilities.

Most colleges require that prospective students take entrance examinations like the Scholastic Aptitude Test, *opposite page,* which assesses skills needed to do well in school. Once accepted, students can sometimes take advanced placement tests, *below,* to see if they know enough about specific subjects to skip basic courses and study at a higher level.

SECTION II

Time—30 minutes

25 QUESTIONS

In this section solve each problem, using any available space on the page for scratchwork. Then decide which is the best of the choices given and blacken the corresponding space on the answer sheet.

The following information is for your reference in solving some of the problems.

Circle of radius r: Area $= \pi r^2$; Circumference $= 2\pi r$
The number of degrees of arc in a circle is 360.
The measure in degrees of a straight angle is 180.

Definitions of symbols:

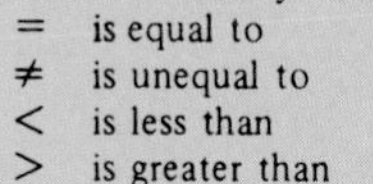

$=$	is equal to	$\leq$	is less than or equal to
$\neq$	is unequal to	$\geq$	is greater than or equal to
$<$	is less than	$\parallel$	is parallel to
$>$	is greater than	$\perp$	is perpendicular to

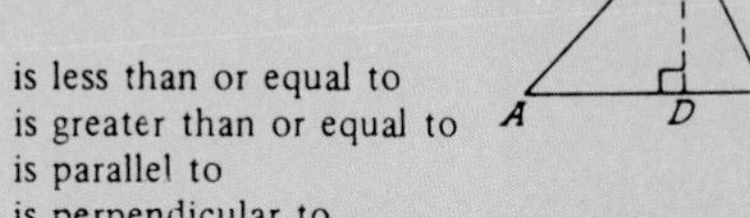

Triangle: The sum of the measures in degrees of the angles of a triangle is 180.

If $\angle CDA$ is a right angle, then

(1) area of $\triangle ABC = \frac{AB \times CD}{2}$

(2) $AC^2 = AD^2 + DC^2$

Note: Figures which accompany problems in this test are intended to provide information useful in solving the problems. They are drawn as accurately as possible EXCEPT when it is stated in a specific problem that its figure is not drawn to scale. All figures lie in a plane unless otherwise indicated. All numbers used are real numbers.

1. If $x^2 - 1 = y$ and $x = 3$, then $y^2 =$

(A) 81 (B) 64 (C) 9 (D) 8 (E) 4

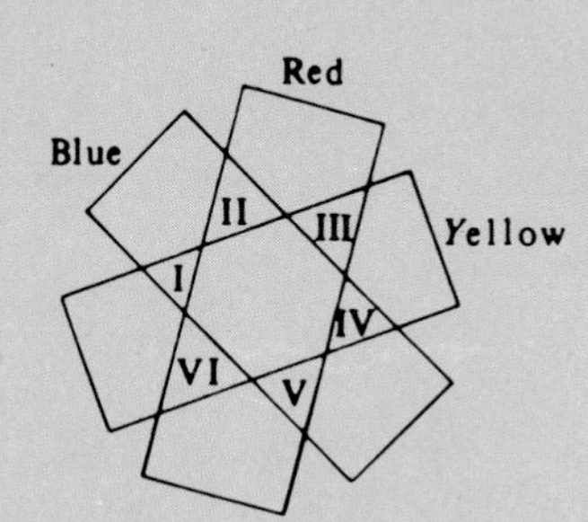

Red + Blue : Purple
Red + Yellow : Orange
Blue + Yellow : Green

2. The figure above shows strips of colored glass that overlap to form other colors as shown by the color chart. Which two labeled triangular regions would be green?

(A) I and III
(B) I and IV
(C) II and V
(D) III and VI
(E) IV and VI

ℓ_1
ℓ_2
ℓ_3
ℓ_4

3. In the figure above, if $\ell_1 \parallel \ell_2$, $\ell_2 \parallel \ell_3$, and $\ell_1 \perp \ell_4$, which of the following statements must be true?

I. $\ell_1 \parallel \ell_3$
II. $\ell_2 \perp \ell_4$
III. $\ell_3 \perp \ell_4$

(A) None (B) I only (C) I and II only
(D) II and III only (E) I, II, and III

4. If $100 \leqq k \leqq 400$ and k is a multiple of 5, 6, 7, and 10, then $k =$

(A) 105
(B) 150
(C) 210
(D) 300
(E) 350

(Answers on page 105)

Electronic instruction offered by a private coaching service helps some college graduates review facts they will need to know to meet entrance requirements for professional studies like law and medicine.

Testing came to be seen as the best tool to reduce guesswork and risk in making selection decisions in schools, factories, and offices.

■ The development of testing also appealed to citizens of democratic societies. Tests emphasized merit rather than privilege or influence as the basis for selection. In addition, many people believed that social progress depended on continually expanding the application of scientific methods and knowledge to human affairs.

■ Tests that certified a person's competency at the end of a formal educational or training program satisfied the need for public accountability. Such tests enabled government authorities to grant licenses to practice various professions on the basis of factual rather than personal evaluations.

Let us consider the nature of tests, who is involved in the testing process, and what standards determine the usefulness of a test. Every test is merely a *sample of behavior;* that is, it is an indication of certain abilities or other characteristics of a person. Most tests measure learning achievements, learning abilities, aptitudes and interests, or personality. In most cases, three parties are involved in testing. The *test developer*, someone like me or one of my colleagues at the Educational Testing Service (often working with a committee of high school and college teachers), for example, designs the specifications for the test, prepares it, and conducts research to ensure that the test meets professional standards. The *test taker*, such as a student or job applicant, answers the test questions, and expects to be told how well he or she performed. The *test user*, such as a school official or personnel officer, uses the scores and other information provided by the test to reach a decision about the person who took it.

To be a good sample of behavior, a test should meet four criteria:

- The test should be *reliable;* that is, the measurement, or score, should be as free from error as possible and be obtained under standard, controlled conditions.
- The test should have *validity*, which means that interpretations, or predictions, based on the score should be accurate and justified. A test may have validity for one purpose but not for another. For example, a test of reading comprehension might validly predict how well a student would do in a history course but have poor validity for predicting the student's success in a mechanical-drawing class.
- The test should be a *sufficient* sample of behavior and therefore cover most of the important aspects of what is being tested. In some cases, obtaining a sufficient sample is fairly straightforward. For example, a test that is a "work sample," such as a typing test, is a sample of the task obtained under standard conditions. In such a complex task as flying an airplane, test developers often study the job carefully by conducting a *job analysis.* They then construct a test or series of tests that reflects each major aspect of the job.
- Finally, *fairness* in a test is critical. No one should have access to the questions or answers ahead of time. In addition, questions that give a person an unfair advantage over others because of social background, race, or sex should be eliminated. In some cases, unfairness can arise through the use of vocabulary that is specific to a particular region, ethnic or social group, or school curriculum.

The goal of test developers is to devise tests that meet the standards of reliability, validity, sufficiency, and fairness. Professional organizations have established technical standards for constructing tests. Most widely used tests have been developed according to these standards and have been evaluated by independent researchers. Every year, even more new tests are devised as personnel, educational, and clinical psychologists seek to extend their usefulness.

The many kinds of tests can be classified in various ways. One classification depends on whether a given test is designed to measure *maximum* or *typical* performance. Tests of maximum performance include *achievement tests* and *aptitude tests*. Such tests yield scores along a scale that ranges from "excellent" or "good" at one end to "unsatisfactory" or "poor" at the other end. Most achievement tests are given at the end of a course. They assess the degree to which the student has mastered a subject, such as history or mathematics.

Aptitude tests help forecast how well a person is likely to do in

An aspiring driver in Illinois must pass three kinds of tests before receiving her license. A paper-and-pencil test, *above,* assesses her knowledge of traffic rules; an eye test, *top right,* checks vision; and a road test, *above right,* demonstrates her ability actually to handle a moving car.

the future. Most of these tests are given to people entering a course of study, applying to a college, or seeking a job. Achievement and aptitude tests differ much less than is often supposed because aptitude, rather than being something you are born with, depends heavily on learning. Indeed, the same test can sometimes be regarded as a measure of prior learning (achievement) or as a predictor of future learning (aptitude), depending on how it is used.

Tests of typical performance assess aspects of personality. They do not use a scale that ranges from "good" to "poor." Instead, neither end of the scale is "good" or "poor"—only different. The assessment reflects personality traits that range, for example, from "cautious" to "impulsive" or from "quick tempered" to "lethargic." Many such assessment tests are questionnaires about a person's preferences, typical attitudes, or dispositions.

School counselors increasingly use *diagnostic tests* in addition to assessment tests. Diagnostic test scores help people understand their strengths and weaknesses. For example, a reading test might identify the sources of a student's reading difficulties. In the case of diagnostic tests, the test taker and the test user are often the same person. In evaluating diagnostic scores, counselors seek to help people reach their own decisions as they plan their educational programs and careers. Interest in diagnostic tests has grown greatly because the test results can strongly influence an individual's future. However, a qualified counselor should supervise and assist the test taking.

Psychiatrists and psychologists sometimes use *projective tests.* In

To show a new employer that her typing skills are transferable to modern technology, a typist prepares a timed "work sample" on a word processor.

these tests, a person is given a task that could have many "answers." For example, the person may be asked to make up a story in response to a picture or to tell what images are suggested by inkblots. Projective tests require skilled interpretation by a specially trained person and are almost always used only by psychologists or psychiatrists to aid diagnosis of personality.

Interpretation of test scores is a critical aspect of testing. Unlike a score on a teacher-made test, a score on a standardized test is almost never directly understood as the number or percentage of items answered correctly. The number of items answered correctly is a *raw score*. To be useful, that raw score must be placed in a context. In many cases, it is placed in context by preparing a *table of norms*, in which the distribution of scores for a large sample of people taking the test is compiled. From this table, it is possible to establish the score levels below which varying percentages of test takers fall. For example, the 30th percentile is the level below which 30 per cent of the scores fall. The score of a particular test taker is converted to a percentile rank. Thus, we might find that a person's raw score of 57, for example, would equal a percentile rank of 30. In other words, the test taker's level of performance exceeded 30 per cent of the total group but fell below 70 per cent of it.

Some tests have their own special score scales. For example, the Scholastic Aptitude Test (SAT) given by the College Entrance Examination Board (usually called the College Board) reports scores on a scale from 200 to 800. Although 500 is the middle of the scale, it is not the average score on the test. The average is about 425. The SAT has no passing grade. Students receive a percentile rank for their scores, and each college has its own standards for interpreting the scores.

Scores achieved on the SAT or the assessment tests of the American College Testing Program (ACT) are highly important to high school students who want to be admitted to college. These students may therefore desire materials or special coaching to prepare for the tests. Test publishers provide free or at small cost complete descriptions and explanations of test items as well as full-length sample tests. These materials may be obtained from the College Entrance Examination Board, 888 Seventh Avenue, New York, N.Y. 10019, or from the American College Testing Program, Box 168, Iowa City, Iowa 52240. Testing agencies encourage students to use the materials to familiarize themselves with the conditions of standardized testing and the kinds of tests they will face.

Many high school students purchase books or the services of commercial coaching firms to help them prepare for college entrance exams. However, parents should know that most students show small improvements in test performance from cramming. Such gains have relatively little effect on admissions to most colleges. The typical result of coaching on the SAT has been a gain of less than 15 points on the verbal section of the exam and less than 20 points on the mathematics section. On the average, these gains represent two or three additional correct items in each section. Some students might benefit much more, however, especially if they have not recently studied mathematics in school.

As the impact of the testing industry on education, business, and government has increased, so has the controversy over some aspects of testing. The three major points of controversy concern test validity, test bias, and truth-in-testing.

Just how valid are tests? In recent years, this question has been applied especially to college admissions tests. Thus, the question might be rephrased: "Just how valid are college admissions tests?"

In evaluating the validity of an admission test, two major sources of evidence must be analyzed. First, the content of the test should be relevant; that is, it should be logically related to what the test users are trying to predict. A careful look at the content of SAT or ACT tests shows that these tests cover such skills as reading, vocabulary, problem solving, and mathematical reasoning—all of which are important tools of learning in college. The second source of evidence of validity is the extent to which test scores predict success in college as measured, for example, by grade-point average for the freshman year. Such predictions are never perfect, however. Errors are unavoidable for reasons ranging from varying motivation of students to mistaken measurements in both the test and grades. Nevertheless, when judged in relation to such predictors as letters of

Opposite page: An aptitude test measures a person's skills and interests and helps identify school courses and jobs he or she might find rewarding.

MECHANICAL REASONING

Description: This test measures how well you understand basic mechanical principles as they apply to machinery, tools, and motion. Since the questions deal with simple or familiar objects, special training in physics or mechanical work will have little effect on your score. People who do well in Mechanical Reasoning usually find it easy to learn how to repair and operate complex devices. Occupations such as carpenter, mechanic, engineer, electrician, and machine operator are among those that require good mechanical reasoning ability.

DIRECTIONS

Find the space for Mechanical Reasoning on the Practice Answer Sheet.

This test consists of a number of pictures and questions about those pictures. Look at the example below, to see just what to do.

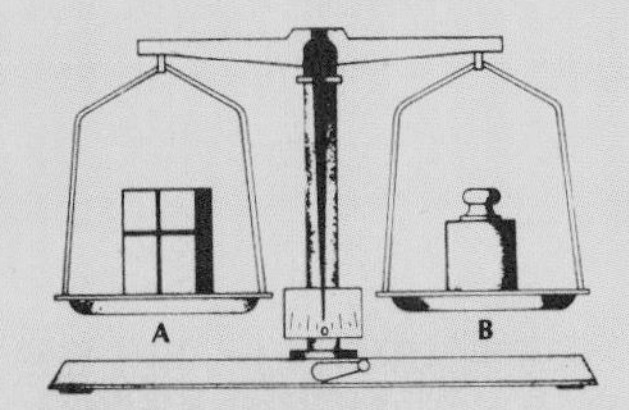

Example Y.

Which weighs more?
(If equal, mark C.)

Example Y asks, **Which weighs more? (If equal, mark C.**) As the scale is perfectly balanced, **A** and **B** must weigh the same, so you should have filled in the circle for C on line Y of your Practice Answer Sheet. Read each following question carefully, look at the picture, and mark your answer on the Practice Answer Sheet. Do not forget that there is a third choice for every question.

PRACTICE QUESTIONS FOR MECHANICAL REASONING

1.

Which horse has to run faster to win the race?
(If neither, mark C.)

2.

Which boat would be easier to tip over?
(If no difference, mark C.)

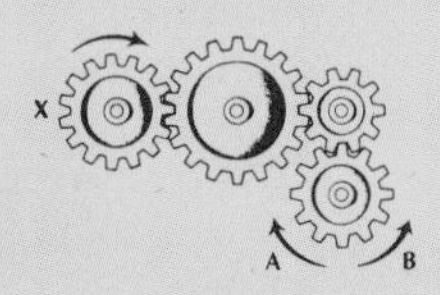

3.

When gear "X" turns in the direction shown, which way does the bottom gear turn?
(If either, mark C.)

(Answers on page 105)

reference and personal interviews, scores on admissions tests stand up well. The typical validity of the SAT is not much lower than the validity of high school grades. Together, admissions tests and high school grades have a strong relation to college grade-point averages.

On the whole, admissions tests are useful predictors. The controversy tends to center on the fact that they are not perfect predictors. Some people fault the tests for not assessing such desirable characteristics as courage, honesty, creativity, and concern for others. Many college admissions officers try to consider such qualities, but the methods of appraising them are unscientific and personal. As a result, many people mistakenly believe that test scores alone determine who gains college acceptance. However, a joint 1979 study by the College Board and the American Association of Collegiate Registrars and Admissions Officers reported that less than 2 per cent of college admissions officers regarded scores as the chief determiners of who is accepted at their schools. A survey made a year earlier by the American Council of Education reported that 95 per cent of all college freshmen attended the college of either their first or second choice. Most students would be reluctant to see admissions tests eliminated as long as high schools differ in grading. These students

Making a night landing in a flight simulator is a "hands-on" test that gauges a pilot's continuing capability to fly an airplane safely.

realize that abandoning the tests would leave those who attended schools with demanding programs at a disadvantage compared with those from schools where most students easily received high grades.

The question of test bias arises because on most educational tests consistent differences have been found between various ethnic and racial groups for many years. The subject received much attention from the news media on Oct. 4, 1982, when the College Board for the first time released a breakdown of SAT scores by minority groups. Those scores were for 1980-1981 and showed that most minorities did less well than white majority students. On October 13, the College Board released the 1981-1982 scores. Although the minority scores were still far below those of the majority, they showed improvement. The average 1981-1982 scores for white students were 444 in the verbal part of the test and 483 in math. For minority groups, they were as follows: blacks, 341 in verbal and 366 in math; American Indians, 388 and 424; Mexican Americans, 377 and 416; Asian Pacific Americans, 398 and 513; and mainland Puerto Ricans, 360 and 403. For all males, the median scores were 431 in verbal and 493 in math. For all females, the scores were 421 and 443.

The minority test scores reflect the unequal opportunities — social, educational, and occupational — that have existed among minorities for generations. Indeed, College Board President George H. Hanford said he hoped that publishing the SAT scores would "illuminate the extent and nature of the educational deficit this nation must overcome." He expressed concern that the relatively low scores for minority youths "lend themselves to misinterpretation by those who seek simple explanations." He emphasized that, despite their situation, "a significant number of minority youths score well on the SAT." In fact, Hanford added, "Our examination of SAT scores since 1976 indicates that, as a whole, minorities are making progress in closing the gap that exists between their scores and those of the white majority."

One common way to evaluate whether admissions tests are biased is to see whether the difference in test scores between groups is reflected in a corresponding difference in later performance in college or graduate school. In other words, in predicting college grades from test scores, does it make any difference whether the score is for a minority student? Most studies have shown that tests predict about equally well for minority and majority students.

Despite these findings, many people still believe that admissions tests must be biased, or else the average differences between minority and majority scores would not be so large and so persistent. To some extent, controversy over test bias is fueled by the mistaken idea that tests measure unchangeable inherited intelligence. However, many years of research have shown that performance on educational tests largely reflects learning and that test performance, at least in the early years of life, can be improved markedly through a better

Testing experts say that, for the most part, students show only small improvements in test performance after cramming. But current classes of students probably will continue to cram, a practice that figures strongly in memories of school days – and nights.

intellectual environment. Rather than assuming that tests are biased, many minority educators now believe that strict standardized tests are the best evidence available concerning the gap to be closed in assuring equal educational opportunities for all children.

We now come to the question of truth-in-testing. The process of developing, standardizing, and validating a test is lengthy and costly. Therefore, testing agencies have generally reported scores to students but have not published the questions or provided students with a copy of their answer sheet. This practice has been challenged as not providing truth-in-testing. It is said to be unfair to the student, who might profit from review of the test and who could, if the answer sheet were available, challenge the accuracy of the scoring or the construction of test items.

In principle, students should be able to review their test answers, simply as a matter of fairness. But to reveal the answers to every test as soon as it is given would require continually creating new tests. This practice might drive up the cost of tests and so hinder the process by which good tests are developed that the entire testing system would be weakened. During the last five years, legislation to require testing agencies to return their tests and answer sheets to test candidates was proposed in New York, California, and many other states. A compromise was finally reached. For the most part, students may now ask for copies of the test questions and of their answer sheets. Surprisingly, relatively few students have done so. Today, truth-in-testing applies almost exclusively to college and graduate school admissions tests. Professional licensing examinations, civil service examinations, and other tests used in employment and education are excluded. The principle of fairness would suggest that truth-in-testing also be applied in these situations.

Truth-in-testing is only one more aspect of the growing concern many people have about the way institutions use tests and other personal information. For example, personality tests have increasingly fallen into disfavor in industry and education because the questions often appear to invade a person's privacy. Invasion of privacy becomes a matter of serious concern if the tests are used by people untrained in clinical psychology, psychiatry, or counseling or if responses to test questions are not kept confidential. Testing has also come under fire in the courts, when unvalidated tests have been required by employers or when tests have been used to screen out minority applicants. Court decisions and state and federal regulations now require employers to develop research data supporting their testing requirements.

Sample Test Answers
Page 93: 1. C; 2. B; 3. B; 4. A; 5. A.
Page 95: 1. B; 2. B; 3. E; 4. C.
Page 101: 1. B; 2. A; 3. B.

The next 10 years are likely to bring about the most far-reaching changes in testing since the introduction of objective, standardized, paper-and-pencil tests. These changes will come about as tests are developed for administration at the computer terminal. Test takers will be able to receive immediate feedback on the correctness of their answers. In addition, the computer can be programmed to select questions at the appropriate level of difficulty for each student—neither too easy nor too hard.

The most promising developments are in increasing the complexity of test questions. A test taker using a terminal can answer "branching questions" in which a sequence of problems is presented, each depending on the preceding response. Most problem solving involves sequential exploration of alternatives. Questions involving sequential problem solving are awkward with paper-and-pencil testing, but the computer terminal makes them possible.

More and more capabilities for improved testing will open up as a result of the coming widespread availability of inexpensive computers, two-way television, and related technological developments. The rapid evolution of electronic communication devices offers a broad new range of possibilities for devising better tests that will provide good assessment and be educational as well. In the future, therefore, testing is likely to become an even more useful tool for both individuals and institutions.

For further reading:

Anastasi, Anne. *Psychological Testing*. Macmillan, 1981.
Dobbin, John. *How to Take a Test*. Educational Testing Service, 1982.
Ebel, Robert. *Essentials of Educational Measurement*. Prentice-Hall, 1979.
Feder, Bernard. *The Complete Guide to Taking Tests*. Prentice-Hall, 1979.
Millman, Jason, and Pauk, Walter. *How to Take Tests*. McGraw-Hill, 1969.
Whimbey, Arthur, and Lochhead, Jack. *Problem Solving and Comprehension*. The Franklin Institute Press, 1981.

The Video Revolution

By Mark Schubin

New technology has transformed the role of the video screen, and even more changes lie ahead

"Jenny, keep your eye on the wall screen or you'll miss the separation of the space telescope from the shuttle arm," Tom Henderson warned.

"I'm watching, Dad," the teen-ager replied, looking up at the television screen that covered much of the Hendersons' living room wall.

"I know you're watching," said Henderson. "Watching your wrist video. Here it is, an important moment in history, the first deployment of a space telescope from the Space Shuttle. But you want to watch something else. What is it?"

"I wasn't really watching my wrist video," Jenny protested. "It's turned to the high school tennis matches, but I only glanced at it."

This scene would have been considered science fiction in 1950 and far-fetched as recently as 1970. Yet it could take place in the 1980s. Researchers in the United States are experimenting with wall-screen television, and a Japanese company has already made a test model wrist TV.

These two developments are only a small part of a great ongoing revolution that has already changed television in many ways. Ten years ago, for example, the typical TV viewer had only six or so channels to choose from—all broadcasting from local stations. The video revolution has made possible such scenes as the following:

- A family in Oklahoma is trying to pick a program to watch on television. No one is interested in what is on the major network stations. However, the family is not discouraged. It has 60 other channels to choose from.
- A sailor on a freighter in the Atlantic Ocean relaxes in front of the ship's television set. He can watch a perfect picture, even though the ship is more than 1,000 miles (1,600 kilometers) from the nearest television station.
- In the United States, hearing-impaired people watch television programs that have captions, while their neighbors watch the same programs on the same channels without the captions.
- In Australia, people wearing special glasses view television shows whose images seem to have three dimensions—depth as well as height and width. When the viewers remove the glasses, the images appear in the two dimensions of ordinary television.

The marvels of the video revolution go on and on. They include the development of videotape, video cassettes and videodiscs, home television cameras, and video games and home computers. In short, the video revolution is rapidly turning the TV set into a home entertainment and information center.

The video revolution began in the 1970s. Before then, television viewers could watch only what was transmitted by the few stations in their area. In 1945, the United States Federal Communications Commission (FCC) had set aside 13 channels—numbers 1 through 13—in the very high frequency (VHF) band of broadcast waves for television. The FCC dropped channel 1 in 1948, however, and broadcasters were not permitted to use more than seven of the remaining channels in an area because transmissions on closely spaced channels interfered with one another.

The author:
Mark Schubin is a technological consultant based in New York City who frequently writes about the world of video.

The FCC made channels 14 through 83 available in the ultrahigh frequency (UHF) band in 1952, and the first UHF television station went on the air in that year. Unfortunately, broadcasters could use only a few UHF channels in a particular area because UHF channels are even more easily affected by interference than are VHF channels. Furthermore, few television sets could receive UHF signals until 1964, when federal law required manufacturers to include UHF tuning in all new sets. Even then, UHF tuning was more difficult than VHF tuning. Finally, new regulations required manufacturers to make UHF and VHF tuning comparable in 1970.

The introduction of *cable television* eventually led to far greater program diversity. Cable TV transmits signals by means of cables rather than through the air. Its original purpose was only to bring television to places that could not receive signals clearly — or at all — through the air because hills and mountains deflected broadcast waves.

The first cable television systems began operating in 1948 in Mahanoy City, Pa., and Astoria, Ore. Each system was little more than an antenna mounted on a hilltop to pick up a TV signal, with cables trailing down to the community it served. Cable systems thus became known as *community antenna television* (CATV).

By 1965, the United States had 1,325 CATV systems, which served about 1.3 million homes. Many of the systems used *microwave radio links* (sets of receiving and transmitting equipment operating at extremely high frequencies) to import broadcasts from distant cities and so increase program diversity.

The CATV systems could use all 12 VHF channels because cable television is not easily subject to interference. In the late 1960s, CATV operators even began to use more than 12 channels, either by running two cables to subscribers or by providing them with converters that shifted signals transmitted outside the VHF range to signals that ordinary TV sets could receive.

In mid-1982, more than 5,000 cable television systems were in operation. They served about 25 million homes. Fifteen systems provided fewer than five channels, while 2,000 offered 20 channels or more. The latest cable systems offer more than 100 channels.

Cable operators are filling the extra channels by means of two breakthroughs in video technology — video cassettes and small satellite antennas. These devices solved production problems that plagued early operators who wanted to set up *pay-TV systems*, on which viewers pay a fee to see certain programs in their homes.

One such operator began a pay-TV experiment with a small Canadian system in 1952. Viewers who wanted to watch special programs had to feed coins into a device attached to the television set. Unfortunately, no workable *videotape-recording system* existed at that time. Videotapes can be played back immediately after recording and provide good quality pictures and sounds. Without a videotape system, all programs had to originate live or be on film. Cable operators trying to produce enough programs to fill their channels found that the production expenses of live entertainment and the cost of renting film were too high, and the pay-TV experiment failed.

A workable videotape recorder, in which the tape was wound on

New video sources provide a variety of home viewing to suit the viewer's needs. A videodisc player, *above left,* supplies images from a store catalog. A video cassette recorder, *above right,* plays a motion picture, while a home computer, *below,* displays instructional material.

Young people meet the video revolution in an arcade, *above,* where they push, pull, and twist mechanical controls in games with computer-generated images.

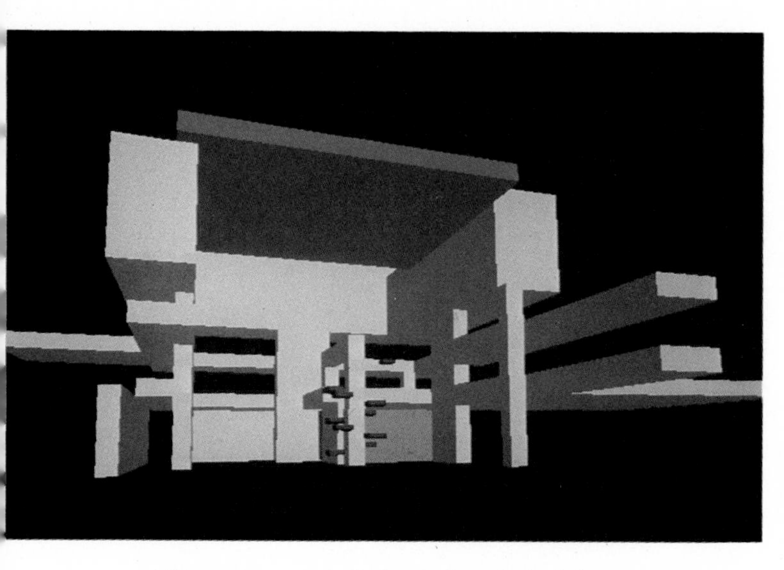

Video screens help in the design of a building, *above,* by showing a computer-generated perspective view, and aid motion-picture animation, *right, top to bottom,* by displaying computer-drawn images.

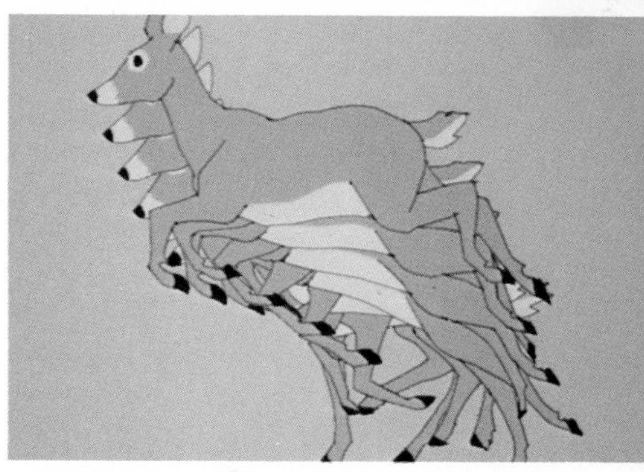

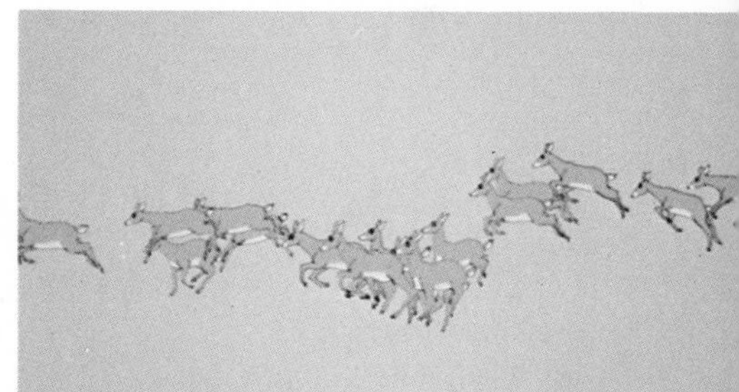

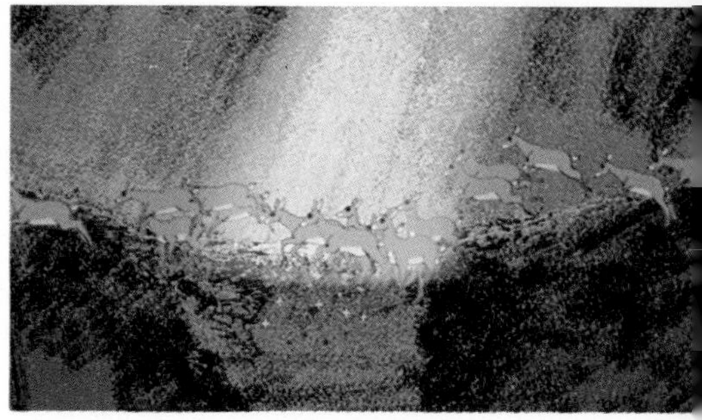

Japan Computer Graphics Lab in conjunction with the New York Institute of Technology Graphics Lab.

open reels, was introduced in 1956. The device was so expensive, however, that CATV systems could not afford it. In the 1960s, the development of a new recording technique reduced the price of an open-reel videotape recorder from about $100,000 to about $1,000. The picture quality was poor, however, and the machine required expert attention.

The introduction of the video cassette recorder (VCR) in 1971 was a milestone in the video revolution and breathed new life into the pay-TV industry. Instead of being wound on open reels, the videotape was enclosed in a cassette. In 1972, more than 40 cable television systems began pay-TV operations using video cassette players and set-top signal-decoding devices that allowed customers to pay a monthly bill instead of keeping a pocketful of change.

In 1973, cable system operators held their annual convention in Anaheim, Calif. Operators who expected to sign contracts with video cassette movie services to get more programs for their systems got a shock. On a truck in the Anaheim Convention Center's parking lot sat a huge, dish-shaped object—an antenna designed to receive signals from a space satellite. Although the antenna was 28 feet (8.5 meters) in diameter, it was small compared with the 100-foot (30-meter) antennas then used for satellite reception. Furthermore, the $100,000 price was a tiny fraction of the cost of the larger antennas. This meant that cable system operators would soon be able to draw on program material beamed to them via satellite.

One pay-TV company, Home Box Office (HBO)—a subsidiary of Time Inc.—began transmitting programs by satellite in 1975, and two cable systems immediately bought dish antennas to receive them. A TV signal is sent from earth to the satellite, which strengthens the signal, changes its frequency, and sends it back to earth. The antenna captures the signal, and it is then sent to viewers by cable. Soon after HBO's debut, more pay-TV companies began to use the satellite, and more cable systems bought dish antennas. Eventually, one satellite was filled to its 24-channel capacity, and a second began to fill.

Opposite page: A wide variety of wires and waves will carry video signals to the home from broadcasting companies and from data services such as computer networks and teletext and videotex facilities. Viewers will receive signals via telephone lines, television cables, and antennas.

Pay-TV companies, which provided chiefly movies and sports programs, were not the only firms that used satellites to transmit signals to cable systems. The second cable system satellite channel was taken by a firm that simply retransmitted the signals of WTCG (now WTBS), a UHF station in Atlanta, Ga. The station carried many movies and sports events. WTCG was difficult to receive over the air in the Atlanta area, but it came in clearly to cable customers throughout the United States. WTCG became known as a *superstation* because of its vast coverage.

Cable system operators today have so much programming available that they offer subscribers a variety of services. All cable systems provide a *universal service* consisting, at a minimum, of the over-the-air stations normally received in an area.

How the Video Revolution Reaches the Home

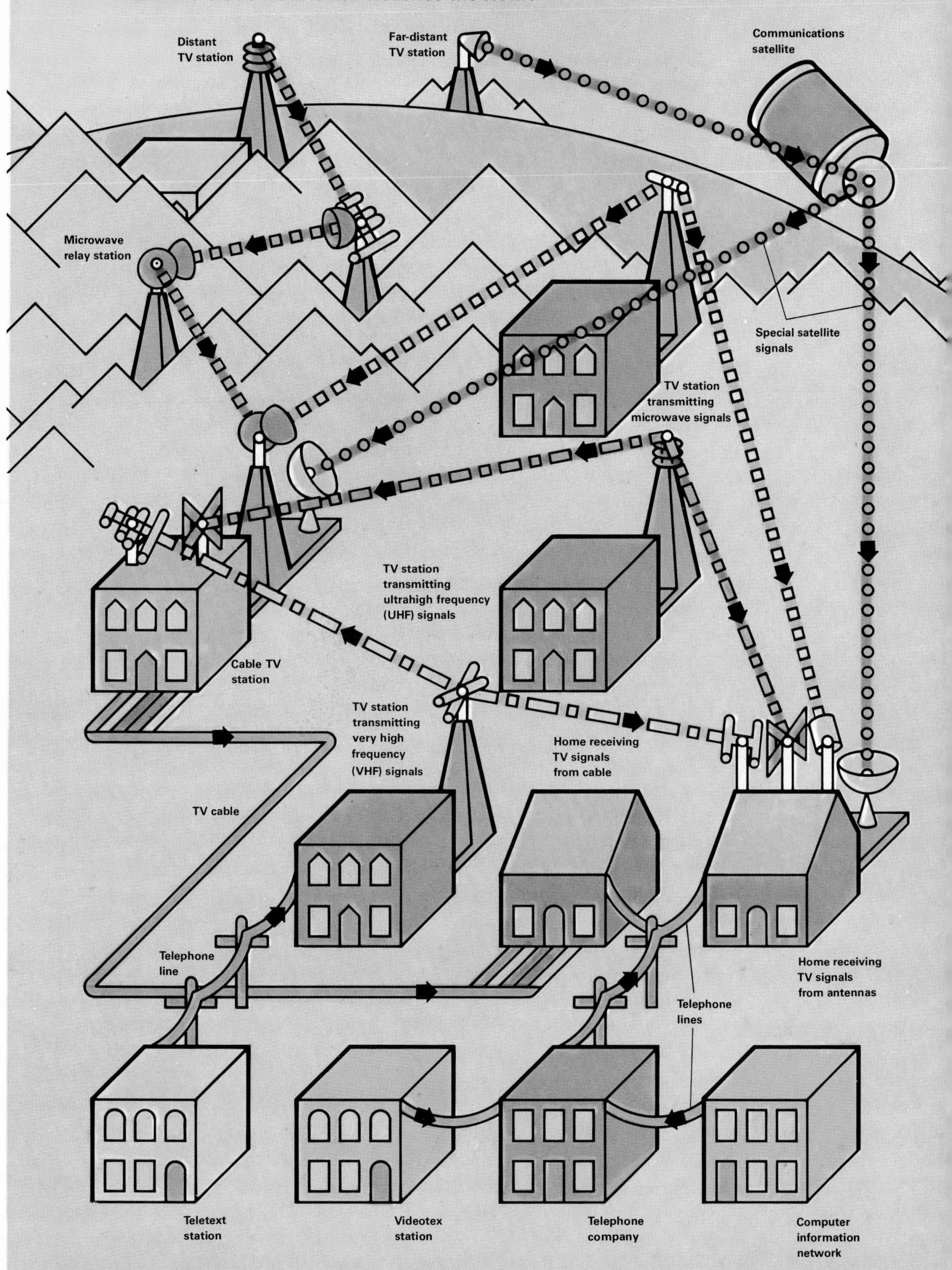

Most cable operators provide *basic service*. For the same monthly fee, subscribers receive universal service plus satellite channels. An operator may also offer individual pay-TV channels, or *premium channels*. The operator may charge a monthly fee for each premium channel or lump the channels into groups, called *tiers*, and charge a single fee for each tier. For example, a subscriber may buy a movie tier. Some subscribers buy a *deluxe tier*, consisting of all the premium channels that the cable operator offers. Certain cable operators charge subscribers a specific fee for each program viewed, a technique called *pay-per-view*. Other operators add pay-per-view charges to a monthly premium charge only for major events, such as boxing matches. To prevent viewers from seeing events they haven't paid for, cable operators sometimes use devices called *addressable decoders*. These devices can turn off a nonpaying subscriber's channel remotely, without affecting anyone else's picture.

Cable operators may soon face competition from companies that send signals to the home by microwaves rather than over cables. Microwave transmission developed from the expansion of pay-TV into hotel in-room movie systems in 1971. In 1973, in-room systems took a step forward when a pay-TV operator began to broadcast microwave signals to two hotels in the Washington, D.C., area from a single location. The transmission system, called Multipoint Distribution Service (MDS), was technically identical to a system that had fed educational programs to schools for years. In 1974, an MDS operator secured an agreement to feed HBO's pay-TV programming to apartment buildings in the New York City area. Microwave transmissions travel in a straight line and are especially convenient when one building—such as a school or an apartment building—can be served by one master antenna. These systems also can use decoders to ensure that only paying customers are able to receive a clear picture.

MDS has been restricted by the FCC to only one or two channels in any area. However, MDS operators are seeking multiple-channel licenses that would enable them to compete more fully with cable systems.

Both cable and MDS got some potentially unwelcome company in 1977. That year, Bob Cooper, a cable television engineer in Oklahoma, installed a satellite antenna in his backyard. Cooper's antenna, which cost $20,000, caused a legal battle when Cooper refused to apply to the FCC to have it licensed. In 1979, the FCC said that a private owner of a satellite antenna needs no license. Viewers who use satellite antennas still are supposed to get the permission of programmers to watch their shows. The price of a *satellite earth station*—the antenna and associated electronic devices—has now declined to about $1,000.

However, even a television viewer who has a satellite earth station, an MDS receiver, and a 100-channel cable feed could still be at the mercy of television programmers. For example, there might be six excellent programs at 8 P.M. and no good ones at 10.

Beginning in the 1960s, manufacturers tried to solve the timing problem with a videotape recorder for consumers. The recorders of the 1960s were too complex, however, and the video cassette recorder introduced in 1971 was too large. A number of home recording systems were developed, but none captured the consumer market. Then, in 1976, Sony Corporation of America introduced Betamax, which caught on. Betamax could record a one-hour program. Later the same year, Japan Victor Corporation (JVC) brought out Video Home System (VHS), which had a two-hour capacity. Sony and JVC then introduced VCR's that recorded more slowly, increasing the recording time. The current champion is the VHS-SLP (Super Long Play), which can record up to eight hours of programming on one cassette.

Most of the first VCR's had a simple timer that enabled them to record a program unattended for later viewing. This feature is called *time-shifting*. Later machines could record up to eight programs at different times and on different channels over a three-week period. Some machines even had automatic cassette changers and so could record or play up to 48 hours of tape continuously.

Soon after the introduction of the VCR's, a huge market for sales and rentals of prerecorded video cassettes emerged. Most of these cassettes are tapes of movies. However, there are also scientific cassettes, art cassettes, and a large variety of instruction cassettes on such diverse subjects as dog training, stained-glass craftwork, tap dancing, and magic. One reference manual lists more than 35,000 titles. Cassettes are widely played by sailors on merchant vessels, workers on oil-drilling platforms, and other people in remote areas out of the range of commercial broadcasting.

VCR's have led to another marvel of the video revolution: the home television camera. Sales of home television cameras to dealers totaled about 115,000 in 1980 and were expected to climb to 400,000 in 1982.

Today's home TV cameras must be operated with separate VCR's. A cable connects the camera to the VCR. The smallest recorders weigh only 5½ pounds (2.5 kilograms). Nevertheless, video recording is still less convenient than using a self-contained movie camera. However, video professionals are already using the *camcorder*, a newly developed combined camera and recorder. The first consumer camcorder is expected to be marketed in 1985. It will record at least one hour on a cassette and be about the size and weight of a super-8-millimeter movie camera.

Another device that plays prerecorded programs on TV is the *videodisc player*, which resembles a phonograph. It plays back material recorded on flat, round platters called *videodiscs*. There are two main kinds of disc systems. One of them uses a stylus that rests on the

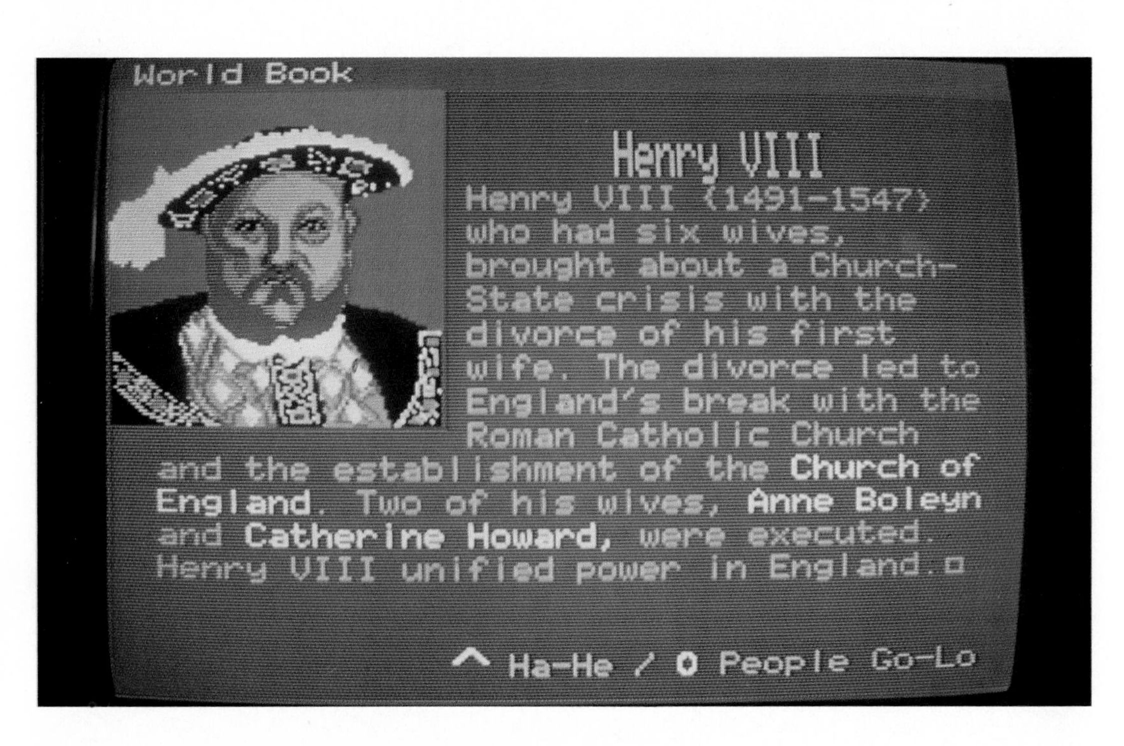

A still picture, called a page, of data can be transmitted as part of an ordinary television broadcast in a system called teletext, *above,* or by telephone lines in a similar system called videotex, *below.*

disc to convert the material recorded on the disc into a TV signal. The other system is an optical system that reads a pattern of reflected light on the disc's surface.

Videodiscs date from the early days of television. They were sold in London in the 1920s and the 1930s. However, the picture quality was poor. From 1936 to 1975, no videodiscs were sold anywhere in the world. During that time, TV producers first used film and then videotape to record programs. The research that produced today's videodisc players was done in the days of expensive videotape recorders. Experts therefore thought that the videodisc player would be the first low-cost playback device. However, Betamax was introduced first.

Today's least expensive videodisc players cost somewhat less than the cheapest VCR's, and videodiscs are much less expensive than prerecorded cassettes. However, videodisc players cannot record programs. Only about 200,000 videodisc players were in use in the United States in 1982, compared with about 4 million VCR's.

Videodiscs have a significant advantage over VCR's for purposes other than entertainment, however. Almost any point on a videodisc can be reached in seconds, while searching through a cassette may take minutes. A computer hooked up to a videodisc player can therefore be instructed to present different pictures according to different viewer responses. One side of a videodisc can contain one or more motion sequences or up to 54,000 *frames* (still pictures).

The cost of the computer might have made a hookup with the videodisc player far too expensive until 1971, when the *microprocessor* was developed. This device, which handles many of the functions of a computer, is built on a silicon chip smaller than a thumbnail.

Many video components contain microprocessors. VCR's use them to control unattended recording, and videodisc players use them to find frames. Experimental television sets use microprocessors to switch channels when viewers give them a spoken command.

However, the microprocessor's most important contribution to the video revolution has been in the development of the home computer, which appeared toward the end of 1974. The home computer is becoming increasingly common. Manufacturers expected to sell 2 million home computers in the United States in 1982.

Actually, the expected sales figures for home computers in 1982 would be higher if they included the sales of some video game consoles. The distinction between home computers and game consoles is rapidly blurring. The first home video game, introduced in 1972, was easy to distinguish from a computer. The game displayed crude pictures and provided only an electronic version of table tennis. It was connected to the antenna terminals of a television set and cost less than $100. Computers, on the other hand, provided detailed pictures. However, they had to be connected to special visual displays called *monitors* and cost thousands of dollars.

Video Components and Services in United States Homes in Mid-1982

Component or service	Number of homes	Percentage of homes
Television set	82,000,000	99+
Option to subscribe to cable TV	49,000,000	60
Cable TV	25,000,000	30
Pay-TV received on cable	17,000,000*	21
Video game	9,000,000	11
Video cassette recorder	4,000,000	5.9
Pay-TV broadcast on regular channels	1,500,000*	1.8
Home computer	1,400,000	1.7
Pay-TV broadcast on microwave	850,000	1.0
Videodisc player	200,000	0.24
Satellite earth station	150,000	0.18
Computer databank	90,000*	0.11

*Number of subscriptions.
Sources: Various industry authorities.

Cable Television Subscribers in the United States

Subscribers as of January 1 (in millions)

1970	1971	1972	1973	1974	1975	1976	1977	1978	1979	1980	1981	1982
4.5	5.3	6.0	7.3	8.7	9.8	10.8	11.9	13.0	14.1	16.0	18.3	21.0

Source: *Television and Cable Factbook.*

Estimated Sales of Video Equipment to Dealers

	1979	1980	1981	1982
Television sets	16,600,000	17,500,000	16,700,000	17,000,000
Video games	400,000	2,200,000	4,200,000	8,000,000
Video cassette recorders	600,000	920,000	1,400,000	2,000,000
Home computers	150,000	325,000	500,000	2,000,000
Home video cameras	Negligible	115,000	185,000	400,000
Videodisc players	Negligible	20,000	175,000	300,000

Sources: Various industry authorities.

A Chronology of Video Firsts

1878—First article about an electronic video system published
1880—First book about video published
1884—First patent for a video camera issued
1900—First use of the word *television*
1925—First recognizable image of a human face viewed on video
1926—First facsimiles of documents transmitted by radio
1927—First broadcasting station devoted to television
1928—First 3-D TV experiments; first successful demonstration of color video; first videodiscs
1929—First movie on television
1930—First video projection in a theater
1941—First licensed commercial television station in the United States
1948—First cable television system
1950—First broadcast pay-TV experiment
1951—First experimental videotape recorder
1952—First UHF television station; first pay-cable TV
1955—First so-called flat television set demonstrated
1962—First video carried by satellite
1963—First microwave television broadcasts
1971—First video cassette recorder sold
1972—First home video game
1973—First demonstration of teletext
1974—First home computer
1975—First microwave pay-TV broadcast directly to homes
1977—First backyard satellite earth station
1978—First random-access videodisc; first TV with stereophonic sound

Today, some computers sell for less than $100, while some video games cost several times that much. A few video games offer accessories that turn them into home computers, and most home computers can be equipped to play games. In fact, the popularity of games seems to be a major reason for the spread of home computers. Most games and computers are now connected to television sets, but some computers can display elaborate, detailed color pictures only if connected to an RGB (Red, Green, Blue) monitor. However, the latest television sets — particularly those whose tuner is a unit separate from the picture tube — have RGB connections that enable them to display computer pictures.

RGB connections can also be used with two advanced computer-related video systems: *teletext* and *videotex*. The two systems transmit still pictures known as *pages* to the home. Researchers in Great Britain developed both systems. Teletext and videotex systems similar to the British versions have also been developed in Canada, France, and Japan.

British teletext, introduced in 1973, transmits TV signals in the form of 36,000 to 216,000 tiny white dots per second in the black bar that is visible when the vertical hold on a television set is misadjusted. Roughly, every group of eight dots represents a letter, a number, a punctuation mark, or a letter-sized piece of a large picture. Teletext does not interfere with the transmission of normal television pictures.

A teletext broadcaster can transmit hundreds of pages at a time. The pages contain a wide variety of information, such as news headlines, racing results, recipes, and airline schedules. A page called the *menu* tells what is on the other pages.

To get the menu, a viewer touches a key on the teletext decoder, which has a keyboard like that of a calculator. The decoder is either built into the TV set or is in a separate case that has a cable running to the set or a tuner. The decoder scans the dots until it finds the sequence that indicates the menu page. It then stores the 8,000 or so dots that represent the menu into a unit called a *memory*. Finally, the decoder interprets the dots and displays the menu on the television screen. The menu can be kept on the screen indefinitely. To change the page, the viewer simply presses the appropriate numbers on the keyboard. Again, the decoder scans the dots to find the desired page. The decoder works almost instantaneously; but there might be a wait of a few seconds until the right dots are transmitted.

Teletext can also provide a means by which foreign-language captions can be displayed on television programs. The captions are transmitted at the same time as the program, and the decoder can be set to put the captions over the pictures on the bottom of the screen. Thus, one viewer might watch a British movie with French captions, another with Spanish captions, and a third with Italian captions — and all on the same channel. In the United States, thanks

Component Video

The video revolution is replacing the ordinary television set with an assembly of components under the control of a device called a switcher. (In actual practice, a switcher that uses cable TV signals will not also take signals from antennas.)

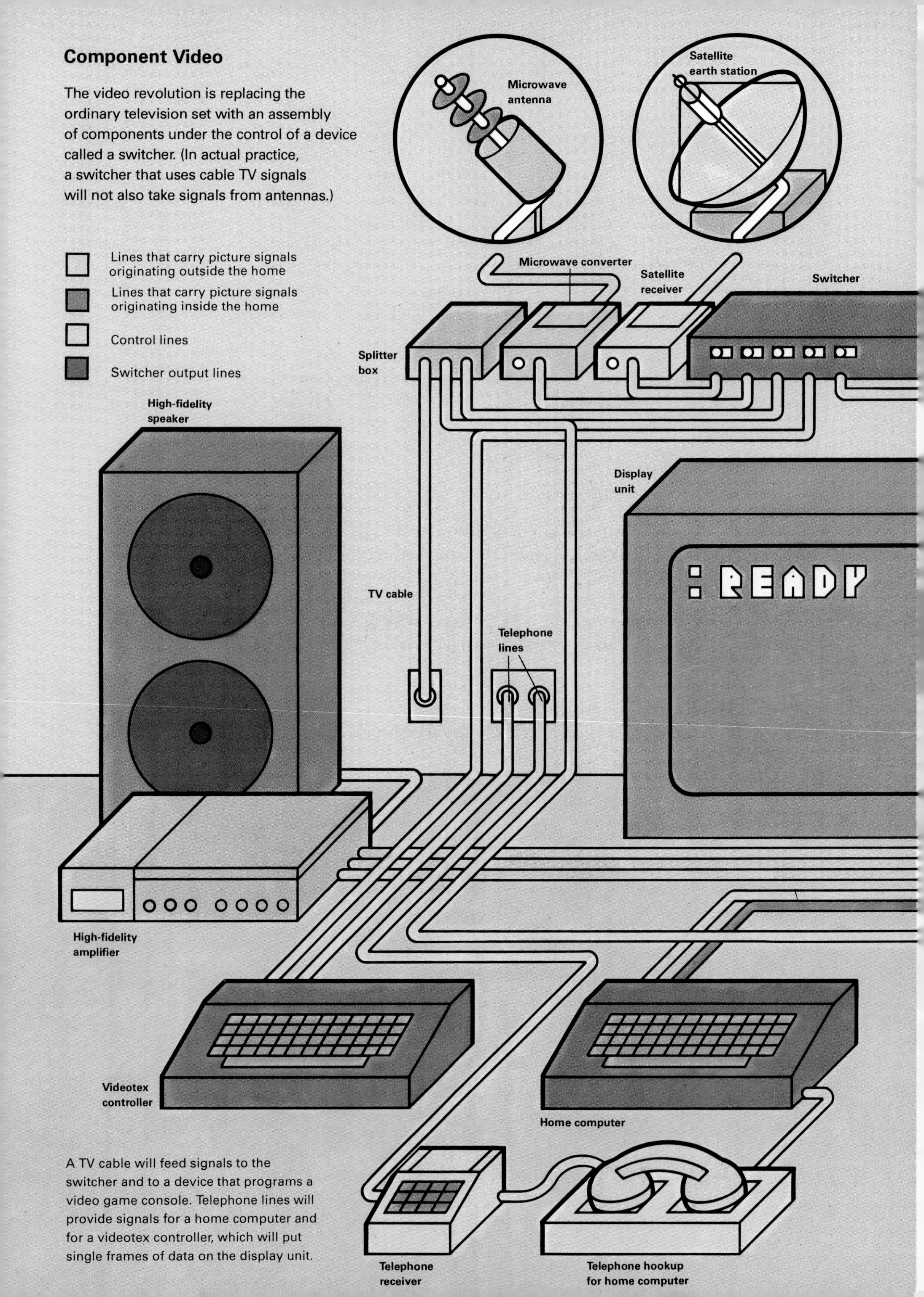

A TV cable will feed signals to the switcher and to a device that programs a video game console. Telephone lines will provide signals for a home computer and for a videotex controller, which will put single frames of data on the display unit.

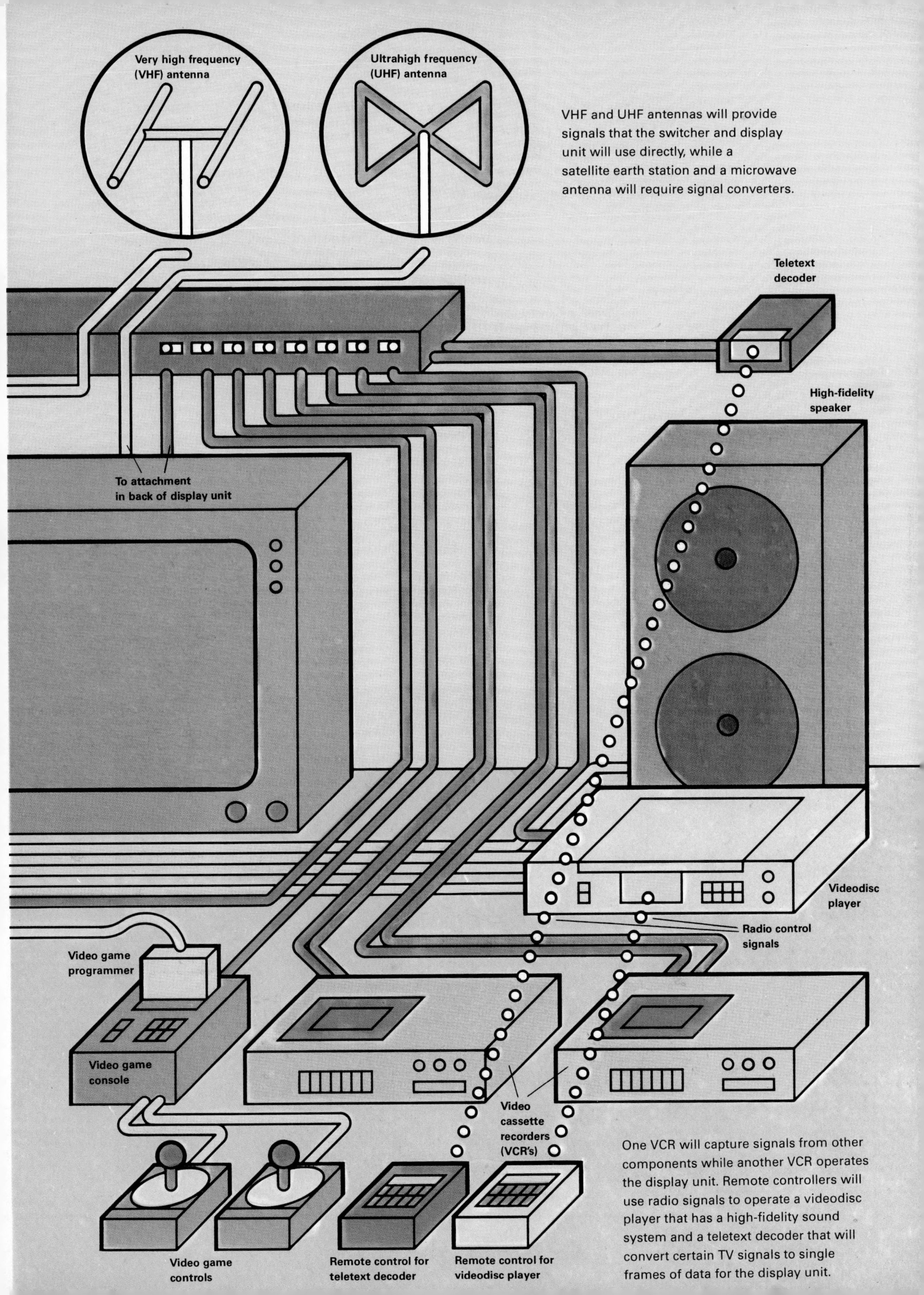
Very high frequency
(VHF) antenna
Ultrahigh frequency
(UHF) antenna
VHF and UHF antennas will provide signals that the switcher and display unit will use directly, while a satellite earth station and a microwave antenna will require signal converters.
Teletext
decoder
High-fidelity
speaker
To attachment
in back of display unit
Videodisc
player
Radio control
signals
Video game
programmer
Video game
console
Video
cassette
recorders
(VCR's)
One VCR will capture signals from other components while another VCR operates the display unit. Remote controllers will use radio signals to operate a videodisc player that has a high-fidelity sound system and a teletext decoder that will convert certain TV signals to single frames of data for the display unit.
Video game
controls
Remote control for
teletext decoder
Remote control for
videodisc player

to a teletextlike system, more than 50,000 hearing-impaired Americans use low-cost decoders to watch their favorite programs with English captions.

The second advanced computer-related video system, videotex, went into operation in 1979. The system operates like teletext from the decoder memory to the TV screen. However, to reach the decoder, videotex uses beeps of sound transmitted over telephone lines instead of dots broadcast in a television signal. Furthermore, a videotex user simply dials the appropriate page rather than waiting for the correct page to turn up.

Beeps cannot be transmitted as quickly as dots. About 3,000 beeps per second is as fast as information can be sent over a telephone line, but 300 beeps per second is much more common. However, videotex has several advantages over teletext. First, an unlimited number of pages can be made available on videotex. Second, a videotex user can send information back to the computer that transmits the page. And, third, almost every home already is hooked up to telephone lines.

The ability of a videotex user to interact with a remote computer offers fantastic possibilities. Someday, for example, television viewers might shop by videotex. They would look at video pages of a catalog and touch a few buttons to place an order. All banking might be conducted by videotex. Even elections could someday be held on videotex.

A viewer in a video laboratory interacts with a videodisc-generated image, center screen, that displays what he would see if he drove a car along a city street. Special controls enable him to simulate turning the car and provide details of buildings on two side screens.

The video revolution advances in the lab, *above,* as a scientist adjusts the picture on a flat video tube. An experimental antenna, *left,* picks up satellite signals that come through the window.

However, you do not need a videotex decoder to obtain many personal services. Home computers can provide them by receiving information from distant electronic libraries called *databases*. The United States lags behind other countries in videotex, but there are more than twice as many U.S. subscribers to databases than there are videotex users throughout the rest of the world. Americans look up restaurants, buy airline tickets, read the daily news, and send and receive messages through home computers.

One major use of databases is to gain access to video games. One video game system even enables an adapter connected to a cable television system to substitute for the usual game cartridge. The use of a cable system to gain access to consumer databases can combine the speed of broadcast teletext with the interactivity of telephone videotex because many cable systems can carry signals both to and from subscribers. The only advantage that telephone connections retain is unlimited capacity in dialing.

In the future, there is likely to be one medium that provides the speed of broadcasting and the interactivity and unlimited capacity of telephone transmission. That medium will be *fiber optics*. Fiber optics uses hair-thin, flexible glass or plastic fibers to carry light in the same way a wire carries electricity. But an optical fiber might carry 1 billion flashes of light per second, compared with the 300 beeps per second for a telephone wire.

Someday, such fibers will replace telephone wires, but it might not happen in this century, if only because there are so many telephones. When the change occurs, the fiber going to a home could carry not only telephone calls and computer information, but also an unlimited number of radio and television signals — all accessible simply by dialing.

Television pictures delivered by fiber could be much sharper than those broadcast today and could be accompanied by high-fidelity stereophonic sound. If the image is viewed in three dimensions it may be difficult to distinguish from reality. Japan and West Germany already have stereophonic television, and it could be available in the United States in 1983. *High-definition television*, as television with sharper pictures is called, and three-dimensional (3-D) TV could be available soon after. CBS hopes to transmit, possibly before 1990, pictures four times as sharp as today's directly from a satellite to homes. Other direct-broadcast satellite systems could go on the air even earlier. These systems would transmit several pay-TV channels to earth stations as small as 60 centimeters (2 feet) in diameter.

Three-dimensional TV has been demonstrated since the 1920s. In Mexico, 3-D TV was broadcast in the early 1950s. Today, eye surgeons regularly use a 3-D TV microscope. Both the microscope and the old 3-D broadcast techniques, however, require the use of special eyeglasses or hoods. Current research centers on systems that provide the 3-D effect without glasses and a technique that presents a

3-D image to viewers wearing glasses and a clear, two-dimensional picture to viewers not wearing them.

The invention of a flat TV set has been difficult to achieve. In 1955, Robert E. Kintner, president of ABC, predicted that by 1965 almost every home in the United States would have a flat color TV measuring 5 by 7½ feet (1.5 by 2.3 meters) hanging on a wall. He was wrong in his prediction, but research is bringing wall-screen TV ever closer to reality. When it is developed, however, it will have to compete with high-quality projection systems, which present greatly enlarged TV pictures.

Predictions of pocket TV sets were also fairly common in the 1950s and 1960s. Those predictions finally came true in the spring of 1982, when Sony put the first flat pocket TV set on sale in Japan. Suwa Seiko Company demonstrated the first television set built into a wrist watch in the summer of 1982 and is scheduled to begin selling them in 1983.

Imagine the home video environment of the future. To decide what program to watch, you simply mention some preferences to your home computer.

"A movie," you might say. Your computer, knowing your tastes, might suggest, "Bogart?"

"Yes."

"*The Maltese Falcon*?"

"No, show me what else you've got."

In a split second, your computer asks all the pay-TV services to which you subscribe for a list of their Bogart movies. It culls the list and projects it on the screen. You pick *Casablanca.*

"Do you want the regular ending?" your computer asks. If you want a new ending for the movie, the computer will make one up, using information stored in it, plus its ability to generate pictures, to create characters and backgrounds that match the original. As you sit back to watch the movie, your computer automatically pays the pay-TV service that is supplying it.

Developments such as these may be a long time in coming. They are not inconceivable, however, now that the video revolution has begun.

For further reading:

Dunton, Mark, and Owen, David. *The Complete Home Video Handbook.* Random House, 1982.

Head, Sydney W., with Sterling, Christopher H. *Broadcasting in America: A Survey of Television, Radio and New Technologies.* Houghton Mifflin, 1982.

Siegel, Efrem (editor). *Videotex: The Coming Revolution in Home/Office Information Retrieval.* Knowledge Industry Publications, 1980.

Siegel, Efrem, et al. *Video Discs: The Technology, the Applications and the Future.* Knowledge Industry Publications, 1980.

The Video Age: Television Technology and Applications in the 1980s. Knowledge Industry Publications, 1982.

The Coming Cropland Crisis

By Lester R. Brown

Wind and water are eroding topsoil so rapidly that the productivity of much of the world's cropland is in jeopardy

"A gentle wind followed the rain clouds, driving them on northward, a wind that softly clashed the drying corn. A day went by and the wind increased, steady, unbroken by gusts. The dust from the roads fluffed up and spread out and fell on the weeds beside the fields, and fell into the fields a little way. Now the wind grew strong and hard and it worked at the rain crust in the corn fields. Little by little the sky was darkened by the mixing dust, and the wind felt over the earth, loosened the dust, and carried it away. The wind grew stronger. The rain crust broke and the dust lifted up out of the fields and drove gray plumes into the air like sluggish smoke. The corn threshed the wind and made a dry, rushing sound. The finest dust did not settle back to earth now, but disappeared into the darkening sky.

"The wind grew stronger, whisked under stones, carried up straws and old leaves, and even little clods, marking its course as it sailed across the fields. The air and the sky darkened and through them the sun shone redly, and there was a raw sting in the air. During a night the wind raced faster over the land, dug cunningly among the rootlets of the corn, and the corn fought the wind with its weakened leaves until the roots were freed by the prying wind and then each stalk settled wearily sideways toward the earth and pointed the direction of the wind.

"The dawn came, but no day. In the gray sky a red sun appeared, a dim red circle that gave a little light, like dusk; and as that day advanced, the dusk slipped back toward darkness, and the wind cried and whimpered over the fallen corn."*

Such were the Dust Bowl days of Oklahoma in the 1930s, as described by John Steinbeck in his novel *The Grapes of Wrath*, which won a Pulitzer Prize. Strong winds blew topsoil from dry land where the protective layer of grass had been plowed under years before, when rainfall had been more plentiful.

Huge clouds of dust blew eastward. The disaster was brought home dramatically to the United States government by a blanket of dust over Washington, D.C., in the summer of 1934. The wind had carried the dust all the way from Oklahoma.

Millions of acres of once-fertile land could no longer provide crops. Farmers went bankrupt by the thousands and had to leave the land. Eventually nature gave back the rain, however, the winds became gentler, and farmers took steps to minimize topsoil loss.

Now, some 40 years later, we are in the midst of another topsoil crisis, this time worldwide. One-fifth, perhaps as much as one-third, of the world's cropland is losing topsoil at a rate that is undermining its long-term productivity. Some of the soil is blown away by the wind and some is washed away by water. In addition, valuable cropland is being converted to building and road sites as the world's population increases. Urban sprawl, village expansion, and highway construction claim several million acres of the world's cropland each year.

Millions of people already go to bed hungry each night, of course, and many starve to death when famines strike. But if the loss of topsoil and cropland continues its steady increase, inevitably food prices will rise and the picture will become even bleaker. Some people will be able to spend a greater percentage of their income on food without changing their life styles significantly. Other people, however, will not be able to do so. Differences in individual income both among and within countries are so extreme that additional millions of people will go hungry while others merely adjust their spending habits. For the poorest—who are already close to the margin of survival—food shortages and price increases will sharpen the pangs of hunger.

The author:
Lester R. Brown is president of Worldwatch Institute in Washington, D.C. Worldwatch is a nonprofit organization that studies uses of the earth's resources.

Soil scientists have only recently begun to monitor soil erosion. Consequently, so little information is available that researchers cannot accurately predict how present rates of soil erosion will affect food production. They do, however, know quite a bit about topsoil and how it erodes, and they have discovered some general relationships between erosion and soil productivity.

Topsoil forms a fertile carpet, usually less than 12 inches deep, over less productive soil. Topsoil's organic matter and other nutrients, its ability to hold water and air, and its firm structure make it ideal for plant growth.

New soil forms naturally at rates of 1 to 5 short tons per acre per year. That is at most about 1/32 of an inch. Soil begins to form when chemical action and environmental factors such as freezing and thawing and rainfall break down rocks on or near the earth's surface. Simple plants and animals soon take up residence on fine particles of the rocks. Eventually, the particles break down into even tinier pieces, while dead plants and animals decompose into organic matter. Topsoil is simply a mixture of particles of inorganic and organic matter.

Soil erosion is a natural process. Topsoil disappears naturally as wind blows it off the surface or water carries it away. There are two kinds of water erosion. In *rill erosion*, water digs rills or rivulets — tiny streams — into the surfaces of sloping fields as it carries topsoil away. The rills form increasingly larger streams. In its most extreme form, rill erosion creates deep gullies. In *sheet erosion*, water removes thin layers of topsoil from relatively flat fields. Unlike rill erosion, sheet erosion leaves no scar on the land. Nevertheless, sheet erosion can tear down a field rapidly.

As a part of the Soil and Water Resources Conservation Act passed in 1977, the Soil Conservation Service (SCS) — an agency of the United States Department of Agriculture (USDA) — studied the condition of the 413 million acres of U.S. cropland. The SCS concluded that more than one-third of this land urgently needs attention. Some 17 million acres on which crops grow continuously are losing topsoil so rapidly that the SCS recommends withdrawing them from farming and planting grass or trees on them. An additional 141 million acres are losing more than 5 short tons of soil per acre every year.

The study revealed "alarmingly high" rates of erosion by water in several states. Tennessee, for example, was losing an average of 14 short tons of topsoil per acre of cropland every year. Missouri and Mississippi were losing about 11 short tons per acre, while the loss in Iowa was almost 10 short tons per acre. Across America, sheet and rill erosion alone annually remove some 2 billion short tons of topsoil from U.S. croplands. That is 1 billion short tons more topsoil than forms each year. Assuming a typical topsoil depth of 8 inches, this loss is equivalent to losing 781,000 acres of cropland per

Water forms small streams in a sloping field, *right,* as it carries away topsoil in a process known as rill erosion. In sheet erosion, *below,* the water removes layers of topsoil from relatively flat land before entering a broad stream.

Irrigation water concentrates soil salts in low areas, *above,* destroying the land's ability to produce crops. The spread of urbanization, *below,* takes prime cropland out of production.

year. Cropland in drier regions is threatened by severe wind erosion, which annually claims almost 15 short tons per acre in Texas and 9 short tons per acre in Colorado.

Natural cover such as grass and trees helps to hold topsoil in place, but even land in grassy fields and in forests erodes. Clearing land and planting crops usually increases the erosion rate. When the pace of erosion exceeds the rate of soil formation — called the tolerance, or T, factor — the land becomes less productive. Eventually, the topsoil can no longer support crops adequately. If nature cannot provide new cover for the land, the topsoil eventually disappears, leaving only subsoil or even bare rock.

Soil scientists know that 1 inch of topsoil lost annually from a thin layer of such soil affects the land's productive potential more than does the same rate of erosion from deeper soil. But increasing the use of fertilizer can disguise declines in natural productivity, complicating the task of relating erosion to productivity. Even so, the USDA estimates that if erosion continues in the U.S. Corn Belt at present rates, "potential corn and soybean yields would probably be reduced by 15 to 30 per cent on some soils by the year 2030." A study of the erosion of certain soils in Georgia showed that a 6-inch loss of topsoil reduced average yields by 41 per cent. Similar erosion in western Tennessee caused a 42 per cent drop in the corn yield.

In 1930, the Congress of the United States appropriated funds to study soil erosion, beginning to recognize that it was, as the secretary of agriculture put it, "a national menace." Erosion control and soil conservation became national policy in 1935, when the federal government created the Soil Conservation Service. In 1936, the Soil Conservation and Domestic Allotment Act established a plan by which the federal government paid part of the farmers' cost of conserving topsoil.

Farmers used many techniques to combat erosion. Some used crop rotation, planting a row crop in a field every other year and using the land as pasture in the alternate years. Using land as pasture builds up the organic content of the soil, increasing the soil's ability to hold water, and thus making it less vulnerable to brief dry spells.

Some farmers used contour plowing, forming ridges across slopes to slow the flow of rain water down the slopes. Some used strip cropping on slopes, planting cover crops such as grass and clover in strips between bands of corn, wheat, and other grain crops. Cover crops hold water better than grain crops do, so strip cropping retards the flow of rain water even more.

To prevent erosion on steep hillsides, farmers cut broad terraces into the hills. The rain then soaked into the terraces, rather than flowing down the hillside carrying topsoil with it. Farmers also planted lines of trees and shrubs that served as wind barriers, greatly decreasing wind erosion.

But much of the progress of the 1930s and 1940s was undone by

Water Erosion of Topsoil in the United States

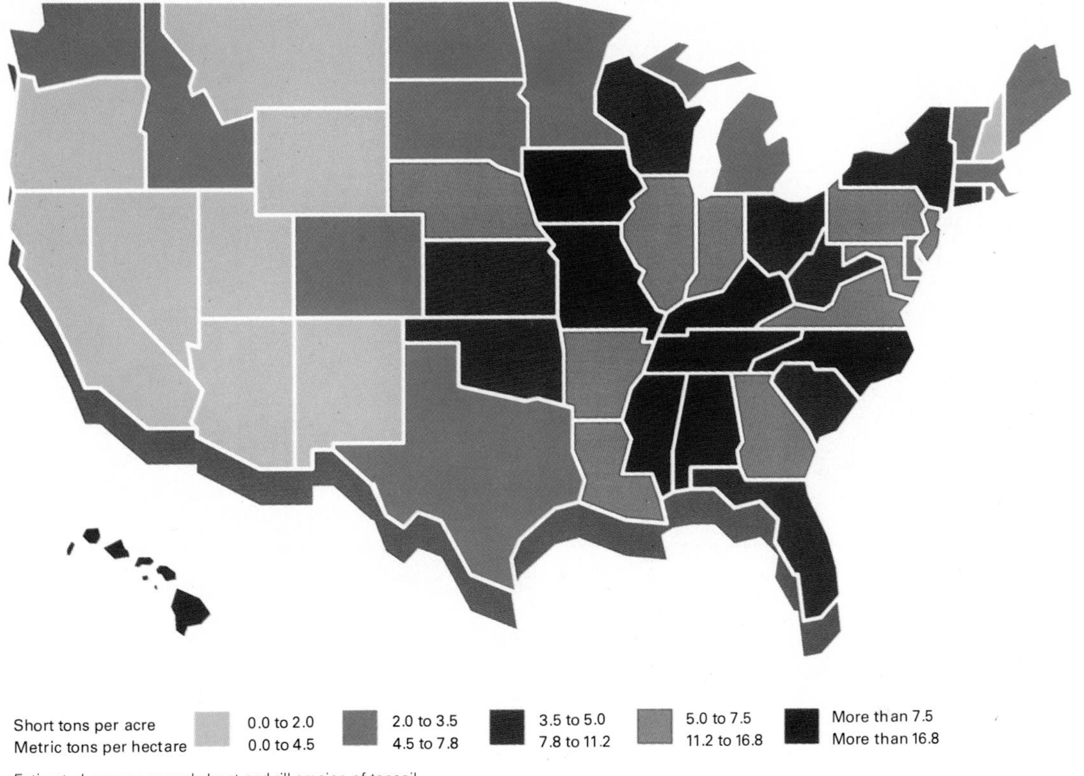

Estimated average annual sheet and rill erosion of topsoil from nonfederal cropland in 1977 (data for Alaska unavailable). Source: U.S. Department of Agriculture.

Much of the rich cropland of the United States suffers from water erosion that exceeds the natural rate of topsoil formation – which is at most 5 short tons per acre per year.

the need to meet a growing population's increasing demand for food. The demand was met with an unprecedented growth in food production. Between 1950 and 1971, grain production doubled, increasing from 696 million short tons to 1.4 billion short tons. Because of population growth, however, production per person went up by only about one-third, increasing from 553 pounds in 1950 to 728 pounds in 1971. Nevertheless, diets improved measurably in many Third World countries.

Since 1971, though, agricultural gains have barely kept pace with population growth. Production per person has fluctuated widely but has shown little increase. Indeed, the per capita grain production of 708 pounds in 1980, an unusually poor year, was lower than the 728 pounds of 1971. And, as food prices climbed, diets deteriorated in some Third World countries, especially among landless laborers and the urban poor.

To achieve the increased food production of the 1950s and 1960s, unfortunately, many farmers changed their techniques. From the beginnings of agriculture until about 1950, most increases in food pro-

How Topsoil Forms

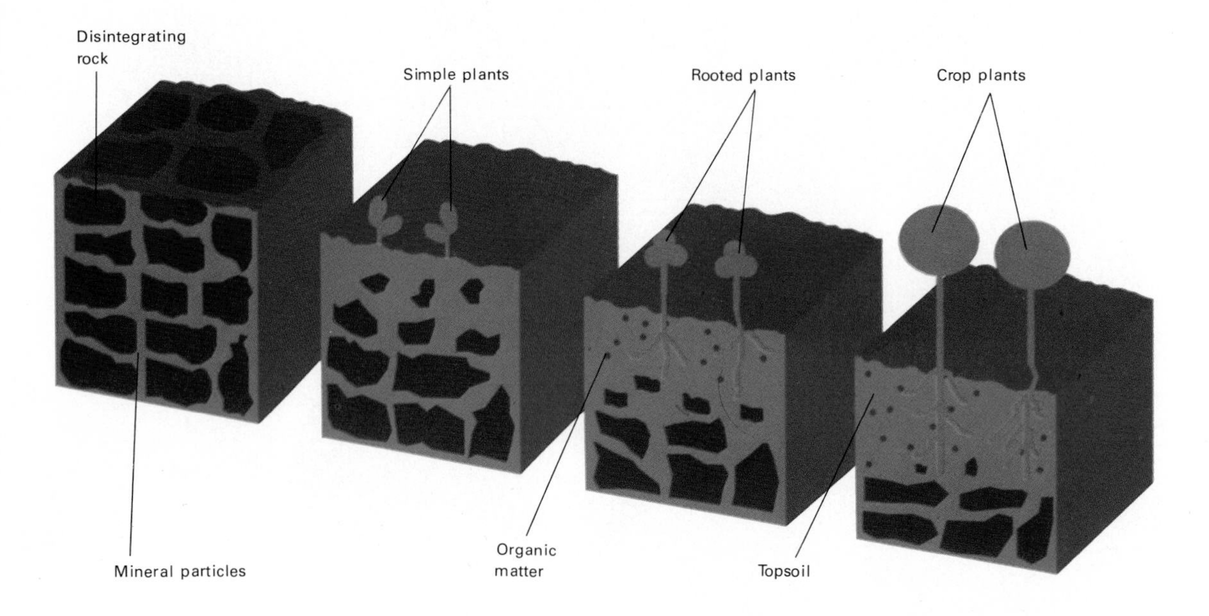

Topsoil formation begins when rock disintegrates into mineral particles. Simple plants then contribute organic matter to the mixture, which eventually becomes so deep that rooted plants grow in it. Finally, it develops into topsoil, with the strength and organic content needed to support and nourish crop plants.

duction came from expanding the area under cultivation. But since then, most increases have come from raising yields on existing cropland.

In the pursuit of increased yields, many farmers abandoned methods of conserving soil. In the United States, for example, the mounting demand for food and the availability of cheap nitrogen fertilizer led farmers to abandon crop rotations that build up the soil's nitrogen content naturally. Instead, they used fertilizer and grew corn and other row crops on the same fields year after year, greatly increasing yields. The price paid in lost topsoil, however, was high. A bulletin published in 1936 by the Missouri Agricultural Experiment Station in Columbia showed that, over a period of 14 years, land planted to a corn-wheat-clover rotation lost an average of less than 3 short tons of topsoil per acre annually through erosion. A 3-ton loss is well within the T factor for this soil. But comparable land on which corn was grown continuously lost nearly 20 short tons per acre each year. This loss would lead to a steady thinning of the topsoil layer. Given that 1 inch of topsoil covering an acre of land weighs 160 short tons, the erosion of 20 tons each year would result in the loss of some 6 inches of topsoil in 50 years.

Farmers could use even more fertilizer to offset declining crop yields. That would not improve the soil's long-term productivity, however. Crop yields increase predictably with each increment of chemical fertilizer—rapidly at first, then more slowly until they eventually level off. Where fertilizer use is intensive, the response is already diminishing. In Japan, the Netherlands, and the U.S. Corn Belt, for example, where the use of chemical fertilizer is close to the saturation point, further increases will not increase yields appreciably. On the other hand, in such countries as Argentina and India, where farmers use little fertilizer, increasing its use still increases yields greatly. However, a great deal of energy is consumed in manufacturing and distributing chemical fertilizer, and the cost of making agriculture more dependent on scarce energy resources may be prohibitive.

The switch from rotation to continuous cropping of row crops was not the only change that increased both food production and erosion. The average size of farms in the United States has more than tripled since 1900. And as farm size increased, so did the size of the equipment used by farmers. The larger tractors—pulling larger plows, threshers, or other machines—needed large open spaces in which to operate efficiently. So did some modern irrigation systems. Terraces or wind barriers that help fight soil erosion only got in the way of such modern equipment, so either they were removed or they were never built.

Some farmers in dry areas of the United States increased crop yields by cutting back on their use of a technique known as summer fallowing. Farmers who use this technique use a variation of strip cropping to do this. They leave every other strip free of vegetation during one crop season in order to store moisture for the next season. However, farmers who abandon this technique and farm all the land continuously are often faced with falling land productivity.

As world wheat prices rose between 1969 and 1974, U.S. wheat farmers decreased the amount of land in summer fallow by 24 per cent—from 42 million acres to 32 million acres. This shrinkage led Kenneth Grant, head of the SCS, to warn farmers in 1975 that the other side of the lure of record wheat prices and short-term gains is the sacrifice of the land's long-term productivity.

The U.S. agricultural attaché in Moscow reported a similar reduction in fallow land in the Soviet Union after a disastrous grain harvest in 1972. The Soviet Union's efforts to increase food production may eventually be stymied by the condition of exhausted and eroded soils. Scientists at the Soil Erosion Laboratory at Moscow University measured the extent of cropland deterioration by looking at the deep gullies that carve themselves into erosion-plagued land. They reported in *Soviet Geography* in March 1979 that while only 2 per cent of the cropland in western Siberia, Kazakhstan, and other parts of central Russia had severe gullies, efforts to intensify agriculture could damage up to 50 per cent of the land by gullying. Thane Gustafson, a scholar at Rand Corporation — a research organization in Santa Monica, Calif., that studies U.S. policy — said in 1977 that the Soviet government had to reckon with "50 years of neglect [that] have left a legacy of badly damaged soils."

Farmers throughout the world, in an effort to increase production, have extended cropping into lands that erode easily, creating potential Dust Bowls. For example, farmers are plowing such lands in northern India, the world's most densely populated dry zone, and possibly the dustiest.

Extending agriculture into marginal areas increases its vulnerability to the weather. Erosion aggravates the soil's instability. When erosion reduces a soil's organic content, the soil's ability to hold water declines, so that the land becomes more vulnerable to short-term dry spells. A 1981 study by the U.S. Center for Environmental Assessment Services showed how erosion affects yields during dry spells. Researchers measured the variation in the yield of an eroded plot of land whose average yield was 70 per cent as large as the yield of a noneroded control plot. The yield of the eroded plot turned out to be four times as variable as the yield of the control plot.

Third World farmers urgently in need of cropland have moved farther and farther up hillsides, chopping trees and planting crops. Villagers searching for firewood have also exposed bare soil to the elements, setting the stage for erosion. As a result of deforestation high in the Himalaya, rivers carry 380 million short tons of valuable soil from Nepal to India annually, making that country the recipient of what has been called Nepal's "most precious export."

Reporting on cropland deterioration in Ethiopia, the U.S. Agency for International Development stated in 1978, "There is an environmental nightmare unfolding before our eyes. . . . It is the result of the acts of millions of Ethiopians struggling for survival: scratching the surface of eroded land and eroding it even further; cutting down the trees for warmth and fuel and leaving the country denuded. . . . Over 1 billion — 1 billion —tons of topsoil flow from Ethiopia's highlands each year."

Cattle, too, contribute to the damage when they are allowed to overgraze delicate grasses near deserts. The animals consume the plants more rapidly than the plants can regenerate. The plants eventually disappear, and so the land loses its protective cover and becomes much more vulnerable to erosion. As soil erodes, the deserts expand.

Overgrazing, deforestation, and overplowing are contributing to the spread of deserts or desertlike conditions in Africa, the Middle East, Iran, Afghanistan, and northwestern India. Of 16 desert countries, per capita grain output has fallen over the past three decades in all but four.

The fragile soil in forested regions of the tropics is losing productivity as land shortages force cultivators to alter traditional practices such as slash-and-burn agriculture. The farmer clears a field of trees and other vegetation and burns the land over before planting. The ashes from the grass and trees help fertilize the soil. The farmer grows crops on the field for several years, and then moves on to clear other fields. Natural vegetation returns to the abandoned field, building up the soil's fertility until the next slash-and-burn cropping cycle begins. Farmers once used 10- to 15-year cycles. Today, however, many farmers are trying to increase food production by shortening the cycles. In some places, farmers have reduced the cropping cycle to five years, thus giving the land less time than it needs to recover its fertility.

The result of shorter cycles is made even worse as marginal lands — those once considered incapable of producing good crops — are put into use. In Nigeria, for example, farmers have both expanded onto previously unfarmed marginal land and reduced the time period between crops. The farmers have grown more food in this way, but their yield per acre has been falling since the early 1960s. A study of Nigeria by the World Bank indicated in 1974 that "fallow periods under shifting cultivation have become too short to restore fertility in some areas."

Solutions to the problem of erosion are the same in the 1980s as they were in the 1930s — terracing, countour farming, strip cropping, cover cropping, rotating crops, fallowing, and planting wind barriers. And newer conservation techniques known as minimum tillage or no-till have shown signs of taking hold in recent years, partly because they help farmers conserve both fuel and topsoil. These two new techniques call for farmers to plow their land infrequently or not at all. Instead, they use herbicides to kill weeds. They leave the crop and weed residues on their fields and plant the next crop through the residues. Less plowing requires less fuel. And leaving plant residues in the fields allows soils to retain more moisture and makes them less vulnerable to erosion. The SCS estimated that farmers would use minimum tillage or no-till on more than 25 per cent of U.S. cropland in 1982.

Many conservation techniques, however, are not economically attractive to farmers. The short-term costs of conservation often exceed the short-term benefits. A 1980 study in Iowa indicated that the immediate cost of controlling erosion so that it would not reduce the soil's inherent productivity would be three times as great as the benefits. Similar financial considerations influence Third World farmers who have little concern about the distant future because their immediate survival is at stake.

Under these circumstances, only the willingness of governments to share the costs of the needed measures will induce farmers to fight erosion on a broad scale. The USDA estimated in 1981 that a detailed national program needed to stabilize U.S. soils over the next

Contour farming, *above,* limits water erosion because the rows of crops act as barriers to the flow of water down slopes. In strip cropping, *right,* rows of a cover crop such as clover alternate with bands of grain crops. The cover crops hold water better than the grain crops do and they contribute organic matter to the topsoil.

Terracing converts a steep, erosion-prone hill into a series of gentle slopes. Contour plowing limits the erosion of topsoil from these slopes.

A farmer using a conservation technique called no-till, *right,* plants seeds under stubble left by the previous crop. The stubble prevents water from carrying away large amounts of topsoil. Rows of trees between fields, *below,* act as barriers that prevent the wind from blowing topsoil away.

50 years would cost $103 billion — about $2 billion per year. Laying the groundwork for such massive financial investments and training people to do the job takes time, but time — unfortunately — is at a premium.

Furthermore, while soil scientists can develop plans of action, they cannot muster the political support needed to finance and carry out such massive plans. Farmers and consumers both know that adopting soil-saving measures would in many cases run counter to their short-term economic interests by raising food production costs and prices. Withdrawing severely erosion-prone land from crop production even temporarily would reduce food supplies, putting more pressure on food prices. Difficult though all this might be to accept, however, the alternative is to do nothing and face reduced food supplies and soaring costs over the long term as soils deteriorate.

At what point will we take action? Soil scientists headed by R. A. Brink of the College of Agriculture and Life Sciences at the University of Wisconsin in Madison suggested in a 1977 article in *Science* magazine that predominantly urban societies may not support soil conservation strongly enough until the food crisis deepens. City dwellers are too far from farms to be directly aware of the topsoil crisis. They can learn about it only by indirect means such as books, articles, and radio and television broadcasts. But even if they understood that soil loss eventually causes lower productivity, which results in less and costlier food, they still might not respond, believing that the problem lies too far in the future to require immediate action. The truth is, however, that the future is rapidly approaching.

For further reading:

Brown, Lester R. *Building a Sustainable Society.* W. W. Norton, 1981.

Eckholm, Erik. *Losing Ground: Environmental Stress and World Food Prospects.* W. W. Norton, 1976.

Final Report 1981. National Agricultural Lands Study. U.S. Department of Agriculture and the Council on Environmental Quality, 1981.

The Global 2000 Report to the President. Council on Environmental Quality and U.S. Department of State, 1980.

Hyams, Edward. *Soil and Civilization.* Harper and Row, 1952.

Impacts of Technology on U.S. Cropland and Rangeland Productivity. U.S. Congress, Office of Technology Assessment, 1982.

Kramer, Mark. *Three Farms: Making Milk, Meat & Money from the American Soil.* Little, Brown, 1980.

Lockeretz, William. "The Lessons of the Dust Bowl," *American Scientist,* September-October 1978.

Sampson, R. Neil. *Farmland or Wasteland: A Time to Choose.* Rodale, 1981.

Soth, Lauren. "The Grain Export Boom: Should It Be Tamed?" *Foreign Affairs,* Spring 1981.

Food, Fads, Fat, and Fitness

By Neil Solomon

Obesity is a serious health problem, and good weight control depends on a lifetime program based on a sensible, nutritious diet and exercise

"Dinner's ready!" Carol Jensen called to her family.

"Smelling that steak frying sure has made me hungry," her husband, Phil, declared, coming through the kitchen door.

"Oh boy, French fries!" cried their 10-year-old son, Robbie.

"I thought you were on a diet, Carol," said Phil, looking at the table laden with food.

"There must be something wrong with my thyroid," Carol sighed. "After a week of just cottage cheese and grapefruit, I've only lost 3 pounds. Besides, I got such a craving for chocolate cake."

"I'm just having salad tonight," announced Betsy, 15, as she sat down at the table. "No dressing."

"You and your diet," her mother said, shaking her head. "By the way, how did you do on your biology test this morning?"

"Well, not so great," Betsy admitted. "And I really did study. I was just so tired I couldn't remember anything."

"Robbie, eat your green beans," Carol scolded. "I told you having that piece of cake before dinner would ruin your appetite. And Betsy, maybe you should eat breakfast once in a while."

"Don't start that again," Betsy said, glaring at her mother. "You know I have to lose 5 pounds before the dance next week. Besides, I take vitamins every day."

"Robbie, did you win your baseball game today?" Phil asked, quickly changing the subject.

"Naw," said Robbie, dejectedly, his mouth full of French fries. "I missed a ground ball that let the winning run score. I just can't run as fast as some of the other guys on the team."

"Don't worry about it," his father consoled him. "Husky boys like you always make better linebackers than outfielders. Only a little piece of cake tonight, Carol. I *have* to get rid of this spare tire."

"Robbie, finish off these French fries. I made them especially for you," Carol said, pushing the plate toward him. "There are children starving in India, you know."

The conversation around the fictional Jensen family's dinner table sounds like something from a television situation comedy. But, unfortunately, many such conversations probably take place every day. The sad fact is that too many people only *think* they know all about nutrition, good diets, and weight control. Actually, all that many of them know is that they don't want to be fat. So they do silly things and jeopardize their health, all in the name of fighting obesity.

The fear of fat has become a national phobia in the United States. Yet obesity is the most serious nutrition problem—and one of the most serious of all health problems—in America. An estimated 40 per cent of American adults, 20 to 30 per cent of American teenagers, and 10 per cent of American children are overweight.

Meanwhile, diet books—some useless at best, potentially dangerous at worst—dominate the lists of best sellers. Dieting may be so popular because Americans are so unsuccessful at it. Too often, our attempts to lose weight consist of a series of depressing cycles. They begin with firm resolutions and unrealistic expectations, then spiral down through boredom, discouragement, and fatigue to end in failure. Then they start all over again with a new batch of firm resolutions. Some victims of this yoyo effect may lose—and regain—hundreds of pounds in their lifetime.

The author:
Neil Solomon, a practicing physician, writes a nationally syndicated newspaper column and is the author of several popular books on nutrition, diet, and weight control.

Sometimes we fail because we diet for the wrong reasons—to look like the willowy models in clothing ads, to win approval from others, or because our 20th high school reunion is coming up. Too often, however, we fail because we rely on fad diets or so-called instant weight-loss pills. To succeed, we have to change the way we think about food. Successful weight control must be a lifetime program based on a sensible, nutritious diet and exercise, and it should begin in infancy.

Obesity is not a disease but a symptom—the all-too-visible con-

Table of Recommended Weights

Height		Men		Women	
Feet	Inches	Average	Range	Average	Range
4	11	....	....	104	94–122
5	0	....	....	107	96–125
5	1	....	....	110	99–128
5	2	123	112–141	113	102–131
5	3	127	115–144	116	105–134
5	4	130	118–148	120	108–138
5	5	133	121–152	123	111–142
5	6	136	124–156	128	114–146
5	7	140	128–161	132	118–150
5	8	145	132–166	136	122–154
5	9	149	136–170	140	126–158
5	10	153	140–174	144	130–163
5	11	158	144–179	148	134–168
6	0	162	148–184	152	138–173
6	1	166	152–189	....	....
6	2	171	156–194	....	....
6	3	176	160–199	....	....
6	4	181	164–204	....	....

Height without shoes; weight without clothes. Table recommended by the Fogarty International Center Conference on Obesity, adapted from the Table of the Metropolitan Life Insurance Co.

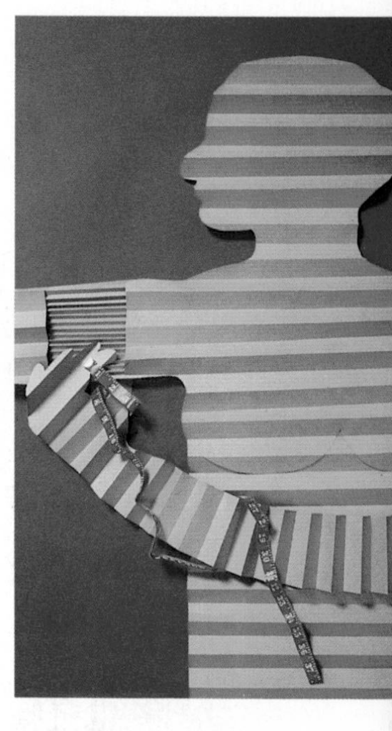

Two ways to determine obesity are by comparing your weight to that on a height-weight chart, *left*, and by doing a pinch test, *above*. To do the pinch test, extend one arm straight out to the side. Then, with the thumb and index finger of the other hand, pinch the skin between the elbow and armpit. If you can pinch more than 1 inch (2.5 centimeters), you are probably obese.

sequences of consuming food that provides more calories than the body can use. Daily caloric requirements vary from person to person. A growing 16-year-old boy, for example, needs almost 3,600 calories a day, while a 65-year-old man needs only 2,500. If they consume more than they need, the result is excess fat. The body of a nonobese man typically consists of from 5 to 10 per cent body fat. In a nonobese woman, the figure may rise to as much as 20 per cent. Many American adults, however, are carrying much more fat than that—perhaps two to three times the body fat they should.

How can you tell if you're fat? One way is to take an honest look at yourself naked in a full-length mirror. If you think you look obese, you probably are. You can also do a pinch test or a waist-height comparison. To do the pinch test, extend one arm straight out to the side. Then, with the thumb and index finger of the other hand, pinch the skin between the elbow and the armpit. If you can pinch more than 1 inch (2.5 centimeters), you probably are too fat. Another way to tell is by subtracting the size of your waist in inches from your height in inches. If the difference is less than 36, it's time to cut back at mealtime.

The most common method of determining obesity is to compare your weight to that listed on a height-weight chart. Such charts pro-

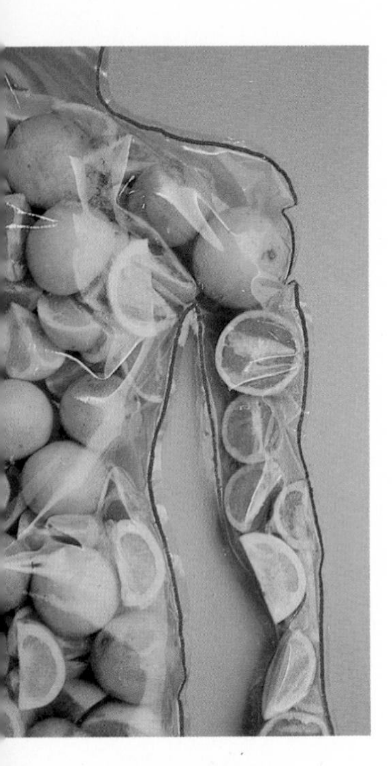

All fad diets, such as the grapefruit diet, deprive the dieter of some essential nutrients, and most are so monotonous that dieters quickly lose interest.

vide a range of ideal weights for a specific height and body frame—large, medium, or small. People who weigh 15 to 20 per cent more than their ideal body weight are generally considered obese.

However, not everyone who exceeds their ideal body weight may be obese. For example, a professional football player weighing 275 pounds (125 kilograms) probably would not be considered obese because his extra weight consists of muscle, not fat. Yet a 275-pound office worker of the same height whose only exercise is walking to and from his car would certainly be considered grossly obese. Height-weight charts may also be misleading for some people because they generally do not provide standards for determining body frame size, and most people don't fall neatly into one category. Nevertheless, the charts are convenient. And if you use them honestly—and don't credit yourself with the wrong body frame size to justify the extra pounds you may be carrying—they can give you a fairly good idea of whether you are obese.

Obesity is risky. About 2,400 years ago, Hippocrates, the father of modern medicine, observed that, "Persons who are naturally fat are apt to die earlier than those who are slender." Hippocrates' words are just as true today. Obesity can also aggravate a host of serious health problems, among them high blood pressure, diseases of the heart and blood vessels, gall bladder and liver disease, degenerative arthritis, and diabetes. Experts have estimated that if all Americans were at their ideal weight, there would be 25 per cent less coronary heart disease, 35 per cent less heart failure and stroke, 50 per cent less diabetes, and an annual 1 per cent increase in life expectancy.

For the vast majority of us, extra pounds are the heavy price we pay for eating too much and exercising too little. In recent years, however, researchers have discovered that there may also be medical reasons why some people seem to gain weight just by sniffing calorie-rich foods while others can eat hot-fudge sundaes with impunity. Here are a few of the theories currently being investigated:

- A defective *enzyme* may be the culprit in some cases. Enzymes are substances in the body that help to break down food so it can be digested and converted to energy. Researchers have found evidence that obese people have lower levels than do nonobese people of adenosine triphosphatase (ATPase), an enzyme that controls the balance of salt in the body's cells. To do its job properly, ATPase requires a lot of energy, which is obtained from calories in food we eat and drink. Some studies suggest that obese people may store as fat many of the calories nonobese people burn to fuel ATPase.
- A team of researchers in Great Britain has theorized that obese people may be the victims of a *brown-fat deficiency*. The body stores fuel in the form of fatty tissue. One form, white fat, makes us obese. Brown fat, however, produces heat to help keep us warm and—in the process—burns off calories. The scientists speculate that obese

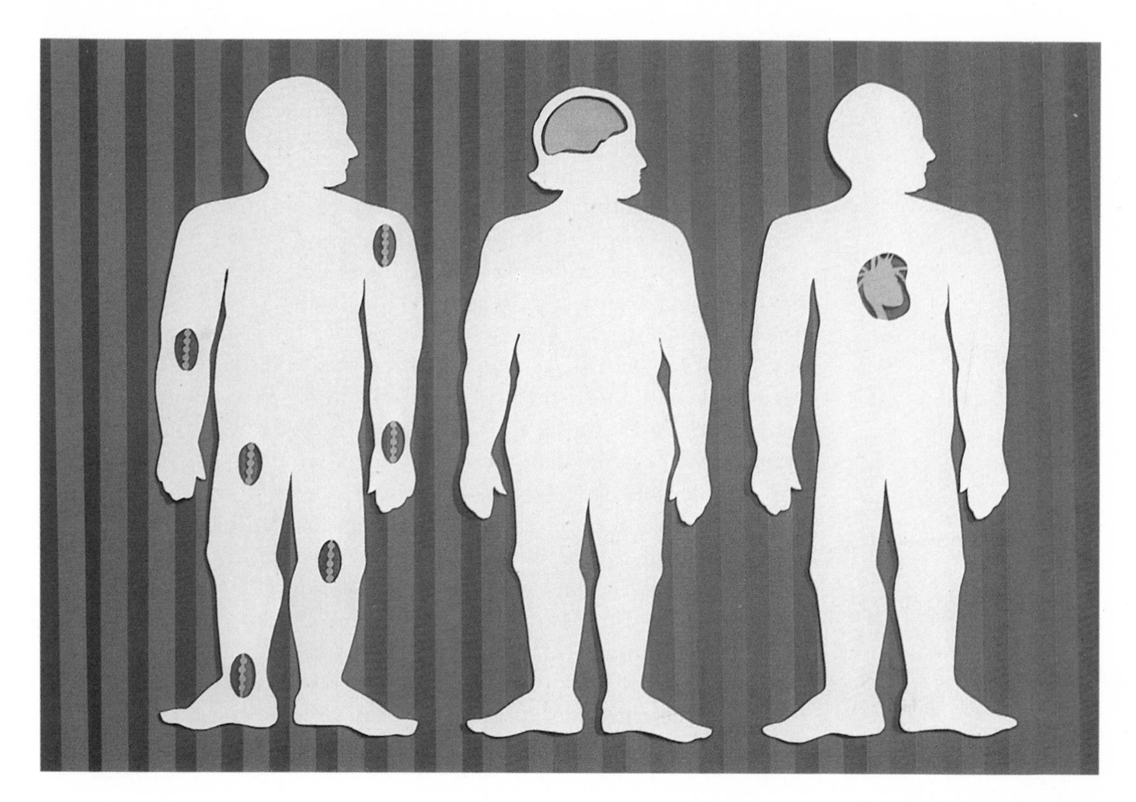

Obesity can be hazardous to your health. It can aggravate such serious medical problems as degenerative arthritis, which affects the joints, *above left,* as well as high blood pressure and diseases of the heart and blood vessels, which can lead to stroke, *above center,* and heart attack, *above right.*

people may have fewer brown fat cells than do nonobese people or that their brown fat cells do not burn calories as efficiently as they should.

■ The brown-fat and ATPase theories are also part of another theory suggesting that a *lipostat,* a set point, regulates body weight. Some researchers suggest that—just like the thermostat on a furnace—our lipostat maintains our body weight at a certain point. Supporting this theory is the observation that many nonobese people can maintain their weight at a fairly constant level despite wide fluctuations in the amount of calories they consume. Researchers speculate that the set point in obese people may simply be higher than that in nonobese people. Thus, for obese people, fewer calories go further. So some obese people may be telling the truth when they lament that they can't lose weight no matter how little they eat.

■ *Hormones* may also play a crucial role in determining our body weight. A hormone is a substance produced in one part of the body that causes some effect in a different part. Experiments with laboratory animals indicate that the pituitary glands of obese rats and mice contained twice as much of a substance called beta endorphin as did the pituitary glands of lean rats and mice. Researchers also discovered that beta endorphin causes the pancreas—a gland in the abdomen—to release insulin, a hormone that can convert sugar to fat. Theoretically at least, this could mean that a person with increased levels of beta endorphin could become obese without overeating. Of course, if a person overeats, as most obese individuals do, additional sugar becomes available to be converted into fat.

Researchers at Johns Hopkins University School of Medicine in Baltimore, on the other hand, have investigated a hormone that seems to do exactly the opposite of what beta endorphin does. In experiments, the scientists found that cholecystokinin (CCK), which is secreted by the brain and small intestine, suppressed monkeys' appetites. Apparently, CCK works by delaying the release of ingested food from the stomach, causing a "full" feeling. Then, at some point, a "satisfied" signal is sent to the brain, inhibiting further eating. Although their work is still in its early stages, the scientists theorize that a lack of CCK may lead to overeating.

Although these medical factors may contribute to obesity in some people, nutrition experts stress that most people get fat simply because they take in more calories than they use up in physical activity. If you want to lose weight, you must cut calories, exercise more frequently, or both. Diet alone and exercise alone may both result in weight loss, but the best results are obtained when the two are combined. In addition to taking off some pounds, exercise will help keep your muscles firm and your heart and blood vessels healthy.

As far as cutting calories goes, the American obsession with losing

Calories in Fast Foods and Favorite Snacks

Food	Calories
McDonald's Big Mac	541
Burger King Whopper	606
Burger Chef Hamburger	258
Dairy Queen Cheese Dog	330
Taco Bell Taco	186
Pizza Hut Thin 'N Crispy Cheese Pizza (1/2 of 10-inch pie)	450
Pizza Hut Thick 'N Chewy Pepperoni Pizza (1/2 of 10-inch pie)	560
Arthur Treacher's Fish Sandwich	440
Burger King Whaler	486
McDonald's Filet-O-Fish	402
Long John Silver's Fish (2 pieces)	318
Kentucky Fried Chicken Original Recipe Dinner	830
Kentucky Fried Chicken Extra Crispy Dinner (3 pieces chicken)	950

Food	Calories
McDonald's Egg McMuffin	352
Burger King French Fries	214
Arthur Treacher's Coleslaw	123
Dairy Queen Onion Rings	300
McDonald's Apple Pie	300
Burger King Vanilla Shake	332
McDonald's Chocolate Shake	364
Dairy Queen Banana Split	540
Hostess Chocolate Cup Cake	205
Almond Joy Candy Bar	132
Oreo Creme Sandwich Cookie	50
Sealtest Ice Cream Sandwich	208
Potato chips, 10 chips	114
Jello Chocolate Pudding, 1/2 cup	168
Kool-Aid, 8-oz. glass	91

Source: Data supplied by the companies to various sources.

weight has spawned a seemingly endless profusion of quick-fix diet plans. There have been grapefruit diets, water diets, rice diets, drinking man's diets, macrobiotic diets, high-protein diets, and low-carbohydrate diets — to name just a few. The trouble with these fad diets is that they don't work — at least not on a permanent basis. If they did, there wouldn't be so many. Because they usually allow fewer than 1,200 calories a day — much less than a body needs — and tell the dieter exactly what to eat at every meal, these fad diets usually ensure that the dieter will lose at least a few pounds. However, most of them are so monotonous — eating the same food three times a day gets boring quickly — that they are soon abandoned. And dieters nearly always regain their lost pounds once they return to their old eating habits. Hence, the yoyo effect I mentioned earlier.

Another big problem with fad diets is that they can be risky. The human body is remarkably adaptable, but it is not immune to damage. The notion that to lose weight people need only take in fewer calories than they expend is not only simplistic but can be downright dangerous. A low-protein diet, for example, forces the body to turn to its own muscle tissue for a source of energy. Over a long period, this could lead to heart attack, kidney failure, or liver disease.

On the other hand, high-protein diets, which are also usually high-fat diets, advocate cutting out nearly all carbohydrates — fruits,

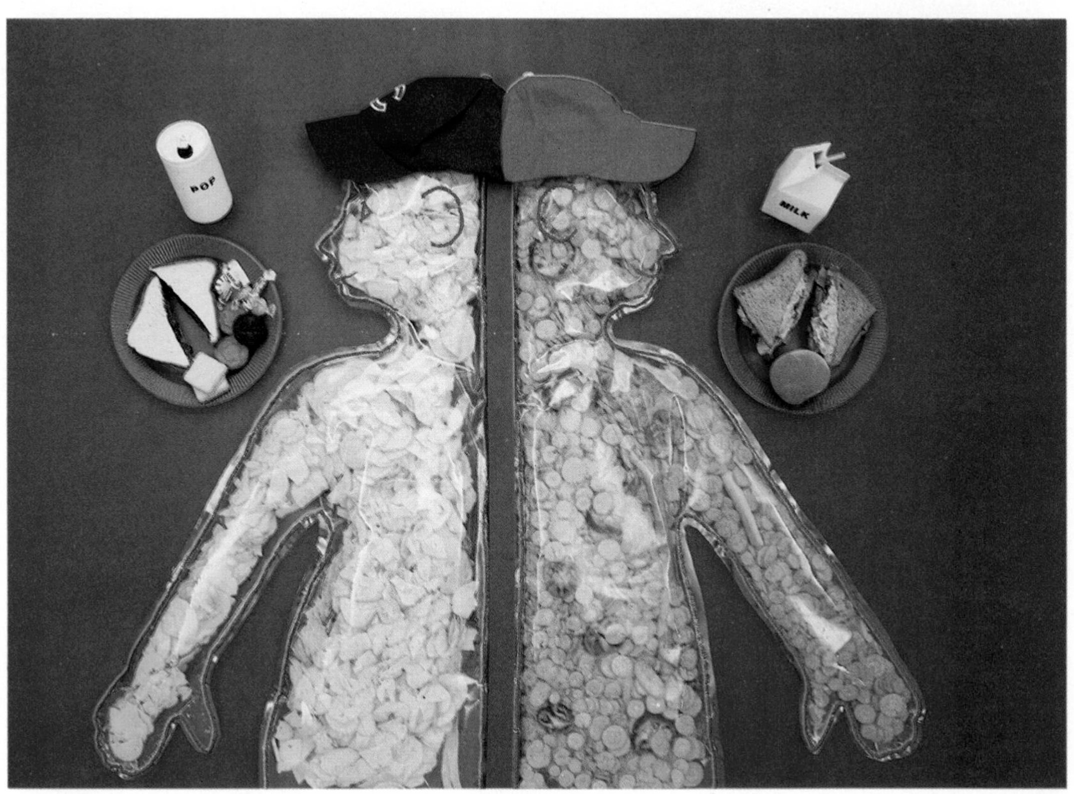

A nutritious lunch, *below right,* can fuel the afternoon's school or play activities and provide the essential nutrients for health and growth. A steady diet of empty calories, *below left,* can lead to fatigue, poor school and work performance, disease, and obesity.

A well-balanced diet, even for those trying to lose weight, should include adequate daily servings from each of the four basic food groups: *above, from left to right,* meats and other proteins, breads and cereals, fruits and vegetables, and milk products.

vegetables, and cereals. But some fruits and vegetables are actually low in carbohydrates and are excellent sources of essential vitamins and minerals. High-protein diets may also force the kidneys to work overtime to eliminate the large amounts of nitrogen wastes produced when protein is broken down in the digestive system.

High-fat, low-carbohydrate diets are often easier to swallow than other diets because your body digests fats more slowly than proteins and carbohydrates and therefore you don't feel hungry so soon after eating. However, in order to burn fats efficiently, the body needs carbohydrates. When the body burns fats without them, acid chemicals called ketone bodies are produced. Ketones can increase the acid level of the urine and lead to serious kidney damage.

People on a high-protein or high-fat, low-carbohydrate diet lose weight because they consume fewer calories, not because eating a lot of protein stimulates some sort of chemical reaction that burns fat more quickly. Most people simply cannot eat as much of the harder-to-digest protein — such foods as cheese, eggs, meat, and milk — as they can of the carbohydrates.

In one way or another, all fad diets deprive the dieter of some

essential nutrients. The real key to a successful weight-loss plan is a varied diet that includes all the nutrients you need. Vitamin supplements are often recommended for pregnant or nursing women, elderly people, and others who may not get all the nutrients they need from a normal diet. But supplements are never a substitute for a well-balanced diet. Betsy Jensen, the dieting teen-ager, is fooling herself if she thinks popping a vitamin pill every day compensates for an inadequate diet consisting chiefly of lettuce. A balanced diet, even for people trying to lose weight, should include adequate daily servings of the three main substances of which food is composed—fats, carbohydrates, and protein.

Fat stored just below the surface of our skin acts as a natural insulator and helps keep our skin soft and our hair glossy. Deposits of fat surrounding our organs insulate them against injury. And fats are needed to help us absorb some vitamins. But most important, fats are the body's most concentrated source of energy. Fats contain about 4,000 calories per pound (9 calories per gram), compared with about 1,800 calories per pound (4 calories per gram) in carbohydrates and proteins.

Savory herbs and tangy flavorings, such as basil, dill, parsley, lemon, garlic, and ginger root, can enliven foods prepared for people on low-sodium diets.

Because the body converts unneeded carbohydrates and proteins to fat and stores it for future use, you can get fat without eating too many fatty foods. However, many Americans eat more fats than they think they are eating because the fat content in some food is not as obvious as it is in others. Butter and some meats obviously are fatty. But many foods — including whole milk, egg yolks, fish, cheese, and nuts — contain large amounts of "invisible" fats. All in all, Americans get about 40 per cent of their total calories from fat, a figure some experts believe is much too high.

In July 1982, the National Research Council (NRC), a part of the National Academy of Sciences, recommended reducing fats to 30 per cent of daily calories. In a report on the relationship between food and cancer, the NRC cited extensive evidence that seems to link high fat consumption with several types of cancer, including cancer of the breast, prostate, and colon.

Diets high in one class of fats — called saturated fats because the fatty acids of which they are composed are saturated with hydrogen—have also been linked to heart disease. Saturated fats seem to increase the amount of cholesterol, a fatty substance in the blood. High cholesterol levels, in turn, appear to be connected to the build-up of cholesterol deposits on the inner walls of the arteries near the heart, a condition that increases the risk of heart attack. Foods high in saturated fats include salami, bologna, and other meats with visible fat; chocolate; vegetable shortening; whole milk; and egg yolks.

Unsaturated fats, in contrast, may even tend to lower the amount of cholesterol in the blood. Foods high in this type of fat include corn oil; mayonnaise; fish; almonds, walnuts, and pecans; and soybean, sunflower, and safflower oil.

The second of the three main components of food is carbohydrates. Carbohydrates, as I've noted, contain fewer calories per pound than do fats. Nevertheless, they are our main source of energy. Americans get about 45 per cent of their daily calories from carbohydrates. Rich in vitamins and minerals, carbohydrates are also our most efficient source of energy. The body can use them completely, without producing the toxic substances that result when proteins are broken down. And although carbohydrates are often one of the first things dieters give up, they can actually help you lose weight—if they are the right kind.

Contrary to popular belief, foods high in natural carbohydrates—those obtained from plants—are not fattening. A medium-sized potato, for example, has only 100 calories, while 1 cup (0.24 liter) of pasta has about 200 calories. In contrast, a broiled, 4-ounce (110-gram) hamburger, without the bun, has about 325 calories. Starchy carbohydrates such as bread and potatoes can also help you lose weight because a little goes a long way. You fill up fast and don't feel hungry so soon after eating. Natural carbohydrates also contain little or no sodium. Research has linked excessive consumption of sodium chloride—table salt—to high blood pressure, heart and kidney disease, and stroke.

People with diets high in natural carbohydrates also seem less prone to diabetes and diseases of the heart and blood vessels. In addition, according to the NRC, a diet rich in whole grain cereals, fruits, and vegetables—particularly those high in vitamin C—seems to reduce the risk of getting certain types of cancer. One reason may be the fiber these foods provide. Fiber is the part of plant foods that is not broken down by digestive enzymes. It is important because it absorbs water in the digestive tract, adding bulk to the feces and allowing them to move more smoothly through the intestine. As a result, potential cancer-causing substances pass through the intestine more quickly and thus are not absorbed as readily. A few studies with laboratory rats have indicated that fiber may also retard the formation of toxic substances in the intestine.

Protein—the third main component of food—is our most versatile nutrient. The 22 amino acids — complex organic building blocks —of which proteins are composed can be assembled into thousands of different proteins needed by the body. Some of these amino acids, called *essential amino acids*, cannot be produced by the body and must be obtained from the food we eat. Foods that contain adequate amounts of these essential amino acids plus some nonessential amino acids are called *complete proteins*. Meat, poultry, eggs, and dairy products are the best sources of complete proteins.

Incomplete proteins, on the other hand, lack one or more of the essential amino acids. However, these proteins — which include beans, nuts, vegetables, and whole grain cereals — can be combined with other incomplete proteins or a small amount of complete protein to form complete proteins. For example, you can create a complete protein by spreading peanut butter on whole wheat bread. Other combinations that provide complete proteins include rice and beans, macaroni and cheese, cereal and milk, and cheese enchiladas with refried beans. The advantage of vegetable proteins is that they are usually low in saturated fats and rich in carbohydrates.

Protein's importance as a nutrient is undisputed, but most Americans eat more than twice as much protein as they need. As a result,

The Exercise Payoff: Calories Burned per Minute of Activity

Activity	Weight in pounds				Activity	Weight in pounds			
	100	120	150	170		100	120	150	170
Bicycling, 5.5 mph	3.1	3.8	4.7	5.3	Skating, moderate	3.6	4.3	5.4	6.1
Bicycling, 10 mph	5.4	6.5	8.1	9.2	Skiing, downhill	6.3	7.6	9.5	10.7
Calisthenics	3.3	3.9	4.9	5.6	Skiing, cross-country	7.2	8.7	10.8	12.3
Golf	3.6	4.3	5.4	6.1	Squash	6.8	8.1	10.2	11.5
Handball	6.3	7.6	9.5	10.7	Swimming, crawl	5.8	6.9	8.7	9.8
Jogging, 11-min. mile	6.1	7.3	9.1	10.4	Tennis	4.5	5.4	6.8	7.7
Running, 8-min. mile	9.4	11.3	14.1	16.0	Volleyball, moderate	2.3	2.7	3.4	3.9
Running, 5-min. mile	13.1	15.7	19.7	22.3	Walking, 3 mph	2.7	3.2	4.0	4.6
Racquetball	6.3	7.6	9.5	10.7	Walking, 4 mph	3.9	4.6	5.8	6.6

Source: Adapted from *The Complete Book of Physical Fitness* by A. Garth Fisher and Robert C. Conlee, Brigham Young University Press, 1979.

they are probably consuming more saturated fats than they should. Also, the body stores excess protein as fat. The Recommended Daily Dietary Allowance of protein for adults is only 0.8 gram per kilogram (0.013 ounce per pound) of ideal body weight. That means that a man who weighs 170 pounds (77 kilograms) needs only 62 grams (2.2 ounces) of protein daily. He could get more than one-third of this amount from only 3 ounces (24 grams) of roast beef.

Although what you eat is certainly basic to any weight control program, how you eat is just as important. For many people, successful weight control requires changing their reasons for eating. The key is learning to eat because you are hungry — not because you are angry, depressed, bored, frustrated, or even happy — and to stop eating as soon as you are not hungry any more.

Successful weight control is also a lifetime program that should begin in infancy because the risk of obesity begins then. Scientists have discovered that obese people fall into two general categories. People in the first category have a normal number of fat cells but the fat cells are larger than normal. Obesity in these people usually started after age 20. The other group has larger-than-normal fat cells as well as an excessive number of them. People in this category usu-

ally became obese before age 13. Unfortunately, obesity that gets such an early start seems to be much more difficult to deal with. People who became fat as children usually do not lose weight as easily as do those who gained their excess pounds as adults. They also tend to regain any lost weight more quickly.

The problem appears to be that no matter how strenuously you diet, you can never reduce the number of fat cells in your body. You can only shrink them. Researchers believe that there are two critical periods — between birth and age 2, and just before adolescence — when the number of fat cells multiplies rapidly. So overfeeding children, especially at those times, could doom them to a lifetime battle of the bulge. One survey, for example, found that 80 per cent of fat 5-year-olds went on to become fat adults.

One way parents can help children form the right attitude toward food is to avoid giving them sweets to reward them for good behavior, to bribe them to obey, or to console them when they are upset. Doing these things can establish a link between food and emotion that may lead children to use food as a refuge all their life.

Parents should also allow children to stop eating when they are full. There certainly are starving children in the world, but that's not a good reason to force children like Robbie Jensen — the husky fan of French fries — to clean an overflowing plate. Of course, parents should make sure their children are getting all the nutrients they need. But most experts in child care agree that the healthy, well-nourished child is lean rather than plump.

For most people, even those who have been victims of the yoyo effect for years, it's never too late to establish a sensible weight-control program. The guiding principle should be common sense. The diet should be based on a wide variety of ordinary foods, including an occasional treat such as chocolate cake. In this way, you can stick with the diet, with slight modifications, once you've lost the weight you want to lose. Ideally, a person trying to lose weight should lose only 1 or 2 pounds a week. A person — such as Carol Jensen — who drops more than that is losing mostly excess fluid, not fat. Moreover, such people usually have trouble keeping those quickly shed pounds off.

One of the worst ways to diet is to skip meals. Passing up breakfast only makes you that much hungrier at lunchtime. Skipping meals also increases the temptation to snack and to make excuses for eating more at the next meal. At least three meals a day are preferred. Some people would rather eat six small meals, which is all right as long as you don't increase your total intake of calories proportionately.

You should also eat slowly. There is a 20-minute lag between the time food is consumed and the time your brain responds. If you eat rapidly, you will tend to eat too much food before your brain registers a "satisfied" signal.

Exercise, an important element in a good weight-control program, provides one obvious benefit and several that are not so obvious. During exercise, you burn calories, of course. For every 3,500 calories you burn, you lose a pound. You could also lose a pound by cutting your calorie intake by 3,500. But exercise provides a weight-control bonus. It appears that the body continues to burn calories at an accelerated rate for some time after you stop exercising.

Exercise also helps compensate for the body's response to reduced food intake. Some studies indicate that when you eat less, your metabolism — the process by which your body turns food into energy — slows, probably as a means of conserving energy. That's why some dieters reach a point at which they seem unable to lose more weight, even though they're restricting their calories. If you exercise while dieting, however, you can help counteract that effect. Exercising also helps you lose the right kind of excess weight. People who exercise while dieting lose more body fat, while people who diet without exercising lose muscle tissue as well.

Almost everyone, no matter how obese, can engage in some type of exercise. However, explosive bursts of activity after years of a relatively sedentary life style can lead to aching muscles and sore joints. Not everyone can run a 4-minute mile or finish a marathon, but neither accomplishment is essential to good health. In fact, for people who are substantially overweight, some forms of exercise, such as running and jumping rope, may actually do more harm than good.

Exercises that are recommended, especially for beginners, include stretching, which can even be done while sitting down, and swimming, which is one of the best all-around exercises and carries a very low risk of injury. Another good exercise is walking, which can be done by nearly everyone in nearly every type of weather. The best rule of thumb is that if you are too exhausted to talk while exercising, you are working too hard. If you are overweight and haven't had much exercise lately, it's a good idea to check with your doctor before starting any exercise program.

Successful weight control provides benefits beyond a trim body and more energy for work and play. An old adage says, "An apple a day keeps the doctor away." That's only part of the story. A nutritious, well-balanced diet and an exercise program appropriate for your age and physical condition are more likely to do the job.

For further reading:

Brody, Jane. *Jane Brody's Nutrition Book.* W. W. Norton & Co., 1981.

Solomon, Neil, and Knudson, Mary. *Doctor Solomon's Easy No-Risk Diet.* Warner Books, 1974.

What's to Eat? And Other Questions Kids Ask About Food. U.S. Department of Agriculture, 1980.

Winick, Myron. *Growing Up Healthy; A Parent's Guide to Good Nutrition.* William Morrow, 1982.

Wurtman, Judith J. *Eating Your Way Through Life.* Raven Press, 1979.

A Year in Perspective

THE YEAR BOOK casts a backward glance at the furors, fancies, and follies of yesteryear. The coincidences of history that are revealed offer substantial proof that the physical world may continually change, but human nature — with all its inventiveness, amiability, and even perversity — remains fairly constant, for better or worse, throughout the years.

PAY NO RENT
AGITATE EDUCATE ORGANIZE
ABOLISH CONVICT LABOR
LABOR CREATES ALL WEALTH
WHO STOLE THE TENEMENT HOUSE REFORM. BILL
ALL MEN ARE BORN EQUAL
THE TRUE REMEDY
ORGANISATION & THE BALLOT
LABOR PAYS ALL TAXES

See page 165.

A Backward Look at 1882

By Sara Dreyfuss

Thousands flocked to see Jumbo the elephant, there was violence in Ireland, and a presidential assassin stood trial

Picnics and circuses were popular entertainment in 1882. Men and women enjoy an elegant picnic, *opposite page,* and a poster advertises Jumbo, *above,* the huge elephant bought that year for P. T. Barnum's circus.

In the United States, a mentally unbalanced young man stood trial for shooting the President, and unemployment was increasing. Great Britain fought a brief, successful war in a distant land. And in Ireland, terrorists pressed their demands by waging a campaign of assassinations and bombings. These top news events sound familiar, but the year was 1882, not 1982. On the other hand, headlines of 1882 also announced that the United States treasury bulged with the largest surplus in its history, and that Chicago's baseball team won its third straight National League pennant.

In the most publicized trial of 1882, Charles J. Guiteau was convicted on January 25 of murdering President James A. Garfield. During Guiteau's trial, the defendant shrieked at the jury and issued lengthy statements that one magazine, *The Nation*, described as "displaying throughout the extraordinary egotism which is one of the prisoner's most prominent characteristics." His attorney argued that

Guiteau was insane, but the jury—and probably most other people—disagreed. Guiteau was hanged on June 30, and *The Nation* commented, "It must long be a cause of shame and regret that the sentence could not have been executed nine months ago." *Frank Leslie's Illustrated Newspaper* grumbled about the expense of the trial—$200,000—and declared, "That is a big sum to pay for the privilege of hanging so monstrous a wretch." A sheet music firm marked the occasion by publishing a song called "Guiteau's March to Hades."

In 1982, another disturbed man, John W. Hinckley, Jr., stood trial for shooting an American President, Ronald Reagan, as well as three other people. The jury in this case found Hinckley not guilty by reason of insanity, and he was committed to a mental hospital for an indefinite period. Hinckley's trial cost more than $2 million, 10 times the price of Guiteau's.

The year 1882 was also rocked by other assassinations and attempted assassinations. On March 2, a grocer's assistant named Roderick Maclean shot at, but missed, Queen Victoria of England. On May 6, two British officials—Lord Frederick C. Cavendish, the chief secretary for Ireland, and Thomas H. Burke, his permanent undersecretary—were brutally murdered, their throats cut, while strolling in Phoenix Park, Dublin's largest park. A group of Irish extremists claimed responsibility for the crime, which the British magazine *The Economist* called an "almost unprecedented atrocity."

In response to the Phoenix Park murders, the British government passed a harsh law called the Prevention of Crimes Bill. It suspended trial by jury for three years and gave the police unlimited power to search and arrest suspected lawbreakers for the same period. Irish extremists retaliated with a campaign of dynamiting public buildings. A hundred years later, in July 1982, Irish terrorists carried out bomb attacks in two London parks, killing nine people and injuring more than 50 others.

Other violence erupted along the Kentucky-West Virginia border in the United States in 1882. Since the 1860s, hostility had simmered between the Hatfield family of West Virginia and the McCoy family of Kentucky. In the early 1880s, two incidents aggravated the tensions: a dispute over the ownership of a half-wild hog, and a love affair between a McCoy girl and a Hatfield boy.

On Aug. 7, 1882, a fight broke out between Ellison Hatfield and Tolbert McCoy. Two other McCoys sprang to Tolbert's aid, and Ellison received multiple stab wounds that left him near death. The enraged Hatfields kidnapped Tolbert and two of his brothers. After Ellison died from his wounds on August 9, the Hatfields tied the McCoy brothers to some bushes and shot them dead. These four murders were the first of more than 50 killings in the famous feud between the Hatfields and McCoys.

In 1982, President Reagan, a conservative Republican, faced the prospect of a record deficit in the federal budget. A century earlier,

The author:
Sara Dreyfuss is Associate Editor of THE WORLD BOOK YEAR BOOK.

another conservative Republican President, Chester A. Arthur, had the opposite problem — a huge surplus. High taxes and import tariffs imposed during the 1860s to pay for the Civil War brought in more money than the government could spend. The overflowing treasury did nothing to help the economy because the surplus funds lay idle instead of being used to finance economic growth.

The labor movement was in its infancy in 1882. Workers were discovering that they had greater bargaining power as a group than as individuals. Most laborers worked 10 or more hours a day, six or seven days a week, with no paid holidays or vacations. The most powerful labor organization was the Knights of Labor, whose goals included an eight-hour workday and the end of child labor.

On May 8, 1882, a New York City labor leader named Peter J. McGuire proposed a national holiday to honor working people. Another labor leader, Matthew Maguire of Paterson, N.J., made a similar suggestion. The Knights of Labor sponsored the first such celebration on September 5. More than 10,000 workers marched around Union Square in New York City, and *Leslie's* newspaper praised their "orderly appearance and sobriety of manner."

Labor Day became a national holiday in 1894, and the labor movement eventually became a powerful economic force, giving workers a higher standard of living than ever before. By 1982, however, the movement faced new challenges as the U.S. economy sagged and unemployment soared to its highest level in more than 40 years, with 1 out of every 10 workers jobless. Unions in automaking and other troubled industries departed from tradition by accepting wage freezes and cuts in benefits.

Unemployment was also high a hundred years before, in 1882, and a huge wave of immigration increased the competition for jobs. Nearly 800,000 newcomers poured into the United States that year, more than twice as many as in 1982. The nation had never limited immigration, but many people began to demand restrictions in 1882. On May 6, President Arthur yielded to the pressure and signed the Chinese Exclusion Act, which temporarily suspended immigration from China. On August 3, another immigration law barred convicts, insane or mentally retarded people, and persons likely to need public care. The act also imposed a 50-cent tax on each new arrival. A hundred years later, Congress considered yet another bill to limit immigration by setting a ceiling of 425,000 immigrants per year and forbidding the hiring of illegal aliens.

Despite the economic problems of 1882, some Americans prospered. The fortunate ones included William H. Vanderbilt, the railroad king, and John D. Rockefeller, owner of the powerful Standard Oil Company. Vanderbilt made headlines on October 8, when a reporter asked him if he ran certain trains for the benefit of the public. Vanderbilt exploded, "The public be damned!" His profanity as well as his arrogance outraged the nation at a time when no polite

An 1882 cartoon in New York City's *Daily Graphic, left,* mocks railroad king William H. Vanderbilt for saying, "The public be damned!" In the same city, electricity begins to flow in September from the Pearl Street Station, *right,* the first commercial power plant in the United States.

person used such strong language. The *Chicago Tribune* refused to print the remark and changed Vanderbilt's reply to "Nonsense!"

Rockefeller made history on January 2, when he set up a simple-looking agreement that created a new type of industrial monopoly called a trust. Stockholders in about 40 oil companies transferred their voting rights to Rockefeller and eight other members of a board of trustees, establishing the Standard Oil Trust, which controlled almost all U.S. oil refining and distribution.

Trials of U.S. federal officials made news in both 1982 and 1882. In 1982, the charges resulted from a Federal Bureau of Investigation (FBI) project known as Abscam, in which an FBI agent posing as a wealthy Arab offered lawmakers bribes in return for favors. In 1882, eight men were charged with cheating the Post Office Department in a scheme called the Star Route Frauds. Two of the accused were postal officials. The other six were private citizens who worked under contract with the Post Office to deliver mail in areas not served by railroads, an arrangement known as star route service.

The Arthur Administration worked vigorously to bring the Star Route defendants to justice. The first trial began on June 1, 1882, and ended on September 10 when the jury failed to agree on a verdict. A second trial lasted from Dec. 7, 1882, to June 14, 1883, when the jury found the defendants not guilty. Nevertheless, public opinion became aroused against official corruption, and Arthur dismissed the accused men from government service. The Senate passed the Pendleton Act, a bill to reform the civil service system, on Dec. 27, 1882; it became law as the Civil Service Act of 1883.

More than 10,000 workers march around New York City's Union Square in the first labor day parade on Sept. 5, 1882.

The Star Route defendants could not match the notoriety of 1882's best-known criminal, Jesse James. The famous bank and train robber was shot in the head and killed on April 3 while standing on a chair dusting pictures in his home in St. Joseph, Mo. He was 34 years old. A member of his own gang, Robert Ford, shot James to collect a reward offered by the governor of Missouri. *The Nation* commented, "Everybody will be pleased to hear that Mr. James died poor after an active and much-respected career."

Criminals like James were not the only source of violence on the Western frontier. The spread of white settlers continued to push the Indians westward, and many tribes fought desperately to hold on to their lands and to avoid being penned up on reservations. In 1882, a Chiricahua Apache chief named Geronimo escaped from a reservation in Arizona. With his band of warriors, Geronimo terrorized the Southwest from hidden camps in Mexico.

An article in *The Atlantic Monthly* charged that the government treated the Apaches too kindly. "The Apache murders our people; therefore we feed and clothe him," the magazine complained. "Nor are we content simply to supply him with the necessities of life; but from the $283,000 which the Interior Department annually furnishes to the agency, the enormous sum of over $19,800 goes for the luxuries of sugar and coffee. . . . " The U.S. Army sent General George Crook, a veteran Indian fighter, to lead the struggle against Geronimo. The chief surrendered in 1883 but later escaped again.

Great Britain's chief foreign affairs crisis in 1882 involved Egypt, which was controlled by Turkey as part of the Ottoman Empire.

Britain owned much of the stock in the company that operated the Suez Canal in Egypt. On June 12, bloody riots broke out in Alexandria, Egypt, started by nationalists who sought to free the country of non-Egyptian control. Britain wanted to protect the Suez Canal, which greatly shortened the water route to its empire in India. The British began to bombard Alexandria on July 11, and they invaded Egypt a few days later. On September 13, British troops, led by Lieutenant-General Sir Garnet J. Wolseley, who had become a national hero following earlier victories in Africa and Asia, defeated the Egyptians at the village of Tel el Kebir. On September 15, the British occupied Cairo, Egypt's capital, and Egypt surrendered. British Prime Minister William E. Gladstone declared, "We have carried on this war from a love of peace."

Another province of the Ottoman Empire, an area called Palestine, also made news in 1882. Young European Jews calling themselves Hoveve-Zion (Lovers of Zion) formed a movement that year to send settlers to Palestine. The new settlers bought land and established farm colonies, joining the approximately 25,000 Jews who were already there. Eventually, in 1948, an independent Jewish nation, Israel, was founded in part of Palestine. In 1982, however, Israel partially reversed its policy of encouraging settlement. The Israeli government uprooted residents from the Sinai Peninsula, an area Israel had seized in 1967, and returned it to Egypt.

In Europe, international tensions were beginning to build in 1882. On May 20, Italy joined the Triple Alliance, a defense agreement with Austria-Hungary and Germany. The three nations agreed to help one another in case of attack by two or more great powers. The treaty resulted largely from brilliant diplomacy by Chancellor Otto von Bismarck of Germany, who wanted to fortify his country against an attack by France or Russia. But the Triple Alliance helped divide Europe into two armed camps and contributed to the frictions that led to the outbreak of World War I in 1914.

There was more friendship than friction on June 16, 1982, however, when a joint French and British study group approved a railroad tunnel, under the English Channel, that would link the two countries. A century earlier, France and Britain had actually started to build such a tunnel, the French digging from Sangatte and the British from Dover. By February 1882, the tunnelers had pushed nearly 1 mile (1.6 kilometers) in each direction. To promote the project, British supporters held lavish parties in the tunnel. Prominent people came to see the excavation machinery and sip champagne under the latest form of illumination—electric lights. Members of Parliament, society leaders, and even the Prince of Wales (later King Edward VII) attended the fashionable tunnel parties.

Despite the promotional efforts, the project met with growing resistance from Britons who feared that a tunnel would increase the chance of invasion from the Continent. General Wolseley, the hero of Africa

Charles J. Guiteau, an accused presidential assassin, shrieks at the court during his 1882 trial, *opposite page, top.* British troops visit the Great Sphinx in Egypt after invading that nation, *center.* Bank and train robber Jesse James is shot while standing on a chair dusting pictures, *bottom left.* Apache chief Geronimo, *bottom right,* terrorized the Southwest.

IOLANTHE

or The Peer & the Peri — A Fairy Opera

Written by W. S. Gilbert · Composed by Arthur Sullivan

Under the Management of Mr. R. D'Oyly Carte.

On SATURDAY EVENING, NOVEMBER 25, at 8.30.

DRAMATIS PERSONÆ.

The Lord Chancellor,	Mr. George Grossmith.
The Earl of Mountararat,	Mr. Rutland Barrington.
The Earl Tolloller,	Mr. Durward Lely.
Private Willis, *of the Grenadier Guards,*	Mr. Charles Manners.
Strephon, *an Arcadian Shepherd,*	Mr. R. Temple.
Queen of the Fairies,	Miss Alice Barnett.
Iolanthe, *a Fairy—Strephon's Mother,*	Miss Jessie Bond.
Celia, *Fairies,*	Miss Fortescue.
Leila, *Fairies,*	Miss Julia Gwynne.
Fleta, *Fairies,*	Miss Sybil Grey.
Phyllis, *an Arcadian Shepherdess and Ward in Chancery,*	Miss Leonora Braham.

CHORUS OF DUKES, MARQUISES, EARLS, VISCOUNTS, BARONS, AND FAIRIES.

Act 1.—An Arcadian Landscape. Act 2.—Palace Yard, Westminster.

Date.—Between 1700 and 1882.

On this occasion the Opera will be conducted by the Composer.

The Opera produced under the personal direction of the Author and Composer. Scenery by Mr. H. Emden. Costumes by Miss Fisher, Messrs. Edr & Sons, Messrs. Frank Smith & Co., Messrs. E. Moses & Son, Mons. Alias, and M.M. Auguste & Cie. Dances arranged by Mr. J. D'Auban. Perruquier, Mr. Clarkson.

Musical Director—Mr. FRANK CELLIER.

NO FEES OF ANY KIND.

Programmes are provided, and Wraps and Umbrellas taken free of charge. Any attendant detected in accepting money from visitors will be instantly dismissed; the public is therefore requested not to tempt the attendants by offering them gratuities. The Refreshment Saloons are under the direct control of the Management, and everything will be found to be of the best quality. All letters on any business connected with the Savoy Theatre should be addressed to Mr. R. D'Oyly Carte, and not to any individual official.

Ellen Terry's expressive face, *left,* makes her one of 1882's most popular actresses. The border on a program for *Iolanthe, right,* an operetta by Sir William S. Gilbert and Sir Arthur S. Sullivan, features the newly invented electric lights that illuminated its first performance in 1882.

and Asia, called the proposed tunnel "a constant inducement for the unscrupulous foreigner to make war upon us." An antitunnel pamphlet predicted, "Dover taken, the garrison butchered, the tunnel vomiting men of all arms, London invaded, England conquered." On April 1, the government's Board of Trade, which supervised coastal waters, ordered the tunnelers to stop until the effects on military security could be studied. Work never resumed, though Britain and France talked about it occasionally over the years.

Other engineering feats also made news in 1882. The St. Gotthard Tunnel, a railroad tunnel through the Alps between Italy and Switzerland, opened in May. In January, a French company headed by Ferdinand Marie de Lesseps, the builder of the Suez Canal, started to dig a canal across Panama. It would have enabled ships to travel between the Atlantic and Pacific oceans without sailing around South America. De Lesseps' firm went bankrupt, however, and an American group finally completed the Panama Canal in 1914.

One technological achievement of 1882 involved electricity, which began to flow from the first commercial power plants in the United States. The great inventor Thomas A. Edison built the first steam-powered plant, the Pearl Street Station in New York City. On September 4, Edison flipped a switch that sent current to about 60 homes and offices in Manhattan. Later that month, in Appleton,

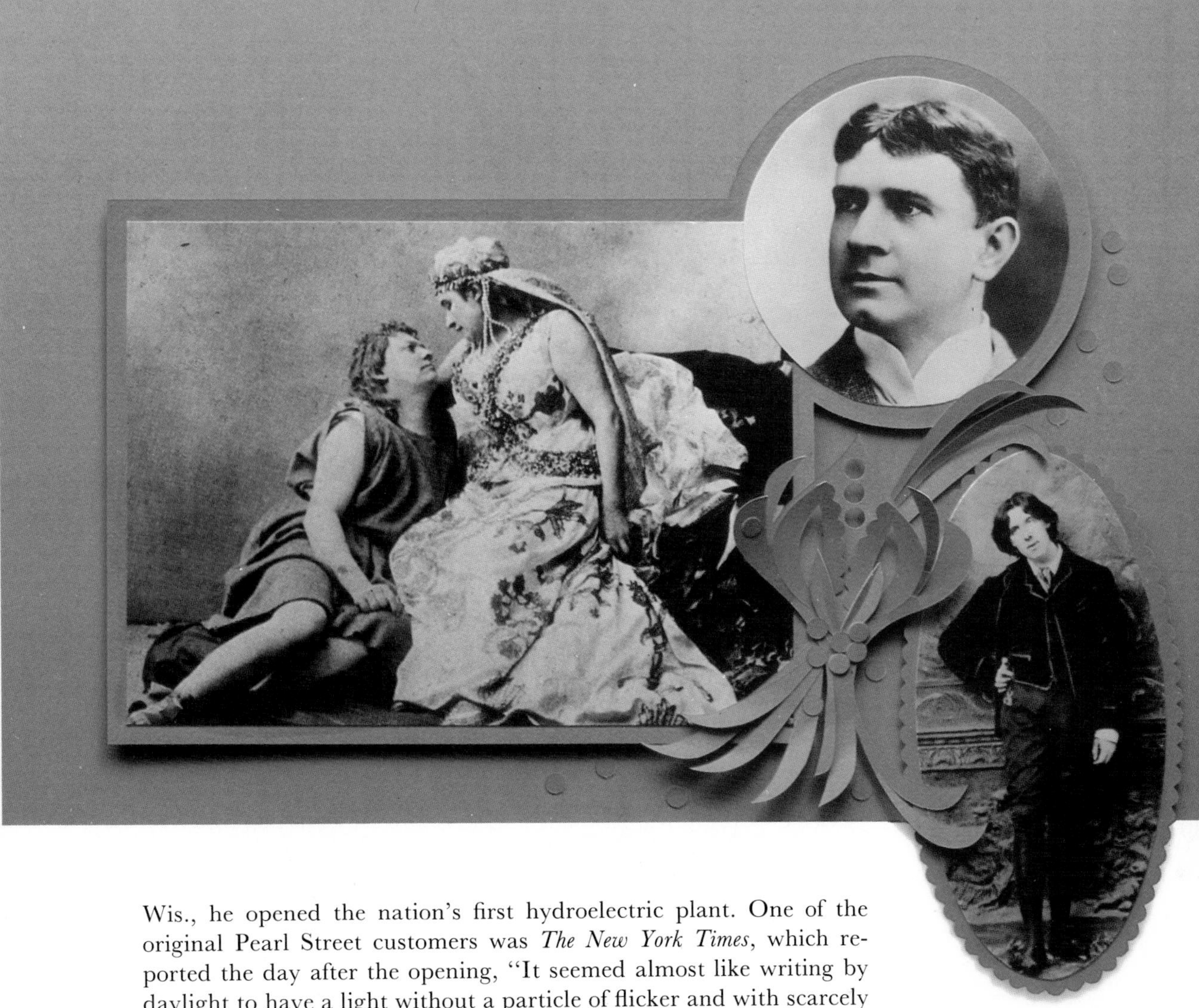

Wis., he opened the nation's first hydroelectric plant. One of the original Pearl Street customers was *The New York Times*, which reported the day after the opening, "It seemed almost like writing by daylight to have a light without a particle of flicker and with scarcely any heat to make the head ache." In 1982, one of Edison's first customers still stood at its original site—Sweet's Restaurant at 2 Fulton Street, New York City.

Edison visited his customers to see how they liked the new lights. One of them, a Mr. Kolb, recalled: "I replied that they were all right but that you couldn't light a cigar from them. Mr. Edison said nothing, but three days later he came back and presented me with an electric cigar lighter."

Inventors found other uses for the new source of power. Henry W. Seely patented the electric iron on June 6, and Schuyler S. Wheeler invented the electric fan. The first theater in the United States to make use of electricity was the Bijou Theatre in Boston. On December 11, more than 650 light bulbs illuminated the Bijou's production of *Iolanthe*, a new operetta by Sir William S. Gilbert and Sir Arthur S. Sullivan.

Gilbert and Sullivan were in their heyday. The D'Oyly Carte Opera Company in London delighted audiences with a new production at the Savoy Theatre almost every year. In 1881, the Savoy had

The opera *Parsifal, left,* the last work by German composer Richard Wagner, premières on July 26, 1882. A theater dynasty is established on February 15, when actor Maurice Barrymore, *top right,* becomes the father of a son, John. British writer Oscar Wilde, *bottom right,* poses in the flamboyant suit he wore for his 1882 tour of the United States.

become the first theater in England lit by electricity. But 101 years later, the lights went out at the Savoy. D'Oyly Carte gave its last performance on Feb. 27, 1982, and disbanded.

The theater was a favorite form of entertainment in 1882. Lillie Langtry, a beautiful British actress known as the Jersey Lily because she was born on the island of Jersey, made her U.S. debut in 1882 in William Shakespeare's *As You Like It.* The public flocked to see her not only because of her beauty, but also because of rumors that she and the Prince of Wales were lovers. Other popular performers included Maurice Barrymore, Sarah Bernhardt, John Drew, Lillian Russell, and Ellen Terry. Maurice Barrymore's son John, who became one of the greatest stars of the stage and early motion pictures, was born on Feb. 15, 1882. John Drew was his uncle. In 1982, John Barrymore's granddaughter, 7-year-old Drew Barrymore, carried on the family tradition in the motion picture *E.T.: The Extra-Terrestrial.*

In 1882, audiences throughout the United States thrilled to various stage versions of Harriet Beecher Stowe's novel *Uncle Tom's Cabin.* One touring company took the play to Tombstone, Ariz., with a live bloodhound in its cast. The dog was trained to chase the heroine, Eliza, as she escaped from slave catchers. When Eliza fled across the stage with the bloodhound baying at her heels, a cowboy in the audience rose to her rescue and shot the dog.

Lecture tours were also a popular source of entertainment and education. Oscar Wilde, the British writer and wit, lectured on aesthetics during a tour of the United States in 1882. Upon his arrival, customs officials asked him if he had anything to declare. Wilde replied, "Only my genius!" When he appeared in Leadville, Colo., a rowdy mining town, the writer entertained his audience by reading passages from the autobiography of Benvenuto Cellini, an Italian sculptor and goldsmith of the 1500s. They enjoyed Cellini so much, Wilde said, "I was reproved by my hearers for not having brought him with me. I explained that he had been dead for some little time, which elicited the inquiry, 'Who shot him?' "

Boxer John L. Sullivan, *opposite page, top,* shows the form that made him heavyweight champion of the world in 1882. The Chicago White Stockings, later called the Cubs, won their third consecutive National League pennant, captained by their star first baseman, Cap Anson, center (number 7). Other popular sports of 1882 are bowling, *bottom left,* and croquet, *bottom right.*

Silver miners at Tabor's Matchless Mine in Leadville invited Wilde into the mine for supper. He was lowered into the shaft in an ore bucket and spent several hours visiting the men. "Having got into the heart of the mountain," Wilde reported, "I had supper, the first course being whisky, the second whisky, and the third whisky." Perhaps with this alcoholic menu in mind, Vermont in 1882 became the first state to require "scientific temperance instruction" — teaching abstinence from alcohol — as part of the public school curriculum.

In many families, a summer evening rarely passed without a game of croquet on the lawn. The National Croquet Association was formed in 1882 to standardize the rules of the game. A hundred years later, croquet was having a revival of popularity, especially among college students. The number of croquet clubs in the United States grew from five in 1977 to more than 100 in 1982.

Another sports organization established in 1882 was the American Association, a group of professional baseball teams organized as a rival to the National League. The Chicago White Stockings—later renamed the Cubs—won their third consecutive National League pennant, an achievement incredible to Cub fans of 100 years later.

Another champion of 1882 was the boxer John L. Sullivan, who defeated Paddy Ryan on February 7 to win the heavyweight championship of the world. The men fought with bare knuckles on the lawn of the Barnes Hotel in Mississippi City, Miss., and Sullivan knocked out Ryan in the ninth round. Sullivan, known to millions as "the Great John L.," held the championship for 10 years.

Perhaps the most dreaded disease in 1882 was tuberculosis (TB), the leading cause of death among young and middle-aged adults. Victims of TB developed a lasting cough and fever, and lost weight so rapidly that they seemed consumed by the disease, which was often called consumption. Most physicians believed that tuberculosis was hereditary because so many cases occurred in the same families. On March 24, however, a German physician, Robert Koch, presented a paper to a Berlin medical society announcing his discovery of the organism that causes tuberculosis. Today, the disease has been nearly wiped out in most industrialized countries.

Another development in health care came when William Horlick of Racine, Wis., combined wheat extract, malted barley, and milk to create a dietary supplement for infants and the sick. Horlick's concoction was the first malted milk.

Three babies born in 1882 became great national leaders during the next century. Franklin Delano Roosevelt, future President of the United States, was born on January 30. The birth of Louis S. St. Laurent, a future prime minister of Canada, came two days later. The Irish leader Eamon de Valera, born on October 14, was three times prime minister and twice president of Ireland.

The world of 1882 could not have recognized the leaders it had gained, but it did know the great artists it had lost. Henry Wadsworth Longfellow, the most famous and popular American poet of the time, died on March 24, 1882. England paid tribute to him two years later by placing a memorial bust in the Poets' Corner of Westminster Abbey, making Longfellow the only American so honored. The English novelist Anthony Trollope died on December 6 of a stroke caused, according to rumor, by hearty laughter. Other writers who died that year included Richard Henry Dana, the American author of *Two Years Before the Mast*, on January 6; Dante Gabriel Rossetti, the English poet and painter, on April 9; and Ralph Waldo Emerson, the American poet and essayist, on April 27.

Literature was in no danger of becoming impoverished, however. Authors born in 1882 included A. A. Milne of England, who wrote the Winnie the Pooh stories, on January 18; Virginia Woolf, also of England, the author of *Orlando* and *To the Lighthouse*, on January 25;

James Joyce of Ireland, who wrote *Ulysses* and *Finnegans Wake*, on February 2; and Sigrid Undset, a Norwegian novelist who won the 1928 Nobel Prize for Literature.

The great German composer Richard Wagner completed his last work, the opera *Parsifal*, in 1882. Its first performance, in Bayreuth, Germany, on July 26, received prolonged applause after each act. Other operas that premièred that year included *The Snow Maiden* by Nicholas Rimsky-Korsakov of Russia and *Françoise de Rimini* by Ambroise Thomas of France. Composer Igor Stravinsky was born in Russia in 1882, and orchestra conductor Leopold Stokowski in England, and the Berlin Philharmonic Orchestra was founded. In the visual arts, artists born in 1882 included Edward Hopper, an American painter famous for his realistic city scenes; Rockwell Kent, the American illustrator and printmaker; and Georges Braque, the French painter who helped develop cubism.

The Victorian Age, with its strict morals, was at its height in 1882. In Philadelphia, the Society for the Suppression of Vice and Immorality tried to stop circulation by mail of Walt Whitman's book of poems, *Leaves of Grass*. Many people considered the book immoral because it glorified both physical and spiritual life. It is now considered a classic. Efforts to ban books were still making news in 1982, as groups of parents in many communities sought to remove such books as Mark Twain's *Huckleberry Finn*, John Steinbeck's *The Grapes of Wrath*, and J. D. Salinger's *The Catcher in the Rye* from school libraries and reading lists.

The year 1882 also saw the publication of *A Modern Instance*, one of the best novels by the American writer William Dean Howells, which dealt with the then-shocking subject of divorce. Robert Louis Stevenson's pirate classic *Treasure Island* appeared in serial form in a boys' magazine. *Two on a Tower*, by the English novelist Thomas Hardy, and *Specimen Days*, a book of Whitman's essays, also were published. One of the year's best sellers was a get-rich-quick book, *The Art of Money-Getting*, by the American showman P. T. Barnum.

Barnum made himself richer—and helped enrich the English language—when he purchased a huge African elephant from the London Zoo. The elephant, named Jumbo from an African word for elephant, was the largest animal in captivity, standing more than 11 feet (3.4 meters) tall. The sale aroused protests from the British public and press, who regarded the giant beast as a national treasure. Jumbo arrived in New York City on April 9, 1882, and quickly became a star of Barnum's circus. The word jumbo, still used in 1982 for almost anything huge, came from the elephant's name.

Jumbo is gone, but his name endures, as do many other innovations of 1882, including Labor Day parades, electric power plants, and malted milks. Like a distant mirror, the similarities of the year in perspective prove once again the words of the French philosopher Voltaire: "History never repeats itself; man always does."

The Year on File

1977
1978
1979
1980
1981
1982

Contributors to THE WORLD BOOK YEAR BOOK report on the major developments of 1982. The contributors' names appear at the end of the articles they have written, and a complete roster of contributors, listing their professional affiliations and the articles they have written, is on pages 6 and 7.

Articles in this section are arranged alphabetically by subject matter. In most cases, the article titles are the same as those of the articles in THE WORLD BOOK ENCYCLOPEDIA that they update. The numerous cross-references (in **bold type**) guide the reader to a subject or information that may be in some other article or that may appear under an alternative title. "See" and "See also" cross-references appear within and at the end of articles to direct the reader to related information elsewhere in THE YEAR BOOK. "In WORLD BOOK, see" references point the reader to articles in the encyclopedia that provide background information to the year's events reported in THE YEAR BOOK.

See "Motion Pictures," page 412.

The Year on File Quiz

THE YEAR BOOK presents a quiz on some events of 1982 as reported in various articles in the Year on File. Answers appear on page 531.

1. Like many travelers, Charles Burton and Sir Ranulph Twisleton-Wykeham-Fiennes journeyed around the world. Why was their trip unusual?
2. In June, the man at the right convinced the right people that he should not be held responsible for his actions. Who is he, and what happened then?

3. Bashir Gemayel was elected president of Lebanon in August, but he was never able to take office. Why not?
4. Many countries got new leaders in 1982. Match the leaders and the countries in the list below.

Hissene Habré	Bangladesh
Yuri V. Andropov	Mexico
Olof Palme	Chad
Amin Gemayel	Sweden
Hussain Muhammad Ershad	Soviet Union
Miguel de la Madrid Hurtado	Lebanon

5. In March, Bertha Wilson of Canada became one woman whose word is law. Why?
6. In the November elections in the United States, only two incumbent senators, one from each party, were defeated. Name them.
7. What animals inspired several best-selling books and a hit Broadway musical in 1982?
8. In June, Congress extended a certain law, first passed in 1965, aimed at ending state practices that discriminate against blacks. What is the law?
9. In February, many residents of a Middle Eastern city united with Muslim rebels to revolt against their national government. What is the city, and what country is it in?
10. Time ran out in June 1982 for a proposal to change a document that has been changed only 26 times in 200 years. What is the document, and what was the proposed change?
11. In October, the Socialist Party won elections in a country where it had been illegal until 1976. What was the country?
12. What do Alexander M. Haig, Jr., Murray L. Weidenbaum, James B. Edwards, and Richard V. Allen have in common?
13. A multinational peacekeeping force withdrew from Lebanon in September, only to return about two weeks later. Why?
14. What visitor from outer space, last seen in 1911, returned within range of astronomers' telescopes in October?
15. A noted actor died just 4½ months after winning an Oscar for best actor. Who was the actor?
16. President Ronald Reagan appointed Donald Paul Hodel to head a government agency that Reagan has pledged to dismantle. Name the agency.
17. The *Mary Rose,* once the pride of the English fleet, was salvaged in October from waters where she had sunk years ago. Which monarch watched her go down?
18. Wayne Gretzky, only 21 years old, eclipsed a hockey record set by Phil Esposito when he was 29. What was the record?
19. The only labor union president to sit on the board of directors of a major U.S. corporation announced in November that he was temporarily stepping down from that board. Who is he, and why did he step down?
20. Kate Smith made a trademark of the song "God Bless America," but in September, America blessed Kate Smith. What happened?
21. Automaker John Z. De Lorean had an especially bad day on October 19. What two things happened to him just hours apart?

22. The city above, once called the Paris of the Middle East, suffered countless bomb attacks in 1982 by one nation directed at a political group. What is the city, who did the bombing, and who were they trying to hit?
23. A motion picture about an ugly but lovable visitor from outer space set box-office records in 1982. What was the picture, and who directed it?
24. In January, the U.S. Department of Justice dropped one antitrust suit seeking to dismember a large corporation and settled a similar action with an agreement to break up another corporation. Which company remained whole, and which was broken up?

25. The space shuttle *Columbia,* on its fifth mission in November, accomplished two firsts but canceled a third. What were they?

26. A demonstration in a Middle Eastern country by hundreds of thousands of people—nearly 10 per cent of the population—may have affected an announcement made by the government several days later. What country is it, what was the protest about, and what was the announcement?

27. What do Laker Airways, Manville Corporation, and Braniff International Corporation have in common?

28. One nation moved closer to its European allies by joining the North Atlantic Treaty Organization in May; another nation voted to withdraw from the European Community in February. What two nations were they?

29. The monarch at the right is presiding over April 17 ceremonies to loosen the ties between her country and another. What is happening?

30. Japan literally rewrote history in 1982, drawing protests from China, South Korea, and other Asian nations. What were the protests about?

31. What was the significance of the phrase "Energy Turns the World" during 1982?

32. Two African nations formed a confederation on February 1. What are the two nations, and what is the confederation called?

33. Archbishop Valerian D. Trifa, spiritual leader of the Romanian Orthodox Episcopate, was deported from the United States. What were the circumstances?

34. France, Great Britain, Italy, and West Germany encountered stiff opposition from their ally the United States for abiding by contracts that they had signed. Why?

35. What man, admired throughout the world, was released from detention in November?

36. By beating the throw, the man below also beat a record established in 1974 by Lou Brock. Who is he, and what was the record?

37. Some tiny islands became the subject of a war between two major powers. Name the islands and the two major powers.

38. In February, a labor union for the first time approved a contract that makes major concessions in wages and benefits. What union and what employer were involved?

39. Former President Richard M. Nixon won one and lost one before the Supreme Court of the United States in 1982. What were the decisions?

40. Representatives of African nations gathered in Libya in August for a meeting of the Organization of African Unity (OAU). But the meeting never took place. Why not?

41. In November, President Reagan announced that he had chosen the so-called dense-pack proposal. The term refers to:
   a. Food and Drug Administration regulations limiting the amount of syrup in canned fruit.
   b. A Department of Defense proposal for basing the MX missile.
   c. A Department of Transportation plan for increasing ridership on urban rapid transit systems.

42. In June, the Department of Agriculture had some advice for needy Americans: "Say cheese!" What did the department do?

43. Seven people in the Chicago area took pain-reliever capsules in September, with tragic results. Explain.

44. Leftist guerrillas in El Salvador received a setback in March elections. Why?

45. A baby boy with three middle names but no last name was born in London in June. Who is he, and why is he important?

46. A two-year-old war between two Middle Eastern countries seemed to change direction in 1982. What are the countries involved?

47. New presidents took office in several Latin American countries in 1982. In the following list, indicate whether the president came to power through an election (E) or a coup (C).
Roberto Suazo Córdova of Honduras
José Efraín Ríos-Montt of Guatemala
Belisario Betancur of Colombia
Hernán Siles Zuazo of Bolivia
Salvador Jorge Blanco of the Dominican Republic

48. By the middle of November, the Chicago Bears football team had lost only two games, but the fans weren't cheering. Why not?

49. Barney B. Clark, a retired dentist, made medical history in December. What did he do?

50. With joblessness in the United States running over 10 per cent, even one member of President Reagan's family was standing in an unemployment line. Who was it?

ADVERTISING. One of the biggest news stories in the United States in 1982 — the Extra-Strength Tylenol poisonings in the Chicago area at the end of September — also proved to be one of the biggest advertising stories of the year. After seven persons died from taking cyanide-contaminated Extra-Strength Tylenol capsules, not only did the Johnson & Johnson pharmaceutical company have to remove the product from stores, but it also had to cut off a multimillion-dollar advertising campaign for the highly successful painkilling product. Less than one month later, the company reported losses in excess of $50 million. The brand, which had captured 37 per cent of the analgesic market, was returned to stores, and advertising, in November, and early sales were good. See CRIME.

Burgers and Bulgers. The always-hot advertising battle among fast-food marketers for a larger share of consumers' dining dollars got considerably hotter in the fall of 1982. Burger King Corporation started airing television commercial spots claiming that its hamburgers were better than those of competitors: that the Whopper tastes better than the Big Mac, and "in a similar test we beat Wendy's single." The McDonald's Corporation and Wendy's International Incorporated filed lawsuits claiming that the Burger King campaign was "false and deceptive."

Calorie-conscious Americans were offered a host of new food and drink products in 1982 to help them maintain better health and fight the "battle of the bulge." Millions of advertising dollars went into the promotion of new low-calorie foods, soft drinks, beers, and wines.

A Devilish Boycott Threat plagued Procter & Gamble Company for more than two years, and in 1982, the company decided to fight back. The boycott was called for by word-of-mouth and by handouts distributed by religious fundamentalists, primarily in so-called Bible Belt states in the South and Midwest. The absolutely untrue claim was that "the owner of Procter & Gamble" had appeared on television programs — "The Phil Donahue Show," "The Merv Griffin Show," and "60 Minutes" were all cited — in a discussion of cults. During this discussion, the owner had supposedly said that as long as cults had come out of the closet, he might as well admit that his company worships Satan. The handouts pictured Procter & Gamble's moon-and-stars trademark, but with the stars connected to form the number "666," which some people believe is associated with the Devil. By July 1982, Procter & Gamble reported it was receiving as many as 12,000 telephone calls per month from concerned consumers on the toll-free numbers it lists on its products. The company

For the first time in its history, the Federal Bureau of Investigation uses billboard advertising to help find one of its "10 most wanted" men.

brought lawsuits against several of the persons responsible, charging them with "libeling the character" of Procter & Gamble by circulating "false and malicious" statements about the company. It dropped two lawsuits on August 12, after the rumormongers publicly apologized, but other libel suits were still pending at year-end.

Advertising Revenue. Late in 1981, Robert J. Coen, senior vice-president of McCann-Erickson USA, predicted that advertising spending in 1982 in major media would increase 11.7 per cent to $68.5 billion. But by mid-1982, Coen had scaled down his estimate about 1 per cent to $68 billion, primarily because of sluggishness in local newspaper and retail advertising. "Our December 1981 projections for 1982 ad expenditures were based upon the then-current consensus of a 9.2 per cent gross national product growth," Coen said. "Current expectations have been lowered to less than 6 per cent. In comparison, ad expenditures will not only continue to grow faster than the economy as a whole, but it is evident that the differential is widening as advertising is increasingly used to solve problems created by the economy. The ratio of advertising-to-sales is expected to rise."

Despite unfavorable exchange rates affecting overseas operations, U.S. advertising agencies had another record year in 1981, with gross income rising to just over $5 billion on worldwide billings of $35.2 billion, according to the annual report published in 1982 by *Advertising Age*. The gross income total for 1981 was a 7.3 per cent increase over the $4.67 billion reported for 1980, and the combined billings figure was up 10.1 per cent from the previous year's total of $31.8 billion. For the second straight year, Young & Rubicam Incorporated posted the top gross income—$353 million on billings of $2.4 billion in 1981. The largest agency in the world continued to be Japan's Dentsu Advertising, which reported gross income for 1981 of $428 million.

The 100 leading advertisers in the United States spent $14.8 billion in 1981, according to the annual *Advertising Age* study of expenditures. This was a rise of 14 per cent from the estimated $13-billion invested in national advertising by the 100 top spenders in 1980. The top advertiser again was Procter & Gamble with $671.9 million.

An Advertising Loss. William Bernbach, a giant of the advertising world, died on October 2 at the age of 71. Since he helped found New York City's Doyle Dane Bernbach International in 1949, Bernbach's name had become synonymous with such classic campaigns as "Think small" for the introduction of the Volkswagen car to the United States; Levy's rye bread, which "You don't have to be Jewish to love"; and the Avis rental car "We try harder" campaign. Jarlath J. Graham

In WORLD BOOK, see ADVERTISING.

AFGHANISTAN. The war against Russian occupation ground on in 1982. Russian forces had invaded the country in 1979 in support of the Communist government of Revolutionary Council President Babrak Karmal. They met armed resistance from Afghan *mujahedeen* (fighters for the faith), who opposed both the government and the invaders. Despite several major offensives by Soviet forces and Afghan Army units in 1982, the mujahedeen continued to control most of the countryside. They also made life difficult for the invaders in the cities, with sabotage of Soviet installations and attacks on military personnel.

A Major Soviet Offensive got underway in May in the strategic Panjshir Valley north of Kabul. More than 12,000 Soviet and Afghan Army troops swept through the valley. Entire villages suspected of harboring the mujahedeen were destroyed and civilians massacred. But the invaders sustained heavy casualties and losses in equipment. Most of the Soviet forces withdrew from the valley in June, and the mujahedeen regained nearly all outposts.

Aside from its impact on civilians—with about one-sixth of the 1979 Afghan population in refugee camps in Pakistan—the war had grim overtones in the alleged use of chemical weapons by Soviet forces. This use included not only crop defoliants, but also lethal nerve gases and toxins. The U.S.

Afghan resistance fighters purchase ammunition in Pakistan to continue their battle against the Soviet forces occupying their country.

Department of State estimated that about 3,000 Afghans died from chemical attacks between the summer of 1979 and the summer of 1981. A Soviet spokesman called the charge a lie.

Efforts Toward a Settlement took at least two directions. On June 16, talks began in Geneva, Switzerland, between representatives of Pakistan and the Karmal government, who met separately with a United Nations intermediary. They agreed on a peace plan that included withdrawal of Soviet troops and guarantees of nonintervention in Afghan affairs by its neighbors.

On July 23, the United States revealed that it had held unpublicized talks with the Soviet Union in the hope of reaching a solution in Afghanistan. Nothing had come of the talks.

Tunnel Disaster. From 300 to 400 Soviet soldiers and from 500 to 800 Afghans were burned to death or died of asphyxiation when they were trapped inside the 1.7-mile (2.7-kilometer) Salang Tunnel near Kabul in early November. A fuel truck collided with the lead vehicle in a Soviet military convoy and exploded. Soviet soldiers guarding the tunnel thought the explosion signaled an attack by resistance fighters and blocked the tunnel entrances, preventing those inside from escaping. William Spencer

See also ASIA (Facts in Brief Table). In WORLD BOOK, see AFGHANISTAN.

AFRICA. Wars or military uprisings occurred in 11 African countries during 1982. Opposition forces waged guerrilla wars against the central governments of Angola, Mozambique, and Uganda. Chad's government was toppled in that country's ongoing civil war, and a military revolt succeeded in Ghana. Abortive uprisings occurred in Kenya and the Central African Republic. Secessionist wars continued in two parts of Ethiopia, and separatists fought Morocco for control of the former Spanish colony of Western Sahara. Black Namibian nationalists continued their long-standing war against South Africa over control of Namibia.

Civil Wars. In Chad's 17-year-old civil war, Muslims from the country's north have fought for control of the government against Christians and other forces from the south. On June 7, an army led by a northerner, Hissene Habré, captured the capital city, N'Djamena, and deposed President Goukouni Weddeye. Habré, a former defense minister and once also prime minister, proclaimed himself interim head of state on June 19. He tried to win the support of a long-time rival, Colonel Wadal Abdelkader Kamougue, Weddeye's vice-president, but the two could not reach accord. Habré became president of the country on October 21. See CHAD.

Guerrilla forces began opposing the government of Uganda's President Milton Obote shortly after he took office in December 1980. The rebels claimed that the elections that put him in office had been rigged. In January 1982, two former presidents of Uganda, Yusufu K. Lule and Godfrey Lukogwa Binaisa, announced that they had formed a united front against Obote. They said Obote was guilty of a more repressive rule than Idi Amin Dada, who headed Uganda until 1979. On February 23, guerrillas belonging to the Uganda Freedom Movement mounted a large-scale attack on the main army barracks in the capital city, Kampala. The fighting lasted from dawn to midafternoon.

Angola's civil war dates from 1975, when the country became independent from Portugal. In 1982, the main opposition to Angola's government came from the National Union for the Total Independence of Angola (UNITA). UNITA forces disrupted road and rail communications and attacked towns in central and southeastern Angola. See ANGOLA.

Guerrilla forces have opposed Mozambique's government since that country gained its independence from Portugal, also in 1975. The rebels belong to the Mozambique National Resistance (MNR), whose forces numbered 3,000 to 5,000 troops and reportedly operated in all of the country's provinces in 1982. They attacked military

Pallbearers carry the body of King Sobhuza II, monarch of Swaziland from age 1 until his death in August at 83, to his funeral service.

garrisons and sabotaged railways, roads, and power facilities.

South Africa's white government provided military support to both the MNR and UNITA. The governments the two rebel groups are trying to overthrow have supported black nationalists opposed to white rule in South Africa and Namibia.

Besides aiding UNITA, South Africa sent its own troops into southern Angola to attack guerrilla bases established there by the principal black movement for the independence of Namibia, the South West Africa People's Organization (SWAPO). In an incursion that began on June 11 and lasted more than two months, South African forces raided various SWAPO facilities.

Namibia. South Africa's military successes against SWAPO caused it to harden its position on independence for Namibia, which is under South African control. Five years of negotiations sponsored by the United States and four other Western powers appeared close to success in June 1982, with SWAPO and South Africa reportedly agreeing on a voting formula for choosing Namibia's constituent assembly. An August 15 cease-fire seemed likely, and the United Nations (UN) began arranging for a peacekeeping force to supervise the cease-fire and subsequent elections.

However, South Africa's government stated that it would not sign any agreement unless Angola first committed itself to the withdrawal of the 15,000 to 20,000 Cuban troops stationed in that country. Angola and SWAPO rejected that condition on the grounds that the Cubans were needed to protect Angola against South African attacks. See NAMIBIA.

The South African government has opposed SWAPO control of Namibia because it expects that SWAPO will support black nationalists committed to ending white-minority rule in South Africa. Whites comprise about 17 per cent of South Africa's population but hold virtually all of the political power. In a move to win support from South Africans of Asian and mixed racial backgrounds, who make up about 12 per cent of the people in the country, the government announced on July 30 that it would establish separate legislative bodies for those two groups. The existing all-white Parliament would share some powers with them. Blacks were still to be excluded from participation in the national government and to remain subject to strict segregation.

Opposition to the government's segregationist policies emerged in the ranks of South Africa's Dutch Reformed Church, the principal church for whites. On June 9, 123 white ministers called for policies of racial equality. See SOUTH AFRICA.

Secessionist Wars. Ethiopia's Marxist central government launched a large-scale offensive in February to end the 20-year armed struggle of separatists to establish an independent state in Ethiopia's northeastern province, Eritrea. Over 70,000 Ethiopian troops, accompanied by 400 military advisers from the Soviet Union, took part in the operation. However, the attack bogged down, and the rebels continued to hold the mountain town, Nakfa. See ETHIOPIA.

Two Nations Form a Confederation

★ National Capital

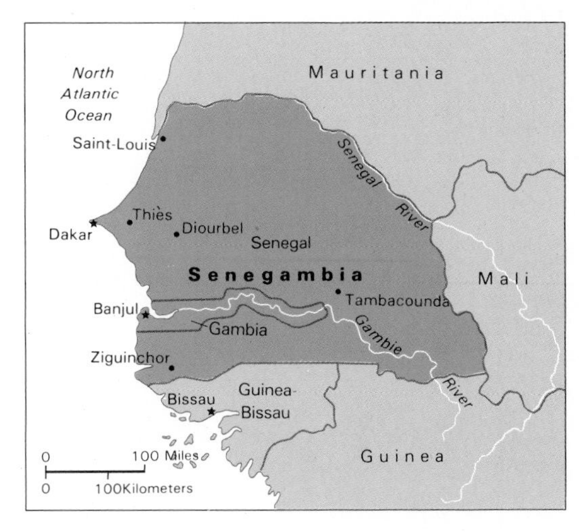

Somali-speaking secessionists in Ethiopia's southeastern region, Ogaden, fought to join their territory to neighboring Somalia. Their major source of military support was Somalia's government, headed by President Mohamed Siad Barre. To weaken that source, Ethiopia provided supplies and bases for two Somali guerrilla groups opposed to Siad Barre. Ethiopian troops joined the guerrillas for an attack in July on two towns. The offensive faltered, and at year-end, the two sides were in a stalemate. See SOMALIA.

Forces of the Polisario Front, a Marxist group dedicated to independence for the one-time Spanish colonial province of Western Sahara (formerly Spanish Sahara), continued to fight against Moroccan annexation of the area. They call the territory the Sahara Arab Democratic Republic (SADR). See MOROCCO.

Organization of African Unity (OAU). Recognition of the Polisario Front's claim to rule Western Sahara badly divided Africa in 1982. At the OAU's February meeting of foreign ministers, 26

Facts in Brief on African Political Units

Country	Population	Government	Monetary Unit*	Foreign Trade (million U.S. $) Exports†	Imports†
Algeria	20,377,000	President Chadli Bendjedid; Prime Minister Mohamed Ben Ahmed Abdelghani	dinar (4.6 = $1)	13,656	10,811
Angola	7,622,000	President José Eduardo dos Santos	kwanza (33.3 = $1)	791	562
Benin	3,875,000	President Mathieu Kerekou	CFA franc (362.3 = $1)	170	410
Bophuthatswana	1,719,000	President & Prime Minister Lucas Mangope	rand (1.1 = $1)	no statistics available	
Botswana	885,000	President Quett K. J. Masire	pula (1.1 = $1)	447	532
Burundi	4,355,000	President Jean-Baptiste Bagaza	franc (87 = $1)	71	167
Cameroon	9,103,000	President Paul Biya; Prime Minister Bello Bouba Maigari	CFA franc (362.3 = $1)	1,384	1,602
Cape Verde	342,000	President Aristides Pereira; Prime Minister Pedro Pires	escudo (54.3 = $1)	3	17
Central African Republic	2,385,000	National Recovery Committee President & Prime Minister André-Dieudonne Kolingba	CFA franc (362.3 = $1)	79	70
Chad	4,843,000	President Hissene Habré	CFA franc (362.3 = $1)	91	180
Ciskei	600,000	President Lennox Sebe	rand (1.1 = $1)	no statistics available	
Comoros	358,000	President Ahmed Abdallah; Prime Minister Ali Mroudjae	CFA franc (362.3 = $1)	12	27
Congo	1,660,000	President Denis Sassou-Nguesso; Prime Minister Louis-Sylvain Goma	CFA franc (362.3 = $1)	510	291
Djibouti	355,000	President Hassan Gouled Aptidon; Prime Minister Barkat Gourad Hamadou	franc (178.3 = $1)	11	184
Egypt	44,697,000	President Mohamed Hosni Mubarak; Prime Minister Ahmad Fouad Moheiddin	pound (1 = $1.43)	3,233	8,839
Equatorial Guinea	389,000	President Obiang Nguema Mbasogo	ekuele (226.4 = $1)	13	37
Ethiopia	33,552,000	Provisional Military Administrative Council Chairman Mengistu Haile-Mariam	birr (2.1 = $1)	408	779
Gabon	569,000	President Omar Bongo; Prime Minister Léon Mebiame	CFA franc (362.3 = $1)	1,477	532
Gambia	653,000	President Sir Dawda Kairaba Jawara	dalasi (2.3 = $1)	27	125
Ghana	12,585,000	Provisional National Defense Council Chairman Jerry John Rawlings	cedi (2.7 = $1)	1,200	1,100
Guinea	5,415,000	President Ahmed Sékou Touré; Prime Minister Lansana Beavogui	syli (22.9 = $1)	385	375
Guinea-Bissau	834,000	Revolutionary Council President João Bernardo Vieira; Vice-President & Prime Minister Victor Saúde Maria	peso (37.8 = $1)	10	48
Ivory Coast	9,018,000	President Félix Houphouët-Boigny	CFA franc (362.3 = $1)	3,000	2,600
Kenya	18,185,000	President Daniel T. arap Moi	shilling (10.1 = $1)	1,172	2,069
Lesotho	1,442,000	King Moshoeshoe II; Prime Minister Leabua Jonathan	loti (1.1 = $1)	36	311
Liberia	2,071,000	Head of State Samuel K. Doe	dollar (1 = $1)	601	535
Libya	3,226,000	Leader of the Revolution Muammar Muhammad al-Qadhafi; General People's Congress General Secretary Muhammad al-Zarruq Rajab; General People's Committee Chairman (Prime Minister) Jadallah Azzuz al-Talhi	dinar (1 = $3.38)	22,578	9,890
Madagascar	9,387,000	President Didier Ratsiraka; Prime Minister Désiré Rakotoarijaona	franc (352 = $1)	402	600

Country	Population	Government	Monetary Unit*	Foreign Trade (million U.S. $) Exports†	Imports†
Malawi	6,427,000	President H. Kamuzu Banda	kwacha (1.1 = $1)	284	362
Mali	7,481,000	President Moussa Traoré	franc (724.6 = $1)	149	359
Mauritania	1,775,000	President Mohamed Khouna Ould Haidalla; Prime Minister Maayouia Ould Sid Ahmed Taya	ouguiya (51 = $1)	194	264
Mauritius	1,003,000	Governor General Sir Dayendranath Burrenchobay; Prime Minister Aneerood Jugnauth	rupee (10.4 = $1)	326	553
Morocco	22,119,000	King Hassan II; Prime Minister Maati Bouabid	dirham (5.9 = $1)	2,500	4,400
Mozambique	12,910,000	President Samora Moisés Machel	metical (30.5 = $1)	150	495
Namibia (South West Africa)	1,097,000	Administrator-General Danie Hough; Ministerial Council Chairman Dirk Mudge	rand (1.1 = $1)	no statistics available	
Niger	5,780,000	Supreme Military Council President Seyni Kountché	CFA franc (362.3 = $1)	433	632
Nigeria	84,721,000	President Shehu Shagari	naira (1 = $1.48)	17,331	10,991
Rwanda	5,450,000	President Juvénal Habyarimana	franc (89.2 = $1)	115	188
São Tomé & Príncipe	88,000	President Manuel Pinto da Costa	dobra (38.8 = $1)	27	16
Senegal	6,114,000	President Abdou Diouf; Prime Minister Habib Thiam	CFA franc (362.3 = $1)	536	931
Seychelles	69,000	President France Albert René	rupee (6.7 = $1)	14	66
Sierra Leone	4,071,000	President Siaka Stevens	leone (1.3 = $1)	206	316
Somalia	3,914,000	President Mohamed Siad Barre	shilling (6.3 = $1)	141	275
South Africa	31,444,000	President Marais Viljoen; Prime Minister Pieter Willem Botha	rand (1.1 = $1)	25,680	19,246
Sudan	20,246,000	President & Prime Minister Gaafar Mohamed Nimeiri	pound (1.3 = $1)	658	1,529
Swaziland	603,000	Queen Regent Dzeliwe; Prime Minister Prince Mabandla Dlamini	lilangeni (1.1 = $1)	235	259
Tanzania	20,629,000	President Julius K. Nyerere; Prime Minister Cleopa David Msuya	shilling (9.3 = $1)	508	1,226
Togo	2,793,000	President Gnassingbe Eyadéma	CFA franc (362.3 = $1)	382	532
Transkei	1,914,000	President Kaiser Matanzima; Prime Minister George Matanzima	rand (1.1 = $1)	no statistics available	
Tunisia	7,083,000	President Habib Bourguiba; Prime Minister Mohamed Mzali	dinar (1 = $1.70)	2,189	3,479
Uganda	15,117,000	President Milton Obote; Prime Minister Erifasi Otema Alimadi	shilling (100 = $1)	315	499
Upper Volta	7,439,000	Provisional Council Chairman Jean Baptiste Ouédraogo	CFA franc (362.3 = $1)	90	358
Venda	320,000	President Patrick Mphephu	rand (1.1 = $1)	no statistics available	
Zaire	30,824,000	President Mobutu Sese Seko; Prime Minister Kengo wa Dondo	zaire (5.8 = $1)	662	672
Zambia	6,243,000	President Kenneth David Kaunda; Prime Minister Nalumino Mundia	kwacha (1 = $1.05)	1,402	1,090
Zimbabwe	7,926,000	President Canaan Banana; Prime Minister Robert Mugabe	dollar (1 = $1.32)	1,423	1,322

*Exchange rates as of Dec. 1, 1982. †Latest available data.

French President François Mitterrand samples camel's milk as he dines on May 26 with President Mohamed Khouna Ould Haidalla of Mauritania.

African governments voted to make SADR the organization's 51st member. Morocco and 18 other countries walked out of the meeting on the grounds that only a two-thirds majority could admit a new member. Most of those 19 states boycotted the OAU heads of state meeting, scheduled for August 5 to 8 in Libya's capital city, Tripoli. Because the organization's charter requires a two-thirds quorum at meetings, the conference had to be postponed, making it the first meeting called off since OAU's founding in 1963.

Morocco and its allies refused to resume participation until the Polisario Front was stripped of its membership. A meeting held in Zaire on October 8 and 9 among 18 French-speaking African states failed to find a compromise for ending the boycott.

The OAU's first-ever peacekeeping force was deployed at the end of 1981 to help restore stability to war-torn Chad. In January, the OAU force blocked an offensive by Hissene Habré's army. However, in June, it apparently did not try to stop Habré's final drive on the capital.

U.S. Relations with Africa. The Administration of United States President Ronald Reagan contributed $12 million toward the maintenance of the OAU force in Chad. It also was actively involved in the negotiations for achieving independence for Namibia.

African leaders criticized the Reagan Administration for being more cooperative than previous administrations toward South Africa's white government. On February 26, the White House relaxed restrictions imposed by the Administration of President Jimmy Carter on the sale to South Africa of communications equipment, chemicals, and other goods. The supplies, though not directly military in character, could be used by that country's armed forces and police. The Reagan Administration also supported South Africa's application to the International Monetary Fund (IMF)—a UN agency that promotes world trade—for a $1.1-billion loan.

These measures were parts of the Reagan Administration's policy of "constructive engagement" toward South Africa. The Administration, in answer to critics of that policy, contended that the United States could do more to encourage black rights in South Africa if it remained on good terms with that country's government.

Military Uprisings. On Dec. 31, 1981, rebel soldiers overthrew Ghana's elected government, headed by President Hilla Limann. The revolt was led by 34-year-old former Ghanaian Air Force Lieutenant Jerry John Rawlings, who named himself chairman of a seven-member ruling council. The coup was the fifth military power seizure in Ghana since 1966. Rawlings had also led the fourth coup, in June 1979. He justified the latest overthrow on the grounds that the Limann government had been corrupt and repressive. On November 24, Rawlings reported that troops loyal to him had crushed a rebellion led by "misguided individuals." See GHANA.

Kenyan Air Force rebels also claimed to be opposing corruption when they tried to overthrow the one-party government of President Daniel T. arap Moi on August 1. However, most of the army remained loyal to Moi and defeated the rebels. Following the coup, the entire 2,100-member air force was arrested. See KENYA.

A coup attempt also failed in the Central African Republic (CAR). On March 3, the CAR's information minister, General François Bozize, apparently tried to seize power with the help of an opposition party, the Movement for the Liberation of the Centrafrican People, led by Ange Patasse. Army and police units loyal to President André-Dieudonne Kolingba rounded up a number of Patasse's supporters, putting some under arrest and shooting as many as 40 others. Patasse fled to the French Embassy.

Elections. The government of Mauritius was replaced peacefully in elections held on June 11. The prime minister since the country gained independence in 1968, Sir Seewoosagur Ramgoolam, was replaced by Aneerood Jugnauth, leader of a two-party socialist alliance that won all 62 seats in the parliament. See MAURITIUS.

Multiparty elections were also held in Gambia, where the party of President Sir Dawda Kairaba Jawara won 27 of the 35 contested parliamentary seats. Jawara, who has headed the country since it gained independence in 1965, was elected to another five-year term. On February 1, Gambia and Senegal joined together in a confederation called Senegambia. While remaining two sovereign states, they pledged to work toward united policies for defense, foreign affairs, finance, and trade.

Decline in Exports. Virtually all African states suffered in 1982 from the economic recessions in Western Europe and North America, because those regions normally buy most of Africa's exports. For example, weak demand for Nigerian crude oil caused that country to cut back its production from an average of about 2.1 million barrels per day (bpd) in 1980 to 725,000 bpd in March 1982. See NIGERIA.

Pope's Visit. Pope John Paul II visited Nigeria, Benin, Gabon, and Equatorial Guinea during a weeklong tour in February. See ROMAN CATHOLIC CHURCH. J. Dixon Esseks

In WORLD BOOK, see AFRICA.

AGRICULTURE. See FARM AND FARMING.

AIR FORCE. See ARMED FORCES.

ALABAMA. See STATE GOVERNMENT.

ALASKA. See STATE GOVERNMENT.

ALBANIA. Adil Çarçani became prime minister in January 1982, succeeding Mehmet Shehu, who was reported to have committed suicide in December 1981. On November 10, Communist Party First Secretary Enver Hoxha said that Shehu had killed himself because of revelations that he had served as an agent for Russia, the United States, and Yugoslavia at various times. Hoxha said that the Yugoslav intelligence service had ordered Shehu to kill him and other Albanian leaders.

After Shehu's death, the government began to purge his relatives and political associates from official posts. Qirjako Mihali replaced Haki Toska as minister of finance. The Communist Party had dropped Toska from its ruling council, the Politburo, at the last party congress in November 1981. Hekuran Isai took over the interior ministry from Feçor Shehu, a relative of Mehmet Shehu. In October, Kadri Hasbiu, minister of defense and a brother-in-law of Mehmet Shehu, disappeared from the list of candidates for election to the People's Assembly. In November, Foreign Minister Nesti Nase reportedly was arrested.

On November 22, Ramiz Alia replaced Haxhi Lleshi as Albania's head of state—officially, as chairman of the Presidium of the People's Assembly (parliament). Lleshi, 69, had held the post since 1953. Western diplomats believed that Albania's leaders were preparing Alia to succeed the 74-year-old Hoxha. Hoxha replaced 10 Cabinet ministers, including Hasbiu and the chairman of the State Planning Commission, on November 23.

Invasion. On September 28, Albanian authorities announced the "liquidation" of a group of exiled Albanians described as "criminals" and alleged to have tried to land on Albania's Adriatic coast three days earlier. The group's leader, Xhevdet Mustafa, was a resident of the United States. Leka, the son of Albania's last king, Zog I, denied involvement in the landing, but said that he supported it. Leka lives in South Africa.

Relations with Yugoslavia. In September, Albania and Yugoslavia signed an agreement to complete a rail link between the two countries by the end of 1983. The railway will be Albania's first direct rail link with the outside world.

Relations between the two countries worsened in October 1982 following speeches critical of Yugoslavia at the congress of Albania's youth movement. The movement's leader referred to "savage persecution" of ethnic Albanian students and intellectuals who live in Yugoslavia's Kosovo region. Hoxha said on November 10 that Yugoslavia had sponsored the September invasion attempt. The official Soviet newspaper *Pravda* said at the end of November that Russia was ready to establish normal relations with Albania. Chris Cviic

See also EUROPE (Facts in Brief Table). In WORLD BOOK, see ALBANIA.

ALBERTA gave an overwhelming victory to Premier Peter Lougheed, 54, and his Progressive Conservative (PC) Party government in an election on Nov. 2, 1982. It was the Lougheed government's fourth election victory, and the premier said it would inaugurate his final term.

The PC, which had won 74 of the legislature's 79 seats in the 1979 election, captured 75 this time. The four opposition seats were won by two members of the New Democratic Party and two Independents. The separatist Western Canada Concept Party, which had dramatically elected its first member in a by-election on February 17, was wiped out despite running candidates in all the province's ridings, or electoral districts. The once-powerful Social Credit Party, which had ruled Alberta for 36 years until its defeat by Lougheed in 1971, was also eliminated as a political force.

Economy. Premier Lougheed dipped into the Alberta Heritage Savings Trust Fund—a public endowment that receives 30 per cent of provincial resource revenues—on September 7 to finance a program to reduce mortgage interest rates to 12.5 per cent. He borrowed the idea from the PC in neighboring Saskatchewan, which had used it to help elect a new government in the spring. Lougheed also promised that business and farm loans would be subsidized in order to lower interest rates to 14.5 per cent. An estimated 225,000 households would be eligible for assistance under the plan. Lougheed planned to reduce the amount of oil and gas revenues that flow into the Heritage Fund to 15 per cent and to spend the difference on the interest rate subsidies. The fund stood at $11 billion (Canadian dollars; $1 = U.S. 81 cents as of Dec. 31, 1982) at the end of March, having made $1 billion in investment earnings during the previous fiscal year, the most in its existence.

The Budget, presented on March 18, estimated 1982-1983 revenue at $7.9 billion but expenditures at $8.7 billion, a 30 per cent increase over the past year. There were no tax increases for individuals.

The government promised to spend more than $5 billion on roads and other capital projects in an effort to stimulate the economy. Alberta's oil royalty structure was overhauled, and Lougheed announced on April 13 that royalties would be reduced to allow a larger share of the proceeds of oil and gas production to go to industry. This would improve cash flows for companies suffering from reduced demands in the industry.

A bitter 23-day strike by 7,000 of Alberta's 9,000 nurses ended on March 11 after the provincial legislature passed a law forcing them to return to work. David M. L. Farr

See also CANADA. In WORLD BOOK, see ALBERTA.

Roland Michener, former governor general of Canada, reaches another peak in July, standing atop the mountain named for him in Nordegg, Alta.

ALGERIA granted asylum to about 600 of the estimated 15,000 Palestine Liberation Organization guerrillas who were evacuated from Lebanon in August 1982 in the wake of the Israeli invasion of that country in June (see MIDDLE EAST). Algeria also gave refuge to President Goukouni Weddeye of Chad after the forces of Chadian rebel leader Hissene Habré ousted him in June (see CHAD).

The government held firm in its support of the Polisario Front fighting for independence from Morocco in Western Sahara. It voted with other members of the Organization of African Unity (OAU) in granting OAU membership to the front's political organization in February.

The Political Scene. The Cabinet was reshuffled in January. President Chadli Bendjedid established a new position of secretary of state for social affairs and gave the top post to a woman. The action underscored government support for the new family code being debated in the National Assembly. The code, still to be enacted at year-end, covers the role of women in Algerian society and other related family matters.

In March elections, the Assembly was enlarged from 261 members to 281. Thus, although all 123 delegates of the ruling National Liberation Front (FLN) were re-elected, they represented a smaller proportion of the Assembly than previously, allowing for freer political debate.

In April, the General Union of Algerian Workers (UGTA) was also reorganized, under a new and enlarged 123-member national executive council. The previous council had been accused of allowing militants who were not FLN members to hold responsible posts and thus dominate union activities. The new UGTA organization is to have eight professional sectors directly under the executive council. Since council members are now required to be FLN members, the change should ensure greater government control over labor.

The Economy. Algeria's banking system was still another target of reorganization during the year. There are to be new national banks parallel to existing banks in each of six sectors of the economy—agriculture, industry, transport, energy, tourism, and service industries. A separate bank was established for housing loans. The first new bank, the Bank for Agricultural and Rural Development, opened in Algiers in April.

The economy remained strong. The country reduced oil prices in June and cut production, but new agreements with the United States, France, Great Britain, and Belgium promised to almost double natural gas exports. William Spencer

See also AFRICA (Facts in Brief Table). In WORLD BOOK, see ALGERIA.

AMERICAN LEGION. See COMMUNITY ORGANIZATIONS.

AMERICAN LIBRARY ASSOCIATION (ALA) in 1982 returned to the city of its birth, Philadelphia, to celebrate its 101st annual conference and 106th year. The meeting, which was held from July 10 to 15 in conjunction with the Pennsylvania Library Association, attracted 12,819 librarians, trustees, and friends of libraries to more than 2,100 meetings and workshops.

During the year, ALA President Elizabeth W. Stone had sought a United States commemorative stamp for libraries, and got it. The first stamp to honor America's libraries was introduced at a special ceremony during the Philadelphia conference. Stone also proposed a national symbol for libraries, and the ALA Council approved both the concept and the design: a stylized drawing of a reader with a book, done in the manner of international road signs.

Carol Nemeyer, associate librarian for national programs at the Library of Congress, took office as the new ALA president. Brooke Sheldon, director of the School of Library Science at Texas Woman's University, was elected ALA vice-president, president-elect.

Public Service Campaigns. Also in 1982, the ALA's Public Information Office received the Silver Anvil Award from the Public Relations Society of America for its marketing program to promote U.S. libraries. The newly formed Coalition for Literacy, which is an alliance of librarians, educators, volunteer groups, and corporate representatives, announced plans for a massive nationwide public-service advertising campaign to promote adult literacy. The ALA led in the development of the coalition, which is seeking solutions to the serious problem of adult functional illiteracy in the United States.

National Awards. The ALA Committee on the Status of Women in Librarianship received the 1982 Bailey K. Howard-World Book Encyclopedia-ALA Goals Award for a study that will assist women librarians re-entering the work force. The Association of College and Research Libraries' Bibliographic Instruction Section received the 1982 J. Morris Jones-World Book Encyclopedia-ALA Goals Award for "Bringing Workshops to Members," a training project.

Nancy Willard, author of *A Visit to William Blake's Inn: Poems for Innocent and Experienced Travelers,* won the 1982 Newbery Medal for the most distinguished contribution to American literature for children. Chris Van Allsburg, author and illustrator of *Jumanji,* won the 1982 Caldecott Medal for the most distinguished American picture book for children. Peggy Barber

See also CANADIAN LIBRARY ASSOCIATION (CLA); LIBRARY; LITERATURE FOR CHILDREN. In WORLD BOOK, see AMERICAN LIBRARY ASSN.

ANDROPOV, YURI V. (1914-), became General Secretary of the Communist Party of the Soviet Union on Nov. 12, 1982. He succeeded Leonid I. Brezhnev, who died on November 10. Speculation that Andropov would succeed Brezhnev had run high since May 24, when Andropov was named to the powerful Secretariat of the Communist Party Central Committee. Two days later, Andropov withdrew from his post as chairman of the KGB, Russia's secret police agency. See RUSSIA.

Yuri Vladimirovich Andropov was born in Nagutskaya, near Mineralnyye Vody, on June 15, 1914. The son of a railway worker, he was educated at a state university in Petrozavodsk near the border with Finland and at a political school. He worked his way up through the party in what was then the Karelo-Finnish Republic and joined the Secretariat staff in 1951.

From 1953 to 1957, he was counselor, then ambassador, to Hungary. He returned to the Secretariat staff in 1957 and became a member of the Central Committee in 1961. Andropov was a member of the Secretariat from 1962 until 1967, when he took the KGB post.

In 1967, he was elected an alternate member of the Politburo, the policymaking body of the Central Committee. He became a full member in 1973. Jay Myers

ANGOLA suffered in 1982 from civil war and related incursions by South African government troops. The National Union for the Total Independence of Angola (UNITA), which has fought the government since 1975, had guerrilla forces in the eastern and southern parts of the country.

South Africa supported UNITA with weapons and other supplies in order to weaken the central government's hold on the southern region of Angola. In that area, the Angolan government has permitted black nationalists from Namibia to establish bases and launch attacks on South African forces in Namibia. On March 13 and again on July 16, South African troops crossed into Angola to raid the Namibian bases. See NAMIBIA.

United States and Angolan government officials met in January and September to discuss Namibian independence from South Africa. The main stumbling block continued to be American and South African insistence that Angola send home the Cuban and East European troops there.

Troubles within the government surfaced on July 16, when the dismissal of three prominent leaders was announced. J. Dixon Esseks

See also AFRICA (Facts in Brief Table). In WORLD BOOK, see ANGOLA.

ANIMAL. See CAT; CONSERVATION; DOG; ZOOLOGY; ZOOS AND AQUARIUMS.

Guerrillas of the South West Africa People's Organization attend a weaponry lecture somewhere in the bush country between Angola and Namibia.

ANTHROPOLOGY. In June 1982, a scientific team under the direction of anthropologist J. Desmond Clark of the University of California at Berkeley announced the discovery of the oldest known fossil bones from a hominid—a human ancestor—and the earliest evidence of upright walking by a hominid. Found in the Middle Awash River Valley in the Afar region of Ethiopia, the fossils have been dated to about 4 million years ago.

The specimens consist of skull fragments and part of a thighbone. Measurements of the skull fragments indicate that the creature had a brain about the size of that of a modern chimpanzee. The thighbone, which is almost certainly from another individual, belonged to an adolescent male that walked upright.

Clark and anthropologist Timothy D. White, another member of the Berkeley team, believe that the fossil bones are from the species *Australopithecus afarensis,* the same species as "Lucy," the 3.5-million-year-old skeleton found nearby in Hadar in 1974. According to the scientists, the absence of significant differences between Lucy and the newly discovered fossils indicates that the species remained relatively the same over a long period of time.

According to Clark and White, the new finds also confirm earlier suggestions that *A. afarensis* was fully adapted to standing and walking upright. In addition, the fossils provide strong evidence for the theory of early human evolution outlined in 1979 by White and anthropologist Donald C. Johanson of the Institute of Human Origins in Berkeley, Calif., who found Lucy. The theory suggests that hominids walked upright for approximately 2 million years before they developed larger brains and the ability to make tools.

Further, the scientists said, the absence of any remains at the site from the genus *Homo,* the line to which human beings belong, supports Johanson and White's contention that *A. afarensis* was the only hominid alive between 3 million and 4 million years ago and so was a direct ancestor of modern human beings. Other anthropologists, notably Richard E. Leakey, director of the National Museums of Kenya in Nairobi, believe the *Homo* line arose before *A. afarensis* and that the species was not a direct human ancestor.

Filling the Fossil Gap. The discovery of the jawbone of a hominoid creature—an ape or prehuman—that may be 8 million years old was announced on August 31 by anthropologist Hidemi Ishida of Osaka University in Japan and Richard Leakey. If the preliminary estimate of the fossil's age is correct, the jawbone would be the first hominoid fossil found from that period—4 million to 12 million years ago. Many anthropologists believe that human ancestors diverged from African apes and began to walk upright during that period.

Part of a thighbone and skull fragments found in Ethiopia and dated to 4 million years ago are the oldest known fossil bones of a human ancestor.

Discovered in the Samburu Hills of north-central Kenya, the fossil consists of an upper left jaw with five excellently preserved teeth. The creature was 18 to 20 years old and about the size of a female gorilla. Ishida and Leakey reported that the jawbone is unlike any hominid or ape fossil previously discovered. But they stressed that further study is needed before they can theorize about whether the fossil was a human ancestor.

***Ramapithecus* Revised.** *Ramapithecus,* previously thought by many anthropologists to be the earliest known hominid, lost its place in the human evolutionary line in 1982. The change resulted from the discovery of an 8-million-year-old partial skull by anthropologist David R. Pilbeam of Harvard University's Peabody Museum in Cambridge, Mass. The fossil skull, which was found on the Potwar Plateau of Pakistan, belonged to a chimpanzee-sized adult ape.

Although Pilbeam classified the fossil as *Sivapithecus indicus,* he and other researchers believe it is identical to *Ramapithecus.* The scientists suggest that because many features of the *Sivapithecus* skull resemble those of modern orang-utans, *Ramapithecus* should no longer be considered a direct human ancestor. Furthermore, Pilbeam suggests that *Sivapithecus* was not a direct ancestor of modern orang-utans either, but a close relative of that ancestor. Paleontologist Peter Andrews of the British Natural History Museum in London contends that the *Sivapithecus* skull indicated that orang-utan ancestors diverged between 8 million and 12 million years ago from the path that led to the development of African apes and humans.

First Scalping. An analysis of a 300,000-year-old hominid skull, reported by Berkeley's Timothy White in June 1982, revealed unmistakable evidence of the first known scalping of one hominid by another. White found extensive cuts on the skull's left cheekbone below the eye socket and across the forehead. White explained that the nature of the marks indicates that they were made by a jagged-edged instrument, such as a stone knife, rather than by the claws or teeth of a carnivore. Since the marks show no signs of having healed, White concluded that they were made just before or shortly after death.

If the individual, called Bodo man after the site in Ethiopia where the skull was found in 1976, died before he was scalped, the finding would also provide the first evidence of the mutilation of a hominid by another after death. White speculated that the scalping was part of a death ritual. However, the skull itself provides no evidence for this theory.

Donald C. Johanson

See also ARCHAEOLOGY. In WORLD BOOK, see ANTHROPOLOGY; PREHISTORIC PEOPLE.

AQUARIUM. See ZOOS AND AQUARIUMS.

ARCHAEOLOGY. Among the most important archaeology exhibits held in the United States in 1982 was a display of ancient Aztec art presented at the American Museum of Natural History in New York City. The artifacts were unearthed during a major archaeology project in the heart of Mexico City, Mexico.

The project was set in motion in 1978, when workers digging a ditch discovered a huge carved stone disk depicting the dismembered body of an Aztec goddess. Mexican archaeologists have since opened up a vast pit, exposing the remains of the most important temple in the ancient Aztec capital of Tenochtitlan, which stood on the site of modern Mexico City. This temple, known in Spanish as the Templo Mayor (Great Temple), loomed 165 feet (50 meters) above street level when it was first seen by Spaniards in the early 1500s.

An eyewitness, Spanish conquistador and writer Bernal Díaz del Castillo, described it as a towering pyramid topped by twin shrines. One shrine was dedicated to the rain god Tláloc; the other, to the war god Huitzilopochtli, who was also the patron god of the Aztec people.

Díaz del Castillo actually saw the latest of 11 temples that had been built on the same spot over a period of two centuries. During each renovation of the temple, the older structures were completely buried within the newest one. The Spaniards, as a part of their campaign to stamp out the pagan religion of the Aztec people, razed the outermost temple and buried the ruins under tons of rubble.

Under the direction of archaeologist Eduardo Matos Moctezuma, modern excavators removed the rubble in order to expose the ruins of the Templo Mayor. They peeled away the outer construction layers, revealing a small early version of the temple that is an exact replica of the later one described by Díaz del Castillo.

During their work, excavators found thousands of artifacts, many with religious significance. Among them was the stone disk, the discovery of which led to the archaeological salvage project. The disk shows the moon goddess Coyolxauhqui after having been dismembered by her war god brother, Huitzilopochtli. According to Aztec myth, Huitzilopochtli killed his sister because she tried to murder their mother, the earth.

When the objects on display in New York City are returned to Mexico City, they will be placed on permanent display with other artifacts from the temple in a new museum at the excavation site. The museum was scheduled to be opened to the public in early 1983. The ruins were opened in November 1982.

Tool Marks. An analysis of ancient stone tools excavated from a cave in Israel that had been continuously occupied by human beings for about 80,000 years has lent support to the theory that modern human beings evolved from Neanderthal ancestors in some areas of the world. In June 1982, archaeologist Arthur J. Jelinek of the University of Arizona published a report on a series of excavations carried out from 1967 to 1972 at Tabun Cave on Mount Carmel. Jelinek's team excavated deposits in one section of the cave floor to a depth of 32 feet (10 meters), unearthing more than 44,000 stone tools and other artifacts. The deposits at the bottom were dated to about 130,000 years ago; those at the top, to about 50,000 years ago.

Jelinek found only minor differences in the stone tools left in the cave. He theorized that only one group of human beings, Neanderthals (*Homo sapiens neanderthalensis*), lived in the eastern Mediterranean area from 100,000 to 40,000 years ago, and that throughout their occupancy of the region, their method of making stone tools remained relatively unchanged. Jelinek supports the theory that in this region, modern human beings (*Homo sapiens sapiens*) evolved from the culturally conservative Neanderthals.

Other scientists see the changes in tools as evidence that both Neanderthals and modern human beings inhabited the region during that period. They believe that Neanderthals and *Homo sapiens sapiens* evolved from the same ancestor and that the Neanderthals died out about 40,000 years ago.

Tudor Treasure Trove. On October 11, the *Mary Rose,* a flagship of King Henry VIII of England, was raised to the surface after spending nearly 450 years in the mud off Portsmouth, England. While Henry watched, the warship sank on July 19, 1545, as it sailed to take action against the French, with at least 650 sailors on board. During the 15-year salvaging effort, archaeologists recovered scores of skeletons and more than 17,000 artifacts.

Cave Art. On December 8, a team from the University of Tennessee in Knoxville announced discovery of a cave in that state decorated with ancient Indian drawings. The artwork dates from the 12th to the 16th centuries. Archaeologist Charles H. Faulkner, who headed the study, called the site "unique in North America."

Oldest Building? The discovery in Chile of the foundation of what could be the oldest known architectural structure in the Americas was announced on February 5 by anthropologist Tom D. Dillehay of the University of Kentucky in Lexington. Unearthed near Monte Verde, Chile, the foundation is made of compacted sand and pebbles and contains the remains of embedded wooden stakes. It is believed to be from 12,000 to 15,000 years old. Previously, the oldest structures in the Americas were thought to be from 6,000 to 8,000 years old. Barbara Voorhies

In WORLD BOOK, see ARCHAEOLOGY.

ARCHITECTURE. The American Institute of Architects (AIA) celebrated its 125th anniversary at its annual meeting held in Honolulu, Hawaii, from June 6 to 9, 1982. If the locale appeared somewhat exotic to many AIA members, the futurist-oriented seminars seemed even more far-fetched to architects attempting to cope with the current reality of tight money. Speakers addressing themselves to exploration of distant planets and 21st-century space colonies drew scant audiences. But seminars on "Computer-Aided Design and Practice" and "Computers for the Small Firm" resulted in standing-room-only attendance.

Architectural Awards. The highest award the AIA bestows, its annual Gold Medal, went in 1982 to New York City architect Romaldo Giurgola. He and Ehrman B. Mitchell, Jr., of Philadelphia, are partners in a firm with offices in both cities. Giurgola's design style is nonrepetitive and invariably relates to other structures in its immediate environment. The award winner has written, "A building is a fragment of the larger environment, which includes other continuously growing structures and the natural scape."

The fourth annual Pritzker Architecture Prize, a $100,000 award that many consider architecture's most prestigious honor, went to architect Kevin Roche of Kevin Roche John Dinkeloo & Associates of Hamden, Conn., on April 14. Roche

The Illinois Regional Library for the Blind and Physically Handicapped in Chicago was designed especially to make it easy for the handicapped to use.

is best known for his John Deere Company West Office Building in Moline, Ill.; the Oakland (Calif.) Museum; and the Ford Foundation headquarters in New York City. Roche announced that he would use the tax-free award to endow a chair of architecture at Yale University in honor of Finnish-born architect Eero Saarinen, for whom he worked until Saarinen's death in 1961. Roche said, "I want to remind the younger generation of his importance."

Expositions and Exhibits. Beginning with the Crystal Palace at the "Exposition of the Industry of All Nations" held in London in 1851, many world's fairs and international exhibitions have been showcases for innovative architectural and engineering ideas. However, the World's Fair held in Knoxville, Tenn., from May 1 to Oct. 31, 1982, contributed little to that tradition. The various national pavilions attempted a not very effective sort of ethnic-modern approach. A striking exception was the United States pavilion, designed by six architects comprising the FABRAP Organization of Atlanta, Ga. The finely detailed steel and glass building was distinguished by cantilevered floors facing a sloping curtain wall that fronted on a reflecting pool.

Visitors at NEOCON (National Exposition of Contract Furnishings), an annual presentation of office furniture and related accessories held in Chicago's Merchandise Mart from June 15 to 18, found showroom architecture outshining the latest chairs and tables. Japanese architect Arata Isozaki's concept for Hauserman Office Interiors was the talk of the show. The 50-year-old designer divided the showroom into three areas: the entry symbolizing the past; the middle area, the present; and the innermost area, the future. A square-colonnaded space led visitors into a barrel-vaulted nave with a series of crossings opening into areas of up-to-date technology. Another innovative showroom was the Italian-government-sponsored Italcenter, designed by Vignelli Associates. Its free-form walls enticed visitors through the various-sized interior spaces, where they viewed office furniture of Italian manufacture.

Three important architectural exhibits were held during 1982. "Mies van der Rohe: Interior Spaces" ran from September 21 through November 4 at the Arts Club of Chicago. The club's interior was designed by the subject of the show, German-born architect Ludwig Mies van der Rohe, who died in 1969. Photographs and drawings, as well as examples of such renowned furniture designs as the Barcelona chair of 1929, detailed Mies's long and influential career.

"The Architecture of Richard Neutra: From International Style to California Modern" opened on July 24 in New York City's Museum of Modern

Art and ran through October 12. Neutra, who was born in 1892 in Vienna, Austria, achieved his greatest fame from the 1920s to the 1940s for a series of private homes built mainly in California. His cool, sleek, monochromatic style is best exemplified by the glass and white-stucco Lovell "Health" House erected in 1929 in Los Angeles.

Notable New Buildings. Two concert halls made news in 1982. The Roy Thomson Hall opened in Toronto, Canada, on September 13. The structure, designed by the Toronto firm of Arthur Erickson-Mathers & Haldenby, is a circular building. Its exterior resembles one of designer Buckminster Fuller's dome-shaped Dymaxion structures with the top of the "bubble" sliced off. Two balconies run around three sides of the 2,812-seat auditorium.

A concert on September 16 inaugurated the Joseph Meyerhoff Symphony Hall in Baltimore. The $22-million, 2,450-seat facility was designed by the Boston firms of Pietro Belluschi Incorporated and Jung/Brannen Associates Incorporated. Resembling a huge oval drum with a sloping top, the building has entrance areas and stairwells ringing the base. The column-free hall is a structural mass supported by perimeter columns. Rob Cuscaden

In WORLD BOOK, see ARCHITECTURE; MIES VAN DER ROHE, LUDWIG; NEUTRA, RICHARD JOSEPH.

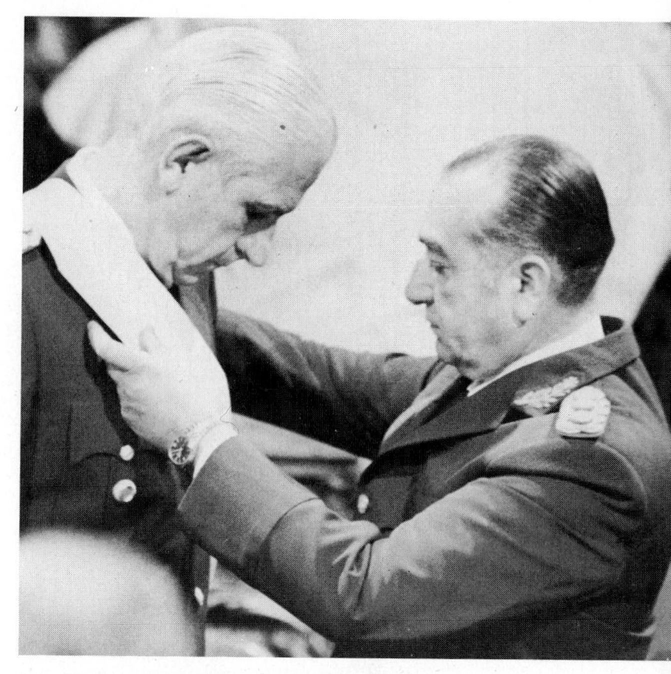

Argentina's new president, Reynaldo Benito Bignone, receives the presidential sash at his inauguration in Buenos Aires on July 1.

ARGENTINA. The war with Great Britain over the Falkland Islands (called *Islas Malvinas* by Argentines) dominated the attention of the people of Argentina in 1982. On April 2, when their troops seized the British-held islands, the mood of Argentines climbed to giddy heights of nationalistic fervor. But their mood turned to despair 10 weeks later, when British troops took the islands back by force. See FALKLAND ISLANDS.

In the aftermath of defeat, the nation's military government was sharply divided over whom to hold responsible. On June 17, three days after the Argentine surrender, President Leopoldo Fortunato Galtieri was forced to resign. Military leaders replaced him with Reynaldo Benito Antonio Bignone, a retired army general. Bignone's key asset for the job was that he had played no role in the Falklands defeat. He was inaugurated on July 1. See BIGNONE, REYNALDO BENITO ANTONIO.

The Argentine Economy was on the brink of collapse going into the war. Coming out of the war, it was in even worse shape. Argentina's foreign debt was estimated at $40 billion. Its annual inflation rate was 137 per cent, the highest in the world. Successive devaluations of the peso had wreaked havoc with the nation's financial and business sectors, as well as with the everyday lives of most citizens. On Dec. 1, 1982, the exchange rate was 39,965 pesos per U.S. $1. By comparison, in December 1981, the rate was 9,875 pesos per U.S. $1. In October 1982, the International Monetary Fund, an agency of the United Nations, agreed to provide $2 billion in loans.

The New Government. Hopes for a quick transition to peaceful reconstruction under Bignone soon turned to deepening despair. A month after Bignone's elevation to power, a Buenos Aires newspaper carried an editorial that said: "Without captains, without rudder, without course, and practically without ship, this country has turned into one of the great refugees of the modern world." Bignone himself soon found that the man with the real power in Argentina was General Cristino Nicolaides, army commander-in-chief.

The new government's official policy line was that the country would gradually return to democratic rule, which it abandoned in 1976. On July 20, the first legal political rally in more than six years of military dictatorship took place in Buenos Aires. Although some observers applauded the lifting of the ban on such gatherings, most Argentines were skeptical, worrying where the new leniency might lead.

Their worries seemed justified when bus and train workers went on strike for higher wages on August 18, causing traffic jams in and around Buenos Aires. Strikes had been outlawed since the military took over the government in 1976.

Bignone pledged in December 1982 to hold general elections in Argentina by late 1983. He also promised an in-depth study of the fate of more than 6,000 people who disappeared while in the custody of government security forces in the mid-1970s. In October and November, the bodies of nearly 1,000 unidentified people were found in unmarked graves near Buenos Aires.

International Relations improved during the second half of the year as Argentina softened its stance on the Falklands issue. Argentine diplomats at the United Nations pushed for a negotiated settlement to the dispute over ownership of the islands. By moderating its formerly stubborn claim to the Falklands, Argentina hoped to patch up its frayed trade relations with the United States and other nations that had sided with Great Britain.

Meanwhile, the situation within Argentina settled down somewhat. Anti-American demonstrations ceased, and United States diplomats and business executives who had fled the country during the war returned. A highly successful tour of Argentina by the New York Philharmonic in September seemed to indicate that relations with the United States would improve. Nathan A. Haverstock

See also LATIN AMERICA (Facts in Brief Table). In WORLD BOOK, see ARGENTINA.

ARIZONA. See STATE GOVERNMENT.

ARKANSAS. See STATE GOVERNMENT.

Opponents of nuclear arms march down New York City's 42nd Street on their way to a massive peace rally in Central Park on June 12.

ARMED FORCES. Partly in response to growing worldwide public demand for a nuclear freeze, the United States and the Soviet Union opened strategic arms reduction talks (START) on June 29, 1982, in Geneva, Switzerland. An arms-control proposal by U.S. President Ronald Reagan preceded the negotiations to reduce nuclear missile and bomber arsenals. In a speech at Eureka College in Eureka, Ill., on May 9, Reagan urged that both superpowers agree to reduce their stockpile of nuclear missile warheads by one-third.

Although Reagan described the Geneva arms talks as "one of the most important tasks of our age," little progress was apparent during the year. As a result, the Reagan Administration proceeded with a massive expansion of U.S. military strength expected to cost $1.6 trillion over five years.

The Administration completed a five-year strategic defense plan in August that broke with precedent by directing the Pentagon to prepare to fight a prolonged nuclear war against the Soviet Union. Previous U.S. war plans had assumed a nuclear conflict would end quickly.

In answer to strong criticism of the plan from some members of Congress and leaders of the peace movement, Secretary of Defense Caspar W. Weinberger insisted that the United States had no interest in fighting a protracted nuclear war and did not believe that such an exchange was "winnable." But he maintained that the Soviets were preparing for just such a conflict, and that only improved U.S. readiness could deter an attack.

MX Problems. Military planners struggled during the year to find a permanent basing system for the controversial MX missile that would be secure from surprise enemy attack and acceptable to congressional critics. The MX is a land-based intercontinental ballistic missile (ICBM) capable of carrying 10 nuclear warheads. In February, the Pentagon dropped plans to place the MX in existing underground missile silos, hardened for protection against nuclear attack. Congressional armed services committees had signaled skepticism for the "hardened silo" concept by limiting development funds.

On November 22, Reagan announced his support for a plan to cluster all the missiles in superhardened silos in a column array 14 miles (22.5 kilometers) long and 1½ miles (2.4 kilometers) wide in Wyoming. Proponents of the "dense pack" idea argued that incoming enemy warheads concentrated on such a small area would destroy one another on impact, allowing some MX's to survive and launch a retaliatory attack. But opponents labeled the plan "dunce pack" and criticized it as technically unfeasible. On December 7, the House of Representatives voted down $988 million in 1983 appropriations for the production of five MX

The WASP II fanjet, described as an individual lifting device, performs midair maneuvers during a demonstration at Fort Benning, Ga., in June.

missiles. The Senate retained the funds but stipulated that they not be spent until Congress approved a basing plan. On December 20, the full Congress passed a compromise measure that eliminated MX production funds from the 1983 military budget and froze most of the $2.5 billion in MX research and development funds until Congress had approved a plan to deploy the missile.

Middle East Role. American forces served in two Middle East peacekeeping roles in 1982. About 1,100 U.S. troops formed the vanguard of a 2,600-member multinational force that began policing a section of the Sinai Peninsula after Israel withdrew the last of its troops on April 25. The force was sent as part of an agreement by which Israel returned remaining portions of the territory captured from Egypt during the 1967 Six-Day War.

As part of an agreement ending bitter fighting in Lebanon between Israeli forces and the Palestine Liberation Organization (PLO), 800 marines landed in Beirut on August 25 to monitor an evacuation of PLO forces. The marines left Beirut three weeks later but returned on September 29 after Israeli troops failed to prevent the massacre of several hundred Palestinians in refugee camps in West Beirut, allegedly by right wing Lebanese Christian militiamen. See MIDDLE EAST.

Defense Budget. On February 8, President Reagan submitted to Congress a Department of Defense budget request for $215.9 billion for the 1983 fiscal year beginning Oct. 1, 1982. The budget request ran $33.1 billion higher than fiscal 1982 outlays, an increase of 10.5 per cent after inflation.

This record peacetime increase in defense spending included huge jumps in funding for major weapons systems. The Pentagon proposed to spend $6.8 billion for two nuclear-powered aircraft carriers, $4.8 billion for the long-range B-1 bomber, $4.5 billion for the MX missile, $4.2 billion for the Trident nuclear-powered submarine and sea-launched missiles, $3 billion for the F-18 Hornet carrier-based attack jet, and $2 billion for the M-1 tank.

Congressional critics complained that the budget proposal was inconsistent with the fiscal austerity Reagan imposed on other government programs. On December 20, Congress approved a $209-billion defense spending bill, which Reagan signed the next day.

Conventional Weapons. The Pentagon dropped plans to develop a new cargo plane and decided instead to buy more C-5 Galaxy jets. The C-5, the world's largest transport plane, was designed to airlift the new Rapid Deployment Force to world trouble spots with a minimum of delay. All military services were ordered to strengthen special operations forces in such areas as sabotage and clandestine operations. The Pentagon prepared to resume production of chemical weapons for the first time in more than a decade. United States military troop strength stood at 2,108,600 troops on September 30, an increase of 26,000 from 1981.

Readiness Improves. Sizable spending hikes for operations and maintenance increased the readiness of the armed forces in 1982. But all military services remained short of skilled career personnel.

The Army again exceeded enlistment and re-enlistment quotas, partly due to an economic slump that made military service an attractive alternative for thousands of unemployed young people. Its recruiting success enabled the Army to accept only high school graduates for the first time in history. In August, the Army announced plans to increase the number of women soldiers by 5,000. At the same time, however, it curtailed women's opportunities by excluding them from 23 combat-related job categories previously open to female soldiers.

Draft Registration. President Reagan ordered an indefinite extension of compulsory draft registration for 18-year-old men on January 7, reversing his 1980 campaign position. Reagan maintained that he would consider a return to conscription "only in the most severe national emergency."

Despite Reagan's professed opposition to the draft, an estimated 700,000 young men refused to register. After warning repeatedly that it would prosecute violators, the government began criminal proceedings against 160 offenders in June. On

October 4, California college student Benjamin H. Sasway became the first American since the Vietnam War to be sentenced to jail for refusing to register for the draft.

On November 15, U.S. District Judge Terry J. Hatter, Jr., ruled in Los Angeles that the draft registration program is illegal. The U.S. Department of Justice asked young men to continue to register while the decision is appealed.

Command Changes. General John W. Vessey, Jr., a former enlisted soldier and Army vice-chief of staff, was named chairman of the Joint Chiefs of Staff on July 1. He replaced retiring Air Force General David C. Jones. General Charles A. Gabriel replaced General Lew Allen, Jr., as Air Force chief of staff, and Admiral James D. Watkins succeeded Admiral Thomas B. Hayward as chief of naval operations. Lieutenant General Roscoe Robinson, Jr., in August became the U.S. Army's first black four-star general (see ROBINSON, ROSCOE, JR.). Admiral Hyman G. Rickover, the father of the nuclear Navy, was forcibly retired from active duty by President Reagan on January 31 after more than 63 years of service. Thomas M. DeFrank

In WORLD BOOK, see the articles on the branches of the armed forces.

ARMY. See ARMED FORCES.

ART. See ARCHITECTURE; DANCING; LITERATURE; MUSIC, CLASSICAL; POETRY; VISUAL ARTS.

ASIA was troubled during 1982 by its usual poverty and by unusual drought, by the harmful effects of a worldwide recession, and by one national war and numerous guerrilla conflicts. On the other hand, regional cooperation flourished, violent political upheavals were avoided, and Asia made new efforts to deal with the problems of refugees and the narcotics trade.

Poverty. The United Nations (UN) Economic and Social Commission for Asia and the Pacific estimated that almost 1 billion of the continent's approximately 2.7 billion people live below what it classified as the poverty line. The commission reported on March 8 that neither local food production nor imported food met the caloric requirements of the people of Afghanistan, Bangladesh, Burma, India, Indonesia, Iran, Nepal, Pakistan, or the Philippines.

The commission's executive secretary, Shah A. M. S. Kibria, said extreme poverty compelled many Asians to overuse farmland, forests, and water resources in order to survive. There was, he said, a "vicious circle in which it is difficult to determine whether the actions of the poor lead to environmental damage or whether lower environmental carrying capacity leads to poverty."

Tropical forests in the region were disappearing at "an alarming rate" of 2 per cent per year, the commission said. On October 10 in Bali, Indonesia, the World Wildlife Fund and other organizations began a joint effort to save Asian forests.

The UN commission estimated that the average annual rate of population growth in Asia had dropped from 2.2 per cent in the early 1970s to 1.9 per cent later in the decade. Population pressure on land and investment capital continued to mount, however. China announced in October that its population on July 1 was 1,008,175,000, almost 25 per cent of all the people on earth and 40 per cent of Asia's population.

The Worst Drought in half a century affected 100 million persons throughout northern India in late 1982. Wells dried up, crops failed, and villagers sold "their cows and goats at throwaway prices to save their families from starvation," an Indian newspaper reported. A two-year drought gripped northeastern Sri Lanka, and northern Malaysia was also hurt by lack of rain.

Asian Economies suffered from a recession in Western industrial countries, which cut back their demand for raw materials and manufactured goods of Asian origin. Asia's declining exports reduced its ability to pay for oil and other imports that most Asian countries needed. Prices of Asian exports were also low, while the prices the region had to pay for industrial imports crept upward.

Within Asia, slow economic changes were tak-

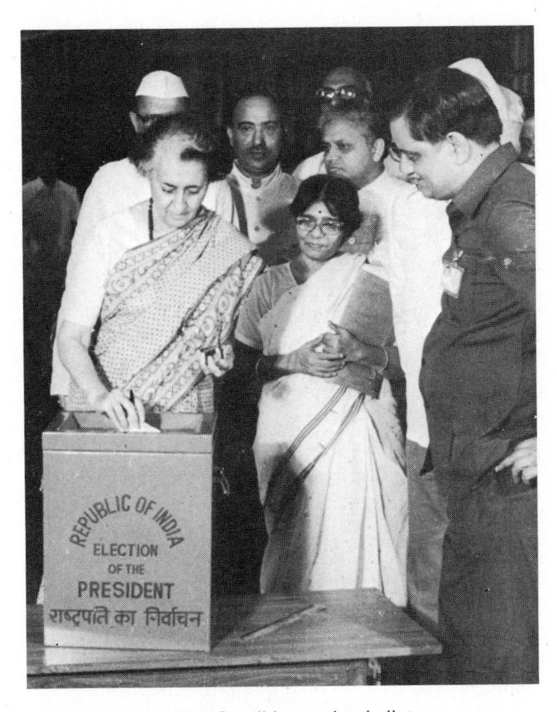

Prime Minister Indira Gandhi casts her ballot in New Delhi, India, as voters choose a new president in July. Zail Singh won the election.

Vietnamese boat people — refugees who have fled their country in small boats and risked their lives at sea — crowd Hong Kong harbor in April.

ing place. Such countries as South Korea, Taiwan, and Singapore had developed their industries on the basis of labor-intensive production during the 1960s and 1970s. As a result, they had improved their living standards and raised their wage levels so much that less-developed countries with lower wages, including Indonesia and some African nations, underpriced them on simple industrial goods.

To improve their balance of trade, some governments encouraged the manufacture of more complex products requiring more capital and greater labor skills. Indonesia moved to restrict the export of timber and to encourage the export of wood products instead, thus providing more jobs for Indonesians.

Regional Cooperation expanded. Leaders of 17 Asian and Pacific members of the Commonwealth of Nations — an association of independent countries and other political units that were once British colonies — met in Suva, Fiji, in October to discuss their concerns. The foreign secretaries of seven southern Asian nations met in Islamabad, Pakistan, on August 8 and made plans for their foreign ministers to meet later. They also decided that representatives of their national planning organizations would meet to coordinate economic plans.

The Association of Southeast Asian Nations (ASEAN) — an organization consisting of Indonesia, Malaysia, the Philippines, Singapore, and Thailand — developed its defense links. However, the members carefully avoided turning ASEAN into a defense organization and focused their international activities on problems in Cambodia, Laos, and Vietnam. ASEAN pressure succeeded in forging a coalition of opponents to the Vietnamese-sponsored government of Heng Samrin in Cambodia.

Regional problems were tackled by both local governments and international organizations. One problem was refugees. The UN High Commissioner for Refugees worked with Pakistan to help the estimated 2.7 million refugees from Afghanistan living in Pakistan, but Afghan refugees in Iran received less international assistance. Millions of Afghans had fled to both countries after the Soviet Union invaded Afghanistan in 1979.

Refugees continued to leave Cambodia, Laos, and Vietnam, fleeing poverty and Communist oppression. However, the number of refugees from those three countries was down by a third in 1982, compared with 1981. Fewer than 50,000 boat people left in small boats during the first 10 months of 1982.

The number of Asian refugees being accepted for permanent settlement in countries outside Asia declined. This created regional concern over being

Facts in Brief on the Asian Countries

Country	Population	Government	Monetary Unit*	Foreign Trade (million U.S. $) Exports†	Imports†
Afghanistan	14,238,000	Revolutionary Council President Babrak Karmal; Prime Minister Sultan Ali Keshtmand	afghani (50 = $1)	729	924
Australia	15,150,000	Governor General Sir Ninian Martin Stephen; Prime Minister Malcolm Fraser	dollar (1.04 = $1)	21,680	23,652
Bangladesh	91,281,000	Chief Martial Law Administrator Hussain Muhammad Ershad; President Abul Fazal Ahsan Uddin Chowdhury	taka (22.6 = $1)	791	2,594
Bhutan	1,390,000	King Jigme Singye Wangchuck	Indian rupee & ngultrum (9.7 = $1)	1	1
Burma	37,670,000	President U San Yu; Prime Minister U Maung Maung Kha	kyat (7.8 = $1)	465	352
Cambodia (Kampuchea)	9,360,000	People's Revolutionary Party Secretary General & Council of State President Heng Samrin (Coalition government: President Norodom Sihanouk; Vice-President Khieu Samphan; Prime Minister Son Sann)	riel (4 = $1)	2	140
China	1,008,175,000	Communist Party General Secretary Hu Yaobang; Communist Party Deputy Chairman Teng Hsiao-ping (Deng Xiaoping); Premier Zhao Ziyang	yuan (1.9 = $1)	18,255	19,530
India	726,154,000	President Zail Singh; Prime Minister Indira Gandhi	rupee (9.7 = $1)	7,560	13,194
Indonesia	156,864,000	President Suharto; Vice-President Adam Malik	rupiah (676.5 = $1)	22,400	15,600
Iran	40,919,000	President Ali Khamenei; Prime Minister Hosein Musavi-Khamenei	rial (86.7 = $1)	14,251	12,247
Japan	120,246,000	Emperor Hirohito; Prime Minister Yasuhiro Nakasone	yen (248.8 = $1)	152,016	143,288
Korea, North	19,291,000	President Kim Il-song; Premier Yi Chong-ok	won (1 = $1)	1,320	1,300
Korea, South	39,275,000	President Chun Doo Hwan; Prime Minister Kim Sang Hyup	won (745.3 = $1)	21,254	26,125
Laos	3,995,000	President Souphanouvong; Prime Minister Kayson Phomvihan	kip (10 = $1)	31	130
Malaysia	14,554,000	Paramount Ruler Ahmad Shah Ibni Al-Marhum Sultan Abu Bakar; Prime Minister Mahathir bin Mohamed	ringgit (2.4 = $1)	14,345	12,139
Maldives	159,000	President Maumoon Abdul Gayoom	rupee (7.1 = $1)	11	27
Mongolia	1,795,000	People's Revolutionary Party First Secretary & Presidium Chairman Yumjaagiyn Tsedenbal; Council of Ministers Chairman Jambyn Batmonh	tughrik (3.3 = $1)	343	497
Nepal	14,955,000	King Birendra Bir Bikram Shah Dev; Prime Minister Surya Bahadur Thapa	rupee (12.8 = $1)	116	373
New Zealand	3,136,000	Governor General Sir David Stuart Beattie; Prime Minister Robert D. Muldoon	dollar (1.4 = $1)	5,563	5,684
Pakistan	89,230,000	President Mohammad Zia-ul-Haq	rupee (12.7 = $1)	2,880	5,348
Papua New Guinea	3,348,000	Governor General Sir Tore Lokoloko; Prime Minister Michael Somare	kina (1 = $1.29)	1,031	1,023
Philippines	58,378,000	President Ferdinand E. Marcos; Prime Minister César E. Virata	peso (8.8 = $1)	5,722	7,946
Russia	272,775,000	Communist Party General Secretary Yuri V. Andropov; Council of Ministers Chairman Nikolay Aleksandrovich Tikhonov	ruble (1 = $1.39)	76,449	68,522
Singapore	2,577,000	President Devan Nair; Prime Minister Lee Kuan Yew	dollar (2.2 = $1)	20,993	27,571
Sri Lanka	15,640,000	President J. R. Jayewardene; Prime Minister R. Premadasa	rupee (20.8 = $1)	1,036	1,803
Taiwan	18,783,000	President Chiang Ching-kuo; Premier Sun Yun-hsuan	new Taiwan dollar (40.6 = $1)	19,838	19,818
Thailand	50,027,000	King Bhumibol Adulyadej; Prime Minister Prem Tinsulanonda	baht (23 = $1)	6,999	9,911
Vietnam	57,990,000	Communist Party Secretary General Le Duan; National Assembly Chairman Nguyen Huu Tho; Prime Minister Pham Van Dong	dong (9 = $1)	535	1,225

*Exchange rates as of Dec. 1, 1982. †Latest available data.

left with unwanted refugees. The United States announced that, as of April 30, refugees from Cambodia, Laos, and Vietnam would "be considered for resettlement in America only if they can demonstrate close links with the United States." After complaints by Thailand, the U.S. government agreed on November 1 to speed up immigration processing of refugees there. More than 210,000 refugees remained in camps in Southeast Asia.

Narcotics were another regional problem. Two of the world's main sources of heroin were the northwest frontier of Pakistan and the so-called Golden Triangle of Thailand, Burma, and Laos. Burma and Thailand cooperated in January and February in a military drive against drug dealers living along their border. Burma also fought guerrilla armies of both Communist and national separatist groups that supported themselves by the narcotics trade. Pakistan promised United States Attorney General William French Smith that it would take steps to control an increase in heroin production. Smith traveled through Asia in October and November to study both the refugee and narcotics problems.

Efforts to Improve International Relations were made in several parts of Asia. China and the Soviet Union in October held their first talks since 1979 in an effort to reduce tensions. China continued occasional talks with India on border disputes that had disturbed their relations since the 1950s. President Mohammad Zia-ul-Haq of Pakistan visited India on November 1 for talks with India's Prime Minister Indira Gandhi—the first time leaders of the two countries had met since 1972. They agreed to establish a joint commission to consider some form of peace treaty or nonaggression pact.

Efforts to End Asian Wars were unsuccessful, however. The war between Iran and Iraq dragged on. Numerous guerrilla conflicts also smoldered, the largest ones in Afghanistan and Cambodia.

The UN sought to arrange a settlement in Afghanistan that would bring a withdrawal of the Soviet Army. The Soviet Union was unwilling to allow its puppet regime there to collapse, however, and the Russians continued to fight against a national resistance movement by the Afghan people. The Soviets also supported Vietnam's occupation of Cambodia and indirectly helped Vietnam suppress resistance in Cambodia and Laos.

Anger flared in several Asian nations over Japan's revision of its school history textbooks. The changes glossed over Japanese aggression against China, Korea, and other countries before and during World War II. China and South Korea protested strongly, and China charged that the revisions were part of a renewed militarization of Japan. Japanese Prime Minister Zenko Suzuki acknowledged on August 23 the validity of the protests, and Japan's Education Ministry pledged to correct the textbooks.

Political Changes occurred peacefully. In Japan, Suzuki announced on October 12 that he would step down from leadership of the ruling Liberal-Democratic Party, which meant resigning as prime minister. In elections on November 24, the party elected Yasuhiro Nakasone as its president, and two days later he became prime minister of Japan.

Hussain Muhammad Ershad, the army chief of staff in Bangladesh, seized control of the country on March 24 without bloodshed. He then replaced President Abdus Sattar with a figurehead president. Prime Minister Lee Kuan Yew of Singapore, one of Asia's most durable leaders, held his office but promoted several younger men to high positions. Other Asian leaders won reaffirmation of their positions. Elections in Malaysia on April 22 gave Prime Minister Mahathir bin Mohamed a strong new declaration of support from Malaysian voters. President J. R. Jayewardene of Sri Lanka won that country's first direct presidential election on October 20. President Suharto's supporters in Indonesia won control of parliament in elections on May 4.

Henry S. Bradsher

See also the various Asian country articles. In the WORLD BOOK SUPPLEMENT section, see JAPAN; THAILAND. In WORLD BOOK, see ASIA.

ASTRONOMY. A team of astronomers from the United States, Great Britain, and Australia discovered the most distant object in the universe on March 25, 1982. The object is a quasar designated PKS 2000-330, and it is 12 billion to 18 billion light-years away from Earth. (A light-year is the distance light travels in a year at a speed of 186,000 miles [300,000 kilometers] per second.)

Quasars are tremendously energetic sources of radio waves, so the search that found the newest one was conducted using the radio antennas of the California Institute of Technology (Caltech) Jet Propulsion Laboratory's (JPL) Deep Space Network at its tracking station in Tidbinbilla, Australia. JPL's Samuel Gilkis and David Jauncey of Cornell University in Ithaca, N.Y., began the work in 1972. They were joined by Australian astronomer Michael Batty, and the team measured the positions of many radio sources. Later, astronomer Anne Savage of the Royal Observatory in Edinburgh, Scotland, matched the radio sources with objects in photographs. Then, Bruce Peterson of the Australian National University's Mount Stromlo Observatory, together with Jauncey, Savage, and Alan E. Wright, used the Anglo-Australian telescope at Mount Stromlo to measure the spectrum of PKS 2000-330 in order to determine from that how far away the object is. It is difficult to measure such things exactly, but the astronomers believe that the newly discovered quasar is at least 12 billion—and very likely as much as 18 billion—light-years distant. In any case, the light arriving at Earth today began its long journey from the quasar billions of years before the solar system and the Milky Way galaxy were formed.

Hail to Halley's Comet. Paradoxically, it was more difficult to detect Halley's Comet at a distance of about 1 billion miles (1.6 billion kilometers) than to observe the most distant object in the universe. The comet is only about 1 mile (1.6 kilometers) in diameter and is made visible only by the sunlight it reflects. Many astronomers hoped to be the first to catch sight of Halley's Comet in 1982 as it came in range of telescopes on Earth for the first time in more than 70 years. Halley's Comet returns to the vicinity of the Sun, and can be seen, every 76 to 79 years. It was near the Sun in 1910 and will be near it again in 1986.

On the night of Oct. 15, 1982, astronomer G. Edward Danielson and graduate student David Jewitt of Caltech succeeded in spotting the comet, using the 200-inch (508-centimeter) telescope on Palomar Mountain, equipped with an electronic sensor called a charge-coupled device. They took photographs with eight-minute exposures. The comet showed up as a faint blur moving to the southwest, as expected, in the constellation Canis Minor. Danielson said amateur astronomers will have to wait until 1985 before Halley's Comet is bright enough to be seen with their telescopes.

And a Thrifty Trip to Another. The U.S. National Aeronautics and Space Administration (NASA) passed up the opportunity to mount a $500-million mission to observe Halley's Comet as it approaches the Sun in 1986, leaving the field—or sky—to the Russians, the Japanese, and the European Space Agency. However, NASA announced in October that it would give the United States a chance to be the first nation to examine one of the icy visitors from the far reaches of the solar system. The agency was in the process of reprogramming a spacecraft that has been in a permanent orbit between the Earth and the Sun since 1978, measuring electric and magnetic fields and charged particles. Engineers redirected the orbit of the International Sun Earth Explorer (ISEE 3) so that it will be able to rendezvous with the Giacobini-Zinner Comet when that object nears the Sun on Sept. 11, 1985.

Although ISEE 3 carries no cameras and therefore will not give us a look at Giacobini-Zinner—which will not be visible to the naked eye—the spacecraft's instruments are expected to return data that will be valuable to scientists studying the interaction between a comet and the Sun. This op-

A unique picture of four stages of the July 6 lunar eclipse results from printing together negatives of the vanishing moon and the Boston skyline.

portunity will be an astronomical bargain at a cost of less than $1.5 million.

The Sky Is (Orangey) Red. Two Russian *Venera* spacecraft landed on Venus during the first week of March 1982 and returned to Earth remarkable color photographs and detailed chemical analyses of the surface of our "sister planet." Soviet geophysicists reported on the results of the mission at the Lunar and Planetary Science Conference in Houston on March 18. They said the photos yielded "convincing proof" that the Venusian sky is reddish-orange and the sandy and rocky area where *Venera 13* landed is dark-brown.

Venera 13 transmitted data for more than two hours, and *Venera 14* functioned for about one hour, before being overcome by the 900°F. (480°C) temperature on the planet's surface. Data they collected revealed that Venus' rocky surface is basaltic, like volcanic rock on Earth. According to astrogeologist Harold Masursky of the United States Geological Survey, "It's as if they had landed on the ocean floor near Hawaii and up on a Hawaiian mountain." The implication of this finding is that the chemical processes at work on Venus and the Earth are quite similar, and scientists must seek other reasons to explain why the two bodies evolved so differently.

Ring Around Neptune? The first tentative evidence for a ring system around the planet Neptune was announced on June 9 at the American Astronomical Society meeting in Troy, N.Y., by astronomers Edward F. Guinan, Craig C. Harris, and Frank P. Maloney of Villanova University in Villanova, Pa. Guinan had made the observations 14 years earlier—on April 7, 1968, at the Mount John Observatory in New Zealand. Investigating Neptune's atmosphere, he recorded the light of the star BD-17°4388 as the planet passed in front of the star and briefly cut off its light. The best data were recorded on a strip chart, which unfortunately was lost. The cruder data, on computer punch cards, were set aside.

Years later, Guinan, working with Harris and Maloney, realized that his punch cards might have recorded the effect of a ring of material around Neptune as it passed in front of the star. When the cards were analyzed, they showed the expected 50 per cent drop in brightness as Neptune passed in front of the star, but they also showed a 30 per cent drop in brightness caused by something else. The astronomers theorized that a ring of material orbiting 2,200 to 5,000 miles (3,500 to 8,000 kilometers) above Neptune's equator could have caused the drop. An unknown satellite would have produced a drop like the one made by Neptune itself. Eric D. Carlson

See also Space Exploration. In World Book, see Astronomy; Halley's Comet; articles on the planets.

AUSTRALIA had a bad year economically in 1982, though the government hoped that conditions would improve when the country's overseas customers pulled out of the recession. The government of Prime Minister Malcolm Fraser suffered some setbacks but remained generally steady.

Fraser faced a challenge on April 8, when the parliamentary Liberal Party voted 54 to 27 to retain him as leader. Andrew Peacock, his opponent, rejoined the Cabinet on October 11 as minister for industry and commerce. Similarly, Bill Hayden, the leader of the Opposition, was challenged on July 16 by Bob Hawke, whom he defeated by 42 votes to 37 in the Labor Party caucus.

There were three state elections in 1982. Voters in Victoria on April 3 elected a Labor government for the first time in 27 years with John Cain at its head. Tasmanian voters on May 15 turned out the Labor government in favor of a Liberal government under Robin Gray. Labor had split badly over the issue of whether hydropower should be developed on the wilderness rivers of southwest Tasmania. In South Australia on November 6, Labor defeated the Liberals.

In Foreign Affairs, the Australian government instituted a ban on Argentine imports after Argentina's seizure of the Falkland Islands, a British dependency in the South Atlantic Ocean. Australia also protested against the Israeli incursion into Lebanon. The prime minister urged upon the developed countries a concerted reduction of tariff protection, in order to provide economic opportunities for the nations of the Third World.

In Regional Affairs, Australia moved to consolidate its connections with other countries in the South Pacific. In October, New Zealand's Prime Minister Robert D. Muldoon said that finishing touches were being put on arrangements for closer economic relations between the two countries. At the South Pacific Forum on August 9, Fraser offered a substantial increase in Australian aid to Pacific Island nations and suggested that an increase in aid to Papua New Guinea would be forthcoming.

The Australian Economy suffered considerably in 1982, mainly because of declining markets abroad, but also because of increasing inflation and unemployment and a widespread drought in eastern Australia that affected the wheat crop. The drought was the worst in history, and the shortage of wheat caused speculation that Australia might have to import wheat—and corn for cattle feed—from the United States.

Contrary to the government's hopes, Australian inflation continued to increase, reaching 10.7 per cent by the time the federal budget was presented on August 17. Unemployment ran at about 7 per cent throughout 1982. In October, however, there was some optimism over the fall in U.S. interest

As Australia experiences the driest winter in history, farmers in New South Wales study the damage done to their land by three years of drought.

rates and the encouraging effects this might have on the Australian economy.

The value of the Australian dollar fell below the U.S. dollar — to 99.68 cents per U.S. $1 — on July 29. By the end of October, it had fallen further, to about 94 cents. Nevertheless, the balance of payments caused little alarm. Capital inflow continued to be strong, offsetting the decline in export sales. Industrial trouble declined during the year, with wage increases moderating as unemployment grew.

The Bureau of Agricultural Economics forecast a deteriorating situation for farmers in 1982-1983, especially in income from crops. Wheat and sugar had particular difficulties. Problems were compounded by a prolonged drought in the states of Queensland, New South Wales, and Victoria, which affected about 60 per cent of Australian farms. The failure of winter rains meant poor germination of cereal grains, endangering the 1982-1983 wheat harvest, lowering farmers' incomes, and creating the need for massive drought-relief programs by state and federal governments. Fortunately, there was a bumper crop of wheat in Western Australia, making it easier to fulfill Australia's export contracts.

On July 19, the prime minister announced that the government had completed a review of its policy toward manufacturing industries. It had decided that, though there would be a gradual reduction in tariff protection, there would also be continued budgetary assistance, including increased depreciation allowances for tax purposes.

Australia's Population passed 15 million toward the end of 1981, and immigration continued to increase in 1982. New guidelines for refugees were announced on March 16. On April 19, Minister for Immigration and Ethnic Affairs Ian McPhee stated that improved opportunities for entry would be provided for brothers, sisters, and nondependent children of people already settled in Australia. But the government said it would adopt harsher measures toward the 50,000 illegal immigrants and the 50,000 visitors unlawfully taking jobs while in the country.

Questions relating to Aborigines occupied much attention and aroused much feeling in 1982, especially in matters relating to land rights in Queensland. Minister for Aboriginal Affairs Ian Wilson said on August 23 that $270 million would be spent on special Aboriginal programs in 1982-1983. (The money values in this article are expressed in Australian dollars; $1 = U.S. 98 cents as of Dec. 31, 1982.) This represented an expenditure of $1,692 on each Aborigine, above what was provided for all Australians. J. D. B. Miller

See also ASIA (Facts in Brief Table). In WORLD BOOK, see AUSTRALIA.

AUSTRIA. Chancellor Bruno Kreisky welcomed Libya's leader, Muammar Muhammad al-Qadhafi, to Austria for a four-day visit that ended on March 13, 1982. Kreisky had invited Qadhafi during a 1975 visit to Tripoli, but Qadhafi accepted the invitation just two days before his visit began.

Qadhafi gave two reasons for his visit. "I want to rectify the picture of Libya," he said in Vienna. "The Americans have my picture all distorted." Qadhafi also wanted to conclude a $1-billion deal with the Austrian state-owned steel company for a steel plant and vocational schools near Tripoli. Kreisky, who in 1979 became the first European leader to formally receive Palestine Liberation Organization chairman Yasir Arafat, defended Qadhafi's visit, saying, "There is no proof that he pulls the strings of international terrorism." But in parliament, opposition leader Alois Mock accused Kreisky of "breaking the international quarantine" of Qadhafi.

Qadhafi spent much of his visit discussing oil. He said that Libya would buy more Austrian goods if Austria increased its purchases of high-priced Libyan oil from the current $200 million worth per year. On the day Qadhafi arrived in Vienna, the United States announced an embargo on Libyan oil imports and banned exports of U.S. technology to Libya.

France's President Francois Mitterrand visited Austria on June 18, becoming the first French head of state to go to Vienna since 1809, when Napoleon traveled there to dictate peace terms. Kreisky seized the opportunity to show his leaning toward the Arab states. He described the Israeli government as "semifascist" and warned that Israel's invasion of Lebanon would lead to a wider conflict. He said he welcomed Mitterrand because the French leader also opposed the Israeli war.

Other Developments. Austria agreed on June 24 to buy from Russia an additional 1.5 billion cubic meters (53 billion cubic feet) of natural gas per year for 25 years beginning in 1984. Russia would ship the gas from Siberia through a pipeline that it is building to central Europe. See PETROLEUM AND GAS; RUSSIA.

Austria's unemployment rate rose to 4.5 per cent in November. This was the country's highest rate since December 1953. The increasing strength of the United States dollar and high oil prices drove inflation to 6.8 per cent at the beginning of 1982, but a drop in imports eased this figure to 5.8 per cent by April.

Zita, the last empress of Austria and queen of Hungary, returned to Austria on May 16 after a 63-year exile. The former empress, aged 90, visited her daughter's grave, then returned to her home in Switzerland. Kenneth Brown

See also EUROPE (Facts in Brief Table). In WORLD BOOK, see AUSTRIA.

AUTOMOBILE. The United States automobile industry staggered through its fourth consecutive year of poor sales in 1982. The recession, high interest rates, and the side effects of a strike by Canadian workers of Chrysler Corporation were blamed for the dreary situation. By late November, the number of U.S. auto workers indefinitely laid off reached a record 264,074, with an additional 21,400 workers temporarily laid off.

Auto Sales by the big three U.S. automakers—Ford Motor Company, General Motors Corporation (GM), and Chrysler—as well as sales by American Motors Corporation (AMC) and Volkswagen of America fell 15.9 per cent during the 1982 model year, which ran from Oct. 1, 1981, to Sept. 30, 1982. During that period, U.S. automakers sold 5.5 million cars, the lowest figure since 1961. Volkswagen of America watched its 1982 sales slump by 38 per cent.

Although imported cars continued to capture a significant share of the U.S. market, hard economic times also put a dent in their sales. During the 1982 model year, foreign car sales accounted for 24.4 per cent of the U.S. market. Foreign carmakers sold 2.1 million cars, 9.3 per cent fewer cars than during the 1981 model year and the lowest number since 1978.

Japanese Quotas. In March, Japan agreed to continue to restrict auto exports to the United States at previously agreed upon levels. In early 1981, Japan had agreed to export no more than 1.68 million cars to the U.S. between April 1, 1981, and March 31, 1982. United States automakers had pressed for continuation of the quotas.

On August 11, Japan agreed to cut auto exports to Canada. The Japanese promised to ship no more than 153,000 cars during 1982, 24 per cent fewer cars than in 1981.

Sales Incentives. To shore up sagging sales, U.S. car manufacturers offered a variety of incentives in 1982. In January, GM sponsored a sweepstakes, and Ford, Chrysler, and AMC offered rebates of up to $2,000 on some models. When the rebates failed to lure customers to dealer showrooms, automakers turned to warranties. For example, Chrysler offered buyers of its domestic autos a five-year or 50,000-mile (80,500-kilometer) warranty on power trains, external body panels, and maintenance.

Instead of warranties, GM announced on March 30 that it would offer new-car customers financing at rates lower than those offered by banks and other lending institutions. Ford offered rebates, warranties, low-cost financing, and free maintenance. Nevertheless, at year-end, dealer lots held an unusually high proportion of 1982 models.

Auto Production in U.S. plants in 1982 sank to the lowest levels in 24 years. During 1982, U.S.

automakers built 5.1 million cars, 19.5 per cent fewer than during 1981. By comparison, in 1978, the year before the current slump began, American automakers built 9.2 million vehicles.

GM, the leading automaker, built 3.2 million cars in 1982, down 18.4 per cent from 1981. Ford produced 1.1 million cars, down 16.5 per cent. On January 14, Ford announced that for the first time since 1956, it would not pay a quarterly dividend to stockholders. Chrysler produced 600,180 cars, down 19.9 per cent.

AMC posted a modest gain in 1982 due to the popularity of its new Renault Alliance. Production during 1982 was 110,262, up almost 1 per cent. AMC was the only U.S. car company to exceed its 1981 production figures. Volkswagen of America reported a 49.5 per cent drop in production, to 84,707 cars.

Labor Agreements. During 1982, the United Automobile Workers (UAW) agreed on renegotiated contracts with Ford, GM, and American Motors. The auto companies had insisted that wage and benefit concessions were necessary in order to make U.S. cars more competitive with imported cars.

On February 28, UAW workers at Ford plants agreed to give up cost-of-living increases for the duration of their new contract, which runs until Sept. 14, 1984, and the equivalent of two weeks of paid holidays per year in return for a moratorium on plant closings. In April, UAW members approved similar agreements with GM and AMC.

Auto workers in December ratified a new pact with Chrysler that included the first wage increase since March 1981. On November 5, 10,000 auto workers struck Chrysler Limited of Canada. The work stoppage dragged on for 38 days, forcing the layoff of 4,600 U.S. auto workers. The strike ended on December 12, when Canadian workers voted to accept a one-year contract offering immediate wage hikes. See LABOR.

Seat Belts. The controversy over automatic passenger restraints—airbags and automatic seat belts—continued during 1982. On August 4, a federal appeals court ruled that all new automobiles sold after December 1983 must be equipped with automatic restraints. The ruling overturned the National Highway Traffic Safety Administration's 1981 decision to rescind the regulation, which originally was to have affected all new large and medium-sized cars in the 1982 model year and all cars made thereafter.

The Administration of President Ronald Reagan scrapped the requirement as part of its effort to deregulate the auto industry. The Administration also argued that installing automatic restraints would cost auto buyers and auto companies $1 billion a year. Insurance companies and consumer groups attacked the decision. On November 8, the Supreme Court of the United States agreed to hear the case.

The last Checker taxi, the victim of rising fuel costs and production problems, rolls off the assembly line in Kalamazoo, Mich., on July 12.

De Lorean Arrest. The De Lorean Motor Company lurched through most of 1982 only to crash in October when John Z. De Lorean, the founder of the company, was arrested on charges of drug trafficking and racketeering. On January 28, the company, whose production plant was in Belfast, Northern Ireland, announced the layoff of 1,100 workers. The company blamed poor economic conditions for the slumping sales of its $25,000 gull-wing sports car and a refusal by Great Britain to provide additional aid. On February 19, the company went into voluntary receivership.

The case took a bizarre turn on October 19 when De Lorean was arrested in Los Angeles and charged with possession of more than 59 pounds (27 kilograms) of cocaine. Federal officials said De Lorean planned to use the money from the sale of the drug to rescue his company. Only hours before De Lorean's arrest, the British government announced that the company's Belfast plant would be closed permanently.

Honda U.S.A. The first American-built cars from Honda of America Manufacturing, Incorporated, rolled off the assembly line in Marysville, Ohio, on November 1. The plant will produce Honda Accords.

Charles C. Cain III

In WORLD BOOK, see AUTOMOBILE.

AUTOMOBILE RACING. Keke Rosberg, a 34-year-old Finn who had never won a Grand Prix race, won only one in 1982. But that victory plus other high finishes helped him win his first world drivers' championship.

The title was decided in 16 races—three in the United States—for the sleek, fast Formula One cars. No driver won more than two races. Rosberg, driving a Williams with a Cosworth engine, won in Switzerland. He finished second in Long Beach, Calif.; Monaco; and Austria.

Rosberg's success was surprising. Although he had won championships in go-carts and Formula Vees, he had never been successful in Formula One cars since he started driving them in 1978. The Fittipaldi team, for which he drove in 1981, was financially unable to keep his car competitive that year.

The drivers for the Williams team in 1981 were Alan Jones of Australia, who won the 1980 world championship, and Carlos Reutemann of Argentina, the 1981 runner-up. Jones retired after the 1981 season, and Rosberg became the team's number-two driver. When Reutemann retired in the 1982 season, Rosberg became number one.

The Ferrari team, with its efficient turbocharged engines, was favored in 1982. However, accidents felled both Ferrari drivers. Gilles Villeneuve of Berthierville, Canada, was fatally injured on May 8 in the Belgian Grand Prix in Zolder, Belgium, and Didier Pironi of France broke both legs on August 7 while practicing for the German Grand Prix in Hockenheim, West Germany. Pironi also was involved in the accident that killed Ricardo Paletti of Italy on June 13 in the Canadian Grand Prix in Montreal, Canada.

Until Pironi was injured, he had a solid lead in the world-championship series. Rosberg moved ahead late in the season and clinched the title by placing fifth in the season's last race, on September 25 in Las Vegas, Nev. Rosberg finished with 42 points to 39 for Pironi and John Watson of Northern Ireland, who drove a McLaren.

Indianapolis 500. The $2-million Indianapolis 500 on May 30 lasted a little more than three hours. It was decided by 0.16 second—slightly more than one car-length—making it the closest of the 66 runnings of the celebrated race.

Gordon Johncock of Coldwater, Mich., driving a Wildcat-Cosworth, won by that slim margin over Rick Mears of Bakersfield, Calif., in a Penske-Ford. Johncock's average speed of 162.026 miles per hour (mph) or 260.756 kilometers per hour (kph) was second only to the 162.962 mph (262.262 kph) by Mark Donohue in 1972.

Four of the 33 starters were knocked out of the

Gordon Johncock crosses the finish line only 0.16 second ahead of Rick Mears to win the closest Indianapolis 500 in history on May 30.

race before it began. The trouble started when Kevin Cogan of Redondo Beach, Calif., driving a Penske-Ford, veered to the right as the field of cars approached the start. He hit A. J. Foyt's March-Cosworth, bounced across the track, and hit Mario Andretti's Wildcat-Cosworth. The cars of Cogan, Andretti, and two other drivers were too damaged to run when the race was restarted. Cogan attributed his sudden move to mechanical trouble. Andretti and Foyt said it was due to Cogan's inexperience. Later in the year, Cogan was dropped from the Penske team.

Other Races. Darrell Waltrip of Franklin, Tenn., won 12 races and Bobby Allison of Hueytown, Ala., took eight on the Grand National circuit of the National Association for Stock Car Auto Racing (NASCAR). Waltrip led in earnings ($691,085) and points in this 31-race series for late-model sedans. Allison won the richest race, the $927,625 Daytona 500 on February 14 in Daytona Beach, Fla., in a Buick.

Porsches were one-two-three in the 24 Hours of Le Mans in June in France, with Jacky Ickx of Belgium and Derek Bell of Great Britain driving the winning car. John Paul, Sr., and John Paul, Jr., of Atlanta, Ga., also in a Porsche, dominated the International Motor Sports Association GT series of endurance races. Frank Litsky

In WORLD BOOK, see AUTOMOBILE RACING.

AVIATION companies in the United States suffered severe financial hardship in 1982. A prolonged recession, fare cutting, overexpansion of routes, and a continuing shortage of air-traffic controllers contributed to the companies' difficulties. The aircraft market slumped. A crash-free stretch of more than two years by major United States carriers ended in January.

Passenger traffic on U.S. domestic airlines through November 1982 was up only 4.7 per cent from the slow pace of the first 11 months of 1981. Air freight declined 8.4 per cent through October, while international air freight rose 5.2 per cent. The International Air Transport Association (IATA) said that airlines carried 2 per cent fewer paying passengers on North Atlantic routes in the first seven months of 1982 than in the same period in 1981. Cargo was also off 2 per cent. International traffic by U.S. airlines was down 4.9 per cent through November.

George W. James, the U.S. airline industry's chief economist, estimated in December that U.S. scheduled carriers would have an operating loss of $400 million to $500 million in 1982, compared with a loss of $428 million in 1981.

Financial Distress. Laker Airways, the British low-fare carrier, went into receivership on February 5, unable to pay its debts. Braniff International Corporation, which had expanded greatly under U.S. deregulation, ran out of cash. Braniff tried to head off collapse by leasing most of its South American routes. The U.S. Civil Aeronautics Board (CAB) rebuffed a proposed lease of the routes to Pan American World Airways (PanAm), but on April 26 approved their transfer to Eastern Air Lines. Braniff filed for bankruptcy on May 13. On December 23, PSA, Incorporated, filed an agreement on a PSA-Braniff joint venture with a bankruptcy court in Fort Worth, Tex. The agreement would establish a PSA division that would lease equipment from Braniff.

Several other airlines had shaky going, including PanAm, Western Airlines, Republic Airlines, World Airways, Air Florida, and three carriers under the Texas Air Corporation mantle—Texas International Airlines, Continental Air Lines, and New York Air. Some airlines, including PanAm, cut routes and flights and sold aircraft to bolster finances. But late in the year, PanAm re-entered Caribbean markets that it had not served since the mid-1970s. After a fast expansion, Air Florida began cutting routes. World Airways, which had pioneered fare cutting, asked the CAB to curb discounts, but the board refused.

Traffic Control Curbs. Federal Aviation Administration (FAA) flight restrictions continued to hurt airlines. The FAA imposed the curbs during the air-traffic controllers strike in 1981. Limits on peak-hour schedules affected traffic, partly by disrupting flight connections. Airlines held onto some lightly patronized connecting flights in order to keep FAA-allocated airport landing "slots" from their competitors. Maintaining these flights caused overcapacity—too many slots and too few passengers—which led to fare cutting.

The FAA continued to train traffic controllers. By late 1982, airline operations were above 90 per cent of the prestrike level. FAA Administrator J. Lynn Helms promised a full level of controllers by April 1983. However, many controllers complained of working long hours with few relief breaks alongside inexperienced personnel, and of tension between managers and controllers.

International Airlines faced a worldwide recession, currency fluctuations, widespread discounting on tickets, and overcapacity. At the IATA annual meeting in Geneva, Switzerland, in November, Armin Baltensweiler, president of IATA and Swissair, said that IATA members would lose $2 billion on world routes in 1982, up from $1.68-billion in 1981. Most of the increase would stem from high interest rates. The IATA voted to curb fare discounting.

The United States and 11 other nations belonging to the European Civil Aviation Conference agreed in May to give carriers wide freedom to raise and lower North Atlantic fares in specified zones without government approval. The pact

Braniff International's terminal at Dallas-Fort Worth Airport looks like a truck stop for jets after the airline filed for bankruptcy in May.

went into effect on August 1, for six months. At the end of October, Air France ended flights of its Concorde supersonic airliner between Paris and Washington, D.C.; and between Paris and Mexico City, Mexico. However, Air France maintained Concorde service to and from New York City.

Fare Trimming. United States airlines slashed fares in 1982, especially on transcontinental routes and flights serving Hawaii, Chicago, Dallas, and Florida. However, carriers boosted prices in smaller markets. They also made some attempts to raise fares generally. In June, for example, American Airlines, PanAm, and Trans World Airlines (TWA) raised fares by up to 40 per cent on many routes on which Braniff had competed.

A fare war in November drove the price of a one-way ticket for most transcontinental flights down to $99. On December 27, PanAm extended its $99 fare to cover all cities it served in the United States and some flights to the Bahamas.

The CAB lowered the basic allowable domestic fare level by 3.4 per cent on July 1. This was the agency's last basic-fare action. At the end of 1982, the CAB lost all power to control U.S. airfares.

Air-travel taxes increased on September 1. The tax on passenger tickets rose from 5 per cent to 8 per cent. The government planned to use the money to help finance a major 20-year program to upgrade its air-traffic-control system.

Safety. The first fatal accident of a major U.S. airliner in more than 26 months occurred on January 13. An Air Florida Boeing 737 that was taking off from Washington National Airport in a snowstorm stalled, crashed into a bridge, and then plunged into the icy Potomac River. Seventy-eight people died as a result of the accident. The National Transportation Safety Board said in August that wing icing and the pilot's decision to take off without being sure the wings were clear of snow or ice contributed to the crash. The board also said the 737 has a tendency to nose up or to roll when the wing's leading edge is contaminated.

On January 23, a World Airways DC-10 skidded off an icy runway while landing at Boston's Logan International Airport. The aircraft broke in two, and the first part skidded into Boston Harbor. Authorities presumed that two passengers missing after the accident drowned.

A PanAm Boeing 727 crashed shortly after take-off during a rainstorm at Kenner, La., near New Orleans, on July 9. The accident caused 153 deaths. Investigators said that the cause of the accident may have been a sudden shift in the wind. A certain kind of wind shift known as wind shear can reduce crucial airplane lift on take-off or landing. Albert R. Karr

See also TRANSPORTATION. In WORLD BOOK, see AVIATION.

AWARDS AND PRIZES presented in 1982 included the following:

Arts Awards

Academy of Motion Picture Arts and Sciences. ***"Oscar" Awards: Best Picture,*** *Chariots of Fire,* David Puttnam, producer. ***Best Actor,*** Henry Fonda, *On Golden Pond.* ***Best Actress,*** Katharine Hepburn, *On Golden Pond.* ***Best Supporting Actor,*** Sir John Gielgud, *Arthur.* ***Best Supporting Actress,*** Maureen Stapleton, *Reds.* ***Best Director,*** Warren Beatty, *Reds.* ***Best Original Screenplay,*** Colin Welland, *Chariots of Fire.* ***Best Screenplay Adaptation,*** Ernest Thompson, *On Golden Pond.* ***Best Cinematography,*** Vittorio Storaro, *Reds.* ***Best Film Editing,*** Michael Kahn, *Raiders of the Lost Ark.* ***Best Original Musical Score,*** Vangelis, *Chariots of Fire.* ***Best Original Song,*** "Arthur's Theme (Best That You Can Do)," from *Arthur,* by Christopher Cross, Burt Bacharach, Carole Bayer Sager, and Peter Allen. ***Best Visual Effects,*** Richard Edlund, Kit West, Bruce Nicholson, and Joe Johnston, *Raiders of the Lost Ark.* ***Best Art Direction,*** Norman Reynolds and Leslie Dilley, *Raiders of the Lost Ark.* ***Best Costume Design,*** Milena Canonero, *Chariots of Fire.* ***Best Makeup,*** Rick Baker, *An American Werewolf in London.* ***Special Achievement for Sound Effects,*** Bill Varney, Steve Maslow, Gregg Landaker, and Roy Charman, *Raiders of the Lost Ark.* ***Best Foreign Language Film,*** *Mephisto* (Hungary). ***Best Documentary Feature,*** *Genocide,* Arnold Schwartzman and Rabbi Marvin Hier, producers. ***Honorary,*** Barbara Stanwyck. See FONDA, HENRY; HEPBURN, KATHARINE.

American Dance Festival. ***Samuel H. Scripps American Dance Festival Award,*** choreographer Merce Cunningham.

American Institute of Architects. ***Honors, New Buildings:*** Bentz/Thompson/Rietow, Incorporated, Minneapolis, Minn., for a residence in Orono, Minn.; Joseph W. Casserly of Stanley Tigerman Associates, Chicago, for the Illinois Regional Library for the Blind and Physically Handicapped in that city; Eisenman Robertson Architects, New York City, for a summer residence in East Hampton, N.Y.; Esherick Homsey Dodge and Davis, San Francisco, for Garfield Elementary School in that city; Robert R. Frankeberger, Phoenix, for the Lath House, a park pavilion in that city; Hood Miller Associates, San Francisco, for the Macondray Terrace condominium complex in that city; Kallmann, McKinnell & Wood, Architects, Incorporated, Boston, for the American Academy of Arts and Sciences building in Cambridge, Mass.; Taft Architects, Houston, for a residence on the Caribbean island of Nevis. ***Honors, Restored or Recycled Buildings:*** Michael Graves, Princeton, N.J., for an addition to a house in that city; Charles Herbert and Associates, Des Moines, Iowa, for restoration of the Valley National Bank in that city; Long Hoeft Architects and McCrystal Design, Denver, for restoring 43 houses in a deteriorating neighborhood in that city; John Vinci, Chicago, for the Scoville Square Building, containing stores and offices, in Oak Park, Ill.

Antoinette Perry (Tony) Awards. ***Drama: Best Play,*** *The Life and Adventures of Nicholas Nickleby,* by David Edgar. ***Best Actor,*** Roger Rees, *The Life and Adventures of Nicholas Nickleby.* ***Best Actress,*** Zoe Caldwell, *Medea.* ***Best Featured Actor,*** Zakes Mokae, *"Master Harold" . . . and the Boys.* ***Best Featured Actress,*** Amanda Plummer, *Agnes of God.* ***Best Director,*** Trevor Nunn and John Caird, *The Life and Adventures of Nicholas Nickleby.* ***Musical: Best Musical,*** *"Nine."* ***Best Actor,*** Ben Harney, *Dreamgirls.* ***Best Actress,*** Jennifer Holliday, *Dreamgirls.* ***Best Featured Actor,*** Cleavant Derricks, *Dreamgirls.* ***Best Featured Actress,*** Liliane Montevecchi, *"Nine."* ***Best Director,*** Tommy Tune, *"Nine."* ***Best Choreography,*** Michael Bennett and Michael Peters, *Dreamgirls.* ***Best Book,*** *Dreamgirls,* by Tom Eyen. ***Best Score,*** *"Nine,"* by Maury Yeston. ***Best Revival of a Play or Musical,*** *Othello.*

Cannes International Film Festival. ***Golden Palm Grand Prize,*** *Missing* (United States) and *Yol* (Turkey). ***Best Actor,*** Jack Lemmon, *Missing.* ***Best Actress,*** Jadwiga Jankowska-Cieslak, *Another Look* (Hungary). ***Best Director,*** Werner Herzog, *Fitzcarraldo* (West Germany). ***Best Screenplay,*** Jerzy Skolomowski, *Moonlighting* (Poland). ***Special Jury Prize,*** Paolo Taviani and Vittorio Taviani, *Night of the Falling Stars* (Italy).

Capezio Dance Foundation. ***Capezio Dance Award,*** American choreographer Alwin Nikolais.

Avery Fisher Music Prize. Horacio Gutiérrez, Cuban-born American pianist.

Hyatt Foundation. ***Pritzker Architecture Prize,*** Kevin Roche, United States, for lifetime achievement.

John F. Kennedy Center for the Performing Arts. ***Honors,*** for contributions to the performing arts, George Abbott, writer and director; Lillian Gish, actress; Benny Goodman, clarinetist; Gene Kelly, dancer, choreographer, and director; and Eugene Ormandy, orchestra conductor.

MacDowell Colony. ***Edward MacDowell Medal,*** American sculptor Isamu Noguchi.

National Academy of Recording Arts and Sciences. ***Grammy Awards: Record of the Year,*** "Bette Davis Eyes," Kim Carnes. ***Album of the Year,*** *Double Fantasy,* John Lennon and Yoko Ono. ***Song of the Year,*** "Bette Davis Eyes," by Donna Weiss and Jackie DeShannon. ***Best New Artist of the Year,*** Sheena Easton. ***Best Jazz Vocal Performance, Female,*** Ella Fitzgerald, *Digital III at Montreux.* ***Male,*** Al Jarreau, "Blue Rondo Ala Turk." ***Best Jazz Instrumental Performance, Solo,*** John Coltrane,"Bye Bye Blackbird." ***Duo or Group with Vocal,*** The Manhattan Transfer, "Until I Met You." ***Group,*** *Chick Corea and Gary Burton in Concert, Zurich, October 28, 1979.* ***Big Band,*** Gerry Mulligan & His Orchestra, *Walk on the Water.* ***Best Jazz Fusion Performance, Vocal or Instrumental,*** Grover Washington, Jr., *Winelight.* ***Best Pop Vocal Performance, Female,*** *Lena Horne: The Lady and Her Music Live on Broadway.* ***Male,*** Al Jarreau, *Breakin' Away.* ***Duo or Group with Vocal,*** The Manhattan Transfer, "Boy from New York City." ***Instrumental,*** "The Theme from Hill Street Blues," Mike Post, featuring Larry Carlton. ***Best Rhythm and Blues Vocal Performance, Female,*** Aretha Franklin, "Hold On, I'm Comin'." ***Male,*** James Ingram, "One Hundred Ways." ***Duo or Group with Vocal,*** Quincy Jones, *The Dude.* ***Instrumental,*** David Sanborn, "All I Need Is You." ***Best Country Vocal Performance, Female,*** Dolly Parton, *9 to 5.* ***Male,*** Ronnie Milsap, *(There's) No Gettin' Over Me.* ***Duo or Group with Vocal,*** The Oak Ridge Boys, "Elvira." ***Instrumental,*** Chet Atkins, *Country—After All These Years.* ***Best Country Song,*** "9 to 5," by Dolly Parton. ***Best Rock Vocal Performance, Female,*** Pat Benatar, "Fire and Ice." ***Male,*** Rick Springfield, "Jessie's Girl." ***Duo or Group with Vocal,*** The Police, "Don't Stand So Close to Me." ***Instrumental,*** The Police, "Behind My Camel." ***Producer of the Year, Nonclassical,*** Quincy Jones. ***Album of the Year, Classical,*** *Mahler: Symphony No. 2 in C Minor,* Sir Georg Solti, conductor. ***Best Classical Orchestra Performance,*** *Mahler: Symphony No. 2 in C Minor,* Sir Georg Solti, conductor. ***Best Opera,*** *Janacek: From the House of the Dead,* Sir Charles Mackerras, conductor. ***Best Classical Choral Performance,*** *Haydn: The Creation,* Neville Marriner, conductor. ***Best Chamber Music Performance,*** Itzhak Perlman, Lynn Harrell, and Vladimir Ashkenazy, *Tchaikovsky: Piano Trio in A Minor.* ***Best Instrumental Solo Performance with Orchestra,*** Isaac Stern, Itzhak Perlman, and Pinchas Zukerman, *Isaac Stern 60th Anniversary Celebration.* ***Best Instrumental Solo Performance,*** Vladimir Horowitz, *The Horowitz Concerts 1979/80.* ***Best Classical Vocal Solo Performance,*** Joan Sutherland, Marilyn Horne, and Luciano Pavarotti, *Live from Lincoln Center: Sutherland—Horne—Pavarotti.*

Performances by Katharine Hepburn and Henry Fonda in *On Golden Pond* won Academy Awards in 1982 for best actress and best actor.

National Academy of Television Arts and Sciences. ***Emmy Awards: Outstanding Comedy Series,*** "Barney Miller." ***Outstanding Actor in a Comedy Series,*** Alan Alda, "M*A*S*H." ***Outstanding Actress in a Comedy Series,*** Carol Kane, "Taxi." ***Outstanding Drama Series,*** "Hill Street Blues." ***Outstanding Actor in a Drama Series,*** Daniel J. Travanti, "Hill Street Blues." ***Outstanding Actress in a Drama Series,*** Michael Learned, "Nurse." ***Outstanding Limited Series,*** "Marco Polo." ***Outstanding Drama Special,*** *A Woman Called Golda.* ***Outstanding Actor in a Limited Series or Special,*** Mickey Rooney, *Bill.* ***Outstanding Actress in a Limited Series or Special,*** Ingrid Bergman, *A Woman Called Golda.* ***Outstanding Variety, Music, or Comedy Program,*** *Night of 100 Stars.*

National Society of Film Critics Awards. ***Best Film,*** *Atlantic City.* ***Best Actor,*** Burt Lancaster, *Atlantic City.* ***Best Actress,*** Marilia Pera, *Pixote.* ***Best Supporting Actor,*** Robert Preston, *S.O.B.* ***Best Supporting Actress,*** Maureen Stapleton, *Reds.* ***Best Director,*** Louis Malle, *Atlantic City.* ***Best Screenwriter,*** John Guare, *Atlantic City.* ***Best Cinematography,*** Gordon Willis, *Pennies From Heaven.*

New York Drama Critics Circle Awards. ***Best New Play,*** *The Life and Adventures of Nicholas Nickleby,* by David Edgar. ***Best New American Play,*** *A Soldier's Play,* by Charles Fuller.

New York Film Critics Circle Awards. ***Best Film,*** *Gandhi.* ***Best Actor,*** Ben Kingsley, *Gandhi.* ***Best Actress,*** Meryl Streep, *Sophie's Choice.* ***Best Supporting Actor,*** John Lithgow, *The World According to Garp.* ***Best Supporting Actress,*** Jessica Lange, *Tootsie.* ***Best Director,*** Sydney Pollack, *Tootsie.* ***Best Screenplay,*** Larry Gelbart and Murray Schisgal, *Tootsie.*

Journalism Awards

American Society of Magazine Editors. ***National Magazine Awards: General Excellence, Circulation over 1 Million,*** *Newsweek;* ***Circulation of 400,000 to 1 Million,*** *Science 81;* ***Circulation of 100,000 to 400,000,*** *Rocky Mountain Magazine;* ***Circulation Under 100,000,*** *Camera Arts.* ***Public Service,*** *The Atlantic.* ***Design,*** *Nautical Quarterly.* ***Fiction,*** *The New Yorker.* ***Reporting,*** *The Washingtonian.* ***Essays and Criticism,*** *The Atlantic.* ***Single Topic Issue,*** *Newsweek.* ***Service to the Individual,*** *Philadelphia.*

Long Island University. ***George Polk Memorial Awards: Local Reporting,*** *The* (Orlando, Fla.) *Sentinel Star* for "The Federal Impact." ***National Reporting,*** Seymour M. Hersh, Jeff Gerth, and Philip Taubman, *The New York Times,* for articles exploring illegal activities of former U.S. intelligence agents. ***Regional Reporting,*** Stephanie Saul and W. Stevens Ricks, *The* (Jackson, Miss.) *Clarion-Ledger,* for "Mississippi Gulf Coast: Wide Open and Wicked." ***Foreign Reporting,*** John Darnton, *The New York Times,* "for reporting the complex story of the Polish crisis with discernment and clarity." ***Consumer Reporting,*** Phil Norman, *The* (Louisville, Ky.) *Courier-Journal,* for "Sacred Cows: Power, Politics, and Prices in the Milk Industry." ***Magazine Reporting,*** William Greider, *The Atlantic,* for "The Education of David Stockman." ***Book,*** Edwin R. Bayley, University of Wisconsin Press, for *Joe McCarthy and the Press.* ***Science Reporting,*** *Science* magazine for "News and Comment." ***Television Documentary,*** Pierre Salinger, ABC News, for "America Held Hostage: The Secret Negotiations." ***Television Reporting,*** Ted Koppel, ABC News, for "Nightline." ***Radio Reporting,*** John Merrow of the Institute for Educational Leadership and National Public Radio for "Juvenile Crime and Juvenile Justice."

The Society of Professional Journalists, Sigma Delta Chi. ***Newspaper Awards: General Reporting,*** David L. Ashenfelter and Sydney P. Freedberg, *The Detroit News,* for exposing Navy cover-ups of circumstances surrounding the deaths of six sailors aboard ship. ***Editorial Writing,*** Jon T. Senderling, *Dallas Times Herald,* for a series on Texas political reform. ***Washington Correspondence,*** Jerome R. Watson, Chicago *Sun-Times,* for a series of articles analyzing the first year of President Ronald Reagan's Administration. ***Foreign Correspondence,*** Richard Ben Cramer, *The Philadelphia Inquirer,* for coverage of the plight of starving refugees in Somalia. ***News Photography,*** Ron Edmonds, Associated Press, for his sequence of pictures of the attempted assassination of President Reagan. ***Editorial Cartooning,*** Paul Conrad, *Los Angeles Times.* ***Public Service in Newspaper Journalism,*** *Los Angeles Times* for a series examining the extent of crime and its effects. ***Magazine Awards: Reporting,*** Seymour M. Hersh, *The New York Times Magazine,* for two reports on the American role in terrorism abroad. ***Public Service in Magazine Journalism,*** *National Geographic* for issues on acid rain and on energy.

Literature Awards

Academy of American Poets. ***Lamont Poetry Selection Award,*** Margaret Gibson, for her book *Long Walks in the Afternoon.* ***Harold Morton Landon Award for Translation,*** Rika Lesser, for translating Gunnar Ekelöf's *Guide to the Underworld.* ***Walt Whitman Award,*** Anthony Petrosky, for his book, *Jurgis Petraskas.*

Academy of the American Book Awards. ***The American Book Awards: Autobiography-Biography,*** *Mornings on Horseback,* by David McCullough. ***Fiction,*** *Rabbit Is Rich,* by John Updike. ***General Nonfiction,*** *The Soul of a New Machine,* by Tracy Kidder. ***First Novel,*** *Dale Loves Sophie to Death,* by Robb Forman Dew. ***History,*** *People of the Sacred Mountain,* by Peter John Powell. ***Science,*** *Lucy,* by Donald C. Johanson and Maitland A. Edey. ***Poetry,*** *Life Supports,* by William Bronk. ***Children's Fiction,*** *Westmark,* by Lloyd Alexander. ***Children's Picture Book,*** *Outside Over There,* by Maurice Sendak. ***Children's Nonfiction,*** *A Penguin Year,* by Susan Bonners. ***Translation,*** *In the Shade of*

Spring Leaves, translated by Robert Lyons Danly; and *The Ten Thousand Leaves,* translated by Ian Hideo Levy. ***The National Medal for Literature,*** John Cheever.

American Library Association (ALA). ***Bailey K. Howard-World Book Encyclopedia-ALA Goals Award,*** Committee on the Status of Women in Librarianship of the ALA. ***J. Morris Jones-World Book Encyclopedia-ALA Goals Award,*** Bibliographic Instruction Section of the Association of College and Research Libraries. ***Newbery Medal,*** *A Visit to William Blake's Inn: Poems for Innocent and Experienced Travelers,* by Nancy Willard. ***Caldecott Medal,*** *Jumanji,* by Chris Van Allsburg.

Canada Council. ***Governor General's Literary Awards, English-Language Works: Fiction,*** *Home Truths: Selected Canadian Stories,* by Mavis Gallant. ***Poetry,*** *The Collected Poems of F. R. Scott,* by F. R. Scott. ***Drama,*** *Blood Relations,* by Sharon Pollock. ***Nonfiction,*** *Caribou and the Barren-Lands,* by George Calef. ***French-Language Works: Fiction,*** *La province lunaire,* by Denys Chabot. ***Poetry,*** *Visages,* by Michel Beaulieu. ***Drama,*** *C'était avant la guerre à l'Anse à Gilles,* by Marie Laberge. ***Nonfiction,*** *L'échappée des discours de l'oeil,* by Madeleine Ouellette-Michalska.

Canadian Library Association. ***Amelia Frances Howard-Gibbon Illustrator's Award,*** Heather Woodall for *Ytek and the Arctic Orchard: An Inuit Legend.* ***Book of the Year for Children Award,*** Janet Lunn for *The Root Cellar.*

National Book Critics Circle. ***National Book Critics Circle Awards: Fiction,*** *Rabbit Is Rich,* by John Updike. ***General Nonfiction,*** *The Mismeasure of Man,* by Stephen Jay Gould. ***Poetry,*** *A Coast of Trees,* by A. R. Ammons. ***Criticism,*** *A Virgil Thomson Reader,* by Virgil Thomson, with an introduction by John Rockwell.

PEN American Center. ***Faulkner Award,*** *The Chaneysville Incident,* by David Bradley.

Royal Society of Canada. ***Lorne Pierce Medal,*** Malcolm Ross, Dalhousie University. ***Tyrrell Medal,*** Jean-Pierre Wallot, Université de Montréal.

Nobel Prizes. See NOBEL PRIZES.

Public Service Awards

American Institute for Public Service. ***Jefferson Awards,*** Senator Howard H. Baker, Jr. (R., Tenn.); Mayor Henry G. Cisneros of San Antonio, Tex.; Dallas Doyle of Butte, Mont.; Richard M. Garrett of Easley, S.C.; Ruth Heinz and Lorraine Schreck of Brookfield, Wis.; comedian Bob Hope; Helena Kyle of Chapel Hill, N.C.; Representative Claude D. Pepper (D., Fla.); Caroline Putnam of Springfield, Mass.

National Association for the Advancement of Colored People. ***Spingarn Medal,*** Benjamin E. Mays, former president of Morehouse College, Atlanta, Ga.

Alexander Onassis Foundation. ***Awards,*** Bernard Kouchner, French physician who founded Doctors of the World; Manolis Andronikos, Greek archaeologist who discovered the tomb of King Philip II of Macedonia.

The Templeton Foundation. ***Templeton Prize,*** Billy Graham, American evangelist.

United States Government. ***Medal of Freedom,*** special United States envoy Philip C. Habib, for negotiating the withdrawal of Palestine Liberation Organization troops from Beirut, Lebanon; singer Kate Smith.

Pulitzer Prizes

Journalism. ***Public Service,*** David L. Ashenfelter and Sydney P. Freedberg, *The Detroit News,* for exposing Navy cover-ups of the circumstances surrounding the deaths of six sailors aboard ship. ***General Local Reporting,*** *The Kansas City* (Mo.) *Star* and *The Kansas City Times* for their coverage of the collapse of two aerial walkways in the Hyatt Regency Hotel in that city. ***Special Local Reporting,*** Paul Henderson, *The Seattle Times,* for proving the innocence of a man convicted of rape. ***National Reporting,*** Rick Atkinson, *The Kansas City Times,* for articles on a variety of subjects, including missile espionage and mismanagement of water resources. ***International Reporting,*** John Darnton, *The New York Times,* for reporting on the Polish crisis. ***Editorial Writing,*** Jack Rosenthal, *The New York Times,* for writing on "a wide range of concerns." ***Editorial Cartooning,*** Ben Sargent, *The* (Austin, Tex.) *American-Statesman.* ***Spot News Photography,*** Ron Edmonds, Associated Press, for his pictures of the attempted assassination of President Reagan. ***Feature Photography,*** John H. White, Chicago *Sun-Times,* for photographs on "a wide range of subjects." ***Commentary,*** Art Buchwald, Los Angeles Times Syndicate, for his columns on political and social concerns. ***Criticism,*** Martin Bernheimer, *Los Angeles Times,* for his music criticism. ***Feature Writing,*** Saul Pett, Associated Press, for a profile of the federal bureaucracy.

Letters. ***Biography,*** William S. McFeely, for *Grant: A Biography.* ***Drama,*** Charles Fuller, for *A Soldier's Play.* ***Fiction,*** John Updike, for *Rabbit Is Rich.* ***General Nonfiction,*** Tracy Kidder, for *The Soul of a New Machine.* ***History,*** C. Vann Woodward, for *Mary Chesnut's Civil War.* ***Poetry,*** Sylvia Plath, for *The Collected Poems.*

Music. ***Music Award,*** Roger Sessions, for *Concerto for Orchestra.* ***Special Citation,*** Milton Babbitt for "his life's work as a distinguished and seminal American composer."

Science and Technology Awards

American Association for the Advancement of Science (AAAS). ***AAAS-Newcomb Cleveland Prize,*** Robert Axelrod and William D. Hamilton, University of Michigan. ***AAAS Socio-Psychological Prize,*** Gary Wayne Strong, University of Louisville.

American Chemical Society. ***Willard Gibbs Medal,*** Gilbert Stork, Columbia University. ***Charles Lathrop Parsons Award,*** Representative James G. Martin (R., N.C.). ***Priestley Medal,*** Robert S. Mulliken, University of Chicago.

Columbia University. ***Louisa Gross Horwitz Prize,*** Barbara McClintock, Carnegie Institution; and Susumu Tonegawa, Massachusetts Institute of Technology.

Gairdner Foundation. ***Gairdner Foundation International Awards,*** G. Gilbert Ashwell, National Institutes of Health; Günter Blobel, Rockefeller University; Arvid Carlson, University of Göteborg, Sweden; Paul Janssen, Janssen Pharmaceutica, Belgium; and Manfred M. Mayer, Johns Hopkins University School of Medicine.

Albert and Mary Lasker Foundation. ***Albert Lasker Basic Medical Research Award,*** J. Michael Bishop and Harold E. Varmus, University of California at San Francisco; Raymond L. Erikson, Harvard University; Robert C. Gallo, National Cancer Institute; Hidesaburo Hanafusa, Rockefeller University. ***Albert Lasker Clinical Medical Research Award,*** Roscoe O. Brady and Elizabeth F. Neufeld, National Institutes of Health.

National Science Foundation. ***Vannevar Bush Award,*** Lee A. Dubridge, former president of California Institute of Technology. ***Alan T. Waterman Award,*** Richard Axel, Columbia University.

Royal Society of Canada. ***Bancroft Award,*** Christopher R. Barnes, Memorial University of Newfoundland. ***Thomas W. Eadie Medal,*** Bernhard Cinader, University of Toronto. ***Flavelle Medal,*** Clayton Person, University of British Columbia. ***McLaughlin Medal,*** John C. Brown, University of British Columbia. ***Rutherford Memorial Medal in Chemistry,*** Geoffrey Ozin, University of Toronto. ***Rutherford Memorial Medal in Physics,*** W. G. Unruh, University of British Columbia.

Sara Dreyfuss

BAHAMAS. See LATIN AMERICA.

BAHRAIN. See MIDDLE EAST.

BALLET. See DANCING.

BANGLADESH. The army chief of staff, Lieutenant General Hussain Muhammad Ershad, seized control of Bangladesh in a bloodless coup on March 24, 1982. Ershad declared martial law, suspended the Constitution, and named himself chief martial law administrator of the country. The government of President Abdus Sattar was removed from office. On March 27, a retired judge, Abul Fazal Ahsan Uddin Chowdhury, was sworn in as a figurehead president. See ERSHAD, HUSSAIN M.

The Coup followed unhappiness in the armed forces over governmental inefficiency and corruption. Under military pressure, Sattar fired his 42-member Cabinet on February 11 and named a new one with 18 members, many drawn from a list approved by the army. But some politicians whom the military disliked stayed in office.

The situation came to a head on March 23, when Vice-President Mirza N. Huda, a nonpartisan professional administrator, resigned. Sattar named a politician, Muhammadullah, to succeed him. The army staged a nonviolent coup early the next morning. Ershad described Sattar as an "honest and honorable man" who could not control the politicians. In a broadcast, Sattar supported martial law, saying increasing corruption made it necessary. Almost 300 politicians were arrested for misuse of power and other offenses.

Bangladesh's new military leader, Hussain Muhammad Ershad, addresses the nation after seizing power in a bloodless coup on March 24.

Ershad promised new elections "as soon as possible." He said later he hoped to return to elective government in two years.

The Economy. The new government reported that prices of Bangladesh's exports fell 17 per cent, while import prices rose 7 per cent, in the fiscal year that ended June 30, 1982. The International Monetary Fund (IMF), a United Nations agency that promotes world trade, confirmed in July that it had canceled about $630 million remaining on an $872-million loan to Bangladesh negotiated in 1980. The IMF explained that Bangladesh had failed to make economic reforms that were a condition of the loan. Ershad's regime began steps to reform the economy by cutting development spending and raising taxes beginning July 1.

Relations with India remained difficult. During a meeting in New Delhi, India, Ershad and India's Prime Minister Indira Gandhi agreed on October 7 to set an 18-month deadline for studies on sharing waters of the Ganges River, which flows from India through Bangladesh. They also agreed to make more surveys of an island in the Bay of Bengal that both nations claim. Bangladesh blamed India for supporting guerrilla resistance by Bangladesh's Chakma tribe. India accused Bangladesh of aiding Mizo rebels in India. Henry S. Bradsher

See also ASIA (Facts in Brief Table). In WORLD BOOK, see BANGLADESH.

BANK. Dramatically falling interest and inflation rates in 1982 signaled the success of the United States Federal Reserve Board (Fed) policy of slowing the growth rate of the U.S. money supply. At the same time, sluggish economic growth and the failure of several important financial institutions indicated all was not well.

The money supply is usually measured in two ways. Narrowly defined as M1 (formerly M1B), it includes currency in the hands of the public and checking-account balances in banks, savings and loan associations (S&L's), credit unions, and similar institutions. More broadly defined as M2, the money supply includes M1 as well as savings-account balances, savings certificates, balances in money market funds (MMF's), and other high-paying assets. The Fed limits interest rates on regular checking accounts to 5½ per cent, but it places higher interest limits on savings certificates and no limits on MMF's. Thus, people hold money only temporarily as cash or in checking accounts counted in M1 but keep money for longer periods in assets counted in M2.

M2 behaved smoothly and within limits set by the Fed by starting 1982 at $1.84 trillion and rising by about 9 per cent during the year. This was slightly slower than its 10 per cent growth during 1981. Most of the growth came in MMF's, which climbed to more than $300 billion.

Stayskal in *Chicago Tribune*

"If you want to close your account you'll have to give us our choice of a toaster, pocket calculator, or clock radio!"

M1 fluctuated as money moved in and out of checking accounts, beginning the year at $448 billion but scarcely growing through the end of March. At that time, it jumped to between $450-billion and $455 billion. It hovered there until the end of June, when it suddenly dipped to $446 billion. M1 rose thereafter and ended the year at $478 billion.

In October, the Fed leaked its new policy of paying less attention to swings in M1 than to swings in M2. Fed Chairman Paul A. Volcker explained why he expected erratic fluctuations in M1. First, many all-savers certificates were about to mature, throwing cash into checking accounts included in M1. Second, the Garn-St. Germain Depository Institutions Act of 1982 permitted banks and S&L's to offer money market accounts with checking privileges and no interest-rate ceilings as of December 14. These accounts would pull money out of checking accounts in M1 and into higher-paying accounts in M2.

Interest and Inflation Rates. Interest rates remained high by historical standards in 1982 but fell several percentage points from their 1981 peaks. The federal funds rate—the rate that banks pay to borrow reserves from other banks—began the year at 12 per cent and peaked at 15.8 per cent early in February. It held steady at about 15 per cent through May, fell during July and August to 9 per cent, rose to 10.8 per cent in October, and finished the year near 9 per cent.

The 90-day Treasury bill (T-bill) rate determines what rate banks and S&L's may pay on certain certificates of deposit. It began the year at 11.2 per cent and peaked at just over 14 per cent early in February. Until mid-July, it stayed near 13 per cent and then fell to 7.6 per cent by the end of August. It stayed near 8 per cent for the rest of the year.

The prime rate, which banks charge their best corporate customers, is the short-term rate that receives most attention. The prime, which hit a record high of 21.5 per cent in 1981, began 1982 at 15.5 per cent and rose to 16.5 per cent by the end of July. During the next three months, banks leapfrogged one another's rates, driving the prime down to 12 per cent by the end of October. The prime rate moves both slower and later than other short-term rates, which hit their lows by the end of September. It fell slowly during the last three months of the year, finishing at 11 to 11.5 per cent.

Lower interest rates in late 1981 and through 1982 had two causes. In the first place, slower money growth since 1979 had contributed to falling inflation rates as measured by increases in the Consumer Price Index (CPI). The CPI, which soared 11.7 per cent in 1980, rose 8.4 per cent in 1981 and only about 5 per cent in 1982. Falling inflation rates eventually cause lenders to lower the interest premium they charge to cover an expected loss in the value of their money.

The second cause of lower interest rates was the slowdown of the economy. When the economy slows, the demand for credit also slows, and interest rates fall. The real rate of interest—the current interest rate minus the inflation rate—remained at 1981's high level of 7 to 9 per cent through the first half of 1982 and fell to between 3 and 4 per cent by the end of August. Compared with rates in the 1960s and 1970s, the real interest rate remained high and may have acted as a drag on the economy. However, it drew closer to the long-term average of 1 to 2 per cent.

Savings and Loans. S&L's continued to be hard-pressed in 1982. Rising interest rates hit S&L's hard in 1980 and 1981 because their earning assets consisted mostly of old mortgages issued over long terms at low, fixed interest rates. High current rates that S&L's had to pay to attract short-term deposits made for losses and forced many failures and mergers. When an S&L fails, the Federal Savings and Loan Insurance Corporation (FSLIC) steps in and either pays depositors up to $100,000 on each account or arranges a merger between the failing S&L and a healthy one. By the end of 1982, there were few healthy S&L's left to merge with, but the government had made life easier for the S&L's in several ways.

Starting in October 1981, Congress allowed banks and S&L's to issue all-savers certificates, which paid 70 per cent of the rate on one-year T-bills with up to $1,000 of interest free of federal income tax. This made all-savers worth more to the depositor than they cost the institution. In addition, in late 1982, the FSLIC began to loan money to ailing S&L's through income capital certificates, which did not have to be paid back until the institutions became profitable again. Finally, the Depository Institutions Act of 1982, signed on October 15, expanded the range of loans S&L's could make to include a greater number of personal loans and some business loans. Because these loans are short-term, they have interest rates that vary with the S&L's cost of funds.

By the end of 1982, the worst was over. S&L's could pay lower interest rates to depositors. Lower mortgage rates—below 14 per cent—made it easier to sell homes. Increased home sales helped S&L's in two ways: They wrote new, higher-rate mortgages and, at the same time, they took old, low-rate mortgages off their books as holders of these mortgages found it easier to sell their homes.

International Banking Scares. The banking system around the world received a string of shocks in 1981 and 1982 when several financial institutions failed unexpectedly and several countries neared default on loans from major banks. By the end of 1982, 43 U.S. banks had failed, beating the previous modern record of 16 in 1976.

More important than the number of bank failures was their nature. On June 18, the chairman of Banco Ambrosiano S.p.A. of Milan, Italy's largest private bank, was found hanged. The bank's operations were suspended the following week, and on August 6, Italy ordered Ambrosiano liquidated. What made this failure unusual was the Italian central bank's refusal to pay off on deposits at Ambrosiano's Luxembourg subsidiary.

United States bank regulators closed Penn Square Bank in Oklahoma City, Okla., on July 5 after it suffered large oil-loan losses. Although the Federal Deposit Insurance Corporation (FDIC) insures accounts only up to $100,000, the Fed had acted in previous failures to cover much larger accounts. This time, however, the Fed did not step in but let the world know that large accounts were now at risk in a bank failure.

Mexico, unable to meet interest payments on its $80-billion foreign debt, closed its foreign exchange markets on August 13. Coming less than a year after Poland's near-default, this crisis signaled that lending to governments might be riskier than supposed. Donald W. Swanton

See also ECONOMICS. In WORLD BOOK, see BANKS.

BARBADOS. See WEST INDIES.

BASEBALL. On the field, the 1982 major-league baseball season was exciting, with close pennant races followed by a seven-game World Series won by the St. Louis Cardinals. Two weeks after the World Series ended, a minority of club owners, dissatisfied with Bowie Kuhn's performance as commissioner, blocked his re-election, meaning that his job would end in August 1983.

All four division races were decided in the final week of the season, two of the four on the final day. None had more twists and turns than the National League's Western Division.

National League. The Atlanta Braves won their first 13 games of the season, a feat never before accomplished. On July 30, the Braves led the San Diego Padres by 9 games, the Los Angeles Dodgers by 10½, and the San Francisco Giants by 13½. Then the Braves lost 11 games in a row and 19 of 21. They fell three games behind the Dodgers with 10 games to go but regained the Western Division lead by winning four of their next five.

The Giants stayed in the race until the next-to-last day of the season. On the last day, with the Braves one game ahead of the Dodgers, the Braves lost to the Padres. The Braves backed into the Western Division title by that one-game margin when the Giants defeated the Dodgers, 5-3, on Joe Morgan's seventh-inning, three-run home run.

The Braves were managed by Joe Torre, who

Rickey Henderson of the Oakland A's steals his 119th base of the season on August 27 to break Lou Brock's major-league record.

had been fired in 1981 as manager of the New York Mets. The Braves had no .300 hitters, no left-handed pitchers, and no consistent starting pitcher except 43-year-old Phil Niekro.

The Cardinals won the National League's Eastern Division by three games over the Philadelphia Phillies. Whitey Herzog, who became the Cardinals' manager and general manager in 1980, had traded players freely and turned the team into speedy, aggressive opportunists. They won 12 straight games in April, fell behind later in the season, and pulled away with eight straight wins in mid-September. Their key player was Bruce Sutter, a relief pitcher who won nine games and saved 36 others.

American League. When the Milwaukee Brewers fell to fifth place early in the season with a 23-24 won-lost record, Bob (Buck) Rodgers was fired as manager and replaced by Harvey Kuenn, a Brewers coach. The new manager told his players to go out and have fun. They did, and they entered the season-ending four-game series against the Baltimore Orioles with a three-game lead over the Orioles. They needed only one victory to win the division title, but when the Orioles won the first three games, the teams began the last day of the season tied for first. The Brewers won that game, 10-2, with four home runs.

The Brewers had relied on power all year. Four Brewers drove in at least 100 runs each, and a fifth drove in 97. Shortstop Robin Yount drove in 114 runs as the second batter in the line-up, led the major leagues in hits (210), tied for the lead in doubles (46), and was second in the American League in batting (.331) and runs scored (129).

Although the California Angels won the Western Division by three games over the Kansas City Royals, they did not clinch the title until the next-to-last day of the season. The Angels got hitting help from 36-year-old Reggie Jackson and late-season pitching help from 39-year-old Tommy John.

Postseason Competition. In the National League play-offs, the Cardinals swept past the Braves in three games. In the American League play-offs, the Angels won the first two games at home from the Brewers. When the series moved to Milwaukee, the Brewers won three straight and the pennant. The Brewers were the first team in either league to overcome a two-game deficit in the 14-year history of the play-offs. They won the fifth and deciding game, 4-3, on Cecil Cooper's seventh-inning two-run single.

In the World Series, the Brewers took a 3-2 lead in games. Then the Cardinals, on their home field, drew even with a 13-1 victory on John Stuper's four-hit pitching. The Cardinals won the seventh game, 6-3, as Sutter retired the last six Brewers in

Final Standings in Major League Baseball

American League

Eastern Division	W.	L.	Pct.	GB.
Milwaukee	95	67	.586	
Baltimore	94	68	.580	1
Boston	89	73	.549	6
Detroit	83	79	.512	12
New York	79	83	.488	16
Cleveland	78	84	.481	17
Toronto	78	84	.481	17
Western Division				
California	93	69	.574	
Kansas City	90	72	.556	3
Chicago	87	75	.537	6
Seattle	76	86	.469	17
Oakland	68	94	.420	25
Texas	64	98	.395	29
Minnesota	60	102	.370	33

Offensive Leaders

Batting Average—Willie Wilson, Kansas City	.332
Runs Scored—Paul Molitor, Milwaukee	136
Home Runs—Reggie Jackson, California; Gorman Thomas, Milwaukee (tie)	39
Runs Batted In—Hal McRae, Kansas City	133
Hits—Robin Yount, Milwaukee	210
Stolen Bases—Rickey Henderson, Oakland	130

Leading Pitchers

Games Won—LaMarr Hoyt, Chicago	19
Win Average—Pete Vuckovich, Milwaukee (18-6); Jim Palmer, Baltimore (15-5) (tie) (162 or more innings)	.750
Earned Run Average—Rick Sutcliffe, Cleveland	2.96
Strikeouts—Floyd Bannister, Seattle	209
Saves—Dan Quisenberry, Kansas City	35

Awards

*Most Valuable Player—Robin Yount, Milwaukee
*Cy Young—Pete Vuckovich, Milwaukee
*Rookie of the Year—Cal Ripken, Jr., Baltimore

National League

Eastern Division	W.	L.	Pct.	GB.
St. Louis	92	70	.568	
Philadelphia	89	73	.549	3
Montreal	86	76	.531	6
Pittsburgh	84	78	.519	8
Chicago	73	89	.451	19
New York	65	97	.401	27
Western Division				
Atlanta	89	73	.549	
Los Angeles	88	74	.543	1
San Francisco	87	75	.537	2
San Diego	81	81	.500	8
Houston	77	85	.475	12
Cincinnati	61	101	.377	28

Offensive Leaders

Batting Average—Al Oliver, Montreal	.331
Runs Scored—Lonnie Smith, St. Louis	120
Home Runs—Dave Kingman, New York	37
Runs Batted In—Dale Murphy, Atlanta; Al Oliver, Montreal (tie)	109
Hits—Al Oliver, Montreal	204
Stolen Bases—Tim Raines, Montreal	78

Leading Pitchers

Games Won—Steve Carlton, Philadelphia	23
Win Average—Phil Niekro, Atlanta (17-4) (162 or more innings)	.810
Earned Run Average—Steve Rogers, Montreal	2.40
Strikeouts—Steve Carlton, Philadelphia	286
Saves—Bruce Sutter, St. Louis	36

Awards

*Most Valuable Player—Dale Murphy, Atlanta
*Cy Young—Steve Carlton, Philadelphia
*Rookie of the Year—Steve Sax, Los Angeles
†Manager of the Year—Whitey Herzog, St. Louis

*Selected by Baseball Writers Association of America.
†Selected by *The Sporting News.*

relief. Darrell Porter, the Cardinals' catcher, was named the series' Most Valuable Player.

Season Highlights. Gaylord Perry, at age 43, pitched the Seattle Mariners to a 7-3 victory over the Yankees on May 6 in Seattle and became the 15th pitcher in major-league history to gain 300 career victories. Pete Rose of the Phillies, at age 41, broke Henry Aaron's National League lifetime record of 3,771 hits and took aim at Ty Cobb's major-league record of 4,191. Steve Carlton of the Phillies, the year's only 20-game winner, struck out 286 batters for a lifetime total of 3,434, only 74 short of Walter Johnson's major-league record. Outfielder Rickey Henderson of the Oakland A's stole 130 bases, breaking Lou Brock's 1974 record of 118. See HENDERSON, RICKEY HENLEY.

With all that excitement, American League attendance reached 23,080,449, and National League attendance totaled 21,504,494, both records. The Dodgers set club records for total attendance (3,608,881) and average (45,111).

Kuhn. In 1969, Bowie Kuhn, a lawyer who had represented the National League, was elected commissioner of baseball. Since the late 1970s, he had come under criticism from newer club owners, many of them businessmen, including George Steinbrenner of the Yankees, Nelson Doubleday of the Mets, Ted Turner of the Braves, and John McMullen of the Houston Astros.

Their objections were varied. Player salaries had rocketed, partly because of the establishment of an arbitration system. Some owners felt baseball management had given away too much in negotiations to the players' union. Others disliked Kuhn's campaign to have teams share cable television revenue equally.

Kuhn's supporters tried to save his job by proposing to hire a business executive to handle the business aspect of the sport, but Kuhn's opponents voted that down. The American League owners finally voted by 11-3 to rehire Kuhn and the National League owners agreed by 7-5, but Kuhn needed three-quarters of the votes from each league and therefore lost his job.

Hall of Fame. Outfielders Henry Aaron and Frank Robinson were voted into the National Baseball Hall of Fame in Cooperstown, N.Y., in 1982. Aaron, the career home run leader with 755, played for the Braves and the Brewers from 1954 to 1976. Robinson hit 586 home runs in 21 years with five teams and became the first black manager in major-league history.

Travis Jackson and Albert B. (Happy) Chandler were selected by a veterans' committee. From 1922 to 1936, Jackson, a shortstop, hit .291 for the New York Giants. Chandler was baseball's commissioner from 1945 to 1951. Frank Litsky

In WORLD BOOK, see BASEBALL.

BASKETBALL. Despite a change of coaches early in the season, the Los Angeles Lakers won the National Basketball Association (NBA) 1981-1982 championship, their second title in three years. For the first time ever under Dean Smith's coaching, North Carolina, which had come close before, won the National Collegiate Athletic Association (NCAA) championship.

The Pro Season. The NBA's 23 teams played 82 games from October 1981 to April 1982. The defending champion Boston Celtics (63-19) had the best record. The Lakers, the Milwaukee Bucks, and the San Antonio Spurs won the other division titles.

The best play-off series was the Eastern Conference finals, in which the Philadelphia 76ers defeated Boston, 4 games to 3. Los Angeles breezed through its first two series, beating the Phoenix Suns in four straight games and San Antonio in another four straight. In the finals, Los Angeles defeated Philadelphia, 4 games to 2.

The Lakers' coaching change also recalled their 1979-1980 championship year. Early that season, after head coach Jack McKinney was seriously injured in a bicycling accident, assistant coach Paul Westhead took over the team. Eleven games into the 1981-1982 season, Lakers guard Earvin (Magic) Johnson asked to be traded because he differed with Westhead over the team's new and complex offensive system. Instead, Jerry Buss, the team owner, fired Westhead and replaced him with Jerry West and Pat Riley as co-coaches. West soon bowed out, and Riley, who had started the season as Westhead's assistant, became coach.

Although most teams were still financially shaky, several developments heartened the NBA. The league set a season attendance record of 9,989,410. Ratings for televised NBA games rose for the third straight year, and the NBA and CBS signed a new four-year contract worth $88 million.

Individual Stars. George Gervin, a San Antonio guard, won the scoring title for the fourth time in six years. Only Wilt Chamberlain, with seven straight titles from 1960 to 1966, had won more. Gervin averaged 32.3 points per game.

Moses Malone of the Houston Rockets was second in scoring with a 31.1-point average. He led the league in rebounding for the second straight year and the third time in four years.

On September 15, after Malone had become a free agent, he was traded to Philadelphia. His contract with the 76ers, worth between $11.8 million and $15 million, made him basketball's highest-paid player.

Malone was voted the league's Most Valuable Player. The all-pro team had Malone at center, Larry Bird of Boston and Julius Erving of Philadelphia at forward, and Gus Williams of the Seattle SuperSonics and Gervin at guard.

James Worthy of North Carolina holds the ball away from Georgetown's Eric Smith as North Carolina wins the NCAA championship in March.

The College Season. North Carolina, as expected, dominated the regular season. The final wire-service polls ranked North Carolina (27-2) first; DePaul (26-1) second; and Virginia (29-3) third.

The NCAA tournament involved 48 teams. The regional winners—North Carolina, Houston, Louisville, and Georgetown of Washington, D.C.—advanced to the national semifinals held on March 27 in New Orleans. North Carolina beat Houston, 68-63, and Georgetown defeated Louisville, 50-46. Thus, North Carolina gained its third final under Smith, and the Tar Heels were favored to beat Georgetown.

On March 29, North Carolina won the final, 63-62, on a jump shot by freshman Michael Jordan with 15 seconds left. James Worthy, a junior forward, led North Carolina with 28 points and was voted Most Valuable Player.

North Carolina, leading by a point in the title game with 5 minutes 50 seconds remaining, had gone into its four-corner offense. That maneuver attempts to spread the defense, and teams that use it often go for minutes without shooting. Such stalling tactics and the difficulty of shooting against zone defenses caused a drop in total scoring nationally for the seventh straight year.

Officials and fans were concerned that basketball games were becoming dull. To counter that,

National Basketball Association Final Standings

Eastern Conference

Atlantic Division	W.	L.	Pct.	GB.
Boston	63	19	.768	
Philadelphia	58	24	.707	5
New Jersey	44	38	.537	19
Washington	43	39	.524	20
New York	33	49	.402	31
Central Division				
Milwaukee	55	27	.671	
Atlanta	42	40	.512	13
Detroit	39	43	.476	16
Indiana	35	47	.427	20
Chicago	34	48	.415	21
Cleveland	15	67	.183	40

Western Conference

Midwest Division	W.	L.	Pct.	GB.
San Antonio	48	34	.585	
Denver	46	36	.561	2
Houston	46	36	.561	2
Kansas City	30	52	.366	18
Dallas	28	54	.341	20
Utah	25	57	.305	23
Pacific Division				
Los Angeles	57	25	.695	
Seattle	52	30	.634	5
Phoenix	46	36	.561	11
Golden State	45	37	.549	12
Portland	42	40	.512	15
San Diego	17	65	.207	40

Individual Leaders

Scoring	G.	FG.	FT.	Pts.	Avg.
George Gervin, San Antonio	79	993	555	2,551	32.3
Moses Malone, Houston	81	945	630	2,520	31.1
Adrian Dantley, Utah	81	904	648	2,457	30.3
Alex English, Denver	82	855	372	2,082	25.4
Julius Erving, Philadelphia	81	780	411	1,974	24.4
Kareem Abdul-Jabbar, Los Angeles	76	753	312	1,818	23.9
Gus Williams, Seattle	80	773	320	1,875	23.4
Bernard King, Golden State	79	740	352	1,833	23.2
Lloyd Free, Golden State	78	650	479	1,789	22.9
Larry Bird, Boston	77	711	328	1,761	22.9

Rebounding	G.	No.	Avg.
Moses Malone, Houston	81	1,188	14.7
Jack Sikma, Seattle	82	1,038	12.7
Buck Williams, New Jersey	82	1,005	12.3
Mychal Thompson, Portland	79	921	11.7
Maurice Lucas, New York	80	903	11.3

College Champions

Conference	School
Atlantic Coast	North Carolina
Big East	Villanova (regular season) Georgetown (Big E tournament)
Big Eight	Missouri
Big Sky	Idaho
Big Ten	Minnesota
East Coast	Temple (regular season) St. Joseph's (EC tournament)
Eastern College Athl. — North	Northeastern
Eastern College Athl. — Metro	Robert Morris
Eastern College Athl. — South	James Madison (regular season) Old Dominion (ECAC-South tournament)
Eastern 8	West Virginia (regular season) Pittsburgh (E-8 tournament)
Ivy League	Pennsylvania
Metro	Memphis State
Metro Atlantic	St. Peter's (regular season) Iona (MA tournament)
Mid-American	Ball State (regular season) Northern Illinois (M-A tournament)
Mid-Eastern	North Carolina A. & T.
Midwestern City	Evansville
Missouri Valley	Bradley (regular season) Tulsa (MV tournament)
Ohio Valley	Murray State-Western Kentucky (tie) (regular season) Middle Tennessee State (OV tournament)
Pacific Coast Athletic	Fresno State
Pacific Ten	Oregon State
Southeastern	Kentucky-Tennessee (tie) (regular season) Alabama (SEC tournament)
Southern	Tennessee (Chattanooga)
Southland	Southwestern Louisiana
Southwest	Arkansas
Southwestern Athletic	Jackson State (regular season) Alcorn State (SW tournament)
Sun Belt	Alabama (Birmingham)
Trans-America Athletic	Arkansas (Little Rock) (regular season) Northeast Louisiana (TA tournament)
West Coast Athletic	Pepperdine
Western Athletic	Wyoming

College Tournament Champions

NCAA (Men) Division I: North Carolina
Division II: District of Columbia
Division III: Wabash (Indiana)
NCAA (Women) Division I: Louisiana Tech
Division II: California Polytechnic (Pomona)
Division III: Elizabethtown (Pennsylvania)
NAIA (Men): South Carolina (Spartanburg)
(Women): Southwestern Oklahoma State
NIT: Bradley
AIAW (Women) Division I: Rutgers
Division II: North Central (Illinois)
Division III. Concordia (Moorhead, Minn.)
Junior College (Men): Midland (Texas)
(Women): Moberly (Missouri)

at least a dozen conferences adopted rules involving a shot clock or a three-point field goal for the 1982-1983 season.

Ralph Sampson, Virginia's 7-foot 4-inch (224-centimeter) junior center, was selected Player of the Year for the second straight year. Others chosen for all-America teams included Worthy, Terry Cummings of DePaul, Kevin Magee of California-Irvine, and Quintin Dailey of San Francisco, all juniors; and Eric (Sleepy) Floyd of Georgetown, a senior. After the season, San Francisco discontinued the sport, partly because an alumnus had been making illegal payments to Dailey.

Women. Drastic changes occurred on the professional and college scene. The professional Women's Basketball League collapsed in January when six of its eight teams dropped out. The Association for Intercollegiate Athletics for Women disbanded shortly after its tournament final. In that final, held in Philadelphia on March 28, Rutgers defeated Texas, 83-77.

The NCAA moved into women's sports in the 1981-1982 college year. Louisiana Tech won the first NCAA women's tournament. It beat Cheyney State College of Cheyney, Pa., 76-62, in the final on March 28 in Norfolk, Va. Louisiana Tech had the best regular-season record (31-1) and extended its winning streak in midseason to 54 games, a women's collegiate record. Frank Litsky

In World Book, see Basketball.

BELGIUM. Prime Minister Wilfried A. E. Martens' center-right coalition government adopted stern measures to avoid economic and financial disaster in 1982. On January 18, the House of Representatives agreed to give the government special emergency powers, nicknamed "the Martens Bulldozer." These powers enabled the Cabinet, in consultation with King Baudouin I, to make financial edicts without parliamentary debate or approval. The Senate approved the legislation on January 31, and the government immediately announced an austerity program. Martens wanted to reduce a budget deficit that was estimated at $2.8-billion for 1982; cut the unemployment rate of 12.5 per cent, the highest in the 10-member European Community (EC or Common Market); and improve a trade situation that had deteriorated as other countries adjusted the relative values of their currencies.

Devaluation. Martens based his program on an 8.5 per cent devaluation of the Belgian franc within the European Monetary System, a program set up by eight of the 10 EC nations in 1979 to stabilize their currencies. The devaluation took effect on February 22.

Martens' most controversial measure was the halting of the automatic adjustment of salaries to changes in the cost-of-living index and the freezing of prices and wages for three months beginning on February 21. Other measures included the cutting of energy prices for industry; the ending of the capital gains tax on building sites; and a decrease from 17 to 6 per cent in the value-added tax, a form of sales tax, on construction.

Strikes. The General Federation of Belgian Labor (FGTB), a Socialist-led labor union, reacted strongly to the austerity measures, calling a general strike on February 8. The strike paralyzed much of southern Belgium's French-speaking Wallonia area, but had little effect in Flanders, the Dutch-speaking region. A March 9 strike brought the Liège area to a standstill when public services closed and pickets prevented people from going into banks, insurance offices, and the university. On March 25, FGTB called a strike that had its strongest effect on the depressed steel-producing regions of Charleroi and Liège.

A steelworkers' rally in Brussels ended in violence on February 11. Marchers threw stones and iron bars at riot police, who used tear gas and water cannons. About 200 people were injured. The workers had come to Brussels to demand that the European Commission, the EC's executive body, approve a Belgian plan to restructure the country's steel industry. Kenneth Brown

See also EUROPE (Facts in Brief Table). In WORLD BOOK, see BELGIUM.

BELIZE. See LATIN AMERICA.

BENIN. See AFRICA.

A demonstrator uses a slingshot to fire a steel ball at a wall of riot police during a steelworkers protest in Brussels, Belgium.

BETANCUR, BELISARIO (1923-), the leader of the Conservative Party, became president of Colombia on Aug. 7, 1982. It was his third try for the office. During the campaign, Betancur pledged to decentralize the government, cut unemployment through tax incentives for business, and increase agricultural production. He also promised to seek a truce with the leftist guerrillas who have been battling the Colombian government for 33 years. See COLOMBIA.

The second of 22 children, Betancur was born in Amagá, near Medellín, Colombia, on Feb. 4, 1923. While working as the assistant editor of the newspaper *La Defensa* in Medellín, Betancur attended Bolívar Pontifical University in that city, earning a law degree in 1947. In 1948, he became editor of the conservative daily *El Siglo* in Bogotá. Between 1953 and 1957, he was jailed 14 times for opposing the country's military government.

In 1958, after the return of civilian rule, Betancur was elected to the Colombian Senate. He later served in the House of Representatives. In 1963, he was appointed minister of labor, and in 1974, he became ambassador to Spain and diplomatic representative to the Arab nations. He ran unsuccessfully for the presidency in 1970 and 1978.

Betancur married Rosa Elena Alvarez in 1945. They have three children. Barbara A. Mayes

BHUTAN. See ASIA.

BIGNONE, REYNALDO BENITO ANTONIO (1928-), a retired army officer, became president of Argentina on July 1, 1982. He succeeded Lieutenant General Leopoldo Fortunato Galtieri, who was forced to resign the presidency after Argentina's defeat by Great Britain in the war over the Falkland Islands. See ARGENTINA; FALKLAND ISLANDS.

Bignone's appointment as president by the army, the most powerful branch of the Argentine armed forces, was opposed by the navy and air force and political and labor leaders, who wanted a civilian named to the post. The army promised to return the country to civilian rule before Bignone's term of office expires in March 1984.

Bignone was born on Jan. 21, 1928. He graduated from the Argentine Military Academy in 1947, then rose through the ranks to become a colonel in 1970. He became secretary to the army general staff in 1972. In 1975, he was appointed director of the Argentine Military Academy and was promoted to brigadier general. He became secretary general of the army in 1978 and was promoted to major general one year later. In 1980, Bignone was named commander of the Argentine Military Institutes Command. He retired from active military service in January 1982.

Bignone is married to the former Nilda Belen. They have three children. Barbara A. Mayes

BIOCHEMISTRY. Recombinant-DNA research in 1982 moved closer to the goal of correcting genetic diseases in human beings. Recombinant-DNA technology involves splicing specific genes from one organism into the genetic material of another.

Using recombinant-DNA technology, biochemist Yuet Wai Kan and his colleagues at the University of California, San Francisco, succeeded for the first time in correcting a defect in a human gene. The faulty gene causes an incurable and often fatal type of anemia known as beta thalassemia. A *mutation* (alteration) in one of the molecular subunits of the gene's DNA results in an incorrect set of instructions for the production of beta-globin, a component of blood hemoglobin. The mutated segment of the gene halts production of the globin, which is formed by linking chemical units called amino acids, at the point where the amino acid lysine should be added.

Because scientists had been unable to correct the mutation in the globin gene itself, the California research team decided instead to try creating a "suppressor" gene to cancel the orders of the first gene. The gene used in the experiment had earlier been isolated by Canadian biochemist Kenneth L. Roy of the University of Alberta. It codes for a type of *transfer RNA* — a substance that carries out DNA's instructions for making specific proteins — that causes lysine to be added to an amino acid chain. The researchers modified the gene so that it would produce a transfer-RNA molecule that would ignore the stop order. To test the gene, the scientists inserted copies of it into the nuclei of frog eggs along with the defective gene. The cells then produced the correct globin molecule, so the suppressor gene had worked.

Gene Transporters. Allan C. Spradling and Gerald M. Rubin of the Carnegie Institution of Washington's Department of Embryology in Baltimore reported in October that they had changed the eye color of a strain of fruit flies — the first time a genetic trait had been altered in a complex organism. Wild fruit flies have red eyes, while inbred strains used for experimentation have brown eyes. Spradling and Rubin inserted the gene for red eyes into a section of genetic material known as a *transposon,* or transposable element — a piece of DNA that is known to move about in chromosomes — and injected copies of the transposon into fly embryos. Up to half of the flies developing from the embryos, and their offspring, had red eyes.

Super Mice. Researchers at four American institutions, working in collaboration, announced in December that they had succeeded in altering the natural growth of mice. The scientists spliced a segment of a mouse gene on to the end of a rat gene that codes for rat growth hormone. Copies of the altered gene were injected into 170 fertilized mouse eggs, which were then implanted into foster

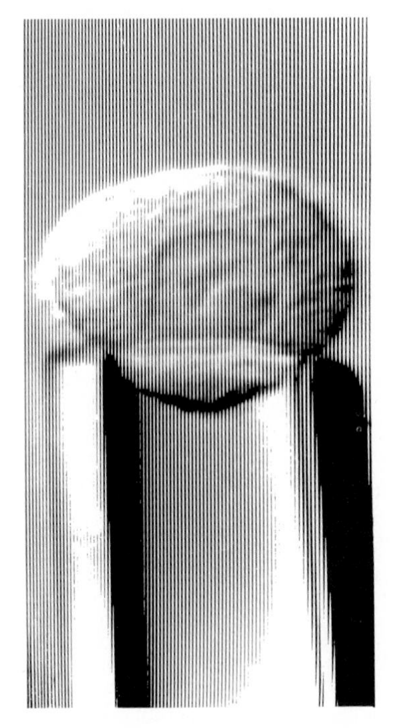

Research photos show how a cancer cell deforms to fit a narrow tube, as it does to travel through capillaries in the human body, then returns to normal shape.

mother mice. Some of the mice that developed from the eggs had incorporated the rat gene. They grew faster, and to a much larger size, than normal mice.

Vaccines. One major use of recombinant-DNA techniques may be to produce vaccines against viruses and bacteria. Scientists are able to insert genes from a disease-causing microorganism into yeast or bacteria to grow large quantities of proteins identical to those found on the surface of the microorganisms. These surface-marker proteins stimulate immunity when administered as a vaccine by causing the patient's immune system to produce antibodies against the proteins.

Investigators have used this technique to produce vaccines against several animal diseases, and research on human vaccines is underway. Merck, Sharp & Dohme Research Laboratories of Rahway, N.J., succeeded in 1982 in producing hepatitis A proteins for a potential vaccine. And in August, Molecular Genetics, Incorporated, of Minnetonka, Minn., announced the production of a protein from the herpes simplex type 2 virus, the cause of sexually transmitted herpes infections. Scientists are uncertain whether the protein will confer immunity against herpes, however.

Regulators. Two substances that regulate bodily functions were discovered in 1982. In June, a team at Harvard Medical School in Boston isolated from human urine a *glycopeptide* (a protein with a portion of a carbohydrate molecule attached) that extends sleep when infused into an animal's brain.

In August, a team at Loma Linda University in California reported the isolation of a protein that stimulates the growth of human and chicken bone cells in the laboratory. The protein appears to participate in regulating the regeneration of bones. It might prove useful in treating bone disorders.

A Potent Mutagen from human feces that may be linked to colon cancer was identified in September by a team at Virginia Polytechnic Institute and State University in Blacksburg. Mutagens are chemicals that cause changes in a cell's genetic information, often resulting in cancer. The new mutagen is produced by bacteria in the intestines.

Amphetamine Receptors. A team of researchers at the National Institutes of Health in Bethesda, Md., reported in October that they had identified specific binding sites, or receptors, in the brain for amphetamines, and that these receptors are linked to appetite control. It is possible that the brain manufactures its own amphetamines. If that is the case, it should help scientists find drugs that reduce appetite. Thomas H. Maugh II

In WORLD BOOK, see BIOCHEMISTRY; CELL.

BIOLOGY. See BIOCHEMISTRY; BOTANY; ENVIRONMENT; OCEAN; PALEONTOLOGY; ZOOLOGY.

BLINDNESS. See HANDICAPPED.

BOATING. Chip Hanauer of Seattle became the United States unlimited hydroplane champion in 1982 after Bill Muncey and Dean Chenoweth, the most successful drivers in the history of the sport, died in race accidents nine months apart.

Nine races for the propeller-driven hydroplanes were held from June to October. The 28-year-old Hanauer won five races in a new boat named *Atlas Van Lines*. Muncey was driving the previous *Atlas Van Lines* when it flipped and killed him in October 1981. The 53-year-old Muncey had won seven national titles and eight Gold Cups, and his 62 career victories far outstripped other drivers.

His widow, Frances, had planned to build a new boat to race in 1983. Instead, as a tribute to her late husband, she had a boat built immediately. This one, powered by a Rolls-Royce Merlin engine, was not ready until 48 hours before the season's first race. Three weeks later, on June 26, Hanauer drove the boat to victory in the Gold Cup race in Detroit.

Chenoweth, a beer distributor from Tallahassee, Fla., won the national titles in 1980 and 1981 in *Miss Budweiser*. He was badly injured in crashes in 1979 and 1980. On July 31, 1982, he was killed instantly when *Miss Budweiser* flipped while traveling at 175 miles (282 kilometers) per hour in a qualifying race in Pasco, Wash. Hanauer won the national title on October 3 in Houston in the season's final race after a new *Miss Budweiser* had run out of fuel and stalled 100 feet (30 meters) short of the finish line.

Other powerboats raced in the eight-race national offshore series from April to September. Jerry Jacoby of Old Westbury, N.Y., won his first national title by finishing fourth in the season's last race at Freeport in the Bahamas. Had Jacoby finished fifth or poorer, 59-year-old defending champion Betty Cook of Newport Beach, Calif., would have kept her title.

Yachting. Dennis Conner of San Diego had a busy year. In February, he sailed the 51-foot (15.5-meter) sloop *Retaliation* to first place overall in the Southern Ocean Racing Conference (SORC) series of six races off Florida and the Bahamas. In the summer, Conner helped the Maritime College Foundation prepare three 12-Meter sloops for the 1983 America's Cup races.

In 1980, the last time the America's Cup was held, Conner sailed *Freedom* to victory. The United States had *Freedom* and three other sloops primed to defend the title in 1983. A record eight challengers were set to compete—three from Australia and one each from Great Britain, Canada, Sweden, Italy, and France.

Frank Litsky

In WORLD BOOK, see BOATING; SAILING.

Dean Chenoweth's *Miss Budweiser* begins to flip while racing in Pasco, Wash., on July 31. The boat landed on top of Chenoweth, killing him instantly.

BOLIVIA. Hernán Siles Zuazo became the president of Bolivia for the second time on Oct. 10, 1982. Bolivians hoped that his election to office by the nation's Congress would end Bolivia's chaotic political changes. During the previous four years, nine presidents had ruled Bolivia as a result of military coups. In addition, Bolivia had been flattened by economic problems.

Bolivia's president when the year began was Celso Torrelio Villa. Torrelio resigned on July 15, and the nation's ruling military junta replaced him with General Guido Vildoso Calderón, chief of staff of the Bolivian Army. Bolivian military commanders ordered Vildoso to step down in September, and Congress elected Siles Zuazo.

Siles Zuazo, a leftist, served previously as president from 1956 to 1960. He was re-elected by Congress in 1980, but the military seized power in a bloody coup before he could start his term. He then spent two years in exile in Peru. See SILES ZUAZO, HERNÁN.

The Bolivian Economy was in a shambles when Siles Zuazo took office in October. State-run industries, including mining companies, petroleum companies, airlines, and railroads, were losing money. Leaders of the Central Bolivian Workers Confederation, which represents about 95 per cent of the country's labor force, were calling for massive strikes for higher wages.

The nation was in default on loans from foreign banks, and consumer prices had increased by 200 per cent in 10 months. The peso, officially pegged at about 44 to U.S. $1, was commonly traded at 200 to the dollar. On November 7, Siles Zuazo announced sweeping austerity measures to turn the Bolivian economy around. The measures included increases in the price of public transportation and gasoline and strict controls on foreign money.

Corruption. The most urgent task of the new government was to restore public confidence in the morality of the nation's leadership. Spawned by a lucrative illegal trade in narcotics, corruption had become firmly established in Bolivia's political system. While in office, the nation's military leaders had enriched themselves by accepting payoffs for ignoring drug operations.

President Siles Zuazo pledged to fight corruption and restore honesty in government. He also pledged to promote the progress of Bolivia's Indians, a long-neglected group that makes up more than half of the population. Nathan A. Haverstock

See also LATIN AMERICA (Facts in Brief Table). IN WORLD BOOK, see BOLIVIA.

BOND. See STOCKS AND BONDS.

BOOKS. See CANADIAN LITERATURE; LITERATURE; LITERATURE FOR CHILDREN; POETRY; PUBLISHING.

BOPHUTHATSWANA. See AFRICA.

BOTANY. Human interferon, an antiviral substance produced by the cells of the body, also has an inhibiting effect on some plant viruses, Israeli scientists announced in April 1982. Patricia Orchansky and Ilan Sela of Hebrew University in Jerusalem and Menachem Rubinstein of the Weizmann Institute of Science in Rehovot tested the ability of interferon to protect tobacco plants against the tobacco mosaic virus.

The researchers chose to study tobacco plants because those plants produce an interferonlike antiviral substance of their own. The scientists found that human interferon suppressed the reproduction of the mosaic virus in tobacco plant leaves. This discovery demonstrated once again the biochemical affinities between all living things.

Nutrients in Leaves. Botanists have often speculated as to why certain trees—oaks and beeches in particular—retain some of their leaves through the winter. Christian Otto and Lars M. Nilsson of the University of Lund, Sweden, reasoned that this might be a mechanism enabling the trees to obtain soluble nutrients from the leaves in the spring, when the leaves are finally shed.

Otto and Nilsson collected leaves still attached to trees and leaves that had fallen to the base of those trees. The scientists soaked each leaf in water for 25 days. They measured the electrical conductivity of each water sample before and after soaking the leaves to determine the increase of ions leached from the leaves. (Ions are atoms and molecules that have gained or lost electrons.)

The conductivity of the water that had contained the attached leaves was twice that of the water that had held the fallen leaves, indicating a much higher availability of leachable nutrients in the leaves still on the trees. Thus, it seems that some trees do indeed save nutrients for themselves by holding onto some of their leaves until spring.

Plant Electrical Activity. Plants that close their leaves in response to touch will also close when stimulated with electricity, but only if the charge is negative, according to British researchers Christine Jones and M. M. Wilson of the University College of North Wales in Bangor. They investigated the effects of temperature and leaf age on the electrical activity of *Biophytum sensitivum*—one of several types of plants that close their leaves when stimulated with electricity. Botanists have known for some time that such a response is associated with electrical activity in the leaf's cell membranes. The finding that only negative, and not positive, charges cause the leaves to contract indicates that a greater negative polarity is necessary to cause the electrical signal to pass down the cell membrane and thereby trigger the closing response. Barbara N. Benson

In WORLD BOOK, see BOTANY; INTERFERON.

BOTSWANA. See AFRICA.

BOWLING. Although Earl Anthony became bowling's first million-dollar career winner in 1982, he shared attention with Glenn Allison's unrecognized perfection.

The 43-year-old Anthony of Dublin, Calif., won three tournaments on the Professional Bowlers Association (PBA) tour during the first three months of the year. The second of these victories came in the $200,000 PBA championship, held from February 21 to 27 in Toledo, Ohio. By winning the PBA title for a record fifth time, Anthony raised his career earnings to $1,012,586. A month later in Milwaukee, he recorded his 39th career triumph, also a record. He ended the year as the leading money winner with $134,760.

Other major winners in 1982 included Dave Husted of Milwaukie, Ore., who won the United States Open; Mike Durbin of Chagrin Falls, Ohio, who won the $200,000 Firestone Tournament of Champions; and Art Trask of Fresno, Calif., who took three winter tournaments. In all, the 36 PBA tournaments were worth almost $5 million. The all-America team chosen by the *Bowlers Journal* consisted of Anthony; Durbin; Trask; Steve Cook of Roseville, Calif.; and Pete Weber of St. Louis.

The 54-Year-Old Allison, a member of the National Bowling Hall of Fame, retired from the tour in 1971. On July 1, 1982, at the 300 Bowl in La Habra, Calif., he bowled in two leagues. In the first, he rolled 578 for three games. In the second, he rolled 36 straight strikes, which meant three straight 300 games, or a perfect score of 900.

In 1981, more than 6,000 bowlers who rolled 300 games in competition had them approved by the American Bowling Congress (ABC), the governing body for men's bowling. Allison had 41 previous 300s approved. But no one had rolled three straight 300s. The three-game record was 886, set by Allie Brandt of Lockport, N.Y., in 1939.

The ABC, following procedure, sent an inspector to determine whether the lane conditions were proper for Allison's 300s. The inspector said he found excessive oil on the center boards, a condition that gives a bowler better control of the ball. The ABC then rejected Allison's record. Allison said the oiling was proper, and sued the ABC.

Women. The Ladies Pro Bowlers Tour conducted 14 tournaments, worth $438,000. Nikki Gianulias of Vallejo, Calif., won four tournaments and set a women's tour record of more than $43,000 in earnings. Shinobu Saitoh of Japan became the first foreign winner of the women's United States Open.

Gianulias was named to the *Bowlers Journal* all-America team along with Donna Adamek of Duarte, Calif.; Pat Costello of Fremont, Calif.; Lorrie Nichols of Island Lake, Ill.; and Cindy Coburn of Buffalo, N.Y.

Frank Litsky

In WORLD BOOK, see BOWLING.

BOXING. The sport's gains in 1982 were outweighed by the retirement of a world champion (Sugar Ray Leonard), the death of a challenger (Duk Koo Kim) after a title fight, and the death of a champion (Salvador Sánchez) in an automobile accident.

Leonard, Sánchez, and Kim. The 26-year-old Leonard, recognized as welterweight champion by both the World Boxing Council (WBC) and the World Boxing Association (WBA), was preparing for a May 14 title fight when his left eye bothered him. An eye specialist determined that the retina was detached, and on May 9 Leonard underwent surgery.

Although the surgeon said Leonard probably could box again, Leonard did not want to risk further injury and perhaps blindness. He had a wife and a son and a beautiful home in Mitchellville, Md.; and he had earned $40 million in six years. On November 9, he made the retirement formal.

Sánchez, 23, the WBC featherweight champion since 1980, was killed on August 12 in a highway accident in Mexico. He had made his ninth successful title defense three weeks before.

On November 13, WBA lightweight champion Ray Mancini of Youngstown, Ohio, knocked out the 23-year-old Kim of South Korea with a hard right to the head in the 14th round of a bout

World Champion Boxers

Division	Champion	Country	Year Won
Heavyweight	†Larry Holmes	U.S.A.	1978
	*Michael Dokes	U.S.A.	1982
Cruiserweight	†S. T. Gordon	U.S.A.	1982
	*Ossie Ocasio	Puerto Rico	1982
Light-heavyweight	†Dwight Muhammad Qawi	U.S.A.	1981
	*Michael Spinks	U.S.A.	1981
Middleweight	Marvin Hagler	U.S.A.	1980
Junior-middleweight	†Thomas Hearns	U.S.A.	1982
	*Davey Moore	U.S.A.	1981
Welterweight	Vacant		
Junior-welterweight	†Leroy Haley	U.S.A.	1982
	*Aaron Pryor	U.S.A.	1980
Lightweight	†Alexis Arguello	Nicaragua	1981
	*Ray Mancini	U.S.A.	1982
Junior-lightweight	†Bobby Chacon	U.S.A.	1982
	*Samuel Serrano	Puerto Rico	1982
Featherweight	†Juan LaPorte	U.S.A.	1982
	*Eusebio Pedroza	Panama	1978
Junior-featherweight	†Wilfredo Gomez	Puerto Rico	1977
	*Leo Cruz	Dominican Republic	1982
Bantamweight	†Lupe Pintor	Mexico	1979
	*Jeff Chandler	U.S.A.	1980
Junior-bantamweight	†Rafael Orono	Venezuela	1982
	*Jiro Watanabe	Japan	1982
Flyweight	†Eleoncio Mercedes	Dominican Republic	1982
	*Santos Laciar	Argentina	1982
Junior-flyweight	†Hilario Zapata	Panama	1982
	*Katsuo Tokashiki	Japan	1981

†Recognized by World Boxing Council, as of Dec. 31, 1982.
*Recognized by World Boxing Association, as of Dec. 31, 1982.

Gerry Cooney falls to the mat after a flurry of punches from Larry Holmes in the 13th round of their June 11 heavyweight title bout. Holmes won.

in Las Vegas. Kim lapsed into a coma seconds after the blow and four days later was declared legally dead.

The Heavyweights. There was an attractive match-up for the WBC heavyweight title on June 11 in Las Vegas, Nev. Larry Holmes of Easton, Pa., the 32-year-old champion, faced 25-year-old Gerry Cooney of Huntington, N.Y. Holmes was black, Cooney white, and both fighters were unbeaten. The gross gate of almost $50 million was the highest in history.

In the 13th round, with Cooney about to be knocked down for the second time, his trainer, Victor Valle, rushed into the ring to stop the fight. The referee complied with eight seconds left in the round.

On November 26 in Houston, Holmes successfully defended his title for the 13th straight time with a unanimous 15-round decision over Randy (Tex) Cobb of Philadelphia.

The WBA heavyweight champion, Mike Weaver of Pomona, Calif., did not make a title defense during the first 11 months of 1982. Then, on December 10 in Las Vegas, he lost his title to Michael Dokes of Akron, Ohio, who stopped him in the first round. Frank Litsky

In WORLD BOOK, see BOXING.

BOY SCOUTS. See YOUTH ORGANIZATIONS.
BOYS CLUBS. See YOUTH ORGANIZATIONS.

BRAZIL took a long step toward the restoration of democracy in 1982 after years of military rule. On November 15, Brazilians took part in the first free elections of state and municipal officials in 17 years. In these elections, government candidates received only about 38 per cent of the vote and won only 13 of Brazil's 23 states. However, they retained control of the electoral college that will choose a new president of Brazil in 1985.

Among the opposition parties was the newly formed Workers Party, led by Luis Inácio da Silva, a charismatic 37-year-old labor leader who lost in his race for governor of São Paulo state. During the campaign, Brazil's Roman Catholic clergy participated at the grass-roots level to help raise political consciousness among young Brazilians, who never before had the chance to vote.

Brazil's Economy. Like other Latin Americans, Brazilians felt the impact of recession. By year-end, Brazil's foreign debt had swelled to nearly $85 billion, the largest of any developing nation. The Brazilian government, crippled by high interest rates and a decline in fresh investment, seemed incapable of recovering its economic momentum. Mid-1982 figures indicated that Brazil had an annual inflation rate of more than 100 per cent—a 20-year high—and a trade surplus of less than $1.5 billion in the first half of the year. To pay its debts, Brazil had to borrow heavily abroad and impose austerity measures. In December, the United States announced that it would lend Brazil $1.23 billion.

Continued Confidence. Despite its economic problems, Brazil remained a country of unbounded confidence in the future. That confidence was exemplified by willingness to plunge into new endeavors to develop the nation's vast and unexploited hinterland. In January, for example, the territory of Rondônia in western Brazil was declared Brazil's 23rd state. To encourage settlement there, the government awarded free tracts of 250 to 610 acres (100 to 250 hectares) to families willing to homestead. The government also launched programs to develop the new state's resources, said to include rubber, cacao, coffee, gold, tin, and iron ore.

Brazil continued to develop its nuclear power industry during the year. Under an agreement with West Germany, work began on four nuclear plants in the state of São Paulo. Plans call for the construction of four more nuclear plants—two in Rio de Janeiro state and two between the cities of São Paulo and Rio de Janeiro. In November, a huge hydroelectric plant at Itaipú, on Brazil's border with Paraguay, went into partial operation. To further reduce its dependence on oil imports for energy, Brazil increased its production of vehicles that can operate on alcohol that is produced from sugar.

A crowd in Rio de Janeiro shows its support of a gubernatorial candidate, center. Brazil held its first free elections in 17 years in November.

Environmental Concern. Environmentalists in Brazil continued to be concerned about the fate of Indians living along the path of the Trans-Amazon Highway, as land-hungry peasants and developers rushed in to stake their claims to the area's vast mineral and farming resources. There was also concern over the proposed use of toxic defoliants to clear a wide swath of Amazon jungle for the construction of the Tucuruí Dam. This mammoth hydroelectric plant is to be built on one of the Amazon River's tributaries and requires the clearing and flooding of 834 square miles (2,160 square kilometers) of land.

Amazon Project Abandoned. Ironically, with so much going on to develop the Amazon in 1982, U.S. shipping magnate and financier Daniel K. Ludwig abandoned the most ambitious effort ever undertaken to develop resources there, reportedly because of mounting financial losses and disputes with government officials. The 84-year-old Ludwig had invested more than $1 billion over 25 years to develop the lumber and farming resources of nearly 4 million acres (1.6 million hectares) of jungle. The site is located in northeastern Brazil where the Amazon and Jari rivers meet, two days by boat from Belém. Nathan A. Haverstock

See also LATIN AMERICA (Facts in Brief Table). In WORLD BOOK, see BRAZIL.

BRIDGE. See BUILDING AND CONSTRUCTION.

BRIDGE, CONTRACT. The United States dominated the 1982 world championships of the World Bridge Federation held in Biarritz, France, in October. Chip Martel of Davis, Calif., and Lew Stansby of Castro Valley, Calif., won the World Open Pair Championship. Victors in the World Women's Pair Championship were Carol Sanders of Nashville, Tenn., and Betty Ann Kennedy of Shreveport, La. Dianna Gordon and George Mittelman of Toronto, Canada, won the World Mixed Pair Championship.

Luella Slaner of Scarsdale, N.Y., was the surprise bridge player of the year. In the prestigious Harold A. Vanderbilt Knockout Team Championship at Niagara Falls, N.Y., in March, she led her team to the finals before losing to a team captained by George Rosenkranz of Mexico City, Mexico. Slaner, not even close to a Life Master, finished second and qualified for the North American International Team Trials.

In American Grand National events in Albuquerque, N. Mex., in July, the team winners were Martel; Stansby; Hugh Ross of Oakland, Calif.; Peter Pender of Guerneville, Calif.; Ronald Von der Porten of San Francisco; and Kyle Larsen of Walnut Creek, Calif. The Open Pairs victors were Ivan H. Scope of San Francisco and Bill Nutting of Kensington, Calif. Henry G. Francis

In WORLD BOOK, see BRIDGE, CONTRACT.

BRITISH COLUMBIA, the most-unionized province in Canada, suffered from serious industrial disputes during the summer of 1982. In early August, 1 in 5 of British Columbia's workers was out of work; 170,000 people were unemployed; and about 100,000 were on strike. Unemployment was caused by drastic declines in the market for wood products, and many of the strikers were engaged in the first provincewide strike of civil servants.

Faced with an unprecedented $1.1-billion deficit (Canadian dollars; $1 = U.S. 81 cents as of Dec. 31, 1982), the Social Credit government of Premier William R. Bennett announced a sweeping program to hold provincial, municipal, and school board budgets to a 12 per cent increase and to limit government employees to a 10 per cent salary raise. The employees responded by closing all but the most essential public services for a week beginning on August 6. An agreement was reached on September 20 that provided an average 6 per cent wage increase and other benefits.

The Budget, presented on April 5, predicted only a $358-million deficit, but this was revised upward to more than $1 billion by the end of the summer as the economic depression continued and government revenues fell. The budget proposed increased corporate taxes for chartered Canadian banks operating in British Columbia and raised the tax rate on rural properties.

A Bright Spot in the economy was the start of the Northeast Coal Development Project, a giant $3-billion industrial development involving the construction of two mines, 78 miles (126 kilometers) of railroad through mountain country, 57 miles (92 kilometers) of paved highway, a new town for 5,000 people, and a 79-mile (127-kilometer) power transmission line. Destined for Japanese steel mills, the first deliveries of coal were scheduled to arrive at a new terminal at Prince Rupert, B.C., by December 1983.

Plans were announced on July 15 for a $3-billion liquefied natural gas plant to be built on the province's north coast by a consortium headed by Dome Petroleum Limited of Calgary, Alta. Five tankers to carry the liquefied gas would also be built. The plant is about 19 miles (31 kilometers) north of Prince Rupert, where a $300-million grain-handling terminal was scheduled to be completed by late 1984.

A Dynamite Explosion on May 31 destroyed four voltage reactors used to stabilize flows of electric current at a power station on central Vancouver Island. Responsibility for the blast was claimed by Direct Action, a protest organization hoping to stop environmental damage. David M. L. Farr

See also CANADA. In WORLD BOOK, see BRITISH COLUMBIA.

BUILDING AND CONSTRUCTION. A weak economy, high interest rates, and government budget cutbacks made 1982 a difficult year for the construction industry in the United States. Construction spending increased from $230 billion in 1980 to $238 billion in 1981, but the United States Bureau of the Census estimated that it would fall to $228.5 billion in 1982. Based on activity during the first seven months of the year, the bureau broke down its estimate into $48.8 billion of public works and $179.7 billion of private building, down from $53 billion and $185 billion, respectively, in 1981.

Private nonresidential construction was estimated at $64 billion, up from $61 billion in 1981. An office building boom and new hospital construction accounted for most of the increase. However, new construction contracts for office buildings began to decline steeply in August due to lack of tenants, a situation attributed to the recession. Residential construction, which totaled $86.5 billion in 1981, dropped to an estimated annual rate of $76.7 billion by July 1982. Multiunit housing starts reached an annual rate of 393,000 units and single-family houses reached 610,000 units in August, only the third time in 13 months that residential construction topped the 1-million mark. The National Association of Home Builders cited

The mail must go through, so when a government workers' strike in August interrupts ferry service in Vancouver, B.C., water taxis float to the rescue.

continuing high interest rates as the prime reason for the slump.

The weak economy and an increase in construction unemployment to 20 per cent slowed the rise in wage increases. Pay increases for skilled trades rose 10 per cent, to about $19 an hour, for the year ending in September, compared with an 11 per cent jump in the same 1980-1981 period. Pay increase rates for laborers were down 1 per cent, and their pay averaged $14.64 per hour. The rise of construction equipment and building materials costs also slowed.

Codes. Codemaking groups rushed to catch up with the fast-paced increase in the construction of atriums, the multistoried open areas at the center or entrance hall of many new hotels and other buildings. They revised atrium fire codes, which have been in existence only since 1980. The three standard building codes and the life-safety code of the National Fire Protection Association now require atrium smoke-exhaust, smoke-detection, and sprinkler systems. The codes also restrict use of atriums to activities that involve little fire hazard.

Owners of buildings more than 100 feet (30 meters) high in New York City must comply with a landmark retroactive fire code—Local Law 5. It applies to 839 existing buildings and requires that they have elevator recall systems, fire-alarm communication systems, compartmentalization or sprinklers, and pressurized stairwells. Retroactive fire codes are being debated elsewhere, so experiences in New York City may guide other cities.

The first deadlines for New York City's pioneering facade-inspection law passed in 1982. The first law of its kind in the United States, it requires owners of buildings six stories or taller to have a registered architect or engineer perform a "critical examination" every five years, or to institute an ongoing maintenance program under supervision of an architect or engineer. Detroit also enacted a law requiring inspection of high-rise building facades every five years.

The Kansas City, Mo., building code called for each rod that supported the walkways over the atrium of the city's Hyatt Regency Hotel to support 68,000 pounds (30,800 kilograms). The two walkways collapsed on July 17, 1981, killing 113 persons, because a design change caused failure when the weight on a crucial rod connection reached about 21,000 pounds (9,500 kilograms), according to a National Bureau of Standards report issued in 1982. The change replaced a single set of rods to suspend both walkways from the ceiling framing with two sets of rods offset from each other. This doubled the stress around each connection under the upper walkway because it had to support the weight of both walkways.

New Techniques. The Hubert H. Humphrey Metrodome, which opened in Minneapolis, Minn., in April, is covered by a roof of 9.5 acres (3.8 hectares) of fabric, the largest such covering ever made. It consists of an outer layer of Teflon-coated fiberglass and an inner layer of acoustical material with air space between for insulation. After a heavy snowfall in December, snow removal equipment tore a hole in the roof and caused it to collapse. The roof had previously caved in under the weight of snow in November 1981, before the structure was completed.

The largest movable water barrier on earth is being built on the Thames River to protect London from a possible tidal surge and flood.

The city of Tacoma, Wash., covered its 25,000-seat stadium with the world's largest wood dome—530 feet (162 meters) in diameter and 157 feet (47.9 meters) high. A deck of waterproofed planking fits beneath supporting beams of wood connected by steel plates.

Adding plastic spheres 0.000008 inch (0.0002 millimeter) in diameter to concrete makes it lighter, a better insulator, and more water-resistant, according to the technique's Swedish inventors. The new concrete, known as 3L, has been used for wall panels in single-family houses and for floor slabs in a four-story town hall in Kungsbacka, Sweden, near Göteborg. Reductions in foundation and reinforcement needs more than compensate for the cost of 3L, builders claim.

Dams. The Itaipú Dam, which will shut off the Paraná River and fill a reservoir on the Brazil-Paraguay border, was partially opened in November. The dam, a component of the world's largest hydroelectric project, is part of a complex of almost 5 miles (8 kilometers) of barriers rising as high as 620 feet (189 meters). The project will generate 12.6 million kilowatts of electricity.

An earth-fill dam in Colorado failed in July, sending a wall of water through the town of Estes Park and killing one person. In September, another earth-fill dam broke in western California, washing away several homes in Bishop.

Tunnels. Work continued in 1982 on the world's longest railroad tunnel—a bore 33.5 miles (53.9 kilometers) long and 800 feet (244 meters) deep—connecting two of Japan's main islands, Honshu and Hokkaido. The tunnel runs under Tsugaru Strait, which is 460 feet (140 meters) deep. Washouts, produced by geologic faults, and cave-ins had killed 33 workers and injured 700 others by late 1982. Completion was expected in 1984.

Soviet engineers completed a tunnel 29 miles (46.7 kilometers) long through the Lesser Caucasus Mountains, providing a channel for an estimated 66 billion gallons (250 billion liters) of water per year to flow from the Apra River into Lake Sevan in Armenia. This is the first step in a project designed to reverse decreasing water levels and reduce pollution of the lake. William J. Cromie

In WORLD BOOK, see BRIDGE; BUILDING CONSTRUCTION; DAM; TUNNEL.

BULGARIA departed somewhat from Russian-style centralized economic management in 1982 but remained strongly loyal to Russia in internal politics and foreign affairs. A government decree that took effect on January 1 made factories, research institutes, and design bureaus financially self-supporting. State subsidies were to be provided only "in exceptional circumstances." In agriculture, the government gave owners of private household plots in the countryside and near cities more freedom to decide what to grow. Bulgaria also granted teams of about 165 workers on state and cooperative farms more independence from the nation's central plan. In industry, the government provided foreign trade offices for enterprises that export their products.

Bulgaria Punished several senior officials for corruption. Zhivko Popov, ambassador to Czechoslovakia, was sentenced to 20 years in prison in March. Three of his associates also received heavy sentences. Peko Takov was dismissed from the Politburo, the most powerful part of the Communist Party Central Committee, as a punishment for his son's smuggling and currency speculation. Takov's son got a 2½-year prison sentence.

Warsaw Pact Nations held military exercises in southern Bulgaria at the end of September. After the exercises, Bulgaria announced that it planned to build a Russian-style broad-gauge railroad between Varna, its main port on the Black Sea, and the rest of the country. There is ferry service between Varna and the Russian port of Odessa.

Other Events. In September, terrorists killed Bora Suelkan, a Turkish consular official, in the port of Burgas. Two Armenian terrorist groups claimed responsibility for the slaying.

Bulgaria and Great Britain announced a joint venture at an international East-West trade and cooperation seminar in Varna in May. The Perkins Engines Company of Great Britain and a Bulgarian enterprise will produce engines for Bulgarian vehicles, including trucks and lift trucks. The Bulgarians will sell the engines in the nations of the Communist bloc's Council for Mutual Economic Assistance (COMECON). Perkins will sell the engines elsewhere. The deal was the first Bulgarian-Western joint venture on Bulgarian soil.

In October, Bulgaria and Yugoslavia concluded a long-term agreement on cooperation in the automobile industry. Bulgaria will import 5,000 to 10,000 Yugoslav Zastava cars per year through 1992. In return, Bulgaria will ship automobile parts to Yugoslavia. Chris Cviic

See also EUROPE (Facts in Brief Table). In WORLD BOOK, see BULGARIA.

BURMA. See ASIA.

BURUNDI. See AFRICA.

BUS. See TRANSIT; TRANSPORTATION.

BUSH, GEORGE H. W. (1924-), 43rd Vice-President of the United States, served in 1982 as a low-key team player for President Ronald Reagan's Administration, visible chiefly as an energetic campaigner for Republican candidates in the midterm elections. Bush side-stepped suggestions by White House aides and Republican National Committee officials that he mount an outspoken, high-profile assault on Democrats.

Representing President Reagan, Bush traveled in Asia from April 23 to May 9, visiting Japan, South Korea, Singapore, Australia, New Zealand, and China. On June 15, he flew to Saudi Arabia as head of a U.S. delegation to express condolences to Saudi leaders on the death of King Khalid. In November, he interrupted a seven-nation African tour to represent the United States at the funeral of Soviet leader Leonid I. Brezhnev.

In one brush with controversy, Bush in April withdrew from an effort to win a continuation of tax breaks for drug companies with operations in Puerto Rico. He had been a director of Eli Lilly & Company, a company that was a beneficiary of the tax incentives. Frank Cormier

See also PRESIDENT OF THE UNITED STATES. In WORLD BOOK, see VICE-PRESIDENT OF THE UNITED STATES.

BUSINESS. See BANK; ECONOMICS; LABOR; MANUFACTURING.

CABINET, UNITED STATES. Several Cabinet-level members of President Ronald Reagan's Administration resigned in 1982, notably Secretary of State Alexander M. Haig, Jr. Although Haig reportedly had threatened several times to quit over what he felt were encroachments on his authority by other Administration officials, his exit on June 25 surprised Americans as well as foreign governments.

In his letter of resignation, Haig told Reagan that, in the previous few months, it had become apparent to him "that the foreign policy on which we embarked together was shifting from that careful course which we laid out." Reagan said he had accepted Haig's resignation with regret, but he reportedly had requested it. At the same time that he disclosed Haig's departure, the President announced that he had named George P. Shultz, a former secretary of the Treasury, as the new head of the State Department. See SHULTZ, GEORGE PRATT.

Earlier in the Year, on January 4, Richard V. Allen resigned as the President's assistant for national security affairs. He had been under investigation by the U.S. Department of Justice and the White House for apparent misconduct in office, including accepting gifts and associating with clients of his former consulting firm. He was cleared but resigned anyway. William P. Clark, assistant secretary of state, succeeded him.

Murray L. Weidenbaum stepped down as chairman of the Council of Economic Advisers on August 25. He was succeeded by Martin S. Feldstein, an economist at Harvard University in Cambridge, Mass.

Other Developments. On November 5, James B. Edwards left office as secretary of energy to head the Medical University of South Carolina in Charleston. His successor was Undersecretary of the Interior Donald P. Hodel (see HODEL, DONALD PAUL). On December 28, Transportation Secretary Andrew L. (Drew) Lewis, Jr., said he would resign as of Feb. 1, 1983.

Throughout much of the year, Secretary of Labor Raymond J. Donovan was under a cloud of suspicion as investigators probed allegations that he had ties to organized crime. The controversy surrounding Donovan began during his Senate confirmation hearings in 1981, when it was reported that he had taken part in an illegal payment to union officials. Further allegations against the labor chief surfaced in 1982, including claims that he had consorted with Mafia figures. The Senate's special prosecutor, Leon Silverman, said in June that he had been unable to substantiate the charges against Donovan. He later reopened the investigation, but in September, he brought it to a close. David L. Dreier

In WORLD BOOK, see CABINET, U.S.

CALIFORNIA. See LOS ANGELES; STATE GOV'T.

CAMBODIA (Kampuchea) had two rival governments in 1982. One had been installed in 1979 by the Vietnamese Army, which continued to occupy the country. With Vietnamese support and under Vietnamese influence, this government controlled most of Cambodia from the capital, Phnom Penh. The other government was created in June 1982 by a coalition of three groups opposed to the Phnom Penh regime. It had only a slight foothold inside Cambodia, but it conducted a guerrilla war against the Vietnamese Army.

The Phnom Penh Government announced on February 10 that Chan Sy had become premier. A former deputy premier and deputy defense minister, he had been acting premier since the removal of Premier Pen Sovan in December 1981.

Heng Samrin continued to hold the two top positions. He was Council of State president and secretary general of the Communist party, the People's Revolutionary Party of Kampuchea.

Up to 200,000 Vietnamese soldiers remained in Cambodia. Vietnam said on July 7 that it would withdraw a "significant number" of troops, and it proposed a demilitarized "safety zone" on the Thai-Cambodian border, across which came support for the opposition guerrillas. Thailand rejected the idea, and Vietnam apparently replaced any withdrawn soldiers.

Efforts by Communist countries to have the Phnom Penh regime seated in the United Nations (UN) failed. The UN continued to recognize the Communist regime led by the Khmer Rouge that had ruled Cambodia from 1975 until 1979.

The Coalition Government was formed when the three opposition groups signed a coalition agreement in Kuala Lumpur, Malaysia, on June 22. Prince Norodom Sihanouk, Cambodia's king for nearly 15 years and later its chief of state, became president of the new government, called Democratic Kampuchea. Its vice-president in charge of foreign affairs was Khieu Samphan, who had been president and prime minister of the Khmer Rouge regime. Son Sann, a former premier and leader of a right wing group called the Khmer People's National Liberation Front, became the coalition government's prime minister.

The coalition symbolically established its presence inside Cambodia at a ceremony on July 7 near the Thai border. Each member's guerrilla force continued separate operations.

Good Harvests reduced the food problem that had long plagued Cambodia, but the country still needed outside food aid. The population, which had been reduced by war and by massacres under the Khmer Rouge, rose again. Henry S. Bradsher

See also ASIA (Facts in Brief Table). In WORLD BOOK, see CAMBODIA.

CAMEROON. See AFRICA.

CAMP FIRE. See YOUTH ORGANIZATIONS.

CANADA

Winds of change blow into Ottawa on April 17 as Prime Minister Pierre Trudeau watches Queen Elizabeth II sign Canada's new Constitution.

With almost a million and a half people out of work, the recession dominated Canadian life during 1982. Prime Minister Pierre Elliott Trudeau's Liberal government failed to inspire confidence in its economic management as it directed its efforts toward fighting inflation. The Trudeau government promoted a climate of restraint on wages and salaries while embarking on an emergency program of job creation. But a fiscal deficit of unprecedented size hampered its freedom of action.

A New Constitution, the Constitution Act, 1982, was formally proclaimed by Great Britain's Queen Elizabeth II, serving in her capacity as Canada's constitutional monarch, in a stirring ceremony in Ottawa, Ont., on April 17 (see Close-Up). The proclamation followed passage of the new act in the British Parliament, the last time that body would be asked to amend a piece of Canadian legislation. The Ottawa ceremony was a proud moment for Prime Minister Trudeau, who had made

Her fellow justices welcome Bertha Wilson, the first woman appointed to the Supreme Court of Canada, at the swearing-in ceremonies on March 30.

the adoption of a truly Canadian constitution his goal ever since he entered public life.

Quebec, the only province that refused to endorse the Constitution Act, continued its opposition to the new Constitution through the courts. But the Quebec Court of Appeal held unanimously on April 7 that the accord reached in November 1981 by Ottawa and nine of the 10 Canadian provinces represented a sufficient demonstration of provincial agreement to sanction major changes. Although the provinces were not uniform in size, they were all on the same footing in legal terms. Thus, Quebec's role as the dominant French-speaking province did not justify its government's claim for special status. The government of Quebec Prime Minister René Lévesque received another setback on September 8, this time from the Quebec Superior Court. Its chief justice ruled that parts of the province's language law were unconstitutional because they conflicted with the new Charter of Rights and Freedoms in the Constitution Act. On December 6, the Supreme Court of Canada rejected Quebec's claim that it had a veto over constitutional change.

Internal Affairs. The damaging economic and social consequences of recession made the tasks of government hard. Finance Minister Allan J. MacEachen received criticism from the business community for his November 1981 budget, and despite presenting a second budget in June 1982, he was transferred to another post. In a Cabinet shuffle on September 10, MacEachen was switched to minister of external affairs, a post he held previously. Marc Lalonde, the minister responsible for the nationalist thrust in Canada's energy program, was appointed to the finance post. Jean Chrétien, minister of justice, became minister of energy, mines, and resources. Mark MacGuigan, secretary of state for external affairs, became minister of justice. Of the 35 ministers in Trudeau's Cabinet, 13 were reassigned. Two Conservatives were given key economic responsibilities, one in economic development and science and technology and the other in industry, trade, and commerce.

The Cabinet changes could not hide the fact that Trudeau's Liberal Party had slipped, by August, to a 24 per cent popularity rating. The Progressive Conservative (PC) Party had moved up to 47 per cent, the highest the party had received since Joseph (Joe) Clark became its leader in 1976. A report that 38 per cent of voters in Quebec, the traditional Liberal stronghold, were undecided worried the Liberals. In Ontario, their popularity dropped to third place behind the PC and the New Democratic Party (NDP). Even so, Trudeau's Liberals held a solid majority in the House of Commons, with 146 of the chamber's

282 seats. The PC held 102 seats; the NDP, 33; and there was 1 Independent. There were no Liberal governments in any of the provinces, however, and no Liberal members of the federal Parliament or provincial legislatures west of Manitoba.

The Parliamentary Session was a bitter one. A two-week impasse occurred starting on March 2, when PC members refused to vote on a motion to adjourn the House of Commons. No business could be transacted during that period. The PC members were objecting to an omnibus energy security bill, which they said should be broken into separate sections for a full examination of its provisions. On March 22, the three parties agreed to split the omnibus measure into eight parts and proceed with its examination. The legislature adjourned for the summer on August 4—having sat for 394 days, the longest session on record—then resumed on October 27 to complete its business. It passed 107 bills, making its session one of the most productive in history. Highlights were the measures providing for a strong Canadian presence in the oil and gas industry and passage of Canada's first freedom of information act.

Prime Minister Trudeau announced the appointment of the first woman to the Supreme Court of Canada on March 4. She is Madame Justice Bertha Wilson of the Ontario Court of Appeal. A widely respected lawyer and judge, Scottish-born Madame Justice Wilson was considered a moderate, with a good grasp of social issues. See WILSON, BERTHA.

The Economy. Canada, in the words of Finance Minister Marc Lalonde, experienced in 1982 "the most severe period of economic turmoil since the 1930s." The gross national product declined 6.2 per cent from the second quarter of 1981 to the same period in 1982. It was expected to reach $344.6 billion (Canadian dollars; $1 = U.S. 81 cents as of Dec. 31, 1982) on an annual basis. Although exports were strong, especially to the United States and Japan, low prices for minerals caused havoc in the mining industry. The housing market collapsed, a victim of high mortgage rates, and consumer and business demand was soft. Unemployment reached 12.8 per cent in December. It had been 8.6 a year earlier. The seasonally adjusted number of unemployed in December 1982 came to 1.53 million.

There were some brighter signs, however. The Trudeau government's war against inflation had some success. Inflation abated, standing at 9.8 per cent in November, well below the 13 per cent level of 1981. Interest rates also fell, with the Bank of Canada lending rate reaching 11.6 per cent in mid-October, its lowest level in two years. Mortgage and loan rates showed the same trend.

The Government's Budgets reflected the difficulty of dealing with such a slump in economic

The Ministry of Canada*
In order of precedence

Pierre Elliott Trudeau, prime minister
Allan Joseph MacEachen, deputy prime minister and secretary of state for external affairs
Jean-Luc Pepin, minister of transport
Jean Chrétien, minister of energy, mines, and resources
John Munro, minister of Indian affairs and northern development
H. A. Olson, leader of the government in the Senate
Herbert Gray, president of the Treasury Board
Eugene Francis Whelan, minister of agriculture
André Ouellet, minister of consumer and corporate affairs
Marc Lalonde, minister of finance
Raymond Joseph Perrault, minister of state for fitness and amateur sport
Roméo LeBlanc, minister of public works
John Roberts, minister of the environment
Monique Bégin, minister of national health and welfare
Jean-Jacques Blais, minister of supply and services
Francis Fox, minister of communications
Gilles Lamontagne, minister of national defence
Pierre De Bané, minister of fisheries and oceans
Hazen Argue, minister of state for the Canadian Wheat Board
Gerald Regan, minister of state for international trade
Mark MacGuigan, minister of justice and attorney general of Canada
Robert Kaplan, solicitor general of Canada
James Fleming, minister of state for multiculturalism
William Rompkey, minister of state for small businesses and tourism
Pierre Bussières, minister of national revenue
Charles Lapointe, minister of state for external relations
Edward Lumley, minister of industry, trade, and commerce and minister of regional economic expansion
Yvon Pinard, president of the queen's privy council for Canada
Donald Johnston, minister of state for economic development and minister of state for science and technology
Lloyd Axworthy, minister of employment and immigration
Paul Cosgrove, minister of state for finance
Judy Erola, minister of state for mines
Jacob Austin, minister of state for social development
Charles L. Caccia, minister of labor
Serge Joyal, secretary of state of Canada
W. Bennett Campbell, minister of veterans affairs

*As of Dec. 31, 1982.

Premiers of Canadian Provinces

Province	Premier
Alberta	Peter Lougheed
British Columbia	William R. Bennett
Manitoba	Howard Pawley
New Brunswick	Richard B. Hatfield
Newfoundland	Brian Peckford
Nova Scotia	John Buchanan
Ontario	William G. Davis
Prince Edward Island	James M. Lee
Quebec	René Lévesque
Saskatchewan	Grant Devine

Commissioners of Territories

Northwest Territories	John H. Parker
Yukon Territory	Douglas Bell

Canada's New Constitution

Until April 17, 1982, Canada, unlike the United States, had never had a single document that could be called its Constitution. Instead, the country, which comprises 10 provinces and two territories, had a collection of rules covering the various elements of its government. Some were British laws, such as the British North America Act, which created the Canadian Confederation in 1867 and served as the formal structure of the Constitution. Some were Canadian laws, such as the 1905 acts establishing the provinces of Alberta and Saskatchewan. Other parts were decisions of British and Canadian courts; for example, rulings affirming freedom of religion and discussion. Then there were fundamental customs and conventions, such as one that when a government loses the support of a majority in the legislature, it must either resign or face the people through an election. Canada has relied on British political traditions during its evolution toward independent national status.

Amendments to the British North America Act could be made only by the British Parliament. Although Canada initiated constitutional changes, it was embarrassing for a mature country to have to go to another nation in order to alter its form of government. And though many provinces had been pushing for changes in the federal system, Canadians could not agree among themselves on a formula for change.

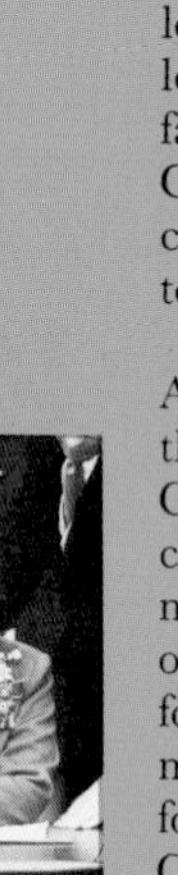
The Constitution is signed.

Prime Minister Pierre Elliott Trudeau, once a professor of constitutional law, broke the impasse in October 1980 when he put forward a plan for a constitutional amending process combined with a charter of fundamental rights. Trudeau's proposal was adopted by Canada's Parliament, whose legal right to initiate changes on behalf of Canada was upheld by the country's Supreme Court in September 1981. Two months later, a historic meeting with the provinces produced a compromise acceptable to all except Quebec. The so-called Constitution Act, 1981, was then duly approved by the British Parliament in London. Amid much pomp and ceremony, the new Constitution—the Constitution Act, 1982—was proclaimed in Ottawa, Ont., by Queen Elizabeth II of Great Britain acting as Queen of Canada on April 17, 1982. After 115 years, the last legal tie with Great Britain was dissolved, and Canada became a fully sovereign state. Queen Elizabeth II, Queen of Canada, remains head of state, with the governor general as her representative in Canada.

The new Constitution contains most of the written parts of the old one, with some important additions. Of prime importance, instead of having to cross the Atlantic Ocean to be altered, the Constitution will hereafter be amended at home.

Trudeau's main interest in changing the Constitution was to see adopted a Charter of Rights and Freedoms. This section sets down, for the first time in Canada's written Constitution, 34 rights and freedoms. They include fundamental freedoms and democratic rights, legal rights, prohibition of racial and other discrimination, official language status for English and French in federal institutions and in New Brunswick, and minority language rights in education depending on a "where numbers warrant" test. These rights are not fully entrenched but can be set aside by Parliament and the provincial legislatures if, for example, they wished to enact "affirmative action" programs.

Other sections of the new Constitution confirm the provinces' control of natural resources and recognize historic rights of aboriginal peoples.

So Canada has a new Constitution—but two controversial areas remain. One is the need for a division of federal and provincial powers that will strike a balance between a strong central economic authority and citizens' loyalties to a closer provincial government. The other area concerns such federal institutions as the Senate and the Supreme Court, where the provinces want to exert a stronger presence. Changing these sections will prove difficult. Still, the Constitution Act, 1982, is a step toward adapting government to changing needs.

David M. L. Farr

activity. After Finance Minister MacEachen's budget of Nov. 12, 1981, failed to inspire confidence, he presented a new budget on June 28, 1982. Its theme was "6 and 5"; that is, wage controls of 6 and 5 per cent for 1982 and 1983, respectively, for all federal employees. The indexing factor for personal income tax exemptions was to be tied to the "6 and 5 formula" rather than to the rate of inflation. Old-age pensions and family allowances were also to be linked to the restraint formula. MacEachen called on the provinces to institute similar restraint measures and asked private industry to adhere voluntarily to the guidelines. Most of the provinces followed his lead.

After Finance Minister Lalonde took over, he presented Parliament with a new economic statement on October 27. Lalonde admitted that conditions had become worse than the government had expected and that the federal deficit, forecast at $19.6 billion, would run to $23.6 billion before year-end. The unemployment insurance fund, facing a staggering deficit, would have to be augmented by premium increases from employees and employers of about 40 per cent. Over the next three years, the government would spend $500-million, which it hoped would establish 60,000 new jobs in the first 18 months. To finance these plans, money would have to come from sums allocated for energy development, defense, and foreign aid. Lalonde promised that for the time being the government would not cut back on social assistance programs.

World Affairs. Canada sided with the United States in imposing sanctions against Poland and the Soviet Union on February 23 to protest the establishment of martial law in Poland. Commercial credits for new Polish purchases in Canada were withdrawn, academic exchanges were suspended, and limits were placed on Polish and Soviet airline flights to Canada. The sanctions did not affect food, Canada's largest export to Poland.

Argentina's use of force in an effort to seize the Falkland Islands, a British dependency in the South Atlantic Ocean, was also met by curbs on imports and exports. On April 12, Canada cut off new credits for exports to Argentina. Not affected were the components for a CANDU nuclear reactor that Canada was building in Argentina. Arms sales to Argentina were banned a week before the commercial embargo was set.

Trudeau paid official visits to Spain and Yugoslavia after he attended the economic summit conference in June at Versailles, France. He also participated in the North Atlantic Treaty Organization meeting in Bonn, West Germany, on June 10, where he criticized allied leaders for failing to confront the real problems of the East-West conflict. He said disarmament talks should not be related to Soviet behavior in other areas.

Members of Parliament pay attention in June as Finance Minister Allan J. MacEachen unveils a new federal budget designed to fight the recession.

The Superpowers, Trudeau told the United Nations (UN) Special Session on Disarmament on June 18, should not impose political conditions on the start of arms talks, nor should they try to use the talks to make strategic gains. He repeated his 1978 call to the UN for a "strategy of suffocation," under which the arms race would be halted in the laboratories where new weapons were conceived.

To many Canadians, Trudeau's words at the UN seemed at variance with his government's decision to allow the testing of unarmed U.S. cruise missiles in northern Alberta, starting in 1984. That plan was announced on March 17, 1982, and permission to test the earth-hugging missile was to be embodied in a bilateral agreement being drafted at year-end. The government defended its decision, saying that testing was in the interest of the military alliance to which Canada owed its defense. But the announcement provoked demonstrations and protest marches in Canada, as well as a bomb blast on October 14 outside the Litton Systems Canada Limited plant, which manufactured guidance devices for the missile. The blast injured seven persons.

The controversial Canadian seal hunt off Newfoundland and Labrador was threatened when the European Parliament, meeting at Strasbourg, France, passed a resolution on March 11 proposing a ban, on moral grounds, of Canadian seal im-

Canada Counts Noses

During 1982, Statistics Canada released final population figures and other results from the 1981 census of Canada. On June 3, 1981, the day the census was conducted, the population of Canada stood at 24,343,181, an increase of 1,350,577 or 5.9 per cent since the 1976 census. (The population was estimated to be 24,541,000 at the end of 1982.) The Census Supplement on the following pages lists official 1981 population figures for provinces and territories, metropolitan areas, and incorporated cities. From 1971 to 1981, the population of Canada grew by 12.9 per cent, the second slowest 10-year growth rate during the 20th century. The only slower growth rate since 1901 occurred during the decade of the Great Depression, the 1930s, when the population increased only 10.9 per cent. The present rate contrasts sharply with the 30.2 per cent growth for 1951-1961 and the 18.3 per cent increase for 1961-1971.

Growth rates for Canada's provinces and territories between 1976 and 1981 showed that the population is moving westward. Alberta, which has most of Canada's oil and gas, and British Columbia, which has the country's mildest climate, recorded growth rates of 21.8 and 11.3 per cent, respectively, for the five-year period, far above the national average of 5.9 per cent. The Atlantic Provinces of New Brunswick, Newfoundland, Nova Scotia, and Prince Edward Island—which have been troubled by economic problems—grew at an average rate of only 2.4 per cent. Canada's largest provinces, Ontario and Quebec, grew by 4.4 and 3.3 per cent, respectively. Manitoba and Saskatchewan grew by 0.5 per cent and 5.1 per cent.

Canada's major metropolitan areas also recorded widely varying rates of growth between 1976 and 1981. Toronto remained the largest metropolitan area, growing by 7 per cent to a population of 2,998,947. The second-largest metropolitan area, Montreal, grew by only 0.9 per cent to 2,828,349. Third-ranked Vancouver was up 8.7 per cent to 1,268,183. The highest metropolitan growth rates were recorded by Edmonton, the capital of Alberta, and Calgary, the center of the province's oil and gas industry. Fifth-ranked Edmonton grew by 18.1 per cent, and sixth-ranked Calgary swelled by 25.7 per cent. Of Canada's 24 census metropolitan areas, eight recorded growth rates below 3 per cent. Sudbury, Ont., recorded an actual population decrease of 4.5 per cent and Windsor, Ont., a loss of 0.6 per cent.

The census figures also revealed that Canada's population is growing older. Between 1976 and 1981, there was a decline of 415,000, or 7 per cent, in the number of children under age 15. At the same time, the number of Canada's elderly, those aged 65 and over, grew by 359,000, or 17.9 per cent—three times the national population growth rate. The median age of all Canadians rose from 27.8 years in 1976 to 29.6 years in 1981. In 1966, the median age was as low as 25.4 years. Statisticians attributed the rise in the median age to a decline in birth rate and to the aging of people born during the post-World War II baby boom that began in the early 1950s.

The 1981 census figures also showed an increase of 65 per cent in the divorced population since 1976. The proportion of married persons declined in every age group, with the most significant decline, 5 per cent, among young adults aged 20-29. The drop in the number of children and the increase in the ranks of senior citizens and divorced or separated persons, many of whom live alone, contributed to a significant decline in the average household size from 3.1 persons in 1976 to 2.9 persons in 1981. Other data showed that in 1981 there were 983 males to every 1,000 females.

Census takers collected information from nearly 100 per cent of Canadian households for the 1981 census. A sample of 20 per cent of the households answered additional questions about education, ethnic origin, jobs, and income. Statistics Canada plans to release data from that sample in 1983.

David Roy

Census Day poster

Census Supplement

This section lists official population figures according to the 1981 census of Canada conducted by Statistics Canada. This page and the following ones give population totals for provinces and territories, metropolitan areas, cities, and other incorporated places. Figures for unincorporated areas were not available for publication.

ALBERTA — Population 2,237,724

METROPOLITAN AREAS

- Calgary* 592,743
- Edmonton 657,057

CITIES, TOWNS, AND VILLAGES

- Acme 457
- Airdrie 8,414
- Alberta Beach 485
- Alix 837
- Alliance 208
- Amisk 196
- Andrew 548
- Arrowwood 156
- Athabasca 1,731
- Barnwell 359
- Barons 318
- Barrhead 3,736
- Bashaw 875
- Bassano 1,200
- Bawlf 350
- Beaumont 2,638
- Beaverlodge 1,937
- Beiseker 580
- Bentley 823
- Berwyn 557
- Big Valley 360
- Birchcliff 55
- Bittern Lake 139
- Black Diamond 1,444
- Blackfalds 1,488
- Blackie 298
- Bon Accord 1,376
- Bonnyville 4,454
- Bonnyville Beach 45
- Botha 172
- Bow Island 1,491
- Bowden 989
- Boyle 638
- Breton 552
- Brooks 9,421
- Bruderheim 1,136
- Burdett 220
- Calgary 592,743
- Calmar 1,003
- Camrose 12,570
- Canmore 3,484
- Carbon 434
- Cardston 3,267
- Carmangay 266
- Caroline 436
- Carstairs 1,587
- Castor 1,123
- Cayley 194
- Cereal 249
- Champion 339
- Chauvin 298
- Chestermere Lake 487
- Chipman 266
- Claresholm 3,493
- Clive 364
- Cluny 92
- Clyde 364
- Coaldale 4,579
- Coalhurst 882
- Cochrane 3,544
- Cold Lake 2,110
- Consort 632
- Coronation 1,309
- Coutts 400
- Cowley 304
- Cremona 382
- Crossfield 1,217
- Crowsnest Pass 7,306
- Crystal Springs 29
- Czar 148
- Daysland 679
- Delburne 574
- Delia 211
- Derwent 142
- Devon 3,885
- Dewberry 163
- Didsbury 3,095
- Donalda 280
- Donnelly 336
- Drayton Valley 5,042
- Drumheller 6,508
- Duchess 429
- Eaglesham 208
- Eckville 870
- Edberg 150
- Edgerton 387
- Edmonton 532,246
- Edmonton Beach 280
- Edson 5,835
- Elk Point 1,022
- Elnora 249
- Empress 200
- Entwistle 462
- Evansburg 779
- Fairview 2,869
- Falher 1,102
- Ferintosh 155
- Foremost 568
- Forestburg 924
- Fort Assiniboine 207
- Fort Macleod 3,139
- Fort McMurray 31,000
- Fort Saskatchewan 12,169
- Fox Creek 1,978
- Gadsby 47
- Galahad 152
- Ghost Lake 42
- Gibbons 2,276
- Girouxville 325
- Gleichen 381
- Glendon 430
- Glenwood 259
- Golden Days 30
- Grand Centre 3,146
- Grande Cache 4,523
- Grande Prairie 24,263
- Grandview 31
- Granum 399
- Grassy Lake 201
- Grimshaw 2,316
- Gull Lake 80
- Hairy Hill 72
- Half Moon Bay 33
- Halkirk 156
- Hanna 2,806
- Hardisty 641
- Hay Lakes 302
- Heisler 212
- High Level 2,194
- High Prairie 2,506
- High River 4,792
- Hill Spring 200
- Hines Creek 575
- Hinton 8,342
- Holden 430
- Hughenden 267
- Hussar 175
- Hythe 639
- Innisfail 5,247
- Innisfree 255
- Irma 474
- Irricana 558
- Irvine 360
- Kapasiwin 22
- Killam 1,005
- Kinuso 285
- Kitscoty 497
- Lac la Biche 2,007
- Lacombe 5,591
- Lakeview 13
- Lamont 1,563
- Lavoy 122
- Leduc 12,471
- Legal 1,022
- Lethbridge 54,072
- Linden 407
- Lloydminster† 8,997
- Lomond 180
- Longview 301
- Lougheed 226
- Magrath 1,576
- Ma-Me-O Beach 82
- Manning 1,173
- Mannville 788
- Marwayne 500
- Mayerthorpe 1,475
- McLennan 1,125
- Medicine Hat 40,380
- Milk River 894
- Millet 1,120
- Milo 100
- Minburn 146
- Mirror 507
- Morinville 4,657
- Morrin 244
- Mundare 604
- Munson 148
- Myrnam 397
- Nampa 334
- Nanton 1,641
- New Norway 291
- New Sarepta 417
- Nobleford 534
- Norglenwold 86
- Okotoks 3,847
- Olds 4,813
- Onoway 621
- Oyen 975
- Paradise Valley 177
- Peace River 5,907
- Pelican Narrows 29
- Penhold 1,531
- Picture Butte 1,404
- Pincher Creek 3,757
- Plamondon 259
- Ponoka 5,221
- Poplar Bay 28
- Provost 1,645
- Radway 192
- Rainbow Lake 504
- Raymond 2,837
- Red Deer 46,393
- Redcliff 3,876
- Redwater 1,932
- Rimbey 1,685
- Rochon Sands 39
- Rocky Mountain House 4,698
- Rockyford 329
- Rosalind 197
- Rosemary 328
- Rumsey 87
- Rycroft 649
- Ryley 483
- St. Albert 31,996
- St. Paul 4,884
- Sangudo 398
- Seba Beach 126
- Sedgewick 879
- Sexsmith 1,180
- Silver Beach 19
- Slave Lake 4,506
- Smoky Lake 1,074
- Spirit River 1,104
- Spruce Grove 10,326
- Standard 379
- Stavely 504
- Stettler 5,136
- Stirling 688
- Stony Plain 4,839
- Strathmore 2,986
- Strome 281
- Sundance Beach 11
- Sundre 1,742
- Swan Hills 2,497
- Sylvan Lake 3,779
- Taber 5,988
- Thorhild 576
- Thorsby 737
- Three Hills 1,787
- Tilley 345
- Tofield 1,504
- Torrington 189
- Trochu 880
- Turner Valley 1,311
- Two Hills 1,193
- Valleyview 2,061
- Vauxhall 1,049
- Vegreville 5,251
- Vermilion 3,766
- Veteran 314
- Viking 1,232
- Vilna 345
- Vulcan 1,489
- Wabamun 662
- Wainwright 4,266
- Wanham 266
- Warburg 501
- Warner 477
- Warspite 96
- Waskatenau 290
- Wembley 1,169
- Westlock 4,424
- Wetaskiwin 9,597
- Whitecourt 5,585
- Wildwood 441
- Willingdon 366
- Youngstown 297

*City and metropolitan area have same boundary and population.
†City on Alberta-Saskatchewan border; total population 15,031.

BRITISH COLUMBIA — Population 2,744,467

METROPOLITAN AREAS

- Vancouver 1,268,183
- Victoria 233,481

REGIONAL DISTRICTS

- Alberni-Clayoquot 32,558
- Bulkley-Nechako 38,309
- Capital 249,473
- Cariboo 59,252
- Central Coast 3,047
- Central Fraser Valley 115,012
- Central Kootenay 52,045
- Central Okanagan 85,237
- Columbia-Shuswap 40,131
- Comox-Strathcona 68,621
- Cowichan Valley 52,701
- Dewdney-Alouette 62,004
- East Kootenay 53,723
- Fraser-Cheam 56,934
- Fraser-Fort George 89,431
- Greater Vancouver 1,169,831
- Kitimat-Stikine 42,400
- Kootenay Boundary 33,232
- Mount Waddington 14,671
- Nanaimo 77,101
- North Okanagan 54,352
- Okanagan-Similkameen 57,185
- Peace River-Liard 55,463
- Powell River 19,364
- Skeena-Queen Charlotte 24,023
- Squamish-Lillooet 18,928
- Stikine 1,953
- Sunshine Coast 15,503
- Thompson-Nicola 101,983

DISTRICT MUNICIPALITIES

- Abbotsford 12,745
- Burnaby 136,494
- Campbell River 15,832
- Central Saanich 9,890
- Chilliwack 40,642
- Coldstream 6,450
- Coquitlam 61,077
- Delta 74,692
- Esquimalt 15,870
- Houston 3,921
- Hudson's Hope 1,365
- Kent 3,394
- Kitimat 12,814
- Langley 44,617
- Mackenzie 5,890
- Maple Ridge 32,232
- Matsqui 42,001
- Mission 20,056
- New Hazelton 712
- North Cowichan 18,210
- North Saanich 6,117
- North Vancouver 65,367
- Oak Bay 16,990
- Okanagan 589
- Peachland 2,865
- Pitt Meadows 6,209
- Port Hardy 5,075
- Powell River 13,423
- Richmond 96,154
- Saanich 78,710
- Salmon Arm 10,780
- Spallumcheen 4,213
- Sparwood 4,157
- Squamish 10,272
- Stewart 1,456
- Summerland 7,473
- Surrey 147,138
- Terrace 10,914
- West Vancouver 35,728
- Whistler 1,365

CITIES, TOWNS, AND VILLAGES

- Alert Bay 626
- Armstrong 2,683
- Ashcroft 2,156
- Belcarra 430
- Burns Lake 1,777
- Cache Creek 1,308
- Castlegar 6,902
- Chase 1,777
- Chetwynd 2,553
- Clinton 804
- Comox 6,607
- Courtenay 8,992
- Cranbrook 15,915
- Creston 4,190
- Cumberland 1,947
- Dawson Creek 11,373
- Duncan 4,228
- Elkford 3,126
- Enderby 1,816
- Fernie 5,444
- Fort Nelson 3,724
- Fort St. James 2,284
- Fort St. John 13,891
- Fraser Lake 1,543
- Fruitvale 1,904
- Gibsons 2,594
- Gold River 2,225
- Golden 3,476
- Grand Forks 3,486
- Granisle 1,430
- Greenwood 856
- Harrison Hot Springs 569
- Hazelton 393
- Hope 3,205
- Houston 3,921
- Invermere 1,969
- Kamloops 64,048
- Kaslo 854
- Kelowna 59,196
- Keremeos 830
- Kimberley 7,375
- Ladysmith 4,558
- Lake Cowichan 2,391
- Langley 15,124
- Lillooet 1,725
- Lion's Bay 1,078
- Logan Lake 2,637
- Lumby 1,266
- Lytton 428
- Masset 1,569
- McBride 641
- Merritt 6,110
- Midway 633
- Montrose 1,229
- Nakusp 1,495
- Nanaimo 47,069
- Nelson 9,143
- New Denver 642
- New Westminster 38,550
- North Vancouver 33,952
- Oliver 1,893
- 100 Mile House 1,925
- Osoyoos 2,738
- Parksville 5,216
- Pemberton 282
- Penticton 23,181
- Port Alberni 19,892
- Port Alice 1,668
- Port Clements 380
- Port Coquitlam 27,535
- Port Edward 989
- Port McNeill 2,474
- Port Moody 14,917
- Pouce Coupe 821
- Prince George 67,559
- Prince Rupert 16,197
- Princeton 3,051
- Qualicum Beach 2,844
- Quesnel 8,240
- Revelstoke 5,544
- Rossland 3,967
- Salmo 1,169
- Sayward 482
- Sechelt 1,096
- Sidney 7,946
- Silverton 280
- Slocan 351
- Smithers 4,570
- Tahsis 1,739
- Taylor 966
- Telkwa 840
- Tofino 705
- Trail 9,599
- Ucluelet 1,593
- Valemount 1,130
- Vancouver 414,281
- Vanderhoof 2,323
- Vernon 19,987
- Victoria 64,379
- Warfield 1,969
- White Rock 13,550
- Williams Lake 8,362
- Zeballos 329

MANITOBA

Population 1,026,241

METROPOLITAN AREA

Winnipeg 584,842

CITIES, TOWNS, AND VILLAGES

Altona 2,757
Arborg 974
Beausejour 2,462
Benito 441
Binscarth. 472
Birtle 887
Boissevain 1,660
Bowsman 454
Brandon 36,242
Carberry 1,510
Carman. 2,408
Cartwright 384
Crystal City 489
Dauphin 8,971
Deloraine 1,136
Dunnottar 287
Elkhorn. 509
Emerson 762
Erickson 540
Ethelbert. 474
Flin Flon* 7,894
Garson. 318
Gilbert Plains 812
Gimli 1,550
Gladstone 964
Glenboro. 741
Grandview. 1,013
Gretna 545
Hamiota 728
Hartney. 490
Killarney 2,342
Lac du Bonnet. . . . 985
Leaf Rapids 2,356
MacGregor 795
Manitou 861
McCreary 618
Melita 1,156
Minitonas 628
Minnedosa. 2,637
Morden. 4,579
Morris 1,570
Napinka 132
Neepawa. 3,425
Niverville. 1,329
Notre Dame de Lourdes 627
Oak Lake 369
Pas, The 6,390
Pilot Mound 838
Pinawa 2,011
Plum Coulee. 592
Portage la Prairie 13,086
Powerview. 691
Rapid City 431
Rivers 1,107
Riverton 657
Roblin 1,953
Rossburn. 696
Russell 1,660
St. Claude 592
St. Lazare 414
St. Pierre-Jolys . . . 919
Ste. Anne 1,338
Ste. Rose du Lac . 1,090
Selkirk 10,037
Shoal Lake. 835
Snow Lake. 1,853
Somerset 596
Souris 1,731
Steinbach 6,676
Stonewall 2,210
Swan River 3,782
Teulon 925
Thompson. 14,288
Treherne. 743
Virden 2,940
Waskada. 239
Wawanesa. 492
Winkler. 5,046
Winnipeg 564,473
Winnipeg Beach. . . 565
Winnipegosis 855

*City on Manitoba-Saskatchewan border; total population 8,261.

NEW BRUNSWICK

Population 696,403

METROPOLITAN AREA

Saint John. . . . 114,048

COUNTIES

Albert. 23,632
Carleton 24,659
Charlotte. 26,571
Gloucester. 86,156
Kent 30,799
Kings 51,114
Madawaska 36,432
Northumberland 54,134
Queens. 12,485
Restigouche 40,593
St. John 86,148
Sunbury 21,012
Victoria. 20,815
Westmorland . . 107,640
York 74,213

CITIES, TOWNS, AND VILLAGES

Alma 329
Aroostook 403
Atholville. 1,694
Baker Brook 527
Balmoral. 1,823
Bas-Caraquet . . . 1,859
Bath 794
Bathurst 15,705
Belledune 690
Beresford 3,652
Bertrand 1,268
Blacks Harbour . . 1,356
Blackville. 892
Bristol 824
Buctouche 2,476
Cambridge-Narrows 433
Campbellton. . . . 9,818
Canterbury. 474
Cap-Pelé 2,199
Caraquet. 4,315
Centreville 577
Charlo 1,603
Chatham 6,779
Chipman 1,829
Clair 915
Dalhousie 4,958
Darlington 749
Dieppe 8,511
Doaktown 1,009
Dorchester. 1,101
Douglastown . . . 1,091
Drummond 849
East Riverside-Kinghurst 989
Edmundston. . . .12,044
Eel River Crossing. 1,431
Fairvale. 3,960
Florenceville. 709
Fredericton 43,723
Fredericton Junction. 711
Gagetown 618
Gondola Point. . . 3,076
Grand Bay 3,173
Grand Falls 6,203
Grand Harbour . . . 614
Grande-Anse 817
Hampton. 3,141
Hartland 846
Harvey 356
Hillsborough. . . . 1,239
Jacquet River 778
Kedgwick 1,222
Lac Baker 292
Lamèque. 1,571
Loggieville. 781
McAdam 1,857
Meductic. 234
Millville. 309
Minto. 3,399
Moncton 54,743
Nackawic. 1,357
Neguac. 1,755
Nelson-Miramichi 1,452
Newcastle 6,284
Nigadoo 1,075
North Head 661
Norton 1,372
Oromocto 9,064
Paquetville. 626
Perth Andover. . . 1,872
Petit-Rocher 1,860
Petitcodiac. 1,401
Plaster Rock 1,222
Pointe-Verte 1,335
Port Elgin 504
Quispamsis 6,022
Renforth 1,490
Rexton 928
Richibucto 1,722
Riverside-Albert. . . 478
Riverview 14,907
Rivière-Verte. . . . 1,054
Rogersville. 1,237
Rothesay. 1,764
Sackville 5,654
St.-André. 385
St. Andrews 1,760
St.-Antoine 1,217
St.-Basile. 3,214
St.-François-de-Madawaska 753
St. George 1,163
St.-Hilaire 244
St.-Jacques 2,297
St. John 80,521
St.-Joseph 630
St.-Léolin. 799
St. Leonard 1,566
St.-Louis-de-Kent 1,166
St. Martins. 530
St.-Quentin 2,334
St. Stephen 5,120
Ste.-Anne-de-Madawaska . . . 1,332
Salisbury. 1,672
Seal Cove 548
Shediac 4,285
Sheila 1,172
Shippegan. 2,471
Stanley. 432
Sussex 3,972
Sussex Corner. . . 1,023
Tide Head 952
Tracadie 2,452
Tracy 636
Verrett 637
Westfield. 1,100
Woodstock. 4,649

NEWFOUNDLAND

Population 567,681

METROPOLITAN AREA

St. John's 154,820

CITIES, TOWNS, AND OTHER MUNICIPALITIES

Appleton. 420
Arnold's Cove . . . 1,124
Avondale. 890
Badger 1,090
Badger's Quay-Valleyfield-Pool's Island . . 1,566
Baie Verte 2,491
Bay de Verde 786
Bay l'Argent 483
Bay Roberts 4,512
Bayview 625
Belleoram 565
Birchy Bay 707
Bishop's Falls . . . 4,395
Bonavista 4,460
Botwood 4,074
Branch 462
Brigus 898
Buchans 1,655
Burgeo 2,504
Burin 2,904
Burnt Islands 991
Campbellton. 703
Carbonear 5,335
Carmanville 966
Cartwright 658
Catalina 1,162
Centreville 604
Chance Cove 498
Change Islands . . . 580
Channel-Port aux Basques 5,988
Chapel Arm 689
Clarenville 2,878
Clarke's Beach. . . 1,009
Colliers. 819
Come-by-Chance . . 337
Conception Bay South 10,856
Conception Harbour 917
Conne River 588
Cook's Harbour . . . 388
Cormack 788
Corner Brook . . .24,339
Cottlesville. 409
Cow Head 695
Cox's Cove. 980
Cupids 706
Daniel's Harbour . . 614
Deer Lake 4,348
Dover. 925
Dunville 1,817
Durrell 1,145
Eastport 597
Elliston. 527
Embree. 846
Englee 998
Flatrock. 808
Fleur de Lys 616
Flower's Cove 459
Fogo 1,105
Fortune. 2,473
Fox Cove-Mortier . . 469
Freshwater. 1,276
Gambo 2,932
Gander. 10,404
Garnish. 761
Gaultois 558
Glenwood 1,129
Glovertown 2,165
Goulds 4,242
Grand Bank 3,901
Grand Falls 8,765
Greenspond 423
Halfway Point-Benoit's Cove-John's Beach . . 2,214
Hampden 838
Hant's Harbour . . . 542
Happy Valley-Goose Bay. . . . 7,103
Harbour Breton . . 2,464
Harbour Grace . . 2,988
Harbour Main-Chapel Cove-Lakeview 1,303
Hare Bay. 1,520
Hawke's Bay. 553
Heart's Content . . . 625
Heart's Delight-Islington 899
Heart's Desire 416
Hogan's Pond 129
Holyrood. 1,789
Hopedale. 425
Howley 456
Isle aux Morts . . . 1,238
Jerseyside 641
Joe Batt's Arm-Barr'd Islands. 1,155
King's Point 825
Kippens 1,219
Labrador City . . .11,538
Lamaline. 548
L'Anse-au-Loup . . . 589
La Scie 1,422
Lawn 999
Lawrence Pond 46
Lewisporte. 3,963
Little Bay Islands . . 407
Little Burnt Bay . . . 482
Little Catalina 750
Long Harbour-Mount Arlington Heights 660
Lumsden. 645
Main Brook 514
Marystown 6,299
Massey Drive 409
Middle Arm, Green Bay. 575
Milltown-Head of Bay d'Espoir 1,376
Mount Carmel-Mitchell's Brook-St. Catherine's . . 699
Mount Moriah. . . . 751
Mount Pearl 11,543
Musgrave Harbour 1,554
Musgravetown . . . 635
Nain 938
New Perlican 350
Newtown 511
Norman's Cove-Long Cove 1,152
Norris Arm. 1,216
Norris Point 1,033
North West River . . 515
Northern Arm-Exploits 298
Old Perlican 709
Pacquet 395
Paradise 2,861
Parson's Pond. . . . 605
Pasadena 2,685
Peterview 1,119
Petty Harbour-Maddox Cove 853
Placentia 2,204
Point Leamington. . 848
Port au Choix . . . 1,311
Port au Port West-Aguathuna-Felix Cove. 938
Port Blandford. . . . 702
Port Rexton 489
Port Saunders. . . . 769
Port Union. 671
Portugal Cove . . . 2,361
Pouch Cove 1,522
Ramea 1,386
Renews-Cappahayden . . . 578
Robert's Arm . . . 1,005
Roddickton 1,142
Rose Blanche-Harbour Le Cou. 975
Rushoon 520
St. Alban's. 1,968
St. Anthony 3,107
St. Bernard's. 696
St. George's 1,756
St. Jacques-Coomb's Cove 1,048
St. John's 83,770
St. John's Area . .24,485
St. Lawrence. . . . 2,012
St. Pauls 454
St. Phillips 1,365
St. Thomas 448
St. Vincent's-St. Stephen-Peter's River . . . 796
Salmon Cove 786
Salvage 244
Seal Cove 751
Seldom-Little Seldom 560
Shoal Harbour. . . 1,000
Small Point-Broad Cove-Blackhead-Adams Cove 539
South Brook, Hall's Bay. 786
South River 645
Southern Harbour . 772
Spaniard's Bay . . 2,125
Springdale. 3,501
Stephenville 8,876
Stephenville Crossing. 2,172
Summerford. . . . 1,198
Summerside. 848
Sunnyside 703
Terrenceville. 796
Tilton. 575
Torbay 3,394
Trepassey 1,473
Trinity, Bonavista Bay. 522
Triton. 1,235
Trout River. 759
Twillingate. 1,506
Upper Island Cove 2,025
Victoria. 1,870
Wabana 4,254
Wabush 3,155
Wareham 458
Wedgewood Park 1,226
Wesleyville 1,225
Whitbourne 1,233
Windsor 5,747
Winterton 753

NORTHWEST TERRITORIES

Population 45,741

Fort Simpson 980
Fort Smith 2,298
Frobisher Bay . . . 2,333
Hay River 2,863
Inuvik. 3,147
Pine Point 1,861
Yellowknife 9,483

NOVA SCOTIA

Population 847,442

METROPOLITAN AREA

Halifax 277,727

COUNTIES

Annapolis 22,522
Antigonish. 18,110
Cape Breton . . . 127,035
Colchester 43,224
Cumberland 35,231
Digby. 21,689
Guysborough . . .12,752
Halifax 288,126
Hants. 33,121
Inverness 22,337
Kings 49,739
Lunenburg. 45,746
Pictou 50,350
Queens. 13,126
Richmond 12,284
Shelburne 17,328
Victoria. 8,432
Yarmouth 26,290

CITIES AND TOWNS

Amherst 9,684
Annapolis Royal. . . 631
Antigonish. 5,205
Bedford 6,777
Berwick. 1,699
Bridgetown 1,047
Bridgewater 6,669
Canso 1,255
Clark's Harbour . . 1,059
Dartmouth 62,277
Digby. 2,558
Dominion 2,856
Glace Bay 21,466
Halifax 114,594
Hantsport 1,395
Kentville 4,974
Liverpool. 3,304
Lockeport 929
Louisbourg 1,410
Lunenburg. 3,014
Mahone Bay. . . . 1,228
Middleton 1,834
Mulgrave. 1,099
New Glasgow . . .10,464
New Waterford . . 8,808
North Sydney . . . 7,820
Oxford 1,470
Parrsboro 1,799
Pictou 4,628
Port Hawkesbury. . . 3,850
Shelburne 2,303
Springhill 4,896
Stellarton 5,435
Stewiacke 1,174
Sydney. 29,444
Sydney Mines. . . 8,501
Trenton. 3,154
Truro 12,552
Westville. 4,522
Windsor 3,646
Wolfville 3,235
Yarmouth 7,475

ONTARIO

Population 8,625,107

METROPOLITAN AREAS

Hamilton. 542,095
Kitchener. 287,801
London. 283,668
Oshawa 154,217
Ottawa-Hull . . . 717,978 (547,399 in Ontario; 170,579 in Quebec)
St. Catharines-Niagara 304,353
Sudbury 149,923
Thunder Bay. . . 121,379
Toronto 2,998,947
Windsor 246,110

COUNTIES

Brant 104,427
Bruce. 60,020
Dufferin 31,145
Dundas. 18,946
Elgin 69,707
Essex. 312,476
Frontenac 108,133
Glengarry 20,254
Grenville. 27,176
Grey 73,824
Haliburton. 11,361
Hastings 106,883
Huron 56,127
Kent 107,022
Lambton 123,445
Lanark 45,676
Leeds. 53,765
Lennox and Addington. . . .33,040
Middlesex 318,184
Northumberland 64,966
Oxford 85,920
Perth 66,096
Peterborough . . 102,452
Prescott 30,365
Prince Edward. . .22,336
Renfrew 87,484
Russell 22,142
Simcoe. 225,071
Stormont. 61,927
Victoria. 47,854
Wellington. . . . 129,432

DISTRICTS

Algoma. 133,533
Cochrane. 96,875
Kenora 59,421
Manitoulin 11,001
Nipissing. 80,268
Parry Sound. . . .33,528
Rainy River 22,798
Sudbury 27,068
Thunder Bay. . . 153,997
Timiskaming. . . .41,288

REGIONAL MUNICIPALITIES

Durham 283,639
Haldimand-Norfolk. 89,456
Halton 253,883
Hamilton-Wentworth . . 411,445
Niagara. 368,288
Ottawa-Carleton 546,849
Peel. 490,731
Sudbury 159,779
Waterloo. 305,496
York 252,053

DISTRICT MUNICIPALITY

Muskoka 38,370

METROPOLITAN MUNICIPALITY

Toronto 2,137,395

CITIES, TOWNS, AND VILLAGES

Ailsa Craig. 765
Ajax. 25,475
Alexandria. 3,271
Alfred. 1,054
Alliston. 4,712
Almonte 3,855
Alvinston. 736
Amherstburg . . . 5,685
Ancaster 14,428
Arkona 473
Arnprior 5,828
Arthur 1,700
Athens 948
Aurora 16,267
Aylmer 5,254
Bancroft 2,329
Barrie. 38,423
Barry's Bay 1,216
Bath 1,071
Bayfield 649
Beachburg 682
Beeton 1,989
Belle River 3,568
Belleville. 34,881
Belmont 831
Blenheim. 4,044
Blind River. 3,444
Bloomfield. 718
Blyth 926
Bobcaygeon 1,625
Bothwell 915
Bracebridge 9,063
Bradford 7,370
Braeside 492
Brampton 149,030
Brantford. 74,315
Brighton 3,147
Brockville 19,896
Bruce Mines. 635
Brussels 962
Burk's Falls 922
Burlington 114,853
Cache Bay 665
Caledon 26,645
Cambridge. 77,183
Campbellford . . . 3,409
Capreol. 3,845
Cardinal 1,753
Carleton Place. . . 5,626
Casselman. 1,675
Chalk River 1,010
Charlton 213
Chatham 40,952
Chatsworth 383
Chesley. 1,840
Chesterville 1,430
Clifford 645
Clinton 3,081
Cobalt 1,759
Cobden. 997
Cobourg 11,385
Cochrane. 4,848
Colborne. 1,796
Coldwater 964
Collingwood. . . .12,064
Cookstown. 918
Cornwall 46,144
Creemore 1,182
Deep River. 5,095
Deloro 235
Deseronto 1,740
Drayton 809
Dresden 2,550
Dryden 6,640
Dundalk 1,250
Dundas. 19,586
Dunnville. 11,353
Durham 2,458
Dutton 1,115
East Gwillimbury. . .12,565
Eganville. 1,245
Elliot Lake 16,723
Elmvale 1,183
Elora 2,666
Englehart 1,689
Erie Beach 244
Erieau 430
Erin. 2,313
Espanola. 5,836
Essex. 6,295
Exeter 3,732
Fenelon Falls . . . 1,701
Fergus 6,064
Finch 353
Flesherton 565
Forest 2,671
Fort Erie 24,096
Fort Frances 8,906
Frankford 1,919
Gananoque 4,863
Geraldton 2,956
Glencoe 1,694
Gloucester. 72,859
Goderich. 7,322
Gore Bay. 777
Grand Bend 680
Grand Valley. . . . 1,226
Gravenhurst. . . . 8,532
Grimsby 15,797
Guelph 71,207
Haileybury 4,925
Haldimand. 16,866
Halton Hills 35,190
Hamilton. 306,434
Hanover 6,316
Harriston. 1,954
Harrow 2,274
Hastings 975
Havelock. 1,385
Hawkesbury 9,877
Hearst 5,533
Hensall 973
Hepworth 393
Highgate 435
Hilton Beach. 228
Huntsville 11,467
Ingersoll 8,494
Iron Bridge. 821
Iroquois 1,211
Iroquois Falls . . . 6,339
Kanata 19,728
Kapuskasing. . . .12,014
Kearney 538
Keewatin. 1,863
Kemptville 2,362
Kenora 9,817
Killaloe Station . . . 634
Kincardine 5,778
Kingston 52,616
Kingsville 5,134
Kirkland Lake . . .12,219
Kitchener. 139,734
Lakefield 2,374
Lanark 753
Lancaster 637
Latchford. 397
Leamington 12,528
Lincoln 14,196
Lindsay. 13,596
Lion's Head 467
Listowel 5,026
Little Current . . . 1,507
London. 254,280
L'Orignal 1,819
Lucan. 1,616
Lucknow 1,088
Madoc 1,249
Magnetawan 208
Markdale. 1,289
Markham. 77,037
Marmora. 1,304
Massey. 1,274
Mattawa 2,652
Maxville 836
Meaford 4,367
Merrickville 984
Midland 12,132
Mildmay 928
Millbrook. 927
Milton 28,067
Milverton 1,463
Mississauga . . . 315,056
Mitchell 2,777
Morrisburg 2,308
Mount Forest . . . 3,474
Nanticoke 19,816
Napanee 4,803
Nepean. 84,361
Neustadt. 511
New Liskeard . . . 5,551
Newboro. 260
Newburgh 617
Newbury. 441
Newcastle 32,229
Newmarket 29,753
Niagara Falls . . .70,960
Niagara-on-the-Lake 12,186
Nickel Centre . . .12,318
North Bay 51,268
North York. . . . 559,521
Norwood. 1,278
Oakville 75,773
Oil Springs. 627
Omemee 819
Onaping Falls . . . 6,198
Orangeville 13,740
Orillia. 23,955
Oshawa 117,519
Ottawa 295,163
Owen Sound . . .19,883
Paisley 1,039
Palmerston 1,989
Paris 7,485
Parkhill. 1,358
Parry Sound. . . . 6,124
Pelham. 11,104
Pembroke 14,026
Penetanguishene 5,315
Perth 5,655
Petawawa 5,520
Peterborough . . .60,620
Petrolia. 4,234
Pickering. 37,754
Picton 4,361
Plantagenet 870
Point Edward . . . 2,383
Port Burwell 655
Port Colborne . . .19,225
Port Elgin 6,131
Port Hope 9,992
Port McNicoll . . . 1,883
Port Stanley 1,891
Powassan 1,169
Prescott 4,670
Rainy River 1,061
Rayside-Balfour. 15,017
Renfrew 8,283
Richmond Hill. . . .37,778
Ridgetown. 3,062
Ripley 591
Rockcliffe Park. . . 1,869
Rockland. 3,961
Rodney. 1,007
Rosseau 218
St. Catharines . . 124,018
St. Clair Beach. . . 2,845
St. Isidore de Prescott 746
St. Mary's 4,883
St. Thomas 28,165
Sarnia 50,892
Sault Ste. Marie. 82,697
Seaforth 2,114
Shallow Lake 418
Shelburne 2,862
Simcoe. 14,326
Sioux Lookout. . . 3,074
Smiths Falls 8,831
Smooth Rock Falls 2,352
South River 1,109
Southampton . . . 2,830
Springfield. 555
Stayner. 2,530
Stirling 1,638
Stoney Creek . . .36,762
Stratford 26,262
Strathroy. 8,748
Sturgeon Falls. . . 6,045
Sturgeon Point 63
Sudbury 91,829
Sundridge 734
Tara. 687
Tecumseh 6,364
Teeswater 1,026
Thamesville 961
Thedford. 694
Thessalon 1,620
Thornbury 1,435
Thornloe. 170
Thorold. 15,412
Thunder Bay. . . 112,486
Tilbury 4,298
Tillsonburg 10,487
Timmins 46,114
Tiverton 806
Toronto 599,217
Tottenham. 3,022
Trenton. 15,085
Trout Creek 652
Tweed 1,574
Valley East. 20,433
Vanier 18,792
Vankleek Hill. . . . 1,774
Vaughan 29,674
Victoria Harbour . 1,125
Vienna 369
Walden. 10,139
Walkerton 4,682
Wallaceburg 11,506
Wardsville 450
Wasaga Beach . . 4,705
Waterloo. 49,428
Watford 1,402
Webbwood 519
Welland 45,448
Wellington. 1,082
West Lorne 1,258
Westport. 621
Wheatley. 1,638
Whitby 36,698
Whitechurch-Stouffville 13,557
Wiarton 2,074
Winchester 2,001
Windsor 192,083
Wingham 2,897
Woodstock. 26,603
Woodville 575
Wyoming 1,682
Zurich 795

PRINCE EDWARD ISLAND

Population 122,506

COUNTIES

Name	Population
Kings	19,215
Prince	42,821
Queens	60,470

CITIES, TOWNS, AND VILLAGES

Name	Population
Abrams Village	351
Alberton	1,020
Bedeque	162
Borden	485
Bunbury	1,024
Cardigan	321
Central Bedeque	185
Charlottetown	15,282
Cornwall	1,838
Crapaud	303
East Royalty	1,696
Georgetown	737
Hills Borough Park	1,227
Hunter River	322
Kensington	1,143
Kinkora	283
Miminigash	304
Miscouche	752
Montague	1,957
Morell	347
Mount Stewart	364
Murray Harbour	443
Murray River	439
North Rustico	688
O'Leary	736
Parkdale	2,018
St. Eleanors	2,716
St. Louis	156
St. Peters	335
Sherwood	5,681
Souris	1,413
Southport	1,313
Summerside	7,828
Tignish	982
Tyne Valley	182
Victoria	163
Wellington	376
West Royalty	1,686
Wilmot	1,563

QUEBEC

Population 6,438,403

METROPOLITAN AREAS

Name	Population
Chicoutimi-Jonquière	135,172
Montreal	2,828,349
Ottawa-Hull (547,399 in Ontario; 170,579 in Quebec)	717,978
Quebec	576,075

COUNTIES

Name	Population
Abitibi	93,529
Argenteuil	32,454
Arthabaska	59,277
Bagot	26,840
Beauce	73,427
Beauharnois	54,034
Bellechasse	23,559
Berthier	31,096
Bonaventure	40,487
Brome	17,436
Chambly	307,090
Champlain	119,595
Charlevoix-Est	17,448
Charlevoix-Ouest	14,172
Châteauguay	59,968
Chicoutimi	174,441
Compton	20,536
Deux-Montagnes	71,252
Dorchester	33,949
Drummond	69,770
Frontenac	26,814
Gaspé-Est	41,173
Gaspé-Ouest	18,943
Gatineau	54,229
Hull	131,213
Huntingdon	16,953
Iberville	23,180
Ile-de-Montréal	1,760,122
Ile-Jésus	268,335
Iles-de-la-Madeleine	14,130
Joliette	60,384
Kamouraska	28,642
Labelle	34,395
Lac-Saint-Jean-Est	47,891
Lac-Saint-Jean-Ouest	62,952
Laprairie	105,962
L'Assomption	109,705
Lévis	94,104
L'Islet	22,062
Lotbinière	29,563
Maskinongé	20,763
Matane	29,955
Matapédia	23,715
Mégantic	57,892
Missisquoi	36,161
Montcalm	27,557
Montmagny	25,678
Montmorency I	23,048
Montmorency II (Ile-d'Orléans)	6,436
Napierville	13,562
Nicolet	33,513
Papineau	37,975
Pontiac	20,283
Portneuf	58,843
Québec	458,980
Richelieu	53,058
Richmond	40,871
Rimouski	69,099
Rivière-du-Loup	41,250
Rouville	42,391
Saguenay	115,881
Saint-Hyacinthe	55,888
Saint-Jean	55,576
Saint-Maurice	107,703
Shefford	70,733
Sherbrooke	115,983
Soulanges	15,429
Stanstead	38,186
Témiscamingue	52,570
Témiscouata	19,479
Terrebonne	193,865
Territoire-du-Nouveau-Quebec	41,140
Vaudreuil	50,043
Verchères	63,353
Wolfe	15,635
Yamaska	14,797

CITIES, TOWNS, AND VILLAGES

Name	Population
Abercorn	320
Acton Vale	4,371
Akulivik	256
Albanel	992
Alma	26,322
Amos	9,421
Amqui	4,048
Ancienne-Lorette	12,935
Andréville	379
Ange-Gardien	495
Angliers	263
Anjou	37,346
Annaville	712
Armagh	902
Arthabaska	6,827
Asbestos	7,967
Aston-Jonction	236
Aupaluk	102
Ayer's Cliff	810
Aylmer	26,695
Baie-Comeau	12,866
Baie-de-Shawinigan	503
Baie-d'Urfé	3,674
Baie-St.-Paul	3,961
Baie-Trinité	749
Baieville	390
Barkmere	51
Barraute	1,273
Beaconsfield	19,613
Beauceville	4,302
Beauharnois	7,025
Beaulac	453
Beauport	60,447
Beaupré	2,740
Bécancour	10,247
Bedford	2,832
Beebe Plain	1,072
Belleterre	475
Beloeil	17,540
Bernierville	2,120
Berthierville	4,049
Bic	2,994
Bishopton	364
Black Lake	5,148
Blainville	14,682
Bois-des-Filion	4,943
Boisbriand	13,471
Boucherville	29,704
Brome	288
Bromont	2,731
Bromptonville	3,035
Brossard	52,232
Brownsburg	2,875
Bryson	809
Buckingham	7,992
Cabano	3,291
Cadillac	840
Calumet	729
Campbell's Bay	1,007
Candiac	8,502
Cap-à-l'Aigle	819
Cap-aux-Meules	1,507
Cap-Chat	3,464
Cap-de-la-Madeleine	32,626
Carignan	4,544
Carillon	302
Carleton	2,710
Causapscal	2,501
Chambly	12,190
Champlain	496
Chandler	3,946
Chapais	3,119
Chapeau	450
Charlemagne	4,827
Charlesbourg	68,326
Charny	8,240
Châteauguay	36,928
Château-Richer	3,628
Chénéville	633
Chesterville	207
Chibougamau	10,732
Chicoutimi	60,064
Chute-aux-Outardes	2,280
Clarenceville	280
Clermont	3,621
Coaticook	6,271
Compton	728
Contrecoeur	5,449
Cookshire	1,480
Coteau-du-Lac	1,247
Coteau-Landing	1,386
Côte-St.-Luc	27,531
Cowansville	12,240
Crabtree	1,950
Danville	2,200
Daveluyville	1,257
Deauville	942
Dégelis	3,477
De Grasse	278
Delson	4,935
Desbiens	1,541
Deschaillons	312
Deschaillons-sur-St.-Laurent	950
Deschambault	977
Deux-Montagnes	9,944
Disraëli	3,181
Dixville	505
Dolbeau	8,766
Dollard-des-Ormeaux	39,940
Donnacona	5,731
Dorion	5,749
Dorval	17,722
Drummondville	27,347
Drummondville-Sud	9,220
Dunham	2,887
Duparquet	581
East Angus	4,016
East Broughton Station	1,302
East Farnham	453
Eastman	612
Estérel	68
Evain	2,657
Farnham	6,498
Ferme-Neuve	2,266
Fermont	4,216
Forestville	4,271
Fort-Coulonge	1,616
Fortierville	509
Fossambault-sur-le-Lac	570
Frelighsburg	292
Gagnon	3,402
Gaspé	17,261
Gatineau	74,988
Godbout	533
Gracefield	869
Granby	38,069
Grande-Rivière	4,420
Grandes-Bergeronnes	748
Grand-Mère	15,442
Greenfield Park	18,527
Grenville	1,417
Hampstead	7,598
Hatley	219
Hauterive	13,995
Hébertville-Station	1,442
Hemmingford	737
Henryville	595
Howick	639
Hudson	4,414
Hull	56,225
Huntingdon	3,018
Iberville	8,587
Ile-Cadieux	99
Ile-D'Entrée	167
Ile-Perrot	5,945
Inukjuak	661
Inverness	329
Joliette	16,987
Jonquière	60,354
Kamouraska	442
Kangiqsualujjuaq	149
Kangiqsujuaq	229
Kingsbury	193
Kingsey Falls	818
Kirkland	10,476
Kuujjuaq	805
Kuujjuarapik	632
La Baie	20,935
Lac-au-Saumon	1,332
Lac-Bouchette	1,703
Lac-Brome	4,319
Lac-Carré	717
Lac-Delage	259
Lac-des-Ecorces	766
Lac-Etchemin	2,729
Lachenaie	8,631
Lachine	37,521
Lachute	11,729
Lac-Mégantic	6,119
Lacolle	1,319
Lac-Poulin	14
Lac-St.-Joseph	75
Lac-Sergent	138
Lafontaine	4,799
La Guadeloupe	1,692
La Malbaie	4,030
L'Annonciation	2,384
La Patrie	413
La Pêche	4,977
La Pérade	1,039
La Pocatière	4,560
La Prairie	10,627
La Reine	333
Larouche	969
LaSalle	76,299
La Sarre	8,861
L'Assomption	4,844
La Station-du-Coteau	892
Laterrière	788
La Tuque	11,556
Laurentides	1,947
Laurier-Station	1,657
Laurierville	939
Lauzon	13,362
Laval	268,335
Lavaltrie	2,422
Lawrenceville	562
Lebel-sur-Quévillon	3,681
Leclercville	352
LeMoyne	6,137
Lennoxville	3,922
L'Epiphanie	2,971
Léry	2,239
Les Becquets	525
Les Cèdres	680
Lévis	17,895
Linière	1,168
L'Islet	1,070
L'Islet-sur-Mer	774
L'Isle-Verte	1,142
Longueuil	124,320
Loretteville	15,060
Lorraine	6,881
Lorrainville	1,144
Lotbinière	1,123
Louiseville	3,735
Luceville	1,524
Macamic	1,791
Magog	13,604
Malartic	4,833
Maniwaki	5,424
Manseau	626
Maple Grove	2,009
Marbleton	522
Marieville	4,877
Marsoui	529
Mascouche	20,345
Maskinongé	1,005
Masson	4,264
Massueville	671
Matagami	3,794
Matane	13,612
McMasterville	3,612
Melbourne	555
Melocheville	1,892
Mercier	6,352
Métabetchouan	3,406
Métis-sur-Mer	194
Mirabel	14,080
Mistassini	6,682
Mont-Gabriel	31
Mont-Joli	6,359
Mont-Laurier	8,405
Mont-Royal	19,247
Mont-St.-Grégoire	740
Mont-St.-Hilaire	10,066
Mont-St.-Pierre	351
Montebello	1,229
Montmagny	12,405
Montreal	980,354
Montréal-Est	3,778
Montréal-Nord	94,914
Montréal-Ouest	5,514
Murdochville	3,396
Napierville	2,343
Neuville	996
New Glasgow	163
New Richmond	4,257
Newport	792
Nicolet	4,880
Noranda	8,767
Norbertville	295
Normandin	4,041
North Hatley	689
Notre-Dame-du-Bon-Conseil	1,089
Notre-Dame-du-Lac	2,258
Omerville	1,398
Ormstown	1,659
Otterburn Park	4,268
Ouiatchouan	1,318
Outremont	24,338
Papineauville	1,481
Parent	439
Percé	4,839
Philipsburg	306
Pierrefonds	38,390
Pierreville	1,212
Pincourt	8,750
Plessisville	7,249
Pohénégamook	3,702
Pointe-au-Pic	1,054
Pointe-aux-Outardes	1,056
Pointe-aux-Trembles	36,270
Pointe-Calumet	2,935
Pointe-Claire	24,571
Pointe-des-Cascades	692
Pointe-du-Moulin	249
Pointe-Fortune	369
Pointe-Lebel	1,573
Pont-Rouge	3,580
Pontiac	3,658
Port-Cartier	8,119
Portage-du-Fort	360
Portneuf	1,333
Price	2,273
Princeville	4,023
Quaqtaq	145
Quebec	166,474
Rawdon	2,958
Repentigny	34,419
Richelieu	1,832
Richmond	3,568
Rigaud	2,268
Rimouski	29,120
Rimouski-Est	2,506
Ripon	620
Rivière-à-Pierre	690
Rivière-Beaudette	224
Rivière-du-Loup	13,459
Robertsonville	1,987
Roberval	11,429
Rock Island	1,179
Rosemère	7,778
Rougemont	972
Rouyn	17,224
Roxboro	6,292
Roxton Falls	1,245
St.-Agapitville	2,954
St.-Alban	673
St.-Alexandre	446
St.-Alexis	482
St.-Ambroise	3,606
St.-André-du-Lac-St.-Jean	582
St.-André-Avellin	1,312
St.-André-Est	1,293
St.-Anselme	1,808
St.-Antoine	7,012
St.-Basile-le-Grand	7,658
St.-Basile-Sud	1,719
St.-Bernard	585
St.-Boniface-de-Shawinigan	3,164
St.-Bruno	2,580
St.-Bruno-de-Montarville	22,880
St.-Casimir	1,133
St.-Casimir-Est	362
St.-Césaire	2,935
St.-Charles	1,019
St.-Charles-des-Grondines	364
St.-Charles-sur-Richelieu	401
St.-Chrysostome	1,018
St.-Constant	9,938
St.-Cyrille	1,041
St.-Damase	1,203
St.-David-de-l'Auberivière	5,380
St.-Denis	861
St.-Dominique	2,068
St.-Elzéar	743
St. Emile	5,216
St.-Ephrem-de-Tring	973
St.-Eustache	29,716
St.-Félicien	9,058
St.-Félix-de-Valois	1,462
St.-Flavien	734
St.-François-du-Lac	942
St.-Gabriel	3,161
St.-Gédéon	1,569
St.-Georges	3,344
St.-Georges	10,342
St.-Georges-de-Cacouna	1,160
St.-Georges-de-Windsor	307
St.-Georges-Ouest	6,378
St.-Gérard	544
St.-Germain-de-Grantham	1,373
St.-Grégoire-de-Greenlay	637
St.-Guillaume	830
St.-Herménégilde	151
St.-Hubert	60,573
St.-Hugues	808
St.-Hyacinthe	38,246
St.-Isidore	811
St.-Jacques	2,152
St.-Jean	35,640
St.-Jean-Chrysostome	6,930
St.-Jean-de-Boischatel	3,345
St.-Jérôme	25,123
St.-Joseph-de-Beauce	3,216
St.-Joseph-de-la-Rive	247
St.-Joseph-de-Sorel	2,545
St.-Jovite	3,841
St.-Lambert	20,557
St.-Laurent	65,900
St.-Léonard	79,429
St.-Léonard-d'Aston	992
St.-Liboire	1,151
St.-Louis-du-Ha! Ha!	1,502
St.-Luc	8,815
St.-Ludger	229
St.-Marc-des-Carrières	2,822
St.-Nicolas	5,074
St.-Noël	666
St.-Ours	625
St.-Pamphile	3,428
St.-Pascal	2,763
St.-Patrice-de-Beaurivage	477
St.-Paulin	663
St.-Pie	1,725
St.-Pierre	5,305
St.-Pierre	400
St.-Placide	278
St.-Polycarpe	602
St.-Prime	2,522
St.-Raphaël	1,346
St.-Raymond	3,605
St.-Rédempteur	4,463
St.-Rémi	5,146
St.-Romuald-d'Etchemin	9,849
St.-Sauveur-des-Monts	2,348

St.-Siméon 1,152
St.-Sylvestre 383
St.-Thomas-Didyme 1,006
St.-Timothée 2,113
St.-Tite 3,031
St.-Ulric 792
St.-Vallier 489
St.-Victor 1,104
St.-Wenceslas 408
St.-Zacharie 1,284
St.-Zotique 1,774
Ste.-Adèle 4,675
Ste.-Agathe 709
Ste.-Agathe-des-Monts 5,641
Ste.-Agathe-Sud . 1,344
Ste.-Angèle-de-Mérici 669
Ste.-Anne-de-Beaupré 3,292
Ste.-Anne-de-Bellevue 3,981
Ste.-Anne-des-Monts 6,062
Ste.-Anne-du-Lac . . . 28
Ste.-Catherine . . . 6,372
Ste.-Clothilde-de-Horton 368
Ste.-Croix 1,814
Ste.-Félicité 711
Ste.-Foy 68,883
Ste.-Geneviève . . 2,573
Ste.-Jeanne-d'Arc 1,047
Ste.-Julie 14,243
Ste.-Madeleine . . 1,361
Ste.-Marie 8,937
Ste.-Marthe-sur-le-Lac 5,586
Ste.-Martine 2,196
Ste.-Monique 201
Ste.-Perpétue . . . 1,037
Ste.-Petronille 982
Ste.-Pudentienne . . 866
Ste.-Rosalie 2,862
Ste.-Thècle 1,703
Ste.-Thérèse 18,750
Salaberry-de-Valleyfield 29,574
Salluit 480
Sault-au-Mouton . . 828
Sawyerville 939
Sayabec 1,721
Schefferville 1,997
Scotstown 762
Scott 554
Senneterre 4,339
Senneville 1,221
Sept-Iles 29,262
Shawinigan 23,011
Shawinigan-Sud 11,325
Shawville 1,608
Sherbrooke 74,075
Sillery 12,825
Sorel 20,347
Stanstead Plain . . 1,093
Stukely-Sud 398
Sutton 1,599
Tadoussac 900
Taschereau 781
Tasiujaq 77
Témiscaming . . . 2,097
Terrebonne 11,769
Thetford Mines . . 19,965
Thurso 2,780
Tracy 12,843
Tring-Jonction . . 1,315
Trois-Pistoles . . . 4,445
Trois-Rivières . . . 50,466
Trois-Rivières-Ouest 13,107
Upton 926
Val-Barrette 609
Val-Bélair 12,695
Val-Brillant 687
Val-David 2,336
Val-des-Monts . . . 4,148
Val-d'Or 21,371
Valcourt 2,601
Vallée-Jonction . . 1,200
Vanier 10,725
Varennes 8,764
Vaudreuil 7,608
Vaudreuil-sur-le-Lac 583
Verchères 4,473
Verdun 61,287
Victoriaville 21,838
Ville-Marie 2,651
Warden 438
Warwick 2,847
Waterloo 4,664
Waterville 1,397
Weedon-Centre . . 1,263
Westmount 20,480
Windsor 5,233
Wottonville 673
Yamachiche 1,258
Yamaska 447
Yamaska-Est 289

SASKATCHEWAN

Population 968,313

METROPOLITAN AREAS

Regina 164,313
Saskatoon* . . . 154,210

CITIES, TOWNS, AND VILLAGES

Abbey 218
Aberdeen 496
Abernethy 300
Admiral 52
Alameda 318
Alida 169
Allan 871
Alsask 652
Alvena 94
Aneroid 129
Annaheim 209
Antler 107
Arborfield 439
Archerwill 286
Arcola 493
Arelee 60
Arran 93
Asquith 507
Assiniboia 2,924
Atwater 64
Avonlea 442
Aylesbury 62
Aylsham 132
B-Say-Tah 112
Balcarres 739
Balgonie 777
Bangor 68
Battleford 3,565
Beatty 108
Beechy 279
Belle Plaine 69
Bengough 536
Benson 90
Bethune 369
Bienfait 835
Big River 819
Biggar 2,561
Birch Hills 957
Birsay 78
Bjorkdale 269
Bladworth 124
Blaine Lake 653
Borden 197
Bounty 35
Bracken 66
Bradwell 168
Bredenbury 467
Briercrest 151
Broadview 840
Brock 184
Broderick 101
Brownlee 99
Bruno 772
Buchanan 392
Buena Vista 112
Bulyea 124
Burstall 550
Cabri 632
Cadillac 173
Calder 164
Cando 163
Canora 2,667
Canwood 340
Carievale 246
Carlyle 1,074
Carmichael 26
Carnduff 1,043
Carragana 92
Carrot River 1,169
Central Butte 548
Ceylon 184
Chamberlain 136
Chaplin 389
Choiceland 543
Churchbridge 972
Clavet 234
Climax 293
Coderre 114
Codette 236
Coleville 383
Colgate 44
Colonsay 594
Conquest 256
Consul 153
Coronach 1,032
Craik 565
Craven 206
Creelman 184
Creighton 1,636
Cudworth 947
Cupar 669
Cut Knife 624
Dalmeny 1,064
Davidson 1,166
Debden 403
Delisle 980
Denholm 95
Denzil 199
Dilke 115
Dinsmore 398
Disley 41
Dodsland 272
Dollard 62
Domremy 209
Drake 211
Drinkwater 78
Dubuc 129
Duck Lake 699
Duff 76
Dundurn 531
Duval 129
Dysart 275
Earl Grey 303
Eastend 723
Eatonia 528
Ebenezer 164
Edam 384
Edenwold 143
Elbow 313
Elfros 199
Elrose 624
Elstow 143
Endeavour 199
Englefeld 271
Ernfold 91
Esterhazy 3,065
Estevan 9,174
Eston 1,413
Evesham 57
Eyebrow 168
Fairlight 74
Fenwood 99
Ferland 71
Fife Lake 81
Fillmore 396
Findlater 69
Flaxcombe 90
Fleming 141
Flin Flon† 367
Foam Lake 1,452
Forget 70
Fort Qu'Appelle . . 1,827
Fosston 105
Fox Valley 380
Francis 182
Frobisher 166
Frontier 619
Gainsborough 308
Gerald 197
Girvin 60
Gladmar 72
Glaslyn 430
Glen Ewen 168
Glenavon 284
Glenside 85
Glentworth 86
Glidden 48
Golden Prairie 83
Goodeve 116
Goodsoil 263
Goodwater 53
Govan 394
Gravelbourg 1,338
Grayson 264
Grenfell 1,307
Guernsey 198
Gull Lake 1,095
Hafford 557
Hague 625
Halbrite 125
Handel 53
Hanley 484
Harris 259
Hawarden 137
Hazenmore 124
Hazlet 132
Hepburn 411
Herbert 1,019
Herschel 65
Heward 54
Hodgeville 329
Holdfast 297
Hubbard 73
Hudson Bay 2,361
Humboldt 4,705
Hyas 165
Imperial 501
Indian Head 1,889
Insinger 39
Invermay 353
Ituna 870
Jansen 223
Jedburgh 52
Kamsack 2,688
Kannata Valley 42
Keeler 50
Kelliher 397
Kelvington 1,054
Kenaston 345
Kendal 92
Kennedy 275
Kerrobert 1,141
Khedive 62
Killaly 112
Kincaid 256
Kindersley 3,969
Kinistino 783
Kinley 54
Kipling 1,016
Kisbey 228
Krydor 73
Kyle 516
Lafleche 583
Laird 233
Lake Alma 101
Lake Lenore 361
Lampman 651
Lancer 156
Landis 277
Lang 219
Langenburg 1,324
Langham 1,151
Lanigan 1,732
La Ronge 2,579
Lashburn 813
Leader 1,108
Leask 478
Lebret 274
Leipzig 29
Lemberg 414
Leoville 393
Leross 94
Leroy 504
Leslie 65
Lestock 402
Liberty 135
Limerick 164
Lintlaw 234
Lipton 364
Lloydminster** . . 6,034
Lockwood 38
Loon Lake 369
Loreburn 201
Love 121
Loverna 37
Lucky Lake 333
Lumsden 1,303
Luseland 704
Macklin 976
MacNutt 127
Macoun 190
Macrorie 133
Madison 41
Maidstone 1,001
Major 119
Makwa 115
Manitou Beach . . . 134
Mankota 375
Manor 368
Maple Creek 2,470
Marcelin 238
Marengo 79
Margo 153
Markinch 80
Marquis 121
Marsden 229
Marshall 453
Martensville 1,966
Maryfield 431
Maymont 212
Mazenod 43
McLean 189
McTaggart 103
Meacham 178
Meadow Lake . . . 3,857
Meath Park 262
Medstead 163
Melfort 6,010
Melville 5,092
Mendham 109
Meota 235
Mervin 155
Meyronne 69
Midale 564
Middle Lake 275
Milden 251
Milestone 602
Minton 131
Mistatim 132
Montmarte 544
Moose Jaw 33,941
Moosomin 2,579
Morse 416
Mortlach 293
Mossbank 464
Muenster 385
Naicam 886
Neilburg 354
Netherhill 55
Neudorf 425
Neville 124
Nipawin 4,376
Nokomis 524
Norquay 552
North Battleford 14,030
North Portal 164
Odessa 232
Ogema 441
Osage 49
Osler 527
Outlook 1,976
Oxbow 1,191
Paddockwood 211
Palmer 56
Pangman 227
Paradise Hill 421
Parkside 104
Paynton 210
Pelly 391
Pennant 202
Pense 472
Penzance 74
Perdue 407
Piapot 101
Pierceland 425
Pilger 150
Pilot Butte 1,255
Plato 38
Plenty 175
Plunkett 150
Ponteix 769
Porcupine Plain . . . 937
Preeceville 1,243
Prelate 317
Primate 54
Prince Albert 31,380
Prud'homme 222
Punnichy 394
Qu'Appelle 653
Quill Lake 514
Quinton 169
Rabbit Lake 159
Radisson 439
Radville 1,012
Rama 133
Raymore 635
Redvers 859
Regina 162,613
Regina Beach 603
Rhein 271
Richmound 188
Ridgedale 134
Riverhurst 193
Robsart 40
Rocanville 834
Roche Percee 142
Rockglen 511
Rockhaven 42
Rose Valley 538
Rosetown 2,664
Rosthern 1,609
Rouleau 443
Rush Lake 101
Ruthilda 47
St. Benedict 157
St. Brieux 401
St. Gregor* 140
St. Louis 448
St. Victor 54
St. Walburg 802
Saltcoats 549
Salvador 48
Saskatoon 154,210
Sceptre 169
Scott 203
Sedley 373
Semans 344
Senlac 96
Shackleton 22
Shamrock 73
Shaunavon 2,112
Sheho 285
Shell Lake 220
Shellbrook 1,228
Silton 59
Simpson 231
Sintaluta 215
Smeaton 246
Smiley 97
Southey 697
Sovereign 55
Spalding 337
Speers 114
Spiritwood 926
Spring Valley 31
Springside 533
Springwater 34
Spruce Lake 78
Spy Hill 354
Star City 527
Stenen 143
Stewart Valley 133
Stockholm 391
Storthoaks 142
Stoughton 716
Strasbourg 842
Strongfield 85
Sturgis 789
Success 63
Swift Current . . . 14,747
Tantallon 196
Tessier 37
Theodore 473
Tisdale 3,107
Togo 181
Tompkins 275
Torquay 311
Tramping Lake . . . 178
Tribune 72
Tugaske 175
Turtleford 505
Tuxford 90
Unity 2,408
Val Marie 238
Valparaiso 43
Vanguard 292
Vanscoy 298
Vawn 81
Veregin 120
Vibank 369
Viceroy 96
Viscount 386
Vonda 313
Wadena 1,495
Wakaw 1,030
Waldeck 292
Waldheim 758
Waldron 50
Wapella 487
Warman 2,076
Waseca 169
Watrous 1,830
Watson 901
Wawota 622
Webb 80
Weekes 113
Weirdale 90
Weldon 279
Welwyn 170
Weyburn 9,523
White City 602
White Fox 394
Whitewood 1,003
Wilcox 202
Wilkie 1,501
Willow Bunch 494
Willowbrook 54
Windthorst 254
Wiseton 195
Wishart 212
Wolseley 904
Wood Mountain 41
Woodrow 68
Wroxton 72
Wynyard 2,147
Yarbo 158
Yellow Creek 131
Yellow Grass 477
Yorkton 15,339
Young 456
Zealandia 114
Zelma 62
Zenon Park 273

*City and metropolitan area have same boundary and population.
†City on Saskatchewan-Manitoba border; total population, 8,261.
**City on Saskatchewan-Alberta border; total population, 15,031.

YUKON

Population 23,153

Dawson 697
Faro 1,652
Whitehorse 14,814

Federal Spending in Canada

Estimated Budget for Fiscal 1983*

	Billions of dollars†
Health and welfare	22.800
Public debt	16.765
Defense	8.335
Economic development and support	7.328
Fiscal transfer payments to provinces	4.678
General government services	3.283
Transportation and communications	2.690
Internal overhead expenses	2.008
Education assistance	1.821
Culture and recreation	1.700
Foreign affairs	1.527
Total	72.935

*April 1, 1982, to March 31, 1983
†Canadian dollars; $1 = U.S. 81 cents as of Dec. 1, 1982.

Spending Since 1977

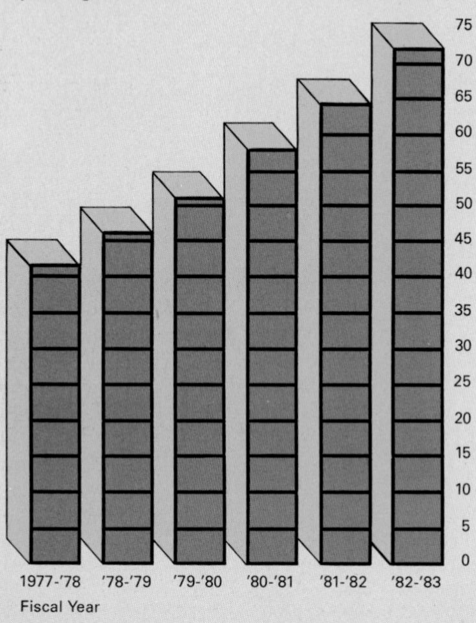

Source: Treasury Board of Canada

ports into the European Community (EC or Common Market). At stake was a $15-million-a-year industry, an important source of livelihood to about 4,500 fishermen in Newfoundland. Canada warned that the EC suspension of seal imports might mean the end of European fishing privileges on Canada's east coast.

International Business Transactions brought both success and failure for Canada in 1982. In October, a record sale was made to the Soviet Union of 8.4 million short tons (7.6 million metric tons) of western Canadian grain. In May, China bought $2.25 billion worth of Canadian wheat, to be shipped over the next three years. Mexico canceled plans on June 10 to acquire more nuclear generating stations, ending Canada's hopes of selling that country a CANDU reactor.

On May 18, Bombardier Incorporated, a Quebec company, announced that it would sell 825 subway cars to New York City. Bombardier's purchase order could reach $1 billion—the largest export contract ever awarded to a Canadian manufacturer—and would create about 15,000 worker-years of Canadian jobs.

Japan agreed on August 11 to limit car exports to Canada to 153,000 vehicles during Japan's 1982 fiscal year, which ends in March 1983—a reduction of 24 per cent from its 1981 fiscal year. Canada secured the cutback by subjecting all Japanese cars entering the country to a detailed and time-consuming customs check.

Canadian-U.S. Relations were in a state of disrepair in 1982, fueled by ideological differences between Trudeau's government and President Ronald Reagan's Administration. While the Canadian government enacted policies that emphasized economic nationalism and government intervention in the economy, the Reagan Administration moved in the opposite direction. It asserted that the role of government should be limited in an effort to bolster the free market economy. Problems between the neighbors centered on Canada's National Energy Program (NEP) of 1980, designed to achieve 50 per cent Canadian ownership of the oil industry by 1990. Under the NEP, preferential treatment is given to Canadian oil companies, and Petro-Canada, the government-owned company, is entitled to a 25 per cent share in new oil resources found on federal land. The United States labeled this policy discriminatory and in contravention of international treaties. Canada considered it a legitimate pursuit of national interests. The Foreign Investment Review Agency (FIRA), a group established in 1974 to screen foreign investments in Canada, was another subject of contention. The United States considered FIRA another discriminatory mechanism and announced in June that it was taking the matter to the council of the General Agreement on Tariffs and Trade. The United States alleged that it was wrong for FIRA to force approved foreign companies doing business in Canada to buy Canadian-made goods.

A spate of protectionist legislation in the U.S. Congress caused Canada some concern. Canadian Ambassador Allen E. Gotlieb reported that 53 so-called protectionist bills were before Congress, many of them potentially damaging to Canada's trade. Valued at over $100 billion per year in two-way traffic, this trade is the largest exchange of goods between any two countries in the world.

Environmental damage also caused hard words. There were signs that the attempt to improve the water quality of the Great Lakes was flagging and that air quality in some congested border areas, such as Windsor and Detroit, had not improved since 1976. Acid rain—caused by sulfur dioxide emissions from industrial plants—was an explosive issue in Canada. When the U.S. Senate Committee on Environment and Public Works voted 15-0 for a program to combat acid rain, the Canadian House of Commons voted on July 22, 1982, to express its formal appreciation. The official United States position on the subject was that more research was necessary before action would be taken. However, the governments of Quebec and New York state signed their own agreement on July 26 to cooperate in dealing with the acid rain problem. A visit to Ottawa by U.S. Secretary of State George P. Shultz in October resulted in an agreement to exchange reports on acid rain before year-end, with the U.S. report focusing on scientific aspects of the problem.

Facts in Brief: Population: 24,541,000. Government: Governor General Edward Richard Schreyer; Prime Minister Pierre Elliott Trudeau. Monetary unit: the Canadian dollar. Foreign trade: exports, $69,922,000,000; and imports, $65,797,000,000. David M. L. Farr

See also Canadian provinces articles; CANADIAN LIBRARY ASSOCIATION (CLA); CANADIAN LITERATURE; SCHREYER, EDWARD RICHARD; TRUDEAU, PIERRE ELLIOTT. In WORLD BOOK, see CANADA; CANADA, GOVERNMENT OF.

CANADIAN LIBRARY ASSOCIATION (CLA) sponsored seven regional seminars in 1982 to alert librarians and library trustees to impending problems in Canada's library system. The expected difficulties, and the steps necessary to avert them, were outlined in the report of a nationwide study called Project: Progress. The report warned that unless public libraries learn to aggressively market their services, they will lose their position as a central information source to private computer-based information services.

Freedom of Information. On June 28, Canada's House of Commons passed the nation's first freedom of information act. Passage of the bill marked the culmination of a seven-year lobbying effort by the CLA and other groups.

At the same time that the CLA was working for freedom of information, it was also working against censorship. The association's board of directors voted $11,500 (Canadian dollars; $1 = U.S. 81 cents on Dec. 31, 1982) in April for a study of censorship and the law. The study is intended to give libraries the legal footing they need to select materials without being hindered by community members who object to the selections.

Annual Conference. Nearly 1,200 delegates attended the 37th annual CLA conference, held in Saskatoon, Sask., from June 10 to 15. Pearce J. Penney, chief provincial librarian of Newfoundland, succeeded Marianne F. Scott of McGill University, Montreal, Que., as CLA president.

Awards. The CLA awarded the Howard V. Phalin-World Book Graduate Scholarship in Library Science ($2,500) to Margaret P. Taylor of Ottawa, Ont.; the H. W. Wilson Education Foundation Scholarship ($2,000) to Gloria Anderson, also of Ottawa; and the CLA/Elizabeth Dafoe Scholarship ($1,750) to Patricia Bellamy of Vancouver, B.C.

The recipients of the CLA Outstanding Service to Librarianship Award for 1982 were Bruce B. Peel of the University of Alberta in Edmonton and Robert H. Blackburn of the University of Toronto in Ontario. The CLA Award for Special Librarianship in Canada went to Susan Klement of Toronto; the CLA school libraries division Margaret B. Scott Award of Merit was awarded to W. Art Forgay of Regina, Sask.; and the Canadian Library Trustees Merit Award went to George Bothwell, also of Regina.

The CLA presented two children's book awards in 1982. The winner of the CLA Book of the Year for Children Award was Janet Lunn, for *The Root Cellar* (Lester & Orpen Dennys). The Amelia Frances Howard-Gibbon Illustrator's Award went to Heather Woodall for her illustrations in *Ytek and the Arctic Orchard* (Douglas & McIntyre). Paul Kitchen

In WORLD BOOK, see CANADIAN LIBRARY ASSN.

CANADIAN LITERATURE continued to demonstrate growth in artistic maturity, if not productivity, in 1982. Canada's Federal Cultural Policy Review Committee made several recommendations for easing the financial plight of writers and publishers, including compensating writers for library lending of their works and expanding direct government subsidy for culturally important books.

Fiction. Graeme Gibson's *Perpetual Motion,* his first novel in 10 years, chronicled the odd obsessions of a 19th-century Ontario settler. At once a parody, a moral tale, and a realistic description of the mechanistic faith of the Victorian Age, it was the most intriguing novel of the year. Joseph Skvorecky's *The Swell Season,* about a young boy growing up during the Nazi occupation of Czechoslovakia, exemplified the Toronto writer's inventive narrative skills. Hugh Hood's *Black and White Keys,* set in Toronto and Europe during World War II, was the fourth novel in his projected 12-volume series documenting the social, intellectual, and political fabric of Canadian society through the fate of three generations of an Ontario family.

Among other notable novels dealing with regional themes and such familiar subjects as women's issues and urban anxiety were Katherine Govier's *Going Through the Motions,* Richard Wright's *The Teacher's Daughter,* Carol Shields's *A Fairly Conventional Woman,* Joan Barfoot's *Dancing in*

Author Mavis Gallant won the Governor General's Literary Award in the English fiction category for her book of short stories *Home Truths.*

the Dark, Aviva Layton's *Nobody's Daughter,* Rachel Wyatt's *Foreign Bodies,* Jack McLeod's *Going Grand,* and John Marlyn's *Putzi, I Love You.*

Convincing evidence of Canadian mastery of the short story was produced by Alice Munro in *The Moons of Jupiter.* Other fine collections were Barry Callaghan's *The Black Queen Stories,* Greg Hollingshead's *Famous Players,* Guy Vanderhaeghe's *Man Descending,* and Keath Fraser's *Taking Cover.*

Biographies and Memoirs. The careers of businessmen and literary and political figures inspired some excellent studies. Peter C. Newman's *The Establishment Man* was a lively examination of the life of Conrad Black, a dominant Canadian financial figure. Simma Holt's *The Other Mrs. Diefenbaker* chronicled the life of Edna May Brower, the mysterious first wife of John G. Diefenbaker, a former Canadian prime minister. Clara Thomas and John Lennox produced *William Arthur Deacon,* about a critic whose career illuminates the development of Canadian literature from 1922 to 1960.

Hugh Keenlyside wrote *On the Bridge of Time,* the second volume of his reminiscences of Canadian international diplomacy, while Margaret Trudeau's *Consequences* sensationalized her life after she separated from Prime Minister Pierre Elliott Trudeau. *The Informer* was Carol de Vault's intriguing acccount of her work as a Quebec police spy during the 1970 terrorist crisis. Among the best literary memoirs was *Letters to the Past* by George Woodcock, Canada's pre-eminent man of letters. It is an account of his involvement in England with the anarchist movement and his friendship with George Orwell and other writers. Poet and novelist Michael Ondaatje contributed *Running in the Family,* a quasifictional memoir of his youth in Ceylon; and novelist Gabrielle Roy's *The Fragile Lights of Earth* contained articles and memories from 1942 to 1972.

History. Christina Newman-McCall's *Grits* was an intimate study of the workings of the Liberal Party, while Charles Taylor's *Radical Tories* sympathetically portrayed Canada's conservative intellectuals, historians, and writers. J. L. Granatstein's *The Ottawa Men* was an admiring study of the civil service elite; and the same author joined Robert Bothwell to edit *The Gouzenko Transcripts,* based on secret testimony given in 1946 to the Royal Commission concerning the Igor Gouzenko spy case. In *The National Deal,* Michael Valpy and Robert Sheppard reconstructed the difficult road toward Canada's new Constitution; and in *The Presidents and Prime Ministers,* Lawrence Martin examined the history of visits between Canadian and United States leaders. Other historical accounts include Michael Bliss's *The Discovery of Insulin,* a study of the controversy surrounding one of Canada's medical milestones. Irving Abella and Harold Troper's *None Too Many* documented Canada's rejection of Jewish refugees from Europe between 1933 and 1948.

Poetry. *The Oxford Book of Canadian Verse,* chosen by Margaret Atwood, was a landmark work demonstrating the regional and universal appeal of Canadian poetry—beginning with Robert Hayman, who died in 1629, and ending with Roo Borson, who was born in 1952. The most interesting individual collection was Gwendolyn MacEwen's *The T. E. Lawrence Poems,* which conjured up startling images of that complex individual.

Miscellaneous. *The Great Code,* an intellectually audacious inquiry into the Bible's imaginative textual unity and into the ways it has influenced writers in theme and structure, enhanced Northrop Frye's considerable reputation as educator and critic. Frye's *Divisions on a Ground* was much lighter, containing 13 witty essays on Canadian literature and society. Margaret Atwood's *Second Words* brought together 50 essays and reviews from the past 20 years, ranging from analyses of writers as diverse as Frye and Sylvia Plath to discussions of such topics as feminism, sexism, and Canadian nationalism. Arousing much interest was Martin Knelman's *Stratford Tempest,* a report on the bitter controversy over the directorship of Canada's major theatrical enterprise, the annual Stratford Festival in Ontario. Pierre Berton's *Why We Act Like Canadians,* presented as informal letters to an

American, explained the differences between Canada and the United States.

Governor General's Literary Awards for books published in 1981 went to Mavis Gallant for *Home Truths* (English fiction); George Calef for *Caribou and the Barren-Lands* (English nonfiction); F. R. Scott for *The Collected Poems of F. R. Scott* (English poetry); Sharon Pollock for *Blood Relations* (English drama); Denys Chabot for *La province lunaire* (French fiction); Madeleine Ouellette-Michalska for *L'échappée des discours de l'oeil* (French nonfiction); Michel Beaulieu for *Visages* (French poetry); and Marie Laberge for *C'était avant la guerre à l'Anse à Gilles* (French drama).

Mervyn Huston won the Stephen Leacock Memorial Award for his novel *Gophers Don't Pay Taxes;* and Jack McClelland won the Molson Prize in recognition of his outstanding contribution to the arts as a Canadian publisher.

Ray Ellenwood won the Canada Council Translation Prize for his English translation of *The Entrails,* a collection of plays and poetry by Claude Gauvreau; and Ivan Steenhout won for the French translation of Donald Creighton's two-volume biography of John A. MacDonald, *The Young Politician* and *The Old Chieftain.* Ken Adachi

See also LITERATURE. In WORLD BOOK, see CANADIAN LITERATURE.

CAPE VERDE. See AFRICA.

CARTER, JAMES EARL, JR. (1924-), the 39th President of the United States, made only a few campaign appearances for Democratic candidates in the 1982 elections. He was far busier promoting his presidential memoirs, *Keeping Faith.*

Carter did not attend his party's midterm conference in Philadelphia in June. But Senator Edward M. Kennedy (D., Mass.), a featured speaker, drew applause by declaring, "I had my disagreements with the last Administration, but on the vital issue of human rights, Ronald Reagan is wrong and Jimmy Carter was right."

Carter voiced criticism of many Reagan policies during the year, including his attempt to thwart construction of a Soviet-European gas pipeline, but he supported the President at several key junctures. Traveling in Europe in May when Reagan proposed a mutual reduction of U.S. and Soviet nuclear arms, Carter termed it "a good move toward peace and better understanding." On September 2, after Israel labeled Reagan's Middle East peace plan a "serious deviation" from the Camp David accords, Carter said there was "absolutely nothing" in it that violated the letter or the spirit of the Camp David agreement. Also in September, Carter became a visiting "distinguished professor" at Emory University in Atlanta, Ga. Frank Cormier

In WORLD BOOK, see CARTER, JAMES EARL, JR.

CAT. The cat continued to grow in popularity as a pet in the United States in 1982. The Pet Food Institute estimated that Americans maintained more than 42 million cats as pets, a 25 per cent increase from 33.8 million a year before. The Cat Fanciers' Association, Incorporated (CFA), registered 45,000 purebred cats in 1981, an increase of 10 per cent from 1980. Persians once again led in number of registrations.

Grand Champion Simbelair Carla of Northbrook, a white female Persian, was awarded the title of National Best Cat by the CFA. Bred by Lois Weston of Mount Hope, near Toronto, Canada, and owned by Peggy and Arnold Blackburn of Winston-Salem, N.C., Carla won 114 best-in-show awards while competing for this title.

The title of National Best Kitten went to Grand Champion South Paw Sunburst, a red male Persian bred and owned by Judy and Greg Brocato of Rome, Ga. Best Altered Cat was Champion and Grand Premier Delite Million Dollar Baby, a blue female Persian bred by Dea Deutsch of Wichita, Kans., and owned by Gordon and Betty Ford of Chatham, Ill. Persians won half the awards given to cats, kittens, and altered cats. A Colorpoint Shorthair, Maine Coon, and Scottish Fold won top national awards for the first time. Thomas H. Dent

In WORLD BOOK, see CAT.

Simbelair Carla of Northbrook poses with owner Peggy Blackburn. Carla was named National Best Cat in 1982 after winning 114 best-in-show awards.

CENSUS. The United States Bureau of the Census continued in 1982 to release information gathered during the 1980 census and from surveys conducted in 1981. By Jan. 1, 1983, the population of the United States was about 232.4 million, some 1.9 million more than a year earlier.

Education Gains. In 1980, for the first time, more than half of Americans over age 25 in all states—66.3 per cent nationally—had completed at least four years of high school.

College enrollment rose dramatically. Between 1970 and 1981, the number of college students jumped 45 per cent, mainly because of the large increase in the number of women students. During that period, the number of college graduates among Americans 25 or older rose from 11 per cent to 17.1 per cent. However, women still lagged behind men, 13.4 per cent to 21.1 per cent.

Family Changes. Between 1970 and 1981, the average size of the American family dropped from 3.58 persons to 3.27 persons. Census officials attributed the decline to lower birth rates and a huge increase in the number of one-parent families. In 1970, 6.3 per cent, or 3.3 million American families, were headed by one parent. By 1981, that figure had almost doubled to 10.4 per cent, or 6.3 million families.

Changes in the traditional family were reflected in statistics concerning children. In 1970, only 8 million American children under 18 lived in a one-parent household. By 1981, the number had increased to 12.6 million.

The Census Bureau reported that the median family income in the United States in 1981 was $22,390, compared with $23,110 (in 1981 dollars) in 1970. Census figures also showed that housing costs rose 112 to 115 per cent for homeowners and 125 per cent for renters during that period.

Other Developments. The Supreme Court of the United States on February 24 unanimously upheld the confidentiality of the Census Bureau's master list of street address numbers and vacant dwellings used in the 1980 census.

A number of large cities had sued the bureau, contending that their minority populations were seriously undercounted. On April 5, census officials estimated that the 1980 census missed counting about 1.3 million blacks, about 4.8 per cent of the total black population of the United States.

The Census Bureau on October 31 announced the reinstatement of several major statistical programs lost to budget cuts in 1980 and 1981. The loss of the programs had alarmed many business and social welfare groups that frequently use government statistics. Mark A. Mangold

See also POPULATION. In WORLD BOOK, see CENSUS; POPULATION.

CENTRAL AFRICAN REPUBLIC. See AFRICA.

CEYLON. See SRI LANKA.

CHAD. On June 7, 1982, about 8,000 guerrillas led by Hissene Habré captured Chad's capital, N'Djamena, after a brief struggle with forces loyal to President Goukouni Weddeye. Weddeye sought refuge in neighboring Cameroon, and, on June 19, Habré declared himself interim head of state. A former minister of defense and once a prime minister of Chad, Habré led one of 11 factions in a civil war that began in 1966.

The major rivalries in that conflict were among northern Muslims, southern Christians, and *animists* (believers in spirits in nature), also from the south. After seizing the capital, Habré, a northerner, appealed to southern leaders to end the civil war. On July 10, he met in Libreville, Gabon, with the principal southern leader, Colonel Wadal Abdelkader Kamougue, who had been Weddeye's vice-president. However, Kamougue insisted on a federal form of government, which Habré rejected. In September, dissidents in Kamougue's own army rebelled and forced him to flee to Cameroon.

Weddeye and other Habré rivals had hoped that the advance of Habré's army on N'Djamena would be blocked by the multinational peacekeeping force deployed in Chad in 1981 by the Organization of African Unity (OAU). However, OAU troops did not intervene. J. Dixon Esseks

See also AFRICA. In WORLD BOOK, see CHAD.

Hissene Habré became the president of Chad on October 21, 4½ months after his forces deposed the former president, Goukouni Weddeye.

CHEMICAL INDUSTRY activity in the United States followed the national business trend in 1982, with slow sales, lower profits, and not much capital spending. The synthetic-fibers industry was especially weak as major producers showed sharp reductions in profits and even losses.

Capital Spending. At the end of 1981, industry experts predicted that plant investment during 1982 would be 5 per cent higher than in 1981, about half the average for all industry. By the end of the first quarter, however, expectations had taken a turn for the better, rising to a predicted $15.2 billion in spending for the year, an increase of almost 11 per cent. But by June, there had been a turn for the worse amid large drops in chemical profits. Spending plans were trimmed to $14.2 billion, up only 4 per cent. By the third quarter, actual and planned spending held steady at about a 3 per cent rise.

The news about funding for research and development (R & D) was better. Early in 1982, chemical companies said that they expected to boost spending by only about 5 per cent over that of 1981. By June, however, McGraw-Hill Publications Company's Department of Economics reported in their 27th annual survey of business plans for R & D spending that the chemical sector planned to increase R & D spending by 19.3 per cent in 1982. Industry representatives said that the Economic Recovery Tax Act was a major factor in the increase. This act, which was passed in August 1981, gives firms a 25 per cent tax credit for their R & D expenditures in excess of the average spent during the three previous years.

Business Was Bad throughout the U.S. chemical industry in 1982. The only bright spots were in such peripheral industries as pharmaceuticals and cosmetics, which were almost alone in showing growth in sales and earnings.

The only ray of hope for the future was the drastic lowering of inventories. With inventories low when demand for chemical products picks up, underutilized capacity will get a sudden boost.

Safety. The U.S. Occupational Safety and Health Administration (OSHA) eased up on companies with good records and continued to rewrite health standards to make them more flexible and easier for industry to obey. The agency moved ahead on a number of safety fronts affecting the chemical industry. It prepared to drop more than 200 unenforceable rules because they use the advisory word "should" instead of the mandatory word "shall."

An apparent OSHA success is its 1978 standard for inorganic arsenic. This standard reduced the permissible amount of the chemical by 98 per cent, from 500-millionths to 10-millionths of a gram per cubic meter of air. Risk-assessment studies completed in May conclude that lung cancer risk among employees exposed to arsenic also has been reduced by 98 per cent.

One of OSHA's major programs—the writing of rules governing carcinogenic substances in the workplace—stalled in an increasingly complex debate on technical and emotional questions. OSHA announced in January that it would revise the rules adopted in 1980, but the evaluation of comments was slowed by the volume of response from people with opinions on the subject.

Bubble Bursts. In August, the U.S. Court of Appeals for the District of Columbia threw out key parts of the *bubble concept.* According to this concept, a number of industrial plants under an imaginary dome-shaped bubble in an area are considered to be a single source of air pollution, rather than several sources. Thus, when one plant under the bubble shuts down or reduces the amount of air pollution that it emits, other plants in the area are allowed to increase their capacity as long as the net amount of pollution remains the same or decreases. The U.S. Environmental Protection Agency (EPA) developed the bubble concept in 1979 as a cost-effective way to control air pollution at chemical and other industrial plants. The court decision blocked as many as 100 bubble proposals that the EPA contended could save industry up to $1 billion. Frederick C. Price

In WORLD BOOK, see CHEMICAL INDUSTRY.

CHEMISTRY. In September 1982, chemists at the University of California's Lawrence Berkeley Laboratory in Berkeley reported what may be a significant advance in using the sun's energy to convert water to hydrogen gas, a useful fuel. Gabor A. Somorjai, Christofer Leygraf, and Monica Hendewerk built an electrochemical cell whose electrodes are disks made of iron oxide.

Common rust is a form of iron oxide. However, the California chemists used a specially treated material. One electrode contained very small amounts of silicon, and the other had tiny amounts of magnesium. These converted the disks into semiconductors—materials that conduct electricity well at high temperatures but poorly at low temperatures.

To build the cell, the chemists connected the disks with a conducting wire of silver epoxy fiber, immersed them in water that contained sodium sulfate or sodium hydroxide, and illuminated them with visible light. Small amounts of hydrogen gas bubbled out of the cell.

The experimental cell makes an extremely small amount of hydrogen for about four hours. Furthermore, only about 0.05 per cent of the energy of the light that strikes the disks is available in the hydrogen fuel that it produces. However, the materials that are used in the cell are inexpensive, and if the efficiency can be improved, hydrogen gas

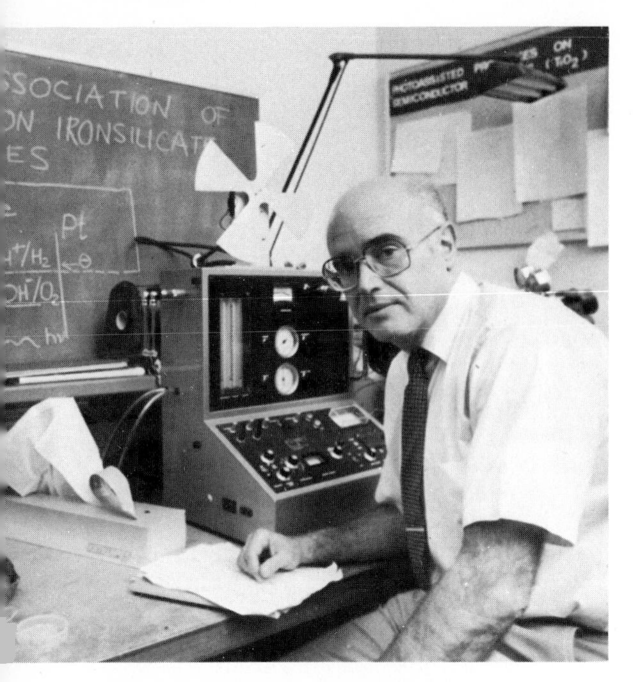

University of California chemist Gabor A. Somorjai headed a research team that found a way to create a cheap source of hydrogen.

may be available cheaply as an important fuel of the future.

High-Energy Molecules. Nien-chu C. Yang, Ming-Jang Chen, Peter Chen, and Kwok Tim Mak of the University of Chicago reported in August 1982 that they had synthesized two high-energy molecules and used them to test a major chemical theory. High-energy molecules release chemical energy by breaking into molecules of lower energy.

The Chicago chemists used two compounds, each made up of benzene and anthracene. Benzene is a molecule consisting of six carbon atoms joined in the shape of a hexagon. Anthracene is a flat molecule consisting of three benzene rings attached to one another side by side. The two compounds, called dimers, differed only in how the benzene ring was attached to the anthracene.

The researchers used the high-energy dimers to test a set of rules that predict how certain types of chemicals will react. The rules are named after their developers, chemists Robert B. Woodward and Roald Hoffmann, then of Harvard University.

Each dimer broke apart into benzene and a high-energy form of anthracene. As the dimers broke apart, one of them changed the structure of its bonds — the connections among its atoms — an even number of times, while the other went through an odd number of bond changes.

The dimer with the even number of bond changes reacted much more rapidly, as the Woodward-Hoffmann rules predicted. Thus, the Chicago chemists extended the scope of the rules.

Möbius Strip Synthesized. In June 1982, chemists at the University of Colorado in Boulder reported that they had synthesized the first organic molecule in the shape of a Möbius strip.

A Möbius strip is a geometric figure that you can make by twisting a strip of paper once and attaching its ends. The strip has the fascinating properties of having only one edge and one surface, both of which are continuous.

Chemists David M. Walba, R. Curtis Haltiwanger, and Rodney M. Richards started with a long, strip-like polyether molecule. Each end of the molecule contained chemical groups that could become hooked together.

The chemists carried out the reaction in a solvent at high dilution so that the polyether molecules were widely separated from one another. This separation minimized the number of reactions between molecules. Instead, in most of the reactions, the head of one molecule hooked up with its own tail. Two products formed — cylinders and the Möbius strips. The strip is of great interest to chemists who study the strengths of chemical bonds. Lawrence P. Verbit

In WORLD BOOK, see CHEMISTRY.

CHESS. Three men's interzonal tournaments held in 1982 produced six candidates for the world championship match that will take place in 1984. The top two finishers at each interzonal advanced to the 1983 candidates' matches that will produce a challenger to world champion Anatoly Karpov of the Soviet Union. Also participating will be the two finalists in the previous championship cycle — Viktor Korchnoi, a Russian now living in Switzerland, and Robert Hübner of West Germany.

Hungarian Zoltan Ribli won the first men's interzonal in Las Palmas, Spain, in July. Former world champion Vassily Smyslov, 61, of the Soviet Union finished second, becoming a candidate at an age when most professional players retire. Another Hungarian, Lajos Portisch, and Filipino Eugenio Torre tied for first place in the second men's interzonal, played in Toluca, Mexico, in August. Teen-age Soviet Gary Kasparov won the third interzonal in Moscow in September. His countryman Alexander Beliavsky finished second.

Two women's interzonal tournaments held in West Germany and the Soviet Union produced six hopefuls for the women's world championship. Joining previous finalists Nana Alexandria and Nana Ioseliani, both of the Soviet Union, in the 1983 candidate matches will be former women's world champion Nona Gaprindashvili and Lidia Semenova, both of the Soviet Union; Tatiana Lematchko of Bulgaria; Margareta Muresan of Romania; Irina Levitina of the Soviet Union; and Liu Shilan of China. Only one winner will emerge from the play-offs to challenge champion Maya Chiburdanidze of the Soviet Union in 1984.

Ninety-two nations competed at the biennial Chess Olympiad in Lucerne, Switzerland, in the fall. The Soviet Union won the gold medal.

Other Tournaments. Andres Soltis of New York City and William Martz of Wauwatosa, Wis., tied for first place at the 1982 U.S. Open Championship in St. Paul, Minn., in August. The World Open, held in Philadelphia in July, ended in a four-way tie for first place among John Fedorowicz and Dmitry Gurevich of New York City; Nick de Firmian of Oakland, Calif.; and Eugene Meyer of Arlington, Va.

Joel Benjamin, 18, of New York City, won his second U.S. Junior Invitational Championship in South Bend, Ind., in July. Benjamin went on to the World Junior Championship in Copenhagen, Denmark, in August, tying for third behind the new world junior champion, Andrea Sokolov of the Soviet Union. Meanwhile, David Gertler of Riverton, N.J., and 13-year-old Stuart Rachels of Birmingham, Ala., the youngest master in U.S. history, won the U.S. Junior Open in Crossville, Tenn., in June. Al Lawrence

CHICAGO. Mayor Jane M. Byrne continued to consolidate her position in 1982 as she prepared her campaign for re-election in 1983. Byrne gave property owners a small amount of tax relief and sponsored a number of citywide festivities during the year, which some observers saw as an effort to woo voters.

On November 12, Byrne submitted a balanced 1983 budget of $1.95 billion, 8 per cent higher than the 1982 budget. It called for reducing property taxes by $22 million, or about 5 per cent, and cutting the "head tax" paid by local businesses from $3 per employee per month to $2. The budget gave raises of 11 per cent to police officers and fire fighters and 5 per cent to most other city employees.

Housing Controversy. The Chicago Housing Authority (CHA), which provides 45,870 public housing units for 142,000 of the city's poor, was accused of mismanagement early in the year by the U.S. Department of Housing and Urban Development (HUD). On March 31, HUD said it would withhold a $14.5-million subsidy until the CHA board was reorganized. The department also demanded the resignation of CHA Chairman Charles R. Swibel, an adviser and fund-raiser for Mayor Byrne. On July 1, the state legislature passed a bill expanding the CHA board from five

Technicians in Chicago test bottles of Extra-Strength Tylenol in October after seven local deaths were traced to cyanide-tainted Tylenol capsules.

members to seven and setting requirements for the chairmanship that, in effect, excluded Swibel. HUD released the money after Byrne promised Swibel would resign. He did so on July 7.

Chicago's Schools opened on schedule on September 8 after the Chicago Teachers Union leadership agreed to a new one-year contract that provided no pay raise for the second straight year. The school board agreed to make the teachers' pension payments for them, an amount equal to 7 per cent of salary.

Transportation. A four-day strike by the Brotherhood of Locomotive Engineers from September 19 to 22 halted almost all commuter trains in the Chicago area and forced an estimated 175,000 riders to find alternate transportation. Other Chicago-area mass transit ran without interruption in 1982, largely because the Regional Transportation Authority won state legislative approval on July 1 to borrow $100 million to cover operating losses of the Chicago Transit Authority, suburban bus lines, and commuter railroads.

Downtown Redevelopment. A 10-year-old plan to redevelop a six-block area of the North Loop, a deteriorating part of Chicago's downtown business district, was delayed again after Hilton Hotels Corporation announced on March 15 that it was abandoning plans for a 1,800-room hotel in the renewal area. On October 12, the city issued new guidelines calling on developers to bid for the land on a piecemeal basis. City officials were disappointed when only one developer submitted a bid for a key site by the December deadline.

Other Developments. Archbishop Joseph L. Bernardin of Cincinnati, Ohio, was installed on August 24 as head of the archdiocese of Chicago, the nation's largest Roman Catholic diocese. Bernardin, 54, succeeded John Patrick Cardinal Cody, who died on April 25 at the age of 74 after 17 years in office. On July 6, a federal grand jury ended its investigation into allegations Cody may have diverted up to $1 million in church funds to his personal use. There were no indictments.

Civic leaders began making plans to hold a world's fair in Chicago in 1992. On December 8, the International Bureau of Expositions in Paris approved both Chicago and Seville, Spain, as sites of fairs in 1992.

The city experienced its coldest day in history on January 10 when the temperature dropped to −26° F. (−32° C) and the wind-chill factor to −81° F. (−63° C). The cold wave was blamed for 24 deaths in the metropolitan area.

Tylenol Deaths. On September 29 and 30, police discovered, seven Chicago-area residents had died after taking capsules of Extra-Strength Tylenol, a popular painkiller, that had been poisoned with cyanide. See CRIME. John Camper

See also CITY. In WORLD BOOK, see CHICAGO.

CHILD WELFARE. The United States Bureau of the Census reported in 1982 that its 1980 census data showed 1 American child in 5 to be living in poverty, a proportion that had changed little in 15 years. In 1982, however, American children were apparently in even more desperate straits.

The Children's Defense Fund, a private, nonprofit children's advocacy organization based in Washington, D.C., reported that 1982 federal funding for important child-welfare programs was cut by $10 billion. The Institute for Research on Poverty at the University of Wisconsin in Madison found that 20 per cent of all American children in 1982 were being raised in families headed by women and that about 45 per cent of those families were living below the poverty line (defined, in late 1982, as an income of about $7,750 for a family of three and $9,950 for a family of four). Other studies by child-welfare groups predicted that federal budget slashing would also halt Medicaid coverage for 661,000 children by the end of 1983 and reduce or eliminate 660,000 grants made to families, including more than 1 million children, under the Aid to Families with Dependent Children program.

Missing Children. On the plus side, President Ronald Reagan on October 12 signed the Missing Children Act. The law ordered the establishment of a national computerized *clearing house* (coordinating center) of information on the approximately 300,000 children and teen-agers who disappear each year in the United States. The clearing house, which will use the Federal Bureau of Investigation (FBI) National Crime Information Center computer, will enable law enforcement officials throughout the country to keep one another informed of missing children. Parents will have access to the network through FBI offices.

Battered Wives. The U.S. Commission on Civil Rights, an independent federal advisory group, criticized the criminal and civil justice systems for the way they deal with women who have been beaten by their husbands. The commission reported that police officers, prosecutors, and judges often treat spouse abuse as a private family matter rather than a crime. In a second report, the commission listed 19 government programs in effect in 1980 to help battered women and noted that budget cuts and the transfer of much social-welfare jurisdiction to the states had reduced the number and funding of such programs. The commission's findings were considered significant from a child-welfare standpoint, because women who cannot find protection from abusive husbands cannot provide a good home environment for their children. Frances A. Mullen

In WORLD BOOK, see CHILD WELFARE.

CHILDREN'S BOOKS. See LITERATURE FOR CHILDREN.

CHILE. The worldwide recession hit Chile head-on in 1982. The nation foundered in a sea of economic woes, including high unemployment and a decline in foreign investments. Chile had relied on foreign earnings to expand its mining industry.

Prior to 1982, the military government of President Augusto Pinochet Ugarte had largely avoided the recessionary troubles that plagued many other nations. Pinochet's regime had won the confidence of most Chileans by cutting federal spending and returning to private ownership companies that had been nationalized by the previous socialist government. The economic reversal, however, caused concern.

Internationally, Chile continued to be branded with a negative image under Pinochet. Other countries protested alleged brutality by Chilean police in putting down dissension and the government's repression of political activities.

To reassure Chileans about the future, Pinochet reaffirmed his pledge to restore democracy in Chile by 1989. But he warned that the nation's political parties would not recover the power they once had.

The Economy. The prices earned by Chile for its major exports—including copper, iron ore, and wood products—sharply declined in 1982. The drop in export earnings affected businesses of all types. In May, 122 Chilean companies declared bankruptcy.

Unemployment in Chile rose to 20 per cent, causing increased labor unrest. Chileans were shocked by the assassination of labor activist Tucapel Jiménez Alfarao in February. The 60-year-old Jiménez had been an outspoken critic of the growing gap between Chile's rich and poor.

Foreign Relations. In an unusual step to help Chile improve its international image, the United States Department of State on February 9 issued a statement condemning the movie *Missing,* starring Jack Lemmon and Sissy Spacek. The documentary-style film attempts to reconstruct the story of Charles Horman. The film alleges that the young American was killed by the Chilean military during the bloody coup of 1973 because he had information on U.S. involvement in the overthrow of President Salvador Allende Gossens.

Chile's relations with Argentina continued to be troubled by a dispute over ownership of territory at the tip of South America. Argentina also was angered by Chile's apparent support of Great Britain in the Falkland Islands war. During that conflict, Argentine forces captured British troops operating on Chilean soil. Nathan A. Haverstock

See also LATIN AMERICA (Facts in Brief Table). In WORLD BOOK, see CHILE.

Chile's President Augusto Pinochet Ugarte gives a speech on September 11 to mark the ninth anniversary of the coup that brought him to power.

CHINA, PEOPLE'S REPUBLIC OF. China conducted the largest census in history in July 1982. On October 27, it announced that the population under control of the government in Peking (Beijing in the phonetic Pinyin alphabet) on July 1 had been 1,008,175,288. Including Taiwan, Hong Kong, and Macao, which Peking considers part of China, the total was 1,031,882,511. China had almost one-fourth of the world's population.

China's Population. The State Statistical Bureau said that 51.5 per cent of the population was male and 48.5 per cent female. The proportion of illiterates and semiliterates had declined from 38.1 per cent in 1964—the year of China's last census—to 23.5 per cent in 1982. The number of people with university educations had risen from 0.4 per cent to 0.6 per cent.

The 1964 census had shown 694,582,000 persons, so China's population rose by 45.1 per cent, an average annual growth rate of 2.1 per cent. Other sources estimated China's population growth to have slowed to 1.4 per cent in 1981 as a result of government efforts to discourage couples from having more than one child. Chinese officials hoped to hold the population in the year 2000 to 1.2 billion.

Economic Problems caused by rapid population growth continued. Use of marginal land to grow crops, overgrazing, and other efforts to expand food production to keep up with the population had by 1982 created widespread erosion and destruction of forests. A shortage of fuel in rural areas caused peasants to burn wastes that were needed as fertilizer. Lakes and rivers were becoming polluted with insecticides.

Unemployment was another problem. The government claimed to have found urban work for 8 million people in 1981, and it sought an additional 5.6 million jobs in 1982. The number of urban residents "waiting for jobs" was reported to be just 3 million, but rural underemployment added to the potential city work force.

On the Brighter Side, the Chinese government created more jobs by relaxing controls on the economy, thus allowing people to try new ways to earn a living. Although the government imposed traditional Communist central planning on some key sectors of the economy, it left a wide range of industrial products and consumer goods relatively free of price controls and production quotas.

The State Economic Commission reported that industrial production in the first nine months of 1982 was up 8.6 per cent over the same period during 1981. It predicted that grain output would break the record of 332.1 million metric tons (366.1 million short tons) set in 1979. Exports

Government officials clean a park in Peking (Beijing), China, in February to launch Civic Virtues Month, promoting cleanliness and politeness.

were up 10.4 per cent and imports down 1.3 per cent. China had a trade surplus, partially a result of new restrictions on importing consumer goods.

China gave a major role in economic growth to foreign investment and cooperative ventures, especially in oil production. In February, the government offered 43 offshore oil fields to international companies for exploration and development on carefully regulated terms.

On November 30, the government presented its overdue five-year economic plan for 1981 through 1985. The plan called for a modest annual growth rate of 4 to 5 per cent. It concentrated investment in the key areas of energy and transportation.

Shrinking the Bureaucracy. As part of the government's efforts to solve economic problems, Premier Zhao Ziyang announced on March 8 plans to reduce the size of the central government to increase efficiency. Twelve ministries were combined into six, the number of deputy premiers cut from 13 to two, the total number of ministers and deputy ministers reduced from 505 to 167, and the size of ministerial staffs slashed from 49,000 to 32,000. The total number of ministries and commissions under the State Council—which carries on the day-to-day affairs of government—was reduced from 52 to 41. The changes lowered the average age of ministers and deputy ministers from 64 to 58, increased the proportion of officials with college educations from 59 to 62 per cent, and doubled the percentage of women in senior jobs.

In another high-level shakeup, China announced on November 19 the appointment of a new minister of foreign affairs, Wu Xueqian, and a new minister of national defense, Zhang Aiping. Both Wu and Zhang were strong supporters of Communist Party Deputy Chairman Teng Hsiao-ping (Deng Xiaoping), China's top leader.

New Constitution. On December 11, China adopted a new national Constitution, the third in seven years. The Constitution revived the position of president, which had been eliminated in 1975. The new president and vice-president were to be chosen for five-year terms, with a limit of two terms for those and other top jobs, including that of premier. This provision represented a major change, because Chinese officials had traditionally held their posts for life unless they were purged or accused of crimes.

The Constitution restored the right to inherit property, which had been abolished in 1978 under the last Constitution. The new charter eliminated the right to strike and the right to a uniquely Chinese form of political expression—putting up posters. The document also reduced people's communes to economic units, taking away their political functions. Formerly, each commune combined economic and political administration for 20 or more villages.

Two Chinese girls try out a Mickey Mouse telephone at the opening of a United States industrial exhibit in Peking in February.

The Communist Party's 12th Congress was held in Peking from September 1 to 11. The congress brought together 1,545 delegates representing more than 39 million party members. It approved basic policy decisions for running China that had been worked out by the nation's senior leaders, headed by Teng.

The congress adopted a new party constitution (not to be confused with the new national Constitution), the ninth since the Communists came to power in China in 1949. The party constitution restructured the group's leadership, abolishing the post of party chairman. The chairmanship had been created for Mao Tse-tung (Mao Zedong) and held by him until his death in 1976. Its abolition was a step further away from Mao's personal style of rule.

The new party constitution also eliminated vice-chairman positions, removing the last important position held by Hua Kuo-feng (Hua Guofeng), Mao's chosen successor. Hu Yaobang, whom Teng promoted in 1981 to the party chairmanship, was named by the congress as general secretary. This became the most powerful position in the party and nation, thus bringing Chinese practice into line with most Communist countries.

The congress named a 28-member Politburo to direct the new 210-member Central Committee. The Politburo's standing committee, with six members, became the nation's key policymaking unit. Teng was elected to it, along with Hu, Zhao, and three elderly leaders who had been expected to step down: Chen Yun and Li Xiannian, both 77 years old, and 85-year-old Ye Jianying. Reports had circulated in Peking that Teng wanted to retire the three officials and a number of other veterans. Teng's goal was to rejuvenate the leadership with new, younger officials who would have better managerial and technical qualifications in addition to party experience.

To encourage older leaders to make room for younger talent, the new party constitution created a central advisory commission of 172 members. The commission would consist of semiretired but honored party elders who would give advice and make recommendations. Teng became its head.

Resistance to Teng's Changes continued to be especially strong in the armed forces. Some old military leaders resented the move away from Mao's concepts. Many high-ranking officers were also displeased that Teng's policies gave a low priority to military modernization and had created such economic incentives for young people to stay on the farm that the army lost much of its appeal.

At the September Communist Party congress, Teng was named chairman of the party's central military commission, keeping his role as overseer of the army. He moved to further restrict army opposition shortly after the congress. On September 27, Teng replaced the army's chief political commissar. Shortly thereafter, many regional military commanders were replaced.

Teng Hsiao-ping (Deng Xiaoping), China's top leader, votes for Communist Party officials at the party's congress in Peking in September.

In another move to suppress political opposition, several followers of the so-called Gang of Four were tried and sent to prison during 1982. The Gang of Four—Mao's widow and three of his prominent associates—remained in prison. They had been convicted of treason in 1981.

The first airplane hijacking reported in the Chinese press occurred on July 25. Five young factory workers armed with knives and explosives tried to divert a domestic flight and force it to Hong Kong or Taiwan. The plane's crew and passengers attacked the hijackers with soft-drink bottles, umbrellas, and other articles. During the flight, the hijackers' explosives blew a hole in the plane's side, but it landed safely in Shanghai. The five were executed on August 18, and the government gave decorations to the plane's crew.

In Foreign Relations, China emphasized its role as a developing nation that identified with poor Third World countries. Some official statements condemned both Soviet and United States policies in equal terms, and some reiterated the 1970s position that the Soviet Union was a more dangerously aggressive power than the United States.

China and the Soviet Union met in Peking from October 5 to 21 for the first governmental talks since 1979, trying to improve relations. China asked the Soviet Union to stop supporting Vietnam's control of Cambodia, to withdraw its troops from Afghanistan, and to reduce its military forces on the Chinese-Soviet border. The Soviets rejected these demands and unsuccessfully sought Chinese agreement to a general statement of principles. Further talks were planned in 1983.

Relations with the United States were troubled by continuing American support for Taiwan. United States Vice-President George H. W. Bush visited China from May 5 to 9 to discuss Taiwan and other subjects. On August 17, China and the United States issued a joint communiqué on Taiwan, in which the United States promised a gradual reduction in arms sales to Taiwan. But some tensions remained.

China's 1982 Constitution included a provision for the establishment of "special administrative regions." The provision was apparently intended to pave the way for Taiwan's reunification with the mainland. Henry S. Bradsher

See also ASIA (Facts in Brief Table); TAIWAN. In WORLD BOOK, see CHINA.

CHURCHES. See EASTERN ORTHODOX CHURCHES; JEWS and JUDAISM; PROTESTANTISM; RELIGION; ROMAN CATHOLIC CHURCH.

CISKEI. See AFRICA.

CITY. The cities of the United States had another difficult year in 1982 as they tried to deal with a nationwide recession coupled with sharp reductions in federal aid.

President Ronald Reagan's National Urban Policy Report, issued on July 9, said cities would have to solve their problems on their own and could no longer depend on as much federal aid as they had grown accustomed to.

"It is the policy of this Administration to return maximum authority over the use of resources to state and local governments," the report said. "The Administration believes that, properly unfettered, they will make better decisions than the federal government acting for them."

Central to That Policy, the report said, was the President's so-called new federalism program, which he announced in his State of the Union message on January 26. As revised later, it called for states and localities to assume the full $47-billion cost of Aid to Families with Dependent Children, the major federal welfare program, and about 40 other federal programs. In return, the federal government would relieve states and localities of their share of the cost of the Medicaid health-care program. State and local governments also would get money from a new temporary trust fund to help them through the changeover.

In a speech to the National Association of Counties on July 13, President Reagan said that under his program "localities will be guaranteed 100 per cent of the funds historically passed to them from the federal government." He added, "States will not be able to opt out of programs until 1985 and, when they do, will be required to consult with local elected officials."

Reagan's other major urban program, which he said would help to solve the problem of high unemployment among blacks, was outlined in a message he sent to Congress on March 23. It would provide extensive tax credits and relief from certain federal regulations to businesses that are located in decaying urban areas designated by the secretary of housing and urban development as urban enterprise zones.

Support and Nonsupport. Many mayors supported the enterprise zone concept but were skeptical of the new federalism, fearing it would leave them at the mercy of state legislatures dominated by rural and suburban interests. Mayor Charles Royer of Seattle told the Joint Economic Committee of Congress on July 13 that the National Urban Policy Report was "a blueprint for surrendering America's cities." Royer, speaking for the National League of Cities, also charged that "the urban policy report and the new federalism initiative are an attempt to rationalize some serious budget cutting with a certain amount of rhetoric."

Detroit Mayor Coleman A. Young, the presi-

The Sunsphere, symbolizing the theme of energy, towers 266 feet (81 meters) over the grounds of the 1982 World's Fair in Knoxville, Tenn.

50 Largest Cities in the United States

Rank	City	Population (a)	Per cent change in population since 1970 census	Mayor or city manager (b)
1.	**New York City**	7,071,639	−10.4	Edward I. Koch (D, 1/86)
2.	**Chicago**	3,005,072	−10.8	Jane M. Byrne (D, 4/83)
3.	**Los Angeles**	2,966,850	+ 5.5	Tom Bradley (NP, 6/85)
4.	**Philadelphia**	1,688,210	−13.4	William J. Green (D, 1/84)
5.	**Houston**	1,595,138	+29.3	Kathryn J. Whitmire (NP, 1/84)
6.	**Detroit**	1,203,339	−20.5	Coleman A. Young (D, 1/86)
7.	**Dallas**	904,078	+ 7.1	*Charles S. Anderson (1981)
8.	**San Diego**	875,538	+25.5	*Ray Blair, Jr. (1978)
9.	**Phoenix**	789,704	+35.2	*Marvin Andrews (1976)
10.	**Baltimore**	786,775	−13.1	William Donald Schaefer (D, 12/83)
11.	**San Antonio**	786,023	+20.2	*Thomas Huebner (1977)
12.	**Indianapolis**	700,807	− 4.9	William H. Hudnut III (R, 12/83)
13.	**San Francisco**	678,974	− 5.1	Dianne Feinstein (NP, 1/84)
14.	**Memphis**	646,174	+ 3.6	Wyeth Chandler (I, 12/83)
15.	**Washington, D.C.**	638,432	−15.6	Marion S. Barry, Jr. (D, 1/87)
16.	**Milwaukee**	636,236	−11.3	Henry W. Maier (D, 4/84)
17.	**San Jose**	629,442	+36.9	*Francis T. Fox (1980)
18.	**Cleveland**	573,822	−23.6	George V. Voinovich (R, 11/83)
19.	**Columbus, Ohio**	565,032	+ 4.6	Tom Moody (R, 12/83)
20.	**Boston**	562,994	−12.2	Kevin H. White (D, 1/84)
21.	**New Orleans**	557,927	− 6.0	Ernest N. Morial (D, 5/86)
22.	**Jacksonville, Fla.**	540,920	+ 7.3	Jake M. Godbold (D, 7/83)
23.	**Seattle**	493,846	− 7.0	Charles Royer (NP, 1/86)
24.	**Denver**	492,365	− 4.3	William H. McNichols, Jr. (D, 6/83)
25.	**Nashville**	455,651	+ 7.0	Richard H. Fulton (D, 9/83)
26.	**St. Louis**	453,085	−27.2	Vincent L. Schoemehl, Jr. (D, 4/85)
27.	**Kansas City, Mo.**	448,159	−11.7	Richard L. Berkley (NP, 4/83)
28.	**El Paso**	425,259	+32.0	Jonathan W. Rogers (NP, 4/83)
29.	**Atlanta**	425,022	−14.1	Andrew J. Young, Jr. (D, 1/86)
30.	**Pittsburgh**	423,959	−18.5	Richard S. Caliguiri (D, 1/86)
31.	**Oklahoma City**	403,136	+ 9.5	*Scott Johnson (1981)
32.	**Cincinnati**	385,457	−15.0	*Sylvester Murray (1979)
33.	**Fort Worth**	385,164	− 2.1	*Robert L. Herchert (1978)
34.	**Minneapolis**	370,951	−14.6	Donald M. Fraser (D, 1/86)
35.	**Portland, Ore.**	366,383	− 3.3	Francis D. Ivancie (NP, 11/84)
36.	**Honolulu**	365,048	+12.4	Eileen Anderson (D, 1/85)
37.	**Long Beach**	361,334	+ 0.7	*John E. Dever (1977)
38.	**Tulsa**	360,919	+ 9.3	James M. Inhofe (R, 5/84)
39.	**Buffalo**	357,870	−22.7	James D. Griffin (D, 12/85)
40.	**Toledo**	354,635	− 7.4	*David Boston (1981)
41.	**Miami**	346,865	+ 3.6	*Howard V. Gary (1981)
42.	**Austin**	345,496	+36.3	*Nicholas Meiszer (1981)
43.	**Oakland**	339,337	− 6.1	*Henry Gardner (1981)
44.	**Albuquerque**	331,767	+35.7	Harry E. Kinney (R, 12/85)
45.	**Tucson**	330,537	+25.7	*Joel D. Valdez (1974)
46.	**Newark**	329,248	−13.8	Kenneth A. Gibson (D, 7/86)
47.	**Charlotte**	314,447	+30.2	*O. Wendell White (1981)
48.	**Omaha**	313,911	− 9.5	Michael Boyle (NP, 6/85)
49.	**Louisville**	298,840	−17.4	Harvey Sloane (D, 12/85)
50.	**Birmingham**	284,413	− 5.5	Richard Arrington, Jr. (NP, 11/83)

Sources:
(a) 1980 census (U.S. Bureau of the Census).
(b) *Asterisk before name denotes city manager; all others are mayors. Dates are those of expiration for mayors and dates of appointment for city managers. D — Democrat, R — Republican, I — Independent, NP — Nonpartisan. (National League of Cities; *Municipal Yearbook 1982,* International City Management Association).
(c) Estimates for autumn, 1981, for Standard Metropolitan Statistical Areas (U.S. Bureau of Labor Statistics). n/a — not available.

Average cost of living (family of 4) (c)	Unemployment rate (d)	Revenue (e)	Gross debt outstanding (e)	Per capita income (f)	Sales tax rate (g)
$29,540	10.7	$19,303,349	$9,898,210	$11,087	8.25%
25,358	10.6	2,050,708	1,199,766	11,394	6%
25,025	9.1	3,206,147	2,859,395	11,350	6%
26,567	8.1	2,143,712	1,859,686	10,142	6%
23,601	7.0	922,591	1,403,984	11,861	5%
25,208	15.2	1,534,685	880,855	11,208	4%
22,678	6.0	508,270	626,863	11,041	5%
24,776	11.0	479,567	132,444	9,962	6%
n/a	8.6	464,049	555,137	9,637	5%
25,114	10.1	1,407,568	717,620	10,016	5%
n/a	7.3	718,939	1,161,510	8,445	5%
n/a	9.1	466,756	311,425	10,082	4%
27,082	8.8	1,466,349	885,753	12,998	6.5%
n/a	9.5	1,070,462	580,172	8,696	6%
27,352	6.0	2,229,119	1,706,219	12,871	6%
26,875	10.9	438,217	368,203	10,906	5%
25,598	11.0	458,602	406,905	11,236	6.5%
n/a	7.8	306,945	164,274	12,297	6.5%
n/a	9.2	317,069	634,750	9,537	5.5%
29,213	6.8	1,064,455	575,784	10,803	5%
n/a	9.7	467,135	530,211	9,791	7%
n/a	6.3	698,258	681,803	8,675	5%
25,881	10.8	506,507	487,124	11,882	5.4%
24,820	6.4	604,679	429,177	11,301	6%
n/a	8.4	792,616	678,665	8,821	6.75%
24,498	9.5	486,833	148,912	10,300	5.625%
24,528	8.4	399,654	261,659	10,550	5.125%
n/a	n/a	168,497	59,794	6,677	5%
23,273	6.1	435,779	1,015,192	9,997	4%
24,717	12.5	265,029	224,037	10,253	6%
n/a	4.5	258,745	394,366	10,394	4%
25,475	10.4	384,141	175,539	9,877	5.5%
22,678	6.0	186,917	205,327	11,041	5%
25,799	6.4	312,507	487,620	11,329	5%
n/a	9.6	246,427	348,359	10,650	—
31,893	7.0	426,941	198,587	10,492	4%
25,025	9.1	441,135	187,247	11,350	6%
n/a	6.4	222,696	505,600	10,359	5%
26,473	11.8	439,904	248,113	9,458	7%
n/a	12.2	189,203	162,899	9,505	5.5%
n/a	7.7	185,435	204,790	9,598	5%
n/a	n/a	415,821	938,736	9,150	5%
27,082	8.8	273,684	364,506	12,998	6.5%
n/a	8.6	178,347	426,885	8,629	4.25%
n/a	10.5	158,367	157,988	8,666	6%
n/a	8.8	425,117	157,719	11,689	5%
n/a	7.4	161,580	239,344	9,528	4%
n/a	6.6	153,314	140,097	10,054	5%
n/a	11.6	222,766	251,872	9,275	5%
n/a	14.2	149,972	302,828	8,909	5%

(d) August 1982 figures for Standard Metropolitan Statistical Areas (U.S. Bureau of Labor Statistics).
(e) Figures in thousands of dollars for 1980-1981 (U.S. Bureau of the Census).
(f) 1980 figures for Standard Metropolitan Statistical Areas (U.S. Bureau of Economic Analysis).
(g) Total sales tax rate, including state, county, city, school district, and special district taxes (The Tax Foundation).

50 Largest Cities in the World

Rank	City	Population
1.	Shanghai, China	10,820,000
2.	Mexico City, Mexico	9,373,353
3.	Seoul, South Korea	8,366,756
4.	Tokyo, Japan	8,349,209
5.	Moscow, Russia	8,099,000
6.	Peking (Beijing), China	7,570,000
7.	New York City, N.Y., U.S.A.	7,071,030
8.	São Paulo, Brazil	7,033,529
9.	London, England	6,696,008
10.	Bombay, India	5,970,575
11.	Jakarta, Indonesia	5,490,000
12.	Hong Kong	5,315,000
13.	Bangkok, Thailand	5,153,902
14.	Rio de Janeiro, Brazil	5,093,232
15.	Cairo, Egypt	5,074,016
16.	Leningrad, Russia	4,638,000
17.	Teheran, Iran	4,496,159
18.	Tientsin (Tianjin), China	4,280,000
19.	Lima, Peru	4,278,000
20.	Santiago, Chile	3,853,275
21.	Karachi, Pakistan	3,515,402
22.	Ho Chi Minh City, Vietnam	3,460,500
23.	Delhi, India	3,287,883
24.	Madrid, Spain	3,201,234
25.	Pusan, South Korea	3,160,276
26.	Calcutta, India	3,148,746
27.	Berlin (East & West), East and West Germany	3,038,689
28.	Chicago, Ill., U.S.A.	3,005,072
29.	Baghdad, Iraq	2,969,000
30.	Los Angeles, Calif., U.S.A.	2,966,763
31.	Buenos Aires, Argentina	2,908,001
32.	Rome, Italy	2,897,505
33.	Sydney, Australia	2,874,415
34.	Bogotá, Colombia	2,850,000
35.	Istanbul, Turkey	2,822,579
36.	Yokohama, Japan	2,773,822
37.	Osaka, Japan	2,648,158
38.	Melbourne, Australia	2,578,527
39.	Pyongyang, North Korea	2,500,000
40.	Madras, India	2,469,449
41.	Shen-yang (Shenyang), China	2,411,000
42.	Singapore, Singapore	2,390,800
43.	Alexandria, Egypt	2,317,705
44.	Paris, France	2,299,830
45.	Rangoon, Burma	2,276,000
46.	Kinshasa, Zaire	2,242,297
47.	Taipei, Taiwan	2,200,427
48.	Kiev, Russia	2,192,000
49.	Lahore, Pakistan	2,169,742
50.	Wu-han (Wuhan), China	2,146,000

Sources: 1980 Bureau of the Census final results for cities of the United States; censuses and estimates from governments or UN *Demographic Yearbook, 1980* for cities of other countries.

dent of the U.S. Conference of Mayors, was equally outspoken. In a speech to the conference, which met in June in Minneapolis, Minn., Young said the Reagan Administration had "washed its hands of the cities," and added, "There is no other major country in the world today whose federal government refuses to help stabilize the economies of its large population centers."

Neither the new federalism nor the enterprise zone plan made it through Congress in 1982. But many mayors were upset by a provision of the $98.3-billion tax-increase bill, approved on August 19, that made it more difficult for cities to issue tax-exempt industrial revenue bonds to lure new industries. The new restrictions on the bonds were expected to save the federal government $863 million in fiscal 1984 and 1985. The bonds would be eliminated after Dec. 1, 1986.

Cities Hike Taxes. Many cities were forced, as they had been in 1981, to raise taxes to make up for declining federal aid. A survey of 301 cities by the Joint Economic Committee of Congress, released on October 16, said federal aid to cities declined by an average of 12 per cent during the federal fiscal year that ended on Sept. 30, 1982, while overall city revenues fell 6 per cent. Forty per cent of the cities reported that their operating expenses and debt payments exceeded income in 1981, and 59 per cent were projecting deficits for 1982.

The report said cities were expecting revenues to increase by an average of only 1.3 per cent in 1982, while expenditures were growing at an average rate of 7.8 per cent. Many cities, the report said, were increasing property taxes, which rose 13.7 per cent from 1980 to 1982, and user fees for services such as garbage collection and recreation, which grew 21 per cent in that two-year period.

Cities also were cutting services, according to a survey of 55 cities issued on October 13 by the U.S. Conference of Mayors. It examined city services in the areas of health care, mental health, day care, welfare, employment, and aid to the elderly and disabled, and concluded that "in not one of the human service areas examined was even 50 per cent of the eligible population served" in fiscal 1981 and 1982.

Some cities sought help from the private sector. In San Francisco, Cleveland, and other cities, committees of business leaders devised plans to reorganize city government and finances. Private funds were helping to build a domed stadium and other sports facilities in Indianapolis and a power plant in Trenton, N.J. Donations were also helping San Francisco to restore its cable car system.

Fewer Strikes. High unemployment combined with a shortage of city revenues had one salutary effect: Public employee strikes, which had plagued cities throughout the 1970s, were practically nonexistent in 1982. Philadelphia's schools, for exam-

Visitors explore the Future World section of Epcot Center, a Walt Disney theme park adjacent to Disney World in Orlando, Fla. It opened October 1.

ple, opened on time in September for the first time in three years. However, Detroit schools were closed for 22 days by a teachers' strike that ended October 5.

The trend in 1982 was toward small pay increases, or even pay freezes, for municipal employees. The Cleveland Regional Transit Authority ended automatic cost-of-living pay raises for its drivers, froze wages for 18 months, and won the right to hire part-time workers. According to the American Public Transit Association, at least 12 cities froze, rolled back, or eliminated cost-of-living adjustments for transit workers, and 10 won the right to hire part-time workers.

At least two cities sought to lure riders to their transit systems by lowering fares. Boston realized a quick 3 per cent increase in riders after it lowered its fare from 75 cents to 60 cents on May 1. Los Angeles reduced its fare from 85 cents to 50 cents on July 1 after the California Supreme Court upheld a measure, approved by Los Angeles County voters in a 1980 referendum, that raised the sales tax from 6 to 6.5 per cent to generate $228 million a year for transit. The fare reduction enabled the system to recover the 200,000 daily riders it lost in 1981, when fares were raised.

Decaying Infrastructure. Mayors and other public officials became increasingly alarmed in 1982 over the decay of public works such as streets, bridges, sewers, and water mains. Economist Pat Choate of the Council of State Planning Agencies estimated that governments would have to spend between $2.5 trillion and $3 trillion in the next 10 years just to repair and maintain public facilities in both urban and rural areas. Choate estimated that city streets would require $600 billion of that total; municipal water systems, $125 billion; and mass-transit systems, $40 billion.

A survey of 28 U.S. cities by the Urban Institute found that 10 of them were losing as much as 10 per cent of their water supply because of leaky pipes. When a water main near Jersey City, N.J., broke on July 16, about 300,000 persons were without water for three days. The Joint Economic Committee of Congress said New York City would have to replace 1,000 bridges, 6,200 miles (10,000 kilometers) of streets, 6,000 miles (9,700 kilometers) of sewers, and 6,000 miles of water lines within the next two decades.

Infrastructure problems were not limited to the older cities of the East and Midwest. Excessive tapping of ground water caused the ground to crack in the Phoenix area and to sink in the Houston area. Houston officials began planning a $1.8-billion rail-transit line to reduce congestion on the city's streets and expressway system. The Houston Chamber of Commerce estimated that traffic delays cost residents $1.9 billion per year.

The Supreme Court of the United States created another problem for mayors when it ruled on January 13 that cities are not immune from antitrust suits unless their state grants them immunity. It ruled that Boulder, Colo., was liable to prosecution under the Sherman Antitrust Act for enacting a 90-day moratorium on the expansion plan of a cable television firm. Mayors feared the decision could limit their power to regulate the building plans of private developers or to grant exclusive franchises to private garbage collectors, bus lines, hospitals, and ambulances.

Natural Disasters added to the problems of some cities. In mid-March, floods in Fort Wayne, Ind., left at least 15,000 people homeless, killed seven, and caused $40 million in damage. Two brushfires raged in the Los Angeles area on the weekend of October 9-10, one of which—in the Santa Monica Mountains—destroyed about 75 homes and caused damage estimated at $4.5 million.

Five big cities lost newspapers in 1982 *The* (Philadelphia) *Bulletin* closed on January 29; *The Cleveland Press* on June 17; the Buffalo, N.Y., *Courier-Express* on September 19; and the *Des Moines* (Iowa) *Tribune* on September 25. *The Minneapolis* (Minn.) *Star* and the *Minneapolis Tribune* merged on April 5.

John Camper

See also articles on individual cities. In WORLD BOOK, see CITY and articles on individual cities.

CIVIL RIGHTS. The Administration of United States President Ronald Reagan on Feb. 7, 1982, released its first report on the status of human rights around the world. The report criticized the erosion of political and economic rights in many countries. Throughout the year, however, many American civil rights groups charged the Administration itself with seriously failing to enforce civil rights in the United States.

The Administration's human rights report covered 158 countries. It found that although human rights violations were still numerous, there was a general reduction in political violence. But it also said the observance of rights was deteriorating in Central America, Taiwan, Zaire, Uganda, and South Africa. In addition, the report was sharply critical of the Soviet Union for its repressive activities in Afghanistan and Poland.

A Mixed Picture. Some improvement in human rights occurred in several Central American countries, but the gains were generally overshadowed by persistent political violence. El Salvador held national elections in March, despite a continuing civil war and a boycott of the voting by leftist opponents of the government. The government reported that more than 900,000 of the estimated 1.3 million eligible voters participated. However, some groups in El Salvador and the United States accused the government of inflating the figures. In addition, human rights and church groups in both countries reported that government security forces as well as rightist and leftist extremists continued to torture and kill political opponents.

In Guatemala, where a coup in March installed a military junta headed by General José Efraín Ríos-Montt, the human rights situation improved significantly for the country's urban middle class, the press, the university, and the Roman Catholic Church. At the same time, however, a U.S. congressional fact-finding team reported in May that the murder of civilians, particularly peasant Indians, by the Guatemalan Army increased after the coup.

Some gains occurred elsewhere in Latin America. On May 16, the Dominican Republic successfully conducted a presidential election that was regarded as the most peaceful and open election in that country since 1961. In Argentina, the ruling military junta lifted its ban on political parties and political gatherings in mid-July. In Bolivia, civilian government returned after years of military rule when Hernán Siles Zuazo was installed as president on October 10.

Soviet Peace Group. A small group of Moscow dissidents who formed the Soviet Union's first independent disarmament movement in 1982 promptly found themselves harassed by government authorities. Members of the group said on July 6 that two of its founders had been placed under virtual house arrest by the KGB, Russia's secret police agency, and that other members were threatened with prosecution and loss of jobs and student stipends.

On September 8, the three remaining members of a Soviet group trying to monitor their country's observance of the 1975 Helsinki Agreement, an international accord on human rights, decided to disband. The decision came after the KGB threatened to arrest an elderly member of the group.

U.S. Civil Rights Groups during 1982 denounced the Reagan Administration for what they charged were attempts to dismantle civil rights laws and programs. In response, the Administration insisted that its civil rights record was stronger than that of any previous administration. Nevertheless, many statements and actions by Administration officials aroused controversy.

An uproar followed the Administration's decision on January 8 to reverse an 11-year-old policy by which the Internal Revenue Service (IRS) denied tax-exempt status to private schools and colleges and other nonprofit institutions that practice racial discrimination. The change benefited the Goldsboro Christian Schools in Goldsboro, N.C., which denies admission to blacks from kindergarten through grade 12, and Bob Jones University in Greenville, S.C., which admits some blacks but prohibits interracial dating and marriage. Reagan

Marchers parade through Montgomery, Ala., in February to show their support for an extension of the Voting Rights Act of 1965.

Administration officials said only Congress, not the IRS, has the authority to determine how tax exemptions should be used to further public policy. Moved by warnings that he would be viewed as racist, however, Reagan on February 25 asked the Supreme Court of the United States to decide whether racially discriminatory private schools are entitled to tax exemptions.

In September, the heads of 33 of the 50 state advisory agencies affiliated with the United States Commission on Civil Rights signed a letter to President Reagan accusing him of responsibility for a "dangerous deterioration in the federal enforcement of civil rights." Clarence M. Pendleton, Jr., the Reagan-appointed chairman of the civil rights commission, which is independent and bipartisan, called the charges "unfounded."

Voting Rights. On June 29, President Reagan signed into law a 25-year extension of the Voting Rights Act of 1965, which has greatly expanded the number of black voters. Intensive grass-roots lobbying prompted the President to abandon an earlier version of the bill that would have made it more difficult to prove voter discrimination.

On June 28, the National Association for the Advancement of Colored People announced the launching of its largest voter education and registration drive. In the November elections, heavy black voter turnout in many areas contributed substantially to Democratic gains in the U.S. House of Representatives and in governorships.

End of an ERA. The long struggle for ratification of the Equal Rights Amendment (ERA) to the U.S. Constitution ended in defeat on June 30, the deadline for its passage. By that date, only 35 of the required 38 state legislatures had ratified the amendment. Eleanor Smeal, president of the National Organization for Women, the largest of the organizations working for ratification, charged that corporate interests had contributed decisively to defeat of the ERA. Smeal said corporations profit from paying lower wages to women, from charging higher insurance rates, and from other discriminatory acts.

During 1982, women's groups complained that the Reagan Administration had slowed enforcement of some antidiscrimination regulations, including those barring schools from discriminating on the basis of sex. They also accused the Administration of attempting to ease affirmative-action guidelines in hiring and promotion for companies doing business with the government and placing the burden of budget cuts in social service programs mainly on women. Louis W. Koenig

See also CONSTITUTION OF THE UNITED STATES; EDUCATION. In WORLD BOOK, see CIVIL RIGHTS.

CLOTHING. See FASHION.

COAL. Despite optimistic predictions about coal's potential for meeting future world energy needs, stagnation prevailed in the United States coal industry during 1982. The National Coal Association (NCA), the major organization of coal producers, reported on September 19 that both domestic coal consumption and coal exports during 1982 could fall below 1981 levels. Unemployment among coal miners remained high, and production lagged.

The president of the NCA, Carl E. Bagge, blamed the situation on the prolonged economic slump, which flattened demand from coal's two biggest customers—the steel industry and electric utilities. In addition, economic problems abroad created a surplus of coal on the export market that industry officials likened to the international glut of crude oil. The NCA forecast that U.S. mines would produce 837 million short tons (759 million metric tons) of coal during 1982. That would be only 22 million short tons (20 million metric tons) more than the amount produced in 1981, when U.S. mines were idle for 72 days because of a strike by the United Mine Workers of America. United States coal exports were expected to reach only 104 million short tons (94 million metric tons), a decrease from the record 110 million short tons (100 million metric tons) exported in 1981. By mid-1982, 40,000 U.S. coal miners were unemployed, almost 20 per cent of the industry's work force.

But some studies foresaw brighter times in 1983 and beyond, coinciding with the hoped-for improvements in the overall U.S. economy. In a long-range forecast released on June 25, 1982, the NCA predicted that domestic coal consumption would rise to 1.3 billion short tons (1.2 billion metric tons) by 1995, up 85 per cent from 1980.

A study published three days later by the International Energy Agency (IEA) echoed that optimism. The IEA, established by 21 industrialized countries in 1974, reported that coal could supply 44 per cent of the increase in world energy demand expected by 1990. The IEA also said that by 1990, coal would supply about 27 per cent of the world's total energy needs, compared with about 22 per cent in 1980.

Boosting Coal Use. The U.S. Department of Energy (DOE) announced on January 21 that it is trying to develop the technology for using mixtures of powdered coal and water as a replacement for oil and natural gas. The DOE said that coal-water mixtures could replace all of the oil now burned by electric utility and industry boilers without major changes in machinery. Mixtures of up to 70 per cent coal powder and 30 per cent

A conveyor belt carries coal for a power plant from a Peabody Coal Company mine in Arizona to a train loading station 14 miles (22 kilometers) away.

water could be used in oil burners, the DOE said.

In another effort to stimulate coal use, the U.S. Department of the Interior said on October 13 that it would sponsor a feasibility study on an unusual coal pipeline stretching from Colorado to the Pacific Coast. The pipeline, which is expected to cost $2 billion, would use undesirable salty water from the Colorado River to carry large plastic bags of coal 1,200 miles (1,900 kilometers) to markets on the West Coast. The packages of coal would be 15 feet (4.6 meters) long and 30 inches (76 centimeters) in diameter.

Slurry Pipelines. Legislation to encourage construction of coal slurry pipelines in the United States was approved by various committees in Congress during 1982 but died with the 97th Congress. The legislation would have removed legal barriers to construction of coal pipelines, which carry a mixture—or slurry—of coal and water. Proponents claim the pipelines would reduce the cost of coal by offering an alternative to rail transportation, which accounts for up to 75 per cent of coal's delivered price.

New Mine Leader. On November 9, lawyer Richard L. Trumka trounced incumbent Sam M. Church, Jr., in a race for the presidency of the United Mine Workers of America. Michael Woods

See also ENERGY; MINING. In WORLD BOOK, see COAL.

A Bureau of the Mint worker handles a large model of the back of the George Washington half dollar, which was introduced in July.

COIN COLLECTING. Although auction prices for rare coins in 1982 were generally lower than the record levels set in 1979 and 1980, the rare-coin market in the United States seemed to be making a definite upturn by midyear. Investors, who had driven prices up in previous years, were less in evidence at 1982 sales. Thus, bidding at auctions was dominated once again by collectors.

Coin Sales at the American Numismatic Association's (ANA) annual August meeting totaled $3.5-million. Notable coins sold at the meeting included a 1796 quarter, which fetched $27,000, and a 1915 gold octagonal $50 piece commemorating the Panama-Pacific Exposition, which brought $20,000. The star attraction at an earlier ANA meeting, in February, was an extremely rare Brasher's doubloon, a gold American coin minted privately in 1787. The purchase price was thought to be considerably less than the $625,000 the seller paid for the doubloon in 1981. At a California auction, an anonymous bidder paid $195,000 for an 1804 silver dollar.

Some coins did bring record prices in 1982. For example, a $3 gold piece struck at the San Francisco mint in 1870 and an 1822 $5 gold piece each sold for $687,500 in October at a New York City auction of the only complete set of U.S. gold coins, owned by the late Louis Eliasberg, Sr., a Baltimore, Md., banker. It was the most ever paid for any regular-issue U.S. coins. A 100-peseta piece issued by the Spanish provisional government in 1870 went for $190,000 in September at a sale held by Stack's in New York City. At a July auction in Zurich, Switzerland, a buyer paid $120,000—the most ever paid for an ancient coin—for a coin minted about A.D. 300 to honor Galerius as heir to the throne of the Roman Empire.

New Commemorative Coins. The first true United States commemorative coin since 1954, the George Washington half dollar, was minted in 1982. The coins were struck on July 1 and honored the 250th anniversary of Washington's birth. On July 22, President Ronald Reagan signed into law the Olympic Commemorative Coin Act. The act calls for the minting of two silver dollars and a $10 gold piece to celebrate and raise funds for the 1984 Summer Olympics in Los Angeles.

Gold Prices hit a three-year low of $296.75 per troy ounce (31.1 grams) in the week ending June 22, but by August prices had risen to above $400. Silver rebounded from a low of $4.81 per troy ounce in June to more than $10. Copper has continued to increase in price in recent years. As a result, the U.S. government in 1982 converted from a bronze-alloy Lincoln cent to one made of copper-plated zinc. Bronze pennies were also minted to avoid a shortage of the coins. Lee Martin

In WORLD BOOK, see COIN COLLECTING.

COLOMBIA. On Aug. 7, 1982, Belisario Betancur of Colombia's Conservative Party took office as the nation's president for a four-year term. In his third try for the presidency, Betancur won a hard-fought contest that saw a record turnout of voters despite threats from guerrillas who burned buses and other targets, including a church, on the eve of the May 30 elections. See BETANCUR, BELISARIO.

Betancur at once set about putting in place a program aimed at achieving economic recovery. The Liberals, who won a majority of the seats in the nation's Congress, pledged to be constructive in their opposition.

During the presidential campaign, the main issue was working out peace with Colombia's armed guerrillas. The most important of the guerrilla groups, in terms of the damage it has done, is the Movement of April 19, also known as M-19. This group is made up of revolutionaries and members of Communist youth groups.

New Policies. As president, Betancur moved to restore full constitutional guarantees and to end the state-of-siege laws that for nearly 30 years have provided the nation's army and police great freedom in fighting crime. To get at the root causes of unrest, the Betancur administration developed programs to reduce Colombia's high rate of inflation—more than 30 per cent annually—and to ease unemployment, which exceeded 20 per cent in 1982. To generate jobs, the Colombian government eased up on credit and adopted incentives for industrial development, including tax credits for foreign investors.

The new president attempted to decentralize public administration by laying more stress on Colombia's network of regional cities in promoting economic progress. He continued policies of the previous administration aimed at reducing Colombia's dependency on imported oil through a balanced program to develop the nation's hydroelectric, natural gas, and coal resources.

Coal Project. During the year, work began on the development of the Cerrejón coal deposits in northern Colombia—part of the largest industrial development project in Colombian history. Open-pit mines are being built at an estimated cost of $3.5 billion. The mines will produce 11 million short tons (10 million metric tons) of coal per year when they reach full production in 1986. Other works under construction during the year include a 90-mile (140-kilometer) railroad and coal-handling and port facilities. Nathan A. Haverstock

See also LATIN AMERICA (Facts in Brief Table). In WORLD BOOK, see COLOMBIA.

COLORADO. See STATE GOVERNMENT.

COMMON MARKET. See EUROPE.

With his wife, Rosa Elena, Colombia's President Belisario Betancur greets a crowd after his inauguration on August 7 in Bogotá.

COMMUNICATIONS. Major public policy decisions and technological expansion dominated communications developments in the United States in 1982. Above all, the year will be remembered for the decision to break up the world's largest communications company—the American Telephone and Telegraph Company (A.T. & T.). The decision, which settled an antitrust suit brought by the federal government in 1974, stunned the nation and set off a series of dramatic changes across the communications industry.

On January 8, President Ronald Reagan's Administration and A.T. & T. announced an agreement ending the eight-year-old suit. Under the pact, A.T. & T. agreed to divest itself of its 22 Bell System local telephone companies. It said it would give them up in exchange for an end to the lawsuit. The consent decree began what will be the most significant and complex restructuring in the history of U.S. business. When implemented in 1984, the action also will change the outlook for the international communications business.

Under the Terms of the decree, which was modified slightly but approved on August 24 by U.S. District Judge Harold H. Greene, A.T. & T. will keep its manufacturing arm, Western Electric Company; its research division, Bell Telephone Laboratories; and its long-distance subsidiary, Long Lines. In addition, it will maintain control

The Breakup of Ma Bell

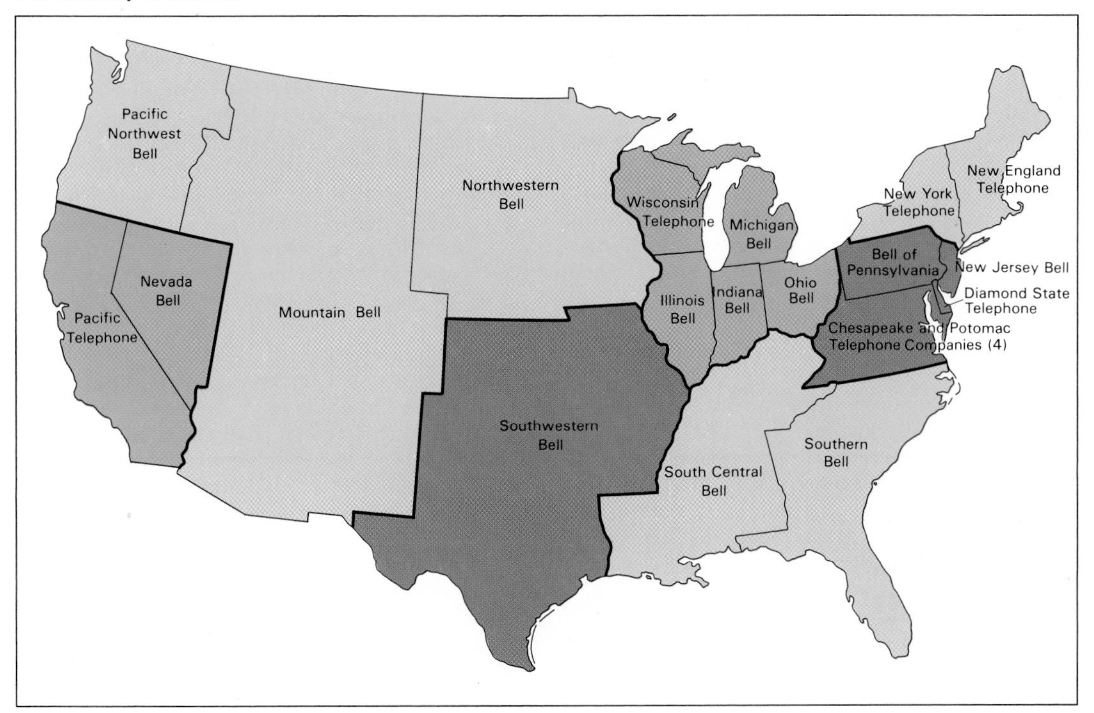

of a new unit, named American Bell Incorporated, to begin offering computerized products and computer services in 1983.

As A.T. & T. and the government were sorting out the complex decision and a series of court actions it spawned, concern that the restructuring might force local companies to raise phone rates in order to remain financially healthy prompted a legislative effort to expand the local phone firms' powers. That effort in the House of Representatives was abandoned in September 1982 when Representative Timothy E. Wirth (D., Colo.), chairman of the House telecommunications subcommittee, withdrew legislation he had introduced after A.T. & T. mounted opposition to the bill.

Several communications industry participants in the suit opposed the settlement. Telecommunications equipment manufacturers had sought the divestiture of Western Electric also, and petitioned for changes in the agreement. The newspaper industry, through the American Newspaper Publishers Association, petitioned for a prohibition on A.T. & T.'s originating news and advertising to consumers. Judge Greene, in revising the settlement, barred A.T. & T. from originating information for home distribution for at least seven years and expanded local companies' powers.

New Services. A series of regulatory actions opened the door for new technologies in other domestic telecommunications. The Federal Communications Commission (FCC) set off an intense scramble in the communications industry when it moved in March to permit the introduction of cellular communications — new mobile telephone service such as portable phones for cars and trucks.

Other developments also signaled the emergence of increased competition and new services in the industry. Companies like MCI Communications Corporation continued dramatic growth, taking away significant pieces of A.T. & T.'s intercity communications dominance. GTE Corporation agreed in October to pay $750 million to purchase Southern Pacific Communications Corporation's long-distance network and also pledged to compete vigorously in the $50-billion long-distance market. Other firms — such as Satellite Business Systems, a partnership involving International Business Machines Corporation —also announced plans to enter the business.

Cable Television continued to expand. A number of large cities, such as Boston and Denver, granted cable franchises, and about 30 million homes in the United States were subscribing to basic cable services by the end of 1982. Dozens of programmers had rushed in 1981 to fill the needs of growing systems, but in 1982, many services either changed direction or folded. For example, after accumulating about $30 million in losses, CBS Inc.

in September abandoned what was perhaps the most ambitious basic cable-programming venture ever undertaken, CBS Cable. Although it was a critically successful, advertiser-supported cultural network specializing in fine arts shows, it failed to meet the corporation's advertising revenue goals.

On the other hand, 1982 also saw the introduction of several new programming services, particularly in the information field. Atlanta, Ga., sports magnate Ted Turner's Cable News Network expanded. American Broadcasting Companies Incorporated and Westinghouse Electric Corporation joined forces to launch a competing 24-hour-a-day cable news service on June 21.

Other technologies offering television services to supplement the over-the-air networks also multiplied. Subscription television, a method of sending scrambled signals that are decoded in the home, expanded in such major metropolitan areas as New York City, Washington, D.C., and Chicago. In addition, the FCC on June 23 gave final approval to Communications Satellite Corporation to offer direct broadcast satellite (DBS) service. Due for distribution in 1986, DBS technology would enable broadcasters to beam their programs to homes via rooftop antennas. Merrill Brown

In the Special Reports section, see THE VIDEO REVOLUTION. In WORLD BOOK, see COMMUNICATIONS; COMMUNICATIONS SATELLITE.

COMMUNITY ORGANIZATIONS. The American Red Cross expanded its activities in the health field in 1982 by undertaking a 10-year public education program to improve the health of every American. The program focuses on the role that individuals can play in reducing major health risks. Health needs to be highlighted include nutrition; physical fitness; reduction of alcohol, tobacco, and drug abuse; accident prevention; stress management; and control of high blood pressure.

The Salvation Army. Commissioner John D. Needham succeeded Commissioner Ernest W. Holz as U.S. commander of the Salvation Army on January 8. Needham, an American, had previously headed Army activities in Great Britain. The organization dedicated new U.S. headquarters in Verona, N.J., on February 13.

YMCA of the USA launched an after-school program for elementary-school children whose parents work. Egie Huff served as the first woman president of the National Council of YMCAs. Publication of *Discovery YMCA,* a magazine for Y volunteers, began in October.

The Young Women's Christian Association of the USA (YWCA) had 2.5 million members and 6,000 centers in 1982. The organization moved in June to temporary quarters in New York City, following the sale of the building that had housed it since 1911. A search for new headquarters began.

Service Organizations. Kiwanis International reported its 1982 membership at more than 300,000 in 8,000 clubs in 75 nations. J. T. Roberts, a chemical engineer from Baton Rouge, La., was elected president in October. He called upon Kiwanis clubs to support the Special Olympics, an athletics program for mentally retarded children and adults. He also announced that clubs would "Share Good Health with Children" by contributing to health care programs for needy children.

Lions Clubs International elected Everett J. Grindstaff, an attorney from Ballinger, Tex., president in June. Grindstaff chose as his theme, "Share the Vision of Service." He urged Lions to support drug awareness programs and to assist the millions of people who have diabetes. Lions membership stood at 1.35 million in 35,750 clubs.

Rotary International had more than 19,800 clubs with some 909,000 members in 157 countries in 1982. The Rotary Foundation sponsored immunization campaigns in Haiti and Bolivia and health projects in Bangladesh, Guatemala, Mali, Mexico, and Pakistan. The foundation also granted more than 1,100 scholarships at a cost of $15.4 million. Virginia E. Anderson

In WORLD BOOK, see the articles on various community organizations.

COMOROS. See AFRICA.

CONGO. See AFRICA.

CONGRESS OF THE UNITED STATES. Confronted with record budget deficits growing out of the worst recession in more than 40 years, Congress in 1982 approved the largest tax increase in United States history in an effort to stem the flood of red ink. Both the Republican-controlled Senate and the Democratic-led House of Representatives showed less deference to President Ronald Reagan during the year. They rejected his budget and worked out an alternative spending plan with a $98.3-billion tax increase over three years that Reagan grudgingly accepted to break a months-long stalemate. It was a sharp contrast to the President's unbroken string of legislative victories in 1981, before the economy started downhill and unemployment increased to double-digit levels.

Although economic issues dominated the lawmakers' agenda, Congress also approved a 25-year extension of the Voting Rights Act, a multibillion-dollar job-training bill, legislation to help ailing savings and loan associations, and an emergency law to stop a strike by locomotive engineers that shut down most of the railroads for four days.

The second session of the 97th Congress was also notable for what it did not do. Efforts by Senator Jesse A. Helms (R., N.C.) and his conservative allies to pass legislation allowing group prayer in public schools and banning abortion were shelved by the Senate after weeks of debate. Congress did nothing to revise the Social Security system, found by a special presidential commission to be headed for a shortfall ranging from $150 billion to $200 billion in the next seven years. Nor was any action taken on President Reagan's highly publicized "new federalism" program to shift federal welfare programs to the states and give the U.S. government responsibility for Medicaid, a program that provides health care to the poor.

Economy Dominates Agenda. But it was the economy that became the overriding issue almost from the moment that Congress convened. With unemployment at 8.9 per cent as the year began, a confident Reagan said the downturn, which started in mid-1981, would soon be over.

Reagan's problems with Congress began when he submitted his budget, with deficits totaling nearly $250 billion over three years. Even before he sent the budget to Capitol Hill on February 8, he was forced to ask Congress for an extra $2.29-billion for unemployment benefits because joblessness was far higher than he had expected.

The budget was greeted with shock and disbelief by conservative Republicans because of its projected deficits. Many Democrats criticized Reagan for requesting a record peacetime increase in military spending while urging a freeze or cutback in social programs. At first, the President refused to consider lower defense outlays or tax increases to reduce the deficits.

As the deadlock continued, leading Republican senators pressed for a change in Reagan's position. Eventually, the President authorized his top White House advisers to meet with a group of Republican and Democratic lawmakers to work out an alternative budget. Talks by the so-called "Gang of 17," however, ended in failure when Reagan and Speaker of the House Thomas P. (Tip) O'Neill, Jr. (D., Mass.), failed to reach agreement at a meeting on April 28. But Senate Republicans later drafted their own version of a budget that was adopted by Congress and endorsed by Reagan.

After a Senate-House conference to reconcile differences, Congress set spending for fiscal year 1983 at $769.8 billion and projected a deficit of $103.9 billion. This budget squeaked through the House on June 22 with only a two-vote margin and was adopted by the Senate the next day.

Tax Hike. Later in the year, on August 19, both houses of Congress, following up on a directive in the budget compromise, passed a tax increase totaling $98.3 billion. The necessity for a tax hike produced an election-year dilemma. Without it, the deficit would have soared by another $20 billion in the next fiscal year, reducing chances for a decline in the abnormally high interest rates that were blocking an economic recovery. But passage of the bill would scale back some of the 1981 business tax cuts and levy new taxes on cigarettes,

Republican San Diego Mayor Pete Wilson claims victory over Democratic California Governor Edmund G. Brown, Jr., in November's Senate race.

telephone service, and air travel shortly before voters were scheduled to go to the polls.

The President got behind the measure, however, and enlisted Speaker O'Neill in a dramatic bipartisan effort. Opposing Reagan were many of the most conservative Republicans in the House, who felt he was, as Representative Jack F. Kemp (R., N.Y.) put it, "making a U-turn" in economic policy by seeking to raise taxes when the economy was in recession.

With Reagan and O'Neill laying their prestige on the line, the tax increase was approved by the House by a surprisingly large margin of 226 to 207, with Democrats providing 123 of the votes needed for passage, compared with 103 for the Republicans. In the Senate, the bill passed 52 to 47, with nine liberal Democrats voting for it.

In addition to scaling back some of the tax breaks for business that were adopted in 1981, the tax bill also imposed a 10 per cent withholding tax on dividends and interest payments. It doubled the tax on cigarettes from 8 to 16 cents a pack; raised the telephone tax from 1 per cent to 3 per cent in 1983, 1984, and 1985; and hiked the airline ticket tax from 5 per cent to 8 per cent. As an added sweetener for doubtful lawmakers, the bill also included an extension of unemployment benefits for up to 10 additional weeks in some states.

"I had to swallow hard," Reagan said in ex-

Members of the United States House of Representatives

The House of Representatives of the first session of the 98th Congress consisted of 269 Democrats and 165 Republicans (not including representatives from American Samoa, the District of Columbia, Guam, Puerto Rico, and the Virgin Islands), with 1 seat vacant, when it convened in January 1983, compared with 241 Democrats and 192 Republicans, with 2 seats vacant, when the second session of the 97th Congress adjourned. This table shows congressional district, legislator, and party affiliation.

Asterisk (*) denotes those who served in the 97th Congress; dagger (†) denotes "at large."

Alabama
1. Jack Edwards, R.*
2. William L. Dickinson, R.*
3. Bill Nichols, D.*
4. Tom Bevill, D.*
5. Ronnie G. Flippo, D.*
6. Ben Erdreich, D.
7. Richard C. Shelby, D.*

Alaska
†Don Young, R.*

Arizona
1. John McCain, R.
2. Morris K. Udall, D.*
3. Bob Stump, R.*
4. Eldon Rudd, R.*
5. Jim McNulty, D.

Arkansas
1. Bill Alexander, D.*
2. Ed Bethune, R.*
3. John Paul Hammerschmidt, R.*
4. Beryl F. Anthony, Jr., D.*

California
1. Douglas H. Bosco, D.
2. Eugene A. Chappie, R.*
3. Robert T. Matsui, D.*
4. Vic Fazio, D.*
5. Phillip Burton, D.*
6. Barbara Boxer, D.
7. George Miller, D.*
8. Ronald V. Dellums, D.*
9. Fortney H. Stark, D.*
10. Don Edwards, D.*
11. Tom Lantos, D.*
12. Ed Zschau, R.
13. Norman Y. Mineta, D.*
14. Norman D. Shumway, R.*
15. Tony Coelho, D.*
16. Leon E. Panetta, D.*
17. Charles Pashayan, Jr., R.*
18. Richard Lehman, D.
19. Robert J. Lagomarsino, R.*
20. William M. Thomas, R.*
21. Bobbi Fiedler, R.*
22. Carlos J. Moorhead, R.*
23. Anthony C. Beilenson, D.*
24. Henry A. Waxman, D.*
25. Edward R. Roybal, D.*
26. Howard Berman, D.
27. Mel Levine, D.
28. Julian C. Dixon, D.*
29. Augustus F. Hawkins, D.*
30. Matthew G. Martinez, D.*
31. Mervyn M. Dymally, D.*
32. Glenn M. Anderson, D.*
33. David Dreier, R.*
34. Esteban Torres, D.
35. Jerry Lewis, R.*
36. George E. Brown, Jr., D.*
37. Al McCandless, R.
38. Jerry M. Patterson, D.*
39. William E. Dannemeyer, R.*
40. Robert E. Badham, R.*
41. Bill Lowery, R.*
42. Dan Lungren, R.*
43. Ron Packard, R.
44. Jim Bates, D.
45. Duncan L. Hunter, R.*

Colorado
1. Patricia Schroeder, D.*
2. Timothy E. Wirth, D.*
3. Ray Kogovsek, D.*
4. Hank Brown, R.*
5. Ken Kramer, R.*
6. Vacant

Connecticut
1. Barbara B. Kennelly, D.*
2. Samuel Gejdenson, D.*
3. Bruce A. Morrison, D.
4. Stewart B. McKinney, R.*
5. William R. Ratchford, D.*
6. Nancy L. Johnson, R.

Delaware
†Thomas R. Carper, D.

Florida
1. Earl D. Hutto, D.*
2. Don Fuqua, D.*
3. Charles E. Bennett, D.*
4. William V. Chappell, Jr., D.*
5. Bill McCollum, R.*
6. Buddy MacKay, D.
7. Sam M. Gibbons, D.*
8. C. W. Young, R.*
9. Michael Bilirakis, R.
10. Andy Ireland, D.*
11. Bill Nelson, D.*
12. Tom Lewis, R.
13. Connie Mack, R.
14. Dan Mica, D.*
15. Clay Shaw, R.*
16. Larry Smith, D.
17. William Lehman, D.*
18. Claude D. Pepper, D.*
19. Dante B. Fascell, D.*

Georgia
1. Lindsay Thomas, D.
2. Charles F. Hatcher, D.*
3. Richard Ray, D.
4. Elliott H. Levitas, D.*
5. Wyche Fowler, Jr., D.*
6. Newt Gingrich, R.*
7. Larry McDonald, D.*
8. J. Roy Rowland, D.
9. Ed Jenkins, D.*
10. Doug Barnard, D.*

Hawaii
1. Cecil Heftel, D.*
2. Daniel K. Akaka, D.*

Idaho
1. Larry Craig, R.*
2. George Hansen, R.*

Illinois
1. Harold Washington, D.*
2. Gus Savage, D.*
3. Martin A. Russo, D.*
4. George M. O'Brien, R.*
5. William O. Lipinski, D.
6. Henry J. Hyde, R.*
7. Cardiss Collins, D.*
8. Dan Rostenkowski, D.*
9. Sidney R. Yates, D.*
10. John Edward Porter, R.*
11. Frank Annunzio, D.*
12. Philip M. Crane, R.*
13. John N. Erlenborn, R.*
14. Tom Corcoran, R.*
15. Edward R. Madigan, R.*
16. Lynn Martin, R.*
17. Lane Evans, D.
18. Robert H. Michel, R.*
19. Daniel B. Crane, R.*
20. Richard Durbin, D.
21. Melvin Price, D.*
22. Paul Simon, D.*

Indiana
1. Katie Hall, D.
2. Philip R. Sharp, D.*
3. John P. Hiler. R.*
4. Dan Coats, R.*
5. Elwood H. Hillis, R.*
6. Dan Burton, R.
7. John T. Myers, R.*
8. Francis X. McCloskey, D.
9. Lee H. Hamilton, D.*
10. Andrew Jacobs, Jr., D.*

Iowa
1. James Leach, R.*
2. Thomas J. Tauke, R.*
3. Cooper Evans, R.*
4. Neal Smith, D.*
5. Tom Harkin, D.*
6. Berkley Bedell, D.*

Kansas
1. Pat Roberts, R.*
2. Jim Slattery, D.
3. Larry Winn, Jr., R.*
4. Dan Glickman, D.*
5. Bob Whittaker, R.*

Kentucky
1. Carroll Hubbard, Jr., D.*
2. William H. Natcher, D.*
3. Romano L. Mazzoli, D.*
4. Gene Snyder, R.*
5. Harold Rogers, R.*
6. Larry J. Hopkins, R.*
7. Carl D. Perkins, D.*

Louisiana
1. Bob Livingston, R.*
2. Lindy Boggs, D.*
3. Billy Tauzin, D.*
4. Charles Roemer, D.*
5. Jerry Huckaby, D.*
6. W. Henson Moore, R.*
7. John B. Breaux, D.*
8. Gillis W. Long, D.*

Maine
1. John R. McKernan, Jr., R.
2. Olympia J. Snowe, R.*

Maryland
1. Roy Dyson, D.*
2. Clarence D. Long, D.*
3. Barbara A. Mikulski, D.*
4. Marjorie S. Holt, R.*
5. Steny H. Hoyer, D.*
6. Beverly Butcher Byron, D.*
7. Parren J. Mitchell, D.*
8. Michael D. Barnes, D.*

Massachusetts
1. Silvio O. Conte, R.*
2. Edward P. Boland, D.*
3. Joseph D. Early, D.*
4. Barney Frank, D.*
5. James M. Shannon, D.*
6. Nicholas Mavroules, D.*
7. Edward J. Markey, D.*
8. Thomas P. O'Neill, Jr., D.*
9. Joe Moakley, D.*
10. Gerry E. Studds, D.*
11. Brian J. Donnelly, D.*

Michigan
1. John Conyers, Jr., D.*
2. Carl D. Pursell, R.*
3. Howard E. Wolpe, D.*
4. Mark D. Siljander, R.*
5. Harold S. Sawyer, R.*
6. Bob Carr, D.
7. Dale E. Kildee, D.*
8. Bob Traxler, D.*
9. Guy Vander Jagt, R.*
10. Donald J. Albosta, D.*
11. Robert W. Davis, R.*
12. David E. Bonior, D.*
13. George W. Crockett, Jr., D.*
14. Dennis M. Hertel, D.*
15. William D. Ford, D.*
16. John D. Dingell, D.*
17. Sander Levin, D.
18. William S. Broomfield, R.*

Minnesota
1. Timothy J. Penny, D.
2. Vin Weber, R.*
3. Bill Frenzel, R.*
4. Bruce F. Vento, D.*
5. Martin O. Sabo, D.*
6. Gerry Sikorski, D.
7. Arlan Stangeland, R.*
8. James L. Oberstar, D.*

Mississippi
1. Jamie L. Whitten, D.*
2. Webb Franklin, R.
3. G. V. Montgomery, D.*
4. Wayne Dowdy, D.*
5. Trent Lott, R.*

Missouri
1. William L. Clay, D.*
2. Robert A. Young, D.*
3. Richard A. Gephardt, D.*
4. Ike Skelton, D.*
5. Alan Wheat, D.
6. E. Thomas Coleman, R.*
7. Gene Taylor, R.*
8. Bill Emerson, R.*
9. Harold L. Volkmer, D.*

Montana
1. Pat Williams, D.*
2. Ron Marlenee, R.*

Nebraska
1. Douglas K. Bereuter, R.*
2. Hal Daub, R.*
3. Virginia Smith, R.*

Nevada
1. Harry Reid, D.
2. Barbara Vucanovich, R.

New Hampshire
1. Norman E. D'Amours, D.*
2. Judd Gregg, R.*

New Jersey
1. James J. Florio, D.*
2. William J. Hughes, D.*
3. James J. Howard, D.*
4. Christopher H. Smith, R.*
5. Marge Roukema, R.*
6. Bernard J. Dwyer, D.*
7. Matthew J. Rinaldo, R.*
8. Robert A. Roe, D.*
9. Robert G. Torricelli, D.
10. Peter W. Rodino, Jr., D.*
11. Joseph G. Minish, D.*
12. James A. Courter, R.*
13. Edwin B. Forsythe, R.*
14. Frank J. Guarini, D.*

New Mexico
1. Manuel Lujan, Jr., R.*
2. Joe Skeen, R.*
3. Bill Richardson, D.

New York
1. William Carney, R.*
2. Thomas J. Downey, D.*
3. Robert J. Mrazek, D.
4. Norman F. Lent, R.*
5. Raymond J. McGrath, R.*
6. Joseph P. Addabbo, D.*
7. Benjamin S. Rosenthal, D.*
8. James H. Scheuer, D.*
9. Geraldine A. Ferraro, D.*
10. Charles E. Schumer, D.*
11. Edolphus Towns, D.
12. Major R. Owens, D.
13. Stephen J. Solarz, D.*
14. Guy V. Molinari, R.*
15. Bill Green, R.*
16. Charles B. Rangel, D.*
17. Ted Weiss, D.*
18. Robert Garcia, D.*
19. Mario Biaggi, D.*
20. Richard L. Ottinger, D.*
21. Hamilton Fish, Jr., R.*
22. Benjamin A. Gilman, R.*
23. Samuel S. Stratton, D.*
24. Gerald B. Solomon, R.*
25. Sherwood L. Boehlert, R.
26. David O'B. Martin, R.*
27. George C. Wortley, R.*
28. Matthew F. McHugh, D.*
29. Frank Horton, R.*
30. Barber B. Conable, Jr., R.*
31. Jack F. Kemp, R.*
32. John J. LaFalce, D.*
33. Henry J. Nowak, D.*
34. Stanley N. Lundine, D.*

North Carolina
1. Walter B. Jones, D.*
2. Tim Valentine, D.
3. Charles Whitley, D.*
4. Ike Andrews, D.*
5. Stephen L. Neal, D.*
6. Charles Robin Britt, D.
7. Charles Rose, D.*
8. W. G. Hefner, D.*
9. James G. Martin, R.*
10. James T. Broyhill, R.*
11. James Clarke, D.

North Dakota
† Byron L. Dorgan, D.*

Ohio
1. Thomas A. Luken, D.*
2. Willis D. Gradison, Jr., R.*
3. Tony P. Hall, D.*
4. Michael G. Oxley, R.*
5. Delbert L. Latta, R.*
6. Bob McEwen, R.*
7. Michael DeWine, R.
8. Thomas N. Kindness, R.*
9. Marcy Kaptur, D.
10. Clarence E. Miller, R.*
11. Dennis E. Eckart, D.*
12. John R. Kasich, R.
13. Donald J. Pease, D.*
14. John F. Seiberling, D.*
15. Chalmers P. Wylie, R.*
16. Ralph Regula, R.*
17. Lyle Williams, R.*
18. Douglas Applegate, D.*
19. Edward F. Feighan, D.
20. Mary Rose Oakar, D.*
21. Louis Stokes, D.*

Oklahoma
1. James R. Jones, D.*
2. Mike Synar, D.*
3. Wes Watkins, D.*
4. Dave McCurdy, D.*
5. Mickey Edwards, R.*
6. Glenn English, D.*

Oregon
1. Les AuCoin, D.*
2. Robert Smith, R.
3. Ron Wyden, D.*
4. James Weaver, D.*
5. Denny Smith, R.*

Pennsylvania
1. Thomas M. Foglietta, D.*
2. William H. Gray III, D.*
3. Robert A. Borski, D.
4. Joseph P. Kolter, D.
5. Richard T. Schulze, R.*
6. Gus Yatron, D.*
7. Bob Edgar, D.*
8. Peter Kostmayer, D.
9. Bud Shuster, R.*
10. Joseph M. McDade, R.*
11. Frank Harrison, D.
12. John P. Murtha, D.*
13. Lawrence Coughlin, R.*
14. William J. Coyne, D.*
15. Don Ritter, R.*
16. Robert S. Walker, R.*
17. George Gekas, R.
18. Doug Walgren, D.*
19. William F. Goodling, R.*
20. Joseph M. Gaydos, D.*
21. Thomas J. Ridge, R.
22. Austin J. Murphy, D.*
23. William F. Clinger, Jr., R.*

Rhode Island
1. Fernand J. St. Germain, D.*
2. Claudine Schneider, R.*

South Carolina
1. Thomas F. Hartnett, R.*
2. Floyd Spence, R.*
3. Butler Derrick, D.*
4. Carroll A. Campbell, Jr., R.*
5. John Spratt, D.
6. Robin Tallon, D.

South Dakota
† Thomas A. Daschle, D.*

Tennessee
1. James H. Quillen, R.*
2. John J. Duncan, R.*
3. Marilyn Lloyd Bouquard, D.*
4. Jim Cooper, D.
5. William H. Boner, D.*
6. Albert Gore, Jr., D.*
7. Don Sundquist, R.
8. Ed Jones, D.*
9. Harold E. Ford, D.*

Texas
1. Sam B. Hall, Jr., D.*
2. Charles Wilson, D.*
3. Steve Bartlett, R.
4. Ralph M. Hall, D.*
5. John Bryant, D.
6. Phil Gramm, D.*
7. Bill Archer, R.*
8. Jack Fields, R.*
9. Jack Brooks, D.*
10. J. J. Pickle, D.*
11. Marvin Leath, D.*
12. Jim Wright, D.*
13. Jack Hightower, D.*
14. Bill Patman, D.*
15. Eligio de la Garza, D.*
16. Ronald Coleman, D.
17. Charles W. Stenholm, D.*
18. Mickey Leland, D.*
19. Kent Hance, D.*
20. Henry B. Gonzalez, D.*
21. Tom Loeffler, R.*
22. Ron Paul, R.*
23. Abraham Kazen, Jr., D.*
24. Martin Frost, D.*
25. Mike Andrews, D.
26. Tom Vandergriff, D.
27. Solomon P. Ortiz, D.

Utah
1. James V. Hansen, R.*
2. Dan Marriott, R.*
3. Howard C. Nielson, R.

Vermont
† James M. Jeffords, R.*

Virginia
1. Herbert H. Bateman, R.
2. G. William Whitehurst, R.*
3. Thomas J. Bliley, Jr., R.*
4. Norman Sisisky, D.
5. Dan Daniel, D.*
6. James R. Olin, D.
7. J. Kenneth Robinson, R.*
8. Stan Parris, R.*
9. Frederick C. Boucher, D.
10. Frank R. Wolf, R.*

Washington
1. Joel Pritchard, R.*
2. Al Swift, D.*
3. Don Bonker, D.*
4. Sid Morrison, R.*
5. Thomas S. Foley, D.*
6. Norman D. Dicks, D.*
7. Mike Lowry, D.*
8. Rod Chandler, R.

West Virginia
1. Alan B. Mollohan, D.
2. Harley O. Staggers, Jr., D.
3. Bob Wise, D.
4. Nick Joe Rahall, D.*

Wisconsin
1. Les Aspin, D.*
2. Robert W. Kastenmeier, D.*
3. Steve Gunderson, R.*
4. Clement J. Zablocki, D.*
5. Jim Moody, D.
6. Thomas E. Petri, R.*
7. David R. Obey, D.*
8. Toby Roth, R.*
9. F. James Sensenbrenner, Jr., R.*

Wyoming
† Richard B. Cheney, R.*

Nonvoting Representatives
American Samoa
Fofo I. F. Sunia, D.*

District of Columbia
Walter E. Fauntroy, D.*

Guam
Antonio Borja Won Pat, D.*

Puerto Rico
Baltasar Corrada, D.*

Virgin Islands
Ron de Lugo, D.*

Members of the United States Senate

The Senate of the first session of the 98th Congress consisted of 54 Republicans and 46 Democrats when it convened in January 1983. Senators shown starting their term in 1983 were elected for the first time in the Nov. 2, 1982, elections. Others shown ending their current terms in 1989 were re-elected to the Senate in the same balloting. The second date in each listing shows when the term of a previously elected senator expires.

State		Term
Alabama		
	Howell T. Heflin, D.	1979—1985
	Jeremiah Denton, R.	1981—1987
Alaska		
	Theodore F. Stevens, R.	1968—1985
	Frank H. Murkowski, R.	1981—1987
Arizona		
	Barry Goldwater, R.	1969—1987
	Dennis DeConcini, D.	1977—1989
Arkansas		
	Dale Bumpers, D.	1975—1987
	David H. Pryor, D.	1979—1985
California		
	Alan Cranston, D.	1969—1987
	Pete Wilson, R.	1983—1989
Colorado		
	Gary Hart, D.	1975—1987
	William L. Armstrong, R.	1979—1985
Connecticut		
	Lowell P. Weicker, Jr., R.	1971—1989
	Christopher J. Dodd, D.	1981—1987
Delaware		
	William V. Roth, Jr., R.	1971—1989
	Joseph R. Biden, Jr., D.	1973—1985
Florida		
	Lawton Chiles, D.	1971—1989
	Paula Hawkins, R.	1981—1987
Georgia		
	Sam Nunn, D.	1972—1985
	Mack Mattingly, R.	1981—1987
Hawaii		
	Daniel K. Inouye, D.	1963—1987
	Spark M. Matsunaga, D.	1977—1989
Idaho		
	James A. McClure, R.	1973—1985
	Steven D. Symms, R.	1981—1987
Illinois		
	Charles H. Percy, R.	1967—1985
	Alan J. Dixon, D.	1981—1987
Indiana		
	Richard G. Lugar, R.	1977—1989
	J. Danforth Quayle, R.	1981—1987
Iowa		
	Roger W. Jepsen, R.	1979—1985
	Charles E. Grassley, R.	1981—1987
Kansas		
	Robert J. Dole, R.	1969—1987
	Nancy Landon Kassebaum, R.	1979—1985
Kentucky		
	Walter Huddleston, D.	1973—1985
	Wendell H. Ford, D.	1975—1987
Louisiana		
	Russell B. Long, D.	1948—1987
	J. Bennett Johnston, Jr., D.	1972—1985
Maine		
	William S. Cohen, R.	1979—1985
	George J. Mitchell, D.	1980—1989
Maryland		
	Charles McC. Mathias, Jr., R.	1969—1987
	Paul S. Sarbanes, D.	1977—1989
Massachusetts		
	Edward M. Kennedy, D.	1962—1989
	Paul E. Tsongas, D.	1979—1985
Michigan		
	Donald W. Riegle, Jr., D.	1977—1989
	Carl M. Levin, D.	1979—1985
Minnesota		
	David F. Durenberger, R.	1978—1989
	Rudolph E. Boschwitz, R.	1979—1985
Mississippi		
	John C. Stennis, D.	1947—1989
	Thad Cochran, R.	1979—1985
Missouri		
	Thomas F. Eagleton, D.	1968—1987
	John C. Danforth, R.	1977—1989
Montana		
	John Melcher, D.	1977—1989
	Max Baucus, D.	1979—1985
Nebraska		
	Edward Zorinsky, D.	1977—1989
	J. James Exon, D.	1979—1985
Nevada		
	Paul Laxalt, R.	1975—1987
	Chic Hecht, R.	1983—1989
New Hampshire		
	Gordon J. Humphrey, R.	1979—1985
	Warren B. Rudman, R.	1981—1987
New Jersey		
	Bill Bradley, D.	1979—1985
	Frank R. Lautenberg, D.	1983—1989
New Mexico		
	Pete V. Domenici, R.	1973—1985
	Jeff Bingaman, D.	1983—1989
New York		
	Daniel P. Moynihan, D.	1977—1989
	Alfonse M. D'Amato, R.	1981—1987
North Carolina		
	Jesse A. Helms, R.	1973—1985
	John P. East, R.	1981—1987
North Dakota		
	Quentin N. Burdick, D.	1960—1989
	Mark Andrews, R.	1981—1987
Ohio		
	John H. Glenn, D.	1975—1987
	Howard M. Metzenbaum, D.	1977—1989
Oklahoma		
	David L. Boren, D.	1979—1985
	Donald L. Nickles, R.	1981—1987
Oregon		
	Mark O. Hatfield, R.	1967—1985
	Robert W. Packwood, R.	1969—1987
Pennsylvania		
	H. John Heinz III, R.	1977—1989
	Arlen Specter, R.	1981—1987
Rhode Island		
	Claiborne Pell, D.	1961—1985
	John H. Chafee, R.	1977—1989
South Carolina		
	Strom Thurmond, R.	1956—1985
	Ernest F. Hollings, D.	1966—1987
South Dakota		
	Larry Pressler, R.	1979—1985
	James Abdnor, R.	1981—1987
Tennessee		
	Howard H. Baker, Jr., R.	1967—1985
	James R. Sasser, D.	1977—1989
Texas		
	John G. Tower, R.	1961—1985
	Lloyd M. Bentsen, D.	1971—1989
Utah		
	Edwin Jacob Garn, R.	1975—1987
	Orrin G. Hatch, R.	1977—1989
Vermont		
	Robert T. Stafford, R.	1971—1989
	Patrick J. Leahy, D.	1975—1987
Virginia		
	John W. Warner, R.	1979—1985
	Paul S. Trible, Jr., R.	1983—1989
Washington		
	Henry M. Jackson, D.	1953—1989
	Slade Gorton, R.	1981—1987
West Virginia		
	Jennings Randolph, D.	1958—1985
	Robert C. Byrd, D.	1959—1989
Wisconsin		
	William Proxmire, D.	1957—1989
	Robert W. Kasten, Jr., R.	1981—1987
Wyoming		
	Malcolm Wallop, R.	1977—1989
	Alan K. Simpson, R.	1979—1985

plaining his turnabout on tax increases. But the measure also included another $17.5 billion in spending reductions to help lower the deficit in the fiscal year starting Oct. 1, 1982. See TAXATION.

In August, the President vetoed a $14.1-billion supplemental appropriations bill that contained funds for education, child nutrition, and other social programs. Although he complained that it would "bust the budget by nearly a billion dollars," Congress in September overrode his veto for the first time on any major legislation.

Amendment Gets Axed. In another setback for Reagan, the balanced budget amendment—which he backed strongly despite presiding over the largest deficit in U.S. history—was rejected by the House on October 1. The President's forces fell 46 votes short of the required two-thirds majority for proposed amendments to the Constitution. The Senate had approved the plan, which would have required Congress to match revenue with expenditures except in times of war or unless three-fifths of each house voted for a deficit budget.

Both the President and congressional Democrats claimed credit for a job-training bill that replaced the Comprehensive Employment and Training Act (CETA), which had channeled $66-billion into public-service jobs and training since it was established in 1973. The new measure, aimed primarily at disadvantaged young people, required that 70 cents of each dollar be used for actual training, with only 15 cents to be spent on supportive services such as transportation payments, child care, or subsistence allowances. The program was expected to cost at least $3 billion in fiscal 1983.

In another move to help struggling savings and loan associations (S&L's), which were caught in a profit squeeze by the relatively low interest rates on mortgage loans of past years and the high interest rates they had to pay for new deposits, Congress authorized a new form of savings account known as a "money market account." The aim was to make the S&L's and banks more competitive with money market funds, which burgeoned rapidly in 1981-1982 and attracted more than $200 billion in savings. See BANK.

Voting Rights Reaffirmed. Congress also approved an extension of the Voting Rights Act of 1965, with the Senate voting 85 to 8 on June 18 in favor of the measure, following House approval in 1981. Senator Robert J. Dole (R., Kans.) worked out a compromise between the Reagan Administration and proponents of the measure in the Senate over standards for court enforcement of the law. Conservatives, including the President, wanted to require judges to find an "intent" to discriminate where a violation of the law was alleged. Others said that would weaken enforcement efforts. The final version of the bill required federal judges to consider a "totality of circumstances," including election outcomes, where discrimination is alleged. It extended for 25 years the requirement that areas where voting discrimination had occurred within the previous 10 years must clear any changes in voting laws with the Department of Justice.

In a setback for the New Right movement, the Senate tabled an antiabortion measure sponsored by Senator Helms by a vote of 47 to 46 on September 15 after weeks of a liberal filibuster. On September 23, a Helms legislative amendment to limit court rulings against voluntary prayer in public schools was defeated on a tabling vote.

Railroad Strike. Congress approved legislation in September to halt a national railroad strike by the Brotherhood of Locomotive Engineers. The union called the strike on September 19 to underscore its demand that the union's 26,000 members continue to receive a pay differential of 15 to 20 per cent more than members of 12 other U.S. railroad unions. Contrary to past practice, the American Federation of Labor and Congress of Industrial Organizations (AFL-CIO) did not oppose the measure, partly because the engineers' union was outside the big labor federation. The strike, which crippled rail traffic in most of the United States, ended on September 22 after President Reagan

Senator Howard W. Cannon (D., Nev.), *above,* and Senator Harrison H. Schmitt (R., N. Mex.) were the only incumbent senators defeated in 1982.

signed the emergency legislation. See LABOR.

In a further move toward deregulation, Congress approved a measure to give intercity bus operators greater freedom to set fares and arrange routes. It also passed an export trading company act, at the President's request, that allowed U.S. companies to combine forces to market their goods overseas without violating antitrust laws. The measure was designed to encourage exports and reduce a rapidly escalating balance-of-trade deficit, which appeared likely to break the record $42.4-billion trade deficit set in 1978.

Crime Bill. The President proposed a five-part crime bill on September 13. It included a proposal to restrict the use of the insanity defense by focusing more attention on whether a person accused of crime was aware of what he or she was doing at the moment of the crime, rather than on whether the person is mentally ill. The proposal came less than three months after a federal jury in Washington, D.C., found John W. Hinckley, Jr., not guilty by reason of insanity in the shooting of Reagan and three others in 1981. White House officials said there was no connection between the verdict and the President's support of the measure.

The Federal Budget Deficit for fiscal year 1982 hit a record $110.7 billion, more than double Reagan's original projection of $45 billion early in his Administration. It also was far above the previous record for red-ink spending of $66.4 billion set six years earlier after the 1974-1975 recession.

Democrats scored major gains in the midterm elections, picking up 26 seats in the House, adding seven governors, and fighting the Republicans to a stand-off in the Senate. As a result, the line-up for the 98th Congress was 269 Democrats and 165 Republicans, with 1 vacancy. In the Senate, the Republicans retained their 54-46 margin of control. See ELECTIONS; DEMOCRATIC PARTY; REPUBLICAN PARTY.

The President, criticizing Congress for passing only two of the 13 regular appropriations bills during the session that adjourned on October 1, demanded a post-election session. It convened on November 29. Before adjourning on December 23, Congress passed seven additional appropriations bills. It also approved a nickel-a-gallon (3.8 liters) increase in the federal gasoline tax, proceeds from which will help finance repairs to the nation's roads, bridges, water mains, and sewer lines.

Members of the House voted themselves a $9,137 pay increase, boosting their annual salary to $69,800. The Senate refused the raise but eliminated a limit on outside income that was scheduled to take effect in January 1983. William J. Eaton

See also UNITED STATES, GOVERNMENT OF THE; PRESIDENT OF THE UNITED STATES. In WORLD BOOK, see CONGRESS OF THE U.S.

CONNECTICUT. See STATE GOVERNMENT.

CONSERVATION. President Ronald Reagan aroused speculation and controversy on Feb. 25, 1982, when he ordered a survey of all federal land to identify any that was surplus and might be sold. Reagan wanted to sell $1 billion worth of surplus property in fiscal year 1983 and $4 billion annually in the next four years to help reduce the national debt.

The federal government owns about one-third of the land area of the United States, about 750 million acres (300 million hectares). On June 10, U.S. Secretary of the Interior James G. Watt said that the government planned to sell about 5 per cent of this land, or about 35 million acres (14 million hectares). The government would not sell national parks and certain other land that it has set aside for special purposes, said Watt. On June 17, the Bureau of Land Management (BLM), the government's largest landholder, reported that it had only 4.3 million acres (1.7 million hectares) that were suitable for disposal.

Most of this available land is in small, isolated tracts, so environmentalists did not object to its sale. However, many conservationists expressed fear that the lack of objection to the initial inventory of lands to be sold would be interpreted as consent to a greatly expanded sell-off.

The program faced a major congressional hurdle. Under present federal law, money from property sales must be used for park acquisition, rather than to reduce the national debt.

Endangered Species. On October 14, President Reagan approved a three-year extension of the Endangered Species Act of 1973 with only minor revisions. Environmentalists hailed the extension as a victory.

The House of Representatives approved the extension on June 8, and the Senate on June 9. The two houses worked out minor differences between the bills, and Congress approved the resulting bill in October.

More than 1,000 leading scientists had urged the extension. They warned that plant and animal species are being destroyed more rapidly than at any other time in history. "Nature can heal many of its wounds," they said, "but extinction is irreversible." The U.S. Fish and Wildlife Service lists 763 species, including 68 plants, 281 mammals, and 213 birds throughout the world as endangered or threatened.

Whaling Moratorium. The International Whaling Commission (IWC), meeting in Brighton, England, voted on July 23 to ban commercial hunting of all whales beginning in 1986. The IWC delayed the moratorium until 1986 to ease the transition for such whaling nations as Japan. The IWC intended to review the ban in 1990 to see whether the whale population had increased enough to permit some whaling.

Conservation groups had sought the moratorium since the early 1970s. Save-the-whale organizations contended that the world's whale population was falling precipitously.

Some observers feared that Japan would react to the ban by withdrawing from the IWC. However, the Reagan Administration backed the moratorium and could impose sanctions against Japanese fishing in U.S. waters if Japan continues to hunt whales. By November 8, Chile, Japan, Norway, Peru, and Russia served notice that they did not consider themselves bound by the treaty.

Barrier Bill. On October 2, Congress approved the Coastal Barrier Resources Act, which cuts off federal subsidies for building on undeveloped barrier islands off the Atlantic and Gulf coasts. Conservationists viewed the act as the most important federal environmental protection law of 1982. President Reagan signed it on October 18.

About 40 per cent of the United States 2,500 miles (4,000 kilometers) of barrier shoreline is either developed or being developed, while about 47 per cent is undeveloped and already protected. The act was expected to discourage development in the remaining 13 per cent. Beginning on Oct. 1, 1983, the government will no longer subsidize such activities as roadbuilding and sewer construction on the islands. Congress weakened the bill by exempting small stretches of beaches in Florida, North Carolina, and Texas.

Wilderness Preservation. Conservationists won a key victory on August 12, when the House voted overwhelmingly to ban oil and gas leasing in the nation's wilderness areas. The Wilderness Act of 1964 allowed mining and oil and gas exploration in wilderness areas until the end of 1983. The government leased a few areas for oil and gas development over the years. However, the leases prohibited the penetration of the earth's surface, thus preventing lessees from building roads or drilling wells. Watt said on entering office that the law did not permit him to deny lease applications solely because they involved wilderness lands.

Aggressive lobbying by environmentalists won support in Congress for an immediate ban on all leases. The success of their efforts was reflected in the lopsided 340 to 58 vote in the House.

On February 21, Watt proposed legislation that would halt wilderness leasing until the year 2000. Environmentalists charged, however, that the bill had too many loopholes and would force quick congressional action on the nearly 40 million acres (16 million hectares) of land under study for wilderness designation.

The wilderness legislation passed by the House was co-sponsored in the Senate by 54 members and called the "most important lands conservation bill of this Congress" by the environmental groups working for its passage. However, James A. McClure (R., Ida.), chairman of the Senate Energy and Natural Resources Committee, said on September 24 that he feared the bill would undermine the drive for energy independence.

A fawn is carried from Florida's Everglades in a thinning-out operation in July. Floods covered much of the herd's food supply.

In testimony on September 23, Assistant Secretary of Agriculture John B. Crowell, Jr., said the Administration was "willing to accept" a permanent ban on oil and gas exploration on wilderness lands. Crowell said, however, that the legislation should include deadlines for congressional action on wilderness recommendations and should authorize the government to use explosive charges to conduct seismic testing in wilderness areas.

On December 27, Watt withdrew more than 800,000 acres (320,000 hectares) of federal land in 10 Western states from consideration as protected wilderness areas. Environmentalists called Watt "a very dangerous man" with "utter contempt of Congress" and demanded that he be replaced.

Volcanic Monument. The site of volcanic eruptions in Washington became a national monument on August 27, when President Reagan signed a bill that designated 110,000 acres (45,000 hectares) of land as the Mount St. Helens National Volcanic Monument. The U.S. Forest Service administers the monument.

Threats to Parks. Environmental organizations became increasingly concerned by what they saw as new threats to national parks in the United

States. "America's national parks are becoming a national disgrace because of the government's neglect," Paul C. Pritchard, president of the National Parks and Conservation Association, said on September 27.

The U.S. National Park System more than doubled to 79 million acres (32 million hectares) from 1971 to 1982. However, the increase in size was not matched by a hike in appropriations for park maintenance. Nevertheless, in 1982, the Interior Department was carrying out a $1-billion, five-year program of park maintenance while holding down purchases of new parklands.

Energy and mineral developments in land next to national parks also threatened the parks. "Either we protect against development in the buffer zones or allow permanent degradation to the parks," Representative Pat Williams (D., Mont.) said on March 30.

Visitors to national parks may be threatened as the result of a dramatic increase in vandalism and crime in parks. The General Accounting Office (GAO) reported in March that violations of federal laws in U.S. parks had tripled since 1969. Assaults were up 400 per cent and vandalism up 220 per cent, the GAO said. Andrew L. Newman

See also ENVIRONMENT. In the Special Reports section, see THE COMING CROPLAND CRISIS. In WORLD BOOK, see CONSERVATION.

Chained together, Equal Rights Amendment (ERA) backers demand that the Illinois legislature pass ERA. They lost, and the amendment died in 1982.

CONSTITUTION OF THE UNITED STATES. The controversial Equal Rights Amendment (ERA) went down to defeat on June 30, 1982, after a 10-year ratification drive. The amendment would have prohibited discrimination on the basis of sex. Last-ditch efforts in Illinois and Florida by the National Organization for Women (NOW) failed, and the amendment remained three states short of the 38 it needed to become law.

Indiana, which ratified ERA in 1977, was the last state to vote in favor of the amendment. ERA was born during a period of liberalism, but its progress during the last few years was halted by a growing tide of conservatism. In fact, five states (Idaho, Nebraska, Tennessee, Kentucky, and South Dakota) had approved ERA and later reversed their votes.

Those votes, still being counted among the 35 in favor of ERA, remained an unresolved issue. A federal judge in Idaho had ruled in 1981 that it was legal for states to withdraw their ratification of ERA. He also ruled that the three-year extension of the ratification deadline granted by Congress in 1979 violated the Constitution.

The amendment's backers vowed to continue their efforts. A similar amendment was introduced when the 98th Congress convened in January 1983.

A Ban on Deficits. A proposed amendment requiring balanced federal budgets received Senate approval on August 4 but was defeated in the House of Representatives, 236-187, on October 1. President Ronald Reagan had urged passage of the amendment. Moreover, 31 states had passed resolutions calling for a constitutional convention to draft a balanced-budget amendment unless Congress passes one. The convention will be held if 34 states pass resolutions.

Other Proposed Amendments. President Reagan in May sent to Congress an amendment, still pending in committee as the 97th Congress died, to allow voluntary individual or group prayer in public schools. The amendment would have overturned a 1962 Supreme Court decision banning organized prayer in public schools.

A proposed amendment that would empower Congress and each state to restrict or prohibit abortion was approved by the Senate Judiciary Committee in March. However, further action was delayed until 1983.

An amendment to give District of Columbia residents full voting representation in Congress was not approved by any additional states in 1982. In 1981, Oregon had become the 10th state to ratify it. David L. Dreier

In the Special Reports section, see THE HIGH COURT: AT THE CENTER OF A STORM AGAIN. In WORLD BOOK, see CONSTITUTION OF THE UNITED STATES; EQUAL RIGHTS AMENDMENT.

CONSUMERISM. Double-digit increases in living costs no longer troubled the United States during 1982. By September, the Consumer Price Index (CPI), the most widely used measure of inflation, stood only 5 per cent above its level a year earlier, largely because of lower energy prices. Medical costs, however, had gone up 11.4 per cent.

Price Increases were held down by the recession, which caused a national unemployment rate of 10.8 per cent in December, the highest since the Great Depression of the 1930s. As a result of the recession, many Americans found it difficult to buy anything beyond basic necessities. Hardest hit were the steel, housing, and automobile industries, but few industries were spared.

As the year drew to a close, there were growing signs of an upturn in the economy, particularly in the housing industry. Mortgage rates turned down—averaging about 14 per cent in October—but they still remained too high for many people to consider buying a home.

Auto manufacturers ended their annual across-the-board price hikes and started selective price cutting after finding that sporadic rebate programs of about $500 on a $10,000 car had lost their pulling power. General Motors Corporation in March lowered its new-car financing rate to 12.8 per cent per year, down from the usual rate of 18 per cent. In November, the company dropped the rate for remaining 1982 models to 10.9 per cent. Competing firms also lowered their rates and tried other tactics, but nothing seemed to help sales.

Ironically, gasoline prices tumbled significantly because of surplus stocks and fuel-efficient cars. In April, Atlantic Richfield Company (Arco) stopped accepting credit cards and cut the price of gasoline by 3 cents per gallon (3.8 liters). Other marketers eventually copied Arco. By year-end, the average price of gasoline was 10 cents lower than a year earlier.

Legislative Actions. Prodded by business interests and the Administration of President Ronald Reagan, Congress continued to push for relaxation of consumer-protection laws in 1982. By a vote of 94 to 0, the Senate in March passed a bill that would force regulators to weigh the financial costs of all proposed rules against the expected benefits; make it easier to challenge such regulations in court; and give the White House more power over regulatory agencies. It also called for broad congressional veto power over virtually all rules passed by agencies of the executive branch, despite some court decisions ruling such vetoes unconstitutional. Efforts to get a similar measure through the Democratic-controlled House of Representatives ran into delays.

Another Senate-passed bill that stalled in the House would require consumers, but not business firms, to repay their debts in bankruptcy cases. Banks and retail firms claimed that many people who declared bankruptcy had the ability to repay their debts. Critics of the bill contended that the flood of bankruptcies resulted from hard times.

The mood of Congress was reflected in its veto of Federal Trade Commission (FTC) regulations requiring dealers to disclose known defects of used cars to buyers. An intensive lobbying effort by auto dealers and allied businesses paid off in May when the Senate rejected the rules 69 to 27 and the House voted against them 286 to 133.

Regulatory Actions. The Reagan Administration continued to press its campaign to reduce regulations affecting business. In August, it reported that 100 major regulations were under review; 51 others had been reviewed and either changed or killed; and countless proposals for regulations had been nipped in the bud. Savings to business firms and taxpayers amounted to $7 billion a year, said Vice-President George H. W. Bush, head of the President's Task Force on Regulatory Relief.

Regulations to protect home buyers from excessive closing fees and fraudulent practices were killed. Automobile-bumper standards were reduced, and a tire-grading system was weakened.

The Administration also eliminated hundreds of government publications—mostly those offering consumer information—to save money. One controversial proposal would have allowed the Department of Health and Human Services (HHS) to change regulations without giving public notice. Efforts were also made to place additional limitations on the kinds of information obtainable under the Freedom of Information Act.

Activity at the FTC, the chief government watch dog of the market place, virtually came to a halt under its Reagan-appointed chairman, James C. Miller III. Miller and his aides managed to kill a number of long-pending actions and to weaken others. But he did not succeed in closing down four of the agency's 10 regional offices.

Carry-over appointees on the FTC occasionally outvoted Miller. For example, in July they approved a watered-down set of rules requiring funeral homes to disclose itemized prices upon request and prohibiting the homes from misrepresenting their services. But the FTC had to submit the rules to Congress, where a veto was considered likely because of the political power of the funeral business.

Meanwhile, the Civil Aeronautics Board relaxed rules requiring airlines to compensate passengers bumped from scheduled flights, and the Interstate Commerce Commission reduced its monitoring of household moving firms. The Department of Agriculture sought to reduce standards for grading meat and inspecting poultry.

Court Decisions. In rulings that affected consumers, the Supreme Court of the United States upheld FTC prohibitions of medical-society restrictions on advertising by physicians; backed bans by savings and loan associations on the assumption of mortgages by home buyers; and allowed victims of fraud and manipulation in commodity trading to bring suit to recover damages.

In October, a federal appeals court rejected the congressional veto of the used-car regulations, paving the way for an eventual Supreme Court ruling on whether such vetoes of regulatory actions are constitutional.

Voluntary Changes. Claims by advocates of deregulation that private initiatives would replace phased-out government programs were proved correct in several instances in 1982. In 1981, the Department of Transportation stopped publishing *The Car Book*, a compendium of crash-test data, repair costs, and other information about specific automobile models. In 1982, a private publisher brought out his own updated version with much publicity. After HHS in September 1982 killed a proposal requiring that manufacturers of widely sold prescription drugs provide buyers with detailed information sheets, the American Medical Association and other groups developed similar inserts for voluntary use by doctors and druggists. After the FTC voted in July 1982 to issue regulations for the funeral industry, the industry voluntarily set up a complaint-handling system in the hope of persuading Congress to veto the rules as unnecessary.

During the 10 years when the government tried to set energy-efficiency standards for home appliances, manufacturers steadily improved efficiency. By the time Reagan took office, efficiency had come close to where the government wanted it, leaving little opposition to the elimination of the proposed standards in April.

Consumer Organizations ran into increasingly hard times in 1982 as a result of deregulation and the elimination of government grants that were a major source of their funding. Like other citizen groups, they formed coalitions to wield greater power. Consumer groups joined labor unions and other groups in opposing government efforts to deregulate fuel prices, commercialize wilderness areas, and relax pollution standards.

Financial pressures caused some local governments to close consumer offices or to cut their budgets. Business firms also took a hard look at the need for consumer advisers and, in many instances, cut down on their services.

Ralph Nader, a long-time consumer advocate, dourly suggested that the Administration abolish its Office of Consumer Affairs. He said it misled "citizens into thinking they have an ear in the White House, into believing that someone is watching out for their rights." Arthur E. Rowse

In WORLD BOOK, see CONSUMERISM.

COSTA RICA. On May 8, 1982, Luis Alberto Monge Alvarez became president of Costa Rica. Monge had bested his nearest rival by nearly a 2 to 1 margin in national elections held three months earlier.

After taking office, Monge and his Party of National Liberation (PLN), faced urgent economic problems. These problems included diminished earnings from the country's coffee exports, a staggering $2.9-billion foreign debt, a threatened cutoff of further credit by international banks, raging inflation, and 20 per cent unemployment. More worrisome still in a country known for its domestic tranquility was a rise in terrorism— fanned, the government charged, by outside forces.

To resolve its troubles, Costa Rica turned to the United States. In June, Monge visited U.S. President Ronald Reagan in Washington, D.C. Reagan pledged his support for Costa Rica's economic recovery. In September, the Congress of the United States approved a bill that provided $70 million in economic aid for Costa Rica. Monge also launched an austerity program, which included a reduction in government spending. Nathan A. Haverstock

See also LATIN AMERICA (Facts in Brief Table). In the Special Reports section, see WHAT WENT WRONG IN CENTRAL AMERICA? In WORLD BOOK, see COSTA RICA.

Costa Rica's new president, Luis Alberto Monge Alvarez, right, receives the presidential sash at his inauguration in San José, the country's capital, on May 8.

COURTS AND LAWS. John W. Hinckley, Jr., who shot U.S. President Ronald Reagan and three others outside the Washington, D.C., Hilton Hotel on March 30, 1981, was found not guilty by reason of insanity on June 21, 1982, after an eight-week trial. The jury, which deliberated for four days after hearing conflicting testimony from 41 witnesses, including 18 physicians, had watched Hinckley lapse into erratic behavior on several occasions during the trial. Hinckley was committed to St. Elizabeth's Hospital, a mental institution in Washington, D.C., on August 9 for an indefinite term. Although he was technically eligible to be considered for release in 60 days, his lawyers indicated they would make no such request in the foreseeable future. Nonetheless, the verdict was greeted by a storm of protest and renewed calls for abolition of the insanity defense. See Close-Up.

Other Important Trials made headlines during 1982. In a 47-day courtroom drama in Newport, R.I., Claus von Bülow, a financial consultant and socialite, was convicted on March 16 of twice attempting to murder his wealthy wife by injecting her with insulin. Judge Thomas H. Needham sentenced Von Bülow on May 7 to 30 years in prison. Von Bülow's lawyers filed an appeal.

Philip B. Cline, who had worked as a busboy at the Las Vegas (Nev.) Hilton Hotel for only two days when a fire broke out there on Feb. 10, 1981, killing eight people and injuring about 200, was convicted on Jan. 15, 1982, of murder and arson. On March 25, a Superior Court judge sentenced Cline to eight life terms in prison.

Jack Henry Abbott, a convicted criminal who was befriended by author Norman Mailer and won parole in 1981, went back to prison. On Jan. 21, 1982, he was convicted of manslaughter after he admitted stabbing a waiter. Abbott was sentenced on April 15 to serve a minimum of 15 years in prison before he can be considered for parole.

The latest chapter in the bizarre story of physician Jeffrey R. MacDonald, a former U.S. Army captain convicted in August 1979 of the 1970 slayings of his wife and two children, was written on Aug. 16, 1982. The United States Court of Appeals for the Fourth Circuit upheld the murder convictions, denying a new appeal based on grounds that the original trial judge had improperly excluded helpful testimony. But in 1980, the same court had reversed the original conviction, on the ground that MacDonald had been denied a speedy trial. On March 31, 1982, the Supreme Court of the United States overturned the 1980 appeal decision and reinstated the murder conviction. MacDonald was then returned to a federal prison in Los Angeles, made and lost the appeal in August, and is now serving a life sentence.

Libel and Liability. A trend toward increased liability for news media in libel cases disturbed press officials during 1982. The *Alton* (Ill.) *Telegraph* on April 14 paid a $1.4-million settlement and went into bankruptcy after an earlier $9.2-million libel judgment was upheld on appeal. The plaintiff in the case claimed that inquiries by newspaper reporters—though nothing was ever published—had ruined his credit and his contracting business. On July 30, a jury assessed *The Washington Post* $2.05 million in damages for a 1979 article that implied the president of Mobil Oil Corporation, William P. Tavoulareas, had used Mobil money to set his son up in business.

Court officers take Wayne B. Williams to prison in February after he is convicted of killing two of 28 young blacks slain in Atlanta, Ga.

In a move that stunned the legal community, the Manville Corporation, the largest U.S. asbestos producer, filed a bankruptcy petition on Aug. 26, 1982, to obtain relief from multiplying lawsuits. Company attorneys said the firm, which posted a net profit of $60.3 million in 1981, was "overwhelmed" by product liability cases. The lawsuits were filed by people unknowingly exposed to health- and life-threatening asbestos particles.

The U.S. Legal Profession recorded mixed progress in dealing with its vexing problems. At the 104th annual meeting of the American Bar Association, held in San Francisco from Aug. 5 to 12, 1982, lawyers failed for the third year to agree on changes in their Model Code of Professional Responsibility, or code of ethics.

The Judicial Conference of the United States, a

An Insane Defense?

"As to the first count, not guilty by reason of insanity." Those words by District Judge Barrington D. Parker, repeated on the evening of June 21, 1982, for each of 13 charges against would-be presidential assassin John W. Hinckley, Jr., set off a storm of outrage across the United States. Critical commentators called for alterations in the laws covering the insanity defense. A United States Senate subcommittee, proposing to change the relevant federal statutes, summoned five of Hinckley's jurors to testify. News reports carried expressions of anger and bewilderment from the public and elected officials alike, along with ideas for reform. The general perception was clear: Another guilty criminal had used expensive lawyers and psychiatrists to exploit a loophole in the judicial system.

The insanity defense has long been an important but controversial part of Anglo-American justice. The rule is that conduct should be punished only when the accused person has, in legal terminology, a *mens rea,* or criminal state of mind.

Hinckley on his way to court

Although English common law first recognized mental incapacity as a defense in the 14th century, the landmark case in insanity was decided in England in 1843. Daniel M'Naghten, a schizophrenic, tried to shoot Prime Minister Robert Peel but killed Peel's secretary instead. M'Naghten was judged innocent on grounds of insanity, causing a furor that encouraged Queen Victoria to demand tighter rules. The result was a new standard called the M'Naghten Rule. Henceforth, a defendant would be found not guilty if he "was laboring under such a defect of reason, from disease of the mind, as not to know the nature and quality of the act he was doing; or if he did know it, that he did not know he was doing what was wrong."

That standard is still used today in Great Britain and in 22 U.S. states, but recently, the rigidity of the law has run headlong into subtle shadings of modern psychiatry. In the process, the strict standard of the M'Naghten Rule has been replaced in 26 states by a vaguer one: To be judged insane, the defendant must have a mental illness so severe that he "lacked substantial capacity to appreciate the wrongfulness of his acts and could no longer control his own conduct." Hinckley was judged under that rule.

Only about 1 per cent of criminal defendants even attempt to plead insanity, and fewer than 25 per cent of those are successful. But the defense is often invoked in high-visibility crimes, and the resulting public disenchantment is fed by the contradictory "scientific" evidence offered by psychiatric witnesses. Jurors in the Hinckley case heard seven separate opinions from seven psychiatrists.

Thoughtful medical and legal leaders have proposed various plans to take psychiatric testimony out of the adversary process while retaining its use in the criminal justice system. Although establishing proof in a criminal case is ordinarily the obligation of the prosecution—the Hinckley prosecutors were called upon to prove Hinckley sane—some states have shifted responsibility for establishing insanity to the defense. Eight states have gone a bit further, setting up a controversial "guilty but mentally ill" verdict that is supposed to lead to medical treatment after conviction but requires serving a set prison term even if the treatment is successful. Two other states have taken reform one step further—Idaho and Montana have banned use of the insanity defense.

Although many legal scholars favor modifications of the insanity defense, an overwhelming majority support its retention. An American Bar Association panel reviewed the issue in 1982 and voted to retain the insanity defense. Said panel chairman Terence F. MacCarthy, "Traditionally, crime involves some element of blameworthiness, and we're not going to hold people responsible for a crime if they don't have this blameworthiness." And New York City forensic psychologist Thomas Litwack concluded that the insanity defense concept "is one of the justice system's reminders that compassion and mercy are high values in American society."

David C. Beckwith

body of 27 federal judges, agreed on September 26 on reforms of trial rules. The most significant was a proposal to increase judges' power to limit the pretrial "discovery" phase in civil trials, which some lawyers abuse. The conference suggested that judges hold lawyers accountable for unnecessary delays, which waste time and money.

The year was one of comparative turmoil for federal courts. The United States Supreme Court on June 28 ruled 6 to 3 that the Bankruptcy Code of 1978 gave federal bankruptcy judges unconstitutionally broad powers. The Supreme Court put the bankruptcy courts out of business but delayed the effective date of the ruling until year-end to give Congress time to amend the code. Two other federal courts, the United States Court of Claims and the United States Court of Customs and Patent Appeals, were replaced on October 1. The new tribunals are the U.S. Claims Court and the U.S. Court of Appeals for the Federal Circuit. The former will have expanded jurisdiction in trade matters and in claims against the U.S. government, and the latter will hear cases dealing with customs and patents. David C. Beckwith

See also CRIME; SUPREME COURT OF THE UNITED STATES. In the Special Reports section, see THE HIGH COURT: AT THE CENTER OF A STORM AGAIN. In WORLD BOOK, see COURT; LAW.

CRIME. The biggest crime story in the United States in 1982 began on September 29, when four Chicago-area people, including three members of one family, died after taking cyanide-laced capsules of Extra-Strength Tylenol, a nonprescription pain reliever. By the next day, such capsules had poisoned three more people, all of whom died.

On September 30, a California man suffered convulsions after taking two Extra-Strength Tylenol capsules. This poisoning led the McNeil Consumer Products division of Johnson & Johnson, the manufacturer of Tylenol, to recall Tylenol capsules from the entire United States. Tylenol capsules returned to the market in mid-November.

In the weeks following the poisonings, police throughout the United States reported more than 90 incidents of "copycat" crimes, typically the adulteration of food and other consumer items. As 1982 drew to a close, no one had been charged with the Tylenol poisonings.

Mass Killings. On September 25, George Banks, a Pennsylvania state prison guard who was under psychiatric care, allegedly went on a rampage in the Wilkes-Barre, Pa., area. Police said that Banks killed 13 people, including four women who had borne him children, before he surrendered. Another mental patient, schoolteacher Carl Robert Brown, shotgunned eight employees of a Miami, Fla., machine shop to death on August 20. Brown

A roadblock set up in April to catch illegal aliens and drug smugglers leaving the Florida Keys causes a 19-mile (31-kilometer) traffic jam.

tried to escape on a bicycle, but a bystander drove after Brown, shot him, and ran over him.

Authorities in Texas and Florida obtained confessions from killers who apparently equaled or exceeded the U.S. record, 33, for multiple slayings. On September 3, a judge in Houston sentenced Coral Eugene Watts to 60 years in prison after Watts pleaded guilty to one count of burglary with intent to commit murder. Watts gave details of 13 murders in return for not being prosecuted for them. Investigators said that Watts may have been responsible for another 20 murders.

Tampa, Fla., police said that Gerald Eugene Stano had admitted slaying 33 women, mostly hitchhikers and prostitutes, in Florida between 1969 and 1980. Stano, 31, is already serving a 75-year sentence on three homicide convictions.

On September 23, Juan V. Corona was convicted for a second time in the killing of 25 migrant workers near Yoruba City, Calif., in 1971. Corona's 1973 conviction for the same offenses had been overturned on appeal. And William G. Bonin, a truckdriver, was sentenced to death after his January 6 conviction for murdering 10 young men and boys in the Los Angeles area over the past decade.

The De Lorean Case. On October 19, federal agents in California arrested John Z. De Lorean, head of an automobile-manufacturing company bearing his name, on drug charges. On October 29, a federal grand jury indicted him on charges of drug trafficking and racketeering. Officials said De Lorean apparently intended to use drug profits to rescue his company, which had been placed in receivership in Northern Ireland.

International Terrorism and violence in the name of political goals continued during 1982. However, only one major aircraft hijacking occurred. On February 2, a self-described "homesick Cuban" diverted a Miami-to-Key West, Fla., flight to Havana, Cuba. The Air Florida crew of five and 71 passengers returned to Miami the same day.

Less Crime. Incidence of crime in the United States began to decline in 1982, reversing a 20-year upward trend. Final figures from the federal Bureau of Justice Statistics indicated that major crime in the United States dropped 2 per cent during 1981. The crime rate declined by 5 per cent during the first six months of 1982, compared with the same period in 1981. Crimes against property decreased by 6 per cent, as burglary declined by 11 per cent and both larceny and motor-vehicle theft were down 3 per cent. Violent crimes generally were down 3 per cent. Specifically, murder decreased by 8 per cent; robbery, 7 per cent; and forcible rape, 6 per cent. Aggravated assault increased by 1 per cent. David C. Beckwith

See also COURTS AND LAWS. In WORLD BOOK, see CRIME.

CUBA, beset by economic problems in 1982, showed signs of easing its support for revolution in Latin America and other regions of the world. The nation particularly felt the pinch from a tightened trade embargo by the United States and resistance by the Soviet Union toward increased aid.

U.S. Relations. Following a meeting between U.S. Ambassador Vernon A. Walters and Cuba's President Fidel Castro in March in Havana, Cuba, an unidentified Cuban official reportedly announced that his country had reduced its aid in arms and troops to revolutionaries of developing nations. The same official—thought by some observers to be Castro himself—said that Cuba wanted to negotiate its differences with the United States and also help in promoting a solution to the guerrilla war in El Salvador.

Having heard such statements from Cuba in the past, the United States government ignored them this time, at least publicly. United States President Ronald Reagan continued to criticize Cuba for maintaining 15,000 troops in Angola. The Reagan Administration announced new restrictions on travel to Cuba, granting visas only to journalists and scholars. In July, two Cuban aides at the United Nations were expelled from the United States for buying electronic equipment in violation of the trade embargo.

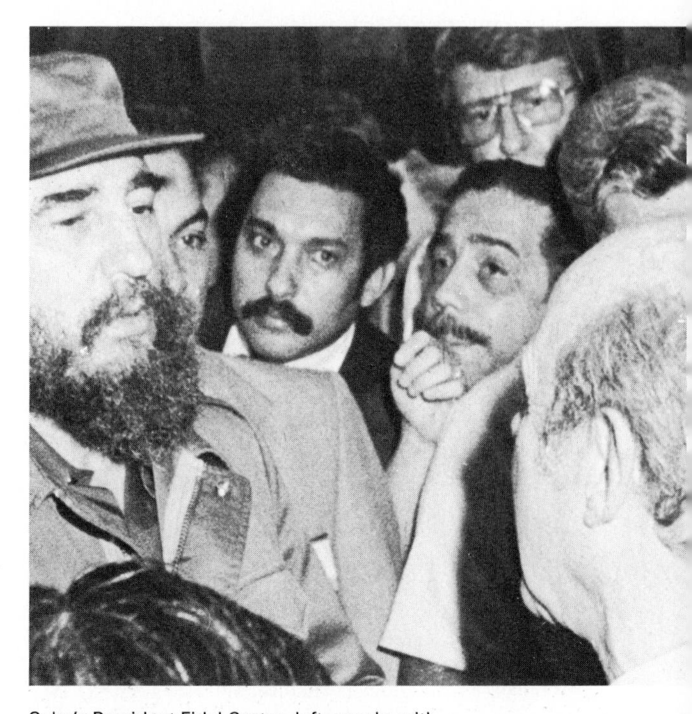

Cuba's President Fidel Castro, left, speaks with Argentina's foreign minister at a meeting of nonaligned nations in Havana, Cuba, in June.

Despite Cuban threats to disrupt American radio broadcasts, U.S. congressional committees approved funds for Radio Martí, a station for broadcasting to the Cuban people. On August 30, broadcasting by the Cuban government disrupted programming in several sections of the United States for four hours.

Cuba hosted a meeting of 94 nonaligned nations in late May and early June in Havana. Many of the attending nations bitterly attacked the United States for siding with Great Britain in the Falkland Islands dispute.

Internal Tension. Reports from Cuba in 1982 indicated that people were growing increasingly uneasy about the regimentation imposed on their lives by the government. Their movements at work and in their neighborhoods were closely watched by groups of their fellow Cubans.

The Cuban economy continued to founder. In September, Cuba was forced to negotiate with foreign bank lenders to delay the repayment of $1.2-billion in loans due before 1986. The bankers required Cuba to regularly publish economic statistics. The first report showed that the nation had $17 million in gold reserves and $643 million in convertible Russian rubles. Nathan A. Haverstock

See also LATIN AMERICA (Facts in Brief Table). In WORLD BOOK, see CUBA.

CYPRUS. See EUROPE.

CZECHOSLOVAKIA suffered from economic deterioration in 1982. Industrial output increased by only 0.4 per cent in the first half of the year, compared with the same period in 1981. The grain harvest was 7 per cent lower than planned, and meat output fell by 8 per cent.

Exports to the non-Communist world declined by 0.7 per cent in the first half of 1982, instead of increasing by 7.5 per cent as planned. Imports from the same area were 9.2 per cent lower than in the first half of 1981. However, trade with Russia increased by 21.2 per cent. In July, Milŏs Jakes, the government's economic chief, revealed that Czechoslovakia would use the entire increase in its national income for the period from 1981 through 1985 to diminish its $3.4-billion hard-currency debt.

Price Hikes. The prices of food and other consumer items were increased by 17 to 47 per cent on January 30, the steepest rise since the Communists seized power in 1948. Meat went up by 41 per cent, meat products by 17 per cent, tobacco by 30 to 39 per cent, and wine by 18 per cent. Food shortages continued throughout 1982. In April, the government allowed the opening of private shops selling fruits and vegetables.

Gold Returned. On January 29, Czechoslovakia, Great Britain, and the United States signed an agreement calling for the two Western nations and France to return to Czechoslovakia 590,000 troy ounces (18,300 kilograms) of gold that Germany had taken during World War II. The gold had fallen into Western hands at the end of the war. The agreement also called for Czechoslovakia to pay British and United States individuals and companies $130 million for property that Czechoslovakia nationalized after the Communists took power.

France had agreed to the return of the gold earlier, but Great Britain and the United States had insisted upon compensation for the nationalized property. The West returned the gold in February.

Church Targets. In January, František Lizna, a Jesuit priest, was sentenced to 19 months in prison for "damaging Czechoslovakia's interests abroad." Lizna had helped to send an underground religious magazine to the West and had met with Western priests in Czechoslovakia.

The government banned the publication of a Vatican decree, issued in March, forbidding priests to belong to clerical associations that serve political ends. One-third of all Roman Catholic priests in the nation belong to one such organization, Pacem in Terris. This organization refused to accept the decree. Chris Cviic

See also EUROPE (Facts in Brief Table). In WORLD BOOK, see CZECHOSLOVAKIA.

DAM. See BUILDING AND CONSTRUCTION.

DANCING. The 100th anniversary of Russian-born composer Igor Stravinsky's birth was celebrated internationally by the dance world in 1982. His music is paramount in the history of ballet. It was largely through his scores for *The Firebird* (1910), *Petrouchka* (1911), and *The Rite of Spring* (1913) that Sergei Diaghilev's company, the Ballets Russes, made its enormous impact on European culture in the early 1900s. Stravinsky continues to be a profound inspiration to the New York City Ballet's artistic director, George Balanchine, who is generally considered the greatest choreographer of the 20th century.

Between June 10 and 18, during its annual spring season at the New York State Theater at Lincoln Center for the Performing Arts, the New York City Ballet staged a Stravinsky Centennial Celebration comprising all the Stravinsky ballets already in its repertoire plus 14 new works. The new ballets were choreographed by Balanchine and company associates Jerome Robbins, Peter Martins, John Taras, and Jacques d'Amboise.

Although the sheer volume of premières was impressive, it was generally conceded that the heart of the festival was the retrospective survey of old Balanchine-Stravinsky works rather than the new creations. Ranging from *Apollo*—called *Apollon Musagète* when Balanchine choreographed the ballet to Stravinsky's music of that name in 1928—

New York City Ballet dancers Heather Watts and Mel Tomlinson rehearse a pas de deux from *Agon* for a Stravinsky Centennial Celebration in June.

through the brilliant *Violin Concerto* of 1972, the festival reconfirmed the sublime affinity between the two artists. However, it was disappointing that none of the new ballets measured up to past achievement. The Stravinsky celebration was subsequently featured in the City Ballet's annual three-week summer season in Saratoga Springs, N.Y., and during a two-week engagement in October at the John F. Kennedy Center for the Performing Arts in Washington, D.C.

For other major ballet companies in the United States, 1982 was a year of transition. In February, the Philadelphia-based Pennsylvania Ballet's Board of Directors decided to relieve Barbara Weisberger, the company's founder and director, of many of her duties. She was charged with financial mismanagement at a time when the Pennsylvania troupe was suffering from severe economic stress. Weisberger resigned on March 2, and associate director Benjamin Harkarvy did the same a few months later when the board refused to rehire him on a long-term basis. In a surprise move, Robert Weiss, a dancer from the New York City Ballet, was named artistic director.

The Joffrey Ballet, which has always been a

New York City company, spent 1982 without a real home base. When not laid off, the company spent most of its time on short tours to 11 cities across the United States. Fund-raising, rather than preparation of new repertory, was the keynote. While money continued to be a problem for the Joffrey, the company at last found a permanent home. On June 29, it announced that it would become the first resident dance troupe of the Los Angeles Music Center.

Labor Problems again plagued American Ballet Theatre (ABT) when its dancers' contracts expired on August 31. American Guild of Musical Artists union officials accused ABT management of refusing to negotiate the dancers' demands for parity with New York City Ballet dancers. The dispute was finally settled on November 8, but ABT was not scheduled to perform until January 1983. Nevertheless, ABT had a fruitful year. The company appeared in Chicago in February 1982 and played a month in California before opening at the Metropolitan Opera House in New York City on April 19 for a two-month season. With superstar Mikhail Baryshnikov sidelined by an injury, the company still drew large audiences, thus enhancing its new image as an ensemble troupe. The repertory chosen by Baryshnikov in his capacity as director was in accord with that image. The new productions—among them Lynne Taylor-Corbett's *Great Galloping Gottschalk,* Choo San Goh's *Configurations,* and revivals of Balanchine's *Bourrée Fantasque* and Merce Cunningham's *Duets*—all featured young soloists.

A New Theater. Large dance groups have had little problem finding suitable theaters across the United States. Middle-sized troupes, however, have faced a squeeze between opera house theaters and small community spaces. The problem has been especially acute in, of all places, the dance capital of the world—New York City. The problem was alleviated on June 2 with the opening of the renovated Joyce Theater. With a seating capacity of 475, the former motion-picture theater became a financially sound showcase for the Feld Ballet, which owns the theater and inaugurated it. The modern dance companies of Murray Louis and José Limon also performed there in November and December.

The most prestigious of the modern dance troupes, the Martha Graham Dance Company, had a relatively fitful year. It toured sporadically in the West in the fall and in the Northeast in the winter and had only a few extended engagements—at the New York City Center for three weeks in June, at Tivoli in Copenhagen, Denmark, from July 8 to 13, and as a festival participant in southern France for the rest of July. Although Graham premièred two works in June, *Dances of the Golden Hall* and *Andromache's Lament,* the pieces that stirred most interest were revivals of *Primitive Mysteries* and *Dark Meadow.* Critics were divided as to whether the current crop of Graham dancers has the force and dramatic conviction of previous generations.

Visitors from Other Countries included the distinguished Royal Danish Ballet. It performed at the Kennedy Center from June 1 to 13 and at the Metropolitan Opera House from June 15 to 26. The tour marked the first time in which the ballets of 19th-century Danish choreographer August Bournonville were featured prominently. Although he is considered one of the world's great masters, the Danes rarely perform Bournonville's work outside their own country. In 1982, Americans saw for the first time the comic *The Kermesse in Bruges* and the rather mystical *A Folk Tale,* which Bournonville considered his masterpiece. In presenting these old, unfamiliar ballets and a yet older one—the 1786 *Whims of Cupid* by Vincenzo Galeotti—the tour was considered a test case. By all accounts, the Royal Danish Ballet won the case. Fans wanting to see more Bournonville could do so during the 50th anniversary season of the Jacob's Pillow Dance Festival in Lee, Mass. During the first week of July, a small contingent of Danish soloists performed excerpts from other, even less familiar, Bournonville ballets. Nancy Goldner

In WORLD BOOK, see BALLET; DANCING.

D'AUBUISSON, ROBERTO (1944?-), became president of El Salvador's Constituent Assembly on April 22, 1982, making him probably the most powerful political leader in that nation. D'Aubuisson headed the Nationalist Republican Alliance, an extreme right wing party that he founded in 1981. It was the largest party in a rightist coalition that controlled the Assembly after elections in March 1982. Because the Assembly has the power to write a new Constitution and schedule elections, and must approve all legislation, D'Aubuisson wielded great power. See EL SALVADOR.

D'Aubuisson was born in Santa Tecla, also called Nueva San Salvador. He graduated from El Salvador's national military academy and then joined the national guard. During the 1970s, he directed Salvadoran Army intelligence under the right wing dictator General Carlos Humberto Romero. In 1979, a group of army officers removed Romero from office and dismissed D'Aubuisson from the armed forces.

In 1980, Archbishop Oscar Arnulfo Romero y Galdamez, an outspoken Roman Catholic leader, was killed by gunfire as he celebrated Mass. D'Aubuisson was arrested carrying papers that indicated he had ordered the killing. He denied the charges and was released.

D'Aubuisson is married to the former Yolanda Munguia. They have four children. Sara Dreyfuss

DEATHS of notable persons in 1982 included those listed below. An asterisk (*) indicates the person is the subject of a biography in THE WORLD BOOK ENCYCLOPEDIA. Those listed were Americans unless otherwise indicated.

Ace, Goodman (1899-March 25), humorist and columnist whose "Easy Aces" radio show, co-starring his wife, Jane, regaled audiences of the 1930s and 1940s.

Adams, Harriet S. (1893-March 27), author of some 200 children's books, including many of the Nancy Drew and Hardy Boys series.

Ashbrook, John M. (1928-April 24), Republican congressman from Ohio since 1961.

Bader, Sir Douglas (1910-Sept. 5), British fighter pilot, noted for his heroism in World War II despite having lost both legs in an accident in 1930.

Balmain, Pierre A. (1914-June 29), French dress designer who pioneered in ready-to-wear adaptations of couture styles.

Barnes, Djuna (1892-June 18), poet and novelist of the 1920s and 1930s, best known for her avant-garde novel *Nightwood* (1937).

Beaumont, Hugh (1909-May 14), actor who played the patient father in the TV series "Leave It to Beaver."

Belushi, John (1949-March 5), comic actor and writer, best known for his outrageous antics on TV's "Saturday Night Live" and in the film *Animal House*.

Benelli, Giovanni Cardinal (1921-Oct. 26), Roman Catholic archbishop of Florence, Italy, since 1977.

Satchel Paige, one of baseball's stars.

John Cheever, noted for his elegant tales of modern life.

John Belushi, a gifted comedian.

Bess Wallace Truman, widow of President Harry S. Truman.

Benet, Brenda (1946-April 7), actress who played the scheming Lee Dumonde in the daytime TV serial "Days of Our Lives."

***Bergman, Ingrid** (1915-Aug. 29), gifted Swedish-born actress noted for her portrayal of women of integrity. She won three Oscars—for best actress in *Gaslight* (1944) and *Anastasia* (1956), and for best supporting actress in *Murder on the Orient Express* (1974).

Bernbach, William (1911-Oct. 2), founder and chairman of Doyle Dane Bernbach International, one of the largest U.S. advertising agencies.

Bettis, Valerie (1920-Sept. 26), dancer and choreographer noted for her exciting technique in such works as a dance version of *A Streetcar Named Desire* in 1952 and the 1948 revue *Inside U.S.A.*

Bishop, Wallace B. (1905-Jan. 15), artist who drew the cartoon strip "Muggs and Skeeter" from 1927 to 1974.

Bloch, Ray (1902-March 29), conductor and composer for TV variety shows starring Ed Sullivan and Jackie Gleason from 1947 to 1971.

Bloomingdale, Alfred S. (1916-Aug. 20), millionaire business executive who gave the world the Diners' Club.

Boyer, Ken (1931-Sept. 7), star third baseman with the St. Louis Cardinals baseball team from 1955 to 1965.

***Brezhnev, Leonid Ilich** (1906-Nov. 10), Russian political leader, head of the Communist Party of the Soviet Union since 1964 and chairman of the Presidium of the Supreme Soviet since 1977 (see Close-Up).

Broderick, James J. (1927-Nov. 1), actor who starred in the 1970s TV series "Family" and in such films as *The Group* (1966) and *Dog Day Afternoon* (1975).

Bruce, Virginia (1909-Feb. 24), Hollywood actress who portrayed the quintessential Ziegfeld showgirl in *The Great Ziegfeld* (1936).

Buono, Victor (1938-Jan. 1), character actor, best known for his performance in the film *Whatever Happened to Baby Jane?* (1962).

Burck, Jacob (1904-May 11), Polish-born artist whose political cartoons appeared in the Chicago *Sun-Times*. He won a Pulitzer Prize in 1941.

Burnett, William R. (1899-April 25), novelist and screenwriter whose 39 books began with the pattern-setting *Little Caesar* in 1929.

Bushmiller, Ernie (1905-Aug. 15), creator of the comic strip "Nancy" in 1940.

Butler, Lord Richard A. (Rab) (1902-March 8), British Conservative leader who narrowly missed becoming head of state on two occasions.

Canham, Erwin D. (1904-Jan. 3), editor of *The Christian Science Monitor* from 1945 to 1964 and editor-in-chief until 1974.

***Case, Clifford P.** (1904-March 5), liberal Republican who championed civil rights legislation as a congressman from New Jersey from 1945 to 1953 and as senator from 1955 to 1979.

Chatfield-Taylor, Brenda Diana Duff Frazier Kelly (Brenda Frazier) (1921-May 3), glittering debutante who captured headlines in the 1930s and 1940s and later wrote that her hedonistic life style had brought her "nothing but despair."

***Cheever, John** (1912-June 18), author who wrote about the delights and despairs of contemporary life in such elegant novels as *The Wapshot Chronicle* and *The Wapshot Scandal* and more than 400 short stories.

Chenoweth, Dean (1938-July 31), powerboat race driver who won the U.S. national hydroplane championship four times.

Chuikov, Marshal Vasily I. (1900-March 18), Russian military leader whose defense of Stalingrad during World War II helped to turn the tide against Adolf Hitler.

Churchill, Sarah (1914-Sept. 24), British actress, daughter of Sir Winston Churchill.

***Cody, John Patrick Cardinal** (1907-April 25), Roman Catholic archbishop of Chicago since 1965.

Conried, Hans (Frank Foster) (1915-Jan. 5), versatile character actor and comedian of stage, radio, and television for more than 40 years.

Coote, Robert (1909-Nov. 25), veteran British actor, best known as Colonel Pickering in the hit musical *My Fair Lady.*

Coslow, Sam (1910-April 2), composer and lyricist whose songs included "Cocktails for Two" and "My Old Flame."

Cox, Allyn (1896-Sept. 26), mural painter whose work adorns the rotunda corridors of the United States Capitol in Washington, D.C.

Crisler, Herbert Orin (Fritz) (1899-Aug. 19), football coach who devised two-platoon football at the University of Michigan in 1945.

Curzon, Sir Clifford (1907-Sept. 1), British concert pianist noted for his impeccable virtuoso technique.

Dannay, Frederic (1905-Sept. 1), co-author with Manfred B. Lee of more than 35 detective novels and many short stories under the pen name of Ellery Queen.

Davis, Loyal (1896-Aug. 19), noted neurosurgeon and father of first lady Nancy Reagan.

Del Monaco, Mario (1915-Oct. 19), Italian tenor, a leading singer at New York City's Metropolitan Opera in the 1950s.

Demara, Ferdinand W. (1922-June 7), whose life provided the inspiration for the film *The Great Impostor.*

Deutsch, Helene R. (1884-March 29), Austrian-born psychoanalyst who was noted for her work in personality disorders and her classic book *The Psychology of Women.*

***Dubinsky, David** (1892-Sept. 17), president of the International Ladies' Garment Workers' Union from 1932 to 1966.

***Dubos, René Jules** (1901-Feb. 20), bacteriologist whose research led to the first commercially produced antibiotic in 1939.

Duffy, Clinton T. (1898-Oct. 11), warden of California's San Quentin prison from 1940 to 1952 and a noted humanitarian.

Eldjárn, Kristján (1916-Sept. 13), president of Iceland from 1968 to 1980.

Farber, Edward R. (1915-Jan. 22), electronic engineer and photographer credited with the invention of the portable flash for still cameras.

Fassbinder, Rainer Werner (1946-June 10), German filmmaker, best known for *The Marriage of Maria Braun* (1979).

Fehr, Howard F. (1902-May 6), mathematician who helped start the new math system of teaching mathematics in the United States in the 1960s.

Feingold, Benjamin F. (1900-March 23), pediatrician and allergist who believed that hyperactivity in some children was caused by synthetic coloring and other additives in their diet.

Feldman, Marty (1934-Dec. 2), bulging-eyed British comic, writer, and director, perhaps best known for his portrayal of Igor in the movie *Young Frankenstein* (1974).

Felici, Pericle Cardinal (1911-March 21), Roman Catholic cardinal noted for his expertise in church law.

Fitzgerald, Edward (1893-March 22), radio commentator best known for his long-time radio show "The Fitzgeralds"—a series of discussions with his wife, Pegeen.

Fitzmaurice, David J. (1913-Nov. 13), president of the International Brotherhood of Electrical Workers.

***Fonda, Henry** (1905-Aug. 12), actor who played the strong, silent type of hero in more than 70 films and many stage plays and TV dramas. He won an Oscar in 1982 for his performance in *On Golden Pond.* See FONDA, HENRY.

***Fortas, Abe** (1910-April 5), associate justice of the Supreme Court of the United States from 1965 to 1969, when he resigned following criticism of his association with a financier who was under federal investigation.

King Khalid, ruler of Saudi Arabia.

Ayn Rand, novelist and social critic.

Ingrid Bergman, gifted Swedish actress who won three Oscars.

John P. Robarts, political figure.

Foster, Harold R. (1892-July 25), artist who created the "Prince Valiant" comic strip in 1937.

Frei Montalva, Eduardo (1911-Jan. 22), president of Chile from 1964 to 1970.

***Freud, Anna** (1895-Oct. 9), Austrian-born psychoanalyst, daughter of Sigmund Freud.

Gallen, Hugh J. (1924-Dec. 29) Democratic governor of New Hampshire since 1979.

Gardner, John (1933-Sept. 14), poet and writer whose philosophical novels include *Grendel* (1971), *The Sunlight Dialogues* (1972), and *October Light* (1976).

Garroway, Dave (1913-July 21), genial low-key star of early television's "Garroway-at-Large" and the first host of the "Today" show in 1952.

Gemayel, Bashir (1947-Sept. 14), president-elect of Lebanon, leader of the Christian Phalangists.

George, Bill (1930-Sept. 30), football player, a linebacker with the Chicago Bears from 1952 to 1965.

Ghotbzadeh, Sadegh (1936-Sept. 15), foreign minister of Iran during the U.S. hostage crisis in 1980.

Giauque, William F. (1895-March 28), Canadian-born chemist who won the Nobel Prize for Chemistry in 1949 for his studies of reactions to extreme cold.

Goldmann, Nahum (1895-Aug. 29), Lithuanian-born Zionist and chief architect of the pact pledging West Germany to pay reparations to Israel.

***Gomułka, Władysław** (1905-Sept. 1), leader of Poland's Communist Party from 1956 to 1970.

Dave Garroway, TV star in the 1950s.

Marty Robbins, country singer.

Anna Freud, eminent child psychoanalyst.

Archibald MacLeish, poet who won three Pulitzer Prizes.

Gosden, Freeman (1899-Dec. 10), who played Amos and Kingfish on the "Amos 'n' Andy" radio show from 1928 to 1960.

***Gould, Glenn** (1932-Oct. 4), Canadian pianist, best known for his Bach interpretations.

Greer, William A. (Sonny) (1903-March 23), original drummer in Duke Ellington's Orchestra. He played with Ellington for more than 30 years.

Gregory, Horace (1898-March 11), poet, winner of the 1965 Bollingen Prize. His eight books include *Another Look* (1976). His wife, poet Marya Zaturenska, died on January 19.

Griffin, Marvin (1907-June 13), Democratic governor of Georgia from 1955 to 1959.

Grosvenor, Melville B. (1901-April 22), president of the National Geographic Society and editor of *National Geographic* magazine from 1957 to 1967.

***Grumman, Leroy R.** (1895-Oct. 4), aeronautical engineer who built Grumman Aircraft Corporation (now the Grumman Corporation).

Guzmán Fernández, Silvestre Antonio (1911-July 4), president of the Dominican Republic since 1978.

Hall, Joyce C. (1891-Oct. 29), founder of Hallmark Greeting Cards Incorporated in 1910.

Hallstein, Walter (1901-March 29), West German lawyer and diplomat. He was the first president and a founding father of the European Community (Common Market).

Harkness, Rebekah W. (1915-June 17), composer and philanthropist who gave millions to the dance and to medicine.

Harman, Fred (1902-Jan. 2), artist who created the cowboy comic strip "Red Ryder" in 1938.

Harrison, Ernest J. (Dutch) (1910-June 19), golfer who won 18 titles on the Professional Golfers' Association (PGA) tour.

Holloway, Stanley (1890-Jan. 30), British actor, best known for his role as Eliza Doolittle's father in both the Broadway production and the film of *My Fair Lady*.

Hopkins, Sam (Lightnin') (1912-Jan. 30), country blues singer and guitarist.

Horikoshi, Jiro (1904-Jan. 11), Japanese aeronautical engineer who designed the Zero fighter plane.

Hughes, Emmet John (1921-Sept. 20), journalist who served as speechwriter for President Dwight D. Eisenhower.

Hugo, Richard F. (1923-Oct. 22), distinguished poet whose works included *31 Letters and 13 Dreams* (1977).

Irish, Edward S. (Ned) (1905-Jan. 21), founder and president of the New York Knickerbockers basketball team from 1946 to 1974.

Janson, Horst W. (1913-Sept. 30), Russian-born art historian whose classic work *History of Art* (1962) was translated into 14 languages.

Jarman, John (1915-Jan. 15), congressman from Oklahoma from 1951 to 1977. He switched from the Democratic Party to the Republican Party in 1975.

Jaworski, Leon (1905-Dec. 9), special Watergate prosecutor who helped force the resignation of President Richard M. Nixon in 1974.

Jensen, Jackie (1927-July 14), baseball player who drove in 667 runs for the Boston Red Sox in six seasons.

Jeritza, Maria (1887-July 10), Czech-born soprano, a prima donna of opera's golden age from 1910 to 1930.

Jessup, Richard (1925-Oct. 22), novelist whose books included *The Cincinnati Kid* (1964).

Johnson, Dame Celia (1908-April 25), British actress, best known for her role in the film *Brief Encounter*.

Jory, Victor (1902-Feb. 11), actor who played the taciturn bad guy in dozens of Hollywood films.

Jurgens, Curt (1915-June 18), German film actor who starred in such films as *Inn of the Sixth Happiness* (1958) and *The Blue Angel* (1959).

Kaufman, Murray (Murray the K) (1922-Feb. 21), disk jockey noted for his breezy style.

***Kelly, Grace P. (Princess Grace of Monaco)** (1929-Sept. 14), actress who won an Oscar in 1954. She married Prince Rainier III of Monaco in 1956.

***Khalid, King** (1913-June 13), king of Saudi Arabia.

King, Henry (1888-June 29), Hollywood film director whose more than 100 films included *Twelve O'Clock High* (1950) and *Love Is a Many-Splendored Thing* (1955).

Kingdon, Kenneth H. (1894-March 9), Jamaica-born physicist, a leader in the development of nuclear energy.

Kistiakowsky, George B. (1900-Dec. 7), Russian-born chemist who helped develop the first atomic bomb. He later was chairman of the Council for a Livable World, an antinuclear group.

Kogan, Leonid (1924-Dec. 17), Russian violinist.

Lamas, Fernando (1915-Oct. 8), Argentine-born actor who played the quintessential Latin lover in numerous 1950s films.

Lawler, Richard H. (1886-July 24), surgeon who performed the world's first kidney transplant in 1950.

Lawrence, Daisy G. (1901-April 26), who became the first Girl Scout in the United States in 1912.

Lockridge, Richard (1898-June 19), writer who with his wife, Frances, created the fictional sleuths Mr. and Mrs. North.

Loughran, Tommy (1903-July 7), world light-heavyweight boxing champion from 1927 to 1929.

Lynd, Helen M. (1896-Jan. 30), sociologist and co-author of the classic sociological studies *Middletown* (1929) and *Middletown in Transition* (1937).

Brezhnev's Legacy

Leonid Brezhnev (1906-1982)

Leonid Ilich Brezhnev, who died on Nov. 10, 1982, brought stability to the Soviet Union when the country needed it badly. Brezhnev's predecessor—the ebullient, original, unpredictable Nikita S. Khrushchev—had disturbed Communist Party bureaucrats by dividing the party machinery into an industrial sector and an agricultural sector, and by intensifying the destalinization campaign, which condemned the policies of Joseph Stalin—Russian dictator from 1929 until his death in 1953. Khrushchev had upset the party's civilian ruling group with his dictatorial methods. And he had alarmed the entire leadership, including the heads of the armed forces, by taking Russia to the brink of nuclear war with the United States over Cuba in 1962 and then pulling back under humiliating circumstances.

Shortly after Brezhnev replaced Khrushchev as party chief in 1964, he reversed the partition of the party and put the brakes on destalinization. Furthermore, Brezhnev shared power with other Communist leaders, ruling by bureaucratic consensus.

Brezhnev gave the Soviet military leaders what they wanted. By 1979, 130 SS-20 nuclear missiles, capable of reaching Western Europe, were installed on Russian soil. That year, the North Atlantic Treaty Organization (NATO) decided to counteract this deployment by installing United States missiles in Western Europe. However, by the time Brezhnev died, Russia had installed 320 SS-20's, while NATO had not deployed a single missile in Western Europe.

Brezhnev was never as powerful as Khrushchev had been, but he enjoyed a personality cult surpassing anything that Khrushchev ever had. In 1976, on Brezhnev's 70th birthday, he was proclaimed *vozhd* (leader), an honorary title previously given only to Stalin and V. I. Lenin—the founder of Russia's Communist Party. In 1979, Brezhnev received the Lenin Prize for Literature, the Soviet Union's highest literary award. Brezhnev's speeches and writings became part of the Marxist-Leninist doctrine quoted by party members to support ideological arguments.

In foreign policy, Brezhnev presided over the crushing of Czechoslovakia's liberal reform experiment in 1968. Russia based this suppression on its self-proclaimed right to exercise a veto over the internal and external policies of other Eastern-bloc nations. This right was part of what became known as the Brezhnev Doctrine of limited sovereignty.

Brezhnev gave high priority to détente between East and West. Détente eased the burden of arms competition and allowed Russia to use Western technology to plug gaps in its own economy. But toward the end of Brezhnev's life, powerful challenges to satellite governments in Afghanistan and Poland threatened détente.

Western economic sanctions imposed in the wake of Russia's invasion of Afghanistan in December 1979 caused some damage to the Soviet Union and its allies. Western counteractions against Russia for its role in Poland's imposition of martial law in December 1981 threatened to spoil the relationship that Russia had established with West Germany.

But perhaps the greatest failure of the Brezhnev era was the Russian economy. The government poured money, resources, and labor into the economy, but industrial growth slowed dramatically during Brezhnev's last years, and food shortages plagued the country. Russia accepted the humiliating and politically risky position of becoming a major importer of grain from the capitalist world. Meanwhile, Russia's East European partners built up large debts to the West.

Brezhnev was the first Soviet leader to preside over almost two stable decades. However, he purchased domestic peace at the price of prosperity. As 1983 approached, political observers wondered how insistent his successor, Yuri V. Andropov, would be about bringing prosperity to the Soviet Union, and what price Andropov would be willing to pay for it.

Chris Cviic

Lynde, Paul (1926-Jan. 9), witty actor and comedian, a regular performer on TV's game show "The Hollywood Squares."

Macdonald, Dwight (1906-Dec. 19), author, essayist, critic, and editor.

Mackin, Catherine (1940-Nov. 20), television news reporter with the American Broadcasting Company.

***MacLeish, Archibald** (1892-April 20), noted poet and dramatist. He won three Pulitzer Prizes: in 1932, for his epic poem *Conquistador;* in 1953, for *Collected Poems, 1917-1952;* and in 1959, for his verse drama *J.B.*

Magee, Patrick (1924-Aug. 14), Irish actor who won a 1965 Tony Award for his performance in *Marat/Sade* (1964).

Manone, Joseph (Wingy) (1904-July 9), one-armed jazz trumpeter, best known for his 1935 swing version of "The Isle of Capri" and "Tar Paper Stomp."

Margulies, Lazar (1895-March 7), Polish-born physician who invented the flexible plastic intrauterine coil for birth control.

Marlowe, Hugh (1911-May 2), stage and screen actor who played the role of Jim Matthews in the daytime TV serial "Another World" since 1969.

Marsh, Dame Ngaio (1899-Feb. 18), New Zealand writer known throughout the world for such detective novels as *A Man Lay Dead* and *Tied Up in Tinsel.*

McGivern, William P. (1922-Nov. 18), writer of 23 mystery novels including *The Big Heat* and *Summit.*

Mendès-France, Pierre (1907-Oct. 18), Socialist premier of France in 1954 and 1955.

Wilfrid Pelletier, Canadian conductor.

Cathleen Nesbitt, a noted British character actress.

Grace Kelly, actress, princess of Monaco.

Thelonious Monk, a brilliant jazz composer and pianist.

Merchant, Vivien (Ada Thompson) (1929-Oct. 3), British actress noted for her brilliant performances in plays written by her former husband Harold Pinter, such as *The Birthday Party* (1958) and *The Homecoming* (1965).

Mills, Harry (1913-June 28), a member of the Mills Brothers singing group, whose many hit records included "Paper Doll" and "Glow Worm."

***Monk, Thelonious** (1917-Feb. 17), jazz composer and pianist noted for his adventurous melodies.

Montessori, Mario (1899-Feb. 9), Italian-born educator and a prominent figure in the Montessori educational system established by his mother, Maria.

Morrow, Vic (1932-July 23), stage and film actor who played Sergeant Chip Saunders on TV's "Combat" series from 1962 to 1969.

Morton, Thruston B. (1907-Aug. 14), Republican congressman from Kentucky from 1947 to 1953 and senator from 1957 to 1969.

Namgyal, Palden Thondup (1923-Jan. 29), king of Sikkim from 1963 to 1975.

Nesbitt, Cathleen (1888-Aug. 2), British actress who epitomized the grande dame. She played Henry Higgins' mother in the Broadway production of the hit musical *My Fair Lady* (1956).

***Nicholson, Ben** (1894-Feb. 6), British artist noted for his abstract paintings.

Noel-Baker, Lord Philip J. (1889-Oct. 8), British statesman, winner of the Nobel Prize for Peace in 1959.

Oates, Warren (1929-April 3), character actor whose films included *In the Heat of the Night* and *Easy Rider.*

O'Brien, Leo W. (1901-May 4), Democratic congressman from New York from 1952 to 1967.

O'Gorman, Juan (1905-Jan. 18), Mexican architect and artist whose work adorns the National Museum of Anthropology and the airport in Mexico City.

Orff, Carl (1895-March 29), German composer, best known for *Carmina Burana* (1937).

***Paige, Leroy (Satchel)** (1905-June 8), baseball player, one of the great pitchers. He was elected to baseball's Hall of Fame in 1971. He was also noted for such homespun aphorisms as, "Don't look back, something may be gaining on you."

Pelletier, Wilfrid (1896-April 9), Canadian symphony conductor whose appointments included the New York Philharmonic and the Quebec Symphony Orchestra.

Poulson, C. Norris (1895-Sept. 25), Republican congressman from California from 1943 to 1945 and 1947 to 1953, and mayor of Los Angeles from 1953 to 1961.

Powell, Eleanor (1912-Feb. 11), tap-dancing star of dozens of Hollywood films in the 1930s and 1940s.

***Primrose, William** (1903-May 1), Scottish violist noted for his outstanding performances in solo concerts.

***Rand, Ayn** (1905-March 6), Russian-born author and social critic who espoused "rational selfishness." Her best-known novel was *The Fountainhead* (1943).

***Rexroth, Kenneth** (1905-June 6), poet and translator, a leading member of the beat generation writers in the 1950s. His books include *Defense of the Earth* (1956).

Robarts, John P. (1917-Oct. 18), Canadian politician, premier of Ontario from 1961 to 1971.

Robbins, Marty (1925-Dec. 8), country music singer best known for his Grammy Award-winning song "El Paso."

***Rubinstein, Arthur** (1887-Dec. 20), Polish-born pianist who played his first formal concert in 1898, when he was 11 years old.

Sackler, Howard (1929-Oct. 14), writer and director whose play *The Great White Hope* won a Pulitzer Prize.

Sakata, Harold T. (1920-July 29), actor best known for his role as Oddjob—the one with the razor-rimmed hat—in the James Bond movie *Goldfinger* (1964).

Sánchez, Salvador (1959-Aug. 12), boxer, holder of the World Boxing Council's featherweight title.

Schaefer, Rudolph J. (1900-Sept. 2), brewery president and sportsman.

Schneider, Romy (1938-May 29), Austrian-born actress who appeared in such films as *The Cardinal* (1963) and *What's New, Pussycat?* (1965).

Sebelius, Keith G. (1916-Sept. 5), Republican congressman from Kansas from 1969 to 1981.

***Selye, Hans** (1907-Oct. 16), Canadian endocrinologist, born in Austria, noted for his pioneering studies of the effects of stress on the human body.

Shimura, Takashi (1905-Feb. 11), Japanese actor who appeared in such films as *Seven Samurai* (1954) and *Godzilla, King of the Monsters* (1956).

Sillman, Leonard (1908-Jan. 23), producer of the New Faces revues on Broadway between 1934 and 1968 that introduced such stars as Henry Fonda, Imogene Coca, and Eartha Kitt.

Simmons, Calvin (1950-Aug. 21), gifted musician and the only black music director of a major symphony in the United States when he became conductor of the Oakland (Calif.) Symphony in 1979.

Slone, Dennis (1930-May 10), South African-born epidemiologist whose *Birth Defects and Drugs in Pregnancy* (1977) was considered the definitive work linking drug use by pregnant women to fetal deformities.

Smiley, Gordon (1949-May 15), race-car driver, killed in the qualifying laps for the Indianapolis 500.

Smith, Walter W. (Red) (1905-Jan. 15), sports columnist for *The New York Times* since 1971, one of the world's most admired sports commentators, and long-time member of the Board of Editors of THE WORLD BOOK YEAR BOOK. He won a Pulitzer Prize in 1976.

Spivak, Charlie (1905-March 1), orchestra leader during the big-band era of the 1940s.

Stitt, Sonny (1925-July 22), jazz alto saxophonist whose style and stature were compared to those of Charlie Parker.

Strasberg, Lee (Israel Strassberg) (1901-Feb. 17), Polish-born stage director and film actor who promoted Stanislavski method acting in America and had a profound influence on theater and films.

Stratton, Monty (1912-Sept. 29), baseball player who pitched for the Chicago White Sox in the 1930s. His comeback after a leg amputation inspired the film *The Stratton Story* (1949).

***Suslov, Mikhail A.** (1902-Jan. 25), Russian politician, chief ideologist of the Soviet Communist Party, and one of the most powerful men in the Kremlin.

***Swigert, John Leonard, Jr. (Jack)** (1931-Dec. 27), former astronaut who was elected to the U.S. House of Representatives on November 2.

Swinnerton, Frank (1884-Nov. 6), British novelist whose work spanned 70 years—from *The Merry Heart* (1908) to *Old Man with Three Daughters* (1979).

Tati, Jacques (Jacques Tatischeff) (1907-Nov. 5), French actor and writer who directed and starred in the film *Mr. Hulot's Holiday* (1954) and won an Oscar in 1958 for *Mon Oncle*.

Terry, Walter (1913-Oct. 4), dance critic with *The New York Herald Tribune* from 1945 to 1966.

Truman, Bess (Elizabeth Virginia Wallace) (1885-Oct. 18), widow of President Harry S. Truman.

Twining, Nathan F. (1897-March 29), U.S. Air Force general and chairman of the Joint Chiefs of Staff from 1957 to 1960.

Vidor, King Wallis (1894-Nov. 2), director of many classic films including his silent films *The Crowd* (1928) and *The Champ* (1931).

Villeneuve, Gilles (1952-May 8), Canadian race-car driver who won six Grand Prix races.

Wakeley, Jimmy (1914-Sept. 23), singing star of numerous Westerns. His hit songs included "Tennessee Waltz" and "Beautiful Brown Eyes."

Abe Fortas, an associate justice of the Supreme Court.

Harriet S. Adams, who wrote books for children.

Red Smith, one of the world's great sports columnists.

Henry Fonda, a star of more than 70 films.

Walker, Fred (Dixie) (1910-May 17), baseball player, hard-hitting outfielder for the Brooklyn Dodgers from 1939 to 1947.

Walters, Charles (1903-Aug. 13), director of such Hollywood musicals as *Meet Me in St. Louis* (1944) and *Easter Parade* (1948).

Waner, Lloyd (Little Poison) (1906-July 22), star outfielder for the Pittsburgh Pirates from 1927 to 1941.

Webb, Jack (1920-Dec. 23), actor and producer best known as Sergeant Joe Friday on the radio and television series "Dragnet.".

Weiss, Peter (1917-May 10), German-born playwright, best known for *Marat/Sade* (1964).

Whitney, John H. (Jock) (1904-Feb. 8), newspaper publisher who served as ambassador to London from 1957 to 1961.

Williams, Gluyas (1888-Feb. 13), artist who satirized suburban life in *New Yorker* cartoons from 1925 to 1953.

Wilson, Don (1900-April 5), announcer who was Jack Benny's foil on radio and TV for more than 40 years.

Zaturenska, Marya (1902-Jan. 19), Russian-born poet whose works included *Cold Morning Sky*, for which she won the Pulitzer Prize in 1938.

Ziolkowski, Korczak (1908-Oct. 20), sculptor who spent 35 years carving a majestic monument to Chief Crazy Horse of the Sioux Indians in a granite mountain in the Black Hills of South Dakota.

***Zworykin, Vladimir K.** (1889-July 29), Russian-born physicist and engineer who developed the first practical television tube.

Irene B. Keller

DE LA ESPRIELLA, RICARDO, JR. (1934-), became president of Panama on July 30, 1982, succeeding Aristides Royo, who resigned. Royo said that he resigned because of a throat affliction, but political observers cited a power struggle between Royo and the head of the National Guard, Brigadier General Rubén Darío Paredes. See PANAMA.

Less than an hour after De la Espriella's inauguration, Paredes held a news conference at which he made "recommendations" and "suggestions" to the new president. De la Espriella apparently carried all of them out.

De la Espriella said that he would maintain Panama's traditional foreign policy. Royo had called for a regional organization that would exclude the United States but include Cuba.

Ricardo de la Espriella, Jr., was born on Sept. 5, 1934, in Panama City. He was educated at the University of Panama, Louisiana State University in Baton Rouge, and Stanford University in Stanford, Calif.

From 1957 to 1962, De la Espriella held an administrative post with the Agency for International Development—a United States government agency that administers foreign aid. He held various banking positions during the 1960s and became general director of the National Bank of Panama in 1970. He left the bank in 1978 to become vice-president of Panama. Jay Myers

DE LA MADRID HURTADO, MIGUEL (1934-), was elected president of Mexico on July 4, 1982, and took office on December 1. He succeeded José López Portillo, who did not run for re-election because Mexico limits presidents to one term. De la Madrid was the candidate of the Institutional Revolutionary Party, which has dominated Mexican politics since 1929. See MEXICO.

Miguel de la Madrid Hurtado was born on Dec. 12, 1934, in the western city of Colima. He was raised in Mexico City and studied law there. He entered the government at the age of 19, working for a state bank.

De la Madrid received a master's degree in public administration from Harvard University in Cambridge, Mass., in 1965. He then returned to Mexico and served as an undersecretary in the Finance Ministry. In 1970, he became assistant director of the state oil company. When López Portillo was named finance minister in 1972, De la Madrid returned to the Finance Ministry. He remained in that ministry when López Portillo became president in 1976.

In 1979, López Portillo appointed De la Madrid to fill the new position of secretary of budget and programming. That year, De la Madrid drafted the Global Development Plan, Mexico's first integrated socioeconomic blueprint. Jay Myers

DELAWARE. See STATE GOVERNMENT.

DEMOCRATIC PARTY candidates, cashing in on voters' anger over economic hard times, scored major gains in the November 1982 midterm elections in the United States. The results were a setback for Republican President Ronald Reagan in the House of Representatives, where the Democrats gained 26 seats. The Republicans fought the Democrats to a stand-off in the Senate. In governors' races, Democrats picked up seven statehouses to strengthen their power base for the 1984 presidential contest.

The 26 seats the Democrats picked up in the House gave them a 267 to 166 advantage over Republicans in the new Congress. The advantage later increased to 269 to 166 when Democrats won in a delayed congressional election in Georgia. The Republican total was cut to 165 when Jack Swigert, a former astronaut elected to the House from Colorado, died on December 27.

The outcome apparently provided a working majority for Speaker of the House Thomas P. (Tip) O'Neill, Jr. (D., Mass.), who termed the election a "devastating defeat" for the President.

In the Senate, the Republicans retained their 54 to 46 edge as 28 of 30 incumbents from both parties won re-election. Senator Howard W. Cannon (D., Nev.) was the only Democrat to lose, bowing to Republican Chic Hecht, a former state senator.

Gubernatorial Elections. In the governors' races, Democrats ran strongest in the industrial Midwest, where the recession had taken a heavy toll. Democrats captured the governorships of Alaska, Arkansas, Texas, Ohio, Michigan, Minnesota, Wisconsin, Nebraska, and Nevada and nearly toppled heavily favored Republican Governor James R. Thompson in Illinois.

Democrats also won control of 11 more state legislative bodies, virtually wiping out GOP gains in recent years. As a result, Democrats control both houses of the legislature in 34 states, compared with 10 states in which the GOP dominates both houses.

New Nominating Rules. Internally, the Democrats adopted new rules on presidential nominations. The rules, which are a retreat from the party's 1970s emphasis on grass-roots participation, strengthened the role of party officeholders and organized labor in the selection process. A commission headed by North Carolina Governor James B. Hunt, Jr., working with backers of Senator Edward M. Kennedy (D., Mass.) and former Vice-President Walter F. Mondale, approved the changes on January 15. The Democratic National Committee ratified them on March 26.

In one major change, about 550 seats at the 1984 national convention, or nearly 15 per cent of the total, were to be reserved for delegates not pledged to any candidate. Another change allows a presidential contender to win all the delegates in

Democratic leaders gather on the rostrum during opening ceremonies of the Democratic National Party Conference in Philadelphia on June 25.

a state's primary election by winning a plurality of votes in each congressional district.

The Democrats also attempted to shorten the presidential primary season. Party caucuses were to be delayed from January to late February in Iowa. The New Hampshire primary, traditionally the first, was put back a week to early March.

In a move expected to affect Democratic presidential maneuvering, the American Federation of Labor and Congress of Industrial Organizations (AFL-CIO) on August 5 adopted a new policy of announcing an endorsement before the primaries if two-thirds of its affiliated unions agree on which candidate to support.

The Democrats showed a rare, and carefully orchestrated, degree of concord during a midterm national conference in Philadelphia from June 25 to 27 when they presented a united front against the Reagan Administration and its economic policies. Delegates declared their backing for a freeze on nuclear-arms production and reaffirmed the party's support for the Equal Rights Amendment.

Kennedy Won't Run. Senator Kennedy said on December 1 that he will not be a candidate for the presidency in 1984. His surprise announcement left Mondale as probably the leading Democratic presidential contender. William J. Eaton

See also REPUBLICAN PARTY; ELECTIONS. In WORLD BOOK, see DEMOCRATIC PARTY.

DENMARK. The Social Democratic minority government of Prime Minister Anker Henrik Jorgensen resigned on Sept. 3, 1982, after failing to agree with opposition parties on an emergency package aimed at saving $1.2 billion in the 1982-1983 budget. Queen Margrethe II then persuaded Poul Schlüter, the Conservative leader, to form a center-right minority coalition government.

Schlüter, heading the second biggest party in the 179-seat Folketing (parliament) with 26 seats, reached an agreement with the Liberals, who had 21 seats, and the Center Democrats and Christian People's Party, with 15 and 4 seats, respectively. This gave the coalition 66 seats in the Folketing. Tacit support from Radical Liberals and the antitax Progress Party increased the coalition's voting power to 91 seats, enough for a narrow majority. The new government took office on September 10. See SCHLÜTER, POUL.

Devaluation. On February 21, Denmark devalued the krone by 3 per cent against seven other currencies of the European Monetary System (EMS), a program set up in 1979 by eight of the 10 nations in the European Community (EC or Common Market) to stabilize currency values. The value of the eighth EMS currency, the Belgian franc, declined by 8.5 per cent. Denmark had asked for a 7 per cent devaluation of the krone, but France and West Germany objected to protect their own currencies.

The Economic Scene. Jorgensen had risked his government's future in May by presenting an $800-million economic package and demanding agreement within 10 days. The package included increased taxes on a wide range of consumer goods. He got reluctant agreement on the package from the Folketing. Unemployment dropped from a peak of 10 per cent in January to 8.5 per cent in June.

On October 17, the Folketing passed Schlüter's austerity package by five votes. The package included an immediate wage freeze and a $2-billion cut in public expenditures, social welfare, and unemployment benefits. On December 16, the Folketing approved a budget with a $7.9-billion deficit.

Greenland Quits EC. Greenland, the icebound North Atlantic territory that gained home rule under the Danish crown in 1979, voted by a narrow margin on February 23 to leave the EC. Greenland and Denmark had joined the EC in 1973 even though 71 per cent of the Greenlanders voting in a 1973 referendum had cast their ballots against joining. The 1982 vote was 52 per cent in favor of leaving the EC to 46 per cent for staying. Greenland is expected to leave the EC by 1985. Its people will seek closer links with Iceland, Norway, and Canada. Kenneth Brown

See also EUROPE (Facts in Brief Table). In WORLD BOOK, see DENMARK.

DENTISTRY. A study by the American Dental Association (ADA) predicted in September 1982 that continued growth of the adult sector of the United States population, particularly in the over-65 category, will have a considerable impact on dental practice during the 1980s. More dental care will be aimed at older age groups, because improved preventive dentistry has enabled a growing percentage of adults to retain their natural teeth. The services older adults require include periodontal, or gum, treatment; endodontic, or root canal, therapy; bridgework; and dentures.

Decay Drops in Children. Tooth decay among schoolchildren has decreased by 25 to 32 per cent in all areas of the United States since the early 1970s, according to a study reported in December 1981 by the National Institute of Dental Research (NIDR) in Bethesda, Md.

The study estimated that almost 17 million U.S. schoolchildren are totally free from dental decay. The study compared 1980 data with those from a 1971-to-1973 survey and found that the average number of decayed, missing, or filled tooth surfaces per child dropped from 7.1 to 4.8. Each tooth has five surfaces.

The percentage of children totally cavity-free ranged from a low of 30 per cent in New England to a high of 45 per cent in the Southwest. NIDR officials credited community water fluoridation, school-based fluoride mouth rinse and tablet programs, and fluoride toothpastes for the declining cavity rate.

Progress in the war against tooth decay may suffer a setback in the near future, according to officials at the U.S. Centers for Disease Control (CDC) in Atlanta, Ga. CDC officials warned in summer 1982 that supplies of fluoride for treating water supplies were running low. They blamed production drops in the chemical fertilizer industry for the shortage, because fluoride is a by-product of phosphate-fertilizer manufacturing.

New Type of Filling. Plastic-resin filling materials that match the color of tooth enamel usually wear better and last longer in front teeth than in molars, where chewing forces can reach thousands of pounds. Therefore, dentists most often fill cavities in molars with a silver-metal amalgam. A more natural-looking filling material for molars may soon be possible, according to a March 1982 report from the University of Virginia in Charlottesville. The new material, aluminum oxide fibers in plastic resin, is reported to be 14 times more resistant to wear than currently available plastic fillings and 22 times more resilient to chewing forces than metal amalgam. However, the material has not yet been tested on dental patients. Lou Joseph

In WORLD BOOK, see DENTISTRY; TEETH.

Quino in *Clarín Revista,* Buenos Aires

DETROIT endured mounting economic problems, declining city services, and City Hall scandals in 1982. But the city managed to keep its $1.6-billion budget in reasonable balance despite an economic slump that produced the highest unemployment levels since the 1930s.

The City's Economic Problems dominated its agenda throughout the year. Unemployment in the Detroit metropolitan area in August was 15.2 per cent, well above the national average. Workers in the slumping automobile industry were especially hard hit, with more than 220,000 on indefinite layoff by autumn.

The business slump depressed tax revenues for both the state and city governments and led to a serious state fiscal crisis, which was resolved only by severe budget cuts and a temporary income tax hike. Detroit's city government, however, avoided serious fiscal problems, largely because it had instituted a municipal tax increase and city-employee wage freeze in 1981. The city finished its 1982 fiscal year on June 30 with a small surplus, its first in five years.

The city's weakened fiscal condition caused a steady erosion in municipal services. A survey by a local newspaper in April found that the number of employees and the level of services had fallen steadily in the past five years in most key city departments. The city's bus system on July 1 increased its basic fare to $1, making Detroit the first city in the continental United States to reach that level.

Twin Scandals. Mayor Coleman A. Young, who had won re-election in 1981, became the longest-serving mayor in the city's history when he took the oath of office for his third 4-year term on Jan. 5, 1982. But his administration was soon embroiled in two scandals involving city contracts. By autumn, both matters were under investigation by federal and county grand juries.

The first scandal involved ongoing allegations that the city's water and sewer chief, Charles Beckham, had accepted kickbacks from sludge-hauling contractors. Beckham strongly denied the charges. In October, Young refused to testify before a grand jury about his knowledge of the case, on the grounds of potential self-incrimination.

The second scandal involved the city's contract for bus fuel. After the city's daily newspapers raised questions about the contract, the city's auditor general, Marie Farrell-Donaldson, reported on May 13 that the city had overpaid the supplier, Magnum Oil Company, $247,897. The auditor also questioned the legality of a $1-million loan made to the fuel company by the city.

On June 2, after weeks of silence, Young admitted that "serious mistakes" had been made by members of his administration, and by October he had replaced or demoted virtually every official who had handled the bus fuel contract. Striking back at his detractors, the mayor, who is black, accused the Detroit newspapers and the auditor (who also is black) of launching a racially motivated attack on his administration.

The unresolved investigations apparently did little to damage the mayor's widespread popularity with Detroit's predominantly black electorate. But the scandals led to increased tension between the mayor and City Council members, who on October 27 approved, over Young's veto, an ordinance guaranteeing themselves a role in contract renewals.

Redevelopment Projects. On June 15, developers broke ground for a high-rise apartment complex on the city's riverfront, and in the fall, work began on a 3-mile (4.8-kilometer) downtown people-mover transit system. But other redevelopment projects—including a downtown shopping center, a subway, and apartment housing—were stalled by the sour economic climate or lack of federal funding. On June 6, Detroit held its first Grand Prix automobile race on a 2½-mile (4-kilometer) course through the downtown area. In the fall, Detroit residents learned that Hudson's, a famous 91-year-old department store in the ailing downtown area, would close its doors after the 1982 Christmas season. Ken Fireman

See also CITY. In WORLD BOOK, see DETROIT.

Race cars make a hairpin turn at the start of the Detroit Grand Prix on June 6. In the background is the city's Renaissance Center.

DISASTERS. What may have been the worst traffic accident in history occurred in Afghanistan in November 1982. From 300 to 400 Soviet soldiers and from 500 to 800 Afghan civilians died when they were trapped inside the 1.7-mile (2.7-kilometer) Salang Tunnel near Kabul.

In the United States, violent storms claimed more than 300 lives in 1982. In January, an Arctic storm bringing heavy snow, high winds, and record low temperatures blanketed 38 states. In April, an early spring storm caused tornadoes, blizzards, fierce winds, and floods from the Sierra Nevada in California to the East Coast.

Poor weather conditions were also a major factor in two U.S. aircraft crashes. In January, an Air Florida 737 jetliner hit a bridge seconds after taking off from Washington's National Airport in a heavy snowstorm. The jet then crashed into the ice-crusted Potomac River. The death toll was 78, including four people on the bridge when the plane hit it. In July, a Pan American 727 jet crashed into a residential neighborhood in Kenner, La., near New Orleans, killing all 145 people aboard and eight more on the ground.

Disasters that resulted in 10 or more deaths in 1982 included the following:

Aircraft Crashes

Jan. 13—Washington, D.C. An Air Florida Boeing 737 struck a bridge, then crashed into the Potomac River shortly after taking off in a heavy snowstorm, killing 78 people, including four people on the bridge.

Jan. 23—Krasnoyarsk, Russia. Approximately 150 people, including two Russian Army officers, died when an Aeroflot jetliner crashed while landing.

Feb. 3—Djibouti. There were no survivors when a French Army plane with 31 French Foreign Legion paratroopers and five crew members crashed into a mountain in the small east African country.

Feb. 5—Seoul, South Korea. All 53 people aboard a South Korean C-123 military transport plane died when sudden winds slammed the plane into that country's highest mountain peak while landing.

Feb. 9—Tokyo. A Japan Air Lines DC-8 crashed into Tokyo Bay 1,000 feet (300 meters) short of the runway, killing 24 passengers.

March 19—Wonder Lake, Ill. An Air National Guard KC-135 tanker jet exploded during a thunderstorm and crashed into a snowy field, killing all 27 people aboard.

March 20—South Sumatra, Indonesia. Twenty-six people died when a P. T. Garuda Indonesia Airways jetliner crashed.

April 2—Crete. A U.S. Navy C-1A cargo-passenger plane from the aircraft carrier *Dwight D. Eisenhower* crashed into a mountain, killing 11 people.

April 13—Near Erzincan, Turkey. All 27 people aboard a U.S. Air Force C-130 cargo plane died when the plane crashed into a mountain.

April 26—Near Kuei-lin (Guilin), China. There were no survivors in the crash of a Chinese airlines Trident jet that went down in poor weather with 112 people aboard.

June 8—Near Fortaleza, Brazil. A Brazilian airlines Boeing 727 slammed into a mountaintop in heavy rain and fog, killing all 137 people aboard.

June 22—Bombay, India. Nineteen people died when an Air India Boeing 707 crashed on landing.

July 6—Moscow. An Aeroflot Ilyushin-62 crashed shortly after take-off, killing all of the estimated 90 people aboard.

July 9—Kenner, La. A Pan American Boeing 727, buffeted by strong winds, crashed into a residential neighborhood shortly after take-off, killing 145 aboard and eight people on the ground.

July 28—Van, Tex. Twelve people, including gospel singer Keith Green and his son and daughter, died when their overloaded twin-engine Cessna crashed.

Sept. 11—Mannheim, West Germany. A U.S. Army Ch-47 Chinook helicopter nose-dived into a highway after a propeller blade broke off, killing 46 people.

Sept. 13—Málaga, Spain. Fifty-six people died when a Spantax Airlines DC-10 jetliner crashed during take-off.

Oct. 17—Taft, Calif. A Beechcraft C-45H plane stalled in the air, crashed into a parachute drop zone, then exploded into flames shortly after take-off, killing all 14 people aboard, including 12 skydivers.

Nov. 17—Off Northern Taiwan. A helicopter ferrying workers from an offshore drilling ship to Chilung (Keelung) crashed into the sea, killing all 15 people aboard.

Nov. 30—Near Bogotá, Colombia. Twenty-two people died when an Aces Airlines Twin-Otter plane crashed into a mountain during a rainstorm.

Dec. 9— Santiago, Chile. An Aeronor Airlines F-27 turboprop crashed on approach to La Serena airport, killing all 46 people aboard.

Dec. 9—Jinotega Province, Nicaragua. A helicopter evacuating children from a war-torn area of the country slammed into a hillside, killing 84 people, including 75 children.

Dec. 24—Canton (Guangzhou), China. Twenty-three people died when fire broke out on a Chinese airlines Ilyushin-18 during landing.

Bus and Truck Crashes

Jan. 26—Near Tuxpan, Mexico. A bus plunged into a river from a bridge after one of its tires blew out. Nineteen people were killed.

March 20—Near Hyderabad, India. A tourist bus was rammed by a passenger train, killing 40 people.

March 27—Near Mexico City, Mexico. Twenty-eight people were killed when a bus collided head-on with a truck on a rain-slicked highway.

March 31—Near Lima, Peru. Twenty-two people died when a bus hurtled into a deep canyon.

July 31—Near Beaune, France. Seven automobiles and three buses collided on a wet highway, killing 53 people, including 44 children on their way to a vacation camp, in the worst traffic accident in French history.

July 31—Near Simla, India. Thirty-three people were killed when an intercity bus plunged down a steep mountain gorge.

Aug. 14—Sukkur, Pakistan. At least 27 people died when their truck ran off the road.

Sept. 11—Punjab State, India. At least 30 prisoners died when a bus taking them to jail was hit by a train.

Sept. 12—Pfäffikon, Switzerland. A bus carrying West German soccer fans home drove through an open railroad barrier and was rammed by a locomotive, killing 39 people.

Nov. 2 or 3?—Near Kabul, Afghanistan. As many as 1,200 people, including from 300 to 400 Russian soldiers and from 500 to 800 Afghan civilians, were killed when a fuel truck collided with the lead vehicle in a Soviet Army convoy in the 1.7-mile (2.7-kilometer) Salang Tunnel. The victims were burned to death or died of asphyxiation when Russian soldiers, believing the explosion of the truck signaled an attack by Afghan rebels, sealed the entrances to the tunnel.

Nov. 25—Southwest India. Eighteen people died when a heavily loaded truck overturned.

Wreathed coffins in a town gymnasium tell the story of a traffic accident that killed 44 children and nine adults near Beaune, France, on July 31.

Earthquakes

June 19—San Salvador, El Salvador. An earthquake measuring 7 on the Richter scale killed at least 14 people in San Salvador and a nearby village.

Dec. 13—Dhamar Province, Yemen (Sana). More than 2,800 people died in an earthquake.

Explosions and Fires

Feb. 8—Tokyo. At least 23 people died when flames engulfed the top floors of a luxury hotel.

March 6—Houston. A cigarette smoldering in a chair grew into a blaze that swept through the Westchase Hilton Hotel, killing 12 people.

April 25—Todi, Italy. At least 33 people died when a 15th-century building exploded and erupted in flames during an antiques exhibition.

Sept. 4—Los Angeles. Fire swept through the hallways of the Dorothy Mae Residence Hotel, killing 24 people, including nine children.

Nov. 11—Tyre, Lebanon. Seventy-five Israelis and 14 Arabs died when an Israeli military headquarters building blew up. A cylinder of cooking gas accidentally exploded, detonating stored munitions and explosives.

Nov. 21—Istanbul, Turkey. A propane gas tank exploded near the only exit of a crowded seaside restaurant, killing 21 and injuring 30.

Dec. 19—Near Caracas, Venezuela. Oil storage tanks caught fire, killing at least 145 people.

Floods

Jan. 23—Near Lima, Peru. The Chontayacu River, fed by torrential rains, overflowed its banks, sweeping away 16 villages and killing at least 600 people.

May 12—Kwangtung (Guangdong) Province, China. Floods caused by torrential rains left at least 430 people dead and 450,000 stranded.

June through August—India. At least 700 people were killed and 17 million left homeless in the north and east sections of the country by floods caused by rains.

June 3—South Sumatra, Indonesia. Touched off by unusually heavy and continuous rains, the worst floods to hit the island this century claimed 225 lives.

June 6—Southern Connecticut. Twelve people died when heavy floods swept across the region, overflowing rivers and washing out roads and bridges.

July 23-24—Nagasaki, Japan. Monsoon rains caused landslides and the country's worst floods in 25 years, resulting in a death toll of at least 307.

Sept. 17-21—El Salvador and Guatemala. A week of torrential rains and flooding claimed at least 600 lives in El Salvador and 560 in neighboring Guatemala. Among the casualties were 60 people who died on September 19 when a mudslide destroyed a church.

Hurricanes, Tornadoes, and Other Storms

Jan. 3-6—San Francisco Area. Violent rainstorms caused mudslides that killed 31 people.

Jan. 9-17—United States. As many as 261 weather-related deaths were reported in 38 states as frigid Arctic air blasted the country.

March 2—Tonga. Cyclone Isaac, the worst storm ever to hit the South Pacific island, claimed about 24 lives.

March 30—Philippines. At least 38 deaths resulted when Typhoon Nelson tore through the central and southern areas of the country.

April 1-10—United States. A storm that spawned 86 tornadoes, snow, fierce winds, and floods swept down from the Sierra Nevada across the Midwest to the East Coast, killing at least 64 people.

May 29—Southern Illinois. A tornado traveled along the ground for 15 miles (24 kilometers), smashing through three towns and killing 10 people.

Wreckage from an Air Florida 737 is hauled from the Potomac River in Washington, D.C. The plane crashed in a snowstorm on January 13, killing 78.

June 4—Orissa State, India. A hurricane ravaged southeast India with tidal waves and winds up to 136 miles (219 kilometers) per hour, killing at least 200.

June 24-29—Nicaragua and Honduras. High winds and heavy rains produced by Tropical Storm Aleta killed at least 226 people and left 80,000 homeless.

June 25-26—Paraná State, Brazil. Winds of up to 90 miles (145 kilometers) per hour killed 43 people, most of whom died when their homes collapsed.

Aug. 2—Honshu Island, Japan. Typhoon Bess tore through the island, claiming at least 80 lives.

Aug. 12-13—South Korea. A typhoon swept over the southwest part of the country, killing at least 38 people.

Sept. 12—Japan. At least 26 people died when a typhoon ripped across the country's main islands, causing extensive flooding.

Nov. 9—Gujarat State, India. A hurricane slammed into India's west coast, causing tidal waves and killing at least 300 people.

Late November-Early December—the United States. At least 34 people died in major storms that swept across the United States, bringing rain and howling winds.

Dec. 24-28—Western and Midwestern United States. At least 31 people died in a winter storm that caused heavy rains on the West Coast, then changed to a blizzard when it hit the Rocky Mountains.

Shipwrecks

Jan. 6—Aleutian Islands. The Japanese fishing boat *Akebono Maru* capsized, drowning 27 fishermen.

Feb. 2—North Atlantic. The Greek tanker *Victory* broke apart in heavy seas and high winds, drowning 15 crew members.

Feb. 15—Off Newfoundland. Eighty-four men drowned when the *Ocean Ranger,* an offshore drilling rig in the North Atlantic, listed and sank during a storm.

Feb. 16—Off Newfoundland. An estimated 32 sailors were lost when the Soviet freighter *Mekhanik Tarasov* sank in a storm and the captain reportedly refused help from a nearby Danish fishing boat.

Feb. 18—Off South Africa. The S.A.S. *President Kruger,* the South African Navy's flagship, collided with the supply ship S.A.S. *Tafelberg* during a gale and sank, killing 16 crew members.

March 28?—Near Rangoon, Burma. A ferry capsized in a canal, killing some 130 people aboard.

April 11—Near Rangoon, Burma. About 160 people drowned when a ferry hit a sandbar in the Irrawaddy River and capsized.

July 25—Manila Bay, Philippines. The tourist ship *Coral Island* caught fire when an engine exploded on a trial run, and 21 crew members died.

Oct. 17—Java Sea, Indonesia. An Indonesian cargo ship sank in relatively calm waters, drowning 89 people.

Trainwrecks

June 15—Near Sigulu, Uganda. About 200 people were killed when a passenger train derailed following an explosion.

July 11—Near Tepic, Mexico. At least 120 lives were lost when the express train La Bala (The Bullet) traveling to Guadalajara derailed after rounding a sharp curve at high speed and plunged down a mountain gorge.

Oct. 17—Near Buenos Aires, Argentina. A speeding passenger train slammed into the rear of a standing passenger train, killing 18 people.

Other Disasters

Jan. 17—Brazil-Paraguay Border. At least 30 tourists died when a suspension footbridge over a scenic waterfall on the Paraná River collapsed.

Jan. 31—Near Salzburg, Austria. An avalanche crashed down on a school group, killing 11 students and a teacher, after two days of unseasonably warm weather.

Feb. 2—Northern Jammu and Kashmir States, India. Twenty-three people were killed in a landslide that followed heavy rains.

Feb. 17—Moscow. An escalator in a suburban subway station collapsed during the evening rush hour, killing at least 15 people.

March 14—Near Grenoble, France. At least 11 skiers died in nine avalanches caused by a thaw.

March 21—Nagano, Japan. Two avalanches claimed at least 13 lives.

March 26—Mount Ararat, Turkey. Fifteen members of two families were killed in a snowslide in the foothills of this peak, where tradition says Noah's ark came to rest.

March 29—Pichucalco, Mexico. El Chichón, a long-dormant volcano, began to erupt, spewing rock and ash over the countryside and killing at least 187 people.

April 15—East Chicago, Ind. Two sections of an unfinished bridge buckled, then crashed 50 feet (15 meters) into an industrial canal, killing 13 workers.

Sept. 4—Kerala State, India. Fifty-four people, most of them agricultural workers, died after drinking poisonous bootleg liquor at a harvest festival.

Oct. 6—Nye Nye, Liberia. At least 45 miners in a mining camp were buried in a landslide when a huge pile of iron ore waste collapsed during heavy rains.

Nov. 17—Cali, Colombia. Twenty-four people attending a soccer match died and 250 were injured on an exit ramp in a human stampede that began when spectators in the upper tiers of a stadium started urinating and throwing firecrackers on the people in the stands below.

Nov. 19—Natal, Brazil. A high-tension wire fell on a crowd watching rescuers pull bodies from a wrecked van, killing at least 29 people.

Barbara A. Mayes

DJIBOUTI. See AFRICA.

DOG. A female Pekingese, Champion St. Aubrey's Dragonora of Elsdon, owned by Anne Snelling of Ottawa, Canada, was chosen best-in-show at the Westminster Kennel Club show in New York City on Feb. 9, 1982. The club's 106th annual competition drew 2,214 entries. Lee-Lee, as the Pekingese is called by her owner, was retired after her triumph. It was the second time a dog owned by Snelling had won the highest award at America's most prestigious dog show.

According to figures released in March, the American Kennel Club (AKC) registered more than 1 million dogs in 1981. Poodles again headed the list of AKC registrations, as they have since 1960. Cocker spaniels moved from third into second place, followed in popularity by Doberman pinschers, German shepherds, Labrador retrievers, golden retrievers, miniature schnauzers, beagles, dachshunds, and Shetland sheepdogs.

The Dog Museum of America opened on Sept. 15, 1982, under the sponsorship of the AKC Foundation. The museum, located at 51 Madison Avenue in New York City, houses works of art and books that relate to dogs. Roberta Vesley

In WORLD BOOK, see DOG.

DOMINICAN REPUBLIC. See WEST INDIES.

DRAMA. See THEATER.

DROUGHT. See WATER; WEATHER.

Angel, a female beagle owned by the Helinek family of Philadelphia, points to the draft registration notice she received in February.

DRUGS. There were several controversies over drugs during 1982, including their promotion and distribution. One controversy involved a new arthritis medication, Oraflex, which had been approved by the United States Food and Drug Administration (FDA) in May. Reports soon surfaced about serious side effects. In Great Britain, where the drug had been used for two years, the Health Ministry suspended promotion of the drug in August because of safety concerns. Oraflex was linked with liver, kidney, and gastrointestinal damage as well as with 61 deaths in Great Britain and 11 in the United States.

The manufacturer of Oraflex, Eli Lilly & Company, had reported booming sales of more than $6-million in the product's first month on the U.S. market. However, the company withdrew the drug in August after several consumer groups went to court seeking a ban on Oraflex. A U.S. government report made public in November indicated that Eli Lilly had withheld information about the drug's potential ill effects.

The FDA took action during the year against Pfizer, Incorporated, the manufacturer of Procardia, a newly approved drug for treating a certain type of angina, or chest pain, caused by a coronary artery spasm. In late August, the FDA accused Pfizer of promoting Procardia for all types of angina, even where research indicated that other drugs were more effective. Pfizer was ordered to revise its promotional materials and to correct its previous advertising statements.

Tylenol Deaths. In late September and early October, seven people in the Chicago area died as the result of cyanide placed in capsules of Extra-Strength Tylenol. This prompted the FDA in November to order tamper-proof packaging for all over-the-counter medicines. See CRIME.

Third World Marketing. Researchers at the University of California at San Francisco in 1982 accused pharmaceutical manufacturers of practicing a "blatant double standard" in selling drugs to developing countries of the Third World. They documented cases in which side-effect warnings were not disclosed, products outlawed or severely restricted in Western nations were dumped onto unregulated markets in developing countries, and products were promoted for inappropriate or unproven uses. The drug industry issued denials. However, in July, U.S. pharmaceutical firms launched an effort to upgrade the quality of information in Third World drug manuals.

Aspirin Warning. In June, the U.S. government ordered labels on all aspirin bottles warning that giving the drug to children with influenza, chicken pox, or other viral diseases could lead to development of Reye's syndrome, a potentially deadly disease. Its symptoms include fever, vomiting, convulsions, and coma.

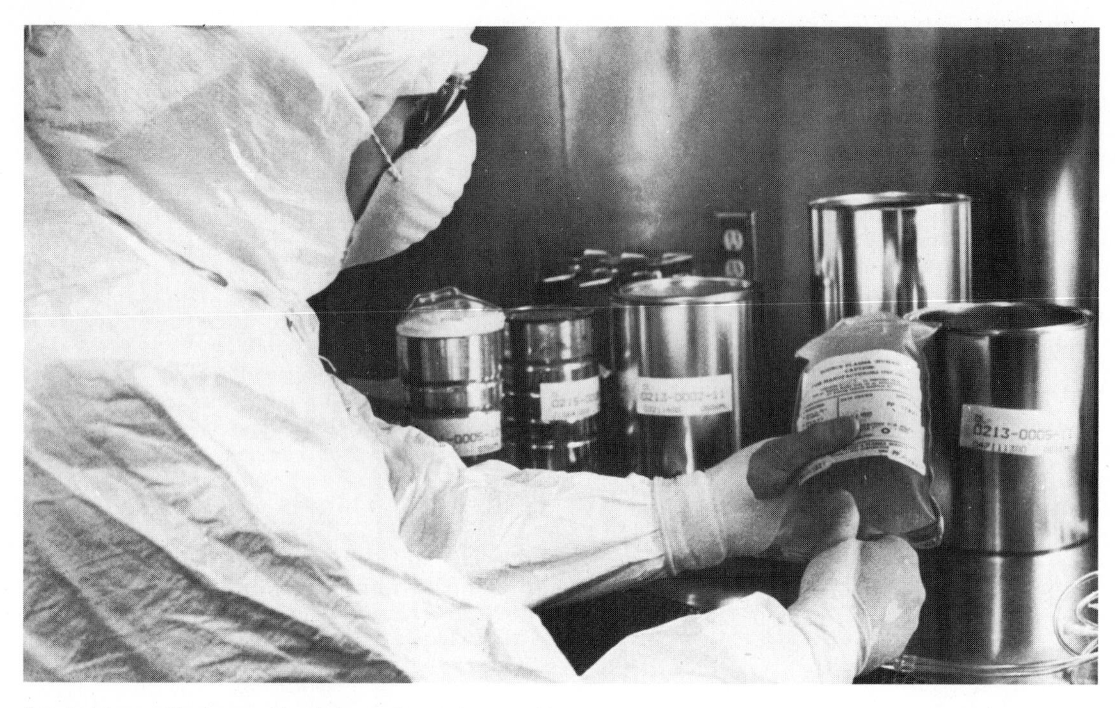

A technician readies human blood plasma for use in preparing hepatitis B vaccine, which first became widely available in 1982.

The label warning had been requested by the U.S. Centers for Disease Control (CDC), the American Academy of Pediatrics, and an FDA task force. CDC researchers reported that children with Reye's syndrome had received aspirin medications for flu more frequently than did children who did not develop the syndrome.

Some physicians criticized the warning as a premature overreaction. They believed that an association between aspirin use and Reye's syndrome had not yet been conclusively proven.

Starch Blockers. Another controversy centered on diet pills called "starch blockers," made from a kidney bean extract. The manufacturers claimed this extract prevented a particular enzyme in the intestine from breaking down starch into sugars. Starch blockers were marketed as a means of cutting calories by preventing digestion of starchy foods, such as pizza.

In July, the FDA issued an indefinite ban on the sale of starch blockers, claiming they were drugs, and required further research. This action followed reports of serious side effects, including vomiting and severe diarrhea. Several manufacturers challenged this ban in court by arguing that starch blockers, because they are made from beans, are a food rather than a drug, and therefore not subject to strict FDA regulation. But in October, a federal court agreed that starch blockers are a drug and granted the FDA's request for a permanent ban.

Marijuana Risks. In February, the Institute of Medicine of the National Academy of Sciences issued a report by 22 scientists who found that what little was known about marijuana use "justified serious national concern." They reported a variety of reversible, short-term effects, such as impaired driving skills and learning ability. However, the scientists said that there was insufficient reliable evidence to allow them to draw conclusions about long-term health hazards.

After 15 months of study, the scientists concluded that marijuana increases the heart rate and that this could be harmful to persons with high blood pressure and cardiovascular disease. They also speculated that the effects of persistent marijuana smoking could be similar to those of tobacco smoking and thus might lead to serious respiratory problems and increase the risk of lung cancer. Because marijuana is the most commonly used illicit drug in the United States, the panel urgently called for more research.

In October, the FDA approved marketing of human insulin produced by bacteria through genetic engineering. It was the first drug so produced to be approved for human use. Dianne Hales

In World Book, see Drug; Drug Abuse.

EARTHQUAKE. See Disasters.

EASTERN ORTHODOX CHURCHES. Efforts to unify the various Orthodox jurisdictions in the United States continued in 1982. The Bilateral Commission, appointed by the Antiochian Orthodox Christian Archdiocese of North America and the Orthodox Church in America (OCA) to lay the groundwork for unification, received the full support of the heads of both groups.

Controversy over the OCA's liturgical calendar, a long-time problem, also continued during the year. For centuries, the Orthodox Church had followed the Julian calendar, even after most people in the Western world changed to the Gregorian calendar. Then, in 1981, OCA bishops decided that all parishes should adopt the Gregorian calendar as of Sept. 1, 1982. Parishes in several states, especially in Pennsylvania, refused to comply and took steps to withdraw from the OCA.

Pimen, the patriarch of Moscow and all Russia, visited New York City in June to attend the United Nations (UN) Special General Assembly on Disarmament. He was the first Russian patriarch ever to visit the United States.

Greece. The Socialist government of Greece made decisive moves in 1982 to bring about a separation of church and state in that country. The Greek Constitution recognizes the Greek Orthodox Church as the nation's official church and provides for its financing. But the government of Prime Minister Andreas Papandreou wanted to separate church and state to end what it regarded as the church's improper involvement in official functions.

After coming to power in October 1981, the Papandreou government obtained approval in Parliament to establish civil marriage and to end the prosecution of adultery as a crime. Although the church opposes most of the projected changes, Archbishop Seraphim, primate of Greece, said he agreed with Papandreou that separation would benefit both church and state. Other Greek Orthodox bishops disagreed, however, and fought the reforms.

Archbishop Deported. In October, the U.S. Department of Justice announced that Valerian D. Trifa, a Romanian Orthodox archbishop, would be deported for concealing war crimes from immigration officials. Archbishop Trifa was accused of being a Nazi sympathizer who incited anti-Jewish riots in Romania during World War II. He immigrated to the United States in 1950. Archbishop Trifa was the spiritual head of the 35,000-member Romanian Orthodox Episcopate based in Grass Lake, Mich. Alexander Schmemann

In WORLD BOOK, see EASTERN ORTHODOX CHURCHES.

In a Moscow church jammed with worshipers, Patriarch Pimen, at right, conducts the Easter Sunday service of the Russian Orthodox Church in April.

ECONOMICS. Unemployment in the United States rose to a post-World War II high of 10.8 per cent near the end of 1982 as the nation, along with the rest of the world, suffered the most serious recession since the 1930s. The U.S. gross national product (GNP) — the total of all the goods and services produced during the year — rose slightly to about $3.05 trillion in 1982, measured in current dollars. But when the effects of inflation were taken into account, the GNP actually decreased slightly from 1981 levels. On the more cheerful side, interest rates fell and the inflation rate was down markedly from 1981 levels. Thus 1982, which had been looked upon as the test year for the so-called supply-side economic program of lower taxes and higher productivity so strongly pushed by President Ronald Reagan, had a mixed record.

Clearly, tax cuts had failed to produce the hoped-for spurt in the United States economic activity. But the reduction in interest rates and lowered inflation gave some promise that a lasting recovery would take place in 1983. The 1982 results came as no surprise because only a handful of economists believed that inflation could be squeezed out of the economy soon enough to permit the optimistic outcome a few supply-side enthusiasts predicted.

On July 22, the chairman of the President's Council of Economic Advisers, Murray L. Weidenbaum, resigned. President Reagan named his successor, Martin S. Feldstein, on August 6, and the Senate confirmed Feldstein's appointment on December 8.

Labor and Production. Nearly 12 million U.S. workers were without jobs at the close of 1982, and unemployment had supplanted inflation as the American people's number-one worry. Workers felt the effects most strongly in the automobile industry, where production was at the lowest level in 20 years; the steel industry, which at year-end was operating at approximately 40 per cent of capacity; and the construction industry, as housing starts remained low for the second consecutive year and business cut back on its expenditures.

All three of these industries are significantly affected by interest-rate levels. Few individuals have the ready cash to purchase an automobile; still fewer have the funds to purchase a new house; and most businesses find it necessary to borrow funds in order to complete an extensive construction program. Thus, high interest rates severely limit people's capacity — and, perhaps even more important, their willingness — to borrow extensively for purchases that can be deferred. See BUILDING AND CONSTRUCTION; HOUSING.

Demonstrators outside the Indiana Capitol show their feelings about the economic state of the nation during a presidential visit in February.

Although 1982 added more than 2 million workers to the unemployment rosters, the number of people at work in the United States expanded very slightly over 1981 levels. Nearly 100 million persons held jobs at year-end. Thanks to an estimated 5 per cent inflation rate, average hourly earnings showed the first improvement in purchasing power in four years, rising by approximately 1.5 per cent. Average weekly earnings continued to rise. However, as a result of shorter hours, paychecks failed to keep pace with inflation and for the fourth consecutive year showed a slight decline—but the smallest of that time span. If inflation can be controlled, or held to a modest 3 or 4 per cent per year, it will mean that the steady upward movement of living standards, which for so many years characterized the American economy, will resume when the recession is ended.

Other bright signs that emerged during 1982 were the smallest increase in labor cost per unit output in almost 10 years and a resumption of the increase in productivity—output per hour—which also was once characteristic of the U.S. economy. From 1979 through 1981, productivity either declined or stayed constant.

Industrial production, as expected, was down sharply in 1982, falling about 9 per cent by year-end from its 1981 level. Profits fell by 20 per cent (measured before taxes), and farm income was down slightly. The principal sufferers from the decline in farm income were Midwestern crop farmers, with corn down below $2 a bushel at local grain elevators. Livestock producers fared somewhat better. However, because farmers had to pay more for goods, the agricultural economy in general was weak in 1982. The only exceptions were a few sectors, such as the dairy industry, in which government price supports kept prices high and tended to produce record surpluses. See FARM AND FARMING.

The Stock Market, somewhat surprisingly, showed a sharp gain of more than 200 points on the Dow Jones average of 30 blue-chip industrial stocks (the Dow). On December 27, the market set a record high on the Dow of 1,070.55. The rally began in August, largely in response to lower interest rates, but the strength of the upswing in the face of a relatively low level of economic activity and sharply reduced profits was unexpected. If, as traders usually assert, the level of stock prices is a leading indicator—that is, a forecast of business conditions six months in the future—then prospects for 1983 were somewhat brighter than most economists projected. A relatively modest recovery was forecast—perhaps a gain of 2.5 per cent in real GNP. Economists expected the rate of inflation to continue to drop but expressed substantial concern about interest levels. See STOCKS AND BONDS.

The federal deficit for fiscal year 1982, ending September 30, was $110.7 billion. Estimates for the 1983 deficit ranged between $150 billion and $200 billion. It was feared that so much federal borrowing added to that of the private sector would prevent further declines in interest rates and might even push them up again toward the high levels of early 1982. If that occurred, the resulting high rates would certainly limit the extent of the recovery and might prevent it entirely. See BANK.

Stresses on Steel. Certainly, rapid revival of the steel and automobile industries did not appear likely at year-end. A few analysts even suggested that two or three bankruptcies in the steel industry would come as no surprise.

At least a part of the problem with steel is that steelworkers are the highest-paid workers in U.S. industry and their wages are almost double the level of the highest-paid steelworkers in other countries. This economic truth, combined with the fact that U.S. steel mills are generally older and less efficient than those abroad, has led to imported steel taking about 20 per cent of the U.S. market despite various protective measures aimed at limiting imports. Another possible factor is that certain overseas steel producers, particularly those in the European Community (EC or Common Market), receive government subsidies that permit them to sell more cheaply than their unsubsidized competition.

Much the same situation prevails in the automobile industry, where imports took about 23 per cent of U.S. car sales in 1982, despite the so-called voluntary restrictions on exports imposed by Japan. In general, auto workers were more willing than steelworkers to reduce their demands, especially those employed by the ailing Chrysler Corporation. In November, the steelworkers rejected a request for concessions from the industry, which increased the likelihood that more jobs would be lost. Chrysler workers in Canada were less willing than their U.S. counterparts to forgo a wage increase and went on strike on November 5. Fortunately for American plants dependent upon parts made in Canada, the Canadian workers voted to accept a new contract on December 12 and returned to work the next day. See AUTOMOBILE; STEEL INDUSTRY.

The Economy Abroad. The extent of the recession was shown by the drop in factory production in most of the industrialized world. Even Japan, one of the fastest-growing developed nations, showed a 1 per cent drop during the first six months of 1982. Great Britain showed a 1 per cent gain, but industrial production there started the year at unusually low levels. France and Canada showed declines of approximately 12 per cent each; and in Italy, the decline was a startling 25

Selected Key U.S. Economic Indicators

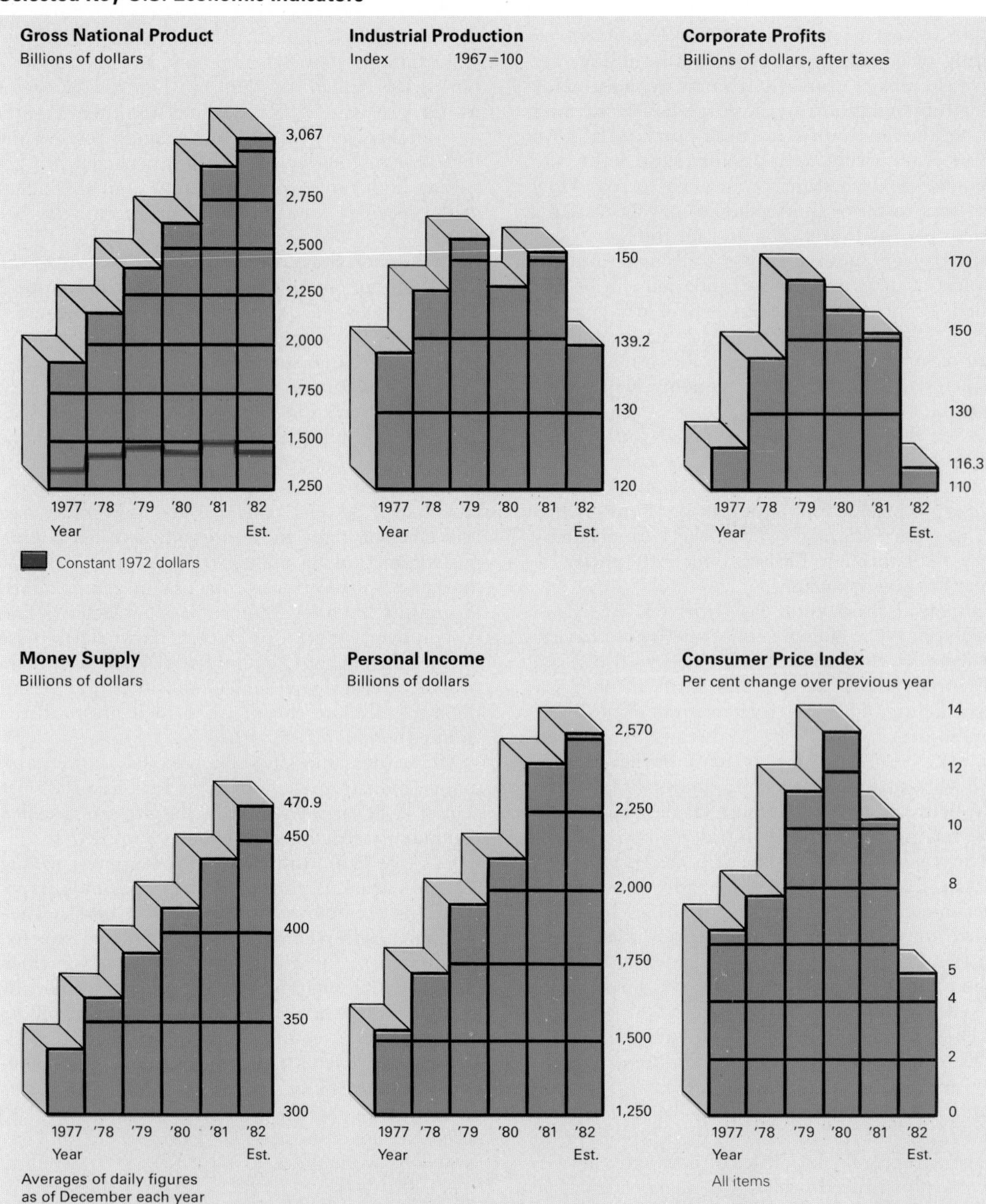

The most comprehensive measure of the nation's total output of goods and services is the *Gross National Product* (GNP). The GNP represents the dollar value in current prices of all goods and services plus the estimated value of certain imputed outputs, such as the rental value of owner-occupied dwellings. *Industrial Production* is a monthly measure of the physical output of manufacturing, mining, and utility industries. *Corporate Profits* are quarterly profit samplings from major industries. *Money Supply* measures the total amount of money in the economy in coin, currency, and demand deposits. *Personal Income* is current income received by persons (including nonprofit institutions and private trust funds) before personal taxes. *Consumer Price Index* (CPI) is a measure of changes in the prices of goods and services consumed by urban families and individuals. CPI includes selected goods and services. All 1982 figures are *Year Book* estimates.

per cent or more. Even in West Germany, whose steady growth was the envy of Europe, output was down by 1 per cent.

At the same time, inflation continued to plague those economies. In France and Italy, the rate was 12 per cent or more, and West Germany showed a rate of approximately 5 per cent. In Great Britain, the rate fell below 10 per cent for the first time in several years. By comparison with less developed countries, and even compared with developing countries, those inflation rates were modest. For example, in Argentina, Brazil, Israel, and Mexico, inflation raged at the rate of more than 100 per cent in 1982.

Oil-Rich Nations of the Organization of Petroleum Exporting Countries (OPEC) also had their difficulties. The recession in the industrial nations sharply reduced the demand for oil, and conservation measures added to the pressure on prices. At year-end, some OPEC countries—notably Iran, Libya, and Nigeria—were substantially undercutting the agreed-upon base price of $34 per barrel. Balance-of-payments problems and reduced demand encouraged such price cutting, and the countries that sold low were substantially exceeding their assigned production quotas.

In an effort to hold OPEC together, Saudi Arabia reduced its output to less than 6 million barrels per day (bpd) from its 10-million bpd level of 1980. OPEC meetings late in 1982 were adjourned twice in order to avoid an open quarrel, with Saudi Arabia threatening to cut the $34 per barrel price for its crude oil and substantially increase output unless the countries that were discounting their prices and exceeding their output quotas fell into line. A real test of OPEC's ability to withstand decreased demand and, at the same time, maintain the price of their product was expected to come in 1983. The history of other international associations formed to control the market for a product indicates that such a combination of events often causes the cartels to break up.

United States imports of oil products were down 45 per cent from 1981 by late 1982, measured in dollar terms—another illustration of recession effects. This astonishing drop, the result of a reduction in both prices and consumption, reduced the total dollar value of oil imports from 29 per cent of U.S. total imports in 1981 to a little less than 24 per cent in 1982. See PETROLEUM AND GAS.

The Food Shortage in Africa south of the Sahara continued to be among the more vexing and difficult economic problems in the less-developed world. Self-sufficient in food during their colonial days, the southern African nations failed to maintain agricultural production after they gained independence. They rushed to adopt one form or another of state-controlled economy and embarked on rapid industrialization. Those programs, though usually unsuccessful, nevertheless attracted large numbers of people into the cities, where they became only consumers of the food they once had produced.

Harvard University economist Martin Feldstein took office in August as head of President Ronald Reagan's Council of Economic Advisers.

Debts and Deficits. A situation of major concern to the financial community was the inability of Brazil, Mexico, and Poland, among other nations, to make the payments due on their foreign debt. Substantial help from the International Monetary Fund (IMF)—an agency of the United Nations that promotes world trade—and agreements among the lending banks promised to solve the immediate problems and avoid default. But the long-run prospects for obtaining the further credit necessary to maintain those countries' economies were slim. Most of the problems arose from overambitious development programs; inefficient economic organization, especially in Poland; and in Mexico, widespread corruption.

Evidence of economic and other events within the Soviet Union is scanty, but the Russians themselves admitted in 1982 to a fourth straight year of failure to meet their grain-raising targets. Most observers believed that Russia would need continuing substantial imports of animal feed to prevent further reduction in the already inadequate meat supply available to the Soviet people. The reportedly widespread shortages of consumer goods may be the major internal weakness in Russia's planned economy. New General Secretary of the Communist Party Yuri V. Andropov acknowledged as much in his first public remarks after becoming head of the Soviet Union following the death of Leonid I. Brezhnev in November.

Social Security. A major problem of the United States that remained unsolved at the end of 1982 was the financing of projected Social Security deficits. For many years, Congress increased Social Security benefits for a variety of purposes never intended in the original act, without making corresponding increases in taxes. The result is that funds in the old-age assistance portion of the program may be completely exhausted by July 1983. Probably the only long-term solutions are to gradually raise the retirement age of U.S. workers and reduce the periodic adjustments for cost-of-living increases. The unpleasant alternative is to increase taxes, thus placing an even greater burden on employment. Both of these proposals met with a storm of protest when they were suggested. But it is as true in the United States as it is in Western Europe that social benefit costs have risen beyond the point where they are consistent with balanced budgets, adequate national defense, and other functions of government. Warren W. Shearer

See also International Trade and Finance and individual country articles. In World Book, see Economics; Gross National Product.

ECUADOR. President Osvaldo Hurtado Larrea struggled in 1982 with economic woes brought on by a drop in Ecuador's oil earnings, amid rising factionalism in the nation's Congress. Hurtado faced an uphill battle to build coalitions around issues facing the nation, including inflation and high unemployment. His own Popular Democracy Party held less than one-fifth of the seats in Congress, not enough to pass legislation in the face of an increasingly troublesome leftist alliance.

Ecuador watched helplessly during the year as prices for its oil plummeted along with production. Foreign oil companies were reluctant to invest in a country divided by a stiffening nationalism and a rise in left wing agitation.

Ecuador's earnings from oil exports during the first six months of the year were off 20 per cent from 1981 levels. By September 1982, the country's financial reserves had slipped to less than $100 million.

Ecuadoreans looked for scapegoats. Hurtado's finance and oil ministers were forced out of office in September by the Concentration of Popular Forces Party in Congress. On October 15, Hurtado announced an austerity program that included the removal of government subsidies on food and gasoline. Nathan A. Haverstock

See also Latin America (Facts in Brief Table). In World Book, see Ecuador.

EDUCATION. The leading barometers of educational achievement in the United States were rising in 1982, but fiscal indicators continued to fall. Reading scores improved in many urban school systems. Scholastic Aptitude Test (SAT) scores showed a slight upturn, the first in 19 years. School violence declined. Although the schools showed clear signs of improvement, public support for education failed to keep pace. Federal subsidies continued to decline, and a troubled economy did not allow state and local governments to make up for the cutbacks.

Private colleges, in particular, felt the impact of the recession and the threat of reduced federal grants and loans. Students turned increasingly to less-expensive public colleges and universities and particularly to two-year community colleges within commuting distance from home.

Efforts mounted to establish partnerships between corporations and public schools. In one such partnership, the Chase Manhattan Bank provided $430,000 for a training program to improve the leadership skills of principals in New York City's 110 high schools. The grant followed the Bank of America's earlier support for California schools. In other cities, corporations backed an "Adopt-a-School" program. This type of partnership provided not only funds, but also the services of corporate staffs and executives, particularly in fields that suffer from an acute teacher shortage, such as mathematics and science.

Total Enrollment in U.S. schools and colleges declined for the 10th consecutive year in 1982. The Department of Education (DOE) expected 57.3 million persons to enroll in formal education programs from kindergarten through graduate school during the 1982-1983 academic year. This represented a decline of 500,000, or about 1 per cent, from the year before. Colleges and universities, however, were expected to enroll 128,000 more students than in 1981. Nearly 61 million Americans were engaged in education as their primary activity, as either teachers or students. In a nation of 233 million people, about 26 per cent took part in the process of education.

Elementary grades enrolled 30.9 million children, 27.3 million of them in public schools. The decline of about 200,000 was smaller than that of previous years. For the mid-1980s, the DOE predicted a reversal of the downward trend in enrollments that began in 1970, with modest increases occurring each year for the remainder of the decade. Nonpublic school enrollments remained stable, at approximately 3.6 million.

High schools enrolled an estimated 13.9 million students in 1982, down from 14.3 million in 1981. Of these, 12.4 million were in public schools. High school enrollments peaked in 1976 and have decreased every year since.

Two of 60 high school students learning computer programming check a printout during a New York University five-week summer course in New York City.

Enrollment in institutions of higher learning reached nearly 12.4 million in 1981. Only a nominal increase to about 12.5 million was expected in 1982. Public institutions accounted for 9.75 million students, an increase of about 100,000. The increase in students at private institutions was not expected to exceed 25,000. Even though the college-age population reached a peak in 1981 and will decline for the remainder of the decade, college enrollments may remain high because of increased attendance by minority groups, women, older students, and part-time students.

The Graduates. About 3 million students graduated from public and private high schools in 1982, down from 3.16 million in the peak year of 1977. The 1983 graduating class was expected to exceed 2.8 million.

Colleges and universities were expected to award 965,000 bachelor's degrees, 307,000 master's degrees, 33,000 doctor's degrees, and 74,000 first professional degrees in 1982-1983. The figures for master's and doctor's degrees have dropped slightly from peaks attained in 1977 and 1973, respectively.

The Bureau of the Census reported that there were approximately 110 million high school graduates in the United States in 1980. Nearly 24 million of these had also completed four or more years of college. The median number of school years completed by persons 25 years old or older was 12½, compared with nine years in 1949. The number of adults with less than five years of schooling decreased by about 54 per cent over the last 30 years, from 9.45 million to 4.32 million.

The Teachers. More than 2.4 million elementary and secondary school teachers were employed as classroom instructors in 1982, a small decrease from 1981. An additional 300,000 worked as superintendents, principals, and supervisors. The number of college-level teachers was expected to rise slightly from 840,000 in 1981 to about 870,000.

Most elementary and secondary school teachers belong to organizations that bargain collectively for them. The National Education Association of the United States has 1.7 million members, and the American Federation of Teachers has approximately 560,000, mostly in urban centers. At the beginning of the school year, the two organizations reported a total of 75 strikes in six states. The largest number occurred in Illinois, Michigan, and Pennsylvania.

Average salaries for teachers in public schools ranged from a high of $31,924 in Alaska to a low of $14,141 in Mississippi. Average salaries exceeded $22,000 in California, the District of Columbia, Hawaii, Michigan, New York, Washington, and Wyoming. Salaries below $15,000 were being paid in Arkansas, New Hampshire, South Dakota, and Vermont, in addition to Mississippi.

Education Expenditures at all levels for the 1982-1983 school year were estimated by the DOE at $215 billion, compared with about $200 billion in 1981-1982. Higher education was to receive almost $80 billion; public elementary and secondary schools, $120 billion. Public institutions at all levels were expected to spend about $173 billion, with the private sector spending about $42 billion.

Of the $215 billion to be spent on education, the federal government was to contribute an estimated 9 per cent, 1 per cent less than the preceding year; state governments were to provide about 39 per cent; and local governments, 25 per cent. Funds from a variety of private sources—including tuition and fees, earnings from endowments, gifts, and grants—were to account for about 27 per cent of expenditures, an increase of 1 per cent over 1981-1982. Total expenditures for education amount to approximately 8 per cent of the gross national product.

The Cost of College Tuition has risen at an average annual rate of 14 per cent during the past decade. The increase for 1982-1983 averaged 20 per cent at public institutions and 13 per cent at private colleges, raising the average tuition at state colleges and universities from $815 to $979 and the average tuition at private institutions from $3,552 to $4,021. The total annual bill, including room, board, and incidental expenses, ranged from about $3,500 to $6,000 at public institutions and from about $6,000 to $12,000 at private ones. At two-year public community colleges, tuition costs ran approximately $600, a $100 increase from 1981.

Sauers in *The Wall Street Journal*

"And as you go out in the world, please remember one thing . . . pay back your government loans."

Tuition increases and general inflation have begun to change the student population at high-prestige private colleges. From 1979 to 1982, the enrollment of students from families with incomes between $6,000 and $24,000 dropped 39 per cent. At the same time, the number of students from higher-income families who receive financial aid increased substantially.

Student Aid from all sources in the 1981-1982 academic year was estimated at about $20 billion. This figure included at least $3 billion provided by the colleges and $1 billion each from state scholarship funds and from employer tuition-aid plans. About 2.2 million students—23 per cent of all those attending public colleges—depend on federal aid to meet their expenses. More than half of such aid goes to families or individuals earning less than $9,287 per year, the figure defined by the U.S. government as the poverty line for a family of four in 1981.

Grants to needy students declined by only $10-million from the 1981 total of $2.29 billion, as a result of congressional action to override President Ronald Reagan's veto of supplementary allocations. However, the Congressional Budget Office estimated that the total amount of low-interest loans will drop from $7.2 billion in 1982 to $4.8-billion in 1993.

Creation-Science Law Overturned. On January 5, a federal district judge struck down an Arkansas law that required schools to teach "creation science" along with the theory of evolution. Creation science claims that the world and all living things originated in an act of creation. The judge ruled that creation science was not science but religion, and that the law violated constitutional guarantees of the separation of church and state.

A similar law, passed by the Louisiana legislature, was overturned in November. The judge ruled in that case that the law violated the state constitution, which empowers only the state Board of Elementary and Secondary Education to order the teaching of a course.

Tax Questions. In February, the Reagan Administration asked the Supreme Court of the United States to decide whether tax exemptions could legally be granted to schools that practice racial discrimination. The government argued that the current law entitles such schools to a tax-exempt status. At year-end, the court had not ruled.

In April, Reagan proposed that families receive

income tax credits for tuition payments to private elementary and secondary schools. His proposal was introduced in Congress in June but did not come to a vote.

Electronic Education. Progress was made during the year in bringing computers to classrooms. International Business Machines Corporation (IBM) allocated funds for a program to teach reading by computer. The New York Academy of Sciences supported a New York City program to equip each pupil in six elementary school classrooms with a microcomputer. Meanwhile, critical reports by Columbia University Teachers College and the Bank Street College of Education warned school administrators about the preponderance of poorly designed computer programs, or software, available for electronic teaching.

Public Attitudes toward the schools, as measured by the 14th annual Gallup Poll, showed that the number of people concerned about inadequate financing of public education grew from 12 per cent in 1981 to 22 per cent in 1982. Nearly all Americans, the poll showed, believed that education was important to their children's future, and 84 per cent believed that building the best possible system of education was more important than building a stronger military force. Fred M. Hechinger

In the Special Reports section, see THE ABC'S OF TESTING. In WORLD BOOK, see EDUCATION.

EGYPT. President Mohamed Hosni Mubarak moved cautiously in 1982 to establish a brand of leadership separate from that of his predecessor, Anwar el-Sadat, who was assassinated in October 1981. Mubarak also attempted to prevent an upsurge of the Islamic extremism that had led to Sadat's assassination. His efforts were helped by improved relations with other Arab states.

After his election in January as head of the ruling National Democratic Party (NDP), Mubarak replaced nine Cabinet ministers and named a new prime minister, Ahmad Fouad Moheiddin. Most of the dismissed ministers were associated with economic corruption and mismanagement prevalent during Sadat's last years. On September 1, Mubarak again reshuffled the Cabinet, this time replacing seven ministers, including the two chiefly responsible for economic affairs.

Fundamentalist Opposition. Mubarak dealt cautiously with the issue of Islamic fundamentalism. On March 6, a military court sentenced five Muslim fundamentalists to death for the assassination of Sadat. Among them was the leader of the group, Lieutenant Khaled Ahmed el-Islambouly. Five other defendants were given life sentences at hard labor. Of the remaining 14 charged in the case, 12 received prison terms ranging from five years to 15 years, and two were acquitted.

The court ignored defense arguments that the trial was illegal because it was not conducted according to Islamic law. During the trial, the defendants declared they had committed no crime because they had acted to rid Egypt of a tyrant.

Mubarak also tried to defuse the fundamentalist opposition by releasing many Egyptians arrested by Sadat during a crackdown on opponents in September 1981 or detained following his assassination. By August, about 1,700 detainees had been set free.

But unrest continued, and Egyptian authorities announced on September 16 the arrest of 58 Muslim fundamentalists for plotting to overthrow the Mubarak government. In October, the government's emergency powers were extended for another year to deal with militant groups. On December 4, 280 Muslim fundamentalists went on trial on charges of plotting to overthrow the government after Sadat's assassination.

Sinai Returned. Israel returned the remaining occupied part of the Sinai Peninsula to Egypt as scheduled on April 25 under the terms of the 1979 peace treaty. But the two countries could agree on little else involving their future relationship. Mubarak canceled an official visit to Israel in March because it would have required meeting Israel's Prime Minister Menachem Begin in Jerusalem, which Egypt does not recognize as Israel's capital.

Egyptian President Mubarak's visit to King Fahd of Saudi Arabia in June was the first meeting of the two countries' leaders since 1979.

Relations worsened after Israel invaded Lebanon in June. Mubarak condemned the invasion and recalled Egypt's ambassador to Israel.

Arab Relations. Mubarak moved to re-establish good relations with other Arab states. In June, he flew to Saudi Arabia on a visit of condolence after the death of King Khalid. It was the first meeting between leaders of the two countries since Saudi Arabia broke diplomatic relations with Egypt in 1979. In addition, Egypt provided $1.5 billion in arms to Iraq after Iranian forces drove into Iraqi territory in July. In October, Egypt signed an agreement with the Sudan to coordinate political and economic policies of the two countries. The agreement called for the establishment of a joint parliament to meet twice yearly.

The Economy remained Mubarak's most pressing long-term problem, as it had been for Sadat. The government hoped that important oil discoveries in February and significant finds of uranium, copper, and chromite would expand exports and reduce the drain on hard-currency reserves. An emergency export program was established in August to reduce dependence on foreign loans. The government predicted it would expand cotton and rice exports and increase oil production by 11 per cent to 650,000 barrels per day. William Spencer

See also MIDDLE EAST (Facts in Brief Table). In WORLD BOOK, see EGYPT.

ELECTIONS. Democrats, blaming President Ronald Reagan for hard times, chalked up major gains in the Nov. 2, 1982, midterm elections in the United States. Only in the Senate did the Democrats have to settle for a draw. In the House of Representatives, they added 26 seats to their majority to achieve working control of one branch of Congress. Democrats also scored a net gain of seven governors' chairs, building a powerful political base for the 1984 elections. In addition, Democrats took control of both legislative bodies in six more states, while Republicans lost five.

President Reagan, who campaigned actively for Republicans and urged voters to "stay the course" with his economic policies, insisted that he was pleased by the outcome, since the GOP retained its 54-46 margin of control in the Senate. However, Speaker of the House Thomas P. (Tip) O'Neill, Jr. (D., Mass.), claimed that it was a "devastating defeat" for the President.

The November elections were notable for big spending. An estimated $300 million—a record amount—was spent by candidates of both parties, with some multimillion-dollar outlays by wealthy contenders.

Voter turnout was heavy for an off-year election. Slightly more than 40 per cent of the nation's eligible voters cast ballots, according to the Committee for the Study of the American Electorate. This reversed a downtrend in voting that was reflected in a 37.9 per cent turnout in the 1978 elections, the lowest figure since 1942.

The House. The Democrats' biggest victory came in the House of Representatives, where they gained 26 seats to raise their margin over the Republicans to 267-166. The Democrats' lead later increased to 269-165, when Democrats retained two seats in Georgia in delayed balloting and Representative-elect Jack Swigert (R., Colo.) died before taking office. Twenty-six GOP incumbents were defeated, compared with just three for the Democrats.

Blacks gained three seats, raising their number to 21 in the new House. The number of women in the House edged up by one, to 20. Three more Hispanics were elected, raising their number to nine. There were to be 80 new faces in the 98th Congress.

Senate. It was a good year for incumbents, with 18 of 19 Democrats and 10 of 11 Republicans winning re-election. The sole Republican casualty was Senator Harrison H. Schmitt of New Mexico, who lost to Democratic state Attorney General Jeff Bingaman. The defeated Democrat was Senator Howard W. Cannon of Nevada, who was ousted by Republican challenger Chic Hecht, a former state senator. In races for three open seats, Republican Paul S. Trible beat Democratic Lieutenant Governor Richard J. Davis in Virginia; Democrat Frank R. Lautenberg beat GOP Representative Millicent Fenwick in New Jersey; and San Diego Republican Mayor Pete Wilson won easily over Democratic Governor Edmund G. (Jerry) Brown, Jr., in California.

Governors. Democrats won 27 of 36 governors' races, scoring heavily in the Midwest, where the recession took a heavy toll on industrial workers and farmers were angry over low prices for their crops. The Democratic gains gave them a total of 34 governorships, to the Republicans' 16. In Ohio, Richard F. Celeste, a former lieutenant governor and Peace Corps director, coasted to victory over Representative Clarence J. Brown, while Representative James J. Blanchard defeated archconservative Richard H. Headlee, an insurance executive, in Michigan. Rudy Perpich, a former Minnesota governor, won in that state; Anthony S. Earl, a onetime state cabinet member, in Wisconsin; and Robert Kerrey, a Vietnam veteran who won the Medal of Honor, in Nebraska.

In New York, Democratic Lieutenant Governor Mario M. Cuomo, who was also the Liberal Party candidate, defeated drugstore magnate Lewis E. Lehrman, who spent $8 million of his own money in the race. The biggest upset occurred in Texas, where Democratic state Attorney General Mark White won despite GOP Governor William P. Clements, Jr., spending an estimated $15 million.

Winners and losers in the November midterm elections include, *clockwise from above,* Democrat Katie Hall, the first black woman to represent Indiana in the House; Republican Governor James R. Thompson, who beat Democrat Adlai E. Stevenson III in the closest governor's race in Illinois history; and Democrat George C. Wallace, re-elected after three years out of office as Alabama's governor.

California was a bright spot for Republicans, with Attorney General George Deukmejian narrowly defeating Los Angeles Mayor Tom Bradley, who had hoped to be the first black governor. In New Hampshire, former state Representative John H. Sununu ousted Governor Hugh J. Gallen, the only Democratic incumbent to lose.

In Illinois, Republican Governor James R. Thompson won by an eyelash over former U.S. Senator Adlai E. Stevenson III. In Alabama, Democratic Governor George C. Wallace disavowed his past segregationist creed to win the support of black voters, who helped to return him to the governor's mansion.

Voters Also Decided a wide variety of ballot questions on November 2. Proposals advocating a U.S.-Soviet freeze on nuclear weapons production were endorsed in eight states and defeated in Arizona. In addition, one state approved the freeze in a primary election.

Proponents of gun control suffered a major setback when a stringent proposal for registration of handguns was defeated in California by a 2 to 1 margin. Voters in New Hampshire and Nevada also approved state constitutional amendments affirming the right to bear arms. William J. Eaton

See also DEMOCRATIC PARTY; REPUBLICAN PARTY. In WORLD BOOK, see ELECTION.

ELECTRIC POWER. See ENERGY.

ELECTRONICS. The long-awaited emergence of computerized communications networks for businesses took place in the United States in 1982. Manufacturers of such data-communications equipment as computers, computer terminals, printers, and telephone systems rushed to put these components together in computerized systems known as *local area networks*.

Some of these networks move information rapidly among widely separated branches of a company or even among different departments in the same office. Other networks enable various companies in a large office building to avoid paperwork that slows the daily routine of doing business. The last obstacle to rapid growth in the number of local area networks is the lack of standards for data-transmission techniques.

Technological and Political developments made major contributions to the emergence of the networks. Very-large-scale integrated (VLSI) circuits containing 100,000 or more transistors on thumbnail-sized silicon chips became available commercially in 1982, while makers of memory devices built chips that could store some 256,000 bits of information.

The U.S. Department of Justice boosted the entire data-communications industry on January 8, when it agreed to drop antitrust cases against International Business Machines Corporation (IBM), the world's largest manufacturer of computers, and American Telephone and Telegraph Company (A.T. & T.). In turn, A.T. & T. agreed to divest itself of its 22 local telephone companies.

However, the decision's real import lay in allowing IBM and A.T. & T. to compete in each other's business. IBM was now allowed to communicate data, while A.T. & T. might generate data. This head-on clash of titans could cause basic changes in how business is transacted throughout the world. See COMMUNICATIONS.

Computers became so small, powerful, and economical that more types of businesses could afford to use them. For example, the local drugstore or barbershop is now a likely site for a computer that helps the owner keep track of business details.

Even more remarkable was the explosive growth of the home computer market. As home computers became less expensive, computer novices bought them to use for more than playing video games. The upshot was rapid growth in *computer literacy*—familiarity with computer concepts and terms, and the ability to use a computer. One big contribution to the market growth came from IBM, which introduced its Personal Computer in August. But industry leaders such as Apple Computer, Incorporated; Tandy Corporation, maker of Radio Shack products; and Commodore International

Timex Corporation introduced a compact, lightweight computer to the United States market, at a price of $99.95, in July.

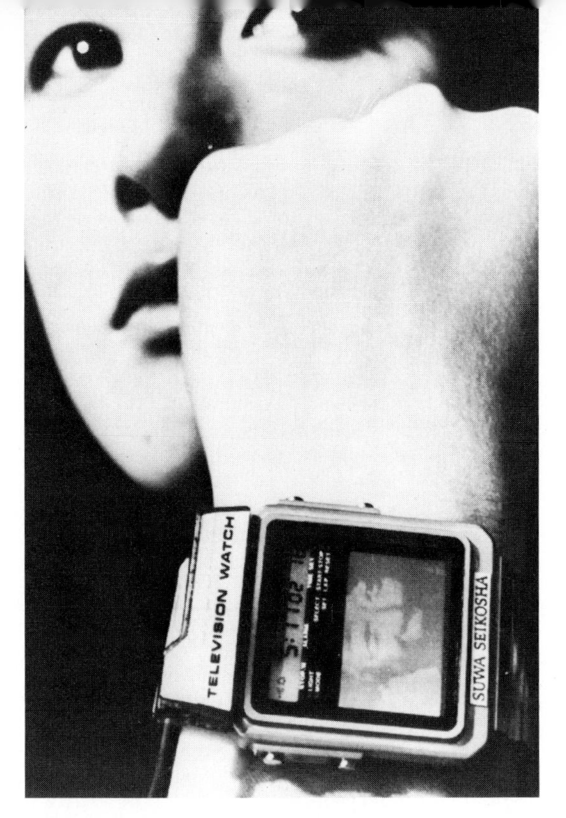

Wrist TV, due on the market in 1983, has a black-and-white display unit. A wallet-sized receiver feeds picture signals to this unit.

Limited were quick to counter IBM by introducing more powerful models.

The surge in computer sales brought a corresponding demand for software — programs — to run those computers. For about five years, there had been a severe shortage of programmers. Makers of microprocessors — the heart of the small computers — spent a great deal of time and money recruiting liberal arts graduates, schoolteachers, and anyone else with an aptitude for the exacting work. However, the shortage began to ease in 1982, as recession-forced layoffs in other industries provided a new group of programmers.

Walk and Watch. Manufacturers of home-entertainment devices turned to the improvement of sound systems in 1982. The major result was a device that plays prerecorded stereophonic cassettes, is small enough to carry in a pocket, and plays through small headphones. The first such device was Sony Corporation's Walkman, which was introduced in the United States in 1980. The next electronic innovation for consumers probably will be the pocket or wrist television set. Prototypes have already been developed. The smaller ones use liquid crystals rather than cathode-ray tubes to display the picture. Howard Wolff

In the Special Reports section, see THE VIDEO REVOLUTION. In WORLD BOOK, see ELECTRONICS.

EL SALVADOR

EL SALVADOR received worldwide acclaim on March 28, 1982, when the people of that war-torn country braved threats of violence to vote in national elections. Rebel leftist guerrillas, who had been battling the government since the late 1970s, boycotted the election and tried to disrupt it with bombings and shootings. However, television cameras recorded the determined mood of Salvadorans as they voted in record numbers, many waiting hours to cast their votes. The elections chose a new Constituent Assembly, a legislative body that was to rewrite the nation's Constitution and provide for the restoration of full democracy.

The Elections failed to provide a clear-cut mandate to any single party or person. They were followed by furious politicking as five right wing parties worked out a coalition that gave them a majority of seats in the Assembly. The Nationalist Republican Alliance, an extreme right wing party founded by Roberto D'Aubuisson, achieved dominance within the coalition despite having won just 29 per cent of the popular vote. Observers both inside and outside El Salvador had hoped that the other four rightist parties — all more moderate than D'Aubuisson's — would exercise more power.

The New Government. Because of the intense infighting, the Constituent Assembly was slow to take form and did not convene until April 19. On

Assembly President Roberto D'Aubuisson, left, sings El Salvador's anthem at the inauguration of Provisional President Magaña, right, in May.

April 22, D'Aubuisson became its president, making him probably the most powerful leader in El Salvador. See D'AUBUISSON, ROBERTO.

On April 29, the Assembly named Alvaro Magaña as provisional president of El Salvador. Magaña, a 56-year-old lawyer and former head of El Salvador's largest mortgage bank, had no affiliation with any political party. At his inauguration on May 2, he called for an end to bickering. "There is no room for resentment, for hatred or for sectarian positions" at a time of "terrible crisis," he declared.

Notwithstanding Magaña's appeal, the right-wing-dominated Assembly in May suspended further redistribution of lands under the country's comprehensive land reform program. However, pressure from the United States—including the threat of a cutoff in economic aid—helped persuade the Assembly to resume land redistribution.

Human Rights. How much progress El Salvador was making on human rights became the subject of a lively debate in the U.S. Congress. Under legislation enacted in 1981, Congress requires certification by the President every six months that El Salvador is making progress in safeguarding human rights as a condition for continued U.S. economic assistance. President Ronald Reagan provided such certification on January 28 and again on July 27, 1982. He also asked for increased financial and military aid to El Salvador as part of U.S. efforts to restore peace in Central America and stem the advance of leftist revolution. In December, Magaña appointed seven leading Salvadorans to a new commission on human rights.

Fighting between leftist guerrillas and government troops continued throughout 1982. On August 31, General José Guillermo García Merino, El Salvador's defense minister, announced that in the 12-month period ending June 30, government forces had suffered nearly 4,000 casualties. About 1 soldier in 5 in the armed forces had been killed or wounded. The United States continued to supply military advisers, said to number about 100.

In September, there were unconfirmed reports that the Salvadoran government, with the quiet backing of the Reagan Administration, had begun indirect talks with guerrilla leaders seeking to end the war. In addition, many Latin American nations and some European countries exerted pressure to help bring an end to the conflict, which had gripped El Salvador for more than three years. Nathan A. Haverstock

See also LATIN AMERICA (Facts in Brief Table). In the Special Reports section, see WHAT WENT WRONG IN CENTRAL AMERICA? In WORLD BOOK, see EL SALVADOR.

EMPLOYMENT. See ECONOMICS; EDUCATION; LABOR; SOCIAL SECURITY; WELFARE.

ENDANGERED SPECIES. See CONSERVATION.

ENERGY. Efforts to develop a synthetic-fuels (synfuels) industry in the United States to reduce U.S. dependence on foreign oil suffered major setbacks during 1982. The synfuels program, the keystone of the energy strategy developed by President Jimmy Carter, was expected to supply the equivalent of 2 million barrels of oil per day (bpd) by 1992. During 1982, such production levels appeared increasingly unlikely.

On May 2, Exxon Corporation, the world's largest energy company, announced that it was abandoning the Colony shale oil project in Colorado. The $5-billion to $6-billion project, the most ambitious U.S. synfuels venture, was a victim of cost overruns that more than doubled its original price, as well as of stable oil prices resulting from the worldwide oil glut.

Another major synfuels project was placed in jeopardy on October 20, when Standard Oil Company (Ohio), also known as Sohio, pulled out. The synfuels plant, to be built near Gillette, Wyo., was to convert coal into 19,000 bpd of gasoline. Sohio also blamed economic factors for its decision, noting that the project no longer appeared profitable.

Synfuels projects failed elsewhere, as well. On April 30, Shell Canada Limited and Gulf Canada Limited ended their participation in the Alsands oil sands project in Canada. The $13.5-billion venture (Canadian dollars; $1 = U.S. 81 cents on Dec. 31, 1982), believed to be the world's largest synfuels development program, was an effort to produce crude oil from tar sands in Alberta. The two firms were the last remaining private investors. The Canadian government said it would not continue Alsands without private participation.

DOE Hangs On. United States President Ronald Reagan remained unsuccessful in his efforts to persuade Congress to abolish the Department of Energy (DOE). Although he sent Congress a revised plan to do so on May 24, it was opposed as strongly as was an earlier plan submitted in 1981. On June 24, DOE Secretary James B. Edwards, who announced his resignation on May 12, told Congress that dismantling the department was his top priority before leaving. However, in November, after Edwards' departure, the DOE still existed and Reagan appointed Donald P. Hodel as energy secretary. See HODEL, DONALD PAUL.

The U.S. General Accounting Office (GAO) completed a study of the DOE on August 1. It found no evidence that abolishing the department would save $2 billion over four years, as the Reagan Administration contended.

Nuclear Milestone. The commercial nuclear power industry in the United States observed its 25th birthday on December 18. America's first commercial nuclear plant, the Shippingport Atomic Power Station near Pittsburgh, Pa., went into operation on that day in 1957. The plant,

The largest magnetic fusion energy test reactor, here being assembled at Princeton University in New Jersey, was tested successfully in December.

which was decommissioned on Oct. 1, 1982, was to be dismantled and its components studied. Shippingport pioneered the pressurized water reactor concept, now used extensively throughout the United States.

Reactor Shutdowns. Declining demand for electricity, tough economic times, and persistent concerns over safety issues combined to make the nuclear power birthday an unhappy one. For the fourth straight year, utilities in 1982 ordered no new nuclear power plants and continued to cancel reactors already under construction. The Tennessee Valley Authority (TVA) announced on March 4 that it would halt construction on three nuclear reactors on which it already had spent $2.1 billion. On August 25, the TVA decided to cancel four other reactors, on which it had spent $1.8 billion. The Duke Power Company announced on November 2 that two large nuclear units it was building in North Carolina would be canceled. Two other nuclear units in Washington state were canceled in January, and construction on a third was suspended on April 29.

Safety Issues. Faulty tubes in steam generators continued to cause problems in nuclear power plants. Leaks in the devices, which carry hot radioactive water from a reactor's core, forced the closing of several plants, including the Robert E. Ginna nuclear power plant in Ontario, N.Y., on January 25. The U.S. Nuclear Regulatory Commission (NRC) reported on March 31 that steam generator tubes were corroding prematurely at about 40 plants. On October 3, the NRC cited 11 nuclear plants that it said needed modifications to prevent ruptures in the reactor walls. According to an NRC study issued on November 1, the chances of the worst possible nuclear accident are 1 in 1 billion per year at each U.S. nuclear plant.

On March 19, Boston Edison Company paid a $550,000 fine for safety violations at its nuclear station near Plymouth, Mass. It was the largest fine ever imposed by the NRC.

The Supreme Court of the United States agreed on November 1 to decide whether the NRC must consider psychological stress on the community when it decides whether to permit the start-up of the undamaged Nuclear Unit Number 1 at the Three Mile Island nuclear plant near Harrisburg, Pa. The NRC previously refused to consider a claim by residents of the area that restarting the plant would aggravate psychological problems arising from the accident there in 1979.

Plant Growth. The DOE unveiled a plan on October 15 to stimulate construction of new nuclear plants. The proposals, requested by President Reagan, would streamline nuclear licensing and regulations, reducing the time and cost involved in building new plants.

The largest private wind turbines in the United States, in the Altamont Pass near Livermore, Calif., began to supply electricity in July.

Planning for the construction of the Clinch River breeder reactor, near Oak Ridge, Tenn., moved ahead slowly during 1982. On August 5, the NRC reversed a March decision and agreed to exempt the project from rules that would have slowed its construction. Congress on December 20 voted to continue funding for the reactor, intended to "breed"—or produce—more nuclear fuel than it consumes. The GAO concluded on December 11 that Clinch River's final costs could exceed $8.5-billion, more than twice as much as previous estimates.

"Energy Turns the World" was the theme of the 1982 World's Fair held in Knoxville, Tenn., from May 1 to October 31. The fair, officially known as the Knoxville International Energy Exposition, featured exhibits of new energy technology.

U.S. Energy Consumption during the first seven months of 1982 totaled 42.4 quadrillion British Thermal Units (BTU's), the DOE reported on November 1. Consumption was 2.6 per cent less than during the same period in 1981. Daily U.S. consumption of petroleum fell 5.1 per cent; natural gas, 4.0 per cent; and coal, 1.2 per cent. Imported energy totaled 4 quadrillion BTU's, 33 per cent below the 1981 level. The sharpest decline, 25 per cent, was in imported oil.

In its first study dealing exclusively with wood energy, the DOE concluded on August 27 that industrial and residential use of wood has increased dramatically. Wood consumption rose by 56 per cent between 1970 and 1981. The DOE said that 130 million short tons (118 million metric tons) of wood were consumed in the United States in 1981, with industry using the largest share. By 1981, 4.5 million households relied upon wood as their major source of heat, and each consumed an average of 4.9 cords. (A cord is a measure of cut wood equal to 128 cubic feet [3.6 cubic meters].)

The DOE and the Edison Electric Institute (EEI), a utility industry group, reported on October 11 that U.S. consumption of electricity declined by an "unprecedented" 1.9 per cent during the first seven months of 1982. As of August 28, 1.55 trillion kilowatt hours of electricity had been used, compared with 1.58 trillion during the same period in 1981. No such decline had occurred since the early 1940s, according to the agencies. They attributed the fall-off to the continuing economic recession, energy conservation measures, and a cool summer that reduced the electricity demand for air conditioning. United States demand for electricity grew at an annual rate of more than 7 per cent during the early 1970s but has been stagnant in recent years. Michael Woods

See also COAL; PETROLEUM AND GAS. In WORLD BOOK, see ENERGY SUPPLY.

ENGINEERING. See BUILDING & CONSTRUCTION.

ENVIRONMENT. The environmental movement in the United States won impressive victories in Congress and in the nation's voting booths in 1982. On March 31, 10 of the largest conservation groups in the United States attacked President Ronald Reagan directly for the first time. They charged his Administration with "a wholesale giveaway to private interests of our most precious natural resources." The organizations had criticized many of the Reagan Administration's policies, but they had previously focused their attacks on Secretary of the Interior James G. Watt and Environmental Protection Agency Administrator Anne M. Gorsuch.

Polls conducted in 1982 confirmed public support for tough regulations to control air and water pollution. Fifty-six per cent of those questioned in a nationwide poll that *The Washington Post* conducted in mid-March said Democrats would protect the environment better than Republicans would; 22 per cent favored the Republicans.

The "Green Vote." Environmentalists responded by launching plans to make 1982 the year of the "green vote." Five national groups—the Sierra Club, Environmental Action, the Solar Lobby, Friends of the Earth, and the League of Conservation Voters—announced on April 20 that they planned to spend more than $2 million to demonstrate their power at the polls.

The Conservation Foundation, an environmental research group that generally avoids political confrontation, charged on June 16 that the Reagan Administration had given priority to deregulation and defunding efforts that broke "the bipartisan consensus that supported federal protection of the environment for more than a decade." The President's Council on Environmental Quality responded with a report that said the United States had made "great progress" on environmental fronts, especially in reducing air pollution. "Regulations should complement, not stifle, market forces in determining the most cost-effective methods of proper environmental management," said Reagan in a letter that accompanied the report.

Election Results. Environmentalists said that the results of the November 2 elections showed the strength of the green vote. Marion B. Edey, director of the League of Conservation Voters, said on November 3 that the environmental movement was second only to the labor movement in turning out volunteers to help candidates. "We won 73 per cent of the 63 races we targeted," Edey said.

Clean Air Bill Deadlock. A two-year battle over revision of the Clean Air Act of 1970 ended indecisively in Congress as the legislation became tangled in a thicket of conflicting interests. When Republicans won the 1980 election, business forces launched a campaign to rewrite the Clean Air Act, which was due for reauthorization. Industry viewed the legislation as a costly multibillion dollar burden and a prime example of the type of regulatory excess that Ronald Reagan had promised to eliminate. However, in 1981, the battle ended with the law extended for one year.

Legislation that would have made major changes in the law ran into trouble on April 29, when John D. Dingell (D., Mich.), chairman of the House Committee on Energy and Commerce, suspended work on the measure. Environmental groups said that the sudden suspension meant the coalition supporting the bill was cracking.

On August 19, the Senate Environment and Public Works Committee sent the full Senate a bipartisan bill that generally pleased environmentalists. Senator Robert T. Stafford (R., Vt.) hailed the bill as rejecting "virtually every major effort to weaken the Clean Air Act."

When Congress recessed on October 2, the House Energy Committee was still divided over the legislation. The Administration threatened to begin cutting off highway and sewage-system construction funds if Congress did not reauthorize the act by December 31, and Congress failed to do so.

Acid Rain. The debate over the need to control sulfur dioxide emissions in order to reduce acid

Trout trapped in a pen die gradually in a study of the chemical effects of acid snow and rain on a stream in New York's Adirondack Mountains.

rain escalated in 1982. Sulfur dioxide combines with moisture in the air to form sulfuric acid, which falls to earth as acid rain. On February 25, Representative Toby Moffett (D., Conn.) released a study documenting what environmentalists say is "severe and widespread damage" to water and soil resources from acid rain. The study was made by the Institute of Ecology, located at Butler University in Indianapolis, Ind. The institute said acid rain had already damaged between 2,400 and 3,600 lakes in the Eastern United States.

The Edison Electric Institute, an association of investor-owned electric companies, responded with advertisements in many newspapers. The ads urged readers "to tell your elected representatives to press for scientific facts before they are stampeded into casting a vote that may not control the acidity of precipitation, but will surely cost electricity customers billions of dollars."

On July 23, the Senate Environment Committee voted 15-0 to begin a program that would cut sulfur dioxide emissions in 31 Eastern states by 50 per cent by 1995. "Acid rain is perhaps the single most important environmental problem in North America," Stafford said. "It is an issue of international importance, seriously affecting relations between the United States and Canada." Richard C. Ayres, chairman of the National Clean Air Coalition, called the committee vote "an eloquent rebuttal to the Reagan Administration and those elements of industry which propose nothing but lengthy studies."

Offshore Leasing Accelerated. On July 21, Secretary Watt adopted an energy development program that called for the offering of oil and gas leases on almost 1 billion acres (400 million hectares) beneath U.S. coastal waters over the next five years. Watt said his program was designed "to protect the environment while making America less dependent on foreign oil sources."

California Governor Edmund G. Brown, Jr., protested the action, and the state filed suit on July 22 to overturn the program. Brown said that Watt was "trying to auction off the patrimony of America precipitously."

Representative Edward J. Markey (D., Mass.) charged at a congressional hearing on September 24 that the Department of the Interior had embarked on a "crash program" based on "an ideology rather than sound economic and environmental principles." Interior officials responded that they wanted to spur offshore development and thus get more oil and gas produced for the American consumer. The officials said that offshore wells have produced more than 4 billion barrels of oil since 1970 and that only 791 barrels of oil have escaped into the sea because of blowouts. On December 19, Congress passed an appropriations bill that included a provision blocking Watt from selling leases off the northern and central coast of California before Oct. 1, 1983. Reagan signed it on December 20.

On October 13, oil companies bid a near-record $2.07 billion for oil leases in the Beaufort Sea off Alaska's North Slope. Interior officials hailed the sale results as a vindication of the five-year leasing program. The tracts are in the Diapir Field near the rich Prudhoe Bay oil field and in an area believed to hold the largest pool of undiscovered oil and gas reserves in North America.

Sea Law. Eight years of diplomatic bargaining climaxed on April 30, when delegates to the United Nations Law of the Sea Conference adopted a comprehensive treaty governing the use of the seas. The treaty included seabed mining rules to which the United States objected. These rules grant control of ocean mining to an international seabed authority.

The United States and three other nations voted against the treaty. Seventeen other nations, most of them industrial countries, abstained in the 130-4 vote. On December 10, 117 nations signed the treaty. The U.S. and other major industrial countries did not sign. See OCEAN. Andrew L. Newman

See also CONSERVATION; PETROLEUM AND GAS. In WORLD BOOK, see ENVIRONMENT; ENVIRONMENTAL POLLUTION.

EQUATORIAL GUINEA. See AFRICA.

ERSHAD, HUSSAIN MUHAMMAD (1930-), a lieutenant general in the Bangladesh Army, seized political power in Bangladesh on March 24, 1982, ousting the administration of President Abdus Sattar. Ershad declared martial law, suspended the Bangladesh Constitution, prohibited all political activity, and named himself chief martial law administrator of the country. He said he acted to end rampant corruption in government and to deal with Bangladesh's bankrupt economy. He said he hoped democracy could be restored in Bangladesh within two years. See BANGLADESH.

Ershad was born on Feb. 1, 1930, in Rangpur, India (now in Bangladesh). He graduated from the University of Dacca in 1950 and two years later received a commission in the Pakistani Army. In the 1971 civil war between East Pakistan and West Pakistan, Ershad commanded an East Pakistani regiment.

After East Pakistan achieved independence and became the nation of Bangladesh, Ershad was promoted to the rank of colonel. He attained the position of army chief of staff in 1978 and the rank of lieutenant general in 1979.

Ershad has been active in athletics all his life. He was a star soccer player in his youth and has served as chairman of the National Sports Control Board and president of the Bangladesh Lawn Tennis Federation. David L. Dreier

ETHIOPIA launched large-scale offensives in 1982 against secessionist forces in two regions of the country. In the northeastern province of Eritrea, the military government faced Muslim separatists who since 1962 had been waging a guerrilla war to establish an independent state. On January 18, the government announced that the secessionist movement had been "effectively smashed." However, on January 22, guerrillas attacked the province's capital city, Asmara, and held part of it for 24 hours.

In mid-February, the government sent more than 70,000 troops, backed by an estimated 400 Soviet advisers, to attack rebel strongholds in Eritrea's mountains. Ethiopia's head of state, Provisional Military Administrative Council Chairman Mengistu Haile-Mariam, personally directed the offensive. However, by early May it had bogged down, and its principal target, the mountain town of Nakfa, remained in guerrilla hands.

The rebel forces, estimated at 30,000 to 40,000 men and women, belonged to the Eritrean People's Liberation Front. A spokesman for the guerrilla group told journalists in New York City that the Ethiopian troops were using chemical weapons, napalm, and nerve gas against the rebels.

War for Ogaden. In Ethiopia's southeastern region, which is known as Ogaden, the central government faced Somali-speaking separatists of the Western Somali Liberation Front, who fought to join Ogaden to neighboring Somalia. Their main source of support was Somalia's pro-Western government, which was led by President Mohamed Siad Barre.

In an effort to weaken or topple the Somali government, Ethiopia provided weapons and other supplies to two anti-Siad Barre Somali rebel movements. On June 30, about 9,000 troops entered Somalia to support the rebels. They seized two towns in Somalia near the border in July. Somali government forces counterattacked in that area a month later, and Somali guerrillas stepped up their attacks inside Ogaden. Ethiopia said that its troops were not involved. See SOMALIA.

Exiles' Status. After the military government took power from Emperor Haile Selassie in 1974, many Ethiopians sought refuge in the United States. In August 1981, President Ronald Reagan's Administration told the thousands of Ethiopians living in the United States to expect to be deported unless they could prove, on a case-by-case basis, that they faced persecution if they returned to Ethiopia. However, in July 1982, after complaints from human rights groups and members of Congress, the U.S. Immigration and Naturalization Service gave the exiles a blanket clearance to stay in the country. J. Dixon Esseks

See also AFRICA (Facts in Brief Table). In WORLD BOOK, see ETHIOPIA.

Cuban troops in Ethiopia confer under the hot African sun. They are suspected of providing weapons and backup support to Somali rebels.

EUROPE

The death of 75-year-old Russian leader Leonid I. Brezhnev on Nov. 10, 1982, gave Europeans a new element to ponder—the possibility of a policy change in the Kremlin. But Soviet policy remained on course during the early days of the leadership of Brezhnev's successor, Yuri V. Andropov, former head of the KGB, the Soviet intelligence and security agency.

The 10-nation European Community (EC or Common Market) began 1982 without an agreement on what to do about Russia's role in the December 1981 imposition of martial law in Poland. The United States had imposed economic sanctions against Russia, but the EC hesitated to follow suit. On January 4, the EC nations pledged not to undercut the U.S. sanctions. Finally, on March 15, the EC decided to curb Russian imports into EC markets by about 1 per cent. The cuts trimmed $145 million from Soviet trade with Western Europe in 1982.

Belgian Prime Minister Wilfried A. E. Martens, visiting Washington, D.C., in February, complained about high United States interest rates. He said that the estimated U.S. budget deficit of $91.5 billion for 1983 would block European economic recovery efforts in 1982. He also blamed the United States for disrupting dollar exchange rates against European currencies.

Production in all Common Market countries was almost stagnant. Unemployment had risen to 10.4 million, or 9.1 per cent of the work force. The EC nations therefore resented what they saw as a hawkish attitude on the part of the United States toward the European nations of the Soviet bloc. The Common Market countries thought that this attitude threatened the benefits of détente with the East.

Trade Relations between the United States and the EC worsened in June, when the United States announced that it would impose import duties on some European steel and widened earlier sanctions against companies supplying parts for a gas pipeline that Russia was building from Siberia to central Europe.

United States President Ronald Reagan visited London from June 7 through 9 but failed to ease U.S. tensions with Great Britain. In an address to both houses of Parliament at the Palace of Westminster, Reagan declared that freedom and democracy "would leave Marxism-Leninism on the ash heap of history."

Russian workers inspect a section of the controversial natural gas pipeline that will carry gas from Siberia to central Europe.

Greenlanders celebrate the results of a February referendum calling for withdrawal from the European Community (Common Market).

On December 10, the United States and the Common Market announced progress in settling their differences over agricultural exports. United States officials had threatened to dump surplus farm products on the world market if the EC continued its policy of subsidizing farm exports. The parties agreed to meet early in 1983 to try to hammer out a settlement.

Pipeline Problem. The worst political storm ever to hit the transatlantic alliance blew up in 1982 when European countries defied the U.S. embargo on supplying parts for Russia's pipeline. The source of the gas, the Urengoyskoye field in western Siberia, is the world's largest. In the 1970s, U.S. companies had negotiated with the Soviet Union about supplying pipeline parts and know-how. However, Russia ended these talks and turned to West Germany.

President Reagan argued at the 1981 economic summit conference of Western leaders that a deal calling for European countries to buy gas from Russia would make the West dangerously dependent on the Soviets. But France, Great Britain, Italy, and West Germany signed contracts worth $3.1 billion for supplying management, computers, pipeline parts, turbines, and compressors for the pipeline.

Facts in Brief on the European Countries

Country	Population	Government	Monetary Unit*	Foreign Trade (million U.S. $)	
				Exports†	Imports†
Albania	2,944,000	Communist Party First Secretary Enver Hoxha; People's Assembly Presidium Chairman Ramiz Alia; Prime Minister Adil Çarçani	lek (5.8 = $1)	151	173
Andorra	39,000	The bishop of Urgel, Spain, and the president of France	French franc & Spanish peseta	no statistics available	
Austria	7,533,000	President Rudolf Kirchschläger; Chancellor Bruno Kreisky	schilling (17.3 = $1)	15,846	21,049
Belgium	9,887,000	King Baudouin I; Prime Minister Wilfried A. E. Martens	franc (48.4 = $1)	55,646 (includes Luxembourg)	62,133
Bulgaria	9,049,000	Communist Party General Secretary & State Council Chairman Todor Zhivkov; Prime Minister Georgi Stanchev Filipov	lev (1 = $1.03)	10,500	9,700
Czechoslovakia	15,682,000	Communist Party General Secretary & President Gustáv Husák; Prime Minister Lubomir Strougal	koruna (12.3 = $1)	14,706	14,958
Denmark	5,169,000	Queen Margrethe II; Prime Minister Poul Schlüter	krone (8.7 = $1)	15,735	17,530
Finland	4,821,000	President Mauno H. Koivisto; Prime Minister Kalevi Sorsa	markka (5.4 = $1)	14,015	14,201
France	54,360,000	President François Mitterrand; Prime Minister Pierre Mauroy	franc (6.9 = $1)	101,392	120,689
Germany, East	16,637,000	Communist Party Secretary General & State Council Chairman Erich Honecker; Prime Minister Willi Stoph	mark (2.4 = $1)	15,063	16,214
Germany, West	61,412,000	President Karl Carstens; Chancellor Helmut Kohl	Deutsche mark (2.5 = $1)	176,085	163,907
Great Britain	55,705,000	Queen Elizabeth II; Prime Minister Margaret Thatcher	pound (1 = $1.63)	115,114	119,925
Greece	9,919,000	President Constantine Karamanlis; Prime Minister Andreas Papandreou	drachma (70.6 = $1)	4,241	8,885
Hungary	10,818,000	Communist Party First Secretary Janos Kadar; President Pal Losonczi; Prime Minister Gyorgy Lazar	forint (35.1 = $1)	8,712	9,128
Iceland	236,000	President Vigdis Finnbogadottir; Prime Minister Gunnar Thoroddsen	krona (14.7 = $1)	887	1,033
Ireland	3,575,000	President Patrick J. Hillery; Prime Minister Garret FitzGerald	pound (1 = $1.36)	7,786	10,596
Italy	57,902,000	President Sandro Pertini; Prime Minister Amintore Fanfani	lira (1,427 = $1)	75,214	91,011
Liechtenstein	28,000	Prince Franz Josef II; Prime Minister Hans Brunhart	Swiss franc	no statistics available	
Luxembourg	368,000	Grand Duke Jean; Prime Minister Pierre Werner	franc (48.4 = $1)	55,646 (includes Belgium)	62,133
Malta	377,000	President Agatha Barbara; Prime Minister Dom Mintoff	franc (1 = $2.41)	475	923
Monaco	27,000	Prince Rainier III	French franc	no statistics available	
Netherlands	14,427,000	Queen Beatrix; Prime Minister Ruud Lubbers	guilder (2.7 = $1)	68,756	66,111
Norway	4,128,000	King Olav V; Prime Minister Kaare Willoch	krone (6.9 = $1)	17,992	15,646
Poland	36,463,000	Communist Party First Secretary & Council of Ministers Chairman Wojciech Jaruzelski; President Henryk Jablonski	zloty (80 = $1)	13,249	15,475
Portugal	10,264,000	President António dos Santos Ramalho Eanes; Prime Minister Francisco Pinto Balsemão	escudo (91.4 = $1)	4,632	9,299
Romania	22,874,000	Communist Party General Secretary & President Nicolae Ceausescu; Prime Minister Constantin Dascalescu	leu (15 = $1)	11,201	12,816
Russia	272,775,000	Communist Party General Secretary Yuri V. Andropov; Council of Ministers Chairman Nikolay Aleksandrovich Tikhonov	ruble (1 = $1.39)	76,449	68,522
San Marino	22,000	2 captains regent appointed by Grand Council every 6 months	Italian lira	no statistics available	
Spain	38,679,000	King Juan Carlos I; Prime Minister Felipe González Márquez	peseta (117.6 = $1)	20,338	32,159
Sweden	8,370,000	King Carl XVI Gustaf; Prime Minister Olof Palme	krona (7.4 = $1)	28,597	28,857
Switzerland	6,348,000	President Pierre Aubert	franc (2.1 = $1)	27,051	30,689
Turkey	48,410,000	President Kenan Evren; Prime Minister Bulend Ulusu	lira (182 = $1)	4,721	8,944
Yugoslavia	23,129,000	President Petar Stambolić; Prime Minister Milka Planinc	dinar (52.9 = $1)	10,929	15,757

*Exchange rates as of Dec. 1, 1982. †Latest available data.

In December 1981, Reagan banned American companies from taking part in the construction of the pipeline. Reagan imposed this embargo because of Russia's role in forcing a military regime on Poland in December 1981. However, the Europeans refused to cooperate. France and West Germany said that signed contracts to take gas from the pipeline when it becomes operational in 1984 must stand.

In June 1982, Reagan extended the embargo to foreign subsidiaries and licensees of U.S. companies. However, West Germany and Italy told their companies to defy this ban. France cited a law giving the government requisitioning powers and ordered its companies to go ahead. British Prime Minister Margaret Thatcher invoked a law that would impose unlimited fines on companies backing out of the deal. The EC said that the U.S. attempts to regulate foreign companies violated international law.

Defiance. The first company to defy the embargo was Dresser (France) S.A., a subsidiary of the multinational corporation Dresser Industries of Dallas. Dresser (France) had Russian orders for 21 compressors. On August 26, the U.S. Department of Commerce suspended export licenses for all U.S. goods bound for Dresser (France). However, on September 1, the United States limited the suspension to licenses for oil and gas equipment.

Italy sent out the first two of 19 pumping stations from Livorno on September 1. On September 9, a Scottish company, John Brown P.L.C., sent off the first six of 21 turbines that it was building for the pipeline. Key parts for the turbines came from a U.S. firm, General Electric Company, so the United States imposed sanctions against John Brown. On November 13, Reagan announced that the United States and its European allies had reached "substantial agreement" on an East-West economic policy, and he lifted all the sanctions.

Falklands Invasion. On March 19, a group of Argentine scrap-metal merchants raised their nation's flag over South Georgia Island, part of Great Britain's Falklands dependency in the South Atlantic Ocean. Argentine troops seized the main Falkland Islands on April 2. The unexpectedness of the action led to the resignation of British Foreign Secretary Lord Carrington on April 5. He was succeeded by Francis Pym.

A British task force including the aircraft carriers H.M.S. *Hermes* and H.M.S. *Invincible* sailed from Portsmouth for the Falklands on April 5. Two days later, Pym announced a 200-mile (320-kilometer) naval blockade around the Falklands beginning on April 12. An air blockade followed on April 30. Peacemaking efforts by U.S. Secretary of State Alexander M. Haig, Jr., resulted only in proposals that were unacceptable to one side or the other.

Representatives of seven Western nations conclude their June economic summit with a dinner in the Palace of Versailles near Paris.

Surrender. The first air battles took place on May 1, and on the following day Britain sank the Argentine cruiser *General Belgrano*. Argentina retaliated by sinking the British destroyer H.M.S. *Sheffield*. On May 21, British troops established a beachhead on East Falkland Island, the more important of the two main islands. After sea, air, and land battles, Argentina surrendered on June 14. See FALKLAND ISLANDS.

The United States imposed military and economic sanctions on Argentina during the Falklands crisis. The EC provided similar support initially, but Italy and Ireland broke ranks. Italy wished to preserve its long-standing ties with Argentina, and Ireland wanted to assert its traditional neutrality.

Farm Deal. Prolonged haggling on EC farm prices for 1982 and 1983 began in January and was complicated by failure to agree on Britain's contribution to the general budget. The European Commission, the EC's governing body, proposed a record $1.46-billion increase in agricultural spending that would add 10.7 per cent to the community's farm budget. Great Britain vetoed the proposal, following the EC tradition that any nation can block a measure it believes is against its national interest. However, the EC ended a two-

NATO Under Stress

The North Atlantic Treaty Organization (NATO) faced unprecedented stresses in 1982, its 33rd year. In February, NATO Secretary-General Joseph M. A. H. Luns appointed six military experts to determine whether NATO "is still up to the task of effective participation in the management of the national security concerns of its members." Their conclusions, published in a special edition of *NATO Review,* were ambivalent.

The six experts had no difficulty in identifying the problems. First was the British air, sea, and land offensive that recaptured the Falkland Islands from Argentina in June. Great Britain's sending a huge task force to the Falklands area seriously weakened NATO's East Atlantic force. From April through June, that NATO force was vulnerable as never before. Furthermore, Great Britain's losses of ships, equipment, and troops were heavy.

However, Britain's resolution stiffened NATO's resolve. And the devastating effect of modern Western nonnuclear weaponry—including that used by Argentina and, later, by Israel against modern Russian weapons in Lebanon—confirmed the West's technological superiority.

Antimissile protest in Great Britain

A more serious problem was the strained relations between Europe and the United States. Differences of opinion ranged over a wide variety of financial and economic matters, but they came to a head in June, when United States President Ronald Reagan slapped an embargo on the supplying of parts for a natural gas pipeline that Russia was building from Siberian gas fields to central Europe. The embargo was a retaliation against Russia for its role in Poland's imposition of military rule in December 1981. Reagan threatened to impose sanctions against foreign subsidiaries and licensees of U.S. companies for violating the embargo. However, the governments of the nations in which the subsidiaries and licensees are located—Britain, France, Italy, and West Germany—ordered them to defy the ban. None of the governments was prepared to sacrifice income and jobs. Reagan withdrew the ban in November. He said that the United States and its European allies had reached "substantial agreement" regarding East-West trade.

A 1979 decision by NATO to install 572 U.S.-built nuclear-armed Pershing II ballistic missiles and cruise missiles in five Western European countries, beginning in late 1983, continued to provoke dissension and riots, particularly in West Germany, the Netherlands, and Britain. Environmentalist and peace groups seemed to have the potential to become strong enough to prevent some governments from allowing missile installations on their soil.

NATO's 1979 decision was coupled with a demand that the Soviet Union and the United States negotiate to reduce the number of nuclear weapons in Europe. Russia was estimated to have 300 mobile SS-20 missile launchers targeted on Western Europe.

NATO came under fire in the United States, too. But U.S. Secretary of State Alexander M. Haig, Jr., strongly defended NATO against its critics in the U.S. Senate Foreign Relations Committee in March. "I do not accept for one moment that the agony and the disarray in the alliance in any way approaches the degree your comments suggest," he told the committee.

So what of the future? Russia's power has grown inexorably, and the Soviet Union has shown clearly that it is willing to use force. Elliot L. Richardson, a former U.S. secretary of defense, said in the February 1982 issue of *NATO Review* that NATO must continue "to provide highly capable and interlinked conventional and nuclear forces so as to deter conflict in the North Atlantic area, and to work for the stability in, and security from Soviet threats to, other vital parts of the globe."

NATO will achieve this only if it works toward consensus among the nations it is designed to defend, and if the balance between benefits and costs continues to be tolerable to the member countries. Kenneth Brown day meeting in Brussels on May 18 by overriding the veto.

EC Budget. Britain continued its three-year struggle for cash rebates to reduce its contributions to the Common Market budget, even though it took $35 million more out of the EC than it contributed in 1981. Britain's contribution for 1982 was estimated at $940 million. After Britain blocked the annual farm price review, the EC decided on May 25 that Britain would receive a rebate of about $850 million over the year, with a greater rebate if its contributions rose above $1.5-billion. On June 30, the presidents of the three EC institutions—the Council of Ministers, the European Parliament, and the Commission—signed new rules designed to end budget squabbles. The rules call for settling all issues by January 31 of each year.

Two Currency Realignments took place in 1982 within the European Monetary System (EMS), a program that eight nations established in 1979 to stabilize their exchange rates. On February 22, Belgium devalued its franc by 8.5 per cent, and Denmark decreased the value of its krona by 3 per cent. On June 13, the French franc was devalued by 5.75 per cent and the Italian lira by 2.75 per cent, while the values of the West German Deutsche mark and the Dutch guilder were increased by 4.25 per cent.

Five Western European nations that are not in the EMS devalued their currencies in 1982. Iceland cut the value of its krona by 13 per cent in January. Portugal devalued the escudo by 9.5 per cent in June. In October, Sweden pegged its krona 16 per cent lower, while Finland devalued the markka twice, by 4 and 6 per cent. And in December, Spain devalued the peseta by 8 per cent.

Steel Crisis. In January, the EC Commission authorized the payment of $1.2 billion to the ailing steel industries of Belgium, France, and Italy. The commission also extended 1981 mandatory quotas for steel production through 1982.

The EC then turned its attention to fighting proposals by President Reagan to impose extra duties on U.S. imports of EC steel. The duties would protect the U.S. steel industry. After six months of negotiations, U.S. and EC officials agreed on August 6 to reduce the European share of the U.S. market to slightly less than 5.8 per cent over three years. However, the U.S. steel industry rejected the pact.

On October 21, the EC agreed to reduce its share of the U.S. market to an average of 5.44 per cent, a value acceptable to the American steelmakers. The EC, in turn, said that it would limit steel imports from such nations as Brazil, East Germany, and South Korea.

Eastern Debt. Western bankers became concerned by the growing debts incurred by the Soviet bloc of 10 countries in the Council for Mutual Economic Assistance (COMECON). The debts reached $90 billion in 1982, and the delicacy of U.S.-Soviet relations added to the debt problem. COMECON reported a decline in industrial growth at its annual conference in Budapest, Hungary, in June. Poland was the worst off. It had to deal with Western sanctions and huge debts.

NATO Difficulties. The North Atlantic Treaty Organization (NATO) condemned Russia for its involvement in the military take-over of Poland but was reluctant to apply sanctions. Britain's action in the Falklands decreased the forces available to NATO, but military experts said that Britain's success eventually would strengthen the alliance. Opposition continued in some European countries, especially West Germany and the Netherlands, to NATO's plan to deploy 572 intermediate-range nuclear missiles in five Western European countries. See Close-Up.

World Cup. Four European teams reached the semifinals of the World Cup soccer tournament in Spain. In semifinal play, Italy defeated Poland, 2-0, and West Germany beat France, 4-3. Italy won the World Cup on July 11, defeating West Germany 3-1. See SOCCER. Kenneth Brown

See also the various European country articles. In WORLD BOOK, see EUROPE.

EXPLOSION. See DISASTERS.

FAHD (1923-) became king of Saudi Arabia on June 13, 1982, when his half brother King Khalid died. During the reign of Khalid, who was often ill, the dynamic Fahd directed much of the day-to-day operation of the government. Fahd named his half brother Abdullah as crown prince and first deputy prime minister. See SAUDI ARABIA.

One of the 43 sons of Ibn Saud, the founder of Saudi Arabia, Fahd bin Abdulaziz al-Saud was born in Riyadh in 1923. From 1953 to 1960, he served as Saudi Arabia's first minister of education and won praise for his development of the country's educational system. He resigned from the government in 1960.

In 1962, Fahd returned to the Cabinet as minister of the interior. In 1967, during the reign of King Faisal, Fahd became second in line to the throne with his appointment as second deputy prime minister. After the assassination of Faisal in 1975, the new king, Khalid, named Fahd crown prince.

Once known for his flamboyant life style, Fahd as crown prince demonstrated an enormous capacity for hard work. Considered to be more pro-Western than was Khalid, he is believed to have been instrumental in efforts to keep oil prices moderate. He also helped arrange a cease-fire between Israel and the Palestine Liberation Organization in Lebanon in 1982. Barbara A. Mayes

FALKLAND ISLANDS. To the surprise of the world, an undeclared 10-week war broke out between Great Britain and Argentina in 1982 over the ownership of the Falkland Islands—called *Islas Malvinas* by the Argentines—inhabited by fewer than 2,000 people. Before the shooting stopped, the casualties on both sides approximated the population of the remote islands, located in the South Atlantic Ocean about 250 miles (400 kilometers) off the southeastern tip of Argentina.

Ever since 1833, when Britain seized the islands, their ownership had been disputed by Argentina. The war of 1982 was touched off by a bizarre incident. On March 19, some Argentine salvage workers raised an Argentine flag on South Georgia Island, a Falkland dependency 800 miles (1,300 kilometers) east of the Falklands. To get even, British residents of the Falklands broke into the office of Argentina's national airline at Stanley, the capital of the islands, and decorated it with a British flag.

The Argentine Take-Over. On April 2, Argentine forces invaded and captured the Falkland Islands after a 3½-hour battle with a small detachment of British marines. The following day, Argentine forces seized South Georgia Island.

Great Britain prepared to recover the islands by force. On April 5, a powerful British naval task force carrying troops set sail for the South Atlantic. On April 12, Britain imposed a blockade around the Falkland Islands.

Heavy Fighting began on April 25, when British commandos recovered South Georgia Island. On May 2, a British submarine sank Argentina's only cruiser, the *General Belgrano*. On May 4, an Argentine fighter plane sank the British destroyer H.M.S. *Sheffield*.

On May 14, British forces established a beachhead on West Falkland, the smaller of the two main islands. They landed on East Falkland a week later. On May 29, the British captured Darwin and Goose Green on East Falkland in a bloody battle that left 250 Argentines and 17 Britons dead. By May 31, British forces had encircled Argentine forces at Stanley. The Argentines surrendered on June 14.

The 74-day war exacted a heavy toll on both sides. British casualties included 255 persons dead or missing and 777 wounded. Argentine losses included approximately 1,200 persons killed or missing and 100 wounded.

UN Resolution. On November 4, the United Nations General Assembly voted to adopt a resolution urging Britain and Argentina to negotiate their dispute over ownership of the Falklands. Britain objected, saying that it was too soon after the war to begin such talks. Nathan A. Haverstock

See also ARGENTINA; LATIN AMERICA. In WORLD BOOK, see FALKLAND ISLANDS.

A British paratrooper has tea with a family of Falklanders, *above*, during a break in the fighting. The Union Jack goes up on South Georgia, *opposite page*, as the British recapture the island on April 25. H.M.S. *Antelope* explodes, *below*, after bombing by Argentine aircraft in May.

The Islands That Caused a War

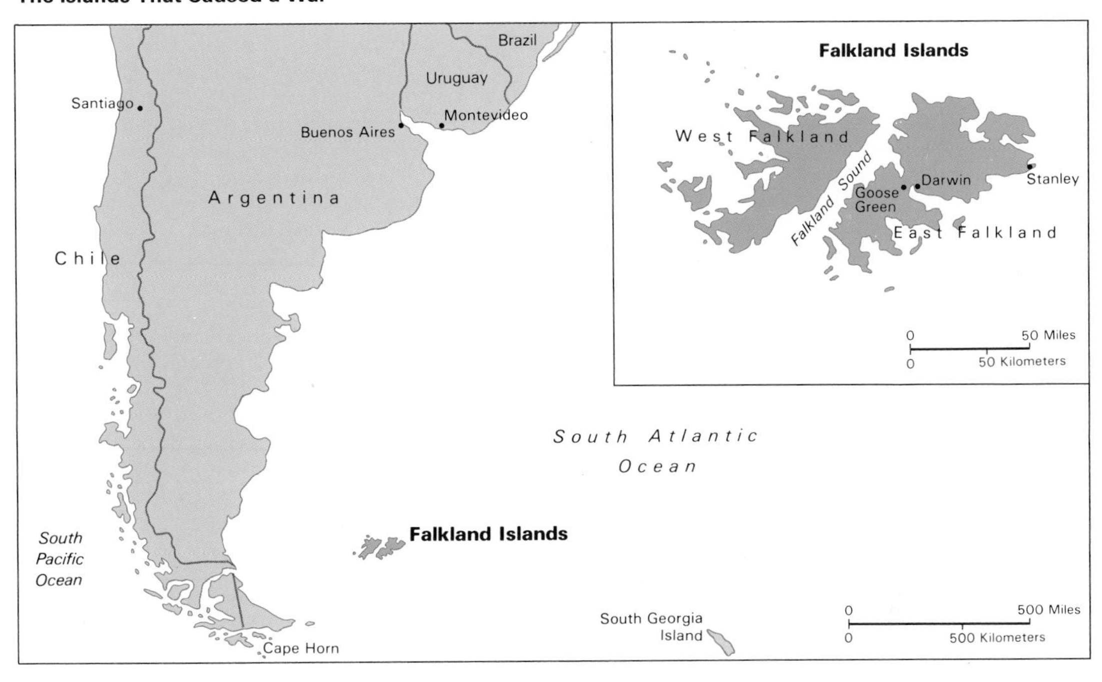

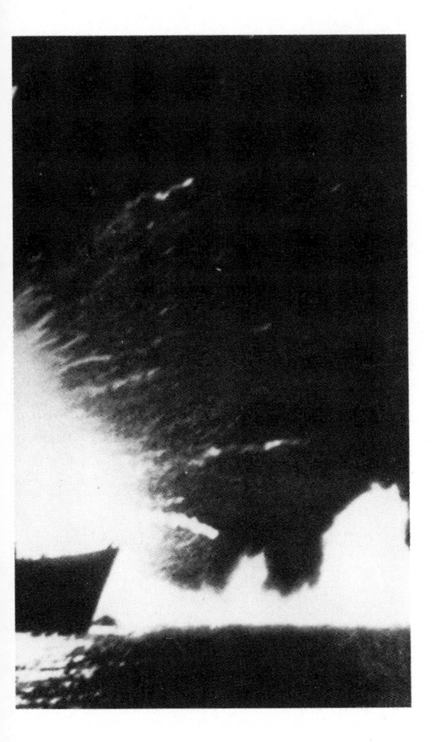

FARM AND FARMING. Farmers in the United States had another bad year in 1982, their third in a row. The cumulative effect of these difficult years left farmers' cash flow weak, and their fixed assets did not sustain modern farms as well as they would have supported farms in the past. The pride American farmers felt in producing abundant crops could not offset their disappointment at lower incomes. They became more cautious, which added to their problems. And, to top it all off, experts predicted another bad year in 1983.

Many U.S. farmers in 1982 felt that their problems were the results of factors outside their control. Congress radically changed a number of commodity programs, a move that some producers felt depersonalized farm policy. Some farmers were hit harder than others by economic problems, and that further undermined the already weakened unity of the traditionally solid farm bloc.

Some developments in 1982 dramatized farmers' economic plight. Farm exports dropped after 12 record-setting years. Land prices, which had risen rapidly for nearly 20 years, also fell. Per capita consumption of meat, a bellwether of U.S. farm success, declined. In addition, an increasing number of farmers filed for bankruptcy, and farm purchasing power was generally conceded to be the lowest since the Great Depression of the 1930s.

Farmers around the world experienced similar problems. Harvests worldwide were erratic, and depressed economic conditions added to the difficulty. Many governments tightened trade barriers to protect domestic agriculture. And although increased food supplies gave some hope of easing current world-hunger problems, available food stocks were poorly distributed, and many developing countries found agricultural development difficult in such depressed times.

U.S. Production fell slightly in 1982, with livestock production down 2 per cent and crops up 1 per cent. Pork production dropped 12 per cent, and turkeys fell 2 per cent. Whole milk was up 2 per cent; veal, 3 per cent; lamb and mutton, 9 per cent; and broilers, 3 per cent. Beef was essentially unchanged. Soybeans were up 15 per cent; oats, 18 per cent; wheat and corn, 1 per cent; and potatoes, 4 per cent. However, rice was down 16 per cent; sorghum, 7 per cent; tobacco, 6 per cent; and cotton, a whopping 27 per cent.

Prices received by U.S. farmers in 1982 dropped 3 per cent from 1981 levels. Although livestock prices rose 2 per cent, all crops were down 10 per cent. Hogs were the major bright spot, with prices climbing 23 per cent between the third quarter of 1981 and the third quarter of 1982. Turkeys were up 4 per cent. But eggs were down 9 per cent;

President Reagan discusses farm problems with Agriculture Secretary John R. Block, left, and Iowa farmer Eric Dee during a tour of Dee's farm in August.

milk, 2 per cent; beef cattle, 4 per cent; and broilers, 6 per cent. Major crop prices plummeted, with wheat down 8 per cent; corn, 19 per cent; soybeans, 16 per cent; and cotton, 15 per cent.

Agricultural Trade. Agricultural exports, which had increased for 12 consecutive years, took an 11 per cent nosedive in 1982, from $43.8 billion to $39.1 billion. Record crops and sluggish economic conditions drove commodity prices down in U.S. markets. However, the higher value of the U.S. dollar on foreign-exchange markets and weak economies abroad discouraged foreign buyers. Wheat and flour exports were down 4 per cent from 1981; rice, 25 per cent; corn and coarse grains, 33 per cent; poultry and poultry products, 24 per cent; horticultural products, 8 per cent; cotton and linters (cotton fibers), 4 per cent; and sugar and tropical products, 39 per cent. Oilseeds—including peanuts, cotton seeds, and linseed—and oilseed products were up 4 per cent; soybeans rose 8 per cent; and tobacco climbed 11 per cent. Overall livestock exports were up slightly. Poultry dropped about 24 per cent, but dairy products soared 53 per cent.

Farm imports dropped from $17.2 billion in 1981 to $15.4 billion in 1982. Although the agricultural trade balance fell from a surplus of $26.6-billion to $23.7 billion during the same period, agricultural exports were still a bright spot in U.S. foreign trade.

World Production. World grain production in 1982 rose by only 600,000 metric tons (660,000 short tons) over the 1.5 billion metric tons (1.6 billion short tons) produced in 1981. Larger U.S. crops accounted for most of this global increase. Harvests were erratic. For example, larger wheat crops were recorded in Argentina, Canada, East Germany, Great Britain, Hungary, Turkey, the United States, and West Germany. On the other hand, Australia's 1982 crop was only half as large as 1981's, and Russia harvested its fourth consecutive poor grain crop.

The world's sugar crop increased 13.3 per cent compared with 1981 and far surpassed the previous record set in 1977. Good weather helped increase world production of oilseed and cotton crops in countries that generally import these crops, and this helped depress U.S. exports. With poor economic conditions flattening food demand, supplies of grain and other food stocks increased in the United States and abroad.

Compared with 1981 levels, world production of wheat rose 6 per cent; corn was up 3 per cent; sugar rose 2 per cent; rice fell 2 per cent; soybeans climbed 13 per cent; cotton fell 4 per cent; and coffee fell 15 per cent. World meat production remained essentially the same as in 1981.

U.S. Farm Finances. Farmers' net income in 1982 dropped 24 per cent to $19 billion. Farm debt continued to increase, rising about 10 per cent. Equity of farmers was down to $770 billion, the lowest since 1979. Cash receipts fell by more than $1 billion from the 1981 total of $143.5 billion. Although a lower U.S. inflation rate and lower interest rates helped slow the increase in production costs and farmers received slightly higher government payments, the rise in expenses still outstripped income increases. Farm land values dropped in 1982 after increasing consistently for nearly 20 years, with the greatest drops occurring in the Corn Belt, the Great Lakes states, and the Southeast.

Farm Policy. On January 29, Secretary of Agriculture John R. Block announced a voluntary pro-

Agricultural Statistics, 1982

World Crop Production
(million units)

Crop	Units	1981	1982*	% U.S. 1982*
Corn	Metric tons	434.7	446.0	47.5
Wheat	Metric tons	445.8	471.0	14.4
Rice (rough)	Metric tons	411.0	399.0	1.7
Barley	Metric tons	162.1	164.0	6.7
Oats	Metric tons	45.6	47.0	19.1
Rye	Metric tons	24.7	27.0	1.9
Soybeans	Metric tons	86.2	97.0	64.9
Cotton	Bales†	71.1	68.0	20.0
Coffee	Bags**	96.9	82.0	4.9
Sugar (centrifugal)	Metric tons	95.8	98.0	5.1

*Preliminary
†480 lbs. (217.7 kilograms) net
**132 lbs. (60 kilograms)

Output of Major U.S. Crops
(millions of bushels)

Crop	1962-1966*	1981	1982†
Corn	3,876	8,201	8,315
Sorghum	595	880	821
Oats	912	508	599
Wheat	1,229	2,793	2,811
Soybeans	769	2,000	2,300
Rice (rough) (a)	742	1,854	1,564
Potatoes (b)	275	295	307
Cotton (c)	140	156	114
Tobacco (d)	2,126	2,046	1,930

*Average; †Preliminary
(a) 100,000 cwt. (4.54 million kilograms)
(b) 1 million cwt. (45.4 million kilograms)
(c) 100,000 bales (50 million lbs.) (22.7 million kilograms)
(d) 1 million lbs. (454,000 kilograms)

U.S. Production of Animal Products
(millions of pounds)

	1957-1959*	1981	1982†
Beef	13,704	22,214	22,315
Veal	1,240	415	428
Lamb & Mutton	711	327	355
Pork	10,957	15,716	13,884
Eggs (a)	5,475	5,800	5,763
Turkey	1,382	2,509	2,469
Total Milk (b)	123	132.6	135.0
Broilers	4,430	11,906	12,249

*Average; †Preliminary
(a) 1 million dozens
(b) Billions of lbs. (454 million kilograms)

Combines harvest winter wheat in southwestern Russia. The Soviet Union's 1982 wheat crop was its fourth consecutive poor crop.

gram to reduce acreage of corn and feed grains by 10 per cent and wheat, cotton, and rice by 15 per cent. The program was intended to reduce farm subsidies, which were estimated at record levels of about $12 billion in 1982. By March, larger-than-expected supplies of grains and cotton led the Agriculture Department to announce new voluntary acreage reduction programs for wheat, feed grains, upland cotton, and rice.

A new sugar price-support program, the first since 1978, was implemented in 1982. In May, President Ronald Reagan established quarterly quotas on U.S. sugar imports and raised the market stabilization price to 19.88 cents per pound (43.88 cents per kilogram) for raw sugar. The decision caused considerable concern in many sugar-exporting countries. The price was later raised to 20.73 cents per pound (45.76 cents per kilogram).

The peanut program was altered substantially, with acreage allotments for the 1982-1985 crops suspended. In May, a national peanut-production quota on the 1982 crop was set 17 per cent below that of 1981. Meat imports for human consumption became subject to the same inspection laws as meat produced in the United States. And new or expanded research programs were authorized for aquaculture, dairy goats, rangeland management, rural development, and small farms.

On July 20, President Reagan signed into law the No Net Cost Tobacco Program Act. The act requires tobacco growers to contribute to a special fund through their cooperatives to cover their losses when the price of tobacco falls below the price-support level.

Cheese Giveaway. With annual dairy price-support payments nearing $3 billion in 1982, the U.S. dairy program was changed substantially. Beginning on December 1, dairy farmers were to be assessed a fee of 50 cents for every 100 pounds (45 kilograms) of milk sold. The fees are to be used to offset price supports paid by the U.S. government. On December 21, however, a federal judge issued a temporary order halting collection of the fees. The government also expanded its giveaway program of surplus dairy products to low-income Americans. Begun in December 1981 with the distribution of 30 million pounds (13.6 million kilograms) of surplus cheese, the program was intended to reduce the mountain of dairy products accumulated by the Agriculture Department's Commodity Credit Corporation in order to support dairy prices. On June 1, 1982, Agriculture Secretary Block announced that an additional 120 million pounds (54 million kilograms) of surplus cheese as well as 50 million pounds (22.7 million kilograms) of surplus butter would be distributed.

Trade Tensions. The Reagan Administration threatened in November to use U.S. surpluses of dairy products to combat European subsidies of farm exports and to retaliate against the import duties imposed on U.S. farm products by some European countries. The United States said it would consider dumping surplus dairy products on the world market to lower prices. The action would also force European governments to pay more in subsidies to their dairy farmers.

Farm Technology. The U.S. Department of Agriculture announced in September that new rice plants created by gene-splicing techniques had 10 per cent more protein than do conventional rice plants. Gene splicing involves the transfer of genes from one organism to another. Rice is the world's third most important grain crop, and improved protein content could mean improved health for many people, especially children.

Sharply reduced prices for computers were welcomed by many U.S. farmers, to whom computers have become as essential a piece of farm equipment as tractors and combines. Farmers increasingly relied on computers to develop long-range plans as well as to coordinate integrated pest-management programs; control water flow in irrigation systems; determine planting schedules for crops; and supervise breeding, feeding, and production for poultry, dairy, and hog operations.

Medfly Conquered. The discovery of a Mediterranean fruit fly in California's San Joaquin Valley on June 24—the first Medfly found in the state since Nov. 20, 1981—sparked fears that the persistent pest had returned. The next day, state officials ordered a resumption of aerial pesticide spraying and imposed a new quarantine. But on Sept. 21, 1982, California officials lifted the quarantine and declared a victory over the pest.

Ozone Damage. Ozone, a major air pollutant, causes from $2 billion to $4.5 billion in damage to U.S. corn, wheat, soybean, and peanut crops each year, according to an analysis by the congressional Office of Technology Assessment released in February. Ozone, a form of oxygen present naturally in the atmosphere, builds up when sunlight acts on nitrogen oxides and hydrocarbons in automobile exhaust fumes and factory emissions.

To determine how ozone affects crop yield, scientists grew crops in clean air and compared them with crops grown in air heavily polluted with ozone. The scientists found that soybean yield dropped 45 per cent; peanut yield, 50 per cent; and winter wheat yield, 30 per cent. Corn yield fell by only 10 per cent. According to one expert, the loss in the four crops from ozone pollution represents as much as 5 per cent of the total annual U.S farm output.

Charles E. French

See also FOOD. In the Special Reports section, see THE COMING CROPLAND CRISIS. In WORLD BOOK, see AGRICULTURE; FARM AND FARMING.

FARM MACHINERY. See MANUFACTURING.

A U.S. inspector checks some of the 120 million pounds (54 million kilograms) of surplus cheese that was given to needy Americans during 1982.

FASHION, traditionally the province of rich and leisured women, subtly changed its focus during 1982. The most successful styles were not the most outrageous or the instantly obsolete. Instead, they were clothes that were moderately subdued, in durable fabrics that required little upkeep, and in quiet, basic colors.

There were two main reasons for this development. The worldwide recession put extravagant clothes out of the reach of a good portion of the population, and a growing number of women continued to join the work force. In the United States, more than 51 per cent of women over the age of 16 were employed outside the home. An increasing number of them were entering professions and moving into executive positions in business. They helped bolster the demand for such clothing as classic suits and softly tailored dresses. Even those who did not pursue a paycheck were influenced by the more sober styles.

American Designers, who generally have been more practical than their European counterparts, were most aware of this trend. Because they developed clothes that were relevant to the 1980s, the Americans played an increasingly significant role in the world's fashion scene. Audiences at their openings were swelled by buyers and fashion reporters from Japan as well as Europe.

There was no prescribed length for hemlines. Perry Ellis, one of the rising stars of American fashion, was successful with his near-ankle lengths. Americans Bill Blass, Adolfo, and James Galanos—all favorites of first lady Nancy Reagan, whose clothes sparked more interest than those of any other President's wife since Jacqueline Kennedy—kept their daytime hems around the knee. Calvin Klein and Ralph Lauren both favored calf-length clothes. The two American designers are leading exponents of the sportswear look—their country's major contribution to the fashion scene. Based on easy-fitting separate parts that can be interchanged to make a modest wardrobe look more extensive, the sportswear concept is well adapted to contemporary needs.

Fashion Follows Finance. While the ready-to-wear houses in Paris and Milan, Italy, lost ground, the exclusive and expensive haute-couture branch of the French fashion industry held its own. It no longer attempted to maintain its 100-year-old position as fashion pacesetter for the rest of the world. Instead, the most expensive fashion houses, concentrating on made-to-order clothes, shifted direction toward turning out super-luxurious styles for the wives of international dignitaries. Neither France nor the United States provided the clients, however. They came from the oil countries of the Middle East; from South America, where French haute couture has traditionally been the fashion mecca; and from developing countries of

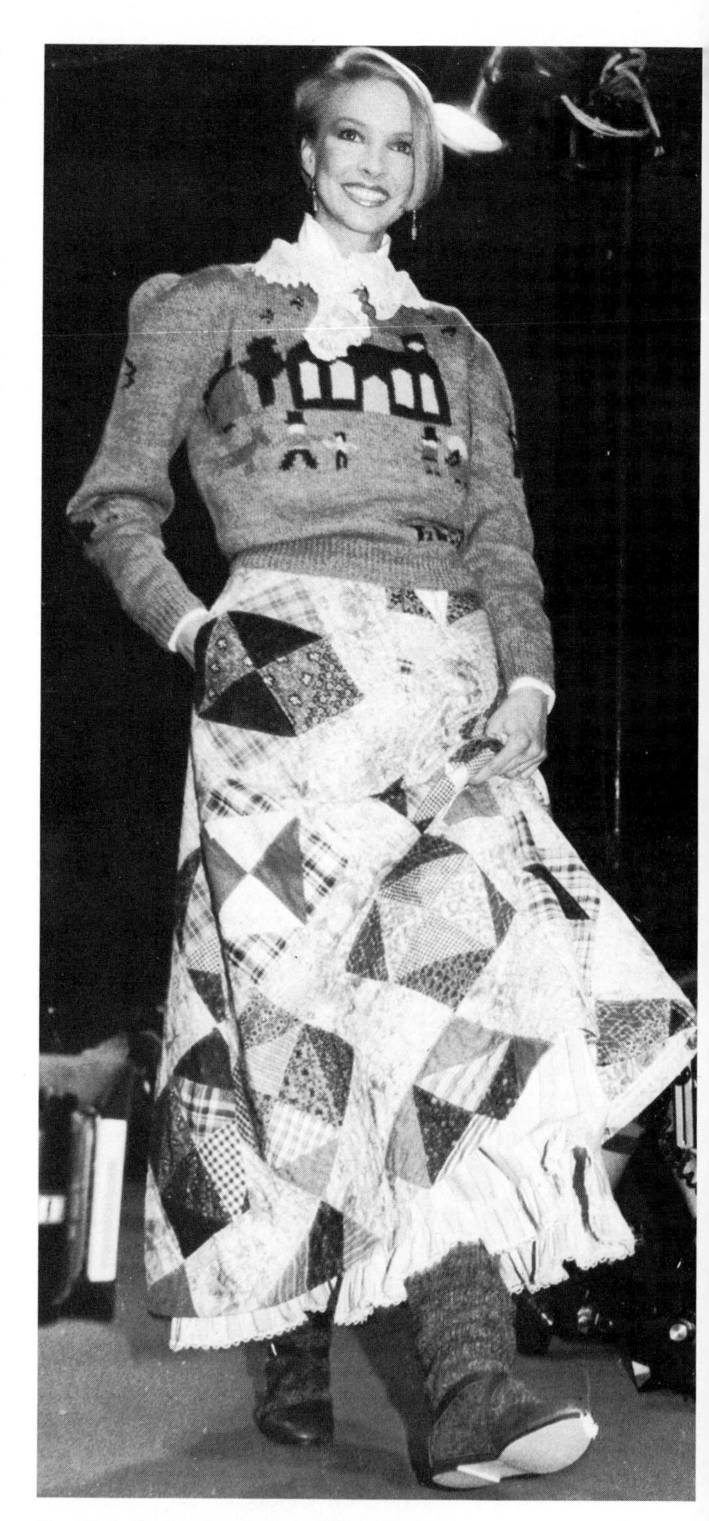

New York City fashion designer Ralph Lauren shows country-fresh inspiration in a "painting" sweater and long, quilted patchwork skirt.

Africa and Asia, where a Paris dress is an effective sign of status.

Feathers were the latest extravagance for fall and winter, supplementing the beads, hand embroidery, sequins, and furs that are an integral part of couture collections. France's Socialist government has encouraged the haute couture as a proven means of drawing foreign visitors to the country. French designer Emanuel Ungaro, with his extravagant mixtures of prints and colors—and such fabrics as cashmere, silk, and wool—is one of the couture stars. In 1982, he joined the houses of Christian Dior, Hubert de Givenchy, and Yves Saint Laurent as a top drawing card.

Coty American Fashion Critics' Awards, sponsored by the cosmetics firm of Coty, Incorporated, in 1982 marked their 40th anniversary. At ceremonies in September in New York City, designers Donna Karan and Louis Dell'Olio of Anne Klein were inducted into the Hall of Fame. A Return Award for women's fashions went to Norma Kamali, and Sal Cesarini received the award for menswear. The young designer Adri won a Winnie Award for outstanding achievement. Coty recognized the enduring elegance of Geoffrey Beene with his sixth citation and of Bill Blass with his second. Jeffrey Banks was a first-time winner in the menswear category. Bernadine Morris

In WORLD BOOK, see FASHION.

FINLAND. Finnish voters chose Prime Minister Mauno H. Koivisto to be their president in indirect elections on Jan. 17 and 18, 1982. The voters elected a 301-member Electoral College, which picked Koivisto on January 26. Koivisto, a Social Democrat, won 43 per cent of the popular vote and 167 electoral votes. See KOIVISTO, MAUNO H.

Koivisto's coalition government with the Center Party, the People's Democratic League, and the Swedish People's Party resigned as a matter of form when Koivisto took office as president on January 27. On February 17, the same coalition announced the formation of a government headed by Prime Minister Kalevi Sorsa, who had been prime minister from 1972 to 1975.

Sorsa resigned on December 30 after his coalition collapsed. However, Koivisto asked him to stay as head of an interim government until elections in March 1983.

Devaluation of the Swedish krona in 1981 had put Finnish pulp and paper mills at a disadvantage in export markets. On October 6, Finland devalued its markka by 4 per cent. Sweden then devalued its currency by 16 per cent on October 8. Finland responded on October 10 by devaluing the markka an additional 6 per cent. Kenneth Brown

See also EUROPE (Facts in Brief Table). In WORLD BOOK, see FINLAND.

FIRE. See DISASTERS.

FISHING. Rich I. Tauber, 24, of Woodland Hills, Calif., won the first prize of $50,000 in the United States Open National Bass Tournament held in August 1982 on Lake Mead near Las Vegas, Nev. A field of 262 anglers shared $303,000 in prize money in the competition, which offered the largest purse in history for a fishing contest. Tauber caught 37.38 pounds (16.96 kilograms) of bass during the four-day contest.

Fishing enthusiasts rallied to protect striped bass in 1982 as evidence mounted that the number of "stripers" was plummeting off both the Atlantic and Pacific coasts. Stripers Unlimited, an organization headquartered in Massachusetts, asked the federal government to declare striped bass an endangered species.

Environmentalist organizations attributed a decline in bass catches of more than 50 per cent to the impact of pesticides, such as DDT, that kill the larvae of the fish. The growing scarcity of bass drove its market price up to $6 per pound (0.45 kilogram) in the fall.

In April, the U.S. Fish and Wildlife Service predicted improved fishing for most species for America's 54 million anglers. The service said Americans in 1980 spent 858 million days fishing. In 1982, the economic slump led many Americans to fish for food as well as for sport. Andrew L. Newman

In WORLD BOOK, see FISHING.

FISHING INDUSTRY. A botulism scare that led to a worldwide recall of defective cans of salmon caused a $100-million blow to Alaska's salmon industry in 1982. Salmon prices dropped sharply after the scare crippled sales.

The salmon crisis started in February when a man in Belgium died of botulism poisoning after eating salmon canned in Alaska. Belgium, Great Britain, and the Netherlands embargoed Alaskan canned salmon, and salmon sales in Europe plummeted. The U.S. Food and Drug Administration (FDA) called back 55 million cans of Alaskan salmon—the second largest canned food recall ever—after FDA inspectors discovered tiny holes in some of the cans. The holes, which had admitted the botulism spores, had apparently been made by a defective machine during canning.

On July 25, two Alaskan canneries sued the American Can Company, charging that faulty machinery it had provided had punctured the cans. The can company denied the charges. The suit was still pending at the end of the year.

The U.S. Fish Catch fell to 6 billion pounds (2.7 billion kilograms) in 1981, the lowest volume since 1977, but it brought a record dockside value of $2.4 billion. Shrimp was the most valuable catch, worth more than $463 million, followed by salmon, $438 million; crab, $297 million; and tuna, $206 million. Louisiana led all states in volume with 1.2 billion pounds (540 million kilograms) landed, followed by Alaska and California. Alaska's catch, which was worth $640 million, was the most valuable.

Whaling Moratorium. A worldwide ban on all commercial whaling beginning in 1986 was approved by a 25 to 7 vote of the International Whaling Commission (IWC) at its annual meeting on July 23. Japan, the world's major whaling nation, strongly opposed the whaling ban. Although the IWC has no enforcement powers, the United States, a supporter of the ban, could invoke sanctions to discourage Japan and other whaling countries from withdrawing from the IWC and continuing to hunt whales.

Under amendments to the Fishery Conservation and Management Act of 1979, the United States can deny fishing rights within its 200-nautical-mile coastal zone to nations that flout IWC rules, as well as halt imports of their fish products. Fishery experts believe that only the threat of sanctions, which could cause a monetary loss much larger than the value of Japan's whale catch, could persuade Japan to abandon whaling. Andrew L. Newman

In the World Book Supplement section, see Fishing Industry.

FLOOD. See Disasters.
FLORIDA. See State Government.
FLOWER. See Gardening.

FONDA, HENRY (1905-1982), received the Academy of Motion Picture Arts and Sciences Award for best actor on March 29, 1982, for his performance as Norman Thayer in *On Golden Pond.* It was the last role of his career, which began at the Omaha (Nebr.) Community Playhouse in 1925 and ended with his death on August 12.

Henry Jaynes Fonda was born in Grand Island, Nebr., on May 16, 1905. On his father's side, the actor who was called "the incarnation of American virtue" was descended from a titled Italian family by way of Holland and New York state. Young Henry grew up in Omaha, then studied journalism at the University of Minnesota. Persuaded to try acting by Dorothy Brando, a family friend and actor Marlon Brando's mother, Fonda proved to be good at it.

Starting in 1929, Fonda had several small roles in Broadway plays, then went to Hollywood in 1934. His first film was *The Farmer Takes a Wife* (1935). Memorable movies included *Young Mr. Lincoln* (1939), *The Grapes of Wrath* (1940), *Mister Roberts* (1955), *Twelve Angry Men* (1957), and *The Best Man* (1964). Among Fonda's stage successes were *Mister Roberts* (1948), *The Caine Mutiny Court Martial* (1953), and *Clarence Darrow* (1974).

Fonda, married five times, was the father of actress-activist Jane, actor-director Peter, and clinical psychologist Amy. Marsha F. Goldsmith

FOOD. Retail food prices in the United States in 1982 experienced the smallest annual increase—4.5 per cent—since 1976. The moderate increase was due not only to the nation's lower inflation rate, but also to the large domestic supplies of grains and soybeans, which depressed livestock feeding costs.

Food Programs. Many Americans continued to feel the effects of changes in federal regulations and budget cuts in U.S. food programs. The 12 per cent drop in the number of students participating in school lunch and breakfast programs was much greater than had been predicted. In addition, poor children made up a disproportionate share of the 3 million students no longer participating in the program.

At the same time, as a result of government price-support programs, enormous surpluses of cheese, butter, and other dairy products continued to accumulate in government warehouses. In June, the government expanded its program, begun in December 1981, of giving surplus cheese to poor Americans.

Food Consumption. Overall, per capita food consumption in the United States was slightly lower in 1982 than in 1981. Pork showed the largest price increase for any food category—and the greatest decrease in consumption. The fall-off in pork consumption—from 65 to 57 pounds (29 to 26 kilograms) per person—brought red-meat consumption in the United States to its lowest level since 1965—144 pounds (65 kilograms) per person. Beef and veal consumption remained the same as in 1981. Poultry consumption continued to increase. For the first time, Americans ate more poultry than pork. Chicken was also the most popular item added to restaurant menus.

Egg consumption, which in 1981 fell to its lowest level since 1935, remained unchanged. Fluid milk consumption declined, but the government distribution of surplus cheese and butter increased total consumption of dairy products. Consumption of fruits and vegetables, whose prices rose by about 6 per cent, declined. For the second consecutive year, a freeze in Florida reduced the production of frozen concentrated orange juice as well as the quantity of fresh oranges on the market. The freeze also damaged a number of vegetable crops. Bad weather in California early in 1982 harmed some crops, but fall harvests were good.

Sugar and sweetener intake remained the same as in 1981 and prices held, even though global production of sugar far exceeded consumption and world sugar prices fell sharply. However, in the United States a sugar price-support program was enacted in 1981, which kept sugar prices stable.

World Food Production. Production of food grains—wheat and rice—declined from 1981 levels, particularly because of a sharp fall in Soviet

A scientist at the Bodega Marine Laboratory in California feeds Maine lobsters whose maturation time has been reduced by half, to 3½ years.

wheat production. However, production exceeded demand, and prices dropped while stocks increased. The United States exported a record volume of 49 million short tons (44 million metric tons) of wheat, even though the per capita consumption of wheat slowed worldwide because of balance-of-payment problems and deteriorating economic conditions in developing countries. For the second consecutive year, world feed-grain production — corn, barley, oats, rye, and sorghum — significantly exceeded consumption. The U.S. exported more than 60 million short tons (54 million metric tons) of feed grains. Despite the excess production, hunger and malnutrition in developing countries continued to rise.

Diet and Cancer. In June, the National Academy of Sciences released a report on the relationship between diet and cancer. The team that conducted the study developed "interim dietary guidelines" that it said are likely to reduce the risk of cancer. The guidelines include suggestions to reduce fat intake from 40 to 30 per cent or less of total calories; include more fruits, vegetables, and whole grains in the diet, especially citrus fruits and vegetables from the cabbage family; minimize consumption of salt-cured, pickled, and smoked foods; and consume alcoholic beverages in moderation. Some scientists as well as representatives of industries that might be affected by the recommendations challenged the report. They said its conclusions were premature and that more research was needed before any diet recommendations could be made to the public.

Sodium Labeling. In June, the Food and Drug Administration (FDA) proposed new regulations for voluntary labeling of the sodium content of food products. The regulations would establish definitions for terms such as "low sodium" and "no salt added" and would require that sodium content be added to nutrition-labeling information.

Diet Aid? A federal judge ruled in October that diet pills called starch blockers were drugs, not foods, and must be tested and proved effective before they can be sold. Manufacturers of the products claimed the starch blockers contained a chemical that inhibited the production of the enzyme that breaks down starch molecules during digestion. As a result, people taking the pills could supposedly eat large quantities of starchy foods without gaining weight. The judge ordered the manufacturers to halt production of the pills. In December, the first major controlled human study of starch blockers as a dietary aid showed the pills were not effective. Katherine L. Clancy

See also FARM AND FARMING; NUTRITION. In the Special Reports section, see FOOD, FADS, FAT, AND FITNESS. In WORLD BOOK, see FOOD; FOOD SUPPLY.

FOOTBALL. The most memorable aspect of the 1982 football season in the United States was not who won or who played, but when they played. The first regular-season players' strike in the 62-year history of the National Football League (NFL) wiped out almost half of the season.

After weeks of no negotiations and then fruitless negotiations, the NFL told hotels in and near Pasadena, Calif., to release the thousands of hotel rooms it had reserved for Super Bowl XVII on Jan. 30, 1983. But the strike was finally settled, a new play-off formula was established, and the Super Bowl went on as scheduled.

The Washington Redskins won the Super Bowl by beating the Miami Dolphins, 27-17, as John Riggins rushed for 166 yards, a Super Bowl record. He also scored one touchdown.

The college season was much simpler. Georgia was ranked first and Penn State second in the wire-service polls taken after the regular season. The two teams met on Jan. 1, 1983, in the Sugar Bowl at New Orleans, and Penn State won, 27-23, and became national champion in the post-bowl polls. The Penn State defense held Herschel Walker, the Georgia running back who had won the Heisman Trophy as the year's outstanding college player, to less than 4 yards per carry.

NFL Strike. The overall contract between the NFL club owners and players expired in July, and

1982 College Conference Champions

Conference	School
Atlantic Coast	Clemson
Big Eight	Nebraska
Big Sky	Idaho, Montana, Montana State (tie)
Big Ten	Michigan
Ivy League	Dartmouth, Harvard, Pennsylvania (tie)
Mid-American	Bowling Green
Missouri Valley	Tulsa
Ohio Valley	Eastern Kentucky
Pacific Coast	Fresno State
Pacific Ten	UCLA
Southeastern	Georgia
Southern	Furman
Southland	Louisiana Tech
Southwest	Southern Methodist
Southwestern	Jackson State
Western Athletic	Brigham Young
Yankee	Boston U., Connecticut, Maine, Massachusetts (tie)

Major Bowl Games

Bowl	Winner	Loser
Aloha	Washington 21	Maryland 20
Amos Alonzo Stagg (Div. III)	West Georgia 14	Augustana (Ill.) 0
Bluebonnet	Arkansas 28	Florida 24
Blue-Gray	Gray 20	Blue 10
California	Fresno State 29	Bowling Green 28
Cotton	Southern Methodist 7	Pittsburgh 3
Fiesta	Arizona State 32	Oklahoma 21
Gator	Florida State 31	West Virginia 12
Hall of Fame	Air Force 36	Vanderbilt 28
Holiday	Ohio State 47	Brigham Young 17
Hula	East 30	West 14
Independence	Wisconsin 14	Kansas State 3
Liberty	Alabama 21	Illinois 15
Orange	Nebraska 21	Louisiana State 20
Palm (Div. II)	Southwest Texas 34	California-Davis 9
Peach	Iowa 28	Tennessee 22
Rose	UCLA 24	Michigan 14
Senior	North 14	South 6
Shrine	East 26	West 25
Sugar	Penn State 27	Georgia 23
Sun	North Carolina 26	Texas 10
Tangerine	Auburn 33	Boston College 26
NCAA Division I-AA	Eastern Kentucky 17	Delaware 14
NAIA Division I	Central State (Okla.) 14	Mesa (Colo.) 11
NAIA Division II	Linfield (Ore.) 33	William Jewell (Mo.) 15

All-America Team (as picked by AP)

Offense

Wide receivers–Anthony Carter, Michigan; Kenny Jackson, Penn State
Tight end–Gordon Hudson, Brigham Young
Tackles–Bill Fralic, Pittsburgh; Don Mosebar, Southern California
Guards–Steve Korte, Arkansas; Bruce Matthews, Southern California
Center–Dave Rimington, Nebraska
Quarterback–John Elway, Stanford
Running backs–Eric Dickerson, Southern Methodist; Herschel Walker, Georgia
Place kicker–Chuck Nelson, Washington

Defense

Ends–Wilber Marshall, Florida; Billy Ray Smith, Arkansas
Tackles–Gary Lewis, Oklahoma State; Gabriel Rivera, Texas Tech
Middle guard–George Achica, Southern California
Linebackers–Ricky Hunley, Arizona; Mark Stewart, Washington; Darryl Talley, West Virginia
Defensive backs–Terry Hoage, Georgia; Terry Kinard, Clemson; Mike Richardson, Arizona State
Punter–Jim Arnold, Vanderbilt

Player Awards

Heisman Trophy (best player)–Herschel Walker, Georgia
Lombardi Award (best lineman)–Dave Rimington, Nebraska
Outland Award (best interior lineman)–Dave Rimington, Nebraska

the players set high goals in negotiations for a new contract. To begin with, their average salary was $83,000 to $90,000, compared with higher averages in major-league baseball ($230,000), basketball ($218,000), and hockey ($120,000).

In addition, the owners had signed in March a $2.076-billion package with CBS, NBC, and ABC for television rights to games for the five seasons from 1982 to 1986. That ensured each team an average of $15 million a year in television revenue, as opposed to the $5.8 million a year of the previous contracts.

The NFL Players Association, the union that represented the 1,500 players, first demanded 55 per cent of the clubs' gross income. It later abandoned that goal in favor of 50 per cent of the television income. Each of those demands involved the creation of a central fund from which payments were to be distributed to players. The union's demands and the concept of a central fund were rejected by the NFL Management Council, which represented the owners.

The scheduled 16-game season began on September 12. On September 21, after two games, the players went on strike. The players set up an all-star league and scheduled 20 games. Only two were played, however, before sparse crowds.

On November 13, former NFL defensive back Paul Martha, the general counsel of the San Francisco 49ers, entered the negotiations as an intermediary. He quickly brought the sides together, and agreement was reached on November 16, the 57th day of the longest strike in the history of major-league sports. The players later approved the new contract by a 3-to-1 margin.

The contract called for the owners to spend $1.6-billion in salaries and benefits from 1983 to 1986, plus $60 million in immediate bonuses to veteran players. Severance pay was created. Salary minimums, play-off money, and medical benefits were increased. The players' union agreed to allow the draft of college players to continue through 1992.

Strike losses totaled about $450 million, including $240 million by the clubs and $72 million by the players. Public interest also suffered, as many ticket holders allowed post-strike seats to go unused. After the strike, fewer than 75 per cent of all seats were filled, as opposed to a 93.8 per cent average for all of the 1981 season.

Revised Play-Off Format. The strike wiped out eight weeks of the season, but one week was recaptured by extending the regular season to Jan. 3, 1983. The play-off format was restructured for one time only, with 16 teams advancing rather than 10 and with the conference finals played on the usually idle Sunday before the Super Bowl.

The eight leading teams in each conference gained the play-offs, led by the Washington Redskins (8-1 won-lost record) in the National Confer-

National Football League Final Standings

The 1982 season was interrupted by a players' strike from September 21 to November 16. Under a revised plan, 16 teams - eight from each conference - qualified for the play-offs. Those teams are indicated by an asterisk (*).

American Conference	W.	L.	T.	Pct.
*Los Angeles Raiders	8	1	0	.889
*Miami Dolphins	7	2	0	.778
*Cincinnati Bengals	7	2	0	.778
*Pittsburgh Steelers	6	3	0	.667
*San Diego Chargers	6	3	0	.667
*New York Jets	6	3	0	.667
*New England Patriots	5	4	0	.556
*Cleveland Browns	4	5	0	.444
Buffalo Bills	4	5	0	.444
Seattle Seahawks	4	5	0	.444
Kansas City Chiefs	3	6	0	.333
Denver Broncos	2	7	0	.222
Houston Oilers	1	8	0	.111
Baltimore Colts	0	8	1	.056

Individual Statistics

Leading Scores	TDs.	E.P.	F.G.	Pts.
Marcus Allen, Los Angeles	14	0	0	84
Rolf Benirschke, San Diego	0	32	16	80
Nick Lowery, Kansas City	0	17	19	74
Jim Breech, Cincinnati	0	25	14	67
Uwe von Schamann, Miami	0	21	15	66

Leading Passers	Att.	Comp.	Yds.	TDs.	Int.
Ken Anderson, Cincinnati	309	218	2,495	12	9
Dan Fouts, San Diego	305	204	2,889	17	11
Richard Todd, New York	261	153	1,961	14	8
Steve Grogan, New England	122	66	930	7	4
Terry Bradshaw, Pittsburgh	240	127	1,768	17	11

Leading Receivers	No. Caught	Total Yds.	Avg. Gain	TDs.
Kellen Winslow, San Diego	54	721	13.4	6
Wes Chandler, San Diego	49	1,032	21.1	9
Chris Collinsworth, Cincinnati	49	700	14.3	1
Ozzie Newsome, Cleveland	49	633	12.9	3
Dan Ross, Cincinnati	47	508	10.8	3

Leading Rushers	No.	Yds.	Avg. Gain	TDs.
Freeman McNeil, New York	151	786	5.2	6
Andra Franklin, Miami	177	701	4.0	7
Marcus Allen, Los Angeles	160	697	4.4	11
Joe Cribbs, Buffalo	134	633	4.7	3
Tony Collins, New England	164	632	3.9	1

Leading Punters	No.	Yds.	Avg.	Longest
Luke Prestridge, Denver	45	2,026	45.0	65
Rohn Stark, Baltimore	46	2,044	44.4	60
Rich Camarillo, New England	49	2,140	43.7	76
Jeff Gossett, Kansas City	33	1,366	41.4	56

Leading Punt Returners	No.	Yds.	Avg.	TDs.
Rick Upchurch, Denver	15	242	16.1	2
James Brooks, San Diego	12	138	11.5	0
Paul Johns, Seattle	19	210	11.1	0
Rick Woods, Pittsburgh	13	142	10.9	0
Tom Vigorito, Miami	20	192	9.6	1

National Conference	W.	L.	T.	Pct.
*Washington Redskins	8	1	0	.889
*Dallas Cowboys	6	3	0	.667
*Green Bay Packers	5	3	1	.611
*Minnesota Vikings	5	4	0	.556
*Atlanta Falcons	5	4	0	.556
*St. Louis Cardinals	5	4	0	.556
*Tampa Bay Buccaneers	5	4	0	.556
*Detroit Lions	4	5	0	.444
New Orleans Saints	4	5	0	.444
New York Giants	4	5	0	.444
San Francisco 49ers	3	6	0	.333
Chicago Bears	3	6	0	.333
Philadelphia Eagles	3	6	0	.333
Los Angeles Rams	2	7	0	.222

Individual Statistics

Leading Scorers	TDs.	E.P.	F.G.	Pts.
Wendell Tyler, Los Angeles	13	0	0	78
Mark Moseley, Washington	0	16	20	76
Bill Capece, Tampa Bay	0	14	18	68
Jan Stenerud, Green Bay	0	25	13	64
Eddie Lee Ivery, Green Bay	10	0	0	60

Leading Passers	Att.	Comp.	Yds.	TDs.	Int.
Joe Theismann, Washington	252	161	2,033	13	9
Danny White, Dallas	247	156	2,079	16	12
Joe Montana, San Francisco	346	213	2,613	17	11
Jim McMahon, Chicago	210	120	1,501	9	7
Steve Bartkowski, Atlanta	262	166	1,905	8	11

Leading Receivers	No. Caught	Total Yds.	Avg. Gain	TDs.
Dwight Clark, San Francisco	60	913	15.2	5
James Wilder, Tampa Bay	53	466	8.8	1
William Andrews, Atlanta	42	503	12.0	2
Wendell Tyler, Los Angeles	38	375	9.9	4
Jeff Moore, San Francisco	37	405	10.9	4

Leading Rushers	No.	Yds.	Av. Gain	TDs.
Tony Dorsett, Dallas	177	745	4.2	5
Billy Sims, Detroit	172	639	3.7	4
Walter Payton, Chicago	148	596	4.0	1
Ottis Anderson, St. Louis	145	587	4.0	3
William Andrews, Atlanta	139	573	4.1	5

Leading Punters	No.	Yds.	Avg.	Longest
Carl Birdsong, St. Louis	54	2,365	43.8	65
John Misko, Los Angeles	45	1,961	43.6	59
Russell Erxleben, New Orleans	46	1,976	43.0	60
Dave Jennings, New York	49	2,096	42.8	73

Leading Punt Returners	No.	Yds.	Avg.	TDs.
Billy Johnson, Atlanta	24	273	11.4	0
LeRoy Irvin, Los Angeles	22	242	11.0	1
Robbie Martin, Detroit	26	275	10.6	0
Freddie Solomon, San Francisco	13	122	9.4	0
Leon Bright, New York	37	325	8.8	0

ence and the relocated Los Angeles Raiders (8-1) in the American Conference.

NFL Under Attack. The NFL faced many other problems in 1982. Over league objections, the Raiders, in federal court, won the right to move from Oakland to Los Angeles and did so, though they still practiced in Oakland and commuted 400 miles (640 kilometers) to their home games. Despite players' objections, the league sought federal antitrust exemption that would prevent lawsuits against it by its teams, such as the one by the Raiders. The NFL acknowledged the existence of drug and alcohol problems among players, and both the league itself and its clubs set up rehabilitation programs.

In addition, a new major professional league, the 12-team United States Football League, was formed during the year. The new league was scheduled to play its first season between March and July 1983.

Canadian Football. The Edmonton Eskimos won their fifth consecutive championship of the Canadian Football League by beating the Toronto Argonauts, 32-16, in the Grey Cup game on Nov. 28, 1982, in Toronto, Ont. Earlier in the year, the nine-team league reclaimed the franchise of the financially troubled Montreal Alouettes and awarded a new franchise to the Montreal Concordes.

College Football. The best regular-season records among major colleges belonged to Georgia

Georgia running back Herschel Walker (34), the 1982 Heisman Trophy winner, rushed for 1,752 yards and scored 16 touchdowns in 11 games.

(11-0), Southern Methodist (10-0-1), Nebraska (11-1), Penn State (10-1), UCLA (9-1-1), and Clemson (9-1-1).

It was a year for the offense. The major colleges, which played in the National Collegiate Athletic Association (NCAA) Division I-A, set record per-game averages for combined total yards by the offense (703.3), combined yards passing (364.8), and combined points (43.8). For the first time since passing became legal in 1906, the average team gained more yards passing per game (182.4) than rushing (169.3), though only 38 per cent of plays were passes.

The continuation of big-time college football as a major television attraction was assured when the NCAA sold network television rights for the 1982 and 1983 seasons to ABC and CBS for $263.5 million. Cable-television rights brought millions more. By the time the network contract expired, major colleges would receive up to $700,000 for each television appearance.

Most of the television money would be shared by fewer colleges because NCAA member colleges voted in January 1982 to reduce Division I-A membership to 96 colleges from 139. Smaller member colleges of Division I-A whose stadiums or crowds were too small were demoted to Division I-AA. Frank Litsky

In WORLD BOOK, see FOOTBALL.

FORD, GERALD RUDOLPH (1913-), the 38th President of the United States, returned to the campaign trail in 1982. Resuming a practice that won him many political allies as a House of Representatives member from Michigan, he campaigned extensively for Republican candidates in the congressional and gubernatorial elections.

Ford met with President Ronald Reagan at the White House on October 25, eight days before the balloting, to report on his campaign activities and offer an assessment of Republican prospects. The former President also briefed Reagan on his October trip to Japan with former Secretary of State Henry A. Kissinger. Ford and Kissinger had conferred with Japanese officials and business leaders and taken part in public affairs forums.

In January, Ford joined former President Jimmy Carter, who defeated him in 1976, in issuing an unusual joint appeal to the legislature in Carter's native Georgia to ratify the Equal Rights Amendment. The Georgia House voted against ratification, 116 to 57.

Ford was also active on the lecture circuit and appeared in celebrity pro-am golf tournaments. In February, he was named a director of the American Express Company. He had earlier been made a director of several other firms. Frank Cormier

In WORLD BOOK, see FORD, GERALD RUDOLPH.

FOREST AND FOREST PRODUCTS. The forest-products industry in the Pacific Northwest faced serious financial problems in 1982 as the United States housing industry slumped to its lowest point since World War II. Lumber companies in the region, which purchase a large part of their timber from federal forests, had signed contracts with federal agencies in the late 1970s, when the housing industry was strong and lumber prices were rising. But lumber prices later dropped sharply as high interest rates undermined home-building. Timber for which companies had contracted to pay about $4 billion was worth only $2-billion at depressed 1982 prices.

Rescue Attempt. In August, legislation was introduced in Congress in an attempt to help rescue the financially distressed wood-product companies. The proposed legislation authorized federal agencies to terminate some of the timber contracts made before 1982 and allowed lumber companies to rebid on the timber at reduced 1982 prices.

The proposals proved controversial. The Congressional Research Service had reported on June 16 that excusing the timber companies from their federal logging contracts could cost the government more than $2 billion in lost income.

Opposition even came from segments of the forest industry. An executive of the National Forest Products Association told a Senate subcommittee on August 12 that his organization opposed any move to "distort the normal competitive market system." The split in the industry on the legislation created a deadlock in Congress.

Increased Harvests. Environmental groups criticized plans to accelerate timber cutting in national forests announced on June 28 by John B. Crowell, Jr., assistant secretary of agriculture for natural resources and environment, who supervises the U.S. Forest Service. The Forest Service said it planned to increase harvests from public lands from 11 billion board feet (26 million cubic meters) in fiscal 1982, which ended September 30, to 12.3 billion board feet (29 million cubic meters) in fiscal 1983.

Crowell, a former general counsel of the Louisiana-Pacific Corporation, a major timber company, argued that accelerated cutting was needed to prepare for a coming boom in the housing market. Some observers expected Congress to enact legislation in 1983 that would spur homebuilding.

Environmental groups opposed lumber industry efforts to increase timber cutting. The Sierra Club called such efforts "a major and direct attack on the nation's entire forest system." Andrew L. Newman

In WORLD BOOK, see FOREST; FOREST PRODUCTS; FORESTRY.

FOUR-H CLUBS. See YOUTH ORGANIZATIONS.

FRANCE became a battleground in the 1982 conflict between Israel and the Palestine Liberation Organization (PLO). From February through July, 15 people died and more than 100 were wounded in 21 terrorist attacks, most of them on Palestinian or Jewish targets. The worst incident occurred on August 9, when six people were killed and 22 wounded as gunmen fired into a crowded Jewish restaurant in Paris.

Group Banned. On August 17, President François Mitterrand set up an antiterrorist force under Joseph Franceschi, who took the new post of secretary of state for public security. Mitterrand also set up a centralized antiterrorist databank, tightened frontier controls, banned the sale of certain weapons, and promised to cooperate more closely with other European nations in dealing with terrorists. But Mitterrand vowed not to change his Middle East policy, considered by some observers as anti-Israeli. On August 18, Mitterrand ordered the dissolution of Direct Action, a leftist group that had claimed responsibility for some anti-Jewish attacks in Paris.

Franc Devalued. On March 22, the franc fell to a record low of 6.2755 francs to U.S. $1. On March 25, its value was at the minimum permitted by the European Monetary System (EMS), a group of eight nations working to stabilize their

A transport plane drops fire retardant on blazing stacks of timber at a lumber mill in Rogue River, Ore. The September fire did $1.5 million in damage.

French farmers demonstrate on Paris' Boulevard Voltaire in March to express anger over continuing decreases in agricultural income.

exchange rates. France devalued the franc by 5.75 per cent within the EMS on June 12.

Price Freeze. The government's economic plans ran into problems in 1982. On January 13, the government reduced the workweek from 40 hours to 39, added a fifth week of paid vacation, and cut the retirement age from 65 to 60. Nevertheless, unemployment reached a postwar record of more than 2 million in March, while an inflation rate of 14 per cent put France at a disadvantage with its trading competitors.

On June 13, the government announced that it would freeze prices and wages from July through October. Fuel and certain foods were exempted from the freeze, and the government would allow scheduled increases in minimum wages, family allowances, housing allotments, and pensions. The government also cut the budget by $2.55 billion to reduce the deficit to 3 per cent of the gross national product. On November 1, the government imposed strict "norms" on wages and prices in order to reduce inflation to 8 per cent in 1983.

The Constitutional Council on January 16 ruled invalid parts of the French law nationalizing 5 leading industrial groups, 36 banks, and 2 holding companies. Mitterrand had the laws redrafted to enable him to proceed with his state take-over.

Gas Deal. On January 23, France signed a contract to buy from Russia 282.5 billion cubic feet (8 billion cubic meters) of natural gas per year for 25 years. Russia will pump the gas from Siberia through a pipeline that it is building to central Europe. The United States had called for reducing trade with Russia to protest the military crackdown in Poland. France signed a contract in February to buy liquefied natural gas from Algeria.

Breach with United States. Mitterrand defied President Ronald Reagan's call for a ban on supplying components for the Siberian gas pipeline. On August 24, Dresser (France) S.A., a subsidiary of a U.S. company, obeyed an order from Mitterrand to deliver compressors for the pipeline, thus risking U.S. sanctions. On August 26, the United States barred the company from buying goods and services from the United States for 30 days.

Reagan lifted the ban on November 13. He said that the U.S. and Western European nations had agreed to new curbs on trade with the Soviet bloc. However, on November 14, France said there was no new agreement. On December 14, the United States and France announced an agreement on an East-West trade strategy. Kenneth Brown

See also EUROPE (Close-Up and Facts in Brief Table). In WORLD BOOK, see FRANCE.

FUTURE FARMERS OF AMERICA (FFA). See YOUTH ORGANIZATIONS.

GABON. See AFRICA.

GAMBIA. See AFRICA.

GAMES AND TOYS. Traditional toy industry sales in the United States rose slightly during 1982. It was generally a year of spotty sales, company acquisitions, and several bankruptcies. However, there were a few bright stars, including top-selling video games and licensed playthings.

Several other companies joined Atari, the leader in the video game arena. Many of them specialized in game cartridges that can be played on a home television screen. The newly available second-generation video systems included one that offered superior graphic resolution, another that had a voice synthesis module, and one that could be played independent of a television screen because it had its own self-contained display screen. The most popular game cartridges were those licensed from coin-operated arcades, such as Donkey Kong and Pac-Man.

For the first time, board-game sales — traditionally one of the strongest categories in the industry — slowed as consumers preferred the sophisticated home video games. However, one board game, Pente, was hailed as the biggest rage since backgammon. Based on the ancient Japanese board game Go, Pente had a strong following among college students and older people.

Licensing, or basing a product on a popular motion-picture, television, comic-strip, or specially created commercial character, continued to make its mark in the toy industry. The coming of E.T. the Extra-Terrestrial, one of the most popular licensed playthings in 1982, gave an extra-timely boost to toy sales at midyear. E.T. toy products, based on the title character in a motion picture about a creature from outer space, ranged from stuffed animals to board games. Some equally stellar licensed performers in the toy industry included Smurfs, Garfield, and Pac-Man.

"E.T." seems to stand for "Every Toy" as the ugly-but-lovable Extra-Terrestrial creature captures the market for licensed playthings.

Headliners. Deely bobbers — squiggly antennae attached to a headband with glittering balls, stars, or pinwheels bobbing on the ends — became a nationwide rage.

G.I. Joe re-enlisted into the toy industry after a seven-year "rest and recuperation." Totally redesigned and with a new assignment, the G.I. Joe dolls, or "action figures," as they are called, are a nine-member U.S. Army-outfitted rapid deployment force that includes a female intelligence officer named Scarlet.

Miniature die-cast cars and trucks, one of the many attractively priced toy items that offer good play value, sold extremely well in 1982. Several toy manufacturers followed the lead of the Strawberry Shortcake doll and produced aromatic playthings. Among them were hula hoops and a teddy bear named Kisses. Donna M. Datre

In World Book, see Doll; Game; Toy.

GARDENING. Mealy bugs increasingly became a cause of despair for windowsill gardeners in the United States in 1982. While favoring select species like jade trees and African violets, the cottony-looking sucking insects attack anything that grows. To combat infestations, horticultural experts recommended several approaches. One remedy consists of applying a mixture made of equal parts of water and rubbing alcohol to which a pesticide — pyrethrin, malathion, or diazinon — is added. Alcohol increases the effectiveness of the pesticide. This mixture, which can be applied with a hand sprayer, must be applied weekly for three weeks. The plants should also be watched carefully for another month for signs of reinfestation.

Horticulturists also revived an old remedy — liquefied Fels Naphtha soap, now available in a commercial version called Safer Agro-Chem's Insecticidal Soap. The insecticide is considered environmentally safe, and comparatively harmless to some touchy plants such as sweet peas and nasturtiums. The product's shortcomings are that it must be used repeatedly to control mealy bugs and that thorough coverage of infected leaves and stems is necessary.

In May 1982, the U.S. Environmental Protection Agency cleared the insecticidal soap for use on edible crops. The agency said the residues of the insecticide, which can be used up to the day of harvest, are considered nontoxic to human beings.

Protecting Endangered Plants. In 1982, horticultural groups hoped that stiff new penalties—the first ever—for the interstate sale of endangered and rare plants would aid plant conservation efforts. On Nov. 16, 1981, President Ronald Reagan signed an amendment to the Lacy Act prohibiting the interstate sale of rare plants collected in violation of state law. The new amendment also covers plants protected by the Convention on International Trade in Endangered Species of Wild Fauna and Flora.

Under the law, sellers of illegally acquired plants worth more than $350 face possible prison terms of up to five years and fines of up to $20,000. Previously, states were frustrated in their attempts to control the interstate traffic in endangered plants because they had no jurisdiction beyond their borders.

Such illegal trafficking seriously endangered some plant species. For example, plant rustlers stole about $500,000 worth of Arizona cacti in 1981, according to the March 1982 issue of *American Horticulturist.* The stolen plants included 400 saguaros, Arizona's state flower.

New Plants. All-America Selections, an organization that evaluates new flower and vegetable seed varieties, observed its 50th anniversary by awarding bronze medals to three flowers and two squash plants. Scarlet Luminette, a tall double carnation, won for earliness, sturdy stems, and heat resistance. Small World Cherry, a dwarf zinnia, was recognized for its masses of blooms, which lighten as they mature. Fantastic Light Pink, a compact zinnia, won for its large flowers on low plants and two-tone color. Winning vegetables were Peter Pan, a bush scallop squash selected for its compactness, hardiness, and long bearing season; and Jersey Golden Acorn, also a bush squash, recognized for its fruits, which are rich in vitamin A and may be eaten fresh or stored for winter.

In its 43rd year of testing roses, All-America Rose Selections, an organization of commercial rose growers, chose just two 1983 winners. Sun Flare, a fragrant, clear-yellow floribunda, was bred by William A. Warriner of Tustin, Calif. Sweet Surrender, a spicy, fragrant, pink hybrid tea, was produced by Ollie L. Weeks of Ontario, Calif.

For the first time in its 83-year history, the American Rose Society (ARS) endorsed a commercial product—Ortho's Funginex. According to ARS tests, the fungicide controls the three major diseases that attack roses—black spot, powdery mildew, and rust. Phil Clark

In WORLD BOOK, see FLOWER; GARDENING.

GAS AND GASOLINE. See ENERGY; PETROLEUM.

GEMAYEL, AMIN (1942-   ), was elected president of Lebanon on Sept. 21, 1982, after his brother, President-elect Bashir Gemayel, was assassinated nine days before he was to have taken office (see LEBANON). A successful businessman and lawyer, Amin Gemayel was known as a moderate and a conciliator. Unlike his militant brother Bashir, the quiet and congenial Amin maintained close contacts with Lebanese Muslims and the Palestinians, even at the height of Lebanon's internal conflicts.

Amin Gemayel, the oldest of five children, was born on Jan. 27, 1942, in Bikfeiya, Lebanon, near Beirut. In his youth, he was groomed for a political career by his father, Pierre, the founder of the Christian Phalangist Party. Amin attended Jesuit-operated elementary and secondary schools and earned a law degree from St. Joseph University in Beirut in 1965.

In 1971, Gemayel was elected to the Lebanese parliament, where he earned a reputation as a thoughtful legislator, an efficient administrator, and an eloquent speaker. He speaks fluent English and French as well as Arabic. In addition to running his family's shipping and insurance interests, Gemayel established the French-language newspaper *Le Réveil* in Beirut.

He is married to the former Joyce Tyan. They have three children. Barbara A. Mayes

GEOLOGY. The eruption of El Chichón, a long-dormant volcano in southeastern Mexico, on March 29, 1982, attracted little scientific attention at the time. Although the volcano continued to erupt during early April, killing 187 people and forcing thousands to flee their homes, the force of the eruption was much less than that of Mount St. Helens, the volcano in Washington state that erupted in May 1980. Scientists soon discovered, however, that El Chichón (The Lump) spewed a surprising amount of dust, ash, and sulfur dioxide into the stratosphere—the layer of the atmosphere that begins from 6 to 10 miles (10 to 16 kilometers) above the earth and extends upward for about 30 miles (48 kilometers).

Initially, the cloud formed by the volcanic material was spread by stratospheric winds into a narrow belt around the earth at a latitude of 20° north. Gradually, however, the belt widened and, by May 15, the northern edge of the cloud reached as far north as New Orleans. By the end of the summer, a thin haze extended over all of the United States, Great Britain, and other countries in the same latitudes. See WEATHER.

Mapping the Ocean Floor. Earth scientists during 1982 received an unexpected benefit from the United States space program. Marine geologists discovered that the *Seasat* satellite, which was used in 1978 to study waves and tides on ocean sur-

A towering plume of ash and steam rises from El Chichón, a long-dormant volcano in southeastern Mexico, which began to erupt in late March.

faces, has also indirectly provided data for maps of ocean floors. The satellite had a downward-looking radar system that measured the distance to the surface of the ocean.

Seamounts—free-standing underwater mountains—and other large features on the sea floor have a tiny indirect effect on the ocean surface. The seamounts exert a gravitational pull on seawater, causing a "bump" to form on the surface above them. Although these bumps are only a few inches high, the satellite's radar system was sensitive enough to register them.

Before *Seasat* data became available, marine geologists could map the ocean floor only by the laborious process of gauging the depth to the bottom from surface ships. To do this, they measured the time it took sound waves transmitted from the ship to echo off the bottom and return.

New maps of the ocean floors, based on *Seasat* data, show nearly every seamount in the ocean. Of particular interest is the contrast between the very rough topography and numerous seamounts in the South Atlantic Ocean, where the motion of the plates that make up the earth's crust is very slow, and the smooth topography and relatively few seamounts in the South Pacific Ocean, where the plates are moving 10 times faster. Kenneth S. Deffeyes

In WORLD BOOK, see GEOLOGY.

GEORGIA. See STATE GOVERNMENT.

GERMANY, EAST. Poland and East Germany improved their relationship in 1982. On March 29, almost all of East Germany's ruling Communist Party Political Bureau welcomed Polish leader Wojciech Jaruzelski to East Berlin. Diplomats saw Jaruzelski's visit as an effort to show East Germany that the Communist Party was again in firm control of Poland.

East Germany's Communist Party Secretary General and State Council Chairman Erich Honecker assured Jaruzelski that Poland's imposition of martial law had his "full understanding." Honecker said that East Germany would continue to support all true Polish patriots and Communists.

Trade Talks. East Germany and Poland agreed on March 30 to increase industrial cooperation in order to fight Western sanctions against the Warsaw military regime and to help overcome Poland's economic problems. The two leaders agreed on the need for "more efficient and planned use of the two states' industrial capabilities to mutual advantage" over the long term. Such cooperation was necessary to provide both countries with adequate supplies of fuel, raw materials, chemical products, machinery, electrical and electronic equipment, and consumer goods.

Travel Eased. East Germany announced on February 11 that it was extending the list of occasions on which it would allow East Germans to visit relatives in West Germany. The new rules allow East Germans to go to West Germany for religious confirmation ceremonies or first communions, and for the 60th, 65th, 70th, 75th, and all subsequent birthdays of close relatives. They had previously been permitted to visit only for births, marriages, 25th and 50th wedding anniversaries, critical illnesses, and deaths. West German Chancellor Helmut Schmidt had requested changes when he visited East Germany in December 1981.

Shooting Escapees. On March 25, East Germany's parliament passed a law instructing border guards to shoot fellow citizens trying to escape into West Berlin. Such shootings had been sanctioned by secret orders for 19 years. Parliament justified the new law on the grounds that it was designed to prevent a crime that is punishable by death in certain cases. Guards were ordered not to fire at children or innocent bystanders and to avoid shooting at women and young people "if possible."

East Germany's population declined by more than 2 million from 1948 to 1980, so the nation has had trouble meeting military-personnel requirements. Consequently, in March the Defense Ministry increased the amount of training for reservists and declared that women could be mobilized in times of crisis. Kenneth Brown

See also EUROPE (Facts in Brief Table). In WORLD BOOK, see GERMANY.

GERMANY, WEST. Chancellor Helmut Schmidt resigned the coalition government of his Social Democratic Party (SDP) and the small Free Democratic Party (FDP) on Sept. 17, 1982, and called for an early general election. He had fought for eight months to keep control until the general election scheduled for 1984. But he gave up after Economics Minister Otto Graf Lambsdorff, a Free Democrat, proposed a radical shift in economic policy that the SDP could not accept. Lambsdorff and the three other FDP ministers left the Cabinet, prompting Schmidt's resignation.

The FDP and the opposition Christian Democratic Union (CDU) formed an alliance that planned to take control of the national government. The new alliance looked forward to state elections in Hesse on September 26 as amounting to a referendum on its plan. The alliance expected the CDU to win heavily in Hesse. However, it suffered a setback as the CDU won only 45.6 per cent of the vote, followed by 42.8 per cent for the SDP.

Nevertheless, the alliance went ahead with its plan. On October 1, the Bundestag (parliament) turned Schmidt out of office and replaced him with Helmut Kohl, the leader of the CDU. Kohl promised to hold general elections on March 6, 1983. See KOHL, HELMUT.

On November 28, left wing Free Democrats who objected strongly to the alliance broke away from the FDP. They formed a new party, the Liberal Democratic Party.

Poland and Jobs. Schmidt had faced his first challenge on January 14, when he was jeered in the Bundestag over his government's attitude toward the December 1981 imposition of martial law in Poland. Schmidt wanted to increase economic aid to Poland if that country adopted a more "circumspect" policy. However, the opposition favored the United States harder line of threatening political and legal sanctions if the Polish regime did not end martial law.

Schmidt won this fight, but his next one, on unemployment, was tougher. On February 5, Schmidt staked his future on a confidence vote on a three-year, $5.3-billion program to create jobs and stimulate the economy. Schmidt won the vote by an overwhelming majority of 43.

Schmidt's program was incorporated in the 1983 budget, the cause of still another crisis. After a 12-hour discussion, during which the coalition seemed on the verge of collapse, the SDP and the FDP reached a compromise on June 30 that did not increase taxes but cut social welfare spending and subsidies to businesses.

In December, West Germany's unemployment rate climbed to 9.1 per cent, with 2.22 million peo-

West German Chancellor Helmut Kohl takes the oath of office on October 1 after the Bundestag (parliament) elected him to replace Helmut Schmidt.

ple out of work. The number of unemployed had not been so high since February 1950.

The Greens, a group pledged to preserve the environment and ban nuclear power and nuclear arms, were hailed as "a new third force" when they won seats in legislatures in Bremen, Baden-Württemberg, West Berlin, Lower Saxony, Hamburg, and Hesse. They won 9 seats in the Hesse elections, as FDP representation fell from 7 seats to 0.

Relations with the United States suffered in 1982. West Germany claimed that interest rates in the United States added to West Germany's economic problems and kept the Deutsche mark low in relation to the dollar.

Another cause of friction was the imposition of sanctions by the United States to protest against martial law in Poland. The United States refused to allow U.S. firms or their foreign subsidiaries to provide components for a gas pipeline that Russia was building from Siberia to central Europe. The United States urged its allies to impose similar sanctions. However, on July 9, Schmidt said, "We will stick to the agreements our firms made with the Soviet Union. This will create some irritation in our relations with the United States, but that will have to be overcome." In November, the United States lifted the sanctions. Kenneth Brown

See also EUROPE (Close-Up and Facts in Brief Table). In WORLD BOOK, see GERMANY.

Jerry Rawlings, head of Ghana's military government, tells Ghanaians on January 8 that they will all have to help grow food.

GHANA was ruled during 1982 by a new military government, its fifth since 1966, that seized power in a coup on Dec. 31, 1981. The coup's instigators were former army personnel who had been forcibly retired by the civilian government. They were joined by some Ghanaian military units and opposed by others.

A critical element in the success of the coup was the popularity of its leader, Jerry John Rawlings, a 34-year-old half-Scottish, half-Ghanaian retired air force flight lieutenant. He had also staged a successful coup in June 1979 and ran Ghana's government for 3½ months before turning power over to a newly elected president, Hilla Limann. Limann was ousted in the 1981 coup and put under house arrest. Rawlings said Limann's regime had been corrupt and had oppressed the people.

Ruling Council Established. On Jan. 12, 1982, Rawlings established a seven-member Provisional National Defense Council, with himself as chairman, to run the country. The council pledged to fight corruption in government and to solve Ghana's economic problems, especially the high rate of inflation and a shortage of basic consumer goods, industrial raw materials, and spare parts.

Nevertheless, shortages and high inflation continued. In October, prices were reported to be increasing at an annual rate of 100 to 120 per cent. A major cause of the scarcities was Ghana's dependence on imported goods for many of its domestic needs. Compounding the country's economic problems was a sharp drop in Ghana's foreign exchange earnings, caused by low market prices for cocoa, the nation's chief export, and a continued decline in cocoa production. Although Ghana produced more than 600,000 short tons (540,000 metric tons) of cocoa in the 1964-1965 crop year, the 1981-1982 harvest was less than 330,000 short tons (300,000 metric tons).

Unlawful Military Actions. Military units acting outside the law were another serious problem for Ghana in 1982. In February, soldiers in Kumasi killed a priest and a policewoman who had allegedly refused to obey their orders. In July, a group of soldiers in Accra kidnapped and killed three justices of Ghana's highest court.

A priest on the Provisional National Defense Council, Vincent Damuah, strongly denounced those and other killings by military personnel. In mid-August, Damuah resigned from the council.

On November 3, the government announced the arrest of senior officials charged with attempting to turn the armed forces against Rawlings. On November 23, elements of the military attempted another coup, but it was crushed. J. Dixon Esseks

See also AFRICA. In WORLD BOOK, see GHANA.

GIRL SCOUTS. See YOUTH ORGANIZATIONS.

GIRLS CLUBS. See YOUTH ORGANIZATIONS.

GOLF. Tom Watson, Craig Stadler, and Ray Floyd gained most of the major honors in men's golf in 1982. Among them, they swept the four Grand Slam tournaments and won 10 of the 44 tournaments on the Professional Golfers Association (PGA) tour. JoAnne Carner, at age 42, and Kathy Whitworth, at age 43, made history on the Ladies Professional Golf Association (LPGA) tour.

The Men. Watson, after having come close in the past, won his first United States Open, held from June 17 to 20 in Pebble Beach, Calif. Four weeks later, in Troon, Scotland, he won his fourth British Open.

In the United States Open, Watson and Jack Nicklaus were tied going to the 17th hole of the final round. Watson put his approach shot in the rough, about 16 feet (5 meters) from the pin, and Nicklaus said, "There's no way in the world he can get close to the pin." At that moment, Watson was telling his caddie, "I'm not going to try to get it close. I'm going to make it."

He did, chipping in for a birdie. Another birdie on the last hole gave Watson a 72-hole score of 282 and a two-stroke victory over Nicklaus.

In the British Open, Watson's 284 defeated Nick Price of South Africa and Peter Oosterhuis of England by a stroke. Price, two strokes ahead with four holes to play, took a double bogey on the 15th hole and a bogey on the 17th.

Stadler dissipated a bigger lead in the Masters, held from April 8 to 11 in Augusta, Ga. He took a six-stroke edge into the last nine holes, but he bogeyed four of those nine holes and finished in a tie at 284 with Dan Pohl, the longest driver on the tour. Stadler won on the first extra hole when Pohl missed a 6-foot (1.8-meter) putt.

In the PGA championship, held from August 5 to 8 in Tulsa, Okla., Floyd started with a 63 that included 10 threes. He led by five strokes going into the final round and finished at 272, three strokes better than runner-up Lanny Wadkins.

Stadler won four tournaments—the Masters; the World Series of Golf with its $100,000 first prize; the Tucson Open; and the Kemper Open. Calvin Peete, who had only one previous tour victory, also won four times, the last two by seven strokes each. In addition to the British Open, Watson won three American tournaments. So did Floyd, Wadkins, and Bob Gilder. Both Jay Haas and Wayne Levi won twice. Stadler led in earnings with $446,462. In all, the PGA tour carried purses of $14.5 million.

As previously decided, 1982 was the last year of the PGA-tour format that allowed lesser golfers to attempt to qualify on the Monday before each tournament. Starting in 1983, the 125 leading money-winners of the previous year and 50 from the PGA school's qualifying tournament would be exempt from qualifying all year. A few players would qualify in other ways, but most who failed to gain a full year's exemption would have to return to the PGA school to qualify there.

The Women. The LPGA's 35 tournaments paid $6.4 million in prize money, a record. Carner also set a record with one-season earnings of $310,399.

Carner won five tournaments, including three in a row in August and September. She raised her career total to 37 victories, gaining the LPGA Hall of Fame automatically with her 35th victory.

Beth Daniel won five tournaments, and Sally Little of South Africa won four. Sandra Haynie, Patty Sheehan, and Hollis Stacy won three each.

Whitworth, the leading money winner eight times in the nine seasons from 1965 to 1973, played as well as ever. She won by nine strokes in April on Hilton Head Island, South Carolina; and by four strokes in May in Atlanta, Ga. That gave her 83 career victories, one more than the record of the retired Mickey Wright. Haynie ranked second among active players with 43.

Janet Alex, who had never won in five years on the tour, made her first victory an important one—the women's United States Open. Jan Stephenson of Australia won the LPGA championship; Little, the Dinah Shore; Haynie, the Peter Jackson Classic; and Carner, the 12-player World Championship of Women's Golf. Frank Litsky

In WORLD BOOK, see GOLF.

GONZÁLEZ MÁRQUEZ, FELIPE (1942-), took office as prime minister of Spain on Dec. 2, 1982. The youngest prime minister in Western Europe, González said, "I have been deeply involved in politics for 20 years. There are few politicians today in Spain who have as much experience as I do with democracy." See SPAIN.

Felipe González Márquez was born on March 5, 1942, in Seville. His father was a cowherd who later started his own small dairy. González went to local schools, then studied at the University of Seville and the Catholic University of Louvain in Belgium. He received his law degree in 1966 and began to practice labor law in Seville.

González gave all his free time to politics, starting with the Young Socialists, the youth wing of the Spanish Socialist Workers Party (PSOE). In 1974, he became secretary-general of the PSOE at an election held in France because the regime of dictator Francisco Franco, which lasted until 1975, had outlawed the party in Spain. Under González' leadership, the PSOE in 1979 dropped its professed affiliation with Marxism, which had alienated many otherwise sympathetic supporters, and became the leading left-of-center political force in Spain.

González promised "*un cambio histórico*" (a historic change) and stressed the importance of developing democracy in Spain. Marsha F. Goldsmith

GREAT BRITAIN

Tied-up traffic on Westminster Bridge is typical of the snarls a combined subway and rail strike caused in London in June and July.

The year was dominated by the Falklands crisis, which began on April 2, 1982, rapidly escalated into war, and produced a tremendous ground swell of popular support for Prime Minister Margaret Thatcher's Conservative government by the time it ended with the Argentine surrender on June 14. What became known as the "Falklands factor" was a key influence on the British political scene. See FALKLAND ISLANDS.

At first the Argentine invasion of the Falkland Islands, South Georgia Island, and the South Sandwich Islands—a British dependency in the South Atlantic Ocean—had a traumatic effect on the Thatcher government. Three ministers resigned on April 5. They were Foreign Secretary Lord Carrington; Richard Luce, a minister of state for foreign and Commonwealth affairs; and Humphrey Atkins, the Lord Privy Seal and, as deputy foreign secretary, the principal government spokesman on foreign affairs in the House of Commons.

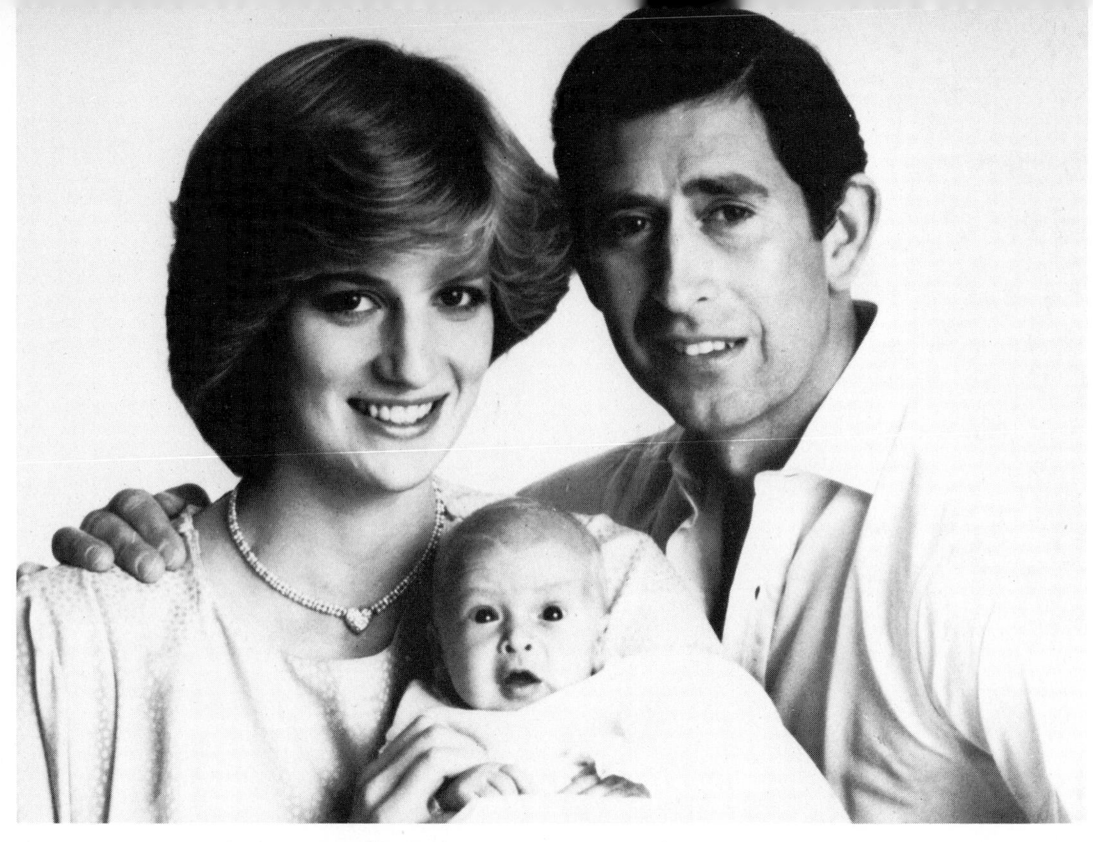

Prince William of Wales smilingly poses for his first official portrait as the Prince and Princess of Wales anticipate their wedding anniversary.

In emergency debates in the House of Commons, the government was severely criticized for failing to prevent the Argentine invasion, and in a national opinion poll in April, 48 per cent of the British people said Thatcher would be remembered as the worst prime minister ever. However, by early May the "Falklands factor" began to work in Thatcher's favor as the majority of the British people rallied behind her.

The Economy. Some political analysts were puzzled by Thatcher's popularity, considering Great Britain's bleak economic outlook. There was no hint of change in the Thatcher government's monetarist economic policies, which were aimed at cutting costs on welfare and other social services, and trying to make industry more competitive by lowering government subsidies and offering fewer government-financed capital programs. By late 1982, Conservative ministers could point to some success. Inflation was down to 7.3 per cent in September, the lowest rate in 10 years. However, unemployment continued to rise, reaching a record total of more than 3 million in September.

British industry continued to stagnate. The most spectacular victim of the harsh economic climate was Sir Freddie Laker, whose Laker Airways had pioneered cut-rate transatlantic fares with its "walk-on" Skytrain. Laker's company crashed on February 5 with debts of $300 million, a victim of the decline in air-passenger traffic. The government continued its policy of selling government-owned enterprises to private owners.

The Labour Party continued its internal wrangles between right and left and, toward the end of 1982, the right succeeded in reversing more than three years of leftist control of key party organs. Much of this struggle centered on what to do about a left wing pressure group within Labour's ranks known as the Militant Tendency, or Militant. The group was thought to number only 5,000 out of an official Labour membership total of 348,156. But it had proved extremely adept at "packing" local Labour committees to vote right wing members of Parliament (M.P.'s) out of office. Right wingers argued that Militant was a party within the Labour Party.

Labour's National Executive Committee (NEC) voted on Dec. 16, 1981, to conduct an inquiry into the activities of Militant. The move was urged by Labour leader Michael Foot, who said the extreme left was gaining excessive influence and that traditional Labour voters were abandoning their loyalty to the party. The inquiry report was presented on June 23, 1982, and the NEC voted to set up a register of groups within the party and reserve for itself the power to decide which organizations were acceptable. It stated that Militant "as at present constituted" would be ineligible.

That would disqualify its acknowledged supporters, including seven parliamentary candidates, from Labour Party membership. The decision was a defeat for Tony Benn, Labour's leading left winger. Militant submitted its application to join Labour's register on October 18, adding that it considered the register unconstitutional.

On September 28, during Labour's annual conference at Blackpool, the right had more successes. Elections for the NEC produced a two-thirds majority for the right. Three of Benn's supporters lost their seats, and the left lost its majority.

Other Party Politics. In December 1981, three more Labour M.P.'s had announced their defection to the Social Democratic Party (SDP), bringing the new center party's strength to 28, and on March 25, 1982, it was increased to 29. The party had formed an alliance with the Liberals, another minority center party, and seemed about to break the two-party mold of British politics.

Then the party's fortunes began to falter. A poll in September found support for the SDP alone down to 4 per cent compared with 26 per cent 11 months earlier, though 27 per cent of voters still said they would vote for the Liberal-SDP alliance. However, the SDP proceeded to elect its first leader on July 2. Roy Jenkins defeated David Owen, another Labour defector, in a poll of the party's 62,000 members. Shirley Williams, also an ex-Labour minister, was elected SDP president on September 23.

On November 30, Foot, Jenkins, Liberal leader David Steel, and a junior minister in the Home Office all received letter bombs sent to the House of Commons. None of them ignited— but a similar one sent to Prime Minister Thatcher went off, slightly injuring an official who checks in the mail.

Papal Visit. The Falklands War had placed in doubt a visit to Great Britain by Pope John Paul II. It would mark the first resumption of full relations with the Roman Catholic Church since King Henry VIII broke away in 1534, setting up the Church of England. After much hesitation, the pope's visit took place from May 28 to June 2.

Royal Events. The British people soon had something else to cheer about. On June 21, Diana, the Princess of Wales, gave birth to a healthy, blue-eyed boy. The baby, second in line to the throne after his father, Prince Charles, was christened William Arthur Philip Louis, and became known as Prince William of Wales.

However, the royal family endured several unhappy incidents during the year. On July 9, a 31-year-old unemployed laborer named Michael Fagan succeeded in climbing over the wall of Buckingham Palace and making his way to the

A crowd of patriots wishes the British warships well as they sail in April for the Falkland Islands in the South Atlantic Ocean.

bedroom of Queen Elizabeth II, where he sat on the queen's bed and insisted on chatting with her. Subsequent howls of public outrage at the laxness of palace security included calls for the resignation of Home Secretary William Whitelaw, whose duties included overall responsibility for palace security. Anger increased when it was learned that Fagan had entered the palace a month previously. On June 7, he had broken in, stolen and drunk half a bottle of wine, and left.

On July 19, the director of public prosecutions announced that Fagan would not be prosecuted for his call on the queen because trespass is not a criminal act in Britain and there was no desire for the queen to be a court witness. But on September 23, Fagan was tried for the earlier break-in and theft—and acquitted. Finally, on October 5, he was ordered sent to a mental hospital after pleading guilty to another, unrelated charge—that of taking a car without the owner's consent.

The Pipeline that is to carry natural gas from Siberia to central Europe caused strain between Britain and the United States. President Ronald Reagan barred all U.S. companies from participating in building the pipeline in protest against the continuation of martial law in Poland, then extended the ban to the sale of goods and services to countries that were involved in the project. When the U.S. Department of Commerce on September 9 announced sanctions against the British engineering company John Brown P.L.C., a representative for the company said, "We've got to fulfill our contract. We're under British Government orders to do so."

A Day of Action, a national walkout on September 22 called by the Trades Union Congress, the national organization of British labor unions, was symbolic of labor strife in Great Britain in 1982. The general strike featured a demonstration in London by about 100,000 people. The walkout was held in support of pay demands by National Health Service Workers, who had been negotiating with the government since April.

Terrorism raised its ugly head again, after a year of inactivity, when bombs planted by the Irish Republican Army exploded on July 20 in two London parks. A total of 11 people died and 51 others were wounded in the surprise attacks.

A Spy Sentenced on November 10 to 35 years in prison for espionage—plus three years for sexual offenses against children—caused another scandal over security. Geoffrey A. Prime, an employee of the Government Communications Headquarters in Cheltenham, was convicted of transmitting to the Soviet Union from 1968 to 1981 secret information that was damaging to the United States as well as Great Britain. Ian Mather

See also ARGENTINA; EUROPE (Facts in Brief Table). In WORLD BOOK, see GREAT BRITAIN.

GREECE. The slogan *"allaghi"* ("change"), used by Prime Minister Andreas Papandreou during the campaign that swept his Pan Hellenic Socialist Movement (Pasok) into power in October 1981, was not implemented in 1982. The promised withdrawal from the European Community (EC or Common Market) did not take place, nor did severance from the North Atlantic Treaty Organization (NATO). And the nationalization of leading banks and industry was not even in the Pasok's legislative program. Papandreou hesitated to bring change because of Greece's economic and financial difficulties and what he saw as the threat of Turkish aggression.

Greek-Turkish Tension increased in the opening months of 1982, and on March 10 Greece warned its NATO partners of the grave consequences that repeated Turkish air violations over the Aegean Sea could bring. But the Turks claimed that Greek oil prospecting in the Aegean continental shelf violated an understanding between the two countries to refrain from "controversial initiatives." The dispute led Greece to withdraw from the NATO military exercise "Distant Drum 82" in May and to declare its national air space out of bounds to other NATO forces. Later in the month, Papandreou ordered the withdrawal of a Greek destroyer from NATO's on-call naval force.

Greece's Prime Minister Andreas Papandreou accepts a bouquet during a visit to the Strovolos Refugee Center on Cyprus in March.

U.S. Relations. United States Secretary of State Alexander M. Haig, Jr., visited Athens on May 15 but failed to resolve differences between the two countries. Papandreou hoped to exchange his shelving of threats to quit NATO and to oust the U.S. from its bases in Greece for Western guarantees to protect Greece in the Aegean. Haig indicated that Greece had already received such guarantees. He said that only Greece's full participation in NATO and bilateral agreement between Greece and Turkey could solve the Aegean problem. In August, Greece dropped its demand for a U.S. guarantee of its Aegean frontiers.

Cyprus Rebuke. Papandreou rebuked President Spyros Kyprianou of Cyprus on April 29 for forming a political alliance with the island's Communist Party. Papandreou said that the alliance could jeopardize an agreement between Greece and Cyprus on the question of unifying Cyprus, which is now divided between Greek and Turkish Cypriots. Papandreou claimed that, by forming the alliance, Kyprianou endorsed Communist support of talks between Cyprus' Greek and Turkish communities. The Greek government said the talks had failed and that international pressure should be brought to bear on the issue. Kenneth Brown

See also EUROPE (Facts in Brief Table). In WORLD BOOK, see CYPRUS; GREECE.

GRENADA. See LATIN AMERICA.

GRETZKY, WAYNE (1961-), star center of the Edmonton Oilers, broke every major single-season scoring record of the National Hockey League (NHL) during the 1981-1982 season. An uncanny stickhandler and shooter, Gretzky amassed 92 goals and 120 assists in 80 regular season games for 212 points. His goal total shattered the record of 76 goals set by Phil Esposito during the 1970-1971 season. Gretzky's assist and point totals surpassed his own records of 109 and 164 set in 1980-1981. In addition, he scored three or more goals in a game 10 times, another record.

Gretzky started his remarkable season by scoring 50 goals in his first 39 games, an unprecedented—and previously inconceivable—achievement. He scored his record-breaking 77th goal on February 24 in his 64th game. Gretzky won the NHL scoring title for the second year in a row. For the third straight year, he won the Hart Trophy as the league's Most Valuable Player.

Born in Brantford, Canada, Gretzky began playing hockey as a small boy. By the age of 11, he had gained national attention in Canada for his scoring feats. His professional career began at age 17 in the now-defunct World Hockey Association. In the 1979-1980 season, his first in the NHL, Gretzky tied for the league scoring title and—at 19—became the youngest player ever to win the Hart Trophy. William T. Graham

GUATEMALA went to the polls on March 7, 1982, to elect a new president. But when the winner—General Angel Aníbal Guevara, the candidate of the country's ruling military clique—was announced, few Guatemalans believed that their ballots had been honestly counted.

Before Guevara could take office, officers of Guatemala's armed forces intervened and staged a coup on March 23. The coup raised to power a three-man junta of military officers. On June 9, two of those officers were forced to resign by the third, retired Brigadier General José Efraín Ríos-Montt, leaving him in sole possession of the presidency. See RÍOS-MONTT, JOSÉ EFRAÍN.

Once in power, Ríos-Montt attempted to restore public confidence in government and to put an end to Guatemala's long-smoldering guerrilla violence. He declared a one-month amnesty for those who had taken up arms against the government, guaranteeing the safety of all who chose to turn in their arms. Ríos-Montt coupled the amnesty with a promise to put an end to repression by government forces. He also pledged his administration to a 14-point program, including the attainment of economic recovery within a free enterprise system and the elimination of corruption.

Government Crackdown. Nevertheless, Ríos-Montt ordered a step-up in the mobilization of the

Troops aim a cannon at the National Palace in Guatemala City, Guatemala, in March, as one group of officers ousts another in a coup.

army "to wipe out subversion" when the 30-day amnesty for guerrillas was over. On June 30, Ríos-Montt suspended civil liberties for 30 days and set up special courts to try persons suspected of subversion, with the death penalty for such crimes as terrorism, kidnapping, and treason. He renewed the decree each month for the rest of the year.

The situation eased up enough in September for the United States Department of State to soften its advisory to Americans warning against travel in Guatemala. But the same month saw the publication of shocking eyewitness accounts of massacres of Guatemalan Indians by the nation's armed forces. From refuge in Mexico, the Indians described the massacres of hundreds of people.

Additional incidents were alleged by Amnesty International, a privately funded human-rights organization. On October 11, Amnesty charged that government forces in Guatemala had killed 2,600 Indians and peasants since Ríos-Montt took power in March. Nathan A. Haverstock

See also LATIN AMERICA (Facts in Brief Table). In the Special Reports section, see WHAT WENT WRONG IN CENTRAL AMERICA? In WORLD BOOK, see GUATEMALA.

GUINEA. See AFRICA.

GUINEA-BISSAU. See AFRICA.

GUYANA. See LATIN AMERICA.

HAITI. See LATIN AMERICA.

United States athletes parade during opening ceremonies of the Pan American Wheelchair Games held in Halifax, Canada, from August 21 to 29.

HANDICAPPED. On June 28, 1982, the Supreme Court of the United States ruled that local school districts are not obliged to provide services that would enable handicapped children to reach their full academic potential. The decision was the first Supreme Court ruling involving the Education for All Handicapped Children Act of 1975, which specifically required that handicapped youngsters be provided an "appropriate" education in the least restrictive environment.

The decision concerned Amy Rowley, a deaf fourth-grader in Peekskill, N.Y. Lower courts agreed with her parents' contention that the school district should provide Amy with a sign-language interpreter.

In reversing the decision of the lower courts, the Supreme Court said that Congress's intent in passing the 1975 act was "more to open the door of public education to handicapped children on appropriate terms than guarantee any particular level of service once inside." The court ruled that although the act entitles handicapped children to a public education from which they can derive "some educational benefit," it does not require school districts to provide services "to maximize each child's potential commensurate with the opportunities provided other children."

The case attracted national attention for another reason. Amy's case was argued by the first deaf lawyer to appear before the court. The justices allowed attorney Michael A. Chatoff to install a special computer-assisted video-transcription system in the courtroom so that he could argue the case more effectively. Questions and comments from the justices were fed into a computer, then displayed almost simultaneously on a video screen for Chatoff to read.

Proposals Dropped. On September 19, Secretary of Education Terrel H. Bell withdrew a number of controversial proposals to ease the rules governing public school education for the 4 million handicapped children in the United States.

The proposals would have reduced the list of health-related services schools must provide for handicapped children and weakened the role of parents in determining the services provided for their children. They also would have made it easier for teachers in regular classrooms to remove handicapped children they considered disruptive.

The Handicapped American of the Year, chosen by the President's Committee on Employment of the Handicapped, was Edward Stiehl-Rios of San Juan, Puerto Rico. A double amputee, Stiehl-Rios works as a psychologist for the Veterans Administration. Virginia E. Anderson

In WORLD BOOK, see HANDICAPPED.

HARNESS RACING. See HORSE RACING.

HAWAII. See STATE GOVERNMENT.

HEALTH AND DISEASE. In February 1982, the surgeon general of the United States, C. Everett Koop, issued the most serious government indictment of smoking to date in a report that concluded: "Cigarette smoking is clearly identified as the chief preventable cause of death in our society and the most important public health issue of our time."

According to the report, men who smoke are twice as likely to die of lung and other cancers as those who do not smoke. The cancer risk among female smokers is 30 per cent greater than among female nonsmokers—and rising. The surgeon general's report expanded the list of cancers associated with smoking. It stated that smoking is the major cause of cancer of the larynx, oral cavity, and esophagus; is a "contributory factor" in cancer of the bladder, pancreas, and kidney; and may be linked with cancer of the stomach and cervix.

Fat Risks. Obesity in adult men and women may be a stronger predictor of cardiovascular disease than smoking, according to an April report by epidemiologist Helen B. Hubert of the National Heart, Lung, and Blood Institute in Bethesda, Md. After reviewing 26 years of data on 5,000 participants in the Framingham (Mass.) Heart Study, Hubert found that weight can contribute directly to heart problems, not just to high blood pressure and cholesterol levels associated with the risk of heart disease.

In February, investigators at the Medical College of Wisconsin in Milwaukee reported that the pattern of body fat in women may be useful in estimating their risk of developing maturity-onset diabetes. Over a six-year period, the researchers observed 52 women with three body types: 25 women were "upper-body obese," with excess weight predominantly in the waist, chest, neck, and arms; 18 were "lower-body obese," with their extra pounds in the hips, buttocks, and thighs; and 9 were of normal weight. Sixty per cent of the upper-body-obese women had a prediabetic condition and 16 per cent had diabetes, but none of the lower-body-obese or normal-weight women showed signs of the disease.

Toxic Shock Syndrome. On June 4, a National Academy of Sciences advisory panel recommended that all women, especially adolescents, "minimize" their use of high-absorbency tampons, which have been linked with the risk of developing Toxic Shock Syndrome (TSS), a rare but sometimes fatal disease. Eighty-five per cent of all cases involved menstruating women. The remainder involved nonmenstruating women, men, or children, half of whom were suffering from skin or surgical wound infections. The panel stated that while the

Steve Kelley in the *San Diego Union*

cause of TSS is not certain, the bacterium *Staphylococcus aureus* was present in most cases.

Scientists speculate that high-absorbency tampons may culture the bacteria that cause TSS. The federal government on June 21 announced it would require warnings on tampon packages.

New Deadly Syndrome. Physicians were baffled and alarmed by the rapid spread in 1982 of a diverse array of medical problems called acquired immune deficiency syndrome (AIDS). These included rare infections and cancers typically found only in the elderly or in the weakened recipients of cancer chemotherapy. Epidemiologist James W. Curran, head of an AIDS task force at the Centers for Disease Control (CDC) in Atlanta, Ga., reported in August that the incidence of AIDS rose from one case per day in the first six months of 1982 to two or three per day in the second half of the year. By October, a total of 684 cases had been reported. About 300 of them were fatal.

Most AIDS victims were previously healthy homosexual men, many of whom reported having numerous sexual partners and using illicit drugs. AIDS also has been diagnosed in several heroin addicts, among a group of Haitian immigrants, and in some hemophiliacs. In December, CDC researchers reported about 20 AIDS cases among children under 2 years of age. Most of the children's mothers were drug abusers; two were Haitian. AIDS victims have immune systems so severely impaired that they cannot fight off diseases and infections. Health officials do not know what causes the syndrome.

Herpes Epidemic. In March, the CDC announced that cases of genital herpes had reached epidemic proportions in the United States. This sexually transmitted disease is caused by herpes simplex viruses and is characterized by painful, recurring sores on the genital organs. Between outbreaks, the virus retreats into nerve cells, where it is safe from the body's immune system.

Researchers continued to search for effective treatments. Acyclovir ointment, the first antiviral drug for the treatment of genital herpes, came on the market in June. According to researchers at the CDC and other centers, acyclovir provides relief of symptoms in first outbreaks of herpes, but it does not prevent recurrences nor relieve symptoms in subsequent outbreaks. In July, scientists at the University of Texas Health Science Center in San Antonio announced development of BIOLF-62, a new drug that might prevent recurrent outbreaks. In December, a herpes research clinic in Seattle announced that it would begin testing a herpes vaccine in 1983. Dianne Hales

See also DRUGS; MEDICINE; PUBLIC HEALTH. In the Special Reports section, see FOOD, FADS, FAT, AND FITNESS. In WORLD BOOK, see HEALTH; DISEASE.

HENDERSON, RICKEY HENLEY (1958-), an Oakland A's outfielder, set a major-league record for stolen bases during the 1982 baseball season. Henderson stole 130 bases, breaking Lou Brock's 1974 record of 118. In addition, he became the first major-league player to steal 100 bases in a season twice.

Unlike Brock, who made a science of stealing bases, Henderson relies chiefly on instinct and speed. Ron Schueler, a coach with the Chicago White Sox, described Henderson's technique by saying: "He simply outruns the ball." Henderson climaxes his steals with a headfirst slide.

Henderson ranks as one of the top leadoff batters in baseball. A right-handed hitter who bats from an exaggerated crouch, he led the major leagues in walks (116) and was fifth in runs scored (119) in 1982. His batting average of .267 was highest on the A's.

Henderson was born on Dec. 25, 1958, in Chicago, and grew up in Oakland, Calif. He starred in baseball and football in high school. In 1980, his first full year in the majors, he stole 100 bases and batted .303. In 1981, he hit .319 and led the American League in hits, runs scored, and stolen bases. That year, he finished second to Rollie Fingers of the Milwaukee Brewers in the voting for the American League's Most Valuable Player Award. William T. Graham

HEPBURN, KATHARINE (1909-), received the Academy of Motion Picture Arts and Sciences Award for best actress on March 29, 1982. She won the Oscar, her fourth, for playing the role of Ethel Thayer in *On Golden Pond.*

Katharine Hepburn was born in Hartford, Conn., on Nov. 8, 1909. She was educated by tutors at home, then at the Hartford School for Girls and Bryn Mawr College, graduating in 1928.

Determined to be an actress, Hepburn went to New York City. By 1932, her Broadway success attracted Hollywood offers. She won her first Oscar the next year, for *Morning Glory.* She originated the role of Tracy Lord in *The Philadelphia Story* on stage, then won a New York Film Critics Award for the movie in 1940.

The actress won her second Oscar for *Guess Who's Coming to Dinner* in 1967. An unprecedented third Academy Award went to Hepburn in 1968 for her performance as Eleanor of Aquitaine in *The Lion in Winter.* She co-starred with John Wayne in a western, *Rooster Cogburn* (1976).

Katharine Hepburn has continued throughout her career to act in plays, notably *Coco* (1969) and *The West Side Waltz* (1981). Marsha F. Goldsmith

HIGHWAY. See BUILDING AND CONSTRUCTION; TRANSPORTATION.

HOBBIES. See COIN COLLECTING; GAMES AND TOYS; STAMP COLLECTING.

HOCKEY. In 1982, for the third consecutive season, the New York Islanders became the National Hockey League (NHL) champions by winning the Stanley Cup. Also for the third consecutive season, Wayne Gretzky of the Edmonton Oilers won the Hart Trophy as the league's Most Valuable Player. The young Edmonton star broke a dozen NHL scoring records (see GRETZKY, WAYNE).

During the regular season, each of the NHL's 21 teams played 80 games from October 1981 to April 1982. The Islanders dominated with 54 victories, 16 defeats, and 10 ties. From January 21 through February 20, they won 15 straight games, breaking the NHL record of 14 set by the Boston Bruins during the 1929-1930 season. The division winners were the Islanders, Edmonton, the Montreal Canadiens, and the Minnesota North Stars.

The Play-Offs. Sixteen teams advanced to the Stanley Cup play-offs. The first round proved harrowing for the favorites. The Islanders needed an overtime goal to beat the lowly Pittsburgh Penguins, 4-3, in the fifth and final game of their series. The Los Angeles Kings eliminated Edmonton in five games, and the Quebec Nordiques upset Montreal in five games. Five of the eight teams in the quarterfinals had losing records, and the Vancouver Canucks reached the finals despite a regular-season record of 30 wins, 33 losses, and 17 ties.

Late in the season, the NHL suspended Vancouver coach Harry Neale for 10 games for grappling with a fan in Quebec. By the time the suspension had ended, interim coach Roger Neilson had the Canucks in the play-offs. Neale, not wanting to interrupt success, exiled himself to the press box, and Neilson remained the coach.

The Vancouver coaching situation made little difference to the Islanders, who swept the Canucks in four games in the finals. The only team to have won more than three straight Stanley Cups was Montreal, which had one streak of five cups (1956-1960) and another of four (1976-1979).

Mike Bossy of the Islanders scored seven goals in the finals, equaling the record set by Jean Beliveau of Montreal in 1956. Bryan Trottier of the Islanders set a play-off record of 23 assists in 19 games.

Gretzky, in his third NHL season, set regular-season records for goals (92), assists (120), points (212), and three-goal games (10). He broke the goals record by 16, the assists record by 11, and the points record by 48. He scored his first 50 goals in 39 games, another record. In January, the 21-year contract he signed in 1979 was renegotiated. His new contract assured him of more than $20 million (Canadian dollars; $1 = U.S. 81 cents on Dec. 31, 1982) over 15 years.

Edmonton Oilers star Wayne Gretzky slips the puck past Don Edwards of the Buffalo Sabres for his record-breaking 77th goal on February 24.

Standings in National Hockey League

Prince of Wales Conference				
Lester Patrick Division	**W.**	**L.**	**T.**	**Pts.**
New York Islanders	54	16	10	118
New York Rangers	39	27	14	92
Philadelphia	38	31	11	87
Pittsburgh	31	36	13	75
Washington	26	41	13	65
Charles F. Adams Division				
Montreal	46	17	17	109
Boston	43	27	10	96
Buffalo	39	26	15	93
Quebec	33	31	16	82
Hartford	21	41	18	60

Clarence Campbell Conference				
James Norris Division	**W.**	**L.**	**T.**	**Pts.**
Minnesota	37	23	20	94
Winnipeg	33	33	14	80
St. Louis	32	40	8	72
Chicago	30	38	12	72
Toronto	20	44	16	56
Detroit	21	47	12	54
Conn Smythe Division				
Edmonton	48	17	15	111
Vancouver	30	33	17	77
Calgary	29	34	17	75
Los Angeles	24	41	15	63
Colorado	18	49	13	49

Scoring Leaders	**Games**	**Goals**	**Assists**	**Points**
Wayne Gretzky, Edmonton	80	92	120	212
Mike Bossy, N.Y. Islanders	80	64	83	147
Peter Stastny, Quebec	80	46	93	139
Dennis Maruk, Washington	80	60	76	136
Bryan Trottier, N.Y. Islanders	80	50	79	129
Denis Savard, Chicago	80	32	87	119
Marcel Dionne, Los Angeles	78	50	67	117
Bobby Smith, Minnesota	80	43	71	114
Dino Ciccarelli, Minnesota	76	55	51	106
Dave Taylor, Los Angeles	78	39	67	106

Leading Goalies (25 or more games)	**Games**	**Goals against**	**Avg.**
Denis Herron, Montreal	27	68	2.64
Rick Wamsley, Montreal	38	101	2.75
Bill Smith, N.Y. Islanders	46	133	2.97
Roland Melanson, N.Y. Islanders	36	114	3.23
Grant Fuhr, Edmonton	48	157	3.31

Awards

Calder Trophy (best rookie) — Dale Hawerchuk, Winnipeg
Hart Trophy (most valuable player) — Wayne Gretzky, Edmonton
Lady Byng Trophy (sportsmanship) — Rick Middleton, Boston
Masterton Trophy (perserverance, dedication to hockey) — Glenn Resch, Colorado
Norris Trophy (best defenseman) — Doug Wilson, Chicago
Ross Trophy (leading scorer) — Wayne Gretzky, Edmonton
Selke Trophy (best defensive forward) — Steve Kasper, Boston
Smythe Trophy (most valuable in Stanley Cup) — Mike Bossy, N.Y. Islanders
Vezina Trophy (most valuable goalie) — Bill Smith, N.Y. Islanders

Gretzky became the first player to win the Hart Trophy by a unanimous vote. He also received the Lester Pearson Award, voted by the players to the person who had contributed most to hockey during the season. The all-star team consisted of Gretzky at center, Bill Smith of the Islanders in goal, Ray Bourque of Boston and Doug Wilson of the Chicago Black Hawks on defense, and Mark Messier of Edmonton and Bossy on wing.

Violence. On January 24, in a game at Vancouver, coach Don Perry of Los Angeles ordered forward Paul Mulvey to join a fight on the ice. Mulvey refused, and the next day Perry told Mulvey he was not wanted on the team. A week later, Mulvey was sent to the minor leagues.

John Ziegler, the NHL president, suspended Perry for 15 games and fined the Kings $5,000. Mulvey felt vindicated, saying, "I'm not going to be a designated assassin who just comes off the bench to fight."

International Competition. The eight-nation world championship took place from April 15 to April 29 in Finland. Russia won the title with nine straight victories and a tie. Czechoslovakia finished second, and Canada, led by Gretzky, placed third. The United States finished last and consequently was not eligible to compete for the 1983 championship. Frank Litsky

In WORLD BOOK, see HOCKEY.

HODEL, DONALD PAUL (1935-), was named secretary of the United States Department of Energy in November 1982 by President Ronald Reagan. Prior to his appointment, Hodel had served as undersecretary of the Department of the Interior. Like Interior Secretary James G. Watt—his close friend for more than a decade—Hodel was distrusted by environmentalists, who said he was indifferent to conserving natural resources.

Hodel was born in Portland, Ore., on May 23, 1935. He graduated from Harvard University in Cambridge, Mass., in 1957 and later earned a law degree at the University of Oregon in Eugene.

In 1969, Hodel became deputy administrator of the Bonneville Power Administration, a huge electric transmission system in the Northwest. As administrator, from 1972 to 1977, he made enemies among environmentalists by minimizing conservation efforts and advocating the construction of nuclear power plants. From 1978 to 1980, Hodel served as president of the National Electric Reliability Council, an organization of electric utilities.

Hodel became undersecretary of the interior in January 1981, when Watt took over that department. Reagan Administration sources said Hodel was chosen to head the Energy Department, in part because he would work hard to carry out the President's desire to abolish it. David L. Dreier

See also CABINET, UNITED STATES.

Major Horse Races of 1982		
Race	Winner	Value to Winner
Belmont Stakes	Conquistador Cielo	$159,720
Benson & Hedges Gold Cup (England)	Assert	139,510
Budweiser Million	Perrault	600,000
Epsom Derby (England)	Golden Fleece	236,217
Grand National Steeplechase (England)	Grittar	99,512
Irish Sweeps Derby	Assert	190,000
Jockey Club Gold Cup	Lemhi Gold	339,000
Kentucky Derby	Gato Del Sol	428,850
King George VI & Queen Elizabeth Diamond Stakes (England)	Kalaglow	224,045
Marlboro Cup Handicap	Lemhi Gold	240,000
Preakness	Aloma's Ruler	209,900
Prix de l'Arc de Triomphe (France)	Akiyda	288,000
Prix du Jockey-Club (France)	Assert	145,985
Rothmans International	Majesty's Prince	251,790
Santa Anita Handicap	John Henry	318,800
Washington, D.C., International	April Run	150,000
Woodward Stakes	Island Whirl	136,500

Major U.S. Harness Races of 1982		
Race	Winner	Value to Winner
Cane Pace	Cam Fella	$153,998
Hambletonian	Speed Bowl	437,500
Little Brown Jug	Merger	99,492
Meadowlands Pace	Hilarion	500,000
Messenger Stakes	Cam Fella	116,809
Roosevelt International	Ideal du Gazeau	125,000
Woodrow Wilson Memorial Pace	Fortune Teller	978,750

HONDURAS. Roberto Suazo Córdova took office on Jan. 27, 1982, as president of Honduras. He was the nation's first elected head of state in 10 years. See SUAZO CÓRDOVA, ROBERTO.

The 54-year-old physician had no sooner taken office and set Honduras on an austerity course than his administration was forced to contend with the threat of war from neighboring Nicaragua. Both sides repeatedly charged the other with armed incursions and other border violations.

The United States, anxious to offset Nicaragua's apparent support for subversion among its Central American neighbors, stepped in to help Honduras. The U.S. supplied arms, military aid, and advisers during the year, and U.S. troops participated with Honduran forces in maneuvers along the Nicaraguan border. Moreover, U.S. officials confirmed that undercover assistance was being provided to Nicaraguan exiles in Honduras who opposed the leftist government in their own country.

The Honduran economy was hit hard by shortfalls in earnings from coffee and bananas, plus the high cost of fuel imports. The number of Hondurans unemployed or working for less than the minimum wage stood at 60 per cent. Nathan A. Haverstock

See also LATIN AMERICA (Facts in Brief Table). In the Special Reports section, see WHAT WENT WRONG IN CENTRAL AMERICA? In WORLD BOOK, see HONDURAS.

HORSE RACING. No outstanding horse dominated thoroughbred racing in 1982. The year was marred by the deaths of two top horses and injuries to several others.

At first, John Henry, the 1981 Horse of the Year, seemed likely to repeat as champion in 1982. On March 7 at Santa Anita Park in Arcadia, Calif., the 7-year-old gelding became the first horse ever to win the Santa Anita Handicap twice. After his next race, however, John Henry was sidelined with an ankle ailment.

Perrault emerged as the probable successor to John Henry by winning the Budweiser Million, held on August 29 at Arlington Park in Illinois. But Perrault was injured in the Marlboro Cup Handicap at Belmont Park near New York City on September 18. Lemhi Gold, winner of that race and the Jockey Club Gold Cup at the same track on October 9, then became a leading candidate for 1982 Horse of the Year honors. Another contender was Copelan, a 2-year-old colt who finished in front in his first six races, though he was disqualified in one of them.

The Triple Crown for 3-year-olds was split among three horses. Gato Del Sol won the Kentucky Derby on May 1, Aloma's Ruler took the Preakness on May 15, and Conquistador Cielo defeated both of them in the Belmont Stakes on June 5. Conquistador Cielo won seven consecutive races during the year but was bothered by strained ligaments. He was retired to stud in August after his syndication for a record $36.4 million, and in January 1983 was named 1982 Horse of the Year.

Timely Writer, the early favorite to win the Kentucky Derby, missed that race because of a severe intestinal ailment. In October, the horse shattered his left foreleg in a spill in the Jockey Club Gold Cup and was humanely destroyed.

Landaluce, a 2-year-old filly sired by 1977 Triple Crown winner Seattle Slew, won her first five races but died of an infection in November.

At the Keeneland sales in Lexington, Ky., on July 19, Englishman Robert Sangster bought a son of Nijinsky II for $4.25 million, the highest price ever paid for an auction yearling.

Harness Racing. Genghis Khan set a world record for a pacer when he ran a mile in 1 minute 51⅕ seconds on August 13 at the Meadowlands in New Jersey. But his record fell on August 22, when the 3-year-old pacer Trenton ran a 1:51⅗ mile at Springfield, Ill. Speed Bowl won the Hambletonian at the Meadowlands on August 7.

Quarter Horse Racing. Mr. Master Bug won the $2.35-million All-American Futurity, held on September 6 at Ruidoso Downs, N. Mex. The horse earned $1 million. Jane Goldstein

In WORLD BOOK, see HARNESS RACING; HORSE RACING.

HOSPITAL. Unions representing almost a million hospital workers in Great Britain staged "industrial actions" throughout 1982 in an attempt to force pay concessions from the British government, sharply curtailing hospital services. The Confederation of Health Service Employees took a variety of job actions, including a five-day walkout in August and a 120,000-person protest march in September to back demands for a 12 per cent pay increase. The government of Prime Minister Margaret Thatcher offered a 7.5 per cent pay hike to nurses and 6 per cent to other employees. The dispute was settled in December when the unions accepted the government's offer.

In the United States, physicians in training at the Brooklyn Veterans Administration (VA) Medical Center in New York City organized the nation's first union of federal hospital physicians in August. The new union joined ranks with the 25-year-old Committee of Interns and Residents, a New York-New Jersey union with 5,000 nonfederal-employee members. Observers believed this action might encourage the more than 7,000 interns and residents who train at VA centers each year—and draw their pay from the federal government—to unionize.

Go-Ahead for CT Scanners. In June, the U.S. government moved to drop its curbs on hospital purchases of computerized tomography (CT) scanners—also known as CAT scanners. Since 1978, hospitals applying for the sophisticated X-ray machines had faced federal rules designed to limit scanner sales to 200 per year. However, a 1981 Consensus Development Conference on CT Scanners, sponsored by the National Institutes of Health, found that CT scanning is often less costly than exploratory surgery and other diagnostic procedures and reported a need for more scanners in both rural and metropolitan areas.

Hospital Costs. While health care costs continued to spiral upward in 1982, the rate of hospital-cost increases for the first quarter of 1982 dropped, according to data reported in September by the American Hospital Association's (AHA) Voluntary Effort to Contain Health Care Costs. AHA officials said total hospital increases had risen 16.8 per cent during the first three months of 1982, compared with increases of 18.6 to 20 per cent per quarter in 1981.

The financial problems of U.S. hospitals, however, will get worse rather than better in the 1980s, according to expert testimony before the National Council for Health Planning and Development, which advises the U.S. Department of Health and Human Services. The council was told that U.S. hospitals will need almost $200 billion in the 1980s to repair and replace deteriorating buildings.

Dianne Hales

In WORLD BOOK, see HOSPITAL.

HOUSING. Homebuilding in 1982 continued a decline that began in 1978 but began to pick up remarkably toward the end of the year as mortgage rates declined. The National Association of Home Builders (NAHB) had predicted that the slump in housing starts during the first eight months of the year would reduce actual starts in 1982 to 1.050 million, down from 1.084 million in 1981 and the lowest annual production in 36 years. Forecasts of a continuing drop in interest rates, however, led the NAHB to predict a "modest recovery" in 1983 to about 1.3 million units, and some builders were predicting 1.5 million. That would raise homebuilding activity to the 1980 level but would be well below the 2 million starts in 1978.

Housing starts during the first nine months of 1982 totaled 758,300, a more than 13 per cent slide from the 873,300 units begun in the same period in 1981. But a decrease in conventional mortgage rates from a historic high of 18.5 per cent in 1981 to 14 per cent or less by September 1982 produced a construction surge during that month. That trend accelerated in October, when starts were up 31 per cent over October 1981.

Home Prices. Buyers of new homes paid a median price of $73,600 in July, up 5.9 per cent from $69,500 in 1981. In September 1982, however, the median price was only $69,000. The median price of houses sold in 1981 was $68,900, an increase of 6.9 per cent over the $64,500 price in 1980.

Existing homes sold at a median price of $69,200 in July 1982. Buyers paid the highest prices in the West ($100,300) and the lowest in the North Central region ($55,300), compared with a nationwide median sales price of $66,400 in 1981. Home resales fell to a seasonally adjusted rate of 1.8 million units in August 1982, 20 per cent below 1981.

The United States Bureau of the Census reported that rental costs, including utilities, rose 81 per cent between 1973 and 1980, from a median of $133 per month to $241. In the same period, renters' median family income increased 46 per cent, from $7,200 to $10,500.

Mortgage Money. Withdrawals exceeded deposits by $15.2 billion at the nation's thrift institutions during the first six months of 1982. This came on top of a $39.3-billion outflow in 1981. The federal government had hoped to increase deposits available for home loans by means of tax-exempt all-savers certificates, but results proved disappointing.

The Federal Home Loan Bank Board (FHLBB) issued regulations in 1981 allowing mortgage rates to fluctuate with the cost of funds to lending institutions. An increasing number of new mortgages used this system in 1982. Indexes used to compute such adjustable mortgages include the rate on six-month Treasury bills and the average rate on ex-

A section of a prefabricated home, an economical housing option, is lowered into place at an Orlando, Fla., building site.

isting home purchases as calculated by the FHLBB.

Alternative Financing Techniques, or creative financing, became a popular means of buying a home in 1982. These financing alternatives include *graduated payment mortgages,* which allow buyers to make smaller monthly payments in the early years of a loan. Payments increase until they reach a fixed amount. Another arrangement permits the buyer to assume an existing mortgage, make a large down payment, and repay the difference on the value of the home with a second loan. When the mortgage is not assumable, sellers can arrange a *wraparound* that combines the old mortgage payment with the new one. Buyers also can enter into a *lease-purchase agreement,* leasing a house for 12 to 18 months and then applying a portion of the rent to a down payment. A *land lease* enables a buyer to own a home but not the land it stands on, which is simply leased to the purchaser. This reduces the down payment required. *Equity sharing* allows a resident owner and an investment owner to share in the purchase of a home. Some builders or developers, acting as bankers, offer *zero-interest mortgages* for part or all of the mortgage term. However, these "buy down," or subsidized, interest rates typically involve a large down payment and, often, a higher base price. William J. Cromie

In WORLD BOOK, see HOUSE; HOUSING.

HOUSTON. Kathryn J. Whitmire, Houston's first woman mayor, took office on Jan. 2, 1982. She promised to improve the city's basic services—to do something about Houston's rising crime rate, pothole-riddled streets, traffic congestion, and inadequate sewage and garbage-collection systems. A certified public accountant and Houston's city controller before being elected mayor, Whitmire stressed the need to run the city like "the large and complex business that it is."

New Police Chief. In March, Whitmire named Atlanta (Ga.) Public Safety Commissioner Lee P. Brown as Houston's first black police chief. Brown, a 22-year law enforcement veteran with a Ph.D. degree in criminology from the University of California at Berkeley, was the first black to become police chief of a large American city where the mayor was not black.

Top police officials in Houston were almost unanimous in opposing Brown's nomination for the $75,000-a-year job and criticized the mayor for not selecting someone from within the 3,200-member Houston Police Department. Some police officials said they did not expect problems because of Brown's race, but others said that acceptance of a black police chief within a department that was only 8 per cent black, with no blacks above the rank of sergeant, might not come easily. The City Council disregarded such cautions and confirmed Brown's appointment.

City Council Actions. In June, the City Council approved an increase in property taxes of 1 cent per $100 of assessed valuation to pay for additional police services. The tax hike was to be used for overtime pay and to hire greater numbers of civilian employees, in order to free up to 300 uniformed officers for patrol duty. The extra police protection was needed; Houston's major crime rate rose 17.7 per cent in 1982, the largest increase for any American city.

A few days later, the council approved a $1.03-billion budget for fiscal 1983, 17.3 per cent higher than for 1982. The new budget included $7 million for merit pay raises for city employees, who traditionally had received cost-of-living raises.

Controlled Development. Because Houstonians historically have rejected every attempt to establish city zoning laws, urban development has often been chaotic. The City Council finally took action on June 22 to control Houston's unbridled growth. The council adopted an ordinance requiring, among other things, that all buildings be set back a minimum distance from streets and that all proposed building projects be reviewed and approved by the City Planning Commission.

Major Construction Projects announced for Houston in 1982 included an 82-story office tower that will be the tallest building in the world outside of New York City and Chicago and a mass

Mayor Kathryn J. Whitmire introduces Lee P. Brown, first black to serve as Houston's police chief, and his wife, Yvonne, in March.

transit rail system designed to relieve the city's critical traffic-congestion problem. The rail system was approved on September 29 by the Metropolitan Transit Authority of Harris County. The still-incomplete plans called for an 18.2-mile (29.3-kilometer) rail line from the city's west side through the downtown area. Transit officials favored an elevated line, rather than a subway, in the central business district because it would be cheaper to build. Downtown merchants, however, spoke out against that proposal, and, on November 30, the City Council rejected it.

Economic Slump. The economic problems that had plagued the rest of the nation for several years finally hit Houston in 1982. The city had seemed immune to recession, thanks to the strength of the energy business, much of which is centered in Houston. But the worldwide crude-oil glut, which led to a severe cutback in oil-well drilling in 1982, combined with the sagging United States economy, caused Houston to start feeling the economic pinch. From January to July, Houston's industrial production declined by 4.1 per cent, the first time since at least the mid-1960s that the city's industrial output had not grown. By September, the unemployment rate in the Houston area had soared to a post-World War II high of 8.2 per cent, compared with 4.8 per cent in September 1981. Pat Reed

See also CITY. In WORLD BOOK, see HOUSTON.

HUNGARY continued its economic reform program in 1982, though economic growth slowed. Western nations helped Hungary overcome serious financial problems during the year. After Poland imposed martial law in December 1981, non-Communist banks withdrew more than $1 billion worth of short-term deposits from Hungary. Hungary's reserves of gold and hard currency fell from $1.8 billion in January 1982 to $374 million at the end of March.

In May, Hungary joined the International Monetary Fund (IMF), a United Nations (UN) agency that seeks to help its member countries achieve economic growth, high employment, and improved standards of living. In July, Hungary affiliated with the World Bank, a UN agency that loans money to countries for development projects. In August, Hungary received a three-year, $260-million loan from a group of Western commercial banks led by Manufacturers Hanover Trust Company of New York City. And in November, Hungary signed an agreement with the IMF for a three-year, $508-million loan. During 1982, Hungary received $510 million in short-term credits from the Bank for International Settlements in Basel, Switzerland—the bank used by various nations' central banks.

Hungary granted foreign trading rights to 27 business enterprises in 1982. In July, the government lifted various restrictions on private retail businesses and on drivers of private taxis and trucks.

Hungary's Exports during the first eight months of 1982 were 1.9 per cent higher than in the same period in 1981. Imports were up 0.6 per cent. Industrial production increased by 1.5 per cent in the first nine months of 1982, compared with the same period in 1981. Hungary's industrial labor force declined by 1.8 per cent during the first nine months of 1982, but productivity increased by 3 per cent. The government hiked consumer prices three times during the year. Hungary reduced its trade deficit with the non-Communist world to $375 million in the first half of 1982, from $406-million a year earlier.

Foreign Relations. Prime Minister Gyorgy Lazar visited Romania in July for talks with that nation's prime minister, Constantin Dascalescu. The two leaders failed to resolve the long-standing dispute over the treatment of the Hungarian minority in the Transylvania area of Romania.

Relations with Czechoslovakia improved. That country had long been a critic of Hungary's economic reforms. In July, Hungary's policies, especially in agriculture, were praised by Gyorgy Aczel, a high-ranking member of Czechoslovakia's Communist Party. Chris Cviic

In WORLD BOOK, see HUNGARY.

HUNTING. In March 1982, the United States Fish and Wildlife Service released statistics from a comprehensive survey on hunting conducted by the U.S. Bureau of the Census. According to the survey, conducted in 1980, 17 million hunters spent $5.5 billion on the sport. The report also revealed that the most popular type of hunting was small-game hunting (12.4 million people), followed by big-game hunting (11.8 million) and migratory bird hunting (5.3 million).

The survey also indicated that hunting was growing in popularity. The United States population grew at an annual rate of 1 per cent, while the number of hunters increased 1.8 per cent.

Many hunters supported legislation introduced in Congress in August that would reopen 12 million acres (4.9 million hectares) of land in Alaska to hunting. A fierce battle over the proposal was expected in 1983. The Alaska National Interest Lands Conservation Act of 1980 permits hunting in about 19 million acres (7.7 million hectares) of land in Alaska's national parks. Hunters complained, however, that some of the best hunting areas remained closed.

High levels of endrin and other toxic pesticides were found in ducks in Montana. Wildlife officials in that state advised hunters to eat only a few waterfowl. Andrew L. Newman

In WORLD BOOK, see AMMUNITION; HUNTING.

ICE SKATING. Sixteen-year-old Elaine Zayak of Paramus, N.J., won her first women's world figure-skating title in 1982 after an uphill struggle. Scott Hamilton, 23, of Denver, won the men's title for the second straight year.

The Winners. The world championships were held from March 9 to 14 near Copenhagen, Denmark. Zayak, the 1981 runner-up, was favored to win the women's title, though she had fallen on three of seven triple jumps in the United States championships six weeks before and finished third.

Zayak fell again during the short program in the world championships and entered the final day's free skating in seventh place. She cried for an hour before that competition because she thought she had no chance to win. But the six leaders faltered, and she did seven successful triple jumps—each better than the one before—and won.

Hamilton also performed seven triple jumps in winning the men's singles title. He and Zayak gave the United States its first singles sweep since David Jenkins and Carol Heiss won in 1959. Sabine Baess and Tassilo Thierbach of East Germany took the pairs championship. The brother-and-sister team of Peter and Caitlin (Kitty) Carruthers of Wilmington, Del., placed third. Christopher Dean and Jayne Torvill of Great Britain retained the dance title.

Scott Hamilton of Denver shows the form that won him the men's world figure-skating title in March. He also won the United States title in January.

In the U.S. championships, held in January in Indianapolis, all the 1981 titlists except Zayak repeated. Hamilton won the men's championship, the Carruthers team won the pairs, and Michael Siebert of Indianapolis and Judy Blumberg of Woodland Hills, Calif., took the dance. Seventeen-year-old Rosalyn Sumners of Edmonds, Wash., succeeded Zayak as the women's titlist.

Speed Skating. The year's four major world championships—men's senior and sprint and women's senior and sprint—took place in February. Hilbert van der Duim, a 24-year-old Dutchman, captured the gold medal in the men's senior championship at Assen, the Netherlands. Karin Busch of East Germany took the women's senior title at Inzell, West Germany. At Alkmaar, the Netherlands, Natalia Petruseva of Russia won the women's sprints and Sergei Khlebnikov took the men's sprints. Gaetan Boucher of Canada finished second in the men's sprints.

The top American finishers were 17-year-old Sarah Docter of Madison, Wis., and 18-year-old Nick Thometz of Minnetonka, Minn. Docter placed fifth in the women's senior, and Thometz finished sixth in the men's sprints. Frank Litsky

In WORLD BOOK, see ICE SKATING.

ICELAND. See EUROPE.
IDAHO. See STATE GOVERNMENT.
ILLINOIS. See CHICAGO; STATE GOVERNMENT.

IMMIGRATION. Congress in 1982 moved closer to enacting a landmark immigration bill to stem the growing influx of illegal aliens, mostly from Mexico, into the United States. Although the Senate passed such legislation, 81-18, on August 17, the House of Representatives version of the bill had still not come to a floor vote by the time Congress adjourned. It was considered likely that an immigration bill would be approved in 1983.

The House and Senate Versions of the bill were broadly similar but differed in many details. Both bills would have granted amnesty to foreigners who had been living illegally in the United States for several years, and both provided penalties for employers who hire illegal aliens. The amnesty provisions of the bills would have established a two-tiered system for granting legal-resident status to aliens who entered the country without permission. Aliens who moved to the United States before Jan. 1, 1977, and had lived there continuously since then would be eligible for permanent-resident status. Those arriving between Jan. 1, 1977, and the end of 1979 could become temporary residents. Temporary residents could become permanent residents after three years. After five years as a permanent resident, an alien could apply for U.S. citizenship. Aliens who arrived in the United States after Jan. 1, 1980, would not be eligible for amnesty and could be deported.

The bills stipulated further that aliens who accepted amnesty would be ineligible for at least three years to receive Medicaid, food stamps, and other federal welfare benefits. Employers hiring aliens who had not received permission to live and work in the United States would be subject to fines and jail sentences. The penalties varied between the House and Senate bills, with the House version being the stronger of the two—providing a maximum sentence for repeat offenders of a year in prison and a fine of $3,000 per illegal alien.

Amerasian Children. On October 22, President Ronald Reagan signed into law an amendment to the Immigration and Nationality Act that will allow thousands of illegitimate Asian-born children of American servicemen to immigrate to the United States. Under the provisions of the amendment, a child born after 1950 in Vietnam, Cambodia, Laos, Thailand, or Korea, and whose American paternity can be proved beyond a reasonable doubt, will be permitted to come to the United States as a permanent resident. Each child must have an American sponsor—a family or charitable agency—that guarantees to support him or her for at least five years, or until the child reaches age 21. Estimates of the number of eligible children range from 20,000 to 80,000.

Haitian Refugees. A yearlong controversy over the treatment of Haitian refugees reached the courts in 1982. Thousands of Haitians come to the United States each year to escape the poverty and political oppression in their country. In 1981, the U.S. government stopped treating the Haitians as political refugees and instead began to hold them in detention camps on charges of illegal entry.

A federal judge in Miami, Fla., on June 29, 1982, ordered the U.S. Department of Justice to release most of the 1,900 Haitians being held in camps. The U.S. Court of Appeals in Atlanta, Ga., upheld the order, and on July 23 the first group of refugees was paroled. By the end of October, all the Haitians had been released. However, at year-end it was still uncertain whether the refugees would be allowed to stay in the United States.

New Commissioner. Alan C. Nelson, a deputy commissioner of the U.S. Immigration and Naturalization Service (INS), was confirmed by the Senate on February 8 as the service's new commissioner.

The INS conducted a roundup of illegal aliens at work sites in nine cities from April 26 to 30, arresting 5,635 persons. Immigration officials persuaded 4,071 of the aliens to leave the country voluntarily. In reply to protests from civil liberties groups and Hispanic leaders, the INS said it was trying to open jobs for Americans. William J. Eaton

In WORLD BOOK, see IMMIGRATION.
INCOME TAX. See TAXATION.

INDIA elected a new president on July 12, 1982—Zail Singh, a former minister of home affairs. Singh was selected by Prime Minister Indira Gandhi, the actual head of the government, to succeed Neelam Sanjiva Reddy in the largely ceremonial position of president. Singh was the first member of India's Sikh religious minority to hold the post.

In Sanjiva Reddy's final Republic Day address—noting the anniversary of India's Constitution—the outgoing president warned on January 25 that Indian democracy was threatened by the growth of violence and corruption. He said that living conditions of the poor had not improved, and "the fruits of development are beyond the reach of a large number." A nationwide strike, resulting in thousands of arrests, had been held on January 19 to protest the government's economic policies.

A Police Revolt in August in Bombay, India's largest city, resulted in five deaths and more than 100 injuries. A commission established by Gandhi's predecessor had investigated police complaints about low pay and bad working conditions. The panel completed its study in 1981, but the Gandhi government had failed to take action on any of its recommendations. Police demonstrations over their grievances erupted into the rioting in Bombay on August 18 and 19. The army was called to restore order. Similar, but less violent, cases of police unrest were reported in other areas.

Corruption in High Places was revealed in Bombay. The high court there convicted the chief minister of Maharashtra state, Abdul R. Antulay, of extortion. Antulay resigned on January 13. He had been a close political associate of Gandhi.

As India's press continued to expose corruption, it was reported in March that the government for the first time banned an article before publication. The article, by *India Today* magazine, examined business dealings of a political ally of Sanjay Gandhi, the prime minister's son, who died in 1980.

Sanjay's Widow, Maneka, sought to keep his political following together, despite Indira Gandhi's desire to fill Sanjay's role as her deputy and political heir with her other son, Rajiv. After Maneka defied Indira by speaking at a rally of Sanjay's supporters, Maneka said in March that she had been driven from the prime minister's household. The ouster created a scandal because Indian customs call for widows to be given shelter and other necessities by their husband's relatives.

On August 26, Maneka formed a political party called Sanjay Vichar Manch (Platform for Sanjay's Views). In September, three party leaders were arrested on a murder charge, and she accused Indira of trying to suppress dissent.

State Elections in four states on May 19 showed that support for Gandhi's Congress-I (I for Indira) Party was slipping. Her party won outright in only one state, Kerala. It failed to win legislative majorities in Haryana or Himachal Pradesh, but in both states it managed to assemble a coalition of minority parties and form a government. In West Bengal, a Marxist-led coalition that had ruled for five years remained in power.

Zail Singh, a member of India's Sikh religious community, accepts congratulations after being elected president of India on July 12.

Demands for an independent Sikh state caused violence in Punjab state and in New Delhi, India's capital. The government banned two extremist Sikh groups on May 2 after a week of violence between Hindus and Sikhs in Punjab. Trouble continued, including three airplane hijackings by Sikhs demanding the release of imprisoned Sikh extremists. When Sikhs tried to storm the parliament building in New Delhi on October 11, police gunfire killed four protesters. Trouble spread to Punjab, adding to violence that killed more than 50 persons during the late summer and fall.

The Economy suffered from a severe drought—the worst in 50 years—that by October had raised fears of starvation for 100 million people. Foreign aid donors promised $3.6 billion for 1982-1983, but India's industrial growth made it difficult to qualify for low-interest loans and other favorable aid terms. India launched its first commercial space satellite in April, but by September the satellite had stopped working. Henry S. Bradsher

See also ASIA (Facts in Brief Table). In WORLD BOOK, see INDIA.

INDIAN, AMERICAN. Plans by the United States Department of the Interior to reorganize the Bureau of Indian Affairs (BIA) were sharply attacked by Indian tribes in 1982. Spokespersons for tribes throughout the country asked Congress on June 11 to head off Interior Secretary James G. Watt's proposal to save $6 million by closing several BIA offices. The Indians charged in testimony before the Senate Select Committee on Indian Affairs that the plan to consolidate 12 area offices into seven regional "service centers" and to lay off 372 BIA employees was put together without adequate consultation with Indians.

The reorganization proposal, hailed as the first major streamlining of BIA in 30 years, was announced on May 28 and promptly condemned by the National Congress of American Indians. Assistant Secretary for Indian Affairs Kenneth L. Smith said some 500 tribal leaders were consulted, but he conceded the tribes "felt we had made reorganization decisions without consultation." Smith is a member of the Wasco tribe, which lives on the Warm Springs Reservation in Oregon. The first American Indian to come directly from a reservation to Washington's top Indian job, Smith said the intent of the plan was to get the tribes to take over much of the work now being done by federal employees. Smith has stressed to tribal leaders that Indians must become less dependent on the federal government.

Sioux Land Demands. The long struggle by the Oglala Sioux tribe to regain ownership of the Black Hills of South Dakota received a fatal blow on January 18 when the Supreme Court of the United States refused to hear their appeal. The tribe had appealed a decision of a lower court that limited the Indians to cash compensation rather than returning the land itself. The Oglalas had asked for the land plus $11 billion.

In 1980, the Supreme Court awarded $122.5-million to eight Sioux tribes as compensation and interest for the federal government's seizure of the Black Hills through an 1877 act of Congress. The Oglala Sioux said they would not be bound by a monetary settlement and would be satisfied only by restoration of the land.

Sioux tribal leaders decided on June 28, 1982, to ask Congress to give them 3.2 million acres (1.3 million hectares) of federal and state land in the Black Hills. They said they wanted to turn the 5,000 square miles (13,000 square kilometers) of land into an Indian park to be used for religious purposes. Federal officials said there is not that much federal land in the area.

Navajo-Hopi Dispute. The Navajo tribe, the largest in the United States, continued to battle the relocation of some tribal members ordered by a 1974 law in an effort to settle a century-old dispute between the Navajos and Hopis over thousands of acres of Arizona desert. The 1974 law split 1.8 million acres (730,000 hectares) between the tribes. About 8,000 Navajo and 100 Hopi Indians living on the wrong side of the dividing line were ordered to move. A federal judge on August 3 ordered the Navajo tribe to pay a $19,000 contempt fine and post a $75,000 bond for failing to comply with a court order in the dispute.

Tribal Taxes Upheld. The Supreme Court ruled on January 25 that Indian tribes can tax the production of oil, gas, and other minerals on their reservations. The 6 to 3 decision gave the tribes the right to impose severance taxes—a tax on the amount of the commodity produced during a certain period—unless explicitly prohibited by Congress. The ruling could cost energy companies millions of dollars. Indian reservations hold significant amounts of coal, oil, gas, and uranium. In 1976, about 30 tribes formed the Council of Energy Resource Tribes and began a vigorous campaign to obtain a maximum financial return from the leasing of their resources. The BIA proposed regulations to prescribe the way Indian tribes can enact severance taxes. The rules require the tribes to prepare an "economic impact" statement to assess the effect of the tax on mineral production, on consumers, and on tribal revenues. Andrew L. Newman

In WORLD BOOK, see INDIAN, AMERICAN.

INDIANA. See STATE GOVERNMENT.

INDONESIA elected a new parliament on May 4, 1982. Sekber Golongan Karya (Golkar), the government-supported political group that technically is not a political party, won 246 of the 364 elected seats in parliament with more than 60 per cent of the votes. An additional 100 members of parliament are appointed by the president, and Golkar had the support of many of the appointees as well.

The bitter and violent 45-day campaign took 59 lives, starting with three deaths during rioting at a Golkar rally in Jakarta, Indonesia's capital, on March 18. No real debate was permitted, and the government banned newspapers from writing about campaign violence. Golkar was opposed by Muslim and nationalist parties, forced to merge under government pressure into two coalitions, one religious and the other nonreligious.

Four Bills passed by the new parliament provided a legal basis for the armed forces' long-time control of both military and civilian affairs in Indonesia. One of the laws gave the armed forces power over the use of strategic materials and over facilities for communications, industry, and agriculture. The law also recognized military control of the police.

Foreign Relations. Indonesia's President Suharto made a two-week trip to Spain, the United States, South Korea, and Japan during October. On October 12, United States President Ronald Reagan

Government troops move in to put down rioting that erupted at a political campaign rally in Jakarta, the capital of Indonesia, on March 18.

named the Department of State's assistant secretary for East Asian and Pacific affairs, John H. Holdridge, as U.S. ambassador to Indonesia. The post had been vacant for almost a year, disturbing U.S.-Indonesian relations.

During Suharto's visit to the United States, Holdridge played down questions about reports of famine and human rights abuses in East Timor. East Timor is a former Portuguese territory that Indonesia invaded in 1975 and annexed in 1976 over American protests. Some guerrilla resistance to Indonesian rule reportedly continued there and in Irian Jaya, the western part of New Guinea.

The Indonesian government expelled a Soviet Embassy military attaché on February 5, accusing him of espionage. As he left the next day, a scuffle at Jakarta airport led to the additional deportation of a Soviet airline representative, also believed connected with Soviet intelligence.

The Economy. The worldwide drop in oil sales and prices during 1982 hurt Indonesia, which depended on oil for 66 per cent of its export earnings in the first half of the year. Exports other than oil and gas dropped 42 per cent from January to June. A foreign exchange surplus of $2.5 billion for the 1980-1981 fiscal year became a $2.5-billion deficit in 1981-1982. Henry S. Bradsher

See also ASIA (Facts in Brief Table). In WORLD BOOK, see INDONESIA.

INSURANCE. For the third year in a row, buoyed by heady investment gains, property and casualty insurance companies in the United States in 1982 continued competitive price cutting on large commercial premiums. At year-end, the underwriting loss, estimated at $10.4 billion, was more than $4.05 billion above the $6.35 billion loss for 1981. This means that insurers' losses exceeded by $10.4 billion the estimated $101.9 billion in premiums earned for 1982. In 1981, losses exceeded the estimated $97.5 billion in earned premiums by $6.35 billion. However, investment gains of $14.9 billion for 1982 and $13.3 billion for 1981 provided operating gains.

Expressed in terms of the combined loss ratio (CLR) — the amount insurance companies pay out for every dollar of premium income — insurance and securities analysts expected 1982 to show even worse results. They projected an average 111 per cent CLR for all of 1982, meaning that some companies would have CLR ratios as high as 115 per cent. For 1981, the CLR average was 106 per cent, with some companies' ratios up to 110 per cent. If a company's CLR overtakes its offsetting investment gain, a negative cash flow results and the company may go bankrupt.

Reorganization Went Ahead despite the bleak outlook. Xerox Corporation on September 21 announced its agreement to acquire Crum & Forster, a giant insurance holding company, for about $1.65 billion. The acquisition was expected to become final in early 1983. Two unusual moves involved major insurance companies taking over major brokerage firms. On November 11, Transamerica Corporation announced an agreement to acquire the fourth largest insurance brokerage company in the United States, Fred S. James & Company, Incorporated. A second such agreement, between Combined International Corporation and Rollins Burdick Hunter Company, also got underway in November.

Legislation. President Ronald Reagan on September 3 signed the voluminous Tax Equity and Fiscal Responsibility Act of 1982, which includes six major areas affecting pension and retirement plans. Effective in stages over a period of years, the law revises the tax status of such programs as individual pension plans and universal-life policies — a new form of insurance combining whole-life features with an investment factor.

On October 12, the President signed the Anti-Arson Act of 1982, a bill strongly supported by the insurance industry. The new law makes arson a crime reportable by the Federal Bureau of Investigation. It broadens federal jurisdiction in arson cases where explosives are used and when the crime affects interstate commerce by occurring, for example, in one hotel of a chain.

On October 15, President Reagan approved the

Garn-St. Germain Depository Institutions Act of 1982. It includes Title VI, which prohibits bank holding companies with assets of $50 million or more from acting as principal, agent, or broker for most types of property and casualty insurance. Among the few exceptions are bank holding companies already engaged in the insurance business and those with approved applications or applications on file with the Federal Reserve Board prior to May 1, 1982.

On October 25, Reagan signed a law authorizing use of $125 million from the Highway Trust Fund to establish a program encouraging states to enact and enforce stiffer drunk-driving laws. The law established minimum standards for the states to follow regarding alcohol content of the blood, suspension of driving privileges, and conviction penalties.

Miscellaneous. The Illinois Insurance Exchange, which functions as a market place for high-risk and hard-to-place insurance, opened its Chicago offices on Jan. 1, 1982. The Insurance Exchange of the Americas, a similar group, opened in October in Miami, Fla. The New York Insurance Exchange, operating in New York City since March 31, 1980, got new powers in 1982 to write excess and surplus risks in all states where it is approved except New York. Emanuel Levy

In WORLD BOOK, see INSURANCE.

INTERNATIONAL TRADE AND FINANCE. The worldwide recession deepened in 1982. For the first time since 1975, the industrial nations registered no overall economic growth. The less developed countries had an equally dismal year—for the first time since World War II, their per capita output declined.

Unemployment worsened. Almost 12 million Americans, nearly 11 per cent of the work force, were jobless at year-end, the highest rate since the Great Depression of the 1930s, when unemployment reached about 25 per cent and remained above 14 per cent through 1940. In the 10-nation European Community (EC or Common Market), about 11.5 million people were unemployed, more than 10 per cent of the work force.

The industrial countries, led by the United States, made substantial progress in reducing inflation, however. The U.S. inflation rate fell to about 5 per cent, the lowest annual rate since 1976. Overall, inflation in the industrial nations averaged about 7 per cent, compared with more than 9 per cent in 1981. In the developing countries, however, inflation rose again, approaching an average of 40 per cent.

Although interest rates in the industrial nations dropped as inflation declined, they remained exceptionally high. United States interest rates, higher than those in other key industrial countries, maintained the attractiveness of the dollar on foreign-exchange markets.

World Trade fell in value for the second successive year. Worldwide government holdings of foreign reserve assets—mainly the dollar, other hard currencies, and gold—declined for the first time since 1965. Primary commodity prices, if adjusted for inflation, were the lowest in more than 30 years. The weighted average price of crude oil on world markets fell by about $1 per barrel early in the year, then stabilized at slightly more than $33 per barrel.

The recession brought changes in international payments patterns. The industrial countries, as a group, moved into a payments surplus on current account, their first since 1978. The current account, one category of the balance of payments, includes exports and imports, foreign aid, income on investments, and tourist spending. Countries belonging to the Organization of Petroleum Exporting Countries (OPEC), the world oil cartel, which had amassed a surplus exceeding $100 billion in 1980, were in a deficit in 1982. Despite lower crude oil prices, the oil-importing, less-developed nations suffered another massive deficit—about $90 billion—and their total foreign debt surpassed $600 billion, much of it due over the next few years.

Bailouts. Mexico, Brazil, and Argentina, their monetary reserves virtually depleted, sought major loans from the International Monetary Fund (IMF), an agency of the United Nations (UN) that works to promote economic growth. They also requested a rescheduling of their debt by foreign lenders. In December, the IMF approved a $4-billion loan to Mexico. In addition, Brazil won emergency aid of $2.4 billion from the United States and other industrial countries.

Summit Agreements. At the economic summit held from June 4 to 6 at Versailles, France, the United States, Great Britain, France, West Germany, Italy, Canada, and Japan agreed to consult more closely on general economic policy and to study the economic impact and potential of high-technology industries. In July, those seven nations and 15 other countries—all members of the Organization for Economic Cooperation and Development—agreed to raise interest rates on government export credits. The United States hailed the move as a step toward ending trade subsidies.

However, the United States and Western Europe plunged into a major dispute on East-West trade policy. In a move that surprised the Western allies of the United States, President Ronald Reagan on June 18 broadened restrictions on the sale of U.S. oil and gas equipment to the Soviet Union for use in building a natural gas pipeline from Siberia to central Europe. The sanctions, which were imposed in December 1981 in response to the

A turbine for use on the Russian gas pipeline is loaded on a Soviet ship in September at a port in Italy, which defied the U.S. pipeline embargo.

imposition of martial law in Poland, were expanded to include equipment manufactured by foreign subsidiaries and licensees of U.S. firms.

In July, however, the President offered to sell as much as 23 million metric tons (25 million short tons) of U.S. grain to the Soviet Union in the 1982-1983 crop year. West Europeans criticized the decision as contradictory to U.S. policy on the pipeline. On November 13, President Reagan lifted the embargo. See EUROPE.

Polish Problems. On October 27, the United States acted against the Polish government for banning the Solidarity labor union by suspending Poland's most-favored-nation status, thus raising U.S. tariffs on most imports from Poland. Meanwhile, Poland continued in virtual default on its foreign debt, estimated at $27 billion, of which more than $10 billion was due in 1982. Western governments, which had rescheduled Poland's 1981 repayments, refused to reschedule 1982 repayments. In November, however, Western banks, trying to avoid calling Poland in default, negotiated a rescheduling of the debt owed them.

Steel Industry Problems further plagued U.S.-West European trade relations during most of 1982. In October, the EC agreed to limit steel exports to the United States through 1985. In return, American steel companies withdrew their charges of unfair steel-pricing practices against European steelmakers, thereby averting the imposition of U.S. import duty penalties. See STEEL.

U.S. Trade Frictions with Canada and Japan persisted. The United States formally complained in January to the General Agreement on Tariffs and Trade (GATT) Council in Geneva, Switzerland, about Canada's foreign investment policies. The GATT is an international agreement to reduce trade barriers among member countries. New Japanese tariff and other trade and investment concessions appeased neither the United States nor Western Europe. The EC charged in the GATT that Japan, through a vast web of nontariff trade barriers, was violating international rules. Japan's trade surplus with the United States reached a record $18 billion in 1982, partly because of the weakening yen. On December 24, Japan announced it would reduce or eliminate tariffs on 315 import items.

GATT Meeting. Trade and finance ministers of 88 nations at a GATT meeting held in Geneva from November 24 to 28 agreed to study ways to strengthen the international trade system. Largely at U.S. urging, they said they would study proposals to limit restrictive import actions, subject services trade to international rules, and liberalize trade in agricultural products. Richard Lawrence

In WORLD BOOK, see INTERNATIONAL TRADE.

IOWA. See STATE GOVERNMENT.

IRAN raised the stakes sharply in its two-year-old war with Iraq in 1982. During the spring, Iranian counterattacks recaptured almost all the territory overrun by Iraq in the early days of the war, including the Iranian oil port of Khorramshahr. On June 29, Iraq's President Saddam Hussein announced that all Iraqi troops had withdrawn from Iran, though Iraqi aircraft continued to raid Iranian cities near the border. However, Iranian officials disputed that claim.

On July 13, Iran mounted a major offensive, sweeping across the Iraqi border and advancing to within a few miles of the Iraqi port city of Basra. The July offensive encountered strong resistance, as Iraqi forces performed better on their own soil than they had in Iran. Large numbers of Iranian troops making human-wave assaults were beaten back, with heavy Iranian casualties. On September 30, Iran launched another major offensive along the Iraqi border, about 100 miles (160 kilometers) northeast of Baghdad, the Iraqi capital. Although the Iraqi government frequently offered during 1982 to agree to a cease-fire, the government of Ayatollah Ruhollah Khomeini refused to negotiate a settlement. It continued to demand the dismissal of Saddam Hussein.

Eliminating the Opposition. The continuing war had the dubious advantage of strengthening the Khomeini regime—the fight against Iraq was seen as a national cause uniting all factions. Public support enabled the regime to press its campaign against political opponents. In February, the capture and execution of a number of top leaders of the main opposition group, the *Mujahedeen-i-khalq* (Fighters for the Faith), seriously weakened the organization. On April 7, Sadegh Ghotbzadeh, a key Khomeini aide as foreign minister in the early days of the 1979 revolution, was arrested and charged with plotting to overthrow Khomeini with the help of army officers. Ghotbzadeh was executed on September 15.

Political Infighting. With the militant opposition decimated, the main challenge to the regime came from within its own ranks. Two factions of the ruling Islamic Republican Party disagreed over the leadership of the government. One faction, Maktabi, favored the continued spread of Shiite Islam—a minority sect of Islam to which most Iranians belong—and the single leadership of Khomeini and his successor as the "supreme Islamic guide." The other faction, Hodjatieh, advocated the establishment of a secular Islamic republic with religious leaders responsible to the Shiite 12th Imam, a religious leader who vanished 1,100 years ago and whose return is expected to bring the Day of Judgment.

Iranian troops gather triumphantly on a disabled Iraqi tank in March after recapturing much of Iran's Khuzistan province, overrun by the Iraqis in 1980.

Law and Order. Iranians, hard-pressed by economic problems, became increasingly subject to stringent Islamic laws. Among these laws, which fell heaviest on the Westernized middle class, were segregation of the sexes in public, enforced veiling of women, tests of religious knowledge for government positions, and a ban on night life and entertainment. Infractions were punished with floggings administered in public.

Economic Progress. The Iranian economy showed surprising resiliency. The $39-billion budget, approved by the *Majlis* (parliament) on March 21, showed a slight decrease from the 1981 budget. To meet an anticipated $8-billion deficit, the government restricted imports to food, medicines, and farming and industrial equipment and cut public sector salaries by 30 per cent.

U.S. Relations. In October, Iran paid $6 million in claims awarded to four U.S. companies that suffered business losses connected with the Iranian revolution. The payments had been authorized by an international tribunal, which had previously assented to payments of $1.75 million to six U.S. companies. Payment was made by the Central Bank of Algiers, which holds Iranian funds in escrow under the terms of the 1981 U.S.-Iran hostage release agreement. William Spencer

See also IRAQ; MIDDLE EAST (Facts in Brief Table). In WORLD BOOK, see IRAN.

IRAQ. The war with neighboring Iran, begun with high hopes in 1980 as Iraqi forces occupied much of western Iran's Khuzistan province, began to turn sour for Iraq in 1982. Two Iranian offensives in the spring recovered much of the 1,100 square miles (2,800 square kilometers) of Iranian territory overrun by Iraqi forces, including the important oil port of Khorramshahr.

On June 20, Iraqi President Saddam Hussein announced a unilateral cease-fire and ordered the withdrawal of Iraqi forces from Iran. Iranian troops ignored the cease-fire and invaded Iraq in July and in August. Operating from well-prepared defensive positions, the Iraqis blunted both counterattacks. In November, the Iranians tried again, this time moving 6 miles (10 kilometers) into Iraq before they were halted. The Iraqis held about 150 square miles (390 square kilometers) of Iranian territory at year-end.

Official Shakeup. The military reversal revived the nationalistic spirit of the Iraqi people. With the nation solidly behind him, Hussein assumed broader powers in June. He reshuffled the three major institutions of government—the Council of Ministers (the Cabinet); the Revolutionary Command Council (RCC), the top policymaking body; and the Baath Party Regional Command, which is responsible for internal administration.

Ten new Cabinet ministers, all Baath Party members, were appointed, reversing a trend in recent years toward multiparty participation in government. Unlike the governmental changes of 1980, when dismissed officials were executed, the outgoing ministers were reassigned to local posts. In addition, the RCC was reduced to 10 members. Finally, Hussein named himself secretary-general of the Regional Command and added seven new members, further tightening party control over the government.

A War Casualty was Iraq's position as the host of the seventh annual summit conference of nonaligned nations. The meeting had been scheduled to take place in September in Baghdad, the Iraqi capital, with Hussein assuming the chairmanship of the 92-nation group. Work was completed in August on a huge conference complex in Baghdad, which included five new hotels and a 90-villa "leisure village" on an island in the Tigris River. But planners feared that Iraq could not provide adequate security for the delegates. These fears, along with diplomatic problems created by the war with Iran, another member state—and threats of a boycott by Iran, Syria, and Libya—led to a change of location. Hussein announced in August that the conference would be held in India, presumably in 1983. However, Hussein was scheduled to remain as chairman.

Rooftop antiaircraft gunners guard Baghdad against possible air raids. Iranian planes bombed the Iraqi capital city in July.

The Iraqi Economy fared reasonably well in 1982 despite the strains of war. The 1982 budget, approved in February by the People's Assembly—the Baath-dominated legislature that approves laws suggested by the RCC—set expenditures at $47.8 billion. Imports were held at the 1981 level of $16.9 billion.

Damage to oil installations by Iranian air raids caused a drop in oil production from a prewar average of 4 million barrels per day (bpd) to 650,000 bpd. Income from oil sales at this level roughly covered the cost of the war for one year. In March, Japan agreed to import 150,000 bpd of Iraqi oil, making Iraq that country's third largest oil supplier. A by-product of the governmental changes in June was the formation of a new Ministry of Light Industry to spur lagging industrial production in the nonoil sector of the economy.

Air attacks by Iran and the diversion of workers from farms to military service also caused a decline in the country's agricultural production. As a result, Iraq was forced to import food, mainly corn and wheat. In June, Saudi Arabia and other Arab countries pledged $25 billion in aid over a two-year period, and Egypt contributed $1.5 billion in weapons after the Iranian summer offensive began. William Spencer

See also IRAN; MIDDLE EAST (Facts in Brief Table). In WORLD BOOK, see IRAQ.

IRELAND held its third general election in 18 months on Nov. 24, 1982, and Garret FitzGerald, leader of the Fine Gael (Gaelic People), was returned to office as prime minister. FitzGerald's party won 70 seats in the Irish Parliament, while the Fianna Fáil (Soldiers of Destiny) of defeated Prime Minister Charles J. Haughey took 75. But the Labour Party, with 16 of Parliament's 166 seats, held the balance of power and entered into a coalition with Fine Gael.

The year's political ups and downs began on January 27 when FitzGerald's Fine Gael-Labour Party coalition government was defeated in the *Dáil Éireann* (House of Deputies) by one vote. FitzGerald resigned, and the second general election in 30 weeks was held on February 18. Fine Gael lost two seats to emerge with 63, and Haughey's Fianna Fáil gained three, bringing its total to 81. Because neither party had an outright majority, intense negotiations took place, focusing on four independents and three members of *Sinn Féin* (Ourselves Alone) the Workers Party (SFWP). The last is distinct from Sinn Féin, the political wing of the outlawed Provisional Irish Republican Army. Sinn Féin—not SFWP—contested the election. It put up candidates in seven constituencies, mainly on a platform of British withdrawal from Northern Ireland, but none was elected. On March 9, Haughey—who had been prime minister from December 1979 until June 1981—secured enough votes and was again elected prime minister. However, less than eight months later, on November 4, he lost a parliamentary vote of confidence 82-80, and resigned.

Fine Gael's January defeat came when it tried to force through severe austerity measures to reduce Ireland's projected budget deficit of $450-million in the first half of 1982. The measures included reduced food subsidies and increases in several taxes, including raising the value-added tax, a kind of sales tax, to 18 per cent. There were also cuts in tax relief on mortgages and an end to short-term welfare benefits.

On taking office, Haughey's deputy premier and finance minister, Ray MacSharry, replaced the gloomy predictions of his predecessor with promises of "bloom and boom." But the government was soon forced to introduce widespread spending cuts in its economic plan. On May 26, Fianna Fáil lost a crucial by-election in a district of Dublin, and the party's continued rule was again placed in doubt.

One individual, however, could count himself a winner. Tony Gregory, 34, the SFWP member of Parliament for central Dublin, had bargained so well before casting his vote for Haughey that he won for Dublin Corporation, which administers local government affairs, a windfall totaling $20-million. His deprived inner-city constituency was to receive free milk for its schoolchildren and lead-free gasoline, and Gregory was to become chairman of a new state agency to develop inner-city areas.

British-Irish Relations deteriorated after the Falklands war crisis as a result of Ireland's decision not to join in European Community (EC or Common Market) sanctions against Argentina. Progress toward setting up an interparliamentary council of elected representatives from the British Parliament in Westminster, the Dáil, and the new Belfast assembly in Northern Ireland ground to a halt. Such a body had been agreed on in principle when British Prime Minister Margaret Thatcher met with Prime Minister FitzGerald in November 1981.

Irish Archaeologists uncovered a unique flint mace head carved into a human mask in a chamber tomb in the Boyne Valley near Drogheda. The object is about 3 inches (7.5 centimeters) long, and radiocarbon dating has placed its origin at 3100 B.C. The director of the excavation, archaeologist George Eogan of the National University of Ireland in Dublin, described it as a "major work of art, the only one of its kind, and of particular significance in its early context." Ian Mather

See also NORTHERN IRELAND. In WORLD BOOK, see IRELAND.

IRON AND STEEL. See STEEL INDUSTRY.

Israeli soldiers climb under cover of foam to evacuate Israeli settlers refusing to leave the Sinai before its return to Egypt in April.

ISRAEL became a deeply divided nation as a result of its invasion and occupation of Lebanon in 1982. The government of Prime Minister Menachem Begin had said that its action would be limited to clearing out Palestine Liberation Organization (PLO) military bases in a 25-mile (40-kilometer) zone north of the Israel-Lebanon border. But once across the border on June 6, the Israeli forces kept on going, all the way to Beirut, the Lebanese capital. It quickly became apparent that the invasion's objective was the complete destruction of the PLO. See MIDDLE EAST.

Although the invasion succeeded in breaking PLO power in Lebanon, it raised serious moral and ethical questions among the Israeli people. Many Israelis felt the invasion was an overreaction to the sporadic assaults on northern Israeli settlements and on Israelis abroad, attacks that the government had cited as the reason for its action. Many Israelis also seriously questioned the enormous destruction of property and the high casualty rates among Lebanese civilians.

Beirut Massacre. Criticism erupted into sometimes violent protest after the massacre of hundreds of Palestinians in the Sabra and Shatila refugee camps in West Beirut from September 16 to 18. Although Lebanese Christian militiamen apparently did the killings, the Israeli Army permitted the militiamen to enter the camps.

Hundreds of thousands of Israelis marched in protest demonstrations, demanding the resignation of Israel's Defense Minister Ariel Sharon and an official inquiry into the massacre. Two ministers resigned from the Cabinet in protest, and a number of high-ranking army officers quit. On September 28, 1,000 army reservists signed a petition refusing to serve in Lebanon. On the same day, Begin yielded to domestic and foreign pressure and approved an official inquiry into the massacre. In late November, a three-member commission warned Begin and eight of his top officials that unless new evidence proved otherwise, they could be found guilty of negligence in the affair, meaning that they had not fulfilled their duty to their country. But the government was adamant in its refusal to withdraw its troops from Lebanon. On October 11, the government announced that 368 Israeli soldiers had been killed during the fighting in Lebanon.

Sinai Withdrawal. Earlier in 1982, Begin had what many called his finest hour when, on April 25, Israel returned the last part of the occupied Sinai Peninsula to Egypt under the terms of the Egyptian-Israeli peace treaty. Ultranationalist Israeli settlers, many of them members of Gush Emunim (Faithful Bloc), attempted to block the return of the Sinai by bringing thousands of squatters to Yamit and other Israeli-developed towns. Israeli soldiers forcibly removed the squatters, without causing casualties, and the region changed hands after a 15-year occupation.

West Bank Control. The Begin government continued to tighten its hold over the occupied West Bank and Gaza Strip. Aside from its historical attachment to these territories, Israel saw important economic reasons for retaining control. Israeli goods sold there generated $600 million a year in revenues, and exports of West Bank produce to nearby Arab states generated $100 million.

By mid-July, Defense Minister Sharon had dismissed the mayors and city councils of seven West Bank cities for alleged PLO connections. Large-scale demonstrations broke out to protest the firings. During a six-week period, more than 100 demonstrators and Israeli soldiers were killed or wounded in the worst outbreak of violence in the area since 1967. Bir Zeit University on the West Bank was closed three times for a total of seven months during the 1981-1982 school year, and Israeli civilian administrators began to enforce a number of military regulations already on the books. These included rules on the appointment of teachers and control of school curriculums.

Troubled Economy. Even before the Lebanese invasion, the Israeli economy struggled with a 135 per cent inflation rate and a foreign debt of $2.5-billion. However, the war in Lebanon added significantly to the country's economic burden. The direct cost of the invasion was estimated at $1 billion, and indirect costs were expected to reach $400 million to $1 billion. On June 13, the government announced new taxes to finance the war. On December 7 and 8, some 400,000 government employees, almost 10 per cent of Israel's population, staged a strike to protest what they considered an inadequate government pay raise offer.

Air Turbulence. On May 2, Begin fulfilled a campaign promise to an ultra-Orthodox political party and banned all flights on the Jewish Sabbath and holy days by El Al, Israel's national airline, which is mostly government-owned. On May 10, Israel's Supreme Court overturned the decision on procedural grounds. Despite the ruling and vocal opposition by El Al employees, the government reinstated the ban on August 25. On September 2, the court again blocked the move.

The dispute was left up in the air, however, when cabin stewards struck the airline on September 13. On November 24, after union and management remained deadlocked, El Al shareholders voted to disband and sell the airline. On December 27, the Israeli labor federation signed a new labor agreement on behalf of El Al employees, but legal difficulties prevented the immediate reversal of the liquidation order. William Spencer

See also MIDDLE EAST (Facts in Brief Table). In WORLD BOOK, see ISRAEL.

Italian police on January 28 rescue Brigadier General James L. Dozier from a terrorist group that had held him captive since Dec. 17, 1981.

ITALY. The five-party coalition government led by Prime Minister Giovanni Spadolini resigned on Aug. 7, 1982, three days after the Chamber of Deputies unexpectedly defeated a bill that would have tightened tax regulations and operating conditions for oil companies. The Christian Democrats abandoned their loyalty to the coalition and voted against the bill. The Socialists, who strongly favored the bill, then withdrew their support from the government, causing the collapse. However, Spadolini resurrected the coalition on August 23.

Spadolini resigned again on November 11. However, in a surprise move, President Sandro Pertini refused to accept the resignation. Instead, he told Spadolini to put the nation's economic issues before Parliament. After two days of parliamentary debate, Spadolini resigned again. At Pertini's request, Christian Democrat leader Amintore Fanfani tried to organize a government. On December 1, Fanfani put together a coalition with the Socialists, Social Democrats, and Liberals.

Economic Troubles. Inflation fell from 20 per cent in 1981 to 16 per cent in June 1982, but the balance-of-payments deficit widened to $2.7 billion. On June 12, Italy devalued the lira by 2.75 per cent within the European Monetary System.

A Bank Scandal erupted in May 1982, when the Bank of Italy demanded information about $1.4-billion in unsecured loans that were on the books of foreign subsidiaries of the nation's largest private bank, Banco Ambrosiano S.p.A. of Milan, but were missing. Ambrosiano's president, Roberto Calvi, refused to provide the information and fled the country. On June 18, his body was found hanging under a bridge in London. A coroner's jury ruled that he had committed suicide.

The Vatican bank, Istituto per le Opere di Religione (IOR), was drawn into the scandal by reports that Archbishop Paul Marcinkus, IOR's chairman, had written letters that the government said represented a form of endorsement of some questionable loans made by Ambrosiano. Italy ordered Ambrosiano liquidated on August 6.

Terrorism. On January 28, special Italian antiterrorist police forces rescued U.S. Army Brigadier General James L. Dozier from an apartment in Padua, where he was a captive of the Red Brigades, a leftist terrorist organization. The Red Brigades had kidnapped Dozier on Dec. 17, 1981.

On November 25, police in Rome arrested Serge Ivanov Antonov, an employee of the Bulgarian national airline and tourist office, and charged him with complicity in the May 1981 attempt on the life of Pope John Paul II. Kenneth Brown

See also EUROPE (Facts in Brief Table). In WORLD BOOK, see ITALY; FANFANI, AMINTORE.

IVORY COAST. See AFRICA.
JAMAICA. See WEST INDIES.

JAPAN. Yasuhiro Nakasone became prime minister of Japan on Nov. 26, 1982. Two days earlier, the ruling Liberal-Democratic Party (LDP)—a conservative party despite its name—had elected him as its president. See NAKASONE, YASUHIRO.

Nakasone succeeded Prime Minister Zenko Suzuki, who unexpectedly announced in October that he would not seek re-election as president of the LDP and would resign as prime minister. Suzuki said he was leaving office to unify his party, some members of which had criticized his failure to deal with what they saw as Japan's mounting economic problems.

The Sluggish Economy had so far created no serious difficulty, but it caused increasing concern about the future. The gap between Japan's relatively healthy economy and the ailing economies of other industrialized nations grew steadily smaller.

A fall in the value of the yen was one of the more visible signs of Japan's economic problems. On October 4, the yen was valued at 272.45 per U.S. $1, the lowest level since 1978.

More significant was the sluggish rate of economic growth. In Japan's 1981 fiscal year, which ended March 31, 1982, the growth rate was 2.7 per cent, falling short of a projected 4.1 per cent.

Domestic automobile sales were slow, and automobile production in September was only 1.1 per cent higher than a year earlier. Economic analysts predicted that Japan's steel production for 1982 would fall below 100 million metric tons (110 million short tons) for the first time in 10 years. A private research group forecast that profits for major companies would decline about 10 per cent in the first half of the 1982 fiscal year, which began April 1, compared with the same period for 1981.

Economic analysts believed that a major problem was the government's budget deficit, which was expected to reach $65 billion by the end of the fiscal year in March 1983. Faced with this and other economic difficulties, Prime Minister Suzuki announced a state of financial emergency in September. In October, the government approved a $7.7-billion economic package designed to stimulate the economy. The funds—all to be spent in the second half of fiscal 1983—were to go for disaster relief, public works, and construction.

In addition to economic problems on the home front, Japan's exports began to fall in 1982, ending several years of rising foreign sales. August 1982 figures were about 10 per cent lower than those of August 1981. Analysts were puzzled by the fact that the fall in the value of the yen, which made Japanese products cheaper for other countries to buy, did not bring a major increase in exports.

Charges of Illegal Trade Practices. The U.S. Department of Justice charged on June 22 that 21 persons, 18 of them Japanese businessmen, had conspired to steal secret computer information from International Business Machines Corporation (IBM). The 18 businessmen were employees of two leading Japanese computer companies, Hitachi Limited and Mitsubishi Electric Corporation. The Justice Department accused Hitachi of paying $622,000 and Mitsubishi of paying $26,000 to an undercover agent for the stolen information.

Protesters calling for a ban on nuclear weapons stage a die-in in March near a memorial to the first atomic bomb attack in Hiroshima, Japan.

Hitachi and Mitsubishi admitted paying $540,000 and $20,000, respectively, for the data. But both firms insisted they never suspected the information was stolen and denied any wrongdoing. In a court brief filed in its defense in late September, Hitachi contended that IBM had played an "improper role" in the case in order to limit possible competition from Hitachi.

In another case, Mitsui & Company (U.S.A.), an American subsidiary of a huge Japanese trading firm, pleaded guilty on July 21 to charges of fraud and conspiracy in selling imported steel below allowable U.S. prices. The company reported falsely inflated prices to the U.S. Customs Service in order to avoid an investigation. The steel was actually priced low enough to set off a probe by the U.S. government, which tries to prevent the sale of foreign steel at unfairly low prices—a practice called dumping. Mitsui agreed to pay $11-million in civil penalties and $210,000 in criminal fines to the U.S. Treasury.

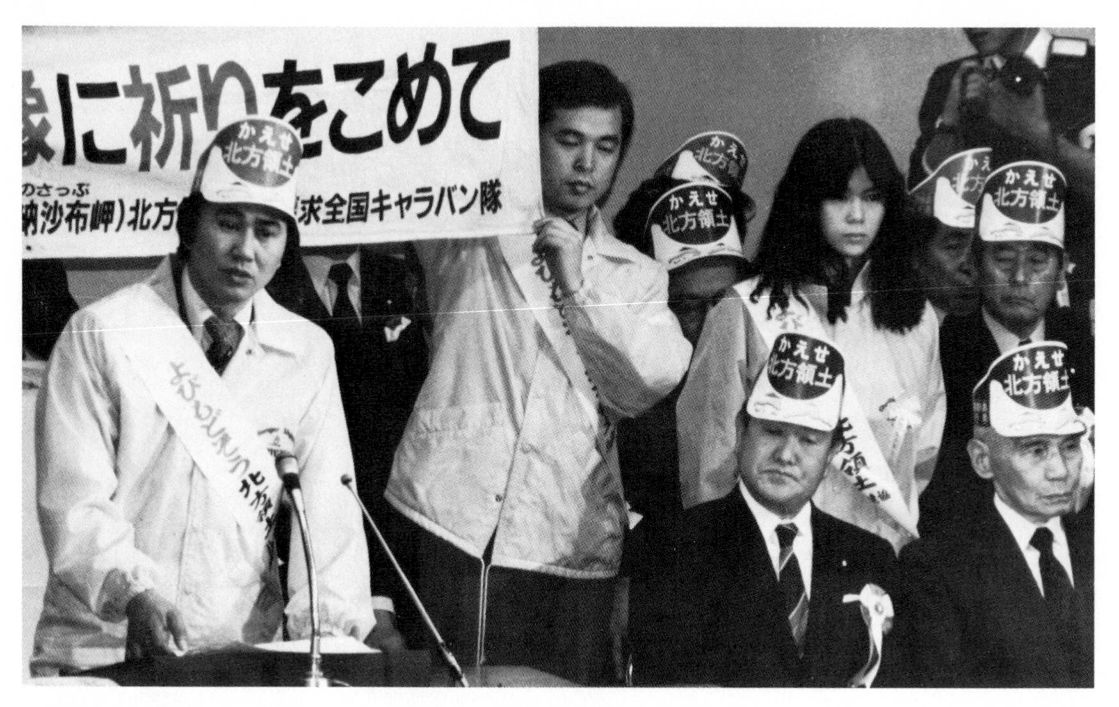

Prime Minister Zenko Suzuki, seated left, attends a rally in February demanding that Russia return the four southern Kuril Islands to Japan.

Trade Agreements. On June 4, Japan and the United States formally adopted a new three-year agreement on airline service between the two countries after 18 months of negotiations. Both sides agreed to increase the number of flights.

The Japanese government announced on March 29 that it would limit the export of automobiles to the United States to 1.68 million cars during the 1982 fiscal year, the same number as in fiscal 1981. On August 11, Japan reached a similar agreement with Canada, limiting its sales to Canadian buyers to 153,000 cars during fiscal 1982.

In response to pressure from the United States, a Japanese government tariff council proposed in December to reduce import duties on about 75 industrial and agricultural products. The tariff cuts, if approved by Japan's parliament, would take effect April 1, 1983.

Military Build-Up. In spite of Japan's economic problems, the country's leaders embarked on a program for expanding its military strength. The government on Dec. 30, 1982, raised the 1983 budget for the Self-Defense Forces—as Japan's armed services are called—to $11.8 billion, an increase of 6.5 per cent. Although this increase was less than the 7.75 per cent boost in the 1982 budget, almost all other government agencies were taking 5 per cent cuts.

The spending hike was the first step in a new five-year plan for a military build-up that is to cost about $64 billion. About $17.4 billion is to go for new weapons.

On September 30, the U.S. Department of Defense announced an agreement with Japan under which it would station F-16 fighter-bombers at the Misawa air base in northeastern Japan. The base lies about 375 miles (600 kilometers) from the Soviet Union. The United States would place 24 F-16s at Misawa in 1985 and double the number later. Russia declared that Japan's decision to permit deployment of the planes was a hostile act.

Textbook Controversy. During the summer of 1982, China, South Korea, and other Asian nations protested revisions in Japan's new government-approved history textbooks. They charged that the books glossed over Japanese military aggression in the 1930s and 1940s. Japan first declared that the schoolbooks would not be revised but finally announced on August 26 that necessary amendments would be made by 1985.

Foreign Visits. President François Mitterrand of France visited Japan in April, and Prime Minister Margaret Thatcher of Great Britain visited in September. Both leaders were principally concerned about their countries' unfavorable balance of trade with Japan. John M. Maki

See also ASIA (Facts in Brief Table). In the WORLD BOOK SUPPLEMENT section, see JAPAN.

JEWS AND JUDAISM. Tensions in the Middle East touched off numerous attacks on Jews in other parts of the world in 1982. Many of the attacks were related to Israel's efforts to oust the Palestine Liberation Organization (PLO) from Lebanon (see MIDDLE EAST).

On January 15, a bomb exploded in a Jewish restaurant in West Berlin, West Germany, killing a baby girl and injuring 24 other people. Palestinians claimed responsibility for the bombing.

On June 3, Shlomo Argov, the Israeli ambassador to Great Britain, was shot in London. Many Jews expressed concern when Argov's assailant was found to be carrying a "hit list" of English Jews. Although the PLO denied involvement, the shooting apparently became a factor in Israel's decision to invade Lebanon on June 6.

Several anti-Semitic incidents rocked Paris during the summer. The worst of these occurred on August 9, when gunmen attacked a kosher restaurant in a Jewish neighborhood, killing six people and injuring 22 others. French authorities blamed the attack on the Fatah Revolutionary Council, a group of Palestinian dissidents.

On October 9, in Rome, Palestinian terrorists tossed grenades and fired submachine guns at worshipers leaving a synagogue. A 2-year-old boy was killed, and 37 other people were injured.

Massacre Denounced. Jews throughout the world denounced the mass slaying of more than 700 Palestinians—allegedly by Lebanese Christian militiamen—in Beirut, Lebanon, from September 16 to 18. On September 25, between 100,000 and 350,000 Israelis and Jews took part in demonstrations to show their revulsion at whatever responsibility Israel might have for the massacre. However, support for Israel among Jews in the United States and other nations remained strong. Israel approved an official inquiry into the incident on September 28. See ISRAEL.

Jewish Emigration from Russia slowed to a trickle in 1982. The Soviet Union allowed only a few hundred Jews to leave the country each month. About 25 per cent of these emigrants moved to Israel, and most of the rest went to the United States. Zionist leaders, troubled by the numbers of Russian Jews immigrating to the United States and other nations, searched for ways to divert more of them to Israel.

Redefining Jewishness. In the United States, Reform rabbis considered a proposal that would liberalize the meaning of Jewishness. The proposal would confer Jewish identity on any child of a mixed marriage, even if the father is the Jewish partner. Under present Jewish law, Jewish identity is granted only if the mother is Jewish.

Paris police officers and medics swarm in front of Jo Goldenberg's, a Jewish restaurant, at right, on August 9, after gunmen killed six people there.

Opponents of the proposal claimed that it would cause a needless confrontation with Orthodox Jews. They also feared the measure would worsen the feud in Israel between the Reform movement and the Orthodox religious establishment. The establishment does not recognize the Reform movement as a legitimate religious group.

Nazi War Criminals. In an interview on the CBS television program "60 Minutes" on May 16, former U.S. Department of Justice prosecutor John J. Loftus charged that government officials smuggled Russian-born Nazi war criminals into the United States after World War II. The Nazis had worked as spies against Russia. In October, Archbishop Valerian D. Trifa, 68-year-old leader of the Romanian Orthodox Episcopate based in Grass Lake, Mich., was deported for concealing war crimes from immigration officials.

New Evidence revealed in March suggested the innocence of Leo Frank, a Jewish factory superintendent convicted of murdering a 14-year-old girl in Atlanta, Ga., in 1913. Frank was lynched by a mob in 1915. In a sworn statement, 83-year-old Alonzo Mann said that he saw another man commit the murder. Mann was a key witness in Frank's trial, which created an anti-Semitic frenzy in Georgia and led to formation of the Anti-Defamation League of B'nai B'rith. Arnold G. Kaiman

In WORLD BOOK, see JEWS; JUDAISM.

Jordan's King Hussein, left, greets U.S. envoy Philip Habib in July during talks to resolve the fate of Palestinian guerrillas in Beirut, Lebanon.

JORDAN. King Hussein I of Jordan marked his 30th anniversary on the throne on Aug. 11, 1982. This made the Jordanian monarch the most enduring head of state in recent Middle Eastern history, having outlasted three Egyptian presidents, numerous Syrian and Iraqi leaders, and four kings of Saudi Arabia.

One key to Hussein's durability was his moderate stance on Israel, which enabled him to remain on good terms with Israel's ally the United States, and his refusal to take actions that Israel might consider provocative. At the same time, however, he continued his support of Palestinian demands for self-rule. After the Israeli invasion of Lebanon in June, world leaders increasingly advocated the establishment of a Palestinian state on the West Bank in federation with Jordan as an alternative to the formation of an independent Palestinian state, which Israel refused to accept.

In August, Jordan agreed to accept 1,000 of the Palestine Liberation Organization (PLO) guerrillas evacuated from Israeli-besieged West Beirut, Lebanon, under the terms of a withdrawal negotiated by the United States. But the offer was limited to those fighters who carried Jordanian passports or visas. In the end, only 265 guerrillas were accepted. Hussein was taking no chances on a recurrence of the 1970 civil war when the PLO, with Syrian aid, attempted to seize control of Jordan.

The Jordanian Economy benefited from noninvolvement in military action, though Jordan remained, in Arab eyes, a front-line state in the struggle with Israel. In January, the government approved a $2.3-billion budget for 1982. It planned to cover an expected deficit of $108 million with foreign loans and a 25 per cent reduction in government subsidies for fuel, electricity, and food.

The 1981-1985 economic development plan was revised upward to reflect improved economic prospects. Expenditures were targeted at $9.9 billion, with an 11 per cent increase in the country's gross national product (GNP).

Exports of phosphates and potash, Jordan's principal mineral resources, continued to increase. In September, a solar-powered potash extraction plant near the Dead Sea began production. In March, a new phosphoric acid-sulfuric acid plant opened at Wadi Two. The first shipment of ammonium phosphate, which is used for fertilizer, went to Italy under a $700,000 order. Also encouraging was the discovery in June of the world's largest artesian well, with a capacity of 98 million cubic yards (75 million cubic meters) of water per year. Water, more than oil, is the key to Jordan's long-range development. William Spencer

See also MIDDLE EAST (Facts in Brief Table). In WORLD BOOK, see JORDAN.

JORGE BLANCO, SALVADOR (1926-), took office as president of the Dominican Republic on Aug. 16, 1982. He succeeded Silvestre Antonio Guzmán Fernández, who died on July 4. See WEST INDIES.

Salvador Jorge Blanco was born in Santiago, a city northwest of the capital city of Santo Domingo, on July 5, 1926. His father was a businessman and his mother a professor. Jorge Blanco was educated in public schools. He went on to receive two doctor of laws degrees, one from the Autonomous University of Santo Domingo in 1950, and the other in 1951 from the Central University of Madrid in Spain.

Returning to Santiago, Jorge Blanco practiced law and taught constitutional law for several years at the Catholic University of Our Mother and Teacher. He became active in politics in 1961, after the assassination of dictator Rafael Leonidas Trujillo Molina. In 1965, Jorge Blanco was appointed attorney general.

Jorge Blanco is married to the former Asela Mera. They have two children. Marsha F. Goldsmith

JUDAISM. See JEWS AND JUDAISM.
JUNIOR ACHIEVEMENT (JA). See YOUTH ORGANIZATIONS.
KAMPUCHEA. See CAMBODIA.
KANSAS. See STATE GOVERNMENT.
KENTUCKY. See STATE GOVERNMENT.

During the suppression of an attempted coup in August, a Kenyan soldier checks the identity cards of persons living in a shantytown near Nairobi.

KENYA. On Aug. 1, 1982, members of Kenya's air force attempted to overthrow the government of President Daniel T. arap Moi. The revolt began at 3 A.M. when rebels took over Eastleigh air base outside the capital city, Nairobi. At 6 A.M., they seized Nairobi's radio station and announced that Moi's government would be replaced by a "People's Redemption Council." The rebel leader was an air force enlisted man, Senior Private Hezekia Ochuka. Loyal army units counterattacked by 10 A.M., and before day's end, Ochuka had fled to neighboring Tanzania.

Air Force Disbanded. On August 21, the government announced that the air force—all of whose members had been arrested—was disbanded and that Major General Mahamoud Mohamed, deputy commander of the Kenyan Army, would organize a new air force.

The rebels' grievances included the government's establishment of a one-party state, censorship of the press, and detention of dissidents without formal charges and trials. On June 9, Kenya's National Assembly had unanimously approved a constitutional amendment making President Moi's Kenya African National Union (KANU) the country's only legal political party. A former vice-president of Kenya, Oginga Odinga, had threatened to establish a competing socialist-leaning party. He was expelled from KANU in May.

Political Detentions. In June, the government detained several persons without trial, including George Anyona, a former member of the National Assembly and a close associate of Odinga, and John Khaminwa, a Nairobi attorney who had represented Odinga and Anyona. These detentions were the first in Kenya since Moi became president in 1978.

A normally pro-government daily newspaper, *The Standard,* published an editorial strongly criticizing the detentions. Under pressure from the government, the paper's owners dismissed its editor, George Githii, on July 21. Among the approximately 1,000 civilians arrested after the August attempted coup and charged with complicity were an editor of *The Sunday Standard,* a son of Odinga, and a University of Nairobi professor.

Turmoil Worries United States. Kenya's political instability worried United States government officials. Kenya has been an important country, both economically and militarily, for the United States. American business investments there totaled about $250 million in 1982, and President Moi's government has permitted United States military forces to use Kenyan air bases and the harbor at Mombasa. J. Dixon Esseks

See also AFRICA. In WORLD BOOK, see KENYA.
KIWANIS INTERNATIONAL. See COMMUNITY ORGANIZATIONS.

KOHL, HELMUT (1930-), leader of the Christian Democratic Union (CDU), became West Germany's sixth chancellor on Oct. 1, 1982. A vote that day in the Bundestag (lower house of parliament) toppled Kohl's predecessor, Social Democrat Helmut Schmidt. Kohl received 256 votes to Schmidt's 235 in a "constructive motion of no-confidence" and became the first chancellor in West Germany's 33-year history elected by this parliamentary procedure. He promised a national election on March 6, 1983. See GERMANY, WEST.

Helmut Michael Kohl was born on April 3, 1930. He studied political science and law at the University of Frankfurt and at the University of Heidelberg, where he received a doctorate in 1958.

Kohl was elected in 1959 to the legislature of his home state, Rhineland-Palatinate. In 1969, the legislature elected him minister president, or head of the state government. Kohl was chosen national chairman of the CDU in 1973 and entered the Bundestag in 1976.

Under Kohl's leadership, membership in the CDU grew rapidly. Kohl's critics labeled him "provincial" and "dull." But many West Germans appeared to respond to the traditional middle-class virtues—punctuality, dependability, savings, and hard work—that he pledged to restore to public life. Kohl married Hannelore Renner in 1960, and they have two sons. Karin C. Rosenberg

KOIVISTO, MAUNO HENRIK (1923-), a popular, plain-speaking outdoorsman, was elected president of Finland on Jan. 26, 1982. A moderate Social Democrat, Koivisto pledged a continuation of "stable and confidential relations with the Soviet Union." See FINLAND.

Koivisto was born in Turku, Finland, on Nov. 25, 1923. Because his family was poor, he had to leave school at the age of 13 and go to work. During World War II, Koivisto fought against the Russian Army, which had invaded Finland. After the war, he resumed his education, working during the day and studying in the evening. He earned a doctorate in sociology at the University of Turku in 1956.

In 1959, Koivisto became a director of one of Finland's largest savings banks. That experience brought him an appointment in 1966 as minister of finance in a coalition government. In a five-party coalition government, formed in 1968, he became prime minister. He returned to private life in 1970 as chairman of the board of the Bank of Finland. In 1972, he served briefly as finance minister and deputy prime minister. In 1979, Koivisto was again named prime minister.

In September 1981, Urho Kekkonen, president of Finland since 1956, was prevented by ill health from fulfilling his duties (he resigned in October), and Koivisto became acting president. David L. Dreier

KOREA, NORTH. Signs of internal dissension came from secretive North Korea during 1982. The son and presumed heir of President Kim Il-song, Kim Chong Il, was elected to parliament on February 28. But when parliament met on April 6, the younger Kim was not named a vice-president as widely expected, and he then disappeared from public view until September. He was not identified as his father's successor during elaborate celebrations of President Kim's 70th birthday on April 15. Unconfirmed reports said 10 generals were purged for opposing the son's promotion, and several other officers fled into exile in China. South Korea charged in April that at least 105,000 political prisoners were held in North Korea.

China's two top leaders, Teng Hsiao-p'ing (Deng Xiaoping) and Hu Yaobang, made a secret visit to North Korea from April 26 to 30. The visit was disclosed when Kim made his first state visit to China since 1975 from September 15 to 26. Hospitality on that trip "surpassed the usual practice in China," the North Korean press reported.

A United States soldier stationed in South Korea, Private First Class Joseph T. White of St. Louis, Mo., defected to the north on August 28. North Korea told U.S. officials that Private White did not want to see them. Henry S. Bradsher

See also ASIA (Facts in Brief Table). In WORLD BOOK, see KOREA.

KOREA, SOUTH. President Chun Doo Hwan shuffled his Cabinet four times during 1982. On January 3, he replaced Prime Minister Nam Duck Woo with Yoo Chang Soon and also changed five other ministers. The announced purpose was to improve economic performance following 1981's trade deficit of $5.3 billion and the nation's rising unemployment. Chun's government took two other steps in January to symbolize a new approach: It lifted for most of the country a midnight-to-4 A.M. curfew that had been in force since the 1940s, and it repealed a regulation requiring short haircuts for schoolchildren.

A Major Financial Scandal led to several corporate bankruptcies during the year and caused three more Cabinet changes. Government prosecutors announced on May 11 the arrest of Lee Chol Hi, a former deputy director of the Korean Central Intelligence Agency, and his wife, Chang Yong Ja. The couple had lent companies money and tricked them into issuing promissory notes worth much more by pledging not to cash the notes. Chang gave businessmen the impression that her brother-in-law, retired General Lee Kyu Kwang—who was also an uncle of President Chun's wife—backed the transactions. The couple then sold the notes, reaping huge profits. When the notes fell due, several firms went bankrupt.

The defendants were found guilty on August 9

President Chun Doo Hwan of South Korea, left, accepts a carved walking stick from the mayor of Nairobi, Kenya, on an August visit to Africa.

of defrauding six companies and several individual investors and were each sentenced to 15 years in prison. General Lee was sentenced to four years and fined. The family and official connections of the swindlers damaged government credibility.

The entire Cabinet offered to resign. On May 21, Chun accepted the resignations of 11 of the 22 ministers. He also fired the five top leaders of his ruling Democratic Justice party, including the secretary-general, Kwong Jung Dal, whose power had seemed second only to Chun's. As public agitation continued, Chun made more Cabinet changes on June 2. Finally, on June 24 he fired Prime Minister Yoo and named a university president, Kim Sang Hyup, to the post. Still another official shakeup came in mid-December, when Chun replaced his two closest advisers.

Crime and Punishment. On March 2, the eve of the first anniversary of his inauguration as president, Chun granted amnesty or reduced sentences to 2,863 prisoners. He also reduced the sentence of opposition political leader Kim Dae Jung from life to 20 years. Kim was convicted in 1980 of charges of trying to overthrow the government. On December 16, he was transferred from prison to a hospital. Officials said the government was suspending Kim's sentence to allow him to fly to the United States for medical treatment. Kim arrived in the U.S. on December 23.

Arsonists burned a United States government information center in Pusan, South Korea, on March 18, killing a Korean visitor. A leaflet distributed nearby criticized United States support of Chun. A Roman Catholic priest and 14 other persons were found guilty on August 11 of setting the fire.

North Korea. Chun proposed on January 22 that North and South Korea set up a consultative conference for national reunification. The conference, composed of representatives from both sides, would draft a new constitution for a united country, hold a referendum on the constitution, and hold free general elections. Chun also offered to meet North Korean President Kim Il-song. North Korea rejected both proposals on January 26.

On April 21, four North Korean soldiers tried to defect across the Demilitarized Zone. Troops on both sides opened fire, leading to a four-hour gun battle in which the four defectors apparently died.

The Economy recovered slowly in 1982 from a recession that had checked the rapid economic growth of the 1970s. In a speech read for him by Prime Minister Kim, Chun said on October 4 that economic growth in 1982 was expected to be 6 per cent, below the planned 8 per cent. Henry S. Bradsher

See also ASIA (Facts in Brief Table); KOREA, NORTH. In WORLD BOOK, see KOREA.

KUWAIT. See MIDDLE EAST.

LABOR. Unemployment in the United States rose quarter by quarter in 1982 as the recession that began in 1981 deepened. By December, the jobless rate had reached 10.8 per cent, the highest since 1940. Nearly 12 million U.S. workers were jobless, up more than 2.2 million since January.

The severe recession muted workers' wage demands and blunted the strike weapon. Job security became more important than added income. Worker concessions to troubled employers ranged from forgoing scheduled wage increases to accepting outright pay cuts to preserve jobs. Some wage concessions were industrywide, but typically, they were agreed to only to prevent plants closing or moving. See MANUFACTURING.

Inflation Eased. The Consumer Price Index (CPI) rose at an annual rate of only 4.6 per cent during the year ending in November 1982, compared with rises of 10.2 per cent in 1981 and 13.5 per cent in 1980. The drop in inflation, in part a result of the recession, contributed to unions and workers accepting lower rates of wage increase.

Preliminary Bureau of Labor Statistics (BLS) data showed that during the first nine months of 1982, wage increases in union contracts covering 1,000 workers or more averaged 3.8 per cent in the first year and 3.5 per cent over the contract's life. In 1981, increases hit 9.8 per cent in the first year and 7.9 per cent over the contract's life. The BLS

Dick Locher, © 1982 *Chicago Tribune*

Employment Cost Index, which measures wage and benefit changes for all private nonfarm workers, increased 5.0 per cent during the first nine months of 1982—for wages and salaries only—contrasted with 6.9 per cent for that span in 1981.

BLS data on major employment changes are summarized below:

	1981	1982*
Total labor force	**110,812,000**	**112,425,000**
Armed forces	2,142,000	2,179,000
Civilian labor force	108,670,000	110,246,000
Total employment	100,397,000	99,530,000
Unemployment	8,273,000	10,716,000
Unemployment rate	7.6%	9.7%
Change in real earnings of production and nonsupervisory workers (private nonfarm sector)†	−2.4%	−0.9%††
Change in output per employee hour (private nonfarm sector)**	1.8%	0.3%

*1982 average, seasonally adjusted except for armed forces data.
†Preliminary data. 1981 change in real earnings in December 1981 from December 1980; 1982 change in October 1982 from the same month a year earlier.
**1981 change in output per employee hour is annual rate; for 1982, change is from the third quarter 1981 to third quarter 1982 (preliminary data).
††September 1982 data.

Trucking Settlements. The International Brotherhood of Teamsters (Teamsters Union) agreed to begin bargaining in December 1981, though their contract did not expire until March 1982. The new National Master Freight Agreement, ratified on March 1, provides that wages increase only to cover inflation. Part of the cost-of-living adjustment (COLA) will be deflected to fund benefits. New truckers will start at 70 per cent of standard rates—which would not be reached until after three years on the job—and "nonstandard" weeks would be used to avoid premium pay. Employers agreed not to move operations to avoid contractual obligations and to a possible reopening of negotiations in April 1984. The contract runs through March 1985 and covers 300,000 workers. Later settlements in the industry followed the pact. See TRUCK AND TRUCKING.

Teamsters President Roy L. Williams finally testified on Dec. 8, 1982, in a trial stemming from his indictment on May 22, 1981, by a federal grand jury in Chicago. Williams and four other men were charged with conspiracy to bribe Senator Howard W. Cannon (D., Nev.), promising him the right to purchase land in Las Vegas in return for help in blocking trucking legislation. The stormy trial ended on December 15 with Williams and the other defendants found guilty.

Automobile Accord. Bargaining on new contracts in automobile manufacturing began on Jan. 13, 1982. The United Automobile Workers

(UAW) agreed on February 28 with Ford Motor Company, which lost more than $1 billion in 1981, on a two-year contract in which wages would increase only with inflation. However, wage raises would not be paid for 18 months. The UAW also agreed to cancellation of "personal" holidays and to lower wages for new employees for longer periods. In exchange, Ford agreed to a two-year moratorium on plant closings, employment counseling for laid-off workers, and a profit-sharing plan to begin in 1983. Also introduced was a new "guaranteed income stream" ensuring that employees with 15 or more years of seniority who are laid off will receive 50 per cent of their pay.

The UAW approved the Ford agreement by a margin of about 3 to 1. By contrast, the union narrowly approved — by 52 per cent — a similar agreement with General Motors Corporation (GM) on April 8, partly because GM had shown a 1981 profit. In exchange for wage concessions and deferrals, GM agreed to open four closed plants, to start a prepaid legal service plan for employees, to share profits above an agreed-upon base, and to try out a pilot program of lifetime job guarantees at four plants. Related agreements were reached with American Motors Corporation (AMC) on April 18. COLA increases were deferred until December 1984. Because of previous concessions to AMC, the contract provided that the company would pay the deferred increases with 10 per cent compound interest. The company also agreed to keep specified plants open until September 1985 except in "grave circumstances."

Even though a September 1982 agreement with a rejuvenated Chrysler Corporation provided the first wage increase granted by that company since March 1981, the UAW rejected the pact. However, workers voted not to strike in 1982 and to resume bargaining early in 1983. In November, 10,000 Canadian workers of Chrysler struck, forcing layoffs of U.S. workers. The strike ended on December 12 with the Canadians gaining a substantial salary increase. See AUTOMOBILE.

Rubber. On April 19, B. F. Goodrich Company and the United Rubber Workers (URW) reached agreement on a three-year contract to replace the pact expiring on April 21. The contract, which became the pattern for the industry, provided no specified wage increase but continued COLA. The union estimated that COLA would provide a 22.5 per cent wage increase over three years, assuming an annual jump of 7 per cent in the CPI. Pensions and other benefits were improved. Goodrich agreed to give the URW early warning of planned plant closures and to start a profit-sharing plan.

United Auto Workers officials, left, and Ford Motor Company executives, right, shake hands after agreeing on a new union contract in February.

Two of 26,000 striking locomotive engineers protest in September before President Reagan signed legislation forcing them back to work.

Telephone Protection. On March 26, the Communication Workers of America agreed with the American Telephone and Telegraph Company on terms to protect 533,000 workers from any negative results of the January decree requiring the company to shed its local affiliates (see COMMUNICATIONS). Protections involved a seven-year guarantee against lost wages and keeping credited service and jobs. Later, the International Brotherhood of Electrical Workers and the Telecommunications International Union assented to similar terms, bringing to 700,000 the number of workers covered by the pact.

Steel Turndown. After bargaining, the United Steelworkers of America (USWA) rebuffed employer proposals for wage concessions to aid an industry troubled by weak domestic demand and strong foreign competition. On July 30, the union's executive board turned down the employers' suggestion for contract modifications to eliminate specified wage increases and to ease COLA's in the contract expiring in July 1983. As a consequence, a scheduled wage increase went into effect the next day. The union rejected similar proposals from aluminum manufacturers on Sept. 2, 1982. See STEEL INDUSTRY.

On the organizing front, the USWA abandoned its effort to organize E. I. du Pont de Nemours & Company. After 14 straight defeats in representation elections, the union threw in the towel before the vote in the 15th election.

Other Settlements. The Oil, Chemical and Atomic Workers International Union on January 11 settled with Gulf Oil Company on an agreement that provided an immediate 9 per cent increase, a 90-cent increase in January 1983 (a raise of about 7.1 per cent), and improvements in health benefits. The settlement ultimately covered 55,000 workers at 400 facilities.

General Electric Company (GE) and three electrical unions agreed on June 29 to immediate wage increases of 7 per cent and 3 per cent in June of 1983 and 1984, respectively. Increases were also programmed under a liberalized COLA plan. Concerning job security, the parties agreed to six-month notice of plant closings and 60 days notice of the introduction of robots or other automated processes. Westinghouse Electric Corporation and the unions agreed on a similar pact after they resolved various problems.

Congress in September legislated a settlement in the dispute between the Brotherhood of Locomotive Engineers and Class I railroads. A four-day strike by the union from September 19 to 22 halted many commuter trains until Congress passed legislation ordering the engineers back to work. The union had resisted accepting the pattern settlement in the industry, which provided for four general wage increases, six COLA increases, and two instances of folding COLA increases into base pay. Union members wanted the right to strike so that they would always be the highest-paid railroad employees. The September law forbade strikes until mid-1984.

National Football League players did not let the depressed economy prevent them from going on a 57-day strike for improved income security. The players walked out on September 21, saying they wanted a guaranteed share of the employers' gross revenues, wage scales based on seniority, and improved minimum salaries. The strike ended in a compromise on November 16, and the season resumed on November 21. See FOOTBALL.

National Policy. President Ronald Reagan's policies of reduction—in income taxes, government spending, and regulation of business—and his defense build-up did not expand the U.S. economy in 1982. Inflation and interest rates moved smartly down, but so did employment, industrial production, and consumer expectations. Economists agreed that it would take a very strong recovery to drive unemployment down.

President Reagan on October 13 signed the Job Training Partnership Act to replace the Comprehensive Employment and Training Act (CETA), which expired on September 30. The legislation will support training for 1 million persons—primarily poor youths—each year. Compared with CETA, the new act reduced the role of the federal government, boosted that of state governors, and provided for an enlarged role for private industry.

Organized labor called for a drastic shift in public policy in the face of high unemployment. It urged that jobs be created by, among other things, revitalizing the housing industry and reconstructing the crumbling infrastructure of the country: its bridges, roads, dams, sewer systems, and other facilities (see BUILDING AND CONSTRUCTION). Labor also demanded tax equity for working people and a halt to cuts in funding of various social welfare programs. Some unions called for protection against "job-stealing" foreign competition.

In a quiet aftermath to 1981's most dramatic labor-management confrontation, the Professional Air Traffic Controllers Organization (PATCO) declared bankruptcy on July 2. PATCO President Gary Eads, who succeeded Robert E. Poli, leader of the 1981 strike, said the union was "finished." After Poli resigned in January, the American Federation of Labor and Congress of Industrial Organizations Executive Council and the Teamsters Union intervened with the Administration on the controllers' behalf. President Reagan agreed that the fired controllers could apply for other federal jobs but said they could not become controllers again. See AVIATION. Robert W. Fisher

See also ECONOMICS. In WORLD BOOK, see LABOR; LABOR FORCE.

LAOS. The Lao People's Revolutionary Party (LPRP) held its first congress in 10 years from April 27 to 30, 1982. The party, a Communist one with close ties to Vietnam, claimed 40,000 members. The congress emphasized the "special relationship" of Laos with Vietnam. Vietnamese advisers reportedly dominated both the Lao party and government.

The April congress did not make any major changes in LPRP leadership. Kayson Phomvihan was renamed secretary-general of the party and continued as prime minister of the government.

However, Laos made a number of governmental changes later in the year. On August 5, the LPRP sent a new Cabinet list to the Supreme People's Council. The council, headed by President Souphanouvong, is theoretically the top government body. It rubber-stamped the party nominations on September 20, and two days later the changes were made. The second-ranked party and government official, Nouhak Phoumsavan, resigned as finance minister. Another LPRP leader, Phoumi Vongvichit, resigned as education minister.

The significance of the Cabinet changes was unclear to outsiders. Nouhak's loss of the finance post might have been related to the Soviet Union's unhappiness about the way economic aid had been used, some observers suggested. An estimated 2,000 Soviet advisers worked in Laos on aid projects during the year.

Opposition. Phoumi Nosavan, a right wing Lao general and vice-premier in the 1960s, announced in Thailand on August 10 that he intended to set up an anti-Communist government somewhere in Laos. Some of the exiled Lao leaders whom he sought to enlist in his effort were reluctant, however. Phoumi claimed to have a large guerrilla army inside Laos fighting the several divisions of Vietnamese troops stationed in the country. He also claimed to be cooperating with the exiled Cambodian coalition government headed by Prince Norodom Sihanouk.

Foreign Relations. The Lao government accused China of giving military training to Lao exiles and sending them into northern Laos. Lao Information Minister Sisana Sisane called China his country's "direct and most dangerous enemy." He said Kong Le, who had commanded a Lao neutralist army in the early 1960s, and former Lao Communist Sisana Saignanouvong were directing operations from China and conducting espionage and psychological warfare.

The United States donated some medical supplies and other civilian aid to Laos. Most outside help came from Vietnam and the Soviet Union. Despite efforts to improve agriculture, Laos remained dependent on foreign aid. Henry S. Bradsher

See also ASIA (Facts in Brief Table). In WORLD BOOK, see LAOS.

LATIN AMERICA

Latin Americans were shocked in 1982 by a bitter 10-week war between Great Britain and Argentina over the Falkland Islands (called *Islas Malvinas* by Argentines). During the conflict, the United States sided with the British to the dismay of an overwhelming majority of its Latin American neighbors. In addition, the worldwide recession caused despair throughout Latin America during the year. The region's earnings from trade fell sharply, forcing governments to redraft budgets.

Elections. Along with new challenges, Latin America experienced political renewal. In 1982, more than two-thirds of Latin America's voters had an opportunity to cast a ballot, and even more of the area's peoples gained new leadership.

In November, voters in Brazil, the most populous Latin American country, went to the polls for the first time in more than 20 years to vote for state and municipal officials. The nation's military regimes had appointed such officials since 1964, when a coup ended democracy in Brazil. According to plans by the Brazilian government, those elected to office in 1982 will, when democracy is completely restored in 1985, pick the country's first civilian president in more than two decades.

Long lines of Salvadorans wait on a street in El Salvador on March 28 to vote in the election for a new Constituent Assembly.

In Uruguay, a somewhat similar process unfolded. Uruguayans went to the polls in November for the first time since 1972 to vote for leaders of political parties, a step aimed at restoring democracy and national elections in 1984.

In 1982, new presidents were elected by the people in Mexico, Colombia, Costa Rica, the Dominican Republic, and Honduras. In Bolivia, at a time of near-total disenchantment with military rule, the nation's Congress elected a former president to the second term previously denied him. In Panama, the vice-president assumed the presidency with a push from the nation's powerful National Guard, which had become irked with his predecessor's flirtation with leftists. In Guatemala, the nation's military took matters into its own hands following massive vote fraud in popular elections and raised to power a general who had been previously denied that high office by vote fraud. In Argentina, following the nation's disastrous military defeat in the Falklands, army leaders elevated to the presidency a retired soldier whose main virtue was that he had nothing to do with the defeat. Among his first statements was a pledge to restore democracy to Argentina by 1984.

But of all the elections in Latin America in 1982, those that most captured the admiration of the world took place in war-torn El Salvador. In record numbers, Salvadorans braved threats of reprisal to vote for a new Constituent Assembly. The results of the election were to some extent inconclusive. But one fact stood out in bold relief—the people of El Salvador voted for peace.

U.S. Relations. Early in his presidency, United States President Ronald Reagan chose to draw the line against foreign subversion in Central America and to use U.S. military power to help create the conditions for the re-establishment of peace there. On March 9, 1982, the Reagan Administration released aerial reconnaissance photographs to document that Nicaragua, with Cuban and Soviet assistance, was building up the largest military force in Central America. At the March briefing, U.S. intelligence officers said that Nicaragua had a standing army of from 25,000 to 35,000 soldiers, equipped with Soviet tanks and helicopters. Nicaragua's total armed forces, including militia, were estimated at nearly 70,000.

In response to the threat posed by Nicaragua's arms build-up and its alleged complicity in funneling Cuban and Soviet arms to rebels in El Salvador, the United States stepped up plans to create a rapid deployment force to operate out of Key West, Fla. Military training provided by the United States to armies of friendly Latin American countries was increased at the U.S.-operated School of the Americas in Panama.

The United States supplied increased military aid in 1982 to countries threatened by the existence of the large Nicaraguan forces. The United States provided military advisers to Honduras and El Salvador, and U.S. forces took part in maneuvers staged by Honduran troops near the Nicaraguan border. In addition, the United States increased its sales of military hardware—including highly advanced weaponry—to friendly Latin American nations.

In September, the U.S. Congress passed a bill that included economic aid under President Rea-

Mexicans vie for copies of the latest foreign exchange rules in August. Mexico made strict rules to stop the flow of pesos out of the country.

gan's Caribbean Basin Initiative plan. The bill provided $350 million in aid for nations of Central America and the Caribbean area.

Falklands War. To the world's surprise, a 10-week war broke out in the South Atlantic Ocean after Argentine forces occupied the Falkland Islands on April 2. The war forced the United States to side with its North Atlantic Treaty Organization ally, Great Britain, an act regarded as betrayal by many Latin American nations. See FALKLAND ISLANDS.

The suddenness with which the Falklands war burst onto the scene, and the inability of the United Nations (UN), the Organization of American States, and negotiators from several well-meaning countries to defuse it, caused a re-examination of the issues involved in a dozen or more other Latin American territorial disputes. Among these disputes—whose solution, according to Thomas O. Enders, assistant secretary of state for inter-American affairs, should have higher priority in U.S. policy—were disagreements pitting Venezuela against Guyana, Argentina against Chile, Peru against Ecuador, Bolivia against Chile, Honduras against El Salvador, and Guatemala against Belize. Any of these disputes might escalate into armed confrontation.

Peace Initiatives. Toward year-end, there were several proposals on ways to bring peace to Central America, in addition to reports of secret negotiations between the government and guerrillas of El Salvador to end the civil war in that country. At Costa Rica's initiative, the concept of a "verifiable and regional accord outlawing arms trafficking, subversion, and foreign military and security advisers" was proposed as a means of reducing tensions between Honduras and Nicaragua. The idea was further refined in a joint Mexican-Venezuelan proposal calling for a negotiated settlement to the border dispute between Honduras and Nicaragua. The United States expressed keen interest in such proposals.

Foreign Debts. Fears of a financial collapse in Latin America mounted in 1982 as country after country reached the brink of bankruptcy. Three main factors were blamed for the economic mess: declines in prices for Latin America's exports, including oil and sugar; overly aggressive lending of large sums of money to developing nations by international banks; and high interest rates, which snowballed the cost of repaying loans. A fourth reason for the region's heavy debt was the massive flight of investment capital out of Latin America.

In all, Latin America's long-term indebtedness reached more than $250 billion during 1982. Payments on long-term and short-term debt represented from 15 to 20 per cent of all earnings by most Latin American countries through international trade. Mexico was forced to devalue its currency by 70 per cent and to seek approximately $12 billion in loans to avoid bankruptcy.

The list of Latin American countries that were forced to reschedule their debts during 1982 was long and varied. It included such democracies as Peru and Costa Rica and such dictatorships as Argentina and Cuba. As the year drew to a close, there was growing concern that some heavily indebted large country—such as Brazil or Mexico—might fail to meet its financial obligations and trigger an international banking collapse. To avoid that catastrophe, various solutions were proposed, including a massive increase in the resources of the International Monetary Fund (IMF), the United Nations agency that helps keep the world's financial payments in order. In December, leading Western nations agreed to raise the IMF's lending capacity by at least 40 per cent.

Big Projects. With funds borrowed largely before the onset of financial difficulties, Latin America launched or completed a number of major projects during 1982. Work began on the development of the enormous coal reserves around Cerrejón in northern Colombia. At a cost of $3.5 billion, the Colombian government, Exxon Corporation, and the Morrison-Knudsen Construction Company are developing open-pit mines there to produce 11 million short tons (10 million metric tons) of high-quality coal annually. Another major mining endeavor was initiated in Carajás, an area that covers 10.5 million acres (4.2 million hectares) of north-central Brazil. Carajás is one of the world's largest untapped sources of iron, copper, bauxite, tin, coal, nickel, manganese, and gold.

In September, a $300-million oil pipeline across the Isthmus of Panama went into operation. A joint project of private companies and the Panamanian government, the pipeline provides for the transfer of crude oil from tankers too large to transit the Panama Canal. In November, the Itaipú hydroelectric dam, built by Brazil and Paraguay on their common border, began partial operation. When it becomes fully operational, the dam will be the world's largest single source of hydroelectric power.

Environment. Expanding development of the Amazon Basin caused environmental concern in 1982. Environmentalists in Brazil and other nations stepped up efforts to ensure that development does not destroy the region's ecology and Indian population.

The environmental movement also gathered momentum elsewhere in Latin America. In Argentina, for example, conservationists denounced commercial plans to kill nearly 50,000 Magellan penguins for their protein-rich meat. The penguins

Guerrillas stand guard near a government truck that they stopped and burned on a road near Usulután, El Salvador, in February.

Facts in Brief on Latin American Political Units

Country	Population	Government	Monetary Unit*	Foreign Trade (million U.S. $) Exports†	Imports†
Antigua & Barbuda	79,000	Governor General Sir Wilfred Ebenezer Jacobs; Prime Minister Vere C. Bird	dollar (2.7 = $1)	1	4
Argentina	28,964,000	President Reynaldo Benito Antonio Bignone	peso (39,965 = $1)	8,054	10,619
Bahamas	240,000	Governor General Sir Gerald C. Cash; Prime Minister Lynden O. Pindling	dollar (1 = $1)	4,834	5,481
Barbados	253,000	Governor General Sir Deighton Harcourt Lisle Ward; Prime Minister J. M. G. Adams	dollar (1.9 = $1)	194	571
Belize	158,000	Governor General Minita Gordon; Prime Minister George Cadle Price	dollar (2 = $1)	102	133
Bolivia	6,048,000	President Hernán Siles Zuazo	peso (44 = $1)	1,033	833
Brazil	127,427,000	President João Baptista de Oliveira Figueiredo	cruzeiro (229 = $1)	22,771	23,543
Chile	11,675,000	President Augusto Pinochet Ugarte	peso (66 = $1)	3,931	6,379
Colombia	29,810,000	President Belisario Betancur	peso (61.05 = $1)	3,925	4,739
Costa Rica	2,411,000	President Luis Alberto Monge Alvarez	colón (40 = $1)	963	1,528
Cuba	10,252,000	President Fidel Castro Ruz	peso (1 = $1.19)	5,652	6,448
Dominica	80,000	President Aurelius Marie; Prime Minister Mary Eugenia Charles	dollar (2.7 = $1)	9	47
Dominican Republic	5,935,000	President Salvador Jorge Blanco	peso (1 = $1)	1,199	1,450
Ecuador	9,235,000	President Osvaldo Hurtado Larrea	sucre (33.1 = $1)	2,459	2,250
El Salvador	5,229,000	Provisional President Alvaro Magaña; Constituent Assembly President Roberto D'Aubuisson	colón (2.5 = $1)	720	976
Grenada	115,000	Governor General Sir Paul Godwin Scoon; Prime Minister Maurice Bishop	dollar (2.7 = $1)	17	49
Guatemala	7,935,000	President José Efraín Ríos-Montt	quetzal (1 = $1)	1,520	1,598
Guyana	919,000	President Forbes Burnham; Prime Minister Ptolemy A. Reid	dollar (2.5 = $1)	389	417
Haiti	5,284,000	President Jean-Claude Duvalier	gourde (5 = $1)	188	266
Honduras	4,104,000	President Roberto Suazo Córdova	lempira (2 = $1)	761	949
Jamaica	2,292,000	Governor General Sir Florizel Glasspole; Prime Minister Edward Seaga	dollar (1.8 = $1)	982	1,509
Mexico	74,507,000	President Miguel de la Madrid Hurtado	peso (70 = $1)	18,973	23,605
Nicaragua	2,980,000	3-member Government of National Reconstruction Junta	córdoba (10.1 = $1)	448	883
Panama	2,013,000	President Ricardo de la Espriella, Jr.	balboa (1 = $1)	315	1,540
Paraguay	3,361,000	President Alfredo Stroessner	guaraní (126 = $1)	296	506
Peru	19,317,000	President Fernando Belaúnde Terry	sol (870.1 = $1)	3,364	2,541
Puerto Rico	3,188,000	Governor Carlos Romero Barceló	U.S. $	6,576	9,018
St. Lucia	121,000	Governor General Boswell Williams; Prime Minister John Compton	dollar (2.7 = $1)	26	115
St. Vincent & the Grenadines	126,000	Governor General Sir Sydney Gunn-Munro; Prime Minister R. Milton Cato	dollar (2.7 = $1)	22	41
Suriname	361,000	President L. F. Ramdat Misier; Prime Minister Henry Neyhorst	guilder (1.8 = $1)	514	504
Trinidad & Tobago	1,232,000	President Ellis Emmanuel Innocent Clarke; Prime Minister George Chambers	dollar (2.4 = $1)	3,763	3,112
Uruguay	2,952,000	President Gregorio C. Alvarez	peso (13.7 = $1)	1,019	1,646
Venezuela	15,202,000	President Luis Herrera Campíns	bolivar (4.3 = $1)	19,221	10,671

*Exchange rates as of Dec. 1, 1982. †Latest available data.

live in the remote southern Argentine province of Chubut.

Environmentalists became increasingly alarmed at conditions in Latin America's cities. In some major cities, headlong urbanization had caused overcrowding verging on anarchy. Demographers predicted that Mexico City, Mexico, will become the world's most populous city by the year 2000 with 31 million people. Mexico City had just 3 million people in 1950. Demographers also predicted that São Paulo, Brazil, will rank second among the world's cities by 2000 with 25.8 million people.

Automobile accidents in Latin American cities skyrocketed during the year. In 1982, the Pan American Health Organization estimated that victims of auto accidents, mostly young people, occupied some 30 per cent of the hospital beds in surgery wards of several Latin American countries. Pollution also gripped some of the area's more industrialized cities.

Cousteau Expedition. On June 2, the French explorer Jacques Cousteau sailed aboard the research yacht *Calypso* from Belém, Brazil, on an expedition to study and film the flora and fauna of the Amazon River and surrounding jungle. He was accompanied by 40 Latin American scientists who were studying the ecological relationship between the Amazon Basin and the Atlantic Ocean, and between the region's Indians and their surroundings. The $4-million expedition, scheduled to last 11 months, included submarines, helicopters, and hovercraft. The project was financed by television networks that will feature the results.

Other Developments. On Jan. 1, 1982, Javier Pérez de Cuéllar of Peru took office as secretary-general of the United Nations. Before year-end, he had earned high praise for his candor in assessing the failures of the UN.

Eduardo Frei Montalva, who was Chile's president from 1964 to 1970 and proclaimed a "Revolution in Liberty," died on January 22 in Santiago, Chile, at age 70. Frei lived to see the collapse of his country's vaunted democracy three years after he left office, when the military overthrew his successor, Salvador Allende Gossens.

On October 21, Colombia's Gabriel García Márquez was awarded the Nobel Prize for Literature. His novels, including *One Hundred Years of Solitude* (1967) and *The Autumn of the Patriarch* (1975), have found a universal audience through translations into many languages. Nathan A. Haverstock

See also articles on the various Latin American countries. In the Special Reports section, see WHAT WENT WRONG IN CENTRAL AMERICA? In WORLD BOOK, see LATIN AMERICA and articles on the individual countries.

LAW. See CIVIL RIGHTS; COURTS AND LAWS; CRIME; SUPREME COURT OF THE UNITED STATES.

LEBANON. Israeli tanks and infantry invaded southern Lebanon on June 6, 1982. Within a week, Israeli forces occupied the entire coast as far north as the Lebanese capital of Beirut, which was placed under siege in a campaign to drive the Palestine Liberation Organization (PLO) out of Lebanon. See MIDDLE EAST.

Because PLO bases and Palestinian refugee camps were located in or close to Lebanese cities, the civilian Lebanese population bore the brunt of the invasion. Such major cities as Tyre and Sidon, as well as Beirut, were devastated. Damage in Sidon was estimated at $320 million, with several thousand shops and homes destroyed. In October, the Lebanese government estimated that reconstruction would cost $10 billion.

More tragic than the loss of property, however, was the loss of life. Although total casualties were impossible to verify, reliable neutral observers estimated that the war left about 18,000 people dead and 30,000 wounded. Included in the count were casualties among Lebanese and Palestinian guerrillas and civilians and Syrian soldiers. In addition, Israel said more than 370 of its soldiers were killed and some 2,400 wounded.

Factional Struggles. The expulsion of the PLO from West Beirut in August eliminated one major factor complicating efforts to restore stability to Lebanon. However, threaded into the web of Israeli-Palestinian conflict in the country was the ongoing struggle between various Lebanese social, ethnic, and religious groups that had set off the 1975-1976 civil war (see MIDDLE EAST [Close-Up]). In April, fighting erupted in southern Lebanon and around Beirut between Shiite Muslim militiamen and several leftist groups, including the Lebanese Communist Party and the PLO.

Nevertheless, after the Israeli invasion, Lebanese leaders set about establishing a "government of national salvation," designed to unite the various factions and work for the withdrawal of all foreign troops. The first step was the election of a new president to succeed Elias Sarkis, whose term expired on September 23.

According to an unwritten agreement, the president of Lebanon must be a Christian and the prime minister a Sunni Muslim, with other government positions allocated according to the size of the religious group. Bashir Gemayel, leader of the Christian Phalangist Party and overall commander of the Lebanese Front Christian militia, was the only candidate for president.

Gemayel was opposed by the majority of Muslim deputies in the Chamber of Deputies, the body responsible for electing the president. They said they would boycott the election until foreign troops left the country. However, after efforts to block a quorum in the chamber failed, Gemayel was elected president. He pledged national unity

Jubilation over Bashir Gemayel's election as president of Lebanon in August turned to mourning weeks later when he was assassinated before taking office.

and urged the Lebanese to forget the past. But Gemayel's suspected involvement in massacres of Palestinians and Muslim leftists during the civil war left him vulnerable to revenge. On September 14—nine days before he was scheduled to take office—he was murdered in a bomb blast at Phalangist headquarters in East Beirut.

The violence escalated from September 16 to 18 when Lebanese Christian militiamen slaughtered hundreds of unarmed Palestinian men, women, and children in the Sabra and Shatila refugee camps in West Beirut. The official death toll compiled by the International Committee of the Red Cross was 328. However, another 991 people were listed as missing, and several hundred bodies were believed to have been carried away by the militiamen. In November, the Lebanese government arrested 12 people in connection with the massacre.

New President. The murder of Gemayel and the massacre of the refugees generated a rare consensus among Lebanese. On September 21, Christian and Muslim groups in the Chamber of Deputies united in electing Amin Gemayel, Bashir's older brother, president by a 77 to 3 vote (see GEMAYEL, AMIN). In a move to satisfy Lebanon's Muslims, Gemayel on October 4 asked Shafiq al-Wazzan, a Sunni Muslim, to remain in his post as prime minister.

The new president issued an eight-point declaration calling for Israel's withdrawal from Lebanon, the subsequent withdrawal of all foreign troops, and the disarming of all armed militias. On November 9, the Lebanese parliament gave the Gemayel government the power to rule by decree for six months.

The declaration also called for the establishment of the authority of the Lebanese Army. In late September, the army disarmed the 1,500-member Sunni Muslim Murabitoun militia, the largest single private army in Beirut. The Lebanese Army began taking control of various sectors of West Beirut in October. On December 26, Israel and Lebanon said they would begin negotiations on December 28 regarding security arrangements and the withdrawal of Israeli troops.

Reconstruction. President Gemayel's official visit to the United States in late October resulted in a pledge of $95 million in aid for Lebanon's reconstruction. As of September, other governments and the United Nations had pledged an additional $90 million. In September, buoyed by the Gemayel election, the Lebanese pound rose to 4.8 to U.S. $1. It had dropped to 5.2 to U.S. $1 during the fighting.

William Spencer

See also ISRAEL; MIDDLE EAST (Facts in Brief Table). In WORLD BOOK, see LEBANON.

LESOTHO. See AFRICA.

LIBERIA. See AFRICA.

LIBRARY. Libraries in the United States attempted to gather increased local support in 1982 to compensate for reductions in library funding by the federal government. Some libraries succeeded. For example, the Houston library received a 34 per cent increase in city funds, enabling it to hire additional staff and provide services to meet the growing and increasingly international population of the city.

On the other hand, libraries in economically depressed areas of the United States suffered losses in revenue. The Detroit Public Library saw its state funds cut from $8.5 million to $7 million. This cutback resulted in staff layoffs, curtailment of services at all library facilities, and a reduction in money allocated to book acquisition. The city of Detroit, reeling under the effects of the automobile industry slump, was unable to significantly increase the library budget. However, wage concessions that were made by library union employees saved several staff positions and preserved some branch services.

The Carnegie Library in Pittsburgh, Pa., opened a used-book store staffed by volunteers to raise money to offset the rising cost of new books and periodicals. The library also hoped income from the store would help compensate for the $432,000 in operating funds that the library requested but did not receive from city and county governments.

New Buildings. A new $6.7-million library at the University of Wisconsin-Stout was dedicated on April 24. The 123,000-square-foot (11,400-square-meter) library provides microcomputers and terminals with access to the university computer center. In addition, an in-house telephone system enables library users to obtain assistance from the circulation and reference desks.

Ground was broken for a three-story, $11.5-million library at Drexel University in Philadelphia. The library will have carrels providing space for individual study for up to 1,350 people. Residents of Anchorage, Alaska, approved a bond sale of $17.1 million to finance construction of a 140,000-square-foot (13,000-square-meter) central library. Voters in Corpus Christi, Tex., also approved city plans to raise $5 million to build a new central library.

Library Meetings. The Canadian Library Association's annual conference was held in Saskatoon, Sask., from June 10 to 15. The International Federation of Library Associations and Institutions' 48th general conference was held in Montreal, Canada, from August 23 to 28. The 101st annual conference of the American Library Association was held in Philadelphia in July. Robert J. Shaw

See also AMERICAN LIBRARY ASSOCIATION; CANADIAN LIBRARY ASSOCIATION. In WORLD BOOK, see LIBRARY.

LIBYA. Leader of the Revolution Muammar Muhammad al-Qadhafi continued to chart an erratic course in foreign policy in 1982. There were as many failures as successes. Relations with Tunisia improved after the Libyan leader's five-day visit there in February. The two nations signed a pact calling for economic and industrial cooperation and coordination of foreign policy. Libya also accepted the decision of the International Court of Justice (ICJ), a United Nations agency, setting the undersea continental shelf boundary between Libya and Tunisia. In March, a week after Qadhafi made a surprise two-hour visit to Malta, the two countries agreed to submit their dispute over offshore oil exploration rights to the ICJ.

Foreign-Policy Failure. Qadhafi suffered a major defeat with the cancellation of the summit meeting of the Organization of African Unity (OAU) scheduled to take place in Tripoli, Libya's capital, in August. A two-thirds quorum of OAU member states could not be mustered. The absentee members boycotted the meeting to support Morocco's opposition to OAU membership for the Polisario Front, a guerrilla group seeking to end Morocco's control of Western Sahara. Libya favored OAU membership for the front. A second attempt to hold the meeting in Tripoli, in November, also failed.

On his first state visit to a Western country, Libyan leader Qadhafi responds to a welcome by Austrian Chancellor Bruno Kreisky in March.

The ongoing dispute with the United States over Qadhafi's alleged support for international terrorism sharpened on March 10 when the Administration of President Ronald Reagan banned all Libyan oil imports and curtailed sales of high-technology items to Libya by U.S. firms.

A Mixed Economic Scene. The cutoff of 150,000 barrels per day (bpd) in oil shipments to the United States had little effect on Libya's economy. New oil agreements with African countries more than made up the difference.

In June, Libya became the first major member of the Organization of Petroleum Exporting Countries to cut oil prices in 1982, from $41 to $39 per barrel. Production was cut to 600,000 bpd, well below the 1.07 million bpd needed for Libya's $62.5-billion 1981-1985 development plan.

Overspending for imports from the industrialized nations caused a loss of credit in July. Italy, Spain, France, Great Britain, and Japan suspended Libyan oil imports pending repayment of debts to exporters in those countries. Italy and Spain resumed imports in August after Libya made scheduled monthly payments. William Spencer

See also AFRICA (Facts in Brief Table). In WORLD BOOK, see LIBYA.

LIECHTENSTEIN. See EUROPE.

LIONS INTERNATIONAL. See COMMUNITY ORGANIZATIONS.

John Updike in April added the 1982 American Book Award to the Pulitzer Prize and National Book Critics Circle awards for *Rabbit Is Rich.*

LITERATURE. Nonfiction captured most of the attention of the United States literary world for the first time in many years in 1982. *The Fate of the Earth,* Jonathan Schell's powerful and disturbing meditation on the consequences of a nuclear holocaust, was easily the most talked-about book of the year. It stood at the head of many new books on nuclear warfare that both capitalized on and led growing public interest in the topic. Other important studies were *The Nuclear Delusion,* by George F. Kennan, and *Beyond the Cold War,* by E. P. Thompson.

Still other significant books about contemporary affairs included *Is There No Place on Earth for Me?,* Susan Sheehan's compelling story of the hopelessness of schizophrenia; *The Underclass,* by Ken Auletta, which asked if the hard-core poor and unemployed could be saved from their lot; and *The Imperious Economy,* by David E. Calleo, exploring the decline of American economic influence.

Some interesting journalistic books were *Indecent Exposure,* by David McClintick, a best-selling exposé of embezzlement and corporate struggle in Hollywood; *The Invisible Bankers: Everything the Insurance Industry Never Wanted You to Know,* by Andrew Tobias; *America in Search of Itself: The Making of the President, 1956-1980,* by Theodore H. White; *American Journey: Traveling with Tocqueville in Search of Democracy in America,* by Richard Reeves; and *Hearts and Minds: The Anatomy of Racism from Roosevelt to Reagan,* by Harry S. Ashmore.

Among the year's volumes on foreign affairs, two dealt with lesser-known aspects of the People's Republic of China. Both Richard Bernstein's *From the Center of the Earth: The Search for Truth About China* and Fox Butterfield's *China: Alive in the Bitter Sea* attempted, largely successfully, to reveal the realities of Chinese society.

Political Biographies followed closely in interest. Lyndon Baines Johnson came under intense scrutiny in two books. Robert A. Caro's controversial *The Path to Power,* the first book in a projected three-volume biography, charged Johnson with overweening, amoral ambition as a congressional secretary and representative from Texas. Ronnie Dugger's *The Politician* contended that Johnson had close and questionable relationships with ruthless Texas businessmen.

Two other important presidential biographies were Robert J. Donovan's *Tumultuous Years: The Presidency of Harry S. Truman, 1949-1953,* filled with new and revealing insights into Truman's upright character; and *Reagan,* by Lou Cannon, exploring the events and forces that shaped the mind of President Ronald Reagan. But Jimmy Carter's memoir, *Keeping Faith,* disappointed those seeking insights into the events of his presidency and into the man.

Other leading political biographies of Americans were *Thomas E. Dewey and His Times,* by Richard Norton Smith, which recalled the 1948 Republican presidential candidate's accomplishments as a politician and public servant; *Earl Warren,* by G. Edward White, a penetrating analysis of the late chief justice's impact on the Supreme Court of the United States as foreshadowed by his earlier career; and *Felix Frankfurter and His Times,* by Michael E. Parrish, a study of the reasons for the Supreme Court justice's eventual political and philosophical turn away from liberalism.

European lives included *Bismarck,* by Edward Crankshaw; *Mussolini,* by Denis Mack Smith; and *Churchill: Young Man in a Hurry,* by Ted Morgan.

Notable Literary Biographies included *Robert Lowell,* by Ian Hamilton; *Katherine Anne Porter: A Life,* by Joan Givner; *Isak Dinesen: The Life of a Storyteller,* by Judith Thurman; *Hannah Arendt: For Love of the World,* by Elisabeth Young-Bruehl; *W. H. Auden,* by Humphrey Carpenter; *Waldo Emerson,* by Gay Wilson Allen; *Kafka,* by Ronald Hayman; *Thomas Hardy,* by Michael Millgate; and *Camus,* by Patrick McCarthy.

Other literary biographies were Australian Patrick White's *Flaws in the Glass: A Self-Portrait,* which revealed the 1973 Nobel Prize winner's homosexuality, important to the development of his literary sensibility; *The Torch in My Ear,* by Elias Canetti, the second volume of memoirs from the winner of the 1981 Nobel Prize for Literature; *Aké: The Years of Childhood,* the autobiography of the splendid Nigerian playwright Wole Soyinka; and *Growing Up,* the charming autobiography of journalist Russell Baker.

Important biographies of figures in the arts were *Seeing Is Forgetting the Name of the Thing One Sees: A Life of Contemporary Artist Robert Irwin,* by Lawrence Weschler; *Nadia Boulanger: A Life in Music,* by Leonie Rosenstiel; *Frederic Remington,* by Peggy Samuels and Harold Samuels; *The Wider Sea: A Life of John Ruskin,* by John Dixon Hunt; and *Mozart,* by Wolfgang Hildesheimer.

Fine memoirs of general interest were *Hunger of Memory: The Education of Richard Rodriguez,* the story of a young Mexican American's rise into the U.S. middle class and the cost to his heritage; *Years of Upheaval,* by Henry A. Kissinger, the second volume of the former U.S. secretary of state's memoirs; and *The Past Has Another Pattern,* the autobiography of diplomat George W. Ball.

Letters and Diaries. *Stravinsky: Selected Correspondence,* edited by Robert Craft, revealed, among other things, the composer's constant search for money to support himself. *The Journals of Sylvia Plath* were scorching self-revelations of the self-destructive poet.

Eleanor Roosevelt's correspondence was mined in two books. *Love, Eleanor,* edited by Joseph Lash and Franklin D. Roosevelt, Jr., revealed her emotional fervor for her friends. *Mother and Daughter,* edited by Bernard Asbell, showed that Eleanor's daughter, Anna, was both her confidante and a rival for Franklin Delano Roosevelt's affections.

The Correspondence of Boris Pasternak and Olga Friedenberg 1910-1954, edited by Elliott Mossman, was a dual self-portrait, in letters, of two gifted artist-cousins trapped under a repressive Soviet regime. *The Diary of Virginia Woolf,* edited by Anne O. Bell, reached the fourth volume, covering the years 1931 to 1935. *Theodore Dreiser: American Diaries 1902-1926,* edited by Thomas T. Riggio, though sometimes unpolished, revealed much about the man and writer as an archetype of the uncultured, rough-hewn American. The second volume of *The Letters of Gustave Flaubert,* edited by Francis Steegmuller, covered the years 1857 to 1880 in the French novelist's life.

History. Among the best of the few important histories to be published in 1982 were the startling *The Auschwitz Album,* pictures by Lili Meier and text by Peter Hellman, a remarkable collection of 188 photographs taken inside the Nazi death camp; *The Complete Anti-Federalist* and *What the Anti-Federalists Were For,* by Herbert J. Storing and Murray Dry, a massive reconstruction of the papers of those who counseled against a federal sys-

Irish President Patrick Hillery unveils a bust of James Joyce in Dublin to mark the centenary of the author whose work celebrated that city.

tem in 1787; *The Vineyard of Liberty,* by James MacGregor Burns, a superb popular history of the United States between the adoption of the Constitution and the declaration of the Emancipation Proclamation; and *The Ruling Race,* by James Oakes, a searching look at the history of American slaveholders.

Science. *The Growth of Biological Thought: Diversity, Evolution and Inheritance,* by Ernst Mayr, was the first of two ambitious volumes on the development of ideas now important in biology. Two other significant books in this category were *Science Observed: Essays Out of My Mind,* by Jeremy Bernstein, and *The Cosmic Code: Quantum Physics as the Language of Nature,* by Heinz R. Pagels.

Fiction. Despite disappointing novels from several of the heavyweights of American letters, younger writers kept the quality of the genre high.

Substandard work came from Saul Bellow, whose *The Dean's December* was fervent but tired, and Bernard Malamud, whose *God's Grace* was excessively preachy. Unhappily, this weakness extended to the valedictory novels of two major writers who died during the year. John Cheever's loving but fragile *Oh What a Paradise It Seems* appeared just before his death in June from cancer, and John Gardner was killed in a motorcycle accident in September shortly after his earnest but clumsy *Mickelsson's Ghosts* appeared.

But John Updike, considered by many critics to be the finest U.S. novelist now working, offered *Bech Is Back,* a sparkling collection of linked comic tales about a failed Jewish novelist. Other highly competent novels by established writers were *Sabbatical: A Romance,* by John Barth; *The Killing Ground,* by Mary Lee Settle; *A Bloodsmoor Romance,* by Joyce Carol Oates; *Grace Abounding,* by Maureen Howard; and *George Mills,* by Stanley Elkin.

Several younger writers began to consolidate their positions as major novelists. Paul Theroux's *The Mosquito Coast* was a brilliant novel about a mad Yankee inventor seeking his fortune in the wilds of Central America, and Gail Godwin's *A Mother and Two Daughters* was a skillful tale of feminine solitude in American life.

The Names, by Don DeLillo, a graceful novel packed with the magic of language, explored the relation of American myths to the rest of the world. *Autumn,* by A. G. Mojtabai, was a deeply felt novel of the emotional awakening of a newly widowed man. Other younger writers who published splendid novels were William Wharton, Anne Tyler, John Gregory Dunne, Alice Hoffman, and Alice Walker.

Important story collections were *The Collected Stories of Isaac Bashevis Singer; Sixty Stories,* by Donald Barthelme; *Levitation: Five Fictions,* by Cynthia Ozick; and *The Burning House,* by Ann Beattie.

The most impressive first novel of the year was *The 13th Valley,* a gritty and authentic tale of combat and disillusionment in Vietnam by John M. Del Vecchio, a former U.S. Army combat correspondent. Other fine first novels came from Ivan Doig, Alice McDermott, Sheilà Ballantyne, Laurel Goldman, and Angela Gardner.

Books from abroad by English-speaking writers included *Schindler's List,* by the Australian Thomas Keneally, a documentary novel of a true-life Sudeten German industrialist who saved 1,200 Jews from the Holocaust; *Monsignor Quixote,* by Great Britain's Graham Greene; *Collected Stories,* by Greene's compatriot V. S. Pritchett; *Beyond the Pale,* short stories by Ireland's William Trevor; *Malgudi Days,* by India's R. K. Narayan; *Bodily Harm,* a novel, and *Dancing Girl and Other Stories,* short stories, by Canada's Margaret Atwood; *Ah, But Your Land Is Beautiful,* by Alan Paton, and *Waiting for the Barbarians,* by J. M. Coetzee, both of South Africa.

Essays. Among the better offerings in this category were *The Tugman's Passage,* by Edward Hoagland; *Abbey's Road,* by Edward Abbey; *The Second American Revolution and Other Essays 1976-1982,* by Gore Vidal; *Pieces and Pontifications,* by Norman Mailer; and *Prejudices: A Philosophical Dictionary,* by Robert Nisbet.

Criticism. Novelist Diane Johnson proved herself a critic of high intelligence with *Terrorists and Novelists,* her first book of literary analysis. William Barrett's *The Truants* took the reader inside the minds of the intellectual circle that published *Partisan Review* immediately after World War II. *Agon: Towards a Theory of Revisionism,* by Harold Bloom, was the newest installment in the critic's theory of creation in poetry as a reaction against those who had gone before.

Miscellaneous. The Library of America, an ambitious enterprise of reprinting the works of classic American writers in sturdy, uniform editions, offered its first eight volumes. They were books by Walt Whitman, Herman Melville, Harriet Beecher Stowe, Nathaniel Hawthorne, Jack London, Mark Twain, and William Dean Howells.

Paperbacks. The 10 best-selling soft-cover books of 1982 were *E.T.,* by William Kotzwinkle; *Gorky Park,* by Martin Cruz Smith; *The Cardinal Sins,* by Andrew Greeley; *The Road to Gandolfo,* by Robert Ludlum; *The Perfect Stranger,* by Danielle Steel; *How to Make Love to a Man,* by Alexandra Penney; *Noble House,* by James Clavell; *Love,* by Leo Buscaglia; *Cujo,* by Stephen King; and *Surrender to Love,* by Rosemary Rogers. Henry Kisor

See also AWARDS AND PRIZES (Literature Awards); CANADIAN LITERATURE; LITERATURE FOR CHILDREN; POETRY; PUBLISHING. In WORLD BOOK, see LITERATURE.

LITERATURE, CANADIAN. See CANADIAN LIBRARY ASSOCIATION; CANADIAN LITERATURE.

LITERATURE FOR CHILDREN. Realistic fiction dominated the list of books for children in 1982. A number of books dealt with relationships between the young and the old. Some stories depicted divided families in which the mother works outside the home and the children make their own adjustments to growing up. Informational books of all kinds continued to be published, with special attention given to ecology and the environment. Fantasy also remained popular, but fewer poetry, folklore, and folk-tale picture books appeared.

Some outstanding books of 1982 were:

Picture Books

Ming Lo Moves the Mountain, by Arnold Lobel (Greenwillow). Disturbed by the presence of a mountain, Ming Lo and his wife seek advice about moving it, with amusing results. Illustrations in soft colors enhance the Chinese flavor of the fantasy. Ages 3 to 8.

Bea and Mr. Jones, by Amy Schwartz (Bradbury). When a bored father and daughter change places, Bea goes to the office and Mr. Jones attends kindergarten. Comical pencil illustrations add to the whimsy. Ages 4 to 8.

Anno's Britain, by Mitsumasa Anno (Philomel). The reader takes a visual trip to Great Britain on beautifully designed, wordless pages where well-known characters appear. Ages 4 and up.

Ernest and Celestine and *Bravo, Ernest and Celestine!,* by Gabrielle Vincent (Greenwillow). These accounts of the friendship between a bear named Ernest and a mouse named Celestine radiate warmth. The homey illustrations show touches of Gallic charm. Ages 3 to 8.

Hetty and Harriet, by Graham Oakley (Atheneum). Marvelous illustrations capture the adventures of two young hens, Hetty and Harriet, as they search for a perfect place. Ages 4 to 9.

A, B, See!, by Tana Hoban (Greenwillow). This handsome alphabet book in black, white, and gray tests a child's powers of observation. Ages 4 to 8.

I Dance in My Red Pajamas, by Edith Thatcher Hurd, illustrated by Emily Arnold McCully (Harper). Jenny spends a joyful day with her grandparents despite her parents' warning about being noisy. Pastel water colors capture characters and events perfectly. Ages 3 to 8.

1 Hunter, by Pat Hutchins (Greenwillow). A determined hunter stalks past an assortment of partially concealed creatures. Vivid illustrations provide the humor in this counting book as the child sees what the hunter does not. Ages 3 to 7.

Alfie Gets in First, by Shirley Hughes (Lothrop). Alfie locks himself inside his house. Realistic, expressive illustrations capture the clamor that follows. Ages 3 to 8.

Sister Sweet Ella, by Rosekrans Hoffman (Morrow). Wadsworth thinks he has turned his new baby sister into a cat. Fanciful illustrations add to the magical quality of the story. Ages 3 to 8.

Good As New, by Barbara Douglass, illustrated by Patience Brewster (Lothrop). Grandpa saves the day when a visiting cousin ruins a boy's teddy bear. Bright pictures capture the warm relationship between grandfather and child. Ages 3 to 8.

The Story of Mr. and Mrs. Vinegar, by Stephen Gammell (Lothrop). A husband and wife set out to seek their fortune in this delightfully retold and illustrated English folk tale. Ages 4 to 8.

The Thingumajig Book of Health and Safety, by Irene Keller, illustrated by Dick Keller (Ideals). Humorous rhymes and pictures teach health and safety rules. Ages 4 to 8.

Cobweb Christmas, by Shirley Climo, illustrated by Joe Lasker (Crowell). A kind old woman finally gets her Christmas wish. The illustrations add warmth and humor. Ages 4 to 8.

The Philharmonic Gets Dressed, by Karla Kuskin, illustrated by Marc Simont (Harper). Preparations for the evening's concert are presented in an informative yet humorous manner. Ages 4 to 8.

Chester's Barn, by Lindee Climo (Tundra). Chester cares for the animals one winter's day. Striking paintings accompany the text. Ages 4 to 8.

Land of Dreams, by Michael Foreman (Holt). An old man and a boy collect dream fragments—

Chris Van Allsburg's illustrations for *Jumanji* won the 1982 Caldecott Medal for the most distinguished American picture book for children.

among them Humpty Dumpty, Babar, and Noah's Ark—in this magnificently illustrated fantasy. Ages 4 and up.

Poetry

Tiny Tim: Verses for Children, chosen by Jill Bennett, illustrated by Helen Oxenbury (Delacorte). Amusing illustrations accompany 20 nonsense verses, primarily about children and animals. Ages 4 to 8.

If I Had a Paka: Poems in Eleven Languages, by Charlotte Pomerantz, illustrated by Nancy Tufari (Greenwillow). Readers "speak" Dutch, Samoan, Swahili, and other languages with the help of well-designed illustrations. All ages.

The Sheriff of Rottenshot, by Jack Prelutsky, illustrated by Victoria Chess (Greenwillow). Hilarious purple illustrations capture whimsical people, animals, and situations. Ages 4 to 10.

The Sun's Asleep Behind the Hill, adapted from an Armenian song by Mirra Ginsburg, illustrated by Paul O. Zelinsky (Greenwillow). This stunning bedtime book shows the child's kinship with nature and the universal need for rest. Ages 3 to 7.

Birds: Poems, by Arnold Adoff, illustrated by Troy Howell (Lippincott). Fine line drawings imaginatively highlight the doings and dangers of familiar as well as unnamed birds. All ages.

Birds, Beasts and the Third Thing: Poems by D. H. Lawrence, selected and illustrated by Alice and Martin Provensen, introduction by Donald Hall (Viking). Illustrations of Nottingham, England, where Lawrence grew up, complement 23 poems on various subjects. Ages 8 and up.

Fantasy

The Guardian of Isis, by Monica Hughes (Atheneum). Adventurous, inventive Jody N'Kumo saves his people in this science-fiction story—but not without help. Ages 12 and up.

Tomorrow's Wizard, by Patricia MacLachlan, illustrated by Kathy Jacobi (Harper). Effective black-and-white illustrations accompany this gentle, humorous fantasy about a wish-granting wizard, his apprentice, and a horse. Ages 9 to 12.

Playing Beatie Bow, by Ruth Park (Atheneum). Abigail goes back to the year 1873 in this engrossing Australian time fantasy. Ages 9 to 12.

Pigs Might Fly, by Dick King-Smith, illustrated by Mary Rayner (Viking). Daggie Dogfoot, a runt pig, has some exciting adventures because of his unusual birth defect. Comical dialogue and humorous drawings add to the fun. Ages 8 to 12.

The Darkangel, by Meredith Ann Pierce (Atlantic-Little). The darkangel, a handsome "vampyre," must have his thirst for blood satisfied by 14 maidens. Aeriel, servant to the 13th bride, attempts to save her mistress and the others in this haunting fantasy set on the moon. Ages 12 and up.

Graven Images, by Paul Fleischman, illustrated by Andrew Glass (Harper). Three very different stories, all set in the past, range from murder to comedy to the supernatural. An eerie illustration precedes each well-told tale. Ages 11 and up.

Dragon's Blood, by Jane Yolen (Delacorte). Jakkin, a boy living in bondage on planet Austar IV, steals a baby dragon in a move to gain his freedom in this tale rich in dragon lore. Ages 12 and up.

The Kestrel, by Lloyd Alexander (Dutton). Mickle, Theo, and their companions react dramatically when the Regians attack. Ages 12 and up.

Sweet Whispers, Brother Rush, by Virginia Hamilton (Philomel). The ghost of Brother Rush reveals family secrets to Theresa, who gains understanding with the knowledge. Ages 12 and up.

Fiction

Witches' Children, by Patricia Clapp (Lothrop). Mary Warren narrates the events leading up to the 1692 Salem witch trials and reveals her own participation and remorse. Ages 11 and up.

Kept in the Dark, by Nina Bawden (Lothrop). Three children and their grandparents are terrorized by David, an older orphan grandson, in this gripping story. Ages 12 and up.

Ask Me No Questions, by Ann Schlee (Holt). In this well-written novel set in the 19th century, Laura and Barty leave London to escape the cholera epidemic. What they encounter is even more horrifying. Ages 10 to 12.

The Hollow Land, by Jane Gardam, illustrated by Janet Rawlins (Greenwillow). A London family rents a home in the country from farmers. This saga comes alive through characterization and a strong sense of place. Ages 12 and up.

Won't Know Till I Get There, by Walter Dean Myers (Viking). Steve's parents adopt a 13-year-old boy with a police record, with amusing results. Fine dialogue captures the interaction between the teen-agers and some elderly people with whom they must work. Ages 12 and up.

What About Grandma?, by Hadley Irwin (Atheneum). This book explores first love and relationships between generations. Ages 12 and up.

Some Glad Morning, by Faye Gibbons (Morrow). Ten-year-old Maude and her mother, brother, and sister must adjust to living in a shack and to relatives who seem dirty and ignorant. Ages 9 to 12.

The Night the Water Came, by Clive King (Crowell). Apu records his first encounters with modern transportation and city life after a cyclone destroys his island home. Ages 9 to 12.

Switching Tracks, by Dean Hughes (Atheneum). After Mark's father dies, his mother goes to work. Lonely and guilt-ridden, Mark gradually becomes friends with old Willard. Ages 12 and up.

Nothing to Be Afraid Of, by Jan Mark (Harper). Seven short stories reveal the various temperaments of children, including 4-year-old Robin, who enjoys being frightened. Ages 9 to 12.

Al(exandra) the Great, by Constance C. Greene (Viking). The narrator reveals her best friend Al's growing maturity and her own occasional jealousy in this warm story of friendship. Ages 9 to 12.

Journey to an 800 Number, by E. L. Konigsburg (Atheneum). Max learns about himself and others when he travels with his father and Ahmed the camel. Unusual characters and situations combine with fast-paced writing. Ages 9 to 12.

Story for a Black Night, by Clayton Bess (Parnassus/Houghton). An African father tells his children a transfixing tale about strangers who brought smallpox to his family. Ages 9 to 12.

Animals, People, Places, and Projects

The Beaver, illustrated by David Nockels, and *The Fish: The Story of the Stickleback,* illustrated by John Butler, both by Margaret Lane (Dial). Each book presents information in an interesting manner accompanied by beautiful illustrations. Ages 8 to 12.

How to Wreck a Building, by Elinor Lander Horwitz, photos by Joshua Horwitz (Pantheon). The demolition of an old school is presented from a child's point of view. Black-and-white photographs accompany clear descriptions of the processes and equipment involved. Ages 8 to 12.

Bluebird Rescue, by Joan Rattner Heilman (Lothrop). In interesting, highly readable prose and beautiful color photographs, the book describes the disappearing bluebird, how to save it, and how to bring it back. Ages 8 to 12.

The Cat's Elbow and Other Secret Languages, collected by Alvin Schwartz, illustrated by Margot Zemach (Farrar, Straus, Giroux). Through riddles and rhymes, the reader learns pig Latin and other "secret" languages. Ages 8 and up.

Lobo of the Tasaday: A Stone Age Boy Meets the Modern World, by John Nance (Pantheon). This fine introduction to a Philippine tribe discovered in the 1970s discloses the people's everyday lives through text and black-and-white photographs. Ages 8 to 12.

Journey to the Planets, by Patricia Lauber (Crown). Clear prose and beautiful black-and-white photos should captivate the reader. All ages.

How to Live with a Single Parent, by Sara Gilbert (Lothrop). In presenting some of the typical feelings experienced by children of single-parent families, the book stresses the importance of communication. A bibliography of related fiction and nonfiction appears at the end. Ages 8 and up.

Saving America's Birds, by Paula Hendrich (Lothrop). In a highly readable style accompanied by black-and-white photographs, the author describes the extinction of some birds and the attempts to save other endangered species. She also suggests ways in which readers can help. Ages 10 and up.

A Visit to William Blake's Inn: Poems for Innocent and Experienced Travelers won the 1982 Newbery Medal for children's literature.

Behind Barbed Wire: The Imprisonment of Japanese Americans During World War II, by Daniel S. Davis (Dutton). Photographs and clear prose eloquently depict people and events. Ages 12 and up.

Seafaring Women, by Linda Grant De Pauw (Houghton). Accounts of female pirates, adventurers, women sailors disguised as men, and wives who raise children at sea are told in fascinating detail. Ages 12 and up.

Awards in 1982 included:

American Library Association/Association for Library Services to Children Awards: The Newbery Medal for "the most distinguished contribution to American literature for children" was awarded to Nancy Willard for *A Visit to William Blake's Inn: Poems for Innocent and Experienced Travelers,* illustrated by Alice and Martin Provensen. The Caldecott Medal for "the most distinguished American picture book for children" went to Chris Van Allsburg for *Jumanji.* The Mildred L. Batchelder Award cited Bradbury Press for its publication of *The Battle Horse,* by Harry Kullman, which was translated from the Swedish by George Blecher and Lone Thygsen-Blecher. Marilyn Fain Apseloff

See also CANADIAN LITERATURE; LITERATURE; POETRY. In WORLD BOOK, see CALDECOTT MEDAL; LITERATURE FOR CHILDREN; NEWBERY MEDAL.

LOS ANGELES won a favorable ruling from the California Supreme Court on April 30, 1982, upholding a county ballot measure that is expected to raise $288 million per year for public transit. The ballot proposition, which passed in November 1980, increased the local sales tax by half a cent.

The transit tax will provide money for a $2-billion subway project between downtown Los Angeles and the suburban San Fernando Valley and for a planned light-rail line between Los Angeles and Long Beach. It also enabled local bus systems to lower their fares to 50 cents beginning July 1 and allowed the Southern California Rapid Transit District (SCRTD), which serves 1.25 million riders, to avert service cutbacks.

The SCRTD, however, encountered a different problem on September 15, when the district's 4,600 bus drivers went on strike in a dispute over contract negotiations. The key issue in the strike was the district's demand that SCRTD be allowed to hire more part-time employees. The five-day walkout ended when United Transportation Union members approved a 32-month contract and returned to work on September 20.

The SCRTD strike was its fifth in 10 years. On November 2, county voters approved a ballot measure urging the state legislature to adopt a law banning the district's employees from striking. Voters also approved another proposition on the same ballot prohibiting county employees from striking and imposing penalties on workers who participate in such labor actions.

School Busing. The Supreme Court of the United States, meanwhile, upheld an earlier measure that ended Los Angeles' court-ordered school busing plan. In siding with the proponents of California's Proposition 1, adopted by voters statewide in 1979, the Supreme Court in June 1982 allowed the city's public schools to continue operating as they have since April 1981, when the mandatory busing program was dismantled. The court decision ended a complex legal battle dating back to 1963 over school desegregation.

Brushfire. A major brushfire that broke out on October 9 charred 45,000 acres (18,000 hectares) in the Dayton Canyon area of the Santa Monica Mountains. No one was injured in the blaze, which was fanned by winds of up to 60 miles (96 kilometers) per hour, but the fire destroyed about 25 houses and 50 mobile homes. Officials placed the property loss at $4.5 million. In signing a state emergency declaration for the area, Governor Edmund G. Brown, Jr., called the fire the worst in the Santa Monica Mountains in 12 years.

The Raiders Move South. Los Angeles, which had been without a professional football team since the National Football League (NFL) Rams moved to Anaheim after the 1979 season, gained a new NFL team in 1982 when the Raiders moved there from Oakland. The Raiders and the Los Angeles Coliseum Commission shared a legal victory on May 7 when a Los Angeles federal court jury decided that the NFL violated antitrust law when it tried to block the Raiders' move.

The Budgets. The Los Angeles County Board of Supervisors on July 6 adopted a $5-billion budget that called for 3,200 fewer county employees during the new fiscal year. In an austerity move, the board also made a number of department cuts, mostly in mental health and social services.

Los Angeles City Council members on July 26 passed a 1982-1983 budget of $1.5 billion. The budget, reflecting a reduction in state aid, included across-the-board cuts in every department except police and sanitation.

Smog Plan. Two Los Angeles-area governmental agencies introduced an air-quality plan in September aimed at cleaning up the region's polluted air. The Draft 1982 Air Quality Management Plan, drawn up by the South Coast Air Quality Management District and the Southern California Association of Governments, outlined strategies for meeting most federal clean-air standards by 1983. The proposal requires approval by the U.S. Environmental Protection Agency. Victor Merina

See also CITY. In WORLD BOOK, see LOS ANGELES.

LOUISIANA. See STATE GOVERNMENT.

LUBBERS, RUUD (1939-), became prime minister of the Netherlands on Nov. 4, 1982. He succeeded Andreas A. M. van Agt, who resigned on October 13. Van Agt recommended that Lubbers replace him as chairman of the Christian Democrats, the leading party in the Netherlands coalition government, and the nomination was accepted unanimously by the party's 45 members in the States-General (parliament).

Rudolph Frans Marie Lubbers was born on May 7, 1939, in Rotterdam. He studied at Canisius College, a grammar school in Nijmegen, and graduated in 1957. Lubbers then studied economics at Erasmus University (then called the Netherlands School of Economics) in Rotterdam, graduating in 1962. He joined his family's firm, becoming secretary to the board of management of Lubbers Hollandia Engineering Works in Krimpen aan de IJssel, and was made co-director of the company in 1965.

Lubbers began his political career as a member of the Catholic People's Party, which later joined with two others to form the Christian Democrats. From 1973 to 1977, he was minister of economic affairs. As a member of the States-General, he was floor leader in the lower house.

Lubbers has been a board member of several civic and cultural organizations. Marsha F. Goldsmith

LUMBER. See FOREST AND FOREST PRODUCTS.

LUXEMBOURG. The economic alliance between Luxembourg and Belgium was threatened on Feb. 21, 1982, when Belgium devalued its franc by 8.5 per cent, carrying the Luxembourg franc with it. Prime Minister Pierre Werner immediately summoned Belgian Prime Minister Wilfried A. E. Martens to tell him the terms by which Luxembourg was prepared to remain part of the Belgian-Luxembourg Economic Union (BLEU).

Luxembourg complained that Belgium informed Luxembourg of its decision to devalue only hours before the action was announced. Belgium argued that the Luxembourg franc, if left at its previous higher value, would be quickly wiped out by speculators. Luxembourg demanded to have the power to veto actions it opposed. It also insisted on a separate valuation of Luxembourg's gold and foreign reserves held in Belgian banks. Luxembourg pointed out that its $348 billion in foreign bank deposits had been a major contribution to BLEU's joint balance of payments. Martens and Werner agreed that, until further discussion, Belgium would keep its franc closer to the rate set by the European Monetary System — an organization to which both nations belong that works to stabilize exchange rates. Kenneth Brown

See also EUROPE (Facts in Brief Table). In WORLD BOOK, see LUXEMBOURG.

MADAGASCAR. See AFRICA.

MAGAZINE. The combined circulation per issue of the 100 leading magazines audited by the Audit Bureau of Circulations (ABC) in the United States showed an increase of 1.4 per cent during the first six months of 1982, compared with the same period in 1981. According to ABC, average paid-subscription circulation per issue increased 2.6 per cent, though average paid single-copy circulation per issue decreased by 1.9 per cent.

In 1977, 50 magazines had circulations of 1 million or more; in 1982, there were 65. The total paid circulation of the 100 leading magazines grew 8.1 per cent from 1977 to 1982. Magazine advertising revenues in the United States increased approximately 5 per cent over 1981's record high, reaching nearly $3.5 billion. An annual survey conducted by the Magazine Publishers Association (MPA) and Price Waterhouse & Company indicated that magazines became more profitable in 1981. The average pretax operating profit for the 170 magazines surveyed increased from 7.77 per cent of total magazine revenues in 1980 to 8.97 per cent in 1981. The magazines' net income for 1981 was about 4.8 per cent.

Awards. The MPA named Andrew Heiskell, former chairman of the board and chief executive officer of Time Incorporated, as the 1982 recipient of the Henry Johnson Fisher Award, the industry's most prestigious honor. The American Society of Magazine Editors presented its National Magazine Awards in April. Among the winning publications were *The Atlantic,* for public service and for essays and criticism; *Newsweek,* for single-topic issue and general excellence for a magazine with a circulation over 1 million; *Camera Arts,* for general excellence, under 100,000 circulation; *Nautical Quarterly,* for design; *The New Yorker,* for fiction; *Philadelphia,* for service to the individual; *Rocky Mountain Magazine,* for general excellence, circulation of 100,000 to 400,000; *Science 81,* for general excellence, circulation of 400,000 to 1 million; and *The Washingtonian,* for reporting.

New Magazines. Among the new magazines introduced in 1982 was *Muppet Magazine,* published by Telepictures Publications, Incorporated. The quarterly appeared on newsstands in November.

Americans' preoccupation with physical fitness prompted the April entry of *Spring* and *American Health. Spring* is published nine times a year by Rodale Press, which also produces *Organic Gardening, Prevention, Bicycling,* and *New Shelter.*

American Health, a bimonthly, was underwritten by Oppenheimer and Company, a venture capital and brokerage house, for approximately $5 million. This was the largest sum ever raised to launch a new magazine. The publisher is Owen Lipstein, former general manager of *Science 81,* and the editor is T. George Harris, former editor of *Psychology Today.*

Whitney Communications Corporation introduced *Corporate Design,* a bimonthly, in January. The magazine is intended for executives who are responsible for company expansion, relocation, furnishing, and renovating.

Changes. In August, *Saturday Review* suspended publication. *Saturday Review*'s owner, Macro Communications Company, had lost $3 million in a two-year effort to reinvigorate the 58-year-old literary and cultural journal. However, on November 10, Jeffrey M. Gluck bought the magazine. The 29-year-old Gluck is the owner and publisher of *The Campus Digest* at the University of Missouri at Columbia and the magazine *Missouri Life.*

Other changes included the November purchase of *The Tatler,* a British monthly magazine devoted to social news, the arts, features, and fashion, by Condé Nast Publications Limited. The Charter Company sold *Ladies' Home Journal* to Family Media Incorporated in July and *Redbook* to The Hearst Corporation in August. In April, CBS Inc. acquired *Cuisine,* a magazine devoted to fine food and gracious living, for $2.7 million. Dow Jones & Company announced that it would cease publication of *Book Digest* in April. Gloria Ricks Dixon

See also PUBLISHING. In WORLD BOOK, see MAGAZINE.

MAINE. See STATE GOVERNMENT.

MALAWI. See AFRICA.

MALAYSIA elected a new national Parliament and state legislatures on April 22, 1982. The National Front, a coalition of 11 political parties led by Prime Minister Mahathir bin Mohamed, won by a landslide. It captured 132 out of 154 seats in Parliament and 312 out of 380 seats in 11 state legislatures, the strongest mandate of any government in Malaysia's 25 years of independence.

The Campaign was fought less on issues than on the new open style of government by Mahathir, the first prime minister not to have served in the British colonial administration before independence. In nine months as head of government, he demanded more polite and efficient work from officials, attacked corruption, tackled urban housing problems, and relaxed internal security restrictions slightly. This approach won support from Malaysia's ethnic Chinese minority group, who had earlier been suspicious of Mahathir's record as an advocate for the ethnic Malay majority.

The New Cabinet of 24 ministers included at least one representative from each of the 11 parties in the National Front. The Cabinet was composed almost entirely of familiar faces, including that of Foreign Minister Muhammad Ghazali bin Shafie. On January 10, Ghazali was reported killed in a plane crash, but the next day he was found alive in the jungle. The two other passengers died.

Internal Security. Despite some relaxation in security rules, the government refused to change its harsh Internal Security Act. The act permits detention of suspects without trial and makes the death penalty mandatory for a variety of offenses, including possession of unlicensed firearms. Home Minister Musa Hitam defended the act as necessary because of possible racial violence and a continued challenge from Communist guerrillas. An estimated 3,000 Communists remained in the jungle fighting the Malaysian government.

More than 30 narcotics dealers had been hanged under Malaysia's strict drug laws. On August 25, however, a Malaysian court spared the life of Beatrice Saubin, the first foreigner sentenced to death under those laws. Saubin, a French-woman was convicted of heroin trafficking. The court commuted her sentence to life in prison.

The Economy. Severe drought in the northern states hurt rice production early in the year. The central bank reported that trade surpluses had turned into deficits as prices for petroleum, rubber, and palm oil exports fell. Demand for these goods, Malaysia's main export earners, dropped because of a worldwide recession. As a result, economic growth slowed. Henry S. Bradsher

See also ASIA (Facts in Brief Table). In WORLD BOOK, see MALAYSIA.

MALDIVES. See AFRICA.

MALI. See AFRICA.

MALTA. See EUROPE.

MANITOBA. Canada's only socialist government, which assumed office in November 1981, followed a different path from the rest of the country in 1982 as its policies emphasized the public rather than the private sector. Premier Howard Pawley and his New Democratic Party (NDP), holding 34 of the 57 seats in the legislature (Progressive Conservatives held the other 23), made good on their campaign promises.

Although their first budget, on May 11, envisaged a record deficit of $335 million (Canadian dollars; $1 = U.S. 81 cents as of Dec. 31, 1982) on expenditures of $2.8 billion, the NDP did not seek to make the taxpayer's plight worse. It limited rent increases on older homes and apartments by law to 9 per cent and set up a $23-million emergency mortgage interest-rate relief plan. It also froze hydropower rates for the fifth consecutive year and restrained civil service salaries.

Hard Hit by the economic recession, Manitoba saw a major project falter in July when a planned $3.3-billion Prairie Power Grid was canceled. The grid would have been based on a large generating station in northern Manitoba, with transmission lines running west to Alberta. But construction costs in the draft agreement were underestimated, and Manitoba's neighboring provinces refused to take on a larger share of the cost. David M. L. Farr

In WORLD BOOK, see MANITOBA.

MANUFACTURING. The crushing worldwide recession, considered mild when it began in July 1981, had a stranglehold on industrial production in the United States in 1982. Inflation was down, but so was business confidence, reflected in reduced capital spending plans and fewer new factory orders. Consumers were more cautious about spending, causing inventories to accumulate. That made manufacturers curtail production and lay off workers. To add to factory owners' woes, interest rates remained far from stable, and even higher government deficits were predicted. In short, as one private investment newsletter put it, manufacturing "was in a shambles." See ECONOMICS.

Factory inventories in October decreased just barely, by less than 0.1 per cent, to an adjusted $272.29 billion, after decreasing a more encouraging 0.7 per cent in September. The inventory-to-shipment ratio in October stood at 1.78, or 1.78 months of shipments still in storage. Manufacturers continued to cut back production until inventories could be sold off.

New Factory Orders fell a hefty 3.9 per cent in October to the lowest level in more than two years, according to a U.S. Department of Commerce report. Factory orders fell to a seasonally adjusted $150.12 billion—the lowest value for new orders since 1980's $145.7 billion. Factory output fell an adjusted 0.8 per cent in October, marking

Bolts of a new fabric called carbon-fiber composite cloth are used to make airplane parts that are lightweight, rustproof, and strong as steel.

the 13th decline in 15 months. Weakness was not limited to one sector of manufacturing, but was apparent everywhere. Orders for durable goods—automobiles, machinery, and furniture—fell 4.7 per cent in October to an adjusted $69.86 billion. Nondurable orders slipped 3.2 per cent to $80.26-billion.

October orders for nondefense capital goods such as buildings, machinery, and tools decreased 0.5 per cent to an adjusted $20.18 billion, after an impressive 7.3 per cent increase in September to an adjusted $20.27 billion. The backlog of manufacturers' orders decreased $3.1 billion, or 1 per cent, to $296 billion for the 14th consecutive monthly decline.

Capital Spending Plans were nothing to base a quick recovery on. According to an October report from the Commerce Department's Bureau of Economic Analysis, U.S. nonfarm business would probably end 1982 having spent $323.7 billion for new plants and equipment, only 0.7 per cent more than the year before. Under more optimistic circumstances, that figure had been estimated at 2.2 per cent in June and 7.3 per cent in March. But many spending plans were shelved as the economy worsened.

Plans for real spending—capital spending adjusted for price changes—declined 4.4 per cent from 1981 to 1982. For 1982, manufacturers estimated a 2 per cent decrease in current-dollar spending.

With inventories at high levels and new orders few and far between, U.S. factories were running at only 68.4 per cent of capacity in October, the lowest level since the Federal Reserve Board started keeping such records in 1948. Hurt by foreign competition, automobile factories were operating at only 49.7 per cent of capacity in October, and the steel industry was operating at only 38 per cent of capacity, the lowest rate since 1938. In July 1981, factories were operating at 79.8 per cent of capacity, having just recovered from the 1980 recession. During the relatively normal years between 1955 and 1979, factory operating rates averaged 83 per cent. Only in wartime does the figure approach 100 per cent.

Factory payrolls dropped 1.2 per cent in October 1982, though total wages and salaries for workers in all sectors of the economy rose 0.1 per cent. The rise was a measure of the great strength of U.S. service industries. See LABOR.

Research and Development (R & D) outlays, despite the recession, jumped a sizable 10.7 per cent in 1982 to an estimated $77.3 billion, compared with $69.8 billion in 1981. That was the report of Battelle Columbus Laboratories, an independent research concern, and the National Science Foundation. Basic research accounted for 12.1 per cent

A simulator and computers at John Deere Technical Center in Moline, Ill., help in studying the interaction between mobile machinery and its users.

of R & D in the United States in 1982, or $9.3-billion. Battelle predicted that R & D expenditures would grow at an annual rate of 3.3 per cent during the 1980s.

Overseas competition and emerging technologies were still the major forces driving R & D. Most R & D funding stemmed from the manufacturing industries, especially electronics, communications, and advanced machinery, with the emphasis on more energy-efficient products and processes. Only 32 per cent of R & D, on the average, was supported by the federal government. Increasingly, R & D funds provided by the government were allocated for weapons research.

Machine Tool builders would like to forget the year 1982. Nine-month net new orders for machine tools were $1.169 billion, down 51 per cent from the first nine months of 1981, according to the National Machine Tool Builders Association. Nine-month shipments were $2.94 billion, off 22 per cent from the first nine months of 1981.

In September 1982, net new orders stood at $86.75 million, a whopping 54 per cent decline from the total a year earlier. And shipments in September were down 38 per cent from the year before. At the end of September, the industry backlog stood at only $1.52 billion, a far cry from the backlog of $3.69 billion in September 1981 and $5.48 billion in 1980.

Rubber. With automobile sales down substantially in 1982 from already depressed 1981 levels, tire manufacturers were forced to diversify. The original equipment manufacturers (OEM) market was weak because Detroit produced fewer cars, but consumers were keeping their old cars longer. That created a strong market for replacement tires to balance out the weak OEM. Stock market analysts estimated that new tire orders from Detroit through the first half of 1982 slipped from 20.4 million in 1981 to 18 million. Replacement tires, however, jumped from 62.8 million in 1981 to 64.1 million. The Rubber Manufacturers Association estimated that 184 million passenger-car, bus, and truck tires were produced in 1982, and 136 million were shipped as of September, compared with 190 million produced in 1981.

In an effort to diversify further and get away from excessive reliance on the automobile industry, rubber producers were bouncing into several new fields. One growth area these producers were considering was long-lasting, single-ply rubber roofing. Some firms had already switched to new products. For example, B. F. Goodrich Company got out of the OEM tire market completely. They now produce polyvinyl chloride, a plastic familiar in such items as floor tiles and phonograph records under its more common name of vinyl. Uniroyal Incorporated expanded its agricultural and chemical lines. General Tire Company diversified but was selling its cable television operations. Goodyear Tire & Rubber Company had not yet diversified in 1982. Perhaps the company did not feel the need, as it enjoyed great success through record sales of its Tiempo all-weather radial tire.

Electrical Equipment sales, like so many others, also slumped in 1982, declining 8.9 per cent, according to the National Electrical Manufacturers Association (NEMA). The only positive showing in 1982, as in 1981, was a projected 12.9 per cent increase in sales of medical diagnostic imaging and therapy systems. These included X-ray machines; computerized tomography (CT) scanners, also known as CAT scanners; and ultrasound and nuclear imaging equipment.

Manufacturers covered under the electronics division of NEMA—making such items as batteries, residential controls, electric indicating instruments, semiconductor power converters and components, electronic power supplies, fire and security signaling systems, and traffic controls—showed sales declines of only 0.8 per cent. Lighting equipment dropped 3 per cent. The greatest decline was in electric wire and cable production, with a total drop of 15.6 per cent from 1981.

Industrial electrical equipment sales slumped as factory expansion plans were tabled. However, there was one hot growth area in that group: Military contracts from the U.S. government increased, because sophisticated electronic guidance systems are vital to modern weapons systems.

Manufacturing Jobs Lost

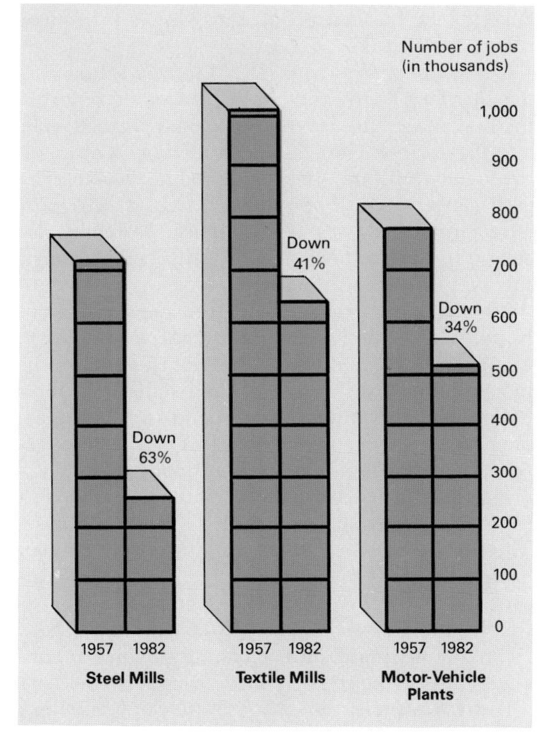

Source: U.S. Department of Labor

Paper and Paperboard. The 1982 recession had a marked impact on the paper industry. A spokesman for the American Paper Institute estimated that the 1982 production of paper and paperboard, excluding the construction and wet machine board grades, amounted to 59.6 million short tons (54 million metric tons), which was 4.4 per cent below the 1981 high. That estimate was based on 10 months actual data. It was also estimated that production of wood pulp in 1982, based on nine months actual data, was approximately 50 million short tons (45 million metric tons), also about 4 per cent below the 1981 total. The wood pulp data excluded pulp for the construction and hard-pressed board grades.

Is America Molting? Amid all the doom and gloom talk of recession, and even depression, came a different interpretation. Some observers believed that the U.S. economy was involved in a great transition period, a revolutionary change similar in nature to, and as broad in scope as, that which forever changed the United States from an agricultural to an industrial society in the 1800s. *Forbes* magazine titled its November 22 cover story "The Molting of America," and opined that the economy was throwing off an old skin and growing a new one. The article said, "The United States, indeed the entire industrial world, is profoundly changing the way it uses men and materials, capital and manufacturing processes."

Electronics and other new technologies have had a tremendous impact on older industries, which are using microelectronics—including many no-longer-exotic robots—to improve productivity, speed up and streamline production methods, and improve quality control. For example, at a General Electric Company plant in Erie, Pa., an automated operation is being updated to turn out one diesel or electric locomotive motor frame each day with no human operators at all. It used to take 68 operators 16 days to accomplish the same task, according to *Forbes*.

Such impressive productivity gains are bound to be felt by the U.S. work force. A Congressional Budget Office study has estimated that microelectronic technology may eliminate 3 million jobs by the end of the 1980s and 7 million by the year 2000, so that many workers will require retraining. Microelectronics is indeed changing the way goods are produced by American industry. Ronald Kolgraf

In WORLD BOOK, see MANUFACTURING.

MARINE CORPS, U.S. See ARMED FORCES.
MARYLAND. See STATE GOVERNMENT.
MASSACHUSETTS. See STATE GOVERNMENT.
MAURITANIA. See AFRICA.

MAURITIUS. A two-party socialist coalition won all 62 seats in the Legislative Assembly of Mauritius in elections held on June 11, 1982. Voters ousted the pro-West government of Prime Minister Sir Seewoosagur Ramgoolam, whose Labour Party had ruled the Rhode Island-sized nation in the Indian Ocean since it gained independence from Great Britain in 1968. Ramgoolam's party was blamed for rapid inflation and an almost 20 per cent rate of unemployment.

The major partner in the new governing coalition was the socialist Militant Mauritian Movement, led by Aneerood Jugnauth, who became prime minister. Jugnauth's government pledged to oppose white-minority rule in South Africa by reducing economic ties with that country.

Jugnauth said the new government would work to establish Mauritian sovereignty over the island of Diego Garcia, a British possession leased to the United States in 1975 for 50 years. Jugnauth's government claimed Diego Garcia because, before Mauritius won its independence, Britain administered the two islands as if they were parts of the same territory. Located about 1,200 miles (1,900 kilometers) northeast of Mauritius, Diego Garcia is the site of the largest U.S. military base in the Indian Ocean. J. Dixon Esseks

See also AFRICA. In WORLD BOOK, see MAURITIUS.

MEDICINE. On Dec. 2, 1982, surgeon William C. DeVries and a 20-member team at the University of Utah in Salt Lake City performed the first permanent artificial heart implant on a human being. The patient was Barney B. Clark, a 61-year-old retired dentist with congestive heart failure.

Just before the operation, Clark was near death. His heart was pumping so little blood that his liver was being damaged and his lungs were filling with fluid. But as soon as the artificial heart began pumping, Clark's blood pressure rose to a healthy level and his organs began to recover.

The plastic heart was operated by a 375-pound (170-kilogram) drive system that included an air compressor and heart monitor. However, the researchers claim that future artificial hearts will be operated by battery-powered microcircuits that will weigh about 5 pounds (2.3 kilograms) and will therefore be portable.

Transplant Success. Both the number of transplant operations and the survival rates for organ recipients surged dramatically in 1982, reflecting advances in surgical techniques and the effectiveness of a new drug, cyclosporin A, in preventing the body's immune system from rejecting the transplanted organ. During the first six months of the year, 56 heart transplants were performed in the United States, compared with an average yearly total of 22 throughout the 1970s.

Researchers at Stanford University Medical Center in California reported that the one-year survival rate for 43 of their transplant patients treated with cyclosporin A was 79 per cent. Before cyclosporin, the one-year survival rate for heart-transplant patients was 65 to 70 per cent. Cyclosporin A also increased survival rates nationwide as of September from 38 to 70 per cent in children receiving liver transplants and from 50 to 80 per cent in people receiving kidneys from cadavers.

Interferon Verdict. The first major scientific meeting on treating patients with the antiviral drug interferon was held in Squaw Valley, California, in March. Physicians reported that although it is an effective fighter against certain cancers and other serious diseases, interferon is probably not the hoped-for cure for cancer. They noted that interferon is a powerful treatment against cytomegalovirus infections in patients with transplanted kidneys and against sometimes fatal cases of chicken pox in patients undergoing cancer chemotherapy. It also reduced tumorous growths in the larynx.

Interferon's effectiveness in fighting cancer was less clear, however, in part because only very limited studies have been done. In the few cases reported, tumors shrank markedly in 25 to 40 per cent of the breast cancer, lymphoma (malignancy of the lymph system), and multiple myeloma (cancer of the blood-forming tissues) treated with interferon. To lesser degrees, interferon had a beneficial effect on cancer of the ovaries, prostate, colon, and cervix.

New Cancer Weapon? In March, scientists at the Stanford University Medical Center reported the first successful use of monoclonal antibodies in treating cancer. Monoclonal antibodies are made by fusing antibody-producing white blood cells with cancer cells. The resulting hybrid cells produce large quantities of antibodies, protein molecules that will attack a malignancy or a foreign substance invading the body.

The Stanford researchers, headed by physician Ronald Levy, designed monoclonal antibodies to attack only the abnormal proteins on cancer cells in the body of a 67-year-old man suffering from a lymphoma that would not respond to other treatment. The cancer disappeared after the man received a series of monoclonal antibody injections.

However, the researchers cautioned that this was an isolated success involving only one case. The highly experimental technique requires much more study and may not work against other cancers. In November, doctors at the Sidney Farber Institute in Boston reported that they had used a technique involving monoclonal antibodies to cure a girl born without any ability to fight disease.

Heart Advances. On May 7, the United States Food and Drug Administration gave its approval to streptokinase, a bacterial protein that can dissolve human blood clots. In prior testing, the drug was used experimentally to treat acute myocardial infarctions (heart attacks caused by clots in coronary arteries) in about 600 patients in the United States and 400 in Europe. The largest U.S. study was carried out at the University of Texas Health Science Center in Houston. The results of this study showed that streptokinase dissolved clots in coronary arteries and allowed blood to resume flowing in 80 per cent of the patients treated.

At the American College of Cardiology meeting in Atlanta, Ga., in July, pioneers in the use of a technique called angioplasty, which employs balloon-tipped catheters to open blocked coronary arteries, reported great success in treating heart patients. They claimed their procedure yielded results comparable to, if not better than, coronary by-pass surgery for at least 20 per cent of patients with one or more blocked arteries. The cardiologists also reported that a combination of balloon angioplasty and streptokinase treatment restored coronary blood flow in 90 per cent of their patients.

Two investigations—one by the U.S. Department of Health and Human Services and the other by the Ralph Nader-affiliated Public Citizen Health Research Group—turned up evidence during the year of widespread overuse of heart pacemakers as well as corrupt practices in selling the devices. The reports noted that 25,000 pacemakers may be implanted unnecessarily each year, risking lives and wasting millions of dollars, mostly from taxpayers' pockets.

Ultrasound Study. The largest epidemiologic study of the effects of ultrasound (high-frequency sound) examinations during pregnancy revealed no significant short-term damage to a fetus, according to a report in March by researchers at the University of Manitoba in Winnipeg, Canada. The study, which began in 1975 and analyzed data on 19,000 pregnancies, found no increases in birth defects or cancers among children who had been exposed to ultrasound as fetuses.

Medical Policy. At its annual meeting in June, the House of Delegates of the American Medical Association (AMA) approved a plan for the AMA to work with hospital, insurance, and other health groups in forging a national health policy. The AMA leadership argued, against stiff opposition from some delegates, that the two-year, $3-million effort would allow physicians to fill the void in medical planning and monitoring left by federal cutbacks. In June, the National Academy of Sciences (NAS) issued a 500-page report on links between diet and cancer. The report urged major changes in eating habits. See NUTRITION. Dianne Hales

See also HEALTH AND DISEASE; PUBLIC HEALTH. In WORLD BOOK, see MEDICINE.

MENTAL HEALTH. Throughout the United States, intense controversy over the insanity defense followed the acquittal of John W. Hinckley, Jr., on June 21, 1982, for the attempted assassination of U.S. President Ronald Reagan in 1981. Hinckley was confined indefinitely to a psychiatric hospital in Washington, D.C. Meanwhile, psychiatrists, lawyers, legislators, and private citizens challenged the basic principle behind his acquittal—that a person should not be punished for crimes deemed to be the product of a sick rather than an evil mind. See COURTS AND LAWS (Close-Up).

Hyperactivity and Diet. In January, a panel of the National Institutes of Health in Bethesda, Md., reviewed the evidence linking diet to childhood hyperactivity. The theory that artificial food flavorings and colorings are a major cause of hyperactivity had been set forth by San Francisco allergist Benjamin F. Feingold in his popular book *Why Your Child Is Hyperactive* (1975). The 14-member panel found no clear scientific proof that the additive-free Feingold diet provides any benefit for the restless, disruptive behavior of hyperactive children. However, the panel concluded after hearing individual testimony that in some cases an additive-free diet might be worth a brief try.

Schizophrenia Research. At the annual meeting of the American Psychiatric Association (APA) in Toronto, Canada, in May, psychiatrist Joannis Nesteros of McGill University reported that high doses of up to 400 milligrams of the widely used tranquilizer Valium (diazepam) dramatically reduced symptoms of paranoid schizophrenia, sometimes within a few hours and after antipsychotic drugs had failed. Eight of nine paranoid patients in a group treated with Valium showed a marked decrease in such symptoms as delusions of persecution, auditory hallucinations, and withdrawal. Within a week, lower doses were sufficient to keep the patients free of these symptoms.

In another report at the meeting, British researcher Eve C. Johnstone suggested that schizophrenia itself, rather than the powerful drugs used to treat it, may cause tardive dyskinesia, a condition characterized by lip smacking and other involuntary movements of the tongue, lips, and head. Johnstone suggested that schizophrenia may be a central nervous system disorder that affects movement as well as mental processes.

Suicide in the Young. Child psychiatrist Perihan Rosenthal from the University of Massachusetts in Amherst reported to the APA in May that children as young as 2½ years old have tried to kill themselves. This report on eight suicidal children between 2½ and 4 years old challenged the conventional belief that suicide in children younger than 6 is rare or nonexistent. Another report at the APA convention described teen-age suicide as an epidemic and noted that suicide has become the most common cause of death among 18- to 24-year-olds in the United States.

New Treatments. Studies at three institutions, reported to the APA in May, indicate that propranolol, a drug first used to treat hypertension and heart disease, can effectively control violent behavior. The drug produced almost complete calm in 75 per cent of the violent mental patients treated with it. The researchers theorize that propranolol reduces the activity of brain cells, thus controlling outbursts of rage.

Another drug that might find application in the mental health area is fenfluramine, used to control appetite in overweight persons. In July, researchers at the University of California and the Veterans Administration Brentwood Medical Center, both located in Los Angeles, reported that fenfluramine may alleviate the withdrawn behavior and boost the intelligence scores of severely autistic children.

A new antidepressant, bupropion, was described at the May APA meeting by psychiatrist Sheldon N. Preskorn of the University of Kansas in Lawrence. Preskorn said bupropion was just as effective as current antidepressant medications but had fewer side effects, such as weight gain, constipation, and low blood pressure. Dianne Hales

See also DRUGS. In WORLD BOOK, see MENTAL HEALTH; MENTAL ILLNESS.

MEXICO. The bottom dropped out of the Mexican economy during the second half of 1982. The suddenness of the collapse stirred fears that Mexico's predicament might touch off a chain reaction leading to international financial chaos.

There were few ominous signals in Mexico early in the year. As the July elections approached, the ruling Institutional Revolutionary Party (PRI) could take pride in its accomplishments. Mexico had risen to fourth place among the world's oil producers. In the four years ending in June 1982, its output of goods and services had increased by almost 40 per cent, and the economy showed an annual growth rate of 8.5 per cent.

With loans amounting to nearly $80 billion on the basis of its high credit rating as an oil exporter, Mexico had increased its farm output by 38 per cent and its electric power generating capacity by 51 per cent. Automobile production was up 133 per cent, with Mexico producing more than half a million cars annually.

On July 4, Miguel de la Madrid Hurtado of the PRI was overwhelmingly elected Mexico's new president with 74 per cent of the popular vote. See DE LA MADRID HURTADO, MIGUEL.

The Economic Collapse came with lightning speed. Between the time of De la Madrid's election and his installment as president on December 1, everything came apart at the seams.

There were two principal reasons for the collapse: a drop in world oil prices and the fact that much higher oil earnings were expected when the Mexican government drew up the country's budget. A third reason was given by outgoing President José López Portillo in September. He said that in the preceding few years Mexicans had taken out of Mexico or invested abroad some $50-billion. The president charged that these Mexicans had been "led, counseled, and supported by the private banks." To solve this problem, López Portillo announced that Mexico's private banks would be nationalized.

By then, Mexico had run out of money twice and had been forced to devalue the peso by more than 70 per cent. The devaluation dealt most Mexicans a severe financial blow, as the value of their earnings and savings plummeted.

In other bad economic news, Mexico's largest privately owned company, Grupo Industrial Alfa, S.A., teetered on the edge of bankruptcy. This development alarmed foreign creditors, who held $2.3 billion of the company's debt.

Austerity Measures. To turn the situation around, the Mexican government pledged to trim its spending. It also pledged to raise additional revenue through hefty increases in the prices of all goods provided by government-run agencies, including basic food staples. In August, prices were raised for everything from railway tickets (up 30 per cent) to telephone calls (up 28 per cent) to gasoline (up 50 per cent).

The United States rushed to help Mexico, paying $1 billion in advance for Mexican oil for the U.S. strategic reserve and buying up more than $1-billion in Mexican pesos. Other nations friendly to Mexico also made large loans to the country. In December, President De la Madrid announced additional austerity measures—including budget cuts, new taxes, and price increases—in return for $3.92 billion in financial help from the International Monetary Fund, an agency of the United Nations.

As Mexico Fell on difficult times, Mexicans became touchy about a wide array of issues that threatened to impinge on their cultural values. For example, Mexican critics decried cultural imperialism when Adventure Kingdom, the first U.S.-style theme park built in Latin America, proved popular after opening near Mexico City in January.

To counterbalance the park's effect, Mexicans thronged to the new Museum of Interventions in Mexico City. The museum is filled with evidence of past foreign meddling in Mexico's affairs. Many of its exhibits play up the U.S. invasions of Mexico in 1846 and 1914. Nathan A. Haverstock

See also LATIN AMERICA (Facts in Brief Table). In WORLD BOOK, see MEXICO.

MICHIGAN. See DETROIT; STATE GOVERNMENT.

MIDDLE EAST

Bombs dropped by Israeli jets explode during an attack on Palestinian guerrilla strongholds in Beirut in June, just before Israel invaded Lebanon.

Israel's invasion of Lebanon in June 1982 introduced a new and disturbing element into the tangled pattern of conflict in the Middle East. The latest outbreak of violence—the fifth Arab-Israeli war to erupt since Israel gained its independence in 1948—became the fourth ongoing conflict in the region. The government of Morocco continued to battle guerrillas challenging its authority in Western Sahara. The confrontation between Iran and Iraq dragged on. And Afghan resistance groups continued to clash with Soviet occupation forces in that country.

Of the four conflicts, the latest Arab-Israeli fighting probably posed the greatest threat to regional stability. Israeli forces invaded Lebanon on June 6. After a quick military victory, however, Israel found itself bogged down in an occupation criticized abroad and unpopular at home.

Israel's stated purpose in launching the invasion was to clear Palestine Liberation Organization

The Scene of Strife

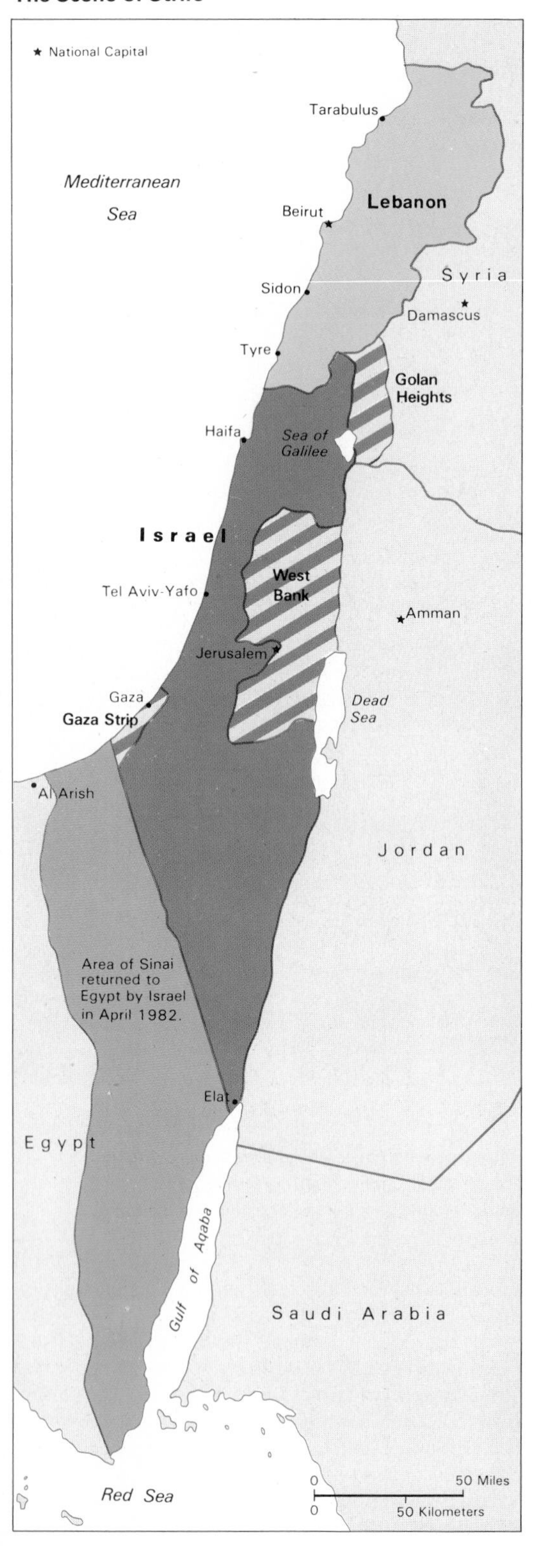

(PLO) units from a 25-mile (40-kilometer) zone north of the Israeli-Lebanon border in order to put Israeli settlements in Galilee out of PLO artillery range. But it became clear that Prime Minister Menachem Begin's government wanted to completely remove the PLO from Lebanon. Israel quickly cleared southern Lebanon of PLO guerrillas. Israeli forces then rolled up the Lebanese coast toward Beirut. Within a week, they had surrounded the Lebanese capital, and all of southern coastal Lebanon was in Israeli hands.

Military Efficiency. As a military operation, the invasion, meticulously planned by Israel's Defense Minister Ariel Sharon and carried out with textbook precision, once again demonstrated Israel's military superiority over its Arab neighbors. Syrian units of the Arab peacekeeping force in Lebanon lost about 400 tanks and armored personnel carriers in intermittent ground battles with Israeli troops, and Israeli planes shot down 86 Soviet-made Syrian jets in aerial dogfights. The Israelis also destroyed all 19 of the Syrian surface-to-air missile sites and batteries in the Al Biqa—or Bekaa—Valley. Deployed in April 1981, the missiles had been a source of tension.

Unfortunately, the quick military victory did not bring Israel a comparable political triumph over the PLO or the long-desired recognition of Israeli independence by the Arab states. Instead, Israel found itself almost universally condemned for the invasion.

Pressure from the United States, among other factors, deterred Israeli forces from attacking West Beirut, the location of PLO headquarters, while U.S. special envoy Philip C. Habib worked out a plan for the evacuation of PLO units from the beleaguered city in August. Most of the 15,000 PLO guerrillas trapped in West Beirut were evacuated to Syria, with smaller contingents going to Tunisia, Algeria, Jordan, Sudan, and North and South Yemen. Except for PLO leader Yasir Arafat, who established temporary headquarters in Tunis, Tunisia, most of the top PLO leaders also went to Syria.

Palestinian Massacre. On September 15, hours after the assassination of Lebanese President-elect Bashir Gemayel, the Israelis moved into West Beirut and stayed there, despite angry protests by the United States. International criticism of Israel reached a peak several days later, when Israeli troops allowed Lebanese Christian militiamen to enter the Sabra and Shatila refugee camps in West Beirut, ostensibly to search for PLO guerrillas hiding there. In a still-unexplained sequence of events, the militiamen massacred hundreds of Palestinian civilians.

After a public outcry and the resignations of several government ministers and high-ranking army officers, the Begin government on September

Lebanon's Legacy of Violence

War-racked Lebanon

The assassination of Lebanon's President-elect Bashir Gemayel and the murder of hundreds of Palestinians in refugee camps in West Beirut in September 1982 were the latest examples of the religious violence and political vendettas that have plagued Lebanon for more than 1,500 years. Lebanon as an entity is a young country in an ancient land. For thousands of years before gaining its independence in 1943, Lebanon was ruled by a succession of foreign powers—including the Egyptians, Assyrians, Greeks, Romans, Ottoman Turks, and French—who were enticed by the country's value as a trading center.

Regardless of the ruler, however, the central fact in Lebanese politics for centuries has been the rivalry between powerful religious sects, chiefly Christians and Muslims. In the best of times, peace in Lebanon has rested precariously on the intricate compromises made by these competing factions. Often, however, religious tensions have plunged the country into civil war.

Most Lebanese believe their first allegiance is to their religious group and family. As a result, despite their independence, the Lebanese have an incomplete sense of national identity and little experience in working together to form a broadly based government.

The three most prominent religious groups in Lebanon are the Maronite Christians, the Muslims, and the Druses. The Maronites, the most powerful group, fled to the mountains of Lebanon in the A.D. 600s to escape religious persecution by their Greek Orthodox rulers. Protected in their mountain stronghold, they resisted the Muslims who invaded the area in the mid-600s, and they retained their religious freedom and a large measure of political autonomy, even during centuries of Muslim rule.

Muslims make up slightly more than 50 per cent of Lebanon's population. When Lebanon gained its independence, its rulers agreed that the country would always have a Maronite Christian president and a Sunni Muslim prime minister and that political power would be apportioned according to population. However, civil war has broken out twice—in 1958 and 1975—chiefly over Muslim demands for more political power.

The Druses practice a religion that is basically Muslim but has many Christian elements. Like the Maronites, they fled to the mountains to escape religious persecution. But the Maronites did not get along with the Druses any better than they did with the Muslims. In the 1840s, bitter conflict arose between the two groups. The conflict erupted into violence in 1860 when Druses massacred many Christians.

Since Lebanon became independent, the turmoil caused by Arab-Israeli conflicts and the arrival of hundreds of thousands of Palestinian refugees in the country has intensified its internal struggles. After Jordan expelled the Palestine Liberation Organization (PLO) in 1970, the PLO established new headquarters in Beirut. From there, the PLO directed attacks against Israel, which retaliated with raids on PLO bases in southern Lebanon. In 1973, the fighting widened into battles between the PLO and the Lebanese Army.

In 1975, Lebanese Muslims again demanded more political power, a move many Palestinians supported. When Lebanese Christians attacked Palestinian commandos, a bloody civil war broke out.

Although a cease-fire was arranged in 1976, fighting soon broke out again between the PLO and Israelis and between the Lebanese Army and Syrian forces. The Syrians had entered the country during the war to try to restore peace, but they often supported the Palestinians. Since then, there have been battles between various Christian groups, between Muslims and the PLO, between Christians and Syrians, and, of course, between Christians and Muslims.

With such a history of religious rivalries, Lebanese could be pardoned for saying to the world, as well as to one another, "A plague on all your houses."

William Spencer

Facts in Brief on the Middle East Countries

Country	Population	Government	Monetary Unit*	Foreign Trade (million U.S. $) Exports†	Imports†
Bahrain	414,000	Amir Isa bin Salman Al-Khalifa; Prime Minister Khalifa bin Salman Al-Khalifa	dinar (1 = $2.66)	3,602	3,484
Cyprus	635,000	President Spyros Kyprianou	pound (1 = $2.02)	562	1,166
Egypt	44,697,000	President Mohamed Hosni Mubarak; Prime Minister Ahmad Fouad Moheiddin	pound (1 = $1.43)	3,233	8,839
Iran	40,919,000	President Ali Khamenei; Prime Minister Hosein Musavi-Khamenei	rial (86.7 = $1)	14,251	12,247
Iraq	14,506,000	President Saddam Hussein	dinar (1 = $3.39)	13,200	17,000
Israel	4,152,000	President Yitzhak Navon; Prime Minister Menachem Begin	shekel (31.3 = $1)	5,416	7,787
Jordan	2,460,000	King Hussein I; Prime Minister Mudhar Badran	dinar (1 = $2.75)	736	3,179
Kuwait	1,610,000	Emir Jabir Al-Ahmad Al-Sabah; Crown Prince & Prime Minister Saad Al-Abdullah Al-Sabah	dinar (1 = $3.40)	19,767	6,560
Lebanon	3,404,000	President Amin Gemayel; Prime Minister Shafiq al-Wazzan	pound (4.1 = $1)	817	3,200
Oman	976,000	Sultan Qaboos bin Said	rial (1 = $2.90)	3,202	1,732
Qatar	242,000	Amir & Prime Minister Khalifa bin Hamad Al-Thani	riyal (3.6 = $1)	5,697	1,527
Saudi Arabia	9,169,000	King & Prime Minister Fahd bin Abdulaziz al-Saud	riyal (3.4 = $1)	120,240	35,244
Sudan	20,246,000	President & Prime Minister Gaafar Mohamed Nimeiri	pound (1.3 = $1)	658	1,529
Syria	9,869,000	President Hafiz al-Assad; Prime Minister Abd al Ra'uf al-Kassem	pound (3.9 = $1)	2,103	5,040
Turkey	48,410,000	President Kenan Evren; Prime Minister Bulend Ulusu	lira (182 = $1)	4,721	8,944
United Arab Emirates	1,256,000	President Zayid bin Sultan Al-Nahayyan; Prime Minister Rashid ibn Said al-Maktum	dirham (3.7 = $1)	20,742	8,752
Yemen (Aden)	2,083,000	Supreme People's Council Presidium Chairman & Council of Ministers Chairman Ali Nasir Muhammad	dinar (1 = $2.90)	248	393
Yemen (Sana)	6,270,000	President Ali Abdallah Salih; Prime Minister Abdul Karim al-Iryani	rial (4.6 = $1)	14	1,492

*Exchange rates as of Dec. 1, 1982. †Latest available data.

28 reluctantly approved a commission of inquiry into alleged Israeli involvement in the massacre. At issue, basically, was whether Israeli officials knew the massacre was taking place and did nothing to prevent it. On December 5, the commission announced that it had found no evidence of involvement in the massacre by one Lebanese Christian militia, that commanded by Major Saad Haddad, a close ally of Israel.

Many Israelis felt that the Begin-Sharon policies in Lebanon were undermining the moral foundation of the Jewish state. And a growing number of Jews abroad questioned what they viewed as the Begin government's stubbornness on the long-term issue of Palestinian rights and its insistence on a military solution to the question of relations with Arab states.

U.S. Mediation. With the Soviet Union largely discredited in the Middle East for a variety of reasons, the United States assumed the major peacekeeping role in Lebanon. In late August, about 800 U.S. Marines, along with French and Italian troops, landed in Beirut to act as a multinational peacekeeping force in the war-ravaged city and supervise the PLO evacuation. Although the troops left on September 10, 4,500 soldiers from the three countries returned in late September, after the massacre of Palestinian refugees. United States paratroopers were also assigned to another multinational force set up to monitor the Egyptian-

Israeli border in the Sinai Peninsula after Israel's withdrawal on April 25.

On September 1, President Ronald Reagan announced a Middle East peace plan that called for the establishment of a Palestinian state federated with Jordan. The next day, the Israeli Cabinet rejected the plan, insisting that a Palestinian state "could create a serious threat to Israel's security."

Arab Peace Proposal. A second plan for a Palestinian-Israeli settlement was announced at the 12th Arab Summit conference, held in Fez, Morocco, from September 6 to 9. Attended by all Arab states except Libya and Egypt, the conference ended with a declaration of principles that was essentially a reworking of the plan proposed by Saudi Arabia in November 1981.

The declaration called on Israel to withdraw from all Arab territories occupied in the 1967 Arab-Israeli war, which included the West Bank, Gaza Strip, and Golan Heights. Under the plan, after a brief transition period under United Nations control, the West Bank and Gaza Strip would become an independent Palestinian state under PLO leadership with East Jerusalem as its capital. The adoption of the proposal was seen as a victory by moderate pro-Western Arab states over Arab hard-liners. On September 10, Israel rejected the proposal.

King Hassan II of Morocco led an Arab delegation to Washington, D.C., in October to explain the Arab position, indicating Arab willingness to recognize Israel if these conditions were met. For his part, Arafat stated in early November that he was ready to consider a Palestinian state federated with Jordan. On November 26, however, the PLO's Central Council, a 60-member consultative group, denounced Reagan's September 1 proposal. The council said the plan did not "satisfy the inalienable national rights of our people" because it did not call for an independent Palestinian state under PLO leadership.

Israeli Settlements. One of the main sticking points between Israel and the United States and Arabs was the issue of continued Jewish settlements on the West Bank. The Reagan plan called for a freeze on further settlements, while the Fez declaration demanded that Israel dismantle existing settlements in the area. Reacting to the Reagan proposal, the Israeli Knesset (parliament) voted 56 to 50 on September 5 to reject the U.S. plan as a basis for peace negotiations. The government then allocated $18.5 million for three new West Bank settlements and announced plans for seven others. The Reagan Administration strongly condemned this move.

In early November, Israeli settlers began reconstructing the old Jewish quarter of Hebron, one of the four cities considered Jewish "holy towns" that have been inhabited exclusively by Arabs

The Israeli flag is lowered during ceremonies marking the return of the last part of the occupied Sinai Peninsula to Egypt on April 25.

U.S. Marines, part of a multinational peacekeeping force, return to Beirut, Lebanon, in late September, after the massacre of Palestinian refugees.

since Jews living there fled after Arab riots in the late 1920s. Israel also revived a law still on the books from the days of the Ottoman Empire, which ended in 1922. The law allows the government to seize all vacant lands, in this case about 65 per cent of the land on the West Bank. The lands confiscated under the law were turned over to private contractors to develop housing subdivisions at building costs one-third below comparable housing in Jerusalem and other Israeli towns. The resulting housing boom could make the settlement question academic even if Begin bowed to Arab and U.S. wishes.

The Iran-Iraq War, though overshadowed by the Lebanese crisis, continued to threaten regional stability. Iranian offensives during the spring recaptured most of the territory lost to Iraq in the early days of the war, which began in 1980. Later counterattacks brought Iranian forces up to its border with Iraq, and in July, the Iranians stormed across. Iraqi tactics of bulldozing such Iranian border towns as Qasr-e Shirin and Musian inflamed Iranian hatred of the Iraqis.

For the Iranians, the war became a Shiite crusade against the Sunni Iraqis, the majority sect in Islam to which the rulers of Iraq belong. Tens of thousands of Iranian *baseejis*—teen-age volunteers—died in human wave attacks against Iraqi positions. Iran rejected all efforts at mediation by outside powers and set reparations and the ouster of Iraq's President Saddam Hussein as its price for peace.

Iran's success sent shudders through the oil-producing Arab states along the Persian Gulf. They feared uprisings of their own large Shiite minorities. In November, the Gulf Cooperation Council, formed in May 1981 by Saudi Arabia, Bahrain, Kuwait, Oman, Qatar, and the United Arab Emirates, agreed on a defense plan backed by the U.S. Rapid Deployment Force based in Oman.

Afghan Impasse. The war between Afghan *mujahedeen* (fighters for the faith) and Soviet occupation forces in Afghanistan ground on. Soviet troops and their Afghan allies were unable to gain the upper hand against the mujahedeen despite superiority in arms and personnel and a policy of massive reprisals—including, reportedly, the use of chemical agents and crop defoliants—against villages suspected of aiding the rebels.

Moroccan Morass. The fighting between the government of Morocco and the Polisario Front guerrilla group in Western Sahara created friction within the Organization of African Unity (OAU). In February, the OAU admitted the Polisario, backed by Libya and Algeria, to membership as the Sahara Arab Democratic Republic. Hassan of Morocco denounced the action as illegal and led a walkout by 19 OAU members. Although the king had agreed in June 1981 to hold a referendum in the territory under OAU supervision and to abide by its results, he insisted that the majority of Western Saharans favored Moroccan rule. With Moroccan forces firmly in control of the settled areas of the territory and the Polisario controlling the open desert, outside mediation seemed the only hope for a solution.

Other Developments. Although peace seemed the exception rather than the rule in the Middle East during 1982, there were some encouraging developments. Saudi Arabia changed kings without incident in June when Crown Prince Fahd succeeded to the throne after the death of his half brother King Khalid. Voters in Turkey on November 7 approved a new Constitution and elected military leader General Kenan Evren to a seven-year term as head of state.

And also in November, Lebanon's new president, Amin Gemayel, was granted power to rule by decree for six months. Like other Middle Eastern leaders before him who were brought to power by the unexpected death of a predecessor, Gemayel had a rare opportunity to turn tragedy into triumph for his country. William Spencer

See also FAHD; GEMAYEL, AMIN; and articles on the various Middle Eastern countries. In WORLD BOOK, see MIDDLE EAST and individual Middle Eastern country articles.

MINING. A major study of mine accidents in the United States concluded on Aug. 1, 1982, that the number of injuries and deaths in underground mines could be reduced substantially if mine owners were more committed to safety. The study, conducted by the National Research Council (NRC), analyzed nearly 40,000 fatalities and injuries occurring in U.S. underground mines between 1978 and 1980. The NRC is the principal operating agency of the National Academy of Sciences, which advises the U.S. government on science and technology. The NRC conducted the study at the request of the U.S. Bureau of Mines, which wanted to know why some underground mines have much better safety records than others.

The NRC found that it is the degree to which management is committed to safety—rather than physical, technical, or geographic factors—that explains the large differences in injury rates among U.S. coal-mining firms. The NRC acknowledged that coal mines are much safer today than they were 10 or 20 years ago.

But the agency said that mining firms with poor safety records could cut their accident rates by 50 per cent by taking relatively simple steps. These include devoting more attention and resources to safety issues, improving cooperation with labor, and lengthening and improving company training programs.

Strategic Minerals Policy. President Ronald Reagan issued a national minerals policy on April 5 that was designed to decrease U.S. dependence on foreign supplies of a number of minerals crucial to industry and the military. The United States currently imports more than half its supplies of 20 of these so-called strategic minerals. They are vital for the manufacture of high-strength steel alloys for jet engines, the production of petroleum products, and many other industrial purposes.

The President's National Materials and Minerals Program, which required congressional approval, encouraged increased production of such minerals. It also recommended major additions to the strategic stockpile of materials that the government maintains for use in case of war or foreign cutoffs, and the opening of public lands to mineral exploration and development.

In addition, Reagan called for steps to eliminate barriers to the mining of manganese and other minerals from deep seabed deposits. The new minerals policy also proposed major revisions in the United Nations Law of the Sea Treaty in order to stimulate deep seabed mining. The White House announced on July 8 that the United States would not sign the treaty, partly out of concern that it would hinder seabed mining activities by U.S. companies. See OCEAN.

Seabed Mineral Find. Discovery of a rich future site for such mining was disclosed on September 22 by the National Oceanic and Atmospheric Administration (NOAA). NOAA reported that an expedition, using the deep-diving research submarine *Alvin,* had located a large mineral deposit in the Atlantic Ocean 1,800 miles (2,900 kilometers) east of Miami, Fla. The deposit was said to be rich in manganese and was believed to contain silver, zinc, and copper. It lies in 10,000 feet (3,000 meters) of water, a depth that NOAA said might be within the reach of future technology.

Restoration Extension. The U.S. Department of the Interior announced on July 30 that it would give mining firms additional time to restore farmland disrupted by surface mining activities. The Administration of President Jimmy Carter had set Aug. 2, 1982, as the date by which such land must be restored to its original condition. But Secretary of the Interior James G. Watt extended the deadline to April 3, 1983, to encourage U.S. mining. Environmental groups objected to the delay. In addition, the American Mining Congress, an industry group that opposes the deadline, promised to begin court action to prevent its implementation. Michael Woods

See also DISASTERS (Mine Disasters). In WORLD BOOK, see MINING.

MINNESOTA. See STATE GOVERNMENT.

MISSISSIPPI. See STATE GOVERNMENT.

MISSOURI. See STATE GOVERNMENT.

MONGE ALVAREZ, LUIS ALBERTO (1925-), became president of Costa Rica on May 8, 1982. He headed the Party of National Liberation (PLN), a liberal political party that he helped found in 1951. The PLN had held power in Costa Rica much of the time since then. In 1978, Monge and the PLN lost the presidential election to Rodrigo Carazo Odio, a conservative candidate. In 1982, however, Costa Rica faced the worst economic crisis in its history, and voters turned again to the PLN, electing Monge to succeed Carazo. See COSTA RICA.

Monge was born on Dec. 29, 1925, in Palmares, near Alajuela. He studied social sciences at the University of Costa Rica near San José and then became active in local and international labor organizations. From 1950 to 1952, he served as a consultant for the International Labor Organization, an agency of the United Nations. From 1953 to 1957, Monge was secretary-general of the Inter-American Regional Organization of Workers, a federation of labor groups in North and South America. He served in Costa Rica's Legislative Assembly from 1958 to 1962 and from 1970 to 1974, the last year as president of the Assembly.

Monge is married to the former Doris Yankelewitz Berger. They have one daughter. Sara Dreyfuss

MONGOLIA. See ASIA.

MONTANA. See STATE GOVERNMENT.

MONTREAL. The regime of long-time Mayor Jean Drapeau faced its first real opposition in three decades in 1982 as Montreal voters expressed their dissatisfaction with the city's economy. After a bitterly fought election campaign, Mayor Drapeau was elected on November 14 to his ninth term, but his Civic Party lost its stranglehold on the City Council. Before the election, the Civic Party held 55 of the 57 seats on the council. After the ballots had been counted, Drapeau's followers had captured only 39 of the seats, with 15 going to the Montreal Citizens Movement (MCM) and 3 to the Municipal Action Group (MAG).

The vote was split largely along linguistic lines, with English-speaking voters backing the opposition parties and much of the French-speaking population remaining loyal to the ruling Civic Party. The city's former police chief, Henri Paul Vignola, made a surprisingly weak showing as head of the right-of-center MAG, while left-leaning Jean Dore did a lot better than expected. MAG got only 15 per cent of the vote; MCM, 37 per cent; and the Civic Party, 48 per cent.

City's Economy Falters. The vote came at a time when Montreal's economy was in even worse shape than that of other cities in Canada.

Local businesses suffered—as did hundreds of thousands of Montreal commuters—when 6,500 transport workers went on strike on January 15 in a wage dispute. The provincial assembly went into special session the same day and passed a law requiring the unions to go back to work. When the unions refused to do so, the government warned of "harsher measures." Faced with this threat, the unions ended the strike on January 20. The bus and subway workers struck again on July 30 and returned to work on August 4 in obedience to an order from the provincial government.

Tourism in Montreal declined by about 10 per cent during the year, making 1982 one of the worst tourist seasons in history. Not a single major hotel made money during the first nine months of the year, and projections for the winter season predicted an occupancy rate of under 50 per cent.

The aerospace business had been one of the bright spots in the local economy, but as the recession took its toll, more than 4,000 aerospace workers were laid off. About 3,000 jobs were lost in the airline industry as Air Canada and several other smaller carriers made staff cutbacks. As the year drew to a close, unemployment in the Montreal area hovered around the 20 per cent mark.

On a brighter note, the port of Montreal held its own, with approximately the same amount of cargo flowing through the city as in previous years. The port is directly responsible for about 10,000 jobs within the city's economy.

Budget Surplus. The city started the year with a cash surplus of $26.4 million (Canadian dollars; $1 = U.S. 81 cents on Dec. 31, 1982). This was the result of revenues in fiscal 1982 of $994 million, or $48-million more than expected. City officials said the excess revenues would be used to pay off some of the $1.03 billion in outstanding civic debt and to hold taxes at the 1982 level. According to an election promise made by the winning party, Montreal taxes, which are already among the highest in North America, will not be raised further and, in some individual cases, may decline. In 1982, the owner of a home valued at $66,500 paid about $1,855 in property and water taxes.

The city's municipal employment rolls shrank by about 2,500 from 1978 to 1982. An expected labor cutback of 500 in 1983 will reduce total Montreal city employment to about 12,800.

Language Problems continued to trouble the city and the region during 1982. Under Quebec's language laws, no sign may be written in a language other than French in most public places, and children of parents who move to the province must be educated in French schools. These laws have made it difficult for companies located in Montreal to recruit management and technical personnel from elsewhere in North America, and many companies have moved their headquarters to other cities. Charles Kendal Windeyer

See also CANADA; QUEBEC. In WORLD BOOK, see MONTREAL.

MOON, SUN MYUNG (1920-), the controversial evangelist and founder of the Unification Church, was convicted on May 18, 1982, of conspiracy to evade paying federal income tax and of filing false tax returns from 1973 to 1975. On July 16, Moon was sentenced to 18 months in prison and fined $25,000. He remained free on bond while appealing his conviction.

Moon was born on Jan. 6, 1920, in Pyung Buk-Do, now in North Korea. He claims that he dedicated his life to religion at age 16 when Jesus Christ appeared to him. Moon began his public ministry in 1946 and was imprisoned by the North Korean government in 1948. Released two years later, he fled to South Korea. There, in 1954, he established the Holy Spirit Association for the Unification of World Christianity.

Moon moved to the United States in 1972. Church membership grew rapidly. However, the organization's recruitment practices and aggressive fund-raising activities aroused considerable controversy. Religious leaders and others also criticized Moon for directing a diverse business empire under the umbrella of the church. The Unification Church has financed publishing, entertainment, fishing, and food retailing operations in the United States.

Moon married Hak-Ja Han in 1960. They have 12 children.

Barbara A. Mayes

King Hassan II of Morocco and President Ronald Reagan ride through the Virginia countryside after a meeting at the White House in May.

MOROCCO received a bitter blow on Feb. 22, 1982, when the Organization of African Unity (OAU) admitted the Polisario Front guerrilla group of Western Sahara as its 51st member. The Polisario was voted into the OAU as the Sahara Arab Democratic Republic. King Hassan II's government had been fighting a desert war with the Polisario since Morocco annexed Western Sahara following Spain's withdrawal in 1976. The Moroccan delegation boycotted the OAU after the February decision, and a vigorous Moroccan campaign wrecked the August 6 OAU summit meeting in Tripoli, Libya, which was canceled because of lack of a quorum.

Hassan, however, was unable to muster support from other African states for Moroccan rights to Western Sahara. This failure was largely due to Morocco's inability to defeat the Polisario. Moroccan control in Western Sahara was limited to a triangle of key towns protected by a 280-mile (450-kilometer) sand wall of 9-foot (2.7-meter) dunes, barbed wire, and minefields. The triangle enclosed only about 8 per cent of the area's 127,000 square miles (329,000 square kilometers). Outside the wall, Polisario units moved at will.

One Bright Spot in Morocco's campaign against the Polisario was the reopening on July 10 of the huge Bou Craa phosphate mine in the protected part of the Sahara. It had been closed since 1976, when guerrillas cut the conveyor belt that carries the phosphate rock about 60 miles (100 kilometers) to loading piers on the Atlantic coast.

Despite the heavy cost of the war and Hassan's inability to win African support for the annexation, he faced very little internal opposition. In March, the king pardoned Abderrahim Bouabid, leader of the opposition Socialist Union of Popular Forces (USFP), and other USFP leaders. They had been sentenced to a year in prison in late 1981 for opposing Hassan's acceptance of an OAU proposal for a referendum on Western Sahara.

In June, a new Moroccan political party, the National Democratic Party, held its first national congress. It had split off from the National Independent Rally, a loose pro-monarchy coalition that developed after the reconciliation between Hassan and his opposition in 1977. The new party, with 57 deputies in the Chamber of Representatives, supports expanded rural development, diversified industries, and social equality.

Economic Woes. The Western Saharan war and declining world phosphate prices were a severe drain on Morocco's economy. The 1982-1983 budget showed a 35 per cent increase in expenditures, to about $8 billion, with defense costs rising to $650 million.

William Spencer

See also AFRICA (Facts in Brief Table). In WORLD BOOK, see MOROCCO.

MOTION PICTURES

Motion pictures in the United States had a year of remarkable commercial highs alternating with discouraging low periods in 1982. From the purely financial viewpoint, the American box office seemed to fluctuate with the changing of the seasons. The winter of 1981-1982 was a disappointment, following the gloomiest box-office Christmas in several years. But spring offered some encouragement, with the extended success of *On Golden Pond* and *Chariots of Fire*, both of which opened in 1981 but were not released nationally until 1982. The summer brought a genuine bonanza that made 1982 a financial banner year for motion pictures. Fall, customarily the blandest season for movies, seemed even more discouraging than usual following the euphoric summer months.

Summer of 1982, however, remained one for the record books, highlighted by the phenomenal success of Steven Spielberg's *E. T.: The Extra-Terrestrial.* The sweet-natured fantasy, about a kindly alien who is stranded on earth and protected by children until he can arrange passage home, struck a responsive chord in people of all ages. It earned $300 million at U.S. box offices by mid-December, tripling the $100-million figure that

Seven-year-old Drew Barrymore makes friends with a kindly creature from outer space in the blockbuster *E. T.: The Extra-Terrestrial.*

traditionally distinguishes commercial blockbusters from mere successes. The film solidified Spielberg's position as a creator of top-grossing, critically acclaimed films. See SPIELBERG, STEVEN.

E. T. also proved a merchandising bonanza. MCA, Incorporated, the parent company of Universal Pictures, the studio that released the Spielberg money-maker, made licensing agreements with 43 firms for E. T. products. The merchandise included lunch boxes, bicycles, and underwear.

Even without *E. T.,* the summer months would have been commercially fruitful for motion pictures. Both *Rocky III* and *An Officer and a Gentleman* exceeded $100 million at the box office.

While the summer lasted, a general state of euphoria existed among exhibitors and distributors. Theater chain executives professed strong hopes that motion pictures would survive the high-technology rivalry of pay-TV and video cassettes. They cited the natural inclination of young people, the most enthusiastic group of filmgoers, to want to get out of the house for entertainment. On a note of optimism, theater executives predicted an end to the building of so-called minicinemas, averaging 150 to 250 seats, and a return to the construction of theaters seating 500 or 600.

The End of the Year brought 1982's two most dynamic performances by actresses, both in roles that were largely tragic. Meryl Streep's portrayal of a lusty concentration camp survivor in *Sophie's Choice* won enormous praise, as did Jessica Lange's delineation of troubled actress Frances Farmer in *Frances.* Paul Newman, a star for more than 25 years, earned some of the best reviews of his career as a struggling, cynical attorney in *The Verdict.* The action-filled *48 Hrs.* promised to launch Eddie Murphy of television's "Saturday Night Live" to big-screen stardom.

The World Film Scene seemed variable. *Diva,* a complex and self-consciously "smart" French thriller from director Jean-Jacques Beineix, drew large crowds and critical praise. So did Wolfgang Petersen's *Das Boot,* the most successful picture in the history of the West German film industry.

On the other hand, Italian director Bernardo Bertolucci failed to win favor with *Tragedy of a Ridiculous Man.* Following the failure of his 1979 picture *Luna,* it continued the downward spiral for the director who created a sensation in 1973 with *Last Tango in Paris.* The Italian film industry was represented more favorably by Francesco Rosi's *Three Brothers,* a gentle film that dealt with three sons of different life styles who return to their native village for the funeral of their mother.

Poland's prime film export of the year was Jerzy Skolimowski's *Moonlighting,* about four Polish workers adrift in London. The film starred Jeremy Irons, who also appeared in the television series "Brideshead Revisited" and the 1981 film *The French Lieutenant's Woman. Moonlighting* proved a magnet at theaters specializing in foreign films.

Yilmaz Guney, the leading figure of the Turkish film industry during the 1960s, was the screenwriter and creative force behind *Yol,* a film about five political prisoners on leave in modern Turkey. It shared the Golden Palm Grand Prize with the American picture *Missing* at the Cannes Film Festival in France in May. But *Yol* was possibly too grim for American audiences.

Sylvester Stallone still packs a wallop. He wrote, directed, and starred in *Rocky III,* which exceeded $115 million at the box office in 1982.

Ironically, the highly romantic French filmmaker Claude Lelouch met a similar fate with his extravagant three-hour *Bolero.* A big hit in Paris, *Bolero* failed to attract American audiences despite the presence of American star James Caan. Lelouch's last true international success was *A Man and a Woman* in 1966. French films that met with a more favorable response than *Bolero* included *L'Adolescente,* with direction by Jeanne Moreau, which transcended the familiar story about a young girl's self-discovery; and *Le Beau Mariage,* in which Eric Rohmer continued his witty, talky "Comedies and Proverbs" series.

Australian films had a lackluster year, particularly considering the critical and commercial attention they enjoyed in 1980 and 1981. Australia enjoyed a healthy box-office year, however. The 1980 American-made comedy *Airplane,* released in Australia as *Flying High,* ran for more than 75 weeks in Perth during 1981 and 1982. *E. T.* was not scheduled to open in Australia until 1983.

The release of Werner Herzog's trouble-plagued *Fitzcarraldo* seemed almost anticlimactic after the years of publicity devoted to its filming in the South American jungles, where it was disrupted by hostile Indians, amebic dysentery, and other difficulties. But the German allegorical adventure enjoyed a respectable run in art houses. In some cities, it was accompanied by the showing of Les Blank's *Burden of Dreams,* a documentary about the making of the Herzog film. In fact, many critics praised Blank's film more than Herzog's.

Mephisto, István Szabó's Hungarian adaptation of Klaus Mann's long-suppressed 1936 German novel, was a surprise Academy Award winner as best foreign film of 1982 and enjoyed a deserved success on the art house circuit. The story of an ambitious actor's rise in Nazi Germany, *Mephisto* benefited from a mesmerizing performance by Klaus Maria Brandauer.

In Great Britain, box-office reports were discouraging. In June, ordinarily a month that registers high attendance figures, average weekly admissions were listed at 860,000, with exhibitors reporting that some films played to empty auditoriums all day. But the British film industry received a shot in the arm with the international success of *Chariots of Fire,* the dark-horse winner of the Oscar for best picture, which opened in many theaters in 1982. *The Long Good Friday,* a drama of the London underworld, drew strong notices and a sturdy list of international bookings. The expected success of *Gandhi,* Sir Richard Attenborough's long-planned film of the life of Indian leader Mohandas K. Gandhi, with Ben Kingsley in the title role, provided another booster shot.

The international motion-picture scene lost one of its most prolific filmmakers on June 10 with the death of West German director Rainer Werner Fassbinder. The 36-year-old director died of a lethal mixture of cocaine and sleeping pills. During his brief career, he had made 41 feature films, including his 1979 success, *The Marriage of Maria Braun.* His next-to-last film, *Veronika Voss,* was perceived by many critics as a dark variation of Billy Wilder's 1950 classic *Sunset Boulevard.*

Old and Young. Major studios continued to make an effort during 1982 to recapture the older audience while catering to the youth market. Three 1981 releases that had most of their bookings in 1982—*On Golden Pond, Chariots of Fire,* and Warren Beatty's *Reds*—had elements that appealed to older viewers. All three films shared a tendency to treat past years with fond regard.

Also appealing to older as well as younger viewers was *An Officer and a Gentleman,* a surprise blockbuster that ultimately was expected to rival the $115-million gross of *Rocky III. Officer* starred Richard Gere as a misunderstood loner redeemed by the love of a good woman and the ministerings of a tough drill sergeant. The boot-camp romance reminded older patrons of earlier military films that might have starred Tyrone Power or Robert Taylor. However, it presented earthy sex that would have been impossible in the old Hollywood.

The Best Little Whorehouse in Texas, a tame version of the stage musical, also proved surprisingly popular with older patrons, particularly in rural areas.

The film paired Burt Reynolds and singing star Dolly Parton. However, its box-office gross of $70-million made it a mild disappointment.

On the other end of the age spectrum, Hollywood continued to attract a youthful audience with movies that adhered to one of two themes: teen-agers indulging in sex (*Porky's, Fast Times at Ridgemont High,* and *Zapped*) and teen-agers being victimized by mad killers (*Friday the 13th, Part III*). The latter, filmed in 3-D, managed a healthy first-week gross and caused reports that 3-D might be a viable commodity in the 1980s.

On the other hand, *Tex,* a sincere study of adolescents in the Southwest, had trouble finding profitable theater dates. More encouraging was the success of *Diner,* a low-budget comedy-drama about young adults reconvening in the haunts where they spent their high school years.

The profitability of the youth market was not limited to the United States. *Porky's* broke records in Belgium, and *Class of 1984,* a violent film that received a mixed critical reception, was a big hit in Italy.

Out of the Closet. Homosexuality was the focus of much attention in 1982 motion pictures. Most earlier movies glossed over homosexuality or used it in minor plot developments. In the few films where homosexuality was the focal point of the plot—such as *The Children's Hour* (1962), *The Fox* (1968), and *The Sergeant* (1969)—it was depicted as a disorder that drove its sufferers to suicide. In 1982, *Personal Best, Partners, Making Love,* and, most successfully, Blake Edwards' *Victor/Victoria* took a sympathetic, nonjudgmental approach to homosexuality. However, none of the films was a commercial breakthrough. At year's end, Sydney Pollack's *Tootsie,* starring Dustin Hoffman as an unemployed heterosexual actor who dons women's clothes to get a part in a soap opera, made telling comments on sexual role-playing.

Failures. Although 1982 was not burdened with a failure as spectacular as Michael Cimino's 1980 flop *Heaven's Gate,* it had its share of disappointments from respected directors. These included Fred Zinnemann's *Five Days One Summer,* Francis Ford Coppola's *One From the Heart,* Woody Allen's *A Midsummer Night's Sex Comedy,* Robert Benton's *Still of the Night,* Don Siegel's *Jinxed,* and Frank Perry's *Monsignor.* Two of the year's biggest flops were *Yes, Giorgio,* an inauspicious film debut for opera star Luciano Pavarotti, and *Inchon,* with Laurence Olivier giving a waxworks impersonation of General Douglas MacArthur. The failures got almost as much media attention as the spectacular successes of the summer. Philip Wuntch

See also AWARDS AND PRIZES (Arts Awards); FONDA, HENRY; HEPBURN, KATHARINE. In WORLD BOOK, see MOTION PICTURE.

MOZAMBIQUE. See AFRICA.

MUSEUM. Funding continued to be a primary concern for museums in the United States in 1982. Federal and state budget cuts and the adverse effects of inflation, recession, and unemployment, which reduced tax revenues, subjected museums to great fiscal stress. Museums supported chiefly by public funds were particularly hard-hit. The elimination of the Comprehensive Employment and Training Act (CETA), a federal employment program that funded the jobs of some museum employees, compounded the difficulty. Outdoor museums also suffered from the decline in travel caused by the tight economy. As a result, museums were forced to reconsider their allotment of funds for the care of collections and for educational programs.

New Buildings and Plans. The Metropolitan Museum of Art in New York City opened the Michael C. Rockefeller Wing for primitive art in February. The Currier Gallery of Art in Manchester, N.H., completed two new wings in April, and the Grand Rapids (Mich.) Art Museum opened a downtown facility in September. A new museum devoted to the works of Spanish painter Salvador Dali opened in St. Petersburg, Fla., in March. The Strong Museum in Rochester, N.Y., opened its new building in October. Barbara A. Mayes

See also VISUAL ARTS. In WORLD BOOK, see MUSEUM.

MUSIC, CLASSICAL. Although financial crises burdened classical music and musicians in 1982, the year had its triumphs and celebrations as well. The most moving victory belonged to pianist Leon Fleisher, who lost the use of his right hand in 1965 because of a mysterious nerve disorder. After 17 years of various sorts of therapy, he made a triumphant comeback on Sept. 16, 1982, at the opening of the Baltimore Symphony's new Joseph Meyerhoff Symphony Hall. Playing César Franck's *Symphonic Variations* and a *Nocturne* by Frédéric Chopin, Fleisher brought the audience to its feet and elicited tears of joy from many listeners.

Canada's Toronto Symphony also gained a home in September, when Roy Thomson Hall opened. One of its festive concerts, featuring Sir William Walton's *Belshazzar's Feast,* marked the composer's 80th birthday. Three other performance halls that opened in September were the refurbished Orpheum Theater in New Orleans, the new home for that city's Philharmonic Orchestra; and two all-purpose theaters—the Eugene (Ore.) Performing Arts Center and the Peoria (Ill.) Civic Center Theater. In London, Barbican Hall, the official home of the London Symphony Orchestra, opened in March as part of Barbican Centre, a $300-million arts complex.

Money, or rather the lack of it, added a sour note to the U.S. musical score in 1982. The pressure of shortages led to disputes and strikes. Two orchestras — the Florida Philharmonic and Kansas City Philharmonic — were disbanded. Music organizations used a variety of fund-raising methods in their efforts to offset the economic slump and reductions in government support. The New York City Opera and the Boston Opera Company cut ticket prices, hoping to increase attendance. The Cleveland Orchestra and others sought corporate support for individual concerts, designating helpful firms in each program. The St. Louis (Mo.) Symphony Orchestra schedule, for example, included "Monsanto Guest Artist" Frederica von Stade. Entertainer Danny Kaye led a fund drive benefit for the Buffalo (N.Y.) Philharmonic Orchestra. The National Symphony Orchestra held a Decorators Show House benefit at a Washington, D.C., department store. Radio marathons continued to play an important part in fund-raising efforts in Chicago and elsewhere, but the New York City Opera took the marathon idea a step further and held a "Fun(d) Run." The San Francisco Opera Company published *What Aria Cooking?* with recipes such as "Die Meistersalad," and *The Washington Cookbook* brought money to the Washington Opera Company.

To be part of the American Telephone and Telegraph (A.T. & T.) Company's "Bell System American Orchestras on Tour" was a sought-after honor. A.T. & T. funds helped 30 orchestras tour 280 cities in 1982.

Premières continued despite money problems. New music introduced by instrumental groups included: Benjamin Lees's *Double Concerto* (American Symphony Orchestra); Jean Eichelberger Ivey's *Sea Change* (Baltimore); Sandor Balassa's *Calls and Cries* and Roger Sessions' *Concerto for Orchestra* (Boston); Doris Hays's *Southern Voices for Orchestra* (Chattanooga, Tenn.); Larry Weiner's *Chipita Rodriguez* (Corpus Christi, Tex.); James Hartway's *City Views* (Detroit); Paul Cooper's *Concerto for Flute and Orchestra* (Houston); John Corigliano's *Pied Piper Fantasy for Flute and Orchestra* and Paul Chihara's *Love Music* (Los Angeles); Olav Thommessen's *Beyond Neon* (Minnesota); Leonardo Balada's *Quasi un paso doble* (New York City); and William Schuman's *American Hymn* (St. Louis).

Opera companies contributed their share of premières. In February, the Charlotte (N.C.) Opera introduced Robert Ward's *Abelard and Heloise,* based on a tragic 12th-century love affair. La Scala of Milan, Italy, gave Luciano Berio's *La vera storia* in March. In April, the Kennedy Center for the Performing Arts in Washington, D.C., premièred Gian Carlo Menotti's one-act opera for

Zubin Mehta conducts the New York Philharmonic in its 10,000th concert, in New York City in March. The orchestra gave its first performance in 1842.

children, *A Bride from Pluto,* replete with robot and spaceship. In June, a Miami (Fla.) Arts Festival included the first performance of Robert Ward's *Minutes Till Midnight,* about a scientist who discovers a more potent energy source than the hydrogen bomb. Also in June, the St. Louis (Mo.) Opera Theatre presented Stephen Paulus' *The Postman Always Rings Twice,* based on the book by James M. Cain. Other summer premières included George Rochberg's musical setting of *The Confidence Man* by Herman Melville at Santa Fe, N. Mex., in July; Kirke Mechem's Molière-inspired *Tartuffe* at the Lake George Opera Festival in New York in August; and Alice Walker's operatic version of *The Ponder Heart* by Eudora Welty in Jackson, Miss., in September. The Portland (Ore.) Opera premièred film composer Bernard Herrmann's *Wuthering Heights* in November.

United States opera companies performed unusual fare as spice for the usual repertory operas. Among works receiving U.S. premières were Arrigo Boïto's *Nerone* (Opera Orchestra of New York); Emmanuel Chabrier's *Gwendoline* (San Diego); Stanislaw Moniuszko's *The Haunted Castle* (Michigan); Wolfgang Amadeus Mozart's *L'Oca del Cairo* (Kansas City); Sergei Prokofiev's *Maddalena* (St. Louis); Giuseppe Verdi's *Il Corsaro* (San Diego); Richard Wagner's *Die Feen* (New York City Opera); Riccardo Zandonai's *Giulietta e Romeo* (San Diego); and Bernd Alois Zimmermann's *Die Soldaten* (Boston).

Notes on Musicians. Eugene Ormandy, retired conductor of the Philadelphia Orchestra, was one of five artistic luminaries honored by the Kennedy Center in December for contributions to the performing arts. Tenor Luciano Pavarotti starred in a prime-time television special in March and in the widely distributed but critically disdained motion picture *Yes, Giorgio.* Tenor Placido Domingo's recordings *Perhaps Love* (with John Denver) and *Domingo Tangos* were best-sellers.

Unusual Musical Events of 1982 included the appearance of baseball player Willie Stargell of the Pittsburgh Pirates narrating the words of Martin Luther King, Jr., in *New Morning for the World* by Joseph Schwantner. The Eastman Philharmonic Orchestra premièred the work at the Kennedy Center on January 15.

In June, the Israel Philharmonic Orchestra and the New York Philharmonic presented a joint concert conducted by Zubin Mehta at Lincoln Center for the Performing Arts in New York City. The University of Cincinnati Orchestra performed Gustav Mahler's revision of Ludwig van Beethoven's *Ninth Symphony* in April. And in November, a rock version of Claudio Monteverdi's 340-year-old opera *The Coronation of Poppea* livened the scene at a New York City discothèque. Peter P. Jacobi

In WORLD BOOK, see MUSIC; OPERA.

MUSIC, POPULAR. Middle-of-the-road music, all but forgotten by the majority of American record companies, made a small but significant comeback in the United States in 1982. Many radio stations suffering from low ratings abandoned rock programming for one of two syndicated services that played music by such nonrock performers as Andy Williams, Steve Lawrence, Eydie Gorme, Frankie Laine, Tony Bennett, Frank Sinatra, and even Glenn Miller. At the same time, a number of record companies brought out LP's by Jack Jones, Mel Torme, Hugo Montenegro, Sammy Davis, Jr., Billy May, and Roger Williams, among others.

No Major New Musical Style emerged in 1982, and in terms of creativity, pop music was in the doldrums. Some record companies attempted to promote hard-driving, new-wave rock bands. But the public had little opportunity to hear most of these bands outside of their own communities because most rock radio stations found their music too violent and chose not to play their recordings.

Record companies searched anxiously for a new sound. However, the only one heard was the robotlike rhythms of the new-wave punk bands patterned after Devo, a seminal band viewed with some alarm by parents when it made its debut several years ago. Devo has since inspired a number of groups, including X, Black Flag, the Plimsouls, and the Go Gos. The Go Gos, an all-woman band, cracked U.S. popularity charts and then suddenly began to abandon their hard-core-punk style.

The diversity of musical styles reflected the wide-ranging taste of the public. It also underscored the lack of a dominant musical style for everyone to copy. In fact, there was really something for everybody in 1982, from reggae to jazz fusion to heavy-metal rock to country rockabilly.

Most Popular Acts of the year, as measured by record sales, were the J. Geils Band, John Cougar, Foreigner, Sheena Easton, Pat Benatar, Joan Jett, Luther Vandross, Duran Duran, the Go Gos, Steve Miller Band, a revitalized Chicago, and Michael McDonald in a solo effort away from the Doobie Brothers.

Black superstar acts declined in popularity in 1982. Only two of them—Diana Ross and Quincy Jones—sold 1 million records to win a platinum-certified LP. In 1981, black pop acts had accounted for 18 per cent of all platinum LP's.

The US Festival, an attempt to re-create the 1968 Woodstock Festival by offering a potpourri of rock names along with exhibits of the latest computer technology, failed at the box office. It racked up an attendance of some 400,000 people and a box-office deficit reported to be $3 million. Such artists as Fleetwood Mac, Tom Petty, Graham Nash, and Jackson Browne failed to lure a large enough audience to recoup the huge cost of staging the out-

The singing group Alabama display their trophies after the Academy of Country Music named them the Top Vocal Group of the year in April.

door concert. Apple Computer co-founder Stephen G. Wozniak financed the Labor Day weekend extravaganza, held near San Bernardino, Calif.

The Apollo Theatre in Harlem, New York City—since 1935 a leading showcase for black talent—was purchased for less than $1 million by the Inner City Broadcasting Company. Programs produced there are to be carried by the Urban Contemporary Music and Entertainment Network, a new cable TV operation that plans to offer "narrowcasting" programs for ethnic audiences.

Teddy Pendergrass was paralyzed from the neck down by injuries suffered in an automobile accident in Philadelphia in March. His doctor said he would eventually be able to sing again.

The Doobie Brothers ended 12 years in show business with a farewell tour of the United States. A concert at the University of California at Berkeley, taped for pay-TV, concluded the tour.

The Who, an influential British rock band, capped its nearly 20-year career with a three-month farewell tour of North America. The band, which had won lasting popularity with American fans, played before an estimated 1.4 million people. The final concert, held in Toronto, Canada, was beamed live to pay-TV audiences in four countries.

Veteran blues singer B. B. King recorded his first country music LP, *Love Me Tender,* in a show of versatility. But the album sold poorly. To commemorate his 35th year in show business, King recorded an LP of his favorite songs with the Crusaders, a jazz-soul group, and the Royal Philharmonic Orchestra at the Royal Festival Hall in London.

One of the oldest and most famous rock nightclubs in the United States, the Whisky, closed in September in Los Angeles. The club opened in the 1960s as the Whisky-A-Go Go, one of the nation's first discothèques. It was forced to close because it could no longer compete with clubs that had larger seating capacities.

Jazz. Because jazz albums cost less to produce than popular recordings, jazz was less severely hit than pop music by economic conditions. In fact, several new jazz-oriented record labels began production in 1982. One of them, Elektra/Musician, released *The Young Lions,* an album featuring probable future stars, among them "vocalese" singer Bobby McFerrin, flutist James Newton, and saxophonist Paquito D'Rivera, who defected from Cuba. Palo Alto Records was launched with a series of albums devoted primarily to bop and swing styles and to vocal jazz.

Concerts and festivals continued to thrive. For the first time, a commercial sponsor—a cigarette company—subsidized major weeklong jazz festivals in 20 U.S. cities between June and November.

In an unusual departure, the Los Angeles festival was devoted to avant-garde music. During the summer, hundreds of American jazz artists played at an estimated 35 jazz festivals in Europe. In September, the first major jazz festival in Israel was staged with American artists.

A slight resurgence of interest in big bands was reflected in the strong sales of *Hooked on Swing*. The album is comprised of early swing and jazz band hits.

Much discussed among new artists was Ronald Shannon Jackson, a drummer who called his small group the Decoding Society. Jackson said that saxophonist Ornette Coleman and pianist Cecil Taylor had inspired his music.

Several second-generation jazz performers gained prominence in 1982. Trumpeter Wynton Marsalis, 20, and his saxophonist brother Branford, 21, are sons of New Orleans pianist Ellis Marsalis. Chico Freeman and his father, Von, both play the saxophone. Guitarist Joe Cohn could be heard on records with his saxophonist father, Al.

The jazz world lost several outstanding artists in 1982, including Thelonious Monk, Art Pepper, and Sonny Stitt. Leonard Feather and Eliot Tiegel

See also AWARDS AND PRIZES (Arts Awards); RECORDINGS. In WORLD BOOK, see COUNTRY MUSIC; JAZZ; POPULAR MUSIC; ROCK MUSIC.

NAKASONE, YASUHIRO (1918-), became prime minister of Japan on Nov. 26, 1982. He succeeded Zenko Suzuki, who resigned. Like Suzuki, Nakasone was president of Japan's ruling Liberal-Democratic Party, a conservative party despite its name. Both leaders were considered pro-Western and supporters of free enterprise. See JAPAN.

Yasuhiro Nakasone was born on May 27, 1918, in Takasaki, Japan, the son of a wealthy lumber dealer. He earned a degree in political science at the University of Tokyo and took a job in Japan's Ministry of Home Affairs. World War II had begun, however, and he was drafted into the Imperial Navy, where he served as a paymaster.

Nakasone was first elected to the House of Representatives, the lower house of Japan's parliament, in 1947. He kept a seat in every election after that. He joined the Cabinet in 1959 as director-general of the Science and Technology Agency and chairman of the Atomic Energy Commission. Altogether, he held five Cabinet-level posts in 23 years, including minister of transport, director-general of the Defense Agency, and minister of international trade and finance.

Nakasone enjoys golf, skiing, swimming, tennis, and oil painting. He and his wife, the former Tsutako Kobayashi, were married in 1945 and live in a suburb of Tokyo. They have three married children and five grandchildren. Sara Dreyfuss

NAMIBIA. During 1982, success continued to elude black nationalists in their long struggle for the independence of Namibia (formerly known as South West Africa). Since 1966, the black nationalist South West Africa People's Organization (SWAPO) had fought South African rule of Namibia through diplomacy and guerrilla warfare.

Since 1978, a group of five Western powers known as the contact group—Canada, France, Great Britain, the United States, and West Germany—had sponsored negotiations about Namibia. The talks involved South Africa's government, SWAPO, and the governments of nearby black-ruled African states that supported SWAPO—the so-called front-line states of Angola, Botswana, Mozambique, Tanzania, Zambia, and Zimbabwe. By 1982, agreement had been reached on most major points, including a cease-fire supervised by the United Nations (UN), followed by elections.

Cuban Troops. On July 13, the contact group reported agreement on what was believed to be the last stumbling block—how members of Namibia's constituent assembly would be chosen. However, one major obstacle remained. South Africa insisted that it would not agree to a settlement unless Angola first committed itself to the withdrawal of the 15,000 to 20,000 Cuban and East European troops stationed in that country.

The United States government supported South Africa on this condition and engaged in intensive diplomatic efforts at the UN and in African capitals to obtain agreement on it. However, Angola and the other front-line states rejected the tying of Namibia's independence to a troop pullout. See ANGOLA.

Successful Attacks by South African forces against SWAPO guerrillas based in southern Angola reduced the pressure on South Africa to agree to a diplomatic settlement. In a raid that began on March 13, South African troops claimed to have killed 201 guerrillas and to have destroyed one of their bases. In another incursion, which started on June 11, South African military units spent more than two months in southern Angola.

SWAPO sent a 100-man raiding party into Namibia from Angola in April. The guerrillas laid land mines and ambushed South African forces.

Namibia's Interim Government, formed after elections in December 1979, which SWAPO boycotted, was supposed to have reached the end of its term on Nov. 21, 1982. South Africa's Prime Minister Pieter Willem Botha extended it until February 1983. The interim government represented moderate blacks, persons of mixed race, and whites, joined in a coalition called the Democratic Turnhalle Alliance (DTA). J. Dixon Esseks

See also AFRICA. In WORLD BOOK, see SOUTH WEST AFRICA.

NATIONAL PTA (NATIONAL CONGRESS OF PARENTS AND TEACHERS) in 1982 formed a television review panel to recommend programs for family viewing. The series "Wild Kingdom" and several specials, including *A Woman Called Golda*, received the panel's approval. In an ongoing effort to reduce TV's negative impact on children, the PTA conducted eight regional workshops to help parents and teachers make instruction in critical TV viewing a part of school curriculums.

In its role as a member of the National Coalition for Public Education and Religious Liberty, the PTA began a nationwide petition campaign opposing tuition tax credits and educational vouchers for parents of children attending private schools.

At the National PTA Convention, held in June in Nashville, Tenn., delegates adopted resolutions calling for programs at the state and local level to deal with the problems of teen-age drug and alcohol abuse. They also urged the federal government to increase Social Security benefits for college and vocational school students. Virginia E. Anderson

In WORLD BOOK, see NATIONAL CONGRESS OF PARENTS AND TEACHERS; PARENT-TEACHER ORGANIZATIONS.

NAVY. See ARMED FORCES.
NEBRASKA. See STATE GOVERNMENT.
NEPAL. See ASIA.

NETHERLANDS. Ruud Lubbers became prime minister of the Netherlands on Nov. 4, 1982, succeeding Andreas A. M. van Agt. Lubbers led a coalition of his Christian Democrats and the right wing Liberal Party. See LUBBERS, RUUD.

The coalition partners held 81 of the 150 seats in the Second Chamber of the States-General (lower house of parliament) as a result of general elections on September 8. Furthermore, they agreed on most political issues. Hence, political observers expected Lubbers' government to remain in power throughout parliament's four-year term. On November 22, the government announced spending cuts for 1983 through 1986 and a freeze on the wages of public employees.

Collapse. The political parties' failure to agree on measures to lift the country out of its economic doldrums caused political instability during most of 1982. Van Agt's center-left coalition government collapsed on May 12, when the Labor Party rejected large-scale spending cuts proposed by his Christian Democrats. Labor's six ministers refused to continue serving in the 15-member Cabinet, so Van Agt resigned. Labor Party leader Joop den Uyl argued that the Christian Democrats and the third party in the coalition, the liberal-progressive Democrats '66, had violated an agreement on the level of spending cuts.

On May 29, Van Agt formed his third government, a minority coalition with the Democrats '66. The two parties controlled only 65 seats. Labor refused to support the coalition, so the government had to rely on the Liberals for its survival.

Van Agt told parliament on June 8 that the Netherlands economy was "going downhill fast." He spoke as unemployment edged toward 525,000, or 10 per cent of the work force, and wages rose by an average of 6.5 per cent—higher than the rate of inflation.

The General Elections on September 8 produced a complex situation. Labor increased its seats in the lower house from 44 to 47. The Christian Democrats had 45 seats; the Liberals, 36; and Democrats '66, 6. Small parties held the remaining 16. Differences between the Christian Democrats and Labor ruled out a coalition.

On October 13, Van Agt resigned as chairman of the Christian Democrats and Lubbers succeeded him. Van Agt said that 11 years in the Cabinet, four of them as prime minister, had sapped his strength.

Queen Beatrix visited the United States in April to mark the 200th anniversary of the establishment of diplomatic relations between that country and the Netherlands. Kenneth Brown

See also EUROPE (Facts in Brief Table). In WORLD BOOK, see NETHERLANDS.
NEVADA. See STATE GOVERNMENT.

NEW BRUNSWICK. Canada's longest-surviving premier won a fourth term after 12 years in office in the election on Oct. 12, 1982. Richard B. Hatfield led the Progressive Conservative (PC) Party as they won 39 seats in the 58-seat legislature. The Liberals dropped to 18 seats, and the New Democratic Party elected a member for the first time in New Brunswick's history. Hatfield's achievement in officially designating New Brunswick a bilingual province was reflected in the PC taking four seats from the Liberals in the French-speaking Acadian district.

Creating New Jobs and preserving existing ones were major concerns for the Hatfield government. Out of a work force of 317,000 persons, 100,000 were unemployed or on social assistance. In the Miramichi region, the heart of the province's forest industry, 1,200 sawmill workers had lost their jobs. A positive note was the completion of a nuclear power reactor at Point Lepreau near Saint John. The plant became operational in late 1982, and will export 295 megawatts of power to three utilities in Massachusetts and Maine. David M. L. Farr

See also CANADA. In WORLD BOOK, see NEW BRUNSWICK.
NEW HAMPSHIRE. See STATE GOVERNMENT.
NEW JERSEY. See STATE GOVERNMENT.
NEW MEXICO. See STATE GOVERNMENT.
NEW YORK. See NEW YORK CITY; STATE GOV'T.

NEW YORK CITY, which had prided itself on an ability to withstand the national recession, began to show signs of a serious economic slump toward the end of 1982. One factor was the sudden decline in Manhattan's white-collar job boom. Manhattan had accounted for 160,600 of the city's 165,900 new jobs between 1977 and 1981. But the United States Bureau of Labor Statistics reported on Nov. 15, 1982, that only 1,600 new jobs had been added in the year ending March 31. Unemployment reached 10.1 per cent in October.

By October, as a result, sales, personal, and business tax revenues fell more than $100 million below projections. Combined with an $850-million fall-off in federal aid over the previous two years, this plunged the city into its deepest fiscal crisis since 1975, when it almost went bankrupt.

Mayor Edward I. Koch announced in early November that the city was facing deficits of $341-million in its $15.5-billion budget for the fiscal year ending June 30, 1983, and $1.3 billion for the 1983-1984 fiscal year. He proposed an austerity program that would raise various city taxes, reduce expenditures, and eliminate many municipal jobs through attrition.

Another factor in the city's fiscal dilemma was a two-year agreement with unions representing 225,000 municipal workers estimated to cost $1.645 billion over the life of the contract. The settlement provided for salary raises of 8 per cent the first year and up to 8 per cent the second year.

Koch Loses in Primary. The contract aroused controversy because it was negotiated during the 1982 primary campaign, in which Koch was seeking the Democratic nomination for governor in a contest with Lieutenant Governor Mario M. Cuomo. Cuomo defeated Koch in the September 23 primary in an upset and went on to narrowly defeat the Republican candidate, Lewis E. Lehrman, in the November 2 general election.

On the same day, voters also elected a new 43-member City Council one year after the original election had been postponed by a U.S. Department of Justice suit. The suit challenged the council's initial redistricting lines as a violation of the Voting Rights Act of 1965.

Real Estate Boom. Despite the stagnant employment picture, the real estate boom continued. Thirteen new skyscrapers, containing a total of 2.5 million square feet (232,000 square meters) of space, were opened in 1982. Another 14 major buildings were scheduled to open in 1983.

The Supreme Court of the United States on March 22 lifted a temporary restraining order blocking the demolition of the historic Helen Hayes and Morosco theaters in the Times Square area to make way for a 50-story, $300-million hotel, the Portman. Destruction of the buildings began at once, despite demonstrations by some 200 Broadway personalities, some of whom were arrested.

Razing of New York City's Morosco Theatre begins on March 22 after the U.S. Supreme Court ruled that it and the Helen Hayes Theatre could be torn down.

In May, after three years of hearings, government agencies adopted a comprehensive zoning plan for midtown Manhattan, the city's first major rezoning in 20 years. The plan is designed to limit high-rise congestion on Manhattan's crowded East Side, encourage new development in the south and west sections of the midtown area, and preserve 44 Broadway theaters.

Deteriorating Subways. Subway ridership continued to decline in 1982. In the year ending June 30, about 992,300,000 passengers used the system, the first time the number of passengers had fallen below 1 billion since 1917. Authorities blamed the fall-off on deteriorating facilities, crime, fare increases, population shifts, greater use of automobiles, and the sluggish economy.

The Metropolitan Transportation Authority (MTA) began a five-year, $7.2-billion capital-improvement program to re-equip New York City's subway and bus system. The MTA touched off a national furor when, for economic and production reasons, the agency passed over United States firms and ordered a total of 1,375 new subway cars from manufacturers in Canada, Japan, and France.

Owen Moritz

See also CITY. In WORLD BOOK, see NEW YORK CITY.

NEW ZEALAND continued to have economic problems in 1982. Poor performance was the rule with regard to growth, inflation, balance of payments, and employment. Although growth in real output improved to about 1 per cent, inflation at 16 per cent for the year remained a major problem. New Zealand's difficult balance-of-payments situation continued, with poor overseas prices for its meat, wool, and dairy products necessitating substantial foreign borrowing. At the end of 1982, interest costs on overseas government debt had risen to about 6 per cent of export receipts. Despite a number of special employment schemes, unemployment rose to nearly 4 per cent of the work force, the highest in New Zealand since the 1930s.

Despite wide opposition from both labor unions and business groups, the government in June introduced a comprehensive 12-month freeze on wages, prices, rents, dividends, and interest rates to combat inflation. The government also ran into difficulty with its so-called think big strategy, an economic growth policy. This strategy was based on 24 major projects with a capital investment of more than $6 billion (New Zealand dollars; $1 = U.S. 73 cents as of Dec. 31, 1982). It was intended to capitalize on New Zealand's large reserves of coal, gas, and hydroelectricity to reduce its dependence on imported fuels.

A proposal for an aluminum smelter to be constructed near Dunedin on the South Island collapsed when overseas partners withdrew because of the decline in the world aluminum market. However, despite industrial problems, work continued on major extensions to the country's only oil refinery and a major synthetic oil plant designed to make New Zealand 50 per cent self-sufficient in motor vehicle fuels by 1986.

The 1982 Budget presented on August 5 provided for an increase of 14 per cent in government outlays and an increase of 16.1 per cent in taxation and other receipts, leaving an estimated budget deficit of nearly $1.9 billion. It provided significant reductions in personal income tax, particularly to families and to people earning middle to high incomes. However, this was offset by significant increases in taxes on alcohol and tobacco products and in motor vehicle fees and charges.

Government. With only a one-seat parliamentary majority, Prime Minister Robert D. Muldoon, the leader of the ruling National Party, survived a major party row over the resignation in June of a senior member of the Cabinet, Derek F. Quigley. Wallace E. Rowling, leader of the opposition Labour Party, also had problems, rating poorly in opinion polls and narrowly surviving a leadership challenge from David Lange, his deputy. David A. Shand

See also ASIA (Facts in Brief Table). In WORLD BOOK, see NEW ZEALAND.

NEWFOUNDLAND. Despite stagnant conditions in the fishing, forestry, and mining industries, and with 34,000 Newfoundlanders out of work, the people of Canada's youngest province gave a solid vote of confidence to 40-year-old Premier Brian Peckford in an April 6 election. The Progressive Conservatives, in power since 1972, took 44 of the 52 seats in the House of Assembly and 60 per cent of the popular vote. Liberal Party support was the lowest in the province's history.

Premier Peckford hammered home the province's demand for control of its offshore oil and gas resources, asking the federal government for legal ownership and 75 per cent of all government revenue from offshore oil and gas until Newfoundland's prosperity equaled that of other provinces. Newfoundland carried its case to its own Court of Appeal, while the federal government referred the issue to the Supreme Court of Canada.

The Worst Maritime Disaster in Canada since World War II occurred when a severe winter storm sank the drilling rig *Ocean Ranger* off Newfoundland on February 15 with the loss of 84 men. A Russian ship that tried to go to the rig's assistance also sank, costing 32 lives. New standards were then announced for oil rigs and drilling ships operating off Newfoundland. David M. L. Farr

See also CANADA. In WORLD BOOK, see NEWFOUNDLAND.

NEWSPAPER mergers made headlines during 1982. Nine United States publishers merged, or announced plans to merge, their competing morning and evening papers into single all-day or morning publications. These newspapers were the *Oakland* (Calif.) *Tribune* and *Eastbay Today;* the *Des Moines* (Iowa) *Tribune* and *The Des Moines Register;* the Portland *Oregon Journal* and *The Oregonian; The Tampa* (Fla.) *Times* and *The Tampa Tribune;* the *Duluth* (Minn.) *News-Tribune* and the *Duluth Herald;* the Sarasota, Fla., *Journal* and the Sarasota *Herald-Tribune; The Daily Peabody* (Mass.) *Times* and the *Beverly* (Mass.) *Times; The Daily News* and *The Sun* of Springfield, Ohio; and *The Minneapolis* (Minn.) *Star* and the *Minneapolis Tribune.* By November, only 29 U.S. cities had two or more completely competitive major newspapers.

The 134-year-old Philadelphia *Bulletin* published its last edition on January 29, after losing $21.5 million in 1981. The 104-year-old *Cleveland Press* suspended operations on June 17, and the financially ailing *Courier-Express* of Buffalo, N.Y., closed its doors on September 19.

New Papers. On a brighter note, industry observers crossed their fingers in September as Gannett Company's new national morning daily, *USA Today,* made its first appearance. Gannett distributed copies in Washington, D.C.; Atlanta, Ga.; Minneapolis; and Pittsburgh, Pa.; and planned to add 10 cities in 1983. *The Washington* (D.C.) *Times,* a Monday-through-Friday paper, made its debut on May 17 with the blessing of the Unification Church's Sun Myung Moon, its founder.

One of the industry's biggest libel cases was resolved in July, when a federal jury awarded Mobil Oil Corporation's President William P. Tavoulareas $2.05 million in damages after concluding that *The Washington Post* libeled him in an article about his business relations with his son.

United Press International, the 75-year-old wire service owned by E. W. Scripps Company and Hearst Corporation, was acquired on June 2 by Media News Corporation, a new company formed by a group of U.S. newspaper, cable, and television station owners.

On the Tube. Newspapers increased their participation in the video revolution in 1982. Field Enterprises, publishers of the Chicago *Sun-Times,* joined the Centel Corporation and Honeywell, Incorporated, to form KEYCOM Electronic Publishing Company. KEYCOM started a national teletext magazine called KEYFAX in November.

In August, CBS Inc. and the American Telephone and Telegraph Company announced a joint videotex venture, Venture One, in Ridgewood, N.J. Several newspapers will provide it with news and information features. Celeste Huenergard

In WORLD BOOK, see JOURNALISM; NEWSPAPER.

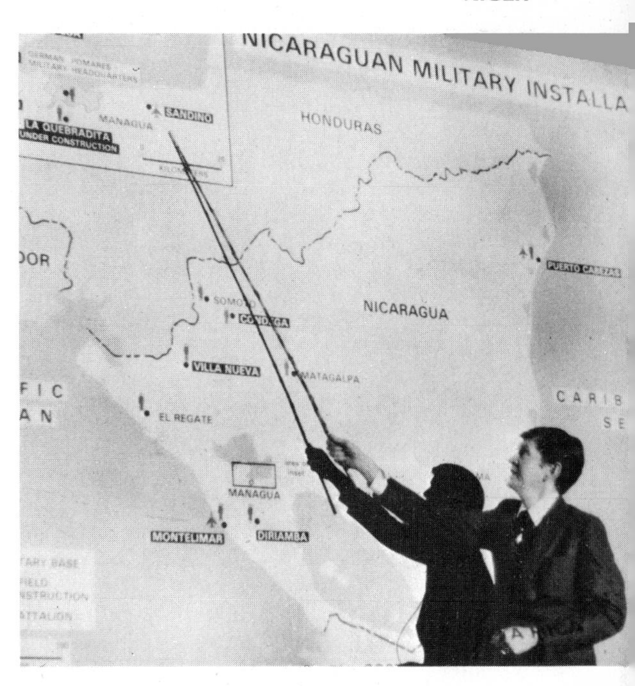

U.S. defense expert John R. Hughes points out Nicaraguan military bases in March as he accuses Nicaragua of a huge military build-up.

NICARAGUA. Three years after seizing control of Nicaragua, the leftist Sandinista National Liberation Front in 1982 found itself mired in economic problems and feuding with its Central American neighbors and the United States. In addition, the people of Nicaragua were beginning to express disillusionment with the Sandinista revolution.

On the Third Anniversary of the revolution, July 19, junta leader Daniel Ortega Saavedra sought to accent the positive. Ortega boasted of such accomplishments as the organization of 133,000 workers into more than 1,000 unions by craft or vocation and a much publicized literacy campaign that he said had lowered the nation's illiteracy rate from 50.3 per cent to 12.9 per cent. Since taking power, he said, the Sandinistas had quadrupled government spending for health. They had also built more than 6,000 homes for low-income families and distributed nearly $90 million worth of food.

But beneath such rosy statistics, opposition to the Sandinista regime grew. Consumers became increasingly disgruntled with the lack of goods in shops and markets. Church leaders were outspoken in their criticism. A protest in Masaya on August 17 left three people dead and six wounded.

There was even rising talk of an armed challenge to the Sandinista regime. Opposition forces coalesced around Edén Pastora Gómez. Pastora, also known as Commander Zero, had been a hero of the Sandinista revolution but defected from the Sandinistas and went into exile in Costa Rica.

In International Relations, there was continuing dismay abroad over alleged government brutality against the Miskito Indians of northern Nicaragua. Many of the Miskitos, burned out of their homes, fled to refugee camps in Honduras.

As relations between Honduras and Nicaragua went from bad to worse, the Sandinistas braced for a possible invasion. Nicaragua drafted and trained the largest army in Central America, with Cuban military advisers. The government also organized part-time militias at the neighborhood level.

The gulf between Nicaragua and the United States widened. On March 9, the Administration of U.S. President Ronald Reagan released aerial photographs supporting its claims of a huge military build-up in Nicaragua, with Cuban and Soviet aid. The Administration also charged the Sandinistas with providing secret assistance to rebels in El Salvador and with allowing their territory to be used for the transhipment of arms from Cuba and the Soviet Union. Nathan A. Haverstock

See also LATIN AMERICA (Facts in Brief Table). In the Special Reports section, see WHAT WENT WRONG IN CENTRAL AMERICA? In WORLD BOOK, see NICARAGUA.

NIGER. See AFRICA.

NIGERIA. Politicians in Nigeria spent much of 1982 preparing for 1983 elections, in which voters are to choose the national president, the state governors, the members of the state assemblies, and both houses of the federal legislature.

In June, President Shehu Shagari was renominated for a second four-year term by a special convention of the National Party of Nigeria. The country's Constitution stipulates that a presidential candidate, to be elected, must receive not only the most total votes, but also a minimum of 25 per cent of the ballots cast in at least two-thirds of Nigeria's 19 states. A bill passed by Nigeria's House of Representatives on June 28 provided for increasing that number by carving new states from existing ones.

Political Alliance. To improve their chances for success in the requisite number of states, four opposition parties formed an electoral partnership in mid-March called the Progressive People's Alliance. The two largest participating parties were the United Party of Nigeria, led by Chief Obafemi Awolowo, and the Nigerian People's Party, headed by Nnamdi Azikiwe, the country's first president.

Awolowo had been Shagari's main rival in the 1979 presidential election and was considered likely to run again in 1983. Azikiwe's party was dominant in three states in 1982, two of which were inhabited mostly by Ibo-speaking peoples. However, in May, President Shagari issued an unconditional pardon for Odumegwu Ojukwu, who led the Ibos from 1967 to 1970 in their unsuccessful struggle to secede from Nigeria and establish the separate country of Biafra. Ojukwu had been living in exile for 12 years in the Ivory Coast. If he formed an alliance with Shagari, Azikiwe faced losing much of his electoral support among Ibos.

Registration of voters for the 1983 elections began in August 1982. About 47 million Nigerians were expected to be enrolled at 127,000 special booths erected throughout the country.

Nigeria's Oil Industry suffered from the economic recession plaguing the United States and other Western countries. Falling demand caused oil production in Nigeria to drop from an average of about 2.1 million barrels per day in 1980 to 725,000 in March 1982. To compensate for lower export earnings, Shagari's government on April 20 imposed stricter curbs on imports.

Religious Violence flared again in northern Nigeria. A total of 452 persons were reported killed in riots in Maiduguri. The disturbances began on October 26, after police tried to arrest 200 followers of Muhammadu Marwa, a Muslim zealot who died in fighting between his supporters and Nigerian forces in 1981. J. Dixon Esseks

See also AFRICA (Facts in Brief Table). In WORLD BOOK, see NIGERIA.

NIXON, RICHARD MILHOUS (1913-), 37th President of the United States, visited China for five days in September 1982 to commemorate the 10th anniversary of the Shanghai Communiqué, the official joint statement that preceded normalization of relations between the United States and China. The country's top leaders received him.

The year 1982 also marked the 10th anniversary of the Watergate break-in at Democratic National Committee headquarters, the event that led to Nixon's resignation from the presidency in 1974.

Officials at Duke University in Durham, N.C., announced on February 26 that they had suspended plans to build a library to house Nixon's archives. They cited a poor economy and an unfavorable political climate as the reasons.

On June 24, the Supreme Court of the United States ruled 5 to 4 that a President cannot be sued for actions taken while in office. The case was brought by A. Ernest Fitzgerald, a civilian Pentagon budget analyst whom Nixon had ordered fired for revealing cost overruns on the C-5A transport plane program to Congress. The Supreme Court on November 29 refused to hear an appeal by Nixon's lawyers to prevent government review, and eventual public release, of his White House tapes.

Nixon's book *Leaders* was published in October. It deals with statesmen he has known. Frank Cormier

In WORLD BOOK, see NIXON, RICHARD M.

NOBEL PRIZES in peace, literature, economics, and sciences were awarded in 1982 by the Norwegian Storting (parliament) in Oslo and by the Royal Academy of Science, the Caroline Institute, and the Swedish Academy of Literature, all in Stockholm, Sweden.

Peace Prize was awarded to Alva R. Myrdal, 80, of Sweden and Alfonso García Robles, 71, of Mexico for their "work to promote peace, disarmament and the brotherhood of mankind." They will share the prize money—equivalent to $157,000 in 1982—which is the same for each Nobel category. Myrdal, the wife of Gunnar Myrdal, who shared the Nobel Prize for Economics in 1974, headed the Swedish delegation to the United Nations (UN) Disarmament Conference in Geneva, Switzerland, from 1962 to 1973. García Robles considers his major achievement the Treaty of Tlatelolco, an antinuclear arms agreement signed in Mexico City, Mexico, in 1967 by 22 Latin American nations. Since 1976, he has represented Mexico at the UN Disarmament Commission in Geneva.

Literature Prize went to Colombian author Gabriel García Márquez, 54, which would not have surprised the citizens of Macondo, the astounding town he created in his novel *One Hundred Years of Solitude* (1967), any more than other remarkable things that happened there. García Márquez, who is regarded as a leader of the rebirth of Latin

American literature, was cited "for his novels and short stories, in which the fantastic and the realistic are combined in a richly composed world of imagination, reflecting a continent's life and conflicts." Works by the best-selling author that have been translated from Spanish into English are *No One Writes to the Colonel and Other Stories* (1968), *Leaf Storm and Other Stories* (1972), and *The Autumn of the Patriarch* (1976).

Chemistry Prize went to Aaron Klug, 56, director of the Medical Research Council's Laboratory of Molecular Biology at the University of Cambridge in England. Klug is noted particularly for three major accomplishments: developing a technique called image reconstruction, which enables scientists to study parts of chromosomes and other cell components; learning the complete composition of the tobacco mosaic virus; and investigating the detailed structure of nucleosome core particles, which make up chromosomes.

Economics Prize was awarded to George J. Stigler, 71, a University of Chicago professor. Described by a colleague as "the archetype conservative economist," Stigler has done research for 50 years on the working of industry and the role of government regulation in the economy. He is considered a pioneer in studying the interaction of economics and law.

Physics Prize rewarded Kenneth G. Wilson, 46, of Cornell University in Ithaca, N.Y., for what colleagues called his "outstanding" and "magnificent" analysis of the way matter changes from one form to another. Wilson's method is based on the use of a mathematical process called renormalization, a way of reducing an infinity of possible calculations in a problem to manageable numbers.

Physiology or Medicine Prize was shared by three researchers for their work on prostaglandins, natural body substances that affect people and other animals in a wide variety of ways. The winners, each of whom studied different aspects of the problem, were Sune Bergstrom, 66, and Bengt Samuelssohn, 48, of Sweden's Caroline Institute, and John R. Vane, 55, research director of the Wellcome Foundation in Beckenham, England. Prostaglandins are fatty acids formed in the cells, and their effects on the body may be good or bad. They play a role in reproduction and heart and lung function, but also cause the aches and pains of many disorders. The Nobel winners' discoveries have greatly increased knowledge of how to control prostaglandins, providing many medical and veterinary health benefits. Marsha F. Goldsmith

In WORLD BOOK, see GARCÍA MÁRQUEZ, GABRIEL JOSÉ; NOBEL PRIZES.

NORTH ATLANTIC TREATY ORGANIZATION (NATO). See EUROPE (Close-Up).

NORTH CAROLINA. See STATE GOVERNMENT.

NORTH DAKOTA. See STATE GOVERNMENT.

NORTHERN IRELAND was dominated in 1982 by the British government's sixth major attempt in 10 years to establish a means for political dialogue between the warring religious and political factions and provide some measure of home rule for Northern Ireland. This effort took the form of holding an election on October 20 for a new 78-seat Northern Ireland assembly, which Great Britain's Secretary for Northern Ireland James Prior hoped would become a working forum where representatives of the Protestant and Roman Catholic communities could resolve their differences.

However, the result of the election was generally considered a disaster for Prior and his plan. Sinn Féin (Ourselves Alone), the legal political wing of the outlawed Irish Republican Army (IRA), taking part in its first across-the-province election, won five seats. This vindicated the party's decision to reverse its previous policy of boycotting elections. The two Protestant parties, representing the majority of voters, won the most seats. The Official Unionist Party took 26 seats and Ian D. Paisley's Democratic Unionist Party took 21—and both were opposed to intercommunity power-sharing. The Catholic minority's Social Democratic and Labour Party, which took 14 seats, had decided, like Sinn Féin, to run in the election but to boycott the assembly.

An immense bomb planted by terrorists in Belfast exploded in June while being defused, damaging 300 houses but killing no one.

The Government's Proposals for the elections were originally unveiled in a policy document on April 5. Voting was to be on a proportional-representation basis, to ensure equality for Northern Ireland's Catholic minority. In the resulting assembly, proposals for devolving power—returning it to Northern Ireland—were to be developed. The object was to gradually end eight years of direct rule from the British Parliament.

Devolutionary powers would be granted from Britain only if they were "likely to command widespread acceptance throughout the community [of Northern Ireland]." But the "rolling devolution" plan was always in trouble. When the bill became law on July 23, the hopes of its sponsors appeared to exceed the likelihood of its fulfilling them.

After the Election, political stability in Northern Ireland was further threatened by a fresh outbreak of sectarian atrocities. On October 22, the IRA kidnapped and killed a Protestant part-time soldier. In retaliation, Protestant Loyalists murdered two Catholics. The outlawed Ulster Volunteer Force claimed responsibility for other killings. On December 6, a bomb planted by the Irish National Liberation Army exploded in a pub in Ballykelly, killing 16 people and injuring 66. Ian Mather

See also GREAT BRITAIN; IRELAND. In WORLD BOOK, see NORTHERN IRELAND.

NORTHWEST TERRITORIES voted narrowly to divide its vast land area in a plebiscite held on April 14, 1982, and on November 26, the federal government agreed to the division. Four land claims and a decision on the boundary remained to be settled. Only about 50 per cent of eligible voters cast their ballots in April, and just 56 per cent of them endorsed the idea.

The strong sentiment for the division of the 1.3-million-square-mile (34-million-square-kilometer) area, a third of Canada's land, came from the 16,000 Inuit (Eskimos) of the eastern Arctic. The eastern Inuit are isolated from the territorial capital at Yellowknife in the west and culturally different from the Indians and *métis* (persons of mixed white and Indian descent) who are dominant in the western region. The Inuit goal is an eastern Arctic province to be called Nunavut.

In the western Arctic, voter turnout was lower, and the white majority in such settlements as Yellowknife and Inuvik voted "no" by a wide margin.

An agreement for educational cooperation was worked out in October between the Northwest Territories and Greenland. Primary school textbooks in the Inuit language will be printed in Greenland and shipped across the Davis Strait for use in Canadian Arctic classrooms. David M. L. Farr

See also CANADA. In WORLD BOOK, see NORTHWEST TERRITORIES.

NORWAY. The minority Conservative government of Prime Minister Kaare Willoch faced economic difficulties in 1982 because Norway's revenue from North Sea oil and gas exports stopped increasing. The 1982 fall in world oil prices threatened to wipe out Norway's 1981 $2.25-million balance-of-payments surplus. The government forecast a 1.4 per cent decline in gross domestic product for 1982, the first fall since 1945.

New Smelter. On June 8, the Storting (parliament) voted by 79 to 76 to cancel the building of a state-owned aluminum plant in Tyssedal, near Bergen. An obsolete aluminum smelter that had employed 262 people had been scrapped there. The government will replace it with a plant that will smelt the mineral ilmenite to obtain titanium and iron. The government claimed that the ilmenite plant would cost less and use less fuel than the canceled aluminum plant and that its products would sell better. Other aluminum smelters in Norway were losing $160 on every metric ton (1.1 short ton) of aluminum produced because there was a global surplus of the metal.

The Labor Party and the Left-Socialist Party opposed the ilmenite smelter because it would provide only 177 jobs. The far-right Progress Party said that both the ilmenite smelter and the canceled aluminum plant were job-creation experiments for which the taxpayer would pay.

Inflation Down. A price freeze from August to December 1981 helped to reduce inflation from 15.5 per cent at the beginning of 1981 to 11.1 per cent in June 1982. Inflation was expected to ease further, though not below 10 per cent. Norway's unemployment rate of 2 per cent remained among the lowest in Europe. On October 6, the government announced that it would cut personal and business taxes in 1983 to stimulate the economy.

Low Production. The 24-nation Organization for Economic Cooperation and Development (OECD) pointed out in March 1982 that Norway's industrial production was lower than it had been in 1973, even though industrial production in the OECD countries as a whole had risen by 10 per cent. The OECD said that Norway's egalitarian wage policies and generous social benefits had reduced incentives to work.

Fishing Ban. On January 1, Norway defied the European Community (EC or Common Market), of which it is not a member, in a fishing dispute. Norway prohibited EC countries from fishing inside its 200-nautical-mile economic zone until the EC implemented a 1981 agreement that specified Norwegian fishing rights in EC waters. The EC reacted quickly, persuading France to withdraw its veto over the agreement. Norway withdrew its ban on January 9. Kenneth Brown

See also EUROPE (Facts in Brief Table). In WORLD BOOK, see NORWAY.

NOVA SCOTIA broke new ground in resource development on March 2, 1982, when the province signed an agreement with the federal government concerning the management and revenue-sharing of oil and gas reserves lying off Nova Scotia's east coast. Without deciding the question of ownership, it was agreed that authority to manage the resources would rest with the federal government in Ottawa, Ont. A five-member board, with three federal appointees, would oversee resource development, and the federal minister of energy would have power to override the board's decisions. The division of revenues will give 30 per cent to Nova Scotia; 13 per cent to Ottawa; 14 per cent to Petro-Canada, the government-owned oil company; and 42 per cent to industry.

The agreement ended 14 years of negotiation with Ottawa and touched off a flurry of activity, with almost $2 billion (Canadian dollars; $1 = U.S. 81 cents as of Dec. 31, 1982) committed for exploration by governments and oil companies.

A 12-day strike at the Sydney Steel Corporation mills on Cape Breton Island ended on May 7. However, the plant closed down for lack of orders, laying off 1,270 workers. The mills reopened on June 11. David M. L. Farr

See also CANADA. In WORLD BOOK, see NOVA SCOTIA.

NUCLEAR ENERGY. See ENERGY.

NUTRITION. What we eat might affect our chances of developing certain kinds of cancer, according to a report issued in June 1982 by a committee of the National Academy of Sciences (NAS). The report, "Diet, Nutrition, and Cancer," was commissioned in 1980 by the National Cancer Institute and is the first official NAS statement that the typical United States diet should be modified to reduce cancer risk.

The committee recommended that the consumption of fat be reduced from the present average of about 40 per cent down to 30 per cent or less of total calories in the diet. This can be accomplished by eating fewer fatty meats, high-fat dairy products, and fats and oils used in cooking. Studies have indicated that a high fat intake is related to cancers of the breast and colon.

The committee also recommended limiting the consumption of salt-cured, salt-pickled, and smoked foods, because they have been associated with cancers of the digestive tract, particularly of the stomach and esophagus. These foods include smoked fish, smoked sausages, ham, and bacon.

Foods to Eat. The committee recommended increased consumption of certain foods that experimental evidence indicates offer protection against various cancers. The committee urged Americans to eat more whole-grain cereals as well as fruits and vegetables, especially those high in vitamin C and beta-carotene, which the body converts to vitamin A. Vegetables in the cabbage family—including broccoli, cauliflower, and Brussels sprouts—also contain cancer-inhibiting substances. Foods containing vitamin C may prevent the formation of cancer-causing chemicals in the body, and foods containing beta-carotene have been associated with reduced risk of lung cancer. Foods high in vitamin C include citrus fruits, tomatoes, and peppers. Carrots and such dark-green leafy vegetables as spinach and broccoli are major sources of beta-carotene. But the committee warned against taking high doses of vitamin pills; some, such as vitamin A, can be toxic.

The committee's recommendations are similar to those issued in 1977 by the U.S. Senate Select Committee on Nutrition and Human Needs and to other earlier guidelines. However, its recommendation to reduce fat in the diet contradicts a 1980 NAS report, "Toward Healthful Diets," which claimed that there was insufficient information to recommend such dietary modifications. The new guidelines were criticized by industry groups, particularly the American Meat Institute. In response, the committee chairman, biologist Clifford Grobstein of the University of California at San Diego, stated that the committee was not putting forth unproven theories. He termed the recommendations "interim guidelines" that are intended to be modified as new information becomes available.

Heart Disease Study. The results of a 10-year study to determine whether reducing heart disease risk factors, such as high blood cholesterol, reduces heart disease deaths were reported in September 1982. The study, sponsored by the National Heart, Lung, and Blood Institute in Bethesda, Md., involved more than 12,000 middle-aged men in the United States who had a high risk of heart attack.

The men were divided into two groups. A special intervention group received blood pressure medication, were urged to quit smoking, and were counseled about a diet to lower blood cholesterol. A control group was only given an annual physical and referred to their personal physicians.

The investigators found that when risk factors such as cigarette smoking and high blood cholesterol were reduced, the death rate from heart disease dropped substantially in the intervention group. But there was also a dramatic drop in the death rate among those in the control group. The scientists speculated that this could have been because their physicians had urged men in the control group to give up smoking and lower their cholesterol levels. Jean Weininger

See also FOOD. In the Special Reports section, see FOOD, FADS, FAT, AND FITNESS. In WORLD BOOK, see DIET; FOOD; NUTRITION.

OCEAN. On April 30, 1982, the United Nations (UN) Law of the Sea Conference approved an international agreement on sea law by a vote of 130 to 4, ending eight years of negotiations. United States President Ronald Reagan rejected the pact, even though three previous U.S. administrations had participated in its drafting.

The Law of the Sea Treaty defines the limits of territorial waters and coastal economic zones. It guarantees safe passage on the high seas and through international straits. The Reagan Administration praised these provisions. But it objected to others setting up procedures by which the treaty could be amended and establishing a global regulatory authority that would control access to valuable minerals at the bottom of the sea. The Administration felt the seabed authority might hinder future commercial seabed mining.

France, Japan, and nearly all of the developing countries adopted the treaty. Great Britain, West Germany, and most of the Soviet bloc were among 17 nations that abstained. Only Israel, Turkey, and Venezuela joined the United States in voting against the plan. It becomes international law one year after ratification by 60 nations.

In September, the United States signed an agreement with France, Great Britain, and West Germany on how to resolve conflicting deep-sea mining claims. Although the agreement in no way indicated a refusal on the part of the European nations to sign the Law of the Sea Treaty, it enhanced U.S. prospects of negotiating separate mining agreements outside the treaty.

On December 10, 117 countries signed the treaty. Twenty-four of the countries that were involved in writing the treaty did not sign it. Among them were the United States, West Germany, Belgium, and Great Britain.

Cleaner Seas. In October, the UN Regional Seas Program released the results of a four-year study on the health of the oceans. The study reported a decrease in the level of toxic substances in the world's oceans over the past decade.

Deep-Sea Vents. In March, scientists discovered new deep-sea hot springs, or vents, in an area of the Pacific Ocean east of the Philippines known as the Mariana Trench. The discovery indicated that vents are more widespread than was thought.

Vents, which erupt from the ocean's crust, deposit mineral-rich sediments on the seabed. They also support previously unknown forms of life that depend not on sunlight but on sulfur-rich nutrients that the vents release. The most recent finds, in the Gulf of California off the coast of Mexico, included black crabs the size of soup plates, white octopuses with heads as big as basketballs, and thick mats of yellow-orange bacteria.

Deep-Sea Drilling. The Deep Sea Drilling Project (DSDP) ship *Glomar Challenger* penetrated deeper

A scientist drills into a coral reef near Puerto Rico to draw out samples. Growth rings in the coral reveal the ocean's recent history.

into the ocean floor in 1982 than ever before and found evidence that seems to confirm a geologic model for the structure of the earth's crust. Samples of crust brought up by the ship suggested that certain geologic formations were thrust up from the ocean floor onto land when two of the plates that make up the earth's surface collided. While drilling along the Middle America Trench off the coast of Costa Rica, scientists encountered a lava layer with veins of metallic sulfides strikingly similar to ores being mined in Central America.

Sea Disaster. The drilling rig *Ocean Ranger* sank about 175 nautical miles east of Newfoundland during a storm on February 15. It took all 84 men aboard to their death. The *Ocean Ranger,* described as the world's largest semisubmersible mobile offshore drilling unit, was built in 1976 by Mitsubishi Heavy Industries Limited in Hiroshima, Japan. Mobil Oil Canada, Limited, operated the rig. The rig was designed to withstand winds of about 115 miles (185 kilometers) per hour and waves up to 110 feet (33.5 meters), but it capsized in 100-mile (160-kilometer) winds and 50-foot (15-meter) waves. Arthur G. Alexiou

In WORLD BOOK, see DEEP SEA DRILLING PROJECT; OCEAN.

OHIO. See STATE GOVERNMENT.

OKLAHOMA. See STATE GOVERNMENT.

OLD AGE. See SOCIAL SECURITY.

OLYMPIC GAMES. Despite severe criticism from the Soviet Union, preparations continued on schedule in 1982 for the 1984 Summer Olympic Games in Los Angeles. Russia complained about plans to house athletes at two university dormitory complexes rather than at one Olympic Village. It also questioned security plans and called medical facilities inadequate.

Some observers saw such criticism as a sign that the Soviet Union and other Communist-bloc countries would boycott the 1984 Summer Olympics in retaliation for the American-led boycott of the 1980 Summer Olympics in Moscow. However, Russia assured Olympic organizers that it would send 1,000 athletes, coaches, and officials, the largest delegation of any visiting nation.

In October 1982, the International Olympic Committee restored the gold medals of Jim Thorpe, an American Indian who in 1912 became the first athlete to win both the decathlon and the pentathlon in the Olympics. The committee's decision ended a long battle by Thorpe's family and friends to have his medals returned. Thorpe, who died in 1953, was stripped of his medals because he had played professional baseball prior to the 1912 games. Frank Litsky

In WORLD BOOK, see OLYMPIC GAMES; THORPE, JIM.

OMAN. See MIDDLE EAST.

ONTARIO, Canada's largest province, representing one-third of the country's economy and one-half of its manufacturing and employment, experienced a severe economic downturn in 1982. One in six jobs in the province was dependent on the slumping automotive industry. Falling United States demand hurt valuable exports of mining and forestry products. At Sudbury, Canada's nickel capital, two major mining companies predicted that 4,400 jobs would be lost permanently over the next five years. The giant Inco mine and smelter suffered a one-month strike in June, followed by a shut-down originally intended to last until January but later extended to April 1983. Another mine also announced layoffs. This was shattering news for a city with a 33 per cent unemployment rate, the highest in Canada.

Two steel producers in Hamilton also announced layoffs late in 1982, bringing employment in the industry to the lowest level in 25 years. The collapse of major energy projects in Western Canada cost Ontario large orders for equipment and services.

Economic Conditions made Ontario's Progressive Conservative (PC) Treasurer Frank Miller introduce a cautious budget emphasizing tax increases on May 13. Consumers were asked to pay $557 million (Canadian dollars; $1 = U.S. 81

Musicians are as pleased as concertgoers with the excellent acoustics and splendid design of Toronto's Roy Thomson Hall, opened in September.

cents as of Dec. 31, 1982) more through a greatly expanded application of the 7 per cent provincial sales tax, higher health insurance premiums, and higher taxes on alcohol and cigarettes. Despite the new taxes, the province's deficit amounted to $2.2-billion on spending of $22.8 billion. To create jobs and ease the tight rental market, a $5,000 interest-free loan was made available to each first-time home buyer. On September 21, Ontario imposed a 5 per cent limit on salary increases for more than 500,000 public employees and banned strikes for up to two years.

The Political Scene. Both the opposition Liberal Party and the New Democratic Party (NDP) changed leaders during 1982 in an attempt to unseat the PC, which had held office in Ontario for almost 40 years. But the PC majority in the provincial parliament remained strong. Holding 70 of the house's 125 seats, they were not affected by a by-election on June 17, which the NDP won at the expense of the Liberals. The NDP held a total of 22 seats and the Liberals, 33. John P. Robarts, premier of Ontario from 1961 to 1971, died in Toronto on October 18. David M. L. Farr

See also CANADA. In WORLD BOOK, see ONTARIO.

OPERA. See MUSIC, CLASSICAL.
OREGON. See STATE GOVERNMENT.

PACIFIC ISLANDS. With all of its near neighbors enjoying newly won independence, French-ruled New Caledonia was again much in the news in 1982. After the French National Assembly decided in December 1981 that New Caledonia should be ruled by decree for 12 months, France moved fast to quiet demands for independence from the country's 55,000 Melanesians. For many of the almost equally large French population, it moved too fast and too far. On July 22, 1982, violence broke out in Nouméa, the capital, when the Territorial Assembly met to debate a French plan to repurchase and return tribal land to the Melanesians.

Elections. The governments of Papua New Guinea, Western Samoa, and French Polynesia were voted out of office in general elections and that of Fiji was narrowly re-elected. In Papua New Guinea, former Prime Minister Michael Somare regained power after a July poll for 108 of the legislature's 109 seats. Somare's Pangu Party won 41 seats, with about 10 each for other major parties. After several weeks of intense lobbying, Parliament voted Somare into office on August 2 by 66 votes to 40. Somare had led his country to independence in 1975 but was deposed in 1980.

Western Samoans went to the polls on Feb. 27, 1982, and toppled the government of Prime Minister Taisi Tupuola Efi. Tupuola, who had served

Facts in Brief on Pacific Island Countries

Country	Population	Government	Monetary Unit*	Foreign Trade (million U.S. $) Exports†	Imports†
Australia	15,150,000	Governor General Sir Ninian Martin Stephen; Prime Minister Malcolm Fraser	dollar (1 = $1.04)	21,680	23,652
Fiji	664,000	Governor General Ratu Sir George Cakobau; Prime Minister Ratu Sir Kamisese Mara	dollar (1 = $1.05)	311	632
Kiribati	56,000	Governor General Reginald James Wallace; President Ieremia Tabai	Australian dollar	23	17
Nauru	8,000	President Hammer DeRoburt	Australian dollar	75	12
New Zealand	3,136,000	Governor General Sir David Stuart Beattie; Prime Minister Robert D. Muldoon	dollar (1.4 = $1)	5,563	5,684
Papua New Guinea	3,348,000	Governor General Sir Tore Lokoloko; Prime Minister Michael Somare	kina (1 = $1.29)	1,031	1,023
Solomon Islands	241,000	Governor General Sir Baddeley Devesi; Prime Minister Solomon Mamaloni	dollar (1 = $1.07)	73	74
Tonga	98,000	King Taufa'ahau Tupou IV; Prime Minister Prince Fatafehi Tu'ipelehake	pa'anga (1 = $1.13)	8	29
Tuvalu	7,000	Governor General Sir Fiatau Penitala Teo; Prime Minister Tomaso Puapua	Australian dollar	0.1	1
Vanuatu	125,000	President Ati George Sokomanu; Prime Minister Walter Lini	vatu (91 = $1)	38	56
Western Samoa	160,000	Head of State Malietoa Tanumafili II; Prime Minister Taisi Tupuola Efi	tala (1.1 = $1)	18	73

*Exchange rates as of Dec. 1, 1982. †Latest available data.

two terms, had become unpopular for mishandling a prolonged public service strike in 1981, a sharp drop in export income, and several scandals involving prominent government figures. However, his successor, Va'ai Kolone, lasted only until September 1982, when his election was voided for electoral malpractice. With several similar cases pending in court, Tupuola was recalled to form a new government.

In Fiji, where the population is almost equally divided between native Fijians and descendants of imported Indian laborers, the largely Fijian Alliance Party of Prime Minister Ratu Sir Kamisese Mara was returned to office by 28 seats to 24 on July 10. The margin in several government-won seats was extremely slim. The election was mainly fought on racial lines and was marked by unprecedented mudslinging and bitterness. Mara, prime minister since 1970, later asked a New Zealand judge to investigate claims of interference by Australia, Russia, and other countries.

In elections in May 1982 for the 30 seats in French Polynesia's Territorial Assembly, no party emerged with a clear majority. But the Gaullist party of Gaston Flosse, which won 13 seats, gained control of the government council by combining with three defectors from the radical party of former council leader Francis A. Sanford. Flosse, who was accused of stealing his opponents' policies, later promised to try to make his country completely autonomous by July 1983.

Good-Will Gestures. Tonga, struck by a devastating hurricane on March 2, 1982, was the scene of its own kind of political revolution a month later. After gathering a petition with 6,500 signatures, 100 citizens led by Roman Catholic Bishop Patelisio Finau marched to the royal palace to protest delays in coping with hurricane relief. The palace was prepared for violence, but, in the end, King Taufa'ahau Tupou IV and his brother, Prime Minister Prince Fatafehi Tu'ipelehake, received the protesters, sitting cross-legged on the veranda in a symbolic gesture of good will. For feudal Tonga, it was a historic moment. Never before had the traditional barrier between monarch and subjects been directly breached.

On October 1, the United States signed a pact giving limited independence to the Federated States of Micronesia.

Landowners of Kwajalein Atoll in the Marshall Islands ended a four-month sit-in on October 20 after the United States agreed to stop using the atoll as an intercontinental missile range in 30 years rather than 50. The United States agreed to make a one-time user-fee payment of $6.5 million and to spend as much as $6 million to upgrade living standards. Robert Langdon

In WORLD BOOK, see PACIFIC ISLANDS.

PAINTING. See VISUAL ARTS.

PAKISTAN in 1982 conducted the first government-authorized debates of public policy in more than four years of military rule. The debates took place in the National Advisory Council, which was inaugurated on January 12. Pakistan's President Mohammad Zia-ul-Haq, who took control of the country as martial law administrator in 1977, appointed nearly 290 members to the council, which was ultimately to have 350 members.

Zia said the council would "help the government in tackling day-to-day problems and stepping up the process of Islamization in the country." The council lacked any legislative powers, but it would be able to make recommendations and perhaps focus national attention on issues. Traditional political parties called on their members to boycott the council, and many experienced politicians denounced it as a mere rubber stamp.

Zia kept in force a ban on political activities. In November, however, he spoke of a return to elected government "within two or three years."

Violence became more common with normal political opposition throttled. Two members of the National Advisory Council were murdered in a wave of bombings and shootings. Terrorists derailed trains, exploded car bombs, and set fire to official buildings. The government blamed a terrorist organization based in Afghanistan called Al Zulfikar, which sought the violent overthrow of Zia's government. Al Zulfikar was reportedly led by two sons of former Prime Minister Zulfikar Ali Bhutto, who was executed in 1979. Pakistan accused the Soviet Union of supporting the group.

On September 27, the government decreed the death penalty for a wide range of antistate activities, including attacks on government facilities and "harming public tranquility." The decree was retroactive, applying to all such actions since 1977.

Amnesty International, a worldwide human rights organization, reported on January 12 that there were 6,000 political prisoners in Pakistan in March 1981. The report also charged that the government practiced torture. Interior Minister Mahmoud A. Haroon denied the charges.

Fighting Sometimes Erupted along the Afghanistan border in areas where Afghan refugees lived. An estimated 2.7 million Afghans had fled to Pakistan since the Soviet Union invaded their country in 1979. Severe food shortages and high prices caused hardships on refugees and local residents.

The Pakistani Rupee was in effect devalued on January 8. The government cut the rupee's tie to the value of the U.S. dollar and pegged it instead to the value of several currencies, including the dollar, weighted in proportion to how much they were used for trade. In December, Zia made his first state visit to the United States. Henry S. Bradsher

See also ASIA (Facts in Brief Table). In WORLD BOOK, see PAKISTAN.

PALEONTOLOGY. One of the most intriguing and persistent puzzles in paleontology—which animal was the source of conodonts—was solved in 1982. Conodonts are tiny toothlike fossils that are abundant in rocks formed during the Cambrian through Triassic periods, from 600 million to 190 million years ago. Although thousands of different types of conodonts have been found, the animal they came from was unknown. Scientists knew, however, that the animal was short-lived, and this has made the fossils important aids in dating the rocks in which they are found.

In August, three British paleontologists announced the discovery of the fossil remains of one species of conodont animal. Euan N. K. Clarkson of the University of Edinburgh found the wormlike fossil in a collection of the Institute of Geological Sciences in Edinburgh, Scotland. Clarkson collaborated with Derek E. G. Briggs of the University of London and Richard J. Aldridge of the University of Nottingham in describing the specimen.

The animal, which is tentatively being classified as *Clydagnathus cavusformis*, is about 1½ inches (4 centimeters) long and has 12 or 13 conodonts arranged near its front end. The fossil also shows that the body of the animal probably consisted of segments. The paleontologists believe the conodonts were used for grasping and tearing prey, and not as tissue-covered supports for some kind of filtering apparatus, which has been a popular hypothesis.

Extinctions. In 1982, paleontologists provided new information to help answer another persistent and controversial question: Has human activity caused mass extinctions of plants and animals only in modern times or did such extinctions occur before industrialization and world population growth? In August 1982, paleontologists Storrs L. Olson and Helen F. James of the National Museum of Natural History in Washington, D.C., reported on their study of thousands of fossil bird bones from Hawaii. Their research indicates that the Polynesian inhabitants caused the extinction of about two-thirds of all bird species on the islands between A.D. 400 and 600, after settling there.

From the fossils, Olson and James were able to identify more than 40 species of land and sea birds—including geese, owls, flightless ibises, crows, and more than 15 species of finches—that became extinct before 1778. In addition, the scientists found that many surviving species now inhabit a smaller area than they did in prehistoric times. The paleontologists theorize that although the chief cause of the extinctions was the burning and clearing of lowland forest, hunting was probably also an important factor.

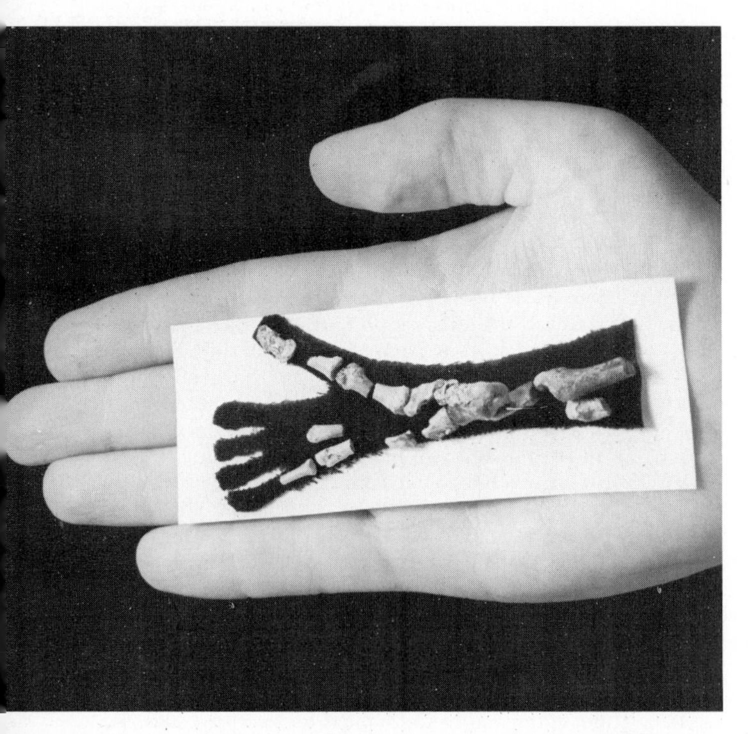

Discovered in Wyoming, the fossil foot bones, *left,* of the earliest known true primate, *reconstructed, right,* date to 50 million years ago.

Earliest Known Primate. The discovery, announced in July 1982, of 50-million-year-old foot bones from the earliest known true primate has shed important light on the early history of primates. The fossil foot bones belonged to *Cantius trigonodus,* an extinct species about the size of a small cat. They were found in the Bighorn Basin of Wyoming by paleontologist Robert T. Bakker of Johns Hopkins University in Baltimore and Julius Goepp, a medical student at the University of Maryland in College Park.

The discovery of the bones is important because they show that *Cantius* had a nail-covered, grasping big toe, which enabled it to climb out on small branches to escape predators and reach food inaccessible to other animals. *Cantius'* closest preprimate ancestors had claws instead of a grasping big toe. The finding lends support to the theory that the development of the grasping big toe, which helped primates escape from predators more easily, led to a slower maturation rate for young primates and, thus, to the evolution of a larger brain.

The scientists also found a partial skull of *Cantius.* The forward-facing eye sockets in the skull show that *Cantius* had stereoscopic vision—and, therefore, depth perception. Earlier preprimates had eyes that faced sideways. Ida Thompson

See also ZOOLOGY. In WORLD BOOK, see PALEONTOLOGY; PRIMATE.

PALME, OLOF (1927-), head of the Social Democratic Party, became prime minister of Sweden on Oct. 7, 1982. He succeeded Thorbjörn Fälldin, who had led a coalition of nonsocialist parties since 1976. Palme had previously served as prime minister from 1969 to 1976, when the socialists lost after 44 years in power. He returned to office on a pledge to increase public spending, create new jobs, and raise funds from taxes for worker-investment in industry. See SWEDEN.

Sven Olof Joachim Palme was born into a well-to-do family in Stockholm, Sweden, on Jan. 30, 1927. He graduated from Kenyon College in Gambier, Ohio, in 1948 and earned a law degree from the University of Stockholm in 1951. He became active in politics as a student, convinced of the justice of the welfare state fathered by Tage Erlander, then Sweden's prime minister.

Palme became Erlander's secretary in 1953. Palme was elected to the Riksdag (parliament) in 1957 and served as minister of transport and communication from 1965 to 1967 and as minister of education and cultural affairs from 1967 to 1969. When Erlander retired in 1969, the Social Democratic Party unanimously elected Palme chairman.

Palme has actively advocated disarmament and increased aid from Western nations to the Third World. He married Lisbeth Beck-Friis in 1956. They have three sons. Karin C. Rosenberg

PANAMA. In what was described as a "constitutional coup d'état," President Aristides Royo of Panama resigned his office on July 30, 1982. That afternoon, Vice-President Ricardo de la Espriella, Jr., was hastily sworn in to take Royo's place. The nation's National Guard reportedly engineered the coup. The National Guard was dissatisfied with Royo's leftist tendencies. See DE LA ESPRIELLA, RICARDO, JR.

On October 1, President De la Espriella visited U.S. President Ronald Reagan at the White House in Washington, D.C. De la Espriella used the occasion to pledge that presidential elections would be held as scheduled in Panama in 1984.

In September, an oil pipeline across the Isthmus of Panama went into operation, facilitating the transfer of Alaskan crude oil from tankers too large for the canal. The $300-million pipeline, financed by private business and the government, helps reduce traffic congestion on the canal.

Panama continued to welcome foreign banks. In the 10 years ending in 1982, the number of foreign banks in Panama grew from 20 to 120. Attracted by laws that encourage secrecy, these banks have assets of $40 billion. Nathan A. Haverstock

See also LATIN AMERICA (Facts in Brief Table). In WORLD BOOK, see PANAMA.

PAPUA NEW GUINEA. See PACIFIC ISLANDS.

Vice-President Ricardo de la Espriella speaks at ceremonies preceding his inauguration as president of Panama on July 30 in Panama City.

PARAGUAY was hit hard in 1982 by a slowdown in the construction of two huge hydroelectric projects on the Paraná River that have provided jobs and fueled the nation's economy in recent years.

Construction declined sharply on the Itaipú dam, which went into partial operation in November 1982. A joint project of Paraguay and Brazil, the Itaipú will be the world's largest single source of hydroelectric power when it is fully operational in 1989. Construction of the Yacyreta hydroelectric project ground to a halt in 1982 because Argentina, Paraguay's partner on the project, was unable to fulfill its obligations.

There were indications during the year that President Alfredo Stroessner would seek another five-year term at elections in early 1983. Stroessner has ruled Paraguay since 1954. Under his dictatorial regime, Paraguay has frequently been criticized for violations of human rights. In 1982, the International League for Human Rights, a privately funded organization, alleged that there had been 17 politically motivated killings in Paraguay in the past two years. Nathan A. Haverstock

See also LATIN AMERICA (Facts in Brief Table). In WORLD BOOK, see PARAGUAY.

PARENTS AND TEACHERS, NATIONAL CONGRESS OF. See NATIONAL PTA.

PENNSYLVANIA. See PHILADELPHIA; STATE GOVT.

Shantytowns cropped up in Asunción, Paraguay, after flooding of the Paraguay River in August forced riverside residents to flee their homes.

PERSONALITIES OF 1982 included the following:

Belafonte, Harry, 55, the singer and actor whose West Indian folk songs and calypso rhythms caused quite a bit of excitement in the 1950s, was recognized for his more solemn endeavors in January. Coretta Scott King awarded Belafonte, a long-time civil rights activist, the 10th annual Martin Luther King, Jr., Nonviolent Peace Prize. At ceremonies in Atlanta, Ga., marking the commemoration of King's birthday, his widow said, "Harry Belafonte has dedicated his life to the struggle for justice, peace, and equality."

Borges, Jorge Luis, 82, the Argentine poet, essayist, and short-story writer, confided in January 1982 that Mark Twain's *Huckleberry Finn* was "the first novel I ever read through." Borges was in New Orleans to lecture and accept awards from two universities.

Capra, Frank, 84, pioneer motion-picture director honored with the American Film Institute's 10th Life Achievement Award on March 4, was the oldest but spryest recipient so far. Striding to the podium, Capra asked, "How in hell did I get up here?" He then went on to reminisce about the eventful life that followed his arrival in America as a 6-year-old Sicilian immigrant. Capra's movies, which generally took the form of romantic comedy, exemplify his sentimental, patriotic, idealistic nature. The ability to turn his love of people and belief in each individual's importance into entertainment earned him three Academy Awards—for *It Happened One Night* (1934), *Mr. Deeds Goes to Town* (1936), and *You Can't Take It With You* (1938). Claudette Colbert, star of the first winner, summed up the films' lasting appeal: "Some people called those pictures Capra-corn," she said. "Today a lot of people call them classics."

Castro, Juanita, 48, of Miami, Fla., furnished new proof in February that family members do not always agree—particularly on questions of political persuasion. Along with 414 other immigrants to the United States, Juanita took the oath of allegiance in the Dade County Auditorium and became a U.S. citizen—while her brother Fidel remained president of Cuba. Referring to that country, the new citizen, who has made her home in Miami for 17 years, said, "My heart is there but my life is here. I wanted to participate fully in the American way of living."

Claiborne, Craig, 62, food editor of *The New York Times* since 1957, hosted a party he called "A Feast Made for Laughter" on September 4 to celebrate his birthday, his silver anniversary at the newspaper, and the publication of his autobiography—which also has that title. From all over the United States and several other countries, 36 chefs gathered at Claiborne's home in East Hampton, Long Island, to prepare their specialties. Maida Heatter, author of four dessert cookbooks, carried

Singer Marie Osmond and Stephen Craig smile for the camera after their June 26 wedding in the Mormon Temple in Salt Lake City, Utah.

the birthday cakes from Miami. Alice Waters brought baskets of vegetables from her Chez Panisse restaurant in Berkeley, Calif. Roger Vergé from the south of France cooked à la Provençal, and Paul Prudhomme from the south of the United States—New Orleans—cooked à la Creole. Pierre Franey, Claiborne's associate, coordinated the activities and saw to it that 400 people from the gastronomic, entertainment, and publishing worlds both feasted and laughed.

Coggeshall, Robert A., a Struthers, Ohio, banker, began to wonder how many other Americans shared his curious cognomen. Knowing that his English ancestor John Coggeshall landed in Boston in 1632 and was head of Providence Plantations in Rhode Island by 1647, the banker placed an ad searching for relatives in *Yankee* magazine. Dozens and dozens of aunts, uncles, and cousins turned up—all descended from John. Robert Coggeshall organized a grand family reunion in July in Portsmouth, R.I., to which almost 700 people of Coggeshall blood came from 36 states and several other countries. They talked about their roots and attended clambakes. But the best part of the gathering for Robert was finding a relative he had not seen since a family split 30 years ago—his own father, Theodore.

Donahue, Wanda and Robert, of Wethersfield, Conn., received a visitor from outer space on November 8. No, it was not E. T.—but it was definitely extraterrestrial. A 6-pound (2.7-kilogram) meteorite from the asteroid belt between Mars and Jupiter crashed through the roof of the Donahue's home. It injured no one but greatly excited scientists—not only because of its rarity, but also because it was the second meteorite to fall in Wethersfield in 11 years, which a geologist called an "almost incomprehensible" coincidence.

Fiennes, Sir Ranulph Twisleton-Wykeham-, 38, and Charles Burton, 40, returned in triumph to Greenwich, England, on August 29 after spending three years making "the last great journey left on earth"—the first trip around the world from pole to pole. Their royal patron, Prince Charles, who saw the adventurers off on Sept. 2, 1979, and greeted them on their return, called the expedition "gloriously mad." Many U.S. and British firms were among the 1,000 sponsors who underwrote the $17.5-million cost of the trek, which was joined by various other daring souls from time to time. Sure to be included in Fiennes' exciting book, *To the Ends of the Earth: The Transglobe Expedition,* will be accounts of their north-to-south crossing of the Sahara followed by—perhaps to cool off—the first crossing of the 9,000-foot (2,700-meter) Scott Glacier in Antarctica, first crossing of the Northwest Passage in small craft, and first crossing of the North and South poles in one journey. During their 55,000-mile (88,000-kilometer) odyssey, the explorers often found themselves in perilous situations, including 99 days of isolation on an ice floe and encounters with hungry polar bears. Summing up three years of experiencing nature's threats and thrills, Fiennes remarked, "Some people would say we have been very lucky, but I would say God has been very good to us."

Nureyev, Rudolf, 42, ended 20 years as a stateless person in 1982. The dancer defected from Russia in 1961 and was a citizen of no country until Austria granted him citizenship in January. For the past few years, he had been traveling with papers of transit from Monaco. How does it feel to be Austrian? "Both as an artist and as a person, I like Vienna and the Viennese," said Nureyev.

Peters, Tara Kathlene, born on March 12 in Redwood City, Calif., represented the sixth living generation in a family line stretching back to 1891. The baby's great-great-great-grandmother, Frankie Underwood, 91, of Fitzgerald, Ga., who has 59 living descendants, said, "The good Lord has blessed me. It's wonderful to be blessed with a family like that." Intervening generations included Tara's mother, Kimberly Kathlene Peters, 19; grandmother Jo Ann Jacobi, 37, of Foster City, Calif.; great-grandmother Kathlene Langella, 55, of Burlingame, Calif.; and great-great-grandmother Olene Cox, 73, of Macon, Ga. Tara's father, George A. Peters, Jr., 21, played a strong supporting role in a documentary film being made about the family.

Rickover, Admiral Hyman G., 82, retired as director of the U.S. Navy's Nuclear Propulsion Program on January 31 and passed up the traditional pomp to make a plea for disarmament. Speaking to House of Representatives and Senate members of the Joint Economic Committee, Rickover showed characteristic bluntness as he attacked defense contractors and nuclear build-up. The man who is known as the father of the nuclear Navy said nothing would please him more than to participate in an international disarmament conference. "Put me in charge of it," he told his listeners. "I'll get you some results."

Rudstrom, Erik, 65, a Norwegian sea captain, steered a dragon ship full of other Viking descendants toward the fulfillment of a dream in July. In 1970, school counselor Robert Asp of Moorhead, Minn., began building a replica of a 10th-century Viking long ship of the type sailed by Norse explorer Leif Ericson. He planned to sail it to Norway. After Asp died in 1980, leaving the *Hjemkomst* (*Homecoming*) not quite completed, his widow, children, and many friends finished outfitting the ship. They hired Rudstrom, who was experienced

Miguel Vazquez comes out of his first flip, turns during his third, and is caught by brother Juan in July in the world's first quadruple somersault.

Explorers Charles Burton and Sir Ranulph Twisleton-Wykeham-Fiennes pause during the Arctic part of their round-both-poles worldwide journey.

in handling open boats in the North Atlantic Ocean, as captain, and the ship left Duluth, Minn., on May 6, 1982. After a trip through the Great Lakes and down the Hudson River to New York City, Rudstrom and the crew of 13 began the ocean crossing on June 14. The 20th-century Vikings took 34 days to complete the voyage. Finally, on July 17, the *Hjemkomst*, powered entirely by sail and strong Scandinavian-American arms, arrived safely "home" in Bergen.

Smith, Kate, 75, of Raleigh, N.C., received the Medal of Freedom from President Ronald Reagan in October. Presenting the nation's highest civilian award to the retired singer, famous for rendering Irving Berlin's "God Bless America" at war-bond rallies during World War II, Reagan said, "Her splendid voice has earned her a place in the history books."

Vazquez, Miguel, 17, flipped—and flipped and flipped and flipped again—at a circus performance on July 10 as he became the first aerialist to achieve the long-attempted quadruple somersault. After being caught by his brother Juan, 31, on that momentous night at the Tucson (Ariz.) Community Center, daring young Miguel said, "I always knew I could do it, but I can't believe I did. It's like the four-minute mile." The stunt is extremely difficult for two reasons: The athlete who "flies" must turn over four times in midair while positioning himself perfectly to be caught by the wrists; and the catcher, hanging upside down, must grasp the flier as he spins out of the final somersault at a speed of 75 miles (120 kilometers) per hour. To all the members of the Ringling Brothers and Barnum & Bailey Circus act called the Flying Vazquez, control is everything. They agree with Miguel that "the quadruple isn't just a physical test; it's also a mental one."

Waldheim, Kurt, 63, who was secretary-general of the United Nations from 1972 until 1982, took on a new job in May. Waldheim, after 37 years as a diplomat, was appointed distinguished university research professor of diplomacy at Georgetown University in Washington, D.C.

Walters, Larry, 33, of North Hollywood, Calif., sat in a lawn chair and looked up at the blue sky one day in July. Nothing odd about that. But attached to the chair were 45 helium-filled weather balloons. At a signal, six of Walter's friends released the restraining ropes they held and launched the lawn chair. Still comfortably seated, Walters soared to 16,000 feet (4,900 meters) for a cloud's-eye view of his backyard. He remained chairborne and airborne for 45 minutes, until he popped the balloons one by one with a pellet gun and drifted slowly to earth. Said Walters, whose flight of fantasy was truly wish fulfillment on a Hollywood scale, "Since I was 13 years old, I've

Denver sixth-grader Molly Dieveney spelled *contretemps* and *psoriasis* correctly and won the 55th U.S. National Spelling Bee in June.

dreamed of going up into the clear blue sky in a weather balloon." However, the Federal Aviation Administration brought Walters back to earth, fining him $4,000 for various airspace violations.

Williams, Kit, an English artist and writer who led readers of his book *Masquerade* (1980) a merry chase for three years, rejoiced when it ended in a sort of hare-and-hound caper on February 24. Williams had hidden a hare-shaped gold filigree pendant set with turquoises, rubies, and moonstones "somewhere in England," then wrote his lavishly illustrated romantic tale filled with clues leading to the buried treasure. Seekers of what the author called "a modern-day Holy Grail" bought a million copies of *Masquerade* and dug holes all over the countryside. At last, a 48-year-old design engineer (who assumed the name Ken Thomas to hide from fellow seekers) followed a clue to the village of Ampthill, 35 miles (56 kilometers) northwest of London. Thomas' dog led the way to a stone cross honoring Catherine of Aragon that served as a pointer to the hidden crypt, and several nights of digging uncovered the treasure. It may be worth about $36,000, but the successful sleuth said he had no plans to sell. Thomas will keep the long-buried hare along with his copy of the book, in which author Williams wrote, "To the keeper of the jewel of the 'Masquerade'—Thanks!!! It's all over." Marsha F. Goldsmith

PERU. On Dec. 12, 1982, Prime Minister Manuel Ulloa Eliás and his 15-member Cabinet resigned in the first major government shakeup since democracy replaced military rule in Peru in 1980. Ulloa, a former Wall Street financier who urged a return to the free market system, had failed in his battle to halt Peru's crippling inflation. He was replaced by Fernando Schwalb Lopez Aldana on Jan 3, 1983.

Throughout 1982, President Fernando Belaúnde Terry waged an uphill struggle to put Peru on the road to economic recovery. Earnings from the nation's mineral exports continued to slide amid international recession. On June 8, the International Monetary Fund, an agency of the United Nations, rescued Peru from bankruptcy by pledging to provide the country with $850 million over a three-year period. The funding was conditional upon the Belaúnde administration's willingness to impose austerity measures.

Factional Disputes erupted within the nation's Congress during the year. Some were generated by opposition groups belonging to the American Popular Revolutionary Alliance, and some by the president's own Popular Action party. Armed uprisings in Peru's countryside resulted in the killing of police officers and soldiers. Nathan A. Haverstock

See also LATIN AMERICA (Facts in Brief Table). In WORLD BOOK, see PERU.

PET. See CAT; DOG.

PETROLEUM AND GAS. The Organization for Economic Cooperation and Development (OECD) warned the world's industrialized nations on Oct. 12, 1982, to avoid complacency over the current glut of crude oil and moderating petroleum prices. The OECD, a group of 24 countries formed in 1961 to promote economic growth, predicted that the oil market will remain "deceptively stable" until the mid-1980s. Thereafter, however, the group forecast growing shortages—of up to 4 million barrels per day (bpd)—as demand for oil increases and production declines in North America, the North Sea, and the Soviet Union.

Cutting Imports. On October 15, the American Petroleum Institute (API), a trade association, reported that during 1982 the United States continued to decrease its dependence on crude oil imported from the Middle East. The API said that Mideast oil imports during the first nine months of 1982 fell by about 1 million bpd, compared with the same period in 1981. An average of 3.3 million barrels of oil were imported each day during 1982, down 22 per cent from 4.3 million bpd in 1981.

The API also cited a significant shift away from previous heavy reliance on imports from the Organization of Petroleum Exporting Countries (OPEC), the world oil cartel. By late 1982, OPEC oil accounted for 45 per cent of U.S. imports, compared with 69 per cent in 1978.

During the first seven months of 1982, U.S. production of crude oil rose 1.1 per cent to 8.7 million bpd. United States production of natural gas during the same period totaled 10.8 trillion cubic feet (306 billion cubic meters), 5.5 per cent less than in 1981, according to the U.S. Department of Energy (DOE). Imports rose 9.1 per cent to 565 billion cubic feet (16 billion cubic meters).

U.S. Reserves. The DOE said on August 31 that proven reserves of crude oil, natural gas, and natural gas liquids in the United States remained virtually stable during 1981 for the second straight year after 10 years of decline. The DOE said that at the beginning of 1982, U.S. proven reserves stood at 29.4 billion barrels of crude oil, 201.7 trillion cubic feet (5.7 trillion cubic meters) of natural gas, and 7.1 billion barrels of natural gas liquids. Proven reserves are known reserves that can be recovered profitably using existing technology.

Pipeline Conflict. President Ronald Reagan on June 18 broadened the embargo on the sale of equipment for construction of a 3,500-mile (5,600-kilometer) Soviet natural gas pipeline that would stretch from Siberia to central Europe. Reagan ordered the embargo of American-made equipment in December 1981 in response to the imposition of martial law in Poland. The 1982 restrictions, which also banned equipment manufactured by foreign subsidiaries and licensees of U.S. companies, triggered sharp criticism from America's allies in Europe.

Although the United States imposed trade sanctions on firms that ignored the embargo, the project moved ahead. On July 13, a group of West German banks formally agreed to extend up to $1.6 billion in credits to the Soviet Union to help finance the pipeline. On November 13, President Reagan announced that he had lifted the embargo after the United States and its allies reached "substantial agreement" on a new economic policy toward the Soviet Union. See EUROPE.

OPEC Problems. Faced with a worldwide oversupply of petroleum that depressed prices, OPEC agreed on March 20 to reduce oil production by about 700,000 bpd. The 13-nation oil cartel met in emergency session on July 20 to consider charges that Iran, Libya, and Nigeria were exceeding production quotas and selling oil below the agreed price. The meeting ended with no solution to the continued oil glut, however. OPEC ministers met again on December 19 in Vienna, Austria, but the meeting also ended in disagreement.

Iranian Imports. The U.S. Department of Defense's $53.1-million purchase of crude oil from Iran on April 22 was the first U.S. purchase of oil from that country since Americans were taken hostage there in late 1979. The 1.8 million barrels of oil were used to help fill the Strategic Petroleum Reserve. The oil stockpile, maintained in underground salt domes in Texas and Louisiana, contained 282 million barrels of oil by mid-October.

An Oil Lease Sale held on October 13 by the U.S. Department of the Interior drew bids totaling $2.07 billion from oil firms eager to drill what is believed to be the largest untapped pool of oil and natural gas in North America. The tracts, in the Beaufort Sea off Alaska's northern coast, contain an estimated 4.7 billion barrels of oil and 1.8 trillion cubic feet (50 billion cubic meters) of natural gas. The total amount bid, a record for any lease sale in Alaska, was hailed by Interior Secretary James G. Watt. Environmentalists, however, challenged Watt's plans for accelerated leasing in other areas, including the scenic coast of northern California. In December, Congress passed an appropriations bill that included a ban on the selling of oil and gas leases off California's central and northern coast. President Reagan signed the bill on December 20.

Alaskan Setbacks. Sponsors of a proposed 4,800-mile (7,700-kilometer) natural gas pipeline from Alaska said early in the year that financing problems would delay completion of the $43-billion project for two years, until about 1989.

Trouble came for another Alaska oil project on April 7 when Governor John D. Spellman of Washington rejected plans for a $2.7-billion oil terminal and a pipeline under Puget Sound. The 1,500-mile (2,400-kilometer) pipeline was planned to carry Alaskan crude oil from supertankers docked at Port Angeles, Wash., to refineries in the Midwest. Spellman cited possible environmental damage to Puget Sound.

Corporate Moves. Gulf Oil Corporation on August 6 retracted a $4.8-billion offer to buy Cities Service Company, citing objections by the Federal Trade Commission (FTC) to the take-over. The FTC charged that the merger of Gulf, the sixth largest U.S. oil company, and Cities Service, the 19th largest, would decrease competition in the petroleum industry. On August 25, Cities Service accepted a $4.05-billion purchase offer from Occidental Petroleum Company.

On March 10, the Reagan Administration imposed an embargo on U.S. imports of Libyan oil, charging that Libya supported international terrorism. However, because Libyan oil accounted for only 2 per cent of U.S. imports, the embargo had little effect on U.S. prices or supplies.

Chinese Developments. On February 16, the People's Republic of China opened 58,000 square miles (150,000 square kilometers) of its offshore waters to oil exploration and development by foreign firms. The newly formed China National Offshore Oil Corporation sent bidding invitations to 46 oil companies that had participated in geologic surveys along China's continental shelf. China estimates that it has offshore oil reserves totaling 100

Controversial Pipeline

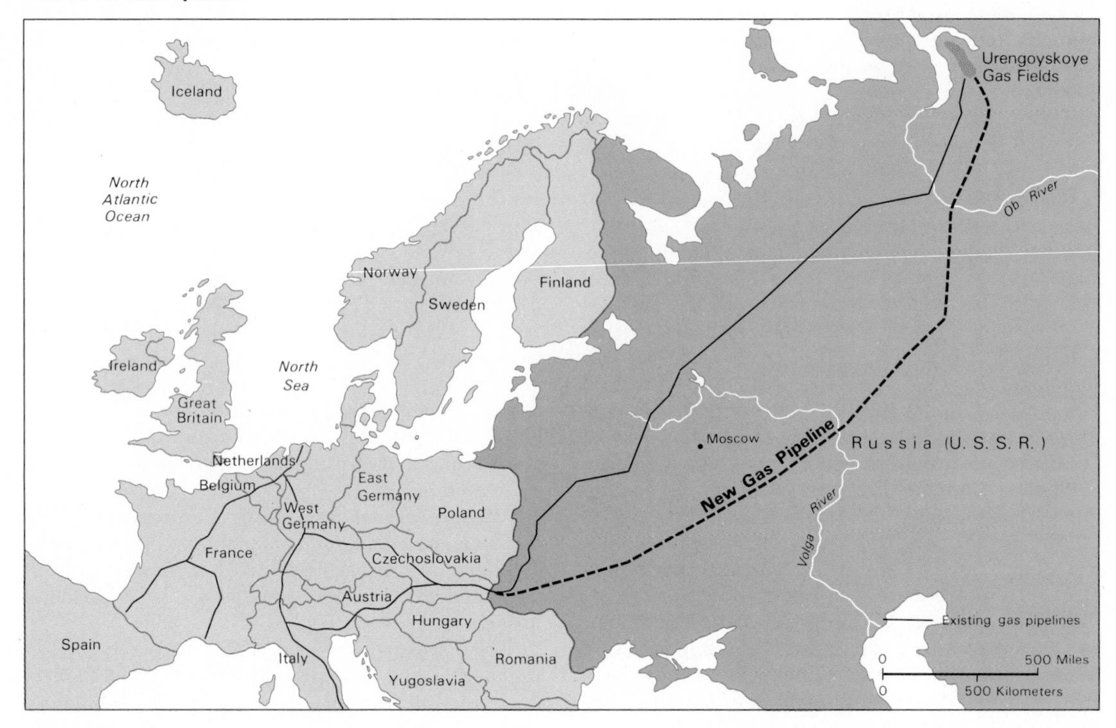

billion barrels, though some Western oil experts believe the amount is much lower.

Canada Gas Venture. A group of Canadian and West German firms reached agreement April 20 on a joint $3-billion project to liquefy natural gas from the Arctic region of Canada and ship it to Western Europe. Partners in the venture are Ruhrgas, West Germany's largest natural gas company; Gelsenberg, A. G., a West German subsidiary of the British Petroleum Company; and Transcanada Pipelines and Petro-Canada.

The project involves construction of natural gas liquefaction facilities in an area of rich gas reserves about 800 miles (1,300 kilometers) north of the Arctic Circle. The liquefied gas will be shipped by special icebreaker tankers to Wilhelmshaven, West Germany. Completion of the project is expected by the late 1980s.

Panama Pipeline. An oil pipeline across the Isthmus of Panama, connecting Pacific and Atlantic ports, went into operation in September. The 80-mile (130-kilometer), $300-million line was built to accommodate modern supertankers too large to use the Panama Canal. The pipeline can carry about 800,000 bpd of oil from the Pacific port of Charco Azul to Chiriquí Grande on the Atlantic Ocean. The oil then moves by tanker to refineries along the U.S. Gulf Coast. Michael Woods

In WORLD BOOK, see GAS; PETROLEUM.

PHILADELPHIA celebrated its 300th birthday in 1982 with a variety of festivities set against a backdrop of municipal belt-tightening that saw no pay increases for the city's major municipal unions. However, the unions—representing police, fire fighters, blue-collar workers, and white-collar workers—won wage increases ranging from 8 to 8.5 per cent in the second year of their contracts.

School Strike Averted. The city's public-school teachers, who had gone without pay raises since 1979, ended a bitter labor dispute on Aug. 31, 1982, when they ratified a contract that provides an 18 per cent salary increase over three years and allows only limited layoffs. The contract agreement avoided a strike, permitting schools to open on schedule for the first time in three years.

To eliminate an $88.8-million operating deficit and help finance the $176-million contract, the Board of Education on October 6 approved an $84.5-million bond issue—part of a refinancing plan for the school system. The bonds are to be paid off with a $38-million real estate tax increase.

The school district entered a new era on October 4, when Constance E. Clayton, associate superintendent for early childhood development, became the first woman and first black named to head the city's school system. The former superintendent, Michael P. Marcase, had been under intense pressure from Mayor William J. Green to resign and agreed on January 27 to step down after the city consented to pay him $108,000 to cover the remaining two years of his contract.

City Budget. The City Council on May 27 approved a $1.3-billion operating budget for fiscal 1983, 8.3 per cent higher than the 1982 budget. The added expenditures were to be financed, in part, by a 25 per cent increase in the tax on businesses' gross sales and by two new levies—a condominium conversion tax and a tax on vacant land to penalize real estate speculation.

The City Council on May 20 unanimously approved the establishment of a four-franchise cable television system. The decision ended a two-year impasse between the council and Mayor Green that left most of the city without cable TV.

Police Hiring. The hiring of minority-group members by the Police Department, a frequent subject of controversy during the past decade, was again raised as an issue by the Guardian Civic League, a group of black police officers. The league urged a boycott of Mayor Green's January 15 prayer breakfast honoring the birthday of civil rights leader Martin Luther King, Jr., contending that the mayor had not done enough to increase the hiring of minority officers. In response to the protest, the mayor appointed a task force to propose a hiring plan. On March 19, however, he rejected its recommendation for a racial quota system that disregarded test scores and proposed instead a quota of 220 additional black officers hired on merit. That would raise the proportion of blacks on the 7,500-member police force from 18 per cent in 1982 to 21 per cent in 1987. Philadelphia's population is 40 per cent black.

Other Happenings. *The Bulletin,* once the largest-selling afternoon newspaper in the United States, ceased publication on January 29 after efforts to sell the 134-year-old paper failed.

In its first ruling in the Abscam case, the Supreme Court of the United States on June 7 let stand the conspiracy and bribery convictions of City Council member Harry P. Jannotti and former Council President George X. Schwartz. Their convictions, overturned by a federal district judge, were reinstated on February 11 by the U.S. Third Circuit Court of Appeals in Philadelphia. On February 26, the council's Ethics Committee voted to let Jannotti retain his seat on the council pending sentencing. Abscam was a Federal Bureau of Investigation (FBI) undercover operation in which an FBI agent posing as a wealthy Arab offered lawmakers bribes in return for favors.

Mayor Green announced in November that he would not seek re-election in 1983. Jan Schaffer

In WORLD BOOK, see PHILADELPHIA.

Fireworks explode over the Delaware River and rigging lights glow on visiting Tall Ships in June during a celebration honoring Philadelphia's 300th birthday.

President Marcos swears in his wife, Imelda, in September as a member of the committee that eventually will supervise the presidential succession.

PHILIPPINES took several steps toward the return of elective government in 1982. On May 17, more than 20 million Filipinos voted in the first nationwide local elections in 10 years. They chose more than 280,000 members for the approximately 40,000 village councils. Legislative assemblies were elected on June 7 in the southern part of the country, where Muslims had been given limited self-government, but few people voted.

On September 11, President Ferdinand E. Marcos signed into law provisions for the presidential succession in case of "permanent disability, death, removal from office, or resignation." A 15-member committee headed by Prime Minister César E. Virata was to supervise the succession. Marcos appointed to the committee his wife, Imelda, and his daughter Imee.

Political Opponents of Marcos joined in February to form a coalition called the United Nationalist Democratic Organization. Marcos charged on August 8 that some opponents planned nationwide strikes, bombings, and assassinations to disrupt his scheduled trip to the United States in September. He ordered the arrest of 39 labor leaders before making his first state visit to Washington, D.C., since 1966.

President Ronald Reagan welcomed Marcos cordially, though some Filipinos in the United States demonstrated against his rule. The visit led to further talks on the use of military facilities in the Philippines by U.S. armed forces. In a report coinciding with Marcos' visit, the human rights group Amnesty International charged that torture, killing, and other abuses continued in the Philippines. In November, Roman Catholic priests in 16 parishes suspended Masses to protest the arrest of a priest on charges of inciting rebellion.

A Filipino defense expert estimated that 20 per cent of the nation's villages were under control of the New People's Army (NPA), a Communist guerrilla force, or soon would be controlled by it. Both the NPA and Muslim separatist guerrillas continued to clash with the Philippine Army.

A Scandal led all 14 members of the Philippine Supreme Court to resign on May 10. The resignations followed charges that the court had regraded the bar examination paper of a justice's son to ensure that he pass. Marcos swore in a new 15-member court on May 14, reappointing 12 of the former judges.

The Economic Situation was the worst in more than a decade during 1982. An austere government budget, presented to the National Assembly on July 27, forecast continued deficits and little improvement in living standards. Henry S. Bradsher

See also ASIA (Facts in Brief Table). In WORLD BOOK, see PHILIPPINES.

PHONOGRAPH. See RECORDINGS.

PHOTOGRAPHY. The Eastman Kodak Company in February 1982 introduced three Kodak Disc cameras and matching Kodacolor HR (high-resolution) film. A bit larger than a cigarette package, the Disc 4000, 6000, and 8000 are highly automated cameras that can make fifteen 8- by 10-millimeter (mm) snapshots on a rotating film disk. Exposure control, flash, and film advance are completely automatic, powered by a sealed lithium battery with a life expectancy of five years. Kodacolor HR film has an ASA/ISO speed of 200 and is finer in grain than other color-negative films. By late 1982, many other manufacturers had brought out cameras, accessories, film, or processing equipment for the disk format.

In October, at the biennial *photokina* trade show in Cologne, West Germany, Kodak introduced Kodacolor VR 1000, a very-high-speed (ASA/ISO 1,000) film of excellent image quality. The company said the film would be available by mid-1983 in the 35-mm format and later in other sizes.

In its continuing effort to gain a larger share of the instant-photography market, Kodak brought out a line of cameras called the Kodamatics. All four new models accept high-speed (ASA/ISO 320) Kodamatic film, three have built-in electronic flash, and the top-of-the-line 98OL also includes Kodak's first autofocus system.

New Polaroid Products. For the first time in its history, Polaroid introduced three films for use in conventional 35-mm cameras. The films—Polachrome Autoprocess color slide film and two black-and-white films—are exposed normally and then processed in just three minutes in a hand-cranked Autoprocessor. The color rendition of Polachrome was not yet equal to that of conventional films.

Closer to Polaroid's traditional line of products was its new SLR 680, an autofocusing single-lens-reflex camera with built-in electronic flash. Like all models that accept Polaroid 600 high-speed self-developing film, the 680 uses flash illumination for every exposure, indoors and out.

Video Photography. The Sony Corporation of Japan unveiled a color video printer, called the Mavigraph, for making paper prints from video images. The device was developed as an accessory to Sony's Mavica camera—which makes color photographs electronically on a magnetic disk for viewing on a television screen—but it may be able to make copies of any still videoscreen image. At a demonstration of the system, the Mavigraph produced prints of inconsistent quality. Sony officials said the printer would be improved before the Mavigraph and the Mavica go on the market sometime in 1983.

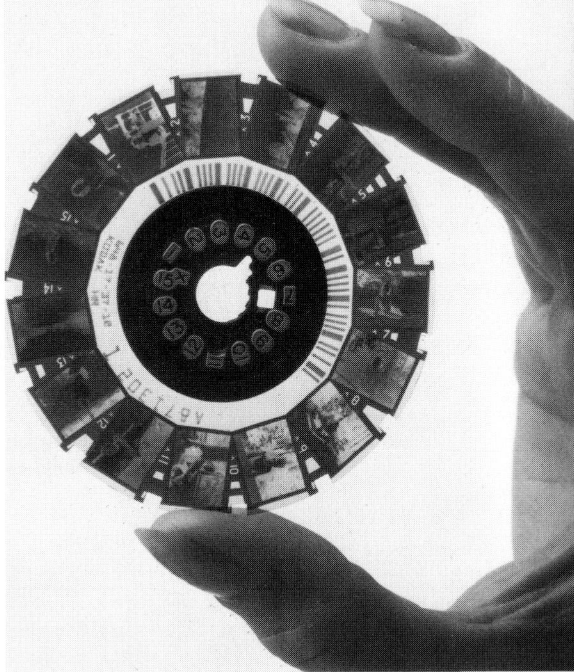

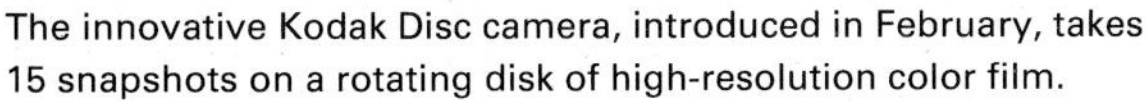
The innovative Kodak Disc camera, introduced in February, takes 15 snapshots on a rotating disk of high-resolution color film.

In answer to the Sony video-photography challenge, Kodak at the *photokina* show exhibited a prototype device for viewing Disc camera negatives on a standard television screen as full-color positives. Kodak said it had no plans to produce a video printer.

At *photokina,* Konica exhibited a small, lightweight color video camera, intended to sell for considerably less than other available models. Throughout the year, various other manufacturers demonstrated prototype compact versions of conventional video cassettes. In each case, the cassette was designed to be exposed in a lightweight combination camera-recorder, then placed in an adapter for playback by a video cassette deck.

Compact Cameras. Several manufacturers in 1982 introduced versions of the compact automatic 35-mm camera. Notable for their unusually low price and simple design were the Canon Snappy 20 and 50 models. New automatic focusing, or at least "guided focus," 35-mm single-lens-reflex cameras included the Canon Al-1, Olympus OM-F, and prototype Nikon F3 AF.

Sales of lower-priced compact cameras remained brisk in 1982, while expensive, sophisticated equipment stayed on the shelf. The market for photographic prints, like those for many other collectibles, became weak. Steve Pollock

In WORLD BOOK, see CAMERA; PHOTOGRAPHY.

Stanford University physicist Blas Cabrera may have detected a magnetic monopole, a very heavy subatomic particle, in February 1982.

PHYSICS experiments reported in 1982 provided strong hints of new phenomena and important confirmation of basic theoretical assumptions. Theoreticians and experimenters shed new light on a phenomenon known as an *anomalous nuclear interaction.* This phenomenon is an extraordinary occurrence that sometimes takes place when scientists expose a piece of photographic film to a beam of high-energy nuclei and then develop the film. Ordinarily, the film's emulsion layer reveals a certain pattern of tracks that the nuclei leave as they interact with nuclei in the emulsion. Typically, a high-energy nucleus that strikes a nucleus in an emulsion breaks into fragments that, in turn, strike other nuclei. The average distance between interactions for a given type of fragment, called its *mean free path,* is fairly predictable.

However, in the 1960s, physicist Barbara Judek of the Canadian National Research Council in Ottawa, Ont., noticed that about 6 per cent of certain fragments seemed to have extremely short mean free paths. This seemed to indicate that the fragments interacted much more strongly than standard nuclear theory predicts.

In January 1982, physicists Sverker Fredericksson and Magnus Jändel of the Royal Institute of Technology in Stockholm, Sweden, suggested that an unusual kind of deuteron, a nucleus composed of a neutron and a proton, might account for extremely short mean free paths. Ordinary neutrons and protons are each composed of three parts called *quarks.* However, the Swedish physicists suggested that a violent collision of a nucleus with other matter might rearrange a deuteron's six quarks into three groups of two quarks. According to nuclear theory, the new particle, called a *demon deuteron,* would interact with great strength.

On February 1, physicists Piyare L. Jain and Gourisankar Das of the State University of New York at Buffalo published results of an exposure of emulsion to high-energy beams of argon and iron nuclei that were produced at Bevelac, an accelerator at the Lawrence Berkeley Laboratory in Berkeley, Calif. Their data added weight to the growing conviction that a new kind of phenomenon is occurring.

EPR Paradox. In 1935, physicists Albert Einstein, Nathan Rosen, and Boris Podolsky published a paper suggesting that quantum mechanics, which seems to govern the behavior of matter, is not a complete theory. The authors were troubled by certain parts of the theory, such as the impossibility of determining simultaneously the precise momentum and position of a particle, and the way in which a measurement of one part of a system apparently causes an instantaneous change in another part. These features of quantum mechanics are so contrary to common sense that writers later referred to them as the Einstein-Podolsky-Rosen (EPR) paradox.

In July 1982, Alain Aspect, Phillipe Graingier, and Gérard Roger of the University of Paris-South in France reported results of the best test of the EPR paradox so far. They measured the polarization—the vibration angle—of each of two particles of light, called *photons,* emitted when radioactive calcium nuclei decayed. Quantum mechanics predicts that the measurement of one photon will affect the polarization direction of the other. The experiment confirmed the theory at an accuracy level of 99 per cent.

Cosmic Monopole? Physicist Blas Cabrera of Stanford University in Stanford, Calif., may have become the first person to detect a magnetic monopole—a particle that has one magnetic pole. All other magnetic objects ever observed have had one or more pairs of poles.

Cabrera reported in May that, on one occasion in February, the current in a shielded and monitored superconducting coil jumped to a new level as if induced to do so by a monopole among cosmic rays passing through the coil. A single event such as this is not sufficient to establish the monopole's existence, but physicists were impressed by Cabrera's report. Thomas Otis White

In WORLD BOOK, see PHYSICS; QUANTUM MECHANICS.

PLANINC, MILKA (1924-), became Yugoslavia's first woman prime minister on May 16, 1982. Planinc (pronounced *plah NEENTZ*) had been president of the Communist Party in Croatia, the second largest of Yugoslavia's six socialist republics, since 1971. She said the overriding concern of her government would be to solve Yugoslavia's serious economic problems. See YUGOSLAVIA.

Planinc was born on Nov. 21, 1924, in the Croatian village of Drnis, near present-day Sibenik, Yugoslavia. She graduated from Zagreb Management School. During World War II, when Yugoslavia was occupied by the Germans, Planinc joined the Partisans, a group led by Josip Broz Tito and the Communist Party.

After 1949, Planinc played an active role in Communist Party politics and held a number of educational, scientific, and cultural posts in Croatia. She rose to prominence as a strong opponent of the Croatian independence movement.

In June, the new prime minister presented her economic stabilization program to the Federal Assembly, Yugoslavia's legislature. It called for discipline and sacrifice on the part of the Yugoslav people and increased foreign competition for the country's industries.

Planinc is married to a retired businessman. They have a son and a daughter. David L. Dreier

POETRY in 1982 was highlighted by several posthumous collections. Notable were Sylvia Plath's *Collected Poems,* which won a Pulitzer Prize; *The Complete Poems* by Anne Sexton, which embodied stark views of personal dilemma; and James Wright's *This Journey,* the final original work of one of the most influential poets in the United States during the last 20 years.

Significant New Works. William Bronk's iconoclastic meditations in *Life Supports* earned an American Book Award. *Recoveries* by Theodore Weiss examined the relationship between visual art and artist. Adrienne Rich addressed feminist issues in *A Wild Patience Has Taken Me This Far.* Carolyn Forché's *The Country Between Us* spoke of political intolerance. Maxine Kumin focused on values of time and place in *Our Ground Time Here Will Be Brief.* Marge Piercy's *Circles on the Water* confronted political, social, and economic realities. William Stafford displayed a gentle concern for the natural world in *A Glass Face in the Rain.* James Dickey's *Puella* reflected a young girl's passage into womanhood. *The Sleeping Beauty* by Hayden Carruth was a book-length poem about love, ecology, and cultural decay. Major translations included Rika Lesser's version of Swedish poet Gunnar Ekelöf's *Guide to the Underworld,* and *From the Country of Eight Islands,* Japanese poetry translated by Kiroaki Sata and Burton Watson.

Awards. Mexican poet Octavio Paz received the Neustadt International Prize for Literature. Richard Hugo and John Frederick Nims were cited by the Academy of American Poets for "distinguished poetic achievement." Brewster Ghiselin's *Windrose* won the William Carlos Williams Award.

The National Poetry Series continued to introduce emerging talents. Winners published in 1982 were *The Mud Actor* by Cyrus Cassells; *Hugging the Jukebox* by Naomi Shihab Nye; *Accidental Weather* by Sherod Santos; *Second Sight* by Jonathan Aaron; and *The Incognito Lounge* by Denis Johnson.

Cathy Song's *From the White Places* was the Yale Younger Poets selection. Other promising new voices included Nicholas Christopher, Katha Pollit, Linda Gregg, Douglas Crase, Brad Leithauser, William Logan, Sonia Gernes, Mary Kinzie, Anthony Petrosky, and Jim Barnes. Anthony Hecht became the 27th consultant in poetry to the Library of Congress, succeeding Maxine Kumin.

The world of poetry was diminished by the death of several distinguished writers in 1982. They included Horace Gregory, 83, the 1965 Bollingen Prizewinner, on March 11; his wife, Marya Zaturenska, 80, a Pulitzer Prizewinner, on January 19; Archibald MacLeish, 89, often called "America's poet laureate," on April 20; Kenneth Rexroth, 76, an early "beat" poet, on June 6; and Richard Hugo, on October 22. G. E. Murray

In WORLD BOOK, see POETRY.

POLAND. The independent labor union Solidarity collapsed in 1982 under severe pressure from the military regime of Wojciech Jaruzelski, the nation's Council of Ministers chairman and first secretary of the Polish United Workers' Party (PZPR), Poland's Communist party.

The government had introduced martial law and arrested Solidarity leaders on Dec. 13, 1981. Four union leaders announced the formation of a provisional underground coordinating commission in April 1982. The commission's first decree called for a 15-minute nationwide strike on May 13. Protests that began on May 1, a holiday honoring workers, turned violent on May 3, when police charged marching demonstrators throughout Poland. The May 13 strike was generally peaceful. Violence erupted again on August 13, the eight-month anniversary of the imposition of martial law, and on August 31, the second anniversary of the signing of the pact whereby the government agreed to recognize independent labor unions.

On October 8, Poland's Sejm (parliament) declared Solidarity and its counterpart in the countryside, Rural Solidarity, illegal. A new law provided for the formation of tightly restricted unions at the factory level. Workers at the Lenin shipyard in Gdańsk protested the Sejm's decision by demonstrating on October 11 and 12. On October 13, the government militarized the shipyard, drafting the workers into the armed service. That day, violence broke out in three other cities.

However, the ban on Solidarity, the police action during the demonstrations, and the militarization of the shipyard seemed to have crushed Solidarity. A Solidarity call for a general strike on November 10 had almost no effect. On November 14, the government released Lech Walesa, who had been chairman of Solidarity, after 11 months of internment. Martial law was suspended at midnight December 30, but the government retained many of the special powers it had assumed.

Government Changes. On June 5, the government appointed Stanislaw Kociolek, a strong opponent of Solidarity, ambassador to Russia. Marian Wozniak replaced Kociolek as secretary of the Warsaw PZPR. On July 16, Wozniak became a full member of the Politburo, the PZPR's policy-making body. Another hard-liner, Stefan Olszowski, became foreign minister on July 16. Olszowski had been a secretary of the PZPR Central Committee. Władysław Gomułka, party leader from 1956 until his dismissal after workers' riots in December 1970, died on Sept. 1, 1982.

Economic Relations with Russia became closer in 1982. However, the West imposed economic sanctions against Poland after Poland's military

Polish riot police chase antigovernment demonstrators in Warsaw in May. Some of the protesters carry banners of the labor union Solidarity.

Internees leave a detention camp near Warsaw in July as Poland eases martial law restrictions that it imposed in December 1981.

crackdown in December 1981. On October 27, United States President Ronald Reagan responded to the dissolution of Solidarity by removing Poland from the list of those countries whose exports to the United States are subject to low tariffs.

On November 3, however, Poland signed an agreement with Western banks for the rescheduling of most of its 1982 debt. Poland will not have to pay any of the $2.3-billion principal for four years. Then, Poland will repay 95 per cent of the principal during the next 3½ years. Poland agreed to pay the $1.1-billion interest by March 1983 and the remaining 5 per cent of principal by Nov. 20, 1983. The banks will loan back $550 million of the interest, creating a debt that Poland must pay off in three years.

Industrial Production declined by 5 per cent from January through October, compared with the first 10 months of 1981. Exports increased by 5.5 per cent, but imports declined by 9 per cent. The grain harvest, at 21 million metric tons (23 million short tons), was higher than in 1981, but the potato harvest was 20 per cent lower. In February, the government raised prices of foods and other goods by up to 400 per cent. Chris Cviic

See also EUROPE (Facts in Brief Table). In WORLD BOOK, see POLAND.

POLLUTION. See ENVIRONMENT.

POPULAR MUSIC. See MUSIC, POPULAR.

POPULATION. World population continued to grow rapidly in 1982, and by midyear there were more than 4.5 billion people on earth, according to an estimate by the private, Washington, D.C.-based Population Reference Bureau. At the current 1.7 per cent annual rate of increase, the world's population would double in about 40 years. However, the worldwide growth rate has been slowly declining—it fell by nearly half a percentage point over the last decade—so that the total world population is expected to stabilize at about 10.5 billion by 2110.

Growth Rates. The population of the industrialized nations, which is now about 25 per cent of the world's total, is increasing at an annual rate of only 0.6 per cent. It is the developing nations, whose growth rates have also declined but still average 2.1 per cent, that account for most of the world's population increase.

Africa, with a birth rate of 46 per 1,000 people and a yearly growth rate of 2.9 per cent, had the world's fastest-increasing population in 1982. Its present population of nearly 500 million could double in 25 years. Latin America, with 378 million people, had a growth rate of 2.3 per cent and will have close to 10 per cent of the world's population by the turn of the century. Asia, with 2.7 billion people, had a growth rate of 1.9 per cent per year. By the year 2000, Asia may have 58 per cent of the total population of the earth.

On the other hand, the slow growth rates of 0.7 per cent in North America and 0.4 per cent in Europe indicate that those areas will continue to decline in their share of world population. By the year 2000, North America may have 5 per cent, and Europe 8 per cent, of the world's people.

China, the earth's most populous country, had more than 1 billion people in 1982, but its growth rate of 1.4 per cent is now lower than the world average. India, in second place with 726 million people, continued to grow by 2 per cent per year, so that by the mid-21st century, India's population may exceed China's. Russia, with 273 million people, and the United States, with 233 million, were third and fourth in population numbers. Both have growth rates below the world average—0.8 per cent and 0.7 per cent, respectively.

Kenya had the world's highest birth rate of 53 births per 1,000 population in 1982; West Germany, the lowest with 10 per 1,000. Canada and the United States averaged 16 births per 1,000.

Life Expectancy. Life expectancy continued to increase in most parts of the world, while death rates declined. Life expectancy at birth is 75 years or more in the Scandinavian countries, Iceland, the Netherlands, and Switzerland. On the other hand, it is little more than half that age in some areas of Africa. Jeanne C. Biggar

In WORLD BOOK, see POPULATION.

PORTUGAL adopted a new Constitution on Aug. 12, 1982, barring all military involvement in government. It also abolished the Revolutionary Council, the military watchdog group set up in 1974 to supervise Portugal's transition to civilian rule. The new Constitution was a preliminary to Portugal's scheduled 1985 entry into the European Community (EC or Common Market).

In instituting the changes, Parliament carried out the wishes of the Portuguese people, expressed at the 1979 general election. The Constitution curtails the authority of President António dos Santos Ramalho Eanes.

Economic Crisis. The government's first task under the new Constitution was to deal with the economy. Portugal's foreign debt of $10 billion at the beginning of 1982 represented half its gross national product (the measure of the value of a country's goods and services). To deal with that debt, and with a balance-of-payments deficit of $2-billion, the budget included austerity measures, with wage increases well below the 20 per cent inflation rate.

Anniversary of the Revolution. The eighth anniversary of the 1974 revolution that toppled Portuguese dictator Marcello Caetano was celebrated on April 25 amid some disharmony. The Democratic Alliance, a union of four political parties that controls Parliament, boycotted a march through Lisbon, the Portuguese capital. Socialist Party leader Mário Soares used the occasion to call for early elections. The public was unenthusiastic about the celebration, having two days earlier suffered a 30 per cent rise in the price of bread.

Strike. The General Confederation of Portuguese Workers, a Communist-led labor group, called Portugal's first general strike on February 12 to protest the government's economic policies. The rival Socialist labor federation said the strike was a political maneuver aimed at disrupting democratic processes.

Other Developments. The Democratic Alliance government survived its first censure motion on March 5 after two days of debate. The Socialist motion charged the government with protecting special-interest groups such as the church, the military, and private industry. The allied forces of Social Democrats, Christian Democrats, and Popular Monarchists outvoted the combined opposition by 130 votes to 116.

On December 19, Prime Minister Francisco Pinto Balsemão resigned after his coalition lost ground to the Socialists in municipal elections. However, he stayed on as head of a caretaker government until the Democratic Alliance and President Eanes could agree on a successor. Kenneth Brown

See also EUROPE (Facts in Brief Table). In WORLD BOOK, see PORTUGAL.

POSTAL SERVICE, UNITED STATES. The U.S. Postal Service ran a bigger surplus than expected in 1982, making it unlikely that a rate increase would be necessary in 1983. A higher volume of mail, along with the 20-cent stamp for first-class letters and other increased postage for second- and third-class mail, contributed to keeping the Postal Service well in the black. Postal officials announced on November 1 that the service's unaudited surplus for the 1982 fiscal year, which ended September 30, was $688 million, more than five times its anticipated surplus of $120 million for that period.

Congress also provided the Postal Service with more funds than President Ronald Reagan had requested. The President had proposed eliminating the public service subsidy that supports Saturday mail delivery, postal service to rural areas, and the operation of smaller post offices. He had also proposed a $500-million ceiling—well below fiscal 1981's $613-million spending level—for subsidizing the mailings of charities and other nonprofit organizations. Both the Senate and House of Representatives Appropriations committees, however, approved a larger postal subsidy payment for nonprofit mailers, $789 million and $708 million, respectively. Either sum would result in a modest rate increase for nonprofit mailers.

Electronic Mail. The Postal Service introduced a new type of electronic mail on January 4 despite the strong opposition of the Department of Justice and the Department of Commerce. The service, known as E-COM, for electronic computer-originated mail, was designed for use by large-volume business mailers. It allows them to transmit address lists and the texts of letters by computer to 25 post offices throughout the United States. At the post offices, the letters are printed out, put into envelopes, and delivered by letter carriers. Delivery within two days is guaranteed. At the outset, 100 companies had signed up for the electronic service for an annual fee of $50. In addition, they were charged 26 cents for the first page of a letter sent by E-COM, plus 5 cents for each additional page.

The Justice and Commerce departments tried to get a court injunction to stop the Postal Service from launching E-COM, but they failed. They argued that E-COM would be subsidized indirectly by regular mail users and that its low charges would discourage private companies from entering the field. However, the U.S. Court of Appeals in Washington, D.C., refused to halt E-COM even though the independent Postal Rate Commission had authorized only a test of the new service. E-COM got off to a slow start, averaging only 6,500 letters per week by late March, but speeded up to 250,000 letters a week by October. Start-up costs were estimated at $35 million.

A U.S. Postal Service employee operates a video terminal to sort and print mail sent by the E-COM system, introduced in January.

Mail Fraud. Congress nearly completed action on a bill to crack down on mail fraud by increasing the subpoena powers of postal inspectors and by raising the penalty for violators. The bill sailed through the Senate on May 19. A different version of the bill was approved by the House, which added safeguards against invasion of privacy to meet objections of civil liberties groups. However, Congress adjourned before both houses reached agreement on the bill, and it died.

Other Developments. The Postal Service's contingency plans for continuing mail service after a nuclear war were ridiculed at a congressional hearing on August 12. The plan called for moving postal headquarters from Washington, D.C., to Memphis or San Bruno, Calif., if the nation's capital were destroyed in a nuclear holocaust. In addition, the Postal Service said it had made plans for circulating emergency change-of-address forms to survivors. Members of Congress greeted the plan with laughter, saying there would be few postal patrons left if a nuclear holocaust occurred.

On October 21, the Postal Service agreed to pay a total of $400 million in back pay to 800,000 of its present and former employees. The payment was for violations of the Fair Labor Standards Act between 1974 and 1978. William J. Eaton

In World Book, see Post Office; Postal Service, United States.

PRESIDENT OF THE UNITED STATES Ronald Reagan spent most of 1982 predicting an economic recovery that never came. The downward spiral of the United States economy bedeviled his Administration's second year, bringing record budget deficits, along with double-digit unemployment rates that put nearly 12 million people out of work by Election Day on November 2. The political fallout was damaging for Republican candidates in the 1982 midterm elections as the Democrats ran hard against "Reaganomics" and recession (see Elections; Republican Party).

As the year ended, Reagan and his advisers appeared to be groping for solutions to offer in 1983, though the President continued to insist that his policies of reducing taxes and government spending and easing federal regulation would work if given enough time. "Stay the course" was his campaign slogan. Reagan pointed out that the inflation rate had declined to about 5 per cent a year and that bank interest rates were falling.

In foreign affairs, the United States relations with its European allies, Israel, Latin America, and the Soviet Union were strained in 1982 for a variety of reasons. The President angered Western Europe when on June 18 he applied trade sanctions against companies in France, West Germany, Italy, and Great Britain that were supplying components and technology to the Soviet Union to help build a natural gas pipeline from Siberia to Europe. Reagan lifted the sanctions on November 13, however, saying that the Europeans had pledged new, more restrictive trade rules to prevent the Soviets from getting advanced technology with military uses.

The long-standing good will between the United States and Israel was strained by the Israeli invasion of Lebanon in June, followed by the bombing of civilian areas in Beirut. Reagan at one point telephoned Israeli Prime Minister Menachem Begin to protest Israeli military actions in Lebanon.

When the President sided with Britain in its war with Argentina over the Falkland Islands, Latin American leaders criticized the United States. Relations with the Soviet Union were notable for a lack of progress on arms control.

Cabinet-Level Changes. For the most part, Reagan's Cabinet and White House teams remained intact through 1982. The President did replace his national security adviser, Richard V. Allen, who had become a source of controversy after it was learned that he had accepted gifts and maintained contact with former business clients. Although cleared of misconduct, Allen resigned on January 4. He was succeeded by William P. Clark, a longtime friend of Reagan's.

In a more important change, Reagan selected George P. Shultz, president of the Bechtel Group of companies, an international construction and

President Ronald Reagan discusses his economic policies with an eighth-grade civics class on April 15 at St. Peter's School in Geneva, Ill.

engineering firm, to be secretary of state after tl June 25 resignation of Alexander M. Haig, Jr from the top diplomatic post. Secretary of Energ James B. Edwards also left the Administration ii November to return to private life. The Presiden selected Donald P. Hodel, undersecretary of the Department of the Interior, to take over from Edwards. On December 28, Secretary of Transportation Andrew L. (Drew) Lewis, Jr., said he was resigning as of Feb. 1, 1983. See CABINET, UNITED STATES; HODEL, DONALD P.; SHULTZ, GEORGE P.

The Sagging Economy. It was the economy, however, that dominated Reagan's second year in office. The most prolonged and severe recession since the Great Depression of the 1930s frustrated the President's hopes of restoring prosperity without inflation. In January, he said the recession would soon go away. His State of the Union message to Congress on January 26 referred only briefly to the decline that had raised unemployment to 8.9 per cent by the start of the year. Reagan devoted most of his address to a proposed "new federalism" plan that would transfer responsibility for welfare payments and food stamps to the states and shift the financing of Medicaid, a health program for the poor, to federal sources. In addition, Reagan proposed the turnover of about 40 other federal programs to the states, along with a federal trust fund to help them pay the bills.

Record Deficits. The President ran into conflict with Congress when he submitted his budget for the 1983 fiscal year on February 6, projecting deficits of nearly $350 billion over three years and giving up on his hope of balancing the budget in his four-year term.

For fiscal 1983, Reagan proposed spending of $757.6 billion with a deficit of $91.5 billion. For a while, he refused to consider modifications, saying the spending plan was a "line drawn in the dirt" to divide the Administration's opponents from its supporters. As for increasing taxes to lower deficits, the President was adamant. "Raising taxes won't balance the budget," he said.

Eventually, however, as his budget went nowhere in either the Senate or the House of Representatives, Reagan changed his mind. With Senate Republicans taking the lead, the President went along with a three-year $98.3-billion tax increase in August. Even so, as the sagging economy reduced federal revenues and added to spending for jobless benefits and welfare payments, the deficit estimates kept rising. By year's end, the Office of Management and Budget was forecasting red-ink spending of $175 billion or more for fiscal year 1983. In the preceding 12-month period, which ended Sept. 30, 1982, the deficit was a record $110.7 billion, compared with the previous record of $66.4 billion in fiscal year 1976.

Reagan becomes the first U.S. President to address both houses of Britain's Parliament when he speaks in London's Palace of Westminster on June 8.

Although Reagan presided over the largest deficits in U.S. history, he went to Capitol Hill on July 19 to endorse a proposed constitutional amendment that generally would require adoption of a balanced budget unless 60 per cent of both the Senate and House agreed to waive the rule. The Senate passed the amendment on August 4 by a vote of 69 to 31, but it fell 46 votes short of passage in the House on October 1. See CONSTITUTION OF THE UNITED STATES.

The economy worsened throughout the year, with unemployment climbing to 10.4 per cent on the eve of the November 2 elections, adding to Republican losses in House races. The jobless rate reached 10.8 per cent in December.

In September, Congress overrode Reagan's veto of a $14.1-billion special appropriations bill—the first time that the House and Senate were able to muster two-thirds majorities to pass a bill into law over Reagan's protest. It may have signaled the end of one of the longest presidential honeymoons in history.

Foreign Relations. The bleak economic picture overshadowed other events during Reagan's second year, though the President attempted fresh starts in other fields. He proposed a major new policy in the Middle East on September 1, suggesting self-government by Palestinians in the Israeli-controlled West Bank and Gaza Strip, in association with Jordan. He stopped short of advocating an independent Palestinian state. Reagan also urged a halt to Israeli settlement of those two areas. Israel rejected the plan, however, contending it would lead to destruction of the Jewish state.

Reagan continued his hard-line approach toward the Soviet Union but took a more conciliatory attitude toward the People's Republic of China, promising a gradual reduction in arms sales to Taiwan if China agreed to use peaceful means to reunite that island with the mainland.

In a speech on May 9 at his alma mater, Eureka College in Eureka, Ill., the President proposed that the Soviet Union and the United States cut their nuclear missile warheads by at least one-third. His suggestion marked a tentative beginning for Strategic Arms Reduction Talks, or START, to replace SALT I and II, the Strategic Arms Limitation Talks. But Reagan was the first President in 20 years to decide against seeking renewed negotiations on a comprehensive nuclear test ban treaty. The President contended on March 31 that the Soviets had a "definite margin of superiority" over the United States in nuclear weapons, but many senators and other authorities on nuclear arms disputed his view. Reagan's invitation to Soviet leader Leonid I. Brezhnev for a meeting in June was spurned by the Kremlin leader.

President Ronald Reagan gives the first of a series of radio broadcasts on August 28 from his ranch near Santa Barbara, Calif.

In another foreign policy move, Reagan proposed in February a Caribbean Basin plan to provide trade and investment incentives to develop that region. It would give an additional $350 million in economic aid for the Caribbean area, which the President declared was vital to U.S. strategic and business interests. Congress passed the aid portion of the plan in September but did not complete work on the trade and investment provisions before adjourning.

Domestic Policies. On the domestic front, there was surprisingly little movement in Congress to pass antirecession legislation. The President and Democratic leaders, however, both claimed credit for a $3.8-billion job-training bill designed to provide work skills to economically disadvantaged young people, victims of the highest jobless rates. The bill, passed in October, stipulated that 70 per cent of the funds would go toward actual training, as opposed to stipends for participants, which Reagan had criticized as wasteful.

After the election, the President reversed himself again on taxes in November, when he came out in favor of a 5-cent-per-gallon (3.8 liters) increase in gasoline taxes to provide $5.5 billion a year for repairs to highways and bridges, along with added funds for mass transit. Congress passed the tax increase on December 23, and Reagan approved it on Jan. 6, 1983. The measure would create an estimated 320,000 jobs, but the President insisted that it was not a quick fix for the unemployment crisis. Earlier, Reagan had said he would not be pushing for any more tax increases unless there was a "palace coup or I'm overthrown."

On another election issue, Reagan seemed out of step with voters. He strongly opposed a U.S.-Soviet freeze on nuclear weapons production, arguing that it would benefit the Soviets because, he insisted, they have an edge in nuclear arms. The President also suggested that Soviet agents were trying to promote the freeze movement in the United States. In the November 2 balloting, however, voters in eight states—and in such major cities as Chicago, Philadelphia, Denver, and Washington, D.C.—approved pro-freeze initiatives. In the House of Representatives, a freeze resolution was defeated by only two votes.

The President generally got his way in Congress on the issue of military spending, with one major defeat. His proposed defense budget figure of $215.9 billion was shaved by just $7 billion, and the lawmakers approved most of the weapons systems he requested, including initial production of the controversial MX missile. The President announced in November that he would request funds for a so-called dense-pack siting of the MX, with 100 missiles placed in silos in a long, narrow, 20-square-mile (52-square-kilometer) area in Wyoming.

At Reagan's request, Congress convened on November 29 for a lame-duck session to consider at least 10 appropriations bills that had not been passed during the regular session, which ended on October 1. The President criticized the House and Senate for approving stopgap financing measures, saying it was "bad economics and bad management" to run the government that way.

On December 20, both houses of Congress passed an emergency spending bill that included $209 billion for defense. Although the legislators refused to approve $988 million that Reagan had requested for production of the first five MX missiles, they appropriated $2.5 billion for continued research on the weapon, including the manufacture of as many as 20 test missiles. Reagan signed the spending bill, which was to finance the federal government through September 1983, on December 21.

For Reagan, 1982 may have marked a low point in his presidency, since his job rating in public-opinion polls dipped as dramatically as the country's economic growth rate. After a year like that, it seemed that he and the economy had nowhere to go but up. William J. Eaton

See also CONGRESS OF THE UNITED STATES; REAGAN, RONALD WILSON; UNITED STATES, GOVERNMENT OF THE. In WORLD BOOK, see PRESIDENT OF THE UNITED STATES.

PRINCE EDWARD ISLAND, Canada's smallest province, with only 85,000 eligible voters, re-elected a Progressive Conservative (PC) government on Feb. 27, 1982. James Lee, 45, who had succeeded as premier on Nov. 17, 1981, after Angus MacLean's retirement, won support in his own right as his party won 22 seats in the legislature to 10 for the Liberals.

A Serious Problem for his government was the high cost of electricity—the highest in Canada—produced almost entirely from oil- and coal-fired plants. The government ordered an inquiry into the operation of the private power utility serving the island in March 1982, after rates had increased 57 per cent over six months. The previous PC administration had turned down a plan to bring nuclear power from New Brunswick's Point Lepreau generating station. Lee stayed with this decision but proposed that the province buy conventional power from Quebec via a corridor through New Brunswick.

The island's economy suffered a heavy blow on October 15 when a large slaughterhouse and meat-processing plant in Charlottetown received a year's notice of closure. About 225 jobs would be lost, a large number for a city of only about 15,000 people. David M. L. Farr

See also CANADA. In WORLD BOOK, see PRINCE EDWARD ISLAND.

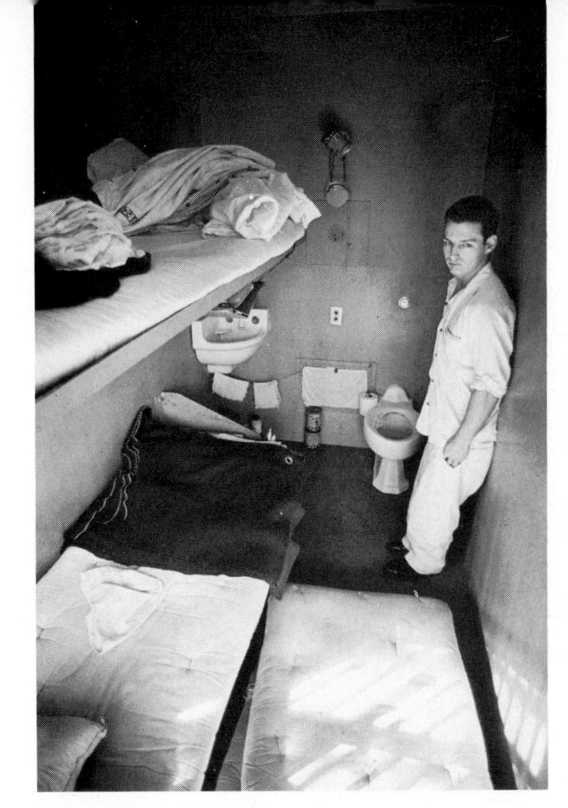

A convict stands in a three-man cell in a Texas prison. Texas is one of 35 states under court order to relieve prison crowding.

PRISON. The population of prisons and jails in the United States grew at a record 14.3 per cent rate in the first half of 1982, further aggravating an already severe overcrowding situation nationwide. A survey by the Bureau of Justice Statistics, a division of the U.S. Department of Justice, found that 394,380 inmates were housed in state and federal prisons at midyear, 25,608 more than at the end of 1981. The bureau attributed the increase to stronger sentencing laws.

Forty-seven states reported a rise in their prison populations. The bureau's survey did not include the approximately 160,000 persons held in local jails, many of which were also reported to be filled beyond their normal capacity because of backup from state facilities. At year-end, 35 states were under some type of court order to relieve overcrowding in their penal institutions.

Death Row. In April, 1,009 men and women were on death rows in 31 states. It was the first time since 1976, when the Supreme Court of the United States reinstated capital punishment laws, that more than 1,000 inmates were awaiting execution in American prisons.

In a 5 to 4 reversal of a Florida decision, the Supreme Court on July 2 ruled that an accomplice to a murder who "did not kill or intend to kill" cannot be executed. However, it was estimated that fewer than 10 death row inmates throughout the United States would be affected by the ruling.

Frank J. Coppola, 38, was executed in the electric chair at the Richmond, Va., state penitentiary on August 10. Coppola, convicted in the 1978 killing of a young woman, was the fifth convict put to death in the United States since 1976.

On December 7, Charles Brooks, Jr.—a convicted murderer on death row in the state prison in Huntsville, Tex.—was executed by an injection of a lethal dose of anesthetics. It was the first such execution in the United States.

Prison Violence. Violence continued to plague overcrowded penal facilities. On February 8, two black prisoners were killed and two others seriously wounded in racial conflict at Brushy Mountain Penitentiary in Petros, Tenn. Other serious racially inspired riots were reported during the year at prisons in Savannah, Ga.; Reidsville, Ga.; Englewood, Colo.; Folsom, Calif.; and at the California State Prison at San Quentin.

In what was called the worst prison incident in Canadian history, three guards were killed and two inmates committed suicide to avoid recapture after a riot on July 25 at Archambault Institution in Anne-des-Plaines, Que. David C. Beckwith

In WORLD BOOK, see PRISON.

PRIZES. See AWARDS AND PRIZES; CANADIAN LIBRARY ASSOCIATION; CANADIAN LITERATURE; NOBEL PRIZES.

PROTESTANTISM

Discussions of merging dominated several Protestant church conventions in the United States in 1982 after some years of quiet on the subject. During simultaneous General Assembly meetings in June, the nation's two largest Presbyterian bodies—the largely southern Presbyterian Church in the United States (PCUS) and the predominantly northern United Presbyterian Church in the U.S.A. (UPUSA)—voted overwhelmingly to reunite. Their division dated from 1861, just after the start of the Civil War. Regional differences had long since healed, but some UPUSA leaders, particularly feminists, worried about the slow pace of change in the PCUS on issues of concern to them. On the other hand, some PCUS conservatives felt that UPUSA was too liberal in theology. The merger would take place in June 1983, if ratified by three-fourths of the church councils in the South and two-thirds in the North.

Three Lutheran Churches also took decisive steps in 1982 toward forming a new, united church. The Lutheran Church in America (LCA), which has its largest constituency in the East; the American Lutheran Church (ALC), strong in the upper Midwest; and the much smaller Association of Evangelical Lutheran Churches (AELC) voted for the merger at their conventions in September. The new church would bring together two-thirds of American Lutherans—about 5½ million people—and would become the third largest Protestant denomination, after the Southern Baptist Convention and the United Methodist Church. A commission was established to write a constitution on which the three churches were to vote in 1987.

The AELC had issued the call for the three to join forces after it split from the conservative Lutheran Church—Missouri Synod in 1976. The Missouri Synod as well as the smaller Wisconsin Evangelical Lutheran Synod were not part of the new Lutheran body. The holdouts feared liberal tendencies in the three merging denominations and disapproved of some of their ecumenical ties.

One of these ties was greatly strengthened in 1982. The LCA, ALC, and AELC resolved at their 1982 conventions to share Eucharist on an interim basis with the Episcopal Church. The Episcopalians reciprocated during their September meeting in New Orleans. Lutherans and Episcopalians differ significantly over practice and doctrine. But in their September actions, they made clear that they formally recognized major signs of the church in each other. They also agreed that Lutheran and Episcopalian clergy could use the rites of either church in joint celebration of the Eucharist and that members of both churches could receive Communion at either church in the services sanctioned by the agreement.

Archbishop of Canterbury Robert Runcie and Pope John Paul II pray in Canterbury Cathedral during the pope's spring visit to Britain.

A Change in Leadership occurred in the National Baptist Convention USA, Inc., an organization of about 5.5 million black Baptists. Joseph H. Jackson, a Chicago pastor and a critic of most features of progressive black movements, had held control for almost 30 years. He was defeated in September at the national convention by Theodore J. Jemison, a minister from Baton Rouge, La. Jemison was the candidate of younger, progressive black leaders who organized carefully to bring about Jackson's defeat by a 3 to 1 majority.

The Southern Baptist Convention (SBC), the largest Protestant group in the United States, had witnessed intense struggles between fundamentalists and moderates in recent years. At the SBC national meeting in New Orleans in June, the assembled delegates seemed reluctant to push for decisive but possibly divisive resolutions of issues. The conservative forces remained clearly in command. But moderates had taken some lessons in counterorganizing and stating their case and were able to prevent purges of theological schools and administrative arms of the SBC. According to archconservatives, these had been infiltrated or taken over by theological liberals. The newly elected SBC president, James T. Draper, a minister from Euless, Tex., and a staunch traditionalist, emphasized that he would not back purges but would try instead to keep the factions together.

The SBC meeting strongly endorsed a proposal for an amendment to the Constitution of the United States that would permit prayer in public schools. The endorsement was opposed by SBC officials in charge of church-state relations and public affairs. They argued that the proposed school prayer amendment denied more than 250 years of Baptist history, which had steadfastly opposed the entry of government into the religious sphere and the movement of formal religion into the governmental sphere. Supporters of the amendment argued that the United States was becoming too godless and that extraordinary measures, which the proposed amendment symbolized, were needed to bring the nation back to God.

Bringing America Back to God had also been considered the major goal of the largely Protestant coalition often called the New Christian Right. The coalition, which became particularly visible during the 1980 election campaigns, included political action groups such as the Moral Majority, Religious Roundtable, and Christian Voice. Un-

Religious leaders including evangelist Billy Graham, right, attend services at Moscow's Russian Orthodox Patriarchal Cathedral on May 9.

der the leadership of television evangelists, these organizations advocated a "social agenda" that included proposals for constitutional amendments against abortion and in favor of school prayer.

Senator Jesse A. Helms (R., N.C.) led social agenda battles in Congress in 1982. He introduced the anti-abortion and voluntary school prayer issues as legislative measures that would restrict the jurisdiction of the Supreme Court of the United States over these issues, rather than as constitutional amendments. Senate debate therefore centered on constitutional questions. President Ronald Reagan backed the Helms measures, but the Protestant Right claimed that his support was late and half-hearted. Filibusters by liberal senators succeeded in tabling the measures in September. Some liberal senators felt that the defeats "broke the back" of the New Christian Right in Congress, but others expected more successful legislative endeavors in the future.

Support for Nuclear Disarmament appeared on the agendas of more liberal Protestant groups in 1982. Much of the leadership on this issue came from Roman Catholic bishops, but they found eager allies in the Protestant peace movements. Disarmament was debated in countless congregations and at numerous national conventions.

The peace cause was also debated in other forums. Enten Eller, a young member of the Church of the Brethren, refused to register for the military draft on grounds of conscience. The court, while expressing respect for his integrity, ruled in August that Eller was guilty of violating the law. On December 8, Eller was ordered to perform two years of unpaid work — alternate service — at a federal institution.

Billy Graham Visits Russia. During a conference on nuclear disarmament in Moscow in May, U.S. evangelist Billy Graham made statements to reporters designed to appear friendly to the Russians. Perhaps with an eye on future evangelistic work in Russia, Graham played down religious persecution in the officially atheistic nation. Graham's remarks provoked vehement criticism from Russian Pentecostals and members of other religious groups who have complained of persecution by the Soviet government. Many Americans also resented Graham's comparison of restrictions on religion in Russia with the fact that Americans are not "free" to pray in public schools.

In time, however, it became clear that some of Graham's remarks had been taken out of context or distorted. The Billy Graham Evangelistic Association reported that mail ran 3 to 1 in support of Graham. Martin E. Marty

See also RELIGION. In WORLD BOOK, see PROTESTANTISM and articles on Protestant denominations.

PSYCHOLOGY. There was "good news and bad news" for victims of common addictions in 1982. Dieters and cigarette smokers could take heart from the research that psychologist Stanley Schachter, of Columbia University in New York City, reported in the April 1982 issue of *American Psychologist*. Schachter reported that success in losing weight and in quitting cigarette smoking may be more common than was believed.

Previous studies had produced discouraging results. Schachter cited one study showing that 98 of 100 obese people in a weight-loss program later regained their weight. Similarly, numerous studies of subjects who tried to quit cigarette smoking showed that more than 80 per cent became addicted again within a year.

These studies are flawed, said Schachter. One problem is that most subjects in addiction research are people who tried unsuccessfully to curb their habits by themselves. They then seek professional help and end up as research subjects. A second flaw is that most studies concentrate on one attempt to quit. Schachter said that many addicted people actually make repeated attempts.

To gather less-biased data, Schachter interviewed two groups of people who might not ordinarily turn up in formal studies of addictive behavior: townspeople in Amagansett, N.Y., and his colleagues in Columbia's Psychology Department.

He found that 62.5 per cent of those with a history of obesity had succeeded in losing substantial amounts of weight. Of the heavy smokers who tried to give up cigarettes, 65.3 per cent were successful, though often not on the first try.

Alcoholics who thought they could become "social drinkers" had less to cheer about in 1982. A widely publicized study supporting that idea was challenged by a team of three researchers: Mary L. Pendery of the San Diego (Calif.) Veterans Administration Medical Center; Irving M. Maltzman of the Department of Psychology at the University of California, Los Angeles (UCLA); and L. Jolyon West of the Department of Psychiatry and Biobehavioral Science at the UCLA School of Medicine. Their article appeared in the July 9 issue of *Science*.

Pendery and her colleagues performed a detailed 10-year follow-up of patients in a controversial "controlled drinking" experiment. These patients had been seriously ill alcoholics when first admitted to Patton State Hospital in San Bernardino, Calif., in 1970 and 1971. After being detoxified, they were given training in moderate "social drinking" by a husband-and-wife team of behavioral psychologists, Mark B. Sobell and Linda C. Sobell. The patients were taught to order mixed rather than straight drinks to moderate the level of alcohol in their bloodstream. They also watched videotapes of their own drunken and nondrunken behavior, and they were trained to make intelligent decisions about when to stop drinking.

A widely cited follow-up study resulted in another research team reporting in 1978 that half of these patients were "100 per cent free" of alcohol-related problems three years after the Sobell treatment—a much better record than that of a control group of former Patton patients. But Pendery and her colleagues disagreed with this conclusion after a 10-year follow-up that included examination of hospital and police records. They found that even at the time of the three-year follow-up, most of the patients in the controlled-drinking group were having severe alcohol-related problems. One patient in the three-year follow-up spent time in a jail and two hospitals because of his behavior while intoxicated. Toward the end of the third year, he was arrested for drunk driving. Nevertheless, he was rated "functioning well 100 per cent of the days in the year" in the 1978 study.

The same pattern was repeated with many other controlled-drinking patients. Only one was truly free of alcoholism 10 years after the study. He was the only one of the original patients who did not show withdrawal symptoms when first admitted to Patton State Hospital, so he might never have been genuinely addicted. Pendery and her group concluded that there is "no evidence" that confirmed alcoholics can learn to engage safely in controlled drinking.

Heroin Addiction was the focus of a surprising Canadian study. Shepard Siegel of the Department of Psychology at McMaster University in Hamilton, Ont., and three other researchers said in the April 23 issue of *Science* that environmental cues are linked to death from heroin overdose.

One of the puzzles about heroin addiction is why an addict may die of a dose that is below levels tolerated on other occasions. Siegel and his colleagues investigated the phenomenon by injecting rats with heroin daily and examining circumstances in which they were likely to die of an overdose. The researchers found that if rats were given increasing doses of heroin in the same place every day—either the rat colony or a room with constant white noise to erase all distracting sounds—their bodies apparently learned to anticipate the drug effects and compensate for them. These rats were less likely to die of an overdose.

However, if a rat was injected in an environment where it had never before received heroin, it was likely to die, even if the dosage was below levels previously tolerated. If the same thing holds true for human beings, it may explain the sudden, unexpected deaths of heroin addicts who depart from their routine and take the drug in an unfamiliar setting. Russell A. Dewey

In WORLD BOOK, see DRUG ABUSE; DRUG ADDICTION; PSYCHOLOGY.

PUBLIC HEALTH officials almost succeeded in meeting their goal of eliminating measles in the United States by Oct. 1, 1982. The 1,284 cases reported during the first 39 weeks of the year were less than 3 per cent of the number of cases reported during the same period in 1977. In the fall of 1982, however, there were outbreaks of measles in Texas and Florida. The nationwide campaign to "make measles a memory" began in October 1978 with a stepped-up effort to immunize all U.S. children.

X-Ray Guidelines. In September, the Council of the American College of Radiology called for a curb on unnecessary chest X rays. The council recommended that routine chest X rays not be given to pregnant patients, new employees undergoing health examinations, or hospital patients without any symptoms or signs of respiratory problems. The council noted that the information gained from such X rays did not justify the risks of radiation exposure and the expense of performing the test.

The council in September also adopted guidelines for *mammography* (X-ray examination of the breast). The guidelines recommended a "baseline" mammogram for all women at age 40, periodic mammograms for screening until age 50, and annual screening mammograms and physical examinations thereafter. They also recommended that all women be taught breast self-examination by age 20 and have an annual physical examination of the breasts after age 35.

The results of a mammography study sponsored by the American Cancer Society (ACS) and involving more than 280,000 U.S. women were reported in July. Mammography was found to be the most effective noninvasive method of diagnosing small breast cancers that could not yet be felt.

Cancer Deaths. In its 1982 edition of *Cancer Facts and Figures,* the ACS estimated that lung cancer would account for 25 per cent of all cancer deaths in 1981 — a sharp rise from 8.7 per cent a generation ago. The ACS estimated that 9,000 more U.S. citizens would die of cancer in 1982 than in 1981. Two-thirds of these additional deaths would be directly attributable to lung cancer (see HEALTH AND DISEASE).

In February, U.S. Surgeon General C. Everett Koop released a new federal report on smoking. It added bladder, kidney, and pancreatic cancers to the list of cancers associated with cigarette use.

Recession Stress. Rising unemployment emerged as a major threat to the well-being of millions of Americans in 1982. The stress caused by unemployment was associated with increases in suicide, homicide, child abuse, depression, liver cirrhosis, heart disease, kidney disorders, and other maladies. In addition, because their insurance and other health benefits were cut off after they became unemployed, many of the jobless did not seek immediate care for physical or psychological problems. Therefore, illnesses that could be easily treated in early stages became potential serious health risks.

Less Salt? At a conference on salt labeling in Washington, D.C., in March, Commissioner Arthur Hull Hayes, Jr., of the U.S. Food and Drug Administration (FDA) estimated that by the end of 1982 one-third to one-half of all canned, processed, and packaged foods monitored by the FDA would have labels revealing their sodium content. Hayes has spearheaded a government effort to increase awareness of potential high blood pressure risks from salt overuse and to encourage everyone to restrict salt intake.

However, the benefits of a low-salt diet were challenged by some high blood pressure experts at a conference in Arlington, Va., in September. Although all agreed that hypertensives should restrict salt intake, the opponents of a low-salt diet for normal individuals pointed out that there is no conclusive evidence that sodium causes high blood pressure, and they claimed that restricting sodium in normal people could throw other minerals out of balance. These scientists called the government's efforts "misguided." Dianne Hales

See also DRUGS; MEDICINE. In WORLD BOOK, see PUBLIC HEALTH.

PUBLISHING. Book sales reflected the shaky economy of the United States as publishers recorded a loss of 2.9 per cent in unit sales to consumers during the first six months of 1982. However, bookstores continued to outpace all other United States retailing concerns by healthy margins. In 1981, U.S. publishers registered net sales of $7.4 billion from the sale of 1.9 billion books.

Courts and Laws. On June 25, the Supreme Court of the United States ordered a lower court to decide whether the Island Trees Board of Education on Long Island, N.Y., violated the First Amendment rights of students by removing books from school libraries. In August, the board decided to restore the books, including Kurt Vonnegut, Jr.'s *Slaughterhouse-Five* (1969). However, the board ordered librarians to notify the parents of children who checked out the books.

In the spring, Congress approved a bill setting penalties for publishing the names of U.S. undercover agents. A court could fine a publisher or an author up to $15,000 and impose a prison sentence of up to three years for this infraction. In June, Congress extended for four years the manufacturing clause of the revised Copyright Act. According to this clause, most books that U.S. authors write in English must be printed and bound in the United States or Canada in order to receive the

Library of America began publishing complete, compact reissues of American classics in 1982. Each volume contains more than 1,300 pages.

full protection of the act. President Ronald Reagan vetoed the extension on July 8, but Congress overrode the veto on July 13.

Changing Hands. Fawcett Publications, formerly one of the top three paperback publishers in the country, announced in February that it would cease to exist as a company and would become an imprint of Ballantine Books when CBS Inc. transferred "substantially all of its assets" to Random House, Incorporated. In May, Putnam Publishing Group, a subsidiary of MCA, Incorporated, agreed in principle to buy Grosset & Dunlap from Filmways, Incorporated. One month later, Putnam and another MCA subsidiary, Berkley/Jove Publishing Group, agreed in principle to buy the book-publishing operations of Playboy Enterprises for an undisclosed sum. MCA completed the purchase in July.

During one week in January, the *Publishers Weekly* best-seller list featured three books on Rubik's Cube and six books on cats, including three by Garfield creator Jim Davis, and the *Second Official I Hate Cats Book* by Skip Morrow. The books consumers made into best sellers during the year included Robert Ludlum's *The Parsifal Mosaic* and *Jane Fonda's Workout Book*. Celeste Huenergard

See also CANADIAN LITERATURE; LITERATURE; MAGAZINE; NEWSPAPER; POETRY. In WORLD BOOK, see BOOK; PUBLISHING.

PUERTO RICO experienced a steady economic downturn in 1982. Conditions on the island, which belongs to the United States, approximated those of a recession.

On January 12, Governor Carlos Romero Barceló and other top Puerto Rican officials met with U.S. President Ronald Reagan in Washington, D.C. The President pledged his support for statehood for Puerto Rico "should the people of that island choose it in a free and democratic election." Under its status as a commonwealth, the island gets important tax benefits. Statehood would make it eligible for federal revenue-sharing programs and help Puerto Rico deal with high unemployment, which reached 30 per cent in 1982.

Much of the island's economic slide was tied to the recession in the United States. Many Puerto Rican factories shut down because American investors lost interest in the island, where wages were higher than elsewhere in the Caribbean. Tourism from the United States slackened. Puerto Rico was also hit hard by federal budget cuts, especially in welfare programs.

In September, the United States helped to defeat a United Nations resolution to have Puerto Rico declared a "colony." Nathan A. Haverstock

See also LATIN AMERICA (Facts in Brief Table). In WORLD BOOK, see PUERTO RICO.

PULITZER PRIZES. See AWARDS AND PRIZES.

QUEBEC. Although the province was beset by economic problems, Prime Minister René Lévesque won an overwhelming vote of confidence from his Parti Québécois (PQ) in an internal referendum in February 1982. The balloting followed a stormy party convention in December 1981 at which Lévesque's moderate position on the possibility of Quebec's future independence from Canada was overruled. He threatened to resign unless his stand was upheld by the party at large. About half the party's 300,000 members mailed in ballots, 95 per cent of them supporting Lévesque.

In two by-elections on April 6, the Liberal Party won two seats. The results gave the Liberals 43 seats in the 122-seat National Assembly and the PQ 79. In June, a PQ member left the party but remained in the Assembly as an Independent.

After the Liberal Party's disastrous defeat in the provincial election in April 1981, Claude Ryan, its leader since 1978, resigned as of Aug. 31, 1982. Gerard D. Lévesque (no relation to the prime minister) was chosen as interim party leader.

Provincial Problems. Neither party's leader was pleased with Canada's new Constitution. In fact, Quebec was the only province to refuse to endorse it, and Lévesque stayed away from the proclamation ceremony (see CANADA [Close-Up]). But that was only one of many problems the province faced

Guards at Archambault Institute, a federal prison near Montreal, stand watch again in the control room after a bloody riot in July.

in 1982. Another was the consequences of its generous treatment of its 350,000 public servants. In 1979, they had been granted contracts that provided the highest salaries in North America. Finance Minister Jacques Parizeau's May 25, 1982, budget projected public spending of $22.6 billion (Canadian dollars; $1 = U.S. 81 cents as of Dec. 31, 1982) but revenues of only $19.6 billion. The deficit would increase Quebec's debt to $15 billion and weaken its credit rating. Therefore, Parizeau announced a detailed wage freeze for 1983 for most of the government's employees. Pension benefits for civil servants would be reduced, state dental programs cut back, and highway tolls increased by 50 per cent.

An Energy Agreement worth $6 billion to the province was signed on March 19 by Hydro-Québec, the government-owned electricity supplier, and the New York State Power Authority. Scheduled to transmit 111 billion kilowatt hours of electricity southward for 13 years beginning in 1984, the agreement represented a 50 per cent increase in the amount of power Quebec had been selling New York. David M. L. Farr

In WORLD BOOK, see QUEBEC.

RACING. See AUTOMOBILE RACING; BOATING; HORSE RACING; ICE SKATING; SKIING; SPORTS; SWIMMING; TRACK AND FIELD.

RADIO. FM radio's steady gain in popularity and AM radio's steady decline continued in the United States during 1982. Some estimates put FM's share of the 1982 radio audience as high as 61 per cent. With a signal that can be received in stereophonic sound, FM has proved vastly superior to AM as a source of music. AM stations have therefore been scrambling for alternative programming, such as news and talk shows, to substitute for music and thus hold on to a share of radio listeners.

The Federal Communications Commission (FCC) gave the AM stations new hope in March 1982 when it authorized the broadcasting of AM-stereo signals. However, the FCC declined to specify what kind of technical equipment was to be used, leaving broadcasters with no clear-cut route to follow. Several different AM-stereo systems are available, and the transmission equipment of one system may not be compatible with another system's receiver. Fearful of choosing a system that would not become the standard, most broadcasters did nothing.

Most AM stations continued during 1982 to drift along old routes, ranging from music to news and talk. There was, however, one hot new format, consisting primarily of music from the 1930s, 1940s, and 1950s. At more than 100 AM stations across the United States, the vintage sound be-

Durable comedians Bob and Ray—Bob Elliott, left, and Ray Goulding—tape one of eight shows broadcast in the fall by American public radio stations.

came highly successful and was continuing to spread as 1982 ended.

National Public Radio, in an effort to find new sources of funding, announced plans in June to begin a service that would use the sidebands of public stations' FM signals for commercial purposes. Those purposes — as proposed to the FCC, whose approval is necessary — might range from providing private networks for professional groups to piping music into offices. Disheartened by the proposal were more than 100 charitable radio reading services. Those services use FM sidebands free of charge to read newspapers and other publications to visually handicapped persons.

Radio Martí. While that controversy simmered, another flared up on August 30 when a government-owned radio station in Cuba began broadcasting radio signals that jammed those of more than 20 U.S. stations, some as distant as Des Moines, Iowa, and Salt Lake City, Utah. The Cuban broadcasts, a mixture of music and propaganda messages, came in apparent retaliation for the U.S. plan to establish Radio Martí to beam political broadcasts into Cuba. Legislation to establish Radio Martí, which was named after the Cuban hero José Martí, was approved by the U.S. House of Representatives but died when the 97th Congress adjourned at year-end. Ron Alridge

In WORLD BOOK, see RADIO.

RAILROAD companies in the United States endured a sharp drop in profits in 1982 amid the economic slump but fared much better than during previous recessions. The Association of American Railroads reported that United States railroad systems earned $747 million in the first nine months of 1982, off 49 per cent from a profit of $1.45 billion through September 1981. Operating revenues were $21 billion, down 9 per cent.

Deregulation Benefits. Railroads continued to take advantage of a 1980 law that deregulated U.S. railroads. In some cases, railroads cut their rates to keep traffic. In other instances, they increased their charges for hauling certain goods. Volume rose in two deregulated categories — piggyback shipments and the transport of perishable commodities. The railroads hiked their general freight rate by 4.7 per cent on Jan. 1, 1982.

Strike. On July 7, the Brotherhood of Locomotive Engineers (BLE) set a strike deadline of July 11 in a dispute over work-rule concessions. President Ronald Reagan averted the strike by declaring a 60-day cooling-off period and appointed an emergency board to investigate the BLE dispute and a larger disagreement involving 12 other unions. The board recommended a wage increase of 28.8 per cent over 39 months for the union workers. All the unions except the BLE agreed to this recommendation. After the cooling-off period

A strike by the Brotherhood of Locomotive Engineers idled much of the United States railroad system for four days in September.

expired at midnight on September 18, 26,000 engineers struck. The Reagan Administration then asked Congress to pass a bill ending the strike. Congress complied on September 22.

Mergers. On September 13, the Interstate Commerce Commission (ICC) approved the merging of the Union Pacific, Missouri Pacific, and Western Pacific railroads. Other railroads fought the ruling in court. The ICC on March 25 approved a merger of the Norfolk and Western Railway and Southern Railway, forming the nation's third largest rail system. Consolidated Rail Corporation (Conrail), the government-owned line, showed a profit of $120 million in the first nine months of 1982, up from a gain of $13 million a year earlier, in spite of a 14 per cent decline in revenues.

Passenger Trains. The National Railroad Passenger Corporation (Amtrak) became more stable in 1982. Amtrak won favorable agreements with rail unions in May and October. The agreements boosted wages by 18.7 per cent over 39 months and changed work rules to increase efficiency. Amtrak ridership declined in 1982. Nevertheless, cost cutting and fare increases enabled Amtrak to trim its deficit, reversing years of climbing losses. The deficit in the fiscal year ending Sept. 30, 1982, was $550 million, down from $720 million the preceding year. Albert R. Karr

In WORLD BOOK, see RAILROAD.

REAGAN, RONALD WILSON (1911-), 40th President of the United States, continued to enjoy personal popularity in 1982, though Republican losses in the November 2 midterm election indicated public unease with some Administration policies. Reagan campaigned extensively, mostly in smaller cities and towns remote from centers of high unemployment. His slogan was "Stay the Course."

Fully recovered from a chest wound suffered in the March 1981 attempt on his life, Reagan enjoyed seemingly robust health at 71. After an April 1 checkup, his physicians reported that all tests were normal. Reagan's assailant, John W. Hinckley, Jr., was found not guilty by reason of insanity on June 21 at a jury trial in the District of Columbia. Hinckley was committed to a federal mental hospital (see COURTS AND LAWS [Close-Up]).

White House Changes. There were significant changes in Reagan's White House high command during the year. On January 4, Richard V. Allen resigned as assistant for national security affairs. He was succeeded by Deputy Secretary of State William P. Clark, a long-time Reagan associate. Because Clark reported directly to Reagan, rather than through Edwin Meese III, counselor to the President, Meese's role was diminished. James A. Baker III, White House chief of staff, came to be seen as the dominant figure in a triumvirate of

Taking a break from pressures of Washington, D.C., President Reagan and his wife, Nancy, relax at the lake on their California ranch in May.

Baker, Meese, and Michael K. Deaver, deputy chief of staff.

Reagan and his wife, Nancy, vacationed often, if briefly, at their 688-acre (278-hectare) ranch near Santa Barbara, Calif. In August, the President postponed for two weeks his longest planned ranch holiday. He remained in Washington, D.C., to lobby, successfully, for a three-year package of tax increases and spending cuts aimed at paring $115.8 billion from federal deficits.

For the first time since taking office, Reagan also vacationed outside the United States. On April 7, the Reagans began a five-day Caribbean holiday. To avert possible criticism for sunning in Barbados while unemployment lines lengthened in the still-frigid North, the President first stopped overnight in Jamaica to meet with Prime Minister Edward Seaga. In Barbados, he conferred with leaders of five eastern Caribbean nations.

California Home Sold. On January 29, the White House announced the sale of the Reagan home at Pacific Palisades, Calif. It had been on the market for a year. Neither the selling price nor the identity of the buyer was disclosed. The property's market value was put at $1.5 million.

The Reagans paid federal taxes on a 1981 income of $418,826, the White House announced on April 16. The couple's income tax bill was $164,291.

Having weathered a 1981 controversy over redecoration of the White House, the Reagans faced fresh criticism in January after a disclosure that Nancy Reagan had received free dresses from American fashion designers. The first lady said she had accepted the outfits to promote the American fashion industry. A month later, she said she would no longer accept such gifts.

Reagan Children Make News. Maureen Reagan, 41, Reagan's daughter by his first wife, Jane Wyman, sought the Republican nomination for U.S. senator from California. She ran fifth, with 5 per cent of the vote, in the June 8 primary.

On October 13, when the President made a televised address to the nation on economic problems, notably unemployment, his 24-year-old son, Ronald P. Reagan, stood in a New York City unemployment line. Temporarily laid off by the Joffrey II Dancers, young Reagan turned down an offer of family help and applied for $125 in weekly jobless benefits.

Later in October, Michael Reagan, 37, the President's adopted son from his first marriage, made headlines during a three-week private vacation in Great Britain with his wife and 4-year-old son. The attention of the British press was caught by the Reagans' entourage of 19 Secret Service agents.

Frank Cormier

See also PRESIDENT OF THE UNITED STATES. In WORLD BOOK, see REAGAN, RONALD WILSON.

RECORDINGS. Record-industry sales in the United States were seriously affected by the depressed economy in 1982, as they had been the year before. Sales totaled about $3.6 billion in 1981, down from the 1980 figure of $4 billion. The gloomy situation caused CBS Records to fire 300 people on Friday, Aug. 13, 1982, and to close 10 of its U.S. offices. Other companies also reduced their staffs.

The decline in sales of long-playing (LP) records also became evident in the number of albums that went gold—that is, sold 500,000 copies. Only 50 LP's went gold in the first half of 1982, down from 72 for the same period in 1981. This was the lowest half-year count since 47 albums went gold in 1971.

Despite the soft market, CBS released 250 LP's in its higher-priced CX system for enhancing sound quality. These included 75 popular and 25 classical titles and such big names as Johnny Cash, Ray Conniff, Miles Davis, and Bob Dylan.

The Single Disk changed in price and concept in 1982. Some stores raised their price for a two-song 45-rpm disk to between $1.69 and $1.99. CBS unveiled a one-sided, single-song 45 record that sold for under $1. It proved so successful that CBS brought out one-sided disks by such powerhouse names as Billy Joel and Teddy Pendergrass.

Some companies developed new kinds of audio

Rick Springfield won a Grammy as best male rock performer from the National Academy of Recording Arts and Sciences in 1982 for "Jessie's Girl."

cassettes. MCA and CBS combined two LP's on one cassette that retailed for $9.98 and $8.98, respectively. Some labels owned by Warner Communications introduced two cassettes for the price of one at $10.98.

This interest in taped products led to record-level sales of blank audiotapes. A Warner Communications home-taping study estimated that record companies lose $3 billion annually because of home dubbing.

Walt Disney Studios rerecorded the sound-track music for *Fantasia* (1940), the first Disney movie recorded in stereophonic sound. The sound track carefully matched Leopold Stokowski's original conducting of the music.

Medleys continued to fascinate record producers. The success of the album *Hooked on Classics* led to *Hooked on Swing*, a medley of early swing and jazz band hits. *Hooked on Country* by the Atlanta Pops followed.

Awards. Quincy Jones ran away with the Grammy Awards, bringing his lifetime total to 11. Jones, a pop-soul producer and arranger and former jazz band leader, won five Grammys in 1982, making him one of only seven artists to win that many in a single year. Leonard Feather and Eliot Tiegel

See also MUSIC, CLASSICAL; MUSIC, POPULAR. In WORLD BOOK, see PHONOGRAPH.

RED CROSS. See COMMUNITY ORGANIZATIONS.

RELIGION. In 1982, Americans had an excellent opportunity to assess the status of religion in the United States. A coalition of religious groups that included the Glenmary Research Center, a Roman Catholic agency, and the interdenominational National Council of Churches issued the joint report that they sponsor each decade.

The 1982 report, which reviewed trends in religion in the United States from 1971 to 1980, indicated that the nation had become more religiously diverse. Mormons remained strong in Utah and the Southwest, Baptists in the South, Methodists along the North-South border, and Lutherans in the upper Midwest, with Roman Catholics strong everywhere else. But population movements and evangelistic efforts had led to an increasing spread of faiths. The regional empires had declined somewhat in strength, and the influence of the dominant groups had extended beyond their historic regions.

Organized Religion experienced some loss of power during the decade, however powerful personal religious faith may have become. Some churches and synagogues increased their membership, but most did not keep pace with the growth of the population. Conservative evangelistic groups registered much of the gain and compensated for some losses in the mainline churches. The two largest Presbyterian bodies, for example,

U.S. Membership Reported for Religious Groups with 150,000 or More Members*

African Methodist Episcopal Church	2,210,000
African Methodist Episcopal Zion Church	1,134,176
American Baptist Association	225,000
American Baptist Churches in the U.S.A.	1,607,541
The American Lutheran Church	2,346,207
The Antiochian Orthodox Christian Archdiocese of North America	152,000
Armenian Church of America, Diocese of the (including Diocese of California)	450,000
Assemblies of God	1,788,394
Baptist Missionary Association of America	228,381
Christian and Missionary Alliance	195,042
Christian Church (Disciples of Christ)	1,173,135
Christian Churches and Churches of Christ	1,063,254
Christian Methodist Episcopal Church	786,707
Christian Reformed Church in North America	215,411
Church of God (Anderson, Ind.)	178,581
Church of God (Cleveland, Tenn.)	456,797
Church of God in Christ	3,709,661
Church of God in Christ, International	200,000
The Church of Jesus Christ of Latter-day Saints	3,490,000
Church of the Brethren	170,267
Church of the Nazarene	492,203
Churches of Christ	1,600,222
Community Churches, National Council of	190,000
Conservative Baptist Association of America	225,000
The Episcopal Church	2,767,440
Free Will Baptists	216,848
General Association of Regular Baptist Churches	300,839
Greek Orthodox Archdiocese of North and South America	1,950,000
Jehovah's Witnesses	588,503
Jews	5,921,829
Lutheran Church in America	2,921,829
The Lutheran Church-Missouri Synod	2,636,715
National Baptist Convention of America	2,688,799
National Baptist Convention, U.S.A., Inc.	5,500,000
National Primitive Baptist Convention	250,000
Orthodox Church in America	1,000,000
Polish National Catholic Church in America	282,411
Presbyterian Church in the United States	823,143
Progressive National Baptist Convention	521,692
Reformed Church in America	345,762
Reorganized Church of Jesus Christ of Latter Day Saints	190,087
The Roman Catholic Church	51,207,579
The Salvation Army	414,999
Seventh-day Adventists	588,536
Southern Baptist Convention	13,782,644
United Church of Christ	1,726,244
The United Methodist Church	9,519,407
United Pentecostal Church, International	465,000
The United Presbyterian Church in the U.S.A.	2,379,249
Wisconsin Evangelical Lutheran Synod	410,288

*Majority of the figures are for the years 1981 and 1982.
Source: National Council of Churches, *Yearbook of American and Canadian Churches* for 1983.

Sun Myung Moon marries more than 4,000 members of his Unification Church in a mass ceremony in New York City's Madison Square Garden on July 1.

lost 16.1 per cent and 9.5 per cent of their membership during the 1970s.

Worldwide Decline. Publication in 1982 of the massive *World Christian Encyclopedia,* edited by David B. Barrett, provided an opportunity to compare the scope of the world's largest religious group, Christianity, with other religions. Barrett noted a decline among all world religions. He estimated that throughout the world the number of believers in a religion had declined from 80.4 per cent of the population in 1970 to 79.2 per cent in 1980, but that their absolute number had increased in this period from 2.9 billion to 3.5 billion. Barrett pointed out that Africa's local traditional religions, which many observers had thought would disappear, persisted and, in some cases, even thrived. Practitioners of such religions, sometimes called shamanists, were expected to drop in number by only 7 million during the 20th century, from 117 million in 1900 to 110 million in the year 2000.

More provocative to the major religions than the survival of traditional local religions was the presence of new "secular quasi-religions," agnosticism and atheism, according to Barrett. In their various guises, these included secularism, scientific materialism, atheistic Communism, nationalism, Nazism, fascism, Maoism, liberal humanism, and numerous other pseudoreligions. In 1900, nonreligious cultures characterized only 0.2 per cent of the world's population, but by 1980 they had attracted 20.8 per cent and were gaining 8.5 million new converts each year.

Shinto, Japan's oldest surviving religion, has experienced a revival. Shinto shrines recently became popular on industrial properties. Executives of investment companies in the city of Osaka, for example, made monthly stops at a shrine at Osaka's securities exchange. The Sogo department store chain included a shrine in a new store for the use of its employees and customers. Shrine headquarters reported requests for 7,000 new shrines during 1981.

News of Religion from around the world often reaches the West as news of military moves by various factions. In 1982, most such reporting came from the Middle East, particularly Lebanon. There, Christian Phalangists, Muslims, Druses, Israeli Jews, and other sects and peoples fought or allied with one another. Doctrine was not at issue as in a conventional holy war. But religion reinforced old hatreds and made resolution of military issues difficult and, on the short pull, perhaps impossible. Martin E. Marty

See also EASTERN ORTHODOX CHURCHES; JEWS AND JUDAISM; MIDDLE EAST; PROTESTANTISM; ROMAN CATHOLIC CHURCH. In WORLD BOOK, see RELIGION and articles on religions.

REPUBLICAN PARTY fortunes suffered a setback in the 1982 midterm elections in the United States despite Republican President Ronald Reagan's active campaigning. Republicans, burdened by recession and high unemployment, dropped 26 seats in the House of Representatives in the November 2 voting, more than double the average loss for off-year elections since the end of World War II. They fought Democrats to a stand-off in Senate races, however, to preserve their 54 to 46 margin of control. At the state level, most GOP gains of recent years were wiped out. The Republicans had a net loss of seven governorships. The Democrats took control of 11 more legislative bodies, while Republicans gained only one.

Ten of 11 GOP senators won re-election, with Senator Harrison H. Schmitt (R., N. Mex.), who was beaten by New Mexico Attorney General Jeff Bingaman, the lone casualty. Only one Republican challenger toppled a Democratic senator in 19 contests. That was in Nevada, where Chic Hecht ousted Senator Howard W. Cannon.

In contests for open Senate seats, U.S. Representative Paul S. Trible, Jr., a Republican, won in Virginia; Democrat Frank R. Lautenberg, a wealthy businessman, beat GOP candidate Millicent Fenwick in New Jersey; and San Diego Republican Mayor Pete Wilson drubbed Democratic Governor Edmund G. Brown, Jr., in California.

House elections proved to be a minor disaster for the Republicans, with 26 GOP incumbents going down to defeat, compared with only 3 Democratic casualties. Moreover, Democrats did better than expected in newly created congressional districts in the Sun Belt states of the South and Southwest, winning 9 of 17 races there.

Governors Races. Republicans also lost control of statehouses in Alaska, Texas, Ohio, Michigan, Minnesota, Wisconsin, Nebraska, Nevada, and Arkansas. They scored a big triumph in California, however, where GOP Attorney General George Deukmejian defeated Los Angeles Democratic Mayor Tom Bradley. In New Hampshire, GOP contender John H. Sununu, a former state representative, unseated Democratic Governor Hugh J. Gallen in the only other Republican turnabout. In Illinois, GOP Governor James R. Thompson barely survived in an extremely close race against former Democratic Senator Adlai E. Stevenson III.

Laxalt Gets Party Post. The Republican Party underwent a major post-election change at national headquarters. At the President's urging, Senator Paul Laxalt (R., Nev.) was selected to fill the newly created post of general chairman of the Republican National Committee (RNC). Laxalt, considered Reagan's closest friend in the Senate, was assigned the role of major party strategist as the 1984 presidential contest approached.

GOP National Committee Chairman Richard Richards gets a cowboy hat from Dallas Mayor Jack Evans after announcing Dallas as site of 1984 GOP convention.

A vacancy in the regular RNC chairmanship was created by the departure on October 4 of Richard Richards, a lawyer from Ogden, Utah, who frequently clashed with White House aides over political matters. Richards also had been in arrears on $300,000 in loans guaranteed by the Small Business Administration during his tenure as GOP chairman, though he later brought his payments up to date. Despite reports that Richards had been forced out, the former chairman said he left of his own accord.

Dallas To Be Convention Site. In other developments, Dallas was chosen as the site of the 1984 Republican Convention, as Reagan had requested. Former California Lieutenant Governor Mike Curb was named finance chairman of the party.

Senator Robert W. Packwood of Oregon made headlines in March by charging that Reagan was out of touch with political reality. "You cannot . . . build a party with white Anglo-Saxon males over 40," he said. "There aren't enough of us left." Packwood later apologized for the remarks. In December, he was defeated by Senator Richard G. Lugar of Indiana in a bid for re-election as chairman of the National Republican Senatorial Committee.

William J. Eaton

In WORLD BOOK, see REPUBLICAN PARTY.

RHODE ISLAND. See STATE GOVERNMENT.
RHODESIA. See ZIMBABWE.

RÍOS-MONTT, JOSÉ EFRAÍN (1926-), a retired brigadier general, was sworn in as president of Guatemala on June 9, 1982. He was previously a member of a three-man junta that had ruled the country since March, when a military coup ousted President Fernando Romeo Lucas García. In June, with the support of the army, Ríos-Montt deposed his two fellow rulers and declared himself president. See GUATEMALA.

Ríos-Montt was born in Huehuetenango, Guatemala, on June 16, 1926. He joined the Guatemalan Army in 1943 and later graduated from the military's Polytechnic Institute. By 1973, he had risen to the post of army chief of staff.

Later that year, the Guatemalan government—worried about the general's liberal tendencies and anxious to get him out of the country—sent him to a post in Washington, D.C. Ríos-Montt returned to Guatemala in 1974 and ran for the presidency. He was defeated, but he and his supporters charged that the government had committed vote fraud.

Ríos-Montt belongs to the Christian Church of the Word, a charismatic sect whose members believe that God gives them the power of prophecy and healing, and he has proclaimed that he attained power through God's will. He pledged an end to violence and corruption. David L. Dreier

ROADS. See TRANSPORTATION.

ROBINSON, ROSCOE, JR. (1928-), a decorated veteran of the Korean and Vietnam wars, became the United States Army's first black four-star general on Aug. 30, 1982. Formerly the commander of Army troops in Japan, Robinson at year's end was serving in Brussels, Belgium, as United States representative to the North Atlantic Treaty Organization Military Committee.

Robinson was born on Oct. 11, 1928, in St. Louis, Mo. He graduated from the U.S. Military Academy at West Point, N.Y., with a bachelor's degree in military engineering and later earned a master's degree in international affairs at the University of Pittsburgh in Pennsylvania.

In the Korean War in the early 1950s, Robinson commanded a rifle company and received the Bronze Star medal. He was awarded the Silver Star for valor during the Vietnam War. From 1973 to 1980, Robinson served as commanding general of the Army garrison on the Pacific island of Okinawa; commanding general of the 82nd Airborne Division at Fort Bragg, N.C.; and deputy chief for operations of Army forces in Europe and the Seventh Army.

Robinson is the second black to attain the rank of four-star general in the U.S. armed forces. The first was Air Force General Daniel James, Jr., who died in 1978 after heading the North American Air Defense Command. David L. Dreier

ROMAN CATHOLIC CHURCH. In 1982, a growing number of Roman Catholic bishops in the United States publicly opposed aspects of U.S. nuclear strategy. In San Francisco on January 20, Archbishop John R. Quinn of San Francisco appeared before the Senate Subcommittee on Arms Control, Oceans, International Operations, and Environment. The archbishop told the subcommittee that the United States and its Western allies should consider a pledge not to use nuclear weapons first in any warfare. Quinn also said that the United States should not deploy its MX missiles or use tactical nuclear weapons. He urged the United States to move toward unilateral nuclear disarmament and warned against a technology "beyond political and moral control."

In the January 28 edition of *Catholic Northwest Progress,* Archbishop Raymond G. Hunthausen of Seattle wrote that he would withhold 50 per cent of his federal income tax to protest government spending for nuclear weapons. The archbishop did not ask other Roman Catholics to follow his lead in holding back tax payments. Rather, he advised "each individual to come to his or her own decision on what should be done to meet the nuclear arms challenge."

On February 13, Bishop Leroy T. Matthiesen of Amarillo, Tex., announced that his diocese would establish a Solidarity Peace Fund to aid workers in nuclear arms plants in Texas. The fund would specifically assist workers who quit their jobs for reasons of conscience. Bishop Matthiesen remarked: "We who believe that we are the stewards of life and creation, not its masters, must use all the religious and moral vision we have to prevent a threat to what God has created, what we could destroy but never re-create."

The bishop said that priests of the Oblates of Mary Immaculate order had given $10,000 to begin the fund, which would be administered by the diocese of Amarillo. Amarillo is the site of a large nuclear arms production facility.

Local officials of the United Way then threatened to withdraw a $61,000 grant to Catholic Family Services, a social service agency also controlled by the Amarillo diocese. The officials worried that the agency would use the money to provide aid for dissatisfied employees of nuclear plants, and thus anger local residents who had pledged money to the United Way and were pronuclear. After meeting with members of Catholic Family Services on February 22, Bishop Matthiesen said he would not ask the agency to manage the peace fund. Nevertheless, the United Way voted to cut off funds to the agency.

Pastoral Letter. Throughout the year, a committee of American bishops worked on a pastoral letter stating the bishops' view on nuclear arms. In June, the committee distributed a draft of the

Security guards surround Pope John Paul II as he waves to a crowd before celebrating a Mass in Ávila, Spain, on November 1.

statement to bishops attending a retreat in Collegeville, Minn. The committee asked the bishops for comments.

Debate over the pastoral letter dominated the four-day National Conference of Catholic Bishops in Washington, D.C., in November. At the conference, Archbishop Joseph L. Bernardin of Chicago, head of the bishops' committee, announced that an informal survey of 278 American bishops showed that more than two-thirds of them approved the statement, which condemned nuclear war. A pastoral letter cannot be sent out in the names of the bishops unless two-thirds of them approve it. The nation's bishops were scheduled to meet in Chicago in May 1983 to vote on the pastoral letter.

Cutbacks Opposed. During 1982, some American Catholics continued to oppose President Ronald Reagan's proposed cutbacks of federal spending for many human services. At a hearing before members of the House of Representatives Budget Committee on February 22, Auxiliary Bishop Joseph M. Sullivan of Brooklyn, N.Y., speaking for the United States Catholic Conference, denounced the proposed cuts. He said that there was an urgent need for continued public support of such services.

Church enterprises felt the pinch of the tighter federal monetary policy when part of the congressional subsidies for classes of mail used by most Catholic newspapers and magazines were ended on January 10. For some publishers, postal costs tripled overnight. Two long-standing national publications, *Catholic Mind* and *Sign*, went out of business. Ten diocesan newspapers reduced the number of issues published per year. On July 28, the postal subsidies were restored.

Ecumenical Efforts. On February 12, a group representing the Roman Catholic and the United Methodist churches announced a general agreement to pursue unification of the two denominations. However, the group admitted that there were substantial areas of disagreement and called for continued discussion.

Ecumenists applauded a meeting of Pope John Paul II and Archbishop of Canterbury Robert Runcie, the spiritual leader of the world's Anglican Communion, in Canterbury, England, on May 29. The meeting came during a six-day papal visit to Great Britain. The two leaders endorsed discussions of the Anglican-Roman Catholic International Commission and called for other Christian churches to move toward unity. In a statement published on March 31, the commission agreed that the pope would be the chief spokesman of Christianity if the two churches reunited. But the commission did not give the papal office all the attributes Roman Catholics traditionally associate with it. The split between Catholics and

New priests prostrate themselves before the papal altar after being ordained by Pope John Paul II in Kaduna, Nigeria, in February.

Anglicans dates from 1534, when King Henry VIII formed the Church of England.

Papal Trips. During his trip to Britain, the pope also visited Queen Elizabeth II in Buckingham Palace in London. But his British trip was overshadowed by Great Britain's war with Argentina over possession of the Falkland Islands (called *Islas Malvinas* by Argentines). John Paul had called Argentine and British church leaders to Rome to pray with him for peace on May 21. On June 11, he arrived in Buenos Aires, Argentina, for a 31-hour stay, during which he again appealed for peace.

Earlier in the year, John Paul traveled to Nigeria and Portugal. During his five-day Nigerian trip in February, he reaffirmed his call for universal human rights. On May 12, while at the shrine to the Virgin Mary in Fátima, Portugal, he was nearly stabbed by a man dressed as a priest. This attack occurred one day before the anniversary of the 1981 attack on the pope's life in Rome. In Fátima, however, he was not harmed.

During the autumn, the pope spent 10 days in Spain and two days in Sicily. In Spain, John Paul condemned weapons research as "the scandal of our time." In Sicily, he spoke strongly against organized crime and the Mafia.

Other Developments. John Patrick Cardinal Cody, the archbishop of Chicago, died of a heart attack in Chicago on April 25. The 74-year-old cardinal had been under investigation by federal authorities after being accused of diverting church funds to his friend and relative Helen Dolan Wilson of St. Louis, Mo. Both the cardinal and Wilson had denied the charges. The case was closed in July without any indictments. On August 24, Archbishop Bernardin succeeded Cardinal Cody in Chicago. Archbishop Bernardin had been archbishop of Cincinnati, Ohio, since 1972.

The Knights of Columbus observed their organization's 100th anniversary in August in Hartford, Conn. President Reagan was the principal guest, and Agostino Cardinal Casaroli, the Vatican's secretary of state, represented Pope John Paul II.

On June 20, the pope canonized his first saint: Crispin of Viterbo, an Italian shoemaker of the 1600s who became a monk. On October 10, Maksymilian Kolbe, a Polish priest who volunteered to die in place of another man in a World War II German concentration camp, was proclaimed a saint. On October 31, John Paul proclaimed two female saints. One of them, Marguerite Bourgeoys, who established the first school in colonial Montreal in the 1600s, is Canada's first female saint. The other, Jeanne Delanoue, worked with the poor in France in the 1600s. Owen F. Campion

In WORLD BOOK, see ROMAN CATHOLIC CHURCH.

ROMANIA struggled with economic difficulties in 1982, while its reputation plummeted because of its repressive internal policies. In June, United States President Ronald Reagan granted Romania most-favored-nation (MFN) status for another year. This status requires the United States to apply its lowest tariff rates to imports from Romania. However, Romania's MFN status was in jeopardy. According to U.S. law, a nation that does not allow its citizens to emigrate freely cannot have MFN status. Reagan warned Romania that the United States might not grant it a further extension unless it improved its emigration policy, particularly on Jewish emigration.

French Plot. In June, France's President François Mitterrand canceled a September trip to Romania as part of a scheme to protect Virgil Tanase, a Romanian exile living in France. Tanase had disappeared on May 20. The French public presumed that the Romanian secret police had kidnapped and killed him because of satirical articles he had published in France about Romania's President Nicolae Ceausescu. Tanase reappeared on August 31, revealing that French security agents had faked his kidnapping. He said that the scheme had protected him and Paul Goma, another Romanian writer living in France, from being murdered. Romania denied that it had plotted to murder the two men.

In October, a group of ethnic Hungarians living in Transylvania, a part of Romania that had been part of Hungary, sent a memorandum to the Madrid conference demanding an international inquiry into what they called a *Romanization* policy. They said that the Romanian government was trying to deprive them of their Hungarian culture.

Romania's economic problems led to a purge of about 250 officials in April and May. These included Prime Minister Ilie Verdet, who was replaced by Constantin Dascalescu.

Industrial Production increased by 3 per cent in the first half of 1982, compared with the first half of 1981. Romania harvested about 21 million short tons (19 million metric tons) of grain in 1982, 5.5 million short tons (5 million metric tons) short of the goal.

In July, Romania requested a rescheduling of its commercial debt to the West. However, negotiations stalled over exact terms. Furthermore, the Western creditors wanted more accurate information about the Romanian economy and wanted Romania to reform its economic system more boldly.

Chris Cviic

See also EUROPE (Facts in Brief Table). In WORLD BOOK, see ROMANIA.

ROTARY INTERNATIONAL. See COMMUNITY ORGANIZATIONS.

ROWING. See SPORTS.

RUBBER. See MANUFACTURING.

RUSSIA lost its leader in 1982. On November 10, Leonid Ilich Brezhnev, 75, general secretary of the Communist Party and chairman of the Presidium of the Supreme Soviet, died of a heart attack. Brezhnev had been party leader since 1964 and chairman—head of state—since 1977. See DEATHS (Close-Up).

Yuri V. Andropov, 68, succeeded Brezhnev as general secretary on November 12. However, as 1982 drew to a close, the Presidium chairmanship was still vacant. See ANDROPOV, YURI V.

The chain of leadership changes that led to the accession of Andropov began with the death on January 25 of Mikhail A. Suslov, 79, the party's chief ideologist and, after Brezhnev, the senior member of the Politburo, the Communist Party's top body. On April 22, Andropov, then chairman of the KGB, Russia's secret police agency, delivered the prestigious address celebrating V. I. Lenin's birthday. On May 24, Andropov became a member of the Secretariat of the Communist Party Central Committee. Vladimir I. Dolgikh, 57, a party official from Siberia, was named a nonvoting member of the Politburo. Dolgikh was put in charge of heavy industry, succeeding Politburo member Andrei P. Kirilenko in this function. On May 26, Andropov relinquished his KGB post, which he had held since 1967. Vitali V. Fedorchuk, 64, succeeded Andropov. Fedorchuk had been KGB chief in the Ukraine.

Changes in leadership continued after Andropov became general secretary. On November 22, the Central Committee appointed Geidar A. Aliyev, 59, a full member of the Politburo. Aliyev had been party secretary in Azerbaijan since 1969. He replaced the 76-year-old Kirilenko, who reportedly retired for health reasons. The Central Committee also promoted Nikolai I. Ryzhkov to the Secretariat. Ryzhkov had been first deputy chairman of Gosplan, the state planning commission. On November 23, the Supreme Soviet elected Andropov to the Presidium and named Aliyev first deputy chairman of the Council of Ministers.

On December 17, Fedorchuk succeeded Nikolai A. Shchelokov, 72, as minister of internal affairs. The Ministry of Internal Affairs is in charge of Russia's uniformed police. Viktor M. Chebrikov, the first deputy chairman of the KGB, succeeded Fedorchuk.

Armaments. Russia and the United States quarreled about nuclear weapons throughout 1982. On March 16, Brezhnev announced that Russia would halt the deployment of medium-range nuclear weapons on its European territory. Brezhnev said that this moratorium would remain in force until Russia and the United States reached an agreement on the reduction of medium-range missiles in Europe or until the United States began "practical preparations" for the deployment of Per-

Flowers, ribbons, and flags decorate the casket of Russian leader Leonid I. Brezhnev at his state funeral in Moscow on November 15.

shing-2 and cruise missiles in Western Europe. He also said that the Soviet Union would withdraw "a certain number" of its medium-range missiles "sometime in 1982," if there were no further aggravation of the world situation. The United States and other members of the North Atlantic Treaty Organization (NATO) viewed Brezhnev's proposal as a propaganda move and ignored it.

On May 9, United States President Ronald Reagan proposed that the United States and Russia reduce the number of their nuclear missile warheads by one-third. On May 18, Brezhnev said that Reagan's proposal was an "insincere position." Brezhnev said that Reagan did not want arms talks to cover the types of weapons the United States was developing most intensively—submarine-launched ballistic missiles and strategic bombers.

Soviet-American talks on strategic arms limitation started in Geneva, Switzerland, in July, but made no progress. In a speech to Soviet military commanders on October 27, Brezhnev drew attention to the fact that NATO powers had begun preparations for installing new medium-range nuclear weapons in Western Europe. He said that Russia therefore considered itself released from the self-imposed "freeze" that he had announced in March. NATO claimed that Russia had continued to deploy SS-20 missiles during the so-called freeze.

Soviet media strongly attacked Reagan's November 22 proposal to deploy 100 MX missiles in a "dense pack" in Wyoming. They said that dense-pack deployment would break the unratified SALT II arms-limitation agreement.

Asia. Brezhnev offered China "unconditional talks on measures to improve relations." In October, Soviet Deputy Foreign Minister Leonid F. Ilyichev visited China to arrange talks. Soviet Foreign Minister Andrei A. Gromyko met with China's Foreign Minister Huang Hua on November 16. Huang was head of the Chinese delegation at Brezhnev's funeral. China replaced Huang on the day of his return to Peking (Beijing). Russia indicated that it would like to end the stalemate over Afghanistan when Andropov held talks in Moscow with President Mohammad Zia-ul-Haq of Pakistan and a visiting Afghan delegation on November 15.

In Europe, Russia's support of Polish efforts to crush the independent labor union Solidarity led to further clashes with the United States. On June 18, President Reagan decided to expand the economic sanctions that he had imposed on Dec. 29, 1981. These sanctions had prohibited U.S. companies from providing equipment for a natural gas pipeline that Russia was building from Siberia to central Europe. The expanded sanctions covered the export of equipment made outside the United

Soviet leader Leonid Brezhnev, far right, hears Yuri V. Andropov speak in April. Brezhnev died in November and was succeeded by Andropov.

States. They prohibited foreign subsidiaries and licensees of U.S. firms from providing equipment for the pipeline. However, on November 13, Reagan lifted the sanctions. He said that the United States had reached an understanding with its Western allies on a set of principles governing future economic relations with the Soviet Union.

Some U.S. allies criticized the United States for excluding grain sales to the Soviet Union from its sanctions. On October 15, President Reagan offered to allow Russia to import from the United States 23 million metric tons (25 million short tons) of grain in the year beginning Oct. 1, 1982, if Russia ordered that amount by Nov. 30, 1982. Russia bought 7.6 million metric tons (8.4 million short tons) of grain from Canada on October 13.

The Middle East. Russia remained on the sidelines in the conflict that developed after Israel invaded Lebanon in June. Russia supported the Palestine Liberation Organization (PLO) verbally. However, Russia's failure to follow this up with action brought bitter criticism from Arab nations.

Economy. Russia experienced serious food shortages during 1982. For the second consecutive year, the Soviet Union did not publish grain harvest figures. However, informed estimates put the 1982 harvest slightly above the 1981 harvest of 170 million metric tons (187 million short tons). Total agricultural production was up about 3.2 per cent.

Industrial production grew by 2.7 per cent from January through September 1982, down 2 percentage points from Russia's production target. The 1982 rate was the lowest since 1946. There were sharp declines in petroleum, chemicals, and some types of machinery.

In May, Brezhnev launched a program calling for the Soviet Union to put one-third of its investment resources into agriculture during the period from 1986 through 1990. The program also included higher wages for workers on collective farms, higher purchase prices for agricultural products beginning in 1983, better mechanical and other services for agriculture, and closer integration of agricultural enterprises at the district level. (A district is roughly equivalent to a U.S. county.)

Dissidents. On September 8, a group set up in 1976 to monitor Russia's compliance with the Helsinki Agreement of 1975 ceased its activities. This agreement, which the Soviet Union signed, dealt with economic and political matters and with human rights. The group stopped its monitoring and disbanded because conditions for its work had become impossible. Ten of the original 20 members of the group had been imprisoned, while others had been forced into exile. Chris Cviic

See also EUROPE (Facts in Brief Table). In WORLD BOOK, see RUSSIA.

RWANDA. See AFRICA.

SAFETY. Seven Chicago-area residents were fatally poisoned in the fall of 1982 after taking cyanide-laced capsules of the top-selling pain reliever, Extra-Strength Tylenol. The poisonings served to remind the public of the hazards to life and health that lurk almost everywhere.

When investigators revealed that the unsealed packages of Tylenol had been tampered with while on store shelves, the public learned the extent of its vulnerability. The pharmaceutical industry, which had fought hard for fewer federal regulations, suddenly demanded nationwide standards for packaging. Without waiting for the new standards, drug manufacturers rushed to put their products in more secure packages. In November, the Department of Health and Human Services issued new regulations designed to protect consumers from product poisoning.

Nuclear Hazards. A study for the Nuclear Regulatory Commission (NRC) suggested that a single accident involving a core meltdown in a nuclear power plant could result in 100,000 deaths and property damage exceeding $300 billion. But the NRC said the chances of such a disaster were only 1 in 1 billion.

Product Safety. Legal claims for injuries instituted against manufacturers of various products rose 474 per cent between 1975 and 1982, providing one measure of the level of product safety.

Many lawsuits involved asbestos, formaldehyde, or automobiles. The number of suits against manufacturers of asbestos, which has been linked to lung cancer, grew so large in 1982 that the principal producer, the Manville Corporation, declared bankruptcy in August in order to avoid paying damages and still remain in business. The move left many people with no way of collecting damages. People who claimed injuries from formaldehyde products faced a similar situation.

The Consumer Product Safety Commission (CPSC) continued to push for voluntary industry action rather than issue mandatory rules. It launched a massive public relations campaign in September to get smoke detectors into more American homes. By 1982, 32 states had some requirements for smoke detectors in residential buildings.

One CPSC mandatory action in 1982 was a requirement that all power mowers have a deadman's control, which automatically turns the machine off when the operator's hand is removed. Another required that citizens band (CB) radio antennas manufactured after Feb. 25, 1983, be insulated to prevent electrocution when they touch power lines during installation.

Vehicle Safety. A major safety issue was whether manufacturers should be required to equip automobiles with automatic seat belts or airbags, as the Administration of President Jimmy Carter had proposed. The Administration of President Ronald Reagan moved quickly to kill the requirement at the request of automakers, but the Administration ran into legal opposition. In August, a federal appeals court ordered manufacturers to install airbags or automatic belts in 1984-model cars. The National Highway Traffic Safety Administration, a government agency, decided to fight the ruling.

Worker Safety. The Occupational Safety and Health Administration (OSHA) also steered toward voluntary cooperation rather than mandatory requirements. It sought to switch responsibility for worker safety as much as possible to the states by certifying state regulatory programs. Many states that had been denied such certification by the Carter Administration won acceptance from Reagan officials.

OSHA proposed in 1982 to reduce the access of workers to their medical records and to stiffen requirements for accepting complaints about unsafe conditions. The agency would thereby cut the number of cases subject to inspection. OSHA claimed in its annual report that employers' objections to OSHA inspections had dropped about 75 per cent in one year. Arthur E. Rowse

In WORLD BOOK, see SAFETY.

SAILING. See BOATING.

SALVATION ARMY. See COMMUNITY ORGANIZATIONS.

SASKATCHEWAN. The 11-year dominance of Saskatchewan political life by Allan E. Blakeney and his New Democratic Party came to a dramatic end in a provincial election on April 26, 1982. The Progressive Conservatives (PC), who had held only 15 seats in the 61-seat legislature, swept the province, winning 55 seats in an expanded 64-seat house. Although Blakeney was re-elected, only two other members of his cabinet were successful, and the party's standing dropped from 44 seats to 9. The Liberals failed to elect a single member, as did the "Unionest Party," committed to Saskatchewan joining the United States. It was a devastating defeat for Blakeney's party, which had governed Saskatchewan for all but seven years since 1944. The new premier was Grant Devine, a 37-year-old agricultural economist. Sworn into office on May 8, he headed the seventh PC administration in control in Canada's 10 provinces.

The new premier convened a two-week session of the legislature on June 17 to put through the most generous mortgage subsidy plan in Canada: 13¼ per cent for three years. The government also won legislative approval for abolishing a 6 cents-per-liter (0.3 gallon) sales tax on gasoline. The Devine government also announced that it would review the operations of 24 provincial corporations, which employ about 170,000 people.

"Wagons ho!" cry the drivers of this outfit and 30 others re-creating in June the historic pioneer journey from Moose Jaw to Saskatoon.

Economic Disaster struck Uranium City when the Eldorado Nuclear mine closed in June after 30 years of operation, putting 800 miners out of work. Earlier, on January 18, Canadian Minister of Employment Lloyd Axworthy had announced that the federal government would spend up to $1.5 million (Canadian dollars; $1 = U.S. 81 cents as of Dec. 31, 1982) to help the miners relocate to find new jobs.

International Events. An economic bright spot was the barter deal arranged in August between the Saskatchewan Potash Corporation and Indonesia. The agreement called for about 84,000 short tons (76,000 metric tons) of bulk potassium chloride to be exchanged for Indonesian rubber, coffee, and cocoa.

More than 2,000 delegates met in Regina from July 18 to 25 for the World Assembly of First Nations, the largest such gathering ever. The delegates, who came from 24 countries, were all native peoples, including Australasian Aborigines, Greenland Eskimos, Scandinavian Lapps, and both North and South American Indians. They adopted an International Covenant on the Rights of Indigenous Peoples, which they hoped to present to the United Nations. David M. L. Farr

See also CANADA. In WORLD BOOK, see SASKATCHEWAN.

SAUDI ARABIA. In contrast to the transfer of power in other Islamic lands, the death of King Khalid on June 13, 1982, caused scarcely a ripple on the surface of Saudi leadership. Khalid's half brother Crown Prince Fahd succeeded him without incident as Fahd's younger half brother Abdullah in turn became the crown prince. Fahd had been active in foreign affairs and in charge of the day-to-day administration of the country, so little change was expected in the direction of Saudi foreign policy or internal development. See FAHD.

Fahd Continued to stress Saudi Arabia's role as a moderate leader in Arab affairs during the year. Saudi Arabia sent a large delegation to the Arab League summit conference in Fez, Morocco, in September. Most elements of the 1981 eight-point "Fahd plan" for an Arab-Israeli peace settlement were incorporated into the Arab League plan adopted at that conference. In July, Saudi negotiators put together a coordinated Arab plan that served as the basis for evacuation of Palestine Liberation Organization guerrillas from Beirut, Lebanon, after the Israeli invasion (see MIDDLE EAST). Saudi Arabia failed in mediation efforts, however, in the war between Iran and Iraq.

In September, Saudi Arabia signed security agreements with the other five members of the Gulf Cooperation Council (GCC) — Bahrain, Ku-

Members of Saudi Arabia's royal family carry the shrouded body of King Khalid through the streets of Riyadh during the monarch's funeral in June.

wait, Oman, Qatar, and the United Arab Emirates—that would allow the use of Saudi forces in the event of an attack by an outside power against any one of the members. King Fahd said the action had been taken to prevent a possible invasion by Iran. The GCC was formed in 1981.

Internal Developments. A new villages law, the first local legislation of its kind in Saudi Arabia, went into effect in September. It established elected village councils and gave women the right to vote in village elections.

King Fahd said that a national consultative assembly would be formed in the near future as the country's first legislative body, but he set no date for its establishment.

The Economic Boom Slowed during the year as oil production was reduced because of a worldwide oil oversupply. Saudi production averaged about 7 million barrels per day (bpd), the lowest output in three years and well below the 10.25 million bpd reached in late 1981. The 1982 budget, introduced in May, was balanced at $91.6-billion, a 5.2 per cent increase over 1981.

In July, liquefied natural gas shipments began from the Red Sea port of Yanbu. A 1,160-kilometer (720-mile) pipeline connects the port with gas fields in eastern Saudi Arabia. William Spencer

See also MIDDLE EAST (Facts in Brief Table). In WORLD BOOK, see SAUDI ARABIA.

SCHLÜTER, POUL (1929-), became prime minister of Denmark on Sept. 10, 1982, heading a four-party minority coalition known as the "four-leaf clover." This was Denmark's first four-party government, consisting of Schlüter's Conservative Party, the Liberals, the Center Democrats, and the Christian People's Party. Schlüter was the nation's first Conservative prime minister since 1901. See DENMARK.

He succeeded Social Democrat Prime Minister Anker Henrik Jorgensen, who had led a center-left minority coalition. Jorgensen resigned on September 3, after failing to muster a majority in the Folketing (parliament) to support his government's plan to deal with Denmark's economic problems.

Poul Schlüter was born on April 3, 1929, in Tønder. When he was 15 years old, he was chosen to lead the Conservative Youth Movement in the town of Haderslev and, at age 22, he became the group's national leader.

Schlüter received a law degree at Copenhagen University in 1957. He was elected to the Folketing in 1964 and later served as deputy mayor of Gladsakse, a suburb of Copenhagen. He returned to the Folketing and became the political spokesman for Conservative members in 1971. In 1974, he became chairman of this group and national chairman of the Conservative Party. Jay Myers

SCHOOL. See CIVIL RIGHTS; EDUCATION.

SCHREYER, EDWARD RICHARD (1935-), Canada's 22nd governor general and representative of Queen Elizabeth II in Canada, carried out a busy round of official duties in 1982. On June 3, Schreyer dedicated the Fountain of Hope, located at the main entrance of Rideau Hall, his residence in Ottawa, Ont. The fountain was named in memory of Terry Fox, the one-legged cancer victim who ran a Marathon of Hope halfway across Canada in 1980 to raise funds for cancer research. On Oct. 28, 1982, the governor general opened the Terry Fox Canadian Youth Centre in Ottawa to house young Canadians and educate them in the country's history, culture, and government.

Schreyer toured parts of Western Canada in February and attended a conference of lieutenant governors, a gathering of those who serve as the Queen's representatives in the provinces. He and his wife, Lily, in August went to Greenland for celebrations marking the 1,000th anniversary of the landing of Norse explorer Eric the Red. They spent October 22 to 26 in New York City, paying the first visit to the United Nations by a Canadian vice-regal representative. David M. L. Farr

See also CANADA.
SCOTLAND. See GREAT BRITAIN.
SCULPTURE. See VISUAL ARTS.
SENEGAL. See AFRICA.
SENEGAMBIA. See AFRICA.

SEYCHELLES. On Aug. 17, 1982, a group of army privates and noncommissioned officers, complaining of maltreatment by their superiors, tried to seize control of this nation of coral islands in the Indian Ocean. The rebels captured the government radio station in the capital city, Victoria. That night, Tanzanian soldiers were flown in to reinforce troops loyal to Seychelles President France Albert René. The uprising ended the next day.

This was the second attempted coup in nine months. On Nov. 25, 1981, a group of about 50 mercenaries from various countries flew by commercial airliner to Seychelles. A customs officer at Mahé Airport discovered weapons in one man's luggage, and a gun battle followed. Most of the mercenaries escaped in a commandeered jetliner to South Africa, where they were arrested.

During their trial, their leader, Michael Hoare, a well-known South African soldier of fortune, testified that South Africa's government had approved their plan to overthrow René and had supplied them with arms. At least six mercenaries failed to escape from Seychelles, and one of them was killed. Another, who admitted to being a South African intelligence officer, was sentenced in July 1982 to 20 years in prison. The four others were given the death penalty. J. Dixon Esseks

See also AFRICA (Facts in Brief Table). In WORLD BOOK, see SEYCHELLES.

SHIP AND SHIPPING. Shipbuilding demand declined throughout most of the world in 1982, but orders rose in the United States. Lloyd's Register of Shipping reported that merchant ships under construction worldwide totaled 1,892 on June 30, up 4 per cent from a year earlier. But orders, including ships being built, fell from 3,291 to 3,190. Tonnage of vessels on order declined to 32.7 million gross tons, 13 per cent below the mid-1981 level.

United States shipbuilders held orders of nearly $18 billion. The Maritime Administration (Marad) of the U.S. Department of Transportation said that commercial ship orders were valued at $1.72 billion on September 1, down from $2.13 billion a year earlier. Thirty-one ships were scheduled for completion by 1984, 10 fewer than on Sept. 1, 1981. Under a 1981 law that expired on Oct. 1, 1982, carriers flying the U.S. flag could get operating subsidies from the federal government even if their ships were built abroad. Marad approved proposals by six shipping lines to construct vessels overseas, including the plan by United States Lines to have 14 container ships built in South Korea for $780.5 million.

The Shipbuilders Council of America estimated that U.S. Navy orders amounted to $16 billion at the end of 1982, up from $11 billion a year before. The government planned to have a 600-vessel naval fleet by the end of the decade, up nearly 150. In July, the Navy selected Litton Industries Incorporated's Ingalls Shipbuilding division and Ogden Corporation's Avondale Shipyard Incorporated unit to modernize the battleship *Iowa* for $411 million. On August 17, the Navy announced $803-million worth of contracts for long-term chartering and conversion of up to 13 cargo ships. And in December, it awarded a $3.1-billion contract to Newport News Shipbuilding and Drydock Company, a unit of Tenneco, Incorporated, for part of the work on two nuclear-powered aircraft carriers.

Aiding the Industry. The Administration of President Ronald Reagan took steps to bolster U.S. shipping lines, but it did not favor the continuation of subsidies for building vessels in domestic yards. Secretary of Transportation Andrew L. (Drew) Lewis, Jr., said in May that the Administration would support policies making it easier for lines to have ships built, repaired, and financed overseas. In August, the Administration boosted by 50 per cent the ceiling on federal guarantees of bonds that finance shipbuilding.

The Administration pushed for legislation to allow carriers to set rates more freely and share business without antitrust prosecution. The House of Representatives approved the bill in September, but it died when Congress adjourned. Albert R. Karr

In WORLD BOOK, see SHIP.

SHOOTING. See HUNTING; SPORTS.

SHULTZ, GEORGE PRATT (1920-), became United States secretary of state on July 16, 1982. His nomination to the post by President Ronald Reagan followed the unexpected resignation on June 25 of Alexander M. Haig, Jr. See CABINET, UNITED STATES.

Shultz was born on Dec. 13, 1920, in New York City and grew up in Englewood, N.J. He graduated from Princeton University in 1942 and earned a Ph.D. in industrial economics from the Massachusetts Institute of Technology (MIT) in 1949. He taught at MIT from 1948 to 1955, and again in 1956 and 1957. In 1957, Shultz became a professor of industrial relations at the University of Chicago Graduate School of Business and, in 1962, was named dean of the school.

In 1969, Shultz became President Richard M. Nixon's secretary of labor. He held that position until June 1970, when he became director of the Office of Management and Budget. In 1972, he became secretary of the Treasury. He resigned in 1974 to join the Bechtel Corporation, now the Bechtel Group, an international engineering firm, and became president of the company in 1975. While at Bechtel, he also negotiated several trade agreements for the United States.

Shultz married Helena M. O'Brien in 1946. They have five children. Barbara A. Mayes

SIERRA LEONE. See AFRICA.

SILES ZUAZO, HERNÁN (1914-), became president of Bolivia again on Oct. 10, 1982, ending 17 years of nearly continuous military rule in that country. He headed the Popular Democratic Union, a coalition of three left-of-center parties. Siles Zuazo succeeded General Guido Vildoso Calderón. To avert a national strike, Bolivia's military leaders promised in September to restore a civilian government and demanded Vildoso's resignation. The congress then elected Siles Zuazo as president. As he took office, he faced an economy in chaos and a nearly bankrupt treasury. See BOLIVIA.

Hernán Siles Zuazo was born on March 19, 1914, in La Paz, Bolivia. His father, Hernando Siles Reyes, was president of Bolivia from 1926 to 1930. Siles Zuazo attended the American Institute in La Paz and received a law degree from the Higher Bolivian University of San Andrés there in 1939. Siles Zuazo served as Bolivia's vice-president from 1952 to 1956 and as president from 1956 to 1960. But after a 1964 military coup, he spent much of the time until October 1982 in exile. Siles Zuazo was again elected president in 1980, but a military coup prevented him from taking office.

He married Maria Teresa Ormachea in 1936. They have three daughters. Karin C. Rosenberg

SINGAPORE. See ASIA.

SKATING. See HOCKEY; ICE SKATING; SPORTS.

SKIING. In 1982, after years of disappointment, the United States Ski Team had its greatest success ever. Phil Mahre of White Pass, Wash., won his second straight World Cup overall title; his twin brother, Steve, won the world giant slalom championship; the American women skied strongly all year; and Bill Koch of Putney, Vt., became America's first World Cup Nordic titlist.

Alpine. The World Cup Alpine series ran from December 1981 to March 1982 in the United States, Canada, and seven European countries. Phil Mahre clinched the championship by midseason because Ingemar Stenmark of Sweden, his main rival, declined to ski downhill races.

Phil Mahre ended the season with 309 points, Stenmark finished second with 211, and Steve Mahre was third with 183. The champions in the individual disciplines were Phil Mahre in the slalom and giant slalom and Steve Podborski of Toronto, Canada, in the downhill.

Erika Hess of Switzerland won the women's overall title with 297 points to 282 for Irene Epple of West Germany. Christin Cooper of Sun Valley, Ida., finished third with 198 points, and Cindy Nelson of Lutsen, Minn., was fifth with 158.

In team competition, the American women were first and the American men placed third, with the Mahres scoring all the points. Americans won almost one-third of the races, including 17 victories by the Mahres. Holly Flanders of Deerfield, N.H., captured two women's downhill races, and Cooper won two slaloms.

The world Alpine championships were held from January 28 to February 7 in Schladming, Austria. Hess was the star, winning the women's slalom, giant slalom, and combined. Steve Mahre won the only American gold medal with his first victory ever in an international giant slalom.

Nordic. The 26-year-old Koch won the World Cup Nordic title in the season's final race. He totaled 121 points to 111 for Thomas Wassberg of Sweden.

Koch was America's only medalist in the world Nordic championships from February 19 to 28 in Oslo, Norway. He won a bronze medal in the 30-kilometer cross-country despite a bad fall. Berit Aunli of Norway won three gold medals and one silver in the four women's races. Norwegians took three of the nine gold medals for men.

Professional. The Professional Ski Racers Association took over the men's tour and conducted 11 events. Edwin Halsnes of Norway was the season point leader and Peter Dodge of Stowe, Vt., led in earnings with $20,500. Toril Forland of Norway took her fourth women's pro title in five years and earned $13,892 in prize money. Frank Litsky

In WORLD BOOK, see SKIING.

Erika Hess of Switzerland races to victory in the combined slalom event on February 6 in the world Alpine championships in Schladming, Austria.

SOCCER. Italy became the surprise winner of the 1982 World Cup in a competition filled with surprises. The Italians defeated West Germany, 3-1, in the final on July 11 in Madrid, Spain, before a crowd of more than 90,000 and an international TV audience of more than 1 billion.

In all, 106 nations took part in the preliminary eliminations in 1980 and 1981. Among them was the United States, which was eliminated by Canada and Mexico in the first round of regional matches. The 22 nations that survived the eliminations qualified for the final rounds along with defending champion Argentina and Spain, the host nation. The final rounds were played at 16 sites in Spain beginning on June 13. Two round robins determined the four semifinalists.

Third World nations not known for soccer prowess made quick impressions. Algeria, in its first cup match ever, upset powerful West Germany, 2-1. Honduras held Spain to a 1-1 tie. Cameroon tied highly regarded Peru, 0-0. Kuwait played a 1-1 tie with strong Czechoslovakia.

Controversy arose in the first round robin when West Germany played Austria. If West Germany lost, it would be eliminated and Algeria would advance. If Austria lost by three or more goals, the Austrians would be eliminated and Algeria would advance. As it turned out, West Germany scored an early goal and beat Austria, 1-0, because neither team made any serious offensive effort after that goal. Spanish spectators, convinced that Algeria was the victim of a conspiracy, waved white handkerchiefs and money at the West German and Austrian teams.

Brazil, the tournament favorite, lost to Italy, 3-2, in the second round and was eliminated. Paolo Rossi scored all three goals for Italy, and he scored both goals in Italy's 2-0 victory over Poland in the semifinals. In the other semifinal, West Germany defeated France in a penalty-kick shootout after they had been tied at 1-1 after regulation time and 3-3 after overtime. In the final, Rossi scored Italy's first goal and set up the decisive second goal.

The NASL. The North American Soccer League (NASL), with 10 teams in the United States and four in Canada, lost $25 million during the year. Six franchises from the 1981 season had disbanded, two others had merged, and attendance fell 20 per cent. Hoping to reverse its fortunes, the league hired former government official and industrialist Howard J. Samuels as its president, with authority over Commissioner Phil Woosnam.

Each of the 14 NASL teams played 32 regular-season games from March to August. The Cosmos (23-9, 203 points), who played in the New York City suburb of East Rutherford, N.J., finished with the best record. The Seattle Sounders (18-14, 165) and the Fort Lauderdale Strikers (18-14, 163) had the next best records.

Those three teams advanced to the play-offs along with the Montreal Manic, the San Diego Sockers, the Toronto Blizzard, the Tulsa Roughnecks, and the Vancouver Whitecaps. The Cosmos gained the final by beating Tulsa in three games and San Diego in two. Seattle beat Toronto and Fort Lauderdale in three games each to make the final.

In the Soccer Bowl, held on September 18 in San Diego, the Cosmos defeated Seattle, 1-0, on a goal by star striker Giorgio Chinaglia. It was the Cosmos' second championship in three years.

The 35-year-old Chinaglia led the league in scoring for the third straight year and was named the Soccer Bowl's Most Valuable Player.

Indoor Soccer. The New York Arrows won their fourth title in the four-year history of the Major Indoor Soccer League (MISL). They beat the St. Louis Steamers, three games to two, in the championship play-off. The San Diego Sockers became champions of the NASL's third indoor season by beating the Tampa Bay Rowdies, 9-7 and 10-5, in the two-game final. The NASL canceled its 1982-1983 indoor season, and three of its teams played in the MISL.

Frank Litsky

In WORLD BOOK, see SOCCER.

A smiling Paolo Rossi watches his winning goal go past goalkeeper Waldir Peres as Italy beats Brazil, 3-2, during World Cup play in July.

SOCIAL SECURITY. The 15-member bipartisan National Commission on Social Security Reform failed during 1982 to come up with a complete set of recommendations for changing the United States Social Security system.

The commission addressed two problems. The first problem was the threat to the system's solvency from 1984 to 1990. This problem stemmed from unemployment and inflation. Payroll-tax increases adopted in 1977 were supposed to keep the system solvent for decades. However, unemployment cut into payroll revenues, and benefits—which are adjusted to compensate for changes in the cost of living—increased with inflation. The Old Age and Survivors Insurance (OASI) trust fund, which pays retirement benefits, ran out of money in 1982. On November 5, the OASI borrowed $581.3 million from the Disability Insurance trust fund.

The Social Security system's other problem was demographic. The percentage of retired persons is expected to increase sharply early in the next century. This problem will become serious by the year 2005, when the ratio of workers to beneficiaries, currently 3.2 to 1, falls to 2.1 to 1.

There are only two ways to solve the two problems. The government must find more money for the OASI fund or must curtail OASI benefits. Options for increasing revenue include raising the payroll tax, bringing federal employees into the Social Security system, taxing benefits, and appropriating general revenue funds. The government can reduce benefits by changing the formula for compensating for changes in the cost of living, by revising the formula that determines a person's initial benefits, and by raising the standard age for retirement.

Benefits Boosted. On July 1, Social Security recipients received a 7.4 per cent increase based on a rise in the cost of living. This adjustment was expected to cost the Social Security system $11.3-billion in the year that began on Oct. 1, 1982.

On March 2, John A. Svahn, the commissioner of Social Security, announced that the Social Security system's antiquated computer and data-processing system, barely able to get 36 million checks in the mail every month, was to be modernized at a cost of $479 million. Net savings to the program should run "in the billions" of dollars and far exceed the total cost of the changes.

The Social Security Administration said on November 8 that $35,700 of an individual's earnings would be subject to the payroll tax in 1983, compared with $32,400 in 1982. The maximum tax that an employee would pay would be $2,391.90, up from $2,170.80 in 1982. Virginia E. Anderson

In WORLD BOOK, see SOCIAL SECURITY.

SOCIAL WELFARE. See WELFARE.

SOMALIA. President Mohamed Siad Barre faced rebellion both inside and outside his autocratic, pro-Western government during 1982. On June 9, five government leaders were arrested on charges of treason. The chief opposition groups outside the government were the Somali National Movement, based in the country's northern region, and the Somali Democratic Salvation Front, in the south.

Ethiopia aided the guerrillas with arms and other supplies, largely because the Siad Barre government supported Somali-speaking secessionists living in the Ethiopian province of Ogaden who wanted to join their region to Somalia.

On June 30, about 9,000 troops, reportedly mostly Ethiopian regulars but including a number of anti-Siad Barre Somali guerrillas, crossed from Ethiopia into Somalia. In mid-July, the invaders captured two towns in the Mudugh area of Somalia. Somali government forces counterattacked in mid-August. The troops withdrew from one of the two towns, Galdogob, but stayed in the vicinity of the other, Balanballe. Ethiopia denied that its forces were involved.

Soon after the invasion began, Siad Barre asked the United States for emergency military aid. On July 24, the U.S. announced that an airlift of supplies to Somalia was underway. J. Dixon Esseks

See also AFRICA. In WORLD BOOK, see SOMALIA.

SOUTH AFRICA. On July 30, 1982, Prime Minister Pieter Willem Botha announced the details of a plan by which the country's white-minority government would share political power with South Africans of mixed race, called Coloreds, and those of Asian backgrounds. Since 1955, only whites had been able to vote for, and serve in, legislative and executive positions at the national and provincial levels of government.

Under the government's proposals, the national Parliament would have three chambers—one each for whites, Coloreds, and Asians. The members of the three chambers would elect the country's president, who would appoint a multiracial Cabinet. A special federal congress of the ruling National Party (NP) approved Botha's proposals on July 31.

Blacks Still Excluded. The plan had been recommended by a 60-member President's Council, appointed in October 1980 to advise the government on constitutional reform. The council's report, issued on May 12, 1982, advocated the continued exclusion of blacks from the national government.

The reform proposals ensured that whites could not be outvoted in Parliament. Even with this veto power, many whites opposed losing their political monopoly. In anticipation of the reform plan, 22

A multiracial crowd watches a cricket match in Johannesburg. Race barriers are falling in South African sports for players and spectators.

NP members of Parliament refused on February 24 to support a vote of confidence in Botha's racial policies. The leader of the dissidents, State Administration Minister Andries P. Treurnicht, resigned his Cabinet post on March 2 and was ousted from the NP the next day. With 15 other right wing NP members, he formed a new opposition party, the Conservative Party.

Ministers Denounce Apartheid. South Africa's all-white Dutch Reformed Church was pressured from inside and outside the country in 1982 to end its support of the government's racial policies. On June 9, 123 ministers and seminary instructors of the church denounced racial separatism. The World Alliance of Reformed Churches, meeting in Ottawa, Canada, voted on August 25 to expel the South African church from the alliance for its support of segregation. Despite those forceful actions, however, when the Dutch Reformed Church held a two-week synod in October, motions to end or soften its support of government racial policies were defeated. J. Dixon Esseks

See also AFRICA. In WORLD BOOK, see SOUTH AFRICA.

SOUTH AMERICA. See LATIN AMERICA and articles on Latin American countries.

SOUTH CAROLINA. See STATE GOVERNMENT.

SOUTH DAKOTA. See STATE GOVERNMENT.

SOUTH WEST AFRICA. See NAMIBIA.

SPACE EXPLORATION. Oct. 4, 1982, was the 25th anniversary of the launch of the first artificial satellite—the Soviet Union's *Sputnik 1.* On that day, two Soviet cosmonauts were en route to a space-endurance record and the United States was preparing for the fifth launch of its first reusable spacecraft, the space shuttle orbiter *Columbia.*

The launch occurred as scheduled on November 11. The five-day mission was the first to employ four astronauts, the first to use *mission specialists* (nonpilot astronauts), and the first in which a shuttle deployed an artificial satellite. In addition, it was to have been the first mission during which astronauts ventured outside a shuttle. However, the astronauts had to cancel the spacewalk.

The orbiter deployed two communications satellites from its cargo bay. The Canadian government owned one of the satellites, and the other was designed to carry communications for U.S. businesses.

Vance D. Brand, mission commander, and Robert F. Overmeyer, pilot, flew *Columbia.* The mission specialists were physicist Joseph P. Allen and electrical engineer William B. Lenoir. The two specialists had to cancel their planned 3½-hour spacewalk when the fan in Allen's suit and Lenoir's oxygen regulator malfunctioned. *Columbia* landed on a concrete runway at Edwards Air Force Base in California on November 16.

The space shuttle *Columbia* blasts off from Kennedy Space Center, Florida, on June 27 for its fourth and final test flight.

This mission was preceded by four test flights—two in 1981, one in March 1982, and the last in June and July 1982.

The payload of the third test flight, launched on March 22, consisted of apparatus and material for 23 scientific experiments. Heavy rains prevented the planned landing at Edwards Air Force Base, and a sandstorm kept astronauts Jack R. Lousma and C. Gordon Fullerton in orbit an extra day until they could land at the White Sands Missile Range in New Mexico on March 30.

Columbia carried military sensors for ground surveillance on its fourth mission, which began on June 27. During this mission, U.S. astronauts conducted military experiments in space for the first time. Astronauts Thomas K. Mattingly II and Henry W. Hartsfield, Jr., ended this mission by landing on a runway at Edwards on July 4. *Columbia*'s previous landings were on a dry lake bed.

Soviet Space Station. On April 19, the Soviet Union launched space station *Salyut 7,* replacing *Salyut 6,* which had been in service from 1977 to 1981. Cosmonauts Anatoly Berezovoy and Valentin Lebedev boarded the space station on May 14 and deployed a 62-pound (28-kilogram) communications satellite from it on May 17. Jean-Loup Chretien of France and Soviets Vladimir A. Dzhanibekov and Aleksandr S. Ivanchenkov visited *Salyut 7* during a mission that began on June 24 and ended on July 2. Leonid I. Popov, Aleksandr Serebrov, and Svetlana Y. Savitskaya boarded the space station on August 20. Savitskaya, 34, became the second woman in space, following Valentina Tereshkova, who orbited Earth in June 1963. Savitskaya and her companions landed on August 27. On November 14, Berezovoy and Lebedev broke the 185-day space-endurance record set by their countrymen Valery Ryumin and Leonid Popov in 1980. The two cosmonauts returned safely to Earth on December 10, after 211 days in orbit.

Two unmanned Soviet craft, *Venera 13* and *14,* landed on Venus on March 1 and 5, respectively. Data radioed to Earth indicated a barren, Moonlike surface under thick clouds. See ASTRONOMY.

Other Activities. The European Space Agency attempted to use its *Ariane* rocket to put a communications satellite and a scientific satellite into orbit on September 10, but the rocket failed 14 minutes into its flight. Space Services Incorporated of America, a Houston-based firm, became the first private company to launch a spacecraft. *Conestoga 1,* a surplus solid-fuel rocket purchased for $365,000, lifted off from Matagorda Island, Texas, on September 9. Its flight path was 196 miles (315 kilometers) high and 321 miles (517 kilometers) downrange. The Houston firm plans to launch a satellite in 1984. William J. Cromie

In WORLD BOOK, see SPACE TRAVEL.

SPAIN. The Socialist Workers' Party (PSOE) swept into power in general elections on Oct. 28, 1982, winning 201 seats, a gain of 80, in the 350-member Chamber of Deputies, the lower house of the Cortes (parliament). The right wing Popular Alliance finished second, gaining 82 seats for a total of 106.

The election was a disaster for the governing Union of the Democratic Center (UCD). The UCD lost 156 seats to finish with 12. The Communists won 5 seats and the new Democratic and Social Center (CDS), led by former Prime Minister Adolfo Suárez González, won only 2.

During the campaign, the PSOE promised to create 800,000 jobs and to reform the armed forces so that promotions would be based on merit rather than seniority. PSOE leader Felipe González Márquez said that he would try to renegotiate the pact under which the United States maintained military bases in Spain and promised a referendum on Spain's membership in the North Atlantic Treaty Organization (NATO).

González took the oath as prime minister on December 2. Only 40 years old, he was Western Europe's youngest prime minister. See GONZÁLEZ MÁRQUEZ, FELIPE.

On December 4, the new government devalued the peseta by 8 per cent.

Breakup. The Suárez government had been in turmoil for most of 1982. In January, it could muster only 151 votes against 153 for the opposition after three deputies defected from the UCD to the right wing Democratic Coalition. Two more deputies quit the UCD on June 17 when the government blocked a proposal to make the province of Segovia, which they represented, an autonomous region. On July 6, the UCD approached breakup when Prime Minister Leopoldo Calvo Sotelo y Bustelo resigned as president of the party. The next day, Calvo Sotelo quarreled with Suárez, his predecessor, over the party's future. Suárez left the UCD on July 28 and formed the CDS on July 29.

Social unrest added to the political turmoil, with both unemployment and inflation at 15 per cent. Calvo Sotelo lost 27 deputies in four weeks. By August 26, he could muster only 123 deputies in the Cortes. On August 27, King Juan Carlos I dissolved the Cortes and ordered the general election at Calvo Sotelo's request.

U.S. Arms and Bases. On July 23, Spain concluded the biggest arms agreement in its history. The $3-billion contract called for McDonnell Douglas Corporation, a United States firm, to deliver 84 F-18A fighter-bombers.

On July 2, Spain and the United States signed a new agreement on the use of U.S. naval and air bases on Spanish soil. However, the pact required parliamentary approval. The Cortes decided to

King Juan Carlos I reviews an honor guard in a parade on May 30, the day on which Spain joined the North Atlantic Treaty Organization.

postpone its decision until after the October general election.

Into NATO. Spain became the 16th member of NATO on May 30, the country's Armed Forces Day. The achieving of membership was a major triumph for the UCD against strong Socialist opposition.

Gibraltar Dispute. Spain's dispute with Great Britain over Gibraltar, the British dependency at Spain's southern tip, continued into 1982. Spain wants to annex Gibraltar. However, the people of Gibraltar voted for continued British rule in 1967. Spain closed its border with Gibraltar in 1969.

Spain had promised to reopen the border in April 1982. However, Britain's defense of the Falkland Islands delayed negotiations. Spain then postponed talks that had been scheduled for June. The Falklands conflict had aroused strong nationalistic feelings in Britain. The Spanish government believed that these feelings would make negotiations on Gibraltar more difficult. Spain finally reopened the border on December 14.

World Cup. Spain was the host for the 1982 World Cup tournament. World Cup tournaments are held every four years to determine the world champion of soccer. Italy won the 1982 tournament on July 11. See SOCCER. Kenneth Brown

See also EUROPE (Close-Up and Facts in Brief Table). In WORLD BOOK, see SPAIN.

SPIELBERG, STEVEN (1947-), enhanced his fame as Hollywood's most brilliant young motion-picture director with the extraordinarily successful film *E. T.: The Extra-Terrestrial* in 1982. The movie, the story of an ugly but lovable superintelligent being from "out there" who shares a bit of his life with some children on earth, continued Spielberg's long-time fascination with astronomy and science fiction.

Steven Spielberg was born on Dec. 18, 1947, in Cincinnati, Ohio, and grew up near Phoenix. He took part in scouting and Little League baseball, but even as a teen-ager his major interest was making films, often starring his sisters.

Spielberg's first commercial film, *Amblin'*, in the late 1960s, brought him two awards and the chance to direct for television. In 1971, he made his first full-length TV film, *Duel*, which won critical raves.

The versatile director's first nationally distributed film, *The Sugarland Express* (1974), also pleased critics, but not movie patrons. Spielberg hit his stride and began to develop his remarkable use of special effects with *Jaws* (1975). He continued to delight moviegoers with *Close Encounters of the Third Kind* (1977), *Raiders of the Lost Ark* (1981), and *Poltergeist* (1982). Steven Spielberg has said, "The only time I feel totally happy is when I'm watching films or making them." Marsha F. Goldsmith

SPORTS. Labor and drug problems beset professional sports in the United States in 1982. The National Football League (NFL) suffered its first regular-season players' strike, and the National Basketball Association (NBA) was threatened by a players' strike. The NFL also was plagued by problems involving the use of cocaine by players.

NFL players went on strike on September 21 after the second game of their 16-game season. The players' overall contract with the league had expired in July, and they sought 55 per cent of the gross income of the NFL clubs. This money was to be distributed to players via a wage scale from a central fund. When the owners rejected the players' demand, the players asked instead for 50 per cent of the league's huge television income. When that demand was also rejected, the players struck. The strike ended 57 days later and play resumed on November 21. See FOOTBALL.

The average salary in the NFL was $83,000 to $90,000. The average salary in the NBA was $218,000, the second highest in sports. But the NBA said two-thirds of its teams lost money during the 1981-1982 season.

The NBA wanted to reduce the 12-man rosters of teams to 10; eliminate guaranteed contracts; change air travel from first class to coach; and require the players to finance their pensions, life insurance, health coverage, and severance pay. The players wanted a share of TV revenue, guaranteed contracts, and increased benefits. The previous contract remained in effect until a new contract was negotiated.

A Drug Scandal erupted in the NFL in June when Don Reese said that widespread use of cocaine "controls and corrupts" the league. Reese, a former defensive end for three NFL teams, had served a year in prison for drug dealing. NFL teams set up rehabilitation programs for players who admitted having drug and alcohol problems.

Carl Lewis of Willingboro, N.J., who won national titles in the long jump and the 100-meter dash in 1981, received the Sullivan Award in February as America's outstanding amateur athlete.

Among the Winners in 1982 were the following:

Fencing. Russia took four gold medals in the world championships in July in Rome but barely won the team title from Italy, 104 points to 102.

Gymnastics. Nineteen-year-old Ni Ling of China dominated the men's events in the World Cup in October in Zagreb, Yugoslavia. He won six gold medals and one bronze. Olga Bicherova and Natalia Yurchenko of Russia won three gold medals each. Two Americans gained bronze medals — Peter Vidmar of Los Angeles in the men's horizontal bar and Julianne McNamara of Danville, Calif., in the women's vault.

Rowing. East Germany won three gold and four silver medals in the eight men's events of the world championships in Lucerne, Switzerland. The United States took two silver medals in women's competition, two silvers in lightweight men's, and two bronzes in heavyweight men's. Yale and California were the best college eights.

Shooting. Sergeant Daniel Carlisle of Fort Benning, Ga., won gold medals in both skeet and Olympic trap in the world championships in November in Caracas, Venezuela. Lieutenant Colonel Lones Wigger of Fort Benning won the small-bore rifle, three-position title for the 7th straight year and the 15th time in 20 years in the national championships at Camp Perry, Ohio.

Weight Lifting. In May, in the Russian championships in Dnepropetrovsk, Anatoly Pisarenko broke all three world records for super heavyweights. He snatched 203 kilograms (446¼ pounds), clean and jerked 258 kilograms (568½ pounds), and totaled 457.5 kilograms (1,008½ pounds). In the world championships in September in Yugoslavia, the gold medals were won by four Russians, including Pisarenko; four Bulgarians; and two Poles.

Wrestling. Russians won medals — seven gold, one silver, and two bronze — in every class in the world championships in Edmonton, Canada. Lee Kemp of Chardon, Ohio, took the 163-pound title for the third time. Greg Gibson of Redding, Calif., won a bronze medal at 220 pounds in these championships and a gold in the world championships of sombo, a form of wrestling.

Other Champions. *Archery,* U.S. champions: men, Rich McKinney, Glendale, Ariz.; women, Luonn Ryon, Parker Dam, Calif. *Badminton,* U.S. champions: men, Gary Higgins, Redondo Beach, Calif.; women, Cheryl Carton, San Diego. *Biathlon,* world champions: 10-kilometer, Erik Kvalfoss, Norway; 20-kilometer, Frank Ullrich, East Germany. *Billiards,* world pocket champions: men, Steve Mizerak, Fords, N.J.; women, Jean Balukas, Brooklyn,

Bernard Hinault of France leads the pack down the Champs Élysées in Paris on July 25 as he wins the 69th annual Tour de France bicycle road race.

N.Y. *Bobsledding,* U.S. champions: two-man, Brent Rushlaw, Saranac Lake, N.Y.; four-man, Bill Renton, Virginia Beach, Va. *Canoeing,* world 500-meter champions: canoe, Olaf Haukrodt, East Germany; men's kayak, Vladimir Parsenovich, Russia; women's kayak, Birgit Fischer, East Germany. *Casting,* U.S. all-around champion: Steve Rajeff, San Francisco. *Court tennis,* U.S. Open champion: Wayne Davies, New York City. *Croquet,* U.S. champion: Archie Peck, Palm Beach, Fla. *Cross-country,* world champions: men, Mohammed Kedir, Ethiopia; women, Maricica Puica, Romania. *Curling,* U.S. champions: men, Madison, Wis.; women, Bemidji, Minn. *Cycling,* world women's champions: sprint, Connie Paraskevin, Detroit; pursuit, Rebecca Twigg, Seattle. *Darts,* U.S. champion: Rick Ney, Schuylkill Haven, Pa. *Equestrian events,* World Cup jumping champion: Melanie Smith, Litchfield, Conn. *Field hockey,* World Cup: Pakistan. *Handball,* U.S. four-wall champion: Naty Alvarado, Hesperia, Calif. *Hang gliding,* U.S. champion: Rich Pfeiffer, San Juan Capistrano, Calif. *Horseshoe pitching,* world champions: men, Dale Lipovsky, Bloomington, Minn.; women, Phyllis Negaard, St. Joseph, Minn. *Judo,* U.S. open champions: men, Mitch Santa Maria, Roselle Park, N.J.; women, Heidi Bauersachs, Brooklyn, N.Y. *Karate,* U.S. open champion: Bob Allen, New Orleans. *Lacrosse,* world champion: United States; U.S. college, North Carolina. *Lawn bowling,* world indoor champion: John Watson, Scotland. *Luge,* U.S. champions: men, Frank Masley, Newark, Del.; women, Erica Terwillegar, Lake Placid, N.Y. *Modern pentathlon,* U.S. champions: men, Bob Nieman, San Antonio; women, Joy Hansen, Phoenix. *Motorcycling,* world champions: 500-cc motocross, Brad Lackey, Concord, Calif.; speedway, Bruce Penhall, Newport Beach, Calif. *Paddle tennis,* U.S. champion: Mark Rifenback, Los Angeles. *Paddleball,* U.S. champion: Larry Fox, Cincinnati. *Parachute jumping,* U.S. champions: men, Justin Shilling, Fort Bragg, N.C.; women, Cheryl Stearns, Fort Bragg. *Polo,* World Cup: Boehm-Palm Beach, Fla. *Racquetball,* U.S. pro champions: men, Marty Hogan, San Diego; women, Lynn Adams, Costa Mesa, Calif. *Racquets,* U.S. open champion: John Prenn, England. *Rodeo,* U.S. all-around champion: Chris Lybbert, Coyote, Calif. *Roller skating,* world artistic champions: men, Tim McGuire, Flint, Mich.; women, Kathleen O'Brien DiFelice, Langhorne, Pa. *Roque,* U.S. champion: Wayne Stephens, Lubbock, Tex. *Rugby,* U.S. champion: Old Blues, Berkeley, Calif. *Shuffleboard,* U.S. doubles champion: Jason Baade and Len deBoer, Lakeland, Fla. *Sled-dog racing,* international champion: Peter Norberg, Tuktoyaktuk, Canada. *Softball,* U.S. fast-pitch champions: men, Peterbilt Western, Seattle; women, Raybestos Brakettes, Stratford, Conn. *Squash racquets,* U.S. champions: men, John Nimick, Narberth, Pa.; women, Alicia McConnell, Brooklyn, N.Y. *Squash tennis,* U.S. champion: Gary Squires, New Haven, Conn. *Surfing,* world amateur champions: men, Tom Curren, Santa Barbara, Calif.; women, Jenny Gill, Australia. *Synchronized swimming,* world champion: Tracie Ruiz, Seattle. *Table tennis,* U.S. open champions: men, Zoran Kosanovic, Canada; women, Kayoko Kawahigashi, Japan. *Taekwondo,* U.S. heavyweight champions: men, Kim Royce, Berkeley, Calif.; women, Lynnette Love, Detroit. *Team handball,* U.S. champions: men, West Coast All-Stars; women, G & D Leisure, Iowa. *Tumbling,* world champions: men, Steve Elliott, Amarillo, Tex.; women, Jill Hollenbeck, Rockford, Ill. *Volleyball,* U.S. champions: men, Chuck's Steak House, Los Angeles; women, Monarch, Honolulu, Hawaii. *Water polo,* world champion: Russia. *Water skiing,* U.S. overall champions: men, Carl Roberge, Orlando, Fla.; women, Cyndi Benzel, Newberry Springs, Calif. Frank Litsky

See also articles on the various sports. In WORLD BOOK, see articles on the various sports.

SRI LANKA held its first direct popular election of a president on Oct. 20, 1982. The incumbent, J. R. Jayewardene, won a new six-year term.

In 1977, Jayewardene had led his United National Party to victory in parliamentary elections and had become prime minister. At that time, Sri Lanka's head of government was a prime minister chosen by the majority party in parliament. The next year, parliament changed the Constitution to establish a presidential system and selected Jayewardene to serve as the first president for a term scheduled to end in February 1984.

On Aug. 27, 1982, parliament passed a constitutional amendment empowering the president to call a presidential election four years after assuming office. Jayewardene immediately called one for October 20 and declared his candidacy.

The Election occurred while Jayewardene's main political opponent, former Prime Minister Sirimavo Bandaranaike, was legally forbidden to run for office. In 1980, the Jayewardene government barred her from politics for seven years on charges that she abused power while prime minister.

In 1982, Bandaranaike's Sri Lanka Freedom Party was split into two factions. Her son, Anura, was denied the party's nomination by quarreling between the factions. The party ran a lesser-known candidate, Hector Kobbekaduwa, for the presidency. He got 39 per cent of the vote to Jayewardene's 53 per cent.

Jayewardene campaigned on his program of relaxing government controls that he said had been strangling Sri Lanka's economy. Unemployment was lower in 1982 than when he took office in 1977, though estimates of joblessness ran as high as 20 per cent. Jayewardene's government had ended scarcities of most consumer goods, but inflation was more than 20 per cent. He had also cut back the nation's welfare system, formerly one of the most generous in the developing world, and he had emphasized free enterprise.

Sri Lanka Suffered during 1982 from severe drought. The lack of rain crippled production of tea, the main export earner, and set back plans to attain self-sufficiency in rice. A worldwide slump in tea prices also hurt Sri Lanka's economy. The government asked foreign food aid for 2 million persons in the northeastern part of the country, which was worst hit by the drought.

A State of Emergency declared on Aug. 17, 1981, because of fighting between the Sinhalese ethnic majority and the Tamil minority was allowed to lapse in January 1982. But the government imposed a new state of emergency on July 30 because of fighting between Muslims and Sinhalese. The government also temporarily introduced press censorship. Henry S. Bradsher

See also ASIA (Facts in Brief Table). In WORLD BOOK, see SRI LANKA.

STAMP COLLECTING. The United States Postal Service on April 14, 1982, issued a commemorative set of fifty 20-cent stamps depicting each state's official bird and flower. Although some collectors complained about the $10 cost of the full sheet of stamps, acceptance of the stamps was generally favorable. Many collectors sought first-day cancellations from state capitals as well as from Washington, D.C. The Postal Service encouraged buyers to keep full panes of the stamps as souvenirs by enclosing them in brightly colored folders.

Other commemorative issues included 20-cent stamps honoring President Franklin D. Roosevelt on the 100th anniversary of his birth; baseball player Jackie Robinson, the first black major-league player; three of the noted Barrymore theatrical family — Ethel, John, and Lionel; and physician and women's rights advocate Mary E. Walker, who received the Medal of Honor in 1865 for her service to the Union as a Civil War surgeon. The 300th anniversary of French explorer Sieur de La Salle's claim to the Mississippi River Basin was commemorated with a 13-cent postal card on April 7, and on August 6 the Postal Service honored the 200th anniversary of the Purple Heart decoration with a 20-cent envelope.

Major Sales. Investors were noticeably less interested in stamps in 1982, so prices were mostly down from previous years. However, there was keen competition among collectors for some seldom-available stamps of exceptional quality.

Two rare United States stamps, both of which had their center illustrations mistakenly printed upside down, sold for record prices in April at the Robert A. Siegel Auction Galleries' Rarities of the World Sale in New York City. An unused 1869 15-cent stamp showing an inverted Christopher Columbus landing in the New World brought $180,000. Only three unused specimens of this stamp are known. A 1918 24-cent airmail stamp with a Curtiss Jenny airplane printed upside down also sold for $180,000. The specimen at the April sale was in extremely fine condition, with all its gum intact.

At a postal history auction at New York City's Christie galleries in April, a fine-quality specimen of the so-called Waterbury, Conn., Running Chicken cancellation on a 3-cent 1869 stamp brought $3,400. The cancellation, depicting a chicken running with its wings outspread, was made by a Waterbury postal clerk, John W. Hill, who carved the design in cork. No more then five such strikes are recorded, all on 1869 stamps. Hill, who became Waterbury postmaster in 1870, carved hundreds of different "fancy cancels" over the next 20 years.

In Canada, the renowned Fur Trade Collection of the late Charles P. De Volpi, a prominent Canadian postal historian, went on the auction block in May in Toronto, Ont. Among the many scarce items from the Canadian frontier was the only surviving soldier's letter bearing a 2-cent Large Queen stamp, which depicts Queen Victoria of England. The letter was written during the first rebellion of the *métis* (Canadians of mixed European and Indian descent), in 1869-1870. The letter fetched $10,000 (Canadian dollars; $1 = U.S. 81 cents on Dec. 31, 1982).

An 1869 fifteen-cent stamp showing an inverted Christopher Columbus landing in the New World sold in April for $180,000 in New York City.

New Stamps. The centennial of German physician Robert Koch's discovery of the organism that causes tuberculosis was commemorated by stamps from a diverse group of countries, including Taiwan, China, Mexico, Belgium, and West Germany. On February 17, Australia issued a multicolored set of four stamps picturing whales that are found in Australian waters. Two of the stamps depict sperm whales and blue whales diving to the ocean depths. The other two stamps show humpback and southern right whales breaking the surface for air.

On February 25, Luxembourg issued, as part of a continuing cultural series, a set of stamps with landscape scenes representing the four seasons. On September 24, the United Nations issued its third annual group of stamps depicting the flags of 16 member nations. Paul A. Larsen

In WORLD BOOK, see STAMP COLLECTING.

STATE GOVERNMENT. The continuing recession in the United States in 1982 and cuts in federal aid forced most states to raise taxes and decrease their budgets to avoid deficits. Even so, six of the 46 states whose fiscal year ended on June 30, 1982, had deficits—Connecticut, Minnesota, New Hampshire, Ohio, Oregon, and Washington.

Twenty-eight states raised taxes, according to the Federation of Tax Administrators, a nonprofit organization of public officials. Twenty-six states cut their budgets, 16 imposed hiring freezes, and 20 laid off workers in the year ending on June 30. Deficits as large as $500 million were being predicted late in 1982 for several states.

The recession hit three regions especially hard: the industrial Midwest, with Michigan leading the nation in unemployment; part of the South, including Alabama, which had the second highest jobless rate; and the Northwest, where Oregon and Washington suffered from the crippling of the timber industry. Oklahoma had a revenue shortfall in September, causing the governor to order 5.5 per cent budget cuts and a hiring freeze.

Michigan's Governor William G. Milliken took severe measures to keep that state economically sound. On April 25, he ordered salary cuts and 700 layoffs of state workers. On May 11, the legislature pushed through a bill raising the state income tax by 22 per cent for six months.

Nevertheless, on May 12, Moody's Investors Service, a company that rates the credit of public and private organizations, reduced Michigan's rating to the lowest of all the states. Milliken took further action on June 8, cutting salaries and ordering 16,000 layoffs. On August 18, the governor ordered all state departments to freeze hiring "except in cases where there is exceptional need."

Sales Taxes rose from 4 to 5 per cent in Florida, Indiana, and Wisconsin; from 5 to 6 per cent in Minnesota and New Jersey; from 3 to 3.5 per cent in Nebraska; and from 3 to 4 per cent in Vermont. Washington levied a 4 per cent surcharge on its taxes and imposed a sales tax on food.

To finance education, Mississippi raised sales and income taxes, and Missouri voters approved a 1 cent sales tax hike. Ohio voted down a sales tax hike for a high-speed train. Authorizing additional local sales taxes were Colorado, Florida, Kansas, and Missouri.

Income Taxes on individual earnings went up in Alabama, Indiana, Michigan, Minnesota, Mississippi, Nebraska, New Jersey, Ohio, Oregon, Rhode Island, and Vermont. Arizona, Indiana, Iowa, Mississippi, and Oregon required speedier payment of income taxes. Maine voted to index income taxes to reflect inflation. However, Massachusetts and Oklahoma increased the value of personal exemptions, and South Carolina increased the amount of tax deduction.

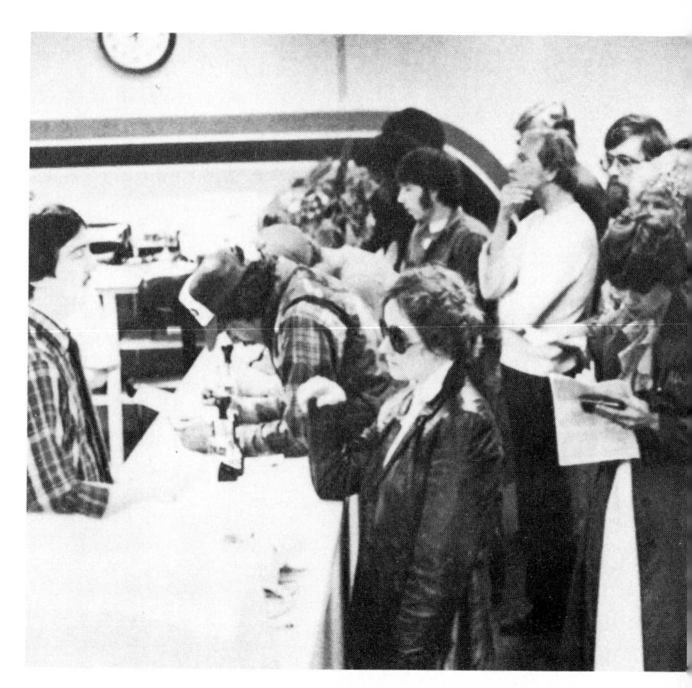

A state office in Anchorage takes applications for shares of Alaska's oil wealth. Alaskans began receiving checks for $1,000 in June.

Florida, Indiana, Iowa, Minnesota, Nebraska, Ohio, and Wisconsin hiked corporate income taxes in response to the federal Economic Recovery Tax Act (ERTA) of 1981. The 45 states that imposed corporate income taxes had tied their depreciation regulations to the federal tax code. ERTA allowed corporations to write off depreciation more rapidly, so the states faced revenue losses. Consequently, 15 of the 45 states decoupled their laws from the federal tax code.

Other Taxes. Motor fuel tax hikes passed in Arizona, Idaho, Kentucky, Maryland, Michigan, Vermont, and Virginia. Voters in Missouri and Oregon defeated increases in gasoline taxes. The District of Columbia, Nebraska, New Mexico, and Ohio increased their variable-rate taxes on motor fuels. These taxes are based on the fuel price. Rhode Island imposed a 1 per cent tax on the gross receipts of oil companies.

Cigarette taxes rose in Michigan, Missouri, Nebraska, New Jersey, Oregon, Rhode Island, Utah, Washington, and Wisconsin. Taxes on alcoholic beverages went up in Alabama, Kentucky, New Mexico, Utah, Virginia, and Washington.

Ballot Issues. Several states resolved tax issues by referendum votes in the November 2 general election. Oregon voters rejected the only property-tax rollback proposition on any state ballot. West Virginia approved a constitutional amendment that allowed local governments to tax property at less than its assessed value. This measure nullified a court order that had compelled local authorities to base taxes on the assessed amount. Utah voters approved a measure that increased property tax relief for homeowners. Wyoming voted to allow higher state property taxes. Voters removed a state property tax from the Texas constitution. The Kansas electorate repealed an intangibles tax.

A court approved a new tax in San Francisco in spite of California's ban on new taxes. Some $3-billion in bonds, half in California, were approved in November voting. On January 5, Governor Edward J. King of Massachusetts signed a bill that permitted communities to override a state law limiting property taxes.

Democrats Won 27 of 36 governors' races in November, bringing the number of Democratic governors to 34. Democrats also gained control of 11 legislative houses, while Republicans picked up one. The elections gave Democrats control of 72 of the 99 houses of state legislatures. (Forty-nine of the state legislatures have two houses, while one—Nebraska—has a single chamber.)

In November, eight states approved ballot issues calling for a nuclear arms freeze. One state approved a freeze issue in a primary election. Arizona defeated a freeze referendum in November. Bills that would have prohibited the use of disposable bottles for beverages lost on ballots in four states.

Thirty-five states and the District of Columbia strengthened drunk driving laws in 1982, according to the Highway Users Federation. Many of the laws required minimum jail terms and fines or license suspensions. Some states raised the drinking age. Only five states still allowed 18-year-olds to drink. The federal government approved a three-year program providing $125 million in incentives to encourage states to enact highway safety measures.

Criminal Justice continued to be a major state concern. In June, California voters approved a Victims' Bill of Rights that required criminals to compensate their victims, called for guaranteed safety in schools, stiffened penalties for repeat offenders, and eased court restrictions on the prosecution of criminals. Laws to aid crime victims or to require courts to consider victims when sentencing criminals passed in Hawaii, Indiana, Kentucky, Louisiana, Maryland, New York, Vermont, and other states. Various laws restricting bail or parole and easing restrictions on law-enforcement measures passed in Arizona, Colorado, Florida, Iowa, Illinois, Kansas, Oklahoma, Vermont, and Wisconsin. Alabama, California, Florida, Kansas,

Bill Garner, *The* (Memphis) *Commercial Appeal*

Selected Statistics on State Governments

State	Resident population (a)	Governor (b)	Legislature (b) House (D)	House (R)	Senate (D)	Senate (R)	State tax revenue (c)	Tax revenue per capita (d)	Public school enrollment (e)	Public school expenditures per pupil in average daily attendance (f)
Alabama	3,917	George C. Wallace (D)	97	8	32	3	$ 2,196	$ 564	743	$1,384
Alaska	412	Bill Sheffield (D)	19	21	9	11	2,539	6,316	91	5,010
Arizona	2,794	Bruce E. Babbitt (D)	21	39	12	18	1,856	683	507	1,914
Arkansas	2,296	Bill Clinton (D)	93	7	32	3	1,264	553	437	1,571
California	24,196	George Deukmejian (R)	48	32	25	15	21,819	922	4,046	2,594
Colorado	2,965	Richard D. Lamm (D)	25	40	14	21	1,690	585	544	2,656
Connecticut	3,134	William A. O'Neill (D)	88	63	23	13	2,340	753	505	2,697
Delaware	598	Charles M. Oberly, III (D)	25	16	13	8	595	1,001	95	2,781
Florida	10,183	Bob Graham (D)	84	36	32	8	5,556	570	1,487	2,262
Georgia	5,574	Joe Frank Harris (D)	156	24	49	7	3,281	601	1,056	1,652
Hawaii	981	George R. Ariyoshi (D)	43	8	20	5	1,066	1,105	163	2,121
Idaho	959	John V. Evans (D)	19	51	14	21	579	613	205	1,780
Illinois	11,462	James R. Thompson (R)	68	49(g)	33	26	7,429	650	1,924	2,441
Indiana	5,468	Robert D. Orr (R)	43	57	18	32	3,064	558	1,025	1,793
Iowa	2,899	Terry E. Branstad (R)	60	40	28	22	1,997	685	516	2,560
Kansas	2,383	John W. Carlin (D)	53	72	16	24	1,443	610	410	2,714
Kentucky	3,662	John Y. Brown, Jr. (D)	76	24	29	9	2,491	681	658	1,569
Louisiana	4,308	David C. Treen (R)	94	10(h)	39	0	3,127	744	782	1,972
Maine	1,133	Joseph E. Brennan (D)	93	57	23	10	730	650	216	2,055
Maryland	4,263	Harry R. Hughes (D)	124	17	41	6	3,193	757	722	2,541
Massachusetts	5,773	Michael S. Dukakis (D)	131	29	33	7	4,804	837	997	3,174
Michigan	9,204	James J. Blanchard (D)	63	47	20	18	6,307	681	1,770	2,461
Minnesota	4,094	Rudy Perpich (DFL)	77	57	42	25	3,799	932	734	2,484
Mississippi	2,531	William F. Winter (D)	116	4	48	4	1,462	580	472	1,536
Missouri	4,941	Christopher S. Bond (R)	110	53	22	12	2,313	470	819	2,079
Montana	793	Ted Schwinden (D)	55	45	24	26	529	672	153	2,948
Nebraska	1,577	Robert Kerrey (D)	49(i)		(unicameral)		861	548	273	2,105
Nevada	845	Richard H. Bryan (D)	23	19	17	4	745	932	151	2,179
New Hampshire	936	John H. Sununu (R)	156	241(g)(j)	9	15	326	353	164	2,033
New Jersey	7,404	Thomas H. Kean (R)	43	37	21	19	5,577	757	1,199	2,791
New Mexico	1,328	Toney Anaya (D)	45	25	23	19	1,228	942	268	2,219
New York	17,602	Mario M. Cuomo (D)	98	51(g)	25	36	15,438	879	2,761	3,358
North Carolina	5,953	James B. Hunt, Jr. (D)	102	18	44	6	3,790	644	1,109	1,992
North Dakota	658	Allen I. Olson (R)	55	51	21	32	533	816	118	2,062
Ohio	10,781	Richard F. Celeste (D)	63	36	17	16	5,819	539	1,909	2,143
Oklahoma	3,100	George P. Nigh (D)	76	25	34	14	2,713	897	583	2,007
Oregon	2,651	Victor G. Atiyeh (R)	36	24	21	9	1,552	590	457	3,049
Pennsylvania	11,871	Dick Thornburgh (R)	102	101	23	27	8,186	690	1,845	2,798
Rhode Island	953	J. Joseph Garrahy (D)	87	13	43	7	675	713	143	2,559
South Carolina	3,167	Dick Riley (D)	103	20(k)	41	5	1,959	628	609	1,560
South Dakota	686	Bill Janklow (R)	16	54	9	26	329	476	126	1,995
Tennessee	4,612	Lamar Alexander (R)	60	38(h)	22	11	2,146	467	838	1,458
Texas	14,766	Mark White (D)	114	36	25	5(k)	9,100	640	2,936	1,955
Utah	1,518	Scott M. Matheson (D)	17	58	5	24	951	651	356	1,742
Vermont	516	Richard A. Snelling (R)	65	83(g)(h)	13	17	332	650	93	2,017
Virginia	5,430	Charles S. Robb (D)	66	33(h)	31	9	3,236	605	990	2,223
Washington	4,217	John D. Spellman (R)	56	42	26	23	3,528	854	750	2,653
West Virginia	1,952	John D. Rockefeller IV (D)	88	12	31	3	1,469	753	378	1,816
Wisconsin	4,742	Anthony S. Earl (D)	58	41	17	16	3,934	836	804	2,769
Wyoming	492	Ed Herschler (D)	25	38(h)	11	19	763	1,622	100	2,596

(a) Number in thousands, 1981 estimates (Bureau of the Census).
(b) As of January 1983.
(c) 1982 preliminary figures in millions (Bureau of the Census).
(d) 1982 preliminary figures (Bureau of the Census).
(e) Number in thousands, fall, 1981 (National Center for Education Statistics).
(f) 1980-1981 (National Center for Education Statistics).
(g) 1 undecided contest.
(h) 1 independent.
(i) Nonpartisan.
(j) 2 independents.
(k) 1 vacancy.

Ohio, Oklahoma, and Texas voted to expand their prisons. Voters approved the death penalty in Massachusetts, while the New Jersey government enacted a death penalty law. Several states passed laws setting forth penalties for making and selling drug paraphernalia and look-alike drugs—legal substances that look like illegal substances. Some states increased penalties for dealing in illegal drugs.

Lawmakers re-evaluated the insanity defense after June 21, when a federal jury found John W. Hinckley, Jr., not guilty by reason of insanity on all charges of shooting President Ronald Reagan and three others in March 1981. At least eight states adopted laws providing for verdicts of guilty but mentally ill, while a few did away with the insanity defense. See COURTS AND LAWS (Close-Up).

Share the Wealth. On June 17, the government of Alaska began mailing $1,000 checks to residents of that state. Money for the payments came from the earnings of the $3.1-billion Alaska Permanent Fund. Money for the fund, in turn, came from the state's oil royalties. Alaska residents who had lived in the state for six months or more were eligible for the payments. More than 400,000 adults and children qualified.

Other Actions. By late October, 36 states had redrawn congressional districts and 39 states had remapped legislative districts in accordance with the 1980 census of the United States. Court challenges or objections by the U.S. Department of Justice were pending against a number of redistricting plans. Colorado, the District of Columbia, and Washington joined the 15 states that had lotteries.

Arizona adopted an unusual medical program for the poor in August. The government pays health-care providers such as physicians and hospitals a fixed fee for supplying medical services to assigned groups of poor people. Adopting this program enabled Arizona to become the 50th state to join the federal Medicaid system.

South Dakota planned to sell Missouri River water for use in a coal-slurry pipeline, but three other states challenged the plan in court. Connecticut legislated that the manufacturer of a new car that requires repeated repairs of one defect must pay for the repairs or replace the car.

The loss of federal aid and the decline in tax revenues shrank state government. The number of workers on state and local government payrolls fell by 212,000 during the year ending on Sept. 30, 1981, according to the Commerce Department's Bureau of the Census. In 1981, state governments employed 3.1 million people. State and local purchases declined from 1979 levels, according to the Bureau of Economic Analysis. Elaine Stuart Knapp

In WORLD BOOK, see STATE GOVERNMENT and articles on the individual states.

STEEL INDUSTRY. Weak domestic demand and strong competition from foreign producers combined to make 1982 a grim year for the United States steel industry. Production, utilization of plant capacity, employment, and other indicators of the industry's health reached their lowest levels in decades.

Production of raw steel by domestic mills during the first eight months of the year totaled 53 million short tons (48.1 million metric tons), compared with 85.7 million short tons (77.7 million metric tons) during the same period in 1981—a decrease of almost 40 per cent. Production in August was the lowest of any month, except for strike periods, since 1940. During the first eight months of 1982, U.S. steel mills operated at 51.8 per cent of capacity, the lowest figure since August 1938, during the Great Depression, when mills operated at only 39.6 per cent of capacity.

Employment in the industry also declined, continuing a long trend. By August 1982, only 283,000 steelworkers were on the job, compared with 402,000 in July 1981.

Dumping Charges. Steel industry executives blamed part of the dreary situation on foreign governments that, they said, subsidize their steel industries, thus allowing foreign producers to sell or "dump" steel products on the U.S. market at artificially low prices. During the first eight months of 1982, imported steel captured 22.6 per cent of the American market, up from 17.6 per cent during the same period in 1981.

The industry responded by filing trade complaints against the European Community (EC or Common Market), and countries outside the EC. On August 25, the U.S. Department of Commerce ruled that European countries were dumping steel on the American market at prices as much as 26 per cent below "fair value." On October 21, the Commerce Department announced that the dispute had been settled, with the EC agreeing to limit some steel exports, eliminating the need for sanctions against the countries involved.

Competitive Bids. General Motors Corporation (GM) announced on March 22 the adoption of a competitive bidding system for buying steel. The new system was intended to reduce GM's costs and improve quality. Previously, each GM plant bought its own steel from a group of about 12 producers, often paying producers' published list prices. GM accounts for about 50 per cent of all steel used by the U.S. automobile industry.

Bethlehem Steel Corporation announced on September 21 that it will end its steelmaking operations on the West Coast. The company, which operates one plant in Los Angeles and another in Seattle, said the closings were part of a strategy to modernize and realign operations. Michael Woods

In WORLD BOOK, see IRON AND STEEL.

STEPHEN, SIR NINIAN MARTIN (1923-), was sworn in as Australia's 20th governor general on July 29, 1982. He succeeded Sir Zelman Cowen. See AUSTRALIA.

Stephen was born on June 15, 1923, near Oxford, England. He was educated first at George Watson's School and Edinburgh Academy in Edinburgh, Scotland, then at St. Paul's School in London and Chillon College in Switzerland.

Arriving in Australia in 1940, Stephen studied law for a year at Melbourne University before serving in the Australian Army from 1941 to 1946. After discharge, he completed his law studies and became a barrister and solicitor.

In 1966, Stephen was appointed queen's counsel and appeared in the Victorian courts, the High Court, and the Privy Council on cases involving constitutional and commercial law and matters of equity and taxation. On June 30, 1970, Stephen was appointed to the Victorian Supreme Court. On March 1, 1972, he became a justice of the High Court of Australia and, in April, was made a Knight of the British Empire. He became a member of the Privy Council in 1979 and of the Judicial Committee in 1981.

Stephen held various posts at Monash University in Melbourne and the University of Melbourne. He married Valery Mary Sinclair in 1949, and they have five daughters. Marsha F. Goldsmith

STOCKS AND BONDS. Recovery from the recession remained just around the corner throughout 1982, but the stock market in the United States saw good news in the future and staged several of the biggest rallies in history. The Dow Jones industrial average, the most widely watched index of the stock market, closed on Dec. 31, 1981, at 875.00, far below the high of 1,051.70 set on Jan. 11, 1973. By early March 1982, the Dow fell to under 800 for the first time since April 1980. A rally carried the Dow to 869 on May 7, but by June 10 it was under 800 again. On July 23, it peaked at 830.57, only to fall once more to the year's low of 776.92 at the close of August 12.

Weeks of Frenzy. Then came the first of the year's "buying panics." The Dow rose 70 points during the week of August 16 with a new one-day record of 132.7 million shares traded on the New York Stock Exchange (NYSE), followed soon by another record of 137.33 million shares on August 26. By the end of August, the Dow was over 900.

The week of October 4 saw an even bigger buying frenzy. The Dow rose 79 points during the week, and another volume record of 147.07 million shares traded was set on October 7. On October 11, the Dow passed 1,000 during a week that set a new weekly volume record of 592.4 million shares.

On November 3, the day after the midterm election, the Dow jumped 43.41 points—a record for one day—and broke through its old high to set a record of 1,065.49. And still another new record volume of 149.35 million shares was set the next day. The market was not done for the year yet, however. It fell below 1,000 in November and December, jumped to another record high of 1,070.55 on December 27, and ended the year at 1,046.54.

Analysts speculated that all this buying amid a recession was caused by lower interest rates, or by the success—or failure—of Reaganomics, or by Democratic gains in the House of Representatives in the November election. No single explanation was agreed on.

Other Indexes. The Dow is the best known of all stock-market indexes, but it covers only 30 stocks of well-established industrial companies. More than 1,500 different stocks are traded on the NYSE, plus many others traded on the American Exchange (AMEX) in New York City, the Midwest Exchange in Chicago, and other exchanges, as well as through dealers in the over-the-counter (OTC) market. Each of these markets has its own index, and while all of the indexes generally move together with highs and lows on about the same dates, they may move at different rates.

Thus, while the Dow fell from 875 to 784 between the end of 1981 and mid-August 1982 for a loss of 10 per cent, the NYSE index covering all

The Dow Sinks, Then Soars

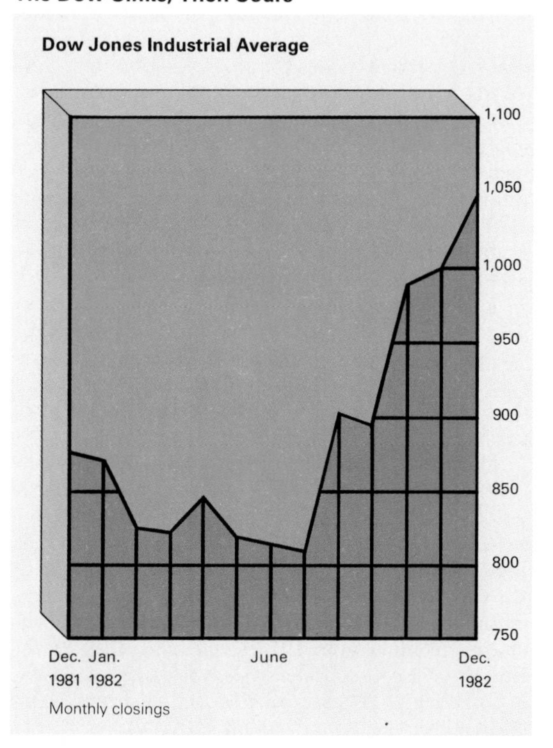

The New York Stock Exchange erupted into buying frenzies from August to December that sent prices soaring and set new volume records.

NYSE stocks fell 17 per cent from 71.1 to 58.8, and the AMEX fell 26 per cent from 321.4 to 237.5. From the bottom of the market in August 1982 to the November peak, the Dow rose 35 per cent while the AMEX climbed 42 per cent and the OTC composite rose 44 per cent. Investors who avoided the blue-chip stocks included in the Dow and bought a more diversified collection of stocks experienced even more violent ups and downs than those who stayed with the Dow.

The Bond Market. As short-term interest rates fell sharply late in 1982, long-term rates fell more slowly. The Bond Buyer Index of corporate AAA bonds began the year with an average yield of 15 per cent. The average yield is the rate of return a buyer would receive by holding newly purchased bonds until their maturity. The index hit a high of 15.5 per cent in mid-February, held between 14 and 15 per cent until the end of July, then fell below 12 per cent by the end of November. Tax-free bond rates followed the same pattern, beginning at 13.1 per cent, dipping in May to 11.9 per cent, remaining between 12 and 13 per cent until August, and dropping below 9 per cent by November. Since bond prices rise when yields fall, the bond market was a cheerful place late in the year. Donald W. Swanton

In WORLD BOOK, see BOND; INVESTMENT; STOCK, CAPITAL.

SUAZO CÓRDOVA, ROBERTO (1927-), a longtime country physician, became the president of Honduras on Jan. 27, 1982. Suazo Córdova was the first civilian to head the government of Honduras, the most impoverished Central American republic, since military rule was imposed in 1972. See HONDURAS.

Suazo Córdova was born on March 17, 1927, in La Paz, Honduras. He graduated from the University of San Carlos, Guatemala, in 1949 and received his medical degree from the University of San Carlos School of Medical Science in 1954. He practiced medicine in La Paz for the next 25 years, while also entering political life.

In 1960, Suazo Córdova became a leader of the moderately conservative Liberal Party, one of the two main political parties in Honduras. Until representative government was abolished in the army power seizure of 1972, Suazo Córdova served often in the Honduran Congress of Deputies. He was also elected as a deputy of the constitutional assemblies of 1957 and 1965, which created new constitutions for Honduras. When, in 1980, the military rulers agreed to re-establish a civilian government, Suazo Córdova served as president of an assembly elected to draft still another constitution.

Suazo Córdova pledged "a revolution of work and honesty" and solutions to the severe economic problems besetting Honduras. David L. Dreier

SUDAN joined other Arab states in providing asylum for Palestine Liberation Organization guerrillas evacuated from Beirut, Lebanon, as a consequence of Israel's invasion of Lebanon on June 6, 1982. About 500 guerrillas arrived in the Sudan in August. See MIDDLE EAST.

President and Prime Minister Gaafar Mohamed Nimeiri also mended fences with several of his African neighbors. The Sudan normalized relations with neighboring Chad in January and supported peace moves between Chad's government and rebel forces. In May, Nimeiri reached an agreement with Ethiopia to close down anti-Sudan and anti-Ethiopian opposition movements in the two countries.

Domestic Troubles. Nimeiri's problems were mainly internal. The dispute continued over reorganization of the southern autonomous region into five subregions. Nimeiri formed a new Higher Executive Council to carry out the changes.

The economy remained the Sudan's major problem. In January, student riots over price increases of 60 per cent for sugar and 30 per cent for gasoline caused the closing of the country's four universities during that month. The increases occurred when the government reduced its subsidies for the two commodities. William Spencer

See also AFRICA (Facts in Brief Table). In WORLD BOOK, see SUDAN.

SUPREME COURT OF THE UNITED STATES. In a term marked by unusual personal acrimony, the Supreme Court established new constitutional rights for illegal aliens and the mentally retarded during 1982. Overall, however, the high court continued its gradual drift to the right. Numerous decisions placed more power in the hands of state and local officials and less in those of the federal government. Several other rulings endorsed the arguments of police, prosecutors, and state judges and rejected those of defendants.

Several court watchers had predicted that the first woman justice, Sandra Day O'Connor, who joined the panel on Sept. 25, 1981, would strengthen the court's political center and diffuse the growing personal friction on the court. In fact, O'Connor quickly joined the court's two most conservative members, Chief Justice Warren E. Burger and fellow Arizonan William H. Rehnquist, and her pro-states' rights views appeared to stir up unprecedented internal warfare in the court's written opinions. Commenting on O'Connor's work at various times, Justice Harry A. Blackmun said it employed "rhetorical devices," "simply and completely misstates the issue," and "only confirms how far removed from the real world" she is. Justice William J. Brennan, Jr., called other O'Connor writings "incomprehensible" and replete with "tortuous reasoning." For her part, the new justice returned the fire, labeling one Blackmun opinion "an absurdity" and writing that Brennan's remarks "carry more rhetorical force than substance."

The tensions were heightened by the court's workload, which grew from 3,900 cases filed in 1975 to nearly 4,500 in the term ending in July 1982. During the year, seven of the nine justices warned that the escalating caseload was leading to a decline in the quality of judging.

Protection of Young People was involved in several court rulings. On July 2, the justices unanimously upheld a New York state law that banned portrayals of sexual activity by persons under 16, regardless of whether the activity in question was legally obscene. In another ruling, a 5 to 4 decision on March 24, the court held that states seeking to take custody of abused children must demonstrate their parents to be unfit using a stricter standard of proof than previously demanded.

Local schools were targets of two important rulings. A 5 to 4 decision on June 25 held that school boards can be sued if they infringe rights of free speech by censoring school library books in a "narrowly partisan or political manner." But the court interpreted a 1975 federal law narrowly in another case. In a 6 to 3 decision on June 28, the court said public schools are not required to provide all services that would allow handicapped children to attain their maximum potential.

In the case of *Plyler v. Doe*, the court decided 5 to 4 on June 15 that states such as Texas must provide free public education to children of illegal aliens. The decision, based on the United States Constitution's 14th Amendment equal protection clause, drew a dissent from Burger, who accused the majority of usurping state authority.

Civil Rights Decisions included a noteworthy ruling written by Justice O'Connor for a 5 to 4 majority on July 1 declaring unconstitutional a state law that excluded men from the Mississippi University for Women School of Nursing. On July 2, the court unanimously threw out a $1.25-million damage award against the National Association for the Advancement of Colored People stemming from its 1966 economic boycott of white merchants in Claiborne County, Mississippi. In still another key case, the court decided by a 6 to 3 vote on July 1 that circumstantial evidence, rather than a so-called smoking gun, is sufficient to prove intentional discrimination in a voting rights complaint.

Claims by criminal defendants fared poorly at the court during 1982. In two rulings, the justices declared that federal courts cannot review issues in habeas corpus petitions that the convicts neglected to raise in earlier stages of their cases. By 6 to 3 on June 1, the court also overturned virtually all barriers to warrantless searches of automobiles, provided that police have cause to suspect the presence of incriminating evidence.

Mentally retarded individuals in state custody have constitutional rights not only to safety and freedom from unreasonable bodily restraint, but also to "minimally adequate or reasonable training to ensure safety and freedom from undue restraint," a unanimous court held in *Youngberg v. Romeo,* decided on June 18.

Other Important Decisions included:

- A 6 to 2 ruling, on June 28, that states cannot ban enforcement of due-on-sale clauses by mortgage lenders. The contract clauses permit lenders to demand full payment if the borrower sells or transfers the mortgaged property.
- A 5 to 4 ruling, on June 24, that former President Richard M. Nixon and other Presidents are immune from civil suits for acts within the "outer perimeter" of their official responsibilities.
- A 6 to 3 ruling, on June 23, reaffirming press access to virtually all criminal trials. The decision overturned a Massachusetts law that closed courtroom doors during testimony of sexual assault victims under 18 years of age.

David C. Beckwith

See also COURTS AND LAWS. In the Special Reports section, see THE HIGH COURT: AT THE CENTER OF A STORM AGAIN. In WORLD BOOK, see SUPREME COURT OF THE UNITED STATES.

SURGERY. See MEDICINE.
SURINAME. See LATIN AMERICA.
SWAZILAND. See AFRICA.

SWEDEN. Swedish voters cast their ballots to end six years of nonsocialist rule in general elections on Sept. 19, 1982. The Social Democrats returned to power by winning 46 per cent of the popular vote, giving them 166 seats, a gain of 12, in the 349-seat *Riksdag* (parliament). The Communists retained their 20 seats.

The Conservatives gained 13 seats, becoming the strongest nonsocialist party. The Centrists, led by Prime Minister Thörbjorn Fälldin, dropped 8 seats, leaving them 56. The Liberals won 6 per cent of the vote and lost 17 seats.

The main issue of the election was a proposal by the Social Democrats' leader, Olof Palme, to introduce wage-earner funds, which would allow representatives of workers to buy private industries. Palme also promised to restore public spending programs that had been cut. He said that the government would pay for the programs by levying a new tax on industrial production and by increasing the value-added tax, a kind of sales tax. Palme took the oath as prime minister October 7. See PALME, OLOF.

Spending Cuts. On January 11, the Fälldin government proposed a budget that would cut public spending by $1.7 billion. The budget provided for cuts in government spending, rent rebates, and public benefits, with higher charges for medical and dental services. The Riksdag approved the budget.

Submarine Summer. On June 17, the Riksdag passed a tough law for dealing with foreign submarines found in its waters. The new law, which was to take effect on July 1, 1983, authorizes the Swedish Navy to force any unknown submarine to the surface and to take it to a safe anchorage.

The new law followed what the Swedish news media called "submarine summer." On June 3, a submarine appeared off Härnösand in the Gulf of Bothnia, which is between Sweden and Finland. The Swedish Navy sealed off most of the gulf, but the submarine slipped out. On June 4, a second submarine was spotted farther south, off Sundsvall. The navy chased this sub back to international waters.

Recovery Program. Sweden devalued its krona by 16 per cent on October 8 as part of a 12-point economic recovery program. The devaluation caused a crisis in the government and angered Norway and Finland. The government also announced a general freeze on prices. On October 11, Sweden increased the value-added tax to 23.5 per cent, cut various tax shelters, and promised to formulate plans to help create jobs. Kenneth Brown

See also EUROPE (Facts in Brief Table). In WORLD BOOK, see SWEDEN.

Schoolchildren dance for Sweden's King Carl XVI Gustaf, far left, and Queen Silvia during the royal couple's visit to Mexico in January.

SWIMMING. The United States, for years the international leader in swimming, suffered a setback in the 1982 world championships. East Germany won 12 gold medals to 8 for the United States, though each nation won a total of 25 medals.

The World Championships were part of the IV World Aquatics Championships, a meet held from July 29 to August 8 in Guayaquil, Ecuador. The meet featured four sports—diving, swimming, synchronized swimming, and water polo. Overall, the leading medal winners were the United States with 34, East Germany with 26, and Russia with 17. The American totals were helped by a sweep of the four gold medals in diving—two by Greg Louganis of El Cajon, Calif., and one each by Megan Neyer and Wendy Wyland, both of Mission Viejo, Calif.

As expected, the East German women did well, winning 10 gold medals to the Americans' 2. The American men won only 6 events, including 3 relays. The only American individual champions were Steve Lundquist of Jonesboro, Ga., in the 100-meter breaststroke; Matt Gribble of Miami, Fla., in the 100-meter butterfly; Rick Carey of Mount Kisco, N.Y., in the 200-meter backstroke; Mary T. Meagher of Louisville, Ky., in the women's 100-meter butterfly; and Kim Linehan of Sarasota, Fla., in the women's 800-meter free-style.

The year's top swimmers were Vladimir Salnikov of Russia among the men and Petra Schneider of East Germany among the women. Salnikov won the world championships in the 400-meter and 1,500-meter free-style, and during the year he broke the world records for 400 meters (3 minutes 49.57 seconds, twice), 800 meters (7:53.83), and 1,500 meters (14:56.35). Schneider gained world titles in the women's 200-meter and 400-meter individual medley. She won the 400-meter race in a world-record time of 4:36.10.

The American Season. The only Americans to set individual world records were Ambrose (Rowdy) Gaines IV of Winter Haven, Fla., in the 200-meter free-style (1:48.93) and Lundquist in the 100-meter breaststroke (1:02.62 and 1:02.53). Gaines won two titles in the United States short-course championships and two in the long-course championships.

Nineteen-year-old Tracy Caulkins of Nashville, Tenn., won the most American titles. She took four titles in the short-course championships and three in the long-course. Her career total of 42 titles broke Johnny Weissmuller's record of 36. Caulkins also won five events in leading Florida to the National Collegiate Athletic Association's first championship for women. UCLA won the men's title. Frank Litsky

In WORLD BOOK, see DIVING; SWIMMING.

Victor Davis of Canada shouts for joy after setting a world record of 2:14.77 in the men's 200-meter breaststroke in Ecuador on August 5.

SWITZERLAND. In a national referendum on June 6, 1982, the Swiss approved, by a margin of almost 2 to 1, penal code changes providing stiffer penalties for terrorism, rioting, and inciting public disorder. The law was drafted in response to youth riots in Zurich in 1981. In another June 6 referendum, the voters narrowly rejected a law that would have made it easier for Switzerland's 795,000 foreign workers to bring their families to Switzerland and to obtain residency permits.

Shortly after approving its stronger penal code, Switzerland experienced its first terrorist incident. On September 6, four armed men, claiming to be members of a Polish paramilitary group, took over the Polish Embassy in Bern. The terrorists took 13 hostages and threatened to blow up the building unless Poland ended martial law and freed its political prisoners. The siege ended on September 9 when Swiss antiterrorist police stormed the embassy, freed the five remaining hostages (eight had been released), and captured the terrorists.

Switzerland may finally become a United Nations member, while maintaining its traditional neutrality. The Federal Assembly was expected to complete membership application procedures by mid-1983, after which the issue would be put to a referendum. Kenneth Brown

See also EUROPE (Facts in Brief Table). In WORLD BOOK, see SWITZERLAND.

SYRIA. A violent uprising in the city of Hama in February 1982 briefly threatened the government of President Hafiz al-Assad before it was put down by army units. The uprising began on February 2 when Syrian security forces raided the city in a search for a suspected arms cache hidden by the Muslim Brotherhood, an organization of fundamentalist Sunni Muslims. Since 1979, the organization has attempted to overthrow Assad's minority Alawi Muslim regime by attacking government officials and members of the Alawi community.

The largely Sunni Muslim population of Hama, angered at what they saw as police and army brutality, united with the rebels. Syrian army units responded by sealing off the city. About 3,000 people were killed or wounded before order was restored in the area.

Conflict with Iraq. The Hama uprising brought to the breaking point Syria's hostile relations with Iraq, whose population is largely Sunni Muslim. Syria accused Iraq of backing the rebels and on April 8 closed its border with that country. Two days later, Syria shut down a pipeline that carried Iraqi crude oil across its territory to the Mediterranean port of Baniyas.

Action in Lebanon. Syria's isolation from other Arab states — a consequence of Syria's support for Iran in its war with Iraq — lessened as a result of the Israeli invasion of Lebanon in June. The invasion papered over some of the cracks in the wall of Arab unity. Although Israel warned Syrian peacekeeping troops stationed in Lebanon to stay out of Israel's battle against the Palestine Liberation Organization (PLO), there was considerable fighting between Israeli and Syrian troops. Syria got the worst of it, as its forces were driven out of the Beirut area and back to the Al Biqa — or Bekaa — Valley, where they dug in and held off the Israelis. During the fighting, the Israelis destroyed 86 of Syria's Soviet-built aircraft and all 19 of its surface-to-air missile sites. In September, however, Russia replaced some Syrian equipment lost in the fighting but delayed aircraft replacement.

Palestinian Refuge. Syria accepted 7,000 to 8,000 PLO guerrillas evacuated in August from West Beirut, Lebanon, more than any other country. It also accepted all top PLO leaders, except Yasir Arafat, who set up new headquarters in Tunisia.

Other Developments. In August, Marathon Oil Company reported a major natural gas discovery in the Hama area. Production of the gas would give a boost to Syria's economy. On March 4, the United States lifted its ban on the sale of civilian aircraft to Syria. William Spencer

See also MIDDLE EAST (Facts in Brief Table). In WORLD BOOK, see SYRIA.

Syrian demonstrators in Damascus proclaim their support for President Hafiz al-Assad, whose troops crushed an uprising in Hama in February.

TABB, MARY DECKER (1958-), of Eugene, Ore., set major records for women's track in 1982. She broke world records in the mile, the 5,000-meter, and the 10,000-meter races. She also set U.S. records for 800 meters and 3,000 meters.

Tabb began the year sensationally, breaking the indoor world record for the mile three times by mid-February. She also set an indoor world record for 3,000 meters. But her biggest records of the year came at outdoor meets because, traditionally, outdoor records are the more important standards.

In June, Tabb ran 5,000 meters in 15 minutes 8.26 seconds. During July, she ran the 800 meters in 1:58.33; the mile in 4:18.08; the 3,000 meters in 8:29.71; and the 10,000 meters in 31:35.3. Her time in the 10,000 meters broke the world record by more than 40 seconds. In September, Maricica Puica of Romania ran the mile in 4:17.44, breaking Tabb's record.

Mary Decker was born in Flemington, N.J., on Aug. 4, 1958. At the age of 13, she was fast enough to qualify for the 1972 U.S. Olympic team, but too young to compete. At 16, she developed shin splints, an injury that kept her out of the 1976 Olympics and threatened her career. In 1977, Decker underwent a then-rare operation on her calf muscles and was competing again within a year. She married Ron Tabb, a top marathon runner, in 1981. William T. Graham

TAIWAN recorded economic growth during 1982, despite a worldwide recession. The nation also maintained internal political calm and weathered another difficult period in its relations with the United States.

President Chiang Ching-kuo continued to maintain political control of the island nation. Families from mainland China who had fled to Taiwan before the Communist victory in 1949 held most of the power, though they made up only 15 per cent of the population. But local Taiwanese increased their role in both political and economic affairs.

Arms Sales. The Nationalist government on Taiwan had hoped that the new Administration of United States President Ronald Reagan would be more supportive than previous administrations had been since the United States began official contacts with the People's Republic of China in 1979. However, in January 1982, the Reagan Administration decided not to sell Taiwan advanced fighter planes that it had requested. "No military need for such an aircraft exists," the United States said. However, it promised to continue to help Taiwan produce the American F-5E jet fighter.

This decision was followed by negotiations between the United States and the People's Republic. On August 17, the two governments issued a joint communiqué on American arms sales to Taiwan. The communiqué declared China's "policy of striving for a peaceful resolution" of its relations with the island. The United States said its arms sales to Taiwan "will not exceed, either in qualitative or in quantitative terms, the level of those supplied in recent years." The United States also promised that arms sales would be reduced slowly.

Taiwan expressed "profound regret" over the communiqué, which it said was "in contradiction of the letter and spirit" of the Taiwan Relations Act of 1979. Taiwan continued to reject suggestions from China that it discuss "unification" with the Communist-ruled mainland.

In early December, the Pentagon announced plans to sell Taiwan $97 million worth of Army vehicles, the first such sale since the communiqué. The U.S. Congress had 30 days to veto the deal.

Taiwan's Economic Growth was about 4 per cent in 1982. Although short of the government's goal of 7.5 per cent, the island's growth rate was better than that of most countries.

By 1982, many of Taiwan's manufactured goods were being produced cheaper in less developed countries. As a result, the government tried to direct industries into higher-value products that would return more profit for Taiwan's skilled labor. Henry S. Bradsher

See also ASIA (Facts in Brief Table); CHINA, PEOPLE'S REPUBLIC OF. In WORLD BOOK, see TAIWAN.

TANZANIA. See AFRICA.

TAXATION. The Tax Equity and Fiscal Responsibility Act of 1982, passed by the United States Congress on August 19 and signed promptly by President Ronald Reagan, repealed some of the record tax cuts of 1981. The measure, which was expected to trim mounting federal budget deficits by $115.8 billion over three years, included tax increases totaling about $91 billion; $17.5 billion in spending cuts, mostly in social programs; and provisions aimed at ensuring greater compliance with tax laws. The total revenue increases were projected to total $98.3 billion.

Reagan told Congress in January, "I will not ask you to balance the budget on the backs of the American taxpayer." However, he adjusted his thinking by midyear under pressure from legislators—Republican as well as Democratic—who were alarmed at the prospect of a succession of record deficits exceeding $100 billion per year.

Some $50 billion of the tax hikes were imposed on business, largely by repealing or restricting tax breaks enacted in 1981, some of which had not yet taken effect. The 1982 act scrapped accelerated depreciation rates for 1985 and 1986. Congress also voted to phase out controversial provisions of the 1981 law that allowed companies to, in effect, sell tax breaks that they could not make use of themselves.

Compliance Measures. Starting July 1, 1983, banks and corporations would be required to withhold 10 per cent from interest and dividend income. However, low-income people, many of the elderly, and the first $150 of income from each account were exempted from the provision.

Consumers were to be directly affected by a tripling, to 3 per cent, of the federal excise tax on telephone service, a doubling of the cigarette tax to 16 cents a pack, and an increase of the tax on airline tickets from 5 per cent to 8 per cent.

Congress also voted to restrict individual tax deductions for medical expenses, effective Jan. 1, 1983. Such expenses would be deductible only if they exceed 5 per cent of a taxpayer's adjusted gross income—up from 3 per cent in the past.

Also restricted, starting in 1983, were deductions for uninsured capital losses. Formerly, losses exceeding $100 were deductible, but under the new law deductible losses must amount to at least $100 plus 10 per cent of adjusted gross income.

The 1982 law did not affect the three-year, 25 per cent reduction in individual income tax rates enacted in 1981. The third installment, of 10 per cent, was scheduled for July 1, 1983.

Congressional leaders of both parties reacted coolly in November when Reagan spoke of possibly advancing the mid-1983 rate cut to January 1 in order to stimulate the recession-battered economy. As Congress convened on November 29 for a post-election session, however, there was broad support for legislation — endorsed by Reagan — to increase the federal gasoline tax by 5 cents per gallon (3.8 liters), to 8 cents. The added receipts of more than $5 billion per year would be earmarked for the rehabilitation of highways, bridges, and urban transit systems. The measure's appeal lay in its creation of an estimated 320,000 jobs. The legislation was passed on December 23.

Social Security Increase. For many American workers, 1983 was to bring an automatic increase in Social Security taxes. Starting on January 1, the 6.7 per cent tax was to be levied on the first $35,700 of annual wages. The wage base, which was $32,400 in 1982, rises each year under a formula tied to average wages. The maximum Social Security tax paid in 1983 was to be $2,391.90, up from $2,170.80. See SOCIAL SECURITY.

Federal Tax Receipts and miscellaneous revenues rose to $617.8 billion in the 1982 fiscal year (ending Sept. 30, 1982). The total for fiscal 1981 was $599.3 billion. Because of the recession and first-time use of more generous depreciation schedules enacted in 1981, corporate income tax receipts fell from $61.1 billion to $49.2 billion. Receipts from individuals rose from $285.6 billion to $298.1 billion. Delinquent taxes rose to $24.6 billion on September 30, up from $20.5 billion a year earlier. The Internal Revenue Service estimated that $97-billion per year in taxes was being evaded.

State Tax Hikes. During 1982, legislatures in 21 states enacted $2.9 billion in tax increases, according to a report by the Tax Foundation, a Washington, D.C.-based organization. Sales-tax increases in seven states, offset in one state by lower property taxes, were projected to yield more than $1.3 billion per year in additional state revenues. Higher personal income taxes in four states accounted for $991 million in new revenues, and seven other states enacted smaller hikes. Minnesota, Ohio, and Wisconsin — among seven states raising corporate taxes — boosted taxes on corporations by an estimated $85.9 million. In addition, six states adjusted individual or corporate tax rates to offset what otherwise would have been automatic revenue losses based on lower federal tax rates.

Nine states increased cigarette taxes to yield an extra $228.4 million annually. Three boosted motor-fuel levies by $76.1 million, and four others passed lesser increases. Taxes on alcoholic beverages were increased in six states.

A 1 per cent increase in Florida's general sales tax was among the largest of the various revenue-raising actions. However, the extra $762 million it was expected to produce would be largely offset by lower property taxes. Other major tax increases were voted by legislatures in Ohio, $544 million; Michigan, $370 million; and Washington state, $266.2 million. Frank Cormier

In WORLD BOOK, see TAXATION.

TELEVISION. Change and turmoil continued to dominate the United States television industry in 1982. A federal government movement to deregulate the industry continued, a consumer boycott was begun, and a labor strike once again caused problems for network programmers. If any major programming trend emerged, it was toward an expanded volume of news and information shows.

FCC Actions. The major deregulation effort accomplished by the Federal Communications Commission (FCC) in 1982 involved pay-TV and cable television. The FCC dropped previous restrictions that required pay-TV stations to broadcast a certain amount of standard, free programming each day in addition to their scrambled-signal programming, which can be received only by paying subscribers.

The FCC also approved a total of eight applications to begin *direct broadcast satellite* (DBS) operations in the United States. Once in place, DBS systems will beam programming directly to viewers who have rooftop dish antennas and whose television sets are equipped to convert the transmissions from the orbiting satellites to the frequencies used by the sets.

The Cable Scene. Meanwhile, a major cable television venture came to an end, raising questions about whether some of the new services launched

Charles Ryder (Jeremy Irons, right) visits the world of Sebastian Flyte (Anthony Andrews) in the British TV series "Brideshead Revisited."

Stacy Keach stars as a Union secret agent in the TV miniseries "The Blue and the Gray." The Civil War drama was shown in the fall on CBS.

during the recent cable boom were about to experience business difficulties. Citing financial losses resulting from weak advertiser support, CBS ceased operating its cultural-programming cable service on December 17. The service had begun in 1981.

At the other extreme, Ted Turner, owner of Cable News Network, announced plans to create a new national network based at his Atlanta, Ga., television station, WTBS. It will transmit programs by satellite to cable TV systems.

A Long-Threatened Boycott designed to change the nature of network programming was called for on March 4 by the National Coalition for Better Television. Led by Donald E. Wildmon, a United Methodist minister from Tupelo, Miss., the organization announced that it was boycotting NBC-TV and its parent company, RCA Corporation. The coalition objected to what its members saw as an excessive amount of sex, violence, and negative values in network programming. An NBC official called the boycott "an obvious attempt at intimidation." As 1982 ended, there was no clear evidence that the boycott was succeeding.

Another organization, the National Coalition on Television Violence, voiced displeasure with the major networks. On May 10, the group reported that the violent acts depicted in network shows had risen by 39 per cent in one year and had reached new highs.

The charge came five days after the National Institute of Mental Health released a report concluding that there was overwhelming scientific evidence that "excessive" television violence could lead to aggressive behavior by children and teenagers. The report was based on some 2,500 publications and studies made since 1970.

Labor Problems Again. For the third consecutive year, a labor strike kept some network programs off the air. This strike, however, was called by the National Football League's (NFL) players rather than by the people who produce or star in television programs. The eight-week strike, which began on September 21 and ended on November 16, halted play in the league—and ABC, CBS, and NBC had to scramble to find programs with which to replace their NFL telecasts. Most of ABC's Monday-night football games were replaced by movies. To replace its Sunday-afternoon games, NBC televised Canadian professional football games for a while but soon dropped the practice because of poor viewer support. CBS used a variety of substitutes, including telecasts of football games played by small colleges seldom if ever seen on national TV.

More Commercials? Despite all their problems, the major networks confidently made plans to sell more advertising than ever. ABC, CBS, and NBC each said they would gradually increase advertising time on their prime-time line-ups.

Danny De Vito, left, and Christopher Lloyd star in the comedy series "Taxi," which was canceled by ABC-TV but picked up by NBC-TV for 1982-1983.

In a separate development, the National Association of Broadcasters (NAB) and the U.S. Department of Justice reached an out-of-court settlement of a 1979 antitrust suit, which could lead to still more commercials on television. The NAB, which for 30 years had been restricting the number of commercials by means of a voluntary code, agreed to stop doing so. The consent decree was signed by U.S. District Judge Harold H. Greene on Nov. 23, 1982. Most industry observers seemed to feel that competitive pressures would prevent broadcasters from adding a large number of commercials to their schedules anytime soon.

The Big Story in Network Programming in 1982 was a major expansion of news, apparently, at least in part, in response to competitive pressures from the various cable news services. ABC, CBS, and NBC added a total of 37½ hours of news programming per week to their schedules, including an expansion of morning news programs by all three networks. Each network also began a new late-night news program. On July 5, NBC launched a one-hour program called "NBC News Overnight." On October 4, CBS began broadcasting its four-hour, post-midnight "CBS News Nightwatch," and on October 25, ABC began its news and information program, "The Last Word."

In Prime-Time Hours, when the bulk of the most expensive and popular entertainment series are broadcast, the 1982-1983 season began on September 27, the beginning of the so-called première week. ABC, CBS, and NBC added a total of 23 new shows to their line-ups during the early days of the season. Six new shows were seen on CBS, the highest rated of the networks during the previous season. ABC, which finished a close second in the ratings in 1981-1982, added seven new shows, while third-rated NBC added 10.

Perhaps, though not admittedly, in response to protests by consumer groups, there was a conspicuous scarcity of sexually suggestive scenes and dialogue in network shows. However, escapist action-adventure shows proliferated, threatening to bring more violence to the airwaves. Shows in that category included ABC's "Tales of the Gold Monkey" and "The Quest"; CBS's "Bring 'Em Back Alive"; and NBC's "Knight Rider," "Voyagers," and "The Powers of Matthew Star." As the year ended and the television season reached its midway point, none of those shows had proved especially popular in the ratings. Several had been canceled, and most of the rest were at or near the bottom of the rankings.

Among the new series, only "Gloria" (with Sally Struthers) and "Newhart" (with Bob Newhart) — both CBS comedies — appeared among the 20 most-popular prime-time series during the first half of the season. Otherwise, such old favorites as

"Dallas," "M*A*S*H," "60 Minutes," and "Three's Company" continued to dominate the popularity charts.

Among the surprises was the sudden popularity of a CBS drama called "Simon & Simon." It received very low ratings during its first season, 1981-1982, and was taken off the air for a while as a result. But the show suddenly soared in 1982-1983, often placing in the top 10 in the weekly ratings. A major reason for the success of the series was its scheduling, which placed it immediately after the network's popular "Magnum, P.I." series. CBS made a noticeable effort to link the two shows in an apparently successful effort to persuade "Magnum" viewers to watch "Simon & Simon" as well.

In Public Television, perhaps the most noteworthy newcomers to the screen were commercials, which cropped up on 10 stations beginning in January as part of an 18-month experiment to explore new sources of funding. The experiment was authorized by the Temporary Commission on Alternative Financing of Public Telecommunications, a panel appointed by Congress. It included members of Congress and of the FCC. Ron Alridge

See also AWARDS AND PRIZES. In the Special Reports section, see THE VIDEO REVOLUTION. In WORLD BOOK, see TELEVISION.

TENNESSEE. See STATE GOVERNMENT.

TENNIS. By competitive standards, the most successful tennis players in 1982 were Jimmy Connors of Belleville, Ill., and Martina Navratilova of Dallas. Financially, Ivan Lendl of Czechoslovakia and Navratilova, born in Czechoslovakia, were the major winners. Each earned more than $1.5 million in tournaments, far more than any of their rivals.

The Men. The two players who had dominated men's tennis—John McEnroe of New York City and Bjorn Borg of Sweden—had trouble in 1982. Borg, at 25, felt he needed a rest, and took five months off from tournaments. He wanted to play only seven Grand Prix tournaments all year, but the rules required him to play at least 10 to avoid having to play qualifying rounds in every tournament. When international officials refused to amend the rules, Borg declined to try for his sixth Wimbledon or seventh French title. Although he played a few tournaments, he sat out most of the year.

McEnroe, who won the Wimbledon and United States Open titles in 1981 at age 22, lost this time to Connors in the Wimbledon final and to Lendl in the United States Open semifinals. Connors beat McEnroe on July 4 at Wimbledon, England, 3-6, 6-3, 6-7, 7-6, 6-4, in 4 hours 14 minutes, the longest Wimbledon final ever.

Lendl skipped Wimbledon because he did not like playing on grass. In the U.S. Open, on asphalt, he eliminated McEnroe, 6-4, 6-4, 7-6. In the final on September 12 in Flushing Meadows, N.Y., Connors defeated Lendl, 6-3, 6-2, 4-6, 6-4. The win gave Connors his fourth U.S. Open title since 1974 and made him the first male tennis player to reach $4 million in career earnings. Navratilova was the only woman at that level.

The brightest newcomer of the year was 17-year-old Mats Wilander of Sweden. He won the French Open by beating four of the world's 10 leading players—Guillermo Vilas and José-Luis Clerc of Argentina; Vitas Gerulaitis of Kings Point, N.Y.; and Lendl. In the final on June 6, Wilander outlasted Vilas, 1-6, 7-6, 6-0, 6-4, in 4 hours 47 minutes, the longest final ever in this championship.

The United States defeated Sweden, 3-2, in the Davis Cup quarterfinals on July 11 in St. Louis when McEnroe beat Wilander, 9-7, 6-2, 15-17, 3-6, 8-6. The match lasted 79 games and 6 hours 35 minutes. The third set alone took 2 hours 29 minutes, a Davis Cup record. In the Davis Cup final, held from November 26 to 28 in Grenoble, France, the United States defeated France, 4-1.

The Women. Navratilova gained her third Wimbledon title with a 6-1, 3-6, 6-2 victory over Chris Evert Lloyd of Fort Lauderdale, Fla. Navratilova

Jimmy Connors rejoices after taking the Wimbledon men's singles title from John McEnroe, 3-6, 6-3, 6-7, 7-6, 6-4, on July 4 in Wimbledon, England.

also won the French Open and the Avon and Toyota finals.

Lloyd won her sixth United States Open by routing Hana Mandlikova of Czechoslovakia, 6-3, 6-1, in 64 minutes. She won her fifth Italian Open and her first Australian Open. She lost to Andrea Jaeger of Lincolnshire, Ill., 6-3, 6-1, in the French Open semifinals, only her fourth defeat in 222 matches on clay since August 1973.

Record Prize Money. There was more money in tennis in 1982 than ever before. The gross purse for the United States Open exceeded $1.5 million, and Wimbledon exceeded $1 million, both records. Tournament prize money worldwide approached $35 million.

The men's circuit remained divided. The Grand Prix international series, featuring 87 major tournaments, paid $17 million in prize money. The other series, World Championship of Tennis, ran 22 tournaments worth $8 million.

The two women's circuits, sponsored indoors by Avon Products, Incorporated, and outdoors by Toyota Motor Company, offered $7.5 million in prize money. Both sponsors failed to renew their contracts. Virginia Slims, a product of Philip Morris, Incorporated, took over the entire 1983 program. Frank Litsky

In WORLD BOOK, see TENNIS.

TEXAS. See HOUSTON; STATE GOVERNMENT.

A parade in Thailand's capital city of Bangkok in April celebrates the 200th anniversary of the Chakri dynasty, which still rules Thailand.

THAILAND in 1982 launched an ambitious project to industrialize the east coast of the Gulf of Thailand by using natural gas from undersea deposits. The project, part of Thailand's five-year economic development plan for 1982-1986, was intended to provide the basis for modernizing the whole economy at a cost of some $4.5 billion. The main goal of the 1982-1986 plan was to improve agriculture. New industries to be developed included fertilizer and petrochemicals.

The Cabinet of Prime Minister Prem Tinsulanonda decided on July 13 to permit export of liquefied natural gas to help pay for imports. Thailand bought more goods abroad during 1982 than it sold, partly because 1981's bumper harvest was followed by smaller crops in 1982. The economy grew by about 5 per cent during the year.

Elections Ahead. Prem—in office since March 1980—became the country's longest-serving prime minister in a decade as he prepared for general elections in 1983. He announced that he would not run for parliament. Under the Thai Constitution, the prime minister is chosen by a joint session of both houses of parliament but need not be a member. Widespread criticism of Prem as indecisive failed to damage his image as an effective politician able to unite others around him.

Prem, who rose to power as an army officer, buttressed his position by promoting General Arthit Kamlang-ek to army commander. Arthit had played a key role in stopping a 1981 attempted coup by officers seeking to oust Prem.

Fighting Along Its Borders continued to concern Thailand during 1982. Resistance fighters attacked the Vietnamese-supported regimes in Cambodia and Laos, and Communist Party guerrillas fought the Malaysian government. Other battles and skirmishes involved opium smugglers of various political persuasions in the so-called Golden Triangle area overlapping the Thai, Burmese, and Laotian borders.

The danger that Thailand might become involved in fighting between the Vietnamese and Cambodian insurgents caused Prem to seek assurances of United States support. Caspar W. Weinberger, the first U.S. secretary of defense to visit Thailand in a decade, reiterated to Prem on November 2 the U.S. commitment to help Thailand. U.S. foreign military sales credits were increased to $80 million in 1982 and $93 million in 1983.

Refugees. Thailand harbored approximately 175,000 refugees from Vietnam, Cambodia, and Laos, with more arriving steadily. The United States agreed to speed up its acceptance of refugees. Henry S. Bradsher

See also ASIA (Facts in Brief Table). In the WORLD BOOK SUPPLEMENT section, see THAILAND.

THEATER

Commercial theater had a nerve-racking season in the United States in 1982. Attendance was down; there were few exciting new shows; and controversy erupted over a mammoth real estate development that caused the demolition of two of the oldest landmark Broadway theaters. On the upside, however, optimists pointed to an influx of imported shows—mostly from London—that significantly raised the quality level on Broadway, record-breaking box-office revenues across the United States, and a resurgence of modestly scaled productions that brought new life to smaller off-Broadway theaters.

Tabulating the trends for the period between June 1, 1981, and May 31, 1982, *Variety,* the weekly show-business publication, dubbed the season a "nervous" one. A respectable number of shows, including *The Life and Adventures of Nicholas Nickleby*, the Royal Shakespeare Company of Great Britain's two-part, 8½-hour panoramic adaptation of the Charles Dickens novel, earned back their production costs. Revenues from Broadway and road shows for the period jumped to a record $470.8 million. Touring companies alone brought in a staggering $249.5 million. However, soaring revenues were attributable mainly to higher ticket prices—the top Broadway price in 1982 climbed to $45—rather than a surge of interest in theater. By year-end, in fact, attendance at Broadway productions was off by about 22 per cent.

Grumbling and Gloom. Theater professionals acknowledged that the tight U.S. economy affected attendance, but they also blamed flagging interest on the artistic decline of new shows. For example, *"Nine,"* the musical version of Federico Fellini's motion picture *8½* (1963), won five Antoinette Perry (Tony) Awards, including best musical and best direction, for its clever staging of the surreal nightmares of a film director (Raul Julia) suffering a mid-life crisis in his career and love life. But many people gave *"Nine"* a zero for content.

Industry grumblings also extended to drama. John Pielmeier's *Agnes of God* featured highly praised performances from Elizabeth Ashley, Geraldine Page, and Amanda Plummer in a contemporary morality tale about an angelic young nun who confounds both her mother superior and a modern-minded psychiatrist with her explanation for the birth and death of the infant she bore in

Cats, a musical based on light verse by T. S. Eliot, dazzles Broadway audiences with its fantastic scenic effects and whimsical costumes.

the convent. But skeptics pointed out that the dramatic situation was basically stagnant, and the thematic content bore more than a glancing resemblance to *Equus,* Peter Shaffer's 1973 play.

Even Charles Fuller's *A Soldier's Play*—which won both the 1982 Pulitzer Prize for drama and the prestigious New York Drama Critics Circle Award for best new American play—elicited some tempered criticism from the theater community. The drama provided a powerful examination of the root causes of racial hatred. But its story of a 1944 U.S. Army investigation into the murder of a black sergeant was structured like a conventional television mystery.

Several other shows that came wrapped in glittering promise provoked disappointment and widespread concern over the faltering standards of commercial theater. In the revival of Neil Simon's 1962 musical comedy *Little Me,* the curious omission of a major star in the role brilliantly created by Sid Caesar seriously marred the production. The star-studded *Come Back to the 5 & Dime, Jimmy Dean, Jimmy Dean,* which featured Cher, Sandy Dennis, and Karen Black, displayed a simplistic and sentimental attitude toward the forlorn remnants of a Texas fan club of the dead star. Jules Feiffer's *Grownups,* though emotionally charged, was essentially a one-note wail of anguish from a journalist mourning the loss of his soul. And a disappointing new play from Pulitzer Prize winner Beth Henley, *The Wake of Jamey Foster,* presented the same kind of Southern eccentrics seen before, caught in a repetitive replay of antics already laughed at once.

Fans await the final performance in February of London's D'Oyly Carte Opera Company, which staged Gilbert and Sullivan operettas for some 100 years.

Typifying the commercial theater's state of artistic crisis was Harold Prince's *A Doll's Life.* A phenomenal $4-million disaster, this ill-conceived operatic "sequel" to Henrik Ibsen's *A Doll's House* (1879) exemplified all the ominous Broadway tendencies toward lavish overproduction and feebleminded content. Although it had some lovely music and a big-voiced chorus to do it justice, the show also had a silly, modernistic plot about "free" women that made a mockery of Ibsen's revolutionary drama.

Land Scrapes. Also casting a pall over the industry was the destruction of two functioning Broadway theaters—the Morosco and the Helen Hayes—which were torn down in March to make way for the new luxury Portman Hotel complex. Industry professionals were divided over the vast real estate project, which will change the face and character of the entire Broadway theater district.

Brighter Lights. Several productions imported from London provided some relief from the gloom. More than spirits rose when *Cats* came to town. Set designers had to remodel the interior of the Winter Garden Theater to accommodate a cat character who ascends to heaven through the theater roof. This dazzling fantasy-musical, based on T. S. Eliot's *Old Possum's Book of Practical Cats* (1939) and set to the melodies of Andrew Lloyd Webber, was the runaway hit of the season.

In contrast, there was the stark and harrowing *Good,* the Royal Shakespeare Company production of C. P. Taylor's provocative drama. On an empty stage, under the glare of a battery of interrogator's lamps, Alan Howard gave a masterful performance as a college professor who allows himself to be seduced into servitude to Nazi political beliefs. Kate Nelligan won rapt attention in another London import, David Hare's *Plenty.* She played a former Resistance fighter unable to adjust to ordinary life in the post-World War II era.

The only other commercial drama worthy of attention in 1982, *"Master Harold" . . . and the Boys,* was also an import, the work of South African playwright-director Athol Fugard. A deeply moving account of the corruptive effects of racism on a white youth and a black man he has known and loved since childhood, the play featured an eloquent performance by Zakes Mokae that won him a Tony Award for best featured actor.

Off-Broadway continued its resurgence with a number of entertaining shows, several of which went on to become larger commercial productions. They included Harvey Fierstein's groundbreaking

Torch Song Trilogy, about the life of a warm-hearted homosexual transvestite, and Jonathan Reynolds' comedy, *Geniuses,* about a movie crew on location in a Philippine jungle during a typhoon. *Little Shop of Horrors,* a delicious horror-musical, starred Ellen Greene and a technicolor man-eating plant. A. R. Gurney, Jr.'s, wryly funny look at upper-middle-class American culture, *The Dining Room,* was ingeniously written and staged.

Around the United States. Theater in some areas of the United States increasingly consisted of a few blockbuster hits playing large-capacity houses in major cities. However, there were some notable exceptions. The Actors Theatre of Louisville in Kentucky continued to hold its biannual new play festivals to showcase the work of such promising American writers as Marsha Norman and Beth Henley. The Arena Stage in Washington, D.C., presented the U.S. première of Tom Stoppard's *On the Razzle* in October. And a newly opened $6.5-million theater at the Old Globe Theater in San Diego debuted with a commitment to new American playwrights. Marilyn Stasio

See also AWARDS AND PRIZES (Arts Awards). In WORLD BOOK, see DRAMA; THEATER.

TIMOR. See ASIA.
TOGO. See AFRICA.
TORNADO. See DISASTERS; WEATHER.
TOYS. See GAMES AND TOYS.

TRACK AND FIELD. The mile heroics of 1981, when Sebastian Coe and Steve Ovett broke the world record three times in 10 days, were expected to continue in 1982. Injuries to the two Englishmen prevented that, but Mary Decker Tabb provided thrills by breaking the women's world records for the mile and two other races.

The 23-year-old Tabb set world records of 15 minutes 8.26 seconds for 5,000 meters on June 5, 4:18.08 for the mile on July 9, and 31:35.3 for 10,000 meters on July 16. Her mile record fell on September 11, when Maricica Puica of Romania ran a 4:17.44 mile in Rieti, Italy.

Tabb's mile record in Paris highlighted a successful European tour, during which she won all five races she entered. The other records were set in Eugene, Ore. A painful Achilles tendon wiped out the latter part of her season. See TABB, MARY DECKER.

Coe and Ovett could not stay healthy either. A stress fracture of the right shin idled Coe for seven weeks in the summer, and Ovett was hampered by knee and hamstring injuries. Both men missed all three races of a series specially set up for them in London; Nice, France; and Eugene. Ovett missed the European championships in September in Athens, Greece; and both runners missed the Commonwealth Games, held from September 30 to October 9 in Brisbane, Australia.

Mary Decker Tabb exults as she sets a new women's mile record of 4 minutes 18.08 seconds in Paris on July 9. Her record fell in September, however.

World Track and Field Records Established in 1982

Men

Event	Holder	Country	Where set	Date	Record
5,000 meters	David Moorcroft	Great Britain	Oslo, Norway	July 7	13:00.42
3,200 meter relay	Peter Elliott, Gary Cook, Steve Cram, Sebastian Coe	Great Britain	London	August 30	7:03.89
Hammer throw	Sergei Litvinov	Russia	Moscow	June 4	275 ft. 6 in. (83.97 m.)
Decathlon	Daley Thompson	Great Britain	Athens, Greece	September 7-8	8,744 points

Women

Event	Holder	Country	Where set	Date	Record
100 meters	Marlies Göhr	East Germany	Karl-Marx-Stadt, East Germany	July 9	*10.88
400 meters	Marita Koch	East Germany	Athens, Greece	September 8	0:48.16
1 mile	Maricica Puica	Romania	Rieti, Italy	September 11	4:17.44
3,000 meters	Svetlana Ulmasova	Russia	Kiev, Russia	July 25	8:26.78
5,000 meters	Mary Decker Tabb	U.S.A.	Eugene, Ore.	June 5	15:08.26
10,000 meters	Mary Decker Tabb	U.S.A.	Eugene, Ore.	July 16	31:35.3
1,600-meter relay	Kirsten Siemon, Sabine Busch, Dagmar Rubsam, Marita Koch	East Germany	Athens, Greece	September 11	3:19.04
High jump	Ulrike Meyfarth	West Germany	Athens, Greece	September 8	6 ft. 7½ in. (2.02 m.)
Long jump	Vali Ionescu	Romania	Bucharest, Romania	August 1	23 ft. 7½ in. (7.20 m.)
Javelin throw	Sofia Sakorafa	Greece	Chanea, Greece	September 26	243 ft. 5 in. (74.20 m.)
Heptathlon	Ramona Neubert	East Germany	Halle, East Germany	June 19-20	6,772 points

m. = meters; *equals record

Even without Coe and Ovett, there was plenty of action in the men's mile. Eleven of the 27 fastest miles ever were run in 1982—including three by Steve Scott of Tempe, Ariz. (3:47.69, 3:48.53, and 3:49.72), and three by Sydney Maree of Bryn Mawr, Pa. (3:48.95, 3:49.44, and 3:49.75). Only Coe's world record of 3:47.33 was faster than Scott's 3:47.69.

European Stars. Although Coe and Ovett had little success, fellow Englishmen Daley Thompson and David Moorcroft excelled. Thompson set two of the year's three world records in the decathlon. He got his first record of the year by scoring 8,704 points in May in Götzis, Austria. In August, in Ulm, West Germany, Jürgen Hingsen of West Germany raised the record to 8,723 points. Thompson reclaimed the record in September by scoring 8,744 points in Athens.

Moorcroft, a successful miler, set a world 5,000-meter record of 13:00.42 on July 7 in Oslo, Norway. He finished the race more than 20 seconds ahead of the runner-up.

In the European championships, Thomas Wessinghage of West Germany beat Moorcroft in the 5,000 meters and Karl-Peter Ferner of West Germany defeated Coe in the 800 meters. The major winners in that meet were West Germany, which won seven men's events, and East Germany, which took six men's and seven women's events.

U.S. Stand-Outs. Carl Lewis of Willingboro, N.J., again won national titles in the long jump and the 100-meter dash. He raised his long-jump best to 28 feet 9 inches (8.76 meters), second only to Bob Beamon's 29 feet 2½ inches (8.90 meters).

Bob Roggy of Santa Barbara, Calif., broke the American record in the javelin throw three times and made the third longest throw in history (314 feet 4 inches, or 95.80 meters). He became the first thrower to surpass 300 feet (91.44 meters) seven times in one year.

The American record in the pole vault fell five times indoors and four times outdoors. At year's end, the indoor record was held by Billy Olson of Abilene, Tex. (18 feet 10 inches, or 5.74 meters—also a world indoor record), and the outdoor record by Dave Volz of Bloomington, Ind. (18 feet 10¼ inches, or 5.75 meters).

Alberto Salazar of Eugene lowered two American records. He ran the 5,000 meters in 13:11.93 and the 10,000 meters in 27:25.61.

In the National Collegiate Athletic Association championships from May 30 to June 5 in Provo, Utah, Canadian jumper Milt Ottey of Texas-El Paso beat Del Davis of UCLA in an exciting high-jump duel. Both men cleared 7 feet 7¼ inches (2.32 meters), the first time two jumpers had cleared that height in one meet. Frank Litsky

In WORLD BOOK, see TRACK AND FIELD.

TRANSIT systems in United States cities struggled to keep operations intact in 1982. Federal, state, and local governments cut their funding of transit systems, so the systems had to cut service and increase fares. These cuts and increases, along with the recession, hurt ridership, and the overall deficit of transit systems climbed.

The American Public Transit Association (APTA) said that ridership on urban mass-transit systems was down for the second straight year after an eight-year rise. The systems carried 6.41 billion passengers in the first 10 months of 1982, 3.7 per cent below the same 1981 period. Through October 1982, New York City ridership declined 3.2 per cent from the first 10 months of 1981. Ridership in Chicago decreased 4.8 per cent, while patronage dropped 6.2 per cent in Boston. But ridership rose 1.0 per cent in Atlanta, Ga., and 9.0 per cent in Orange County, California, which includes San Bernardino.

Financing for Transit stayed tight, but with bright spots. The Administration of President Ronald Reagan pushed for a three-year phase-out of federal subsidies for transit operations, and the subsidies quit growing. President Reagan said on November 23 that he would support an increase of 5 cents per gallon (3.8 liters) in the federal tax on gasoline. The government would spend 1 cent out of every 5 on subways and other capital projects for transit systems. Congress passed the gas tax increase on December 23.

Many state and local governments had trouble funding their transit systems. But voters in Youngstown, Ohio, passed a new transit-aid tax in February. That city's bus system had closed for a month in 1981 after a tax measure failed. The Metropolitan Transportation Authority (MTA) in New York City, and transit systems in Los Angeles, Boston, and San Diego, bolstered finances by using *safe harbor leasing* under a new tax law. A safe harbor law permits a business to sell rights to write off depreciation to profit-making firms.

Pushing for Efficiency. Transit managers worked to make their operations more self-sustaining. Many systems won basic-wage restraints from jobs-conscious unions.

Service reductions, which became common in 1981, became even more widespread in 1982. Many cities said that they would have to trim operations drastically or even close down if federal operating aid were withdrawn. Some systems anticipated the trimming of federal subsidies and cut service.

The recent trend toward higher fares continued. The Greater Cleveland Regional Transit Authority boosted its local fare from 60 cents to 85 cents.

San Francisco cable cars take their last runs for 20 months. The 109-year-old transit system shut down on September 22 for repairs.

On January 1, Tacoma, Wash., ended its 25-cent fare after 26 years, raising its peak fare to 50 cents. But some cities, including Boston and Los Angeles, decreased fares, boosting ridership.

Buying Abroad. The purchase of subway cars and buses from foreign suppliers expanded substantially in 1982, as transit systems shopped for lower prices and higher quality. In May, the New York MTA picked Bombardier Incorporated of Montreal, Canada, to build 825 subway cars for $821 million. Escalator clauses in the deal could push the total to $1 billion. Budd Company, a United States firm though West German-owned, lost the bid. Budd charged Bombardier with unfair trade practices, citing low-interest financing that the Canadian government gave Bombardier. The U.S. Department of Commerce ruled in a preliminary finding on November 22 that the interest aid totaled $137 million in unfair subsidies by Canada. This ruling could lead to U.S. customs duties on the cars.

Rail Transit. Cities moved along with subway systems, despite a general Administration policy against new rail starts. San Francisco's fabled wooden cable cars were taken out of service for 20 months on September 22. The 109-year-old system is being rebuilt. Albert R. Karr

In WORLD BOOK, see TRANSIT.

TRANSKEI. See AFRICA.

TRANSPORTATION. Economic hard times and the effects of deregulation caused financial difficulties for United States transportation industries in 1982. Many airlines and truckers lost heavily, while the earnings of many railroads and some bus companies plunged. Shipping lines and mass-transit systems continued to have financial problems.

On December 28, Secretary of Transportation Andrew L. (Drew) Lewis, Jr., announced that he would leave the Cabinet on Feb. 1, 1983.

Difficult Year. Airlines registered combined operating losses for the third straight year. Some had added many routes after the federal government deregulated commercial aviation in 1978. The route additions and the recession left the airlines with too few passengers and too many routes. Carriers slashed fares to use up their overcapacity.

More companies entered the trucking business and began competing for a shrinking amount of freight business. Many companies expanded service by using new market entry rights that the 1980 deregulation of the trucking industry made available. Companies cut rates sharply. Bankruptcies mounted.

Railroad earnings declined, but the railroads did relatively well despite a lower volume of freight. Railroads opposed legislation that would give builders of coal-slurry pipelines the privilege of invoking the principle of federal eminent domain in dealing for rights of way for their lines. Generally, eminent domain is the right of a government to take private property for public use, after paying the property owner. Slurry pipelines would be privately owned but, say their backers, would serve a public interest.

On September 20, President Ronald Reagan signed a bill deregulating the intercity bus industry. The new law gave bus companies considerable freedom to expand routes, drop unprofitable service, and raise or trim fares. Meanwhile, two big bus firms—Greyhound Corporation and Trailways Incorporated—fought a fare war.

Ocean shipping suffered from low volume worldwide and persistent excess capacity. Shipbuilding orders declined.

Transit systems were plagued by the recession as ridership dropped and financing sources became stingier. There were more fare hikes and service cuts to help keep deficits in check.

Frank Smith, senior vice-president of the Transportation Association of America (TAA), estimated U.S. transportation revenues at $630 billion for 1982, up 4 per cent from 1981. But mainland intercity freight, measured in ton-miles, declined 7 per cent, with truck freight off 5 per cent, railroads 12 per cent, pipelines 3 per cent, air freight 9 per cent, rivers and canals 10 per cent, and Great Lakes traffic 10 to 15 per cent.

Intercity passenger traffic rose by 2 per cent, as motorists drove slightly more. Automobile travel was up 1.7 per cent, and air travel rose 4.5 per cent. But railroad passenger traffic fell about 8 per cent, while bus traffic was up 2 per cent.

New Financing. President Reagan said on November 23 that he would propose an increase of 5 cents per gallon (3.8 liters) in the federal tax on gasoline. The tax hike would generate about $5.5-billion of revenue per year. Most of the new funds would go to rehabilitate roads and bridges. Twenty per cent of the money would finance subways and other capital projects for transit systems. Congress passed the tax increase on December 23, and Reagan signed it on Jan. 6, 1983.

Highway Safety. In October 1982, Congress passed a law to induce states to enact stricter laws against drunk driving. In 1981, Raymond A. Peck, head of the National Highway Traffic Safety Administration, revoked a requirement that automakers install airbags or automatic safety belts in new cars. Decisions by a federal appeals court on June 1 and Aug. 3, 1982, reinstated the rule. On November 8, the Supreme Court of the United States agreed to review the lower-court decision, delaying implementation of the rule. Albert R. Karr

See also AUTOMOBILE; AVIATION; RAILROAD; SHIP; TRANSIT; TRUCK. In WORLD BOOK, see TRANSPORTATION.

TRINIDAD AND TOBAGO. See LATIN AMERICA.

TRUCK AND TRUCKING. The prolonged recession and a scramble for new business caused hardship for many United States trucking firms in 1982. Ronald Roth, an industry economist, estimated in December that trucks would haul 715 million short tons (649 million metric tons) in 1982, down 10 per cent from 1981. Roth said that revenues would be about $44 billion, off 6 per cent; that operating profits would decline 70 per cent, to $450 million; and that ordinary income after taxes would be down $210 million, off 75 per cent.

Extraordinary tax items increased net income slightly in 1982, after boosting net profit considerably in 1981. These items were effects of 1980 write-offs of operating-rights certificates, which allow companies to enter the trucking business or expand their participation in it. The 1980 law that deregulated the trucking industry made the certificates easy to get, so old certificates lost most of their monetary value. Therefore, a trucking company that held an old certificate could write off most of the old value as an extraordinary loss.

Financial Distress. Freight volume lagged, for-hire motor carriers lost more hauls to manufacturers' and retailers' private fleets under liberalized regulation, and the increase in market-entry rights heightened competition. Freight-rate discounting was rampant, as shippers used their new market clout to seek better pricing deals from truckers.

In March, the International Brotherhood of Teamsters and major trucking firms signed an agreement that granted concessions to the companies and a cost-of-living payment of 47 cents per hour to the drivers.

On December 23, Congress approved a law establishing a national standard for truck sizes and weights. The law compels states to allow trucks up to 80,000 pounds (36,000 kilograms) in weight, up to 102 inches (259 centimeters) in width, and up to 65 feet (19.8 meters) long in double-trailer combinations to operate throughout the interstate highway system and on certain other roads.

Turmoil at the ICC. The Administration of President Ronald Reagan, including some new Interstate Commerce Commission (ICC) commissioners Reagan had appointed, promoted deregulation vigorously. The trucking industry asked the ICC to curb freight-rate discounts, but the ICC ruled against the industry in May and July. In November, the ICC decided to explore the impact of widespread rate-cutting. The ICC approved general rate increases of 1½ to 10 per cent, effective on April 1, and additional hikes of 1 to 10 per cent in October and November.

Albert R. Karr

See also TRANSPORTATION. In WORLD BOOK, see TRUCK.

The Megatruck, designed to provide at least 1 million miles (1.6 million kilometers) of service, rolled off the production line in 1982.

TRUDEAU, PIERRE ELLIOTT (1919-   ), saw his personal popularity fall steeply in his 14th year as prime minister of Canada. A Gallup Poll in September 1982 revealed that Trudeau and the Liberal Party had slipped in popular esteem to the lowest level since World War II. Much of Trudeau's loss of favor could be attributed to the recession, in which 1.5 million Canadians found themselves jobless. The prime minister and his government were widely perceived as having mismanaged the economy and lost the confidence of both business and labor. Even the adoption of a new Canadian Constitution in 1982, Trudeau's cherished goal for many years, did not win him general approval (see CANADA [Close-Up]). He was seen as too rigid in his pursuit of his own constitutional aims and too ready to indulge in confrontation with the provinces.

Yet Trudeau still possessed the personal magnetism that was his hallmark ever since he came to office in 1968. His temperament was volatile. Seen as sophisticated, witty, and thoughtful, he could also be glib and indecisive. He could both arouse and repel. He dominated his party and did not take criticism gracefully, but he was never dull. For all his faults, Trudeau remained the most compelling politician in Canada. David M. L. Farr

See also CANADA. In WORLD BOOK, see TRUDEAU, PIERRE ELLIOTT.

TUNISIA. About 1,100 Palestine Liberation Organization (PLO) guerrillas arrived in Tunis on Aug. 26, 1982, and the Tunisian capital was designated as temporary world PLO headquarters by PLO Chairman Yasir Arafat. The guerrillas were some of the 15,000 PLO members evacuated from Beirut, Lebanon, after being forced into West Beirut when Israel invaded Lebanon in June (see MIDDLE EAST). Tunisian President Habib Bourguiba angrily denounced the Israeli invasion.

Relations with neighboring Libya improved sharply in 1982. Libya's head of state, Muammar Muhammad al-Qadhafi, visited Tunisia for five days in February. The two nations signed a pact providing for coordination of their foreign policy and their plans for agricultural, electrical, and industrial production. The accord also called for linking their communication, rail, and road networks.

Also in February, the International Court of Justice, an agency of the United Nations, issued a decision on Tunisia's four-year-long dispute with Libya over undersea continental shelf boundaries. The court's decision gave the majority of offshore-oil concession areas in the Mediterranean Sea to Libya, but Tunisia said it would abide by the verdict and sign a formal boundary treaty.

Internal Problems. Israel's invasion of Lebanon drew attention away from Tunisia's continued economic difficulties and the lingering political uneasiness caused by the shift in 1981 from a single-party to a multiparty political system.

There were strikes in several sectors of the economy, notably transportation, as workers demanded wage increases and other benefits to keep pace with inflation. As a first step toward the reestablishment of good relations between the government and labor in the effort to develop the country, Bourguiba in February pardoned Habib Achour, former secretary-general of the General Union of Tunisian Workers. Achour, who had been imprisoned in 1980 for criticism of the single-party system of the ruling Socialist Destour Party, returned to his union post.

The Economy. In June, the National Assembly approved an ambitious five-year plan calling for the investment of about $14 billion from 1982 to 1986. The plan was expected to create 300,000 new jobs to provide for about 90 per cent of the expected increase in the country's labor force. It is to be funded largely from foreign sources. But the United States, though providing $82 million in military sales, reduced direct economic aid in 1982 from $40 million to $31 million. William Spencer

See also AFRICA (Facts in Brief Table). In WORLD BOOK, see TUNISIA.

TUNNEL. See BUILDING AND CONSTRUCTION.

After expulsion from Lebanon, PLO leader Yasir Arafat, center, rides to new headquarters in Tunis with Tunisian President Bourguiba in September.

TURKEY took a long stride in 1982 toward the return to constitutional government and civilian rule promised by military leaders after they seized power in September 1980. In September 1982, a temporary Consultative Assembly approved a new Constitution to replace the 1961 Constitution, which was suspended after the military take-over. The new Constitution was approved in October by the ruling National Security Council (NSC), composed of Turkey's top military leaders and headed by General Kenan Evren. It was then overwhelmingly approved in a national referendum that was held on November 7. At the same time, voters elected Evren to a seven-year term as president.

The new Constitution differs significantly from its predecessor in the powers given to the president. Those powers include the right to veto constitutional amendments and to appoint the prime minister and all military and civilian judges.

In addition, the president was given the power to veto legislation and even dissolve the Grand National Assembly, the new parliament. The members of the Assembly will be elected to five-year terms. Once the parliament is elected, possibly in 1983, the other four generals on the NSC will form a Presidential Council, ensuring military control over Turkey's fledgling democracy for the rest of Evren's term.

Other constitutional provisions permit political parties to operate as long as they do not advocate Communism, fascism, government by Islamic religious leaders, or any form of dictatorship. However, political activity by leaders of the civilian government before the 1980 coup, such as former Prime Ministers Süleyman Demirel and Bülent Ecevit, was prohibited for 10 years. Labor unions would be allowed but would be prohibited from striking over political issues.

Terrorism Crackdown. Turkey's military rulers continued to crack down on terrorism, holding state trials of both leftist and rightist groups throughout the year. In September, the NSC announced that during its two years in power, 20 terrorists had been executed and 25,000 persons had received jail sentences.

Violence by Armenian terrorists sworn to revenge for the genocide of the Armenian population, which reached a peak during World War I, continued to plague Turkey. During 1982, Armenian terrorists killed two Turkish officials in the United States, two in Canada, one in Portugal, and one in Bulgaria. William Spencer

See Middle East (Facts in Brief Table). In World Book, see Turkey.

UGANDA. See Africa.

UNEMPLOYMENT. See Economics; Labor.

UNION OF SOVIET SOCIALIST REPUBLICS (U.S.S.R.). See Russia.

UNITED NATIONS (UN) institutions in 1982 dealt with new wars in the Falkland Islands and Lebanon and continuing conflicts in El Salvador, Afghanistan, Cambodia, Iran, and Iraq.

On April 1, Great Britain asked for a meeting of the UN Security Council. Britain said that it expected Argentina to invade the Falkland Islands. The same day, the Security Council called on Argentina and Britain to avoid force and seek a diplomatic solution to their dispute. However, Argentina invaded the Falklands on April 2. By April 3, Argentine troops had overrun the islands.

On April 3, the Council adopted a British resolution demanding an immediate end to hostilities, withdrawal of Argentine forces, and a diplomatic solution. The vote was 10 to 1 with 4 abstentions. Great Britain, France, Ireland, the United States, Guyana, Japan, Jordan, Togo, Uganda, and Zaire voted for the resolution. Panama voted against the measure, while China, Poland, the Soviet Union, and Spain abstained.

United States Secretary of State Alexander M. Haig, Jr., tried to settle the dispute on trips to London and to Buenos Aires, Argentina's capital, between April 8 and 19. He failed but sent his ideas to UN Secretary-General Javier Pérez de Cuéllar.

Great Britain begain its counter-invasion on April 25. Pérez de Cuéllar worked out his own proposal for a settlement, calling for both sides to agree to withdraw their forces from the islands and start negotiating. On May 2, the secretary-general gave his plan to British Foreign Secretary Francis Pym and Argentine Ambassador Eduardo Roca. On May 5, Argentina agreed to negotiate on the plan. Great Britain agreed on May 6. On May 7, Argentina's Deputy Foreign Minister Enrique Jorge Ros arrived at UN Headquarters in New York City. In the next two weeks, Pérez de Cuéllar had some 30 meetings with Ros and Britain's UN ambassador, Sir Anthony Parsons.

Impasse. The Council, convened at the request of Ireland and Panama, held six meetings between May 21 and 26. The secretary-general said on May 21 that the talks were stalled. He said that both sides had agreed there should be a cease-fire, a phased withdrawal of forces supervised by the UN, and interim administration of the islands by the UN while he conducted negotiations for a full settlement by Dec. 31, 1982. However, Argentina and Great Britain disagreed over details. Pérez de Cuéllar reported that he had telephoned both Argentine President Leopoldo Fortunato Galtieri and British Prime Minister Margaret Thatcher, but could not resolve the disagreements. On May 26, the Security Council adopted a resolution sponsored by Guyana, Ireland, Jordan, Togo, Uganda, and Zaire asking Pérez de Cuéllar to seek a cease-fire. The vote was 15 to 0.

Britain's ambassador to the UN, Sir Anthony Parsons, and U.S. Ambassador Jeane J. Kirkpatrick chat during a May meeting on the Falklands crisis.

At Panama's request, the Council met again on June 4, 5, and 6. On June 4, the United States and Great Britain vetoed a Panamanian-Spanish resolution that would have asked Argentina and Britain to cease fire. The vote was 9 to 2, with 4 abstentions. Soon after the vote, U.S. Ambassador Jeane J. Kirkpatrick told the Council her government had just instructed her to say that the United States would change its vote to abstention if it could. However, Security Council votes cannot be changed. Kirkpatrick explained to reporters that her final instructions came late because Haig was attending a conference in Versailles, France.

Meanwhile, Britain won the islands back. Argentine troops surrendered on June 14, and the war was over.

Central America was the subject of debate, at Nicaragua's request, at eight Council meetings between March 25 and April 2. Daniel Ortega Saavedra, head of Nicaragua's left wing Government of National Reconstruction Junta, accused the United States of "destabilizing actions" against Nicaragua. He demanded that the United States promise not to attack Nicaragua if the March 28 election in El Salvador did not go as the United States wished.

Kirkpatrick replied that the United States was not about to invade anyone. She charged that Nicaragua had agreed to pass arms from Cuba to rebels in Guatemala, Costa Rica, and El Salvador. On April 2, the United States vetoed a Guyanan-Panamanian resolution that would have had the Council appeal to all UN members "to refrain from the direct, indirect, overt, or covert use of force against any country of Central America and the Caribbean."

Lebanon. On June 4, Israeli aircraft bombed Beirut, the capital of Lebanon; Israeli ships shelled the south Lebanon coast; and artillery in Israel fired across Lebanon's southern border. At Lebanon's request, the Council met on June 5. Israel's Ambassador Yehuda Blum said that if Lebanon would not or could not prevent the Palestine Liberation Organization (PLO) from using Lebanese territory as a base, Lebanon ran the risk of Israeli counteraction. The Council adopted by a vote of 15 to 0 a Japanese resolution expressing deep concern at the new situation and calling on all parties to the conflict to cease all military activities both in Lebanon and across the Lebanese-Israeli border by 6 A.M. local time on June 6.

On that date, Pérez de Cuéllar reported to the Council that Israeli troops in "overwhelming strength" had "overrun or by-passed" UN troops and moved into southern Lebanon that morning. That night, the Council unanimously adopted an Irish resolution demanding that Israel withdraw from Lebanon and that all parties observe the previously demanded cease-fire and notify the secretary-general of their acceptance of the resolution within 24 hours.

Israel Stays. On June 8, Pérez de Cuéllar reported that the PLO and its Lebanese allies had accepted the cease-fire, but that Israel would not withdraw until permanent arrangements were made in Lebanon to prevent hostile action against Israelis by "terrorists operating from that country." Later that day, the United States vetoed a Spanish resolution calling for "practical action"—a hint of sanctions—unless all parties ceased fire in six hours and Israel withdrew from Lebanon.

On June 26, the United States vetoed a French resolution seeking a cease-fire throughout Lebanon, the withdrawal of Israeli and Palestinian forces from Beirut, and the stationing of Lebanese troops and UN military observers in Beirut. The resolution would have called on "armed elements in the Beirut area" to abide by the Lebanese government's authority. A U.S. delegate, Charles Lichenstein, said that the resolution should have sought to rid all Lebanon of such elements.

On July 4, on a Jordanian initiative, the Council called unanimously for respect for civilians' rights in Lebanon and for the restoration of water, electricity, food, and medical supplies throughout Lebanon. On July 29, a Spanish resolution demanding that Israel allow supplies for civilians to go into Beirut passed by a vote of 14 to 0, with the United States not participating in the vote.

Lebanon Requested on August 1 that the UN deploy cease-fire observers in Beirut. That day, the Council unanimously passed a resolution voicing alarm at "intensification of military activities around Beirut," demanding a cease-fire, calling for deployment of UN observers in Beirut, and asking the secretary-general to report the results of the resolution in four hours. The report showed that Lebanon and the PLO had accepted the resolution and that Israel was studying it.

On August 3, Pérez de Cuéllar reported that Israel was delaying its reply until it held a Cabinet meeting four days later. He said that Israeli guards had stopped UN observers but that the observers got into West Beirut later and, on his order, established an observation post on Lebanese-controlled territory. Ambassador Blum protested against the order. That night, the Council urged all sides to let supplies into Beirut and allow effective deployment of UN observers.

The Council held two meetings on August 4. By a 14 to 0 vote with the United States abstaining, it adopted a Jordanian-Spanish resolution expressing shock at Israel's invasion of West Beirut earlier that day. The resolution noted that the PLO had decided to move out of its base in West Beirut, called for Israeli troops to pull back to August 1 positions, and asked the secretary-general to report Israel's response to the Council on the next day.

On August 6, Pérez de Cuéllar reported a negative response from Israel. The Council met and, on an 11 to 1 vote with 3 abstentions, the United States vetoed a Soviet resolution calling for a ban on military aid to Israel until it withdrew from Lebanon. Great Britain, Togo, and Zaire abstained. On August 12, the Council unanimously adopted a resolution demanding an end to all military activities in Lebanon, especially Beirut, and free entry of supplies for civilians in Beirut. PLO leader Yasir Arafat sailed for Greece on August 30 on his way to live in Tunis, Tunisia.

Lebanon's President-Elect, Bashir Gemayel, died in a bomb explosion on September 14 at his headquarters in East Beirut. The next day, the Israelis began to overrun West Beirut. Between September 16 and 18, Israeli troops allowed Lebanese Christian militiamen to pass through Israeli lines into two Palestinian refugee camps, Sabra and Shatila, in Beirut. The militiamen killed hundreds of civilians. The Security Council obtained a UN military observers' report on the killings, then met past midnight on Saturday, September 18. The Council drafted and unanimously adopted a resolution condemning "the criminal massacre of Palestinian civilians" and authorizing the UN ob-

United Nations Secretary-General Javier Pérez de Cuéllar, left, meets Soviet leader Leonid Brezhnev during a September visit to Russia.

server group in Beirut to be raised from 10 to 50. On September 17, the Council had unanimously condemned the Israeli invasion of West Beirut and demanded an immediate pullback.

Freeze Talk. The 157-nation UN General Assembly held a special session on disarmament from June 7 to July 10. On June 15, Soviet Foreign Minister Andrei A. Gromyko proposed that, in starting talks on reducing strategic arms, the Soviet Union and the United States freeze the number of such arms in their possession. U.S. President Ronald Reagan, speaking on June 17, said talks were to begin in less than two weeks.

The 37th Session of the General Assembly began on September 21. The Assembly elected Hungary's Deputy Foreign Minister Imre Hollai as president. On October 4, the Council called unanimously for a cease-fire in the war between Iran and Iraq. On October 22, the Assembly called for a cease-fire in that war. The vote was 119 to 1 with Iran opposed and 15 abstentions.

On October 28, the Assembly voted, 105 to 23 with 20 abstentions, in favor of the withdrawal of foreign forces from Cambodia. Vietnamese troops occupied most of Cambodia.

On November 29, the Assembly voted, 114 to 21 with 13 abstentions, to demand that foreign troops leave Afghanistan. Soviet soldiers were fighting Afghan rebels there.

On December 6, the UN published a report of an investigation of charges that Russia and its allies had been waging chemical warfare in Afghanistan and Southeast Asia. The report said that "while the group [of UN investigators] could not state that these allegations had been proven, nevertheless it could not disregard the circumstantial evidence suggestive of the possible use of some sort of toxic chemical substances in some instances."

On October 21, at the request of African countries upset over South Africa's segregation policies, the General Assembly adopted a resolution asking the International Monetary Fund (IMF) to refuse South Africa a $1-billion credit that it had requested. The vote was 121 to 3, with 23 abstentions. Great Britain, the United States, and West Germany voted against the resolution. Opponents of the resolution argued that the IMF, though linked with the United Nations, was an independent, specialized agency. On November 3, the IMF granted the credit to South Africa.

A Sea Law Treaty worked out at an intermittent eight-year conference won approval at a session at UN Headquarters on April 30. The vote was 130 to 4, with 17 abstentions. Israel, Turkey, the United States, and Venezuela voted against the treaty. On December 10, 117 nations signed the treaty. The United States and other major industrial countries did not sign. William N. Oatis

In WORLD BOOK, see UNITED NATIONS.

UNITED STATES, GOVERNMENT OF THE. Burgeoning federal budget deficits dictated the domestic policy agendas of the United States government's executive and legislative branches in 1982. President Ronald Reagan, forced by fiscal realities to abandon his 1980 campaign goal of balancing the budget during his four-year term, tried without success to shift the national dialogue away from deficits. In his January 26 State of the Union message, Reagan called for a "new federalism"—a gradual reshuffling of responsibility for major social programs among federal, state, and local governments. The plan evoked scant enthusiasm in Congress, and, on August 9, the White House conceded it was a dead issue for 1982.

Budget Battle. Public and congressional attention was fixed, instead, on Reagan's proposed budget for the 1983 fiscal year starting Oct. 1, 1982. Submitted on February 6, it projected outlays of $757.6 billion, revenues of $666.1 billion, and a record deficit of $91.5 billion. The deficit estimate soon proved to be unrealistic, and, on May 21, the Republican-controlled Senate adopted, 49-43, a budget resolution projecting a deficit of $116 billion. Within the week, however, the Democratic-controlled House of Representatives rejected four successive resolutions, in part because some 50 conservative Republicans recoiled from the massive deficits that each entailed.

The prospective sea of red ink was attributed to several factors: the deepening recession, which cut revenues while boosting outlays for unemployment compensation and other social programs; Reagan's record tax cut of 1981 and his unprecedented defense build-up; and high interest rates, which, while countering inflation, aggravated the recession and added to the cost of financing the national debt.

The budget battle finally ended on June 23 when the Senate adopted, 54-45, a compromise budget resolution that the House had narrowly approved, 210-208, a day earlier. The resolution projected a deficit of $103.9 billion.

To effect the compromise, Reagan agreed reluctantly to press for a tax bill that would trim deficits by $98.3 billion over three years (see TAXATION). With some of the President's conservative allies opposing any tax increase, Reagan postponed an August vacation for two weeks so that he could lobby directly for the legislation. At the same time, he acknowledged antideficit fever by endorsing a proposed constitutional amendment to require a balanced budget in every peacetime year except when Congress voted to by-pass the requirement. The measure was passed by the Senate but defeated in the House (see CONSTITUTION OF THE UNITED STATES).

On August 19, the House approved the tax-hike bill, which also included spending cuts totaling

Federal Spending | **U.S Income and Outlays**

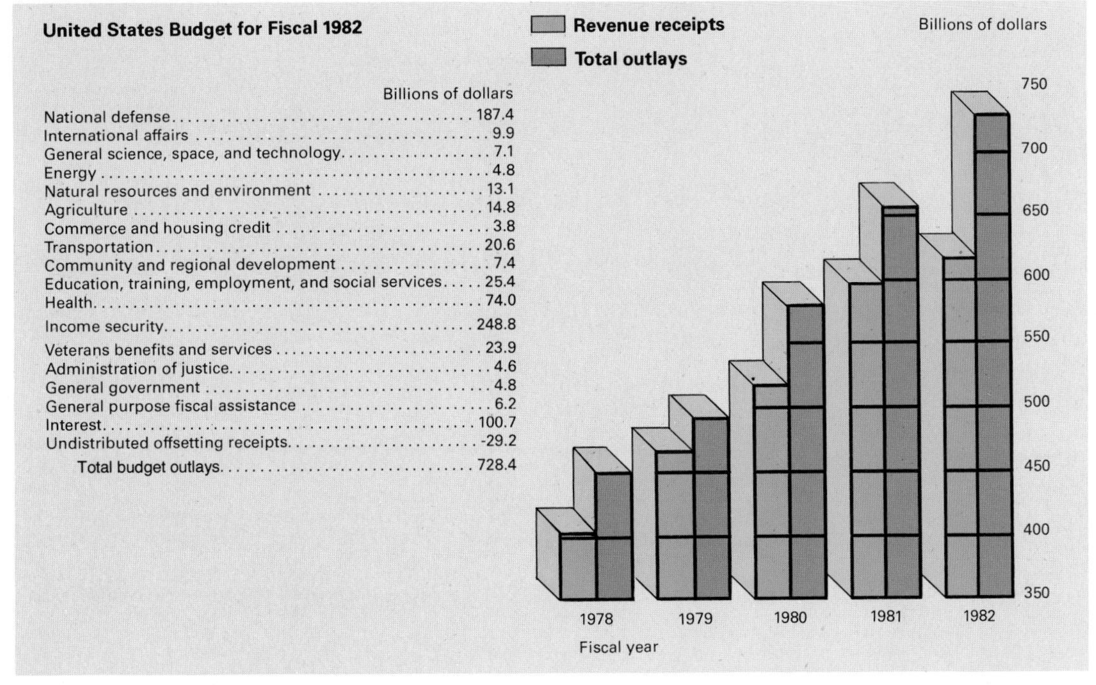

United States Budget for Fiscal 1982

	Billions of dollars
National defense	187.4
International affairs	9.9
General science, space, and technology	7.1
Energy	4.8
Natural resources and environment	13.1
Agriculture	14.8
Commerce and housing credit	3.8
Transportation	20.6
Community and regional development	7.4
Education, training, employment, and social services	25.4
Health	74.0
Income security	248.8
Veterans benefits and services	23.9
Administration of justice	4.6
General government	4.8
General purpose fiscal assistance	6.2
Interest	100.7
Undistributed offsetting receipts	-29.2
Total budget outlays	728.4

Source: U.S. Department of the Treasury

$17.5 billion, by a vote of 226-207, with more Democrats than Republicans voting in its favor. On the same day, the Senate added its approval, 52-47. Nevertheless, the Congressional Budget Office predicted the deficit would balloon to a startling $155 billion unless further steps were taken.

Another major legislative action came on June 23, when the House joined the Senate in passing a 25-year extension of the Voting Rights Act of 1965. But Congress sidetracked a Reagan proposal to offer federal tax credits for tuition paid to private and parochial secondary schools. On the plus side—from the Administration's standpoint—the House defeated by two votes a nonbinding resolution calling for a freeze on U.S. and Soviet nuclear arsenals.

President's Support Wanes. During Reagan's first 19 months in office, Congress gave him virtually everything he requested. But his support began ebbing in September after he vetoed as a "budget buster" a $14.1-billion supplemental appropriation for fiscal 1982. Even Republicans were angered by the action because the bill contained $1.3 billion less than Reagan had requested. On September 9, the House voted to override the veto, and the Senate did the same the next day.

Fresh setbacks followed. The Senate adopted the balanced-budget amendment, but, on October 1, the House rejected it. The Senate also put aside two other Reagan-endorsed proposals that would ban abortion and permit voluntary prayer in public schools.

Throughout the year, the Administration continued its drive to reduce the burden of federal regulation. In November, the Supreme Court of the United States agreed to rule on an Administration move to scrap a requirement that all new cars, beginning with 1984 models, be equipped with airbags or automatic seat belts. The Administration also reduced the speed at which bumpers on autos be required to withstand collisions from 5 miles per hour to 2½ miles per hour (from 8 kilometers per hour to 4 kilometers per hour). Consumer and insurance groups were seeking a federal court decision on that ruling as well.

Many deep cuts in social programs took full effect during the year, but adverse effects were judged to be less widespread than many critics had feared. For example, the number of students included in the school lunch program declined by 3.1 million during the 1981-1982 school year, but only one-third of those affected were from low-income families.

Social Security Deficits. As the year ended, Congress faced the prospect of grappling in 1983 with looming deficits in the Social Security program. Shortly before recommendations were due from a bipartisan National Commission on Social Secu-

Major Agencies and Bureaus of the U.S. Government*

Executive Office of the President

President, Ronald Reagan
- Vice-President, George H. W. Bush
- White House Chief of Staff, James A. Baker III
- Presidential Press Secretary, James S. Brady
- Central Intelligence Agency – William J. Casey, Director
- Council of Economic Advisers – Martin S. Feldstein, Chairman
- Council on Environmental Quality – A. Alan Hill, Chairman
- Office of Management and Budget – David A. Stockman, Director
- Office of Science and Technology Policy – George A. Keyworth II, Director

The Supreme Court of the United States

Chief Justice of the United States, Warren E. Burger

Associate Justices

William J. Brennan, Jr.	Lewis F. Powell, Jr.
Byron R. White	William H. Rehnquist
Thurgood Marshall	John Paul Stevens
Harry A. Blackmun	Sandra Day O'Connor

State Department

Secretary of State, George P. Shultz
- U.S. Representative to the United Nations – Jeane J. Kirkpatrick

Department of the Treasury

Secretary of the Treasury, Donald T. Regan
- Bureau of Alcohol, Tobacco, and Firearms – Stephen E. Higgins, Acting Director
- Bureau of Engraving and Printing – Robert J. Leuver, Acting Director
- Bureau of the Mint – Donna Pope, Director
- Comptroller of the Currency – C. T. Conover
- Internal Revenue Service – Roscoe L. Egger, Jr., Commissioner
- Treasurer of the United States – Angela M. Buchanan
- U.S. Customs Service – William von Raab, Commissioner
- U.S. Secret Service – John R. Simpson, Director

Department of Commerce

Secretary of Commerce, Malcolm Baldrige
- Bureau of the Census – Bruce K. Chapman, Director
- Economic Development Administration – Carlos C. Campbell, Administrator
- National Bureau of Standards – Ernest Ambler, Director
- National Oceanic and Atmospheric Administration – John V. Byrne, Administrator
- Minority Business Development Agency – Victor M. Rivera, Director
- Patent and Trademark Office – Gerald J. Mossinghoff, Commissioner

Department of Labor

Secretary of Labor, Raymond J. Donovan
- Bureau of Labor Statistics – Janet L. Norwood, Commissioner
- Employment and Training Administration – Albert Angrisani, Administrator
- Employment Standards Administration – Robert Burns Collyer, Administrator
- Labor-Management Services Administration – vacant
- Mine Safety and Health Administration – Ford B. Ford, Administrator
- Occupational Safety and Health Administration – Thorne G. Auchter, Administrator
- Women's Bureau – Lenora Cole-Alexander, Director

Department of Health and Human Services

Secretary of Health and Human Services, Richard S. Schweiker
- Administration for Children, Youth and Families – Clarence E. Hodges, Commissioner
- Administration on Aging – Lennie-Marie P. Tolliver, Commissioner
- Alcohol, Drug Abuse, and Mental Health Administration – William E. Mayer, Administrator
- Centers for Disease Control – William H. Foege, Director
- Food and Drug Administration – Arthur Hull Hayes, Jr., Commissioner
- Health Care Financing Administration – Carolyne K. Davis, Administrator
- Health Resources Administration – Robert Graham, Acting Administrator
- Health Services Administration – John H. Kelso, Acting Administrator
- National Institutes of Health – James B. Wyngaarden, Director
- Office of Consumer Affairs – Virginia Knauer, Director
- Public Health Service – C. Everett Koop, Director
- Social Security Administration – John A. Svahn, Commissioner

Department of Defense

Secretary of Defense, Caspar W. Weinberger
- Joint Chiefs of Staff – General John W. Vessey, Chairman
- Secretary of the Air Force – Verne L. Orr
- Secretary of the Army – John O. Marsh, Jr.
- Secretary of the Navy – John F. Lehman, Jr.

Department of Justice

Attorney General, William French Smith
- Bureau of Prisons – Norman A. Carlson, Director
- Drug Enforcement Administration – Francis M. Mullen, Jr., Administrator
- Federal Bureau of Investigation – William H. Webster, Director
- Immigration and Naturalization Service – Alan C. Nelson, Commissioner
- Office of Justice Assistance, Research, and Statistics – Robert F. Diegelman, Acting Director
- Solicitor General – Rex E. Lee

Department of the Interior

Secretary of the Interior, James G. Watt
- Assistant Secretary for Indian Affairs – Kenneth L. Smith
- Bureau of Land Management – Robert F. Burford, Director
- Bureau of Mines – Robert C. Horton, Director
- Bureau of Reclamation – Robert N. Broadbent, Commissioner
- Geological Survey – Dallas L. Peck, Director
- National Park Service – Russell E. Dickenson, Director
- Office of Territorial Affairs – Pedro A. Sanjuan, Director
- U.S. Fish and Wildlife Service – Robert A. Jantzen, Director

Department of Agriculture

Secretary of Agriculture, John R. Block
- Agricultural Economics – William Gene Lesher, Director
- Agricultural Marketing Service – Vern Highley, Administrator
- Agricultural Stabilization and Conservation Service – Everett G. Rank, Administrator
- Farmers Home Administration – Charles W. Shuman, Administrator
- Federal Crop Insurance Corporation – Merritt Sprague, Manager
- Food and Consumer Services – Mary C. Jarratt, Administrator
- Food and Nutrition Service – Samuel J. Cornelius, Administrator
- Forest Service – R. Max Peterson, Chief
- Rural Electrification Administration – Harold V. Hunter, Administrator
- Soil Conservation Service – Peter C. Myers, Chief

Department of Housing and Urban Development

Secretary of Housing and Urban Development, Samuel R. Pierce, Jr.
- Community Planning and Development – Stephen J. Bollinger, Administrator
- Federal Housing Commissioner – Philip Abrams
- Government National Mortgage Association – Robert W. Karpe, President
- New Community Development Corporation – Warren T. Lindquist, General Manager

Department of Transportation

Secretary of Transportation, Andrew L. Lewis, Jr.
- Federal Aviation Administration – J. Lynn Helms, Administrator
- Federal Highway Administration – Ray A. Barnhart, Administrator
- Federal Railroad Administration – Robert W. Blanchette, Administrator
- Maritime Administration – Harold E. Shear, Administrator
- National Highway Traffic Safety Administration – Raymond A. Peck, Jr., Administrator
- U.S. Coast Guard – Admiral James S. Gracey, Commandant
- Urban Mass Transportation Administration – Arthur E. Teele, Jr., Administrator

Department of Energy

Secretary of Energy, Donald Paul Hodel
- Economic Regulatory Administration – Rayburn D. Hanzlik, Administrator
- Energy Information Administration – J. Erich Evered, Administrator
- Federal Energy Regulatory Commission – Charles M. Butler III, Chairman
- Office of Energy Research – Alvin W. Trivelpiece, Director

Department of Education

Secretary of Education, Terrel H. Bell
National Institute of Education – Manuel J. Justiz, Director

Congressional Officials

President of the Senate pro tempore – Strom Thurmond
Speaker of the House – Thomas P. O'Neill, Jr.
Architect of the Capitol – George M. White
Comptroller General of the U.S. – Charles A. Bowsher
Congressional Budget Office – Alice M. Rivlin, Director
Librarian of Congress – Daniel J. Boorstin
Office of Technology Assessment – John H. Gibbons, Director
Public Printer of the U.S. – Danford L. Sawyer, Jr.

Independent Agencies

ACTION – Thomas W. Pauken, Director
Civil Aeronautics Board – C. Dan McKinnon, Chairman
Commodity Futures Trading Commission – Philip F. Johnson, Chairman
Consumer Product Safety Commission – Nancy Harvey Steorts, Chairman
Environmental Protection Agency – Anne McGill Gorsuch, Administrator
Equal Employment Opportunity Commission – Clarence Thomas, Chairman
Export-Import Bank – William H. Draper III, President
Farm Credit Administration – Donald E. Wilkinson, Governor
Federal Communications Commission – Mark S. Fowler, Chairman
Federal Deposit Insurance Corporation – William M. Isaac, Chairman
Federal Election Commission – Frank P. Reiche, Chairman
Federal Emergency Management Agency – Louis O. Giuffrida, Director
Federal Home Loan Bank Board – Richard T. Pratt, Chairman
Federal Maritime Commission – Alan Green, Jr., Chairman
Federal Mediation and Conciliation Service – Kay McMurray, Director
Federal Reserve System – Paul A. Volcker, Board of Governors Chairman
Federal Trade Commission – James C. Miller III, Chairman
General Services Administration – Gerald P. Carmen, Administrator
Interstate Commerce Commission – Reese H. Taylor, Jr., Chairman
National Aeronautics and Space Administration – James M. Beggs, Administrator
National Credit Union Administration – Edgar F. Callahan, Chairman
National Endowment for the Arts – Frank Hodsoll, Chairman
National Endowment for the Humanities – William J. Bennett, Chairman
National Labor Relations Board – Donald L. Dotson,† Chairman
National Mediation Board – Robert O. Harris, Chairman
National Railroad Passenger Corporation (Amtrak) – W. Graham Claytor, Jr., President
National Science Foundation – Edward A. Knapp,† Director
National Transportation Safety Board – James E. Burnett, Jr., Chairman
Nuclear Regulatory Commission – Nunzio J. Palladino, Chairman
Occupational Safety and Health Review Commission – Robert A. Rowland, Chairman
Office of Personnel Management – Donald J. Devine, Director
Panama Canal Commission – Dennis P. McAuliffe, Administrator
Peace Corps – Loret Miller Ruppe, Director
Securities and Exchange Commission – John S. R. Shad, Chairman
Small Business Administration – James C. Sanders, Administrator
Smithsonian Institution – S. Dillon Ripley, Secretary
Synthetic Fuels Corporation – Edward E. Noble, Chairman
Tennessee Valley Authority – Charles H. Dean, Jr., Chairman
U.S. Arms Control and Disarmament Agency – Eugene V. Rostow, Director
U.S. Commission on Civil Rights – Clarence M. Pendleton, Jr., Chairman
U.S. Information Agency – Charles Z. Wick, Director
U.S. International Development Cooperation Agency – M. Peter McPherson, Acting Director
U.S. International Trade Commission – Alfred Eckes, Chairman
U.S. Postal Service – William F. Bolger, Postmaster General
Veterans Administration – Harry N. Walters, Administrator

*As of Jan. 1, 1983. †Nominated but not yet confirmed.

rity Reform, the retirement and survivors fund was forced to borrow $581.3 million from the disability fund to cover benefit checks for November.

The Administration pressed ahead with its proposal to abolish the Department of Energy. On May 24, Reagan submitted to Congress a revised blueprint for transferring nearly all Energy Department functions to the Department of Commerce. He said the action would save $2 billion over four years, mainly in salaries. Congress took no action on the plan.

Cabinet Changes. The Administration's first Cabinet resignation was announced on May 12. Secretary of Energy James B. Edwards said he would step down in the fall to become president of the Medical University of South Carolina in Charleston. On November 5, he was succeeded by Donald P. Hodel, a former utility manager and consultant who had been Reagan's undersecretary of the interior. See HODEL, DONALD P.

On June 25, Alexander M. Haig, Jr., resigned as secretary of state, citing unspecified foreign policy differences. He was succeeded by George P. Shultz, a business executive and a former secretary of labor and of the Treasury. Shultz soon ranked among Reagan's top advisers on economic as well as diplomatic affairs. Secretary of Transportation Andrew L. (Drew) Lewis, Jr., said in December that he was resigning as of Feb. 1, 1983.

A special prosecutor twice ruled that he found "insufficient credible evidence" that Secretary of Labor Raymond J. Donovan had illegal ties with organized crime. See CABINET, UNITED STATES.

Supreme Court. An issue of increasing importance to justices of the U.S. Supreme Court was their workload. In the 1981-1982 term, the court issued 141 opinions and heard arguments in 184 cases—the most in several decades.

On August 6, Justice John Paul Stevens gave the court's internal problems a rare public airing in an address in San Francisco to the American Judicature Society, an organization of judges. Declaring that the quality of the court's work was being impaired, he suggested remedies that included the creation of a new court to screen cases intended for the Supreme Court.

Several other justices were disturbed about the caseload, and, Stevens reported, a conference had been planned on the subject. None was held, he said, because "we were too busy to decide whether there was anything we could do about the problem of being too busy." Frank Cormier

In the Special Reports section, see THE HIGH COURT: AT THE CENTER OF A STORM AGAIN. In WORLD BOOK, see UNITED STATES, GOVERNMENT OF THE.

UNITED STATES CONSTITUTION. See CONSTITUTION OF THE UNITED STATES.

UPPER VOLTA. See AFRICA.

URUGUAY. On Nov. 28, 1982, elections were held in Uruguay for the first time since the military took control of the government in 1973. In the elections, at which Uruguayans picked leaders for their political parties, candidates who opposed the military regime captured more than 70 per cent of the vote. The elections were part of a plan providing for a gradual restoration of democracy, including national elections in 1984.

Participation in the elections was limited to just three parties, the government's own Unión Cívica, and the traditional Colorado and Blanco parties. In accord with rules imposed by Uruguay's military government headed by President Gregorio C. Alvarez, all so-called leftist parties were excluded.

Even under this highly controlled system, however, Uruguayans thronged the streets for political rallies, particularly those held in Montevideo, the nation's capital. The enthusiasm of Uruguayans reflected a widespread disenchantment with military rule. About 60 per cent of Uruguay's eligible voters took part in the elections. Nathan A. Haverstock

See also LATIN AMERICA (Facts in Brief Table). In WORLD BOOK, see URUGUAY.

UTAH. See STATE GOVERNMENT.

UTILITIES. See COMMUNICATIONS; ENERGY; PETROLEUM AND GAS.

VANUATU. See PACIFIC ISLANDS.

VENDA. See AFRICA.

VENEZUELA. The value of Venezuela's oil exports, which account for 95 per cent of the nation's earnings from trade, fell sharply in 1982 despite stepped-up production that reached 2 million barrels per day late in the year. Venezuela expected to earn only $14 billion from oil in 1982, about $6-billion less than it earned in 1981.

The drop in oil earnings—which alone pay more than 70 per cent of the federal budget—caused cutbacks in many government programs, including welfare services. The cutbacks became political dynamite as campaigning began for Venezuela's 1983 national elections.

Political Rallies blossomed, particularly in Caracas, the capital, whose voters historically sway the outcome of elections. The incumbent Social Christian Party, after a bruising intraparty fight, selected Rafael Caldera as their presidential candidate. Caldera had served one term as president previously, from 1969 to 1974. The Democratic Action Party chose Jaime Lusinchi, who had long headed his party's congressional delegation.

The campaigning opened against the backdrop of war between Great Britain and Argentina in the Falkland Islands. Both candidates were outspoken in their criticism of the British, and of the United States for siding with Britain. Of all Latin American countries, none—with the possible exceptions of Cuba and Nicaragua—was more vehement than Venezuela in its denunciation of what it called Anglo-Saxon aggression in the Americas.

Oil Money Transferred. Venezuela's strong private sector was taken aback at what looked like government designs on the resources of the state-owned oil monopoly. When Venezuela completed nationalization of its oil industry in 1976, the government had pledged not to use the oil earnings to pay for politically motivated programs. But with the election year approaching, resources of the oil company were transferred to the Central Bank of Venezuela, raising fears that the government would use them to buttress the country's out-of-balance budget.

Other Developments. Venezuela's territorial dispute with neighboring Guyana continued in 1982, with Venezuela pledging itself to a negotiated settlement of the issue. But some Venezuelans felt that the government was using the issue only to distract public attention from the worsening economic situation.

The nation's government continued to pin future hopes on developing the belt of heavy crude oil in the Orinoco River Basin. But first Venezuela had to develop economical ways to refine oil from the mineral-laden deposits. Nathan A. Haverstock

See also LATIN AMERICA (Facts in Brief Table). In WORLD BOOK, see VENEZUELA.

VERMONT. See STATE GOVERNMENT.

VETERANS. A five-day "National Salute to Vietnam Veterans" held in Washington, D.C., culminated on Nov. 13, 1982, in the dedication of a memorial honoring U.S. military personnel who served in that war. The memorial consists of two black granite walls that bear the names of the 57,792 Americans killed or missing in Vietnam. The memorial, like the war, stirred controversy. Critics, who felt that the starkly simple monument failed to express the heroism of those who served, persuaded the Federal Fine Arts Commission to add a flagpole and a statue of three soldiers to the memorial area. Funds to build the $7-million memorial were raised privately by veterans' organizations. The government provided the site in Constitution Gardens near the Lincoln Memorial.

On November 22, President Ronald Reagan named Harry N. Walters, an assistant secretary of the Army, to succeed Robert P. Nimmo as director of the Veterans Administration (VA). Nimmo had resigned in October.

Studies continued on the effects of Agent Orange, a controversial herbicide used to defoliate forests during the Vietnam War. But findings were not yet available. Virginia E. Anderson

In WORLD BOOK, see VETERANS ADMINISTRATION; VETERANS' ORGANIZATIONS.

VICE-PRESIDENT OF THE UNITED STATES. See BUSH, GEORGE H. W.

The Vietnam Veterans Memorial in Washington, D.C., dedicated in November, honors members of the United States armed forces who served in that war.

VIETNAM changed some middle-level leaders in March 1982 in an attempt to overcome economic and other problems. The Communist Party newspaper explained the need for changes by saying, "In wartime, we had enough to eat and were successful. In peace, we are hungry and failing."

The Shakeup left Vietnam's aging top leadership intact, however. Le Duan, 74 years old, continued as Communist Party secretary general, Vietnam's most powerful leader.

Among those dropped from the party's Politburo were former economic planner Le Thanh Nghi and General Vo Nguyen Giap, who defeated the French at Dien Bien Phu in 1954 and won many victories over United States forces during the Vietnam War. Xuan Thuy, who headed the North Vietnamese delegation to the Paris peace talks in the late 1960s, was also demoted. The new members appointed to the Politburo were professional administrators with better management skills than the party veterans they replaced.

At the Vietnamese Communist Party's fifth congress, held in the capital city of Hanoi from March 27 to 31, Le Duan told party members that there were "serious imbalances in our national economy," with "shortages of food, clothing materials, and other essential consumer goods." Although the strains of war were partly to blame, he said, "the difficulties have also stemmed from the shortcomings and mistakes of the party and state agencies . . . in leadership and management."

In another move apparently inspired by economic problems, Vietnam reshuffled 14 of its 42 Cabinet posts on April 24. Almost all of the 14 posts dealt with economic affairs.

Economic Planning was reduced to short-term goals because of uncertainty about resources. In April, Vietnam sought to delay payment of its $1.4-billion foreign debt.

Vietnam's main source of aid, the Soviet Union, tightened up on economic support amid signs of Moscow's unhappiness over past waste. Hanoi denied reports that it was sending forced labor to Siberia to help pay its Soviet debt. Moscow said in May that 11,000 Vietnamese were working in the Soviet Union to learn economic skills.

Other Developments. On CBS television's "60 Minutes" on June 13, Foreign Minister Nguyen Co Thach said that all prison camp inmates in Vietnam could go to America "if America would like to have them." Estimates of the number of political prisoners in Vietnam ranged from 20,000 to 200,000. Only some of them would qualify for immigration to the United States under present laws, however. Henry S. Bradsher

See also ASIA (Facts in Brief Table). In WORLD BOOK, see VIETNAM.

VIRGINIA. See STATE GOVERNMENT.

VISUAL ARTS. Exhibitions of old masters highlighted the art scene in the United States in 1982 as they had not done for many years. The foremost of those shows—all produced with complex financial support from federal, corporate, and private agencies—was organized by the Toledo (Ohio) Museum of Art together with the National Gallery of Art in Washington, D.C., and the Prado in Madrid, Spain. The event was the first international exhibition of major paintings by 16th-century mystic artist El Greco of Toledo. El Greco was a Greek named Domenikos Theotokopoulas, born on the island of Crete and trained in Italy, who painted in Spain. Equally compelling was the assemblage of paintings of the great 17th-century Dutch landscapist Jacob van Ruisdael. The show was seen at one of the premier university art museums, the Fogg Museum at Harvard University in Cambridge, Mass.

The wealth and depth of American art holdings was confirmed in "France in the Golden Age: 17th Century French Paintings from American Collections," organized by the Metropolitan Museum of Art in New York City. To honor the 300th anniversary of the death of 17th-century French landscape artist Claude—also known as Claude Lorrain—the National Gallery of Art presented the largest exhibition of his work ever assembled.

Large exhibitions also featured modern masters. The Albright-Knox Art Gallery in Buffalo, N.Y., presented the technology-influenced paintings of French artist Fernand Léger. In New York City, the Museum of Modern Art displayed works by the pioneer of dreamlike art, Italian painter Giorgio de Chirico, while at the Guggenheim Museum, "Kandinsky in Munich 1896-1914" was the first of three exhibitions to survey the entire career of Russian abstract painter Wassily Kandinsky. "Braque: Papiers Collés," at the National Gallery of Art, celebrated the 100th birthday anniversary of French cubist Georges Braque, presenting him as the inventor of collage in 1912.

Other exhibitions honored artists more recent in the evolution of a modern vision. The pioneer American abstract painter Milton Avery was featured at New York City's Whitney Museum of American Art, and the 1930s were the focus of "Precisionist Painting and American Photography" at the San Francisco Museum of Modern Art. The Aspen (Colo.) Center for the Visual Arts marked a now-distinct era in American art in its "Castelli and His Artists"—a tribute to the 25-year-old New York City gallery of Leo Castelli, where the careers of such artists as Andy Warhol and Robert Rauschenberg began.

New Museum Structures became so abundant in 1982 that if the importance of visual art to American society were measurable by their numbers, it would have to be termed very high. The Baltimore Museum of Art completed a three-year renovation with the opening of a new wing. The Metropolitan Museum of Art opened its $18.5-million Michael C. Rockefeller Wing to house its collections of primitive art. Other structures were underway, such as the $11.8-million Hood Museum of Art at Dartmouth College in Hanover, N.H., and the new Dallas Museum of Fine Arts. Buildings in advanced planning stages included the Fogg Museum addition at Harvard University, the Museum of Contemporary Art in Los Angeles, the Virginia Museum of Fine Arts in Richmond, and the Des Moines (Iowa) Art Center addition.

In St. Petersburg, Fla., a showing of the A. Reynolds Morse Collection, the world's largest group of works by Salvador Dali, opened the Salvador Dali Institute on March 10. The renovated $2-million structure is devoted to works by the Spanish surrealist. The Daniel J. Terra Museum of American Art, operating in suburban Evanston, Ill., since 1980, acquired a downtown Chicago site for the construction of a major facility, which was expected to open by 1987. And in Malibu, Calif., the J. Paul Getty Museum—which became the richest museum in the world in March when it received $1 billion from the estate of its founder—announced that it would build three institutions in nearby Los Angeles. There will be conservation and study centers and a new museum.

Major Museum Acquisitions included *Pasiphaë*, a 1943 painting by American abstract expressionist Jackson Pollock, which the Metropolitan Museum of Art bought for $1 million. In Chicago, Daniel J. Terra, founder of the museum bearing his name, purchased for $3.25 million a remarkable picture by 19th-century painter and inventor Samuel F. B. Morse and presented it to the museum. The picture, which Morse painted in 1832, is called *The Gallery of the Louvre*. It depicts 38 European masterpieces, each an exact tiny copy of its original. The work was in the collections of Syracuse University in New York since 1884.

The Metropolitan Museum of Art received as gifts two truly fantastic collections: 500 Renaissance and baroque three-dimensional, small-scale works from the Jack and Belle Linsky Collection—appraised at $60 million—and the $18-million John M. Crawford, Jr., collection of Chinese painting. Less generously gifted, the Whitney Museum of American Art raised $1.25 million in 15 days to buy American sculptor Alexander Calder's 50-piece wire-and-cloth construction *Circus*.

Significant Sculpture Shows included the rare importation at the Kimball Art Museum in Fort Worth, Tex., "Great Age of Japanese Buddhist Sculpture, 600-1300 A.D." The first large museum exhibition of the work of French-born artist Louise Bourgeois, who has worked in the United States since 1938, opened at the Museum of Modern Art

Artist Georgia O'Keeffe, newly a sculptor at age 95, shows her painted cast-aluminum *Abstraction* at the San Francisco Museum of Modern Art.

in November. In Washington, D.C., two complementary shows presented various aspects of the steel works of American sculptor David Smith. Both the National Gallery of Art and the Hirshhorn Museum and Sculpture Garden exhibited Smith's work.

Major American Artists were honored with large museum exhibitions. The 100th anniversary of the birth of Ashcan School artist George Wesley Bellows was celebrated in "Bellows: The Boxing Pictures" at the National Gallery of Art and with an exhibition of his lithographs at the Metropolitan Museum of Art. One of the first important American artists, 18th-century painter Charles Willson Peale, was seen at the National Portrait Gallery in Washington, D.C., while "Thomas Eakins: Artist of Philadelphia," at the Philadelphia Museum of Art, honored that city's greatest artist.

Current European Art enjoyed accelerating interest—perhaps due to a lapse in American creativity. This was reflected in the U.S. debuts, in private galleries, of about 100 artists from Italy, West Germany, and France. Several museum shows also surveyed this new area. The Milwaukee Art Museum displayed "New Figuration from Europe," and the Guggenheim Museum presented "New Art from Italy," while Chicago's Museum of Contemporary Art showed "Contemporary Art from the Netherlands."

The Decorative Arts were featured in several large exhibitions. The master jeweler to the early 20th-century aristocracy of Europe was seen in "Louis Cartier: Masterworks of Art Deco, 1915-1935" at the Los Angeles County Museum of Art. At the Cincinnati Art Museum, "Treasures from the Tower of London," a display of arms and armor, was the first such loan in the Tower's 900-year history. At Chicago's Museum of Science and Industry, the Morse Foundation Collection of the magnificent stained-glass creations of American glassmaker Louis Comfort Tiffany was presented as "The Treasures of Tiffany." And the Cooper-Hewitt Museum of Design and Decorative Arts in New York City organized "Scandinavian Design 1880-1980."

The important exhibition at the Walker Art Center in Minneapolis, Minn., "De Stijl 1917-1931, Visions of Utopia," presented two aspects of the circa-1917 group that originated in the Netherlands. The show included both fine art and examples of the theory and form that characterized De Stijl (The Style) in the "useful arts," such as furniture and architecture. Joshua B. Kind

In WORLD BOOK, see ART AND THE ARTS; PAINTING; SCULPTURE.

VITAL STATISTICS. See CENSUS; POPULATION.

WALES. See GREAT BRITAIN.

WASHINGTON. See STATE GOVERNMENT.

WASHINGTON, D.C., started 1982 with a record cold spell and two tragic accidents. On January 13, an Air Florida Boeing 737 jetliner taking off from Washington's National Airport on a flight to Tampa, Fla., hit the 14th Street bridge and plunged into the frozen Potomac River. All but five of the 79 persons aboard, and four persons on the bridge, were killed. A passer-by, Lenny Skutnik, became a national hero when he threw off his coat and boots and dived into the icy water to save a flight attendant from drowning.

Just half an hour after the plane crash, three persons were killed and 25 injured in a mishap in the Metro subway. The accident, the first in the system's five years of operation, occurred when a train was being backed up in a tunnel. One car derailed and was split open by a tunnel divider.

Another kind of crisis occurred on December 8, when a man named Norman Mayer drove a van up to the Washington Monument and threatened to blow it up unless the United States took steps to stop the nuclear arms race. He claimed the van contained dynamite. After holding the monument hostage for 10 hours, Mayer tried to drive away and was killed by police gunfire. There were no explosives in the van.

Statehood for D.C.? Washington planned hopefully for possible statehood as the first District of Columbia statehood convention convened at the

A customer at a Washington, D.C., liquor store buys a string of lottery tickets on August 25, the day the city began running a lottery.

end of January. During three months of sometimes angry debate, the 45 delegates drafted a constitution, which district voters approved in November. The convention also chose a name for the proposed 51st state—New Columbia. The statehood drive faced an uncertain future in Congress, which would have to approve the constitution as part of a bill granting statehood.

Lottery. Washington started its first legal lottery on August 25, with 750,000 tickets sold the first day. In November, two $1-million winners—a security guard with eight children and a widowed part-time bartender—were picked at a drawing.

Elections. The city held elections in 1982 for its mayor, City Council, and delegate to Congress. The primary election, on September 14, was marred by confusion, long lines at polling places, and flaring tempers. The names of some 20,000 voters—17 per cent of those who went to the polls—were missing from the computerized voter-registration lists.

Mayor Marion S. Barry, Jr., won the primary, which in effect returned him to office in the overwhelmingly Democratic city. His victory became official on November 2, when he breezed into a second term with 80 per cent of the vote.

In February, Barry's former wife, Mary Treadwell, was indicted along with four other persons on a charge of stealing thousands of dollars from three federally funded low-income housing projects. The mayor was not implicated.

Vietnam Memorial Dedicated. On November 13, about 15,000 Vietnam War veterans marched down Constitution Avenue to the Mall for the dedication of the Vietnam Veterans Memorial as a crowd of 150,000 watched. The ceremony was the culmination of a five-day salute to Vietnam War veterans.

In contrast to the harmony and reconciliation symbolized by that gathering, a demonstration on November 27 to protest a planned march of Ku Klux Klan members erupted into violence. Hundreds of the estimated 3,000 anti-Klan demonstrators went on a rampage, injuring 12 police officers and a number of other protesters, smashing store windows, and looting. The police subdued the rioters with tear gas.

Other News. *The Washington Times,* a new daily newspaper, made its debut on May 17. The paper is owned by the Unification Church, led by Sun Myung Moon.

In the first major step toward devising a master plan for the city, district planning officials unveiled a comprehensive land-use proposal. The plan would restrict most commercial growth to downtown and most industrial development to the city's northeast section. Sandra Evans Teeley

In WORLD BOOK, see WASHINGTON, D.C.

WATER. United States Secretary of the Interior James G. Watt said on April 28, 1982, that the nation's most serious domestic crisis of the next decade will involve water because the country lacks the billions of dollars needed to solve its water problems. Plentiful spring rains ended the prolonged drought that had plagued such areas as Florida and New Jersey in 1981. But water experts said that the nation was overusing its reserve supply of underground water. For every 100 gallons taken out, only 74 gallons were being returned. (One gallon equals 3.8 liters.)

In March, the sudden melting of the snows of a severe Midwest winter caused damaging floods that forced the evacuation of thousands of people from their homes in Ohio, Michigan, and Indiana. On March 16, President Ronald Reagan visited Fort Wayne, Ind., which was the city hardest hit by that state's worst flooding in almost 70 years. Heavy rainstorms in early December brought flooding that drove at least 25,000 people from their homes in the Mississippi Valley. In late December, severe floods caused at least six deaths in Louisiana and Mississippi.

Water Projects. The United States government spent more than $45 billion from 1950 to 1975 to develop and maintain the nation's water resources. Nevertheless, representatives of 17 Western states, which consume 84 per cent of the nation's water supply, complained that Congress had not cleared an omnibus water project bill since 1976. The Reagan Administration was expected to propose legislation requiring the states that benefit from reclamation projects to pay a greater share of the costs. In exchange, the Administration said that it would back some new water projects in the West.

Reclamation Reform. A five-year congressional battle over the size of farms allowed to use low-cost federal irrigation water ended on October 12, when President Reagan signed a compromise bill that revised the Reclamation Act of 1902. The act helped settle the West by authorizing the federal government to build irrigation projects subsidized by taxpayers and to sell the irrigation water from the projects to settlers at bargain rates. It entitled one person to buy water from federal irrigation projects to irrigate 160 acres (65 hectares) and a husband and wife to buy federal water to irrigate 320 acres (130 hectares).

In 1977, owners of large farms won a delay of a court order that would have required the secretary of the interior to enforce the 160-acre limit. About 97 per cent of irrigation farmers complied with the limit in 1982. However, the small number of large farms not in compliance occupy 30 per cent of the land receiving subsidized water.

On May 6, the House of Representatives voted 228 to 117 to increase the acreage limit to 960 acres (389 hectares). The Senate voted 49 to 13 on July 16 to set the limit at 1,280 acres (518 hectares) per family. The compromise measure signed by Reagan provided subsidized water for farming operations of 960 acres. The law permits large growers to lease unlimited amounts of additional land, as before. However, the grower must pay interest on the cost of the facilities the government built to deliver water to the extra land.

Water Transfers. On July 2, the Supreme Court of the United States ruled by a 7 to 2 vote that states cannot outlaw the shipment of underground water supplies across their borders. The ruling favored two farmers seeking to pipe water from Nebraska to Colorado. The decision cast doubt on the constitutionality of laws in Western states that ban out-of-state use of their ground water resources.

Peripheral Canal Rejected. On June 8, by the stunning margin of 67 to 33 per cent, California voters rejected a proposal to build a 43-mile (69-kilometer) waterway from reservoirs in the water-rich northern part of that state to the canal system feeding the parched south. The so-called Peripheral Canal would have cost $1.3 billion. California political observers had expected approval of the initiative because of southern California's larger population. Andrew L. Newman

In WORLD BOOK, see WATER.

WEATHER. The weather was severe in the Central and Eastern parts of the United States early in 1982. Many weather stations reported record low temperatures. The most extreme departures from normal occurred in a belt stretching from Iowa to western Ohio. Chicago, for example, broke a 109-year-old record on January 10 with a temperature of −26° F. (−32° C). Winter precipitation was especially heavy in the Southeast, which had been plagued by drought.

Cold weather in the spring caused considerable damage to fruit in the Southeast. Subsequently, however, warmer-than-normal temperatures dominated the Eastern half of the United States. Precipitation and severe weather were especially prevalent in the central states from Texas up to South Dakota. Heavy rains and a sudden thawing of snow caused severe flooding in the Midwest in mid-March. Rivers in Indiana, Michigan, and Ohio overflowed in the region's worst flooding since 1913. A record number of tornadoes were reported in May.

In summer and fall, temperatures averaged near normal and precipitation was slightly above normal over most sections of the United States.

On November 23, the first hurricane in 23 years struck the island of Kauai in Hawaii, causing property damage estimated at $180 million. During the week before Christmas, a storm battered

A building of icicles is the aftermath of a fire on January 10, Chicago's coldest day. The temperature dipped to −26° F. (−32° C).

the West Coast with hurricane-force winds and rain, then turned into a blizzard over the Rocky Mountain States. At year's end, rains brought severe flooding to Louisiana and Mississippi.

El Chichón, a Mexican volcano, began to erupt on March 29, sending a cloud of dust and gases 14 to 20 miles (22 to 32 kilometers) into the stratosphere. This was one of the largest volcanic clouds of this century. It was about 20 times as massive as the cloud that issued from Mount St. Helens in Washington when that volcano erupted in May 1980. Within a few weeks, the cloud from El Chichón spread into a band stretching around the earth from the equator to 30 degrees north latitude.

The cloud's effect on the earth's climate depends upon the amount of sulfur dioxide gas in the cloud. Sunlight turns this gas into tiny droplets of sulfuric acid that remain in the stratosphere for more than a year. When sunlight strikes these droplets, the drops scatter the light and reflect it, rather than allowing the rays to warm the earth. Meteorologists suspect that the cloud has the potential of reducing the mean temperature of the earth by several tenths of a degree over a period of one to three years.

Cloud Seeding. Many scientists have experimented with cloud seeding at subfreezing temperatures since Irving Langmuir and Vincent J. Schaefer—chemists at the General Electric Company laboratories—discovered the technique in 1946. The introduction of finely ground solid carbon dioxide—dry ice—into clouds at subfreezing temperatures causes the clouds to precipitate as snow. Cloud seeding has tremendous commercial potential. Because of this potential, scientists conducted many experiments before they thoroughly understood the process.

In 1982, scientists re-examined a number of experiments. Many claims that the original researchers had made were not confirmed in the light of strict scientific standards.

The difficulty of drawing conclusions from cloud-seeding experiments stems from the fact that clouds differ a great deal from one another. Therefore, scientists must experiment with large numbers of clouds and then apply statistical techniques to their results. The scientists must consider the probability that a certain number of clouds would have precipitated even without seeding. Unfortunately, precipitation averages tend to be heavily influenced by a few heavy storms. Scientists believed that they had to eliminate some of the results of these storms in order to draw meaningful conclusions about cloud seeding. Researchers now view this practice as unsound. Today's researchers suggest that few cloud-seeding experiments conducted over the past 35 years demonstrated success for the methods used.

Airflow. In 1982, scientists concluded two programs on airflow in mountainous areas. The first study, conducted in the Geysers area of central California, measured the airflow in sloping valleys at night. In such a situation, air that has been cooled by contact with radiating slopes drains down into creek and river valleys. The air continues down the sloping valley bottoms, entering low-lying areas. Pollutants trapped in these airflows may travel long distances. Furthermore, the cool, heavy air does not mix vertically with warmer, lighter air above it. Consequently, the pollutants may increase to objectionable concentrations.

The second program, the international Alpine Experiment (ALPEX), covered a wide variety of phenomena, from how a large mountain mass influences winter cyclones to how air flows through individual valleys. Scientists took five years to plan ALPEX. It was part of the Global Atmospheric Research Program, a joint project of the World Meteorological Organization and the International Council of Scientific Unions. About 100 ground stations in Switzerland and surrounding countries, along with satellites, special aircraft, ships in the Mediterranean Sea, and balloons, collected data in March and April. Alfred K. Blackadar

In WORLD BOOK, see METEOROLOGY; WEATHER.

WEIGHT LIFTING. See SPORTS.

WELFARE. In his State of the Union message on Jan. 26, 1982, President Ronald Reagan proposed to transfer control of a number of United States welfare programs from the federal government to state and local governments. He claimed that this plan, which he called the "new federalism," would "make welfare less costly and more responsive to genuine need."

Under the plan, the federal government would give the states responsibility for two major welfare programs—food stamps and Aid to Families with Dependent Children (AFDC)—along with other programs. In return, the federal government would relieve state governments of all financial responsibility for Medicaid, a program to provide medical care to the poor.

The cost to the states of $46.7 billion would be offset by savings of $19.1 billion from the transfer of Medicaid and by a $28-billion trust fund created from federal excise and windfall-profits taxes. The trust fund would serve to ease the transition but would be phased out by 1991. The President maintained that the transfer would not result in a net financial gain or loss to any of the states.

Reagan's New Federalism was greeted with skepticism by many governors and members of Congress who feared their states might lose money in the swap. Some opponents claimed that responsibility for programs linked to nationwide economic conditions properly belongs to the federal government. Costs of food-stamp programs and AFDC, for example, would rise sharply during a period of deep recession.

On April 6, the Reagan Administration said it had suspended efforts to draft legislation implementing the transfer. But on June 23, the White House announced a revised plan that would keep the food-stamp program and most of Medicaid under federal control. In August, the Administration said it would not submit the plan to Congress until 1983.

Eight former secretaries of the Department of Health, Education, and Welfare—now the Department of Health and Human Services and the Department of Education—made public in September a report entitled "Welfare Policy in the United States." Their recommendations ran counter to the Reagan Administration's new federalism by proposing nationwide eligibility standards and minimum benefit payments to reduce inequities among states in AFDC programs.

Welfare Cuts. Welfare programs bore the brunt of spending cuts to reduce the budget deficit for fiscal 1982, which ended on September 30. But in preparing the budget for fiscal 1983, Congress resisted pressure from the White House to make further deep cuts in welfare spending.

In the AFDC program, Reagan proposed budget cuts totaling $3.3 billion over three years, but Congress approved only $342 million in cuts. Reagan had asked for an $8-billion reduction in Medicaid over three years, but Congress gave him only a $1.1-billion cut. In the food-stamp program, Congress approved only $1.9 billion of the $7.1-billion reduction requested by Reagan. Because of high unemployment, the number of recipients of these benefits did not drop as much as Reagan had hoped. But only Medicaid rolls registered a slight increase.

Policy Shift. Reagan's attempts to trim welfare spending were seen by some observers as a fundamental shift in U.S. domestic policy. For years, welfare spending had been increased annually. But in its 1982 report to Congress, the President's Council of Economic Advisers stated, "Income redistribution is not a compelling justification for federal taxing and spending programs. The federal government serves the poor better by assuring strong economic growth and reducing inflation than by distributing social welfare benefits."

Poverty Increases. The U.S. Bureau of the Census reported in July that more than 2.2 million Americans joined the ranks of the poor in 1981, an increase of 7.4 per cent over 1980. According to census figures, 31.8 million Americans, or 1 person in 7, lived below the poverty line of a $9,287 annual income for a family of four. Virginia E. Anderson

In WORLD BOOK, see WELFARE.

WEST INDIES. The Caribbean Basin Initiative—a program devised jointly by the United States, Canada, Mexico, Venezuela, and Colombia—spotlighted the problems of small countries in the Caribbean and Central America in 1982. President Ronald Reagan announced U.S. participation in the program in a February 24 address to the Organization of American States (OAS). He said the Caribbean area needs the trade and investment help the program promised because it has been particularly hard hit by the high cost of importing oil, along with declining prices for such major exports as sugar; coffee; and bauxite, a mineral from which aluminum is obtained.

To implement the President's program, the U.S. Congress approved $350 million in emergency assistance for nations in dire straits. Congress failed to pass what the President called "the centerpiece" of the program, the proposed one-way free trade for a 12-year period—except for trade in textiles and apparel—for Caribbean nations friendly to the United States. That part of the program includes provision of tax credits of up to 10 per cent for U.S. companies investing in Caribbean ventures. Many members of Congress believed it would create jobs abroad at a time when they were needed at home. President Reagan vowed to reintroduce the measure in the next Congress, in 1983.

President Reagan took a five-day working vacation in the Caribbean in April. En route, the President stopped in Jamaica to express his continued support for the government of Prime Minister Edward Seaga. Later, while relaxing in Barbados, Reagan met with the heads of five poor eastern Caribbean countries in an effort to enlist their support for his initiative program.

Among those meeting with the President was Prime Minister Mary Eugenia Charles of Dominica. The tiny island nation of 80,000 residents had still not recovered fully from the devastating effects of Hurricane David, which struck in August 1979. Like other areas to be reached by the Caribbean Basin Initiative, Dominica has few resources.

The Dominican Republic inaugurated as president on August 16 Salvador Jorge Blanco, a lawyer from the city of Santiago. Jorge Blanco belongs to the Dominican Revolutionary Party of his predecessor, Silvestre Antonio Guzmán Fernández, who committed suicide in July.

President Jorge Blanco set an austerity course for his country, cutting all government salaries, including his own. Like other Latin American leaders, he blamed hard times on external forces, including declining sugar prices, high interest rates, and a rising protectionist trend in industrialized nations. See JORGE BLANCO, SALVADOR.

Haitian Unrest. During his time in office from February to July 1982, Haiti's Minister of Finance and National Economy Marc D. Bazin waged a campaign against corruption at the highest levels of the government of President Jean-Claude Duvalier. For his troubles, including efforts to collect overdue taxes from Duvalier's friends and relations, and attempts to bring the country's budget under control, Bazin was dismissed.

United States-Grenada Relations remained cool in 1982. Displeasure on the part of the United States stemmed from Prime Minister Maurice Bishop's introduction of a Soviet-style Politburo and Central Committee to rule Grenada, and his acceptance of Cuban assistance to build an airport of alleged military usefulness.

Guyana, a Caribbean nation located on the South American mainland, declared itself a "cooperative republic" in 1966. Few observers at the time believed that either that status or its leader, then-Prime Minister Forbes Burnham, would last. But Burnham kept his position until he was elected president in 1980, and in 1982 he was still pushing what he called cooperative socialism. Although Guyana has paid for its nonalignment in the loss of earnings from bauxite and foreign aid, it has created an impressive sense of self-sufficiency among its citizens. Nathan A. Haverstock

See also LATIN AMERICA (Facts in Brief Table). In WORLD BOOK, see WEST INDIES.

WEST VIRGINIA. See STATE GOVERNMENT.

WILSON, BERTHA (1923-   ), was sworn in as the first woman to serve on the Supreme Court of Canada on March 30, 1982. She succeeded Justice Ronald Martland, who retired on February 10.

Bertha Wernham was born to Christina and Archibald Wernham on Sept. 18, 1923, in Kirkcaldy, Scotland. She was educated at Central Secondary School, the University of Aberdeen, and the Training College for Teachers, all in Aberdeen, Scotland. In 1945, Bertha Wernham married John Wilson, a Presbyterian minister, and four years later the couple immigrated to Canada. Bertha Wilson graduated from Dalhousie University Law School in Nova Scotia in 1958.

She joined the Toronto, Ont., law firm of Osler, Hoskin, and Harcourt in 1958, became a partner in 1968, was appointed queen's counsel in 1973, and remained until 1975. In 1976, Wilson became the first woman justice of the Ontario Court of Appeal, where she served until being appointed to the Supreme Court. Marsha F. Goldsmith

WISCONSIN. See STATE GOVERNMENT.

WYOMING. See STATE GOVERNMENT.

YEMEN (ADEN). See MIDDLE EAST.

YEMEN (SANA). See MIDDLE EAST.

YMCA OF THE USA. See COMMUNITY ORGANIZATIONS.

YOUNG WOMEN'S CHRISTIAN ASSOCIATION (YWCA). See COMMUNITY ORGANIZATIONS.

YOUTH ORGANIZATIONS. The Boy Scouts of America (BSA) announced on Sept. 14, 1982, that 13-year-old Alexander M. Holsinger of Normal, Ill., had become the millionth Eagle Scout. The first Eagle badge was awarded in 1912.

In October, the BSA announced the creation of an emblem for Cub Scouts of the Islamic faith. In addition, the former *Pro Deo et Patria* (For God and Country) badge earned by Lutheran Boy Scouts was redesigned and retitled the Living Faith Award. The BSA also announced the establishment of a project to help the children of working parents become more independent.

Boys Clubs of America (BCA) launched a new health program, "Superfit Allstars," in 1982. Funded by PepsiCo, Incorporated, the program is designed to promote fitness evaluations and exercise. More than 200 boys clubs around the country were expected to take part during 1982. More than 360 BCA executives and program personnel were trained to conduct another program, "The Body Works," which was in its second year. It stressed preventive health care, nutrition, personal safety, and mental health. On September 22, Edward Alameda, a 16-year-old member of the Boys Club of Tucson, Ariz., was named 1982-1983 National Boy of the Year.

Camp Fire received a $58,000 grant from the National Endowment for the Humanities for the project "Many Cultures Make Up Our World." The project includes activities that help children take pride in their own heritage and appreciate the customs and traditions of other cultures.

In March, 115 bluebird nesting boxes, built by Camp Fire members in 31 states, were placed on the grounds of the United States Air Force Academy near Colorado Springs, Colo., in a joint Camp Fire-Air Force conservation effort. Also in 1982, Wanderer Books, a division of Simon & Schuster, published *The Bobbsey Twins: Camp Fire Mystery*. The book is set at a Camp Fire camp in New Mexico.

4-H Clubs introduced *4-H: An American Idea—1900-1980,* an official history, during ceremonies at the U.S. Department of Agriculture on June 24.

A National 4-H Youth Employment and Career Education Pilot Program, conducted in cooperation with the National Collaboration for Youth, an association of youth organizations, and the U.S. Department of Labor, was completed in early 1982. The program was designed to help economically disadvantaged and other young people learn about jobs and careers and develop work skills.

Future Farmers of America (FFA). The 475,000 members of FFA took part in a program emphasizing community leadership and agricultural involvement in 1982. The organization's 1982-1983 theme was "Vocational Agriculture—Educating Through Experience."

On July 27, more than 100 FFA officers met with President Ronald Reagan, Secretary of Agriculture John R. Block, and Secretary of Education Terrel H. Bell at the White House in Washington, D.C. The officers, in Washington to attend conferences on vocational agriculture, also attended dedication ceremonies for the FFA National Hall of Achievement at FFA headquarters in Alexandria, Va.

Nearly 23,000 FFA members and supporters attended the 55th annual national convention in Kansas City, Mo., from November 11 to 13. Kevin Robinson of Eskridge, Kans., was named Star Farmer of America, and Elmer Zimmerman of Lowellville, Ohio, was designated Star Agribusinessman of America.

Girl Scouts of the United States of America (GSUSA) celebrated its 70th birthday by announcing its "Gift of Water" to the United States. The project is related to the United Nations (UN) designation of 1981-1990 as a decade of effort to assure clean, safe water everywhere.

To launch the year's activities, GSUSA conducted a symbolic ceremony at UN headquarters in New York City. Water samples gathered by Girl Scouts from the 50 states and Puerto Rico were mingled to represent the waters of the nation and Girl Scouting's commitment to preserving and protecting them. As part of the project, Girl

Alexander M. Holsinger, 13, of Normal, Ill., became the millionth Eagle Scout in September. The first Eagle badge was awarded in 1912.

Scouts carried out a wide variety of community services.

Girls Clubs of America (GCA). During 1982, the GCA National Youth Employment and Children's Creative Theater projects involved 1,000 and 3,295 girls, respectively, in special training programs. GCA received funding from the U.S. Department of Health and Human Services for a project entitled "Family Life Education for Adolescents." In addition, during 1982, every member club offered programs in the arts, and more than 90 per cent conducted programs in health education, sports, and cooking. Career development and employment programs were also offered in most clubs.

Junior Achievement (JA) set new records during the 1981-1982 academic year as nearly 500,000 young people from fifth grade through college participated in one of the four major programs offered by the organization. JA's eighth annual National Business Leadership Conference and Business Hall of Fame induction ceremony attracted 2,200 JA business executives to Pittsburgh, Pa., in March. Among the laureates named to the Business Hall of Fame were Adolph S. Ochs, founder of *The New York Times*, and Charles F. Kettering of General Motors Corporation. Virginia E. Anderson

In WORLD BOOK, see entries on the individual organizations.

YUGOSLAVIA suffered economically and financially in 1982 amid growing disunity in its ruling party, the League of Communists of Yugoslavia. In May, the collective state Presidency elected Petar Stambolić, a Serb, president for one year. The Presidency also nominated a new federal government, led by Prime Minister Milka Planinc. The Federal Assembly (parliament) then approved the nominations. Planinc was Yugoslavia's first woman prime minister. See PLANINC, MILKA.

Stane Dolanc, a Slovene,was appointed minister of the interior. He had been League Presidium secretary from 1972 until 1978. Lazar Mojsov, a Macedonian and Presidium chairman in 1980 and 1981, became foreign minister. The new defense minister was Admiral Branko Mamula, a Serb from Croatia. Mamula replaced General Nikola Ljubičič, a Serb who had held the post since 1967. Ljubičič became president of the Republic of Serbia.

Ethnic Problems. The political situation in Kosovo, a self-governing province of Serbia, was tense throughout 1982. About 80 per cent of Kosovo's people are ethnic Albanians. Many of these people want Yugoslavia to elevate Kosovo to the status of a republic.

Kosovo was the scene of widespread nationalist riots in the spring of 1981. In the first 10 months of 1982, police arrested 700 people for political offenses in Kosovo, and courts sentenced 332 of them. In October, the Federal Assembly, Yugoslavia's parliament, adopted measures to prevent Serbs and Montenegrins from emigrating from Kosovo. The tough policy in Kosovo continued to draw criticism from some of the other republics. Three bombs exploded in Priština, the province's capital, in November.

Money Problems. In May, the Federal Assembly passed a law that increased the federal government's holdings of hard currency. The government needed hard currency to repay more than $5 billion in principal and interest on Yugoslavia's $18.5-billion foreign debt. The new law ordered business enterprises to exchange 77 per cent of their hard currency for dinars. The law caused much controversy, particularly in the western republics of Slovenia and Croatia. Those republics have large export earnings and heavy income from tourism. In addition, Croatia receives money from Croatians who work in the West. On July 31, Yugoslavia froze prices for six months. In October, Yugoslavia devalued the dinar by 20 per cent and introduced an austerity program.

Industrial output increased by 0.6 per cent in the first 10 months of 1982, the lowest growth figure since 1945. Inflation was about 30 per cent throughout the year. Chris Cviic

See also EUROPE (Facts in Brief Table). In WORLD BOOK, see YUGOSLAVIA.

YUKON TERRITORY. The Liberal Party in Canada lost its last elected representatives west of Winnipeg, Man., on June 7, 1982, when Yukon territorial elections ousted the only two Liberal Party members. The Progressive Conservative Party took 9 of the 16 seats, and its head, Christopher Pearson, continued as government leader in the legislature. The New Democratic Party took 6 seats, and 1 seat went to an Independent.

The Yukon's Fragile Economy faced collapse as 1982 ended and slumping world metal prices and high labor costs closed the mining industry. The Cyprus Anvil Mining Corporation's lead and zinc mine at Faro extended a summer shut-down to the spring of 1983, and the United Keno Hill Mines silver mine at Elsa began an indefinite shut-down in July. For the first time since the 1898 Klondike gold rush, there would be no winter mining in the Yukon. The White Pass and Yukon Railway shut down indefinitely on September 30 because its main winter customer had been Cyprus Anvil. Cyprus Anvil's closing meant a loss of 40 per cent of the Yukon's revenue, and it was predicted that 5,000 of the territory's 24,000 people would leave because of lack of work. David M. L. Farr

See also CANADA. In WORLD BOOK, see YUKON TERRITORY.

ZAIRE. See AFRICA.
ZAMBIA. See AFRICA.

ZIMBABWE. Strife erupted in 1982 between Zimbabwe's two largest black groups after the February 17 ouster of Joshua Nkomo from Prime Minister Robert Mugabe's Cabinet. Mugabe, leader of the majority Mashona group, charged that Nkomo, head of the Matabele people, was plotting to overthrow the government.

Dismissed along with Nkomo were three other ministers of Nkomo's Patriotic Front (formerly the Zimbabwe African People's Union). In addition, two top Matabele military leaders were arrested. Mugabe justified his action by saying that Nkomo had been caught with a large cache of Russian-made weapons.

The Patriotic Front's Central Committee met on February 27 and voted to remain in the coalition government with Mugabe's party, the Zimbabwe African National Union. However, more than 1,000 of Nkomo's followers deserted the national army and began reprisals against Mugabe's government. The rebels, perhaps aided by South African agents, sabotaged power facilities and railroad lines and damaged 13 military aircraft.

Kidnapped Tourists. On July 23, six tourists—two Americans, two Australians, and two Britons—were abducted by pro-Nkomo forces. The kidnappers threatened to kill the tourists unless Mugabe released about 200 jailed Nkomo followers. At year-end, the tourists' fate was still unknown. Three other British tourists, missing for two weeks, were found dead on August 1.

Mugabe and Nkomo met on August 2 to discuss ways to restore order. White farmers, who grow most of the country's crops, told Mugabe on September 18 that many whites would flee their farms if they continued to fear for their safety.

Whites in Government. Mugabe tried to reassure whites about their political future in Zimbabwe. On April 16, he appointed whites to two vacancies in his government. In early September, he announced that his own party would nominate white candidates for some constituencies in the next parliamentary election, scheduled for 1985.

Zimbabwe's 1980 Constitution reserves 20 of the Parliament's 100 seats for whites. All of those seats were won in 1980 by the Rhodesian Front, led by Ian D. Smith, who had headed a white minority government that ruled the country (then called Rhodesia) from 1965 to 1979. However, early in March 1982, nine white members of Parliament resigned from Smith's party, renamed the Republican Front, criticizing Smith for his party's hostility to the Mugabe government.

In April, Zimbabwe's capital city, Salisbury, was renamed Harare, the name of a 19th-century Zimbabwean leader. J. Dixon Esseks

See also AFRICA (Facts in Brief Table). In WORLD BOOK, see ZIMBABWE.

The only king penguins artificially incubated and hand reared, King George and King Tut were born in February at Sea World in San Diego.

ZOOLOGY. The temperature of egg incubation determines the sex of alligators, according to an April 1982 report by biologists Mark W. J. Ferguson of The Queens University of Belfast in Northern Ireland, and Ted Joanen of the Louisiana Wildlife and Fisheries Commission in Grand Chenier. The scientists' observations, made in the Louisiana swamps and in the laboratory, resulted in the discovery that female alligators hatch from eggs incubated at a temperature of 30°C (86°F.) or lower, and males from eggs incubated at 34°C (93.2°F.) or higher. At a temperature of 32°C (89.6°F.), the sex ratio is about 6 females to 1 male.

Because nests built on levees, or embankments, are hotter than nests constructed on wet marshes, levee nests hatch males and marsh nests hatch females. Incubation at the lower temperatures results in slower metabolism and less demand by the developing embryo for nutrients stored in the egg. So more egg yolk remains in the gut of newly hatched females, and they weigh more than males and mature sooner. The earlier maturation of females helps alligators to survive, because they remain functionally reproductive only about half as long as males.

Because alligators are believed to be descended from dinosaurs, Ferguson and Joanen speculated that dinosaur reproduction may have worked the same way, and a sudden temperature change during the age of dinosaurs might have been a factor in their extinction.

Tiny New Old Mammal. Paleontologists on a dinosaur dig in China's Szechwan (Sichuan) Province in 1982 found the fossil jawbone of a mammal unlike any previously known. Because the bone is only 2.5 centimeters (1 inch) long, the mammal was probably about the size of a small mouse.

The jawbone was sent to the National Museum of Victoria in Melbourne, Australia, where scientists concluded that its tiny owner lived in the Jurassic Period, 180 million to 130 million years ago. It must have split off from the mammalian line of evolution 30 million years before the two major types of present-day mammals — pouched and placental — diverged.

The scientists named the creature *Yinotheres,* meaning *reflection beast,* in reference to its unique tooth arrangement. Two major characteristics of the jaw are unique. Other mammalian lower molars have a depression for the upper molars to rest upon behind the major grinding part of the tooth, but in *Yinotheres* the depression is on the opposite, or reflecting, side — toward the front of the tooth. A second odd fact about *Yinotheres* is that the lower jaw has more than one bone, as living lizards — but no mammals — do. Barbara N. Benson

See also PALEONTOLOGY; ZOOS AND AQUARIUMS. In WORLD BOOK, see ZOOLOGY.

ZOOS AND AQUARIUMS. The New York Zoological Society announced plans on April 16, 1982, for a $15-million renovation of New York City's Central Park Zoo. The zoo, which will be divided into tropical, temperate, and polar zones, will feature environments similar to the animals' natural habitats and house 240 animals of 60 species.

Giant Pandas. In January, Cancún, a naturally conceived panda born in captivity and the first panda ever born outside China, made his public debut at his home in the Chapultepec Zoo in Mexico City, Mexico. The chubby cub turned somersaults, cavorted, and hid behind his mother.

The National Zoological Park in Washington, D.C., tried unsuccessfully in 1982 to artificially inseminate its female giant panda, Ling-Ling. However, Shao-Shao, the female panda at the zoo in Madrid, Spain, gave birth to twins on September 4, following artificial insemination. Only one cub survived.

Rhino Review. The plight of the five species of rhinoceroses was examined at a symposium at the Zoological Society of London in August. While the black, white, and Indian rhinos are breeding in captivity, their numbers are not sufficient to maintain genetically diverse zoo populations.

The Javan rhino appears to be on the verge of extinction, especially after disease decimated the already small population living in Java on one of the few reserves devoted to the animal. Scientists at the conference also discussed the need to capture and breed Sumatran rhinos.

New Exhibits. On June 11, the Bronx Zoo in New York City opened the $2.5-million James and Margaret Carter Giraffe Building. The 11 giraffes, along with the cheetahs, ostriches, and gazelles housed in the 5-acre (2-hectare) pavilion, can roam through outdoor enclosures and a building 21 feet (6 meters) high topped by skylights. The zoo also opened an outdoor aviary for sea birds.

The Brookfield (Ill.) Zoo opened the African section of Tropic World, an indoor simulation of a rain forest, in May. Sharing the forest are seven species of primates, including gorillas, and 12 species of birds. Lincoln Park Zoo in Chicago opened an antelope and zebra area and a $14-million complex for large mammals.

The National Aquarium in Washington, D.C., was kept open by a last-ditch effort. The 109-year-old aquarium, in the Commerce Department building, lost its government funding after a new National Aquarium opened in Baltimore in 1981. In March 1982, a private, nonprofit organization called the National Aquarium Society took over the old aquarium.

George B. Rabb

In WORLD BOOK, see AQUARIUM; ZOO.

A gorilla mother and baby sit placidly in Tropic World, an indoor version of a rain forest, which opened in May at the Brookfield (Ill.) Zoo.

Answers to the Quiz

1. They traveled from pole to pole.
2. He is John W. Hinckley, Jr. A jury found him not guilty by reason of insanity on charges of shooting President Ronald Reagan in 1981.
3. Gemayel was assassinated in September.
4. Habré, Chad; Andropov, Soviet Union; Palme, Sweden; Gemayel, Lebanon; Ershad, Bangladesh; De la Madrid, Mexico.
5. Wilson was the first woman appointed to the Canadian Supreme Court.
6. Howard W. Cannon (D., Nev.) and Harrison H. Schmitt (R., N. Mex.).
7. Cats.
8. The Voting Rights Act of 1965.
9. Hama, Syria.
10. The document is the Constitution of the United States. The proposed change was the Equal Rights Amendment.
11. Spain.
12. They all resigned from high-level posts in the Reagan Administration in 1982.
13. After the peacekeeping force withdrew, Lebanese Christian militiamen killed hundreds of unarmed Palestinians in refugee camps.
14. Halley's Comet.
15. Henry Fonda.
16. The Department of Energy.
17. King Henry VIII of England.
18. The National Hockey League record for most goals in a season.
19. To avoid a conflict of interest, Douglas A. Fraser, head of the United Auto Workers, stepped down from Chrysler Corporation's board until a new labor contract was signed.
20. Smith received the Medal of Freedom, the United States highest civilian award.
21. The British government announced that it would permanently close the De Lorean Motor Cars Limited assembly plant in Northern Ireland. Hours later, De Lorean was arrested on charges of drug trafficking.
22. The city is Beirut, Lebanon. Israel bombed it, trying to destroy strongholds of the Palestine Liberation Organization (PLO).
23. The picture was *E. T.: The Extra-Terrestrial,* directed by Steven Spielberg.
24. International Business Machines Corporation remained whole; American Telephone and Telegraph Company agreed to divest itself of 22 subsidiaries.
25. *Columbia* flew with the first four-man crew and accomplished the first launching of a satellite from space but canceled what would have been the first spacewalk from a shuttle.
26. Protesters in Israel demanded an inquiry into the Beirut massacre. Bowing to pressure, Prime Minister Menachem Begin appointed a commission to investigate the incident.
27. They all declared bankruptcy in 1982.
28. Spain and Greenland, respectively.
29. Queen Elizabeth II of Great Britain is signing the Constitution Act, 1982, which will make Canada fully independent of Great Britain.
30. New government-approved history textbooks glossed over Japanese military aggression in the 1930s and 1940s.
31. It was the theme of the World's Fair held in Knoxville, Tenn.
32. Senegal and Gambia formed Senegambia.
33. Trifa was the first person to be deported for concealing war crimes from immigration officials. He was accused of inciting anti-Jewish riots during World War II (1939-1945).
34. The contracts called for them to supply pipeline parts to Russia. In June, President Reagan banned all subsidiaries and licensees of American companies from taking part in the construction because of Russia's role in forcing a military regime on Poland in 1981.
35. Lech Walesa.
36. Rickey Henderson broke the major league record for most stolen bases in a season.
37. Argentina and Great Britain went to war over the Falkland Islands.
38. The United Auto Workers at Ford Motor Company approved the concessions—the first union contract that makes such concessions in the history of the industry.
39. In June, the Supreme Court ruled that a President cannot be sued for actions taken while in office. The case involved a suit against Nixon. In November, the court refused to hear arguments by Nixon's lawyers trying to prevent release of his White House tape recordings.
40. So many members boycotted the meeting to protest admission of the Polisario Front to the OAU that the meeting could not be held.
41. b.
42. The department began distributing 120 million pounds (54 million kilograms) of surplus cheese free to low-income Americans.
43. The capsules (of Extra-Strength Tylenol) were tainted with cyanide, killing all seven people.
44. Voters turned out in unexpectedly large numbers despite a leftist boycott of the elections.
45. He is William Arthur Philip Louis, second in line of succession to the British throne.
46. Iran and Iraq.
47. Suazo Córdova, E; Ríos-Montt, C; Betancur, E; Siles Zuazo, E; Jorge Blanco, E.
48. A strike by the National Football League players interrupted the season after only two games and lasted until mid-November.
49. Clark became the first human recipient of a permanent artificial heart.
50. The President's son Ronald P. Reagan was laid off briefly by the Joffrey II dancers in October and applied for jobless benefits.

1977
1978
1979
1980
1981
1982

World Book Supplement 1982

To help WORLD BOOK owners keep their encyclopedias up to date, the following new or revised articles are reprinted from the 1983 edition of the encyclopedia.

See "Japan," page 545.

© Paul D. Thrash

Majestic Mount Fuji, framed by gorgeous cherry blossoms, symbolizes the great natural beauty of Japan. The country's spectacular scenery attracts tourists from all parts of the world.

JAPAN

JAPAN is an island country in the North Pacific Ocean. It lies off the northeast coast of mainland Asia and faces Russia, Korea, and China. Four large islands and thousands of smaller ones make up Japan. The four major islands—Hokkaido, Honshu, Kyushu, and Shikoku—form a curve about 1,200 miles (1,900 kilometers) long. But all the islands of Japan together have a land area slightly smaller than that of California. Crowded on these islands are about five times as many people as in California.

The Japanese call their country Nippon or Nihon, which means *source of the sun.* The name *Japan* may have come from *Cipango*, the Italian name given to the country by Marco Polo, a Venetian traveler of the late 1200's. Polo had heard of the Japanese islands while traveling through China.

Mountains and hills cover most of Japan, making it a country of great beauty. But the mountains and hills take up so much land that the great majority of the people live on narrow plains along the coasts. These coastal plains have much of Japan's best farmland and most of the country's major cities. More than three-fourths of the people live in urban areas. Japan's big cities are busy, modern centers of culture, commerce, and industry. Tokyo is the capital and largest city.

Japan is one of the world's industrial giants. Its industrial production is exceeded only by that of the United States and Russia. The Japanese manufacture a wide variety of products, including automobiles, computers, iron and steel, plastics, radios, and television sets. The country's factories have some of the most advanced equipment in the world. Japan became a major economic power even though it has few natural resources. It must import many of the raw materials needed for manufacturing.

The contributors of this article are Kenneth B. Pyle, Professor of History and Director of the School of International Studies at the University of Washington; Michael Robinson, Assistant Professor of History at the University of Southern California; and Jay Rubin, Associate Professor of Japanese Literature at the University of Washington.

Facts in Brief

Capital: Tokyo.

Official Language: Japanese.

Form of Government: Constitutional monarchy. *Symbol of State*—Emperor. *Head of Government*—Prime minister.

Area: 145,834 sq. mi. (377,708 km²). The four main islands—Hokkaido, Honshu, Kyushu, Shikoku—stretch about 1,200 mi. (1,900 km) from northeast to southwest. *Coastline*—5,857 mi. (9,426 km).

Elevation: *Highest*—Mount Fuji, 12,388 ft. (3,776 m) above sea level. *Lowest*—sea level.

Population: *Estimated 1983 Population*—120,246,000; distribution, 78 per cent urban, 22 per cent rural; density, 824 persons per sq. mi. (318 persons per km²). *1980 Census*—117,057,485. *Estimated 1988 Population*—125,756,000.

Chief Products: *Agriculture*—rice, wheat, barley, potatoes, soybeans, sweet potatoes, fruits, tea, tobacco. *Fishing Industry*—sardines, cod, mackerel, squid, tuna, shellfish, halibut, salmon, whales. *Manufacturing*—transportation equipment; machinery; electronic equipment; precision instruments; iron and steel; chemicals; textiles. *Mining*—coal, zinc, manganese, copper, lead, silver, tin, gold.

National Anthem: "Kimigayo" ("The Reign of Our Emperor").

Main Holidays: Emperor's Birthday—April 29; New Year's Day—January 1; Constitution Day—May 3.

Money: *Basic Unit*—yen. For the value of the yen in U.S. dollars, see MONEY (table: Exchange Rates). See also YEN.

© Milt and Joan Mann

The Streets of Tokyo, Japan's capital and largest city, are usually crowded. The Ginza, *above,* is a famous shopping district.

© Noriyuki Yoshida from Scott Henriquez

Rice Fields cover many hillsides in rural Japan. Farmers carve terraces in hillsides to make greater use of the limited farmland.

Life in Japan reflects the culture of both the East and the West. For example, baseball games and exhibitions of *sumo,* an ancient Japanese style of wrestling, are the favorite sporting events in the country. Although many Japanese wear Western-style clothing, almost all the people dress in traditional kimonos during festivals, on holidays, and on other special occasions. The Japanese *no* and *kabuki* dramas, both hundreds of years old, remain popular. But the Japanese people also flock to see motion pictures and the latest Western plays. Many Japanese artists combine traditional and Western styles and themes in their works.

Early Japan was greatly influenced by the neighboring Chinese civilization. From the late A.D. 400's to the early 800's, the Japanese borrowed heavily from Chinese art, government, language, religion, and technology. During the mid-1500's, the first Europeans arrived in Japan. Trade began with several European countries, and Christian missionaries from Europe converted many Japanese. During the early 1600's, however, the rulers of Japan decided to cut the country's ties with the rest of the world. They wanted to keep Japan free from outside influences.

Japan's isolation lasted until 1853, when Commodore Matthew C. Perry of the United States sailed his warships into Tokyo Bay. As a result of Perry's show of force, Japan agreed in 1854 to open two ports to U.S. trade. During the 1870's, the Japanese government began a major drive to modernize the country. New ideas and manufacturing methods were imported from Western countries. By the early 1900's, Japan had become an industrial and military power.

During the 1930's, Japan's military leaders gained control of the government. They set Japan on a program of conquest. On Dec. 7, 1941, Japan attacked United States military bases at Pearl Harbor in Hawaii, bringing the United States into World War II. The Japanese won many early victories, but then the tide turned in favor of the United States and the other Allied nations. In August 1945, U.S. planes dropped the first atomic bombs used in warfare on the Japanese cities of Hiroshima and Nagasaki. On Sept. 2, 1945, Japan officially surrendered, and World War II ended.

World War II left Japan completely defeated. Many Japanese cities lay in ruins, industries were shattered, and Allied forces occupied the country. But the skillful Japanese people worked hard to overcome the effects of the war. By the late 1960's, Japan had become a great industrial nation. The success of the Japanese economy has won the admiration of countries throughout the world. Today, few people enjoy a higher standard of living than do the Japanese.

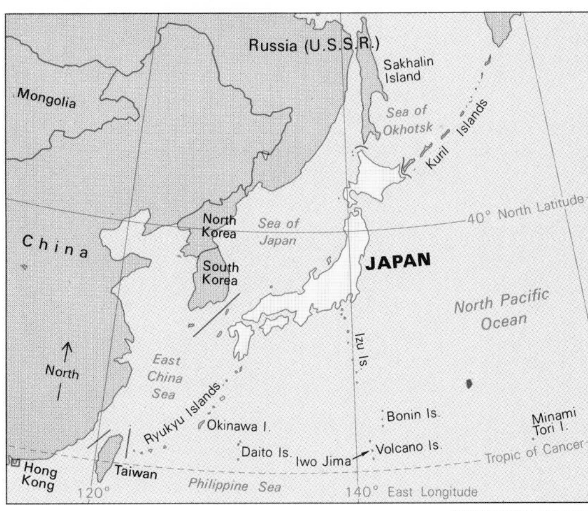

WORLD BOOK map

Japan lies in the North Pacific Ocean off the northeast coast of mainland Asia. It faces Russia, Korea, and China.

Japan Map Index

Cities and Towns

Abashiri . . . . . . 44,777 . . B 9
Abiko* . . . . . . 101,061 . . G 7
Ageo* . . . . . . 166,244 . . G 7
Aizuwaka-
matsu . . . . 114,534 . . F 7
Akashi* . . . . . 254,873 . . H 4
Akishima* . . . . 89,343 . . G 7
Akita . . . . 284,830 . . D 7
Ako . . . . 51,046 . . H 4
Amagasaki . . 523,657 . . H 5
Anan . . . . 61,253 . . H 4
Anjo . . . . 123,842 . . H 6
Aomori . . . . . . 287,609 . . D 7
Arida . . . . 35,685 . . H 5
Asahigawa . . 352,620 . . B 8
Asaka* . . . . . . 90,088 . . G 7
Ashikaga* . . . 165,756 . . G 7
Ashiya* . . . . . . 81,741 . . H 4
Atsugi* . . . . . 145,387 . . G 7
Beppu . . . . . . 136,488 . . I 3
Bibai . . . . 38,554 . . B 8
Bizen . . . . 33,032 . . H 4
Chiba . . . . 746,428 . . G 7
Chichibu* . . . . 61,284 . . G 7
Chigasaki* . . 171,013 . . G 7
Chitose* . . . . . 66,788 . . B 8
Chofu* . . . . . . 180,535 . . G 7
Choshi . . . . 89,415 . . G 7
Daito* . . . . . . 116,625 . . H 5
Ebetsu . . . . 86,349 . . B 8
Ebina* . . . . 77,499 . . G 7
Fuchu* . . . . . . 191,980 . . G 7
Fuji . . . . 205,752 . . H 6
Fujieda* . . . . . 103,224 . . H 6
Fujimi* . . . . 79,591 . . G 7
Fujinomiya* . 108,208 . . H 6
Fujisawa . . . . 300,181 . . G 7
Fukaya* . . . . . . 82,243 . . G 7
Fukui . . . . 240,964 . . G 5
Fukuoka . . 1,088,617 . . I 2
Fukushima . . 262,847 . . F 7
Fukuyama . . . 346,031 . . H 4
Funabashi . . . 479,437 . . G 7
Gamagori* . . . 85,294 . . H 6
Gifu . . . . 410,368 . . G 5
Gobo . . . . 30,400 . . I 5
Gyoda* . . . . 73,205 . . G 7
Habikino* . . . 103,147 . . H 5
Hachinohe . . . 238,208 . . D 8
Hachioji . . . . . 387,162 . . G 7
Hadano* . . . . . 123,130 . . G 7
Hagi . . . . 53,692 . . H 3
Hakodate . . . 320,152 . . C 7
Hamada . . . . . . 50,800 . . H 3
Hamakita* . . . . 72,472 . . H 6
Hamamatsu . 490,827 . . H 6
Hanamaki . . . . 68,875 . . E 7
Handa . . . . 89,328 . . H 5
Higashihiro-
shima* . . . . . 75,810 . . H 3
Higashi-
kurume* . . 106,521 . . G 7
Higashimatsu-
yama* . . . . . 63,889 . . G 7
Higashi-
murayama* 119,382 . . G 7
Higashi-
osaka . . . . . 521,635 . . H 5
Higashi-
yamato* . . . 65,415 . . G 7
Hikone . . . . 89,698 . . G 5
Himeji . . . . . . 446,255 . . H 4
Hino* . . . . 145,417 . . G 7
Hirakata* . . . 353,360 . . H 5
Hiratsuka . . . 214,299 . . G 7
Hirosaki . . . . . 175,330 . . D 7
Hiroshima . . . 899,394 . . H 3
Hitachi . . . . . . 204,612 . . G 7
Hofu . . . . 111,471 . . H 3
Hoya* . . . . 91,251 . . G 7
Ibaraki* . . . . . 234,059 . . H 5
Ichihara* . . . . 216,395 . . G 7
Ichikawa* . . . 364,244 . . G 7
Ichinomiya . . 253,138 . . G 5
Iida* . . . . 78,515 . . G 6
Iizuka . . . . 80,288 . . J 2
Ikeda* . . . . 101,116 . . H 5
Ikoma* . . . . 70,456 . . H 5
Imabari* . . . . 123,237 . . I 3
Inazawa* . . . . . 90,892 . . H 6
Iruma* . . . . . . 104,034 . . G 7
Isahaya . . . . . . 83,725 . . I 2
Ise . . . . 105,621 . . H 5
Isehara* . . . . . . 70,052 . . G 7
Isesaki* . . . . . 105,728 . . G 6
Ishinomaki . . 120,698 . . E 8
Itami* . . . . 178,229 . . H 4
Ito . . . . 69,638 . . H 7
Iwaki . . . . 342,076 . . F 7
Iwakuni . . . . . 112,527 . . H 3
Iwamizawa . . . 78,311 . . B 8
Iwate* . . . . 75,810 . . H 6
Iwatsuki* . . . . . 94,695 . . G 7
Izumi* . . . . 98,015 . . E 7
Izumi . . . . 124,322 . . H 5
Izumisano* . . . 90,684 . . H 5
Izumo . . . . 77,301 . . G 3
Joetsu . . . . . . 127,843 . . F 6
Joyo* . . . . 74,350 . . H 5
Kadoma* . . . . 138,901 . . H 5
Kagoshima . . 505,077 . . J 2
Kaizuka* . . . . . . 81,162 . . H 5
Kakamiga-
hara* . . . . . 114,751 . . G 5
Kakogawa* . . 212,232 . . H 4
Kamagawa . . . 31,680 . . H 7
Kamagaya* . . . 76,157 . . G 7
Kamaishi . . . . . 65,250 . . E 8
Kamakura* . . 172,612 . . G 7
Kanazawa . . . 417,681 . . G 5
Kanoya* . . . . . . 73,243 . . J 2
Karatsu* . . . . . . 77,712 . . I 2
Kariya* . . . . . 105,643 . . H 6
Kashihara* . . 107,320 . . H 5
Kashiwa* . . . . 239,199 . . G 7
Kashiwaziki . . . 83,499 . . F 6
Kasugai . . . . . 244,114 . . G 5
Kasukabe* . . 155,556 . . G 7
Katsuta* . . . . . . 92,620 . . G 7
Kawachina-
gano* . . . . . . 78,573 . . H 5
Kawagoe . . . . 259,317 . . G 7
Kawaguchi . . 379,357 . . G 7
Kawanishi* . . 129,834 . . H 4
Kawasaki . . 1,040,698 . . G 7
Kesennuma* . . 68,559 . . E 7
Kimitsu* . . . . . . 77,286 . . G 7
Kiryu . . . . 132,888 . . G 7
Kisarazu* . . . 110,711 . . G 7
Kishiwada . . . 180,317 . . H 5
Kitakyushu 1,065,084 . . H 2
Kitami . . . . . . 102,915 . . B 9
Kobe . . . . . 1,367,392 . . H 5
Kochi . . . . 300,830 . . I 4
Kodaira* . . . . 154,610 . . G 7
Kofu . . . . 199,272 . . G 6
Koganei* . . . . 102,412 . . G 7
Kokubunji* . . . 91,014 . . G 7
Komai* . . . . 70,824 . . G 7
Komaki* . . . . . 103,234 . . H 6
Komatsu . . . . 104,327 . . G 5
Konan* . . . . 92,141 . . H 6
Koriyama . . . . 286,497 . . F 7
Koshigaya* . . 223,243 . . G 7
Kumagaya . . . 136,807 . . G 7
Kumamoto . . 525,613 . . I 2
Kunitachi* . . . . 64,154 . . G 7
Kurashiki . . . . 403,785 . . H 4
Kurayoshi . . . . 52,271 . . G 4
Kure . . . . 234,550 . . H 3
Kuroiso . . . . . . 46,573 . . F 7
Kurume . . . . . 216,974 . . I 2
Kusatsu* . . . . . . 77,008 . . H 5
Kushiro . . . . . 214,694 . . B 9
Kuwana* . . . . . . 86,606 . . H 5
Kyoto . . . . . 1,472,993 . . H 5
Machida* . . . . 295,354 . . G 7
Maebashi . . . 265,171 . . G 6
Maizuru . . . . . . 97,579 . . G 5
Marugame . . . 70,840 . . H 4
Masuda . . . . . . 52,753 . . H 3
Matsubara* . . 135,852 . . H 5
Matsudo* . . . 400,870 . . G 7
Matsue . . . . . 135,563 . . G 3
Matsumoto . . 192,086 . . G 6
Matsuyama . . 401,682 . . H 3
Matsuzaka . . 113,481 . . H 5
Mihara* . . . . . . 84,450 . . H 3
Miki* . . . . 70,201 . . H 4
Minoo* . . . . . . 104,113 . . H 5
Misato* . . . . 98,222 . . G 7
Mishima* . . . . . 94,613 . . H 6
Mitaka* . . . . . 164,449 . . G 7
Mito . . . . 215,563 . . G 7
Miyako* . . . . . . 62,478 . . E 8
Miyakonojo . . 129,006 . . J 2
Miyazaki . . . . 264,858 . . J 3
Miyoshi . . . . . . 37,875 . . H 3
Mobara* . . . . . . 71,521 . . G 7
Moriguchi* . . 165,635 . . H 5
Morioka . . . . . 229,123 . . D 7
Muroran . . . . 150,200 . . C 7
Musashino* . 136,895 . . G 7
Nagano . . . . . 324,360 . . G 6
Nagaoka . . . . 180,258 . . F 6
Nagaokakyo* . 71,447 . . H 5
Nagare-
yama* . . . . 106,635 . . G 7
Nagasaki . . . . 447,091 . . I 2
Nagoya . . . 2,087,884 . . H 5
Naha† 295,801
Nara . . . . 297,893 . . H 5
Narishino* . . . 125,154 . . G 7
Narita* . . . . 68,419 . . G 7
Nayoro . . . . 35,031 . . A 8
Nemuru . . . . . . 42,881 . . B 10
Neyagawa* . . 255,864 . . H 5
Niigata . . . . . . 457,783 . . F 6
Niihama . . . . . 132,352 . . H 4
Niiza* . . . . 119,312 . . G 7
Nishino-
miya* . . . . . 410,329 . . H 4
Nishio* . . . . 86,524 . . H 6
Nobeoka . . . . 136,595 . . I 3
Noda* . . . . 93,958 . . G 7
Noshiro . . . . . . 60,682 . . D 7
Numazu . . . . . 203,699 . . H 6
Obihiro . . . . . . 153,862 . . B 8
Odate* . . . . 72,480 . . E 7
Odawara . . . . 177,469 . . G 6
Ogaki . . . . 143,151 . . G 5
Oita . . . . 360,166 . . I 3
Okayama . . . . 545,737 . . H 4
Okazaki . . . . . 262,370 . . H 6
Okaya . . . . 62,210 . . G 6
Okinawa† 94,851
Ome* . . . . 98,991 . . G 7
Omiya . . . . . . 354,082 . . G 7
Omuta . . . . . . 163,007 . . I 2
Onomichi . . . . 102,056 . . H 4
Osaka . . . . 2,648,158 . . H 5
Ota* . . . . 123,115 . . G 6
Otaru . . . . 180,728 . . B 7
Otsu . . . . 215,318 . . H 5
Oyama . . . . . . 127,230 . . G 7
Saga . . . . 163,762 . . I 2
Sagamihara* 439,257 . . G 7
Saiki . . . . 54,306 . . I 3
Sakado* . . . . . . 77,334 . . G 7
Sakai . . . . 810,120 . . H 5
Sakata . . . . . . 102,600 . . E 7
Sakura* . . . . . 101,180 . . G 7
Sanjo . . . . 85,276 . . F 6
Sano* . . . . 78,351 . . H 5
Sapporo . . . 1,401,758 . . B 7
Sasebo . . . . . . 251,118 . . I 2
Sayama* . . . . 124,025 . . G 7
Sendai . . . . . . 664,799 . . E 7
Seto . . . . 120,775 . . G 6
Settsu* . . . . 80,686 . . H 5
Shibata . . . . . . 76,210 . . F 7
Shimada* . . . . . 70,705 . . H 6
Shimizu . . . . . 241,578 . . H 6
Shimono-
seki . . . . . . 268,964 . . H 2
Shingu . . . . 39,992 . . I 5
Shiogama . . . . . 61,039 . . F 7
Shizouka . . . . 458,342 . . H 6
Soka* . . . . 186,618 . . G 7
Soma . . . . 38,335 . . F 7
Suita* . . . . . . 332,413 . . H 5
Suzuka . . . . . 156,249 . . H 5
Tachikawa* . . 142,600 . . G 7
Tajimi* . . . . 74,311 . . G 5
Takamatsu . . 316,662 . . H 4
Takaoka . . . . 175,055 . . F 5
Takara-
zuka* . . . . . 183,628 . . H 4
Takasago* . . . 85,463 . . H 4
Takasaki . . . . 221,432 . . G 6
Takasuki* . . . 340,722 . . H 5
Takefu . . . . 67,104 . . G 5
Takikawa . . . . . 51,192 . . B 8
Tama* . . . . 95,248 . . G 7
Tamano* . . . . . . 77,807 . . H 4
Tanabe . . . . 69,550 . . I 5
Tatebay-
shi* . . . . 70,246 . . G 6
Tateyama . . . . 56,256 . . H 7
Tochigi* . . . . . . 85,592 . . G 7
Toda* . . . . 78,343 . . G 7
Tokai* . . . . 96,049 . . H 6
Tokoro-
zawa* . . . . 236,477 . . G 7
Tokushima . . 249,343 . . H 4
Tokuyama* . . 111,468 . . H 2
Tokyo 8,349,209
. . . . . *11,468,516 . . G 7
Tomakomai . . 151,969 . . B 8
Tondabaya-
shi* . . . . 97,423 . . H 5
Toride* . . . . 71,246 . . G 7
Tottori . . . . . . 131,375 . . G 4
Toyama . . . . . 305,054 . . G 6
Toyohashi . . . 304,274 . . H 6
Toyokawa* . . 103,097 . . H 6
Toyonaka* . . 403,185 . . H 5
Toyota* . . . . . 281,609 . . H 6
Tsu . . . . 144,991 . . H 5
Tsuchiura* . . 112,517 . . G 7
Tsuruga . . . . . . 61,844 . . G 5
Tsuruoka . . . . . 99,751 . . E 7
Tsuyama . . . . . 83,140 . . H 4
Ube . . . . 168,960 . . H 2
Ueda* . . . . . . 111,540 . . G 6
Uji* . . . . 152,689 . . H 5
Urasoe† 71,286
Urawa . . . . . . 358,180 . . G 7
Usa . . . . 51,579 . . J 2
Utsunomiya . 377,748 . . G 7
Uwajima* . . . . . 71,592 . . I 3
Wajima . . . . 32,662 . . F 5
Wakayama . . 401,462 . . H 5
Wakkanai . . . . . 53,471 . . A 8
Warabi* . . . . . . 70,876 . . G 7
Yachiyo* . . . . 134,479 . . G 7
Yaizu* . . . . . . 104,362 . . H 6
Yamagata . . . 236,984 . . E 7
Yamaguchi . . 114,744 . . H 3
Yamato* . . . . 167,934 . . G 7
Yamatokori-
yama* . . . . . 81,262 . . H 5
Yao* . . . . 272,706 . . H 5
Yatsushiro . . . 108,194 . . I 2
Yokkaichi . . . 255,442 . . H 5
Yokohama . 2,773,822 . . G 7
Yokosuka . . . 421,112 . . G 7
Yonago . . . . . 127,375 . . G 4
Yonezawa . . . . 92,824 . . F 7
Yono* . . . . 72,326 . . G 7
Yubari . . . . 41,715 . . B 8
Zama* . . . . 93,501 . . G 7

*Does not appear on map; key shows general location.
†Does not appear on map; in Ryukyu Islands.
•Population of metropolitan area, including suburbs.
Source: 1980 census.

Japan Political Map

National park (N.P.)
International boundary
Expressway
Road
Railroad
National capital
Prefectural capital
Other city or town

WORLD BOOK map

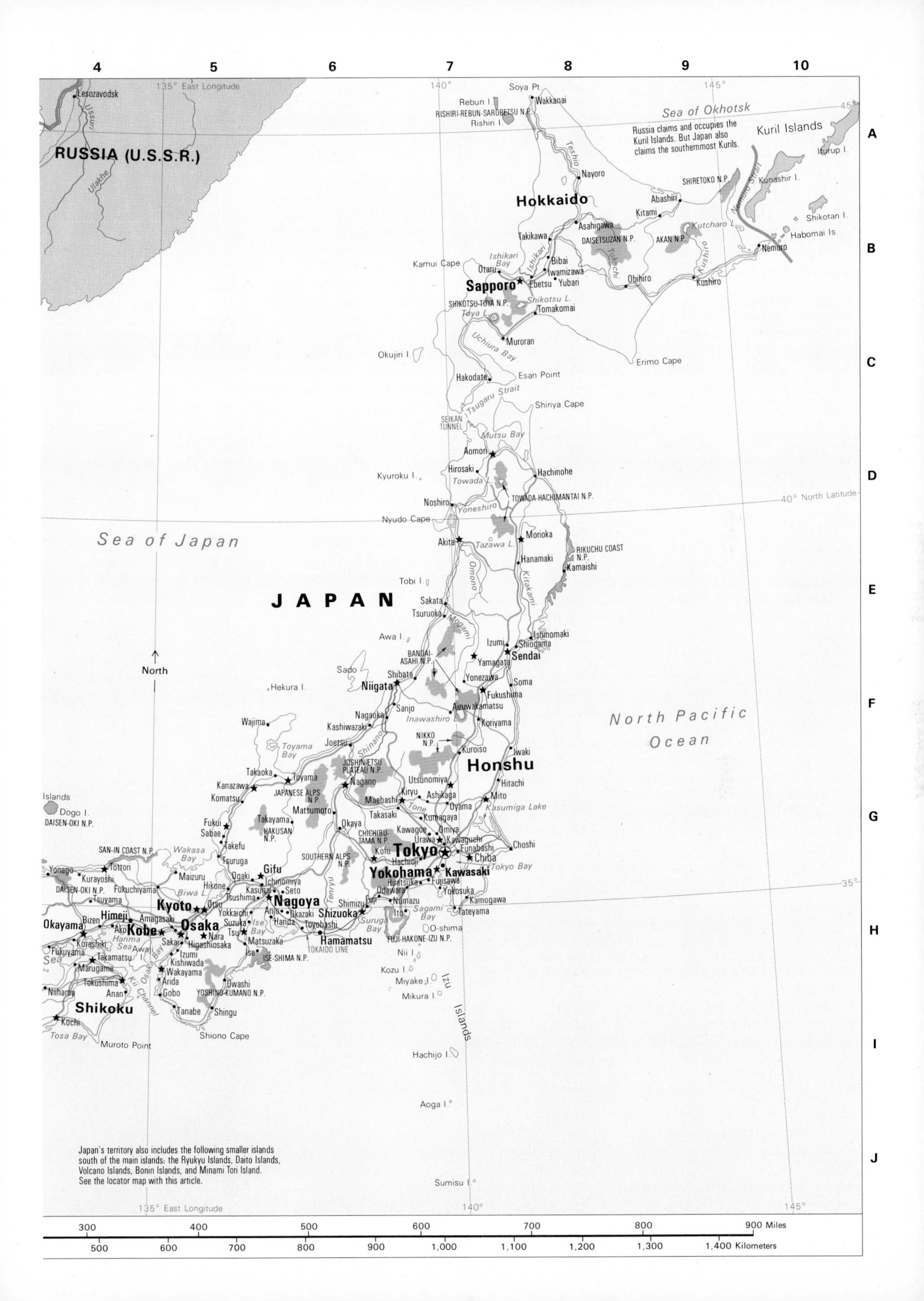

Sea of Japan
JAPAN
RUSSIA (U.S.S.R.)
Sea of Okhotsk
Russia claims and occupies the Kuril Islands. But Japan also claims the southernmost Kurils.
Kuril Islands
North Pacific Ocean
Hokkaido
Honshu
Shikoku
Tokyo
Osaka
Kyoto
Nagoya
Yokohama
Kobe
Sapporo
Sendai
Niigata
Izu Islands
Japan's territory also includes the following smaller islands south of the main islands: the Ryukyu Islands, Daito Islands, Volcano Islands, Bonin Islands, and Minami Tori Island. See the locator map with this article.
135° East Longitude
140°
145°
40° North Latitude
North
300 400 500 600 700 800 900 Miles
500 600 700 800 900 1,000 1,100 1,200 1,300 1,400 Kilometers

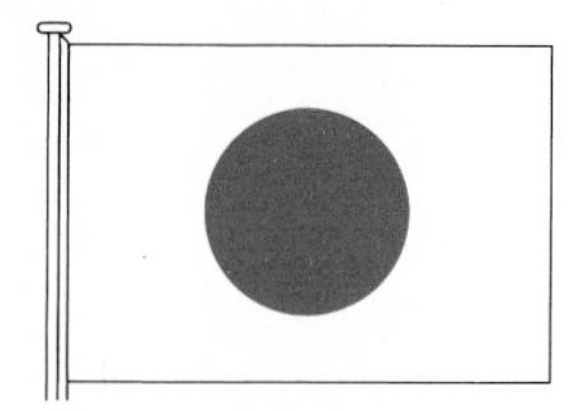

Japan's Flag, adopted in 1854, is a red sun on a white background. The Japanese call the country Nippon or Nihon, meaning *source of the sun.*

The Imperial Coat of Arms consists of a chrysanthemum with 16 petals. This symbol of the imperial family dates back hundreds of years.

Japan's present Constitution was drawn up by the Allied occupation forces and went into effect on May 3, 1947. This democratic Constitution completely changed the Japanese government. The country's first Constitution, proclaimed in 1889, gave ruling power to the emperor of Japan. The 1947 Constitution transferred that power to the Japanese people. It also guarantees the people many human liberties, such as freedom of speech, of religion, of the press, and of assembly. The Constitution provides for three branches of government—legislative, executive, and judicial. All Japanese citizens 20 years and older may vote. The 1947 Constitution granted women the right to vote.

The Emperor. At various times in Japan's history, emperors held great power. However, the 1947 Constitution states: "The Emperor shall be the symbol of the State and of the unity of the people, deriving his position from the will of the people with whom resides sovereign power." The emperor's duties, therefore, are entirely ceremonial. He inherits his throne.

The Diet makes Japan's laws. It consists of two houses. The House of Representatives has 511 members. They are elected to four-year terms from electoral districts. The House of Councillors has 252 members. Half the councillors are elected every three years to six-year terms. Of the councillors, 100 are elected from the country as a whole, and 152 are chosen from 47 political divisions called *prefectures.*

The Prime Minister, Japan's chief executive officer, is chosen by the Diet from among its members. The prime minister is usually the leader of the political party that has the most seats in the Diet. A Cabinet assists the prime minister in carrying out the operations of the government. The prime minister appoints the members of the Cabinet. More than half the Cabinet ministers must be selected from the Diet.

Local Government. The voters in each of Japan's 47 prefectures elect a governor and an assembly. The prefectures are further divided into cities, towns, and villages. The people in each of these smaller units elect a mayor and a local assembly.

Politics. Japan has several political parties. The most successful is the Liberal-Democratic Party (LDP), which has held a majority of seats in the Diet since 1955. The LDP is a conservative party. It has traditionally represented rural areas of Japan and depended heavily on big business for financial support. However, the party has been gaining strength in the cities, particularly among clerical and professional workers. The chief opposition party, the Japan Socialist Party, receives most of its support from labor groups. Smaller parties include the *Komeito* (Clean Government Party); the Democratic Socialist Party; and the Japan Communist Party.

Courts. Japan's highest court, the Supreme Court, consists of a chief justice and 14 other judges. The Cabinet names the chief justice, who is then appointed by the emperor. The Cabinet appoints the 14 other judges. The Supreme Court is the final court in determining questions of constitutionality. Lower Japanese courts are 8 regional high courts; 50 district courts; numerous summary courts, which deal with minor offenses and small claims; and many family courts, which handle domestic cases.

Armed Forces. Japan's Constitution states that the country does not have the right to wage war or to have air, ground, or sea forces for that purpose. However, Japan maintains air, ground, and sea forces for self-defense. Most Japanese believe that these forces are not unconstitutional. Japan's self-defense forces have about 270,000 members. Service is voluntary.

Japan's Prefectures

Prefectures are the largest units of local government in Japan. The map below shows the country's 47 prefectures. Each of them is numbered to correspond to its listing in the table.

1. Aichi
2. Akita
3. Aomori
4. Chiba
5. Ehime
6. Fukui
7. Fukuoka
8. Fukushima
9. Gifu
10. Gumma
11. Hiroshima
12. Hokkaido
13. Hyogo
14. Ibaraki
15. Ishikawa
16. Iwate
17. Kagawa
18. Kagoshima
19. Kanagawa
20. Kochi
21. Kumamoto
22. Kyoto
23. Mie
24. Miyagi
25. Miyazaki
26. Nagano
27. Nagasaki
28. Nara
29. Niigata
30. Oita
31. Okayama
32. Okinawa
33. Osaka
34. Saga
35. Saitama
36. Shiga
37. Shimane
38. Shizuoka
39. Tochigi
40. Tokushima
41. Tokyo
42. Tottori
43. Toyama
44. Wakayama
45. Yamagata
46. Yamaguchi
47. Yamanashi

WORLD BOOK map

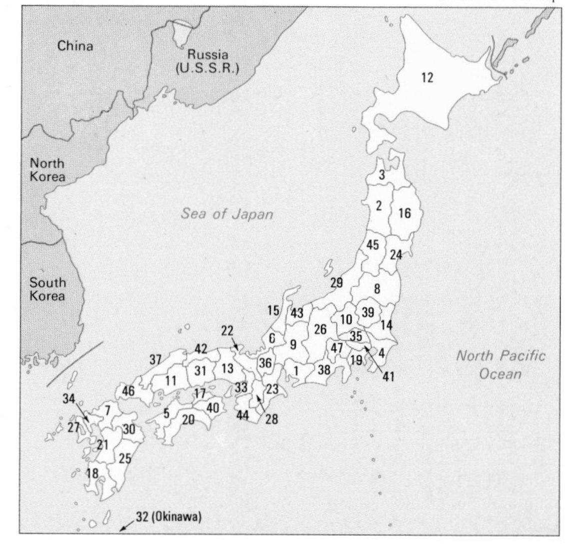

© Milt and Joan Mann

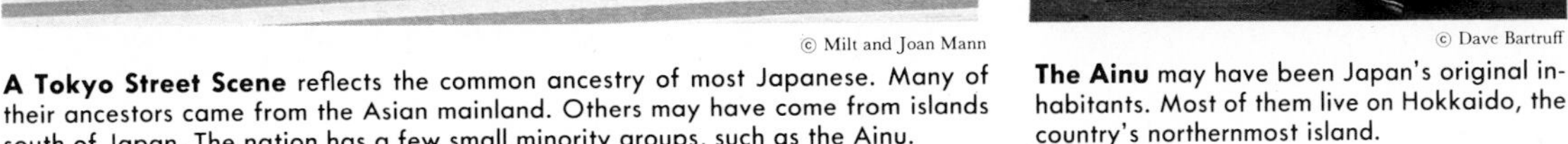

A Tokyo Street Scene reflects the common ancestry of most Japanese. Many of their ancestors came from the Asian mainland. Others may have come from islands south of Japan. The nation has a few small minority groups, such as the Ainu.

© Dave Bartruff

The Ainu may have been Japan's original inhabitants. Most of them live on Hokkaido, the country's northernmost island.

Population. About 120 million people live in Japan, making it the world's seventh largest nation in population. During the period from 1870 to 1970, Japan's population more than tripled. It increased from about 30 million to over 100 million. Since 1970, however, a low birth rate has slowed the population growth, which now averages less than 1 per cent a year.

Japan is one of the world's most densely populated countries. If the people of Japan were distributed evenly throughout the country, there would be about 824 persons per square mile (318 per square kilometer). But parts of Japan are actually much more crowded. About 90 per cent of the people live on the coastal plains, which make up only about 20 per cent of Japan's territory. These plains rank among the most thickly populated places on the earth.

Millions of people crowd the big cities along Japan's coasts. About $8\frac{1}{3}$ million people live in Tokyo, the country's capital and largest city. Tokyo is the third largest city in the world. Only Shanghai and Mexico City have more people. Tokyo has an average of about 37,000 persons per square mile (14,000 per square kilometer). Japan has nine other cities with a million or more people.

Ancestry. Scientists have found evidence that the Japanese are descended from various peoples who migrated to the islands from other parts of Asia. Many of these peoples came in waves from the northeastern part of the Asian mainland, passing through the Korean Peninsula. Some of the ancestors of the Japanese may have come from islands south of Japan.

Scientists do not know for certain when people first arrived in Japan. But as early as 4500 B.C., the Japanese islands were inhabited by people who hunted, fished, and gathered fruits and plants for food. This early culture is known as the *Jomon*, which means *cord pattern*, because the people made pottery that was decorated with rope-like designs.

During the 200's B.C., more major waves of migration must have occurred because a new, settled agricultural society replaced the Jomon. This culture is called the *Yayoi*, after the section of modern Tokyo where remains of the culture were found. The Yayoi people grew rice in irrigated fields and established villages along streams and on coastal plains. The Japanese people of today are probably descended from the Yayoi. In fact, scientists believe that by A.D. 100 the people living throughout the islands closely resembled the present-day Japanese in language and appearance.

The Japanese people belong to the Asian geographical race (see RACES, HUMAN). Chinese, Koreans, and a group of people called the *Ainu* make up the largest minority groups in Japan. The country has about 53,000 Chinese, about 665,000 Koreans, and about 15,000 Ainu. Most of the Ainu live on Hokkaido, the northernmost of Japan's main islands. Many Ainu have intermarried with the Japanese and adopted the Japanese culture. The rest of the Ainu are racially and culturally different from the Japanese. Some scientists believe that the Ainu were Japan's original inhabitants, who were pushed northward by the ancestors of the present-day Japanese people. See AINU.

Japan's minority groups suffer from prejudice. But the people who have suffered the most injustices are a

Where the People of Japan Live

Most of Japan's people live near the coasts. The Pacific coast from Tokyo to Kobe is the most densely populated area. The mountainous interiors of the islands are thinly settled.

WORLD BOOK map

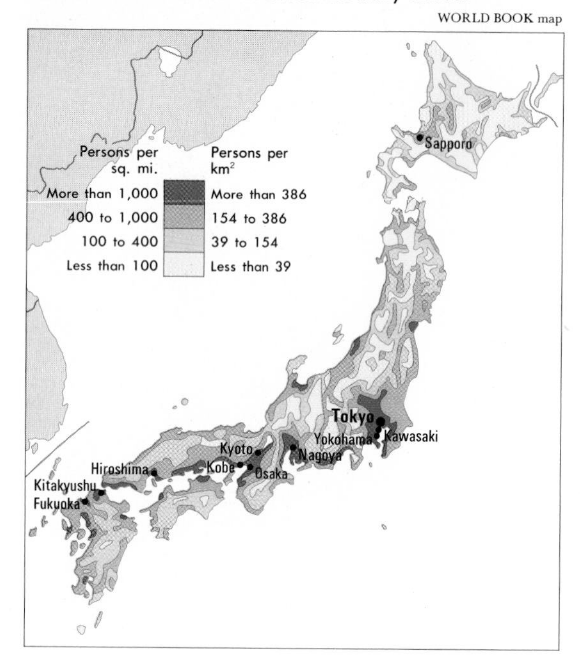

group of Japanese known as the *burakumin* or *eta*. The burakumin number about 1,120,000. They come from villages traditionally associated with such tasks as the execution of criminals, the slaughter of cattle, and the tanning of leather. According to Buddhism, one of the major religions in Japan, these tasks and the people who perform them are considered unclean. As a result, the burakumin—though not ethnically different from other Japanese—have long been discriminated against. Many of the burakumin live in segregated urban slums or special villages. The burakumin have started an active social movement to achieve fair treatment, but they have had only limited success so far.

Language. Japanese is the official language of Japan. Spoken Japanese has many local dialects. These local dialects differ greatly in pronunciation. However, the Tokyo dialect is the standard form of spoken Japanese. Almost all the people understand the Tokyo dialect, which is used in schools and on radio and television. Most of the Japanese people can also speak English to some extent. A number of Japanese words, such as *aisu kuriimu* (ice cream) and *guruupu* (group), are based on the English language.

Written Japanese is considered to be one of the most difficult writing systems in the world. It uses Japanese *phonetic symbols* that represent sounds as well as Chinese *characters*. Each character is a symbol that stands for a complete word or syllable. Schools in Japan also teach students to write the Japanese language with the letters of the Roman alphabet. For additional information, see the article JAPANESE LANGUAGE.

JAPAN/Way of Life

City Life. About 78 per cent of the Japanese people live in urban areas. A large share of the urban population is concentrated in the three major metropolitan areas of Tokyo, Osaka, and Nagoya—all on the island of Honshu. In many ways, Japan's big cities resemble those of Western countries. Tall concrete and steel office buildings crowd commercial districts. Traffic fills wide expressways during rush hours. Modern elevated and subway trains carry millions of people to and from work. Numerous restaurants serve everything from such American favorites as hamburgers, hot dogs, and pizza to the finest European dishes. Many large Japanese cities offer the latest motion pictures, music, and plays from all parts of the world.

Even in the biggest Japanese cities, however, many old customs still flourish. Tiny shops on narrow side streets specialize in traditional items, such as straw mats called *tatami*, which are used as floor coverings. Modern stationery stores sell not only ballpoint pens but also special brushes and sticks of ink for Japanese *calligraphy* (the art of fine handwriting). Toyshops have the latest electronic games, as well as dolls dressed in traditional Japanese clothing. Even the most crowded cities have beautiful gardens, parks, and shrines—all of which reflect the Japanese love of nature. Many city residents attend performances of traditional Japanese drama and music and take part in traditional festivals, some of which date back hundreds of years.

Most Japanese city dwellers enjoy a comfortable standard of living. There are some poor neighborhoods but few slums. Many city people work in banks, factories, hotels, offices, restaurants, and stores. Some own businesses. Others hold government or professional jobs. Japan has a low unemployment rate. The Japanese economy is so strong that most people can find jobs. In addition, some large corporations in Japan guarantee their workers lifetime employment.

City housing includes modern apartment buildings and traditional Japanese houses. Most traditional houses are simple one- or two-story wooden buildings

© John Launois, Black Star

A Traditional Japanese House blends with the natural beauty around it. Many such houses feature lovely gardens, graceful tile roofs, and sliding paper screens between rooms.

© Milt and Joan Mann

A Traditional Japanese Meal is served in attractively arranged dishes that emphasize the colors and shapes of the foods. Most such meals are eaten with chopsticks at low tables.

© Bernard Pierre Wolff, Photo Researchers

A Modern Dining Area in a Tokyo office building reflects Western eating habits. Many Japanese workers buy their lunch at fast-food restaurants like those in Western countries.

with graceful tile roofs. Many of the houses are set within walled gardens. The floor level of a traditional house is above that of the entrance. People leave their shoes in an entranceway and put on slippers after they step up into the main living area. Rooms are separated by sliding paper screens, which can be rearranged to change the size or shape of the rooms. Some people remove these screens in the summer to allow breezes to blow through the house.

In traditional Japanese rooms, tatami cover the floors. The people sit on cushions and spread out quilts for bedding. The principal room in a traditional house has a *tokonoma* (nook) in one wall. A decorative scroll hangs there, with a flower arrangement in front of it. Many apartments and houses have one or more rooms with Western-style furniture and with carpets instead of tatami.

Japan's big cities, like big cities in many other countries, face such serious problems as housing shortages, overcrowded streets and highways, and air and water pollution. However, crime is not as serious a problem in Japan as it is in most Western countries. The crime rate in the major Japanese cities is much lower than the rate in large Western cities. In Tokyo, for example, it is safe to ride public transportation and to walk on most city streets at any hour of the day or night.

© R. L. Zentmaier, Photo Researchers

New Apartment Buildings provide homes for many Japanese city dwellers. However, construction has not kept pace with demand, and many Japanese cities have severe housing shortages.

Rural Life. Only about 22 per cent of the Japanese people live in rural areas. Farmers and their families make up most of the rural population. In rural areas along the coasts, some Japanese make their living by fishing and harvesting edible seaweeds. Most rural workers do not earn as much as city dwellers. But the standard of living in rural Japan has increased steadily since World War II. Almost all rural families have at least one color television set, and many have an automobile. Most rural houses are equipped with a refrigerator and other modern appliances.

Almost all Japanese farmers own their land. Most families can afford some farm machinery. Even on tiny farms, small gasoline-powered tractors have replaced the oxen once used in plowing fields. Japanese farms are extremely productive because of the use of chemical fertilizers, insecticides, and advanced agricultural methods. Among most farm families, at least one member adds to the family income by holding a part-time job in a nearby city or town. Some industries have established factories in rural areas because of the availability of these part-time laborers.

Most rural families live in traditional Japanese-style wooden houses much like those in the cities. The country houses have one to four rooms. Older dwellings have thatched roofs. Newer ones have metal or tile roofs.

Since the late 1950's, many of Japan's rural people have moved to urban areas to seek better-paying jobs in business and industry. Farming has increasingly become an occupation for older men and women as the sons and daughters of farmers leave home to look for work in the cities.

Family Life has always been important in Japan. Before 1945, many Japanese lived in large family units that included grandparents, parents, children, and sometimes uncles and their families. Japanese families were bound together by a strict set of customs. Husbands had complete authority over their wives, and children were expected to show unquestioning obedience to their parents. When a child was old enough to marry, the parents selected a suitable marriage partner. In some cases, the young bride and groom had never met before the wedding ceremony.

Today, most Japanese live in smaller family units that consist of only parents and children. The Japanese still have strong family ties and a deep respect for authority. But since the end of World War II, relationships within Japanese families have become less formal and more democratic. Children are given much greater freedom. Some parents still play a role in arranging their children's marriages. However, most young people now select their own marriage partners on the basis of shared interests and mutual attraction. In some families, the oldest son is expected to carry on the father's profession. But many parents allow their sons to choose their own careers.

The Constitution of 1947 guarantees equal rights for women in all fields. Today, more and more Japanese women are taking jobs outside the home. Many women work until marriage and return to work after their children have started school. Some Japanese women are active in social and political organizations.

Clothing. The Japanese have always placed great importance on their clothes. Today, most of the people wear Western-style clothing outside the home. Many city dwellers keep up with the newest styles by Japanese, American, and European fashion designers. Some Japanese, especially older people, still wear traditional

© Joseph F. Viesti

Skiers flock to Japan's many ski resorts every winter. Skiing and ice skating are favorite winter sports in the country. Japan's numerous snow-covered mountains provide superb ski areas.

© Fred Ward, Black Star

A Three-Decker Driving Range enables large crowds of Japanese golfers to practice their shots. Golf is a popular sport in Japan, and the country has hundreds of golf courses.

clothing at home. But even in the home, casual Western clothes are becoming more and more popular.

The traditional Japanese garment of both men and women is the kimono. It is tied around the waist with a sash called an *obi*. Almost all Japanese wear kimonos during festivals, on holidays, and on other special occasions. On extremely formal occasions, a Japanese man may wear wide, pleated trousers called *hakama* with a short, wide-sleeved coat called a *haori*.

Traditional Japanese footwear includes wooden clogs called *geta* and flat sandals known as *zori*. Leather shoes are worn with Western-style clothing. The Japanese remove all outdoor footwear when entering a house. Only slippers are worn indoors.

Food and Drink. The main food of the Japanese people is rice. It is often simply boiled and eaten with pickled vegetables, such as pickled cabbage, cucumbers, eggplant, or radishes. The Japanese people serve rice at almost every meal.

Fish provides the chief source of protein in the Japanese diet. A favorite method of preparing fish is to salt it and then broil it over an open flame. The people also enjoy raw fish. A popular Japanese dish called *sushi* consists of rice flavored with vinegar and topped with slices of raw fish and horseradish. Other traditional dishes include *sukiyaki* (beef cooked with vegetables) and *tempura* (fish and vegetables fried in batter). Tea has long been the favorite beverage in Japan. Popular alcoholic drinks include *sake*, a winelike beverage made from rice, and beer.

Soybeans are another major source of protein in Japan. Many dishes contain *miso* (soybean paste) or *tofu* (soybean curd cake). Soy sauce—a salty, brown sauce made from soybeans—is widely used to flavor foods. The Japanese people also eat many types of fruits and several varieties of seaweed.

Fresh ingredients are highly important in Japanese cooking because cooks try to bring out the natural flavor of foods rather than use sauces or spices. Meals are usually eaten at low tables. The Japanese take great care to

© Orion Press from The Stock House

Huge Wrestlers parade around the ring before an exhibition of *sumo,* a Japanese style of wrestling. Sumo tournaments attract big, enthusiastic crowds. Many matches are televised.

arrange foods attractively in lacquer or porcelain dishes. Each kind of food is served in a separate dish, which is chosen to emphasize the food's color, shape, and texture. The Japanese eat with chopsticks.

Since the 1950's, the Japanese diet has been changing. The people are eating more meat and dairy products, and many Japanese are substituting bread for rice at some meals. The diet of most of the people supplies all the important nutritional elements. Few Japanese suffer from malnutrition.

Recreation. The Japanese people enjoy a wide variety of sports, hobbies, and other leisure-time activities. Their favorite spectator sports are baseball and a Japanese form of wrestling called *sumo*. Other popular sports include bowling, golf, ice skating, skiing, table tennis, and tennis. Many Japanese practice *aikido*, *judo*, and *karate*, traditional Oriental martial arts that involve fighting without weapons. Another popular sport is *kendo*, a Japanese form of fencing in which bamboo or wooden sticks are used for swords. Many Japanese also fish, hunt, jog, and go mountain climbing.

Calligraphy and traditional chanting and dancing are favorite pastimes in Japan. Some Japanese play traditional or Western musical instruments for recreation. Japan has many clubs for the writing of *haiku* and *tanka*, two forms of Japanese poetry. Members gather to compose poems and to judge one another's work. The Japanese like to travel in their beautiful country, which has numerous inns, hot spring resorts, and other lodging places for vacationers. Many people in cities play a pinball game called *pachinko*. Tokyo alone has about 1,000 pachinko parlors.

Concerts, plays, and motion pictures attract large audiences in Japan. Coffee houses and tearooms are popular places for friends to meet. Many Japanese enjoy dining in restaurants. At some of the older Japanese-style restaurants, young women called *geisha* entertain patrons. The geisha have been trained from childhood in the arts of conversation, dance, and music.

The Japanese celebrate many festivals during the year. One of the most popular celebrations is the New Year's Day Festival, which begins on January 1. On this day, the Japanese dress in their fanciest, most colorful kimonos. People visit their friends and relatives and exchange gifts. Dances, parades, and many exciting sporting events are held throughout the country. At home, families enjoy delicious feasts and play traditional games. Although the festival officially ends on January 3, some celebrations continue until the middle of the month.

Religion. Japan's oldest religion is Shinto, which means *the way of the gods*. It is the native religion of Japan and dates from prehistoric times. Shintoists worship many gods, called *kami*, which are found in mountains, rivers, rocks, trees, and other parts of nature. Shinto also involves ancestor worship. In 1868, the Japanese government established an official religion called State Shinto. State Shinto stressed patriotism and the

© Milt and Joan Mann

© Fred J. Maroon from Louis Mercier

Buddhism and Shinto have millions of followers in Japan. Many Japanese Buddhists visit the *Great Buddha,* a huge bronze statue of the religion's founder in Kamakura, *left.* Shinto is the native religion of Japan. The procession at the right is part of a Shinto festival.

© Milt and Joan Mann

A Calligraphy Class teaches Japanese elementary school students the art of fine handwriting. Students spend much time learning to read and write the difficult Japanese language.

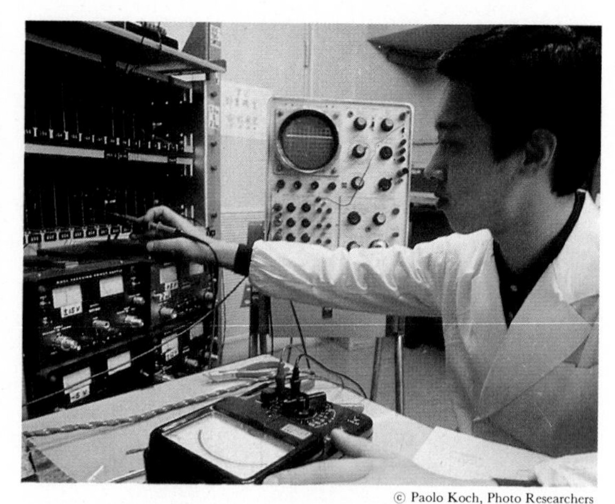

© Paolo Koch, Photo Researchers

An Electronics Laboratory at the University of Tokyo helps prepare students for jobs in industry. The University of Tokyo is Japan's best-known institution of higher learning.

worship of the emperor as a divine being. The government abolished State Shinto after World War II, and the emperor declared that he was not divine.

Many characteristics of the Japanese people—such as their love of cleanliness and of simple, natural things—originate from Shinto. About 84 per cent of Japan's population are Shintoists. But almost all Japanese, regardless of their religion, perform some of the daily and seasonal acts and ceremonies of Shinto. See SHINTO.

About 75 per cent of the Japanese people practice Buddhism. Many of these people also follow Shinto. In fact, most Shintoists and Buddhists in Japan observe elements of both religions. For example, they may celebrate births and marriages with Shinto ceremonies but observe funerals with Buddhist ceremonies. Buddhism came to Japan from China and Korea about A.D. 552. Generally, Buddhists believe that a person can obtain perfect peace and happiness by leading a life of virtue and wisdom. Buddhism stresses the unimportance of worldly things. Much of Japanese culture reflects Buddhist philosophy. See BUDDHISM.

Christians make up less than 1 per cent of Japan's population. Spanish and Portuguese missionaries first brought Christianity to Japan about 1550. Protestants slightly outnumber Roman Catholics among Japanese Christians. Since World War II, religious sects called *New Religions* have developed in Japan. Some of these sects contain elements of Buddhism, Christianity, or Shinto. Others combine beliefs from all three. The largest of the New Religions is the *Sokagakkai*, a Buddhist sect.

Confucianism, a Chinese religion, has had great influence in Japan, though it never became strongly organized there. Confucianism stresses the importance of moral standards and of respect for authority. It also emphasizes reverence for one's ancestors and for the past. The Japanese have adopted many Confucian ideas in their moral teachings. See CONFUCIANISM.

Education. Japanese law requires children to complete six years of elementary school and three years of junior high school. Education at public schools is free during these nine years for children from 6 through 14 years of age. Almost all Japanese children complete the education requirements. Students attend classes $5\frac{1}{2}$ days a week. The Japanese school year runs from April through March of the following year, with a vacation from late July through August.

Japanese elementary and junior high school students study such subjects as art, the Japanese language, mathematics, music, physical education, science, and social studies. Many junior high school students also study English or another foreign language. Much time is spent learning to read and write Japanese because the language is so difficult. The country has an exceptionally high literacy rate. Almost all Japanese aged 15 or older can read and write.

After junior high school, students may attend senior high school for three years. To enter senior high school, they must pass an entrance examination. Classes include many of the same subjects studied in junior high school. But senior high schools also offer courses to prepare students for college or to train them for jobs. About 94 per cent of junior high school graduates go on to senior high school.

Japan has about 450 universities and about 520 junior and technical colleges. The largest university is Nihon University in Tokyo, which has about 110,000 students. The country has more than 90 National Universities, which are supported by the government. Some of these universities—such as the University of Tokyo and the University of Kyoto—have exceptionally high reputations. Highly regarded private universities include Doshisha University in Kyoto and Keio University and Waseda University in Tokyo.

Senior high school graduates who want to attend a college or university must pass the entrance examination given by the school of their choice. Large numbers of students compete for admission to the top Japanese universities. About 37 per cent of senior high school graduates go on to an institution of higher learning.

For hundreds of years, Chinese arts had a great influence on Japanese arts. A Western influence began about 1870. However, there has always been a distinctive Japanese quality about the country's art.

Music. Traditional Japanese music may sound thin compared with the rich harmonies of Western music. Most forms of Japanese music feature one instrument or voice or a group of instruments that follows the same melodic line instead of blending in harmony. Japanese instruments include the lutelike *biwa;* the zitherlike *koto;* and the three-stringed banjolike *samisen*, or *shamisen*. Traditional music also features drums, flutes, and gongs. Performances of traditional music draw large crowds in Japan. Most types of Western music are also popular. Many Japanese cities have their own professional symphony orchestras that specialize in Western music. See MUSIC (Japanese Music).

Theater. The oldest form of traditional Japanese drama is the *no* play, which developed during the 1300's. No plays are serious treatments of history and legend. Masked actors perform the story with carefully controlled gestures and movements. A chorus chants most of the important lines in the play.

Two other forms of traditional Japanese drama—the *puppet* theater and the *kabuki* play—developed during the late 1600's. In the puppet theater, a narrator recites the story, which is acted out by large, lifelike puppets. The puppet handlers work silently on the stage in view of the audience. Kabuki plays are melodramatic representations of historical or domestic events. Kabuki features colorful costumes and makeup, spectacular scenery, and a lively and exaggerated acting style. See DRAMA (Japan; picture).

The traditional types of theater remain popular in Japan. But the people also enjoy new dramas by Japanese playwrights, as well as Western plays.

Literature. Japan has a rich literary heritage. Much of the country's literature deals with the fleeting quality of human life and the never-ending flow of time. *The Tale of Genji*, a long novel written during the early 1000's, is generally considered the greatest work of Japanese fiction. For detailed information on Japan's literary tradition, see JAPANESE LITERATURE.

© Mike Yamashita, Woodfin Camp, Inc.

Court Musicians perform *gagaku,* the official music of the imperial court and one of the oldest forms of Japanese music. The musicians are playing traditional wind instruments made of bamboo.

Sculpture. Some of the earliest Japanese sculptures were *haniwa*, small clay figures made from the A.D. 200's to 500's. Haniwa were placed in the burial mounds of important Japanese. The figures represented animals, servants, warriors, and objects of everyday use. Japanese sculptors created some of their finest works for Buddhist temples. The sculptors worked chiefly with wood, but they also used clay and bronze. The most famous bronze statue in Japan, the *Great Buddha* at Kamakura, was cast during the 1200's. See SCULPTURE (Japan; picture).

Painting. Early Japanese painting dealt with Buddhist subjects, using compositions and techniques from China. From the late 1100's to the early 1300's, many Japanese artists painted long picture scrolls. These scrolls realistically portrayed historical tales, legends, and other stories in a series of pictures. Ink painting

© Paolo Koch, Photo Researchers

Kabuki, a traditional form of Japanese drama, features chanting, colorful costumes and makeup, music, and a lively and exaggerated acting style. Kabuki plays are melodramatic portrayals of historical or domestic events. The Japanese developed kabuki theater during the late 1600's.

flourished in Japan from the early 1300's to the mid-1500's. Many of these paintings featured black brushstrokes on a white background.

During the mid-1500's and early 1600's, a decorative style of painting developed in Japan. Artists used bright colors and elaborate designs and added gold leaf to their paintings. From the 1600's to the late 1800's, artists created colorful wood-block prints. Printmaking is still popular in Japan. See PAINTING (Japanese Painting; pictures); JAPANESE PRINT.

Architecture. Many architectural monuments in Japan are Buddhist temples. These temples have large tile roofs with extending edges that curve gracefully upward. Traditional Shinto shrines are wooden frame structures noted for their graceful lines and sense of proportion. The simple style of Shinto architecture has influenced the design of many modern buildings in Japan. Japanese architecture emphasizes harmony between buildings and the natural beauty around them. Landscape gardening is a highly developed art in Japan. See ARCHITECTURE (Japanese Architecture; picture).

Other Arts. Japan ranks among the world's leading producers of motion pictures. Many Japanese films have earned international praise. The Japanese have long been famous for their ceramics, ivory carving, lacquer ware, and silk weaving and embroidery. Other traditional arts include *cloisonné* (a type of decorative enameling); flower arranging; and *origami* (the art of folding paper into decorative objects). See LACQUER WARE; FLOWER (Flower Arranging; pictures); ORIGAMI.

Detail of *The Siege of Osaka Castle* (1615), a painting on a paper screen by Kuroda Nagamasa; Kuroda Collection, Japan (Werner Forman Archive)

Decorative Painting flourished in Japan from the mid-1500's to the early 1600's. This painted screen shows the lavish use of gold leaf characteristic of many works from this period.

Robert Glaze, Artstreet

The National Stadium of Tokyo shows the influence of traditional Japanese architecture in the gracefully curving lines of the structure's roof. The stadium, designed by the Japanese architect Kenzo Tange, was constructed in 1964 for the Summer Olympic Games held in Tokyo that year.

Japan is a land of great natural beauty. Mountains and hills cover about 70 per cent of the country. In fact, the Japanese islands consist of the rugged upper part of a great mountain range that rises from the floor of the North Pacific Ocean. Jagged peaks, rocky gorges, and thundering mountain waterfalls provide some of the country's most spectacular scenery. Thick forests thrive on the mountainsides, adding to the scenic beauty of the Japanese islands. Forests cover about 68 per cent of the country's land.

Japan lies on an extremely unstable part of the earth's crust. As a result, the land is constantly shifting. This shifting causes two of Japan's most striking natural features—earthquakes and volcanoes. The Japanese islands have about 1,500 earthquakes a year. Most of them are minor tremors that cause little damage, but severe earthquakes occur every few years. Undersea quakes sometimes cause huge, destructive tidal waves, called *tsunami*, along Japan's Pacific coast. The Japanese islands have more than 150 major volcanoes. Over 60 of these volcanoes are active.

Numerous short, swift rivers cross Japan's rugged surface. Most of the rivers are too shallow and steep to be navigated. But their waters are used to irrigate farmland, and their rapids and falls supply power for hydroelectric plants. Many lakes nestle among the Japanese mountains. Some lie in the craters of extinct volcanoes. A large number of hot springs gush from the ground throughout the country.

The Japanese islands have a total land area of about 145,834 square miles (377,708 square kilometers). The four main islands, in order of size, are Honshu, Hokkaido, Kyushu, and Shikoku. Thousands of smaller islands and islets lie near these major islands. Japan's territory also includes the Ryukyu and Bonin island chains. The Pacific Ocean lies to the east and south of Japan. The Sea of Japan washes the country's west coast. Japan's four chief islands have 4,628 miles (7,448 kilometers) of coastline.

The Japanese Alps are the highest mountains in Japan. Their towering peaks rise in central Honshu, the country's largest island. Thick forests thrive on the mountainsides.

Honshu, Japan's largest island, has an area of 87,805 square miles (227,414 square kilometers). About 80 per cent of the Japanese people live on Honshu.

Three mountain ranges run side by side across northern Honshu. Most of the people in this area live in small mountain valleys. Agriculture is the chief occupation. East of the ranges, along the Pacific, lies the Sendai Plain. West of the mountains, the Echigo Plain extends to the Sea of Japan.

The towering peaks of the Japanese Alps, Japan's highest mountains, rise in central Honshu. East of these mountains, a chain of volcanoes cuts across the center

The Ishikari Plain is the largest lowland and the chief farming region on Hokkaido, the northernmost of the four main Japanese islands. The Ishikari River cuts across the plain. Much of the rest of Hokkaido consists of forested mountains and hills.

of the island. Japan's tallest and most famous peak, Mount Fuji, or Fujiyama, is one of these volcanoes. Mount Fuji, which is inactive, rises 12,388 feet (3,776 meters) above sea level. The Kanto Plain, the country's largest lowland, spreads east from the Japanese Alps to the Pacific. This lowland is an important center of agriculture and industry. Tokyo stands on the Kanto Plain. Two other major agricultural and industrial lowlands —the Nobi Plain and Osaka Plain—lie south and west of the Kanto region.

Most of southwestern Honshu consists of rugged, mountainous land. Farming and fishing villages and some industrial cities lie on small lowlands scattered throughout this region.

Hokkaido, the northernmost of Japan's four major islands, covers 30,144 square miles (78,073 square kilometers). It is the country's second largest island but has only about 5 per cent of Japan's total population. Much of the island consists of forested mountains and hills. A hilly, curved peninsula extends from southwestern Hokkaido. Northeast of this peninsula is the Ishikari Plain, Hokkaido's largest lowland and chief agricultural region. Smaller plains border the island's east coast. The economy of Hokkaido depends mainly on dairy farming, fishing, and forestry. The island is also a popular recreational area. Long winters and heavy snowfall make Hokkaido ideal for winter sports.

Kyushu, the southernmost of the main islands, occupies 14,114 square miles (36,554 square kilometers). After Honshu, Kyushu is Japan's most heavily populated island, with about 11 per cent of the population. A chain of steep-walled, heavily forested mountains runs down the center of the island. Northwestern Kyushu consists of rolling hills and wide plains. Many cities are found in this heavily industrialized area. Kyushu's largest plain and chief farming district is located along the west coast.

© Burt Glinn, Magnum

Rugged Terrain covers much of Kyushu, the southernmost of Japan's chief islands. Wooded islands lie in the small natural harbors along Kyushu's jagged west coast.

© Noriyuki Yoshida from Scott Henriquez

Scenic Farms dot many hillsides on Shikoku, the smallest of the main Japanese islands. Shikoku has no large lowlands for farming. Mountains and hills cover much of the island.

The northeastern and southern sections of Kyushu have many volcanoes, high lava plateaus, and large deposits of volcanic ash. In both regions, only small patches of land along the coasts and inland can be farmed. Farmers grow some crops on level strips of land cut out from the steep sides of the lava plateaus.

Shikoku, the smallest of the main Japanese islands, covers 7,049 square miles (18,256 square kilometers). About 4 per cent of the Japanese people live on the island. Shikoku has no large lowlands. Mountains cross the island from east to west. Most of the people live in northern Shikoku, where the land slopes downward to the Inland Sea. Hundreds of hilly, wooded islands dot this beautiful body of water. Farmers grow rice and a variety of fruits on the fertile land along the Inland Sea. Copper mining is also important in this area. A narrow plain borders Shikoku's south coast. There, farmers grow rice and many kinds of vegetables.

The Ryukyu and Bonin Islands belonged to Japan until after World War II, when the United States took control of them. The United States returned the northern Ryukyus to Japan in 1953 and the Bonins in 1968. In 1972, it returned the rest of the Ryukyu Islands, including Okinawa, the largest and most important island of the group.

More than 100 islands make up the Ryukyus. They extend from Kyushu to Taiwan and have about a million people. The Ryukyu Islands consist of the peaks of a submerged mountain range. Some of the islands have active volcanoes. The Bonins lie about 600 miles (970 kilometers) southeast of Japan and consist of 97 volcanic islands. About 800 people live on the islands. See Ryukyu Islands; Bonin Islands.

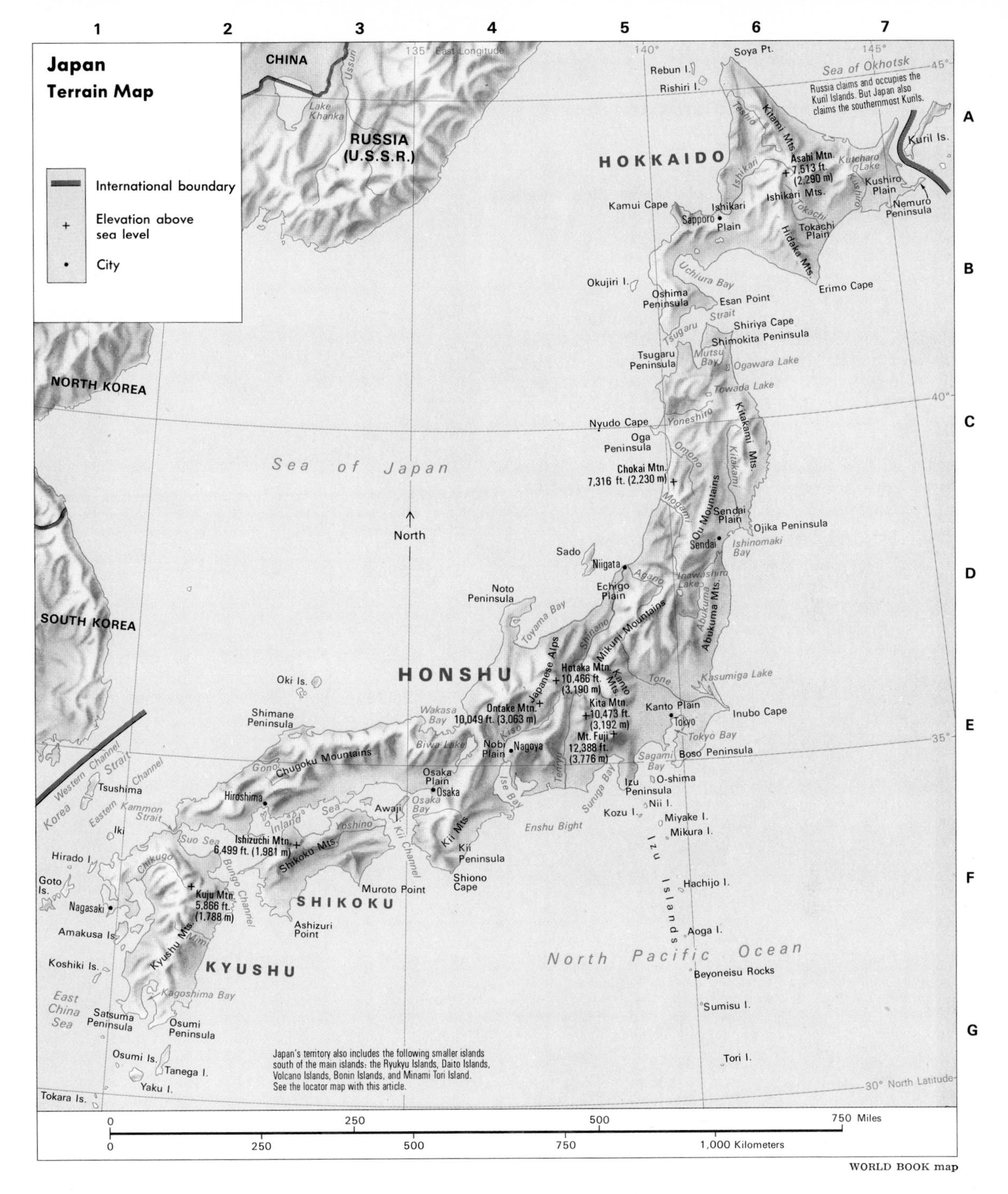

Physical Features

Abukuma Mountains .... D 6
Agano River .... D 5
Amakusa Islands ...... F 1
Asahi Mountain .... A 6
Awaji Island .... F 3
Biwa Lake .... E 4
Boso Peninsula .... E 5
Bungo Channel .... F 2
Chugoku Mountains .... E 3
Echigo Plain .... D 5
Enshu Bight .... F 4
Erimo Cape .... B 6
Esan Point .... B 6
Goto Islands .... F 1
Hidaka Mountains ...... B 6
Hokkaido (Island) ...... A 6
Honshu (Island) .... E 4
Inawashiro Lake .... D 5
Inland Sea .... F 2
Ise Bay .... E 4
Ishikari Plain .... B 6
Ishinomaki Bay .... D 6
Izu Islands .... F 5
Izu Peninsula .... E 5
Japanese Alps .... E 4
Kagoshima Bay .... G 1
Kammon Strait .... F 1
Kanto Mountains .... E 5
Kanto Plain .... E 5
Kasumiga Lake .... E 6
Kii Channel .... F 3
Kii Mountains .... F 4
Kii Peninsula .... F 4
Kitakami Mountains .... C 6
Kitami Mountains .... A 6
Korea Strait .... E 1
Kushiro Plain .... A 7
Kyushu (Island) .... G 2
Kyushu Mountains ...... G 1
Mikuni Mountains ...... D 5
Mount Fuji .... E 5
Mutsu Bay .... C 6
Nemuro Peninsula ...... A 7
Nobi Plain .... E 4
Noto Peninsula .... D 4
Oga Peninsula .... C 5
Ojika Peninsula .... D 6
Oki Islands .... E 3
Okujiri Island .... B 5
Osaka Plain .... E 4
O-shima (Island) .... E 5
Oshima Peninsula ...... B 5
Osumi Islands .... G 1
Osumi Peninsula .... G 2
Ou Mountains .... D 6
Sado (Island) .... D 5
Sagami Bay .... E 5
Satsuma Peninsula ..... G 1
Sea of Japan .... C 3
Sendai Plain .... D 6
Shikoku (Island) .... F 3
Shikoku Mountains ..... F 3
Shimane Peninsula ..... E 2
Shimokita Peninsula .... B 6
Shiono Cape .... F 4
Soya Point .... A 6
Suo Sea .... F 2
Suruga Bay .... E 5
Tanega Island .... G 2
Tokachi Plain .... B 6
Tokyo Bay .... E 5
Tone River .... E 5
Toyama Bay .... D 4
Tsugaru Peninsula ...... C 5
Tsugaru Strait .... B 5
Tsushima (Islands) ..... E 1
Uchiura Bay .... B 5
Wakasa Bay .... E 4
Yaku Island .... G 1

Regional climates in Japan can be compared to those of the East Coast of the United States. Kyushu and Shikoku have a climate much like that of Florida. The islands have long, hot summers and mild winters. Honshu's climate resembles that of the Middle Atlantic States. The island generally has warm, humid summers. Winters are mild in the south and cold and snowy in the north. Honshu has balmy, sunny autumns and springs. Hokkaido, like the state of Maine, has cool summers and cold winters.

Two Pacific Ocean currents—the Japan Current and the Oyashio Current—influence Japan's climate. The warm, dark-blue Japan Current flows northward along the country's south coast and along the east coast as far north as Tokyo (see JAPAN CURRENT). The current has a warming effect on the climate of these regions. The cold Oyashio Current flows southward along the east coasts of Hokkaido and northern Honshu, cooling these areas.

Robert Harding Picture Library

Cherry Blossoms mark the coming of spring weather in Japan. The time when the blooms appear ranges from March in the warm, southern regions to late May in the colder regions of the north.

AVERAGE MONTHLY WEATHER

Tokyo	Temperatures F° High	Temperatures F° Low	Temperatures C° High	Temperatures C° Low	Days of Rain or Snow
JAN.	46	30	8	−1	8
FEB.	48	30	9	−1	8
MAR.	54	36	12	2	13
APR.	63	46	17	8	14
MAY	70	54	21	12	14
JUNE	75	63	24	17	16
JULY	82	70	28	21	14
AUG.	86	72	30	22	13
SEPT.	79	66	26	19	17
OCT.	68	54	20	12	14
NOV.	61	43	16	6	10
DEC.	52	34	11	1	7

Sapporo	Temperatures F° High	Temperatures F° Low	Temperatures C° High	Temperatures C° Low	Days of Rain or Snow
JAN.	28	12	−2	−11	26
FEB.	30	12	−1	−11	23
MAR.	36	19	2	−7	23
APR.	52	32	11	0	13
MAY	61	41	16	5	14
JUNE	68	50	20	10	13
JULY	75	59	24	15	13
AUG.	79	61	26	16	13
SEPT.	72	52	22	11	17
OCT.	61	39	16	4	17
NOV.	46	28	8	−2	19
DEC.	34	18	1	−8	25

Seasonal winds called *monsoons* also affect Japan's climate. In winter, monsoons from the northwest bring cold air to northern Japan. These winds, which gather moisture as they cross the Sea of Japan, deposit heavy snows on the country's northwest coast. In summer, monsoons blow from the southeast, carrying warm, moist air from the Pacific Ocean. Summer monsoons cause hot, humid weather in central and southern Japan.

Rain is abundant throughout most of Japan. All areas of the country—except eastern Hokkaido—receive at least 40 inches (100 centimeters) of rain yearly. Japan has two major rainy seasons—from mid-June to early July and from September to October. Several typhoons strike the country each year, chiefly in late summer and early fall. The heavy rains and violent winds of these storms often do great damage to houses and crops. See TYPHOON.

Average January Temperatures

In winter, winds from the mainland of Asia bring cold weather to northern Japan. Winters are much milder in the south.

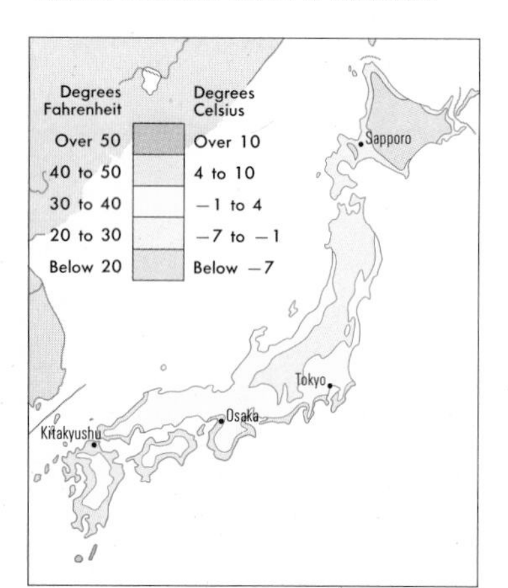

Average August Temperatures

In summer, most of Japan has hot, humid weather. Ocean currents flowing near the islands bring warm, moist air.

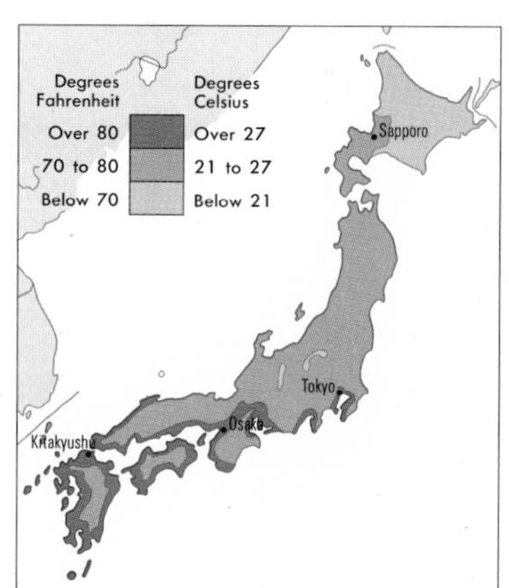

Average Yearly Precipitation

Japan has abundant rainfall. Winds called *monsoons* bring rain in summer. In winter, snow falls over much of Japan.

WORLD BOOK maps

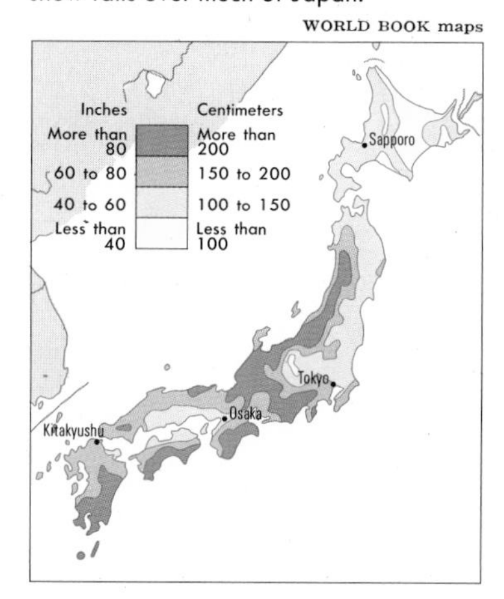

Since the end of World War II, Japan has become a major economic power. The country has the world's third largest economy in terms of its *gross national product* (GNP). The GNP is the total value of all goods and services produced in a country yearly. Only the United States and Russia have a greater GNP than Japan has. Japan has developed a strong, rapidly growing economy in spite of very limited natural resources. The country must import many of the raw materials needed by its industries. To pay for these materials, Japan sells the products of its factories to many other countries throughout the world. Thus, the Japanese economy depends heavily on foreign trade.

Japan's defeat in World War II severely damaged its economy. Many of the country's factories were destroyed. But the Japanese amazed the world by quickly overcoming the effects of the war. The United States provided financial aid to help Japan rebuild its factories. The Japanese invested in the latest technology to make their postwar industries highly productive. Japan soon began to sell high-quality manufactured items to other countries. By the late 1960's, the hardworking, skillful Japanese people had rebuilt their country into a leading industrial nation.

Manufacturing is the single most important economic activity in Japan. It accounts for approximately 39 per cent of the country's gross national product and employs about 25 per cent of all workers. Japan's industrial growth rate ranks among the highest in the world. From 1970 to 1980, the country's industrial output more than tripled.

Japan's manufactured products, which range from tiny electronic devices to huge oil tankers, are world famous for their high quality and standards of performance. Japanese factories use the most advanced equipment and processes, and manufacturers continually invest in new technology to make production cheaper and more efficient. As a result, Japan exports its goods at competitive prices. Japanese products are in great demand on the world market.

The production of transportation equipment is the most important Japanese industry. Japan is the world's leading shipbuilding country. It accounts for about half the total gross tonnage of ships launched annually. Japan also produces about 7 million automobiles a year. Only the United States manufactures more passenger cars. One of Japan's fastest-growing industries is the production of machinery, including heavy electric and nonelectric machines, electrical appliances, and electronic equipment. Large quantities of Japanese electronics products, such as calculators, computers, radios, tape recorders, and television sets, are sold throughout the world. Japan is also noted for its production of high-quality precision instruments, such as binoculars, cameras, and clocks and watches.

© Orion Press

Thousands of Japanese Cars await shipment to other countries at a huge wharf near Nagoya, *above.* The production of automobiles ranks as one of Japan's leading industries.

© Donald Smetzer, Click/Chicago

Advanced Technology has helped make Japan a major industrial country. At the automobile-manufacturing plant above, robots on the assembly line weld car bodies.

Japan is one of the top producers of iron and steel. The country's annual steel output totals more than 120 million short tons (109 million metric tons). Much of this steel is exported. Japan has a thriving chemical industry. Important products of this industry include *petrochemicals* (chemicals made from petroleum or natural gas) and petrochemical products, such as plastics and synthetic fibers. In addition, Japan is one of the leading producers of ceramics, clothing, fabricated metal products, lumber and wood products, paper products, raw silk, and textiles.

Manufacturing in Japan is concentrated in six main regions. For the location of each region and a listing of its main products, see the map titled *Economy of Japan* in this section of the article.

Agriculture accounts for about 4 per cent of Japan's gross national product and employs about 10 per cent of the nation's workers. Only about 15 per cent of the land in Japan can be cultivated. Nevertheless, Japanese farmers produce about 70 per cent of the food needed to feed the nation's people. Japan imports the rest.

Japanese farms average only about 2.4 acres (1 hectare). But they produce extremely high yields per unit of land. Japanese farmers make their land as productive as possible through the use of irrigation, improved seed varieties, and modern agricultural chemicals and machinery. The Japanese islands are so mountainous that level farmland is scarce. Farmers therefore grow some crops on *terraced fields*—that is, on level strips of land cut out of the hillsides.

The most important crop in Japan is rice. Japan is one of the world's leading rice-producing countries. Rice fields occupy more than 50 per cent of the country's farmland. Japanese farmers also raise a wide variety of other crops, including barley, sugar beets, sugar cane, tea, tobacco, and wheat. Mulberry bushes are grown on some hillsides. The leaves of these bushes are used to feed silkworms. Many types of fruits, including apples, mandarin oranges, pears, and persimmons, are grown in Japan. Common vegetables include cabbage, cucumbers, potatoes, radishes, soybeans, and sweet potatoes. Since the 1950's, the Japanese have been eating increasing amounts of dairy products, eggs, and meat. As a result, more and more of the nation's farmers are raising beef and dairy cattle, chickens, and hogs.

Before World War II, many Japanese farmers rented all or part of their land from large landholders. These tenant farmers paid their landlords as much as 50 per cent of their harvest in rent. After the war, a large land-reform program reduced the holdings of the landlords and enabled tenant farmers to buy the land they worked. As a result, about 90 per cent of Japanese farmers today own their land.

Fishing Industry. Japan has the world's largest fishing industry. It employs only about 1 per cent of the nation's workers, but they catch about 10,986,000 short tons (9,966,000 metric tons) of fish yearly. Japan has over 400,000 fishing vessels, more than any other country. Japanese fishing fleets sail in the country's coastal

© Donald Smetzer, Click/Chicago

Japanese Agriculture produces very high yields from tiny farms because the land is made as productive as possible. However, food must still be imported. These women are picking tea leaves.

Japan's Gross National Product

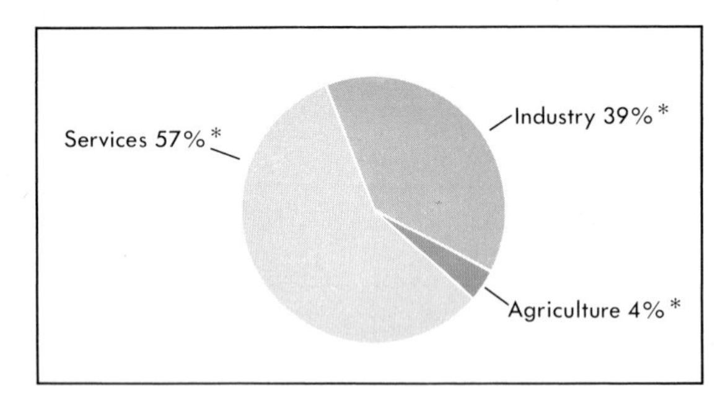

Japan's gross national product (GNP) was $1,161,389,000,000 in 1980. The GNP is the total value of goods and services produced by a country in a year. The GNP measures a nation's total economic performance and can also be used to compare the economic output and growth of countries.

Production and Workers by Economic Activities

Economic Activities	Per Cent of GDP* Produced	Employed Workers: Number of Persons	Employed Workers: Per Cent of Total
Manufacturing	29	13,670,000	25
Community, Social, & Personal Services	17	10,010,000	18
Finance, Insurance, & Real Estate	14	1,910,000	3
Wholesale & Retail Trade	12	12,480,000	22
Construction	9	5,480,000	10
Transportation & Communication	7	3,500,000	6
Government	5	1,990,000	4
Agriculture	4	5,230,000	10
Utilities	2	410,000	1
Mining	1	†	†
Fishing	**	450,000	1
Total	100	55,220,000	100

*Based on gross domestic product (GDP) in 1979. GDP is gross national product adjusted for net income sent or received from abroad.
†Included with utilities.
**Included with Agriculture.

Sources: International Monetary Fund; Statistics Bureau, Tokyo.

© Paul Chesley

The Fishing Industry of Japan ranks as the world's largest. Fish are the chief source of animal protein in the Japanese diet. The dockworkers above are handling an enormous tuna catch.

waters and in many other fishing grounds throughout the world.

Japan leads the world in tuna fishing and ranks second to the United States in the amount of salmon caught. Japan and Russia account for more than half the whales killed each year. Other products of Japan's fishing industry include cod, halibut, mackerel, pollack, sardines, saury, and trout. Japanese fishing crews also catch large quantities of octopus, squid, and crabs, shrimp, and other shellfish.

During the 1970's, almost all nations bordering the sea claimed authority over fishing zones extending 200 nautical miles (370 kilometers) off their shores. The establishment of these zones excluded Japanese fleets from some of their valuable fishing grounds, thus reducing Japan's annual catch of fish. Industrial pollution has further reduced the annual catch by destroying fishing areas in the country's coastal waters. In addition, Japan has limited its catch of whales and of certain species of fish in response to international conservation regulations. The decline in Japan's production has caused the country to import some seafood to meet the high domestic demand.

Mining. Japan has a wide variety of minerals, but the quantities of most of the minerals are too small to satisfy the country's needs. The chief products of Japan's mines include coal, copper, gold, lead, manganese, silver, tin, and zinc. Many of the minerals required by Japan's industries must be imported. For example, the country buys nearly all the bauxite, copper, and petroleum it needs from other countries. Most of the coking coal and iron ore required by Japan's iron and steel industry must also be imported.

Service Industries is a general name for a large, varied category of economic activities. Altogether, service industries account for about 57 per cent of Japan's gross national product and employ about 54 per cent of the country's workers. Service industries include government agencies, hospitals, schools, and other institutions that provide important community services. Financial institutions, such as banks and insurance companies, form another major group of service industries. Advertising agencies, data-processing services, real estate companies, restaurants, and many other business establishments also supply essential business, community, or personal services. Other service industries

Economy of Japan

Manufacturing is the single most important economic activity in Japan. This map shows the nation's six major industrial regions and lists the chief products of each region. Japan's croplands, forest lands, mineral deposits, and fishing products are also indicated on the map.

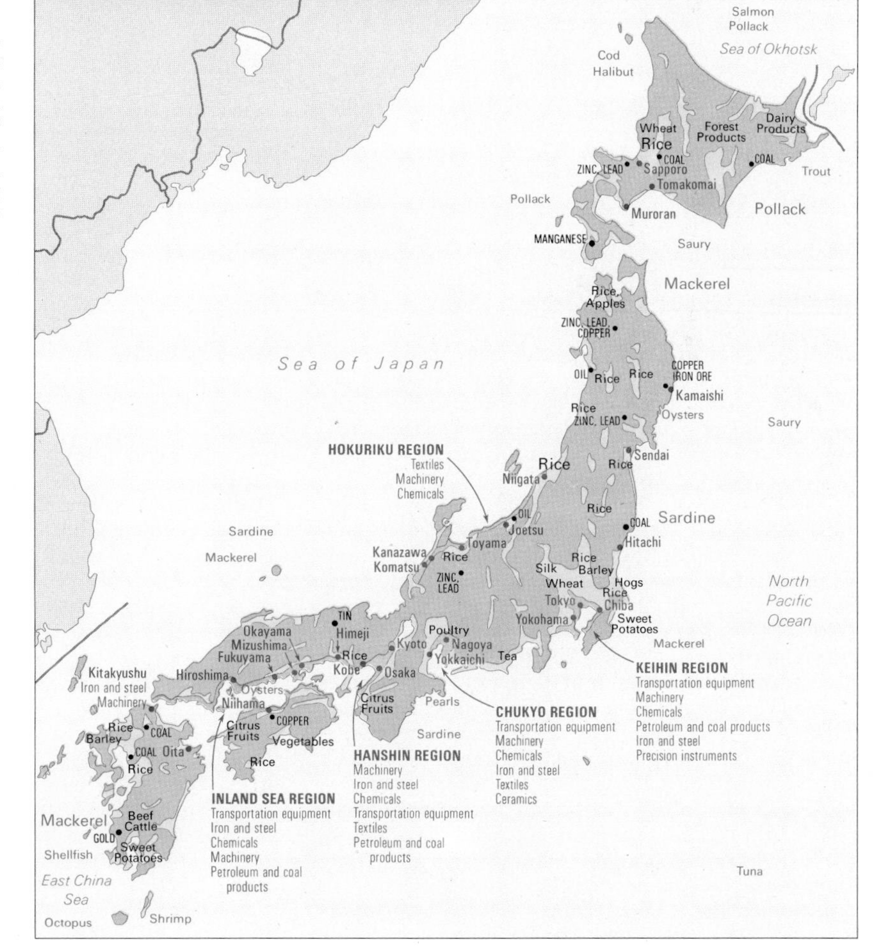

Chiefly cropland

Chiefly forest land

Fishing

Industrial region

• Industrial center

WORLD BOOK map

include trade, transportation, and communication.

Energy Sources. Japan requires vast amounts of energy for its farms, factories, households, and motor vehicles. The country ranks among the world's leading producers of electric power. Its power plants generate about 550 billion kilowatt-hours of electricity yearly.

Petroleum and natural gas provide about 70 per cent of Japan's energy. The country imports nearly all its petroleum and all its natural gas. Domestic oil production meets less than 1 per cent of the country's needs.

Japan spends more than $55 billion a year on oil imports. The country buys much of its oil from Middle Eastern nations. Since the mid-1970's, the rising cost of oil has contributed to inflation in Japan. Japan also faces possible fuel shortages if political instability in the Middle East interrupts supplies of oil. To avoid such shortages, the nation buys some petroleum from several countries outside the Middle East. In addition, Japan is exploring possible offshore sources of oil in the Korea Strait and the Sea of Japan.

Japan has fairly large deposits of coal on Hokkaido and Kyushu. However, the quality of much of the coal is poor. In addition, many coal deposits are thin, tilted, and badly broken—all of which make mining difficult and costly. As a result, petroleum has increasingly replaced coal as a source of power. Coal meets only about 15 per cent of Japan's energy needs.

Electricity generated by hydroelectric and nuclear power plants furnishes about 15 per cent of Japan's energy. The country has about 25 million kilowatt-hours of hydroelectric capacity. Japan's nuclear generators produce about 83 billion kilowatt-hours of power.

© Milt and Joan Mann

Japan's Rail Network is world famous. The bullet-shaped, high-speed electric train above is part of a large fleet of superexpresses that runs the length of the main island of Honshu.

Foreign Trade. Japan is one of the world's leading trading nations. Its imports and exports total more than $200 billion annually. The country's main exports, in terms of value, are passenger cars, iron and steel, and ships. Other leading exports include electric and nonelectric machinery, electronic equipment, motorcycles and trucks, plastics, precision instruments, and synthetic fiber fabrics. Petroleum is Japan's chief import. It accounts for about 50 per cent of the total value of the country's imports. Other major imports include coal, iron ore and other minerals, meat, natural gas, sugar, timber, wheat, and wool.

The United States is Japan's main trading partner. Japan is second to Canada as the principal trading partner of the United States. Japan's other leading trading partners include Australia, Canada, China, Indonesia, South Korea, Saudi Arabia, and West Germany.

Most of the time since the mid-1960's, Japan has had a favorable *balance of trade*—that is, the value of its exports has exceeded the value of its imports. Japan maintains a favorable trade balance by (1) exporting manufactured products throughout the world at competitive prices and (2) restricting imports by means of various trade barriers. The trade barriers include *tariffs* and *quotas*. Tariffs are taxes levied on imports to make them more expensive and thus encourage consumers to buy domestic products. A quota is a trade restriction that limits the quantity of imports allowed.

Japan's trade policies have contributed to unfavorable trade balances for countries that import large quantities of Japanese goods but face barriers to exporting their own goods to Japan. In the late 1970's and early 1980's, a number of Japan's trading partners began criticizing the country's trade practices. They asked Japan to limit some of its exports and to lift obstacles to imports. To maintain good trade relations, Japan has begun responding to these requests. For example, it has reduced its exports of automobiles to the United States and has relaxed restrictions on imports of U.S. food products. However, U.S. officials continue to complain about the serious trade imbalance that remains in Japan's favor.

Transportation and Communication. Japan has a modern, highly efficient transportation system. Its railroad network has about 17,000 miles (27,000 kilometers) of track. Japanese rail lines handle about 10 per cent of the nation's freight traffic and about 40 per cent of its passenger traffic. The government-owned Japan National Railways operates about 75 per cent of the railroads. Many small privately owned lines connect with the national system.

Motor vehicles drive on about 712,700 miles (1,147,000 kilometers) of highways, roads, and streets in Japan. About 300,000 miles (480,000 kilometers) are paved. Japan ranks second to the United States in registered passenger cars. It has more than 22 million automobiles. Trucks carry about 40 per cent of the freight in Japan.

Japan's merchant fleet totals more than 40 million gross tons. Only Liberia and Greece have larger fleets.

Japan's chief ports are Kobe, Nagoya, and Yokohama. Hundreds of smaller ports and harbors enable coastal shippers to serve every major city in Japan.

The principal Japanese airline is Japan Air Lines, which operates both domestic and international flights. Three other domestic airlines and about 35 foreign airlines also serve Japan.

Japan has thriving publishing and broadcasting industries. The country has more than 125 daily newspapers, with a total circulation of about 46 million copies. More than 2,300 magazines are published in Japan, and about 130 publishing houses produce more than 40,000 books annually. Almost every Japanese household has at least one television set—usually a color set—and one or more radios.

The Japanese government operates the country's telephone, telegraph, and postal systems. About 70 per cent of all Japanese households have a telephone.

JAPAN/*History*

Early Days. Historians know little about the earliest days of Japan. The country's oldest written histories are the *Kojiki* (*Record of Ancient Matters*), dated A.D. 712, and the *Nihongi* or *Nihonshoki* (*Chronicles of Japan*), dated A.D. 720. However, these histories consist chiefly of myths and legends. They trace the origin of Japan to a divine brother and sister who gave birth to the Japanese islands and to Amaterasu, the sun goddess. According to legend, Jimmu Tenno, a descendant of the sun goddess, became the first emperor of Japan in 660 B.C. (see JIMMU TENNO).

The origins of the Japanese remain largely a mystery. However, scientists know that people who hunted, fished, and gathered plant foods lived on the islands at least 6,500 years ago. By 200 B.C., farming was practiced, and the people lived in villages. For more information on what is known about earliest Japan, see the subsection *Ancestry* earlier in this article.

Beginning in the A.D. 200's, Japan was controlled by warring *clans* (related families), each headed by a chief. Most of the clans lived on Kyushu and along the Inland Sea to what is now the city of Kyoto. By about 400, the Yamato clan had become the most powerful one in central Japan. The chiefs of the clan are considered the ancestors of Japan's imperial family. See YAMATO PERIOD.

Influence of Chinese Culture. During the late 400's, new ideas and technology began arriving in Japan from China. The Japanese borrowed the Chinese system of writing and adopted their advanced methods of calculating the calendar. Confucianism was introduced from China and began to spread throughout Japan. About 552, Buddhism came to the country from China and Korea.

Prince Shotoku, who ruled Japan from 593 until his death in 622, encouraged the Japanese to adopt Chinese ideas. Shotoku wanted to increase the power of the Japanese emperor by adopting the Chinese system of centralized imperial rule. In 645, Kotoku became emperor. The next year, he and his advisers began the Taika Reform, a program that introduced more features of the Chinese model of government. Japan was divided into provinces, districts, and villages. The provinces were controlled by governors, who reported to the emperor. The Taika Reform also introduced a central system of taxation and a land distribution program.

In 794, the Japanese capital was established at Heian, later called Kyoto. Shortly after completion of the capital, the form of government adopted from China began to weaken. In 858, the emperor and his court fell under the control of the Fujiwaras, a powerful aristocratic family.

The Fujiwaras gained power over the emperor and the court nobility by intermarrying with the imperial family. In addition, the Fujiwaras, as well as other aristocratic families, got control of much of the countryside

Important Dates in Japan

660 B.C. According to legend, Jimmu Tenno became Japan's first emperor.

A.D. 400's New ideas and technology began arriving in Japan from China.

646 The Taika Reform began. It set up a central government controlled by the emperor.

858 The Fujiwara family gained control of the imperial court.

1192 Yoritomo became the first shogun.

1543 Portuguese sailors became the first Europeans to reach Japan.

1603 The Tokugawa family began its more than 250-year rule of Japan.

1630's Japan cut its ties with the outside world.

1853 and **1854** Commodore Matthew C. Perry of the United States visited Japan and opened two ports to U.S. trade.

1867 Emperor Mutsuhito regained his traditional powers.

1894-1895 Japan quickly won a war with China.

1904-1905 Japan's defeat of Russia in the Russo-Japanese War established the country as a world power.

1923 An earthquake destroyed much of Tokyo and Yokohama.

1931 Japan seized the Chinese province of Manchuria.

1937 Japan began a war with China. The fighting became part of World War II.

1941 Japan attacked U. S. bases at Pearl Harbor in Hawaii.

1945 The United States dropped atomic bombs on Hiroshima and Nagasaki. Japan surrendered to the Allies, and the Allied occupation of Japan began.

1947 Japan's democratic Constitution went into effect.

1951 Japan signed a general peace treaty and a security treaty with the United States.

1952 The Allied occupation of Japan ended.

1960 Japan signed the Treaty of Mutual Cooperation and Security with the United States.

1981 Japan agreed to limit its exports of automobiles to Canada, the United States, and West Germany.

by establishing great private estates. The Fujiwara family ruled Japan for about 300 years. During this time, the emperors lost all real power, though they still officially reigned.

Rise of the Shoguns. During the 1000's, the Japanese imperial government continued to lose power over the countryside as the great estates became increasingly independent. The lords who controlled the estates were called *daimyo*. The daimyo hired bands of warriors to protect their lands and the peasants who worked them. These warriors became known as *samurai*. See SAMURAI.

Two of the most powerful bands of samurai were headed by the Taira family and the Minamoto family. These families fought for control of the imperial court in Kyoto. In 1160, the Taira family seized ruling power from the Fujiwaras. But Taira control ended in 1185, when the family was defeated in an Inland Sea naval battle by the Minamoto clan. The Minamoto family, headed by Yoritomo, had clearly become the strongest family in the country. Yoritomo set up his military headquarters in Kamakura.

Yoritomo claimed to be the protector of the emperor and ruled in his name. In 1192, the emperor gave Yoritomo the title *shogun* (general). Yoritomo's military government became known as the *shogunate*. Shogun rule lasted until 1867. Each shogun, or his advisers, controlled Japan—but always in the name of the emperor. See SHOGUN.

As time went on, the Minamoto shogunate found it increasingly difficult to keep the country's many daimyo and their samurai bands united. In 1336, a samurai leader named Takauji Ashikaga gained control of Kyoto. In 1338, he had the emperor name him shogun and established the shogunate in Kyoto. The Ashikaga family governed Japan for almost 235 years. But the family's control was weak, and the last 100 years of Ashikaga rule was marked by constant warfare among local samurai bands.

Foreign Relations. Japan's early relations with other countries chiefly involved adopting features of their cultures. The Japanese felt safe from attack by foreign powers because of their country's isolated island position. In 1274, however, the Mongol conqueror Kublai Khan sent a fleet to conquer Japan. The invaders landed on Kyushu, but they withdrew when an approaching typhoon threatened their ships. In 1281, Kublai Khan again tried to invade Japan. He sent a great fleet with a force of more than 140,000 men. The invasion failed when a typhoon destroyed the fleet. The Japanese attributed the defeat of the Mongols to this typhoon, which they called *kamikaze* (divine wind).

Europeans first heard of Japan from Marco Polo, a Venetian traveler of the late 1200's. He returned to Europe from China with tales he had been told of Japan. Polo called the country *Cipango*, meaning *country where the sun rises*. He said it was a land of gold and riches. Later, explorers tried to reach this country. When Christopher Columbus sailed west from Europe in 1492, he hoped to land in Japan or the East Indies.

In 1543, Portuguese sailors became the first Europeans to reach Japan. In 1549, a Spanish priest, Saint Francis Xavier, came to Kagoshima in southern Kyushu. He began to preach the Roman Catholic religion. The Japanese welcomed the priest, and he converted many of them. Other missionaries from Spain and Portugal followed him, and traders came with them. During the early 1600's, traders arrived from The Netherlands and England.

Tokugawa Period. A great warrior named Hideyoshi controlled Japan from 1585 until his death in 1598. He planned to build an empire that included China, but his armies got only as far as Korea. In 1592 and in 1597, Hideyoshi tried to conquer Korea but failed.

In 1603, Ieyasu, Hideyoshi's chief deputy in eastern Japan, became shogun. His family, the Tokugawas, ruled Japan for more than 250 years. Ieyasu was a brilliant statesman. He was determined to end the warfare among the local samurai bands. Ieyasu built a castle and established his shogunate in Edo (renamed Tokyo in 1868). Under his rule, Japan was divided into about 250 regions called *domains*, each headed by a daimyo who swore allegiance to the Tokugawa shogunate.

Ieyasu feared that the Christian missionaries might soon bring European armies with them to conquer

Detail of *The Burning of the Sanjo Palace* (late 1200's), an ink painting with colors on paper by an unknown Japanese artist; Museum of Fine Arts, Boston, Fenollosa-Weld Collection

Rival Families fought for control of the Japanese government during the 1100's. Two of the country's most powerful families—the Taira and the Minamoto—met in battle in 1160, *left.* The Tairas won and ruled Japan until the Minamotos defeated them in a sea battle in 1185. In 1192, the emperor named Yoritomo, leader of the Minamoto family, *shogun* (general). For the next 675 years, shoguns were the actual rulers of Japan.

Japan. Ieyasu and the rulers who followed him gradually put down the Christian movement. They ordered all missionaries to leave the country. They also forced all Japanese converts to give up their new faith. Those who refused were persecuted or killed. By 1650, Christianity had been almost eliminated.

The Tokugawa government believed that contact with the outside world must end to keep order within the country. During the 1630's, it therefore cut ties with other nations. Japan became isolated from the rest of the world. The Japanese could not leave the country, and those who lived abroad were forbidden to return. Some foreign sailors who had been shipwrecked on Japan's shores were killed. All European traders except the Dutch had to leave. The government had less fear of the Dutch because they had not helped spread Christianity. The Dutch were permitted a small trading station on the tiny island Deshima in the harbor at Nagasaki. The Tokugawa government allowed one Dutch ship to come to the trading station each year.

Renewed Relations with the West. During the early 1800's, the United States became increasingly concerned over Japan's mistreatment of American sailors who had been shipwrecked on the Japanese islands. In 1853, an American mission headed by Commodore Matthew C. Perry was sent to Japan. Perry's orders were to open diplomatic and trade relations with Japan and to ensure good treatment for shipwrecked Americans.

On July 8, 1853, Perry sailed four warships into the bay at Edo (Tokyo). He presented the U.S. demands to Japanese officials and said he would return for their reply. In February 1854, Perry reentered Edo Bay with more warships. A few weeks later, the Tokugawa government signed a treaty with the United States. The treaty provided for an American diplomat to reside in Japan and guaranteed better treatment for American sailors forced to land on the islands. It also granted the United States trading rights in two Japanese ports, Hakodate and Shimoda. Great Britain, The Netherlands, and Russia soon signed similar trade treaties with Japan. See PERRY (Matthew Calbraith).

In 1858, Townsend Harris, the first U.S. diplomatic representative in Japan, arranged a more extensive trade treaty with the Japanese. That same year, Great Britain, France, The Netherlands, and Russia also signed general commercial treaties with the Japanese. Most of these treaties granted the foreigners the right of *extraterritoriality*—that is, foreigners were allowed to live in Japan and be subject only to the laws of their own nations (see EXTRATERRITORIALITY).

The treaties signed in the 1850's were called *unequal treaties*. They gave the foreign powers rights not granted to Japan in return. The enemies of the Tokugawa shogunate sharply criticized the government for having signed the treaties. Several important daimyo from western Japan plotted to overthrow the shogunate and restore the emperor to power. In 1867, troops of the daimyo forced the shogun to resign. On Jan. 3, 1868, the daimyo had Emperor Mutsuhito, then a teen-ager, officially announce the return of imperial rule.

Meiji Period. In 1868, Japan's capital was moved from Kyoto to Edo, which was renamed Tokyo. Emperor Mutsuhito adopted as his title *Meiji*, meaning *enlightened rule*. The years in which he reigned, from 1867 to 1912, are known as the *Meiji period*. During the Meiji period, Japan developed into a modern industrial and military power. Most of the work of the Meiji government was actually carried out by the daimyo who had overthrown the Tokugawa shogunate. But the emperor became the symbol of the new age.

In April 1868, the emperor issued the Imperial Charter Oath, which announced the government's intention to modernize Japan and to turn to the Western countries for new ideas and technology. The Meiji leaders set up a system of required education and built thousands of schoolhouses. They abolished the samurai and established a modern army and navy. The government instituted a telegraph network and began railroad construction. It also set up modern systems of banking and taxation.

The Meiji leaders encouraged industrialization. The government established a number of experimental industrial projects to serve as models for new industries in Japan. American and European experts in many fields

Detail of *The Opening of Japan* (mid-1920's?), a water color by Ogata Gassan; Kurihama Administration Center (International Society for Educational Information, Tokyo, from the Consulate General of Japan, Chicago)

An American Mission led by Commodore Matthew C. Perry arrived in Japan in 1853. The United States government sent Perry to open diplomatic and trade relations with the Japanese. The mission ended Japan's isolation from the rest of the world. In 1854, Japan signed a treaty opening two ports to U.S. trade.

were hired to teach Western knowledge and methods to the Japanese people. By the 1920's, the economic system set up by the Meiji leaders was controlled by the *zaibatsu*, huge corporations owned by single families. These firms operated banks, factories, mines, trading companies, and many other businesses.

In 1882, Hirobomi Ito, one of the greatest of the Meiji leaders, was sent to Europe to study constitutional systems of government. In 1889, Japan's first Constitution was proclaimed. Under this document, the emperor became the head of state and the supreme commander of the army and navy. He appointed all important government ministers, who were, in turn, responsible to him. The Meiji Constitution also provided for a two-house parliament called the Diet.

Imperialism. During the 1890's, Japan succeeded in revising the unequal treaties of the 1850's. The Westerners gave up their privilege of extraterritoriality. About this same time, the Japanese government began a policy of imperialistic expansion. Japan wanted to gain control of Korean trade and industry. It also wanted to increase its influence in China.

In July 1894, Japan went to war with China over control of Korea, which had been ruled by China for many hundreds of years. Japan quickly defeated China. The Treaty of Shimonoseki, signed on April 17, 1895, gave Japan Taiwan and the Liaotung Peninsula, the southernmost tip of Manchuria. But within a week, France, Germany, and Russia forced Japan to return Liaotung to China. The Treaty of Shimonoseki also granted Korea independence, thus leaving the country open to Japanese influence. See CHINESE-JAPANESE WARS.

During the late 1800's, rivalry developed between Japan and Russia, especially over conflicting interests in Korea and Manchuria. England supported Japan in this rivalry and made an alliance with the Japanese in 1902. In 1904, Japan declared war on Russia. The Japanese forces soon won many battles on land and sea, but the war was extremely costly for both countries. President Theodore Roosevelt of the United States helped persuade Japan and Russia to end the war after more than a year of heavy fighting. A peace treaty was signed in Portsmouth, N.H., in 1905.

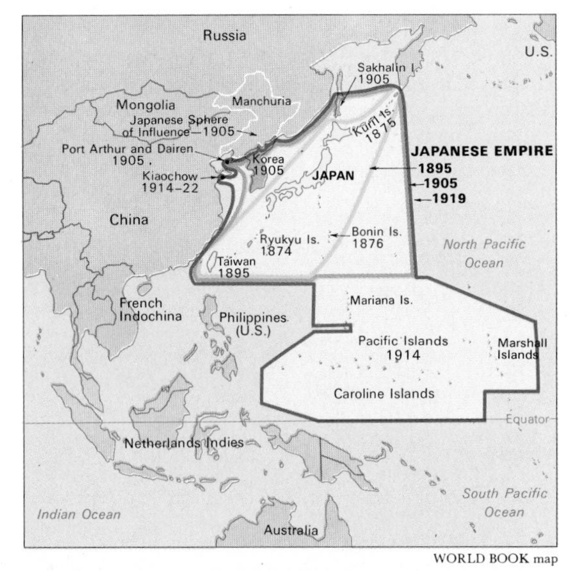

WORLD BOOK map

Japanese Expansion Until 1919. Japan expanded its territory as a result of three wars: the Chinese-Japanese War (1894-1895), the Russo-Japanese War (1904-1905), and World War I (1914-1918). By 1919, Japan was a world power.

The Treaty of Portsmouth gave Japan the Liaotung Peninsula, which Russia had leased from China. In addition, Russia recognized Japanese supremacy in Korea. Japan also received the southern half of Sakhalin Island and railway rights in southern Manchuria. The Russo-Japanese War established Japan as a world power. In 1910, Japan formally annexed Korea as a colony. See RUSSO-JAPANESE WAR.

World War I began in 1914. Japan, as an ally of England, at once declared war on Germany. The war gave Japan an opportunity to enlarge its empire. Japan seized the German holdings on the Shantung Peninsula in China. It also took the German-owned islands in the western Pacific—the Caroline, Mariana, and Marshall groups.

After World War I, Japan adopted a foreign policy that emphasized the development of trade, rather than the expansion of empire. The country strongly supported many measures for world peace. It became an original member of the League of Nations in 1920.

Rise of Militarism. After the Meiji Constitution was proclaimed in 1889, political parties began to gain increasing importance in Japan. During the 1920's, the leader of the majority party in the Diet was commonly selected as prime minister.

Japan's political parties began to win power during a time of great difficulties. On Sept. 1, 1923, a terrible earthquake struck the Tokyo-Yokohama area. The quake, and the fires and tidal waves that followed it, killed about 143,000 people. A worldwide depression during the late 1920's seriously damaged the Japanese economy. About this same time, China began to strengthen its administration in Manchuria. Japan feared that it might lose its Manchurian rights gained in the Russo-Japanese War. The political parties that had only recently gained power could not deal with the problems troubling Japan. Officers in the Japanese army decided to take matters into their own hands.

In 1931, Japanese forces occupied all Manchuria and made it a puppet state called *Manchukuo.* They then extended their influence into Inner Mongolia and other parts of northern China. At home, nationalist groups threatened members of the civilian government who opposed the army's actions. On May 15, 1932, nationalists assassinated Prime Minister Tsuyoshi Inukai.

The League of Nations condemned Japan's actions in Manchuria. Japan withdrew from the League in 1933. On Feb. 26, 1936, an army revolt to establish a more nationalistic government failed. But three leading members of the civilian government were killed during the uprising. Japan's military leaders now held firm control of the government.

In 1937, a small fight between Japanese and Chinese

Wide World

Emperor Hirohito reviewed part of Japan's armed forces in January 1938. In 1939, World War II broke out in Europe. Japanese armies invaded and occupied French Indochina the next year. Japanese aggression led to increased tension with the United States. On Dec. 7, 1941, Japanese bombers attacked U.S. military bases at Pearl Harbor in Hawaii.

troops stationed at the Marco Polo Bridge near Peking, China, flared into open warfare between Japan and China. Japanese armies controlled most of eastern China by the end of 1938. Japanese militarists began to speak of establishing the Greater East Asia Co-Prosperity Sphere, which would unite all eastern Asia under Japanese control. Meanwhile, Japan had moved toward closer relations with Nazi Germany and Fascist Italy by signing anti-Communist pacts with them.

World War II began in Europe in September 1939. In September 1940, Japan invaded and occupied the northern part of French Indochina. That same month, Japanese leaders signed an agreement with Germany and Italy, strengthening the alliance between the three countries. The expansion of Japanese power in Asia created increasing tension with the United States. In July 1941, Japanese troops entered southern Indochina. In response, the United States cut off all exports to Japan. In the fall of 1941, General Hideki Tojo became prime minister of Japan. The Japanese military leaders began planning for war with the United States.

Japan struck on Dec. 7, 1941. Japanese bombers attacked U.S. military bases at Pearl Harbor in Hawaii. They also bombed U.S. bases on Guam and Midway and in the Philippines. The Japanese quickly won dramatic victories in Southeast Asia and in the South Pacific. Japan achieved its greatest expansion early in 1942. The country controlled an area from the Aleutian Islands south about 4,500 miles (7,240 kilometers) to the Solomon Islands and from Wake Island west about 4,700 miles (7,560 kilometers) to Burma.

The Japanese fleet suffered its first major defeat in May 1942, when the United States won the Battle of the Coral Sea. The U.S. victory in the Battle of Midway the following month helped turn the tide in favor of the United States. As Japanese defeats increased, political discontent in Japan grew. On July 18, 1944, Prime Minister Tojo's Cabinet fell.

Early in 1945, the battle for the Japanese homeland began. American bombers hit industrial targets, and warships pounded coastal cities. American submarines cut off the shipping of vital supplies to Japan. On August 6, the United States dropped the first atomic bomb used in warfare on the city of Hiroshima. Two days later, Russia declared war on Japan and invaded Manchuria and Korea. The next day, on August 9, American fliers dropped a second and larger atomic bomb on Nagasaki.

Japanese leaders realized that their country had lost the war. On August 14, Japan agreed to surrender. At noon the next day, Emperor Hirohito announced to his people that Japan had agreed to end the war. On Sept. 2, 1945, the Japanese officially surrendered aboard the battleship U.S.S. *Missouri* in Tokyo Bay.

Japan lost all its territory on the mainland of Asia. It also lost all the islands it had governed in the Pacific—Iwo Jima, the Kurils, southern Sakhalin, the Ryukyus, and Taiwan. Japan kept only its four main is-

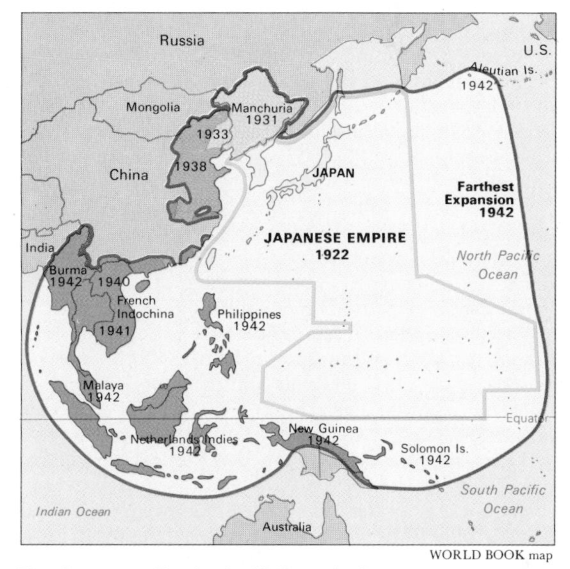

WORLD BOOK map

The Japanese Empire in 1942 reached its greatest extent. In 1931, Japan conquered Manchuria and then advanced into other parts of China and Southeast Asia. The map above shows the stages of Japanese expansion from 1931 to 1942.

lands and small islands nearby. Military and civilian casualties numbered in the millions. Except for Kyoto, all major Japanese cities had suffered heavy damage from air attacks. Japan's economy was shattered. For more detailed information on Japan's role in World War II, see World War II.

Allied Military Occupation of Japan began in late August 1945. The chief goals of the occupation were to end Japanese militarism and to create a democratic government in the country. Almost all the occupation forces were Americans. General Douglas MacArthur of the United States, as supreme commander for the Allied powers, administered Japan during the occupation. The Japanese government served only to carry out MacArthur's orders.

Under the occupation, more than 5 million Japanese troops were disarmed and released from service. The Allies tried 25 top Japanese leaders for war crimes. Seven of the leaders, including former Prime Minister Tojo, were executed. The rest received prison sentences. About 200,000 Japanese were declared ineligible for political office in the future because they had supported militarism and nationalism.

In 1946, MacArthur and his advisers drafted a new Japanese Constitution, which the Japanese government quickly accepted. The document went into effect on May 3, 1947. The Constitution transferred all political power from the emperor to the Japanese people. It abolished the army and navy and stated that Japan would give up the use of war as a political weapon.

Economic reforms also were made during the occupation. A huge land reform program enabled Japanese farmers to own their land. The powerful zaibatsu firms were broken up. Labor unions were established.

In 1949, MacArthur declared that the basic aims of the occupation had been achieved. He began to ease the controls over the Japanese people. On Sept. 8, 1951, Japan signed a peace treaty with 48 nations at San Francisco. That same day, a security treaty was signed between Japan and the United States. The treaty permitted the United States to have military bases and troops in Japan. The San Francisco peace treaty went into effect on April 28, 1952, and the Allied occupation officially ended that day.

Japan tried to join the United Nations (UN) in 1952 but failed because of Russian protests. Russia had not signed the 1951 peace treaty. In 1956, Japan and Russia signed an agreement ending the state of war between them. Japan gained UN membership later that year.

Postwar Boom. Japan made an extraordinary economic recovery in the 25 years after World War II ended. By the mid-1950's, its industrial production had returned to prewar levels. From 1960 to 1970, economic output increased at an average rate of 10 per cent a year.

There were several reasons for Japan's rapid economic recovery. After the war, Japan imported at relatively low cost all the modern technology that the West had to offer. The Japanese invested heavily in new plants and equipment. They focused their energies on the development of industries that produced goods for the world market. Japan also had a hard-working, well-trained work force. In addition, international trade grew rapidly in the postwar years. Thus, Japan was able to export its finished goods and to import the raw materials that it needed.

Many social changes also occurred in postwar Japan. As the country became more prosperous, the people wanted improved consumer goods, such as automobiles, refrigerators, and color television sets. In 1959, Crown Prince Akihito broke tradition by marrying a commoner, Michiko Shoda, the daughter of a wealthy industrialist. In 1971, Emperor Hirohito and Empress Nagako visited Western Europe. Their trip marked the first time a reigning emperor had ever left Japan.

In 1955, members of competing Japanese political groups united and formed the Liberal-Democratic Party. This conservative party has controlled Japan's national government ever since. Japan's greatest postwar political crisis occurred in 1960, after it signed the Treaty of Mutual Cooperation and Security with the United States. This treaty replaced the 1951 security agreement between Japan and the United States. The continued presence of U.S. bases and troops on the islands angered many Japanese. Widespread rioting in protest against the 1960 treaty led President Dwight D. Eisenhower to cancel a visit to Japan. The treaty was renewed in 1970, however, with little opposition.

In 1968, the United States returned the Bonin Islands and Iwo Jima to Japan. The United States had returned the northern Ryukyus in 1953. In 1972, it returned the southern Ryukyus. Russia still claims and occupies the Kuril Islands. But Japan also claims the southernmost Kurils—Iturup, Kunashir, Shikotan, and the Habomai group. The Japanese refer to these islands as the Northern Territories (see Kuril Islands).

Japan Today has the highest rate of economic growth among the world's leading industrialized nations. By the late 1970's, the success of the Japanese economy was attracting worldwide attention. For more than a century, Japan had been learning from the West, adopting its ideas and technology. But in the early 1980's, Western nations were looking to Japan for ways to improve their own economies.

In spite of its remarkable economic success, Japan faces challenging problems today. The country's rapid industrial development has created such problems as severe housing shortages in urban areas and widespread pollution. In addition, the Japanese government faces growing pressure from its allies to increase defense spending and to take a more active part in regional defense arrangements.

Japan's prosperity depends on the export of large quantities of manufactured products in exchange for raw materials. During the early 1980's, however, tensions mounted between Japan and some of its chief trading partners. These countries complained that competition from Japanese goods was damaging some of their home industries. They also criticized Japanese trade barriers that limited the amount and types of imports into the country. To help improve trade relations, Japan agreed in 1981 to limit its exports of automobiles to Canada, the United States, and West Germany. It also began to remove some restrictions on imports.

Kenneth B. Pyle, Michael Robinson, and Jay Rubin

JAPAN/*Study Aids*

Related Articles in WORLD BOOK include:

BIOGRAPHIES

Akihito
Hideyoshi
Hirohito
Jimmu Tenno
Kitasato, Shibasaburo
Kurosawa, Akira
Mutsuhito
Tojo, Hideki
Tomonaga, Sin-itiro
Yamamoto, Isoroku
Yamashita, Tomobumi
Yukawa, Hideki

CITIES

Hiroshima
Kobe
Nagasaki
Nagoya
Osaka
Sapporo
Tokyo
Yokohama

HISTORY

Boxer Rebellion
China (History)
Chinese-Japanese Wars
Colombo Plan
Kamakura Period
Kamikaze
MacArthur, Douglas
Manchuria
Mikado
Perry (Matthew Calbraith)
Russo-Japanese War
Samurai
Shogun
Taira
World War I (The War Begins; Results of the War)
World War II
Yamato Period

ARTS AND RECREATION

Architecture (Japanese Architecture; picture)
Dancing (Oriental Dancing; picture)
Doll (Doll Festivals and Customs; picture)
Drama (Japan; picture)
Flower (Flower Arranging; pictures)
Furniture (Japan)
Japanese Literature
Japanese Print
Judo
Kite
Lacquer Ware
Motion Picture (Postwar Asian Movies)
Origami
Painting (Japanese Painting; pictures)
Sculpture (Japan; picture)

OTHER RELATED ARTICLES

Ainu
Asia (Way of Life in East Asia)
Bamboo
Chrysanthemum
Clothing (pictures)
Far East
Flag (color picture: Historical Flags of the World)
Food (pictures)
Hara-Kiri
Japan, Sea of
Japanese Language
Jinrikisha
Kyodo
Labor Movement (Labor Around the World)
Library (Australia and the Far East)
Mount Fuji
Navy (Navies in the Two World Wars)
Nisei
Okinawa
Pearl (pictures)
Ryukyu Islands
Woman (In Other Countries)

Outline

I. Government
A. The Emperor
B. The Diet
C. The Prime Minister
D. Local Government
E. Politics
F. Courts
G. Armed Forces

II. People
A. Population
B. Ancestry
C. Language

III. Way of Life
A. City Life
B. Rural Life
C. Family Life
D. Clothing
E. Food and Drink
F. Recreation
G. Religion
H. Education

IV. The Arts
A. Music
B. Theater
C. Literature
D. Sculpture
E. Painting
F. Architecture
G. Other Arts

V. The Land
A. Honshu
B. Hokkaido
C. Kyushu
D. Shikoku
E. The Ryukyu and Bonin Islands

VI. Climate

VII. Economy
A. Manufacturing
B. Agriculture
C. Fishing Industry
D. Mining
E. Service Industries
F. Energy Sources
G. Foreign Trade
H. Transportation and Communication

VIII. History

Questions

How has family life in Japan changed since the end of World War II?

Why does Japan have many earthquakes each year?

How does the Japanese economy depend on foreign trade?

Who are the *burakumin* or *eta*? Why have they been the victims of discrimination?

What were the chief goals of the Allied occupation of Japan?

How do monsoons affect Japan's climate?

How did the Constitution of 1947 change Japan's government?

What percentage of Japan's land can be cultivated? How do Japanese farmers make their land as productive as possible?

Why did the Tokugawa shogunate cut Japan's ties with the outside world? How did the Tokugawa rulers restrict trade?

What were some reasons for Japan's rapid economic recovery after World War II?

Reading and Study Guide

See *Japan* in the RESEARCH GUIDE/INDEX, Volume 22, for a *Reading and Study Guide*.

Additional Resources

Level I

BOLITHO, HAROLD. *Meiji Japan*. Lerner, 1980.
DILTS, MARION M. *The Pageant of Japanese History*. McKay, 1961.
SPENCER, CORNELIA. *Made in Japan*. Knopf, 1963.
TAMES, RICHARD. *Japan in the Twentieth Century*. David & Charles, 1981.
VAUGHAN, JOSEPHINE B. *The Land and People of Japan*. Rev. ed. Lippincott, 1972.

Level II

IENAGA, SABURO. *Japanese Art: A Cultural Appreciation*. Tuttle, 1979.
LEBRA, TAKIE S. *Japanese Patterns of Behavior*. Univ. Press of Hawaii, 1976.
LEONARD, JONATHAN N. *Early Japan*. Time Inc., 1968.
PYLE, KENNETH B. *The Making of Modern Japan*. Heath, 1978.
REISCHAUER, EDWIN O. *The Japanese*. Harvard, 1977. *Japan: The Story of a Nation*. 3rd ed. Knopf, 1981.
SANSOM, GEORGE B. *Japan: A Short Cultural History*. Rev. ed. Stanford, 1952.

Rus Arnold

The Boats of Merchants and Shoppers jam a canal in Bangkok, Thailand's capital and largest city. This traditional "floating market" is one of the city's most picturesque features.

THAILAND

THAILAND, *TY land,* is a country in Southeast Asia. It is a wet, tropical land with many rivers, forests, and mountains. The people of Thailand are called *Thai.* Most of them live in villages and farm the land. But many villagers move to Thailand's cities each year, and so the urban areas are growing rapidly. Bangkok is the capital and largest city.

Thailand is the only nation in Southeast Asia that has never been ruled by a Western power. Local peoples established the first Thai nation in A.D. 1238. The country was called Siam from 1782 to 1939, when it became known as Thailand. Its name in the Thai language is *Muang Thai,* which means *Land of the Free.*

Government

National Government. Thailand is a constitutional monarchy. The nation's Constitution of 1978 provides for a monarch, a prime minister, and a legislature called the National Assembly. Until 1980, only males could serve as monarch. But a law passed that year allows either males or females to hold the office.

Thailand's monarch has an advisory role as chief of state, but the prime minister actually heads the nation's government. The National Assembly nominates the prime minister, who is then formally appointed by the monarch. The prime minister selects a cabinet, called the Council of Ministers, which may have a maximum of 44 members.

The National Assembly consists of a Senate of 225 members and a House of Representatives with 301 members. The senators are selected by the prime minister with the approval of the monarch and may be replaced

Herbert P. Phillips, the contributor of this article, is Professor of Anthropology at the University of California, Berkeley, and the author of Thai Peasant Personality.

Facts in Brief

Capital: Bangkok.

Official Language: Thai.

Official Name: Muang Thai (Land of the Free).

Form of Government: Constitutional monarchy.

Area: 198,457 sq. mi. (514,000 km²). *Greatest Distances*—north-south, 1,100 mi. (1,770 km); east-west, 480 mi. (772 km). *Coastline*—1,635 mi. (2,631 km).

Elevation: *Highest*—Inthanon Mountain, 8,514 ft. (2,595 m). *Lowest*—sea level.

Population: *Estimated 1983 Population*—50,027,000; distribution, 86 per cent rural, 14 per cent urban; density, 251 persons per sq. mi. (97 per km²). *1979 Census*—46,113,756. *Estimated 1988 Population*—56,601,000.

Chief Products: *Agriculture*—rice, cassava, corn, cotton, rubber, sugar cane, tobacco. *Manufacturing*—automobiles, cement, drugs, electronic equipment, food products, paper, plywood, textiles. *Forestry and Fishing*—teak, bamboo, rattan, anchovies, mackerel, shellfish. *Mining*—tin, bauxite, iron ore, lead, manganese, natural gas, precious stones, tungsten.

National Anthem: "Pleng Chart" ("National Anthem of Thailand").

Money: *Basic Unit*—baht. For its value in U.S. dollars, see MONEY (table: Exchange Rates).

Thailand's Flag was adopted in 1917. The red represents the nation; the white, purity; and the blue, the monarchy.

The Coat of Arms, adopted in 1910, features the *garuda,* a mythical birdlike creature in the Buddhist religion.

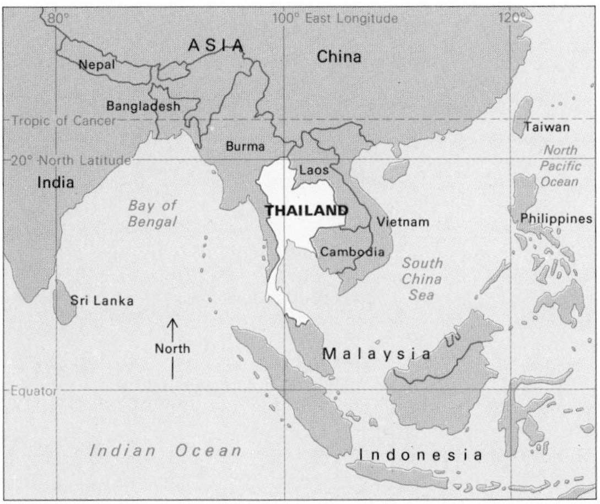

WORLD BOOK map

Thailand, a country in Southeast Asia, lies mostly on the Asian mainland. Southern Thailand extends along the Malay Peninsula.

at any time. The representatives are elected by the people to four-year terms.

Local Government. Thailand is divided into 72 provinces, which, in turn, are divided into 576 districts. Each province has a governor, and every district has a district officer. All these officials are appointed by the minister of the interior. Thailand also has more than 5,300 smaller divisions called *communes,* which consist of a total of almost 50,000 villages. The people of each village elect their own headman. The headmen then choose a *kamnan* from among themselves to serve as the chief administrator of their commune. Every city in Thailand is governed by a mayor and a council, both elected by the people.

Politics. In most cases, a Thai political party comes into power through an election or by a *coup* (sudden revolt) against the ruling party. Thailand has several major political parties and a number of smaller parties. Citizens who are at least 18 years old may vote if they can read and write in Thai.

Courts. The Supreme Court, called the *Sarn Dika,* is the highest court in Thailand. It consists of a chief justice and 21 judges. The Court of Appeals, the second highest court, reviews decisions made by lower courts. All judges of the Supreme Court, and all head judges of the other courts, are appointed by the monarch on the advice of the prime minister.

The Armed Forces of Thailand consist of an army, a navy, an air force, a national police force, and a village defense corps. The forces have a total membership of more than 200,000. Men from 21 to 30 years old may be drafted for at least two years of military duty.

The People

Population and Ancestry. Thailand has approximately 50 million people. About 86 per cent of the Thai live in rural areas. More than 5 million people make their homes in Bangkok.

The majority of the Thai are descendants of Thai-speaking peoples who migrated from southern China between the time period of the A.D. 100's and 900's. Chinese people make up the second largest population group. Most of the rest of the people are immigrants—or descendants of immigrants—from Burma, Cambodia, Malaysia, or Vietnam. The population also includes some European, Indian, and Japanese people—most of whom live in Bangkok. Small groups of peoples who follow tribal ways of life live in the country's northern mountains.

Way of Life. More than 75 per cent of Thailand's people make their living by farming. Large numbers of Thai also work in the fishing, lumbering, and mining industries. In the cities, many have jobs in factories. The nation's Chinese work mainly in commerce.

Most Thai live in villages that range in size from a few hundred to a few thousand people. The villagers raise almost all their own food, including corn, fruit, rice, and *cassava*—a tropical plant used in making tapioca. Every village has a school and a *wat* (Buddhist temple), which serves as the religious and social center of the community. The people enjoy village fairs, harvest celebrations, and other festive occasions.

Maurice G. G. Harvey, Alan Hutchison Library Ltd.

Modern Stores and Offices line the busy streets of the main business districts of Bangkok. The city is Thailand's chief commercial, cultural, and industrial center.

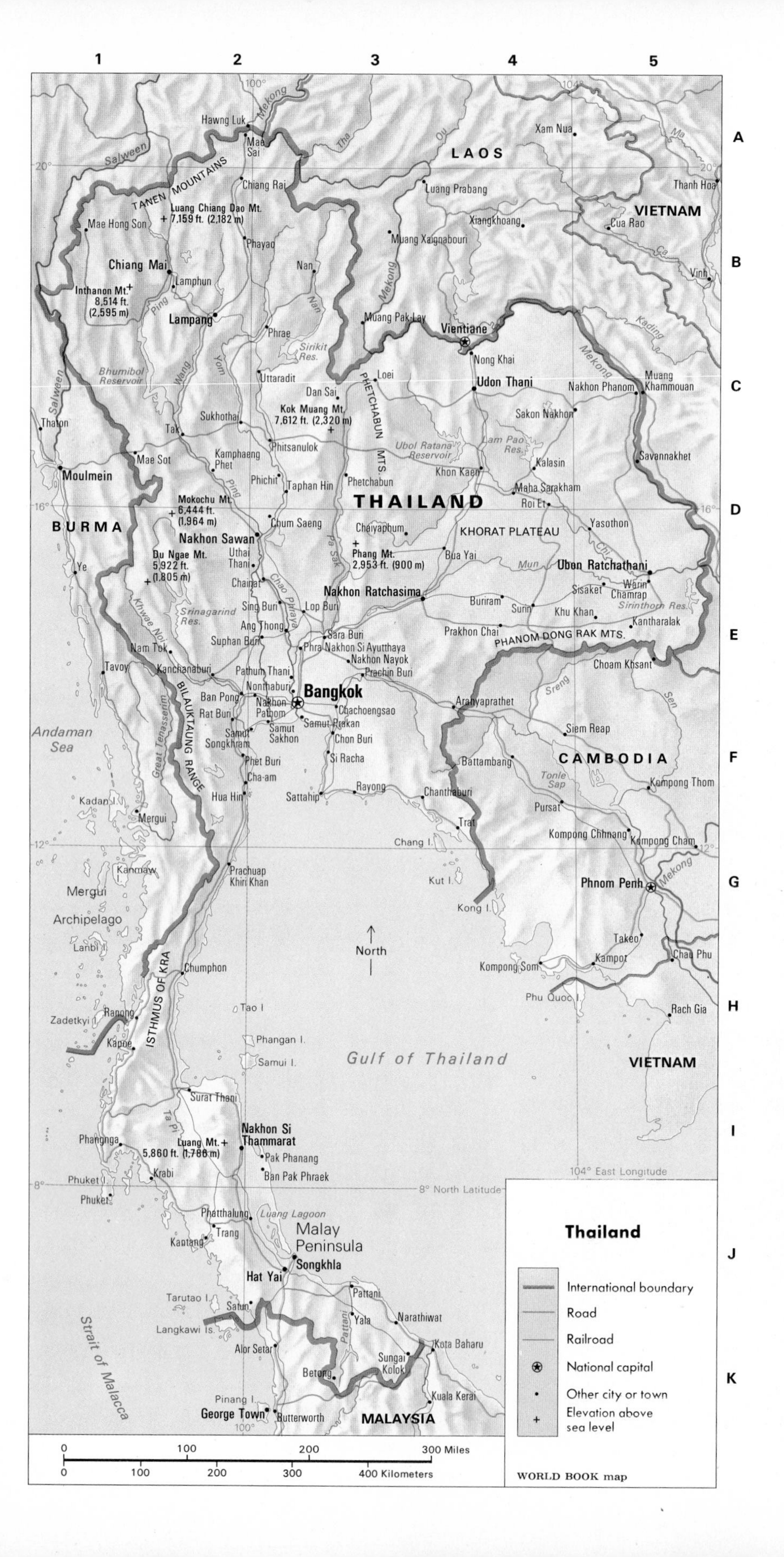

Cities and Towns

Physical Features

Source: 1980 census.

Saul Lockhardt, Advertasia Co., Ltd.

Middle-Class Housing in Thailand consists mainly of small, neat, single-family dwellings. The houses at the left are in a suburb of Bangkok.

Since the early 1960's, large numbers of Thai—especially young people—have moved from rural areas to cities in search of jobs and educational opportunities. The rapid growth of Thailand's cities has led to unemployment, crowded living conditions, and other serious problems.

The women of Thailand have more freedom than those of many other Asian nations. Numerous Thai women have jobs in business, education, government, and medicine.

Most urban Thai people wear Western-style clothing. In rural areas, many people—both males and females—wear the traditional *panung*, a colorful cotton or silk garment. A panung, which consists of a piece of cloth, is wrapped tightly around the body. A male's panung extends from the hips to the ankles, and a female's from above the chest to the ankles. For pictures of other Thai clothing, see CLOTHING (Traditional Costumes).

Housing. Most Thai villagers live in houses of wood or thatch that stand along rivers and canals. The homes are built on stilts to raise them above the ground for protection against flooding. Families use the area under their house as a shelter for farm animals. A high roof of tile or thatch helps keep the interior cool.

In the cities, many people live in small wooden or stucco houses. A number of the Chinese own shops and live in apartments above them. Some wealthy Thai have beautiful mansions. Poor communities in Thai cities consist either of slums or of housing projects built by the government.

Food. Thai people eat rice with almost every meal. Favorite foods served with rice include *curries* (spicy stews) and salads of meat, fish, and vegetables. The Thai take great pride in their *cuisine* (style of cooking and preparing food). Some communities are famous for their special dishes, and people often travel long distances just to taste these specialties.

Recreation. The Thai enjoy such sports as soccer and *Thai-style boxing*, in which opponents fight with both their hands and feet. In another popular sport, called

© Horst Gossler, The Stock House

Thai-Style Boxing, in which opponents use their feet as well as their hands, is a popular sport throughout Thailand.

Orion Press from Katherine Young

Buddhist Monks are dwarfed by a statue that guards the Temple of the Emerald Buddha in Bangkok.

Saul Lockhardt, Advertasia Co., Ltd.

Thai Classical Dancers act out traditional stories with religious themes. Jewels and embroidery decorate their costumes.

takraw, the players try to keep a wicker ball in the air by using their heads, legs, and feet. Many Thai play *mak ruk*, a type of chess. Favorite forms of recreation involving gambling include cockfights and fish fights, in which male Siamese fighting fish attack each other in jars (see FIGHTING FISH). Card games and betting on the national lottery are also popular.

Languages. About 90 per cent of Thailand's people speak Thai, the official language. Thai has four main regional dialects. The dialect of central Thailand is the most common form of the language. A small number of Thai speak Malay and various dialects of Chinese. Many of the nation's secondary schools teach English, but few of the nation's people actually use it.

Religion. More than 95 per cent of the Thai people are Buddhists. They are members of the Therevada school of Buddhism (see BUDDHISM [Buddhist Schools]). According to custom, men over the age of 20 are expected to serve in the Buddhist monkhood for at least a few months, and more than 40 per cent of them actually do. Most of the Chinese in Thailand practice Confucianism, and the majority of the Malays are Muslims. Hinduism is the main religion among the Indians of Thailand. Most of the Europeans, as well as some of the Chinese and Vietnamese, belong to a Christian faith.

Education. More than 80 per cent of Thailand's people can read and write. The Thai government operates free elementary schools throughout the country, and all children are required by law to attend school for at least four years. However, most of Thailand's high schools are privately owned and charge tuition. Only about 10 per cent of the people have graduated from high school. Thailand has 14 universities, 43 teachers colleges, and 179 vocational schools. But only about 1 per cent of the people are university or teachers college graduates.

The Arts in Thailand are greatly influenced by Buddhism. The image of Buddha appears in many Thai paintings and sculptures. The nation's Buddhist temples rank among the best examples of Thai architecture, which combines traditional and modern styles.

Thai literature is divided into two groups, *wannakhadi* and *wannakam*. Wannakhadi consist of classical dramas and epic poems that were originally written and performed for royalty. Wannakam consist of novels, poems, and short stories about modern Thailand. Most of these works center on the problems and pleasures of everyday life.

The Land

Thailand covers 198,457 square miles (514,000 square kilometers). The country has four main land regions: (1) the Northern Mountains, (2) the Khorat Plateau, (3) the Central Plain, and (4) the Southern Peninsula.

The Northern Mountains occupy northwest Thailand and extend along the country's western border to the Malay Peninsula. They are covered by thick forests of evergreen and teak trees, which provide valuable timber. The mountains include Inthanon Mountain, the tallest peak, which rises 8,514 feet (2,595 meters) above sea level.

Many streams flow south from the mountains to the Gulf of Thailand. These streams deposit mud and sand along their banks and help make the soil fertile. Farmers grow rice in the narrow mountain valleys. The region has deposits of copper, iron, and lead.

The Khorat Plateau, which lies in the northeastern part of Thailand, makes up about 30 per cent of the country's land area. It is also the country's most heavily populated region. The plateau is bordered by mountains on the south and west and by the Mekong River on the north and east.

Most of the plateau has sandy soil that holds little moisture. The Mekong, Chi, and Mun rivers provide irrigation water for the farming that takes place there. Rice is the principal crop.

The Central Plain extends between the foothills of the Northern Mountains region and the Gulf of Thailand. The fertile soil of the Central Plain enables farmers to raise more rice there than anywhere else in Thailand. Four rivers—the Nan, Ping, Wang, and Yom—unite in the northern part of the plain and become the Chao Phraya River, which is the country's chief transportation route.

The Southern Peninsula, which forms part of the Malay Peninsula, consists mainly of jungle, with some mountains and rolling hills. Many streams flow through the narrow valleys and flood small coastal plains. In the northern part of this region, Thailand and Burma share the Malay Peninsula. There, only a narrow strip of land belongs to Thailand.

The southern part of the region occupies the entire width of the Malay Peninsula. This mountainous area has fertile soil, and rubber trees thrive there. It also has large deposits of tin.

Animal Life. Thailand's forest and jungle areas abound with boars, crocodiles, deer, tigers, and such poisonous snakes as banded kraits and cobras—including king cobras. In the past, many elephants lived in the wild in Thailand. However, today most of the country's elephants have been domesticated. They serve as beasts of burden.

Climate

Thailand has a tropical climate. Most of the country has three seasons—a hot dry spring, a hot wet summer, and a mild winter. Bangkok has an average temperature of 62° F. (17° C) in January and 98° F. (37° C) in May. The Northern Mountains region is cooler, with temperatures averaging 32° F. (0° C) in January and 90° F. (32° C) in May.

From July to December, winds called *monsoons* cause heavy rains throughout Thailand. The Southern Peninsula region receives an average of about 100 inches (254 centimeters) of rain yearly. Bangkok has an average annual rainfall of 55 inches (140 centimeters).

Economy

Thailand has a developing economy that depends mainly on agriculture and manufacturing. More than 75 per cent of the nation's workers make their living by farming, compared with only about 7 per cent in manufacturing. However, manufactured agricultural products contribute about equally to the Thai economy. Large numbers of people have jobs in the fishing, forestry, and mining industries, and many work in commerce,

© Stephanie Colasanti

In Thailand's Teak Forests, elephants haul heavy logs to rivers to be floated downstream to sawmills. Strong and durable, teak is used mainly for shipbuilding and making fine furniture.

Charles Marden Fitch

Tin Mining contributes greatly to Thailand's foreign trade. Most of the country's tin mines, including the one shown here, are in the mountains of the Southern Peninsula region.

government, and tourism. The economy operates as a free enterprise system, though the government sets prices for such important goods as rice and gasoline.

Agriculture. Thai farmers cultivate about 25 per cent of the nation's land, mostly to grow rice. Other leading crops include cassava, corn, cotton, rubber, sugar cane, and tobacco. Thailand also produces bananas, coconuts, pineapples, silk, soybeans, and *jute*, a fiber plant used in making rope. Farms in Thailand average about 6 acres (2 hectares), and more than 75 per cent of the farmers own their land.

Manufacturing has become increasingly important in Thailand since 1960. The nation's leading industries produce cement, food products, paper, plywood, and textiles. Many international companies operate factories in the Bangkok area. These plants assemble automobiles and electronic equipment, and manufacture drugs and other products.

Forestry and Fishing. Forests cover about 60 per cent of Thailand. Teak is the chief forest product. Elephants move the heavy teak logs to rivers, and the timber is floated downstream to lumber mills for sawing and shipping. Other important forest products include bamboo and *rattan*, a tough, stringy material that comes from the stems of certain palm trees.

Anchovies, mackerel, and such shellfish as crabs and shrimp are caught in Thailand's rivers and coastal waters. Most Thai farmers raise fish and shellfish in ponds that they build on their property.

Mining. Tin is Thailand's most important mineral, and the nation ranks among the world's leading tin producers. Mines in Thailand also provide large amounts of bauxite, iron ore, lead, manganese, precious stones, and tungsten. Natural gas is obtained from deposits in the Gulf of Thailand.

Foreign Trade. Thailand's chief exports include rice, rubber, tapioca products, teak, and tin. The Thai also export corn, sugar, and tobacco. The nation imports such products as chemicals, fuels, and machinery. Thailand trades mainly with Japan, the United States, and China.

Transportation in Thailand ranks among the best in Southeast Asia. The country has about 8,100 miles (13,000 kilometers) of paved roads and more than 2,400 miles (3,800 kilometers) of railroad track. Rivers and canals in Thailand provide local transportation for passengers and cargo. Bangkok is the country's largest and busiest port.

Four international airports provide daily flights between Thailand and other Asian nations, various European countries, and Australia. Local airlines serve the nation's major cities.

Communication. Thailand has approximately 50 daily newspapers, about 20 of which are published in Bangkok. Most of the newspapers are published in Thai, and the rest in Chinese or English. Telegraph and telephone systems link the principal cities. The nation has 4 major television networks and more than 200 radio stations. The government owns and operates all the TV and radio stations.

History

Early Days. People have lived in what is now Thailand for more than 5,000 years. Archaeological evidence indicates that people in what is now the northeastern Thai village of Non Nok Tha grew rice for food more than 5,000 years ago. The evidence is the world's first known record of the cultivation of rice—the most widely eaten of all human foods. The ancestors of most present-day Thai probably moved into the region from southern China between the time period of the A.D. 100's and 900's. They established many settlements, and in 1238, the Thai formed the first Thai nation. They named it *Sukothai*, which means *Dawn of Happiness*. King Ramkhamhaeng, one of the early rulers of Sukothai, invented the Thai alphabet. Sukothai expanded and prospered and, by 1350, occupied most of what became Thailand.

Invasions and Wars. In 1350, a group of Thai people established the kingdom and the city of Ayutthaya in what is now the central region of Thailand. By the late 1300's, Sukothai had declined in importance. The Ayutthaya kingdom absorbed it. The city of Ayutthaya served as the Thai capital from the mid-1300's to the mid-1700's. During that period, the kingdom of Ayutthaya fought numerous wars with the Malays to the south, the Burmese to the west, and the Khmer of Cambodia to the east. In 1431, Thai forces invaded Cambodia and captured its capital, Angkor.

European Contact for the Thai began when Portuguese traders came to Ayutthaya in the early 1500's. During the 1600's, Spain, England, France, Japan, and The Netherlands also established trade there. The Thai granted some nations—including France, England, and The Netherlands—*rights of extraterritoriality*. These rights allowed the people of the foreign nations to live in Ayutthaya under the laws of their own countries (see EXTRATERRITORIALITY).

During the late 1600's, many young Thai began going to schools in Europe, where they learned Western ideas and customs. At the same time, European powers began to interfere in Ayutthaya's internal affairs. This interference angered the Thai. They forced all Europeans to leave the country, canceled the extraterritorial rights of some of the European nations, and resisted any contact with Western nations.

A New Dynasty. Burmese troops invaded Ayutthaya in 1767 and destroyed the capital. But Thai forces, led by General Phyra Taksin, soon drove the Burmese out of the country. Taksin became king and established a new capital at Thonburi.

In 1782, General Phyra Chakri replaced Taksin as king. Chakri took the title Rama I and established the Chakri dynasty, which still reigns in Thailand. In 1782, the nation's name was changed to Siam and the Thai capital was moved from Thonburi across the Chao Phraya River to Bangkok.

King Mongkut (Rama IV), who ruled from 1851 to 1868, was one of Siam's most influential monarchs. He employed advisers from Western nations and encouraged his people to study Western languages and modern science. Mongkut also resumed trade relations with France, Great Britain, and other countries, and granted them extraterritorial rights.

King Chulalongkorn (Rama V), Mongkut's son, continued the social reforms started by his father. During his reign, from 1873 to 1910, Chulalongkorn abolished slavery in Siam, reorganized the government, and established a public education system.

World War I and World War II. During World War I (1914-1918), Siam supported France and Great Britain against Germany and Austria-Hungary. Some Thai soldiers fought in Europe. In return for Siam's help in the war, France and Great Britain gave up their rights of extraterritoriality.

In 1932, a group of Thai who had been educated in France revolted against King Prajadhipok (Rama VII). They forced him to change the government from an absolute monarchy to a constitutional monarchy. In 1935, Prajadhipok gave up the throne in favor of his 10-year-old nephew, Ananda Mahidol (Rama VIII). A *regency* (group of temporary rulers) governed the country for the young king. Some members of the government were military officials, and others were civilians. The civilians held control at first, but the military officers took over in 1938. The country's name was changed to Thailand in 1939.

In 1940, during World War II, Thailand demanded the return of land that King Chulalongkorn had given French Indochina before World War I. Japan supported Thailand's demand and forced Indochina to return the land. In 1941, Japan invaded Thailand. The Thai resisted for a few hours but then signed a treaty of alliance with Japan. That same year, the Japanese attacked the United States military bases at Pearl Harbor in Hawaii, and the United States went to war against Japan. Thailand declared war on the United States and Great Britain in 1942. During the war, a Free Thai Movement worked against the Japanese within Thailand.

After World War II. Field Marshal Pibul Songgram, who had served as prime minister during the Japanese occupation, ruled Thailand from 1946 to 1957. He was overthrown by Field Marshal Sarit Thanarat, who ruled the country until his death in 1963. Sarit brought widespread economic development to Thailand and strengthened the nation's ties with the United States. His successor, Field Marshal Thanom Kittikachorn, continued these policies. Thanom permitted the United States to build air bases in Thailand. In 1965, during the Vietnam War, United States forces began using the air bases to attack Communist forces in Vietnam, Cambodia, and Laos. Thailand also sent troops to Vietnam to fight on the side of South Vietnam and the United States.

In 1967, Thailand, Indonesia, Malaysia, the Philippines, and Singapore formed the Association of Southeast Asian Nations (ASEAN). This organization promotes economic, cultural, and social cooperation among its members.

In 1973, university students in Thailand led a civilian revolt against the Thai government. For the next three years, Thailand had a series of democratically elected governments. This democratic period ended in October 1976 after conservative groups attacked radical students at Thammasat University in Bangkok. About 40 persons died in the fighting, and thousands of others were arrested. Military leaders then took control of the government again.

Thailand Today is one of the most prosperous nations in Southeast Asia, but it faces many serious problems. Some Malay Muslims in southern Thailand want to establish an independent nation, and they started to revolt against the Thai government in the late 1960's. Communist forces in the northeast areas of Thailand are a constant threat to the government.

Since 1975, after the end of the Vietnam War, thousands of refugees have moved to Thailand from Cambodia, Laos, and Vietnam. The Thai government provides the refugees with food, clothing, and shelter—a considerable drain on the nation's economy. In addition, continued conflicts between Vietnamese and Cambodians near Thailand's borders represent a constant threat to the peace and security of the nation. HERBERT P. PHILLIPS

Related Articles in WORLD BOOK include:

Asia (pictures: A Buddhist Monk; River Transportation)
Association of Southeast Asian Nations
Bangkok
Buddhism
Clothing (pictures: Clothing for Work; Religious Clothing)
Mekong River
Rice (graph)
Rubber (graph)
Southeast Asia Treaty Organization
Teak
Tin (graph)

ANGUILLA, *ang GWIHL uh,* is an island in the Caribbean Sea. It is a dependency of Great Britain. For location, see West Indies (map). Anguilla has an area of 35 square miles (91 square kilometers) and a population of about 7,000. It is mostly flat and has a dry, sunny climate. Tourism and fishing rank as major industries of the dependency. A community called The Valley serves as the unofficial capital.

Carib Indians were probably the first inhabitants of Anguilla. The island became a colony of Britain in 1650. In 1882, Britain made Anguilla and the Caribbean islands of St. Christopher (St. Kitts) and Nevis a single colony. The colony became an associated state of Britain in 1967. But most Anguillans favored separation from St. Christopher and Nevis. In 1976, Anguilla became—in effect—a separate British dependency. Its status was officially changed to a separate dependency in 1980 (see West Indies [History]). Thomas G. Mathews

ANTIGUA AND BARBUDA, *an TEE gwuh, bahr BOO duh,* is an island country in the Caribbean Sea. It consists of three islands—Antigua, Barbuda, and Redonda. The islands lie about 430 miles (692 kilometers) north of Venezuela. For location, see West Indies (map).

Antigua and Barbuda has a total land area of 171 square miles (442 square kilometers) and a population of 79,000. The island of Antigua covers 108 square miles (280 square kilometers); Barbuda, 62 square miles (161 square kilometers); and Redonda, only $\frac{1}{2}$ square mile (1.3 square kilometers). About 98 per cent of the people live on Antigua and 2 per cent on Barbuda. Redonda is uninhabited. St. John's (pop. 24,000), on the northwest coast of Antigua, is the country's capital and largest city. The East Caribbean dollar is the country's basic unit of currency. For a picture of the flag of Antigua and Barbuda, see Flag (Flags of the Americas).

Government. Antigua and Barbuda is a constitutional monarchy and a member of the Commonwealth of Nations (see Commonwealth of Nations). A prime minister heads the government. The prime minister and a Cabinet conduct the operations of the government. A 17-member Parliament—composed of a House of Representatives and Senate—makes the country's laws. The people elect the Parliament members. The head of the majority party of the House of Representatives serves as prime minister. The prime minister appoints the Cabinet members.

People. The vast majority of the people of Antigua and Barbuda are descendants of black Africans. About a third of the people live in St. John's, and most of the rest live in rural areas. Most of the people live in small wooden huts. They wear clothing similar to that worn in the United States and other Western nations. Their main foods include beans, fish, lobsters, and sweet potatoes.

Almost all the people of Antigua and Barbuda speak English, the nation's official language. Most of the people are Protestants. Anglicans make up the largest Protestant group. Antigua and Barbuda has well-developed primary and secondary educational systems.

Land and Climate. The islands of Antigua and Barbuda are mostly flat. They were formed from volcanoes that were worn down by wind and rain. The islands have beautiful beaches covered with white sand. Antigua's coast has numerous bays and inlets. Redonda is rocky, and has little plant life.

The average temperature of the islands is 80° F. (27° C). The islands receive about 45 inches (114 centimeters) of rain annually. However, long periods of drought strike the area from time to time.

Economy. Tourism and the production of sugar rank as the major economic activities of Antigua and Barbuda. The country's beaches, resorts, and warm sunny climate attract tourists from many lands. The tourist industry employs most of Antigua and Barbuda's people. Farmers raise sugar cane and processors refine it into sugar in the country. Cotton is another important product. The country's crop production is frequently harmed by droughts. As a result, the government encourages the development of small industries to strengthen the economy. The country's industries include the production of clothing, paint, and such appliances as refrigerators and stoves.

History. Carib Indians were the first inhabitants of Antigua and Barbuda. In 1493, Christopher Columbus became the first European to reach Antigua. British settlers established a colony on Antigua in 1632. The colony, which later also included Barbuda and Redonda, was called Antigua. The British brought African slaves to the islands to work on sugar cane plantations. The slaves were freed in 1834. Most of the British people eventually left the islands, but Britain retained control of the colony.

In 1967, the colony of Antigua became part of the West Indies Associated States and gained control of its internal affairs. It became the independent nation of Antigua and Barbuda on Nov. 1, 1981. Thomas G. Mathews

J. Alex Langley, DPI

Antigua and Barbuda is a nation in the Caribbean Sea that consists of three islands. Many tourists visit the islands each year to enjoy the beautiful beaches, clear water, and warm, sunny climate.

BELIZE, *beh LEEZ,* is a small country in Central America. It lies on the southeast coast of the Yucatán Peninsula. It borders Guatemala on the west, Mexico on the north, and the Caribbean Sea on the east. Belize covers 8,867 square miles (22,965 square kilometers) and has a population of about 158,000. It ranks as Central America's most thinly populated country. More than half of its people live along the Caribbean coast. Belize City, on the coast, with a population of about 50,000, is the country's largest city. Belmopan, an inland town with only about 4,000 people, is the capital.

Belize became an independent nation in 1981. It had been ruled by Great Britain since the mid-1800's. From the mid-1800's until 1973, it was called *British Honduras.*

Government. Belize is a constitutional monarchy that functions as a parliamentary democracy. It is a member of the Commonwealth of Nations (see COMMONWEALTH OF NATIONS). A prime minister heads the government. The prime minister, with the aid of 12 Cabinet ministers, carries out the operations of the government. A National Assembly, which consists of an 18-member House of Representatives and an 8-member Senate, makes the country's laws.

The people elect the House members. The governor general, who serves as head of state and represents the British monarch, appoints the senators and Cabinet ministers on the advice of the prime minister. The leader of the political party that wins the most seats in the House of Representatives serves as prime minister.

People. Belize has a racially mixed population. About half of its people have full or partial black African ancestry. About a fifth are descended from Carib, Maya, or other Indian groups. *Mestizos,* people of mixed European and Indian ancestry, also account for about a fifth of the population. Most of the rest of the people are of European, East Indian, Chinese, or Lebanese descent.

English is the country's official language. It is also the most widely used language, followed by Spanish. Many people speak both English and Spanish. Some people

Facts in Brief

Capital: Belmopan.

Official Language: English.

Form of Government: Constitutional monarchy.

Area: 8,867 sq. mi. (22,965 km²). *Greatest Distances*—north-south, 180 mi. (290 km); east-west, 85 mi. (137 km). *Coastline*—220 mi. (354 km).

Elevation: *Highest*—Victoria Peak, 3,680 ft. (1,122 m) above sea level. *Lowest*—sea level along the coast.

Population: *Estimated 1983 Population*—158,000; distribution, 62 per cent urban, 38 per cent rural; density, 18 persons per sq. mi. (7 persons per km²). *1980 Census*—144,857. *Estimated 1988 Population*—184,000.

Chief Products: *Agriculture and Forestry*—sugar cane, bananas, grapefruit, oranges, beans, beef cattle, corn, honey, poultry, rice, cedar, mahogany. *Fishing Industry*—crabs, crayfish, groupers, lobsters, mullets, snappers. *Manufacturing and Processing*—clothing, construction materials, processed foods.

National Anthem: "Land of the Free."

Flag: A wide horizontal blue stripe is bordered by narrow horizontal red stripes at the top and bottom. The country's coat of arms appears on the blue stripe. See FLAG (picture: Flags of the Americas).

Money: *Basic Unit*—Belizean dollar.

© Peter Arnold, Inc.

Belize City is the largest city of Belize. The scene above shows part of the city's downtown area.

© Karl Kummels, Shostal

Mahogany Logs from a Belizean forest are loaded onto a truck for transport to a lumber mill. Lumber ranks as a major product in Belize.

speak Maya Indian languages. About half of the people are Roman Catholics. Most of the rest are Protestants. Anglicans form the largest Protestant group.

About 60 per cent of Belize's people live in urban areas, and about 40 per cent live in rural areas. Most Belizeans are poor. Unemployment in the cities and low farm production in rural areas are major problems.

Belizean children between the ages of 6 and 14 must attend school. Belize has four colleges. The country faces shortages of technicians and of professionals, especially doctors. Many Belizeans who learn such occupations move to other English-speaking countries in search of advancement.

Land and Climate. Most of the coastal area of Belize is a swampy lowland. A barrier reef and numerous small islands lie offshore. Inland, in the south, the land rises gradually to the low peaks of the Maya Mountains. This range includes the country's highest point—Victoria Peak—which rises 3,680 feet (1,122 meters) above sea level. Northern Belize is generally flat. The country has much forest land. But large forest areas have been cut down for lumber and other products. The 180-mile (290-kilometer) Belize River, the chief waterway, cuts across the country from west to east.

Belize has a hot, humid climate. Temperatures range from 60° to 90° F. (15.6° to 32° C) along the coast, but are often higher inland. Annual average rainfall measures from 50 inches (130 centimeters) in the north to more than 150 inches (380 centimeters) in the south. From May to February, rain falls almost every day. Hurricanes sometimes strike Belize.

Belize

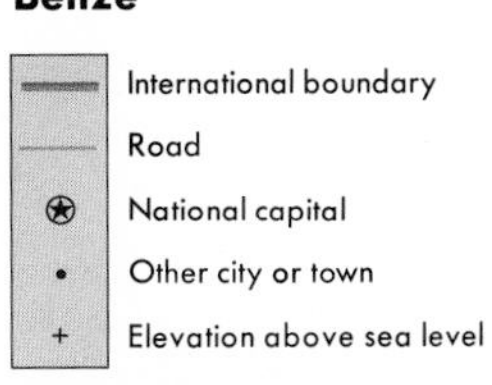

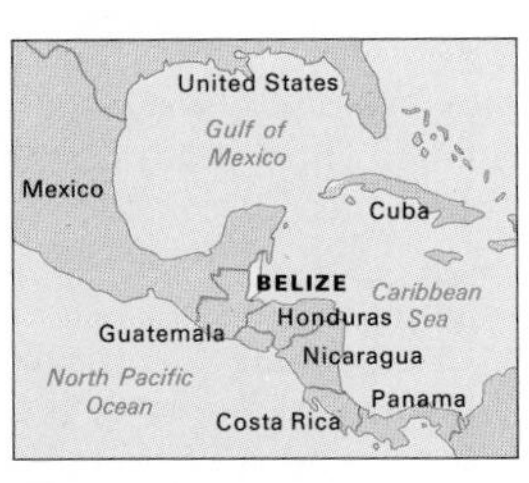

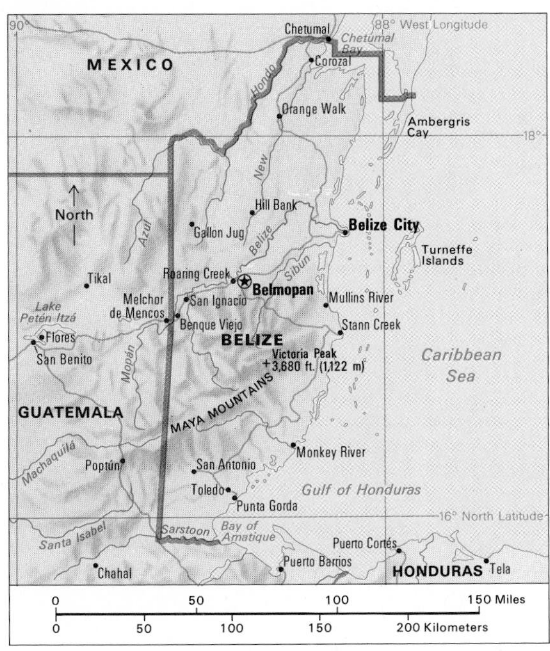

WORLD BOOK map

Economy. Belize is a developing country. Its economy is based on agriculture. Sugar cane, which is raised on plantations, ranks as the country's chief crop and product. Bananas, grapefruits, oranges, and other fruits are also important farm products. Other farm products include beans, beef cattle, corn, honey, poultry, and rice. The country's forests yield lumber, including cedar and mahogany. The Caribbean Sea provides fish and lobsters. Most of Belize's industries are small.

Belize has an international airport and about 1,600 miles (2,600 kilometers) of roads. Belize has one radio station, but no television stations.

History. Between 1500 B.C. and A.D. 300, Maya Indian civilization spread into what is now Belize from the northern part of the Yucatán Peninsula. Maya civilization flourished in the Belize area until about A.D. 1000. Historians know little about life in Belize from that time until the early 1500's, when Spaniards reached the coastal area.

In the 1520's, Spain claimed the Belize area and made it a part of the Captaincy General of Guatemala. In 1638, shipwrecked British sailors established the first known European settlement in Belize. During the next 150 years, the British established several more settlements in the region. Spain did little to exercise its rule, and Britain gradually gained control of it. In 1862, Britain named the area the Colony of British Honduras.

Great Britain made British Honduras a self-governing territory in 1964. George C. Price of the People's United Party became prime minister. In 1973, British Honduras changed its name to Belize. Belize gained independence from Britain on Sept. 21, 1981. Price remained as prime minister. Guatemala had gained independence from Spain in 1821. Since then, it has claimed Belize. Guatemala strongly protested Britain's granting of independence to Belize. NATHAN A. HAVERSTOCK

SAINT CHRISTOPHER-NEVIS, *NEE vihs* or *NEHV uhs*, is an island state in the Caribbean Sea. It is an associated state of Great Britain. As an associated state, St. Christopher-Nevis directs its internal affairs, but Britain handles the state's foreign affairs and defense. St. Christopher-Nevis is composed of two islands. They are St. Christopher (which is commonly called St. Kitts) and Nevis. For the location of St. Christopher-Nevis, see WEST INDIES (map). Basseterre, on St. Christopher, is the capital and largest city.

St. Christopher covers 65 square miles (168 square kilometers) and has a population of 35,104. Nevis has an area of 36 square miles (91 square kilometers) and a population of 9,300. Most of the people of St. Christopher-Nevis are of black African descent. The growing and processing of sugar cane is a major activity on St. Christopher. Most of the people who live on Nevis raise cotton and other crops.

Carib Indians were the first inhabitants of St. Christopher-Nevis. Britain claimed the islands in the early 1600's. In 1882, Britain made St. Christopher, Nevis, and the island of Anguilla a colony. The colony became an associated state of Britain in 1967. Anguilla later became a separate British dependency. THOMAS G. MATHEWS

J. R. Eyerman, Black Star

© David Falconer

Various Types of Fishing Gear and Vessels are used to catch fish. Much of the world's commercial catch is harvested with huge nets like the one being used at the left to haul in tuna. Many fishing vessels, such as the Russian *stern trawler* above, also carry equipment on board to process fish after they have been caught.

FISHING INDUSTRY

FISHING INDUSTRY is an important economic activity that provides food and jobs for millions of people. The fishing industry includes all the activities involved in the commercial and recreational production of fish and shellfish. The catching, processing, marketing, and conservation of fish and shellfish are all parts of the industry. The industry also provides various other products from the sea, such as seaweeds.

Fish are an excellent source of protein, one of the chief *nutrients* (nourishing substances) that people need for a good diet. As the world's population has grown, so has the demand for food—especially food rich in protein. The fishing industry has increased its annual catch to help meet this demand.

The fishing industry markets food fish in a variety of forms. The fish are sold fresh, canned, cured, and frozen. In addition, about a third of the world's fish catch is used to produce high-quality animal feed and various industrial products.

The oceans are by far the main source of fish. Only a small portion of the world's commercial fish catch comes from such inland waters as lakes and rivers. An even smaller portion of the catch comes from *fish farms.* Fish farms are enclosed areas in marine and inland waters where fish are raised commercially for food.

The fishing industry catches many kinds of fish. Such fish as anchovies, capelin, herring, mackerel, sardines, and tuna are caught near the surface of oceans. Such fish as cod, flounder, hake, and pollack are harvested near the ocean floor. Freshwater fish, such as carp, catfish, and whitefish, are caught in inland waters.

Gary D. Stauffer, the contributor of this article, is a Fishery Biologist for the United States National Marine Fisheries Service.

During the late 1970's, the worldwide fish catch totaled more than 78 million short tons (71 million metric tons) annually. Japan is the leading fishing country, followed by Russia, China, Peru, the United States, and Norway. United States fishing fleets harvest about 3.9 million short tons (3.5 million metric tons) yearly. Canada ranks 15th in the world in fish production. Its annual catch totals about 1.4 million short tons (1.3 million metric tons).

The fishing industry employs more than 6 million people worldwide. In the United States, about 193,000 people work on fishing boats and about 103,000 work in fish-processing plants and in other areas of the industry. The Canadian fishing industry employs a total of about 80,000 workers.

People have fished for thousands of years. Through the centuries, they have used hooks, spears, nets, and traps to capture fish. Such equipment is still used, but commercial fishing crews now harvest most of their catch with huge nets. In addition, modern fishing vessels have various devices that make fishing more efficient. For example, advanced navigational aids and fish-finding equipment enable fishing crews to range far from their home ports and to pinpoint schools of fish. Refrigeration systems aboard the vessels help prevent the catch from spoiling. These vessels can remain at sea longer than those without refrigeration.

After World War II ended in 1945, many countries expanded their fishing fleets. These fleets increased their fish catch along their home coasts as well as in distant waters. As a result, the fish harvest generally increased year after year. At the same time, however, overfishing severely reduced the stocks of some kinds of fish. Disputes also arose among countries over the ownership of fish resources. Traditionally, fish have been considered common property—that is, no one owned them until they were caught. The fish then became the property of whoever caught them. After the development of long-range fishing fleets, many nations became concerned with protecting the fish resources along their coasts from fleets of other countries. As a result, a number of international commissions were formed to promote fish conservation and to help settle disputes over fishing rights.

During the 1970's, almost all nations bordering the sea established *fishery conservation zones* in further efforts to conserve and protect their fish resources. These zones extend 200 nautical miles (370 kilometers) from a nation's coast. Countries that have adopted such zones claim authority over all fishing—and ownership of all fish—within the zones.

Where Fish Are Caught

Areas where fish are caught commercially or recreationally are called *fisheries*. The term is also used for the act of harvesting fish. In many cases, more than one species of fish is harvested from a particular fishery. A fishery may be a small lake. Or it may extend across an enormous section of an ocean. For example, the tuna fishery that lies off the west coast of Central and South America covers about 5 million square miles (13 million square kilometers).

Ocean Fisheries provide most of the world's commercial fish catch. About 70 million short tons (64 million metric tons) of fish—or about 89 per cent of the total world harvest—is taken from the oceans annually. This figure includes the production from marine fish farms. Almost all the ocean catch comes from waters near seacoasts, especially the shallow waters over the *continental shelf*. The continental shelf consists of submerged land along the coasts of the continents. In some places, the shelf extends great distances out into the ocean.

A large amount of the fish caught in waters over the continental shelf is taken from regions of *upwelling*. Upwelling occurs during certain seasons when winds blow surface waters near the coast offshore. The colder bottom waters, which are rich in nutrients, then rise to the

Worldwide Fish and Shellfish Catch

Chief Kinds	Annual Catch	
	In short tons	In metric tons
Sardine and pilchard	8,850,000	8,029,000
Pollack	4,863,000	4,412,000
Mackerel	3,994,000	3,623,000
Cod	3,606,000	3,271,000
Anchovy and anchovetta	3,352,000	3,041,000
Smelt	3,288,000	2,983,000
Jack mackerel	2,875,000	2,608,000
Tuna	1,888,000	1,713,000
Shrimp and prawn	1,682,000	1,526,000
Hake	1,617,000	1,467,000
Menhaden	1,312,000	1,190,000
Squid	1,207,000	1,094,000
Clam	1,195,000	1,084,000
Herring	1,139,000	1,033,000
Oyster	962,000	873,000
Crab	908,000	824,000
Shad	892,000	809,000
Sandeel	817,000	741,000
Sprat	729,000	661,000
Salmon	689,000	625,000

Figures are for 1979.
Source: *Yearbook of Fishery Statistics, 1979*, FAO.

Chief Commercial Fishing Areas This map shows the world's major commercial fishing areas. Most lie along the *continental shelf*, the submerged land around the continents. Inland fishing areas include rivers and lakes. The map also shows the chief fish and shellfish, with the most valuable catches in boldface type.

WORLD BOOK map

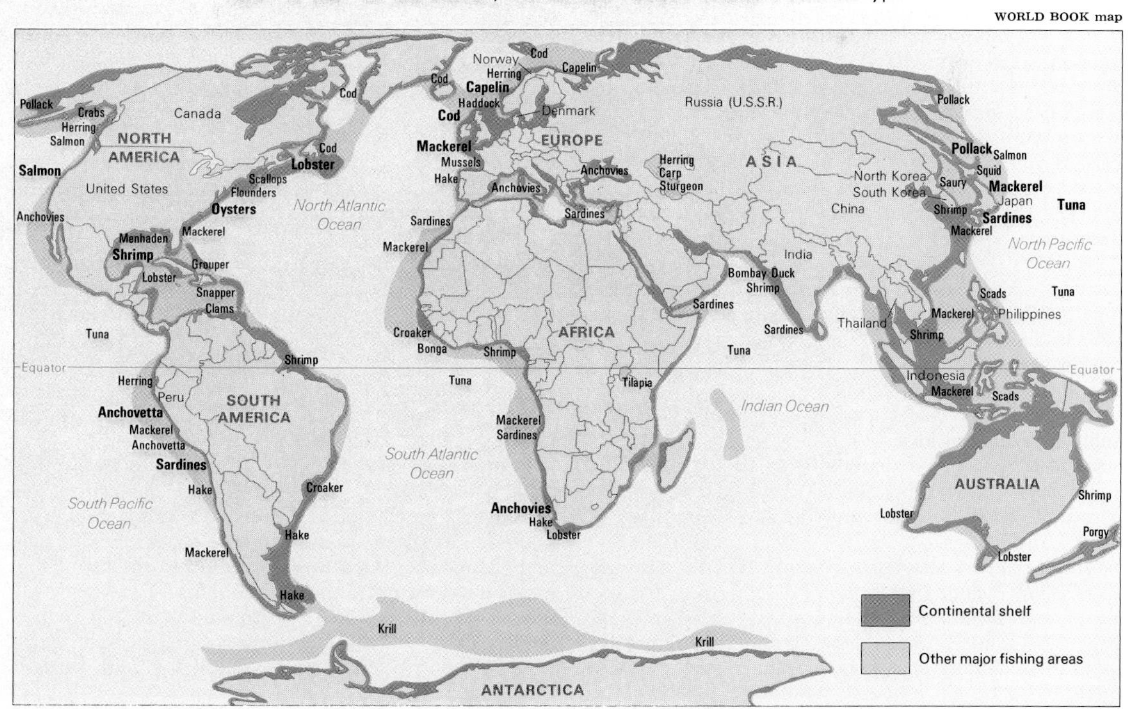

Leading Fishing States and Provinces
Tons of fish and shellfish caught each year

Louisiana	712,000 short tons (646,000 metric tons)
Alaska	527,000 short tons (478,000 metric tons)
Newfoundland	513,000 short tons (465,000 metric tons)
Nova Scotia	481,000 short tons (437,000 metric tons)
California	402,000 short tons (365,000 metric tons)
Virginia	319,000 short tons (289,000 metric tons)
Massachusetts	219,000 short tons (199,000 metric tons)
North Carolina	178,000 short tons (161,000 metric tons)
Mississippi	169,000 short tons (153,000 metric tons)
British Columbia	143,000 short tons (130,000 metric tons)

Sources: National Marine Fisheries Service; Statistics Canada. Figures are for 1980.

Leading Fishing Countries
Tons of fish and shellfish caught each year

Japan	10,986,000 short tons (9,966,000 metric tons)
Russia	10,046,000 short tons (9,114,000 metric tons)
China	4,469,000 short tons (4,054,000 metric tons)
Peru	4,059,000 short tons (3,682,000 metric tons)
United States	3,870,000 short tons (3,511,000 metric tons)
Norway	2,923,000 short tons (2,652,000 metric tons)
Chile	2,902,000 short tons (2,633,000 metric tons)
India	2,583,000 short tons (2,343,000 metric tons)
South Korea	2,383,000 short tons (2,162,000 metric tons)
Denmark	1,916,000 short tons (1,738,000 metric tons)

Source: *Yearbook of Fishery Statistics, 1979,* FAO. Figures are for 1979.

surface near the coast. This upwelling of bottom waters provides nutrients for the growth of microscopic plants and animals that fish feed on, thus promoting growth of the fish population. Upwelling occurs chiefly along the coasts of Peru, California, northwest and southwest Africa, Somalia, the Arabian Peninsula, and Antarctica.

Atlantic Ocean Fisheries. The major U.S. and Canadian fisheries in the Atlantic include the coastal waters from Newfoundland to New England and the *Grand Banks.* The Grand Banks is a stretch of shallow waters southeast of Newfoundland. The Grand Banks and the other waters of the northwest Atlantic rank among the best fishing grounds in the world. The area provides great quantities of cod and herring, as well as flounder, lobsters, and scallops.

Cod is the chief catch of the Canadian fishing industry. The nation's fishing crews harvest about 395,000 short tons (358,000 metric tons) of cod yearly in the northwest Atlantic. The area provides the U.S. fishing industry with an annual cod catch of about 49,000 short tons (44,000 metric tons). Canada also harvests about 159,000 short tons (144,000 metric tons) of herring from the northwest Atlantic each year. It leads the world in the production of Atlantic herring.

The Gulf of Mexico, an arm of the Atlantic Ocean, is another productive area for the U.S. fishing industry. It ranks as the nation's main menhaden fishery, providing about 890,000 short tons (807,000 metric tons) yearly. The Gulf of Mexico also provides large quantities of shrimp and lobsters.

The Atlantic Ocean has several other rich fishing areas. They include the northeast Atlantic near Iceland and Great Britain and the southwest Atlantic near Argentina and Brazil. Crews from a number of nations—including the Soviet Union, Norway, Denmark, Great Britain, and Iceland—fish the waters of the northeast Atlantic. They catch herring, capelin, cod, haddock, mackerel, and many other types of fish. The chief fish caught in the southwest Atlantic include croaker, hake, and sardines.

Pacific Ocean Fisheries. The major U.S. and Canadian fisheries in the Pacific include the Bering Sea, the Gulf of Alaska, and the waters off the coast of California. The chief fish caught in the Bering Sea, the Gulf of Alaska, and other areas of the North Pacific include pollack, salmon, hake, and sole. The United States is the leading salmon-fishing country. It catches about 155,000 short tons (140,000 metric tons) yearly. Canada is also a major salmon-fishing country, ranking behind the United States, Japan, and Russia. It harvests about 65,000 short tons (59,000 metric tons) a year. The waters off the California coast and to the immediate south are harvested for such fish as anchovies, herring, mackerel, and tuna.

The Pacific Ocean also has a number of other productive fisheries. They include the waters of the southeast Pacific off the coast of South America and the coastal seas of the western Pacific from Indonesia to Japan. The fisheries off the west coast of South America provide anchovettas, anchovies, hake, mackerel, and sardines. The coastal seas from Indonesia to Japan are fished for anchovies, mackerel, sardines, scads, shrimp, and tuna.

Inland Fisheries. About 8.3 million short tons (7.5 million metric tons) of fish—or about 11 per cent of the commercial catch worldwide—is harvested yearly from ponds, lakes, rivers, streams, and fish farms in inland waters. China and India lead the world in the fish catch from inland waters. China's annual freshwater catch totals about 1.2 million short tons (1.1 million metric tons). India's catch totals about 935,000 short tons (848,000 metric tons). Both countries chiefly harvest carp, tilapia, and other plant-eating fish.

The Soviet Union ranks third in the production of freshwater fish with an annual catch of about 888,000 short tons (805,000 metric tons). The Caspian Sea provides much of the nation's harvest of fish from inland waters. The main species caught in the Caspian Sea are bream, carp, salmon, and sturgeon. In addition, the rivers that flow into the Caspian yield most of the annual Soviet harvest of sturgeon. The Soviet Union produces about 28,000 short tons (25,000 metric tons) of sturgeon a year, or about 89 per cent of the world total.

The U.S. fishing industry produces about 72,000 short tons (65,000 metric tons) of fish from inland waters yearly. The major freshwater fisheries of the United States include the inland waters of the Southern States and the Great Lakes. The inland waters of the South provide buffalo fish, carp, and catfish. Most of the world's harvest of crayfish comes from Louisiana, which produces more than 10,000 short tons (9,000 metric tons) a year. The Great Lakes are fished chiefly for alewives, whitefish, smelt, and carp.

Canada harvests about 54,000 short tons (49,000 metric tons) of freshwater fish annually. The chief fish caught include alewives, northern pike, smelt, whitefish, and yellow perch. The Great Lakes are the center of the freshwater fishing industry in Canada.

Fish Farms account for about 7 per cent of the world's annual commercial fish harvest. Each year, they produce about 5.3 million short tons (4.8 million metric tons) of fish, shellfish, and *aquatic plants* (plants that live in water). Fish farming is also called *aquaculture*.

Fish farms range from simple ponds or flooded rice fields to highly engineered hatcheries in which the environment is almost completely controlled. Fish farmers try to eliminate harmful environmental conditions so fish can flourish. They provide fish with proper nutrients and protect them from animals that prey on them. Aquaculture is commonly used to rebuild salmon and trout stocks that have been severely reduced.

The chief fish raised on fish farms throughout the world include carp, catfish, gourami, milkfish, salmon, tilapia, and trout. China leads all countries in aquaculture production. It has an annual harvest of about 2.8 million short tons (2.5 million metric tons), or almost 50 per cent of the world total.

The main fish and shellfish raised on fish farms in the United States include catfish, crayfish, oysters, salmon, and trout. The nation's fish farms produce about 150,000 short tons (136,000 metric tons) of fish, shellfish, and aquatic plants yearly. Canadian fish farms raise chiefly salmon, trout, and oysters. Canada's aquaculture production totals about 6,200 short tons (5,600 metric tons) annually.

How Fish Are Caught

Fishing vessels vary greatly in size and in the number of crew members they carry. Vessels in coastal fishing fleets are 25 to 130 feet (8 to 40 meters) long. Their crews consist of as many as 20 to 25 people or as few as 1 or 2, depending on the fishing method being used. Coastal vessels can remain at sea for several days or weeks. The fish catch is stored in holds chilled by either ice or refrigeration systems.

Long-range fishing fleets stay at sea for months at a time and travel great distances from their home ports. Many modern fleets, particularly Russian fleets, include *processing-catcher vessels*, as well as processors, refrigerated transporters, and supply ships. Processing-catcher vessels, which measure about 260 feet (80 meters) in length, are used for both catching fish and processing the harvest into various products. Their crews have from 50 to 100 members and in most cases include a number of women.

Fishing crews use a variety of gear to catch fish. The equipment used depends on the behavior of the fish being sought and the nature of the fishing grounds. The chief types of gear include (1) nets, (2) hooks, (3) traps, and (4) harpoons.

Nets. Most of the world's commercial fish catch is taken in by huge nets. There are three main types of nets: (1) seines, (2) trawls, and (3) gill nets.

Seines (pronounced *saynz*) account for more than a third of the world's fish catch. Over half the U.S. harvest and about a seventh of the Canadian landings are hauled in with this type of net. Fishing crews use seines chiefly to catch anchovies, capelin, herring, mackerel, menhaden, sardines, tuna, and other *pelagic* schooling fish. Pelagic fish swim near the surface of the water.

The most widely used seine is the rectangular *purse*

Michael Friedel

Fish Farmers raise fish in lakes, ponds, reservoirs, and similar bodies of water. The farmers help fish flourish by supplying them with nourishing foods and by protecting them from harmful environmental conditions. The men at the left are harvesting milkfish from a huge fish farm in Laguna de Bay, a lake in the Philippines.

seine. Purse seines range from about 660 to 6,600 feet (200 to 2,000 meters) in length. They have floats along the top. Weights and rings are attached along the bottom edge. A rope or cable called a *purse line* runs through the rings.

A purse seine is set into the water from a large vessel called a *seiner* with the aid of a small, high-powered boat called a *skiff*. After a school of fish is spotted, the skiff is launched from the seiner with one end of the net attached. The seiner speeds ahead, encircling the school and playing out the net as it goes. The bottom of the seine is then closed off with the purse line, capturing the school. Seiners vary from about 30 to 230 feet (10 to 70 meters) in length and carry crews of 12 to 20 people.

Trawls are funnel-shaped nets that are closed off at the bottom end, where the fish collect, and open at the mouth. The most commonly used trawl is the *otter trawl*. The net has floats along the top edge of the mouth and weights on the bottom end. The net is attached by two long towing cables to the back of a vessel called a

© David Falconer

A Large Japanese *Factory Ship*, *above,* processes fish caught off the Aleutian Islands. Such ships are an important part of many fishing fleets that range far from their home ports.

C. C. Lockwood, Earth Scenes

Small U.S. Shrimp Boats, *above,* drag nets over the sea bottom to harvest shrimp. The catch is quickly frozen or canned on the boats or onshore to prevent it from spoiling.

Common Types of Fishing Nets

WORLD BOOK illustrations by Bill and Judie Anderson

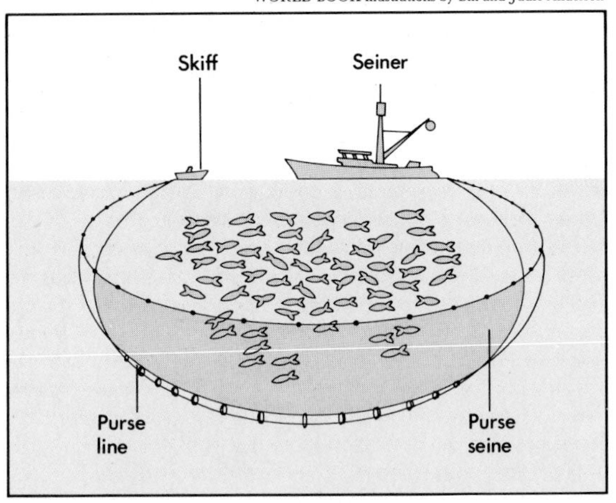

A Purse Seine is set from a vessel called a *seiner* by a *skiff* (small boat). Fish are caught by surrounding them with the net and then closing off its bottom with a rope or cable called a *purse line.*

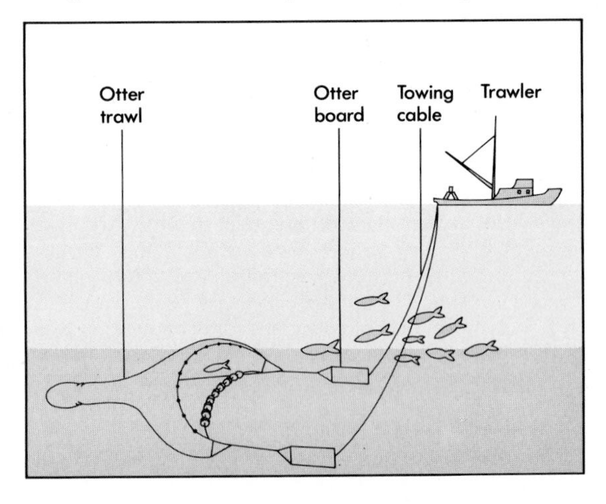

An Otter Trawl is towed by a vessel called a *trawler* or *stern trawler.* The towing causes two doorlike *otter boards* near the mouth of the net to hold the net open to capture fish.

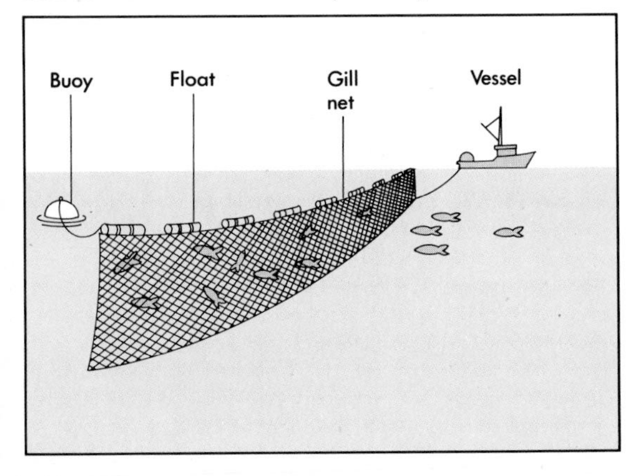

A Gill Net forms a wall of webbing that entangles fish when they swim into it. The size of the open spaces of gill nets varies according to the type of fish being sought.

stern trawler or *trawler*. A large doorlike *otter board* is attached to each towing cable near the open end of the net. As the trawler tows the net, the water forces the otter boards to spread apart, holding the net open to capture the fish. The mouth of some otter trawls can be spread to a width of 120 feet (37 meters).

Trawls are used to catch cod, flounder, hake, pollack, red snapper, scallops, shrimp, and other fish and shellfish that live on or near the ocean floor. Most trawling is done over the continental shelf in waters less than 660 feet (200 meters) deep. However, some stern trawlers fish in waters as deep as 3,300 feet (1,000 meters). Trawlers use sonar and other advanced equipment to locate concentrations of fish (see SONAR). A small trawler needs only a four-member crew. Most trawlers more than 150 feet (45 meters) long carry processing equipment. Such trawlers require larger crews.

Trawling accounts for about a third of the world's fish harvest. Trawls haul in about 20 per cent of the U.S. fish catch and about 35 per cent of Canada's catch. The otter trawl is the chief fishing gear of the distant-water fleets of European and Asian nations.

Gill Nets are long rectangular nets with floats on top and weights on the bottom. They range from 50 to 1,200 feet (15 to 370 meters) in length. The nets are hung in the water near the surface or close to the ocean floor. A gill net is made of thin twine and is nearly invisible in the water. The net is set in the path of migrating fish and forms a wall of webbing that entangles fish when they swim into it. The open spaces of a gill net allow fish to thrust only their heads into the net. The entangled fish try to swim through the net, thrashing about and becoming more entangled.

Gill nets are used to catch billfish, herring, salmon, sharks, and a number of bottom fish. However, all these fish can also be caught with other types of gear. As a result, the total catch with gill nets makes up less than 5 per cent of the world harvest. Only about $4\frac{1}{2}$ per cent of the U.S. and 17 per cent of the Canadian fish catch are brought in with gill nets. Most vessels equipped with such nets measure less than 50 feet (15 meters) long and have crews of one or two people.

Hooks take advantage of the feeding behavior of fish. Bait or lures attached to a hook tempt fish to bite the hook. Hooks account for only a small percentage of the world's fish catch. The most common hooking methods used by commercial fishing crews are (1) bait fishing, (2) trolling, and (3) long-lining.

Bait Fishing. In bait fishing, after a school of fish is sighted, the crew throws live bait or ground-up fish into the water from the fishing boat. The bait attracts schools of tuna or other species that feed on smaller fish to the surface near the boat. As the fish feed greedily on the bait, the crew uses bare hooks and lines to haul them in. Most bait boats have a walkway around the stern from which a crew of as many as 20 people pull in the fish.

Trolling involves towing as many as six fishing lines from two long poles. One pole extends from each side of a vessel. In many cases, metal flashers or feather lures are attached to the lines to attract fish.

A large fleet of *trollers* (trolling vessels) fishes for albacore and salmon off the coasts of British Columbia and the Western United States. Billfish and tuna are also caught by trolling. Most trollers have crews of only two people.

Common Methods of Hooking and Trapping

Honolulu Laboratory, Southwest Fisheries Center, National Marine Fisheries Service

Bait Fishing involves throwing bait into the water to attract fish. As the fish feed greedily on the bait, crew members on a walkway around the stern can use bare hooks to haul them in.

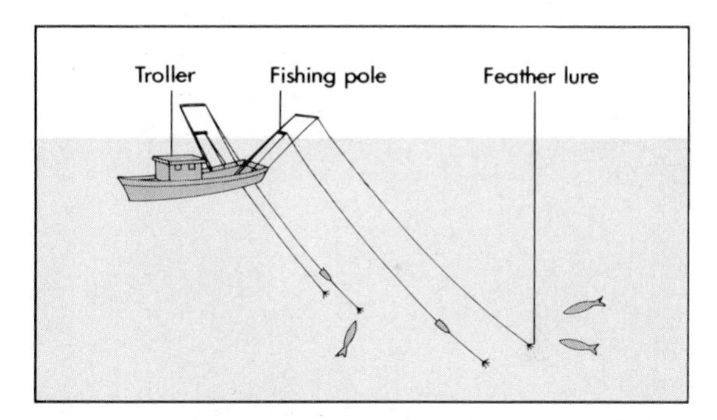

Trolling involves towing fishing lines from poles that extend from the sides of a *troller* (trolling vessel). Feather lures are often attached to the ends of the lines to attract fish.

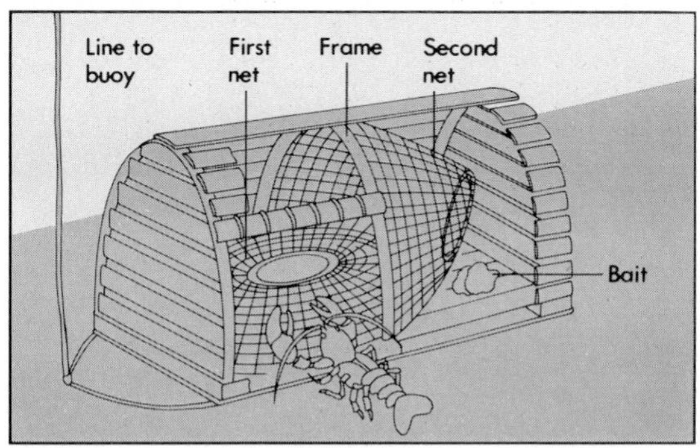

WORLD BOOK illustrations by Bill and Judie Anderson

Trapping is often used to catch lobsters and other shellfish. Traps are designed so that once a fish or shellfish reaches the bait, it has little chance of escaping.

Long-Lining involves using an extremely long *main line* with attached short *dropper lines*. The main line may be stretched across the surface of the water to catch such pelagic fish as billfish, sharks, and tuna or near the ocean floor to catch such bottom fish as cod and halibut. As many as 2,000 dropper lines with baited hooks hang from the main line. Some pelagic lines may be as long as 50 nautical miles (93 kilometers). Bottom long-lines are much shorter. A small long-line vessel needs a crew of only 3 or 4 persons. Large Japanese tuna vessels carry crews of 20 to 45.

Traps depend on the migratory or feeding habits of fish. Most traps contain bait or lures to attract fish into the devices. Only a small fraction of the worldwide fish harvest is taken by means of traps.

A fish trap has an entry consisting of a funnellike tunnel or ramp. This entry directs fish through a small opening in the side of the trap. After fish are inside the trap, they have little chance of finding the opening again and escaping.

Small, baited, boxlike traps are used chiefly to capture shellfish, such as crabs, lobsters, shrimp, and crayfish. These traps are placed on the bottom of the ocean or a lake or stream. Larger, stationary traps are floated near shore in the path of migrating fish. These traps are anchored in place or fastened to wooden pilings driven into the seabed. They are used mainly to catch herring and salmon.

Harpoons are barbed spears connected by a rope to a vessel or large float. They may be shot from a cannon or hurled by a crew member. Harpoons are used mainly to kill whales. For more information on whaling and the use of harpoons, see WHALE (Modern Whaling).

How Fish Are Processed and Marketed

Methods of Processing. The quality of fish declines rapidly after they die. Bacteria that can cause spoilage immediately begin to attack the fish, and enzymes start to break down the protein in fish tissues. As a result, a number of processing methods have been developed over the years to keep fish from spoiling.

Drying, Salt Curing, and Smoking have been used to process fish for thousands of years. All three methods reduce the moisture content of fish and thus slow the growth of bacteria and the breakdown of protein.

Drying fish in the open air for six weeks or more removes most of the water from them. Drying is generally used along with salt curing or smoking.

In salt curing, processors first cut open the fish and remove the head and backbone. They then cover the fish with salt, which draws out the moisture and produces a salty solution called *brine*. Next, the fish are *dry-salted* or *pickled*. In dry-salting, the brine is drained off and the fish are hung up to dry. In pickling, the fish are stored in the brine.

To smoke fish, processors first cut up the fish and soak them in brine. They then place the fish in a large oven, where smoke and heat from smoldering wood chips dries the fish. Processors use this method chiefly to improve the flavor of fish.

© David Falconer

Processing Fish Aboard Ship helps prevent them from spoiling. The man at the left is cleaning and cutting up fish on a Japanese factory ship shortly after they were caught. The fish are then quickly frozen and stored in freezer compartments, *right*.

Ted Spiegel, Black Star

Onshore Processing of Fish is done in fishing ports. These workers at a plant in Prince Rupert, Canada, are preparing deboned, meal-sized portions of fish for shipment to inland markets.

Canning involves sealing cut up fish in metal or glass containers and then cooking the contents under pressure. The high temperature and pressure kill bacteria and halt protein breakdown.

Freezing also prevents the growth of bacteria and protein breakdown. The quickly frozen fish are packaged in airtight wrappers or covered with a thin layer of ice. They are stored at −20°F. (−29°C) or lower. Much of the catch of such fish as cod and flounder is *filleted* (deboned) and frozen. Often, the individual fillets are frozen together in large blocks of fish. These blocks may then be made into fish sticks and meal-sized portions of breaded fish.

Other Processing Methods are used to produce meal and oil from fish. These industrial products are made from such species as anchovies, capelin, herring, menhaden, and sardines. To produce fish meal and fish oil, processors first cook the fish with steam. They then squeeze out most of the water and oil. The remaining solid material is dried and ground into meal. Fish oil is obtained by separating the oil from the water in a whirling device called a *centrifuge*.

Fish meal is added to livestock feed and dry pet food. It is also fed to trout and salmon raised in hatcheries. Manufacturers use fish oil to make a number of products. The most important are glue, paint, lubricants, and ink.

Marketing. Fresh fish may be sold daily in fishing ports located near fishing areas. However, fish and fish products to be sold in distant markets must first be processed to prevent spoilage.

Most fish processors operate in fishing ports. Many fishing crews sell their catches to processors at auctions after fishing trips. The price a catch commands depends on the supply of fish at the market and the demand for it. A fishing crew does not know in advance what a harvest will earn—if it is sold at all. The uncertainty of the auction market has led some fishing crews to form *marketing cooperatives*. Cooperatives enable their members to know, before they leave port, how much fish to catch and how much the harvest will earn. Processors place orders with the cooperative for a specific quantity of fish before a fishing trip. At the same time, both sides agree on the price to be paid for the catch.

Processors sell most of their fish products to fish brokers in large cities. The brokers, in turn, sell the products to restaurants and food stores.

Fishery Conservation

Countless fish die of natural causes or are eaten by animals that prey on them. Nevertheless, a rich fishery will continue to support good catches as long as the stock can produce large numbers of young annually. Problems arise chiefly as a result of overfishing and the polluting of the waters in which the fish live. Fishery conservation seeks to control the human activities that can severely reduce a fish stock.

Government Regulation. Most major fishing nations have laws to conserve and protect their fish resources. The United States, Canada, and almost all other nations that border the sea have established authority over fishery conservation zones extending 200 nautical miles (370 kilometers) from their shores. These zones are intended to protect the nations' coastal fishing industries by controlling the harvest of fleets of other countries. They also enable the nations to pass conservation laws affecting the areas.

The Magnuson Fishery Conservation and Management Act of 1976 established the 200-mile fishery conservation zone off the shores of the United States. Since the passage of this act, various regulations have been adopted to conserve fish within the zone. Some regulations set quotas that limit the total catch of certain species in a fishery and in a few cases limit the number of fishing vessels permitted in an area. Other regulations restrict the areas and the time of year in which crews may fish. The size and type of fishing gear that may be used in a fishery are also regulated.

Water pollution controls also aid in fishery conservation. Such controls limit the amount of harmful materials that may be released into inland and coastal waters. These materials can kill fish or the plants and animals on which fish feed.

International Commissions and Treaties. Through the years, fishing nations have agreed to work together in managing fishery resources in international waters. A number of commissions have been established to protect a particular species of fish or all species in a certain area. For example, the International Pacific Halibut Commission helps regulate halibut fishing off the west coasts of Canada and the United States. The International North Pacific Fisheries Commission promotes the conservation of all fish species in the North Pacific Ocean.

Most international commissions devoted to fishery conservation operate in a similar manner. Scientists from the member nations or from the organization itself gather statistics on the size of the catch and conduct other research regarding a particular fishery or species of fish. The commissions meet annually to review the results of these studies and to recommend ways of managing fishery resources. Each member nation then has the responsibility of passing and enforcing laws based on the recommendations.

Many nations also make *bilateral treaties* to manage fishery resources in international waters. Under such treaties, two nations agree to meet periodically to exchange information on fisheries of interest to both countries and to discuss conservation measures.

Scientific Research involves many activities to improve the harvest of the world's fishery resources. Researchers determine the maximum number of fish that can be harvested annually without severely damaging the stock. Researchers often rely on records of the harvest in a fishery to check changes in the abundance of stocks from year to year. By analyzing these records, the researchers can judge whether fishing should be increased or decreased.

Scientists study the effects of the environment on changes in fish abundance and the effects of fishing on other species. Most fish feed on other fish. Dolphins, seals, and marine birds also prey on fish. Overfishing of prey species, such as anchovies, herring, and sardines, reduces the food supply of predator species. However, overfishing of predator species, such as cod, salmon, and tuna, increases the supply of prey species.

Some researchers work to increase the rates of survival and growth of fish. Such research especially helps fish farmers. Commercially raised fish have greatly increased fish resources, chiefly in Asia and Europe. In addition, some researchers are studying unharvested types of fish to develop new products and markets. Such efforts seek to both increase the world's food supply and promote fish conservation. Through the development of new fish resources, the world's total catch can remain constant—or even be increased—without overfishing individual stocks.

GARY D. STAUFFER

Michael Friedel

Scientific Research can help fish farmers. This West German researcher is seeking to make carp grow faster by feeding them a high-protein diet and raising the water temperature in the tank.

Related Articles in WORLD BOOK. Many articles on countries, states, and provinces have a section on fishing industry. See, for example, JAPAN (Fishing Industry); ALABAMA (Fishing Industry). See also:

SOME FOOD FISHES

Anchovy	Haddock	Pompano	Sprat
Bass	Hake	Redfish	Sturgeon
Carp	Halibut	Rosefish	Swordfish
Catfish	Herring	Salmon	Trout
Cod	Mackerel	Sardine	Tuna
Dogfish	Menhaden	Shad	Turbot
Drum	Mullet	Smelt	Weakfish
Flounder	Perch	Snapper	Whitefish
Grouper	Pollack	Sole	

OTHER SEAFOODS

Abalone	Crayfish	Oyster	Shrimp
Clam	Lobster	Scallop	Squid
Crab	Mussel		

OTHER RELATED ARTICLES

Aquaculture	Food Preservation	Net
Cormorant	Grand Banks	Pearl
Fish	Gulf Stream	Sponge
Fishing	Krill	Whale

Outline

I. Where Fish Are Caught
A. Ocean Fisheries
B. Inland Fisheries
C. Fish Farms

II. How Fish Are Caught
A. Nets
B. Hooks
C. Traps
D. Harpoons

III. How Fish Are Processed and Marketed
A. Methods of Processing
B. Marketing

IV. Fishery Conservation
A. Government Regulation
B. International Commissions and Treaties
C. Scientific Research

Questions

What types of fisheries provide most of the world's commercial fish catch?

Why are fish a valuable food?

What is upwelling? How does it help the fish population in an area grow?

How does the marketing cooperative method of selling a fish catch differ from the auction method?

What are fish farms?

Which are the world's leading fishing countries?

What is a purse seine? How does it work?

How may overfishing of one species of fish affect the populations of other species?

What are fish meal and fish oil? What are they used for?

How do fishery conservation zones aid in fish conservation?

Additional Resources

BELL, FREDERICK W. *Food from the Sea: The Economics and Politics of Ocean Fisheries.* Westview, 1978.

EVERHART, W. HARRY, and others. *Principles of Fishery Science.* 2nd ed. Cornell Univ. Press, 1981.

GULLAND, J. A., ed. *The Fish Resources of the Ocean.* Fishing News (Books) Ltd., 1971. Pub. by arrangement with the UN Food and Agriculture Organization.

IDYLL, C. P. *The Sea Against Hunger.* Rev. ed. Crowell, 1978.

MELTZER, MICHAEL. *The World of the Small Commercial Fishermen: Their Lives and Their Boats.* Dover, 1980.

ROTHSCHILD, BRIAN J., ed. *World Fisheries Policy: Multidisciplinary Views.* Univ. of Washington Press, 1972.

Dictionary Supplement

1978
1979
1980
1981
1982

This section lists important words from the 1983 edition of THE WORLD BOOK DICTIONARY. This dictionary, first published in 1963, keeps abreast of our living language with a program of continuous editorial revision. The following supplement has been prepared under the direction of the editors of THE WORLD BOOK ENCYCLOPEDIA and Clarence L. Barnhart, editor in chief of THE WORLD BOOK DICTIONARY. It is presented as a service to owners of the dictionary and as an informative feature to subscribers to THE WORLD BOOK YEAR BOOK.

A a

ac|cess (*n.* ak′ses; *v.* ak′səs, ak ses′), *n., v.* **—*v.t.* 1** to obtain access to; reach: *The pallets run ... in open, parallel passageways, which can only be accessed from each end* (New Scientist). **2** to retrieve (data) from a computer.

accretion disk or **disc**, *Astronomy.* a disk-shaped formation of gases or other interstellar matter around a black hole, neutron star, or other celestial body: *This formation, called an accretion disk, may be very important in some stellar birth sequences. In our own solar system ... the planets and asteroids formed from the accretion disk as the sun grew in the embryo core* (Stephen P. Maran).

action level, the level of concentration at which a toxic or other unwanted substance in a food or other product is considered hazardous enough to public health to warrant government action: *In Washington, a spokesman for the Food and Drug Administration said that last May the agency established an "action level" of 0.1 part per million for Mirex in fish. Fish containing that level or more will be seized if shipped in interstate commerce* (New York Times).

address, *v.t.* **11** to provide or gain access to (the location of stored information) in a computer: *The hardware is amazingly cheap—and the size of control task is limited only by the amount of memory which can be addressed (a 10 bit address handles 1024 program steps)* (New Scientist).

Am|es|lan (am′əs lan), *n.* = American Sign Language: *Among the sign languages, the deaf in the United States use two principal means of communication, Ameslan and finger-spelling* (Eugene Linden).

anabolic steroid, any of a group of synthetic hormones that increase the size and strength of muscles, often used by athletes during training: *Earlier in the year the IOC [International Olympic Committee] added anabolic steroids, the so-called body-building drugs, to the list of prohibited substances at the Olympic Games* (D. K. R. Phillips).

ap|ple-pie (ap′əl pī′), *adj.* having or showing traditional American values and traits: *[He] trades frankly on the appeal of his Horatio Alger career and apple-pie patriotism* (Time). *The three California women ... were apple-pie sorority sisters at Berkeley who were more or less radicalized by the spirit of the times* (New Yorker). [< the notion that apple pie is a typical old-fashioned American food]

as|par|tame (as par′tām), *n.* an artificial sweetener, several hundred times sweeter than sugar, obtained from aspartic acid and used as a substitute for sugar or saccharin. *Formula:* $C_{14}H_{18}N_2O_5$

au|to|fo|cus (ô′tə fō′kəs), *adj., n., v. Photography.* **—*adj.*** that can focus automatically: *autofocus cameras.*
—*n.* automatic focusing of a camera lens: *Autofocus ... allows you to concentrate more completely on taking pictures because you're less distracted by setting the lens* (Lou Jacobs, Jr.).
—*v.i., v.t.* to focus automatically.

B b

back-of-the-en|ve|lope (bak′əv ᴛʜə en′və lōp, -än′-), *adj.* quickly and easily determined; not requiring elaborate calculations: *A simple back-of-the-envelope sum illustrates the problem* (New Scientist).

Bahasa Ma|lay|sia (mə lā′zhə, -shə), the official language of Malaysia, an adaptation of Malay.

bankable, *adj.* **2** certain to produce box-office success and profits: *[He] has become a "bankable" superstar, whose commitment to a project means that a film will be made and will be guaranteed a certain success* (New York Times Magazine).

bec|que|rel (bek′ə rel′, bek rel′), *n.* the international unit of radioactivity, equal to one disintegration per second. It is intended to replace the curie. *Among the SI's [Système International] derived units with special names are those for ... radioactivity (the becquerel, or spontaneous nuclear transitions per second) and absorbed dose of radiation (the gray, or joules per kilogram)* (Scientific American). [< Antoine H. *Becquerel,* 1852-1908, a French physicist]

bench scientist, a scientist who works in a laboratory; research scientist: *There is no longer any talk of 'wasting your education' or 'prostituting your science' if you prefer not to be a bench scientist* (Science Journal).

best boy, the assistant of the lighting supervisor on a motion-picture or television set; gaffer's assistant.

be|ta-block|ing (bā′tə blok′ing, bē′-), *adj.* of or designating a drug that relieves stress on the heart by preventing absorption of adrenalin in the heart cells and blood vessels.

bi|di|a|lec|tal (bī dī′ə lek′təl), *adj.* using or able to use two dialects of a language: *The public schools continue to vacillate between the old line, "Talk American, boy, American," and the more cosmopolitan line, "Are our er um Black students ahh bilingual or um bidialectal?"* (New York Times Book Review).

bionic, *adj.* **2** consisting of electronic or mechanical parts that enhance anatomical structures to produce extraordinary powers: *The Steve Austin doll ... has a "bionic grip" that can be closed to grasp a girder (supplied with the doll)* (Consumer Reports). **3** *Figurative.* having extraordinary ability: *His awed colleagues in the federal Liberal caucus call Jamieson "the bionic mouth" in tribute to his oratorial skills* (Maclean's).
—bi|on′i|cal|ly, *adv.*

C c

CAD (no periods), computer-aided design.

cal|zone (kal zō′nē, kal zōn′), *n.* a dome-shaped baked pie filled usually with cheese: *I went partway down into the valley and stopped at a pizzeria called the Capri, where I had a calzone* (Alex Shoumatoff). [< Italian]

camel's nose, *U.S.* a small part of something large, especially something difficult or unpleasant to deal with: *Even this amount ... represents merely the camel's nose of the modernization program planned* (Scientific American).

card¹, **play the ______ card**, to use a (specified) tactic to gain an advantage: *He plays the human rights card by noting that violators such as Argentina ... and Ethiopia were recipients of some $600 millions* (Manchester Guardian Weekly).

chip¹, *n.* **4b** = bargaining chip: *The President could have used the need for grain as a chip in the ongoing SALT negotiations* (Maclean's).

choke point, or **choke|point** (chōk′point′), *n.* a narrow route or passageway, especially at sea: *The Soviet access to the open seas passes through a number of choke points (such as the Bosphorus, Gibraltar, and the Greenland-Iceland-United Kingdom gap)* (London Times).

collective behavior, *Sociology.* the behavior of a group of people reacting to a common influence or stimulus. Fads and riots are examples of collective behavior.

co|man|age|ment (kō man′ij mənt), *n.* = worker participation.

come, come down, d *U.S. Slang.* to happen; occur: *What's the government doing for all those families; is it telling anybody what really came down there?* (Harper's).

crisis center, a headquarters from which a disaster is monitored, emergency relief is controlled, psychological counseling is available, or other assistance is given during a time of difficulty: *[She] describes Poe as a kind of crisis center where pregnant teen-agers can count on support* (Tuscaloosa News).

cry|o|pro|tec|tive (krī′ō prə tek′tiv), *adj., n.* **—*adj.*** providing protection against supercooling: *They found that embryos exposed to ... a cryoprotective (antifreeze) agent ... gave the best chances of survival* (Science News).
—*n.* a cryoprotective agent.

D d

Da|lek or **da|lek** (dä′lek), *n. British.* a robot that talks with a rasping, monotonous voice: *Like programmed daleks, the French military planners proceed to their "second generation" ... of 18 intermediate range ballistic missiles* (London Times). [< the name of a robot on "Dr. Who," a BBC science-fiction television series]

de|ni|a|bil|i|ty (di nī′ə bil′ə tē), *n. U.S.* the ability to deny having any knowledge or connection with an illegal or improper activity: *The use of middlemen, of trusted aides-de-camp, of cash instead of checks are all techniques that give the political figure who gets the money "deniability"—he can say he knows nothing about the matter* (Nicholas M. Horrock).

diesel, *n., adj.* **—*v.i.*** (of an internal combustion engine) to continue firing after the ignition has been shut off: *When hot, the engine would diesel ... after the ignition was switched off* (Popular Science).

E e

en|thal|pi|met|ry (en thal′pə met′rē), *n.* the measurement of total heat content generated or absorbed by a substance, used especially to follow the progress of a chemical reaction: *Enthalpimetry depends on the fact that almost all reactions are associated with the evolution or absorption of heat* (New Scientist). [< *enthalpy* + *-metry*]

ept (ept), *adj.* capable; clever; effective: *It is different because it is inept, and those other businesses are very ept indeed. They are eptest at getting what they want* *from the Administration* (Atlantic). [back formation < *inept*]

erg² (ėrg), *n.* a desert area of shifting sand dunes, especially in the Sahara Desert. [< French *erg* < Arabic (North Africa) *'irj*]

es|ky (es′kē), *n., pl.* **-kies.** *Australian.* **1** a portable container for keeping drinks cold: *No less popular is Rugby League football, where raucous fans with well-stocked "eskies"—beer coolers—scream and swill and brawl* (National Geographic). **2 Esky,** a trademark for such a container. [probably < *Eskimo*]

event horizon, *Astronomy.* the inner surface of a black hole, below the ergosphere, from which no energy can escape: *The gravitational field inside the event horizon has become so powerful that even light itself is inevitably dragged inward* (Scientific American).

Ff

fan|tas|mo (fan taz′mō), *adj. Informal.* supremely fantastic: *The figures that populate his [Richard Condon's] books are ... fantasmo embodiments of various sorts of foaming mania* (Time). *Antioch College, Yellow Springs, Ohio, [is] the absolute fantasmo super-pinnacle of academic liberalism* (National Review). [< fantas*tic* + *-mo,* as in *supremo*]

Gg

gag order, *U.S.* a court order prohibiting reporting or public comments on a case before a court of law: *The Supreme Court ... refused to interfere with a judge's gag order on lawyers and other participants in a criminal trial* (C. Herman Pritchett).

gate¹, *n.* **14** one of the locations in the nervous system at which the sensation of pain is blocked: *This theory ... postulates the existence within the nervous system of "gates" that modulate or close off pain signals, either as a result of neurophysiological changes or through brain activity* (Emanuel M. Papper).

genetic screening, study of the genetic makeup of an individual to detect inheritable defects that may be transmitted to offspring: *The best known ... type of genetic screening is ... for the condition known as PKU ... The ill effects [of which] are preventable ... if the dieting begins early enough in infancy* (New York Times).

glitch, *n., v. Slang.* ***—n.*** **2** a sudden irregularity, such as a change in rotation, shown by a celestial body: *Some of these glitches were traced to terrestrial interference sources such as aircraft, while others remain a mystery* (New Scientist).
—v.i. to show or undergo a glitch: *Several times ... the Crab and Vela pulsars were observed to begin suddenly to pulse faster, or "glitch"* (Kenneth Brecher).

grandfather, *n., adj., v.* ***—adj.*** *U.S.* having to do with or based on a grandfather clause: *a grandfather exemption from a new law.*
—v.t. *U.S.* to exempt under a grandfather clause: *As a subdivision that had been filed before the new laws went into effect, Chambers Point was exempt from their requirements—what real estate people call "grandfathered"* (New Yorker).

green currency, any of various artificial rates of exchange, such as the green pound, created to protect the European Economic Community's common agricultural prices from the fluctuations in exchange value of the currencies of its member nations: *It is claimed that the green currency system is used by the West German Government to keep up the incomes of part-time smallholders* (Hugh Clayton).

grunge (grunj), *n. U.S. Slang.* something bad, inferior, or ugly: *Your average American rock-and-roll fan can stand the Dolls' brand of high-strung urban grunge only if it comes from somewhere besides New York—preferably England* (New Yorker). [origin uncertain]

Hh

handoff, *n.* **2** the condition or period in which control of an aircraft is transferred from one airport's control tower to another: *On handoff from Los Angeles' FAA air-route traffic center to San Diego's FAA Approach Control Facility, he [the pilot] reported Lindbergh Field in sight* (Science).

hard-wired (härd′wīrd′), *adj.* **1** wired directly to a computer: *The decoding of the instructions can be done in ... a hard-wired decoder ... for each combination of bits in the operation code* (Scientific American). **2** *Figurative: The facial expressions of human beings really appear to be hard-wired ... comparable to those found in the chimpanzee* (New York Times).

high-tech|nol|o|gy (hī′tek nol′ə jē), *adj.* of or having to do with advanced, highly specialized, and sophisticated technology: *High-technology goods such as computers, aircraft and electronics comprise the most vital part of the U.S. export mix* (Newsweek).

hooker¹, *n.* **4** *Slang.* **a** a hidden difficulty; catch: *Canada can be trusted by nearly everyone. But—and this is the hooker—Canadian statesmen will only be effective if they speak softly* (Maclean's). **b** something to catch the imagination or attract attention: *The structure of a television program ... should have a hooker, a teaser and a conclusion* (New York Times).

Ii

inside skinny, *U.S. Slang.* secret or confidential information: *To get the real inside skinny we shall have to wait until you-know-who's memoirs tell us what the butler really saw* (National Review). [probably from the idea of getting *inside the skin* of a subject]

Jj

ja|mais vu (zhä′me vü′; *French* zha me vʏ′), the illusion of having never experienced the situation one is in, although it is in fact a familiar situation: *The experience of having been somewhere before—déjà vu—is said to be a purely physical experience which affects the frontal lobe of the brain which provides the impression that one has dreamt the identical situation previously. The same explanation is applied to the opposite feeling—jamais vu—when one momentarily fails to recognize a familiar situation* (Auckland Star, New Zealand). [< French *jamais vu* never seen]

jeaned (jēnd), *adj.* wearing jeans: *They're 22, ... jeaned and meticulously casual; perfectly young* (Maclean's). Also, **bejeaned.**

jitterbug, *n.* **3** *Informal.* a jittery person: *Meany despised politicians and power-brokers whose positions seemed to bend with every shift of public opinion or the latest headlines. He dismissed them contemptuously as "jitterbugs"* (Time).

Kk

ku|mi|te (kü mē′tā, -tē), *n.* a sparring event or exhibition in karate, in which blows are stopped just short of contact with the opponent's body: *Free-style combinations of techniques come in kumite, in which two people (karateka) spar with each other* (New Scientist). [< Japanese *kumite* (literally) set hand]

Ll

longitudinal, *adj.* **4** extended over a long period; long-term: *He draws on several longitudinal studies of children in sole custody to make a compelling case for joint custody* (New York Times Magazine).

love bug, a small, black fly of the southeastern United States that appears in the spring in very large numbers, often covering the windshields and clogging the radiators of automobiles: *The love bug population ... is on the increase and is spreading down the Florida peninsula at the rate of 20 miles every year* (Sunday Times).

Mm

magic bullet, a drug or treatment that selectively attacks disease germs, cancer cells, or the like without any harm to the patient: *Another important factor in the development of an effective cancer therapy is that it should act like a "magic bullet," killing cancer cells while doing a minimum of damage to normal ones* (Scientific American). [originally used in reference to the efforts of the German biochemist Paul Ehrlich (1854-1915) to discover a chemical that would kill bacteria without harming the infected person]

Nn

New Federalism, a policy of shifting responsibilities such as social welfare programs from the federal government to the states, advocated by Presidents Richard Nixon and Ronald Reagan: *The President's decision to press forward with the New Federalism ... reflects his optimism that Reaganomics will eventually bear fruit* (Time).

no-growth (nō′grōth′), *adj.* designed to prevent, decrease, or restrict growth: *California's legal system is ... clogged with lawsuits provoked by local zoning restric-*

tions or "no growth" rulings (Atlantic). *An upper-class ecofreak* [*was*] *expounding on the dangers of nuclear power and the wonders of a no-growth economy* (Detroit Free Press).

O o

Ock|er or **ock|er** (ok′ər), *n. Australian Slang.* a type of boorish, self-righteous, and often bigoted Australian man. [colloquial Australian variant of *Oscar*]

or|tho|pho|to (ôr′thō fō′tō), *n.* a composite photograph of terrain, made by joining narrow strips of other photographs so that the finished picture is fully corrected in scale, position, etc.: *Whereas an aerial photograph of rolling or mountainous terrain will have inherent scale and angular distortions, the orthophoto is true to scale; shapes, angles, and distances are correct* (George G. Alexandridis).

o|ver|mike (ō′vər mīk′), *v.t. U.S. Informal.* to amplify too much with a microphone: *Because the show, like all Broadway shows, is damnably overmiked, it is hard to tell what the quality of her voice may be* (New Yorker).

P p

performance art, a form of theatrical performance which combines dancing and acting with music, photography, films, and other art forms: *Performance art. Distinctions between painting, sculpture, theater, and choreography were merged and blurred* (New York Post). **—performance artist**.

proved or **proven reserves**, the amount of oil or natural gas that can be removed profitably from available sources: *In considering resources of oil and gas one encounters a category that has no exact counterpart in world coal statistics; the concept of "proved reserves." The term refers to discovered and well-delineated reserves that can be extracted by available techniques at current costs and sold at current prices* (Scientific American).

psy|cho|ge|net|ics (sī′kō jə net′iks), *n.* **1** the study of the genetic components of mental disorders. **2** the study of psychogenesis.

Q q

quas|qui|cen|ten|ni|al (kwäs′kwē sen ten′ē əl), *adj., n.* **—*adj.*** of or having to do with 125 years or a 125th anniversary. **—*n.*** **1** a 125th anniversary. **2** a celebration of a 125th anniversary. [patterned on *sesquicentennial*]

R r

ratchet effect, intermittent advance, increase growth, or the like: *It appears that there has been a ratchet effect in employment in the service industries* (B. R. Lerner).

Rea|gan|om|ics (rā′gə nom′iks, rē′-), *n.* the economic policies of President Ronald Reagan: *Higher federal deficits and nine-per-cent unemployment ... were precisely the consequences critics of Reaganomics had repeatedly forecast* (Maclean's). [< *Reagan* + (econ)*omics*]

reeducate, *v.t.* **2** to train or drill in a program of political indoctrination, especially in a communist country: *In Vietnam, Laos, and Cambodia ... major efforts were made to revive the rural economy and to "reeducate" former opponents, but the Cambodians were clearly the most draconian in their approach* (David L. Williams).

re|tard|a|taire (rə tàr dà ter′), *adj.* (in the arts) behind the times; lagging behind: *English art had always been retardataire ... the Pre-Raphaelites were repeating things which had already been done a generation before by the German Nazarenes* (Edward Lucie-Smith). [< French *retardataire* < *retarder* to retard]

ripple control, a method by which an electric company reduces the cost of power to individual users by automatically turning off their supply when electricity is most expensive, as during periods of peak consumer demand: *So far, ripple control has worked: according to test results, the system has saved roughly $60 a year per heater in electricity costs* (Time).

rum|dum (rum′dum′), *adj., n. U.S. Slang.* **—*adj.*** ordinary; average: *Ponicsan finds surprising depth and touching delicacy in the rumdum lives he weaves together—dime-store and dinner women, odd-job truckers ...* (Newsweek). **—*n.*** a person who is ordinary or average: *I would still rather look good than win, which is what I usually do: look good and lose. I beat the rumdums but go down before quality players* (Harper's). [origin uncertain]

S s

secondhand smoke, smoke inhaled unintentionally by nonsmokers: *There is little evidence that healthy adults are significantly harmed by ... secondhand smoke* (New York Times).

sin|do|nol|o|gy (sin′də nol′ə jē), *n.* the scientific study of the shroud of Turin, a cloth bearing the image of a life-size figure of a man thought to be Jesus Christ, kept in a chapel in Turin, Italy, since the 1500's: *Sindonology is the study of the shroud—a lifelong romance with the paradox—and in particular two questions: what is the image composed of, and by what mysterious if not miraculous process was it formed? Sindonology is the physics of miracles* (Rolling Stone). [< (archaic or obsolete) *sindon* a shroud < Latin, < Greek *sindṓn* + *-logy*] **—sin′do|nol′o|gist**, *n.*

subduct, *v.t., v.i.* **3** *Geology.* to sink or cause to sink under the margin or edge of a crustal plate: *When an oceanic plate collides with a continental one, the oceanic plate usually dives toward the mantle and is subducted. That is because the continental plates are thicker and more buoyant* (Scientific American).

T t

ta|phon|o|my (tə fon′ə mē), *n.* **1** the processes and conditions of fossilization: *A survey ... on the taphonomy and population dynamics of an early Pliocene* (W. E. Swinton). **2** the study of fossilization: *workers from many ... different disciplines: ... paleontology, anatomy, archaeology, ecology and taphonomy* (Scientific American). [< Greek *táphos* tomb + *-nómos* arranging, managing] **—ta|phon′o|mist**, *n.*

technology transfer, the transfer of new or advanced technological information, especially from the developed to the less developed countries of the world: *Technology transfer is sometimes used to describe information dissemination, but this is only a part of the technology transfer process* (Science).

tel|e|con|fer|ence (tel′ə kon′fər əns, -frens), *n.* a conference of a group of people linked by telephone or television: *The engineers want to establish optical fibre video channels linking homes and offices so that people can ... join in face-to-face "teleconferences"* (New Scientist).

tertiary recovery, any method used to take oil from a well after secondary recovery has failed: *Oil companies are testing a number of tertiary recovery techniques to get at previously unrecoverable reserves ... By injecting air into oil-bearing rocks, it is possible to ignite some of the oil, making the rest thin enough for water-flooding* (J. Tesar).

U u

un|con|struct|ed (un′kən struk′tid), *adj.* (of clothes) not having interfacing, lining, or padding in order to produce a pliant or supple effect: *The classic, unconstructed jacket with lapels and one, two, or three buttons can be adapted to many uses, many occasions* (New York Daily News).

V v

var (vär), *n. Electricity.* the unit of reactive power. [< *v*(olt)-*a*(mpere) *r*(eactive)]

W w

warehouse, *n.* **3** *U.S.* any large public facility for the care of people, especially the mentally ill, the aged, or the poor: *We ought to protect our families ... from the misery of their simply "existing"* (not living) *in a nearby "warehouse" or public institution* (Joseph Fletcher).

war|fight|ing (wär′fī′ting), *n.* combat between ballistic missiles; warfare conducted by using missiles to attack or intercept enemy missiles. [probably < *war*(head) + *fighting*]

Wic|ca or **wic|ca** (wik′ə), *n.* the practice or cult of witchcraft: *Witches call their religion Wicca, from the Anglo-Saxon word meaning wisdom, which is the root of such words as witch, wizard and wicked* (Sunday Post-Herald). [Old English *wicca* (masculine) wizard]

Pronunciation Key: hat, **ā**ge, c**ã**re, f**ä**r; let, **ē**qual, t**ė**rm; **i**t, **ī**ce; h**o**t, **ō**pen, **ô**rder; **oi**l, **ou**t; cup, p**u̇**t, r**ü**le; **ch**ild; lo**ng**; **th**in; **ᴛʜ**en; **zh**, measure; **ə** represents **a** in about, **e** in taken, **i** in pencil, **o** in lemon, **u** in circus.

1977
1978
1979
1980
1981
1982

Index

How to Use the Index
This index covers the contents of the 1981, 1982, and 1983 editions of THE WORLD BOOK YEAR BOOK.

Each index entry is followed by the edition year (in *italics*) and the page number, as:

ADVERTISING, *83*-178, *82*-172, *81*-172

This means, for example, that information about Advertising begins on page 178 in the 1983 edition of THE YEAR BOOK.

An index entry that is the title of an article appearing in THE YEAR BOOK is printed in capital letters, as: **AUTOMOBILE.** An entry that is not an article title, but a subject discussed in an article of some other title, is printed: **Mean free path.**

The various "See" and "See also" cross references in the index list are to other entries within the index. Clue words or phrases are used when two or more references to the same subject appear in the same edition of THE YEAR BOOK. These make it easy to locate the material on the page, since they refer to an article title or article subsection in which the reference appears, as:

Videodisc: *il., 82*-483; video, *Special Report, 83*-115

The indication *"il."* means that the reference is to an illustration only. An index entry in capital letters followed by *"WBE"* refers to a new or revised WORLD BOOK ENCYCLOPEDIA article in the supplement section, as:

JAPAN, *WBE, 83*-534

A

C

D

E

F

G

H

I

J

K

L

M

N

O

P

Q

R

T

U

V

Acknowledgments

The publishers acknowledge the following sources for illustrations. Credits read from top to bottom, left to right, on their respective pages. An asterisk (*) denotes illustrations and photographs that are the exclusive property of THE YEAR BOOK. All maps, charts, and diagrams were prepared by THE YEAR BOOK staff unless otherwise noted.

3 Martha Swope
9 John Bryson, Sygma
10 Diana Walker, Gamma/Liaison
11 © Sipa Press from Black Star
12 William, Sygma; Dennis Brack, Black Star
13 Randy Taylor, Sygma; Bruce Bennett, *Time* Magazine; Lionel Cherruault, Camera Press
14 P. J. Sloan, Camera Press; R. Cruz, Gamma/Liaison; Laffaille, Sipa Press from Black Star; John Bryson, Sygma
15 Rafael Wollmann, Gamma/Liaison; Jonathan Wenk, Black Star; James Nachtwey, Black Star
16 Michael Patrick, Picture Group; Wide World; Shelly Katz, Black Star
17 Nik Wheeler, Sipa Press from Black Star; Moshe Milner, Sygma; Francis Apesteguy, Gamma/Liaison; John Troha, Black Star
18 Antonio Suarez, Wheeler Pictures; Sergio Dorantes, Wheeler Pictures
19 Campion, Gamma/Liaison; Chris Niedenthal, Black Star; Stephen R. Brown, *U.S. News & World Report*
20 Alain Mingam, Gamma/Liaison
21 Laffaille, Black Star; Randy Taylor, Sygma; Focus on Sports
22 John Bryson, Sygma; Diana Walker, Gamma/Liaison
23 Brad Nelson, University of Utah Medical Center
25 Paul Conklin*
26 © John Hillery, Picture Group; WORLD BOOK photo; WORLD BOOK photo; © Sygma
27-29 Paul Conklin*
31 © David Hume Kennerly, Gamma/Liaison
32 Paul Conklin*
33 © John Hillery, Picture Group; Paul Conklin*
34-36 Paul Conklin*
37-41 WORLD BOOK photos
42-43 Paul Conklin*
44 Artstreet
46 © Randy Taylor, Sygma
47 © Michael Grecco, Picture Group
48-50 Paul Conklin*
51 © Sygma
55 Ferorelli, Wheeler Pictures
56 Cameron Gerlach*
59 Supreme Court Historical Society
60 Cameron Gerlach*
63 Supreme Court Historical Society
64-69 Cameron Gerlach*
71 Peter Gridley, Alpha
74 R. Cruz, Gamma/Liaison
80 Susan Meiselas, Magnum
82 Alon Reininger, Contact; Alain Keler, Sygma
84 Alon Reininger, Contact; Alain Keler, Sygma
85 J. P. Laffont, Sygma; Jules Bucher, Photo Researchers
86 John Hoagland, Gamma/Liaison
87 Alain Keler,* Sygma
88 Etienne Montes, Gamma/Liaison
90 Timothy Eagan, Woodfin Camp, Inc.
92 Sepp Seitz, Woodfin Camp, Inc.
93 Florida Student Assessment Test, Florida Department of Education
94 Ferorelli, Wheeler Pictures
95 The indicated SAT test questions are from *Taking the SAT*, College Entrance Examination Board, 1981. Reprinted by permission of Educational Testing Service, copyright owner of the sample questions.
96 Stanley H. Kaplan Educational Center, Chicago (Steve Hale*)
98 Office of the Illinois Secretary of State (Steve Hale*)
99 Steve Hansen, Stock, Boston
101 Practice Questions from the Differential Aptitude Tests, Mechanical Reasoning reproduced by permission. Copyright © 1982, 1980, 1975, 1973, 1972 by The Psychological Corporation. All rights reserved.
102 United Airlines
104 John Lei, Stock, Boston
106 John Craig*
110 WORLD BOOK photo by Milt and Joan Mann; WORLD BOOK photo by Milt and Joan Mann; Dan Miller*
111 © Mario Ruiz; Japan Computer Graphics Laboratory in conjunction with the New York Institute of Technology Graphics Laboratory
113 John Craig*
116 WORLD BOOK photo
120 John Craig*
122 © Most Media
123 Radio Corporation of America; Department of Communications, Ottawa, Ontario
126 James Sugar, Woodfin Camp, Inc.
130 Grant Heilman; Tim McCabe, Soil Conservation Service, USDA
131 Milt and Joan Mann; Landslides
138 Soil Conservation Service, USDA; Grant Heilman
139 Tim McCabe, Soil Conservation Service, USDA; Grant Heilman
140 Soil Conservation Service, USDA; Landslides
142-155 Steve Hale*
159 Newberry Library, Chicago
160 Gersheim Collection, Humanities Research Center, University of Texas at Austin; Construction by Timothy Evans (Steve Hale*)
161 Granger Collection; Construction by Timothy Evans (Steve Hale*)
164 New York Public Library; Bettmann Archive; Construction by Timothy Evans (Steve Hale*)
165 Newberry Library, Chicago; Construction by Timothy Evans (Steve Hale*)
167 Newberry Library, Chicago; BBC Hulton Picture Library; Brown Brothers; Bettmann Archive; Construction by Timothy Evans (Steve Hale*)
168 Historical Pictures Service; Gilbert and Sullivan Collection, Pierpont Morgan Library, New York City; Construction by Timothy Evans (Steve Hale*)
169 Historical Pictures Service; Bettmann Archive; International Museum of Photography, George Eastman House; Construction by Timothy Evans (Steve Hale*)
171 Culver Pictures; Newberry Library, Chicago; Bettmann Archive; Construction by Timothy Evans (Steve Hale*)
175 © 1982 by Universal Pictures, a division of Universal City Studios, Inc., courtesy of MCA Publishing, a division of MCA Communications, Inc.
176 Wide World
177 Canapress; Wide World
178 Wide World
179 © Edward E. Grazda
180-184 Wide World
186 Bill Corbett, *Edmonton Journal*
188 United Press Int.
189 University of California at Berkeley
191 © Howard N. Kaplan
192 Wide World
193-195 United Press Int.
196 Wide World
199 United Press Int.
201 John Carnemolla, Australian Picture Library
203 Wide World
204-206 United Press Int.
208 © John Bryson, Sygma
210 Wide World
211 Wayne Stayskall, © 1982 *Chicago Tribune*. Used with permission
213-217 Wide World
219 University of British Columbia
220 Merrill Oliver, *Tri-City Herald*
223-224 United Press Int.
225 Canadian Press
226 Wide World
229 Canapress
230 United Press Int.
232 Canapress
233 Wide World
234 Statistics Canada
242 The Canada Council
243-247 Wide World

249 United Press Int.
250-252 Wide World
253 United Press Int.
257 © Walt Disney Productions
259 Wide World
260 Peabody Coal Company
261 James F. Lowney
262-265 Wide World
269 Don Ploke, *Las Vegas Sun*
271-272 Wide World
274-275 United Press Int.
276 Wide World
277 Marice Cohn, *Miami Herald*
278 Wide World
280 Martha Swope
282 © Mark Petty, Black Star; Ken Regan, Camera 5; United Press Int.; United Press Int.
283 Regis Bossu, Sygma; Francis C. Fuerst, Black Star; Theo Westenberger, Gamma/Liaison; *The Globe and Mail,* Toronto, Canada
284 Archie Lieberman, Black Star; Wide World; Wide World; United Press Int.
285 United Press Int.
286 Canapress; Wide World; United Press Int.; United Press Int.
287 United Press Int.; Wide World; United Press Int.; © Sipa Press from Black Star
289 D. Gorton, NYT Pictures
290 Quino, *Clarín Revista,* Buenos Aires, Argentina. Reprinted in *World Press Review,* April 1982
291 Wide World
293 United Press Int.
294 © Dennis Brack, Black Star
295 Wide World
296 Merck Sharp & Dohme
297 Wide World
298 D. Todd Moore, *Time* Magazine
301 © Rick Friedman, Black Star
303 Wide World
304 *The Wall Street Journal,* by permission of Cartoon Features Syndicate
305 Ibrahim, Sipa Press from Black Star
307 Wide World; Wide World; United Press Int.; United Press Int.
308 © Robert R. McElroy, *Newsweek*
309 Wide World
311 Plasma Physics Laboratory, Princeton University
312 United Press Int.
313 Ted Spiegel, Black Star
315 Bernard Couret, Gamma/Liaison
316-319 United Press Int.
320 Stuart Franklin, Sygma
322 Wide World
323 United Press Int.
324 Wide World
326 Sovfoto
327 Brad Bower, Picture Group
328-331 United Press Int.
334 Focus on Sports
335 Wide World
336 United Press Int.
337 Wide World
339-341 United Press Int.
343 John Sturrock, Network
344 Lord Snowdon from United Press Int.
345 Michael Walker
346 Wide World
347 United Press Int.
348 Canapress
349 Steve Kelley, © 1982 *San Diego Union.* Reprinted by permission of Field Newspaper Syndicate
351 United Press Int.
355 Cardinal Industries
356 © Fred Bunch, *The Houston Post*
357 Focus on Sports
359-361 United Press Int.
363 Wide World
364 Françoise DeMulder, *Time* Magazine
365 © J. Pavlovsky, Sygma
366 United Press Int.
367 Wide World
368 © Giansanti, Sygma
369-370 Wide World
371 Keystone
372 Wide World
373 Duncan Willetts, Camerapix from Keystone
375 Wide World
376 Dick Locher, © 1982 *Chicago Tribune.* Used with permission
377-378 Wide World
380 R. Cruz, Gamma/Liaison
382-383 United Press Int.
386-387 Wide World
388 © Peter Simon, Black Star
389 Terry Smith, *Time* Magazine
391 From *Jumanji* by Chris Van Allsburg. © 1981 by Chris Van Allsburg. Reprinted by permission of Houghton Mifflin Company
393 Steve Hale*
397 © Lester Sloan, *Newsweek*
398 John Deere Technical Center
403-405 Wide World
407 United Press Int.
408-411 Wide World
412 © 1982 by Universal Pictures, a division of Universal City Studios, Inc., courtesy of MCA Publishing, a division of MCA Communications, Inc.
414 © 1982 United Artists Corporation. All rights reserved
416 © Marilynn K. Yee, NYT Pictures
418 Wide World
421-425 United Press Int.
428 © James P. Sterba, NYT Pictures
429 Canapress
432 Johns Hopkins University
433-435 Wide World
436 Ringling Bros. and Barnum & Bailey Circus
437-441 Wide World
442 Shooters from *Time* Magazine
443 Kodak Corporation
444 Stanford University
446 United Press Int.
447 Wide World
449 U. S. Postal Service
450 © David Hume Kennerly
451 United Press Int.
452 The White House
453 Tomás Pantin, *Texas Monthly*
454-456 Birkett, © 1982 *Punch* from Rothco Cartoons
458 Steve Hale*
459 United Press Canada
460 © David Gahr
461 Peter Main, *The Christian Science Monitor*
462 Michael Evans, The White House
463 Wide World
465 United Press Int.
466 Wide World
468-469 United Press Int.
471 John Bryson, Sygma
473 Peter Wilson, *Saskatoon Star-Phoenix*
474 Gamma/Liaison
477 Wide World
478 United Press Int.
479 Bob Thomas
480 Wide World
482-483 United Press Int.
485 Courtesy of Robert A. Siegel Auction Galleries
486 Wide World
487 Bill Garner, *The Commercial Appeal,* Memphis
491 Wide World
493-494 United Press Int.
495 Martel, Gamma/Liaison
497 Granada Television
498 CBS Entertainment
499 National Broadcasting Company, Inc.
500 United Press Int.
501 Roland Neveu, Gamma/Liaison
502 Martha Swope
504-505 Wide World
507 Keystone
509 Ruan Transport Corp.
510 Wide World
512-513 United Press Int.
519 Diana Walker, Gamma/Liaison
521 © Rick Browne
522 Chick Harrity, *U. S. News & World Report*
524 United Press Int.
527 Boy Scouts of America
529 Wide World
530 Karen M. Koblik
533 © Paolo Koch, Photo Researchers

A Preview of 1983

January

						1
2	3	4	5	6	7	8
9	10	11	12	13	14	15
16	17	18	19	20	21	22
23	24	25	26	27	28	29
30	31					

1 **New Year's Day.**
St. Basil's Day, Eastern Orthodox feast day.

6 **Epiphany,** 12th day of Christmas, celebrates the visit of the Three Wise Men to the infant Jesus.

15 **Martin Luther King, Jr.'s Birthday,** honoring the slain civil rights leader, celebrated on this day in 12 states and the District of Columbia.

29 **Tu B'Shebat,** Jewish arbor festival, observed by donating trees to Israel.

30 **Super Bowl XVII,** the National Football League's championship game, in Pasadena, Calif.

31 **Australia Day** marks Captain Arthur Phillip's landing in 1788 where Sydney now stands. The actual anniversary is January 26.

February

		1	2	3	4	5
6	7	8	9	10	11	12
13	14	15	16	17	18	19
20	21	22	23	24	25	26
27	28					

2 **Ground-Hog Day.** Legend says six weeks of winter weather will follow if the ground hog sees its shadow.

8 **Boy Scouts of America Birthday Anniversary** marks the founding of the organization in 1910.

12 **Abraham Lincoln's Birthday,** observed in most states.

13 **Chinese New Year** begins year 4681, the Year of the Pig, on the ancient Chinese calendar.

14 **Valentine's Day,** festival of romance and affection.

15 **Mardi Gras,** celebrated in New Orleans and many Roman Catholic countries, is the last merrymaking before Lent.

16 **Ash Wednesday,** first day of Lent for Christians, begins the period of repentance that precedes Easter.

21 **George Washington's Birthday,** according to law, is celebrated on the third Monday in February. The actual anniversary is February 22.
Easter Seal Campaign through April 3.

27 **Purim,** Jewish festival commemorating how Esther saved the Jews from the tyrant Haman.

March

		1	2	3	4	5
6	7	8	9	10	11	12
13	14	15	16	17	18	19
20	21	22	23	24	25	26
27	28	29	30	31		

1 **Red Cross Month** through March 31.

6 **Girl Scout Week,** through March 12, marks the group's 71st birthday.

13 **Camp Fire Birthday Week,** through March 19, marks the 73rd anniversary of the organization.

17 **St. Patrick's Day,** honoring the patron saint of Ireland.

19 **Swallows Return to San Juan Capistrano,** California, from their winter homes.
St. Joseph's Day, Roman Catholic feast day honoring the husband of the Virgin Mary.

20 **First Day of Spring,** 11:39 P.M. E.S.T.

27 **Palm Sunday** marks Jesus Christ's last entry into Jerusalem, where people covered His path with palm branches.

29 **Passover,** Jewish festival that celebrates the exodus of the Jews from bondage in Egypt.

31 **Maundy Thursday,** Christian celebration of Christ's commandment to love others.

April

					1	2
3	4	5	6	7	8	9
10	11	12	13	14	15	16
17	18	19	20	21	22	23
24	25	26	27	28	29	30

1 **April Fool's Day,** a traditional day for jokes and tricks.
Good Friday marks the death of Jesus on the cross. It is a public holiday in many countries and several states of the United States.

3 **Easter Sunday,** commemorating the Resurrection of Jesus Christ.

4 **Opening Day** of the major league baseball season.

11 **Academy Awards Night,** when the Academy of Motion Picture Arts and Sciences presents the Oscars.

15 **Income Tax Day** in the United States.

17 **National Library Week** through April 23.

24 **Daylight-Saving Time** begins at 2 A.M.

30 **Walpurgis Night,** when witches gather in East Germany's Harz Mountains, according to legend.

May

1	2	3	4	5	6	7
8	9	10	11	12	13	14
15	16	17	18	19	20	21
22	23	24	25	26	27	28
29	30	31				

1 **May Day,** observed as a festival of spring in many countries and as a holiday honoring workers in socialist and Communist countries.
Law Day U.S.A.
National Music Week through May 8.

7 **Kentucky Derby,** thoroughbred horse race at Churchill Downs in Louisville, Ky.

8 **Mother's Day.**

12 **Ascension Day,** or Holy Thursday, 40 days after Easter, celebrates the ascent of Jesus Christ into heaven.

18 **Shabuot,** Jewish Feast of Weeks, marks the revealing of the Ten Commandments to Moses on Mount Sinai.

21 **Armed Forces Day** honors all branches of the armed forces in the United States.

22 **Pentecost,** or Whitsunday, the seventh Sunday after Easter, commemorates the descent of the Holy Spirit upon the 12 disciples.

23 **Victoria Day,** in Canada, marks the official birthday of the reigning monarch.

29 **Trinity Sunday,** the eighth Sunday after Easter, honors the union of the Father, the Son, and the Holy Spirit.

30 **Memorial Day,** by law, is the last Monday in May.

June

			1	2	3	4
5	6	7	8	9	10	11
12	13	14	15	16	17	18
19	20	21	22	23	24	25
26	27	28	29	30		

5 **Stratford Festival,** drama and music, through late October in Stratford, Canada.

6 **D-Day** commemorates the Allied landing in Normandy in 1944, during World War II.

12 **First Day of Ramadan,** the Islamic holy month, observed by fasting.

14 **Flag Day.**

19 **Father's Day.**

21 **First Day of Summer,** 7:09 P.M. E.D.T.

23 **Midsummer Day,** summer celebration in many European countries.

July

					1	2
3	4	5	6	7	8	9
10	11	12	13	14	15	16
17	18	19	20	21	22	23
24	25	26	27	28	29	30
31						

1 **Dominion Day,** in Canada, celebrates the confederation of the provinces in 1867.
4 **Independence Day,** in the United States, the anniversary of the day on which the Continental Congress adopted the Declaration of Independence in 1776.
6 **Baseball All-Star Game,** Chicago.
14 **Bastille Day,** in France, commemorates the uprising of the people of Paris against King Louis XVI in 1789 and their seizure of the Bastille, the hated Paris prison.
15 **St. Swithin's Day.** According to legend, if it rains on this day, it will rain for 40 more.
19 **Tishah B' Ab,** Jewish holy day, marks the destruction of the first and second temples in Jerusalem in 587 B.C. and A.D. 70.
25 **Puerto Rico Constitution Day.**
28 **Terry Fox Day,** in Canada, commemorates the birthday of the young man who ran across Canada to raise funds for cancer research after losing a leg to the disease.

August

	1	2	3	4	5	6
7	8	9	10	11	12	13
14	15	16	17	18	19	20
21	22	23	24	25	26	27
28	29	30	31			

6 **Hiroshima Day,** memorial observance for victims of the first atomic bombing in Hiroshima, Japan, in 1945.
11 **Perseid Meteor Shower,** through August 13.
15 **Feast of the Assumption,** Roman Catholic and Eastern Orthodox holy day, celebrates the ascent of the Virgin Mary into heaven.
19 **National Aviation Day** commemorates the birthday of pioneer pilot Orville Wright in 1871.
21 **Edinburgh International Festival,** music, drama, and film, through September 10 in Edinburgh, Scotland.
26 **Women's Equality Day** commemorates the enactment of the 19th Amendment in 1920 giving women the vote.
30 **United States Open Tennis Championship,** through September 11 in Flushing Meadows, N.Y.

September

				1	2	3
4	5	6	7	8	9	10
11	12	13	14	15	16	17
18	19	20	21	22	23	24
25	26	27	28	29	30	

5 **Labor Day** in the United States and Canada.
8 **Rosh Hashanah,** or Jewish New Year, beginning the year 5744, according to the Jewish calendar.
17 **Citizenship Day** celebrates the rights and duties of U.S. citizens.
Yom Kippur, or Day of Atonement, the most solemn day in the Jewish calendar.
22 **Sukkot,** or Feast of Tabernacles, begins — Jewish festival that originally marked the harvest season.
23 **First Day of Fall,** 10:42 A.M. E.D.T.
Native American Day honors American Indians.
29 **Shemini Atzeret,** the eighth day of Sukkot, marked with a special prayer for rain.
30 **Simhat Torah,** Jewish festival of rejoicing in God's law, marks the end of the annual cycle of Scripture readings.

October

						1
2	3	4	5	6	7	8
9	10	11	12	13	14	15
16	17	18	19	20	21	22
23	24	25	26	27	28	29
30	31					

2 **National 4-H Week** through October 8.
3 **Child Health Day.**
9 **Fire Prevention Week** through October 15.
10 **Columbus Day** commemorates Christopher Columbus' landing in America in 1492. Celebrated in Latin American countries on October 12, the actual anniversary.
Thanksgiving Day in Canada.
11 **Baseball's World Series** begins.
16 **World Food Day,** sponsored by the United Nations (UN) Food and Agriculture Organization to heighten awareness of world hunger.
National Handicapped Awareness Week, through October 22.
24 **United Nations Day** commemorates the founding of the UN in 1945.
30 **Standard Time Resumes** at 2 A.M.
31 **Halloween.**
UN Children's Fund (UNICEF) Day.
Reformation Day, celebrated by Protestants, marks the day in 1517 when Reformation leader Martin Luther posted his Ninety-Five Theses.

November

		1	2	3	4	5
6	7	8	9	10	11	12
13	14	15	16	17	18	19
20	21	22	23	24	25	26
27	28	29	30			

1 **All Saints' Day,** observed by the Roman Catholic Church.
5 **Guy Fawkes Day,** in Great Britain, marks the failure of a plot to blow up King James I and Parliament in 1605.
8 **Election Day** in the United States.
11 **Veterans Day** in the United States.
Remembrance Day in Canada.
14 **American Education Week** through November 20.
Children's Book Week through November 20.
24 **Thanksgiving Day** in the United States.
27 **Advent** begins, first of the four Sundays in the season before Christmas.
30 **St. Andrew's Day,** feast day of the patron saint of Scotland.

December

				1	2	3
4	5	6	7	8	9	10
11	12	13	14	15	16	17
18	19	20	21	22	23	24
25	26	27	28	29	30	31

1 **Hanukkah,** or Feast of Lights, eight-day Jewish festival that celebrates the defeat of the Syrian tyrant King Antiochus IV in 165 B.C.
6 **St. Nicholas Day,** when children in many European countries receive gifts.
10 **Nobel Prize Ceremony** in Stockholm, Sweden.
13 **St. Lucia Day,** in Sweden, celebrates the return of light after the darkest time of the year.
15 **Bill of Rights Day** marks the ratification of that document in 1791.
16 **Beethoven's Birthday,** anniversary of the birth of German composer Ludwig van Beethoven in 1770.
22 **First Day of Winter,** 5:30 A.M. E.S.T.
24 **Christmas Eve.**
25 **Christmas Day.**
26 **Kwanzaa,** black American holiday based on a traditional African harvest festival, through January 1.
Boxing Day in Canada and Great Britain.
31 **New Year's Eve.**

Cyclo-teacher® The easy-to-use learning system

Features hundreds of cycles from seven valuable learning areas

Here's how Cyclo-teacher works—in 3 easy steps!

Step 1—Asks a new question or poses a problem.

Step 2—Learner writes in answer or response.

Step 3—Learner checks his or her answer against correct response by flipping a lever.

Cyclo-teacher—the remarkable learning system based on the techniques of programmed instruction—comes right into your home to help stimulate and accelerate the learning of basic skills, concepts, and information. Housed in a specially designed file box are the Cyclo-teacher machine, Study Wheels, Answer Wheels, a Manual, a Contents and Instruction Card, and Achievement Record sheets.

Your child will find Cyclo-teacher to be a new and fascinating way to learn—much like playing a game. Only, Cyclo-teacher is much more than a game—it teaches new things . . . reinforces learning . . . and challenges a youngster to go beyond!

Features hundreds of study cycles to meet the individual needs of students—your entire family—just as *Year Book* is a valuable learning aid. And, best of all, lets you track your own progress—advance at your own pace! Cyclo-teacher is available by writing us at the address below:

The World Book Year Book
Post Office Box 3564
Chicago, IL 60654

These beautiful bookstands-

specially designed to hold your entire program, including your editions of *Year Book*.

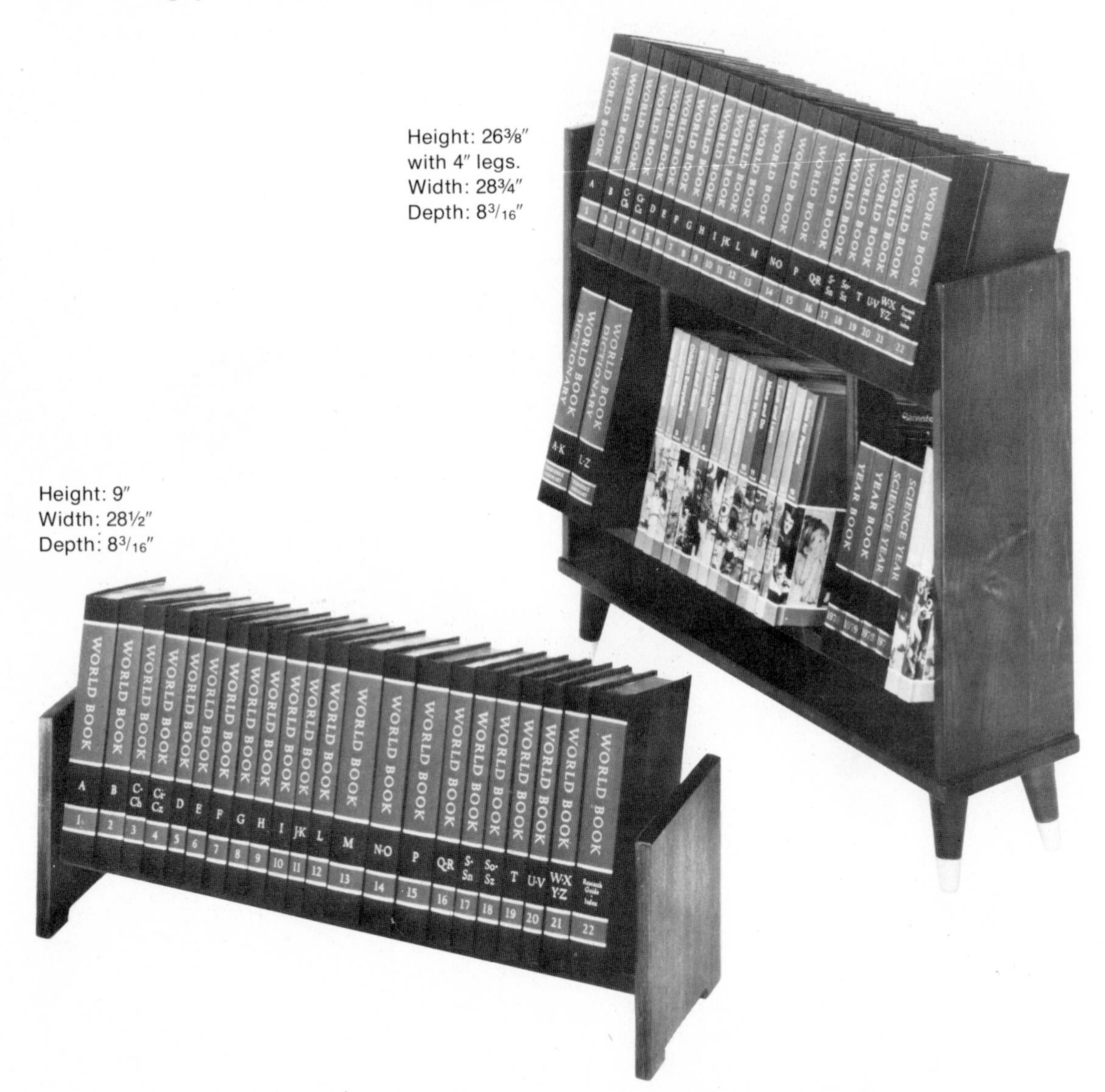

Most parents like having a convenient place to house their *Year Book* editions and their *World Book Encyclopedia*. A beautiful floor-model bookstand—constructed of solid hardwood—is available in either walnut or fruitwood finish.

You might prefer the attractive hardwood table racks, also available in either walnut or fruitwood finish. Let us know by writing us at the following address:

The World Book Year Book
Post Office Box 3564
Chicago, IL 60654